RENAISSANCE HUMANISM&

Volume 3

RENAISSANCE HUMANISM

FOUNDATIONS, FORMS, AND LEGACY

VOLUME 3 • HUMANISM AND THE DISCIPLINES

Edited by Albert Rabil, Jr.

UNIVERSITY OF PENNSYLVANIA PRESS
PHILADELPHIA

Library of Congress Cataloging-in-Publication Data

Renaissance humanism.
   Bibliography: p.
   Includes index.
   Contents: v. 1. Humanism in Italy—v. 2. Humanism
beyond Italy—v. 3. Humanism and the disciplines.
   1. Humanism. 2. Renaissance—Italy. I. Rabil, Albert.
B778.R43   1988   001.1'094   87-13928
ISBN 0-8122-1400-5 (set)
ISBN 0-8122-1372-6 (v. 1)
ISBN 0-8122-1373-4 (v. 2)
ISBN 0-8122-1374-2 (v. 3)

To
MARISTELLA LORCH
Catalyst Among Scholars
Whose Initial Idea Has Developed into These Volumes

CONTENTS

VOLUME 2 ❧ HUMANISM BEYOND ITALY

PART 3 • HUMANISM BEYOND ITALY

VOLUME 3 HUMANISM AND THE DISCIPLINES

PART 5 • THE LEGACY OF HUMANISM

ILLUSTRATIONS

PREFACE

The study of Renaissance humanism became a recognized scholarly enterprise after the publication of Georg Voigt's *The Revival of Classical Antiquity or the First Century of Humanism* (1859) and, more significantly, of Jacob Burckhardt's *The Civilization of the Renaissance in Italy* (1860). Both writers maintained that the Italian Renaissance gave rise to a new personality type, one who had a thirst for fame and adopted a naturalistic attitude toward the world. Burckhardt called this new person a "spiritual individual," which meant, variously, a self-centered person, one who embodied a new kind of moral autonomy or emancipation from traditional religious standards and political authorities, or one always seeking to give full expression to his personality. Accordingly, for a long period the great debate was over the nature and cultural significance of the new kind of consciousness embodied by the humanists. Wilhelm Dilthey, Giovanni Gentile, and Ernst Cassirer, writing during the earlier decades of the twentieth century, regarded humanism as a new philosophy of human values, the chief among which were those values of individualism, secularism, and moral autonomy which had been identified by Burckhardt. The implication of this view was that humanism was hostile to Christianity and, indeed, initiated the development of modern paganism. This view was challenged in 1952 by Giuseppe Toffanin, who argued that far from being pagan and heterodox, Renaissance humanism was the champion of the authentic Latin-Catholic tradition against late medieval Aristotelian science.

These parameters of interpretation have largely been supplanted by the work of Paul Oskar Kristeller during the past generation. On the basis of the most comprehensive study of its sources ever undertaken, Kristeller has effectively established the claim that humanism is part of a rhetorical tradition that has been a continuous aspect of western civilization since classical antiquity. Moreover, humanism has specific roots in the medieval culture from which it arose, notably in the theory and practice of letter and speech writing, the study of classical poetry, prose, and grammar in the cathedral schools of France, and the study of Greek. That the humanists belong to a rhetorical tradition is now generally accepted, though different constructions are placed on what this means. Kristeller has gone on to argue that a study of the humanists' works leads one away from the conclusion that they were professional philosophers. They have no consistent philosophical position and are not concerned with philosophy in the traditional sense. Their preoccupations were those of the rhetorical tradition from which they emerged: grammar, poetry, history, rhetoric, and moral philosophy. Kristeller's formulations constitute the most widely accepted paradigm of humanist studies today. Most of the essays in these volumes reflect adherence to it in one way or another. This paradigm has had a profound impact on the earlier debates about the nature of humanism. The idea that humanism is either a radical departure from the past or a radical defense of traditional values has given way to more mediate studies, which have attempted to reveal the specific relations of the humanists to institutions and their specific ideas on particular issues. This more nuanced discussion of their relationships and ideas is reflected in many of the essays collected here.

Among Kristeller's generation of scholars, his definition of humanism has been challenged by the leading Italian scholar in the field, Eugenio Garin, who regards Renaissance philosophy (for example, Platonism and Aristotelianism) as integral to humanism and treats the philosophers as part of the humanist tradition. While widely respected, Garin's views have not found general acceptance; the writings of the humanists in their various forms and locations bear out to most interpreters the general applicability of Kristeller's paradigm, as the great majority of the essays in these volumes make clear.

Garin has exercised more influence in incorporating the notion of "civic humanism"—first formulated by Hans Baron to designate a specific historical situation in early Quattrocento Florence—into a broader view of humanism and Renaissance thought. He began with the questions: What inspired the humanists to turn from medieval rhetoric to the classical tradition? What motivated their commitment to the disciplines in which they were most interested? Both Garin and Baron believe that humanism as a cultural movement cannot be understood apart from the social and political conditions under which it arose. Their exploration of these conditions, especially in medieval and Renaissance Florence, has led to the recognition of a greater variety within the humanist movement than was previously suspected. Civic humanism, which is explored in these volumes, does not, however, replace Kristeller's paradigm, inasmuch as it applies only to a small group of humanists largely in one location and for a limited period. But it is an important contribution to our understanding of humanism itself and, equally important, to its legacy.

*   *   *

The initial idea for these volumes grew from a course on "Renaissance Humanism" taught at Barnard College/Columbia University by Professor Maristella Lorch and me in the spring of 1979, one of several courses developed through an institutional grant from the National Endowment for the Humanities. We used funds made available through that grant to invite a number of distinguished scholars in Renaissance humanist studies to participate in the course. Professor Lorch suggested the idea of a textbook based on the course, and her initial idea has developed, through several permutations, into the present collection.

We believe we have produced something unique and uniquely valuable for students of the Renaissance at all levels. During the past generation our knowledge of Renaissance humanism in its particular manifestations has grown so vast and at such a rate that the kinds of syntheses mentioned earlier by scholars of a past generation would be much more difficult today, especially if humanism is conceived as a Europe-wide movement interacting with other major movements and institutions. What we have done here is to bring specialists together to accomplish what no one scholar working alone could have achieved.

Each writer, a close student of the field about which he or she writes, was instructed to synthesize the state of the field on the assigned topic. In some cases this task involved a study of what other scholars have discovered, in others an attempt to create a synthesis that has not existed or been perceived before. In a number of cases the articles here represent condensations of book-length studies, which are themselves the major statements of the topics in those areas, for example, the articles by Marianna D. Birnbaum, John F. D'Amico on Rome, Margaret L. King on Venice, Claude V. Palisca, Mario Santoro, Retha M. Warnicke, and Ronald G. Witt. With five exceptions, the forty-one essays published here were written explicitly for these volumes. The five exceptions are Kristeller's essay on humanism and moral philosophy, King's on women and humanism in Italy, and the essays by Deno J. Geanakoplos, Anthony Grafton, and David B. Ruderman. Three of these (King, Geanakoplos, Ruderman) are not readily available; one has been expanded (Ruderman), and in all five the notes have been updated. In very large part, then, this is an originally conceived and executed collaborative scholarly project.

Each essay is addressed to a wide audience. Undergraduates studying in this field for the first time will find here the closest approximation to a textbook that is available in the field. The various essays will introduce a student to any topic that might be addressed in a course on humanism and to the various contemporary interpretations of humanism. The volumes should be of equal or greater value to advanced students, including college and university teachers, whether scholars in the field or not, who want to introduce themselves and their students to Renaissance humanism. We have tried to ensure that all essays are clear, and to this end all quotations have been translated into English. At the same time, all studies relevant to a topic have been included in each essay, regardless of the language in which they were written; many of these are repeated in several essays, and all, both books and articles, have been included in the bibliography located at the end of Volume 3.

A word should be said about the title of these volumes and the scope they promise. The "foundations" and "forms" of humanism are treated in comprehensive fashion. In the "foundations" section, classical, patristic, and medieval backgrounds to humanism are dealt with, and Petrarch, the "father" of humanism, is treated in relation to his ties to all three backgrounds. The forms of humanism have been divided into two frames of reference, geographical (Volumes 1 and 2) and disciplinary (Volume 3). The geographical is further divided into Italian (Volume 1) and European outside Italy (Volume 2). These proceed in chronological fashion, the essays on Italian humanism focusing primarily on the Quattrocento and those on humanism in other countries including the fifteenth century but also extending into and often proceeding to the end of the sixteenth. The disciplinary frame of reference cuts across geographical regions, and each essay proceeds in chronological order, sometimes up to 1700.

The section on the "legacy" of humanism is confined to one essay by Kristeller, a general overview. Actually, the legacy of humanism may be said to involve in part its impact on art, law, music, science, and theology, topics addressed in the final sections of the disciplinary treatment of humanism. It also involves, of course, the impact of humanism on the development of classical scholarship and of the disciplines central to the *studia humanitatis,* all of which are treated in the section on disciplines and institutions. The legacy has thus been more broadly confronted than the one essay in the "legacy" section implies. At the same time, the focus has been placed deliberately on humanism itself, tracing its development as long as it is discernible as a movement in European culture. To trace the impact of humanism after it merged into the broader currents of European culture is a very large task, perhaps as large as the task undertaken here. All readers should therefore be aware that although the legacy of humanism is addressed in various ways in these volumes, the topic itself is not systematically analyzed to the same extent as the foundations and forms of humanism.

*   *   *

Editing these volumes has been at times a trying, but at times also, and ultimately, a rewarding experience. I would like to thank the National Endowment for the Humanities, which provided not only the institutional grant through which this project was initiated but also a personal research fellowship during 1981 and 1982, which enabled me to complete an initial draft of several essays I have contributed, to edit essays in hand, and to enlist many new contributors.

I would like to thank two secretaries at the State University College at Old Westbury: Marion Pensabene, who typed about half of the essays in their final form, and Rosemary Smith, who entered the bibliography in its various phases into a computer; and a colleague, Professor Michael Taves, for help in generating the index on a computer. In addition, I would like to thank the College at Old Westbury for extensive support with respect to the copying and mailing costs involved in bringing the manuscript to its completed form. Most especially, I owe a deep debt of gratitude to Selby Hickey, the college's academic vice-president, through whose efforts the college has contributed toward underwriting the costs of producing these volumes. An underwriting grant has also been received from the Center for International Scholarly Exchange at Barnard College/Columbia University, whose help is here gratefully acknowledged. In addition, several individuals have contributed significantly toward underwriting the costs of publication, and to all of them I extend a deepfelt thanks.

My greatest debt of gratitude is to Paul Oskar Kristeller. These volumes themselves are in an important way a tribute to his scholarship. But in a more personal sense, I am grateful for his constant counsel through letters and (more frequently) telephone conversations. In addition to helping frame the general outline of these volumes, he assisted in the solicitation of contributors—especially during the early stages of the project—and he has read a number of the essays. His graciousness to younger scholars working in the field has become legendary in his own time; this project is certainly a wonderful instance of it.

The volumes are dedicated to Maristella Lorch, the initiator of the original course and the instigator of the idea that has now become this anthology. As the concept of the project matured, we have tried it out together in subsequent incarnations of our initial course on humanism. Without her patient and enduring goodwill and her genius for bringing people together this project would never have been begun, let alone completed.

ALBERT RABIL, JR.

RENAISSANCE HUMANISM

Volume 3

PART IV

HUMANISM AND THE DISCIPLINES

A HUMANIST PEDAGOGY

B THE *STUDIA HUMANITATIS*

C HUMANISM AND THE PROFESSIONS

D HUMANISM, THE ARTS, AND SCIENCE

A 🕊 HUMANIST PEDAGOGY

27 🕊 HUMANISM AND EDUCATION
Benjamin G. Kohl

THE TITLE *MAGISTER—MAESTRO—MASTER:* THIS WAS THE ONE most commonly given to those men of the Italian Renaissance whom we now usually call humanists. In the academic sense the title *magister* usually denoted both some university training, perhaps up to the degree of master of arts, and the position of schoolmaster, tutor, or university lecturer in the liberal arts. A survey of the standard biographical dictionary of Italian humanists by Mario Cosenza shows that of the 1,412 humanists who flourished from 1300 to the sack of Rome in 1527 (one of the most common dates for the end of the Renaissance in Italy), 533 had been at one time or another in their lives schoolmasters, tutors, university lecturers, or professors.[1] In other words, roughly 31 percent of all those usually termed humanists in the Italian Renaissance had made their living as teachers at some point in their careers. This intimate connection between humanists and schooling entails three concerns that will be the subject of this essay: the development of a curriculum for beginning students in Latin authors; the problems and status of being a schoolmaster; and the place of the liberal arts and new humanist educational ideals in the secondary schools and university instruction of the fifteenth century.

*   *   *

Medieval education was founded on the study of the seven liberal arts, of which the trivium—grammar, logic, rhetoric—constituted the verbal arts, a concept of basic training continued with some modification into the Renaissance. Lay schools existed in almost all Italian cities during the thirteenth century, providing basic instruction in Latin grammar and the classical authors. In Florence at the time of Dante, according to the famous estimate of the chronicler Giovanni Villani, out of a population of ninety thousand, some eight thousand to ten thousand boys and girls attended schools for basic instruction in reading and writing in the vernacular. Those boys destined for a career as merchant shopkeeper— about a thousand—received training in arithmetic and the use of the abacus, while perhaps five hundred to six hundred males of the school-age population attended four schools of Latin grammar.[2] In these schools the future administrators of Florence, its notaries, lawyers, judges, and magistrates, received the elements of Latin learning. Such was the education Dante received, as also such Trecento giants as Petrarch, Boccaccio, and humanists of the next generation, including Coluccio Salutati, Giovanni Conversini of Ravenna, and Pier Paolo Vergerio the Elder.[3] The elementary Latin curriculum in Italy indeed continued with few changes until well into the fifteenth century, so that several generations of humanists were nurtured on the same texts and on similar assumptions regarding the mixing of Latin grammatical instruction with basic Christian morality.

This very conservative program began with the study of the Psalter, coupled with instruction in the parts of speech from Donatus, the most famous Latin grammarian of late antiquity. Along with the Psalter, other rhymed elementary Latin works were used, probably to aid in the inculcation of basic religious ideas and Stoic concepts of virtue. The principal ancient text studied was the *Disticha Catonis,* an anonymous third-century collection of proverbial wisdom, attributed to the Roman Stoic Cato the Elder. Its couplets were probably memorized by young students, giving them an innate understanding of Latin accent and grammar as well as proverbs for use in argument and for the embellishment of letters. After Cato, most students read the *Sententiae* of St. Augustine, in the rhymed version of Prosper of Aquitaine. Other basic texts included some of Aesop's fables, again in verse, the *Dittochaeum* of Prosper of Aquitaine, called usually the *Eva columba* from the first words of that poem, and animal stories from the *Physiologus,* attributed to Theobaldus, a twelfth-century author, and called *Tres leo naturas,* from the beginning words of the poem. The last and most difficult text in the first course of Latin authors was Boethius's *Consolation of Philosophy,* which was perhaps read only selectively.[4]

Further study in the liberal arts entailed reading the great works of Latin literature in both philosophy and poetry. By the turn of the fourteenth century the Latin poets were established as a core of literary study. The canonical three were Vergil, Ovid's *Metamorphoses,* and Horace, to which Statius's *Thebiad* and Lucan's *De bello civili* were usually added. Of the philosophers, Cicero and Seneca headed the list. Other poetry read included the satires of Juvenal and the comedies of Terence. Other Roman prose authors, mainly historians, included Livy, Caesar, the collective biographies of the later Roman emperors known as *Scriptores historiae augustae,* Sallust, Suetonius, and Valerius Maximus. Of these most except Valerius Maximus were studied as the corpus for the narrative history of the Roman republic and empire. Valerius Maximus's *Facta et dicta memorabilia,* a collection of memorable deeds and sayings from both Greek and Roman history, organized by topic rather than chronologically, wielded enormous influence as a source for anecdotes. That work inspired university courses, commentaries, and imitations by both Petrarch and Giovanni Conversini. After grammar, Christian authors, and study of the classics usually came the study of rhetoric, itself leading frequently to the notarial arts or the study in civil or canon law. The basic texts here were the pseudo-Ciceronian *Rhetorica ad Herennium* and Cicero's own elementary *De inventione.* These treatises informed both the format and the style of the early humanists' orations and letters. This art of composing letters, called the *ars dictaminis,* flourished at the universities, such as Bologna and Padua, where the new professional classes of the early Renaissance were being trained.[5]

*   *   *

By the turn of the fourteenth century, these jurists, judges, and notaries, trained in rhetoric which was in turn embellished and enriched by the study of Latin poetry, history, and philosophy, developed in northern Italian cities a new enthusiasm for the independent study of Roman literature and for ancient history, archaeology, and the early traditions of their own localities. This group, called the prehumanists, formed at Padua around the figures of Albertino Mussato and Lovato Lovati as a study group bent on recovering lost Latin works and writing good Latin in the ancient style.[6] Thanks to the efforts of the Paduan prehumanists, the poetic corpus of Tibullus and Catullus was recovered as well as Varro, *De re rustica,* and texts of Roman history. Seneca's tragedies were studied, edited, and eventually imitated in the *Ecerinis* of Albertino Mussato, first performed in Padua around 1315. This spontaneous rekindling of interest in the classics had a profound effect on manuscript hunting and manuscript correction by the great scholars of the next generation. To give only the most famous example of continuing self-education: Petrarch discovered in Verona in 1345 a text of the formerly lost Cicero's *Epistulae ad Atticum,* which transformed the humanist's opinion of the great Roman orator, politician, and sage. To this discovery were added others by Boccaccio, the *Metamorphoses* of Apuleius and Tacitus's historical works at Monte Cassino, and by Salutati of Cicero's *Epistulae familiares.* In other words, from the classical and rhetorical education in Italy of the early fourteenth century there emerged a number of mature lawyer-humanists who in their spare moments studied ancient literature and attempted to write history, poetry, and drama after the ancient manner, using Seneca as their stylistic model. From their example derived the more creative and far-reaching reinterpretation of the legacy of antiquity by such giants as Petrarch and Boccaccio.

Yet despite the strides made in the recovery of ancient texts and the reinterpretation of the classical heritage in the fourteenth century, the content and methods of instruction in the classics remained strangely constant until the next century. An examination of the education, careers, and libraries of three humanist schoolmasters of the period will illustrate this conservatism in education.[7] The best known of the three, Giovanni Conversini of Ravenna (1343–1408), provides a fine example of the juncture of the older classical education with the new humanistic ideals. Orphaned at an early age, Giovanni received an indifferent elementary education from several masters in precisely the texts mentioned above. At sixteen he studied rhetoric at Bologna, following lectures on the medieval textbook of Giovanni di Bonandrea, the *Bononianatus*, in the fall term, and progressing to lectures on the so-called new Cicero, the pseudo-Ciceronian *Rhetorica ad Herennium* in the spring. But the requirements of providing for his young wife and child forced Giovanni to follow the more practical course of *ars notaria* for the next two years. After completing this course he soon returned to the study of literature as a member of Pietro da Moglio's household in Padua. At the age of twenty Giovanni began his own career as a teacher, lecturing in Bologna on the works of the Roman historian Valerius Maximus.

Most of Giovanni's teaching career, however, was spent as a tutor in the households of various ruling families of Italian cities, beginning with the Este in Ferrara and ending with the Carrara in Padua, or as schoolmaster in the communal Latin schools of the small cities of northeastern Italy. In this capacity Giovanni taught Latin at Treviso, Belluno, Conegliano, and Udine, usually discharged after disputes with students or their parents. Only one year did he enjoy the post of university lecturer, commenting on the Latin poets and teaching rhetoric at Padua in 1392–93, numbering Sicco Polenton and perhaps Guarino of Verona among his pupils. But even when Giovanni served the Carrara *signoria* in Padua from 1393 to 1404 as its chancellor, he continued to tutor students such as Pier Paolo Vergerio the Elder and Vittorino da Feltre. When Giovanni left the service of the lord of Padua at the beginning of his final war with Venice in 1404, it was perhaps inevitable that he turned to tutoring, this time the sons of Venetian noble families, as his means of support. For those humanists of the Trecento without clerical benefices or lordly patronage, as in the case of Petrarch, teaching or service in a court, lay or ecclesiastical, was the usual occupation. And even Petrarch was at least tempted by the offer of a post lecturing in the Florentine *studium* in 1350, while Boccaccio accepted just such a post, commenting on Dante's *Divine Comedy* toward the end of his life. If teaching was often a sometime activity for the most prestigious humanists, for humbler ones schoolmastering was a sure way of making a living.

The career of Giovanni Travesi of Cremona (d. 1418) illustrates the calling of one of these humbler humanists. A student at Pavia, Travesi received his first degree, the license in rhetoric, in 1372, after passing the private examination by commenting on two passages before the entire college of doctors in the arts. The passages were from the two standard texts of the day, the old Cicero, *De inventione,* and the so-called new Cicero, the *Rhetorica ad Herennium.* Thereafter, in a public ceremony and examination at the cathedral, the candidate received his doctorate in rhetoric from the bishop of Pavia. Not satisfied with one doctorate, Travesi sought the highest degree in the other two parts of the trivium, making a comment and exposition on a portion of Priscian, a standard ancient grammarian, and on a part of Aristotle's *Prior and Posterior Analytics,* the standard university logical text. By 1375, having gained all three doctorates, Travesi became himself an examiner of other students and took the post of extraordinary lecturer in arts. This position below the rank of ordinary, or regular, professor, required the giving of optional lectures, usually in the afternoon, to students who needed instruction in addition to the regular course given in the morning. Late in the Trecento the lord of Lombardy, Giangaleazzo Visconti, called Travesi to the position of lecturer in grammar, rhetoric, and classical authors at the University of Pavia. At the same time, Travesi kept private students in his own home, providing them with instruction in the rudiments of Latin grammar while he taught more advanced subjects at the university. Thus, at Pavia near the end of the fourteenth century, the beginning course was the same as the one Giovanni Conversini had studied at the middle of the century. Beginners worked on the basic Latin grammar and the Psalter, while the next grade, called Donatists, studied the Donatus minor, introductory catechism on the eight parts of speech of the late antique grammarian. The end of grammatical study came with the Christian texts mentioned above, together with certain medieval authors, such as the *Doctrinale* of Alexander of Villedieu and Priscian's extensive *Institutiones grammaticae,* which illustrated the parts of speech and points of syntax with copious quotations from standard school authors. Next Travesi instructed his pupils in the so-called *magni auctores,* the Latin greats, including Vergil, Ovid, Horace, Lucan, Statius, and the tragedies of Seneca, leaving instruction in rhetoric to another professor. Thus did this minor humanist spend his life in Pavia until his death in 1418.

This basic Latin curriculum survived well into the fifteenth century, to judge from an inventory of the private library of a schoolmaster in Cividale in northeastern Italy, one Giovanni d'Amato, who died in 1430. The testament of this obscure teacher in the communal school of Cividale gives an insight into the texts owned and presumably used in teaching, and to classical and modern authors studied or at least read by Giovanni himself. Among grammar texts all the medieval favorites are present: Donatus, Priscian, Prosper of Aquitane's *Sententiae*, Évrard de Béthune's *Grecismus,* from the twelfth century, and a grammatical work by Albertus Magnus from the thirteenth. Reference works and other texts included Nonius Marcellus's *De proprietate vocabulorum,* Boethius's *De disciplina scholarium,* Geoffrey of Vinsauf's *Poetria nova,* and John of Garland's logical text, *De modis significandi.* From the ancient poets, Giovanni owned Vergil's *Aeneid,* Statius's *Thebaid,* Horace's poetry, and works by Ovid and Lucan—the canonical five poets of Dante's Florence. In addition, there were copies of Cicero's orations and certain of Seneca's moral essays. From more recent authors he owned the rhetorical works of Bene of Florence, works of grammar by Francesco da Buti and Guarino of Verona, Petrarch's *De vita solitaria,* Boccaccio's *De genealogia deorum,* and several works by Giovanni Conversini, including the *Drammalogia* and his autobiography, *Rationarium vite.* Though interested in the earlier generation of Italian humanists, Giovanni d'Amato possessed for teaching Latin grammar and authors the basic library of thirteenth-century schools in Florence, Arezzo, or Bologna.

*   *   *

The strains and difficulties of being a good schoolmaster and the ambiguous standing of the learned humanist in the public world were not lost on the humanists themselves. Both Petrarch and Giovanni Conversini treated the theme of schoolmastering and the humanist educator in their major works. In his philosophical treatise, *De remediis utriusque fortune* or *On the Remedies for Both Sorts of Fortune,* Petrarch devotes two dialogues to refuting the supposed benefits of being a great teacher or having fine students.[8] Here Petrarch argues that a fine schoolmaster may have only dullards as students, or, conversely, that fine students, such as Vergil, really need no formal instruction to achieve their predestined greatness. In a famous case, Cicero wasted a superb education on his degenerate son, whom no amount of education would have saved from being a drunkard and a fool. In another dialogue (1.82), Petrarch has reason show that even a great master may be unequal to the task, for at the same time he has to "profit the child, to please the parents, and to render account to the commonwealth."[9]

In his discussion of seemingly adverse fortune, in a mirror image of the earlier dialogues, Petrarch treats the stock figure of an unlearned schoolmaster and of the inept young pupil, vainly proud of what are in reality his very meager accomplishments. The upshot is that Petrarch urges on the schoolmaster the Stoic acceptance of the slow, the nasty boy as the usual pupil. Overdrawn no doubt for Petrarch's purposes in depicting the necessity of accepting adverse fortune, still these dialogues present the humanist teacher as many in the Trecento saw him—a sad figure burdened with unruly charges, beating Latin into intractable students for little pay.

Others, such as Giovanni Conversini, who had themselves spent most of their lives teaching school, attempted to portray the function of master in a more favorable light. His *Dialogue on the Preferable Way of Life,* written in 1404, is cast as a series of discussions between a Paduan and a Venetian on matters of mutual concern arising from the author's recent dismissal from the Carrara court.[10] In arguing that it was no demotion for Giovanni to change from courtier to schoolmaster after leaving the employ of the Carrara lord, the pair move to a discussion of the difference in status and accomplishment of a lord, or political leader (*dominus*) and schoolmaster, or learned scholar (*magister*). The argument put forth by the Paduan is completely in favor of the superiority of the life of scholarship, learning, and contemplation over that of politics, governing, and activity. He points out that a leader may easily lose his political power, or even be stupid and ignorant, while a master by definition must possess learning, a quality that he can never lose. Further, through education, a master may aid the leader to rule the commonwealth well, and polish rusty minds to high wisdom. In arguing for the greatness of learning and contemplation, he states:

> How much the office of master excels in greatness is evident also in that every pursuit of learning has reference to either practice or theory, one of which is perfected in knowledge of truth, the other in operation. From these also comes the twofold function of life, the active and the contemplative. Concerning the superiority of the life of contemplation, there ought not to be any doubt, because of Christ's praise of Mary. Furthermore, a very learned man demonstrated the same thing in his *Consolation of Philosophy* by placing books in the right hand and a scepter in the left. This means that the vocation of government is designed on the left, and that of study on the right. Since government gives the name of lord, and study the name of master, the primacy of the position of master is clear.[11]

This strange argument from Scripture and Boethius for the superiority of the master over the lord leads to other correspondences: wisdom over action, education over law, and our rational, bright natures over our bodily, dark ones. Finally, the Paduan argues for the greatness of teaching, the need for the ruler to support scholarship and learning through patronage. The result is a convincing (if self-serving) argument for the need of learned men in government, and for the disinterested patronage of humanists for the general good they confer.

*　　*　　*

At the same time that Giovanni Conversini was completing this dialogue, his younger friend and fellow tutor at the same Carrara court in Padua, Pier Paolo Vergerio the Elder (1370–1444), was beginning to circulate what was to become the most influential educational tract of the Renaissance, *De ingenuis moribus*. Written in 1403 for Ubertino of Carrara— son of the ruling *signore* of Padua, Francesco Novello—who was to be executed in a Venetian prison three years later, this treatise embodied the program for the humanist concept of education.[12] But Vergerio's programmatic definition of the humanist education was in many ways only a reworking of the older concept of the seven liberal arts, the verbal arts of the trivium and the quantitative arts of the quadrivium. In his scheme of education Vergerio did, however, ascribe a new importance to history and moral philosophy. For to the arts of communication, of grammar and rhetoric, informed by the argumentation gained from logic, Vergerio added history as the source of all knowledge of human achievement and moral philosophy as a guide to right conduct in this life. In summarizing his position Vergerio wrote:

> By philosophy we learn the essential truth of things, which by eloquence we so exhibit in orderly adornment as to bring conviction to differing minds. And history provides the light of experience—a cumulative wisdom fit to supplement the force of reason and the persuasion of eloquence. For we allow that soundness of judgment, wisdom of speech, and integrity of conduct are the marks of a truly liberal temper.[13]

For teaching these subjects to a child, Vergerio also advised a novel method. He posited differing aptitudes for differing children and, hence, suggested that instruction needed to be tailored to the individual child. In general two great mistakes were made in instruction: too much material was presented at one time and the treatment was often too superficial. Vergerio remedied this situation by suggesting that one subject be taught at a time—thus, the student would be able to devote all energy to one discipline before moving on to another.

In this treatment Vergerio also evaluated the ancient Greek ideal of education for his new program. Of the four subjects of Greek education—literature, gymnastics, music, and drawing—Vergerio excluded the last. He placed poetry on a par with music and extended gymnastics to include the martial arts. Vergerio saw the future leaders of Italian city-states as military leaders and advised physical endurance and skill at arms as prerequisite for success in adult life. Hence, luxury and abundance of goods were to be avoided, while the ideal pupil devoted himself to bodily exercise and the study of letters. Thus, Vergerio counseled the development of the complete person, trained in body as well as mind, in morality as well as literature. But in view of the popularity of this treatise (at least one hundred manuscript copies survive and more than thirty printed editions appeared before the end of the fifteenth century), it must have appealed to more than just the scions of the ruling dynasties of Renaissance city-states. Recently David Robey has suggested that *De ingenuis moribus* has its value in advancing the classical revival to a new level.[14] Previous discussion of the study of the classics had always stressed their study in relation to Christian doctrine. But in this treatise, Robey suggests, there is no "attempt to justify secular learning against the criticisms of the church fathers or in relation to biblical beliefs; the assumption that secular learning is intrinsically desirable is at no point either explicitly or implicitly called into question."[15] In other words, Vergerio separated for the first time the study of the classics from their medieval Christian coloring. In so doing, he created an educational program that was to enjoy an enormous popularity among those pursuing learning for its own sake as well as those motivated by Vergerio's civic ideals.

Back in Florence, Vergerio's older friend and mentor, the chancellor Coluccio Salutati (1331–1406), was forced to respond to just the sort of attacks on the new learning that Vergerio was blithely disregarding in his treatise. Two Florentine clerics, Giovanni of San Miniato and the Dominican friar, Giovanni Dominici, had criticized Salutati's enthusiasm for reading the ancient pagan poets. In two letters replying to these attacks Salutati developed his own rationale for liberal studies, arguing the essential harmony of Christian teaching, especially that of the Bible and great church fathers, with the insights of the great Roman poets—Vergil, Horace, and Ovid. Further, the liberal arts were themselves merely propaedeutic to the ends of greater and higher understanding. As such they were free, according to Salutati, of any values that might impair the living of a Christian life, of acting against the teachings of the Bible. Finally, ancient poets wrote with a twofold meaning, and since God's word was expressed precisely in these two ways, the fictions of poetry were an indispensable aid in the understanding of Christian truth.[16]

*　　*　　*

To Salutati's defense of the liberal arts as an aid to Christian living and Vergerio's new program of a secular classical education founded mainly on Roman authors, there was added at the turn of the fifteenth century the possibility of education in a new body of classics: ancient Greek authors from Homer to Plutarch. Interest in the Greek classics had been keen among earlier generations of Italian humanists: both Petrarch and Boccaccio had commissioned translations of Homer, and Salutati had developed an early interest in Plutarch's *Moralia* and *Vitae*. Humanists saw, too, the need for fresh Latin translations of the works of Aristotle and of many of Plato's dialogues that were not yet available in any western language. Instruction in Greek grammar and literature was introduced in Italy by the Byzantine diplomat Manuel Chrysoloras, who came to the West as an ambassador for his emperor and was then persuaded by Salutati to lecture in Florence from 1397 to 1400. Here Chrysoloras numbered among his students of Greek Vergerio, Guarino of Verona, Leonardo Bruni, Roberto Rossi, Uberto Decembrio, and others. The result of this brief university teaching of Greek literature was the training of native Italian Hellenists who were to continue the work of translating the Greek classics and of instruction in Greek grammar on their own. To this twofold program, Chrysoloras himself contributed an elementary Greek grammar, *Erotemata,* cast in the usual question-and-answer form. And translations followed in profusion from Chrysoloras's circle of students: Leonardo Bruni was foremost in this endeavor, contributing Latin versions of works of Greek Fathers as well as of works by Xenophon, Aristotle, and Plutarch. For the next half-century translations of the Greek classics continued to appear, so that by 1475 Latin versions of most of the Greek authors were available to the scholarly public, and training in Greek grammar became a standard facet of humanist education.[17]

*　　*　　*

The institutional framework of the new educational ideas was probably first the *contubernium,* the boarding school within the master's house, where daily living and instruction in the Latin classics were thoroughly mixed. This arrangement had been usual for the great schoolmasters of the Trecento, such as Giovanni Conversini of Ravenna in Padua, 1378–81 and after 1391. A close connection between living and learning also received impetus on the university level with the establishment of a collegial system at many Italian universities in the late fourteenth century.[18] Hence, the new idea of classical study, put forth by Vergerio and others, found supporters in both the Italian university and the courts and boarding schools of the early Renaissance.

The career of the Latin grammar teacher Gasparino Barzizza (1360–1430) admirably demonstrates that the same scholar-teacher could hold positions in both the university and the Latin school world. Barzizza received some of his education at Padua under Giovanni Conversini and later at Pavia and was perhaps the last product of the older scholastic education, with its set medieval authors and emphasis on Christian morality. Barzizza taught afterward in his own household school in Verona and as a tutor in the Visconti court in Pavia before settling at Padua in 1407 as a university lecturer. There Barzizza instituted new grammatical and rhetorical instruction based on the study of Cicero's works as models and a new approach to Latin grammar. Barzizza introduced the study of grammar and letters to boys as preparation for the arts course of the university. He broke down the discipline into four parts—orthography, prosody, etymology, and syntax—thereby reworking but not completely overturning the older scholastic methods. In addition to his instruction in grammar, Barzizza sought in the university setting to introduce a searching reappraisal of the language, literature, and culture of classical antiquity to mature students. At the same time, he based Latin prose composition on the Ciceronian model, thus initiating debate on the correct model for Latin style that was to continue into the high Renaissance.[19]

The most famous examples of schools that attempted this union of philosophy and rhetoric in the education of the Italian elite were the establishments of Vittorino da Feltre (1370–1446) at Mantua and Guarino of Verona (1374–1460) at Ferrara.[20] Both of these humanists had studied under Giovanni Conversini of Ravenna at Padua in the late Trecento; both had mastered Greek, though Guarino was far more proficient in that language than Vittorino; and both had taught in communal Latin schools and household schools before establishing their famous boarding schools attached to the courts of the Gonzaga dynasty and the Este of Ferrara, respectively. In fact both the famous *Giocosa* of Vittorino and the school of Guarino at Ferrara grew out of the older tradition of hiring eminent humanists as tutors to the scions of leading Renaissance dynasties. Both, too, followed in method and spirit the prescriptions of Vergerio on the education of young noblemen outlined above. Finally, both knew, admired, and emulated the new Latin curriculum as developed by Gasparino Barzizza at Padua. But in practice, and to some extent in theory, the schools of Vittorino and Guarino differed.

Vittorino da Feltre's early instruction had been in mathematics and geometry as much as grammar and Latin authors, so he maintained a central place for these studies in the program of *La Giocosa*. Vittorino's formative years as a teacher were spent in Padua where he set up his own *contubernium*, numbering among his students the Greek émigré scholar George of Trebizond and the Venetian aristocrat Francesco Barbaro. In this context Vittorino was much influenced by the new works of Cicero then being discovered: the complete text of his most detailed work of rhetorical theory, *De oratore*, and his little-known orations as commented upon by the Vicentine humanist Antonio Loschi. Soon a devotee of Cicero, Vittorino departed from Padua for Venice soon after his mentor Gasparino Barzizza left for Pavia. In 1423 he accepted a call as tutor to the Gonzaga court at Mantua. There Vittorino included among his students some of the future political and intellectual leaders of Italy, including the condottiere Federigo da Montefeltro and the philosopher and philologist Lorenzo Valla. Setting up school in a spacious but sparsely furnished palace, *La Giocosa*, Vittorino insisted on temperance in eating and drinking, regular hours, and cold rooms, but he refrained from the use of corporal punishment. He held that artificial heat pampered the young student, so he permitted no fires; he also insisted on regular exercise and silence at meals while ancient authors were read aloud to his pupils.

Vittorino's school required the use of Latin from the beginning in speech as well as in writing, though Italian was permitted in informal conversation and on the playing fields. Latin grammar was taught by dictation and recitation, requiring that large portions of major authors, especially Vergil, be committed to memory. Memorization was followed by detailed comment on the poets Lucan and Ovid, with the teacher first giving attention to the sense of words, then style, rhythm, allusions, and character. History and moral philosophy were taught from Valerius Maximus, Caesar, Livy, and Cicero, with similar attention to detailed understanding. Accent, quantity, and enunciation of Latin poetry and prose were ensured by requiring that passages of Vergil and Cicero be memorized. After Latin came Greek grammar, taught from the medieval texts as well as from Chrysoloras's recent *Erotemata*. In some cases Greek authors were consciously chosen to parallel reading in Latin genres: Homer complemented Vergil in epic poetry, Demosthenes matched with Cicero in rhetoric. In other cases there was no such parallelism: the historians were Xenophon and Herodotus, while Aristophanes and the tragedies represented drama. (Thucydides was as yet little studied as a Greek historian, just as the Roman historian Tacitus was neglected.) After these authors came the study of Stoic philosophers and especially the works of Plato and Aristotle. Rounding out these studies was rigorous physical education and a daily regimen founded on self-restraint and the molding of character. Although Vittorino's school did help to educate important scholars like Lorenzo Valla and Filippo Filelfo, its main emphasis was on the training of the future Gonzaga lords of Mantua and other Italian princes.

After Latin study under Conversini and Barzizza at Padua and Greek under Chrysoloras at Constantinople, Guarino made his early reputation as an accurate translator of the Greek classics and as tutor to such Venetian patricians as Francesco Barbaro, who himself made Latin translations of Plutarch under Guarino's guidance and wrote a widely read treatise on wifely duties (*De re uxoria*), which borrowed most of its ideas on household management and child rearing from Plutarch's *Moralia*. After returning for a time to run a household in his native Verona, Guarino answered the call to set up a school at the Este court in Ferrara as a tutor to the heir apparent, Leonello, and other noble boys of the region. Although Guarino's school always numbered future princes among its pupils, there was more emphasis here than at Mantua on the training of scholars for professional careers in law, administration, and the teaching of the *studia humanitatis*.[21] Thus Guarino's school was closer to contemporary university standards of humanistic scholarship than any of the other boarding schools.

Guarino himself left few records of his methods, but the curriculum of the school at Ferrara is recorded in a general treatise on studies (*De ordine docendi et studendi*) composed in 1459 by his son Battista Guarini.[22] In this handbook the study of Latin grammar is divided into two parts, roughly corresponding to method (*methodice*) and content (*historice*). In the beginning, Latin grammar and the parts of speech were studied and continuous prose composition taught, all from Guarino's own manual, *Regulae*. Memorization of parts of Vergil was required, but for examples of correct style he had recourse to such ancient textbooks as Priscian's *Institutiones grammaticae*. After Latin came (as under Vittorino) the study of the Greek language and literature, with emphasis on the fact that the Greek genres should provide models for the Latin as they had in antiquity. For example, the reading of Homer, the tragedians, and Aristophanes would provide a better understanding of Vergil, Seneca, Plautus, and Terence. The part on content (*historice*) encouraged the reading of both prose and poetry: starting with Valerius Maximus, the student progressed to the canonical poets of the scholastic age: Vergil, Statius, Lucan, and Ovid's *Metamorphoses*. Cicero's orations and dialogues formed the basis for the study of rhetoric and moral philosophy, while increasingly Greek authors formed the basis for the sciences: Strabo in geography and Ptolemy in astronomy. Advanced students were encouraged to engage in independent study with a view to tutoring, on the premise that a student learns best if he knows that he must teach the subject some day.[23] The general rule was to reserve part of each day for study so that the student would develop a love of books used at leisure, and thus a lifelong habit of private reading and interest in humanistic studies.

*   *   *

Not all parts of the Italian population received these new studies with the same enthusiasm. Although the daughters of the Mantuan aristocracy were permitted to frequent the school of Vittorino, in general women were denied access to humanistic learning. Leonardo Bruni did write about 1405 a treatise on women's education (*De studiis et literis*), addressed to Battista Montefeltro Malatesta, but he specifically charged that her program of studies must differ from that of a man.[24] Battista was urged to start her studies with a sound and thorough knowledge of Latin, based on the grammarians Donatus, Servius, and Priscian, but her next reading should be in the works of the church fathers. Certain classical authors—Cicero, Vergil, Livy, and Sallust—were then advised, but the study of rhetoric was expressly forbidden as both unbecoming and useless (for a woman in the Renaissance would never be able to make a public speech).[25] The history of Italy and tales of achievements of kings and peoples were encouraged; besides, it was easy to understand and would provide a sense of good style. In sum, knowledge and the power of expression were held to be the two sides of learning, though these accomplishments addressed more the needs of men than those of women.

*   *   *

For some scholars, notably Eugenio Garin, the new humanistic education brought about a new human ideal, the complete man, good citizen, and if need be a good soldier, who was at the same time a man of culture, taste, and discernment.[26] This portrait may have been the ideal for some students in the fifteenth century, but generally education, even humanistic education, had a more practical bent. At Venice, for example, the school at the Rialto, with its emphasis on the abacus, Aristotelian science, and practical Latin prose, remained active until well into the fifteenth century and in general hostile to the aims of humanistic education.[27] Further, after the changes in Latin curriculum under Gasparino Barzizza, the University of Padua became a conservative center of education for the Venetian aristocracy, concentrating on law and medicine. And the most popular treatise by an Italian humanist at mid-century, *De liberorum educatione* by Aeneas Silvius Piccolomini, the future Pope Pius II, was written as a manual of instruction for a future king of Bohemia and Hungary.[28] This work, along with the contemporary treatise of Maffeo Vegio, repeated the ideas of Vergerio and the practices of Vittorino da Feltre and Guarino of Verona established decades before. In short, humanist education as a program of study for the so-called "universal man" attracted only a few adherents.

Its value lay rather in establishing a radically new system of education for the professional scholars, and to a lesser extent for professionals in law, medicine, and government. The ideas put forth by Vergerio and his followers on the knowledge of both Greek and Latin and on a new Latin style derived from the study and memorization of the best of the Roman authors. The new Latin, based primarily but not exclusively on Cicero, now known in his complete modern corpus, led, by the end of the fifteenth century, to a diction and syntax unmistakably classical. The result was the emergence of a new type of university student, the *humanista*, alongside the older teachers and students of Roman and canon law, *civilista* and *canonista*, and of the liberal arts, *artista*.[29] By the beginning of the next century the humanist (as a type of student) was a fixture in the university system and as a professional quite often (as the statistics provided at the beginning of this essay suggest) a schoolmaster or university lecturer. But both culmination and first repudiation of this new educational ideal occurred north of the Alps. The ideal reached its fruition in Erasmus's treatises, especially his *De copia*, which became the standard Latin manual for humanist study.[30] The repudiation came with the Lutheran Reformation, when the basic purpose of classical learning was put to new and original use—the training of educated laymen for offices in the new Protestant states and even more of ministers to preach the Gospel and the theology of the reformers.[31] The new humanist education exerted an enormous influence in Europe and beyond. But that education, establishing a finer and more scholarly appreciation of antiquity in all its facets, was over the centuries put to many strange and novel purposes that the humanists of the Italian Renaissance could themselves never have imagined.

NOTES

1. See M. Cosenza, *Biographical and Bibliographical Dictionary of Italian Humanists of the World of Classical Scholarship, 1300–1800,* vol. 5 (Boston, 1967), synopsis, passim. I am indebted to my son, Benjamin G. Kohl, Jr., for compiling the statistics upon which this figure is based.
2. G. Villani, *Cronica* 11.94, ed. F. G. Dragomanni (Florence, 1845), 3:324, cited by C. T. Davis, "Education in Dante's Florence," *Speculum* 40 (1965): 415.
3. For thirteenth-century Italian education, see H. Wieruszowski, "Rhetoric and the Classics in Italian Education of the Thirteenth Century," in her *Politics and Culture of Medieval Spain and Italy* (Rome, 1971), 589–624. On Dante's knowledge of the classics, see, most conveniently, E. Moore, *Studies in Dante, First Series, Scripture and Classical Authors in Dante* (Oxford, 1896; reprinted with new intro. by C. Hardie, Oxford 1969).
4. For a description of the texts of medieval, scholastic Latin education, see E. Garin, ed., *Il pensiero pedagogico dell'umanesimo* (Florence, 1958), 92–103.
5. On university training in the arts and rhetoric in the early fourteenth century, see N. G. Siraisi, *Arts and Sciences at Padua: The Studium of Padua Before 1350* (Toronto, 1973), chaps. 2–3; and J. R. Banker, "The Ars Dictaminis and Rhetorical Textbooks at the Bolognese University in the Fourteenth Century," *Mediaevalia et humanistica* n.s. 5 (1974): 153–68.
6. On the Paduan prehumanists, see R. Weiss, "The Dawn of Humanism in Italy," *Bulletin of the Institute of Historical Research* 42 (1969): 1–16, and literature there cited.
7. The following discussions are based on the accounts in R. Sabbadini, *Giovanni da Ravenna, insigne figura d'umanista (1343–1406)* (Como, 1924); V. Rossi, "Un grammatico cremonese [Travesi] a Pavia nella prima età del Rinascimento," *Bollettino della Società Pavese di storia patria* 1 (1901): 16–46; and A. Battistella, "Un inventario d'un maestro friuliano del Quattrocento," *Memorie storiche foroguiliesi* 21 (1925): 137–59.
8. I used the Elizabethan translation of *De remediis,* Petrarch, *Phisicke Against Fortune,* trans. T. Twyne (London, 1579; reprinted with intro. by B. G. Kohl, Delmar, NY, 1980), fols. 103–4v, 216v–18.
9. Ibid., fol. 104v.
10. See Giovanni Conversini of Ravenna, *Dragmalogia de eligibili vite genere,* ed. and trans. H. L. Eaker, intro. and notes B. G. Kohl (London and Lewisburg, PA, 1980).
11. Ibid., 151.
12. The treatise is translated in *Vittorino da Feltre and Other Humanist Educators:* ed. W. H. Woodward (Cambridge, 1897; reprinted with intro. by E. F. Rice, Jr., New York, 1963), 93–118.
13. Ibid., 106–7.

14. D. Robey, "Humanism and Education in the Early Quattrocento: The *De ingenuis moribus* of P. P. Vergerio," *Bibliothèque d'humanisme et Renaissance* 42 (1980): 27–58.
15. Ibid., 56.
16. Salutati's texts are available in English translation in *Humanism and Tyranny: Studies in the Italian Trecento,* ed. E. Emerton (Cambridge, MA. 1925), 312–41, 344–77.
17. On Chrysoloras and the introduction of Greek studies in Italy, see I. Thompson, "Manuel Chrysoloras and the Early Italian Renaissance," *Greek, Roman and Byzantine Studies* 7 (1966): 63–82, and numerous studies by D. J. Geanakoplos, most recently his *Interaction of the "Sibling" Byzantine and Western Cultures in the Middle Ages and Italian Renaissance (330–1600)* (New Haven, 1976).
18. See Sabbadini, *Giovanni da Ravenna,* chaps. 6, 9; and on the colleges, see P. Kibre, *Scholarly Privileges in the Middle Ages* (Cambridge, MA, 1962), 66–68.
19. See the recent monograph by R. G. G. Mercer, *The Teaching of Gasparino Barzizza with Special Reference to His Place in Paduan Humanism* (London, 1979).
20. On Vittorino, see *Vittorino da Feltre,* ed. Woodward, 1–92, and on Guarino, W. H. Woodward, *Studies in Education During the Age of the Renaissance, 1400–1600* (Cambridge, 1906, reprinted New York, 1967), 26–47.
21. Woodward, *Studies in Education,* 34.
22. English version in *Vittorino da Feltre,* ed. Woodward, 159–78.
23. See ibid., 172.
24. English version ibid., 123–33.
25. Bruni proved incorrect in this conclusion. See now on the role of the learned woman in Quattrocento Italy, *Her Immaculate Hand: Selected Works by and About the Women Humanists of Quattrocento Italy,* ed. M. L. King and A. Rabil, Jr. (Binghamton, NY, 1983).
26. See, for instance, E. Garin, *Educazione umanistica in Italia* (Bari, 1966), 7ff.; and idem, *Italian Humanism: Philosophy and Civic Life in the Renaissance,* trans. P. Munz (New York, 1965), 77.
27. On schools in Venice, see J. B. Ross, "Venetian Schools and Teachers, Fourteenth to Early Sixteenth Century: A Survey and a Study of Giovanni Battista Egnazio," *Renaissance Quarterly* 29 (1976): 521–66.
28. English text of this treatise in *Vittorino da Feltre,* ed. Woodward, 136–58, and for discussion of Piccolomini's ideas, see S. G. Santayana, *Two Renaissance Educators: Alberti and Piccolomini* (Boston, 1930), 95–114.
29. See A. Campana, "The Origin of the Word 'Humanist,' " *Journal of the Warburg and Courtauld Institutes* 9 (1946): 60–73, and the discussion in P. O. Kristeller, *Renaissance Thought: The Classic, Scholastic, and Humanist Strains* (New York, 1961), 9–13.
30. See R. R. Bolgar, *The Classical Heritage and Its Beneficiaries* (Cambridge, 1954), chaps. 7–8, and for Erasmus's treatise in English, *De copia/De ra-*

tione studii, ed. and trans. C. R. Thompson, in *Collected Works of Erasmus,* vol. 24 (Toronto, 1978).

31. On Lutheran theories of education, see now G. Strauss, *Luther's House of Learning: Indoctrination of the Young in the German Reformation* (Baltimore and London, 1978).

28 ❧ QUATTROCENTO HUMANISM AND CLASSICAL SCHOLARSHIP
Anthony Grafton

T HE HUMANISTS OF THE PERIOD 1400 TO 1460 WISHED ABOVE all to revive classical Latin culture.[1] In pursuit of this goal they hunted down, corrected, and copied manuscripts of previously little-known texts. They translated Greek works that filled gaps in the Latin culture of their time—above all, works of history, geography, and moral philosophy. They wrote their own treatises on grammar, usage, and style, ranging in size and originality from Guarino of Verona's various brief textbooks to Lorenzo Valla's *Elegantiae* and Giovanni Tortelli's *De orthographia,* in which independent learning and acute criticism were combined to produce grammatical works more sophisticated and comprehensive than those the ancients themselves had compiled.[2] They applied the factual and stylistic knowledge they had acquired in writing letters, dialogues, polemical pamphlets, and histories of their cities and even of all Italy.

The emendation and interpretation of particular texts naturally held a relatively minor place in this panoply of interests. Commentaries were written, but for the most part only on texts that could be used in teaching rhetoric: Cicero's speeches on the one hand, the manuals of Quintilian and the author of the *Rhetorica ad Herennium* on the other.[3] The commentators aimed to produce not independent works of scholarship but simple guides to the texts; they were interested not in technical problems of exegesis but in showing their students how to grasp the rhetorical structure that an author had employed. And, like most arts teachers throughout history, they did not make any pretense of originality. Where possible, they borrowed the matter and even the words of their comments directly from ancient and twelfth-century commentaries on the same texts.

When the early humanists addressed themselves to specific scholarly problems, moreover, they did so in a social context highly charged with

Earlier versions of this essay appeared in the *Journal of the Warburg and Courtauld Institutes* 40 (1977), and as chapter 1 of A. Grafton, *Joseph Scaliger: A Study in the History of Classical Scholarship,* vol. 1 (Oxford, 1983). It is reprinted here by permission of the editors of the *Journal* and of the Oxford-Warburg series of monographs.

personal and intellectual rivalry. The humanists tended to emend their texts in semipublic sessions—the circles that met in both Florence and Naples during the 1430s and 1440s to discuss critical problems in Livy are famous. Membership in these groups was a path to fame and patronage, but it was won less by solidity of results than by eloquent delivery and facility in argument. And in any case, such gatherings did not confine their discussions to questions of fact or interpretation. In 1450, for example, Valla and George of Trebizond held a day-long disputation about a remarkable topic, which had much exercised Livy: had Alexander the Great chanced to have a battle with the Romans, who would have won?[4] In this context, the emendation and the interpretation of texts were not independent activities. They formed part of the humanist's arsenal of techniques for public disputation. Philology was very literally the handmaiden of rhetoric, and it served not so much to promote the advancement of knowledge as to discredit particular humanists in the eyes of a circumscribed audience of patrons and other humanists. It is no accident that Valla's *Emendationes* were published as one part of a much larger polemical work against his detractors.[5]

Even when the humanists got down to the discussion of a specific passage, it was inevitable that conjectural emendation would attract much of their energy. The elegant restoration of sense to corrupt passages was the field in which talent and intellect could make themselves most apparent. Mere explication of difficulties or collation of manuscripts could never create as strong an impression of effortless ingenuity. It was in this field that Lorenzo Valla first distinguished himself among his contemporaries; and many of the emendations he devised still win modern classicists' respect. But Valla's concentration on conjectural emendation limited the range and influence of his achievement. Conjectural emendation is a matter of talent. It can be practiced with great success by scholars who have neither a strong intellect nor a historical understanding of the texts they correct, as long as they have a good knowledge of the language and a knack for solving puzzles. Knacks, however, cannot be explained or taught. They obviously cannot become the basis for professional training and practice. And in any case, conjectural emendation can solve only a limited number of textual problems. Brilliant though they were, Valla's Livian conjectures were a purely personal achievement. There was no generally applicable method that underlay them and that could be passed on to disciples or grasped by readers.[6]

Purely technical factors limited the influence of Valla's work even more. On the one hand, the range of materials available to Valla and his contemporaries was necessarily narrow, in view of the difficulties of travel and the instability of libraries. Only a lucky chance gave Valla access to

Petrarch's codex of Livy. In his day, the great public libraries did not yet exist. Extensive collation of manuscripts was wildly difficult. Moreover, in a world of manuscripts, the role of collation was at best problematic. There was no uniform base text against which collations could be made. And even when a manuscript had been collated against an older one, one could not publish the variants except by having them copied, and so introducing fresh errors and confusions into the text.[7]

On the other hand, the conditions of publication also served to inhibit the diffusion of new ideas or methods. In 1446 to 1447 Valla put Panormita and Bartolomeo Facio to shame before Alfonso of Naples by demolishing the corrections they had rashly entered in decade 3 of the Codex Regius of Livy. But in 1448 he left Naples for Rome, and his adversaries simply removed the third decade from the manuscript and substituted a new one that did not contain the corrections Valla had shown to be unsound.[8] In an age of manuscripts there could be no proof of what had happened, and readers had no way of knowing on whose side truth stood. Indeed, Valla's own emendations in the Harleian Livy were lost to sight until modern editors of Livy began to examine them. And even his *Emendationes,* highly polemical and intended for publication, did not find readers in Valla's time, but only "at the height of the Cinquecento, because they were then printed"—in short, when a new generation, schooled by others in philological method, was ready to greet in Valla a forerunner but not a master.[9]

*   *   *

After the middle of the century, however, three momentous changes took place in the context and character of humanism. In the first place, humanistically educated princes and prelates began to assemble manuscripts into more or less accessible collections, above all, the new library of the Vatican and the Medicean public library of San Marco in Florence. Most classical manuscripts did not find secure homes at once: the Medicean Vergil and the Codex Bembinus of Terence led active lives of travel until far into the sixteenth century. Moreover, even the richest collections did not always attract scholarly attention. But in Florence and Rome at least, rich and relatively stable lodes of material now offered themselves up to the spade of anyone lucky enough to be given permission to dig them.[10]

In the second place, the invention of printing made possible a new level of precision in textual scholarship. True, the texts that appeared in the first editions of Giovanni Andrea de Bussi and others were corrupt. Certainly they had the misfortune of being reproduced uncritically, and so turned into a permanent vulgate with an unjustified air of authority.[11]

But at least there were now some hundreds of copies of any work that happened to be printed. Humanists all over Italy could now have access to generally uniform copies of most classical texts, and, within a few years, of commentaries on many of them as well. Falsification became harder, though by no means impossible. More important, a rudimentary standardization of references became possible. A printed text provided a standard for collation, and a collation in the margins of one printed book could be transferred to those of another with relative speed and accuracy. Textual commentaries like Ermolao Barbaro the Younger's famous one on Pliny could now be keyed to a specific edition. The very existence of standardized texts ensured that the same critical problems would attract the attention of humanists all over Italy at the same time. Far more humanists than could have crowded into one of Alfonso's *ore del libro* could now engage in collective debate on specific technical points.

Most important of all, a change had taken place in the direction of many humanists' scholarly work.[12] Thanks to the heroic work of the early humanists, one could now master Latin grammar and rhetoric with relatively little expenditure of time and effort—often after only a few years in a grammar school or university arts course. And as these studies lost their challenge, they also lost something of the absorbing interest that they had held for the pioneers of humanist education.

*   *   *

At the same time, a new generation of humanists appeared. The new men were born in the 1430s and 1440s. Domizio Calderini, Giulio Pomponio Leto, Giorgio Merula, Niccolò Perotti, Giovanni Sulpizio, and their like formed the crest of the mid-century new wave. Like other groups of impatient young intellectuals—like Poggio Bracciolini and Niccolò Niccoli fifty years before—they assimilated what their elders had to offer and thereafter took it for granted. Simple prose texts interested them less than Latin poetry—especially the works of the satirists, studded as they were with allusions and obscurities. When they studied prose at all, they preferred the elder Pliny's *Natural History,* as difficult as the verse of the satirists and more rewarding to the student. Unlike their predecessors, they came to maturity in a world in which such recondite interests could be pursued with ease. They grew up accustomed to the existence of humanist schools and arts faculties, in which they expected to find jobs as lecturers. They were also accustomed to the existence of the printing press and expected to serve the printers, not without remuneration, as editors of texts. Their students could be expected to attain a high level of linguistic proficiency quite soon. It is not surprising that the line-by-line commentary soon became the dominant form of humanist literature—

the form by which reputations were lost and won. For it was by writing and publishing commentaries that the men of the new generation could best demonstrate their independence from the work of their immediate predecessors, while at the same time winning their colleagues' attention and serving the needs of their students, who shared their interest in poetry and Pliny.

Considered as a literary form, the detailed commentary had a number of advantages. In the first place, it was itself the revival of an ancient genre. There were many ancient or old line-by-line commentaries on standard authors: Servius on Vergil, Donatus on Terence, Porphyrion and pseudo-Acro on Horace, the old scholia on Juvenal and Persius, the twelfth-century commentaries on Cicero. These works provided the starting point for the earliest humanist commentaries on the works they dealt with; often the humanists did little more than repeat what their ancient predecessors had said, merely taking care to conceal the extent of their indebtedness. The first humanist commentary on Vergil, that by Pomponio Leto, relied very heavily on an interpolated text of Servius; Gaspare de' Tirimbocchi, the first humanist commentator on the *Ibis,* relied equally heavily on the extant scholia.[13] Where there was no ancient or pseudo-ancient commentary, there was sometimes a later one of similar form and method, for example, the twelfth-century commentary by "Alanus" on the *Rhetorica ad Herennium,* which Guarino sedulously pillaged for his lectures.[14] Moreover, even for those commenting on texts that were not adorned with ancient scholia, the ancient commentaries provided an obvious model of style and method; they were readily accessible and at the same time satisfactorily different from the style of the late medieval classicizing friars.[15]

This style had other advantages as well. Line-by-line commentaries inevitably bulk as large as or larger than the texts they treat. The commentator, in other words, was expected to fill a large amount of space. His audience expected him to turn any suitable word or phrase into the occasion for an extended digression: into the etymology of a word, into the formation of compounds from it, into its shades of meaning; most often, perhaps into the justification in terms of formal rhetoric for its appearance in the passage in question. Many digressions departed even farther from the text, into mythological, geographical, antiquarian, and even scientific matters. A commentary on almost any ancient author could thus become an introduction to classical literature, history, and culture. In short, the commentary was a highly flexible instrument of instruction. Here too the humanists followed their ancient models. Servius, in particular, used the medium of a commentary on Vergil to impart quantities of information on almost every conceivable subject.[16]

Finally, this style was attractive to students. Since the commentator felt obliged to gloss every word that might present a difficulty, he generally made his text accessible even to students of mean intelligence or poor preparation. At the same time, the student who could write quickly enough to keep up with his teacher ended up with an invaluable possession. When he himself went out to teach, he could simply base his lectures on those of his teacher and so avoid the trouble of independent preparation. It is hardly surprising that students came to demand lectures of this kind; what student would not have his teacher do all the work? As Martino Filetico, an unwilling practitioner of this style of commentary, wrote: "At that time [ca. 1468–73] certain very learned men had made the young accustomed not to want to listen to anything unless they added a definition on almost every word. . . . I therefore had to follow their customs."[17] The style was long-lived. Angelo Poliziano himself employed various forms of it in his lectures, adapting the content of the excursuses to the needs of his hearers.[18] Its most preposterous result did not appear until 1489, namely, Perotti's *Cornucopiae,* in which a thousand folio columns served to elucidate one book of Martial.

But the style had disadvantages as well as advantages. It forced the commentator to deal with every problem, the boringly simple as well as the interestingly complex. It also forced him to waste time and pages on the donkey-work of listing synonyms—which is all that thousands of the humanists' short glosses amount to.[19] Worst of all, in a period of intense literary competition the commentary made it impossible for its author to shine. For the most noticeable aspect of all the humanists' commentaries is their similarity to one another. Especially in their printed form, the so-called *modus modernus,* the commentaries are nearly indistinguishable. Waves of notes printed in minute type break on all sides of a small island of text set in large roman.[20] Even numerous digressions into one's field of expertise could not make one commentary distinctively superior to its fellows, for they were hidden by the mass of trivial glosses.

*   *   *

In the mid-1470s several humanists became aware of the drawbacks of the exhaustive commentary and began to move away from it. In 1475, for example, Domizio Calderini wrote: "Hereafter, I shall not be much concerned with commentaries." Rather, he explained, he would concentrate on translation from the Greek and on another work,

> which we have entitled "Observations," in three books of which
> the first contains explications of three hundred passages from
> Pliny; the second whatever we have noted as omitted by others in

[explicating] the poets; the third what we have gathered and observed in Cicero, Quintilian, Livy, and all other prose writers.[21]

The pattern that Calderini sketched became the normal one. Instead of continuing to work through every detail of entire texts, he and others began to produce selective treatments of what they described as difficult and interesting passages—books, in short, written by and for scholars; books composed with publication in mind rather than as by-products of teaching. Most of these works took one of two forms. The majority of them consisted of brief sets of annotations on one text. Calderini published an "Explication of certain particularly difficult passages in Propertius"; Filippo Beroaldo the Elder brought out a short collection of "Annotations against Servius"; more than half a dozen others wrote short treatises on selected passages in Pliny.[22] Others were miscellanies of short chapters, modeled above all on the *Noctes Atticae* of Aulus Gellius. Such works represented an effort to break away entirely from the commentary, tied as it was to a single text. Calderini himself published one, in the shape of a few selections "ex tertio libro Observationum"; Beroaldo's first major piece of work was his more or less miscellaneous *Annotationes centum*. It would be wrong to draw too sharp a distinction between the two new sorts of publication. Calderini's *Observationes* were less a methodological departure than an advertisement for himself, in which he quoted from his own commentaries at length and with relish.[23] And even though Beroaldo's preface contained a modish apology for the selective and disorderly character of his *Annotationes*, the work itself was little more than a collection of short treatises, each dealing with several passages in a text; author followed author in a most logical and orderly succession.[24] Even though the genres were not very clearly defined, the works that fell within them bore unmistakable marks of family resemblance. They were short, specialized, and polemical. Many of them were written by humanists at the very beginnings of their careers. And like other manifestoes by intellectuals, before and since, they were intended above all to win reputations for their authors as rapidly as possible—generally at the expense of the reputations of others.

Beroaldo, for example, began his literary career with his *Annotationes contra Servium*. Here he set out, not weighed down as yet by any great baggage of learning, to win a reputation by the simple expedient of abusing the best ancient commentator on Vergil. Some of his points were well worth making. His knowledge of Latin usage, already solid and independent, enabled him to prove that some of the fine lexical distinctions Servius laid down were not supported by the practices of Latin writers.[25] By drawing on Greek historians and geographers, especially

Strabo, he was able to correct Servius on a fair number of miscellaneous points of fact.[26] But much of what Beroaldo had to say was neither original nor enlightening. Often, following Macrobius, he rebuked Servius for failing to recognize Vergil's allusions to esoteric philosophical doctrines: Servius should have known that Vergil was an expert in all forms of *remotior doctrina*. And he could have drawn the material for such explications from the same philosophical sources on which Macrobius had drawn. The duty of a good commentator was to include as many interpretations as possible of the work with which he was concerned; this Servius had failed to do.[27] It is hard to feel much sympathy for a man who criticizes Servius for being too concise. Yet Beroaldo's tactics had a certain logic. By showing where Servius had gone wrong, he could prove that he himself understood perfectly the duties of the commentator. But he could do so without burying the pearls of his—and Macrobius's—cleverness in the mudbank of a full-scale commentary.

Others, less discreet than Beroaldo, aimed their guns at the vulnerable living rather than the honored dead. Giorgio Merula had won his reputation in the 1470s by attacking Domizio Calderini and Francesco Filelfo. In 1481 to 1482 he himself received a vicious broadside from Cornelio Vitelli, who set himself to avenge both Calderini and Martial for Merula's mistreatment of them. He accused Merula of committing wholesale plagiarism, corrupting the texts he set out to correct, and killing Filelfo by his vicious mistreatment of him. Merula, he quipped—and the joke is no unfair indicator of the intellectual qualities of such debates—should really have been named Merdula. And Vitelli was in turn answered by a student of Merula, as well as by Ermolao Barbaro the Younger, whose refusal to discuss Vitelli's objections to Merula was in itself an imposing rebuttal.[28] Often these critics were competing for the support of a limited number of local patrons, which made their quarrels hot and frequent.

At first reading, most of these works reveal few virtues to accompany their obvious vices. Their repugnant moral defects compete with their amateurish scholarship for the reader's disapproval. If their literary form is new, the philological methods employed in them are often old indeed. For their authors were still, for the most part, employed as teachers, and their monographs bear the stamp of their profession. Their methods were formed not in the study but in the lecture hall. They never acquired the habit of full or precise quotation from their sources, for such precision was impossible to attain if they were to lecture comprehensively on the wide variety of topics that their texts suggested. In particular, they seldom quoted Greek extensively, as Greek would have been unintelligible to most of their students and unmanageable for most printers. Instead, they usually provided vague paraphrases, together with imprecise indications of sources. Worse still, like their ancient exemplars, they often invented explanations by back-formation from the texts they claimed to be elucidating: "misinformation is often elicited from the text by aid of unjustified inferences."[29]

When the members of this generation turned from the commentary to the collection of precise *Annotationes,* they did abandon one bad habit that had characterized their lectures. They no longer set out two alternative solutions of a problem without choosing between them—a maddening habit that had characterized the classroom lecture since the Hellenistic period.[30] Indeed, the whole point of their new genre was to show off their ability at solving problems once and for all. Unfortunately, most of them did not abandon their other habits of sloppy, inaccurate citation and unjustified back-formation. Perotti, who tried to be honest, abbreviated the names of the authors he cited even when the resulting forms were ambiguous, for example, "Lu." Moreover, he usually failed to inform his readers whether the verses he cited came to him at first or second hand, though often he was citing not a line from an extant work but a fragment preserved by Festus or Nonius Marcellus, and sometimes he was citing verses from standard works at second hand.[31] Calderini, as A. J. Dunston and S. Timpanaro have shown, knew Plautus only at second hand, though his words suggest firsthand knowledge.[32] Many of Perotti's contemporaries were dishonest as well as sloppy. Pomponio Leto gave out in his lectures that he had a complete text of Ennius. Calderini falsified his notes on Martial to refute a justified attack by Perotti. Worse, he invented a Roman writer, Marius Rusticus, from whom he claimed to derive disquieting information about the youth of Suetonius.[33]

Yet it would be wrong to dismiss these works as unimportant. Their authors were unscrupulous, but by no means ignorant; and they often found that providing some of the new interpretations or information that they promised was an effective polemical tactic. In a more general sense, too, these treatises represented something new and vital: they were the first technical philological treatises since antiquity. This new literary genre made it possible for the humanists to engage in and publish the results of minute research. The existence of this literature proved a vital precondition for the rise of something like a profession of classical philologists. Like the scholarly journals of more recent times, it provided a convenient and inexpensive forum for widespread, technical debates about problems of both fact and method. Only two things were lacking: a literary form entirely divorced from dependence on specific texts and a set of standards by which the value of individual theses could be assessed. In 1489, Poliziano's *Miscellanea* provided both.

*   *   *

Poliziano was following some well-trodden paths. Like all of his contemporaries, he was bent on making a reputation. Like them, he went about this self-imposed task above all by directing fierce polemics against his predecessors. Merula, Calderini, and other representatives of what he called *semidocta sedulitas,* he hammered without mercy. His disdain for competitors in scholarship was equaled in fervor only by his tail-wagging eagerness to praise his patron, Lorenzo de' Medici. These similarities, though important, are less striking than the differences. In scope, method, and results, the *Miscellanea* was a brilliantly original work, which fully deserved to exert widespread influence.

In the first place, the *Miscellanea* provided a novel and extremely versatile form for presenting philological material. Unlike his predecessors, Poliziano set out deliberately to imitate one ancient work, the *Noctes Atticae* of Gellius.[34] And Gellius's work had several features that no humanist before Poliziano had thought to resurrect. It was entirely miscellaneous in character; by imitating it, Poliziano was able to break completely with the commentary tradition while still following a good ancient model. Moreover, it was laid out in an elegant and useful fashion. Each chapter was set off from the others and provided with a summary title; and a list of all the chapters occurred at the beginning of the work. Strange as it may seem, Poliziano's predecessors knew about but failed to imitate these practices. By adopting them, Poliziano made his work much easier than the others to consult; and his creative imitation of Gellius soon found its own imitators among the other humanists, as the form he had recreated became the normal one.

Second, and more important, Poliziano took over from Gellius and greatly elaborated a new set of rules for judging his own and others' attempts to correct and explicate texts. He placed a new emphasis on the quality and quantity of his sources. From the preface onward he attacked his predecessors' methods and treated his own as exemplary. He took great pains to state that he had cited only genuine works by genuine ancient authors:

> But lest those men who are ill employed with leisure think that we
> have drawn [our conclusions] . . . from the dregs, and that we have
> not leaped across the boundaries of the grammarians, we have at
> the outset followed Pliny's example. We have put at the beginning
> the names of the authors—but only ancient and honorable ones—
> by whom these [conclusions] are justified, and from whom we have
> borrowed. But [we have not put down] the names of those whom
> others have only cited, while their works have disappeared, but

those whose treasures we ourselves have handled, through whose writings we have wandered.[35]

Poliziano was hardly the first to claim that his researches had brought to light fascinating new material long hidden in rare sources. Calderini, for example, had this to say of his commentary on the *Ibis:*

> Ovid's work is full of anger and obscurity. As for me, I have gathered either from the Greeks Apollodorus, Lycophron, Pausanias, Strabo, Apollonius and his scholiast, and other writers, or from Latins, whatever seemed relevant to its explication, into the present short work.[36]

But Poliziano turned Calderini's boasts into an indictment:

> Domizio expounded Ovid's *Ibis*. He began by saying that he wrote matter drawn from Apollodorus, Lycophron, Pausanias, Strabo, Apollonius, and other Greeks, and Latins as well. In that commentary he invents many vain and ridiculous things, and makes them up extemporaneously and at his own convenience. By doing so he proves either that he has completely lost his mind, or that, as someone says, there was so great a distance between his mind and his tongue that his mind could not restrain his tongue.[37]

He backed up this tirade by dissecting Calderini's work on one line. Calderini had taken *Ibis* 569 as reading "Utque loquax in equo est elisus guttur Agenor" (And as the talkative Agenor was strangled in the horse). "As the result of a fall from a horse," he explained, "Agenor's hand became stuck in his mouth and he perished."[38] This explanation, Poliziano insisted, was Calderini's own invention. In fact, the line must be emended to read "Utque loquax in equo est elisus guttur acerno" (And as the talkative one was strangled in the maple-wood horse). Citing passages from real sources, Homer and Tryphiodorus, Poliziano explained the line as an allusion to the death of Anticlus, one of the Greeks who had entered Troy in the Trojan horse, whom Odysseus had strangled to prevent him from revealing their presence prematurely.[39] The moral of the episode was clear.

As one would expect, in view of the polemical tendencies we have seen in action, there was nothing new in accusing one's predecessors of inventing sources. Calderini had done the same. In his commentary on Quintilian Valla had referred to an oration of Cicero *pro Scauro.* "Indeed," wrote Calderini,

> I have read in Valerius Maximus and Pedianus that the case of
> Scaurus was tried in Cicero's presence. But I have never read that
> Cicero delivered the oration on his behalf from which Lorenzo
> claims that he drew these words. Nor do I believe that it exists.
> And I am afraid that Lorenzo recited these words following some
> ignoble grammarian, rather than reading them anywhere in
> Cicero.[40]

So much Poliziano might have said. The difference lies in two things: in
the truthfulness of the attacks, and even more in their consistency with
the attacker's actual practices. Calderini's attack was not in fact justified,
for Valla had taken his quotation from the *pro Scauro* from a fairly reliable source: Isidore's *Etymologiae*. Moreover, the commentary of Asconius Pedianus—which Calderini himself cited—clearly indicates that
Cicero delivered a speech *pro Scauro*. More important, Calderini's attack
on Valla was inconsistent with his own practice. For in the very next
section of the *Observationes* he enthusiastically retailed what he had
read about Simonides "in a Greek writer"—"apud Graecum scriptorem."[41] One whose own references were so slipshod had no business
correcting other people's footnotes—and can hardly have been uphold-
ing a personal ideal of full, clear, and accurate citation.

Poliziano normally used the principles by which he judged others.
He identified the sources he drew on with elaborate, almost finicky precision. And even when he quoted a text at second hand, he generally
pointed out that he was doing so and identified the intermediary source.
In 1.91, for example, he quoted some verses of the comic poet Eupolis.
He then wrote: "Now we did not draw these verses of the poet Eupolis
from the original source, since his works have been lost. But we derived
them partly from a remarkably accurate commentator on the Rhetor
Aristides, partly from a letter of the younger Pliny."[42] Poliziano's attacks
on the practices of his predecessors, then, were traditional only in form.
They stemmed not only from a desire to gain a reputation and to destroy
those of others, but also from a genuine desire to reform the current
method of citation. Poliziano's habits in drawing inferences from sources
were as novel as his precision in identifying them. He compared and
evaluated them in a consistently historical way, that is, by establishing
their relations to one another before he drew inferences from them. His
sources presented him with various kinds of problems, some of which
were fairly trivial. For example, he not uncommonly encountered ancient
sources that contradicted one another about historical or mythological
details. The solution in such cases was usually obvious. It was only natural to follow the most authoritative source, which in most cases simply

meant the oldest one. And that was just what he did when, for example, he preferred Homer's testimony about the ages of Achilles and Patroclus to those of Aeschylus and Statius.[43]

*   *   *

So far there is nothing new here. Petrarch had encountered contradictions in his ancient sources while compiling the *De viris illustribus.* Salutati and Bruni had uncovered discrepancies in the ancient histories of republican Rome. Flavio Biondo had found ancient authors contradicting one another about the functions of certain ancient buildings.[44] And all of them had found it possible to resolve such contradictions. They assumed that the older or otherwise more authoritative source was correct. The divergent accounts in other texts must have resulted either from scribal errors, in which case they could be emended, or from simple slips on the part of the less authoritative writer, due to bias or bad memory.[45]

Poliziano, however, saw that even a group of sources that agreed still posed a problem. Given three sources *A, B,* and *C,* all of which agreed on a given point; if *B* and *C* depended entirely on *A* for their information, should they be considered to add any weight to *A*'s testimony? Poliziano insisted that they should not. In other words, even a group of concordant sources must be investigated, and those which were entirely derived from others must be identified and eliminated from consideration. The way to perform such an investigation was to arrange the sources genealogically, and then to pay attention only to the source from which the others were derived.

Poliziano stated this principle in *Miscellanea* 1.39 while explaining a riddle. In *Epistola* 14.74 Ausonius had employed the expression "Cadmi nigellas filias"—"little black daughters of Cadmus." Poliziano explained that it referred to the letters of the alphabet: "For Cadmus was the first to bring letters into Greece from Phoenicia."[46] Since the Latin letters were directly derived from the Greek, Ausonius could refer to them too as "daughters of Cadmus." Poliziano cited Herodotus as his authority for stating that Cadmus had imported the alphabet. He admitted that other ancient writers had said the same. But he argues that all of them were simply repeating what Herodotus had said. Since their testimony was entirely derivative, it must be ignored:

> I omit Pliny and very many others, who say that Cadmus brought them into Greece. For since these different men recalled indiscriminately what they had read in Herodotus, I think it enough to have restored these matters to his authority. For in my opinion the testi-

monies of the ancients should not so much be counted up as weighed.[47]

It is easy to show how original Poliziano's thinking is here. Beroaldo discussed the same riddle from Ausonius in chapter 99 of the *Annotationes*. He solved it in the same way. And he too cited the sources that had informed him about Cadmus and the alphabet:

> He [Ausonius] calls the letters "daughters of Cadmus" because Cadmus is said to have been the inventor of letters. In book 7 of the *Natural History* Pliny says that he brought sixteen letters from Phoenicia into Greece. Therefore the ancient Greeks called the letters Phoenician, according to Herodotus in book 5. The same writer says that he saw "Cadmean letters," very similar to Ionian letters, incised on certain tripods in the temple of Apollo. Furthermore, Cornelius Tacitus avers that Cadmus was the author of letters, while the Greek peoples were still uncultured.[48]

Beroaldo does not investigate the dependence or independence of his sources. Pliny is evidently as reliable as Herodotus, and Herodotus no more reliable than Tacitus. Since they all agree on the main point in question, he cites all of them. And he omits other accounts not because they are derivative but because they seem to him irrelevant.

What Poliziano has done is to view the problem of the reliability of sources from a new direction. For him, the question is no longer, as it was for Beroaldo, simply to amass evidence, but to discriminate, to reduce the number of witnesses that the scholar need take into account. To be sure, we know now that Poliziano's argument was not completely sound. Herodotus was not the sole source for later traditions about the origins of the Greek alphabet, and even as late a writer as Tacitus may preserve useful information not transmitted by older sources. In some sense, then, Beroaldo was "correct" to draw his information eclectically from a wide range of texts. But in this case, as in many in the history of scholarship, it is deceptive to pay too much attention to the validity in modern terms of particular arguments. If Beroaldo was "correct," it was for the wrong reasons. He cited Tacitus not because he had grounds for doing so but because he knew no better. Poliziano, by contrast, was attacking the evidence with a novel tool. And, in view of the texts available to him, there was no reason not to conclude that Herodotus was the sole source on whom later writers had drawn. Considered in its context, Poliziano's overzealous application of a new and valid method is far more important historically than the "correct" results into which Beroaldo blundered. For in Poliziano's hands, systematic source criticism led to a transformation in the central methods of classical philology.[49]

Poliziano's best-known application of his principles was in the field of textual criticism.[50] Here too he strove to arrive at the independent sources from which later ones were wholly derived. When he found what seemed to him to be corruptions in recent manuscripts or printed versions of classical writings, he did not try to emend them by conjecture. He went back to the oldest sources, that is, to the oldest manuscripts. He recognized that they were not free from errors. But he insisted that they were the closest extant approximation to what the ancient authors had really written. The newer texts—notably the printed ones—were removed by more stages of copying from antiquity, and any apparently correct readings they contained were merely the results of attempts at conjectural emendation. Such alluring but historically unjustifiable readings offered the textual critic less of value than did the errors of the old manuscripts, for they at least "preserve some fairly clear traces of the true reading which we must restore. Dishonest scribes have expunged these completely from the new texts."[51]

Poliziano employed this method throughout the *Miscellanea*. In the vulgate text of Vergil, for example, he found *Aeneid* 8.402 in a metrically impossible form: "Quod fieri ferro, liquidove potestur electro." He consulted the Codex Romanus, and, as he wrote: "In that volume, which is in the inner library of the Vatican, which is remarkably old, and written in capitals, you will find not 'potestur' but 'potest,' a word more commonly used."[52] Again, in the vulgate text of Suetonius he was troubled by a meaningless clause in *Claudius* 34: "si aut ornatum, aut pegma, vel quid tale aliud parum cessisset." In what he called the "veri integrique codices," however, he found not "aut ornatum" but "automaton," a reading which made perfect sense: Claudius made his stage carpenters fight in the arena "if a stage machine, or trap, or something else of the sort failed to work." And he took care to identify the codices on whose testimony he relied:

> Look at the Bologna manuscript from the library of St. Dominic, or another one at Florence from the Library of St. Mark . . .; both are old. But there is another one, older than either, which we ourselves now have at home . . . you will find this latter reading in all of them.[53]

To get a clear impression of the number and accuracy of Poliziano's citations of manuscripts, there is no better way than to read the collection of material in Silvia Rizzo, *Il lessico filologico degli umanisti*.[54]

This new method could not have been more in contrast with the practices of Poliziano's predecessors. Beroaldo, for example, relied almost exclusively on conjecture. And even when he cited manuscripts he identified them only in vague terms.[55] Here, for example, is the way he gives the manuscript readings of a line in Juvenal:

The verse is to be read as follows:

> *Turgida nec prodest condita pyxide Lyde* [*Sat.* II.141].

There "condita" is in the ablative and is connected with "pyxide." Quite recently I found that verse written thus in a very old manuscript. And some time ago Angelo Poliziano . . . told me that he had noted the passage written that way in a manuscript of unimpeachable fidelity.[56]

Here is the way Poliziano described the latter manuscript:

We found the same reading [*cacoethes* (*Sat.* VII.52)] in an old manuscript written in Lombardic script, which Francesco Gaddi . . . made available to me for study. But that [other] verse is also as follows in this codex:

> *Turgida nec prodest condita pyxide Lyde.*[57]

Poliziano's description includes the name of the manuscript's owner and a classification of its script. Beroaldo's citation—which is, if anything, unusually precise for him—gives neither.

In most cases the old manuscripts were more trustworthy than the new merely because they were older, and therefore fewer stages of transmission intervened between them and the author. But Poliziano was able to analyze some textual traditions in a more complex and more decisive way. He applied his genealogical method of source criticism to the manuscripts of certain texts and proved that one of them was the parent of the rest. In such cases, he argued, the parent must be the sole source used in establishing the text.

One case, as Timpanaro has shown, was that of Cicero's *Familiares*.[58] Poliziano had at his disposal in the library of St. Mark the ninth-century Vercelli manuscript (Laur. 49,9 = *M*) and a fourteenth-century manuscript, which he wrongly believed might have been written by Petrarch (Laur. 49,7 = *P*). He also consulted an unspecified number of more recent texts. In *Miscellanea* 1.25 he argued that the fourteenth-century manuscript, in which a gathering had been transposed because of an error in binding, was the parent of all the more recent manuscripts, for the same transposition occurred in all of them, without any evidence of physical damage to account for it. He also asserted, without giving the evidence, that the fourteenth-century manuscript was itself a copy of the ninth-century one. And he concluded that since the ninth-century manuscript was the source of all the others, it alone should be employed in correcting the text of the *Familiares*. As he wrote:

> I have obtained a very old volume of Cicero's *Epistolae Familiares* . . . and another one copied from it, as some think, by the hand of Francesco Petrarca. There is much evidence, which I shall now omit, that the one is copied from the other. But the latter manuscript . . . was bound in such a way by a careless bookbinder that we can see from the numbers [of the gatherings] that one gathering has clearly been transposed. Now the book is in the public library of the Medici family. From this one, then, so far as I can tell, are derived all the extant manuscripts of these letters, as if from a spring and fountainhead. And all of them have the text in that ridiculous and confused order which I must now put into proper form and, as it were, restore.[59]

A second case was that of Justinian's *Digest* or *Pandects*. Here Poliziano used a different method to identify one manuscript as the parent of the rest. He received permission through his patron, Lorenzo, to collate the famous Florentine manuscript of the *Digest*. He noticed certain erasures and additions in the preface which, he thought, must have been made "by an author, and one thinking and composing, rather than by a scribe and copyist."[60] And he inferred from these signs that this manuscript must be the very one that Justinian's commissioners first wrote. If the Florentine manuscript was the author's copy, it must obviously be the archetype. Consequently, all texts of the *Digest* ought to be emended in accordance with the text of the Florentine manuscript. In *Miscellanea* 1.41, for example, he replaced the vulgate reading "diffusum" with "diffisum," the reading of the Florentine manuscript, in *Digest* 2.11.2(3): "Et ideo etiam lex xii. tabularum, si iudex vel alteruter ex litigatoribus morbo sontico impediatur, iubet diem iudicii esse diffisum." The passage thus made perfect sense: the Law of the Twelve Tables orders that, if the judge or either of the litigants is prevented by illness from attending court, the day of the trial is to be "postponed" (*diffisum*).[61] Again, in 1.78 Poliziano examined the reading of the Florentine manuscript at *Digest* 1.16.12: "Legatus mandata sibi iurisdictione iudicis dandi ius habet"—"A deputy on whom jurisdiction has been conferred has the right to appoint judges" (trans. S. P. Scott). Here some of the vulgate manuscripts read "ius non habet." Both readings could be supported by parallels from other parts of the *Corpus iuris,* and Accursius had discussed both readings and the juristic problems each of them posed.[62] For Poliziano, however, the passage presented no problem. It could not. If the reading of the archetype made grammatical and juristic sense, it must be right. Divergent readings in later codices could by definition be nothing but alterations introduced by scribes or jurists. As he put it, "in those Florentine Pandects, which, indeed, we believe to be the original ones, there is no negative at all. Therefore the Florentine jurisconsult Accursius, who also had a faulty codex, torments himself—I almost might say wretchedly."[63] In this case elimination of *codices descripti* apparently leads to the elimination of medieval legal science. There was nothing new in attacking medieval jurists—Valla and Beroaldo had done the same.[64] But the method underlying the attack was unprecedented.

Here Poliziano was both imitating and improving on his literary model. Gellius frequently consulted older manuscripts in order to correct errors in newer ones. Thus, he defended a reading in Cicero's fifth oration *In Verrem* in part because he had found it so written in "a copy of unimpeachable fidelity, because it was the result of Tiro's careful scholarship."[65] Again, he argued that scribes had replaced the unfamiliar archaic genitive "facies" with the later form "faciei" in a work by Claudius Quadrigarius. In the oldest manuscripts, he said, he had found the old reading "facies"; in certain "corrupt manuscripts," on the other hand, he had found "facies" erased and "faciei" written in.[66] But Gellius had not cited his evidence with Poliziano's precision, or evaluated it with Poliziano's discernment.

Humanists from Petrarch on had also sought out and copied or collated old manuscripts. Some had even studied the genealogy of manuscripts. Guarino's friend Giovanni Lamola, for example, set out in 1428 to collate the codex of Cicero's rhetorical works that had been discovered seven years before in the cathedral archive at Lodi. This manuscript contained complete texts of Cicero's *De oratore* and *Orator,* which had previously been known only in mutilated texts, and of his *Brutus,* which had previously been unknown.[67] All these works were fundamental for the rhetorical teaching of the humanists. Consequently, the discovery attracted attention immediately: Poggio Bracciolini, who was then in England, knew of it within a year.[68] And many copies of the new texts were soon in circulation. But as the Lodi manuscript was written in what the humanists called "Lombardic script," that is, an unfamiliar minuscule, they found it hard to read and made their copies not from the original but from other humanists' copies. As a result both of inevitable mistakes in transcription and of equally inevitable attempts at conjectural emendation, the texts in circulation soon became extremely corrupt.[69] Lamola declared that it was necessary to return to the original source. He wrote to Guarino that he had "restored the whole work according to the earlier text."[70] He knew that the Lodi manuscript was very ancient from its unusual script: he described it as "summae quidem venerationis et antiquitatis non vulgaris effigies" (not an ordinary copy but of the highest quality and very old). More important, its discovery had created a sensation only a few years before, and no other complete manuscript of the works it contained had been discovered. Therefore, Lamola, like every other humanist of his time, knew that the Lodi manuscript must be the archetype: "From that accurate exemplar they copied the text which is now commonly accepted."[71] He decided that any attempt to emend the text must be based on a collation of this manuscript. He even maintained that the errors in the Lodi manuscript required preservation and study. For even the errors of so old a manuscript were preferable to the conjectures of later scribes:

> I also took care [he wrote] to represent everything in accord with the old [manuscript] down to the smallest dot, even where it contained certain old absurdities. For I'd rather be absurd with that old manuscript than be wise with these diligent fellows.[72]

Similarly Giorgio Merula pointed out in his 1472 edition of Plautus that all the extant manuscripts of twelve of the comedies were descended from one parent: "There was only one manuscript, from which, as if from an archetype, all the extant manuscripts are derived."[73] The archetype to which he referred was the eleventh-century Orsini manuscript of Plautus (Vat. Lat. 3870), brought to Rome in 1429 by Nicholas of Cusa.[74] Like the Lodi manuscript, it had created a sensation among the humanists, for twelve of the sixteen plays it contained had previously been unknown.[75] Hence, it too was widely known to be the source from which the rest had come. Merula could not collate the Orsini manuscript himself and had to content himself with reconstructing its readings by collating copies of it.[76] But even though he failed to act on his knowledge of the textual tradition, Merula too understood that the manuscripts of one text could be arranged genealogically, and that the text should be based on the parent if it were extant and identifiable.

Both Lamola and Merula, then, had noticed that all the manuscripts of some works were descended from one parent manuscript. Both had agreed that in such cases the text should be based on the parent. And one of them, Lamola, had made a full collation of the parent, recording even its errors.

Poliziano, however, showed how to examine a group of manuscripts and discover their relations to one another. He taught that in some cases an examination could identify an archetype that was not commonly recognized as such. And he maintained that even where the genealogy of the manuscripts could not be established, "conjectural emendation must start from the earliest recoverable stage of the tradition."[77] Moreover, he backed up his statements about the history of texts with precise identifications and evaluations of the manuscripts he used. His consistently methodical approach to the recension of manuscripts went far beyond the isolated insights of Lamola and Merula.

Had Poliziano completed and published the second century of the *Miscellanea,* the novelty of his genealogical method would have stood out even more clearly. In 2.1 we see him suggesting, though in somewhat unclear terms, that even when an archetype was lost, something could still be learned about it from examination of the extant manuscripts. In this chapter he identified and corrected the transposition of Cicero *De natura deorum* 2.16–86 and 2.86–156. The transposed passages were of virtually identical length. Poliziano therefore conjectured that the same thing had happened here as in the *Familiares;* gatherings in the archetype had been transposed because of an error in binding:

> The fact that we have never had to turn over more or less than eleven [pages; i.e., eleven pages in the text that Poliziano had at his disposal when writing] unquestionably shows us that an error has taken place like the one that we previously revealed in the letters: the gatherings were transposed by a bookbinder.[78]

Again, in 2.2 Poliziano proved that a manuscript of the *Argonauticon* of Valerius Flaccus was the parent of the rest. All the manuscripts contained transposed passages; these passages, in turn, were uniformly either fifty lines or multiples of fifty lines in length. Now the pages of the manuscript that he believed to be the parent were fifty lines long, twenty-five to a side. And in this manuscript the pages corresponding to the passages in question themselves had been transposed. Later scribes—including, to Poliziano's evident surprise, Niccolò Niccoli—had mistakenly copied the codes in the order in which they found it.[79] Such mathematical precision in the recension of manuscripts was not seen again until the nineteenth century. These chapters, with their startling anticipations of later discoveries, remained unpublished during the Renaissance; but Poliziano's new

method was still revealed for those with eyes to see by the first century
of the *Miscellanea*.

Poliziano also employed collateral forms of evidence to support or
modify that of manuscripts. In particular, he followed Tortelli in recognizing that inscriptions provided the most reliable evidence for establishing ancient orthographic practices. Tortelli had collected inscriptions to
prove that the Latin name of Rome should be spelled "Roma," rather
than "Rhoma." Poliziano used inscriptions as well as the Florentine Pandects and the codex Romanus of Vergil to show that the proper spelling
of the poet's name was "Vergilius." What was new in Poliziano's work
was not that he employed inscriptions but the manner in which he did
so. For he used them as critically as he did manuscripts. He took care to
show that he had studied the most up-to-date sylloge of inscriptions,
which the highly proficient epigrapher Fra Giovanni Giocondo had presented to Lorenzo. And he followed Giocondo in making an explicit distinction between inscriptions he had inspected and those he knew only
at second hand.[80] In short, he showed that the most sophisticated epigraphic techniques of his time could be joined with his palaeographical
expertise and applied to the solution of technical, philological problems.

*   *   *

The historical approach to source criticism was applicable to literary
works themselves as well as to manuscripts. Poliziano knew that the
Latin poets, whose works were his primary interest, had drawn heavily
on Greek sources in a variety of ways. And he showed that only a critic
who had mastered Greek literature could hope to deal competently with
Latin.

He realized, first of all, that the comparative study of Latin and
Greek was yet another tool for the textual critic—one that could be applied in cases in which the manuscripts afforded no help. In *Miscellanea*
1.27, for example, Poliziano was able to explain some puzzling lines in
Cicero, *Familiares* 7.6.1. He recognized that they were lines of verse, and
more important, that they were a translation of a passage from Euripides's *Medea* (214ff.). He knew that Ennius had written a Latin adaptation of the *Medea,* and he rightly argued that the lines must be a
quotation from Ennius's work.[81] In this case, knowledge of Cicero's
Greek source enabled Poliziano to set out as verse lines that would otherwise have remained incomprehensible when set as prose. As a by-
product he was able to reconstruct a forgotten chapter of early Roman
literary history.

Elsewhere, recourse to Greek sources enabled him to defend Latin forms of Greek words, which others had wrongly held to be corrupt: for example, "crepidas . . . carbatinas" in Catullus 98.4 and Oarion (for Orion) in 66.94.[82] His neatest application of this method was at 66.48. Catullus himself had explained that poem 66 was a translation of a poem by Callimachus, *The Lock of Berenice,* which was lost. But Poliziano found one line from it quoted in an ancient scholium: χαλύβων ὡς ἀπό-λοιτο γένος. He realized that it corresponded to line 48 of the Latin: "Iupiter ut caelitum omne genus pereat." And he also realized that "cae-litum," which made little sense in that context, must be a scribal corruption of the unfamiliar word "Chalybon," which Catullus had simply transliterated. So emended, the Latin became perfectly clear: Berenice's lock, wishing to be back on Berenice's head, prays that the race of Chalybes—a people famous for making metal tools, including the scissors that had cut the lock—may perish.[83] Poliziano had had predecessors in the use of Greek texts to correct Latin ones—notably his Florentine rival Bartolomeo della Fonte.[84] But in erudition and virtuosity he was matchless.

Yet the most striking effects of his comparative method were not in the field of textual criticism but in that of exegesis. For he insisted that proper exegesis of Latin writers must begin from the identification of the Greek sources they had drawn upon for both language and content. In 1.26, for example, he pointed out that Ovid, *Fasti,* 1.357–58 was adapted from an epigram in the Greek Anthology (*AP* 9.75). Ovid had translated the Greek "as literally as possible"—"quam potuit ad unguem"—but he had still failed to capture all the nuances of the original: "The Latin poet did not even touch that—if I may so call it—transmarine charm."[85] Juxtaposition of details inspired some sweeping critical judgments. Quintilian had characterized Ovid's style as "lascivus"—"abundant," "Asiatic." Poliziano argued, on the basis of his comparison, that Ovid was unable to equal his Greek model not from lack of ability, but because the Latin language itself ran counter to his special stylistic gifts: "This is the fault of the [Latin] language, not so much because it is lacking in words as because it allows less freedom for verbal play."[86]

In other cases Poliziano was able to connect the study of verbal borrowings to that of intellectual ones. Tacitly following Cristoforo Landino, he showed that Persius had modeled his fourth satire on the Platonic dialogue *Alcibiades 1.* Persius had drawn the entire philosophical message of his poem from the dialogue: "It is clear that Persius . . . drew from it the discussions which Socrates there holds with Alcibiades about the just and unjust, and about self-knowledge."[87] Indeed, Poliziano said, the words "Tecum habita," with which Persius's poem ended, were a good summary of the dialogue as well.

When he says "tecum habita," doesn't he seem to have understood the meaning of that dialogue clearly—if indeed, as the commentator Proclus affirms, Plato here had in mind precisely that Delphic writing which admonishes every man to know himself.[88]

At the same time, he was able to point out that Persius had alluded directly to individual lines in the dialogue.[89] Persius is an extremely obscure and allusive poet. Medieval readers, at a loss to understand the satires, had invented wild explanations for them. Persius was said to be attacking "leccatores"—gossips, gluttons, bishops, and abbots who failed to live up to their vows.[90] Only after Poliziano's explanation appeared could Persius's poem begin to be read as its author had intended.

Poliziano, of course, was hardly the first to point out that Latin poetry was heavily dependent on Greek models. Latin poets themselves generally claimed to be not the first to write a particular Greek style or verse form into Latin.[91] Moreover, Gellius had regularly compared passages from Latin poetry with the Greek originals from which they had been adapted, and had drawn broad conclusions from the exercise:

> Whenever striking expressions are to be translated and imitated from Greek poems, it is said that we should not always strive to render every single word with literal exactness. For many things lose their charm if they are translated too forcibly—as it were, unwillingly and reluctantly. Virgil therefore showed skill and good judgement in omitting some things and rendering others when he was dealing with passages of Homer or Hesiod or Apollonius or Parthenius or Callimachus or Theocritus or some other poet.[92]

Similar information and arguments appeared in other classics, for example, the *Saturnalia* of Macrobius, where Vergil and Homer are compared at length, and the commentaries of Servius.[93]

These texts, in turn, attracted the attention of medieval and Renaissance scholars before Poliziano. Richard de Bury, bishop of Durham in the fourteenth century, had read his Gellius and Macrobius.[94] In consequence, it is not surprising to find him asking, in his *Philobiblon*,

> What would Virgil, the chief poet among the Latins, have achieved, if he had not despoiled Theocritus, Lucretius, and Homer, and had not ploughed with their heifer? What, unless again and again he had read somewhat of Parthenius and Pindar, whose eloquence he could by no means imitate?[95]

And it was a commonplace among humanist teachers in the fifteenth century that only those who had a sound knowledge of Greek literature could properly understand Latin.[96]

Calderini, moreover, had given detailed attention and much effort to the comparative study of Greek and Latin. In his brief commentary on Propertius, for example, he arrived several times at novel and interesting results.[97] He pointed out that Propertius 1.20 is to some extent modeled on Theocritus 13: "In this passage his particular aim is to imitate and adapt Theocritus, on the story of Hylas."[98] And his wide reading in Greek scholiasts, geographers, and historians enabled him to unravel a number of Propertius's mythological and geographical allusions. For example, he rightly interpreted the phrase "Theseae bracchia longa viae" in Propertius 3.21.24: "He means the long walls, which were called μακρὰ τείχη in Greek. They ran from the city [of Athens] up to the Piraeus; a careful account is to be found in Thucydides."[99] He also noticed that Propertius often made use of variant forms of well-known myths. Thus, in 1.12.21 Propertius described the river god Enipeus as Thessalian. Calderini rightly pointed out that other ancient writers located Enipeus not in Thessaly but in Elis.[100]

Despite its qualities, this commentary reveals the gulf that separated even Calderini from Poliziano. In 4.1.64, Propertius calls himself "the Roman Callimachus."[101] The phrase is not as simple as it appears; when a Roman poet claims a particular Greek poet as his model, he may mean that he has derived his subject or his meter from the Greek, but he may also mean simply that he is as innovative, learned, and subtle as the Greek had been. Calderini, however, took Propertius at his word. He assumed that Propertius must have written direct adaptations from Callimachus: "[Propertius] calls himself the Roman Callimachus. For he sets out Callimachus, a Greek poet, in Latin verse."[102] And he applied this interpretation at least once in a most unfortunate way. In 1.2.1 Propertius calls his mistress Cynthia "vita"—"my life." "The word," wrote Calderini, "is drawn from Callimachus, who is Propertius's chief model. For he too, while flattering his mistress, calls her by the Greek word [for life, i.e., ζωή]."[103]

Calderini's arguments clearly found some acceptance, for Beroaldo repeated them—without acknowledgment—in his own commentary on Propertius, which first appeared in 1487. He too argued that Propertius had taken Callimachus as his model, his "archetypon." And he too described Propertius's use of "vita" in 1.2.1 as an imitation of Callimachus.[104]

The notes of Calderini and Beroaldo stimulated Poliziano to produce a splendid rebuttal in *Miscellanea* 1.80, where he raised an overstated, but nonetheless crushing objection to both Calderini's general interpretation and his reading of 1.2.1, namely, that there was not one shred of evidence that Callimachus had written any love poetry at all, much less a love poem in which ζωή was used as an endearment:

> I find it astonishing that Domizio and some others after him . . .
> dare to write that Propertius says this or that in imitation of Calli-
> machus. For beyond a few hymns nothing at all remains to us of
> that poet, and certainly there is nothing at all that treats of love.[105]

Poliziano certainly had the best in the exchange. There is little reason to think that Calderini had found evidence to back up his theory. As a commentator on Juvenal, Calderini knew from *Satires* 6.195 that ζωή was sometimes used as an endearment. As to the notion that Callimachus had used the word in that sense, it was probably a clever guess.[106] But Poliziano's rebuttal is even more significant when read in the light of the chapter in which it occurred. There he not only attacked Calderini but gave an elegant demonstration of just how one should use Greek poetry to illustrate Propertius. In 4.9.57–58 Propertius alludes to the myth of Tiresias's encounter with Pallas while she was bathing.[107] To illustrate the myth Poliziano published, along with much other material, the first edition of Callimachus's entire poem on the bath of Pallas, which he also translated word-for-word.[108] The Alexandrian poets, in other words, could be used to illuminate Propertius's mythological allusions. But they could not be used to explicate the verbal details of his poems. In *Miscellanea* 1.80, then, Poliziano showed that he understood more than just the virtues of the comparative method in exegesis—he understood its limitations as well. He understood that different Latin poets had used their Greek sources in different ways, and that the exegete must take these differences in poetic method into account when making his comparisons.[109] For all Calderini's reading in Greek prose texts and genuine sensitivity to the nuances of Latin poetry, he could not rival Poliziano in the methodical application of source criticism or the systematic comparison of Latin and Greek poetry. Yet he was the most sophisticated of Poliziano's predecessors. In exegesis as in textual criticism, then, Poliziano's methodological innovations marked nothing less than a revolution.

Modern scholars still begin the study of Latin poems by looking for possible Greek sources and models. To be sure, when they find a model they compare it with the Latin in a far more detailed manner than Poliziano did. We want to know not only that Ennius translated Euripides, and that in doing so he made alterations, but also what specific changes he made, and what purposes they were meant to serve.[110] But it would be unhistorical to reproach Poliziano for not carrying his comparisons far enough. After all, he took them almost as far as had his model Gellius. Rather, Poliziano's work on the comparative method should be seen in the same perspective as his work on manuscripts: as the lineal ancestor of the methods that are still employed.

*   *   *

Poliziano's thoroughness in the study of Greek sources paid off in novel results of other sorts. He mastered not only the whole body of Greek literary texts, but also the huge mass of scholarly material that had grown up among and around them since Hellenistic times, above all the scholia on such Hellenistic poets as Aratus and Apollonius of Rhodes. And by drawing on this material, he was sometimes able to move from the comparison of Latin and Greek to the partial reconstruction of lost Greek works. In 1.24 he discussed the myth of Theseus's encounter with Hecale. Beroaldo had already pointed out, drawing on testimonies in both Latin and Greek texts, that Callimachus had written a poem about Hecale. But Poliziano was able to go much further. He found in a scholium on Callimachus what is still the only information about the exact nature of the poem and the reasons why Callimachus wrote it:

> Where Callimachus says, in his *Hymn to Apollo*, "Envy whispered in Apollo's ear, I do not love the poet whose song is not as vast as the ocean"—the scholiast there writes more or less as follows: "Here he attacks those who mocked him for being unable to write a large poem. That is why he was forced to write the Hecale." [111]

Here too, none of Poliziano's rivals could match either his mastery of recondite materials or his use of them to recreate what had seemed irrevocably lost.

Poliziano's detailed improvements to the art of criticism, finally, stood out all the more because he consistently used them as arguments in favor of an ambitious program for the refinement of the *studia humanitatis*. He made new claims for the status of the critic and his importance for those studies. The competent critic must be more than a mere technician. Like Varro, he must have mastered not only Latin and Greek, but law, medicine, and dialectic, in short, all the disciplines, and philosophy above all. [112] Such a critic, Poliziano showed by precept and example, need not confine his talents to rhetorical and poetic texts. After all, the ancient philosophers as well as the poets were known only through imperfectly transmitted texts. Some of the most puzzling antinomies these presented were really corruptions, which the philosophers' logic could not resolve—but which the philologist's tools could readily eliminate.

John Argyropoulos, a philosopher of high repute in the Florence of the 1450s and 1460s, had criticized Cicero for saying (*Tusculan Disputations* 1.20.22) that Aristotle's term for "mind" was ἐνδελέχεια (continuous motion). Aristotle had denied motion to the mind, and the manuscripts of his *De anima* gave the philosophically more satisfactory term ἐντελέχεια (perfection).[113] In the very first chapter of the *Miscellanea* Poliziano contested this view. The manuscripts of Aristotle, he pointed out, were notoriously corrupt, and Strabo's account of their vicissitudes above and below ground showed that they had first been published in an inaccurate and interpolated form. Moreover, he asked, "is it not possible that Cicero himself saw the archetype of Aristotle's works, which were published in his time?"[114] In that case, his testimony would carry more weight than that of Byzantine manuscripts. Study of the history of texts could thus be a powerful reinforcement for the many humanists who, like Poliziano himself and his friend Ermolao Barbaro the Younger, hoped to wrest the discipline of philosophy from the control of the scholastic professionals.[115]

Even more important, Poliziano showed that the critic's tasks included creation as well as study. His prose and poetry ranged from brief epigrams in Greek and Latin through longer translations of Greek texts to the extended prolusions in prose and verse with which he began his university lecture courses.[116] Into these works he fitted with the delicacy of a jeweler his linguistic, prosodic, mythological, and even text-critical discoveries. His preface to Leon Battista Alberti's *De re aedificatoria*, to take a simple example, announced four years before the *Miscellanea* that he had reworked the text of Suetonius, *Claudius*, 34:

> Ita perscrutatus antiquitatis vestigia est, ut omnem veterum architectandi rationem et deprehenderit et in exemplum revocaverit, sic ut non solum machinas et *pegmata automataque* permulta, sed formas quoque aedificiorum admirabilis excogitaverit.[117] [He examined the traces of antiquity in such a way that he might both detect every method of building [employed by] the ancients and recover them as models, and in order to devise not only machines, trap doors and devices but, in addition, types of buildings worthy of admiration.]

And his poems, naturally, were chock-a-block with every sort of learned allusion. Such Alexandrian refinement of allusion and imitation was just what Poliziano's audience expected from these splendid formal exer-

cises.[118] Codro Urceo of Bologna not only urged Poliziano to publish the
Greek epigrams of which he had been sent a sample, but also analyzed
in detail Poliziano's adaptation of particularly elegant metrical practices
from the best ancient authors, for example, his habit of composing hexameter verses from a large number of short words *scatentibus dactylis,*
after the manner of the first line of the *Odyssey.*[119]

To the intimate connection between his scholarship and his style
Poliziano repeatedly called attention. In *Miscellanea* 1.17 he wrote:

> In Seneca's tragedy entitled *Hercules furens* the following *senari-
> olus* occurs:
>
> > *Sublimis altas luna concipiat feras.*
>
> But the old manuscript in the public library of the Medici reads
> *alias,* not *altas,* as in the common text. [The emended text reads:
> "The lofty moon may bring forth more wild beasts."] You will not
> easily find the sense of this passage anywhere save in Achilles, an
> author whom Firmicus Maternus both cities and praises in his
> *Mathesis.* While discussing the moon in his commentary on Aratus,
> he says: "It is also inhabited, and has rivers and everything else
> found on earth, and they tell the story that the Nemean lion fell
> from it." . . . Whence I [wrote] in the *Nutricia:*
>
> *Nemeaeaque tesqua*
> *Lunigenam mentita feram* [568–569].[120]

Here Poliziano took his own place with aplomb in the poetic genealogy
that his scholarly researches had established. Just as Seneca had displayed his knowledge of Greek myth, so Poliziano—appropriately describing Pindar—invokes at once the Greek myth and the Latin allusion
to it, and by doing so links his poetic method with that of the ancients.
Moreover, his translations from the Greek—especially the version of the
Lavacra Palladis that he printed in the *Miscellanea*—also enabled him to
combine accurate philology with poetic originality. Poliziano's letters became models of Neolatin prose.[121] His poems were considered classical
enough to be the subject of university courses.[122] And his translations set
the standard for all others for a century and more.[123] It is not surprising,
then, that his success as a stylist did much to help his technical methods
and standards impose themselves.

*   *   *

Poliziano was more, of course, than a scholar trying to set new standards
for the selection, citation, and interpretation of sources. Like Calderini

and the rest, he was a writer and teacher who needed financial support and public acclaim. He had to show that his brand of scholarship deserved the protection of Lorenzo, the most discriminating of patrons, and the applause of Florentines, the most critical of audiences. His self-conscious adoption of a new standard of accuracy and precision enabled him to do just that. His constant references to rare materials both enriched his work and enabled him to give thanks in public to the noble friends who had made them available to him. In particular, he could thank Lorenzo, who "in his service to scholars lowered himself" even to arranging access to manuscripts, coins, and inscriptions.[124] Some of Poliziano's distinctive technical innovations, in particular, his efforts to identify parent manuscripts, also amounted to elegant new forms of flattery.

Poliziano's environment exerted pressure on his scholarship at other levels as well. By treating the study of antiquity as irrelevant to civic life and by insisting that only a tiny elite could study the ancient world with adequate rigor, he set himself apart from the earlier tradition of classical studies in Florence. Earlier Florentine scholars, men like Leonardo Bruni and Donato Acciaiuoli, had studied the ancient world in order to become better men and citizens. They wanted to recover the experience of classical republicanism in order to build a sound republic in their own time. Poliziano evidently believed that one must study the ancient world for its own sake, and the exhaustive preparation that he demanded left little time for good citizenship.[125] Moreover, when he set ancient works back into their full historical context Poliziano eliminated whatever contemporary relevance they might have had. It was by misreading the satires of Persius that early medieval clerics had made them useful. Poliziano's historical reading clearly showed that the satires did not concern any problem contemporary with him. The only use that one could make of Latin poetry, analyzed by his methods, was a purely literary one: as sources to be drawn on and models to be imitated in one's own artificial, allusive verse—verse of just the sort that a cultivated elite of patrons will enjoy. As we have seen, that was precisely the practical application that Poliziano made of the new tools he forged.[126] In short, by eliminating moral interpretations and contemporary applications from classical studies, Poliziano made them an object for Medici patronage as decorative, harmless, and sophisticated as the elegant nonsense of the Neoplatonists.

But Poliziano's general intellectual environment did as much as his social and political milieu to shape his work. As we have seen, he belonged to a whole generation of humanists who turned—in Rome and Venice as well as in Florence—from the oration to the emendation, from an audience of eager young citizens to a reading public of crabbed, jeal-

ous scholars.[127] Like Calderini, Merula, and the rest, Poliziano was possessed by the need to excel the competition. Accordingly, his work
sometimes resembled theirs in tone as much as it differed in substance.
And because Poliziano started from so polemical a stance, the course he
followed in argument sometimes wavered from the straight path that his
principles laid down. He did not always confine himself to fair comment
or treat his adversaries with as much attention as the ancient sources.
Sometimes Calderini really had discovered in classical texts the facts that
Poliziano accused him of inventing, for example, the material about rhi-
noceroses with two horns that Poliziano dismissed as error and confusion, and which Calderini had really found in Pausanias and rightly
applied to Martial.[128] Sometimes Calderini really had seen the sense in
passages that Poliziano treated as corrupt, for example, his explanation
of Martial's *Atlas cum compare gibbo* (6.77.7)—which Poliziano wanted
to emend to *Atlas cum compare mulo*—as referring to a camel (a "hump-
backed beast").[129] Sometimes, too, Poliziano did not subject his own conjectures to the harsh scrutiny he turned on those of others, for example,
his argument that Statius had married Lucan's widow, Polla Argentaria,
which he maintained for more than a decade despite the textual evidence
that Statius's wife was named Claudia.[130] These errors and exaggerations
did not stop Poliziano from devising more solid, original, and ingenious
critical methods than anyone else of his generation. But they did infuse
his prose with an acid and unpleasant tone.

Poliziano knew that his scholarly writing struck readers he respected
as too polemical. Jacopo Antiquario, after reading the *Miscellanea,*
wrote to praise its content and deplore its style: "Domizio did what he
could for literature."[131] But Poliziano conceded nothing: "I hold Domizio
up to students as I would a pitfall to travelers."[132] And he made clear
that he saw scholarship not the way an ancient grammarian like Donatus
had, as a collaborative, cumulative enterprise, but rather as the poets
of the Roman Golden Age had seen their art: as a field for personal
triumphs over predecessors and rivals. Why write at all unless to criticize
what others had written?

> My action is supported by prominent examples, unless one thinks
> Horace an insignificant author—Horace, who slaughters Ennius,
> Plautus, Lucilius, Dossennus, and that whole troop of ancient
> poets all at once, though the people opposed him. What? Does
> Aulus Gellius not also attack Seneca with great freedom of speech?
> . . . Do all the schools of philosophers not cross swords above all
> with their predecessors?[133]

Poliziano, then, saw the bitter, eristic style of the *Miscellanea* as an essential component of the scholarship he wanted to produce. That in turn meant not only that he would commit some errors as serious as those he exposed, but also that he would inspire rebuttals as fierce as anything he could compose. And that meant that his complex of new methods would not be adopted as a whole.

Naturally some of Poliziano's results were accepted. Reading the editions of the *Familiares* that appeared after 1489, he congratulated himself: "My restoration, so to speak, has now been accepted, as far as I can see. Texts are printed everywhere in the form that I had prescribed from the old manuscripts."[134] Much of the mail that the *Miscellanea* elicited was favorable. Young men took it apart so that several could read different gatherings at the same time; old men were overwhelmed by its wealth of new material.[135]

But, as might have been expected from its tone and standpoint, the *Miscellanea* also generated anger and abuse. Michael Marullus, Poliziano's rival in both scholarship and poetry, ridiculed in biting epigrams his exaggerated claims of novelty, his obstinate refusal to accept perfectly plausible vulgate readings, and his strained efforts to interpret standard texts in novel ways.[136] Merula attacked the *Miscellanea* point by point, claiming that much of Poliziano's new material was stolen from himself and others.[137] Others, less engaged, criticized Poliziano even more obtusely. Why, they asked, should so able a poet waste his time in blowing dust from old manuscripts when much more legible new ones were available, neatly written in humanistic script?[138] Poliziano's burning rhetoric seemed as forced and curious to such readers as his technical arguments.

External factors joined with these internal ones to divert scholars from the path Poliziano had blazed. The political upheaval that Italy suffered in the 1490s created a sense of new needs and new men to fill them. The terrible years 1493 and 1494 brought the French into Italy, drove the Medici from Florence, and killed off Poliziano and Barbaro. No one had time after 1494 for the precision work that had been their speciality. Readers wanted encyclopaedias, like the *Commentarii urbani* of Raffaele Maffei, who reduced the whole corpus of Greek works on history and geography into an orderly, accessible, and fairly compact form, and plain texts like those of Aldo Manuzio, who saw the creation of a new philology as a task less pressing than that of providing the raw materials from which a new civilization could be built. Italian Latinists turned away from the experimental and eclectic prose of Poliziano's generation to a new ideal of pure imitation of Cicero. And even Poliziano's disciples did not carry on their master's enterprise. Jacopo Modesti of Prato, who had collated manuscripts with Poliziano, published no learned works of his own. Pietro Crinito, who did publish, deliberately rejected Poliziano's methods in order to build a distinctive monument of his own, the mistitled *De honesta disciplina*. Eventually, to be sure, Poliziano's new methods took root again, both in Italy and in France. His Italian heirs concentrated on his method of manuscript recension, his French ones on his comparative approach to exegesis. And by the 1560s and 1570s efforts were underway to revive and extend his methods as a whole. But that story, which is that of the transformation of humanist scholarship into a quasi-professional philology, lies outside the field of this essay.

NOTES

1. For the general context and development of humanist scholarship, see P. Burke, *The Renaissance Sense of the Past* (London, 1969), D. R. Kelley, *Foundations of Modern Historical Scholarship: Language, Law, and History in the French Renaissance* (New York and London, 1970), and L. D. Reynolds and N. G. Wilson, *Scribes and Scholars* (Oxford, 2d ed. 1974). The development of editorial method is surveyed by S. Timpanaro, *La genesi del metodo del Lachmann* (Padua, 2d ed., reprinted 1985), E. J. Kenney, *The Classical Text* (Berkeley, 1974), and A. Grafton, *Joseph Scaliger: A Study in the History of Classical Scholarship,* vol. 1 (Oxford, 1983), chaps. 1–3. Studies of some of the more influential scholars discussed below include: for Petrarch, G. Billanovich, "Petrarch and the Textual Tradition of Livy," *Journal of the Warburg and Courtauld Institutes* 14 (1951): 137–208, and P. de Nolhac, *Pétrarque et l'humanisme* (Paris, 2d ed. 1907); for Salutati, B. L. Ullman, *The Humanism of Coluccio Salutati* (Padua, 1963), and R. G. Witt, *Hercules at the Crossroads: The Life, Works, and Thought of Coluccio Salutati* (Durham, NC, 1983); for Valla, Billanovich, "Petrarch," and J. H. Bentley, *Humanists and Holy Writ: New Testament Scholarship in the Renaissance* (Princeton, 1983). The development of textual explication has been less systematically studied than that of textual criticism, but see the stimulating article by L. Panizza, "Textual Interpretation in Italy, 1350–1450: Seneca's Letter I to Lucilius," *Journal of the Warburg and Courtauld Institutes* 46 (1983): 40–62, and S. Timpanaro, "Atlas cum compare gibbo," *Rinascimento* 2d ser. 2 (1951): 311–18. The most accessible study of one of the early humanist printers is M. J. C. Lowry, *The World of Aldus Manutius: Business and Scholarship in Renaissance Venice* (Ithaca, NY, 1979). And two indispensable collections of information are R. Sabbadini, *Il metodo degli umanisti* (Florence, 1922), and S. Rizzo, *Il lessico filologico degli umanisti* (Rome, 1973).

2. For Valla's method in the *Elegantiae* see, e.g., M. Baxandall, *Giotto and the Orators* (Oxford, 1971), 3–11; H. J. Stevens, Jr., "Lorenzo Valla and Isidore of Seville," *Traditio* 31 (1975): 343–48. For Tortelli's *De orthographia,* see R. P. Oliver, "Giovanni Tortelli," in *Studies Presented to David Moore Robinson* (St. Louis, 1953), 2:1257–71. And on the intellectual

relations between Valla and Tortelli, which at times amounted to collaboration, see O. Besomi, "Dai 'Gesta Ferdinandi regis Aragonum' del Valla al 'De orthographia' del Tortelli," in *Italia medioevale e umanistica* 9 (1966): 75–121.

3. For what follows see J. Monfasani, *George of Trebizond: A Biography and a Study of His Rhetoric and Logic* (Leiden, 1976), 262–65, 289–94, where it is also shown that George of Trebizond was, unlike his predecessors, independent of older traditions of commentary on Cicero.

4. See L. Frati, "Le polemiche umanistiche di Benedetto Morandi," *Giornale storico della letteratura italiana* 75 (1920): 32ff. Cf. Livy, 9.17–19.

5. On the roles of philology and rhetoric in Valla's thought, see H. H. Gray, "Renaissance Humanism: The Pursuit of Eloquence," *Journal of the History of Ideas* 24 (1963): 497–514, esp. 511–12; idem, "Valla's *Encomium of St. Thomas Aquinas* and the Humanist Conception of Christian Antiquity," in *Essays in History and Literature Presented by the Fellows of the Newberry Library to Stanley Pargellis*, ed. H. Bluhm (Chicago, 1965), 37–51, esp. 49–50.

6. For a contrary view of the nature of conjectural criticism, see Kenney, *The Classical Text.*

7. It is significant that modern textual critics refer to a manuscript that has been corrected against another as one that has suffered "contamination."

8. G. Billanovich and M. Ferraris, "Le 'Emendationes in T. Livium' del Valla e il Codex Regius di Livio," *Italia medioevale e umanistica* 1 (1958): 245–64.

9. Billanovich, "Petrarch," 178–79.

10. See e.g. Reynolds and Wilson, *Scribes and Scholars.*

11. Cf. Kenney, *The Classical Text*, chap. 1.

12. This generational change in the character of Italian humanism has often been remarked on: see, e.g., C. Marchesi, *Bartolomeo della Fonte (Bartholemaeus Fontius): Contributo alla storia degli studi classici in Firenze nella seconda metà del Quattrocento* (Catania, 1900), 2; F. Gilbert, "Biondo, Sabellico, and the Beginnings of Venetian Official Historiography," *Florilegium Historiale: Essays Presented to Wallace K. Ferguson*, ed. J. G. Rowe and W. H. Stockdale (Toronto, 1971), 275–93.

13. On Pomponio Leto, see V. Zabughin, *Vergilio nel Rinascimento italiano da Dante a Torquato Tasso*, 2 vols. (Bologna, 1921), 1:188, 192. On Gaspare de' Tirimbocchi, see *Scholia in P. Ovidi Nasonis Ibin*, ed. A. La Penna (Florence, 1959), xxxix–xl.

14. See H. Caplan, *Of Eloquence: Studies in Ancient and Medieval Rhetoric*, ed. A. King and H. North (Ithaca, NY, 1970), 268. In fact, these humanists were imitating their ancient models here too, for the commentators and scholiasts of late antiquity had also cannibalized the works of their predecessors. This fact is hardly surprising, considering that in both cases the commentators were practicing arts teachers who had to cover a vast amount of material in their lectures and could hardly have done original research to support all or even most of what they said (nor is the situation very different

in modern arts teaching; after all, normal twentieth-century school commentaries are mostly derivative in content). On ancient commentators' use
of their sources, see J. E. G. Zetzel, "On the History of Latin Scholia," *Harvard Studies in Classical Philology* 79 (1975): 335–54.

15. On the classical scholarship of the late medieval friars, see B. Smalley, *English Friars and Antiquity in the Early Fourteenth Century* (Oxford, 1960).

16. A good account of Servius's method is given by R. R. Bolgar, *The Classical
Heritage and Its Beneficiaries* (Cambridge, 1954), 396, n. Despite its un-
trustworthiness on many points of detail, this work contains many interesting remarks on the history of the commentary, which should not be ignored.

17. Martino Filetico, dedicatory letter to Cardinal Giovanni Colonna in Filetico's edition with notes of selected letters of Cicero, quoted by G. Mercati,
"Tre dettati universitari dell'umanista Martino Filetico sopra Persio, Giovenale et Orazio," in *Classical and Mediaeval Studies in Honor of Edward
Kennard Rand,* ed. L. W. Jones (New York, 1938), 228, n. 46; and by C.
Dionisotti, " 'Lavinia venit litora': Polemica virgiliana di M. Filetico," *Italia
medioevale e umanistica* 1 (1958): 307.

18. See esp. Poliziano, *Commento inedito alle Selve di Stazio,* ed. L. Cesarini
Martinelli (Florence, 1978), 20.

19. Here too, the humanists were doing what their classical predecessors had
done; many of the shorter glosses in Servius are merely synonyms or peri-
phrases of a word in the text. The inherent defects of the humanists' style
of commentary have often been discussed: see, e.g., *Scholia in Ovidi Ibin,*
ed. La Penna, xlvii and n. 6; Ermolao Barbaro the Younger, *Castigationes
Plinianae et in Pomponium Melam,* ed. G. Pozzi (Padua, 1973), "Introduzione," cxlix–cl.

20. On the *modus modernus,* which was first used for civil and canon law texts,
see K. Haebler, *The Study of Incunabula,* trans. L. E. Osborne (New York,
1933), 91.

21. Domizio Calderini, "Epilogus et προσφώνησις de observationibus," 1475,
quoted by C. Dionisotti, "Calderini, Poliziano e altri," *Italia medioevale e
umanistica* 11 (1968): 167. This paragraph and the following one are based
on Dionisotti's article; cf. also Barbaro, *Castigationes Plinianae,* 1, "Introduzione," chap. 5, "Il Barbaro e gli umanisti," cxii–clxviii, esp. cxlix–cl,
clxiv. For a fifteenth-century assessment of Calderini that stresses his ability
to solve technical problems of interpretation—as well as his lack of scruple—see Paolo Cortesi, *De hominibus doctis dialogus,* ed. and trans. M. T.
Graziosi (Rome, 1973), 54.

22. On Plinian studies in the later fifteenth century, see Barbaro, *Castigationes
Plinianae,* ed. Pozzi.

23. Domizio Calderini, "Ex tertio libro observationum," in *Lampas, sive fax
artium liberalium, hoc est, thesaurus criticus,* ed. J. Gruter (Frankfurt,
1602), 1:316: "*Harpastrum* quid sit longa commentatione Graecis auctoribus explicamus in Epistolam quarti libri sylvarum, multaque de eo docui-
mus, quae adhuc (ut opinor) incognita fuerunt, ea siquis volet legere, illic
requiret"; and 1:314: "Repetamus praeterea particulam commentariorum

nostrorum in Iuvenalem, ubi carmen exit illud in mulierem curantem cutem et expolientem faciem in gratiam adulteri:

Interea foeda aspectu ridendaque multo
Pane tumet facies, et pinguia popeana spirat.

(Juv. Sat. VI, 461–63)

... Haec scripsi, siqui fortasse Iuvenalis carmen parum intellige[ntes] de Popeano ambigant, quod ego, ut arbitror, primus fortasse elucubravi, ut sexcenta alia, quae in commentationibus nostris requires."

24. Filippo Beroaldo the Elder, Annotationes centum, Gesamtkatalog der Wiegendrucke 4113 (Bologna, 1488), fol. a ii v: "Sane has annotationes nullo servato rerum ordine confecimus, utpote tumultuario sermone dictantes, et perinde ut cuiuslibet loci veniebat in mentem, ut quilibet liber sumebatur in manus, ita indistincte atque promiscue excerpentes annotantesque. Fetus hic plane precox fuit, utpote intra menstruum tempus et conceptus et editus." To be sure, this statement may be merely a commonplace, an imitation of Gellius's similar confession of haste and disorderliness (Noctes Atticae, praefatio, x). Nonetheless, Beroaldo seems genuinely less bold than Poliziano in asserting the merits of the new genre; and this difference in tone probably does reflect some difference in opinion.

25. Filippo Beroaldo, Annotationes in commentarios Servii Virgiliani commentatoris, Gesamt katalog der Wiegendrucke (4115 (Bologna, 1482), sigs. [a vi v–a vii r], against Servius on Aeneid 1.373; [a vii r–v] against Servius on Aeneid 1.410; b iii v–b iiii r, against Servius on Aen. 2.707; e ii r–v, against Servius on Georgics 3.124. I give one example of Beroaldo's method [a vii r–v] aginst Servius on Aeneid 1.410:

SERVIVS. Incusare proprie est superiorem arguere; accusare vero vel parem vel inferiorem.

PHILIPPVS. Quis non videt falsam ac penitus inanem esse differentiam, quam Servius nobis persuadere contendit? Nemo fere eruditorum in latina lingua ita loquitur. Nemo hanc differentiam observat: quinimo saepissime secus legitur. Caesar in primo Commentario, omnium ordinum adhibitis ad id consilium centurionibus, vehementer eos incusavit. Certe Caesar militibus suis maior est non minor, et tamen contra Servii disciplinam dicit se illos incusasse, et profecto latinissime locutus est. Incusare enim significat reprehendere vel culpare sine aliquo discrimine. . . . Accusare vero ab auctoribus idoneis usurpatur, nusquam observata fetutina illa et rancida Servii observatione; qua de re exempla ideo ponere supersedeo, quia talibus scatent scriptorum cuncta volumina.

This observation was well worth making, considering that the standard contemporary work on Latin usage—Giuniano Maio, De priscorum proprietate verborum (Naples, 1475)—reproduced Servius's words without comment (admittedly, this was the author's normal practice); see sigs. [a vi ra; s vii rb].

26. Beroaldo, *Annotationes contra Servium,* fols. a iii v–a iiii r, b ii r–v, b iiii v, [b vi r–v], c ii v–c iii r, [c iv r–v], etc.

27. Ibid., fol. [b vii r–v]: "In illo quoque versu Maroniano, Explebo numerum reddarque tenebris [*Aeneid* 6.545], admiror Servium, cum more diligentis commentatoris varias interpretationes attulerit, omisisse id, quod a Macrobio relatum est, quod eruditionem maximam prae se fert, et Virgilianae sententiae optime quadrat. . . . [There follows a summary of Macrobius, *In somnium Scripionis,* 1.13.11–12.] Haec Macrobii interpretatio, tam subtilis, tam elegans, tam erudita, praetermitti non debuit a curioso commentatore, qui ex fontibus philosophorum, unde hauserat Macrobius, haurire potuisset; praesertim cum multa undique exquisiverit. Sed ut mihi videtur, nihil est cum praedicta Macrobii expositione comparandum."

28. Barbaro, *Castigationes Plinianae,* ed. Pozzi, cxxvi–vii.

29. W. G. Rutherford, *Scholia Aristophanica,* 3 vols. (London, 1896–1905), 3:387.

30. Ibid., 3:67–72; cf. N. G. Wilson, "A Chapter in the History of Scholia," *Classical Quarterly* 17 (1967): 244–56.

31. R. P. Oliver, " 'New Fragments' of Latin Authors in Perotti's *Cornucopiae,*" *Transactions of the American Philological Association* 78 (1947): 390–93, 405–6, 411, 412–24, and passim. This article is very useful as an analysis of Perotti's sources and methods.

32. A. J. Dunston, "Studies in Domizio Calderini," *Italia medioevale e umanistica* 11 (1968): 144–49; S. Timpanaro, "Noterelle au Domizio Calderini e Pietro Giordani," in *Tra Latino e Volgare: Per Carlo Dionisotti,* ed. G. B. Trezzini et al. (Padua, 1974), 709–12.

33. On Leto and Ennius, see J. Dunston, "A Student's Notes of Lectures by Julio Pomponio Leto," *Antichthon* 1 (1967): 86–94. On Calderini's falsification of his note on Martial 14.41, see Dunston, "Studies in Domizio Calderini," 134–37, correcting and amplifying R. Sabbadini, *Classici e umanisti da codici Ambrosiani* (Florence, 1933), 59–62. On Marius Rusticus, see Dunston, "Studies in Domizio Calderini," 138–42, and G. Brugnoli, "La 'Praefatio in Suetonium' del Poliziano," *Giornale italiano di filologia* 10 (1957): 211–20, esp. 216, 219–20; but see above all the new information and the suggestion for a new interpretation of the incident in A. Perosa, "Due lettere di Domizio Calderini," *Rinascimento* 2d ser. 13 (1973): 6, 13–15.

34. See L. Ruberto, "Studi sul Poliziano filologo," *Rivista di filologia e d'istruzione classica* 12 (1884): 235–37.

35. Poliziano, *Miscellanea,* "Praefatio ad Laurentium Medicem," in *Opera* (Basel, 1553), 216. Cf. Pliny, *Natural History,* praef., 21: ". . . auctorum nomina praetexui."

36. Calderini, *Commentarioli in Ibyn Ovidii,* Hain 4242 (Rome, 1474), preface, fol. 2v.

37. Poliziano, *Miscellanea,* 1.75, in *Opera,* 285.

38. Calderini, *Commentarioli in Ibyn Ovidii,* fol. 25r *ad* 569: "Agenor lapsu equi inserta ori manu extinctus est."

39. The passages in question are *Odyssey*, 4.285ff. and Tryphiodorus, Ἰλίου ἅλωσις, 476ff.; see *Publi Ovidi Nasonis Ibis*, ed. A. La Penna (Florence, 1957), 153–54. cf. *Scholia in P. Ovidi Nasonis Ibin*, ed. La Penna, xlviii.

40. Calderini, "Ex tertio libro observationum," in *Lampas*, ed. Gruter, 1:316–17: "Incidi nuper in quasdam Laurentii commentatiunculas, quas in Fabium composuit, in quibus cum alia desideravi tum testium, quos citat aliquando, fidem atque adeo, ut unum subiiciamus, ubi Fabius de verbis peregrinis ita scribit: *Nam Mastrugam, quod Sardum est illudens Cicero ex industria dixit* [*Inst. or.* 1.5.8], Laurentius, locum indicans ubi id Cicero dixerit, haec addit: *Cicero pro Scauro, quem purpura regalis non commovit, eum Sardorum Mastruga mutavit* [*Quintiliani institutiones cum commento Laurentii Vallensis, Pomponii, ac Sulpitii*, Proctor 4865, Venice 18.vii.1494, sig. c iiii r, quoting Isidore, *Origines* 19.23.5]. Equidem *Scauri caussam* actam fuisse apud Ciceronem, legi apud Valerium Max. et Pedianum: *Orationem* vero a Cicerone pro illo habitam, unde se haec accipere Laurentius profitetur, legi nusquam, neque exstare arbitror, vereorque ne Grammaticum aliquem ignobilem secutus haec verba recitaverit potius, quam legerit usquam apud Ciceronem."

41. Ibid., 317: "Mendosa est dictio [*medico*, for *melico*] apud Plinium, ut ego quidem arbitror, et heri observavi, cum de Simonide nonnulla apud Graecum scriptorem legi." The "Greek writer" is merely the *Suda, s.v.* Σιμωνίδης.

42. Poliziano, *Opera*, 304.

43. Poliziano, *Miscellanea*, 1.45, in *Opera*, 263: "Patroclo iuniorem Achillem, contra quam aut Aeschylus prodiderit, aut vulgo existimetur."

44. Petrarch said that he followed those "whose verisimilitude or greater authority demands that they be given greater credence"—"Ego ... eorum imitator sum, quibus vel similitudo vel autoritas maior ut eis potissimum stetur impetrat." The translation is that of B. G. Kohl, "Petrarch's Prefaces to *De viris illustribus*," *History and Theory* 14 (1974): 139; the original is from Petrarch, *Prose*, ed. G. Martellotti et al. (Milan, 1955), 220. Petrarch uses much the same formula in his *Epistula posteritati*, where he says that in his study of history he occasionally followed "quo me vel veri similitudo rerum vel scribentium traxit autoritas" (*Prose*, ed. Martellotti et al., 6). For examples of Petrarch's use of historical sources see H. J. Erasmus, *The Origins of Rome in Historiography from Petrarch to Perizonius* (Assen, 1962), 8–11; S. Prete, *Observations on the History of Textual Criticism in the Medieval and Renaissance Periods* (Collegeville, MN, n.d.), 19–20. On Salutati, see A. Von Martin, *Coluccio Salutati's Traktat "Vom Tyrannen." Eine kulturgeschichtliche Untersuchung nebst Textedition* (Berlin, 1913): "Exkurs: Salutati als philologisch-historischer Kritiker," 77–98; Ullman, *Humanism of Coluccio Salutati*, 95–99. On Bruni, see A. D. Momigliano, "Polybius' Reappearance in Western Europe," in *Polybe* (Vandoeuvres, 1974), 356–57. And for a brief but helpful discussion of Biondo, see D. M. Robathan, "Flavio Biondo's *Roma instaurata*," *Medievalia et humanistica* n.s. 1 (1970): 204.

45. In general, the humanists hesitated to attribute error to ancient writers. Thus, Salutati argues in *De tyranno* that a statement in Valerius Maximus must be wrong, since there is incontrovertible evidence to the contrary in Livy. He explicitly states that in such cases it is proper to assume that the error is a textual corruption: "et potius credant textum Valerii fuisse corruptum, quam eum in tam supinum errorem, qui in tante scientie virum cadere non debuit, incidisse." And he concludes by saying that Valerius Maximus should be emended to agree with Livy. (Salutati, *Il trattato "De Tyranno" e lettere scelte*, ed. F. Ercole [Bologna, 1942], 15.) There were some exceptions. Valla set out to expose a genealogical error in Livy; see Erasmus, *Origins of Rome*, 28–29. And Poliziano argued in *Miscellanea*, 1.53 (in *Opera*, 268–69), that Cicero had wrongly attributed a speech of Odysseus to Agamemnon. For the most part, however, the humanists failed to make a sufficiently clear distinction between straight textual criticism—the restoration of corrupt passages, and historical criticism—reconstruction of events. As a result, they often did the latter while thinking that they were doing the former. I would like to thank H. J. de Jonge for making this point to me.

46. Poliziano, *Opera*, 259. For Greek traditions on the origin of the alphabet, see R. Pfeiffer, *History of Classical Scholarship from 1300 to 1850* (Oxford, 1976), 19–22.

47. Poliziano, *Opera*, 259. Poliziano here alludes to Pliny, *Epistolae*, 2.12.5: "Numerantur enim sententiae, non ponderantur."

48. Beroaldo, *Annotationes centum*, sig. h i v.

49. In maintaining that Poliziano revolutionized philological method, I do not wish to imply that his emendations and interpretations were always superior to those his predecessors had proposed. See my text below, at notes 125ff.

50. Kenney, *The Classical Text*, 5–6.

51. Poliziano, *Miscellanea*, 1.57, in *Opera*, 271, quoted by Rizzo, *Lessico filologico degli umanisti*, 162.

52. Poliziano, *Miscellanea*, 1.71, in *Opera*, 282.

53. Ibid., 1.97 (307).

54. Rizzo, *Lessico filologico degli umanisti*, 147–64.

55. Ibid., 233–34, 257, 271.

56. Beroaldo, *Annotationes centum*, sig. [b vi r].

57. Poliziano, *Miscellanea*, 1.46, in *Opera*, 263. The manuscript mentioned is now Vat. lat. 3286; it is in Beneventan script and was written in the eleventh century. See Rizzo, *Lessico filologico degli umanisti*, 124–25.

58. Timpanaro, *Genesi del metodo del Lachmann;* cf. G. Kirner, "Contributo alla critica del testo delle *Epistolae ad familiares* di Cicerone (1.IX–XVI)," *Studi italiani di filologia classica* 9 (1901): 400–406.

59. Poliziano, *Opera*, 246–47.

60. Ibid., 260.

61. Ibid., 261: "Igitur in Pandectis his, non iam Pisanis, ut quondam, sed Florentinis, in quibus pura sunt verba: nec ut in caeteris plena maculis et scabie,

diffusum [ed. 1498; diffissum 1553] reperio, non diffusum." Cf. ibid., 260. The point was hardly important except from a philological viewpoint, as the passage had been understood even in the corrupt form.

62. See H. E. Troje, *Graeca leguntur* (Cologne, 1971), 21–22, though Troje's interpretation of the episode differs from that proposed here.

63. Poliziano, *Opera*, 287.

64. On Valla's attacks on medieval jurisprudence, see M. P. Gilmore, "The Renaissance Conception of the Lessons of History," in *Facets of the Renaissance*, ed. W. H. Werkmeister (New York, 2d ed. 1963), 92–95; Kelley, *Foundations of Modern Historical Scholarship*, 39–43. For Beroaldo, see *Annotationes centum*, sig. [h iii r]: "Sexcenta sunt id genus apud iurisconsultos ab Acursio perperam enarrata."

65. Aulus Gellius, *Noctes Atticae*, 1.7.1 (trans. J. C. Rolfe). To be sure, many of the manuscripts that Gellius and his fellow antiquaries prized seem to have been forgeries, but Poliziano had no way of knowing that. Cf. J. E. G. Zetzel, "*Emendavi ad Tironem*: Some Notes on Scholarship in the Second Century A.D.," *Harvard Studies in Classical Philology* 77 (1973): 225–43.

66. Aulus Gellius, *Noctes Atticae*, 9.14.1–4.

67. R. Sabbadini, *Storia e critica di alcuni testi latini* (Padua, 2d ed. 1971), 77–108.

68. See *Two Renaissance Book Hunters: The Letters of Poggius Bracciolini to Nicolaus de Niccolis*, ed. and trans. P. W. G. Gordan (New York, 1974), 74, 76–78.

69. G. Pasquali, *Storia della tradizione e critica del testo* (Florence, 2d ed. 1952), 61–63.

70. Giovanni Lamola to Guarino of Verona, 31 May 1428, quoted in Sabbadini, *Storia e critica*, 106.

71. Ibid.

72. Ibid. This letter is quoted in part and its sources and significance discussed in Rizzo, *Lessico filologico degli umanisti*, 175–77.

73. Giorgio Merula, preface to his edition of Plautus (Venice, 1472), quoted by Rizzo, *Lessico filologico degli umanisti*, 314.

74. Sabbadini, *Storia e critica*, 241.

75. Ibid., 241–57; C. Questa, *Per la storia del testo di Plauto nell'umanesimo*, vol. 1, *La "recensio" di Poggio Bracciolini* (Rome, 1986), 7–21.

76. Rizzo, *Lessico filologico degli umanisti*, 314–15.

77. Reynolds and Wilson, *Scribes and Scholars*, 128.

78. Poliziano, *Miscellaneorum centuria secunda*, ed. V. Branca and M. Pastore Stocchi (Florence, 1972), iv, 5. See A. J. Hunt, "Three New Incunables with Marginalia by Politian," *Rinascimento* 2d ser. 24 (1984): 251–59, at 257–58.

79. Ibid., 7.

80. Poliziano, *Miscellanea*, 1.77, in *Opera*, 286–87. Poliziano used the first recension of Fra Giocondo's sylloge (1478–ca. 1489), which was dedicated to Lorenzo; in it there were separate sections for inscriptions that Giocondo had seen and those that he had found in other sylloges, or that had been

reported to him by others. After citing two inscriptions in which the form "Vergilius" appears, and carefully specifying their locations, Poliziano writes (*Opera*, 286): "Idque nos utrinque non sine aliquot arbitris etiam de proximo inspeximus. Neque enim antiquarum duntaxat inspectionum auriti testes, sed et oculati esse concupivimus." On his use of Giocondo's sylloge, he says (ibid., 287): "In collectaneis autem, quae nuperrime ad Laurentium Medicem Iucundus misit, vir unus, ut opinor, titulorum monimentorumque veterum supra mortales caeteros non diligentissimus solum, sed etiam sine controversia peritissimus, relata quoque invenio elogia duo, quae Romae (sicut ille indicat) in marmoribus inveniuntur." On Giocondo, see R. Weiss, *The Renaissance Discovery of Classical Antiquity* (Oxford, 1969), 150–51.

81. Poliziano, *Opera*, 248–49; cf. *The Tragedies of Ennius: The Fragments*, ed. H. D. Jocelyn (Cambridge, 1967), frag. CV a, 118–19; cf. 347.

82. Poliziano, *Miscellanea*, 1.2, in *Opera*, 228; 1.69, in *Opera*, 282.

83. Ibid., 1.68 (282).

84. Marchesi, *Bartolomeo della Fonte*.

85. Poliziano, *Opera*, 247–48.

86. Ibid. Cf. Quintilian, 4.1.77: "Ovidius lascivere in Metamorphosesin solet"; cf. also 10.1.88, 93.

87. Poliziano, *Miscellanea*, 1.4, in *Opera*, 229–30. Cf. *Auli Persii Flacci Satirarum liber*, ed. O. Jahn (Leipzig, 1843), 166–67; R. Cardini, *La critica del Landino* (Florence, 1973), 173 n.

88. Poliziano, *Miscellanea*, 1:4. Cf. Proclus Diadochus, *Commentary on the First Alcibiades of Plato*, ed. I. G. Westerink (Amsterdam, 1954), sect. 6, 11; sect. 19, 11–15.

89. Poliziano, *Miscellanea*, 1:4. "Sic item, *Dinomaches ego sum*, ductum ex eo quod apud Platonem sic est, ὦ φίλε παῖ κλεινίου καὶ δεινομάχης [Persius, 4.20; Alcibiades, 1.105D]."

90. B. Bischoff, "Living with the Satirists," in *Classical Influences on European Culture, A.D. 500–1500*, ed. R. R. Bolgar (Cambridge, 1971), 83–94.

91. F. Jacoby, "Zur Entstehung der römischen Elegie," *Rheinisches Museum für Philologie* n.s. 60 (1905): 38 and n. 1.

92. Aulus Gellius, *Noctes Atticae*, 9.9.1–3 (trans. J. C. Rolfe, slightly altered).

93. See esp. Macrobius, *Saturnalia*, 5.2–22. Cf. in general P. Courcelle, *Late Latin Writers and Their Greek Sources*, trans. H. E. Wedeck (Cambridge, MA, 1969), 13–26.

94. De Bury probably knew only the preface and books 1–7 of Gellius; see R. Sabbadini, *Le scoperte dei codici latini e greci ne' secoli XIV e XV*, 2 vols. (Florence, 1905–14), 2:9 and n. 40.

95. Richard de Bury, *Philobiblon*, ed. and trans. E. C. Thomas and M. Maclagan (Oxford, 1960), 111.

96. For an example, see R. Sabbadini, *La scuola e gli studi di Guarino Guarini Veronese* (Catania, 1896), 219.

97. Domizio Calderini, *Elucubratio in quaedam Propertii loca quae difficiliora videantur*, first published at Rome on 13.viii.1475 (*Repertorium Biblio-*

graphicum 14983); my references are to the edition of the same collection of Calderini's works that was published at Brescia on 8.vi.1476 (Hain-Reichling 4244; Proctor 6949).

98. Calderini, *Elucubratio*, sig. [c6 r], *ad* 1.20: "Theocritum in primis hoc loco imitatur et transfert, de fabula Hylae."

99. Ibid., *ad* 3.21.24: "Theseae brachia longa viae. Muros longos intelligit: qui Graece [τὰ μακρὰ τείχη] dicebantur. Ii ex urba in Pyreum usque excurrebant. Historia est apud Thucydidem diligentissime perscripta."

100. Calderini, *Elucubratio*, sig. [c5 r], *ad* 1.13.21: "Hemonio: id est Thessalo. Sed dissentit a Strabone Propertius: nam Enipeum amatum a puella scribit Strabo esse in Pisana regione, cum tamen alter sit in Thessalia." Cf. Strabo, 8.3.32; 9.5.6. Strabo places a river Enipeus or Eniseus in Thessaly, but the river Enipeus with which Tyro fell in love he situates in Elis.

101. See in general D. O. Ross, Jr., *Backgrounds to Augustan Poetry: Gallus, Elegy and Rome* (Cambridge, 1975). The passage 4.1.64 is normally interpreted as a statement of Propertius's intention to write etiological poems about Rome, modeled in scope and method on the *Aetia* of Callimachus; see, e.g., *The Elegies of Propertius,* ed. H. E. Butler and E. A. Barber (Oxford, 1933), lxvi, 322.

102. Calderini, *Elucubratio,* sigs. [d5v–d6r], *ad* 4.1.64: "Romani Callimachi. Se Romanum Callimachum appellat. Nam Callimachum, poetam Graecum, versibus Latinis explicat."

103. Ibid., sig. c2v, *ad* 1.2.1: "Vita. Ex Callimacho, quom praecipue imitatur, verbum deductum est. Nam et ille blandiens Graeca voce amicam [Ζωήν] appellat."

104. Beroaldo's note on 4.1.64 reads as follows (Tibullus, Catullus, Propertius [Venice, 9.xii.1491], Hain* 4763; Proctor 5029, sig. [s vi v]): "Vmbria Romani. Appellat se Romanum Callimachum: quoniam qualis est apud Graecos Callimachus scriptor elegiarum, talis est apud Romanos Propertius: qui in primis Callimachum aemulatus est, et illum in scribendo habet archetypon. Ita Virgilius dictus est Mantuanus Homerus: cuius emulatus est non modo magnitudinem, sed simplicitatem orationis, tacitamque maiestatem." The same point is made in his introductory remarks, ibid., sig 1r. On *vita,* see sig. 1 ii r, *ad* 1.2.1: "Vita. Vox est amatoria. Graece a Iuvenale dictum est [Ζωή], idest, vita et anima. Id genus multa reperies apud Plautum. Imitatio est Callimachi, a quo [Ζωή], id est, vita, amica appellatur."

105. Poliziano, *Miscellanea,* 1.80, in *Opera,* 289.

106. Calderini's own commentary on Juvenal—which A. C. Dionisotti kindly consulted when no copy was accessible to me—does not discuss the word in question.

107. Propertius, 4.9.57–58:

> Magnam Tiresias aspexit Pallada vates,
>   Fortita dum posita Gorgone membra lavat.

108. Poliziano, *Opera,* 288–95.

109. For the later history of the debate on the origins of Latin love-elegy, see A.

Cartault, *À propos du Corpus Tibullianum: Un siècle de philologie latine classique* (Paris, 1906), 518.

110. For a modern comparative discussion of the Euripides and Ennius passages that Poliziano treated in *Miscellanea*, 1.27, see O. Skutsch, *Studia Enniana* (London, 1968), 166–69.

111. Poliziano, *Miscellanea*, 1.24, in *Opera*, 246.

112. Before revealing the Platonic source of Persius's fourth satire, Poliziano makes the general claim that a good critic must also have complete mastery of all other disciplines: "Qui poetarum interpretationem suscipit, eum non scolium (quod dicitur) ad Aristophanis lucernam, sed etiam ad Cleanthis oportet lucubrasse. Nec prospiciendae autem philosophorum modo familiae, sed et iureconsultorum, et medicorum item, et dialecticorum, et quicunque doctrinae illum orbem faciunt, quae vocamus Encyclia, sed et philologorum [ed. 1498; philosophorum 1553] quoque omnium. Nec prospiciendae tantum, verum introspiciendae magis, neque (quod dicitur), ab limine ac vestibulo salutandae, sed arcessendae potius in penetralia, et in intimam familiaritatem, si rem iuvare Latinam studemus, et inscitiam quotidie invalescentem profligare; alioqui semidocta sedulitas cum magna sui persuasione detrimento sit [om. ed. 1498], non usui" (*Miscellanea*, 1.4, in *Opera*, 229). His reference to Cleanthes and Aristophanes is also an allusion to Varro's similarly phrased claim that a good grammarian must have mastered all existing approaches to the study of etymology: "Quod non solum ad Aristophanis lucernam, sed etiam ad Cleanthis lucubravi" (*De lingua Latina* 5.9)—a much-controverted passage. Poliziano also advances a polemical claim for the status of criticism by implication in his discussion of the relative ages of Patroclus and Achilles (*Miscellanea* 1.45); for this was one of the very topics that Seneca had ridiculed grammarians for discussing in *Epistulae morales* 88.6. To take the question seriously was also to deny Seneca's assessment of its worth.

113. On Argyropoulos see J. E. Seigel, "The Teaching of Argyropoulos and the Rhetoric of the First Humanists," in *Action and Conviction in Early Modern Europe; Essays in Memory of E. H. Harbison*, ed. T. K. Rabb and J. E. Seigel (Princeton, 1969), 237–60; on this controversy, see the excellent study by E. Garin, "Ἐνδελέχεια ε Ἐντελέχεια nelle discussioni umanistiche," *Atene e Roma* 3d ser. 5 (1937): 177–87.

114. Poliziano, *Miscellanea*, 1.1, in *Opera*, 227.

115. Naturally I cannot enter here into the important controversies about the philosophical aspirations and achievements of the humanists; see in general C. B. Schmitt, *A Critical Survey and Bibliography of Studies on Renaissance Aristotelianism, 1958–1969* (Padua, 1971), for an orientation into some of the major issues. I am inclined to take the humanists' claims somewhat more seriously than does the leading American authority, Professor Kristeller, and a bit less seriously than does the leading Italian authority, Professor Garin.

116. See in general E. Bigi, *La cultura del Poliziano e altri studi umanistici* (Pisa, 1967).

117. Poliziano, dedicatory epistle in Leon Battista Alberti, *De re aedificatoria, Gesamtkatalog der Wiegendrucke 579* (Florence, 29 Dec. 1485), sig. a v.

118. On what Renaissance readers expected from Neolatin poetry—and on its general social and cultural functions—see the excellent treatment in *The Poems of Desiderius Erasmus,* ed. and intro. C. Reedijk (Leiden, 1956), chap. 2: "Not From Mere Foolishness. . . ."

119. See J. Hutton, *The Greek Anthology in Italy to the Year 1800* (Ithaca, NY, 1935).

120. Poliziano, *Opera,* 241.

121. See, e.g., Erasmus, *De conscribendis epistolis,* in *Opera omnia Des. Erasmi Roterodami,* 13 vols. to date (Amsterdam, 1969–), 1.2.266: "Caeterum cui palma debeatur in hoc genere, non est huius instituti pluribus verbis persequi. Si quis omissis Graecis, patiatur quenquam ullo in genere anteponi, M. Tullio, et Plinio, et Politiano primas detulerim. Sed hac sane in re fruatur suo quisque iudicio." Cf. also the *index nominum,* under Poliziano and Agnolo Ambrogini.

122. F. Simone, "La notion d'Encyclopédie: Élément caractéristique de la Renaissance française," in *French Renaissance Studies 1540–1570,* ed. P. Sharratt (Edinburgh, 1976), 245, 259–60, nn. 78–82.

123. Grafton, *Joseph Scaliger,* chap. 7.

124. Poliziano, *Miscellanea,* 1.41, in *Opera,* 261.

125. I follow, with reservations, H. Baron, *The Crisis of the Early Italian Renaissance,* 2 vols. in 1 (Princeton, rev. ed. 1966); for an important critique, see Q. Skinner, *The Foundations of Modern Political Thought,* vol. 1, *The Renaissance* (Cambridge, 1978), pts. 1 and 2. And see in these volumes, the essay on Florentine civic humanism.

126. For the poetic uses to which Poliziano put his scholarship, see, e.g., A. Perosa, "Febris: A Poetic Myth Created by Poliziano," *Journal of the Warburg and Courtauld Institutes* 9 (1946): 74–95; Bigi, *Cultura del Poliziano,* 89–90 and n. 50; M. Martelli, "La semantica di Poliziano e la *Centuria secunda* dei Rinascimento," *Rinascimento* 2d ser. 13 (1973): 21–84; L. Cesarini Martinelli, "In margine al commento di Angelo Poliziano alle *Selve* di Stazio," *Interpres* 1 (1978): 96–145. My view is indebted especially to D. Quint's introduction to his translation of *The "Stanze" of Angelo Poliziano* (Amherst, MA, 1979); for a very different view, see Cardini, *Critica del Landino,* 48ff.

127. See above, text to notes 2ff.

128. See Dunston, "Studies in Domizio Calderini," 143–44.

129. Timpanaro, "Atlas cum compare gibbo."

130. Poliziano, *Commento inedito alle Selve di Stazio,* 5–7; *Miscellanea,* 2.48, *Miscellaneorum centuria secunda,* 4:86–89.

131. Poliziano, *Epistolario,* 3.18: "Iuvit enim, quantum potuit, rem literariam."

132. Ibid., 3.19: "Ego vero sic Domitium studiosis, quasi foveam viatoribus ostendo."

133. Ibid.

134. *Miscellanea,* 2.1: 4:3.

135. See, e.g., Poliziano, *Epistolario*, 3.18, and the others listed by Branca and Pastore Stocchi in their "Introduzione" to *Miscellanea II, ed. minor*, separately paginated, 3, n. 3.

136. See *Michaelis Marulli Carmina*, ed. A. Perosa (Zurich, 1951), 59, 66, 67, 73, 76, 78–79, 88–89, 185; cf. 218.

137. See L. Perotto Sali, "L'opusculo inedito di Giorgio Merula contro i *Miscellanea* di Angelo Poliziano," *Interpres* 1 (1978): 146ff.

138. See Dionisotti, "Calderini, Poliziano e altri," 183–85 (on Matteo Bosso, who wrote: "Solet enim Policianus codices, quasi vina, magis vetustate quam ratione probare, ut cum eo ridens ingessi quandoque ioco mordaci").

B 🙶 THE *STUDIA HUMANITATIS*

29 🙶 RENAISSANCE GRAMMAR
W. Keith Percival

IRONICALLY, THE EXPRESSION "RENAISSANCE GRAMMAR" AMOUNTS almost to a contradiction in terms, for the term "Renaissance" connotes the reawakening or revival of certain cultural traditions of classical antiquity that occurred from about the middle of the fourteenth century after a long period during which these traditions had been in a state of decline or had virtually ceased to exist. In the case of grammar as it was practiced during the Renaissance, however, nothing could be farther from the truth. First, the study of grammar had been in a perfectly healthy state in the Middle Ages and hence was in no need of renewal. Second, it had always been based on classical models: there was, therefore, no question of reestablishing contact with something which had lain submerged for centuries.[1]

What can be said with some justice, however, is that grammar, like other aspects of Renaissance culture, underwent a gradual transformation in the course of the fifteenth century. Specifically, there is a clear sense in which the approach to antiquity on the part of grammarians changed. To this extent, the traditional connotations of the term "Renaissance" are applicable to grammar, though perhaps not so felicitously as in some other areas.

A further obstacle in the way of understanding Renaissance grammar may be caused by the word "grammar" itself. Nowadays, professional linguists—and also to a considerable extent the general public—apply the term to a set of rules that account for or "describe" the regularities of some language; in practice, grammar embraces everything the learner needs to know about the language he is studying except for the meanings of individual words. In the Renaissance, by contrast, the notion of grammar as a neutral description of the structure of some language was unknown: throughout that period, "grammar" named part of the school curriculum, namely, the portion devoted to the inculcation of the skills of speaking and writing a specific language—Latin—and by a natural semantic extension, it also applied to the knowledge students gained in that process.

We can obtain an approximate idea of what Renaissance humanists understood by grammar by examining a typical definition of "grammar" that occurs in many fifteenth-century grammatical texts: "Grammar is the knowledge (*scientia*) of how to speak correctly and write correctly, the origin and basis of all the liberal arts."[2] The aim of grammatical instruction was to inculcate linguistic competence. It was also understood that Latin was the language in which the student was to become proficient, so well understood that the word Latin did not need to be explicitly mentioned. Furthermore, the enterprise was prescriptive, not descriptive (witness the word "correctly"): grammar was unequivocally an *art,* that is, a set of prescriptions imparted in a systematic fashion. Finally, it was regarded as the gateway to the liberal arts. Indeed, grammar was itself one of the liberal arts, and with logic and rhetoric it belonged in the trivium, the lower of the two major divisions of the liberal arts.

The liberal arts, however, did not stand on their own but were regarded as a preparation for more advanced study, namely, for one of the two learned professions, law and medicine. Within the trivium, in turn, grammar was preparatory to rhetoric and logic because it taught the elementary linguistic skills without which the student could study neither of those two subjects, still less proceed to the two worldly disciplines. As one medieval grammarian put it: "Grammar is justifiably the first of the liberal arts because without it the latter cannot be known."[3] In the hierarchy of scholarly disciplines, therefore, grammar stood at the very base.

This propaedeutic function of grammar was a consequence of the fact that throughout the Renaissance the entire educational system in western Europe continued to use Latin as its medium of communication: all professional literature consulted by lawyers and physicians and utilized in their training was in Latin, and formal proceedings at the university level were carried on in Latin.

It is worthwhile to emphasize that in spite of the steady rise in status of the vernaculars from about the thirteenth century the dominant position of Latin in the school curriculum remained unchallenged throughout the Renaissance. The vernaculars, in fact, competed with Latin only in two areas, namely belles-lettres and secular administration. Thus, it was not customary to compose major philosophical works in the vernacular until the seventeenth century; one thinks, for instance, of Galileo's *Il saggiatore* (Rome, 1623) and René Descartes's *Discours de la méthode* (Leiden, 1637). But as late as the final decades of the eighteenth century Immanuel Kant's *Critique of Pure Reason* (Riga, 1781) was soon translated into Latin, as *Critica rationis purae* (Leipzig, 1796), for the benefit of readers not familiar with German, while translations into the modern languages were much slower to appear (the first French translation, for example, was not published until 1835).

*   *   *

Traditionally, grammar was divided into four parts: orthography, prosody, etymology, and syntax, each being concerned with one of the four basic linguistic units, namely, orthography with letters, prosody with syllables, etymology with words, and syntax with sentences. Orthography comprised a classification of the sounds of Latin into vowels, consonants, semivowels, mutes, liquids, and so on, and it also included prescriptions on correct spelling (in particular, thorny problems such as the correct use of *h*, consonant gemination, the spelling or transliteration of Greek words). Etymology covered what linguists nowadays call morphology, in other words, nominal declensions and verbal conjugations, presented in the form of paradigms. Syntax was concerned, in theory, with the correct arrangement of words in sentences; in practice, it consisted of the rules of agreement and government, such as the rule that Latin adjectives agree with the nouns they accompany in gender, number, and case. Prosody dealt with the nature of the syllable and usually comprised a study of vowel length (rules to predict the length of Latin vowels, along with lists of examples and exceptions to such rules). Related to prosody was metrics, the study of the structure of Latin verse.

The only textbook widely used throughout the Middle Ages and the Renaissance that covered the whole field of grammar was the massive *Institutio de arte grammatica* by Priscian, a work compiled in Constantinople in the early sixth century that remained popular for more than a millennium. A much shorter work, the so-called *Ars minor* of Donatus (mid-fourth century), served as a beginner's manual—it provided nothing more than a definitional framework conveniently formulated in question-and-answer format for use in the classroom. Ideally, therefore, the beginning student first committed Donatus's definitions to memory and then proceeded to study Priscian's *Institutio*.

Not all grammatical manuals treated the four central parts of the subject, nor when they were all present were they necessarily treated in the order I have just mentioned. Treatises on separate parts of grammar were common, as were treatments in which morphological and syntactic material was blended. This situation is what the Renaissance humanists inherited from the immediate past, for in the Middle Ages comprehensive treatments of the whole of grammar were seldom attempted, probably because a systematic coverage of the entire discipline was available to all scholars in Priscian's *Institutio*. To a large extent, therefore, grammatical writing in the late Middle Ages and early Renaissance was intended to supplement, not to supplant, Priscian's work.

This tradition was followed in the fifteenth century by the great educator Guarino of Verona (1374–1460) in his grammatical writings and by the grammatical writers who followed immediately after him.[4] Guarino's *Regulae grammaticales,* for example, explicitly excludes any consideration of prosody, has the barest outline of an orthography, and does not even present definitions of the parts of speech or the most useful nominal and verbal paradigms. These omissions were possible because teachers of grammar used more than one text to teach Latin. Guarino, for example, taught his beginning students grammar from a medieval text that contained definitions of the parts of speech and sets of paradigms, and wrote new grammatical manuals for the benefit of his more advanced students.[5]

Attempts to produce comprehensive Latin grammars were not made until the second half of the fifteenth century. The first example is the *Rudimenta grammatices* by Niccolò Perotti (1429–1480), which was completed in 1468 and first appeared in printed form in Rome five years later.[6] Perotti's grammar starts out with a complete morphology, based for the most part on Priscian, with the rules in the form of questions and answers, as in Donatus's *Ars minor.* The second third of the *Rudimenta* is a Latin syntax on the model of Guarino's *Regulae,* but going into more detail. Perotti's work is, moreover, peculiar in that the final third is a manual of epistolary composition; in other words, Perotti incorporated rhetoric into grammar. The subsequent popularity of the *Rudimenta* was probably due to the fact that it could be used as the basis for a complete course of Latin instruction.

However, Perotti's experiment in combining a grammatical and a rhetorical manual seems not to have started a trend. Thus, the Spanish humanist Antonio de Nebrija, though he produced a grammatical manual that was even more detailed and comprehensive than Perotti's (it was entitled *Introductiones Latinae explicitae* and was first printed in Salamanca in 1481), never attempted a rhetoric. It is also significant that Perotti made a considerable contribution to Latin metrics in the form of two short treatises written in his youth, and that he contributed signally to Latin lexicography with his so-called *Cornucopiae,* which took the form of an extensive commentary on Martial's poems, again as a separate work.

In the early sixteenth century, a figure such as Johannes Despauterius, active in the Low Countries, wrote separate treatises on all branches of grammar, but it is noteworthy that the Parisian printer Robert Estienne put all these ingredients together in a single large volume, entitled

Commentarii grammatici (Paris, 1537). Other comprehensive grammars of Latin were written later in the sixteenth century, perhaps the most notable being the monumental *De institutione grammatica* by the Jesuit Emmanuel Alvares (Lisbon, 1572), which continued to be the official grammatical textbook of the Society of Jesus for more than two centuries.

Theoretical treatises on grammar, popular in the High Middle Ages, were a rare occurrence in the fifteenth century, but by the sixteenth century the interest in general works on grammar had revived. The earliest one is *De rebus non vulgaribus* by Curio Lancellotti Pasi (Reggio, 1504). It was followed by a more influential work by the English humanist Thomas Linacre (*De emendata structura Latini sermonis*, London 1524). The work in this genre that had the greatest impact was *De causis linguae Latinae* by Julius Caesar Scaliger (1484–1558), a grandiose attempt to criticize traditional grammatical terms and categories from an Aristotelian point of view.[7] The educational reformer Pierre de la Ramée (Petrus Ramus) also applied his pedagogical theories to the teaching of languages and composed grammars of Latin, Greek, and his native French in the mid-sixteenth century.[8] Later in the century, the Spanish humanist Francisco Sánchez de las Brozas (Franciscus Sanctius Brocensis) effected a synthesis of the ideas of Linacre, Scaliger, and Ramus in a pungently written grammatical treatise entitled *Minerva seu de causis linguae Latinae* (Salamanca, 1587), which, though relatively uninfluential immediately after its appearance, became an extremely popular textbook from about the middle of the seventeenth century for approximately a further two hundred years.[9]

*   *   *

It would obviously be a mistake to equate Renaissance grammar with the material contained in the new textbooks produced in that period. As I have already hinted, grammarians in the fifteenth century, like their medieval predecessors and scholastic counterparts, continued to utilize pedagogical material that had been inherited, in an unbroken tradition, from late antiquity, namely, the manuals of Donatus (ca. A.D. 350) and Priscian (ca. A.D. 500). As we have seen, the former was a beginner's manual, while the latter served as a reference work for the advanced student and the teacher. In neither of them is there an attempt to grade the material to ease the learning process, as is customarily done in language textbooks nowadays. Instead, the point of departure in both is a set of basic definitions of the fundamental linguistic units (letter, sound, word, sentence) and the so-called parts of speech: noun, pronoun, verb, adverb, and so on. Inflections are presented by means of paradigms, which the student was expected to learn by heart, in addition, of course, to the basic definitions. Priscian's grammar enumerates all regular inflectional patterns and all inflectional irregularities, but for the most part in a piecemeal fashion. What theoretical discussion there is in that work is concerned for the most part with the rationale of the definitions presented. Donatus's grammar does not even contain a skeletal outline of Latin morphology, but confines itself to basic definitions and examples of the major grammatical categories. It is important to note that the grammars of Donatus and Priscian had formed the basis of grammatical instruction for about a millennium. Other components of the textbook literature, however, were of more recent origin.

During the Middle Ages, the grammars of Donatus and Priscian had spawned a vast literature of commentaries, aimed at elucidating them for the benefit of the student and the advanced scholar. Indeed, the commentary was to a large degree the preferred mode of grammatical literature. A significant innovation of the Renaissance humanists was to deemphasize the grammatical commentary.

From the thirteenth century on, another genre of grammatical literature had arisen, namely, metrical treatises, in other words, grammars written entirely in verse. Two of these metrical grammars, the *Doctrinale* by Alexander of Villedieu and the *Graecismus* of Évrard de Béthune, were especially popular as intermediate-level textbooks.[10] Like the grammars of Donatus and Priscian, they gave rise to a large number of commentaries.

Parallel to and deriving from the grammatical commentaries, there also arose, especially from the thirteenth century on and in northern Europe, a considerable literature of independent theoretical treatises on grammatical topics, bearing the stamp of the scholastic method. These so-called speculative grammars were designed to elevate grammar to the level of an apodictic science on a par with logic. Medieval grammarians of Latin may also lay claim to have elaborated the rather disorganized account of sentence structure found in the two final books of Priscian's *Institutio*. In northern Europe, medieval syntactic theory was influenced by contemporary scholastic logic, while in southern Europe rhetorical considerations seem to have played an important role, as exemplified by a number of encyclopedic lexica that appeared in that period, the most notable being the *Catholicon* of Giovanni Balbi from the late thirteenth century.

With the general rejection of scholastic methodology by the early Renaissance humanists, the distinctively medieval grammatical literature gradually lost its popularity, especially the independent "speculative" treatises produced during the Middle Ages. The verse grammars continued to be used by the early humanists, and likewise the medieval lexica (the *Catholicon,* for example, went through more than thirty printed editions between 1460 and 1520). It is also significant that in Italy, the cradle of humanism, there was initially little overt hostility expressed against medieval grammarians. This circumstance may be in part due to the fact that it had always been customary for the grammarians o. each generation to write new textbook material for their students: in this respect, the humanist grammarians were doing what grammarians had always done. Second, however, we must remember that a grammatical manual, especially a primer, was not used as a vehicle for linguistic speculation but had a strictly utilitarian function: doctrinal discussion was no doubt felt to be out of place in such a pedagogical tool. It was especially so in the environment of the new humanistic pedagogy, in contradistinction to scholastic education with its emphasis on dialectical disputation.

*   *   *

It is time to consider the question of the Renaissance humanists' attitude to medieval and ancient grammar. In this regard, one can roughly divide the tradition of Latin grammatical writing in the Renaissance into three stages. In the first stage, many of the standard grammatical textbooks current in the Middle Ages remained in use, and the only areas in which the humanists made any contribution were metrics and orthography. The early humanists, in particular the Paduan circle grouped around Lovato de Lovati (ca. 1240–1309) and Albertino Mussato (1261–1329), contributed nothing to the central areas of grammar. One assumes that they were largely satisfied with the grammatical literature available at the time. Lovati wrote a short account of Senecan meters, which reflects an interest in Latin verse composition in general but was also an attempt to broaden knowledge of the metrical repertoire—Latin poets in the Middle Ages had largely confined themselves to two verse patterns, the pentameter and the hexameter.[11]

In the case of Petrarch (1304–1374), there is some evidence of a positive attitude toward the current grammatical literature. In listing his favorite books, he mentioned not only the two ancient grammarians Donatus and Priscian, but also the *Catholicon* of Giovanni Balbi and an earlier encyclopedic dictionary, the *Papias* (mid-eleventh century). He also on occasion compared grammar and medicine as disciplines and gave his approval to the former while denigrating the latter.[12]

Petrarch's protégé Coluccio Salutati (1331–1406) seems to have been the first humanist to censure medieval standards of Latin orthography and phraseology.[13] The ideal of a Latin style purged of nonclassical words and constructions and observing classical orthographical conventions received its first clear expression with him. Those who followed him quickly accepted the challenge.

In the second period, which coincides more or less with Guarino of Verona's active years (to wit, between about 1420 and 1460), new grammatical textbooks were produced for the first time, but no hostility to medieval grammatical literature is expressed in them. Guarino's grammatical writings are, however, characterized by extreme conciseness of formulation and a complete lack of the dialectical subtleties that had been such a noticeable feature of not only the speculative grammatical literature but also many of the pedagogical grammars of the High Middle Ages. Indeed, the coverage of grammatical facts in Guarino's main work, the *Regulae grammaticales,* is so limited that it is difficult to imagine how beginners could learn a language as complicated as Latin from such a textbook. A conspicuous trait of Guarino's grammatical opus is the extent to which it is based, in many instances verbatim, on medieval grammatical manuals, especially on the *Graecismus.*[14] We know from a remark made by Guarino's son Battista in a pedagogical treatise published in 1459 that Guarino did not disdain to teach from the other major medieval verse grammar, the *Doctrinale.*

In the area of orthography, the first new work of the second period was the *Orthographia* of Gasparino Barzizza, which was written about 1418. In the late 1440s, Giovanni Tortelli wrote his massive *Orthographia* (published in 1453), which was designed to standardize the spelling of the many Greek words and proper names in common use in Latin prose and verse.[15]

In the third stage, which is exemplified in Lorenzo Valla's *Elegantiae linguae Latinae* (completed in the mid-1440s), a distinctively humanistic approach to Latin composition became more clearly defined, and criticism of medieval grammar and lexicography became more acrimonious.[16] In the *Elegantiae* and elsewhere, Valla not only pours scorn on the medieval lexica but explicitly links medieval grammar to scholastic doctrine. The two most salient features of the grammars produced toward the end of the fifteenth century are their increasingly comprehensive coverage and their explicit attempt to use ancient usage as a yardstick. Valla's *Elegantiae* is chiefly concerned with the meaning and correct use of individual words—it does not touch on the problem of sentence structure. Later grammarians were quick to combine Guarino's approach to grammatical rules with Valla's precision in stylistic matters. In southern Europe, the most successful grammars of this period were two works already mentioned, the *Rudimenta grammatices* of Niccolò Perotti

(1468) and the grammatical manual of the Spanish humanist Antonio de Nebrija.[17]

In the meantime, manuscripts of a number of ancient grammars unknown or little known during the Middle Ages, works by Caper, Charisius, Diomedes, Probus, and others, had been rediscovered along with Latin belletristic literature (for example, Lucretius, Martial, Plautus, Tacitus). The new grammatical literature exerted a leavening influence on humanist grammarians in that it introduced them to a wider variety of grammatical doctrine than had previously been available. Among these noncanonical grammatical works the one that had the greatest impact was Varro's *De lingua Latina* (first century B.C.). Known to Lorenzo Valla and Giovanni Tortelli, it was first put to systematic use by Giulio Pomponio Leto in a series of grammatical works that circulated in manuscript from the 1460s on. Based on them, Pomponio published a complete grammar of his own (Venice, 1484), but it seems to have had little success, perhaps because it deviated too much from established practice by incorporating Varro's terminology, which differed appreciably from the standard terms found in the works of Donatus and Priscian.[18] It is curious that the only innovation of Pomponio's that other Latin grammarians increasingly adopted was the practice of arranging morphological paradigms in tabular form: Nebrija already followed suit in the first edition of his *Introductiones* (1481).

*   *   *

In the area of individual words and phraseology, the seminal work was Valla's *Elegantiae linguae Latinae*. It is hard for us nowadays to appreciate the revolutionary nature of this work. The most distinctive feature of Valla's method was made possible by the fact that he was so familiar with Latin literature that he was able to cite passages from classical authors whenever he needed an authority to support his prescriptions. This procedure was undoubtedly inspired by the example of Priscian's *Institutio,* but it had never been used before Valla in the Middle Ages or the early Renaissance, and it started a trend of great historical importance. Grammarians had always paid lip service to the notion that grammar should be based on usage (*usus*), but none had hitherto attempted to do what Valla did, namely, to show specifically how to use Latin words correctly by quoting relevant examples from Roman authors. As a glance at any reputable comprehensive Latin grammar current today will show, this procedure is the one still followed by classical scholars writing on the Latin language.

But it is important to pause a moment to examine the meaning of the term usage, as understood by Valla. It might seem as if Valla would lend support to any locution citable anywhere in an ancient author, but he did not do so. He was perfectly aware that the usage of different ancient writers varied. For instance, in the first chapter of the *Elegantiae,* Valla enumerates the feminine nouns that take *-abus* in the dative and ablative plural (instead of the normal ending *-is*). Having done so, he immediately concedes that one may on occasion encounter an author whose usage violates the rule he has just stated, but he hastens to add: "I am discussing good usage (*usus*) not bad (*abusus*)." [19] Neither was it a question of claiming that usage had no underlying basis in rationality—that question was never raised by Valla. In this respect, he was not a grammatical theorist at all, but contented himself with the task of establishing classical standards of usage. In other words, Valla's espousal of usage was not motivated by any deeper philosophical considerations.

*   *   *

The most signal innovation of Renaissance humanism in the area of grammar was the incorporation of Greek instruction into the curriculum. This change must be regarded as profound in the western pedagogical tradition for the simple reason that it represents the first time that a second language was taught alongside Latin. [20] The reason Renaissance humanists were convinced that the study of Greek should be made an integral part of the *studia humanitatis* was that the Latin writers of antiquity had so often emphasized the indispensability of a knowledge of that language for the serious writer, and, as was well known, Greek instruction had formed the basis of the education of aristocratic Romans in antiquity.

We can distinguish roughly three stages in the assimilation of Greek into western education. At first, isolated individuals attempted to learn the language from native speakers resident in the West. Thus, Petrarch attempted (with little success) to learn Greek from a Calabrian monk. The second period was marked by two developments: a handful of outstanding Italian humanists (among them Guarino of Verona and Francesco Filelfo) traveled to Constantinople and, having learned Greek by immersion, returned to Italy and taught the language with great success to their pupils. At the same time, a steadily increasing stream of Greek emigrants appeared in Italy and likewise began teaching the language. In the final stage, the teaching of Greek became a more or less regular part of the arts curriculum in the West, and instruction was usually imparted by the same teachers who taught Latin.

The paucity and unsuitability of the existing textbook material was a serious problem facing teachers and students of Greek. The Greek grammars current in the Byzantine Empire, like their Latin counterparts, had never been designed with the needs of nonnative speakers in mind. The textbook composed by Manuel Chrysoloras, who taught Greek in Florence and elsewhere from 1397 on, was the first attempt to simplify the presentation of Greek grammar for the needs of the western student, but it was composed entirely in Greek. Guarino, who had studied under Chrysoloras in Constantinople, later summarized this manual, and the summary having been translated into Latin, the resulting bilingual text was the first Greek grammar to appear in printed form many years later (ca. 1475).

The next stage was reached when Greek exiles in Italy began to write introductory Greek manuals themselves. Constantine Lascaris's *Epitome* appeared in its first printed edition in Milan in the mid-1470s, and was soon translated into Latin and thereafter published in bilingual form. Similarly, Theodore Gaza produced an introductory textbook entitled *Eisagoge,* which was published in printed form by the great Venetian printer Aldo Manuzio in 1495. By the end of the fifteenth century, therefore, a number of elementary Greek textbooks were available, and Greek instruction was provided in a number of educational centers in Italy. The extent of the average humanist's knowledge of the language should, however, not be overestimated. The textbook material was still forbiddingly difficult for the uninitiated, and an effective method for inculcating knowledge of a second language did not exist. Much use was made of bilingual texts in an effort to impart the new language inductively.

A further problem faced by learners of Greek was the paucity of Greek literature available at that time. The authors most commonly studied together with one of the grammatical primers were Aesop, Hesiod, Homer, Plutarch (especially the *Moralia*), Lucian, and Aristophanes. Customarily, only selections from these works were attempted, after the manner of the Byzantine chrestomathies. It is unlikely, therefore, that the average student had a clear idea of the immense range of classical Greek literature. Thus, much of the best Greek literature, in particular the works of the great tragedians, was hardly known in the fifteenth century.

The average educated man gained whatever knowledge he had of Greek literature in the main from reading Latin translations, not the originals, and many professional humanists spent a great deal of their time translating Greek authors into Latin. Thus, Guarino translated Strabo's *Geography,* Valla translated Aesop, Xenophon, and Homer, and Perotti translated Epictetus's *Enchiridion.*[21] Perhaps the greatest achievement of fifteenth-century humanism in this area was Marsilio Ficino's translation of, and commentary on, the entire Platonic corpus. This monumental edition first appeared in print in Florence in 1484–85 and was destined to remain in constant use for more than three hundred years.

*   *   *

It seems fair to say, in conclusion, that what distinguishes grammar in the Renaissance is that it was studied not only to give the student access to the higher curricular subjects and eventually to the professions of law and medicine, as had been the case in the Middle Ages, but also to enable him to read and enjoy Latin literature. It is perhaps no accident that this widening of interest is reflected in some of the definitions of grammar to be found in fifteenth-century manuals, which explicitly divide grammar into two parts, the first comprising the art of speaking and writing correctly, and the second the interpretation of literary texts.[22] This enlargement of grammar's scope had the effect of bringing it into closer relation with rhetoric, and we must not forget that rhetoric was no longer confined, as it had been previously, to the art of composition (the medieval *ars dictaminis*). It is not surprising, for instance, that the final decades of the fifteenth century saw the beginnings of textual criticism, the conceptual foundations of which had been laid by Lorenzo Valla but which came to practical fruition in the work of Angelo Poliziano (1454–1494) and many eminent scholars in the sixteenth and later centuries.[23]

Thus, insofar as Renaissance grammar had any distinctive features at all, it was due to its close association with the revivified *studia humanitatis,* which constitute the distinctive feature of the movement we call Renaissance humanism. But despite the close relation between grammar and literature in the period under consideration, most students of grammar probably did not attain a high level of literary appreciation in the modern sense of that term. What passed for interpretation was for the most part confined to the elucidation of unusual words and the literal meaning of sentences, as one quickly discovers if one examines humanistic commentaries of classical works: there is in fact no discussion of literary values or aesthetic matters to be found in them.[24]

Moreover, literature, as understood during the Renaissance, was by no means equivalent to what we would nowadays call belles-lettres. Fifteenth-century humanist teachers and their students read not only the poets Vergil, Lucan, Ovid, and the like, and the prose writers Cicero, Livy, Tacitus, and so forth, but also the Latin-speaking church fathers (in particular St. Augustine), the textbook writers of Roman antiquity (such as the naturalist Pliny the Elder, the geographer Pomponius Mela, the practical farmers Columella and Varro, and the architect and engineer Vitruvius), and last but not least the philosophers of antiquity, in particular Aristotle and Plato. To an extent difficult for us to appreciate and estimate, the Renaissance humanists read Latin literature for its factual content as much as for its aesthetic qualities. Thus, the reading list of the average Renaissance humanist scholar or student would strike a modern classical scholar (and a fortiori the average educated reader of today) as extremely bizarre.

At the same time, the Renaissance humanist was not satisfied with a passive knowledge of the Latin language, that is, a knowledge just adequate to permit him to read authors with understanding: he also put his Latin knowledge to practical use. The consummate Latinist aspired to compose his own orations, elegies, epics, and so forth, and to engage in correspondence with colleagues, and even in learned debates and controversies. From the range of Latin vocabulary the student was expected to master it is clear that the language was intended to serve all the communicative needs of its users. This goal contrasts markedly with the functions that a knowledge of Latin serves for students today. To this extent, the Renaissance humanist was much more intimately familiar with and more thoroughly at home in Latin than it is usual for classicists in our own century to be.

NOTES

1. For the history of grammar in general, a useful starting point is R. H. Robins, *A Short History of Linguistics* (London and New York, 2d ed. 1979). On linguistic studies during the Renaissance, see W. K. Percival, "The Grammatical Tradition and the Rise of the Vernaculars," *Current Trends in Linguistics* 13 (1975): 231–75, and the bibliography contained therein. Another helpful source of bibliographical information may be found in A. D. Scaglione, *Ars grammatica* (The Hague, 1970), esp. 11–43, and my review article devoted to that work in *Language* 51 (1975): 440–56, esp. 444. On grammar in the period immediately preceding the Renaissance, see J. Pinborg, *Die Entwicklung der Sprachtheorie im Mittelalter* (Münster and Copenhagen, 1967), vol. 2, and the same author's *Logik und Semantik im Mittelalter: Ein Überblick* (Stuttgart and Bad Cannstatt, 1972). Especially valuable is C. Thurot, *Extraits de divers manuscrits latins pour servir à l'histoire des doctrines grammaticales au Moyen Âge* (Paris, 1869; reprinted Frankfurt, 1964), which includes a discussion of Renaissance grammar; see 485–500. On grammar in the late Renaissance and the seventeenth century, see G. A. Padley, *Grammatical Theory in Western Europe, 1500–1700* (Cambridge, 1976). I discuss the relation of grammar to rhetoric in "Grammar and Rhetoric in the Renaissance," in *Studies in the Theory and Practice of Renaissance Eloquence,* ed. J. J. Murphy (Berkeley, 1983), 303–30.

2. The Latin original reads: "Grammatica est scientia recte loquendi recteque scribendi, origo et fundamentum omnium liberalium artium." For a representative sample of definitions of grammar current in the Middle Ages, see

Thurot, *Extraits*, 121–22. The same definition of grammar may be found, for instance, in the *Catholicon* of Giovanni Balbi (John of Genoa), a widely disseminated encyclopedic dictionary from the late thirteenth century; and indeed similar definitions occur as far back as Cassiodorus: see the edition of his *Institutiones* by R. A. B. Mynors (Oxford, 1937), 91, 3–5.

3. "Gramatica iure artium liberalium prima est, quia illa sine ipsa sciri non possunt" (quoted in Thurot, *Extraits*, 45).

4. On Guarino's grammatical writings, see R. Sabbadini, *La scuola e gli studi di Guarino Guarini Veronese* (Catania, 1896); reprinted in *Guariniana*, ed. M. Sancipriano (Turin, 1964), 38–58; idem, "Dei metodi nell'insegnamento della sintassi latina," *Rivista di filologia* 30 (1902): 304–14; idem, "Elementi nazionali nella teoria grammaticale dei Romani," *Studi italiani di filologia classica* 14 (1906): 113–25; W. K. Percival, "The Historical Sources of Guarino's Regulae grammaticales: A Reconsideration of Sabbadini's Evidence," *Civiltà dell'umanesimo: Atti del VI, VII, VIII Convegno del Centro di Studi Umanistici "Angelo Poliziano"* (Florence, 1972), 263–84; idem, "Textual Problems in the Latin Grammar of Guarino Veronese," *Res publica litterarum* 1 (1978): 241–54.

5. See Sabbadini, *La scuola e gli studi*, 38–47. The introductory manual that Guarino used was a medieval work, which in the Renaissance was still being ascribed to Donatus. For a modern edition, see W. O. Schmitt, "Die Ianua (Donatus)—Ein Beitrag zur lateinischen Schulgrammatik des Mittelalters und der Renaissance," *Beiträge zur Inkunabelkunde* 3d ser. 4 (1969): 43–80.

6. On Perotti, see G. Mercati, *Per la cronologia della vita e degli scritti di Niccolò Perotti, arcivescovo di Siponto* (Rome, 1925); W. K. Percival, "The Place of the *Rudimenta grammatices* in the History of Latin Grammar," *Res publica litterarum* 4 (1981): 233–64. A list of Perotti's publications may be found in R. P. Oliver, *Niccolò Perotti's Version of the Enchiridion of Epictetus* (Urbana, IL, 1954), 137–66.

7. On the elder Scaliger, see Padley, *Grammatical Theory*, 58–77. On Pasi and Linacre, see G. J. Luhrman, *C. L. Pasius, T. Linacre, J. C. Scaliger en hun beschouwing van het werkwoord: Een kritisch-vergelijkende studie omtrent XVI^{de} eeuwse taalkundige theorievorming* (Groningen, 1984).

8. There is a large literature on Ramus. For primary orientation, see W. J. Ong, S. J., *Ramus, Method, and the Decay of Dialogue* (Cambridge, MA, 1983). Ramus's grammatical notions are discussed in Padley, *Grammatical Theory*, 77–96.

9. On the *Minerva*, see Padley, *Grammatical Theory*, 97–110. Perhaps the most important analytical contribution made by the *Minerva* was the theory of ellipsis, which Sánchez had taken over from Linacre. This procedure involved explaining the grammatical structure of many Latin sentences on the assumption that they contain "understood" or unexpressed words. Thus, a sentence such as *Digitorum medius est longior* 'The middle one of the fingers is longer' could be analyzed as an elliptical version of *Ex numero digitorum medius digitus est longior quam ceteri digiti sint longi* 'Among

the fingers the middle finger is longer than the other fingers are long' (*Minerva,* book 4, chap. 2, sig. X5r). This analytical procedure was adopted and exploited in the next century by Antoine Arnauld and Claude Lancelot in their influential *Grammaire générale et raisonnée* (Paris, 1660), the so-called Port-Royal Grammar. Indeed, the theory of ellipsis retained its popularity until well into the nineteenth century.

10. Both works have been edited in modern times; see Evrard de Béthune, *Eberhardi Bethuniensis Graecismus,* ed. J. Wrobel (Breslau, 1887); Alexander of Villedieu, *Das doctrinale des Alexander de Villa-Dei,* ed. D. Reichling (Berlin, 1893).

11. Lovato de Lovati, *De Senecae tragoediarum lectione vulgata,* ed. R. Peiper (Breslau, 1893), 32–35.

12. See B. L. Ullman, "Petrarch's Favorite Books," in his *Studies in the Italian Renaissance* (Rome, 2d ed. 1973), 113–33; Petrarch, *Epistolae seniles,* 12.2, on which see *Francisci Petrarchae Operum tomus II* (Basel, 1554), sigs. AA2v–AA3r.

13. *Epistolario di Coluccio Salutati,* ed. F. Novati, 5 vols. (Rome, 1891–1911), 4:217.

14. This fact, which may seem surprising to students of the Renaissance, was well documented by Sabbadini in *La scuola e gli studi,* 57. My own research has amply confirmed Sabbadini's position.

15. On the study of orthography in the fifteenth century, see Sabbadini, *La scuola e gli studi,* 47–58. On Barzizza's contribution, see R. G. G. Mercer, *The Teaching of Gasparino Barzizza with Special Reference to His Place in Paduan Humanism* (London, 1979). In the early years of the sixteenth century, Nebrija published an important orthographical treatise (*De vi ac potestate litterarum* [Salamanca, 1503]), based on lectures he had given in 1486, in which he argued that it was incorrect to soften the pronunciation of *c* and *g* before front vowels and to pronounce *ae* and *oe* as monophthongs, which had been customary for centuries in the Latin West. Hence, what came subsequently to be termed the "Erasmian" pronunciation of Latin and Greek, on the strength of Erasmus's famous dialogue on orthography, which was first published in Basel in 1528, originated more than forty years earlier. Here as in some other areas, Erasmus functioned as the brilliant disseminator of other scholars' ideas. For a critical edition of Erasmus's dialogue, see "De recta Latini Graecique sermonis pronuntiatione," ed. M. Cytowska, in *Opera omnia Des. Erasmi Roterodami,* 13 vols. to date (Amsterdam, 1969–), 1.4.1–103. On Nebrija, see F. Rico, *Nebrija frente a los bárbaros* (Salamanca, 1978); on his orthographical treatise, see W. K. Percival, "Antonio de Nebrija and the Dawn of Modern Phonetics," *Res publica litterarum* 5 (1982): 221–32.

16. The standard edition of Valla's works is *Opera omnia,* ed. E. Garin, 2 vols. (Turin, 1962), which includes, in vol. 1 (1–235), the standard sixteenth-century edition of Valla's works, *Laurentii Vallae Opera* (Basel: Henricus Petrus, 1540). The secondary literature on Valla is vast. A useful point of departure is L. Barozzi and R. Sabbadini, *Studi sul Panormita e sul Valla*

(Florence, 1891). The only comprehensive biography is still G. Mancini, *Vita di Lorenzo Valla* (Florence, 1891). Important recent works on Valla are the following: M. Fois, *Il pensiero cristiano di Lorenzo Valla nel quadro storico-culturale del suo ambiente* (Rome, 1969); S. Camporeale, *L. Valla, umanesimo e teologia* (Florence, 1972). The text of the prefaces to all six books of the *Elegantiae* with an Italian translation may be found in E. Garin, ed., *Prosatori latini del Quattrocento* (Milan, 1952), 594–631. Valla wrote an influential treatise on logic, entitled *Dialecticae disputationes,* in which he censured scholastic approaches to language. See C. Vasoli, "Le *Dialecticae disputationes* del Valla e la critica umanistica della logica aristotelica," *Rivista critica di storia della filosofia* 12 (1957): 412–34; 13 (1958): 27–46; G. Zippel, "Note sulle redazioni della Dialectica di Lorenzo Valla," *Archivio storico per le province parmensi* 4th ser. 9 (1957): 301–15; L. Jardine, "Lorenzo Valla and the Intellectual Origins of Humanist Dialectic," *Journal of the History of Philosophy* 15 (1977): 143–64. On the *Elegantiae,* see A. Casacci, "Gli *Elegantiarum libri* di Lorenzo Valla," *Atene e Roma* 2d ser. 7 (1926): 187–203; D. Marsh, "Grammar, Method, and Polemic in Lorenzo Valla's *Elegantiae,*" *Rinascimento* 19 (1979): 91–116; L. Cesarini Martinelli, "Note sulla polemica Poggio–Valla e sulla fortuna delle *Elegantiae,*" *Interpres* 3 (1980): 29–79. A short grammatical work in verse by Valla is discussed in P. Casciano, "Appunti grammaticali di Lorenzo Valla," *A.I.O.N.: Annali dell'Istituto Universitario Orientale di Napoli* 2– 3 (1980–81): 233–67.

17. For a description of the contents of Perotti's grammar, see Percival, "Place of the *Rudimenta grammatices.*" A study of Nebrija's influential *Introductiones* (1st ed. Salamanca, 1481) is an urgent desideratum. The work went through a number of different stages before attaining its final shape in the Salamanca edition of 1495. Sixteenth-century editions included a number of Nebrija's opuscula, including his treatise on Latin and Greek pronunciation; see note 15 above.

18. See J. Ruysschaert, "Les manuels de grammaire latine composés par Pomponio Leto," *Scriptorium* 8 (1954): 98–107; idem, "A propos des trois premières grammaires latines de Pomponio Leto," *Scriptorium* 15 (1961): 68–75.

19. "Quod si qui per licentiam aliter loquuntur, non est mirandum. . . . Sed ego de usu loquendi disputo, non de abusu" (*Opera,* sig. A3r). Many scholars have cited Valla's dictum "Quod ad elegantiam pertinet, ego pro lege accipio quicquid magnis auctoribus placuit" (*Elegantiae,* 3.17; *Opera,* sig. F6v). However, they have failed to notice that this sentence does not occur as an independent categorical statement but is contained in a concessive clause. What Valla is really asserting here is that *despite* the general principle that anything favored by the great authors of antiquity should be regarded as authoritative, he nevertheless advises against following the lead of certain ancient authors in the particular instance he is discussing, and against violating the general rule he has just stated.

20. On Greek grammars of the Renaissance, see A. Pertusi, "*Erotemata:* Per la

storia e le fonti delle prime grmmatiche greche e stampa," *Italia medioevale e umanistica* 5 (1962): 321–51.

21. On Guarino's translations, see Sabbadini, *La scuola e gli studi,* 124–35. On Perotti's translation of the *Enchiridion,* see Oliver, *Niccolò Perotti's Version.*

22. The earliest explicit definition of this type that I have encountered is in a manuscript of Pomponio Leto's grammar, transcribed in 1466. It reads as follows: "Grammatice est scientia recte loquendi scribendique, verborumque interpretandi rationem" (Venice, Biblioteca Marciana, MS lat. XIV [= 4623], fol. 33r). It obviously owes much to Quintilian's definition of grammar in the *Institutio oratoria:* "Haec igitur professio, cum brevissime in duas partes dividatur, recte loquendi scientiam et poetarum enarrationem, plus habet in recessu quam fronte promittit" (1.4.2). But the general notion that the function of grammar extends beyond the traditional art of correct speaking and writing was expressed earlier by a number of authors. Thus Tortelli, in his *Orthographia,* says with regard to the grammarian's province: "Quod vero ad significate et ornate dicendum aut scribendum spectat, maiori competit articifi, quamquam et a grammaticis auferri non debeat" (*Ioannis Tortellii Arretini Commentaria grammatica de orthographia dictionum e Graecis tractarum* [Vicenza, 1480], sig. e2r). It is interesting to observe in this connection that Poliziano, Nebřija, and Erasmus, whose activities clearly transcended grammar in the narrow sense, were nevertheless proud to call themselves *grammatici.* In the sixteenth century, however, this enlargement of the grammarian's purview came eventually to be deplored. Julius Caesar Scaliger, for example, explicitly removes the interpretation of subject matter from the province of the grammarian and transfers it to the province of the relevant expert: "Postremo, quod officium interpretandorum auctorum annumerarunt, id sane grammatici non est, sed sapientis pro cuiusquam rei captu" (*De causis linguae Latinae* [Lyons, 1540], sig. a2r). The same idea was vigorously promoted by Ramus and his followers; see Petrus Ramus, *Rhetoricae distinctiones in Quintilianum ad Carolum Lotharingum Cardinalem* (Paris, 1559), 30–31; Francisco Sánchez de las Brozas, *Minerva* (Salamanca, 1587), book 1, chap. 2, sigs. A8r–A8v.

23. On the respective contributions of Valla and Poliziano to textual criticism, see A. Grafton, *Joseph Scaliger: A Study in the History of Classical Scholarship,* vol. 1, *Textual Criticism and Exegesis* (Oxford, 1983), 9–10. With regard to Poliziano, see also the same author's article "On the Scholarship of Politian and Its Context," *Journal of the Warburg and Courtauld Institutes* 40 (1977): 150–88. I have not had access to K. Krautter, "Der 'grammaticus' Poliziano in der Auseinandersetzung mit zeitgenössischen Humanisten," in *Die Antike-Rezeption in den Wissenschaften während der Renaissance,* ed. A. Buck and K. Heitmann (Weinheim, 1983), 103–16.

24. I do not mean to say, however, that humanists were uninterested in such problems as, for instance, the nature of poetic language. On this topic, see E. Grassi, *Heidegger and the Question of Renaissance Humanism* (Binghamton, NY, 1983); idem, *Einführung in philosophische Probleme des Humanismus* (Darmstadt, 1986).

30 ❧ HUMANISM AND POETICS
Danilo Aguzzi-Barbagli

IN ONE OF HIS TYPICALLY TERSE AND BRILLIANTLY ACCURATE SUM-
mations, P. O. Kristeller recently stated: "For the humanist poetry is
a prominent part of the *studia humanitatis,* and in praising and defending poetry the humanists are actually defending their own intellectual domain."[1] In order to appreciate fully in their proper historical
background the defenses of the classical Greek and Latin poetic heritage
passionately elaborated by the representatives of the new humanistic culture, we must first of all bear in mind some relevant facts about the
identity of their opponents.

The more vocal among these antagonists of ancient poetry were, for
the great majority, members of the Dominican Order, men deeply familiar not only with the doctrines of the earlier Christian thinkers, but also
bound to follow the teaching of St. Thomas Aquinas.[2] Medieval thought
had inherited from St. Augustine an attitude toward poetry that provided
a corroboration in Christian terms of the validity of the positions stated
by Plato in the *Republic* and his banishment of poets from the ideal state.[3]
But the views on problems of aesthetics and poetics formulated by St.
Thomas were not organized in a unified system and thus could be com-
pressed or inflated, according to the polemical drive motivating some of
his followers.[4] In his commentary on the *Metaphysics* of Aristotle, Aquinas analyzed passages of this work destined to attract the attention of
students of poetics throughout the Renaissance, namely, Aristotle's remarks on the early Greek poet-theologians like Hesiod, and his refusal
to grant poetry rational validity. This last position, according to Aquinas,
can be held as a rejection of poetry itself. In the interpretation of the
medieval philosopher, Aristotle's statement that "poets lie" justifies negative conclusions as to the content of poetry and its veracity. Discussions
about poetry also appear in several sections of the *Summa theologiae;*
here Aquinas studies the differences between poetic and biblical allegory
and defines poetry as "the lowest of all sciences."[5] Thus for the great
Dominican thinker poetry is far from occupying a prominent position in
the system of sciences; as a matter of fact its place remains well below
the supreme science of theology and its related field of metaphysical speculation.

In view of the particular structure of the intellectual training among the Dominicans, the theories on poetry formulated by Aquinas were bound to be elaborated in a negative direction by some members of his order, who opposed the humanistic cult of classical poetry. The first celebrated encounter between representatives of the new humanistic tendencies and those who viewed as a serious danger the growing deference toward the poetic achievements of the ancient Greeks and Romans occurred in 1315–16.[6] This debate took place in Padua, a center of prehumanistic studies; not far from that center personalities like Ferreto de' Ferreti had already praised the unique formative power of ancient poetry.[7] During the course of a sermon, delivered on Christmas day of 1315, the Dominican Giovannio of Mantua questioned the veracity of all sciences, but he abstained from mentioning poetry. The poet and scholar Albertino Mussato[8] immediately observed that the friar did not mention this art, simply because poetry can be considered a form of theology. The Dominican promptly objected to this conclusion and stated that poetry deserves the same type of consideration as the other sciences. The documents illustrating the ensuing diatribe between the two include a prose answer by Giovannino of Mantua to an initial epistle of Mussato and the defense of poetry outlined by the latter in the first, fourth, seventh, and eighteenth of his epistles.[9] The Dominican's objections can be reduced to a fundamental one: poetry cannot be granted the same degree of dignity as theology. It cannot be related to theology, since it is pure fiction; it is totally devoid of truth, and therefore it can be considered only as the product of a lower moment of human spirituality. In his counterattack Albertino defends the divine origin of poetry, confirmed by the recognition granted to primitive poets, and maintains that it is possible to establish a strict relationship between the revelation of Genesis and the myths of the primitive poets of Greece. Poetry for Mussato is a form of philosophy; the poet, however, is not aware of his own wisdom. His purpose is to teach and to delight through the use of a unique language, enriched by musical components so singular and powerful as to deserve comparison with the harmonies of the heavens. Thus in Mussato's opinion poetry, far from deserving the qualification of a lower science, is an expression of the human yearning toward the divine, an actual link between the terrestrial and the celestial.

Humanistic ideals, already transparent in the intellectual activity of Albertino Mussato, are pursued a few decades later by Petrarch with such range, clarity, and depth that contemporary scholarship regards him as the father of humanism.[10] Problems of poetics are debated by him[11] in the third book of his *Invective contra medicum;*[12] relevant statements about the art of poetry are scattered in his letters; in the *Collatio laureationis* he speaks of the power of poetic language and of the necessity of a force of divine origin to attain the control of its modulations.[13] Petrarch clearly perceives the possibility of reconciling poetry and theology and envisages no contrast between the message contained at the core of great poetry and the divine message revealed by Scripture. He maintains that an adequate knowledge of the mechanisms of allegory is required in order to penetrate the inner truths contained in classical poetry. Except for the more systematic arrangement of the defense outlined in the *Invective contra medicum* Petrarch's statements are not organized in the format of a treatise; considered in their totality, however, they indicate clearly that the humanist upholds the superior dignity of poetry in the system of the arts and sees its relationship to history. His familiarity with Horace's *Ars poetica* is demonstrated by numerous quotations recurring in his work, and with particular intensity in the *Invective contra medicum,* where we find also a reference to Aristotle's *Poetics.*

Impulses of a Petrarchan nature were used and made available to ever-larger audiences in the defenses of poetry composed during the later decades of the fourteenth century and the earlier part of the following century. It must be noted also that an inner link connects the theories of Mussato, Petrarch, and Boccaccio. As indicated before, Mussato based his equation of poetry to theology on a statement made by Aristotle in the *Metaphysics.* During a visit to Padua Petrarch became familiar with the positions assumed by Mussato in his polemic with Giovannino of Mantua and used the pivotal assertion of Aristotle on primitive poets in the letter to his brother Gherardo.[14] In turn the theoretical significance of this Petrarchan epistle was revealed and appreciated by Boccaccio, who read it during his visit to Petrarch in Padua in 1351.[15] The further spread of the influence of Petrarch's theories on poetry is testified by a letter to Boccaccio from the Neapolitan jurist Pietro Piccolo da Monforte, some of whose ideas were elaborated by the same Boccaccio in the definitive version of the final chapter of his *Genealogie deorum gentilium.*[16]

The defense of poetry in Boccaccio's *Genealogie*[17] may be regarded as a summa of the doctrines in favor of that art and of the argumentations in praise of the relevance to contemporary intellectual interests of the literary heritage transmitted by the ancient Greeks and Romans formulated during the course of the fourteenth century. The reflection on poetics is one of the major interests revealed by Boccaccio during the later period of his life. In his *Trattatello in laude di Dante*[18] the writer quotes again the passage on the poet-theologians of the *Metaphysics,* appraises the civilizing effects of archaic poetic language from the sociological and moralistic viewpoints, establishes analogies between the inner meanings of pagan myths and those disclosed by some episodes of the Bible, and formulates the following axiom: "Theology is nothing but the poetry of God."[19] Consequently the importance of allegorical interpretation is essential; allegory can provide the key to unveil the truth hidden in the language of the ancient poets.

The *Genealogie deorum gentilium* is an encyclopedia of interpretations of classical myths, intended as an instrument both to understand the fables of pagan poetry and to illustrate the wisdom concealed in ancient myths. A carefully structured defense of poetry appears in the last two books of the work. Here Boccaccio identifies the contemporary enemies of poetry and rebukes their objections; he proves the usefulness of the poetic language and illustrates its peculiar characteristics. He defines the poet as a man endowed with a divine gift, a power of celestial origin, which kindles his inspiration. Allegory is extensively discussed in the last part of the *Genealogie* as an essential instrument to penetrate the inner meaning—the true subject matter, as it were—of both theology and poetry. The obscurity of scriptural and poetic texts is only apparent; in reality it is an element intentionally introduced in both cases to increase the dignity of a language revelatory of sublime truths. The doctrines of those who consider poetry as a sort of evil seduction and the poets as apes of the philosophers are erroneous. Poetry, says Boccaccio, must be regarded as "a faithful guardian of truth" even though it is based on images and relies on verbal structures that do not follow the techniques of expression typical of philosophical discourse. The condemnations of poetry by Plato and by Boethius are applicable only to dramatic poetry, says Boccaccio, who firmly believes that the process of familiarization with the poetical legacy of classical times will never lead Christians astray from the doctrines of their faith.

*   *   *

The effort to legitimize poetry as a language uniquely suited to render in sublime images moments of human experience of universal validity, and thus to place it above the reproach of religious censorship, together with a firm commitment to defend the poetical heritage of classical times, are strongly sustained in the humanistic circle of Coluccio Salutati.[20] The defense of poetry is a recurrent theme in Salutati's work. The most important texts that develop his ideas on this issue are two letters to Giuliano Zonarini,[21] the initial chapter of *De laboribus Herculis*,[22] a letter to Pellegrino Zambeccari,[23] two letters to Giovanni of San Miniato,[24] and one letter to Giovanni Dominici.[25] Seen in their general lines of evolution Salutati's defenses are inconspicuous for their doctrinal novelty: most of the motifs utilized for their development had already been used by Petrarch and Boccaccio, authors well known to the humanist, who deeply

admired their contributions.[26] This limitation does not impair the validity of Salutati's position among the earlier supporters of the central role
of ancient poetry in humanistic studies, since in this case the historically
significant fact is the emphasis he places on certain aspects and motives
of the traditional defenses. Salutati's attention is focused with particular
intensity on the problem of the origins of poetry and of the divine nature
of the poetic inspiration, on the power of poetic language to seal the
truth in images that find precise concordance in worldly music and in the
music of the spheres, on the educational values of that language, and on
its relation to philosophy.

"Poetry is a bilingual art and faculty."[27] This declaration can be
found in Coluccio's letter to the Dominican Giovanni Dominici,[28] a for-
midable opponent, who in his *Lucula noctis* had condemned pagan poetry as a body of literature deeply influenced by a heathen theology. Like
Petrarch and Boccaccio, Salutati considers allegory an indispensable tool
of poetic exegesis. Polemically the humanist demonstrates that the use of
allegory becomes inevitable for the proper interpretation of some images
used in Scripture, or to understand correctly some parts of the Bible, like
the *Song of Songs,* which at the literal level can be classified among
the "most erotic and lascivious" poetry.[29] The ancient Greek poet-
theologians invented a language capable of giving divine semblance to
physical forces and of extolling the virtue of excellent men. Their power
was inherited by the prophets, who were inspired by the Holy Spirit to
celebrate the ineffable mysteries of true divinity. During the last part of
his life Salutati revived the theories formulated by Petrarch and Boccaccio on the secret monotheism of the great pagan poets and combined this
idea with the thesis that human conceptions of the divine tend to be
rendered in anthropomorphic terms. This combination provided firmer
foundations to his interpretations of the polytheistic fables of ancient
poets as myths concealing invaluable wisdom.

Presumably in the year 1400 Francesco da Fiano, a friend of Salutati, composed a defense of poetry entitled *Contra oblocutores et detractores poetarum* and dedicated it to a personnage qualified as "the
cardinal of Bologna."[30] This prelate has been recently identified as Cosimo Migliorati,[31] who became Pope Innocent VII and who greatly contributed to transforming the city of Rome into a major center of
Renaissance culture. Francesco da Fiano's work was motivated by the
objections raised by members of the papal curia against the wealth of
quotations from ancient poets contained in a speech delivered by the
rhetorician Stefano d'Arezzo. In his defense of ancient poetry da Fiano
energetically adopts motifs already used by Boccaccio and Salutati; he
declares that pagan myths contain truths detectable through the proper

use of allegorical exegesis and strives to show the inner connection between the fables of the Greek and Roman classics, natural philosophy and ethics. In addition to the traditional observations about the images appearing in the language of Scripture, *Contra oblocutores* contains definitions of poetry as an art concerned with "praise and blame," derived from Averroës's paraphrase of Aristotle's *Poetics;* as well as echoes from Horace's *Ars poetica* and statements on the divine origin of poetry, possibly deduced from Cicero's *Pro Archia.*

After Salutati's death a new, philologically more qualified generation of humanists continued the polemic against opponents of the classical heritage which he had so firmly sustained. Their knowledge of Greek allowed some of them to add new documents of paramount importance to the defense of poetry. At the same time ancient poetry began to be systematically incorporated into the programs of humanistic schools. The body of literature in favor of classical culture left by the church fathers and the early Christian writers was enriched by Leonardo Bruni's translation into Latin of the homily of Basil the Great, *De legendis libris gentilium,*[32] a work that long enjoyed exceptional favor in humanistic circles. Bruni, the translator of Aristotle's *Nicomachean Ethics,* was also the author of a treatise *De studiis et litteris,* initially conceived as a letter to Battista Montefeltro Malatesta.[33] In *De studiis et litteris* the humanist maintains that the school of the great poets of antiquity provides a secure guide to practical wisdom and ethical balance. The subject matter chosen by pagan poets cannot be condemned, even when on the surface it appears to be immoral, as in the case of the myths of Vulcan and Venus. The literal meaning is not the most important part of a poetical composition. Particular attention must be given to the artistry of the poet, and admiration must be paid to the formal perfection of his creations. Bruni discusses at length the problems of the divine nature of poetry, of furor and poetic frenzy; he analyzes the Horatian concept of poetry as inspiration leading to the creation of verbal structures brought to perfection through the use of consummate mastery of style, and thus he investigates the problem of the relation between rhetoric and the language of poetry. In the *Dialogi ad Petrum Histrum*[34] Bruni sees the poet as a man endowed with an exceptional power of invention, as an artist capable of revealing the power of the word with a skill similar to that of the orator, and as an extremely learned individual, whose range of knowledge confers on him the type of intellectual supremacy attained by the philosopher.

Poetry is included in the programs of studies outlined by the educator Pier Paolo Vergerio the Elder[35] and by Maffeo Vegio who, in his treatise *De liberorum educatione et eorum claris moribus,*[36] rebukes the attacks of a contemporary against ancient lyric and satirical poetry. Vegio maintains that while poets like Homer and Vergil may be read without restrictions, discriminating criteria should be adopted in the selection of works from classical erotic, satirical, and comic literature. The same type of moderation is advocated by Aeneas Silvius Piccolomini in his *Tractatus de liberorum educatione;*[37] here the humanist says that the excesses of some ancient poets cannot justify the rejection of all ancient poetry advocated by some theologians. It is necessary, however, to include, in a program of studies for the young, ancient works suited to foster moral edification.

The role of classical poetry as a primary educational instrument is decisively confirmed by Guarino of Verona, a philologist well known as one of the most prominent humanistic educators. In Guarino's work we can find one of the last defenses of poetry from the Italian fifteenth century. The friar Giovanni of Prato, in a sermon delivered in Ferrara during Lent of 1450, violently attacked pagan poetry for its presumed immorality. Guarino's reaction is contained in a group of letters[38] in which he acknowledges the supremacy of theology but does not agree with the view of the theologians who considered poetry as the lowest of all arts. Guarino asserts that theology itself cannot fulfill all its functions without the help of other arts, including poetry. The proper interpretation of the Bible, for instance, requires a remarkable degree of grammatical knowledge and stylistic competence. Guarino reminds his opponent that men as important in the history of Christianity as Jerome, Augustine, Basil, and Gregory the Great had extensive knowledge of classical literatures and maintains that Basil's homily can provide proper guidance for the reading of ancient poetry. Comedy and dramatic literature are not excluded from Guarino's educational program; particularly interesting is his defense of Terence and of the pedagogical value of his comedies.[39]

A more conservative approach to poetry is shown by one of the pupils of Guarino, Ermolao Barbaro the Elder, who became bishop of Verona and formed in that city an active intellectual circle.[40] Between 1455 and 1459 Barbaro composed two *Orationes contra poetas,* in which he contested the theories on poetry stated in a letter by Bartolomeo da Lendinara.[41] Barbaro's approach to the question of the legitimacy of studying pagan poetry is considerably influenced by moralistic preoccupations and by his responsibilities and allegiances as a prelate. Nonetheless his humanistic education and his admiration for ancient philosophy and eloquence led him to adopt a moderate attitude, a conciliary tone quite distant from the intransigent attitude expressed by Giovanni Dominici and other members of the Dominican Order. Barbaro declares that poetry is devoid of truth; its cognitive value cannot be rescued through recourse to allegorical interpretation, which in some cases may even become ridiculous because of its artificiality. Thus the reading of ancient poetry, especially comedies, can be pernicious to Christians. It is possible, however, to peruse the body of ancient literature in the light of selective principles, which may allow the reading of poets like Vergil and Horace.

*   *   *

It is apparent from the development of the previous discussion that during the first half of the fifteenth century the major representatives of civic humanism, the new educators and moral philosophers, attributed to poetry a function of a practical nature. Humanists like Vergerio, Guarino, Bruni, Piccolomini, Angelo Decembrio, and Battista Guarino consider the *studia humanitatis* as solid instruments for the formation of character. Poetry, an integral part of the *studia humanitatis,* together with history and moral philosophy, was viewed primarily as a pedagogical instrument, well suited to foster the intellectual and moral autonomy of man and consequently to prepare him for his personal activities and his political responsibilities. During the second half of the century the study of the problem of poetics is enriched by new theoretical elements of fundamental importance. The intensive study of Plato's works, promoted by Ficino and the Neoplatonic school, determined discussions of such problems as the divine origin of poetry, the uniqueness of poetic inspiration, the nature of enthusiasm, the role of the poet in the progress of civilization. Equally relevant for the future development of literary criticism was the revival of the study of the works of Aristotle, advocated by Ermolao Barbaro the Younger. Barbaro predicated the necessity to analyze directly Aristotle's *Poetics,* a text utilized by earlier humanists only in a very sporadic manner, often by mere reference to its title or by repeated quotations of an extremely limited number of passages derived from the translation by Hermann the German of Averroës's commentary.

New and important positions on the problem of poetics were developed by Cristoforo Landino in his lectures at the *studium* of Florence and in the published volumes of his theoretical works.[42] The basic tenets of Landino's system were already established in his *Praefatio in Virgilio* of 1462.[43] The humanist discussed the poetry of Petrarch in 1467 and devoted his attention to Dante's *Divine Comedy* in 1478.[44] The first edition of his *Disputationes Camaldulenses*—a dialogue in which the author, after detailed debates on the merits of the active and the contemplative lives, discusses the nature of poetry and its characteristics—appeared in about 1480.[45] The same themes reemerge in his *Comento sopra la Comedia* of 1481,[46] one of the most relevant exegetical works on

Dante's masterpiece of the entire Renaissance. The tradition of Horatian criticism was enriched by Landino with his *In Q. Horatii Flacci libros omnes interpretationes* of 1482, followed in 1488 by his commentaries on Vergil (*In P. Virgilii Maronis opera interpretationes*).

As early as the *Praefatio in Virgilio* Landino placed poetry above all other liberal disciplines. He embraced the Platonic doctrine of enthusiasm and assumed positions contrasting not only with those held by some major representatives of civic humanism, but also with conclusions reached by philologists like Lorenzo Valla. By combining poetry, history, and moral philosophy as pedagogical instruments, humanists of the earlier generation in effect had relegated the first of these disciplines to a partial and subordinate role. Thinkers like Valla, by contrast, advocated a new philosophy and a new logic, rooted in a strict relationship among rhetoric, philosophy, and history. The scope of poetry, in the opinion of Valla, is limited to the sphere of the subjective and the contingent; therefore its validity is drastically limited at the cognitive level.

In his attempt to restore the eminence of poetry above all the liberal arts, Landino was not unmindful of the previous humanist tradition of study on the subject. Highly sensitive to the new cultural orientations taking shape in Florence during his time, Landino nonetheless did not hesitate to criticize the positions reached by his predecessors, and he searched the works of Plato for elements that might be suitable to corroborate a theoretical justification of the cognitive validity of the poetic language. The authority of Plato had already been invoked by Bruni. In the *Vita di Dante* he distinguished between poets who attain excellence on the strength of furor, "an internal agitation and application of the mind," and another type who achieved poetical distinction with the help of "science, study, discipline, art, and prudence."[47] In Bruni's view Dante belongs to this second category. As early as 1457 Marsilio Ficino, in his *De divino furore*, had defined enthusiasm as the instrument available to men in order to ascend from physical reality to the contemplation of the perfect ideal world. Ontologically the process followed by the inspired poet is analogous to the ascent that brings the philosopher to the vision of the ultimate truth. Thus, according to Ficino, true poets are not those who hope to succeed on the strength of "some learned techniques," but those "who, aided by the divine spirit" and "imitating the divine and heavenly harmony, order and compose in verses and feet and measures what they have a hint of through the sense and notion of their inner reason."[48] It is evident that the positions reached by Ficino on the supremacy of inspiration as the motivating factor of the loftiest poetic production are diametrically opposed to those held by Bruni.

The impact of Ficino's theories on Landino's poetics is combined with preoccupations of a different nature. The humanist could not accept the contrast established by Ficino between divine inspiration and human art, nor the related argumentation that led the Neoplatonic philosopher to define poetry as the handmaiden of philosophy (*ancilla philosophiae*). For Landino poetry cannot be considered exclusively as an expression of the internal elevation of the soul. It must be recognized as an instrument of communication, as a lofty tool of persuasion in a social context, and therefore it must be charged with some of the powers pertaining to eloquence. The multilateral urges at the core of Landino's thought on poetics are combined in the famous passage in the *Comento sopra la Comedia di Dante*, where he states that "whoever wishes to become a poet without this divine furor labors in vain," and in the declaration: "God is the supreme poet and the world is his poem. And as God organizes creation, *idest*, the visible and invisible world which is his work, with a recourse to number, measure, and weight, and therefore the prophet said *Deus omnia fecit numero, mensura et pondo*, so the poets with the number of the feet, the measure of brief and long syllables and the weight of the maxims and of the sentiments compose their poems."[49] As a human creator the poet cannot operate *ex nihilo*, like the divine creator. Moreover, the material at his disposal for the composition of his artistic microcosm can be used also by the historian; as a result differences must be established between poetic and historical discourse. Poetic language becomes fixed when it is channeled in its proper metrical rhythms, while the weight of the *sententie* and the *affetti* molds the subject matter so intimately as to charge it with philosophical significance. The process described in the *Comento* is further clarified by passages in the proem to the *Aeneid*, where Landino refers again to the analogy between divine and poetic creation. Here the humanist affirms that the language of great poetry is secretly and almost "dissimulatingly" enriched with profound meanings.[50]

In Landino's system of poetics the stylistic and rhetorical analysis of ancient and modern texts become matters of primary interest. Especially during the later years of his activity, he combines this type of exegesis with allegorical interpretations conceived within the categories of moral philosophy. Regardless of Ficino's negative attitude toward the cultural and technical components interacting at the genetic stage of poetic creativity, Landino considers doctrine, accompanied by a highly refined mastery of stylistic skill, as indispensable for poetic composition. His most extensive and definitive argument on the nature and function of allegory may be found in the prologue to the *Comento* and in the third and fourth books of the *Disputationes Camaldulenses*. He does not use allegory as a tool for the defense of poetry, a necessity that in his time had become obsolete, despite the survival of some opponents of pagan poetry.[51] Instead of physical allegory Landino favors moral allegory, which in his view offers the key for an understanding of how the greatest poems ever written—the masterpieces of Homer, Vergil, and Dante—provide sublime representations of the condition and the destiny of man, of his quest for the *summum bonum*. In the prologue to the fourth book of the *Disputationes* Landino asserts that fragmentary interpretations of great pagan poetry in the mode still followed by Salutati and Bruni—the reduction of ancient gods and ancient myths to physical forces or physical phenomena—cannot disclose in its fullness the significance of the unique and complex poetical messages. The proper identification of these inner meanings makes the reading of poetry as relevant as pondering the conclusions of the moral philosopher, while the pleasure offered by the poetic language is indeed superior to the stimulation provided by the arid and abstract argumentations presented in philosophical contexts.

* * *

Landino's extensive study of the art of poetry reflects interests widely shared in the most advanced intellectual circles of Florence during the second half of the fifteenth century. The treatment of poetry as a subject of philosophical analysis, conducted by Landino's friend Marsilio Ficino, is an event of unique historical importance for its intrinsic merits and for its influence on the later developments of literary criticism. Though not a humanist in the strict sense of the term, Ficino was affected by humanistic culture and contributed to its development.[52] His correspondence shows that students of poetics of the stature of Ermolao Barbaro the Younger and Angelo Poliziano recognized the importance of his contributions to the definition of that problem[53] In Ficino's work the theories on the sublime wisdom of the ancient Greek poets—the so-called *prisci theologi*, like Orpheus, Linus, Musaeus—and the debate on the proximity of their messages to the revelations of such forerunners of Christianity as Moses, are extensively developed. Moreover, the allegorical interpretation necessary to penetrate the meaning of that wealth of wisdom is further justified on philosophical grounds. Still at the philosophical level, Ficino demonstrates the proximity of music and poetry.[54] Ficino's views on poetic inspiration and furor have already been mentioned; actually, in his system of metaphysics, love, poetry, and prophecy constitute manifestations of furor deriving from the divine fountainhead. The Neoplatonic philosopher maintains that poetry is endowed with cognitive power; however, the very nature of his speculation leads him to assign to that art an ancillary status in relation to philosophy.

Recently the work of Poliziano (Angelo Ambrogini), his merits as a poet, a philologist, and a literary critic have been the object of attentive analysis,[55] permitting us to understand with greater clarity his extraordinary contributions to the development of Renaissance culture. One of the problems discussed in contemporary scholarship is related to the progressive interest in the works of Aristotle manifested by Poliziano, especially during the later part of his life. It appears that these Aristotelian studies contributed to the materialization of an approach to the problem of poetics in terms considerably different from those adopted by Landino, Ficino, and Giovanni Pico della Mirandola.[56] Through allegorization Ficino and Pico resolve the poetic image into a philosophical concept. Consequently they tend to bring poetry within the territory of philosophy; viewed from such a perspective the artistic creation loses its importance as a human creation dependent on factors like the diversity of languages and circumstantial elements of a historical or sociological nature. Poliziano's studies reveal an increasing aversion to burdening the discussion of poetics with preoccupations of a philosophical nature (*miscere poetica philosophicis*),[57] while they show an extraordinary sensitivity to the word, to the specific nature of the poetic language and its power to reveal the world of man and its history. It certainly cannot be denied that Poliziano was very close to the Florentine Neoplatonic circles, but it must also be recognized that his capacity to assume independent positions was sustained with remarkable vitality.

In 1480 Poliziano was granted a chair at the *studium* of Florence, a position he held until his death in 1494. This last period of his life was immediately preceded by voyages in the north of Italy and by direct contacts with the Aristotelian circles of Padua and Venice, where Ermolao Barbaro the Younger was the dominant figure. The humanist's conception of poetry changed around the 1480s;[58] Neoplatonic ideologies were at the core of Poliziano's *Stanze* (1475–78) and found an explicit materialization in the allegorical and symbolic structures present in that poetry. In his later years Poliziano confessed to Ficino that he abandoned Plato, beloved by the philosopher (*Platonem semper tuum*), in favor of Aristotle (*Aristotelem iam meum*).[59] Poliziano did not write a specific treatise on the art of poetry. His most relevant conclusions must be gathered from the *Miscellanea,* a work containing some of the more outstanding evidence of his acumen as a philologist. More specifically, in the prolusion *Manto* (1482) the humanist discusses the poetry of Vergil in general; *Rusticus* (1483) is an introduction to Hesiod and Vergil's *Georgics; Ambra* (1485) contains an analysis of the poetry of Homer; *Nutricia* (1486) presents a history of some literary genres of antiquity, with references to modern poets such as Dante, Guido Cavalcanti, and Petrarch. Relevant notations on poetics may also be found in *Panepistemon* (1490–91) and in his commentary on the *Andria* of Terence.

The theme of poetic frenzy is discussed by Poliziano in *Nutricia* and more extensively in *Ambra,* where he appeals directly to the doctrines expounded by Plato in the *Ion.* The humanist discusses the question of the civilizing effects of poetry and the proximity of this art to music. As already indicated, Poliziano's theories on poetry can be fully appreciated only if we bear in mind the primary value conferred by the humanist on the word as "an equivalent of the *res,*" as the main tool of creation.[60] This overriding interest was closely related to the impact exerted on Poliziano by Aristotle, the philosopher favored by his friend Barbaro, who wished to restore to their original purity the Aristotelian texts and thereby allow the doctrines they contained to be reconstructed without recourse to medieval versions and commentaries.[61] Poliziano was the first scholar in fifteenth-century Florence to own a copy of the *Poetics.*[62] His care in reading this text is underscored by a series of autograph marginal annotations. The Poliziano codex containing the *Poetics* also includes Plutarch's *Quomodo adulescens poetas audire debeat* and Demetrius Phalereus's *De elocutione,* two treatises extensively used by later theorists. It has been recently affirmed that the Aristotelian principle, which establishes the universal as the aim of poetry, is "singularly present" in important passages of *Manto, Nutricia,* and *Panepistemon.*[63] Frequent references to the *Poetics* appear in Poliziano's commentary on Terence's *Andria;* in this work the humanist states that the origin of poetry is due to imitation, and he supports this conclusion with the authority of Aristotle. Further evidence of Poliziano's knowledge and use of the *Poetics* is provided by his *Enarratio in Sapphus epistolam* and by his *Oratio supra Fabio Quintiliano.*[64]

The historical importance of Barbaro's and Poliziano's intuitions of the profound significance of Aristotle's doctrines on poetry is further confirmed by the links connecting these fifteenth-century humanists with the two earlier translators of the *Poetics:* Giorgio Valla and Alessandro de' Pazzi. Alessandro de' Pazzi, a cousin of Clement VII and a friend of members of Venetian intellectual circles such as Leonico Tomeo and Gasparo Contarini, stated that Ermolao Barbaro either translated or intended to translate the Aristotelian treatise.[65] Giorgio Valla, a protégé of Barbaro in the earlier phases of his career, probably lectured on the *Poetics* in Venice about 1485.[66] The translation of *Poetics* 1448b, 4–24, appearing in Poliziano's commentary on the *Andria,* bears striking similarities to Pazzi's translation of the same passage.[67] At the time (ca. 1485)

that Poliziano was using the *Poetics* in comments on Terence's comedy,
Giorgio Valla was exploring the same text to formulate his conclusions
on poetry contained in the treatise *De expetendis et fugiendis rebus* (published posthumously in 1501).[68]

*   *   *

Bartolomeo della Fonte (Fontius), Landino's student and later his and
Poliziano's colleague at the *studium* of Florence, is considered a minor
figure in the intellectual history of the Renaissance.[69] The general aspects
of della Fonte's activity are not of a quality to warrant a position of
prestige comparable to the reputation secured by the merits of his former
teacher, or by the multiple achievements of Poliziano. Nonetheless, the
significance and originality of his contributions to the tradition of humanistic studies on the problem of poetics deserve proper recognition,
which is now made possible by the recent publication of his *De poetice*
by Charles Trinkaus.[70]

We have seen how Ermolao Barbaro's and Poliziano's interest in Aristotle's *Poetics* established factors of unique importance for the precise
reconstruction of the process of continuity linking fifteenth-century critical speculation to the flourishing of Aristotelian criticism in the later
Renaissance. In an analogous manner, the more original sections of della
Fonte's *De poetice* continue in humanistic terms a lively medieval tradition of Horatian influence and at the same time become a fifteenth-
century antecedent of later Renaissance treatises that exclusively utilize
the *Ars poetica* for the formulation of literary doctrines.[71] It is this characteristic, in conjunction with the fact that the specific nature of late
Renaissance Aristotelian criticism cannot be understood without taking
into consideration the fusion of Horatian elements operating in it, which
confer on della Fonte's treatise its singular historical significance. The
latter is further enhanced by the realization that *De poetice* is the first
Renaissance treatise entirely devoted to the problem of poetics.[72]

The composition of the treatise was preceded by a long period of
study on a variety of critical issues, as Trinkaus has shown in an analysis
of a series of pertinent documents, including della Fonte's student notes
on Landino's exposition of the *Ars poetica*.[73] The treatise was completed
between the summer of 1490 and the spring of 1492.[74] Arranged in dialogue form, the material is divided into three books.

The first book of *De poetice* is the least original. Della Fonte adheres
to the theory of the poet's divine inspiration, but his argumentation on
its veracity depends more on that long (early Christian to early Renaissance) tradition of discussions on poetry as a spark originally kindled in
the heavens than on the doctrines on furor proposed by Ficino and his

circle. Considerable attention is devoted to the problem of poetry's position among the arts and sciences, to the issues related to its utility, to the "images of the poets," and to the moral values upheld by the superior forms of poetic expression. As a defense of poetry, however, this first book lacks conceptual novelty.

Trinkaus asserts that "if the priority of Fontius' *Poetics* is to be upheld . . . the claim must rest on what he does in his second book."[75] It is here that the author formulates a system of poetics based on Horace's *Ars poetica*, internally structured according to the model provided by the dialectical scheme established in the Latin text, and yet not bound to that archetype by absolute fidelity in the sequence of the argumentation. As a result the second book does not assume the aspect of a commentary, but emerges as an independent art of poetry, where classical doctrines are recast and submitted as valid guides to contemporary artists. In spite of della Fonte's familiarity with the patterns of rhetorical analysis, his discussion does not progress from the study of invention to the consideration of the categories of disposition and elocution.

He emphasizes the need of the poet to know himself as an artist and to realize fully in what fields his talent can best manifest itself. Having done this, the poet must then consider the internal organization of the work; he must decide how to "distribute and divide the invented and undertaken content,"[76] how to confer on this structure a unique poetical character. Style and ornamentation are essential ingredients in the creation of poetic language, and the proper use of these elements requires a degree of technical skill, which the author, in typical Horatian fashion, considers indispensable. A central point in the discussions on the art of poetry from a Horatian perspective is the analysis of the relation between innate talent and acquired doctrine combined with the knowledge of the techniques of expression. This issue is attentively examined by della Fonte, and he strongly underscores the importance of doctrine as an attribute of the poet, despite his praise of divine inspiration in the first book.

In his treatment of verisimilitude—a topic of intense debate in Renaissance critical literature—della Fonte abundantly exemplifies from Vergil, and consequently advocates, a principle of internal coherence. And while fantastic elements may be introduced in the poem, "something contrary to all historical truth . . . should be depicted most accurately of all, so that it will appear to be done for just and necessary causes."[77]

It has been observed that della Fonte is particularly sensitive to demands of an aesthetic nature, unavoidable in the consideration of the results of artistic endeavors. This tendency manifests itself even when the discussion is channeled in the order of ideas disclosed by the famous statements: "Aut prodesse volunt aut delectare poetae . . . omne tulit punctum qui miscuit utile dulci" ("Poets wish either to be useful or to please; the one who joined the useful with the pleasant carried every point").[78] Fully aware of the moral and didactic responsibilities of the poet, it is the aesthetic effectiveness of the poem that remains one of the principal concerns in della Fonte's system of poetics.

In the last part of the second book the author devotes a great deal of attention to the question of imitation from classical models, discusses the relation between poetry and philosophy, analyzes the differences between oratorical and poetic language, and examines the ethical relevance of great poetry.

The third book of *De poetice* has been adroitly described as an embryonic treatise on the history of poetry. The sources used by della Fonte for his compilation include the tenth book of Quintilian's *Institutio oratoria,* the third book of Diomedes's *De arte grammatica,* the *De musica* attributed to Plutarch, Eusebius's *Chronicon,* and possibly Suidas's lexicon. Compared to the number of classical authorities used by Francesco Patrizi of Cherso about a century later for his history of poetry in the *Deca historiale,* the ancient sources employed by della Fonte are indeed limited in number, a fact, however, that does nòt diminish the historical importance of the third book. In effect the history of poetry there contained increases the originality of *De poetice* when viewed as a theoretical discussion that may be considered as an immediate antecedent of sixteenth-century texts on literary theories.

Important observations on the art of poetry are contained in Giovanni Pontano's *De sermone* and *Aegidius.*[79] His poetics, however, finds a more complete and systematic formulation in the dialogue *Actius.* Here the humanist, through his efforts to define the specific nature of the poetic language and to outline the elements effective in determining its difference from the discourse of the orator and the narration of the historian, approaches problems destined to acquire major relevance in the critical debate of the sixteenth century. Pontano finds numerous analogies among poetry, oratory, and history. These arts have similar ends as they all intend to "teach, delight, and move";[80] all retain the basic structure provided by invention, disposition, and elocution. The orator is heard from the forum and the senate and his aim is to "persuade the judge; the poet wishes to obtain the admiration of the listener and the reader . . . and he strives for fame and glory."[81] The narration of the historian, however, must adhere to truth and be "chaste"[82] in the severity of its formal mode of expression. Poetry can encompass the probable, the fantastic, and occasionally elements distant from the verisimilar. The historian is bound to a sequential narrative order. The poet can begin *in medias res;* his divinely inspired talent is enriched with a deep knowledge of the techniques suited to increase the power of the word to imitate nature.

The element of *admiratio,* that idea of the wonderful bound to become a central theme in some late Renaissance poetics, is considered by Pontano as the end of poetry. *Admiratio* is heightened by *novitas,*[83] that is, the capacity to surprise the reader through the revelation of unknown facts and through the appeal exerted by the inner strength of imaginary creations. At the end of the *Actius* Pontano praises poetry as "the mother of all doctrines" and as a guide toward the sublime.

This final hymn to poetry could well be taken as a culminating tribute of the humanistic culture of the Italian fifteenth century to an art so profoundly revered for its uninterrupted eminence as a civilizing instrument throughout the history of mankind.

*   *   *

The vast and complex body of critical literature produced by the sixteenth century can be considered as one of the highest achievements of Italian Renaissance culture and as one of the instruments whereby the civilization of the Italian Cinquecento exerted its influence across the Alps. Principles elaborated by Italian theorists on the art of poetry— supplemented by the works of Italian theorists on painting, sculpture, and architecture—stand as initial milestones in the history of modern European aesthetics. Italian literary doctrines were known in England from the time of Sir Philip Sidney; the rise of French classicism in the seventeenth century cannot be understood unless we take into consideration basic intellectual stimulants coming from Italy; throughout the seventeenth century European treatises on the art of poetry are replete with references to positions established by the late Renaissance critics, even if the intention of the author is to affirm polemically a liberation from their norms, as in the case of Lope de Vega's *Arte nuevo de hacer comedias.*

For at least three centuries European theorists concentrated some of their major efforts on problems identified and defined by their Italian predecessors. Subjects of critical speculation included the concept of poetry as an agent of human progress and civilization, intimately motivated by ethical and pedagogical aims, which derived from Horace's *Ars poetica.* Another pole of critical meditation was set through the revival of the Aristotelian principle of mimesis. The acceptance of this principle entails a conception of art as imitation of nature and consequently as a fusion of realistic and fantastic elements organically balanced to the degree necessary to assure universal validity for the artistic product. Fidelity to metaphysical tenets of a Neoplatonic nature led some Italian theorists to speculate on the principles of furor, genius, and enthusiasm, and to emphasize the power of inspiration as a gift of supernatural origin and as a prime mover of artistic creativity.

In order to facilitate a systematic presentation of the development of literary criticism in the sixteenth century within the limits of the present work, it may be useful to subdivide this material into separate categories, in accordance with the main characteristics of the specific critical trends established during that period. Following these criteria I shall distinguish within the corpus of sixteenth-century criticism: (a) a tradition based on Horace's *Ars poetica;* (b) a tradition based on Aristotle's *Poetics;* (c) a tradition applying principles derived from the works of Plato; and (d) a tradition formed by the so-called new arts of poetry. This expression indicates "the general treatises that attempted to present a total conception of the art, rather than to discuss an individual point, or to elucidate some phase of ancient doctrine." [84]

Practical criticism forms a large and important part of the critical literature of the late Italian Renaissance. Literary theorists discussed at length poems, dramas, and prose narratives composed by classical Greek and Roman writers, and in many cases they also devoted their efforts to the analysis of works belonging to Italian literature. Differences of opinion determined extensive and complicated polemics. The main focal points of critical debates at the practical level were the querelles over Dante, over the *Canace* of Sperone Speroni, over Lodovico Ariosto and Torquato Tasso, over Battista Guarino's *Pastor Fido.* The wide discussion of these issues frequently led theorists to reach more precise ideas about tragedy, comedy, the epic poem, tragicomedy, and pastoral drama. Thus strictly related to the literary disputes on works from ancient and contemporary Italian literature was the codification of theories on literary genres.

Seen from a general point of view the emergence of literary quarrels considerably complicated the development of late Renaissance critical thought. It has been correctly stated that "whereas early in the (sixteenth) century criticism had been the work of scholars, it became, as the century wore on, every man's domain; . . . new talents, new backgrounds, new types of literary experience were added as sources. . . . The result of this expansion of the literary world was a constantly increased diversification of the approaches to literary theory and criticism." [85] These later developments of intellectual orientations inherited from the humanistic tradition of the fifteenth century fall beyond the scope of this presentation. Nevertheless, while the late sixteenth-century literary querelles and the formation of the theories of literary genres will not be treated,[86] the chronological limits here implicitly set will be violated in order to include the discussion of the doctrines on poetics formulated by

Francesco Patrizi of Cherso. His system may be considered as a Renaissance culmination of the critical tradition based on Neoplatonic tenets. As such it is intimately linked with the metaphysical positions established by Ficino and adopted by the Neoplatonists of the fifteenth century.

*   *   *

The continuing popularity of Horace as one of the main authorities for Renaissance theorists of the art of poetry is a phenomenon easily explainable. The *Ars poetica* is a relatively simple document to read; the text does not present difficult problems of interpretation at the linguistic level, and it is arranged in the rhythms of the Latin epistle so familiar to fifteenth- and sixteenth-century Italian scholars. Horace develops his argumentation in a clear and consequential manner and is capable of retaining the attention of the reader through the additional charm of his stylistic urbanity, highlighted by moments of humor and intelligent wit. He does not see literature in the abstract: the poetical expression—be it drama or the epic—is considered in a precise and realistic framework. The intention of the writer in fact is to serve the cause of the amelioration of Roman literature, to encourage the efforts of Roman writers to attain the standards of perfection reached in Greek literature. The necessity felt by Horace to ennoble Latin literature, the nationalistic pride motivating this urgency, have precise analogies among the representatives of Renaissance culture in Italy and elsewhere in Europe, as—to quote only one example—the desire to produce a modern national epic is sufficient to demonstrate.

The nationalistic and sociological components traceable in the conception of the *Ars poetica* are among the factors leading a modern student of Renaissance literary criticism to underscore the rhetorical character of Horace's doctrines on poetry and to reach the following conclusions: "In Horace's theory, the internal characteristics of the poem are determined largely, if not exclusively, by the external demands of the audience"; and "In theories of this kind, the determining factor in the production of the work is not an internal principle of structural perfection, but rather an assumption that all these elements are included in the work that will be susceptible of producing the desired effect upon the audience envisaged."[87] The relation between rhetoric and poetics is a problem of primary importance, especially in relation to the history of Renaissance criticism. The conclusions quoted above are based on an interpretation of the *Ars poetica* that has been debated and rejected by other modern critics. While in the present context it is impossible to dwell on the discussion of the theoretical problems determined by the presence of rhetorical components in any particular system of aesthetics, some observations appear to be in order. The most convincing opinion on this issue appears to be the one maintained by those modern scholars who observe that elements of a rhetorical nature appear also in Aristotle's *Poetics* and furthermore affirm that "their presence in a discussion of poetry does not . . . *ipso facto* reduce poetics to something indistinguishable from rhetoric." [88] Secondarily it is legitimate to recognize that Horace's rhetorical tendencies have a definite appeal to Renaissance theorists. Equally strong was the appeal of the Horatian doctrines concerning the social and didactic responsibilities of the poet and the continuing impact of the principles relative to the unique power of art to attain the combination of *utile* and *dulce*. The Renaissance reader could find in the *Ars poetica* a solution to the problem of the end of poetry with considerable ease and expediency; moreover the moralistic overtones of the Horatian doctrines could promptly become instrumental in the continuing process of the legitimation of literary activity, during a period in which the impending Council of Trent and the decisions on censorship taken during its course imposed upon writers careful consideration of the ethical standards set by the religious authorities.

At the beginning of the sixteenth century Horatian critics were in actuality continuing and developing a firmly established tradition. They had easy access to the late classical commentaries on the *Ars poetica* by Acron and Porphyrion; they could avail themselves of the notations of the grammarians Demetrius and Donatus; they could read more recent commentaries, like the one published by Landino, or they could utilize the exegetical work on the *Ars poetica* published by Josse Bade (Iodocus Badius Ascensius) in 1500.[89] During the earlier decades of the century the theories of Horace were discussed and popularized in Pomponio Gaurico's *Super arte poetica Horatii* (ca. 1510),[90] Vittore Fausto's *De comoedia libellus* (1511),[91] Nicolò Liburnio's *Selvette* (1513),[92] and the extensive commentary of Giovanni Britannica of Brescia (1518).[93]

In 1531 Aulo Giano Parrasio published his vast commentary on the *Ars poetica*:[94] this commentary was frequently reprinted in late Renaissance editions of Horace's works. The increasing popularity of Horace's doctrines is further testified by the translation into Italian of the *Ars poetica* by Lodovico Dolce (1535),[95] who in his prefatory letter to Pietro Aretino discusses the importance of Horatian theories in the cultural environment of his times. Horatian premises are at the core of Bartolomeo Ricci's *De imitatione libri tres* (1541),[96] and they can also be detected in the theoretical foundation upon which rests the structure of Lilio Gregorio Giraldi's *Historia poetarum* (1545).[97]

The cultural repercussions of the publication of Pazzi's translation of the *Poetics* will be the object of a more detailed analysis later in this

study. However, it is important to note here that the increasing popularity of Aristotle's treatise had an impact on Italian Renaissance critical
thought even before the appearance of the so-called great commentaries
on the Aristotelian pamphlet. Comparisons between the positions maintained by Aristotle and Horace began to appear in Horatian critical
literature around the 1540s, together with a tendency to juxtapose principles derived from both classical writers. This type of comparison and
juxtaposition may be found in the *Ecphrasis in Horatii Flacci Artem poeticam* (1546)[98] by Francesco Filippo Pedemonte and, even more significantly, in the works of two theorists better known for their monumental
contributions to the analysis of the *Poetics,* namely, Francesco Robortello
and Vincenzo Maggi. In the appendix to his commentary on the Aristotelian treatise Robortello included a *Paraphrasis in libellum Horatii qui
vulgo de arte poetica ad Pisones inscribitur.*[99] As the title indicates, this
short work is a paraphrase of the *Ars poetica;* the author cites a number
of passages in which, in his opinion, the ideas of the two classical theorists run parallel. Vincenzo Maggi's *In Q. Horatii Flacci De arte poetica
librum ad Pisones interpretationes* is similarly appended to his commentary on the *Poetics.*[100] Maggi maintains that Horace was directly dependent on Aristotle for the conception of several aspects of his theories on
poetry. One of these is the question of decorum, a principle widely debated by Renaissance critics in the Horatian mode. According to Maggi,
Horace's recommendations to attribute to each personage appearing in a
literary work qualities consonant with his status in society can be closely
related to Aristotle's precepts on the outline of character.

The long commentary by Iacopo Grifoli, entitled *In artem poeticam
Horatii interpretatio,*[101] appeared in 1550. Here the author maintains the
singular position that Horace in fact is reorganizing and rearranging in
a more synthetic fashion Aristotle's central ideas on the art of poetry.
Grifoli's outlandish conclusions were rebuked by Giason de Nores in his
In epistolam Q. Horatii Flacci de arte poetica interpretatio (1553).[102] De
Nores focused his attention mainly on the problems of invention, disposition, and elocution, while Francesco Lovisini, in his *In librum Q.
Horatii Flacci De arte poetica commentarius* (1554),[103] displays an impressive wealth of erudition, which does not, however, foster the profundity of his critical conclusions. This phase of Horatian criticism
is further enriched by Benedetto Varchi's *Lettioni della poetica* (1553
and 1554),[104] Alessandro Lionardi's *Dialogi della inventione poetica*
(1554), [105] Giovambattista Giraldi Cinzio's *Lettera a Bernardo Tasso*
(1557)[106] and the treatise *Della imitatione poetica* (1560),[107] by Bernardino Partenio, which deals at length with the differences between poetic
and rhetorical imitation. The longest commentary on the *Ars poetica*

written in the sixteenth century is Giovanni Battista Pigna's *Poetica horatiana* (1561).[108] One of Pigna's main preoccupations is to reduce Horace's poetics to a theory of genres, corresponding to those identified by Aristotle: epic, tragedy, lyric poetry, and comedy. The theory of decorum is again with Pigna a central concern; he identifies the end of poetry with pleasure accompanied by utility, and he frequently appeals to the authority of Aristotle to sustain his arguments, although his general approach remains faithful to the Horatian mode.

The development of Horatian criticism during the sixteenth century is enlivened by debates that parallel the discussions arising among the interpreters of the *Poetics* and among the theorists who follow an Aristotelian orientation. These debates provide an index of the interest gained by the study of critical problems, not only among a restricted public of specialists, but in the life of the cultural institutions known as academies. The origins of Italian Cinquecento academies, their significance as centers of intellectual progress, and their paradigmatic function as models for similar institutions later founded in other parts of Europe, are subjects not directly related to the present study.[109] It must be remembered, however, that a variety of problems directly connected with the art of poetry, and issues debated in practical criticism during the course of the great literary polemics waged during the later part of the sixteenth century, are some of the most important issues discussed at the meetings of several Italian Cinquecento academies. A considerable contribution to the tradition of Horatian criticism in the 1560s was originally presented to the members of a literary academy in a series of lectures delivered by Bartolomeo Maranta to the Accademia Napoletana.[110] On this occasion Maranta criticized the conclusions reached by Pigna in his *Poetica horatiana,* and those appearing in the commentaries on Horace written by Robortello and Maggi. Maranta devoted a considerable degree of attention to the problem of the choice of plot in a poetic composition and to the manners best suited to secure its unity.

In 1566 Giovanni Fabrini published the first commentary in Italian of the *Ars poetica*[111] to appear in the sixteenth century. His exegetical standpoint is clarified at the beginning of the work when he says: "It seems that Horace . . . imitated Aristotle, or rather, that poetics is one single art which has only one single path from the beginning to the end, and that he who has perfect knowledge of it, wishing to discourse about it, can discourse about it only in one way; for in truth it is seen that Aristotle and Horace have, from the beginning to the end, proceeded at the same pace, with the same order, and with the same arrangement."[112] The last commentary on the *Ars poetica* belonging to this phase of the Horatian critical tradition was published by Aldo Manuzio the Younger in 1576. Manuzio's originality is highly questionable: his observations echo for the most part conclusions reached by previous interpreters.

Looking in retrospect at the evolution of the Horatian critical tradition from the beginning of the sixteenth century to the late 1560s, we may observe that the legacy of fifteenth-century humanistic culture persevered among commentators and critics as far as the techniques of textual interpretation are concerned and also in relation to the specific interpretations given to the Horatian doctrines. The authority of Horace was incessantly invoked to justify the moralistic end of poetry; *prodesse* and *delectare* were consistently considered as the ultimate task of the poet. Another central issue in Horatian criticism was the concept of decorum, and the discussion of this problem was connected with the structural analysis of the poetic composition, with questions of style, and with the study of the most effective manner of fostering the general ends of poetry. According to Cinquecento Horatian critics obeisance to the rules of decorum increases the instructive potentials of the poetic text, since the proper conduct of fictional characters may acquire exemplary value, but the presentation of improper conduct can also be charged with didactic value. Concerns of a structural nature were incessantly kindled by discussions on the Horatian principles relative to invention and disposition; moreover, the attempts to define the methods to attain the internal harmony of the composition were corroborated through the assimilation into the Horatian tradition of ideas of Aristotelian origin on the relations of plot, character, and diction.

In the last decades of the century the lectures of Francesco Bonciani (1578)[113] and the publication of Pino da Cagli's treatises (1578)[114] open a new phase in the tradition of Horatian criticism. As has been noted, "the theoretical materials . . . are still only secondarily devoted to commentary on the *Ars poetica*. . . . Instead theorists produce a large number of short treatises on particular genres—the madrigal, the sonnet, the elegy, the comedy, the verse romance—in which they apply Horatian principles to these special forms."[115] The discussion of these last developments falls outside the intellectual directives established in this study.

*   *   *

While the tradition of Horatian criticism emerged from the fifteenth into the sixteenth century as an intellectual trend resting on established foundations and thus as a cultural approach endowed with inner powers of expansion, the Cinquecento tradition of Aristotelian criticism had slow and hesitant beginnings. It is a known and puzzling fact that Aristotle's treatise was used to a very minor extent in classical antiquity. Using an apparently daring, but in reality correct image, B. Hathaway declared that the sixteenth-century Italians can be said to have invented the *Poetics* of Aristotle.[116] Obviously the seminal power contained in a book becomes effective when the text is read and naturally increases with the growing number of its readers and thus with the realization of its validity. From this point of view it appears legitimate to define the *Poetics* as an "invention" of Italian Cinquecento theorists, due to the massive process of revitalization attained through their analysis of its content and through their use of the principles therein to satisfy cultural exigencies urgent in their time.

Initially the reading of the *Poetics* presented serious problems. Aristotle's treatise is the only work to reach us from classical antiquity that contains the codification of an organic system of literary theory intimately connected to a solid system of metaphysics, rather than to premises of a rhetorical nature, as happens in the case of the critical precepts formulated by Cicero, Quintilian, and, to some extent, Horace. The Greek philosopher takes into consideration the audience in whom poetry produces its proper effect, and he discusses the natural reality presented in the work of art. His main concern, however, is "to discover how a poem, produced by imitation and representing some aspect of a natural object—its form—in the artificial medium of poetry, may so achieve perfection of that form in the medium that the desired aesthetic effect results."[117] Aristotle's general conception of aesthetics comprises such factors as the end of poetry, the nature of imitation, the relation of artificial to natural objects, the connection between the work and its contemplator, and the general criteria for artistic achievement. In the course of his argumentation he refers to a variety of works from Greek literature and thus verifies the validity of his aesthetic principles.

At the beginning of the sixteenth century classical sources provided very little guidance to the reader of the *Poetics;* he was faced with a text containing many corrupt passages, and the help to understanding offered by exemplification was considerably reduced by the fact that Greek literature was still imperfectly known at the time. In 1481 the commentary to the *Poetics,* written in Arabic by Averroës in the twelfth century and translated into Latin by Hermann the German in the thirteenth century, was published in Venice with the title *Determinatio in poetria Aristotelis.*[118] The perusal of this work could only lead to a distorted impression of the content of the *Poetics.* In the *Determinatio* poetry is presented as an instrument of moral edification, facilitated by the use of rhetorical devices, such as figures of speech and ornaments of various kinds.

The arduous conquest of the *Poetics* began to take shape with the Latin translation of the Aristotelian treatise published in Venice by

Giorgio Valla in 1498.[119] Valla's translation is free from any bias of an interpretative nature. The translator renders in Latin, a language more familiar at his time than Greek, a text containing specialized terminology, syntactical complication, lacunas, and abrupt transitions. Some conspicuous errors are present in Valla's work; for instance περιπατεία, at 1447 b 26 of the original text, is rendered as *petulantia,* and even worse, at 1559 b 11 the same Greek term is rendered as *procacitas.*[120] Despite these occasional errors, Valla is quite successful in rendering key terms of the original and demonstrates remarkable precision in transposing into Latin the argumentations relative to the central issues of the treatise.

The first edition of the Greek text of the *Poetics* was published in Venice by Aldo Manuzio in 1508 in a miscellaneous volume with the singular title *Rhetores in hoc volumine habentur hi,* followed by the names of the authors of the works included.[121] The editor of the Aristotelian treatise was Demetrius Ducas and not Janus Lascaris as suggested by several scholars, including B. Weinberg.[122] As far as present scholarship has been able to determine, both the translation of Valla and Aldo's edition failed to raise an immediate interest in the theories discussed in the *Poetics.* References to Aristotle's literary theories may be found in the work of Pomponio Gaurico and Vittore Fausto[123] and even more extensively in Lodovico Ricchieri's *Lectionum antiquarum libri XXX* (1516).[124] A passage from Averroës's commentary was quoted by Pietro Pomponazzi in his *De incantationibus* (1520),[125] and three years later the same commentary was translated into Latin by Abraham de Balmes, who for this purpose used the fourteenth-century Hebrew translation of Todros Todrosi.[126]

One of the most interesting personalities in the initial phase of Cinquecento Aristotelian criticism is undoubtedly Giangiorgio Trissino.[127] An aristocrat by birth, well known in the intellectual circles of Rome, Florence, and northern Italy, a Maecenas who protected in the earlier stages of his career Andrea di Pietro and coined for him the name Palladio,[128] Trissino fully merits greater recognition from contemporary students of the Renaissance. His multiple activity deserves to be analyzed in greater depth from perspectives unaffected by critical preconceptions and must be attentively evaluated in relation to the more innovative currents in the culture of his time.[129]

Trissino's *Sofonisba* was saluted by his Italian contemporaries[130] as the first regular tragedy in Italian literature and was regarded abroad as a model of dramatic composition.[131] His *Italia liberata dai Goti* was one of the new epic poems studied by Tasso during the period of critical reflection preceding his composition of the *Gerusalemme liberata.*[132] The mediocrity of Trissino's talents as a poet may have overshadowed the significance of his contributions as an advocate for the implementation of critical principles derived from classical antiquity to secure the artistic validity of modern forms of literary expression.

Trissino's *Sofonisba* was composed in Rome during the years 1513–14. It was published in 1524 and performed for the first time in Vicenza in 1556 with sets designed by Palladio. The text of the tragedy is preceded by a dedicatory letter to Leo X. In this brief document we find the first extensive Renaissance attempt to utilize Aristotelian doctrines to define the nature and the characteristics of a literary composition. Under the direct influence of the *Poetics* Trissino discusses the differences between tragedy and comedy, briefly defines the proper magnitude of the tragic structure, its necessary parts, and the linguistic level best suited to confirm its superior position in the order of literary genres. He explains and justifies his use of Italian as a necessity of primary importance for the materialization of the ends of tragedy. These ends are conceived from Horatian perspectives as "universal utility and pleasure"; such goals cannot be attained unless the tragic performance is held in a language familiar to the audience. The *Sofonisba* is written in unrhymed endecasyllables. Trissino justifies the use of this verse on psychological grounds. He maintains that rhyming demands a type of intellectual effort contrasting with the spontaneity of the language employed by tragic characters as they express their passions and their sorrows. The structure of the *Sofonisba* reveals strict adherence to the principles of unity of action and unity of time, while the unity of place is violated. It is evident that in the arrangement of his tragedy's subject matter Trissino was very conscious of examples provided by Greek dramatic literature, particularly Sophocles's *Antigone* and Euripides's *Alcestis*.

In 1529 Trissino published the first section of his *Poetica*.[133] Despite his knowledge of Aristotle, in this part of his work the author refers to the *Poetics* only twice: at the beginning of his discussion of diction and during the course of his debate on the choice of words. Diction and rhyme are the main subjects analyzed in this part of the *Poetica;* here Trissino's sources are the rhetoricians and the works of writers on prosody like Antonio da Tempo.

A singular coincidence makes the date 1524 quite memorable in the history of Aristotelian criticism in Italy, for in that year Alessandro de' Pazzi had prepared in Rome his translation of the *Poetics*, as he states in the dedication, although it appeared posthumously in 1536, the year the celebrated edition of the Greek text prepared by Giovanni Francesco Trincavelli was published.[134] Pazzi's translation met with extraordinary success; reprinted in Basel in 1537 and in Paris in 1538, it had no fewer than twelve additional editions before the end of the century.[135] This success may be explained in the light of some acute typographical and editorial criteria adopted by Pazzi and by his acumen as a translator. Although Nicolò Leonico Tomeo and Gasparo Contarini had been asked to read and correct Pazzi's work, some of the errors committed by Giorgio Valla reappeared in the version of his Cinquecento successor. Nevertheless the superiority of Pazzi's translation over the translation of Valla is unquestionable.

Following the publication of Alessandro de' Pazzi's basic contribution, the most notable developments in the study of the *Poetics* are the public lectures on the Aristotelian system of aesthetics given at Padua by Bartolomeo Lombardi in 1541.[136] Lombardi died shortly after, and among his papers he left a text and translation of the *Poetics*, with extensive annotations. Vincenzo Maggi, one of Lombardi's friends and a professor of philosophy at the *studium* of Ferrara,[137] included the *Poetics* among the subjects of his courses. The notes of Maggi's lectures on the art of poetry, taken by his pupil Alessandro Sardi, bear the date 1546.[138] The interest devoted by Lombardi and Maggi to Aristotle as the classical authority providing the most secure guidance for the understanding and the solution of problems related to poetics, can be classified as an immediate prelude to the fundamental development in the tradition of Aristotle promoted by the so-called great Cinquecento commentaries on the *Poetics*.

The series of these works began in 1548, the publication date of Francesco Robortello's *In librum Aristotelis de arte poetica explicationes*.[139] It was followed in 1550 by the commentary of Maggi and Lombardi: *Vincentii Madii Brixiani et Bartholomaei Lombardi Veronensis in Aristotelis librum de poetica communes explanationes*.[140] In 1560 the Florentine publishers Giunti presented to the public Pietro Vettori's *Commentarii in primum librum Aristotelis de arte poetarum*.[141] The series of commentaries on the *Poetics* in Italian was inaugurated ten years later by Lodovico Castelvetro's *Poetica d'Aristotele vulgarizzata et sposta*,[142] followed in 1575 by Alessandro Piccolomini's *Annotazioni nel libro della Poetica d'Aristotele*.[143] During the last part of the sixteenth century the most important commentaries on the Aristotelian treatise were those of Antonio Riccoboni (1585)[144] in Latin and Lionardo Salviati (1586)[145] in Italian. The impulse given by the great commentaries to the study of the Aristotelian doctrines on poetry was further enhanced by Italian versions of the text of the *Poetics*. The Italian translation published by Bernardo Segni in 1549 was the first to be published in a modern vernacular.[146] It was followed by the translations of Alessandro Piccolomini (1572)[147] and Lorenzo Giacomini Tebalducci (1573);[148] while in 1579 Antonio Riccoboni published a new Latin translation of the Greek treatise.[149]

The great commentaries may well be defined as the internal supporting structure, the skeleton as it were, of the entire body of Renaissance critical literature in the Aristotelian mode. They stand as poles of reference for questions of textual criticism and verbal interpretations; they provide explanations of the Aristotelian doctrines from a position of authority always recognized, even when it is not followed. The method of presentation and analysis of the material adopted in the earlier great commentaries could be considered as a continuation of the expansion of the method followed by the humanists of the fifteenth century. This method has been recently analyzed in detail, and it has been considered to be one of the elements leading to a defective understanding of the doctrines contained in the *Poetics,* to a shift from Aristotle to pseudo-Aristotle.[150] Regardless of the merits of this interpretation, the full understanding of the total value of these works, their function in determining future readings of the text of Aristotle, cannot be understood if we consider them merely as commentaries and cannot find the key to read them also as independent arts of poetry. In their interpretations of Aristotle the commentators were frequently influenced by the thought of other classical authorities: this type of eclecticism is a common Renaissance phenomenon, and in practice it fosters the efforts of these interpreters to outline systems of poetics compatible with the exigencies of their time.

In his commentary Robortello maintains that the end of poetry is threefold: pleasure, utility, and imitation.[151] He studies at length the public of poetry and the impact of the literary work on the soul of the reader. In order to be acceptable the work of art must respect truth; having established this fundamental principle, Robortello is obliged to confront the problem of verisimilitude, to debate the relation between the rational and irrational components of the poetic creation. For this purpose he avails himself of the Aristotelian arguments on the difference between history and poetry, supplementing this part of his speculation with an analysis of the possible and the probable as subjects of literary creativity. Holding fast to the idea that the false cannot motivate poetic expressions, Robortello defines the limits within which the poet may utilize fantastic elements. Indeed the imagination inevitably contributes to the dynamics of the process of artistic metamorphosis. However, in his discriminating choice of fantastic elements the poet is allowed to derive them from established traditions, myths or popular lore; if he invents them anew, he must render them probable by balancing the drive of his fantasy with the proper respect of the laws of verisimilitude. Plot, character, and form of expression, the fundamental triad of the components of tragedy codified by Aristotle, tend to be envisioned by Robortello from a rhetorical standpoint as factors enhancing the process of persuasion. Veracity and verisimilitude augment the plot's power of conviction; the character can serve as an example of moral conduct; consequently evil must be punished or exposed to the ridicule of comedy.[152]

The *Prolegomena* to the commentary on the *Poetics* of Maggi and Lombardi[153] already reveal an intellectual framework characterized by the same moralistic concerns uppermost in Robortello's mind. In the prefatory remarks of the commentary Maggi states that "the end of poetry itself is, by imitating human actions in delightful discourse, to render the soul refined."[154] Such a utilitarian concept of poetry is confirmed through the analysis of all literary genres. One of the notable differences between the positions of Robortello and those held by Maggi is illustrated by their respective interpretations of the Aristotelian principle of catharsis. Maggi does not consider this effect of tragedy merely as a purgation of the passions of pity and fear, but rather as a form of moral lesson on the perils of indulging one's passions, especially those pertaining to the order of the "concupiscible and the irascible."[155] The audience of poetry, according to Maggi, may not be limited to an intellectual elite, since it includes the common people. Thus if the literary work is conceived as an instrument of moral edification for large sections of society, the poet's credibility must reckon with an uncultured audience's limited power of imagination. Hence the poet will be constrained to adhere to truth or to themes not liable to violate popular opinion. Therefore the subjects of poetry must be chosen within the categories of the natural, the necessary, and the verisimilar. Maggi strongly upholds the principle of decorum; in his view dramatic suitability of speech and behavior to character is a powerful factor in determining the artistic validity of tragedy and its acceptability on the part of the audience. These positions provide clear evidence of the fact that in Maggi's system the poet's liberty of choice is considerably reduced. The moralistic tendencies of the commentator are combined with a strong rationalistic urge, which in turn determines a tendency to transform into laws some Aristotelian statements originally intended as mere observations. This normative attitude is particularly evident in the discussion of the unity of time in tragedy, where Maggi leans toward positions later elaborated by Castelvetro.

In his commentary Pietro Vettori displays a degree of erudition and philological preparation considerably superior to that demonstrated by Robortello and Maggi-Lombardi.[156] Since Vettori was in fact more a philologist than a literary theorist, his commentary becomes extremely significant in relation to the textual history of the *Poetics,* because of the suggestions provided therein to improve the text itself through a series of authoritative emendations. In the course of his analysis Vettori expresses his views on problems of poetics. In so doing he follows a moralistic and rhetorical line of interpretation and continues to consider poetry as a sublime retainer of models of human conduct.

Lodovico Castelvetro's commentary on the *Poetics* was defined by a modern scholar as "a landmark or turning point in the development of literary criticism in the sixteenth century."[157] A strong and uncompromising personality and an "acute" thinker (as he was defined by Francesco Patrizi, one of his contemporary opponents), a theorist profoundly admired into the eighteenth century (when one of the era's most representative students of poetics defined him as "the prince of critics"), Castelvetro stands as an impressive, and yet somewhat solitary, figure in the history of Renaissance aesthetics and literary criticism.[158] While the majority of Italian Cinquecento critics remained within the boundaries of Catholic orthodoxy and formulated doctrines in general agreement with the spirit of the Counter-Reformation, Castelvetro was accused of inclining toward Protestant positions. In 1560 he was condemned as a heretic and left Italy to avoid complications with the ecclesiastical authorities.[159] Some of his critical analyses degenerated into violent polemics and transformed well-known writers—like Benedetto Varchi and Annibal Caro—into some of his most bitter enemies. While commentators like Robortello, Maggi, Lombardi, and—to a lesser degree—Vettori maintained a reverential attitude toward Aristotle and the text of the *Poetics*, instead of regarding him as the undisputed authority Castelvetro placed himself in a position of parity with the ancient philosopher from the very outset of his commentary.[160] In so doing Castelvetro retained and developed an attitude toward the classics typical of the more vital among the fifteenth-century humanists. From that position classical culture, the writing of the ancients and their artistic heritage as a whole, is not viewed as an incentive to passive imitation; it is considered instead as a source of stimulation toward self-realization; it is regarded as a catalyst activating a type of self-expression endowed with structural harmony and formal perfection and at the same time inwardly animated by the necessity to comply with the urgencies dictated by present historical factors. Such fidelity to this epistemological directive was one of the forces cementing the argumentation developed in Castelvetro's commentary and strongly contributing to its originality.

Castelvetro's humanistic learning is immediately revealed by his approach to the text of the *Poetics* at the linguistic level. The commentator first of all was a rigorous translator: on the one hand he indicated the errors, the lacunas, the contradictions present in the text and, on the other, he discussed the mistakes made by previous interpreters in their rendering of several passages of the ancient treatise.

Judgment about Castelvetro's system of poetics among modern

students is not unanimous. An attentive consideration of the Renaissance theorist's work, however, does not legitimate the claim that "Castelvetro transposes the whole of the analysis from the world of art to the world of reality, . . . works are treated [by Castelvetro] as if they were natural objects, objects themselves remain unchanged as they pass into the work." [161] Instead of accepting this interpretation, a correct understanding of Castelvetro's system may profit from the advice to pay attentive consideration to Castelvetro's debates on the relation between rhetoric and poetry [162] and on the problem of the analogies and differences between history and poetry. [163]

For Castelvetro the priority of history over poetry is not merely a postulate advanced to sustain a system of poetics, but a consequence of deeply rooted philosophical convictions. He firmly believes that in the order of reality first come the objects and then their representation in the work of art: truth comes first and then it is followed by the verisimilar. Consequently history is strictly related to the domain of reality and nature; poetry instead is rigorously confined to the domain of representation. Thus with Castelvetro the distance between the two disciplines becomes absolute and unbridgeable.

Rationalistic exigencies are uppermost in Castelvetro's mind; a rationalistic urge motivates his critique and his radical rejection of the concept of furor and leads him to formulate the deep-seated conviction that poetry is essentially the product of "art," the fruit of labor and technical skill, the work of "wit" (ingegno). The term ingegno—destined to reappear with such frequency in the poetics of the Baroque age—is frequently invoked by Castelvetro in his definitions of the supreme achievements of the poetic talent. Ingegno cannot be merely classified as a natural gift; it is a form of intellectual power secured through the mastery of all the skills required by the art of poetry and refined through practice.

The poetics of Castelvetro is unequivocally oriented toward the public: "Poetry was invented for the pleasure of the ignorant multitude and the common people, and not for the pleasure of the educated. . . . Poetry was invented exclusively to delight and to give recreation." [164] By assigning to poetry ends strictly limited to the category of pleasure—even if they include the more refined hedonistic gratification provided by the learning of things unknown—Castelvetro drastically reduces the pedagogical potentials of the poetic language so strongly defended by the humanistic culture of the fifteenth century and abandons the moralistic concerns of the previous commentators in Latin on the Poetics.

Concerns of a rhetorical character are present in Castelvetro's system. Rhetoric maintains its domain in the sphere of the expression; its impact, however, extends also to the choice of the plot, the invention. A plausible fictional case must unfold in a suitably persuasive language. Moreover, in order to captivate the audience it becomes imperative to study its nature. Castelvetro believes that the public of poetry is singularly devoid of imagination, and he himself is rationalistically wary of the imaginative faculties. In his opinion common people formulate their judgments on the basis of sense perception: "No deception can take place in them, which the senses recognize as such." [165] And further: "Incredible things cannot engender the marvellous"; [166] one cannot be astonished by the flights of Daedalus if one does not believe that Daedalus can fly: "The marvellous must originate from credible things." [167]

Premises of this nature place Castelvetro's poet before a series of difficult challenges. His aim is the attainment of the artistically astonishing, and yet he must draw his material from the order of reality: thus his creativity is both constrained and challenged by the demands of verisimilitude. "Poetry derives all its light from history," says Castelvetro and adds: "Poetry is similitude or resemblance of history." [168] It would be very misleading to take these statements out of context. Castelvetro clearly distinguishes between historical and poetic representation. Subject matter and form of expression are principal parts of both history and poetry; the subject matter of history, however, is not invention, a choice determined on the strength of creative criteria, but external data, which come into being through the interaction of forces ruling human events, be they destiny or the will of God. The language of history must be couched in the rhythms of prose; the rhetoric of ornamentation cannot transfer it into registers too removed from conversational modes. "The subject matter of poetry is found and imagined by the wit of the poet, and [poetry] does not have words identical to those used in conversation, . . . but arranged in verses by the wit of the poet. . . . The subject matter of poetry must be similar to the subject matter of history, but it must not be identical, because if it were exactly the same it would not be similar and it would not resemble it." [169] If the subject matter of poetry were to be identical to the subject matter of history, "the poet . . . would not have labored to find it, nor would he have shown the acuteness of his wit, and therefore he would not deserve praise; and especially he would not deserve the praise by which he is reputed to be more a divine than a human thing, being able to organize a story imagined by himself and no less delightful nor less verisimilar than the progress of human events or the infinite providence of God." [170] It is quite evident that passages of this nature can by no means legitimize the conclusion that in Castelvetro's system we witness a transposal of "the object into the work of art." [171]

Lodovico Castelvetro is best known as the Renaissance critic who surpassed Aristotle in his normative zeal and codified the law of the three dramatic unities.[172] Indeed in Castelvetro's commentary we find definitions of the unity of time that run as follows: "The perceptible end of tragedy has found its proper compass within the revolution of the sun over the earth."[173] One of the formulations of the unity of place reads: "Tragedy must have as its subject an action accomplished in a small area of place and in a small space of time, that is, in that place and in that time where and when the actors remain engaged in acting, and not in any other place or in any other time."[174] A certain degree of flexibility is shown by Castelvetro in relation to the unity of action, as we can deduce from statements of this nature: "Even if it were conceded [to poetry] to relate many actions of many persons, or of many people, I do not see that any blame should come to it for this reason."[175] It has been observed that this type of concession is another violation of basic principles established by Aristotle, who regarded unity of action as "the very essence of the work of art."[176] This objection may be dismissed as irrelevant: Castelvetro himself made it abundantly clear in the dedicatory letter and throughout his commentary that his guiding concern was not to provide a faithful interpretation of the Aristotelian doctrines, or to regard them as unconditionally acceptable. The Italian critic intended to build a coherent system of poetics, availing himself of ideas derived from Aristotle, without renouncing his own vision of reality, his personal approach to art, his preoccupation to establish principles suited to the needs of his contemporaries and applicable in his own time. Castelvetro's rationalistic and realistic tendencies led him to conceive the artistic process as a difficult and challenging activity, aimed at the attainment of a proper and convincing balance between elements provided by external reality and elements provided by imagination and skill. The Italian critic was not at all concerned with the taste, the expectations, and the psychology of the original public of Greek tragedy, and in his view tragedy was first of all theater, spectacle, and not merely literature. Therefore he considered the possibility of having a tragedy with a complex plot, simply because that type of structure might provide "more pleasure, greatness, and magnificence"[177] when performed before the public he contemplated. Castelvetro's final choice of a single plot, unity of action, was based on a double motivation: a single plot is more viable in terms of the various necessities of the living theater; moreover, "in presenting the single action of one person, which at first sight does not seem to have the power to retain the souls to listen with pleasure,"[178] the poet shows once again the power of his talent, the force of his wit in overcoming another artistic challenge.

The effect of tragedy, or what is known as the Aristotelian concept of catharsis, is interpreted by Castelvetro as a reaction determined by the process of the public's identification with the dramatic action. In "feeling displeasure at the unjustly suffered unhappiness of others, we recognize that we ourselves are good, since unjust things displease us, a recognition—because of the natural love that we have for ourselves—that is a source of great pleasure to us." [179] Tragedy and the epic poem are the only two genres extensively taken into consideration in the *Poetics* of Castelvetro. Comparing these two forms of poetic expression, the theorist concludes that the dramatist faces challenges more arduous than the heroic poet; furthermore in his opinion the pleasure provided by tragedy, in its final and complete aspect revealed by a staged performance, is greater than the pleasure derived from the reading of heroic poetry. [180]

A subtle critique of Castelvetro's position is elaborated in the *Annotazioni alla Poetica di Aristotele* (1575) by Alessandro Piccolomini, the second of the "great commentators" in Italian. A playwright, essayist, and moral philosopher, Piccolomini was also a consummate philologist. [181] His translation of the *Poetics* (1572) may be regarded under some aspects as an improvement on Castelvetro's version. Piccolomini approached the original text with a greater sense of freedom than his predecessor, with the result that, while his renderings may be more diffuse, their significance is clearer. In contrast to Castelvetro's tendency to preserve the density of the Greek original and in the process maintain syntactical structures alien to Italian, Piccolomini does not hesitate to render single words with phrases and to clarify, through paraphrase, the more synthetic locutions used by Aristotle.

In the prologue to the *Annotazioni* Piccolomini states that poetry must be subordinate to the architectonic discipline of politics, as we learn from Aristotle's *Ethics*. This prefatory remark could impress the reader as a prelude to a system of poetics conceived from intellectual perspectives analogous to those leading Plato to define the role of poetry in the society described in his *Republic*. Piccolomini, however, reverts to general orientations typical of the Aristotelian tradition. He defines poetry as "an imitation, not only of things either natural or artificial, but mainly of human actions, characters, and passions, done mostly by means of language and diction . . . in order to give pleasure and by giving pleasure ultimately to benefit human life." [182] Castelvetro's rebellious attitude toward Aristotle is abandoned by Piccolomini, who nevertheless does not strictly follow the text of the *Poetics* and introduces digressions, in which he discusses at length problems considered by Aristotle only in a brief and synthetic manner. Like Robortello and more extensively Castelvetro, Piccolomini is concerned with the psychology of the audience of poetry. A basic principle guiding this aspect of his investigation is the belief that the highest good conceivable by man is "the possession of a true tranquility of spirit." [183] Art can become an aid to materialize that aspiration. The function of tragedy is "to purge the soul mainly of the excess of those passions, which have as their objects evil and fear." [184] Unlike Castelvetro, Piccolomini believes that the public of tragedy is endowed with a considerable degree of imagination; the use of this faculty allows the spectators to understand clearly the distance separating artistic imitation and actual reality.

The relationship between the poet and his audience, or if we prefer between the text and the reader, is debated in new and extremely interesting terms by Piccolomini. Through his reevaluation of the public's imaginative powers, the critic is led to depart again from Castelvetro and to approach the problem of verisimilitude from different angles. In his opinion the task of the poet is not so much to adhere to truth as to attain the metamorphosis of actual, or historical, truth into artistic verisimilitude. Unfortunately these intuitions are not developed in depth, and he falls back into positions not conducive to the formulation of principles proclaiming the freedom of artistic creativity. Piccolomini states that facts are more convincing than fictional actions devised in obedience to the law of probability. Therefore tragedies based on historical material are preferable to those developing purely imaginary themes. Following the concepts developed by exponents of both the Aristotelian and the Horatian traditions, Piccolomini advocates the principle of decorum and defends its necessity as a rule governing aspects of characterization, in accord with the expectations of the public.

Castelvetro's disparaging attitude toward Aristotle is rejected by Antonio Riccoboni in his *Poetica*, one of the last "great commentaries" of the Italian sixteenth century.[185] A professor of humanities at the University of Padua, Riccoboni wrote his commentary in Latin and focused the greater part of his discussion on the problem of the objects of imitation. Riccoboni maintained that verse is necessary in poetry and declared that its ends are utility, pleasure, imitation, and the plot. The arrangement of a particular subject into a poetic structure can be a source of delight: "Poetics is the art of executing plots, or the faculty of imitating in verse; or the organic habit of seeing, in human actions, whatever is suitable for fashioning a plot." [186] The pleasure provided by the plot is always associated with some form of utility. Lessons of utility may be learned from poetic fables; terrible and pitiable actions determine the purgation of pity, and "the poet must bring pleasure through imitation out of pity and fear; this must be achieved by the actions." [187]

A partial translation of and commentary on the *Poetics*, extending from the beginning of the text to 1449 b 9, was completed by Lionardo

Salviati in 1586.[188] Salviati's translation is characterized by an effort to achieve a greater degree of accuracy than his Cinquecento predecessors. In his commentary he observes that the *Poetics* is a rather limited treatise, as far as the method of argumentation is concerned; he believes that in his discussion of problems related to the art of poetry Aristotle does not demonstrate the same degree of dialectical rigor exemplified by his scientific works. According to Salviati also the content of the *Poetics* may be considered as partial. Aristotle in fact discusses only epic, tragedy, comedy, dithyramb, auletic, and citharistic poetry; his principles therefore would be inadequate as a guide to the analysis of such works as Petrarch's *Trionfi* or Boccaccio's *Amorosa visione*. The commentator considers the *Poetics* "as a precious and most useful book,"[189] but he also believes that its usefulness may be increased through revision and incrementation of its doctrinal content.

Salviati defines poetry as "an imitation of the verisimilar expressed through ornamented language"[190] and devotes considerable attention to the analysis of the concept of imitation. He observes that it is not "enough to say that imitation is the form of the poem; for in order to make the composite, form in itself is not sufficient, but there must also be the matter and not every matter, but the proper matter, which (speaking of the extrinsic one) in poetry is verse."[191] In Salviati's opinion the ends of poetry are utility and pleasure. He discusses at length the types of pleasure derived from the various literary genres and tends to reject the position of those Cinquecento critics who identified moral instruction as the end of poetry.

It has been correctly stated that, from a historical point of view, the greatest merit of the Italian Cinquecento tradition of study on the *Poetics* consists in the effort to present "in a rationally clear and systematic fashion the problem of the practical function of artistic representation."[192] The Aristotelian critical orientation allowed the reduction of art into the sphere of the "cognitive activities and legitimized it by attributing to it a precise instrumental, educational and moral function in perfect agreement with the traditional themes of humanistic thought and with the canons of neo-classical taste."[193] The doctrinal content of the *Poetics* was at times misunderstood; in other cases it was distorted, or it was seen through preconceived perspectives. The Aristotelian treatise nevertheless became a major incentive and a solid term of reference for investigations, discussion, polemics on the most varied and fundamental aspects of the problem of aesthetics; it was effective as a guide to place "in a new light the humanistic concept of poetry as imitation (in its double sense of imitation of nature and imitation of the classics)"; it sustained the effort "to define a first criterion of distinction between poetry, science and history, which had been barely hinted at in the discussions of the fifteenth century."[194]

*   *   *

It has been correctly stated that the Cinquecento literary theorist who followed a Platonic orientation was basically a man without a text.[195] This image acquires its proper and adequate meaning once we consider the fact that exponents of the Horatian and Aristotelian traditions could concentrate their exegetical efforts on a central text; they could strive to find answers to questions of a theoretical and technical nature through the study of one single and unified document, organically treating problems related to poetics. Plato did not write an art of poetry. The general principles about literature and art formulated by the Greek philosopher may be reconstructed by piecing together a series of passages scattered in several of his dialogues, such as the *Phaedrus*, the *Ion*, and the *Republic*.[196] Plato's main interest, however, was not focused on questions related to the organization of the poem and to the practice of art; his attention was primarily directed toward the analysis of the relation between poetic language and truth, or the educational necessities arising in an ideal society, or the powers of divine inspiration.

The Platonic tenets that primarily polarized the attention of Italian Cinquecento students of poetics were the question of furor, the treatment of the concept of imitation, and the argumentation leading to the banishment of poets from the ideal state. Frequently ideas of Platonic origin were fused with influences from other sources. During the later part of the Cinquecento the Platonic tradition assumed clearer connotations; it acquired a polemical drive directed against the surge of Aristotelian critical thought, promoted by the great commentaries of the 1560s and 1570s. At this point there was a strong revival of interest in the concept of furor. The validity of this principle is based on historical grounds through a process sustained by a singular form of syncretism between Greco-Roman mythology and Hebrew theology, through the widening of the interests in hermetic literature formerly kindled by the Neoplatonists of the fifteenth century, and through the emphasis on the significance of mythical personages like Orpheus, Linus, and Musaeus in the initial phases of human civilization. The identification of sibyls, prophets, primitive lawgivers as poets inspired by God, using a language replete with images readily accessible for their appeal to the faculty of imagination and yet containing messages of profound wisdom, provides the basis for the establishment of a variety of focal points at the theoretical level. Thus the idea of divine inspiration promotes increasing diffidence in relation to the Aristotelian concepts of mimesis and of the verisimilar; it raises doubts about the validity of the Aristotelian critics' conclusions on the rapport between external reality and artistic representation; and at the same time it promotes deeper considerations of the links between poetry and truth, extensive speculation on the function of imagination in the creative process, on the role of the literary theorist, and on the question of the dominance of canons of literary composition over the inspired freedom of the creative act. These last concepts are widely developed in Patrizi's *Della poetica*, a work of capital importance in the history of the Renaissance Platonic tradition, but also a work that may be considered in the category of the new arts of poetry, where it will be discussed.

Some elements of Platonic origin are traceable in Lodovico Ricchieri's *Lectionum antiquarum libri XXX*, already mentioned in relation to the earlier developments of the Aristotelian tradition; Gasparo Contarini's *De officio episcopi* (ca. 1520); Mario Equicola's *Libro de natura de amore* (1525); Francesco Berni's *Dialogo contra i poeti* (1526); and Giovanni Bernardino Fuscano's *De la oratoria et poetica facoltà* (1531). A lively discussion of the question of the poet's banishment from the ideal state appears in Jacopo Sadoleto's treatise *De liberis recte instituendis liber* (1533).[197] The *Ragionamenti della lingua toscana* (1545) of Bernardino Tomitano[198] has been defined as the first nearly complete art of poetry in the present group of Platonic treatises. One of Tomitano's main concerns is to demonstrate that the "perfect orator and poet" must have a profound philosophical background in order to present truth in pleasant and appealing images. In Tomitano's *Ragionamenti* oratory and poetry are frequently associated as two arts closely allied, since they both aim at the same ends of utility and pleasure, and they share the same qualitative parts of invention, disposition, and elocution. Tomitano recognizes that versification and the use of images and fables confer on poetic language a unique character; however, he tends toward the unification of all arts, using words as materials of construction, and sees in their specific language the most relevant and distinctive element. For Tomitano the excellence of any kind of discourse is achieved through the effort to attain an intimate combination of eloquence and philosophy.

The *Orationes et praefationes* of Antonio Maria Conti (Marcantonio Maioragio)[199] published posthumously in 1582, but presumably composed around 1550, include the oration *De arte poetica*, in which the author praises poetry as the most divine of all arts: "Better than any philosopher, poets taught principles and rules of good living and precepts of moral conduct."[200] The philosophical and moral content of the poetic language is also praised by Maioragio in his prefaces to the *Iliad* and the *Odyssey*, while in his *In tres Aristotelis libros de arte rhetorica* (published posthumously in 1572) he discusses some aspects of Plato's theory of imitation.[201] The moral and educational responsibilities of the poet are studied also in the *Dialogi della inventione poetica* of Alessandro Lionardi,[202] A work already mentioned in relation to the Horatian tradition. In Lionardi's *Dialogi* Horatian, Aristotelian, and Platonic influences are fused in a comprehensive theory of essentially rhetorical character. The poet's qualifications are outlined through references to the *Republic*, the *Phaedo*, and the *Ion*, which appear among the sources employed also by Iacopo Grifoli in his *Oratio de laudibus poetarum* (1557).[203] During this period the tradition of Platonic criticism is enriched by Scipione Ammirato with his dialogue *Il Dedalione overo del poeta* (1560),[204] where the major themes of discussion are the question of the relation between poetry and truth and the problem of the doctrine possessed by the inspired poet. Bernardino Partenio's *Della imitazione poetica*[205] has been listed as a document belonging to the Horatian tradition; it can be observed, however, that Partenio follows a Platonic mode in his praise of Homer and in his discussion of the antiquity of poetry. Other significant documents in relation to the progress of the Platonic tradition in the 1560s are Bernardo Tasso's *Ragionamento della poesia* (1560), Benedetto Grasso's *Oratione contra gli Terentiani* (1566), Lucio Olimpio Giraldi's *Ragionamento in difesa di Terentio* (1566), Orazio Toscanella's *Osservazioni sopra Virgilio* (1566), and Frosino Lapini's *Lettione nella quale si ragiona in universale del fine della poesia*, a lecture delivered before the Accademia Fiorentina in 1567.[206]

The effect of the Council of Trent on Italian cultural and artistic life has been the subject of long and complex chapters in political histories, and histories of philosophy, literature, theater, music, and the visual arts.[207] The reforms advocated by the Tridentine council had an impact also on the development of critical thought during the last part of the sixteenth century. A correspondence between the positions taken by the ecclesiastical authorities and the new attitudes assumed in the speculation on the problem of poetics may be traced in Antonio Viperano's *De scribendis virorum illustrium vitis* (1570).[208] Although this work is specifically devoted to the art of biography, the author analyzes the similarity between the task of the biographer and the task of the poet. In his view both writers "rescue the deeds of great men from oblivion . . . and at the same time they sow them far and wide in the memory of all people." In *De scribendis vitis* Viperano reveals a Platonic tendency in attributing to all arts common ends and in assigning them pedagogical functions.

Despite their eclectic overtones, the *Lezioni sopra le cose pertinenti alla poetica*, delivered by Agnolo Segni before the Accademia Florentina in 1573 and published posthumously in 1581, retain a Platonic framework.[209] Divine furor, according to Segni, is the primary cause of poetry, and its scope is the moral amelioration of the public. The *Tractatio de perfecta poëseos ratione* (1576) of Lorenzo Gambara reflects the views of a man who in his youth wrote profane poetry and later regarded that type of activity as a serious error.[210] In the *Tractatio* the true end assigned to poetry is the glorification of God and the moral improvement of human society. Gambara envisions a Christian state in which the obscene fables of the poets and the licentious images of the painters are not admissible. The literary heritage of the classics must be considered with great caution: the task of the new poet, the Christian poet, is "to see whatever is appropriate to the imitation of each action, passion, character, by means of beautiful language in order to improve life and to live well and happily."[211] A new Christian poetry is advocated by Gambara in these terms: ". . . epic without adulation and without damage to the truth; tragedy presenting the praise of Christian religion; satire without bitterness. . . . A vast field is opened for writing poems without falsehood, without ineptitudes, without mordacity, without foulness, but with faith, majesty, gravity, acumen, charity."[212] Aside from their pietistic overtones, Gambara's doctrines are historically significant as evidence of the efforts toward the complete Christianization of the Platonic point of view sustained by a group of exponents of the critical tradition based on tenets derived from the works of Plato. At the same time Gambara's conclusions are important as preludes to the formulation of doctrines on the Christian epic, as they appear in Tasso's critical works. One should note here that specific references to the twenty-fifth session of the Council of Trent (1563) and the decisions taken at that meeting in relation to obscene literary production are discussed in a letter of Francesco Panigarola of 1576.[213]

The central issues debated in Girolamo Frachetta's *Dialogo del furore poetico* (1581)[214] are the theory of furor, its validity, and its relationship with the doctrines relative to the banishment of the poets from an ideal society. Frachetta maintains that the forms of poetic expression are intimately related to the type of inspiration that dictates them. Under the influence of divine furor the poet adheres to truth; when he speaks in allegorical terms, however, his message is no longer accessible to the ignorant and the young. Consequently this last type of poetry must be excluded from the ideal state, where only the perfect is admissible. The inspiration provided to the poet solely by his human capacities may lead into error; under its influence the poet may choose to give pleasure to the audience with dramatic literature, in violation of the canons of his fundamental mission. Elements of Platonic origin are combined with principles of an Aristotelian nature in Lorenzo Giacomini Tebalducci's *Sopra la purgazione della tragedia* (1586)[215] and Giason de Nores's *Discorso* (1586),[216] while a more consistently Platonic orientation is maintained in Tommaso Correa's *De antiquitate dignitateque poesis et poetarum differentia* (1586).[217] In Correa's opinion the most praiseworthy of all poets are those who were most beneficial to the moral welfare of mankind through their praise of past men's great deeds, inspired by the divine furor described by Plato. Correa also believed that human faculties can motivate a type of poetic language still endowed with educational power, since it illustrates the nature of things, while he maintains that the lowest form of poetry is based on opinion and is sustained through imitation.

Looking in retrospect at the evolution of the Platonic critical tradition during the Cinquecento, and particularly at its development in the later part of the century, several observations are in order. Some theorists, like Correa and the Jesuit Francesco Benci,[218] display a moderate degree of originality at the doctrinal level. Their contribution to the progress of critical thought is indeed limited. Much more significant are the theorists who analyze the relation between poetry and the state, and those who debate the poet's ethical responsibilities. The insistence on these problems inevitably calls to mind the directions taken by the Catholic church during the period of the Counter-Reformation in relation to literary censorship. Filippo Massini, "a full-blown Platonist," in the conclusion of a lecture dealing with the theme of divine aid to poets, declared: "indeed all these things and any others which are not consonant with what the Catholic Church approves, I want to be considered false and not uttered."[219] The critical literature of the 1580s and 1590s, when insinuations of heresy become quite frequent, shows a remarkable number of "protective clauses" added to treatises and lectures. It is quite true that Platonic orientations met with considerable favor among leading members of the Catholic church, but the history of the Neoplatonic critical tradition during the period of the Counter-Reformation still needs to be studied in greater depth.

Undeniably, extreme Christian theorists vigorously elaborated the theme of the banishment of the poets. It has been stated that thinkers like Gambara, Panigarola, and Antonio Possevino[220] see the art of poetry in the theological context of Catholicism; it is also true that from this critical perspective good poetry may be produced only by orthodox Christians, and even the poetry of antiquity can become an object of condemnation. Moderate theorists, like Giovambattista Strozzi,[221] still abide in general terms by these principles. The analysis of the ethical potentials of poetry inevitably leads to the consideration of its public. A theorist like Jacopo Mazzoni,[222] whose thought is deeply influenced by Platonic tenets, divides the audience of poetry into various classes; he identifies for each class a particularly useful form of poetry and outlines a specific poetic for each genre.

Eclecticism is again prevalent in the Neoplatonic tradition of the late sixteenth century. The concept of the pleasure derived from poetry, as an instrument of the utility provided by that art, determines the formulation of positions close to those established by representatives of the Horatian tradition. Moreover, the increasing popularity of the *Poetics* leads some theorists to solve doubts with the aid of Aristotle and to invoke this philosopher's authority in equivocal situations. The Neoplatonic critic remains a man without a text.[223] Patrizi's grandiose attempt to formulate a definitive and exhaustive system of poetics is at the same time an original elaboration of motives dominant in the Neoplatonic tradition, a massive critique of the foundations of the Aristotelian conception of art, and a genial defense of the autonomy of the creative act, fully consonant with the conclusions reached by Giordano Bruno in his *Eroici furori*.

*   *   *

The category of the new arts of poetry comprises critical documents of the sixteenth century that attempt to build systems of poetics in which the individual authors organize their material independently, without adhering to the dialectical framework established by a particular classical text. Analysis of these documents reveals various degrees of assimilation and original elaboration of principles derived from the ancients; it shows differing amounts of concern for problems determined by the evolution of contemporary literary forms; in some cases the attention of the author is drawn with special intensity toward the discussion of particular issues, or to the development of singular critical orientations. Nonetheless, instead of paraphrases of, or commentaries on, ancient texts, more than specialized studies of specific problems related to poetics or individual issues raised by the meditation on ancient doctrines, these treatises are intended as complete and comprehensive arts of poetry; they are conceived in modern terms, and they are organically constructed in order to acquire practical value as guides to literary composition and interpretation. Seen as a whole body of critical literature, the new arts of poetry reveal the force of penetration of principles elaborated by individual critical traditions, the merging of different traditions, and, at times, the effort to reach new critical viewpoints outside the influence of classical thought or even in direct opposition to some of its tenets.

Until the recent discovery and evaluation of the historical significance of Bartolomeo della Fonte's *De poetice*, cultural historians could correctly claim that the first new art of poetry of the Italian Renaissance was Marco Girolamo Vida's *De arte poetica*.[224] Although this primacy can no longer be acknowledged, *De arte poetica* retains a singular position in the development of Italian Renaissance critical thought. Published for the first time in Rome in 1527,[225] it went through an extraordinary number of editions during the sixteenth century and was later partially imitated by Nicolas Boileau and Alexander Pope.[226] The internal structure of *De arte poetica* has recently been the subject of dissent among students of Vida's work. In a modern history of Renaissance criticism, Horace's *Ars poetica* is defined as the "basic model" of Vida's work.[227] More accurately and convincingly, another scholar concluded that *De arte poetica* appears to be patterned after Vergil's *Georgics*.[228]

De arte poetica is a didactic poem in Latin hexameters divided into three books. It has been correctly observed that critics may be misled by the title of the composition, and consequently they may tend to consider this work in anachronistic terms. *De arte poetica* does not contain the theoretical distinctions and the elaborate analysis of problems in poetics that appear in the more critically mature treatises produced later in the sixteenth century. According to Vida humanistic poetry is one of the highest forms of activity, and the most praiseworthy goal of the humanistic poet is the composition of a Christian epic; *De arte poetica* is conceived by its author as "a general work, which itself a work of art, will guide a youth into worthwhile poetical activity."[229]

The first book of Vida's poem is devoted to the theme of the poet's education, and it also contains an evaluative history of poetry; the second treats the subject of invention and disposition; the third is dedicated to the analysis of elocution. Vida considers the poet a recipient of divine inspiration; however, despite his acceptance of the Neoplatonic concept of *mania,* he insists on the importance of "art." Consequently he declares that the poet must be endowed with a deep knowledge of classical literary masterpieces; he must conquer and master the skills of invention and the techniques of disposition and elocution. Vida asserts that one of the principal aims of the poet is the imitation of nature; nevertheless, he also believes that the best way to attain this goal is to accept the guidance of classical poets and profitably imitate their language and style.

In 1529 Giangiorgio Trissino published the first four books of his *La poetica,* a work previously mentioned,[230] and it was followed in the series of the new arts of poetry by Bernardino Daniello's *La poetica* (1536). In this treatise Daniello derives motives from Horace's *Ars poetica* to praise the antiquity and nobility of poetry; moreover he maintains that philosophical discourse, since it is devoid of formal beauty and power of persuasion, is not as effective as the poetic language as a pleasurable instrument of instruction and edification.[231]

The most celebrated among the new arts of poetry written during the first half of the sixteenth century is undoubtedly Girolamo Fracastoro's dialogue *Naugerius sive de poetica* (1540).[232] The author begins his argumentation with a critique of the more current solutions to the problem of the end of poetry as an introduction to the discussion of the specific nature of the art. Initially the theorist dismisses as untenable the position of the Horatian critics who maintain that the fundamental task of the poet is to provide pleasure and utility. According to Navagero, if pleasure were the aim of poetry, the poet would be in effect an extravagant individual devoting major studies and energies to frivolous ends; if, however, the poet's intention is educational, the uniqueness of his contributions may be doubted, since he shares pedagogical purposes with the historian and the scientist. In agreement with positions of Aristotelian origin, Fracastoro declares that the poet, unlike the scientist, imitates nature and human character. Subsequently, through a broad interpretation of Aristotelian discussions of the differences between poetry and history, the critic reaches the conclusion that poets aim at the universal, while the interest of other writers is focused on the particular. Having established this antecedent, Fracastoro first states that poetic imitation does not have as an object things as they are, but rather things as they should be, or the idea of things; second, he affirms that the beautiful, in the absolute sense of the idea of beauty, is the real subject of poetry, and therefore it must be expressed in forms equally beautiful and perfect. The beauty of the poetic language, in Francastoro's opinion, is intimately connected with the principle of decorum, to avoid at the aesthetic level the type of incongruity that would occur if a garment woven in gold were worn by a peasant.

The idea of beauty is a pervasive motif in the system of poetics outlined by Fracastoro, and it is made inseparable from the ideas of goodness and nobility. This expansion of the significance of the concept of beauty allows the critic to approach from a new perspective the problems of the veracity and utility of poetic language. Fracastoro examines and rejects Plato's condemnation of poetry; he maintains that the poet is capable of attaining a superior type of knowledge and believes that only poets who abuse their art should be banished from the ideal society. A definition of the aim of poetry, formulated toward the end of the *Naugerius,* may well be considered as one of the more significant Renaissance attempts to reconcile fundamental positions reached within the rhetorical, Horatian, Aristotelian, and Platonic traditions. Here Fracastoro abandons his initial reservations about the utilitarian purposes of poetic language and states: "We shall say that the end of the poet is to give pleasure and to profit by imitating in any particular object the best and most beautiful aspects, in an absolutely beautiful style, chosen from among those appropriate to the subject."[233]

The *Arte poetica* published in 1551 by Girolamo Muzio[234] is a didactic poem devoid both of the formal elegance of Vida's *De arte poetica* and of the doctrinal depth of Fracastoro's *Naugerius*. Muzio derives some suggestions from Aristotle's *Poetics,* and even more consistently he profits by the doctrinal content of Horace's *Ars poetica*. In general terms, however, his *Arte poetica* may be regarded as a vulgarization of principles of poetics current at his time, without any serious attempt to speculate on their validity from a theoretical point of view.

A much more profound and original personality is revealed by the treatise *Della vera poetica,*[235] published in 1555 by Giovanni Pietro Capriano. In *Della vera poetica* the author's attention is focused mainly on the problem of imitation. The discussion of this subject is followed by the analysis of other issues of primary relevance in the debates on poetics during the 1550s. Capriano in fact discusses the question of the eminence of poetry over the other arts, distinguishes poets and poetry according to the categories of the "natural and moral," defends "against Aristotle" the priority of the epic as the highest form of "moral poetry," analyzes the issue of Vergil's superiority over Homer, deals with matters of versification, and finishes his work with a debate on the poetry of Petrarch.

At the beginning of his argumentation Capriano defines imitation as "a representation of a thing through an appearance, not of truth, because the appearance of truth is not an imitation, but what is feigned and simulated."[236] This definition is a prelude to a distinction between "noble arts of imitation," which exert their appeal on noble faculties, and "ignoble arts of imitation," which stimulate physical faculties. Poetry imitating "natural things with fictions" contains fantastic elements and freely enters the domain of the marvellous. Poetry that instead imitates and represents things that are moral and pertain only to human actions and operations and to the moral improvement and use of life,[237] must adhere to the laws of verisimilitude in order to secure its acceptability in practical terms and fulfill its scope, which is to provide pleasure and utility. The ethical function of "moral imitation" renders it superior to the imitation aimed at natural objects. Moralistic and aesthetic preoccupations are combined by Capriano with remarkable intelligence. The theorist utilizes Aristotle's doctrines on the unity of action and on the relation of the component parts of the plot to the whole; he insists on the necessity to confer "symmetry" to the poetic composition, to intensify its effectiveness through the proper use of versification and the adequate choice of images. Capriano's argument on the priority of Vergil over Homer is a significant anticipation of the debates on the same issue in the critical literature of the late seventeenth and early eighteenth centuries; and while he never relinquished his moralistic preoccupations, his capacity to combine them with acute analyses of the factors necessary to secure the structural and formal beauty of the poetic language transforms *Della vera poetica* into one of the more significant documents in the history of Renaissance poetics and aesthetics.

One of the most prominent theorists of the late Italian Renaissance is undoubtedly Sebastiano Minturno, whose treatises became quite influential in Italy and abroad. In his *Art poétique françoise* Vauquelin de la Fresnaye mentioned him as one of his sources;[238] students of Sir Philip Sidney have traced the impact of some of Minturno's ideas in several passages of the *Defense of Poesy*.[239] Minturno's critical treatises may be defined as a compendium of Italian critical theories of the mid-sixteenth century. They contain elements derived from the rhetorical, Horatian, Aristotelian, and Platonic traditions combined in a vast and exhaustive argumentation, where nevertheless the author's eclectic tendencies are not consistently reconciled.

Minturno's major critical works are *De poeta* (1559) and the *Arte poetica thoscana* (1563).[240] The material of *De poeta* is subdivided into six books; in the *Arte poetica thoscana* the author omits a considerable portion of the theoretical discussion contained in the previous treatise, but adds an analysis of the poetic genres employed by Italian poets. Thus the *Arte poetica thoscana* can be considered as a continuation of, or as pendant from, *De poeta*.

According to Minturno the function of poetry is pedagogical; the critic develops the traditional theme of poetry's civilizing power and sees this art as a branch of civil philosophy. The specific tasks assigned to the poet are to teach, to delight, and to move.[241] One of the clearest illustrations of Minturno's conception of the ends of poetry is when he discusses the principle of purgation in tragedy. Here catharsis is approached from ethical and medical perspectives: "In order to shake off any illness that is similar to poisoning, a force is induced by a medicine of potent and noxious nature, and this excites the body's functions; ought not the mind be roused to the expulsion of its infirmities?"[242] The aims of the poet are secured through a variety of means. In Minturno's opinion, verse is an indispensable tool of poetic imitation, and imitation itself is viewed in terms not precisely corresponding to those established by Aristotle.[243] Minturno maintains that the poet is allowed to imitate not only the actions of men, but also "all things both private and public . . . all kinds of knowledge, all variety of writing in abundance."[244] Truly the poet ought above all see to it that he imitates, "in each of those whom he has undertaken to present by art, whatever about them most nearly approaches the truth of what they actually were as people."[245]

In Minturno's view the poetic faculty is tripartite and is compounded by invention, disposition, and elocution. Invention determines the selection of the material, and it is thus related to verisimilitude, the organic harmony of the composition and its beauty. Disposition rules over the structure of the plot and the proper arrangement of its component parts. The pertinence of elocution is the language, the choice of words, rhymes, and meters best suited to the subject matter. These rhetorical preoccupations are combined in Minturno's system with a pervasive interest in the subject matter of poetry and consequently in the problem of genres. *De poeta* presents an elaborate classification of poetic genres. They are distributed into three main categories: epic, scenic, and melic poetry. Within these original families individual genres are distinguished according to the object of imitation or to the style suited to them. A minute set of rules is provided in order to conform to the demands of each specific genre and by so doing compose a beautiful poem. Implicitly for Minturno conformity to standard generic requirements is the secret to the work's validity and its success. Despite these variants some criteria must be satisfied in all forms of poetry. The poet must be a very learned man; his knowledge, his fidelity to truth, and his wisdom will greatly contribute to recognition as "a good man and an expert in the arts of expression and of imitation";[246] like the Ciceronian orator, he will be capable of reaching the public's heart and intellect; in addition, the force of the poetic language will confer on his message a unique power of penetration.

During the same period in which Minturno was composing his *De poeta,* the colorful and learned Julius Caesar Scaliger,[247] an Italian who had migrated to France, was assembling the material destined to be part of his voluminous *Poetices libri septem.*[248] Known for his adventurous life, his erudition, and his attacks against Erasmus, Scaliger long enjoyed the reputation of one of the most significant literary theorists of the sixteenth century. A late nineteenth-century scholar labeled him "the founder of French classicism";[249] but the merits of this qualification have recently been questioned in a perceptive and attentive study.[250] Moreover, a modern historian of Italian Renaissance criticism opens his account of Scaliger's contributions by correctly remarking that this theorist elaborated his doctrine outside the Italian cultural environment and then rather gratuitously stating that the *Poetice* are "a summa of all possible themes ... somewhat mindful of a rigid medieval scholastic structure."[251] These different lines of interpretation may have been determined by methodological preconceptions in approaching the text[252] or by the difficulties presented by the text itself, in which, at times, an overbearing display of erudition retards the movement of the theoretical argumentation. Despite these difficulties the *Poetice* remains a monument of critical literature, and Scaliger's stature as a theorist increases when it is seen in its proper historical and intellectual perspectives.

In the first chapter of the second book of the *Poetice*, Scaliger formulates some principles of essential importance for the correct understanding of his system. He declares that poetry is compounded of two fundamental parts, matter, or "material"—as some interpreters prefer to say—and form.[253] The material of poetry is the language, or, in other terms, "the material of poetry is provided by the image of the thing represented, that is to say, by the word."[254] These statements place Scaliger in a singular position in relation to both Platonic and Aristotelian metaphysics. While for Plato the idea is immutable and detached from things, for Aristotle the idea is within things, and the artist strives to capture this universal element in perceptible reality and to transpose it into the artistic creation. On the issue of matter and form Scaliger is in substantial agreement with Aristotle, and the critic increases his distance from the Platonic aesthetics when he maintains the superiority of art over nature. Poetry does not of necessity depend on nature; the skilled artist determines his choice according to qualitative and quantitative criteria.[255] "Poetry fashions images more beautiful than reality of those things which are, as well as images of things which are not; . . .[it does not seem] as in the case of other arts, to narrate things like an actor, but like another God to produce the things themselves."[256] This echo of the Neoplatonic image of the poet as a creator similar to God does not mean that Scaliger accepts the concept of furor and divine inspiration. In the second chapter of the first book he follows a Neoplatonic trend as he undertakes the analysis of primitive poetry, concentrating mainly on the origins of Greek literature; in his opinion, poets began to recognize their exceptional stature in society when they became aware of the superiority of their talent as creators of a musical language in relation to the potentials of mere versifiers of elementary rhythmic structures like nursery rhymes. Scaliger repeatedly states that the power of poetic meters is the basic factor conferring on poetry its singular nature. Ancient poets, says Scaliger, claimed to be under the tutelage and patronage of the Muses;[257] this intuition, however, is not developed at the ontological level, as happens with theorists speculating in a more orthodox Neoplatonic orientation. Though not entirely discarded, inspiration retains secondary importance in Scaliger's system, where it is clearly connected with the faculty and practice of invention. The artist's discretion, his judgment, is revealed by his capacity to choose subjects suitable to the proper codification of ethical messages within a poetic context. Seen from a historical perspective, the first stage of the artistic process took place with the discovery of truths hidden in the physical world, and it was followed by a second and more important phase, namely, the moment that criteria of evaluation began to prevail and the artist determined whether the nature of the material was good or bad, necessary or unessential. Scaliger does not conceive of the poet as an inventor or an imitator, but as the man who creates reality anew. Consequently, he refuses to accept Aristotle's principle of mimesis. The end of poetry, in Scaliger's view, is not imitation but the mode of instruction that may lead man toward a perfect type of activity.[258] Still in opposition to Aristotle, Scaliger believes that verse pertains to the essence of poetry, that not only the universal, but also the particular, are legitimately within the proper confines of the art; moreover, he declares that all poetry has a moralistic power; therefore, Aristotle is incorrect when he assigns cathartic functions only to tragedy.[259] Scaliger is not in favor of imitation of other authors except Vergil.[260] The models of imitation are to be found in the physical world. The best form of imitation is the capacity to capture the types of relations in the world of nature, which are hidden to the ignorant and become clear to the poet as *Alter Deus;* these norms are perfectly represented in the *Aeneid.* Thus only the *Alter Deus* Vergil deserves to be imitated.[261] The greatness of the Latin poet is based above all on his superior judgments in choosing his material in the light of its ethical effectiveness. Ethics and aesthetics remain indissolubly united in Scaliger's system of poetics; his conception of the influence of poetry in society brings him closer to positions established by Aristotle in the *Nicomachean Ethics* and in the *Politics* than to the general orientations of Platonic aesthetics.[262] His vision of art as the model of life in its most noble and elevated forms is another general principle contributing to confirm Scaliger as one of the most original and intellectually stimulating theorists in the history of Renaissance criticism.

De poetica libri tres, published by Giovanni Antonio Viperano in 1578,[263] is not as monumental in size, varied in content, or challenging for the complexity of its theoretical structure as Scaliger's *Poetice.* Despite the brevity of his work, Viperano builds a system of poetics patterned on a basic Aristotelian framework and still unencumbered by an unconditional acceptance of Aristotle's authority. It is evident that the author of *De poetica* is familiar with the development of critical thought and with the conclusions reached by contemporary exponents of the various critical traditions; nevertheless, he is able to attain a considerable degree of originality and to amalgamate elements derived from various sources into an organized and exhaustive discussion sustained by the clarity of his personal conception of the art of poetry.

In his system Viperano combines ethical and aesthetic concerns under the common denominator of a rhetorical concept of poetic language. Basically the theorist considers poetry a unique instrument of persuasion. The substance of the poet's message is analogous to the lesson given by the moral philosopher; consequently, poetry assumes the qualifications of an art singularly effective in providing guidance toward the acquisition and confirmation of the habit of virtue.[264] The poet's sublime educational responsibilities are illustrated by Viperano with references to Homer and Vergil. He interprets the *Aeneid* and the Homeric poems in the traditional terms of moral allegory and sees them as exemplifications of the journey toward the conquest of virtue and moral wisdom.[265] While retaining its philosophical and formative substance, the poem must also be pleasing on the strength of its formal beauty. According to Viperano, the harmony of the poetic composition's internal structure can be secured through the application of Aristotle's doctrines on the proper magnitude of the artistic whole and through the respect for norms on the distribution of episodes according to the principle of necessity. Moreover, aesthetic and ethical interests may be simultaneously fostered by the acceptance of Plato's conception of the beautiful as an idea strictly related to the good and engendering a type of sublime pleasure.[266]

Since the poet's language cannot be sustained by proofs as can the demonstrations of the logician, or embellished with the type of ornamentation used by the orator, Viperano emphasizes the importance of imagination as the instrument whereby poetic expression acquires its specific character and intensifies its impact on the audience. The fantasy of the poet cannot violate the laws of decorum and the requirements of verisimilitude; nevertheless, the search for novelty and the use of the marvellous, in Viperano's view, are consistent with the inner logic of poetry,[267] and in fact they increase its power of persuasion. As a subordinate end, the marvellous is defined by Viperano[268] within an ideological field in which the limiting force of rationalistic constraints is still effective; nevertheless, his insistence on the importance of this element in the poetical discourse provides additional evidence of the progressive interest in the balance between irrational and rational components of the artistic product, confirmed by the critical speculation of the late sixteenth century.

It seems particularly appropriate to end this discussion of the vast and complex problem of the development of humanistic thought on poetics with a brief study of the contributions of Francesco Patrizi of

Cherso.[269] Patrizi died in 1597 at Rome, where he had been called by Pope Clement VIII to teach Platonic philosophy at the university. At the time of his death profound changes were taking place in Italian culture. Galileo, another admirer of Plato and the genius who revolutionized scientific methodology, was a young professor at the University of Padua; Giovan Battista Marino, who boldly declared that the end of poetry is the marvellous, had begun a career that would lead to his recognition as one of the major European exponents of the Baroque literary modes; in the Roman church of San Luigi de' Francesi a young painter, Michelangelo Merisi da Caravaggio, was breaking academic conventions with the genial and daring naturalism of his canvases. Giovanni de' Bardi, one of Patrizi's friends, had already left Florence; but in his native city musicians and poets continued the meditations he had so strongly promoted on the Renaissance ideal of the poet-composer-musician, based on Neoplatonic premises and enthusiastically shared by Patrizi.[270] The crowning result of their efforts was the creation of opera, a dramatic form unknown to the ancients and destined to transform the theater into a magnetic pole of artistic creativity in corroboration with its Baroque, eighteenth-century, neoclassical, and Romantic triumphs. Three years after Patrizi's death, Giordano Bruno, at times one of his most severe critics, was burned alive, but the fires of the Inquisition did not destroy his contributions to the progress of philosophical speculation and among them his view of great poetry as a manifestation of creative power, antecedent to the formulation of the laws of poetics—a conclusion autonomously reached by the same Patrizi.

In Patrizi's system of poetics an impressive background of humanistic learning is employed to legitimize poetic creativity as an act that cannot be subjugated to norms deduced *post factum* from the analysis of poetical literature; to expand the field in which the poet could exercise his talent far beyond the limits imposed by the observance of the laws of imitation and verisimilitude; to demonstrate the inadequacy of the principle of mimesis as the foundation of aesthetic activity and judgment; to reevaluate the irrational as proper subject of poetic language; to substantiate the theory that the "image" does not necessarily "presuppose an anterior thing,"[271] but that the language of the poet expresses reality and does not specularly represent reality. Patrizi brought to this impressive task a profound knowledge of classical languages, classical literatures, and thought; he was, besides, versed in the humanistic skills of textual criticism and was conversant with the development of the philosophical and critical traditions established by both the Renaissance Neoplatonists and the Aristotelians.

Patrizi's doctrines on the art of poetry bear the imprint of some of the main directives of his thought. Already at the very beginning of the first part of *Della poetica*—namely *La deca istoriale*—the philosopher polemically observes that contemporary critics are better disposed to believe "more in authorities than in facts and reasons." [272] This desire for independence from the authority of the ancients is a trait of Patrizi's mentality that he shares with other thinkers of the period, like Bernardino Telesio, one of the so-called philosophers of nature, and Bruno. [273] It is also a position reached through a long speculative process testified by earlier work. [274] By the same token Patrizi's opposition to Aristotle and his preference for Plato are by no means positions reached and newly developed in *Della poetica,* but are rather the result of years of meditation and study. [275] *Della poetica* itself may be considered the final attempt to organize a system of doctrines on the art of poetry and thus bring to their definitive conclusion a trend of intellectual interests cultivated since the earlier period of his activity. [276] The fundamental principles at the basis of Patrizi's *Della poetica* are indeed derived from Plato and from the main exponents of the Renaissance Neoplatonic school, like Ficino. Nevertheless, Patrizi consistently tends to verify the material drawn from other sources. Furthermore, the impact of Plato and of the Neoplatonists on his poetics is combined with motives deduced from other authors. Among others, the philosopher considers attentively the treatise attributed to Longinus, and his extensive use of *On the Sublime* is a fact of considerable historical significance, in view of the importance acquired by that work in the critical speculation of the seventeenth and eighteenth centuries.

Plans to write a treatise on the art of poetry were conceived by Patrizi as early as 1555, but the two initial sections of *Della poetica—Deca istoriale* and *Deca disputata*—were completed and published only in 1586. In 1587 and 1588 the philosopher wrote the *Deca ammirabile, Deca plastica, Deca dogmatica universale, Deca sacra,* and *Deca semisacra.* These last five parts of *Della poetica* were left unpublished by the author; their recent discovery and publication allows modern scholars to acquire an understanding of Patrizi's poetics previously unattainable. [277] Departing from polemical positions directly aimed at the representatives of the Horatian and Aristotelian traditions, Patrizi states that a methodologically sound investigation of the problems of poetics must have its foundation on documentary evidence. This foundation can be provided only by study of the origins of poetic language, identification of the poets who created that language, analysis of the progressive development of poetic forms of expression and their metrical structures, and knowledge of the functions of poetry in civilized society. This preliminary documentation is presented in the *Deca istoriale,* which could be considered as a history of Greek and Latin literatures. This *deca*, however, is conceived as a basic point of reference in the logical structure of the entire *Della poetica;* as a factual illustration of the antiquity, variety, and complexity of the language of poetry it is intended to demonstrate that Aristotle in the *Poetics* abstained from taking into consideration all possible aspects of poetic creativity and based his doctrines on principles deduced from only two genres, tragedy and epic poem. Moreover, this initial *deca* provides the historical evidence necessary to substantiate another basic tenet of Patrizi's system. He believes that poetry was born and acquired recognition as a sublime civilizing factor in human society before the invention of poetics; the moment of creativity precedes the moment of reflection on the product of creation and the consequent deduction of rules to define the modalities of poetic expression. Developing principles of Platonic origin, Patrizi insists that nature, or genius, is the activating force of poetic language: "all that is great is without art" he repeatedly exclaims,[278] using an axiom attributed to Aristides the Rhetorician; and in total agreement with previous Renaissance Neoplatonists, he maintains that primitive Greek poetry contained a wealth of sublime wisdom.

The purpose of the *Deca disputata* is to clear the way to a definitive discussion of the art of poetry through a critique of ancient and modern literary doctrines. At the beginning of this second part of *Della poetica*, Patrizi states in direct opposition to Castelvetro that the origin of poetry was due to *enthusiasmos*, inspiration.[279] Poetry, therefore, is considered a legitimate expression of moments of irrationality and emotionalism; consequently, this activity cannot be viewed from the same perspectives as other arts or sciences based on unequivocally rational foundations. The full acceptance of the doctrine of enthusiasm leads the philosopher to an equally uncompromising rejection of the Aristotelian principle of mimesis as the pivotal concept in aesthetic judgment. While Castelvetro declared: "Imitation gives form and being to all poetry," Patrizi, adopting locutions typical of the Aristotelian metaphysical terminology, maintains: "The marvellous is the essential form of poetry, and it is also its end."[280] In another part of the *Deca disputata* Patrizi states: "Words [in the poetic context] are . . . symbols and signals and expressions of the concepts and of the movements of the soul . . . and not imitations of them."[281] The frontal collision between the positions held by Castelvetro and those held by Patrizi is a motive running through the entire argumentation of *Della Poetica*, and its motivation may be reduced to this fundamental difference: for Castelvetro art is representation, while for Patrizi art is expression. Patrizi conceives the poet as the creator of a highly specific language, whose main end is the marvellous. Verse is essential to the language of poetry: "The poet," says Patrizi, "is a maker of the marvellous in verse . . . the poet is a maker of the marvellous in marvellous language . . . the poet is a maker of marvellous concepts and marvellous words." [282] Having excluded the possibility of identifying the ends of poetry with motives pertaining to the categories of utility and ethics, Patrizi strives to define the marvellous at the metaphysical level. This element, according to the philosopher, is an intermediate faculty [283] that accompanies both cognitive and affective faculties: "The marvellous is a motion of the faculty of marveling, stimulated by knowledge and altogether denying full knowledge of causes and producing doubt and credence and lack of credence and pleasure." [284] The psychological effect of poetry on the audience is studied by Patrizi on several occasions; again he argues against Castelvetro and rejects his view that poetry is destined for an uncouth and unimaginative audience. Patrizi believes that there is a kind of poetry for all classes of people, from the child to the philosopher. In Patrizi's view imagination, the liberty to invent what the laws of verisimilitude cannot justify, is an indispensable ingredient of poetry. The poet, therefore, cannot be bound by rules such as the law of the three dramatic unities, and in the epic and narrative poem he can disregard the law of unity of action. The concept of magnitude, the idea that the beautiful results from the balance of proportional elements chosen in the median range, thus avoiding the excessively small and excessively large, is rejected by Patrizi as a valid criterion of aesthetic judgment. "Raphael," he says, "painted small and large images, receiving equal praise in both cases." [285] This consideration becomes one of the factors leading the philosopher to dismiss as false and misleading any attempt to classify poetic genres according to their importance.

The Aristotelian conception of the plot as the "soul," the activating element, of the poetical composition, is also rejected by Patrizi. In the *Deca plastica* the philosopher defines plot not as imitation, but as invention. "We shall say," he states, "that the poetic fable is the invention of a marvellous history or a marvellous event." [286] Thus the marvellous is seen as the catalyst in the organization of the poem. Patrizi devotes considerable effort to defining the manner by which it operates in the composition: how it can be made to penetrate every component part of the structure, from the more outstanding—the subject matter—to the most elementary—the semantic unit. The marvellous, that which captivates and astonishes, cannot be founded on entirely believable elements, nor can it be based on elements that are completely unbelievable. Therefore Patrizi establishes two categories: one for the sources of believable subjects; and, opposite to this, one for the sources of unbelievable subjects— what he calls *fonti topici*. Poetic invention will originate and multiply by joining elements of the two orders. Developing these premises, Patrizi establishes that an extraordinary number of combinations is possible. Free from preoccupations of a thematic nature, not bound by any rigid law of verisimilitude, allowed to unbridle his fantasy to increase the thematic range and the inner magnetism of his compositions, the poet envisioned by Patrizi is led to organize his work according to a principle qualified as *convenevole di natura*,[287] a rather uncommon locution translatable as artistic necessity. In fact the poem, says Patrizi, can be compared to an organism, and as such it must have its own specific organic structure. The perfection of an animal cannot be determined in relation to the species to which it belongs, but rather in relation to the effectiveness of the parts composing its body. The philosopher maintains that the theory of the hierarchy of the literary genres favored by the Aristotelians is untenable. The greatness of a poem must be evaluated in relation to its internal nature and, as in the case of animals, in view of the effectiveness of its parts. As an example Patrizi affirms that on its own merits an epigram may attain the same degree of perfection as the *Iliad*.

The vigorous and stimulating personality of Francesco Patrizi flourished during a period traditionally considered the historical moment at which the civilization of the Renaissance began to be superseded by other currents of cultural and artistic expression. It is my opinion, shared by other students of literary criticism, that the revolutionary opposition against the Aristotelian principle of imitation, his conception of poetry as expression, is a direct antecedent of trends taken in the debates on poetics during the Baroque age. This assessment has met with some opposition;[288] however, the elucidation of specific issues may profit from the analysis of controversial points in a broader context. It is undeniable that the system of poetics outlined by Patrizi testifies to the vitality of principles already established—be it at the genetic stage—by fifteenth-century humanism. This original intellectual impulse is sustained and refined by Patrizi. Traces of the original humanistic methodology in the approach to the problem of poetics become apparent even in the best-known treatise on the art of poetry of the Italian Baroque, when Emanuele Tesauro attentively inscribes in the margin of the pages of his *Canocchiale aristotelico* passages from Aristotle's *Poetics, Rhetoric, Ethics, De anima,* and *De interpretatione* as integrations of the text, as graphic visualizations of authoritative positions established by the ancient classics. Stimulants of humanistic origin are leaven in the aesthetics of Giambattista Vico; they acquire new vitality in the discussions on the nature and the ends of poetry conducted by Gravina and Muratori in the light of eighteenth-century rationalism.

Ending the account of the attitudes toward poetry established by humanistic culture with Patrizi simply means closing a chapter of a widely articulated intellectual movement at a chronologically suitable moment. Other chapters might be added to illustrate the continuing impact of the initial humanistic urge to analyze poetry as a sublime civilizing factor in the history of mankind, confirming thereby once again the importance of Italian humanism in the culture of western Europe.

NOTES

For the study of the problem of poetics in the culture of the late Middle Ages, see K. Vossler, *Poetische Theorien in der Italienischen Frührenaissance* (Berlin, 1900); E. Faral, *Les arts poétiques du XIIe et du XIIIe siècle* (Paris, 1924); C. S. Baldwin, *Medieval Rhetoric and Poetic* (New York, 1928); E. R. Curtius, *European Literature in the Latin Middle Ages* (New York, 1963); A. Viscardi, "Idee estetiche e letteratura militante nel Medioevo," in *Momenti e problemi di storia dell'estetica* (Milan, 1959), 231–52; G. Barberi Squarotti, "Le poetiche del Trecento in Italia," in *Momenti e problemi di storia dell'estetica* (Milan, 1959), 255–324; G. Dahan, "Notes et textes sur la poétique au Moyen Âge," *Archives d'histoire doctrinale et littéraire du Moyen Âge* 55 (1981): 171–239; W. F. Bogges, "Aristotle's Poetics in the Fourteenth Century," *Studies in Philology* 67 (1970): 278–94; L. Minio-Paluello, "Guglielmo di Moerbecke traduttore della 'Poetica' di Aristotele (1278)," *Rivista di filosofia neo-scolastica* 39 (1947): 1–17; E. Lobel, "The Medieval Latin Poetics," *Proceedings of the British Academy* 17 (1931): 309–34; *Aristoteles Latinus XXXIII. De arte poetica. Translatio Guillelmi de Moerbecke*, ed. L. Minio-Paluello (Leiden, 1968); J. Mariétan, *Problème de la classification des sciences d'Aristote à Saint Thomas* (Paris, 1901); J. A. Weisheipl, "Classification of Sciences in Medieval Thought," *Medieval Studies* 25 (1965): 54–90; P. O. Kristeller, "The Modern System of the Arts," in *Renaissance Thought II: Papers on Humanism and the Arts* (New York, 1965), especially 166–78; E. R. Curtius, "Theologische Poetik im italienischen Trecento," *Zeitschrift für Romanische Philologie* 60 (1940): 1–15.

For the problem of poetics in the fifteenth century, see P. O. Kristeller, *The Classics and Renaissance Thought* (Cambridge, MA, 1955); idem, *Studies in Renaissance Thought and Letters,* 2 vols. (Rome, 1956–85); E. Garin, *Italian Humanism: Philosophy and Civic Life in the Renaissance,* trans. P. Munz (New York, 1965); E. L. Spingarn, *Literary Criticism in the Renaissance* (New York, 1899); G. Saintsbury, *A History of Criticism and Literary Taste in Europe from the Earliest Texts to the Present Day* (Edinburgh and London, 1900–1904); C. Trabalza, *La critica letteraria nel Rinascimento* (Milan, 1915); A. Buck, *Italienische Dichtungslehren vom Mittelalter bis zum Ausgang der Renaissance* (Tübingen, 1952); C. Vasoli, "L'estetica dell'umanesimo e del Rinascimento," in *Momenti e problemi di storia dell'estetica* (Milan, 1959), 348–433; F. Tateo, *Retorica e poetica fra Medioevo e Rinascimento* (Bari, 1960); C. Trinkaus, *In Our Image and Likeness: Humanity and Divinity in Italian Humanist Thought,* 2 vols. (Chicago, 1970); C. C. Greenfield, *Humanist and Scholastic Poetics, 1250–1500* (Lewisburg, PA, 1981); V. Branca, "Umanesimo della parola tra poesia, filologia, filosofia e scoperta della 'Poetica' aristotelica," in *Poliziano e l'umanesimo della parola* (Turin, 1983).

For the history of literary criticism in the Italian sixteenth century, see M. T. Herrick, *The Fusion of Horatian and Aristotelian Criticism, 1531–1555* (Urbana, IL, 1946); idem, *Italian Comedy in the Renaissance* (Urbana, IL, 1960); idem, *Italian Tragedy in the Renaissance* (Urbana, IL, 1965); B. Weinberg, *A History of Literary Criticism in the Italian Renaissance* (Chicago, 1961); B. Hathaway, *The Age of Criticism: The Late Renaissance in Italy* (Ithaca, 1962); R. Barilli, *Poetica e retorica* (Milan, 1969).

1. P. O. Kristeller, "Foreword," in Greenfield, *Humanist and Scholastic Poetics,* 9.
2. See P. O. Kristeller, "The Contributions of Religious Orders to Renaissance Thought and Learning," *American Benedictine Review* 21 (1970): 1–55; reprinted in *Medieval Aspects of Renaissance Learning* (Durham, NC, 1974).
3. *De civitate Dei,* 2.14.
4. For the problem of aesthetics in St. Augustine and St. Thomas, see K. Svaboda, *L'esthétique de Saint Augustin et ses sources* (Brno, 1933); J. Maritain, *Art et scholastique* (Paris, 1935); J. P. Trudel, *St. Augustin humaniste* (Trois Rivières, 1954); U. Eco, *Il problema estetico in Tommaso d'Aquino* (Milan, 1970); M. de Munnynck, "L'esthétique de Saint Thomas d'Aquin," in *San Tommaso d'Aquino: Pubblicazione commemorativa del sesto centenario della canonizzazione* (Milan, 1923).
5. *Summa theologiae,* 1.1.9.
6. Vossler, *Poetische Theorien,* 4.
7. For the activity of Ferreto de' Ferreti, see C. Cipolla, "Studi su Ferreto de' Ferreti," *Giornale storico della letteratura italiana* 6 (1885): 103–12.
8. For Albertino Mussato and his views on poetry, see A. Galletti, "La ragione poetica di Albertino Mussato e i poeti teologi," in *Scritti vari in onore di R. Renier* (Turin, 1912), 331–59; G. Vinay, "Il Mussato e l'estetica medievale," *Giornale storico della letteratura italiana* 126 (1949): 113–59; E. Garin, *L'educazione in Europa* (Bari, 1957), 69–80; *Il pensiero pedagogico dell'umanesimo,* ed. E. Garin (Florence, 1958) 3–19; Vasoli, *L'estetica dell' 'umanesimo,* 328–31; M. Dazzi, *Il Mussato preumanista, 1261–1329: L'ambiente e l'opera* (Venice, 1964); G. Ronconi, *Le origini delle dispute umanistiche sulla poesia* (Rome, 1975); Greenfield, *Humanist and Scholastic Poetics,* 78–95.
9. For Musato's epistles, see *Albertini Musati Patavini tragoediae . . . cum notis Nicolai Villani . . . ut et alia auctoris poémata,* in J. G. Graevius, *Thesaurus antiquitatum et historiarum Italiae* (Leiden, 1722), 6.2.34–62. The letter of Giovannino of Mantua, reproduced in Graevius's *Thesaurus,* 6.2.54–62, is reprinted with an Italian translation in *Pensiero pedagogico dell'umanesimo,* ed. Garin, 3–12.
10. P. de Nolhac, *Pétrarque et l'humanisme* (Paris, 2d ed. 1907), 22–31. On Petrarch and humanism, see also G. Martellotti, "Linee di sviluppo dell'umanesimo petrarchesco," *Studi petrarcheschi* 2 (1949): 51–80; U. Bosco,

"Il Petrarca e l'Umanesimo filologico," *Giornale storico della letteratura italiana* 119 (1942): 1–55; G. Billanovich, *Petrarca letterato*, vol. 1, *Lo scrittoio del Petrarca* (Rome, 1947); P. O. Kristeller, "Il Petrarca, l'umanesimo e la scolastica," *Lettere italiane* 7 (1955): 367–88; idem, "Petrarch," in *Eight Philosophers of the Italian Renaissance* (Stanford, 1964), 1–18. See in these volumes the three essays on Petrarch.

11. For the problem of Petrarch's attitude toward poetics and his defense of poetry, see G. Billanovich, "Pietro Piccolo da Monforte tra il Petrarca e il Boccaccio," in *Medioevo e Rinascimento: Studi in onore di Bruno Nardi*, 2 vols. (Florence, 1955), 1:3–76; idem, *Petrarca letterato*, passim; Vasoli, *L'estetica dell'umanesimo*, 328–31. Ronconi, *Origini delle dispute*, passim; Greenfield, *Humanist and Scholastic Poetics*, 96–106. The reference to Petrarch's letters used in the present study is *Familiares*, 10.3 in Francesco Petrarca, *Le familiari*, ed. V. Rossi (Florence, 1934), 2:286–300; *Familiares*, 10.4 in Petrarca, *Le familiari*, 2:268–300. See also *Seniles*, 12.2 and 15.11; *Metrica*, 2.10.188–91.

12. *Invective contra medicum* were edited by P. G. Ricci and published with an Italian translation by D. Silvestri (Rome, 1950). The third book of the *Invective* appears in Francesco Petrarca, *Prose*, ed. G. Martellotti et al. (Milan, 1955). The edition of the *Invective* used in the present study is Francesco Petrarca, *Invettive contro un medico*, ed. M. Schiavone (Milan, 1972). For the text of the *Collatio laureationis* see C. Godi, "La Collatio laureationis del Petrarca," *Italia medioevale e umanistica* 13 (1970): 1–27.

13. *Collatio laureationis*, 14. See also 20–21 for a discussion of the questions of allegorical interpretation and the relation between poetry and history.

14. On the relationship between Mussato's defense of poetry and Petrarch's positions on the same issue see Billanovich, *Petrarca letterato*, 69, 103, 122; Billanovich, *Pietro Piccolo da Monforte*, 19.

15. Billanovich, *Pietro Piccolo da Monforte*, 19.

16. Ibid. Pietro Piccolo da Monforte was a friend of Barbato of Sulmona, who validly contributed to the initial spread of Petrarch's reputation in southern Italy. Boccaccio met Pietro Piccolo during his residence in Naples from the autumn of 1370 to May 1371. On this occasion Boccaccio left a copy of the *Genealogie deorum gentilium*, which was read and corrected by a personage identified by Billanovich as the same Pietro Piccolo. On 2 February 1372 Pietro sent Boccaccio a letter that contains the treatise *In defensione et laude poesis*. In this defense Pietro Piccolo does not appeal to the passage in Aristotle's *Metaphysics* on primitive poets; his arguments on the superior dignity of poetry are supported by references to the Bible and by quotations from early Christian writers, St. Jerome, Boethius, and Dionysius the Areopagite. For the passages of *In defensione et laude poesis* echoed in Boccaccio's *Genealogie* see G. Billanovich, *Pietro Piccolo da Monforte*, 55–76.

17. For the text of the *Genealogie*, see Giovanni Boccaccio, *Genealogie deorum gentilium libri*, ed. V. Romano (Bari, 1951), trans. C. G. Osgood, *On Poetry: Being the Preface and the Fourteenth and Fifteenth Books of Boccac-*

cio's *"Genealogia deorum gentilium"* (Indianapolis, 1956). On Boccaccio's defense of poetry, see F. Woodbridge, "Boccaccio's Defense of Poetry in the XIVth Book of the Genealogiis," *PMLA* 13 (1925): 61–80; E. Garin, *Medioevo e Rinascimento* (Bari, 1954), 66–89; V. Branca, *Boccaccio medievale* (Florence, 1956), passim; Tateo, *Retorica e poetica*, passim; G. Martellotti, "La difesa della poesia nel Boccaccio e un giudizio su Lucano," *Studi sul Boccaccio* 4 (1967): 265–79; Vasoli, *L'estetica dell'umanesimo*, 331; R. Stefanelli, *Boccaccio e la poesi* (Naples, 1978); Greenfield, *Humanist and Scholastic Poetics*, 110–28.

18. For the bibliography and the chronology of Boccaccio studies on Dante, see Giovanni Boccaccio, *Il comento alla Divina Commedia e gli altri scritti intorno a Dante*, ed. D. Guerri (Bari, 1918), 1:39–45, 85–95 and passim; idem, *Esposizioni sopra la "Comedia" di Dante*, ed. G. Padoan (Milan, 1965); idem, *Opere minori in volgare*, ed. M. Marti (Milan, 1969), 1:65–66. See also "Trattatello in laude di Dante," ed. P. G. Ricci, in Giovanni Boccaccio, *Tutte le opere* (Milan, 1974), 3:427.

19. ". . . dico più: che la teologia niuna altra cosa è che una poesia di Dio," Boccaccio, *Opere minori in volgare*, 1:362.

20. The position of Salutati in the development of humanistic civilization is discussed in the works of Kristeller, Garin, and Billanovich cited above. For Salutati, see also E. Walser, *Gesammelte Studien zur Geistesgeschichte der Renaissance* (Berlin, 1932); A. von Martin, *Mittelalterliche Welt und Lebensanschauungen im Spiegel der Schriften Coluccio Salutatis* (Berlin, 1916); idem, *Coluccio Salutati und das Lebensideal* (Berlin, 1916); G. M. Sciacca, *La visione della vita nell'umanesimo di Coluccio Salutati* (Palermo, 1954); B. L. Ullman, *The Humanism of Coluccio Salutati* (Padua, 1963); R. G. Witt, *Coluccio Salutati and His Public Letters* (Geneva, 1976).

21. The letters to Zonarini are dated 25 October 1378 and 5 May 1397; Coluccio Salutati, *Epistolario*, ed. F. Novati, 5 vols. (Rome, 1891–1911), 1:298–307, 321–29.

22. Coluccio Salutati, *De laboribus Herculis,* ed. B. L. Ullman (Zurich, 1951). The first version of *De laboribus* was composed during the years 1378–83; the humanist continued to work on this treatise till the later years of his life. See Ullman, *Humanism of Coluccio Salutati*, 22.

23. The date of this letter is 23 April 1398; the text may be found in *Epistolario*, 3:285–308.

24. Ibid., 3:530–43; 4:170–205. The dates assigned to those letters are 21 September 1401 and 25 January 1405 or 1406, respectively.

25. Ibid., 4:205–40. This letter was written in the winter of 1406; "Coluccio was probably at work on this unfinished letter to Dominici when he died," Ullman states in *Humanism of Coluccio Salutati*, 69.

26. For a detailed discussion of Salutati's defense of poetry, in addition to the works quoted above, see H. Baron, *The Crisis of the Early Italian Renaissance,* 2 vols. in 1 (Princeton, rev. ed. 1966), 295–300 and passim; Garin,

Medioevo e Rinascimento, 63–84; J. Cinquino, "Coluccio Salutati Defender of Poetry," *Italica* 26 (1953): 131–35; Vasoli, *L'estetica dell'umanesimo,* 331–33; J. R. O'Donnel, "Coluccio Salutati on the Poet Teacher," *Medieval Studies* 22 (1960): 240–56; Greenfield, *Humanist and Scholastic Poetics,* 129–45.

27. *Epistolario,* 4:233.

28. The works of Giovanni Dominici and the bibliography on his activity are listed in P. da Prati, *Giovanni Dominici e l'umanesimo* (Rome, 1965). For his attack on poetry see also Giovanni Dominici, *Lucula noctis,* ed. E. Hunt (Indianapolis, 1940).

29. *Epistolario,* 4:198, 236.

30. The treatise of Francesco da Fiano has recently appeared in two editions: "Un opuscolo inedito di Francesco da Fiano in difesa della poesia," ed. M. L. Plaisant, *Rinascimento* 2d ser. 1 (1961): 119–62; "Il 'Contra oblocutores et detractores poetarum' di Francesco da Fiano," ed. I. Taù, *Archivio italiano per la storia della pietà* 4 (1965): 256–350. On Francesco da Fiano see Baron, *Crisis of the Early Italian Renaissance,* 270–84; R. Weiss, "Poesie religiose di Francesco da Fiano," *Archivio italiano per la storia della pietà* 2 (1957): 201–2; G. Radetti, "Le origini dell'Umanesimo civile fiorentino nel Quattrocento," *Giornale critico della filosofia italiana* 38 (1959): 115–17; A. Stäuble, "Francesco da Fiano in difesa della poesia," *Bibliothèque d'humanisme et Renaissance* 26 (1964): 256–59; G. Ronconi, "F. da Fiano, 'Contra oblocutores et detractores poetarum' a cura di I. Taù," *Studi sul Boccaccio* 3 (1965): 403–11.

31. *Contra oblocutores,* ed. Taù, 264–67.

32. *De legendis libris gentilium* appeared in print for the first time in Milan in 1474. During the fifteenth century it enjoyed wide circulation in manuscript; see P. O. Kristeller, *Iter Italicum, a Finding List of Uncatalogued or Incompletely Catalogued Humanistic Manuscripts of the Renaissance in Italian and Other Libraries,* 3 vols. to date (Leiden and London, 1963–83), passim. Still during the fifteenth century it was translated into Italian by Lorenzo Ridolfi and Donato Cocchi; see Garin, *Pensiero pedagogico dell'umanesimo,* 118–19. On *De legendis libris gentilium* see L. Schucan, *Das Nachleben von Basilius Magnus "Ad adulescentes"* (Geneva, 1973).

33. The text of *De studiis et litteris* appears in *Leonardo Bruni Aretino. Humanistisch-philologische Schriften mit einer Chronologie seiner Werke und Briefe,* ed. H. Baron (Leipzig and Berlin, 1928), 5–19. For an English translation of the treatise, see *Vittorino da Feltre and Other Humanist Educators: Essays and Versions,* ed. W. H. Woodward (Cambridge, 1897; reprinted with intro. by E. F. Rice, Jr., New York, 1963). For the question of poetics in Bruni, Vergerio, Vegio, Piccolomini, and Guarino, see also Greenfield, *Humanist and Scholastic Poetics,* 178–94; Vasoli, *L'estetica dell'umanesimo,* 340–41.

34. Sections of this work dealing with poetry appear both in the original and in

Italian translation in *Prosatori latini del Quattrocento,* ed. E. Garin (Milan, 1952).

35. See "Pier Paolo Vergerio, *De ingenuis moribus,*" ed. A. Gnesotto, *Atti e memorie della R. Accademia di scienze, lettere ed arti, Padova,* n.s. 34 (1918). On Vergerio, Guarino, and Vittorino da Feltre, see Garin, *L'educazione in Europa,* 119–59; idem, *Il pensiero pedagogico dell'umanesimo,* 305. See also Angelo Decembrio, *Politiae literariae libri septem* (Augsburg, 1540) and on this work A. della Guardia, *La "Politica litteraria" di Angelo Decembrio e l'umanesimo a Ferrara nella prima metà del sec. XV* (Modena, 1910); M. A. Di Cesare, *Vida's "Christiad" and Vergilian Epic* (New York, 1964), 51–58.

36. Maffeo Vegio, *De educatione liberorum et eorum claris moribus, libri sex,* books 1–3 ed. Sister M. W. Fanning (Washington, DC, 1933); books 4–6 ed. A. S. Sullivan (Washington, DC, 1936).

37. Aeneas Silvius Piccolomini, "*Tractatus de liberorum educatione,*" *Fontes rerum Austriacarum* 61, 62, 67, 68 (1909–18).

38. *Epistolario di Guarino Veronese,* ed. R. Sabbadini (Venice, 1915–19), 2:519–32; 3:419–23.

39. Battista Guarino, the son of Guarino of Verona, also discussed poetry in his *De ordine docendi et discendi.* For the text of this work, see Garin, *Il pensiero pedagogico dell'umanesimo,* 434–70.

40. The bibliography on Ermolao Barbaro the Elder is extremely limited. See the article by E. Bigi in *Dizionario biografico degli italiani* (Rome, 1964), 6:96–99; and the introduction to Ermolao Barbaro il Vecchio, *Orationes contra poetas (with Epistolae),* ed. G. Ronconi (Florence, 1972). Pages 9–14 of this introduction contain a brief, but very accurate summary of the development of the defenses of poetry during the earlier part of the humanistic movement. On Ermolao Barbaro the Elder, see also Greenfield, *Humanist and Scholastic Poetics,* 195–213.

41. For this letter, see Barbaro, *Orationes,* 14. Timoteo Maffei, a member of Barbaro's circle, wrote a defense of literary studies entitled *In sanctam rusticitatem litteras impugnantem,* and Antonio Beccaria, another member of the same circle, wrote in his *Orationes defensoriae* in praise of eloquence and poetry. For these works, see Barbaro, *Orationes,* 8, 14–15.

42. Cristoforo Landino taught poetry and rhetoric at the *studium* of Florence from 1458 until about 1498. On the critical thought of Landino, see Garin, *Italian Humanism,* 84–88; idem, *Prosatori latini del Quattrocento,* 715–91; A. Buck, "Dichtung und Dichter bei Cristoforo Landino. Ein Beitrag zur Dichtungslehre des italienischen Humanismus," *Romanische Forschungen* 58–59 (1947): 233–46; R. Cardini, "Il Landino e la poesia," *Rassegna della letteratura italiana* 74 (1970): 273–97. The latter study is now included in the volume R. Cardini, *La critica del Landino* (Florence, 1973), 85–113.

43. For the text of the *Praefatio in Virgilio,* see Cristoforo Landino, *Scritti critici e teorici,* ed. R. Cardini (Rome, 1974), 1:17–28.

44. See Cardini, *Critica del Landino,* 327–54, 355–71. The *Prolusione petrarchesca* and *Prolusione dantesca* are included in Landino, *Scritti critici e teorici.* See also A. Field, "A Manuscript of Cristoforo Landino's First Lectures on Virgil, 1462–63," *Renaissance Quarterly* 31 (1978): 17–20; idem, "An Inaugural Oration by Cristoforo Landino in Praise of Virgil," *Rinascimento* 21 (1981): 235–45; idem, "The 'Studium Florentinum' Controversy, 1455," *History of Universities* 3 (1983): 31–59; idem, "Cristoforo Landino's First Lectures on Dante," *Renaissance Quarterly* 39 (1986): 16–48.

45. The manuscript tradition and the history of the text of the *Disputationes Camaldulenses* is described in Cristoforo Landino, *Disputationes Camaldulenses,* ed. P. Lohe (Florence, 1980), ix–xxxviii.

46. On the *Comento sopra la Comedia* see the following recent studies: C. Dionisotti, "Dante nel Quattrocento," *Atti del Congresso Internazionale di Studi Danteschi* (Florence, 1965), 1:360–78; M. Lentzen, *Studien zur Dante Exegese C. Landinos* (Cologne and Vienna, 1971); Cardini, *Critica del Landino,* 192–232. For an extensive bibliography of the works on Landino, see E. Garin, "Nota bibliografica su Cristoforo Landino," in his *Testi inediti e rari di Cristoforo Landino e Francesco Filelfo* (Florence, 1949).

47. "Una spezie adunque di poeti è per interna astrazione e agitazione di mente; l'altra spezie è per iscienza, per istudio, per disciplina ed arte e prudenzia. E di questa seconda spezie fu Dante," *Leonardo Bruni Aretino. Humanistisch-philologische Schriften,* 59–60. See also Bruni's letter to Marrasio, entitled "Qualem furorem poetis adesse debeat," in Leonardo Bruni, *Epistularum libri VIII,* ed. L. Mehus (Florence, 1741), 2:36–40.

48. Marsilio Ficino, *Opera omnia,* 2 vols (Basel, 2d ed., 1576, reprinted Turin, 1959), 1:614. On *De divino furore* see: S. Gentile, "In margine all'epistola 'De divino furore' di Marsilio Ficino," *Rinascimento* 23 (1983): 33–77.

49. Landino, *Scritti critici,* 1:142. My translation differs from that offered in Greenfield, *Humanist and Scholastic Poetics,* 216, 226, n. 7, where the text is defectively reproduced and the interpretation of some key terms is incorrect. For the history of the idea that the poet, insofar as he creates a world of his own, can be compared to God who created the world, see E. N. Tigerstedt, "The Poet as a Creator: Origins of a Metaphor," *Comparative Literature Studies* 4 (1968): 455–88.

50. Landino, *Scritti critici,* 1:228.

51. Serious criticism of the humanistic attitudes toward poetry was formulated in Florence during the later part of the fifteenth century by Girolamo Savonarola, a personage well known in the intellectual circle of Ficino, Landino, and Poliziano. In his *Apologeticus de ratione poeticae artis* (published for the first time in Pescia in 1492), Savonarola elaborated the principle, derived from Aquinas, according to which poetry occupies the lowest place among the liberal arts and outlined a clear and harmonious system of poetics, founded on criteria typical of the Thomistic tradition. On Savonarola as a theorist on the art of poetry, see G. Berzero, "Girolamo Savonarola," in *Orientamenti culturali. Letteratura italiana. I Minori* (Milan, 1969),

1:743–67; E. N. Gerardi, "Lo 'Apologetico' del Savonarola e il problema di una poesia cristiana," *Rivista di filologia neo-scolastica* 44 (1952): 412–30; Greenfield, *Humanist and Scholastic Poetics,* 246–56.

52. Of fundamental importance for the study of Ficino are the works of P. O. Kristeller, always enriched by exhaustive bibliographical references. For the purpose of examination of the problem of poetics in Ficino, see among his work, P. O. Kristeller, *The Philosophy of Marsilio Ficino* (New York, 1943); idem, "Marsilio Ficino as a Man of Letters and the Glosses Attributed to Him in the Caetani Codex of Dante," *Renaissance Quarterly* 36 (1983): 1–44. See also A. Chastel, *Marsile Ficin et l'art* (Paris, 1954). For the text of the works of Ficino, see *Opera omnia* (Basel, 1576 and the anastatic reprint of this edition, Turin, 1959); *Supplementum Ficinianum,* ed. P. O. Kristeller, 2 vols. (Florence, 1937).

53. *Opera omnia,* 239, 277–79; *Supplementum Ficinianum,* 212–16.

54. See P. O. Kristeller, "Music and Learning in the Early Italian Renaissance," *Journal of Renaissance and Baroque Music* 1 (1947): 255–74; D. P. Walker, "Le chant orphique de Marsile Ficin," *Musique et poésie au XVIᵉ siècle,* ed. J. Jacquot (Paris, 1954), 17–33; idem, "Ficino's Spiritus and Music," *Annales musicologiques* 1 (1951): 131–50; idem, *The Ancient Theology: Studies in Christian Platonism from the Fifteenth to the Eighteenth Century* (Ithaca, NY, 1972); Greenfield, *Humanist and Scholastic Poetics,* 230–37.

55. For a general bibliography on Poliziano, see B. Maier, "Agnolo Poliziano," in *Orientamenti culturali. Letteratura italiana. I maggiori* (Milan, 1969), 300–305; the article on Poliziano (Angelo Ambrogini) by E. Bigi in *Dizionario biografico degli italiani* (Rome, 1961), 2:691–702. The complete edition of Poliziano's Latin and Greek works is the Aldine: *Opera omnia* (Venice, 1498), to be supplemented with *Angeli Politiani Opera omnia* (Basel, 1553). Several prolusions of Poliziano's courses at the *studium* of Florence were immediately published by the printer Miscomini; see Angelo Poliziano, *Le Selve e La Strega,* ed. I. del Lungo (Florence, 1925), x–xi, 231–41. See also I. del Lungo, *Florentia* (Florence, 1897). For other important recent editions of Poliziano's works, see *Sylva in scabiem,* ed. A. Perosa (Rome, 1954); *Della congiura dei Pazzi (Coniurationis commentarium),* ed. A. Perosa (Padua, 1958); *Epigrammi greci,* ed. A. Ardizzoni (Florence, 1951); *Miscellaneorum centuria prima,* ed. H. Katayama (Tokyo, 1981); *Miscellaneorum centuria secunda,* ed. M. Pastore Stocchi and V. Branca (Florence, 1972); and *La commedia e l'Andria di Terenzio,* ed. R. L. Roselli (Florence, 1973). See also A. Perosa, "Studi sulla tradizione delle poesie del Poliziano," in *Studi in onore di U. E. Paoli* (Florence, 1956), 539–62; idem, "Contributi e proposte per la pubblicazione delle opere latine del Poliziano," in *Poliziano e il suo tempo: Atti del VI convegno internazionale di studi sul Rinascimento* (Florence, 1957), 89–100; I. Maïer, *Les manuscrits d'Ange Politien* (Geneva, 1965); eadem, *Ange Politien: La formation d'un poète humaniste, 1469–1480* (Geneva, 1966). On Poliziano and poetry see also: Vasoli, *L'estetica dell'umanesimo,* 343; Greenfield, *Humanist and Scholastic Poetics,* 257–73.

56. For Pico della Mirandola's attitude toward poetry, his commentary on Gi-rolamo Benivieni's *Canzone d'amore*, and his allegorical interpretations of Genesis 1:1–27, see Weinberg, *History of Literary Criticism*, 255–57; E. Garin, "Filologia e poesia in Angelo Poliziano," *La rassegna della litteratura italiana* 58 (1954): 350; idem, "Poliziano e il suo ambiente," in *Ritratti di umanisti* (Florence, 1967), 131–62; the studies included in the volume *Convegno internazionale per il V centenario della nascita di G. Pico della Mirandola* (Florence, 1965); Q. Breen, "Giovanni Pico della Mirandola on the Conflict of Philosophy and Rhetoric," *Journal of the History of Ideas* 13 (1952): 384–412; and idem, *Christianity and Humanism: Studies in the History of Ideas*, ed. N. P. Ross (Grand Rapids, MI, 1968), 1–68. See also Greenfield, *Humanist and Scholastic Poetics*, 237–41.

57. Quoted in Branca, *Poliziano e l'umanesimo della parola*, 15. On this issue, see also E. Garin, *La cultura filosofica del Rinascimento italiano* (Florence, 1979), 335; C. Vasoli, *La dialettica e la retorica dell'umanesimo* (Milan, 1968), 116.

58. "La concezione dei valori e delle vie stesse della poesia muta dunque nel Poliziano attorno agli anni Ottanta" (Branca, *Poliziano e l'Umanesimo della parola*, 15). On Poliziano's studies on the art of poetry see also E. Bigi, "Il Poliziano critico," *La rassegna della letteratura italiana* 58 (1954): 367–76; idem, "La cultura del Poliziano," *Belfagor* 9 (1954): 633–53; Greenfield, *Humanist and Scholastic Poetics*, 257–73.

59. Quoted from *Epistolae* 10.14 in V. Branca, *Poliziano e l'umanesimo della parola*, 16. On this issue, see also L. Cesarini Martinelli, "In margine al commento di Angelo Poliziano alle *Selve* di Stazio," *Interpres* 1 (1978): 105.

60. Branca, *Poliziano e l'umanesimo della parola*, 15.

61. The historical significance of the relationship between Poliziano and Ermolao Barbaro is clearly emphasized by Vittore Branca in the first chapter of his volume *Poliziano e l'umanesimo della parola*. As an "absolute novelty" Barbaro included the *Poetics* in his expositions of the works of Aristotle, as we learn from the program outlined in his *Oratio ad discipulos* (3): "Credo polliceri vobis posse duas res. Alteram, interpretaturum me vobis intra triennium, vel summum, quadriennium, Aristotelis omnia volumina. Hoc est, quicquid ad dialecticen et philosophiam naturalem, quicquid ad transnaturalem pertinet, item quicquid ad moralem, ad rhetoricen, ad poeticen; nam de omnibus his Aristotelem scripsisse constat" (quoted in Branca, *Poliziano e l'umanesimo della parola*, 31, n. 31). In one of his letters Barbaro stated: "Omnes Aristotelis libros converto et quanta possum luce, proprietate, cultu exorno"; Ermolao Barbaro the Younger, *Epistolae, orationes, carmina*, ed. V. Branca (Florence, 1943), 2:90.

62. *Mostra del Poliziano*, ed. A. Perosa (Florence, 1955), 72–73; Maïer, *Manuscrits d'Ange Politien*, 336. On the question of Poliziano's use of the *Poetics*, see also E. N. Tigerstedt, "Observations on the Reception of the Aristotelian 'Poetics' in the Latin West," *Studies in the Renaissance* 15 (1968): 7–24; E. Garin, "La diffusione della 'Poetica' di Aristotele dal secolo XV in poi," *Rivista critica di storia della filosofia* 28 (1973): 449–50.

63. Branca, *Poliziano e l'umanesimo della parola,* 15.
64. Ibid.
65. Garin, *Diffusione della 'Poetica,'* 448.
66. Ibid.
67. Ibid., 449.
68. Ibid., 450.
69. On della Fonte see C. Marchesi, *Bartolomeo della Fonte (Bartholemaeus Fontius): Contributo alla storia degli studi classici in Firenze nella seconda metà del Quattrocento* (Catania, 1900); C. Trinkaus, "A Humanist's Image of Humanism: The Inaugural Orations of Bartolommeo Della Fonte," *Studies in the Renaissance* 7 (1960): 90–105; idem, *In Our Image and Likeness,* 626–33 and passim; idem, *The Scope of Renaissance Humanism* (Ann Arbor, MI, 1983), 52–87, 88–139; Greenfield, *Humanist and Scholastic Poetics,* 283–307.
70. C. Trinkaus, "The Unknown Quattrocento Poetics of Bartolommeo Della Fonte," *Studies in the Renaissance* 13 (1966): 40–122; the text of della Fonte's *De poetice* appears on pp. 95–122.
71. On this issue, see L. Traube, *Einleitung in die lateinische Philologie des Mittelalters* (Munich, 1911); A. Monteverdi, "Orazio nel Medioevo," *Studi medievali* 7 (1934): 162–80; C. O. Brink, *Horace on Poetry,* 3 vols. (Cambridge, 1971–82).
72. Trinkaus, "Unknown Quattrocento Poetics," 45–46.
73. Ibid., 46.
74. Ibid., 45.
75. Ibid., 69.
76. Ibid., 107.
77. Ibid., 110.
78. *Ars poetica,* 333, 343.
79. For the vast bibliography on Pontano see the treatises on Italian humanism quoted above and the works cited in F. Tateo, *L'umanesimo etico di Giovanni Pontano* (Lecce, 1972). Particularly relevant is the chapter in this volume entitled: "La 'Medietas' dell'arte e il sublime della poesia," where Tateo discusses Pontano's attitude toward poetry. On this issue see also Vasoli, *L'estetica dell'umanesimo,* 344–45; Greenfield, *Humanist and Scholastic Poetics,* 276–81.
80. Giovanni Pontano, *I dialoghi,* ed. C. Previtera (Florence, 1943), 193.
81. Ibid.
82. Ibid.
83. Ibid., 146.
84. Weinberg, *History of Literary Criticism,* 715. This subdivision of the material compounding the body of sixteenth-century critical literature is in agreement with the presentational criteria followed by Weinberg in his *History of Literary Criticism.* Similarly, the critical literature of the Italian Cinquecento is subdivided into four groups by R. Barilli, "Le poetiche e la critica d'arte," in *Il Cinquecento: Dal Rinascimento alla Controriforma* (Bari, 1973), 506–71. Barilli (p. 508) distinguishes: "1. il gruppo dei trattati

in cui la poetica è strettamente associata alla retorica; 2. quello di una di-
retta ortodossia aristotelica; 3. quello della rivolta contro Aristotele in
nome del furor platonico. Tra i gruppi 1 e 2 aggiungeremo un sottogruppo
di trattatisti relativamente autonomi."

85. Weinberg, *History of Literary Criticism*, 811–12.
86. Detailed discussions of the late Renaissance literary quarrels appear in
    Weinberg, *History of Literary Criticism*. For the quarrel over Dante, see
    819–911; for the quarrel over Speroni's *Canace*, 912–53; for the quarrel
    over Ariosto and Tasso, 954–1073; for the quarrel over Guarino's *Pastor
    fido*, 1074–1105. For the history of the theory of genres, see 635–714. On
    these issues, see also Hathaway, *Age of Criticism*, passim.
87. Weinberg, *History of Literary Criticism*, 71–72. For a different interpreta-
    tion of the *Ars poetica*, see Brink, *Horace on Poetry*, 79–84, 99–102, and
    passim. For a critique of Weinberg's position on this issue and a discussion
    of the methodological limitation peculiar to his analyses see Trinkaus, "Un-
    known Quattrocento Poetics," 41, 80–82. Trinkaus adroitly describes
    Weinberg's *History* as a work "monumental in its scope but monolithic in
    maintaining its author's point of view, which is that of the so-called 'Chi-
    cago school' of Aristotelianism." The limitations of the methodology fol-
    lowed by Weinberg in his studies of Renaissance critical theories are again
    intelligently analyzed in R. M. Ferraro, *Giudizi critici e criteri estetici nei
    Poetices libri septem (1561) di Giulio Cesare Scaligero rispetto alla teoria
    letteraria del Rinascimento* (Chapel Hill, 1971), 37: "Il pensiero del Wein-
    berg è minato dal difetto organico di rimaner inceppato nel metodo." For
    the relation between rhetoric and poetics see the introductory essay of G.
    della Volpe to his *Poetica del Cinquecento* (Bari, 1954), 12–51. This work
    of della Volpe was violently reviewed by B. Weinberg in *Comparative Lit-
    erature* 8 (1956): 170–74.
88. Trinkaus, "Unknown Quattrocento Poetics," 82.
89. Josse Bade (Iodocus Badius Ascensius), *Quinti Horatii Flacci opusculum
    aureum* (Paris, 1500). On Bade, see B. Weinberg, *History of Literary Criti-
    cism*, 81–88; idem, "Badius Ascentius and the Transmission of Medieval
    Literary Criticism," *Romance Philology* 9 (1955): 209–16.
90. *Pomponii Gaurici de arte Poetica* (n. loc., n.d.). According to B. Weinberg
    the date of this extremely rare edition is ca. 1510. The work of Gaurico is
    also available in the following edition: *Pomponius Gauricus Super arte poe-
    tica Horatii* (Rome, 1541). On Gaurico, see Weinberg, *History of Literary
    Criticism*, 88–90.
91. *Hoc pugillari Terentius numeris concinatus, et L. Victoris Fausti De com-
    oedia libellus* (Venice, 1515); see also Weinberg, *History of Literary Criti-
    cism*, 90.
92. *Le Seluette di Messer Nicolao Lyburnio* (Venice, 1513); Weinberg, *History
    of Literary Criticism*, 90–91.
93. *Horatii Flacci poemata: Cum commentariis eruditissimorum grammatico-
    rum reconditissimis: Antonii Mancinelli Jodoci Badij Ascensii & Joannis
    Britannici* (Milan, 1518); Weinberg, *History of Literary Criticism*, 92–94.

94. *A. Iani Parrhasii Cosentini in Q. Horatii Flacci Artem Poeticam commentaria locupletissima* (Naples, 1531); Weinberg, *History of Literary Criticism*, 96–101.

95. *La Poetica d'Horatio tradotta per Messer Lodovico Dolce* (Venice, 1535); Weinberg, *History of Literary Criticism*, 101–2.

96. Bartolomeo Ricci, *De imitatione libri tres* (Venice, 1545). See Weinberg, *History of Literary Criticism*, 102–4; Hathaway, *Age of Criticism*, 443–44; Barilli, *Poetiche e la critica d'arte*, 512–13. The edition of Ricci's *De imitatione* of 1541 is listed by A. A. Renouard, *Annales de l'imprimerie des Alde* (Paris, 2d. ed. 1953), 1:292–93. See also Weinberg, *History of Literary Criticism*, 1144; A. Lazzari, "Un umanista romagnolo alla corte d'Ercole II d'Este, B. Ricci da Lugo," *Atti e memorie della Deputazione ferrarese di storia patria* 13 (1913): 3–240. A modern edition of the first book of Bartolomeo Ricci's *De imitatione* appears in *Trattati di poetica e retorica del Cinquecento*, ed. B. Weinberg (Bari, 1970), 1:415–49. During this period the question of imitation is discussed in *Due trattati dell'Eccellentissimo M. Iulio Camillo: L'uno delle materie che possono venir sotto lo stile dell'eloquente: L'altro della imitatione* (Venice, 1544). On Giulio Camillo Delminio, see Barilli, *Poetiche e la critica d'arte*, 513–15.

97. *Historiae poetarum tam Graecorum quam Latinorum Dialogi decem . . . L. Greg. Gyraldo Ferrariensi autore* (Basel, 1545); Weinberg, *History of Literary Criticism*, 104–6.

98. Francesco Filippo Pedemonte, *Ecphrasis in Horatii Flacci Artem poeticam* (Venice, 1546); Weinberg, *History of Literary Criticism*, 111–17.

99. "Paraphrasis in libellum Horatii qui vulgo de arte poetica inscribitur," in *Francisci Robortelli Utinensis in librum Aristotelis De arte poetica explicationes* (Florence, 1548), aa ii 1–25.

100. "Vincentii Madii Brixiani in Q. Horatii Flacci de arte poetica librum ad Pisones interpretatio," in *Vincentii Madii Brixiani et Bartholomaei Lombardi Veronensis in Aristotelis librum de poetica communes explanationes* (Venice, 1550), 328–69; Weinberg, *History of Literary Criticism*, 118–22.

101. *Q. Horatii Flacci Liber de arte poetica Iacobi Grifoli Lucinianensis interpretatione explicatus* (Florence, 1550); Weinberg, *History of Literary Criticism*, 122–27. Some passages relevant to poetics may be found in *Lilii Gregorii Gyraldi Ferrariensis Dialogi duo de poëtis nostrorum temporum* (Florence, 1551). See Weinberg, *History of Literary Criticism*, 127–28.

102. *In epistolam Q. Horatii Flacci de arte poetica Iasonis de Nores Ciprij ex quotidianis Tryphonis Gabrielij sermonibus interpretatio* (Venice, 1553); Weinberg, *History of Literary Criticism*, 128–30; F. E. Budd, "A Minor Italian Critic of the Sixteenth Century: Jason Denores," *Modern Language Review* 22 (1927): 421–34.

103. *Francisci Luisini Utinensis in librum Q. Horatii Flacci de arte poetica commentarius* (Venice, 1554); Weinberg, *History of Literary Criticism*, 130–34.

104. These lectures were delivered by Benedetto Varchi at the Accademia Fiorentina and were published only in 1590 in *Lezzioni di M. Benedetto Varchi Accademico Fiorentino, lette da lui pubblicamente nell'Accademia Fioren-*

tina (Florence, 1590); see Weinberg, *History of Literary Criticism*, 135–37. From the vast bibliography on Varchi, see G. Manacorda, *Benedetto Varchi, l'uomo, il poeta, il critico* (Pisa, 1903); Vasoli, *L'estetica dell'umanesimo*, 423 and passim; Hathaway, *Age of Criticism*, 81–82, 339–41, 445–46 and passim.

105. *Dialogi di Messer Alessandro Lionardi Della inventione poetica* (Venice, 1554). For a modern edition of Lionardi's *Dialogi*, see Weinberg, *Trattati di poetica e di retorica*, 2:211–92. On Lionardi, see Weinberg, *History of Literary Criticism*, 137–38 and Barilli, *Poetiche e la critica d'arte*, 511–12. Problems of poetics are debated also in *Le osservationi grammaticali e poetiche della lingua italiana del Signor Matteo Conte di San Martino e di Vische* (Rome, 1555); see Weinberg, *History of Literary Criticism*, 138–40.

106. See *Lettere di XIII huomini illustri*, ed. Thomaso Porcacchi (Venice, 1565), 867–900; Weinberg, *History of Literary Criticism*, 140–42. On the critical writings of Giovambattista Giraldi Cinzio, see also Hathaway, *Age of Criticism*, 92–93, 444–45 and passim. For an extensive bibliography on Giraldi Cinzio and the theories on tragedy, see C. Lucas, *De l'horreur au "lieto fine": Le contrôle du discours tragique dans le théâtre de Giraldi Cinzio* (Rome, 1984), 206–8.

107. *Della imitatione poetica di M. Bernardino Parthenio* (Venice, 1560); Weinberg, *History of Literary Criticism*, 145–47; Hathaway, *Age of Criticism*, 70, 82, 434. For a modern edition of Partenio's *Della imitatione*, see Weinberg, *Trattati di poetica e di retorica*, 2:519–58. Documents related to Partenio's *Della imitatione* are Giulio Camillo Delminio, "Discorso sopra l'idee di Hermogene," in *Il secondo tomo dell'opere di M. Giulio Camillo Delminio* (Venice, 1560), 111–43, and Francesco Sansovino's "Un discorso in materia della satira," in: Francesco Sansovino, *Sette libri di satire* (Venice, 1560), 5–7. For a modern edition of Sansovino's work see Weinberg, *Trattati di poetica e di retorica*, 2:513–18.

108. *Ion. Baptistae Pignae Poetica horatiana* (Venice, 1561); Weinberg, *History of Literary Criticism*, 157–62. For the activity of Pigna as a critic see also Hathaway, *Age of Criticism*, 30–31, 190–91, and passim.

109. For the history of Italian academies, see M. Maylender, *Storia delle accademie d'Italia* 5 vols. (Bologna, 1926–30); *Università, accademie e società scientifiche in Italia e in Germania dal Cinquecento al Settecento*, ed. L. Boehm and E. Raimondi (Bologna, 1981). The activity of an Italian Cinquecento academy, where problems of poetics were frequent subjects of discussion, is admirably studied in B. Weinberg, "Argomenti di discussione letteraria nell'Accademia degli Alterati (1570–1600)," *Giornale storico della letteratura italiana* 131 (1954): 175–94.

110. The series is composed of six lectures. The texts of these documents are unpublished and they may be found in MSS R. 118 Sup. and R. 126 Sup. in the Biblioteca Ambrosiana of Milan. For the identification of the manuscripts see B. Weinberg, "Bartolomeo Maranta: nuovi manoscritti di critica letteraria," *Annali della Scuola Normale Superiore di Pisa* 24 (1955): 115–25; idem, *History of Literary Criticism*, 162–63.

111. *L'opere d'Orazio poeta lirico comentate da Giovanni Fabrini da Fighine in lingua vulgare toscana* (Venice, 1566); Weinberg, *History of Literary Criticism,* 179–83.

112. *L'opere d'Orazio,* 355v. A theoretical document of some interest composed during this period is the treatise of Orazio Toscanella, *Precetti necessari sopra diverse cose pertinenti alla grammatica, poetica, retorica, historia, loica, et ad altre facoltà* (Venice, 1562); see Weinberg, *History of Literary Criticism,* 167–71. A modern edition of Toscanella's *Precetti* may be found in Weinberg, *Trattati di poetica e retorica,* 2:559–66.

113. In 1578 Francesco Bonciani read before the Accademia Fiorentina a *Lettione della proposopopea,* which has been recently defined as "a poetics in little." The text of this *Lettione* is in MS Ricc. 1539, fols. 132–44, of the Biblioteca Riccardiana, Florence. On this manuscript, see Weinberg, "Nuove attribuzioni di manoscritti di critica letteraria del Cinquecento," *Rinascimento* 3 (1952): 249–50; idem, *History of Literary Criticism,* 201–2.

114. Bernardo Pino da Cagli, *Discorso intorno al componimento della comedia de' nostri tempi* (Venice, 1578); Weinberg, *History of Literary Criticism,* 203–4.

115. Weinberg, *History of Literary Criticism,* 201; for a discussion of the last developments on Horatian criticism in the Italian sixteenth century, see 201–49.

116. Hathaway, *Age of Criticism,* 4–5. See also G. Mazzacurati, "Prologo e promemoria sulla 'scoperta' della Poetica (1500–1540)," in *Conflitti di cultura nel Cinquecento* (Naples, 1977), 1–41.

117. Weinberg, *History of Literary Criticism,* 350–51.

118. Averroës's commentary on the *Poetics* was translated by Hermann the German in 1256. *Aristoteles Latinus,* xxiii–xxvi, lists more than twenty manuscripts of Hermann's translation; some of them were written during the fifteenth century and two are from Padua. See Branca, *Poliziano e l'umanesimo della parola,* 32. In 1278 William of Moerbeke translated the text of the *Poetics.* This translation had an extremely limited circulation, as demonstrated by the fact that the text is transmitted by only two manuscripts; see Garin, *La diffusione della Poetica,* 447. On the problem of the *Poetics* in medieval times, see also E. Lobel, *The Medieval Latin Poetics* (New York, 1972); E. Franceschini, "La Poetica di Aristotele nel secolo XIII," *Atti del R. Istituto Veneto di Lettere, Scienze ed Arti* 94 (1935): 523–48; idem, *Studi e note di filologia latina medioevale* (Milan, 1938), 143–59; Minio-Paluello, "Guglielmo di Moerbeke traduttore"; Tigerstedt, "Observations on the Reception of the Aristotelian Poetics"; Bogges, "Aristotle's Poetics in the Fourteenth Century"; Dahan, "Notes et textes sur la poétique au Moyen Âge." Cardinal Bessarion in the fifteenth century had a copy of the *Poetics* transcribed for his library; see L. Labowsky, *Bessarion's Library* (Rome, 1979), 15 and n. 43. On Averroës's paraphrase see also Weinberg, *History of Literary Criticism,* 352–61.

119. On Giorgio Valla, see J. B. Heiberg, "Beiträge zur Geschichte Georg Vallas und seiner Bibliothek," *Centralblatt für Bibliothekswesen* 16 (1896): 1–

129; Tigerstedt, "Observations on the Reception of the Aristotelian Poetics," 16–24. For the relationship between Giorgio Valla and Ermolao Barbaro the Younger, see Ermolao Barbaro, *Epistolae,* 92, 99, 135; V. Branca, "Ermolao Barbaro e l'umanesimo veneziano," in *Umanesimo europeo, e umanesimo veneziano,* ed. V. Branca (Florence, 1963), 193–212; V. Branca, "L'umanesimo veneziano alla fine del Quattrocento: Ermolao Barbaro," in *Storia della cultura veneta* (Vicenza, 1980), 3.1. See also *Giorgio Valla tra scienza e sapienza: Studi di G. Gardenal, P. Landucci Ruffo, C. Vasoli,* ed. V. Branca (Florence, 1981); Weinberg *History of Literary Criticism,* 361–66; C. Vasoli, "Note su Giorgio Valla e il suo 'Sistema' delle 'Arti' del discorso," *Interpres* 4 (1982): 247–61.

120. See Weinberg, *History of Literary Criticism,* 364. Some of Valla's errors may be due to the deficiencies of the manuscript used by the translator. This manuscript has been identified as the Estensis Gr. 100 of the Biblioteca Estense, Modena.

121. See Weinberg, *History of Literary Criticism,* 366–67.

122. See E. Legrand, *Bibliographie hellénique ou description raisonnée des ouvrages publiés en grec par des grecs au XVᵉ et XVIᵉ siècles* (Paris, 1885), 1:82; Aristotle, *The Poetics,* trans. D. S. Margoliouth (London, 1911), 97; L. Cooper and A. Gudeman, *A Bibliography of the Poetics of Aristotle* (New Haven, 1928), 1; D. J. Geanakoplos, *Greek Scholars in Venice: Studies in the Dissemination of Greek Learning from Byzantium to the West* (Cambridge, MA, 1962), 226; Weinberg, *History of Literary Criticism,* 366–67; Tigerstedt, "Observations on the Reception of the Aristotelian Poetics," 15.

123. See Winberg, *History of Literary Criticism,* 367.

124. Ibid., 367–68.

125. Ibid., 368.

126. Ibid., 369, 1115. Averroës's commentary was translated again by Jacob Mantino in 1550, and this translation, like Balmes's, was based on Todros Todrosi's version. Balmes's translation was reprinted in 1560 and Mantino's in 1562.

127. On Trissino, see B. Morsolin, *Giangiorgio Trissino: Monografia d'un gentiluomo letterato del secolo XVI* (Florence, 1894); P. Palumbo, "Giangiorgio Trissino," in *Orientamenti culturali. Letteratura italiana. I minori* (Milan, 1969), 2:873–89; E. Proto, "Sulla poetica di G. G. Trissino," *Studi di letteratura italiana* 6 (1944–46): 197–298; A. Scarpa, *Giangiorgio Trissino vicentino* (Vicenza, 1950); Weinberg, *History of Literary Criticism,* 369–70; Barilli, *Poetiche e la critica d'arte,* 526–27; Hathaway, *Age of Criticism,* 26–28, 138–39, 211–12, and passim.

128. On the relationship between Trissino and Palladio and on Trissino's interests in Vitruvius and architecture, see R. Pane, *Andrea Palladio* (Turin, 1961), 43–45, 73–75, and passim.

129. The necessity to reevaluate Trissino's contributions was also emphasized during the course of a recent symposium on his work. See *Atti del convegno di studi su Giangiorgio Trissino* (Vicenza, 1980), 5 and passim.

130. Giraldi in the prologue to his tragedy *Orbecche* wrote: "il Trissino gentil

che col suo canto / Prima d'ognun del Tebro e dell'Ilisso / Già trasse la tragedia all'onde d'Arno." See Palumbo, *Giangiorgio Trissino,* 878.

131. Trissino's *Sofonisba* was translated into French by Melin de Saint Gelais in 1559 and in 1584 by Claude Mermet. The *Sophonisbe* of Jean Mairet is also an imitation of Trissino's tragedy. See Nicolas de Montreux, *La Sophonisbe,* ed D. Stone, Jr. (Geneva, 1976), 5–6; and Palumbo, *Giangiorgio Trissino,* 878. For the relations between Trissino and French Renaissance culture and drama, see C. Ricci, *Sophonisbe dans la tragédie classique italienne et française* (Turin, 1904); M. J. Wolff, "Die Theorie der italienischen Tragödie im 16 Jahrhunderts," *Archiv für das Studium der neueren Sprachen und Literaturen* 128 (1912): 161–83; E. Preston-Dargan, "Trissino a Possible Source for the Pléiade," *Modern Philology* 13 (1916): 685–88.

132. For Tasso's annotations to the works of Trissino, see Giangiorgio Trissino, *La Sofonisba con note di Torquato Tasso,* ed. F. Paglierani (Bologna, 1884), iii–x; E. Williamson, "Tasso's Annotations to Trissino's Poetics," *Modern Language Notes* 63 (1948): 153–58. A. M. Carini, "Le postille del Tasso al Trissino," *Studi tassiani* 7 (1957): 31–73.

133. *La Pωetica di M. Giωvan Giorgiω Trissinω* (Vicenza, 1529). In this and other works a special type was cast for Trissino. Closed *o* was represented by an omega, closed *e* by an epsilon. This volume contains parts 1–4 of the *Poetica.* The two remaining parts appeared posthumously in 1562: *La quinta e la sesta divisione della poetica del Trissino* (Venice, 1562). In the final sections of the *Poetica* Trissino devotes part 5 to the issues discussed by Aristotle in the first chapters of the *Poetics.* In part 6 the critic discusses the epic, comedy, the pastoral eclogue, and the lyric genres. See Weinberg, *History of Literary Criticism,* 750–55. A modern edition of both sections of Trissino's *Poetica* is in Weinberg, *Trattati di poetica e di retorica,* 1:21–158; 2:5–91.

134. See Cooper and Gudeman, *Bibliography of the Poetics,* 2; Vasoli, *L'estetica dell'umanesimo,* 377.

135. *Aristotelis poetica per Alexandrum Paccium patritium florentinum in latinum conversa; eadem graece* (Venice, 1536). For the other editions of Pazzi's translation see Cooper and Gudeman, *Bibliography of the Poetics,* 1–6. On Pazzi see Weinberg, *History of Literary Criticism,* 371–73; Barilli, *Poetiche e la critica d'arte,* 525.

136. For Lombardi's lectures see F. V. Cerreta, "An Account of the Early Life of the Accademia degli Infiammati in the Letters of Alessandro Piccolomini to Benedetto Varchi," *Romanic Review* 48 (1957): 253–64; Weinberg, *History of Literary Criticism,* 373; Hathaway, *Age of Criticism,* 221.

137. On Maggi see G. Bertoni, "Nota su Vincenzo Maggi," *Giornale storico della letteratura italiana* 96 (1930): 325–27. Bertoni criticized some positions stated by G. Toffanin, who devoted a chapter to Maggi in his *La fine dell'umanesimo* (Turin, 1920). Toffanin answered in "Pro Pio Madio," *La cultura* 10 (1931): 239–45. For additional bibliographical information on Maggi and for his relations with Erasmus, see D. Aguzzi-Barbagli, "Vin-

cenzo Maggi," in *Contemporaries of Erasmus,* ed. P. G. Bietenholz and T. B. Deutscher (Toronto, 1986), 2:367–68.

138. These notes are in MS lat. 88 (Alpha Q.6.14) in Modena (Kristeller, *Iter Italicum,* 1:369); Weinberg, *History of Literary Criticism,* 373–77, 871–73.

139. See note 99.

140. See note 100.

141. Pietro Vettori, *Commentarii in primum librum Aristotelis de arte poetarum* (Florence, 1560).

142. Lodovico Castelvetro, *Poetica d'Aristotele vulgarizzata et sposta* (Vienna, 1570). A second edition of Castelvetro's *Poetica* was published in Basel in 1576. The relationship between these two editions is discussed in Lodovico Castelvetro, *La poetica d'Aristotele vulgarizzata e sposta,* ed. W. Romani (Bari, 1979), 2:386–94. Subsequent quotations from Castelvetro's *Poetica* are from Romani's edition.

143. *Annotationi di M. Alessandro Piccolomini nel libro della Poetica d'Aristotele* (Venice, 1575).

144. *Poetica Antonii Riccoboni poeticam Aristotelis per paraphrasim explicans & nonnullas Ludouici Castelvetrij captiones refellens. Eiusdem ex Aristotele ars comica* (Vicenza, 1585).

145. Lionardo Salviati, *Parafrasi e commento della Poetica d'Aristotile,* MS II.II.11, Biblioteca Nazionale, Florence. This manuscript carries two dates: 26 January 1585 and 28 January 1586. See Weinberg, *History of Literary Criticism,* 1147.

146. *Rettorica et Poetica d'Aristotele tradotte di greco in lingua vulgare fiorentina da Bernardo Segni* (Florence, 1549). A second edition of Segni's translation was published in 1551.

147. *Il libro della Poetica d'Aristotele tradotto di greca lingua in volgare da M. Alessandro Piccolomini* (Siena, 1572).

148. The translation of Lorenzo Giacomini Tebalducci is in MS Laur. Ash. 531. For an account of this manuscript and a discussion of Giacomini Tebalducci's translation, see Weinberg, "Nuove attribuzioni di manoscritti," 245–46; idem, *History of Literary Criticism,* 523–27, 1129.

149. *Aristotelis liber de poetica ab Antonio Riccobono . . . latine conversus* (Venice, 1589). The translations of Segni, Piccolomini, Giacomini Tebalducci, and Riccoboni were issued separately and without a commentary. Vettori and Castelvetro also translated the *Poetics,* into Latin and Italian, respectively, and they incorporated these translations into their commentaries.

150. See B. Weinberg, "From Aristotle to Pseudo-Aristotle," *Comparative Literature* 5 (1952): 97–104; idem, "The Methodology of the Theorists," in *History of Literary Criticism,* 38–70.

151. The merits of Robortello in the history of Renaissance literary criticism are not limited to his contributions to both the Horatian and the Aristotelian traditions, they also include his work as a philologist. Some of his philological endeavors are described by Robortello himself in the preface *Ad lectorem* of his *De arte poetica explicationes.* Here among other things he states

that in Florence he consulted a manuscript of the *Poetics,* formerly analyzed by Poliziano: "Quatuor enim ego usus sum libris, tribus manuscriptis, quarum duo sunt in Medicea Bibliotheca; alter quidem Politiani manu descriptus; alter vero multo vetustior; plurimum enim tribuendum illi puto, propter Politiani singularem doctrinam et acre iudicium." See notes 61 and 62 on Poliziano's manuscripts of the *Poetics.* In 1554 Robortello found in Padua and published in Basel a manuscript of the treatise *On the Sublime* attributed to Longinus, which was the first edition of the work. Through this contribution Robortello was making available to the larger public a classical source destined to have a profound impact on the evolution of European critical thought as it was developed by personalities like Du Bos, Baumgarten, Pope, and Vico. Initially the process of assimilation of the Longinian theories was slow. About 1570 Franciscus Portus wrote a *Commentarius in Longinum* and, shortly after, the *Sublime* was extensively utilized by Francesco Patrizi of Cherso. On Robortello and the first edition of the *Sublime,* see B. Weinberg, "Translations and Commentaries of Longinus' *On the Sublime* to 1600: A Bibliography," *Modern Philology* 47 (1950): 145–51; *Catalogus Translationum et Commentatiorum, Medieval and Renaissance Latin Translations and Commentaries,* ed. P. O. Kristeller, E. F. Cranz, and V. Brown (Washington, DC, 1971), 2:193–98; Pseudo-Longinus, *Del sublime,* ed. G. Martano (Bari, 1965), xv, xlii–xliii. On Franciscus Portus and his *Commentarius,* see Weinberg, *Translations and Commentaries of Longinus,* 149; idem, *History of Literary Criticism,* 188–90.

152. On Robortello's commentary on the *Poetics* see B. Weinberg, "Robortello on the Poetics," in *Critics and Criticism: Ancient and Modern,* ed. R. S. Crane (Chicago, 1952), 319–48; idem, *History of Literary Criticism,* 388–99; Hathaway, *Age of Criticism,* 214–21; Barilli, *Poetiche e la critica d'arte,* 528–29; C. Diano, "Francesco Robortello interprete della catarsi," in *Aristotelismo padovano e filosofia aristotelica. Atti del XII Congresso Internazionale di Filosofia* (Florence, 1960), 71–79.

153. The volume containing the *Explanationes* of Maggi and Lombardi opens with a dedicatory letter from Maggi to the bishop Cristoforo Madrucci. The writer explains the manner whereby he intends to honor the memory of his dead friend and collaborator Bartolomeo Lombardi: "Ut igitur amici viventis honori ac dignitati nunquam defui, ita sane vita functo deesse nolui, nam quos in Aristotelis de Poetica librum commentarios una scribere coeperamus, ut tenebris nomen eius . . . eriperem . . . summis laboribus atque vigiliis ad finem perduxi." The text of the commentary to the *Poetics* is preceded by *Bartholomaei Lombardi Veronensis in Aristotelis librum de poetica ad Academicos Inflammatos praefatio* and by *Vincentii Madii Brixiani in Aristotelis librum de poetica prolegomena.* Here Maggi explains that while he was finishing the work on the *Explanationes* Robertello published his commentary and devotes a section of his introduction to a violent attack against his rival: "Objectiones quaedam adversus Robortelli explicationem in primum Aristotelis contextum." It is thus evident that Maggi is respon-

sible for the final elaboration of the *Explanationes* and for the greater part of its content. For the textual history of the *Explanationes* and Maggi's diatribe against Robortello, see Weinberg, *History of Literary Criticism*, 373, 406.

154. *Explanationes (Prolegomena)*, 13. It is a known fact that the Plutarchan pamphlet *De audiendis poetis* was widely read during the Renaissance. Maggi's quotation of this work in the passage cited provides one of the many examples of the type of eclecticism previously mentioned in relation to the attitudes of the commentators on the *Poetics*.

155. *Explanationes*, 97. On the commentary of Maggi and Lombardi, see Hathaway, *Age of Criticism*, 221–24 and passim; Weinberg, *History of Literary Criticism*, 406–18; Barilli *Poetiche e la critica d'arte*, 529.

156. On Vettori, see W. Rüdiger, *Pietro Vettori aus Florenz* (Halle, 1896); F. Niccolai, *Pietro Vettori* (Florence, 1912); Weinberg, *History of Literary Criticism*, 461–66; Hathaway, *Age of Criticism*, 88–89, 292–93, and passim; Barilli, *Poetiche e la critica d'arte*, 530. For an important contribution to the study of Pietro Vettori, see A. Grafton, *Joseph Scaliger: A Study in the History of Classical Scholarship* (Oxford, 1983), 53–70. A copy of Vettori's commentary to the *Poetics* was owned and heavily annotated by Jean Racine. See Jean Racine, *Principes de la tragédie*, ed. E. Vinaver (Manchester and Paris, 1951), 29 and passim.

157. Hathaway, *Age of Criticism*, 37.

158. An extensive bibliography on Castelvetro may be found in P. Mazzamuto, "Lodovico Castelvetro," *Orientamenti culturali. Letteratura italiana. I minori*, 1236–37. For the bibliographical information on Castelvetro, see G. Gavazzuti, *Lodovico Castelvetro* (Modena, 1903); T. Sandonnini, *Lodovico Castelvetro e la sua famiglia* (Bologna, 1882); V. Marchetti and G. Patrizi, "Castelvetro, Ludovico," in *Dizionario biografico degli italiani*, 22 (Rome, 1979), 8–21. On Castelvetro's poetics, see H. B. Charlton, *Castelvetro's Theory of Poetry* (Manchester, 1913); R. Scrivano, "Il razionalismo critico di L. Castelvetro," in *Cultura e letteratura nel Cinquecento* (Rome, 1966), 169–94; B. Weinberg, "Castelvetro's Theory of Poetics," in *Critics and Criticism*, ed. Crane, 349–71; idem, *A History of Literary Criticism*, 502; Barilli, *Poetica e retorica*, 79–117; idem, *Le poetiche e la critica d'arte*, 531–34; Hathaway, *Age of Criticism*, 37–43, 85–90, 95–104, 177–88, 448–51, and passim. See also Vincenzo Gravina, *Della ragione poetica libri due* (Rome, 1708), 139–40.

159. According to Sandonnini the Inquisition found 107 heretical statements in Castelvetro's commentary on the *Poetics* and 117 in his commentary on Petrarch's *Canzoniere*. See Sandonnini, *Lodovico Castelvetro*, 190–91.

160. In the dedicatory letter to Maximilian II, Castelvetro declares that he considers the *Poetics*, in their present form, a "first version, rough, imperfect and not polished of the art of poetry." He declares also that he intends not only to write a commentary on the text, but also "to render the art of poetry clear, showing not only what was handed down to us in these few pages by that greatest of all philosophers, but also whatever should or could have

been written for the full benefit of those who might wish to know how one should go about composing poems correctly and how one should judge properly whether those already written do or do not have what they ought to have" (*La poetica,* 3).

161. Weinberg, *History of Literary Criticism,* 503–4.

162. See W. Romani, "Nota critico filologica," in Castelvetro, *La poetica,* 377.

163. Weinberg's interpretation of Castelvetro's theories is analyzed and rejected as inaccurate by Barilli, *Poetica e retorica,* 81 and passim. An interpretation of Castelvetro's doctrines quite different from that given by Weinberg may also be found in Hathaway, *Age of Criticism.*

164. Castelvetro, *La poetica,* 1:46, 345.

165. Ibid., 1:149.

166. Ibid., 2:254.

167. Ibid.

168. Ibid., 1:14, 44.

169. Ibid., 1:44.

170. Ibid.

171. See above, note 161.

172. The question of the unity of time was debated by Giambattista Giraldi Cinzio in his *Discorso sulle tragedie e sulle commedie,* published in 1554. See his *Scritti estetici* (Milan, 1864), 2:20. On Cinzio and his doctrines on dramatic poetry, see Weinberg, *History of Literary Criticism,* 439–42 and passim; Hathaway, *Age of Criticism,* 92–93, 444–45, and passim; Lucas, *De l'horreur au "lieto fine,"* 206–8 has an ample bibliography on the subject.

173. Castelvetro, *La poetica,* 2:149–50.

174. Ibid., 1:149.

175. Ibid., 1:240.

176. Weinberg, *History of Literary Criticism,* 409–10.

177. Castelvetro, *La poetica,* 1:241.

178. Ibid., 1:241.

179. Ibid., 1:391.

180. Ibid., 2:368. An illustrious Cinquecento reader of Castelvetro's *Poetica* was Torquato Tasso, who wrote a series of comments on it. These annotations were published in 1875 under the title *Estratti dalla Poetica di Lodovico Castelvetro,* in Torquato Tasso, *Prose diverse,* ed. C. Guasti (Florence, 1875), 1:275–95; see Weinberg, *History of Literary Criticism,* 570–72. Castelvetro's *Poetica* is quoted in Tasso's *Discorsi del poema eroico;* see Torquato Tasso, *Discorsi dell'arte poetica e del poema eroico,* ed. L. Poma (Bari, 1964), 75, 121, 149, 166, 248. On Tasso and his theories on poetry, see B. T. Sozzi, *Nuovi studi sul Tasso* (Bergamo, 1955); Weinberg, *History of Literary Criticism,* 339–41 and passim; Hathaway, *Age of Criticism,* 150–57, 390–96, 450–53, and passim; Barilli, *Poetiche e la critica d'arte,* 543–45.

181. On Piccolomini and his theories of poetry, see F. V. Cerreta, *Alessandro Piccolomini letterato e filosofo senese del Cinquecento* (Siena, 1960); idem, "Alessandro Piccolomini on the Poetics of Aristotle," *Studies in the Renais-*

sance 4 (1957): 139–68; R. Scrivano, "Alessandro Piccolomini," in *Cultura e letteratura*, 14–50; Weinberg, *History of Literary Criticism*, 543–53 and passim; Hathaway, *Age of Criticism*, 83–84, 160–61, 239–40, and passim; M. Celse, "Alessandro Piccolomini, l'homme du ralliement," in *Les écrivains et le pouvoir en Italie à l'époque de la Renaissance*, ed. A. Rochon (Paris, 1973), 7–76; G. Breitenbürger, *Metaphora. Die Rezeption des aristotelischen Begriffs in den Poetiken des Cinquecento* (Kronberg, 1975), 137–50.

182. Alessandro Piccolomini, *Annotazioni,***5.

183. Ibid., 101.

184. Ibid., 103.

185. On Riccoboni, see G. Mazzacurati, *La crisi della retorica umanistica nel Cinquecento: Antonio Riccobono* (Naples, 1961); Weinberg, *History of Literary Criticism*, 603–8; Hathaway, *Age of Criticism*, 288–89 and passim.

186. *Poetica*, 7.

187. Ibid., 66.

188. On Salviati, see P. M. Brown, "Una grammatichetta inedita del Cavalier Lionardo Salviati," *Giornale storico della letteratura italiana* 133 (1956): 544–72; idem, "I veri promotori della 'rassettatura' del 'Decamerone' nel 1582," *Giornale storico della letteratura italiana* 134 (1957): 314–32; idem, "Manoscritti e stampe delle poesie edite ed inedite del Cavalier Lionardo Salviati," *Giornale storico della letteratura italiana* 146 (1969): 530–49; S. Pasquazi, *Rinascimento ferrarese* (Caltanisetta, 1957), passim; Weinberg, *History of Literary Criticism*, 609–20 and passim; Hathaway, *Age of Criticism*, 99–102, 391–93, and passim; Barilli, *Poetiche e la critica d'arte*, 536–38. Salviati's commentary on the *Poetics* is contained in MS II.II.11 of the Biblioteca Nazionale, Florence. In an added title page it bears the title *Poetica d'Aristotile parafrasata e commentata*. For a description of this manuscript, see Weinberg, *History of Literary Criticism*, 1147. Salviati's commentary will henceforth be indicated with the title *Poetica*.

189. *Poetica*, 6v–7.

190. Ibid., 10.

191. Ibid., 131v.

192. Vasoli, *L'estetica dell'umanesimo*, 377.

193. Ibid., 377–78.

194. Ibid., 378. For an analysis of the documents illustrating the development of the first theoretical applications of principles derived from the *Poetics*, see Weinberg, *History of Literary Criticism*, 424–77; Hathaway, *Age of Criticism*, passim; Vasoli, *L'estetica dell'umanesimo*, 390–400. The study of the Italian vernacular commentaries on the *Poetics* can be implemented by a consideration of Orazio Toscanella's *Precetti necessari* (1562) and Sperone Speroni's *Discorsi sopra Virgilio* (1564). Highly relevant are also the series of three lectures by Lionardo Salviati, known collectively under the title *Trattato della poetica* (1564); the three lectures of Baccio Neroni on the topic *Se il verso è necessario alla poesia* (1571); Filippo Sassetti's *Sopra*

Dante (1573); Giulio del Bene's *Che egli è necessario all'esser poeta imitare actioni* (1574) and *Che favola de la commedia vuole essere honesta et non contenere mali costumi* (1574); Sperone Speroni's *Apologia dei dialogi* (1574–75?); and Filippo Sassetti's *Discorso* (1575). For the impact of the literary quarrels on the interpretation of the *Poetics* during the last quarter of the sixteenth century, the reader is referred to Weinberg, *History of Literary Criticism*, 564–634; Hathaway, *Age of Criticism*, passim. In addition to the above, see also the Latin works of Carlo Sigonio: *Emendationum libri duo* (1557) and *De dialogo* (1562); Bartolomeo Maranta, *Lucullianae quaestiones* (1564); Nicasius Ellebodius, *In Aristotelis librum de poetica paraphrasis* (1572). For the relations between the Italian commentators of the *Poetics*, in Latin and in the vernacular, and the culture of northern Europe, see J. H. Meter, *The Literary Theories of Daniel Heinsius* (Assen, 1984), passim.

195. Weinberg, *History of Literary Criticism*, 250.

196. *Phaedrus*, 245a, 265b; *Ion*, 534; *Republic*, books 2, 3, 10.

197. For a detailed discussion of this group of works, see Weinberg, *History of Literary Criticism*, 257–64.

198. *Ragionamenti della lingua toscana . . . dell'eccelente medico e filosofo Bernardino Tomitano* (Venice, 1545). On Tomitano, see Vasoli, *L'estetica dell-'umanesimo*, 379; Weinberg, *History of Literary Criticism*, 264–67; Hathaway, *Age of Criticism*, 67–68, 310–16, 442–43, and passim. On Tomitano, see also L. de Benedictis, *Della vita e delle opere di Bernardino Tomitano* (Padua, 1903).

199. *M. Antonii Maioragii orationes et praefationes omnes* (Venice, 1582). On Maioragio, see Weinberg, *History of Literary Criticism*, 267–69; Barilli, *Poetiche e la critica d'arte*, 511.

200. Antonio Maria Conti (Marcantonio Maioragio), "De arte poetica (Oratio XXIV)," in Weinberg, *Trattati di poetica e di retorica*, 2:131.

201. *M. Antonii Maioragii in tres Aristotelis libros de arte rhetorica* (Venice, 1572). References to the Platonic theory of imitation may also be found in Sperone Speroni's *Discorso in lode della pittura;* Platonic elements appear also in Giovanni Giacomo Leonardi's *Discorso qual sia più utile al mondo o l'historia o la poesia* (1550–60). See Weinberg, *History of Literary Criticism*, 269–72.

202. On these aspects of Lionardi's *Dialogi*, see Weinberg, *History of Literary Criticism*, 273–74; Hathaway, *Age of Criticism*, 32–33, 146–47, and passim; Barilli, *Poetiche e la critica d'arte*, 511–12.

203. "Oratio de laudibus poetarum," in *Iacobi Grifoli Lucinianensis orationes variae variis in locis habitae* (Venice, 1557), 45–66. On Grifoli's *Oratio*, see Weinberg, *History of Literary Criticism*, 275–77.

204. "Il Dedalione overo del poeta dialogo," in *Opuscoli del Signor Scipione Ammirato*, 3 vols. (Florence, 1642), 3:353–94. For a modern edition of Ammirato's *Il Dedalione*, see Weinberg, *Trattati di poetica e di retorica*, 2:477–512. Ideas on poetry are expressed by Ammirato also in *Il Rota overo dell'imprese dialogo* (Naples, 1562). For Ammirato and his role in

the Florentine culture of his time, see the penetrating chapter "How Ammirato Solved Just About All the Problems of His Age," in E. Cochrane, *Florence in the Forgotten Centuries, 1527–1800* (Chicago, 1973), 95–161. For Ammirato's theories on poetics, see Weinberg, *History of Literary Criticism,* 277–80; Vasoli, *L'estetica dell'umanesimo,* 379; Barilli, *Poetiche e la critica d'arte,* 542. See also R. de Mattei, "Ammirato, Scipione," in *Dizionario biografico degli italiani,* 3 (Rome, 1961), 1–4.

205. On this work of Partenio see Weinberg, *History of Literary Criticism,* 280–81.

206. For the works of Bernardo Tasso, Benedetto Grasso, Lucio Olimpio Giraldi, Orazio Toscanella, and Frosino Lapini mentioned in this part of the text see Weinberg, *History of Literary Criticism,* 282–93.

207. On this issue, see C. Dejob, *De l'influence de Concile de Trente sur la littérature et les beaux arts chez les peuples catholiques* (Paris, 1884); Hathaway, *Age of Criticism,* 408, 436, 447; Weinberg, *History of Literary Criticism,* 796–98 and passim.

208. *Io. Antonii Viperani de scribendis virorum illustrium vitis sermo* (Perugia, 1570); see Weinberg, *History of Literary Criticism,* 297–98.

209. *Ragionamento di M. Agnolo Segni gentilhuomo fiorentino sopra le cose pertinenti alla poetica* (Florence, 1581); see Weinberg, *History of Literary Criticism,* 299–304.

210. *Laurentii Gambarae Brixiani tractatio* (Rome, 1576). For the modern edition of Gambara's *Tractatio* used in the present study, see Weinberg, *Trattati di poetica e retorica,* 3:205–34. On Gambara see Weinberg, *History of Literary Criticism,* 305–8.

211. *Tractatio,* 227.

212. Ibid., 230.

213. See Weinberg, *History of Literary Criticism,* 308–9.

214. *Dialogo del furore poetico di Girolamo Frachetta da Rovigo* (Padua, 1581). On Frachetta, see Weinberg, *History of Literary Criticism,* 311–13; Hathaway, *Age of Criticism,* 345–46 and passim; Barilli, *Poetiche e la critica d'arte,* 541.

215. "De la purgazione de la tragedia," in *Orationi e discorsi di Lorenzo Giacomini Tebalducci Malespini* (Florence, 1597), 29–52; Weinberg, *History of Literary Criticism,* 315–16. For a modern edition of Giacomini Tebalducci's *De la purgazione de la tragedia* see Weinberg, *Trattati di poetica e retorica,* 3:345–71.

216. *Discorso di Iason Denores intorno a que principi, cause et accrescimenti, che la comedia, la tragedia et il poema heroico ricevono dalla philosophia morale e civile e da governatori delle repubbliche* (Padua, 1586); Weinberg, *History of Literary Criticism,* 316–19.

217. "De antiquitate dignitateque poesis et poetarum differentia," in Tommaso Correa, *Globus canonum et arcanorum linguae sanctae ac Divine Scripturae* (Rome, 1586), 674–83. On Correa, see Weinberg *History of Literary Criticism,* 319–22.

218. Benci's observations on the art of poetry are in *Francisci Benci ab Aqua*

Pendente e Societate Iesu orationes XXII (Rome, 1590), 6 and 7. On Benci, see Weinberg, *History of Literary Criticism,* 334; R. Negri, "Benci, Francesco," in *Dizionario biografico degli italiani,* 8 (Rome, 1966), 192–93.

219. Filippo Massini, *Lettioni dell'estatico insensato* (Perugia, 1588), 100; quoted in Hathaway, *Age of Criticism,* 408. On Massini, see also Weinberg, *History of Literary Criticism,* 207–9, 865–66.

220. See *Antonii Possevini Societatis Iesu tractatio de poesi et pictura ethnica, humana et fabulosa collata cum sacra* (Rome, 1593). In his views on poetry Possevino maintains an extreme Christian position, which leads him to declare that only Christian poetry is acceptable. On Possevino, see Weinberg, *History of Literary Criticism,* 335–39.

221. The question whether modern poets should use pagan myths is debated by Giovambattista Strozzi in a lecture delivered before the Accademia Fiorentina in 1588 and entitled *Se sia bene il servirsi delle favole delli antichi.* This lecture is published in *Orazioni et altre prose del Signor Giovambattista di Lorenzo Strozzi* (Rome, 1635), 126–38. On Strozzi see Weinberg, *History of Literary Criticism,* 330 and passim.

222. Mazzoni's major contribution to Italian critical literature is his *Della difesa della Comedia di Dante,* a long treatise probably finished in 1585 and published in 1587: Jacopo Mazzoni (pseud. Donato Rofia), *Della difesa della Comedia di Dante* (Cesena, 1587). The work of Mazzoni is particularly relevant for the study of genre theory and of the querelle on the *Divine Comedy.* Because of the predominance of these themes, a detailed treatment of Mazzoni's treatise has been omitted in the present study. Nonetheless, detailed analyses of the development of the Platonic critical tradition in the later part of the sixteenth century should include serious consideration of Mazzoni's *Difesa.*

223. For an expanded treatment of the progress of the Platonic tradition during the last years of the Cinquecento, the following documents should also be considered: Andrea Menechini, *Delle lodi della poesia d'Omero et di Virgilio* (Venice, 1572); Francesco Bonciani, "Lezione della prosopopea," in Weinberg, *Trattati di poetica e retorica,* 3:237–53; Filippo Mocenigo, *Universales institutiones ad hominum perfectionem* (Venice, 1581); Lionardo Salviati, *Il Lasca dialogo* (Florence, 1583); Lorenzo Giacomini Tebalducci, "Del furor poetico," in Weinberg, *Trattati di poetica e di retorica,* 3:421–44; Anonimo (Federico Ceruti?), "De re poetica libellus." in Weinberg, *Trattati di poetica e retorica,* 3:445–83; Giuseppe Malatesta, *Della nuova poesia* (Verona, 1589); Diomede Borghesi, *Oratione intorno a gli onori et ai pregi della poesia e della eloquenza* (Siena, 1596); and Paolo Beni, *Disputatio* (Padua, 1600). On the works listed here, see Weinberg, *History of Literary Criticism,* 310, 311, 312–14, 322, 328, 332–33. Hathaway, *Age of Criticism,* 409, presents a discussion of Giovanni Maria Verdizzotti, *Genius, sive de furore poetico* (Venice, 1575). This work is not analyzed in Weinberg, *History of Literary Criticism,* where only one of Verdizzotti's works is discussed, namely: Giovanni Mario [sic] Verdizzotti, *Breve discorso intorno alla narratione poetica* (Venice, 1588), reprinted in Weinberg,

Trattati di poetica e retorica, 4:5–12. In the "Nota filologica" of this volume Weinberg states: "In una delle sue poesie latine (Verdizzotti) trattò un argomento letterario, *De furore poetico,*" p. 339. For an interesting aspect of the development of the Neoplatonic tradition in the late sixteenth century, see A. M. Patterson, "Tasso and Neoplatonism: The Growth of His Epic Theory," *Studies in the Renaissance* 18 (1971): 105–33.

224. On Vida, see V. Lancetti, *Della vita e degli scritti di Girolamo Vida* (Naples, 1904); N. Salvatore, *L'arte poetica di Marco Girolamo Vida* (Foligno, 1912); Di Cesare, *Vida's "Christiad" and Vergilian Epic,* 40–86; Weinberg, *History of Literary Criticism,* 715–19; Barilli, *Poetiche e la critica d'arte,* 517–18; R. G. Williams, "Introduction," in Marco Girolamo Vida, *The De Arte Poetica,* ed. and trans. R. G. Williams (New York, 1976), xi–li.

225. *Marci Hieronymi Vidae Cremonensis De arte poetica lib. III* (Rome, 1527). For a detailed list of editions and translations of Vida's *De arte poetica,* see M. A. Di Cesare, *Bibliotheca Vidiana: A Bibliography of Marco Girolamo Vida* (Florence, 1974), 167–98.

226. Boileau, *L'art poétique,* 165–70; Alexander Pope, *An Essay on Criticism,* 705–8; see also Vida, *The De arte poetica,* 183–85.

227. Weinberg, *History of Literary Criticism,* 715.

228. R. G. Williams, "Introduction," xxix and n. 45: "Weinberg . . . is largely interested . . . in a diachronic analysis of the discussion in the cinquecento of particular concepts. . . . His methodology serves him . . . ill here . . . and Weinberg poses questions to which Vida really never intended to address himself systematically. . . . Curiously Weinberg preserves the idea that Vida's model is Horace's *Ars poetica,* ignoring the basic difference between the two works. . . . Vida's poem is in many respects patterned rather after Virgil's *Georgics.*" On this issue see also L. Borsetto, "Il fiuto di Prometeo: struttura e scrittura nei 'Poeticorum libri' di M. G. Vida," *Rassegna della letteratura italiana* 85 (1981): 93–108.

229. R. G. Williams, "Introduction," xxxvii.

230. See note 133 above.

231. *La poetica di Bernardino Daniello* (Venice, 1536). For a recent edition of this work see Weinberg, *Trattati di poetica e retorica,* 1:227–318. On Daniello, see R. G. Williams, "The Originality of Daniello," *Romanic Review* 15 (1924): 121–22; Weinberg, *History of Literary Criticism,* 721–24; Hathaway, *Age of Criticism,* 211; Vasoli, *L'estetica dell'umanesimo* 378–79; Barilli, *Poetiche e la critica d'arte,* 510–11.

232. The *Naugerius* was published posthumously in *Hieronymi Fracastorii Veronensis opera omnia* (Venice, 1555), 153–64v. The text of this edition was reproduced with an English translation by R. Kelso and an introduction by M. W. Mundy in Girolamo Fracastoro, *Naugerius sive de poetica dialogus* (Urbana, IL, 1924). For other editions see Girolamo Fracastoro, *Il Naugerio,* trans. G. Preti (Milan, 1945); idem, *Il Navagero ovvero dialogo sulla poetica,* trans. A. Gandolfo (Bari, 1947). For the date of composition of the *Naugerius* see L. Firpo, "Introduzione," in Tommaso Campanella, *Poetica,*

ed. L. Firpo (Rome, 1944), 9. On Fracastoro and his poetics see E. Barboran, *Girolamo Fracastoro e le sue opere* (Verona, 1897); G. Gianturco,
"La poetica di Girolamo Fracastoro," *Logos* (1932): 1–16; G. Saitta, "Il
pensiero di Giralamo Fracastoro," *Atti dell'Accademia di Agricoltura,
Scienze e Lettere di Verona* (1924): 155–93; *Scritti di varia letteratura e
critica*, ed. A. Scolari (Bologna, 1937); F. Pellegrini, *Fracastoro* (Trieste,
1948); Barilli, "Girolamo Fracastoro," in *Poetica e retorica*, 57–77; idem,
Poetiche e la critica d'arte, 515–16; Vasoli, *L'estetica dell'umanesimo*, 385–
86; Hathaway, *Age of Criticism*, 316–28; Weinberg, *History of Literary
Criticism*, 725–29; B. Maier, "La poetica di Girolamo Fracastoro," *Annali
dell'Università di Trieste* 19 (1949): 29–55.
233. *H. Fracastori opera omnia*, 164.
234. Girolamo Muzio, "Tre libri di arte poetica," in *Rime diverse del Mutio Ius-
tinopolitano* (Venice, 1551), 68–94v. For a modern edition of this work see
Weinberg, *Trattati di poetica e retorica*, 2:163–209. On Muzio as a theorist
see Weinberg, *History of Literary Criticism*, 729–31; Hathaway, *Age of
Criticism*, 12, 107, 132, and passim; Barilli, *Poetiche e la critica d'arte*,
518–19; Ferraro, *Giudizi critici e criteri estetici*, 23–24.
235. *Di Gio. Pietro Capriano bresciano della vera poetica libro uno* (Venice,
1555); a modern edition of the work is in Weinberg, *Trattati di poetica e di
retorica*, 2:293–334. Capriano remains a mysterious personage; nothing is
known about his life, and his only known work is *Della vera poetica*. On
this treatise, see Weinberg, *History of Literary Criticism*, 732–37; Hathaway, *Age of Criticism*, 34–35, 70–71, 138–39, and passim; Barilli, *Poetiche
e la critica d'arte*, 531; Ferraro, *Giudizi critici e criteri estetici*, 24–25.
236. Capriano, *Della vera poetica*, 295.
237. Ibid., 299.
238. Vauquelin de la Fresnaye, *L'art poétique françoise*, 62–65.
239. See *Elizabethan Critical Essays*, ed. G. C. Smith (Oxford, 1904), 1:389,
392; *Sir Philip Sidney's Defense of Poesy*, ed. L. Loens (Lincoln, NE, 1970),
65, 66, 69, 71.
240. *Antonii Sebastiani Minturni De poeta* (Venice, 1559); *L'arte poetica del Sig.
Antonio Minturno* (Venice, 1564). Copies of *L'arte poetica* at the Newberry
Library and the British Library bear the title *Arte poetica thoscana* (the
same title used by Minturno in his references to this work) and the date
1563. It has been concluded that the edition of 1564 is a reissue of the
original edition published the year before; see B. Weinberg, "The Poetic
Theories of Minturno," in *Studies in Honor of F. L. Shipley* (Washington,
DC, 1942), 101–29. On Minturno, see R. Calderini, *A. S. Minturno, vita e
opere* (Aversa, 1921); Hathaway, *Age of Criticism*, 35–37, 93–94, 172–73,
229–30, 234–35, 422–23, 435–36, 446–50, and passim; Weinberg, *History of Literary Criticism*, 737–43; Ferraro, *Giudizi critici e criteri estetici*,
26–27.
241. *De poeta*, 8–9.
242. Ibid., 64.

243. Ibid., 9.

244. Ibid., 11.

245. Ibid., 26.

246. Ibid., 79.

247. For biographical studies on Scaliger, see V. Hall, "Life of Julius-Caesar Scaliger," *Transactions of the American Philosophical Society* 40 (1950): 86–170; M. Billanovich, "Benedetto Bordon e Giulio Cesare Scaligero," *Italia medioevale e umanistica* 11 (1968): 187–256; Grafton, *Joseph Scaliger,* passim. On Scaliger and poetics, see E. Brinkschulte, *J. C. Scaliger's kunsttheoretische Anschauungen* (Bonn, 1913); L. B. Campbell, "A Note on Scaliger's Poetics," *Modern Philology* 20 (1922–23): 375–78; H. Nibley, "New Light on Scaliger," *Classical Journal* 37 (1942): 291–95; V. Hall, "Preface to Scaliger's 'Poetices libri septem,' " *Modern Language Notes* 40 (1945): 445–543; idem, "Scaliger's Defense of Poetry," *Proceedings of the Modern Language Association* 63 (1948): 1125–30; R. Clements, "Literary Theory and Criticism in Scaliger's Poemata," *Studies in Philology* 51 (1954): 561–84; idem, "The Peregrine Muse," *North Carolina University Studies in the Romance Languages and Literatures* 31 (1959) [monograph]; M. Costanzo, *Dallo Scaligero al Quadrio* (Milan, 1961); S. Shepard, "Scaliger on Homer and Virgil: A Study of Literary Prejudice," *Emerita* 29 (1961): 313–40; Hathaway, *Age of Criticism,* 60–70 and passim.

248. *Iulii Caesaris Scaligeri viri clarissimi poetices libri septem* (Lyons, 1561). Scaliger died in 1558 and his *Poetices* were published posthumously.

249. E. Lintilhac, "Un coup d'état dans la république des lettres: Jules-César Scaliger fondateur du 'Classicisme' cent ans avant Boileau," *La nouvelle revue* 64 (1890): 333–46, 528–47.

250. Ferraro, *Giudizi critici e criteri estetici,* 45–49.

251. Barilli, *Poetiche e la critica d'arte,* 524.

252. In this category can be classified the interpretations contained in B. Weinberg, "Scaliger Versus Aristotle on Poetics," *Modern Philology* 39 (1942): 337–60; and idem, *History of Literary Criticism,* 743–50. For an intelligent analysis and a rebuke of Weinberg's interpretation, see Ferraro, *Giudizi critici e criteri estetici,* 37, n. 79, 555–61, and passim.

253. Scaliger, *Poetice,* 137–38.

254. Ferraro, *Giudizi critici e criteri estetici,* 67. On Scaliger's thought, see also A. Corsano, "Studi sul pensiero del tardo Rinascimento: G. C. Scaligero," *Giornale critico della filosofia italiana* 37 (1958): 34–63.

255. On this issue, see Ferraro, *Giudizi critici e criteri estetici,* 69.

256. Quoted in M. H. Abrams, *The Mirror and the Lamp: Romantic Theory and the Critical Tradition* (Oxford, 1974), 273. On the same passage, see Ferraro, *Giudizi critici e criteri estetici,* 82.

257. Scaliger, *Poetice,* 7.

258. Ibid., 900–901.

259. Ibid., 903.

260. Ibid., 83.

261. Ferraro, *Giudizi critici e criteri estetici,* 172. On this issue, see also Weinberg, *History of Literary Criticism,* 747.
262. Ferraro, *Giudizi critici e criteri estetici,* 106, 167, and passim.
263. *Io. Antonii Viperani De poetica libri tres* (Antwerp, 1579). On Viperano, see Weinberg, *History of Literary Criticism,* 759–65; Vasoli, *L'estetica dell-'umanesimo,* 380; Barilli, *Poetiche e la critica d'arte,* 530–31.
264. Viperano, *De poetica,* 6.
265. Ibid., 6.
266. Ibid., 9.
267. Ibid., 19.
268. Ibid., 46–47.
269. On Patrizi and his system of poetics, see P. M. Arcari, *Il pensiero politico di Francesco Patrizi da Cherso* (Rome, 1935); E. Jacobs, "Francesco Patrizi und seine Sammlung griechischer Handschriften," *Zentralblatt für Bibliothekswesen* 25 (1908): 19–47; B. Brickman, "An Introduction to Francesco Patrizi's Nova de universis philosophia" (Ph.D. diss., Columbia University, New York, 1941); P. I. Kamalic, *F. Patrizi nella cultura e sopratutto nella poetica cinquecentesca* (Freiburg, 1930); L. Firpo, "Filosofia italiana e Controriforma," *Rivista di filosofia* 46 (1950): 150–73, and 47 (1951): 30–47; L. Menapace-Brisca, "La retorica di F. Patrizio o del platonismo antiaristotelico," *Aevum* 26 (1952): 434–61; E. Garin, "Nota su alcuni aspetti delle retoriche rinascimentali e sulla 'Retorica' del Patrizi," *Archivio di filosofia: Testi umanistici sulla retorica* (Rome, 1953), 7–47; T. Gregory, "La 'Apologia ad censuram' di Francesco Patrizi," *Rinascimento* 4 (1953): 89–104; idem, "La 'Apologia' e le 'Declarationes' di Francesco Patrizi," in *Medioevo e Rinascimento: Studi in onore di Bruno Nardi* (Florence, 1954), 1:387–442; R. Scrivano, *Il manierismo nella letteratura del Cinquecento* (Padua, 1959), 55–66; P. Zambelli, "Aneddoti patriziani," *Rinascimento* 7 (1967): 309–18; "F. Patrizi, Emendatio in libros suos Novae philosophiae," ed. P. O. Kristeller, *Rinascimento* 10 (1970): 215–18; G. Cotroneo, *I trattatisti dell'"Ars historica"* (Naples, 1971), 205–67; D. Aguzzi-Barbagli, "Un contributo di Francesco Patrizi alle dottrine rinascimentali sull'amore," *Yearbook of Italian Studies* 2 (1972): 19–50; Barilli, "Francesco Patrizi," in *Poetica e retorica,* 119–44; idem, *Poetiche e la critica d'arte,* 539–41; M. A. del Torre, "Di alcuni problemi della 'Historia' in Francesco Patrizi," *Atti del XXIV Congresso Nazionale di Filosofia* (Rome, 1974), 2:387–95; M. Muccillo, "La storia della filosofia presocratica nelle 'Discussiones Peripateticae' di Francesco Patrizi da Cherso," *La cultura* 13 (1975): 48–105; eadem, "La vita e le opere di Aristotele nelle 'Discussiones Peripateticae' di Francesco Patrizi da Cherso," *Rinascimento* 22 (1981): 53–119; F. Purnell, "Francesco Patrizi and the Critics of Hermes Trismegistus," *Journal of Medieval and Renaissance Studies* 6 (1976): 155–78; P. Rossi, "La negazione delle sfere e l'astrobiologia di Francesco Patrizi," *Il Rinascimento nelle corti padane: Società e cultura* (Bari, 1977), 401–37; S. Cella, "Recenti studi sul Patrizi," *Pagine istriane* 8–9 (1980): 11–22; E. Garin, "Note alla 'Retorica' de Francesco Patrizi da Cherso," in *Umanesimo e Rinascimento:*

Studi offerti a Paul Oskar Kristeller (Florence, 1980), 155–65; L. Bolzoni, "La 'Poetica' di Francesco Patrizi da Cherso: Il progetto di un modello universale della poesia," *Giornale storico della letteratura italiana* 151 (1974): 357–82, continued in 152 (1975): 33–56; eadem, "La poesia e le 'imagini de' sognati' (Una risposta inedita del Patrizi al Cremonini)," *Rinascimento* 19 (1979): 171–88; eadem, *L'universo dei poemi possibili: Studi su Francesco Patrizi* (Rome, 1980); eadem, "Il segretario neoplatonico (F. Patrizi, A. Querenghi, V. Gramigna)," in *Centro Studi Europa delle Corti: La Corte e il "Cortegiano"* (Rome, 1980), 2:133–69; eadem, "Il 'Badoaro' di Francesco Patrizi e l'Accademia Veneziana della Fama," *Giornale storico della letteratura italiana* 158 (1981): 71–101; eadem, "Ercole e i pigmei, ovvero Controriforma e intellettuali neoplatonici," *Rinascimento* 21 (1981): 285–96; eadem, "La 'Poetica' del Patrizi e la cultura veneta del primo Cinquecento," in *L'umanesimo e l'Istria,* ed. V. Branca and S. Graciotti (Florence, 1983), 19–35; C. Vasoli, "Francesco Patrizi e la tradizione ermetica," *Nuova rivista storica* 45 (1980): 25–40; idem, "A proposito di Francesco Patrizi, Gian Giorgio Patrizi, Baldo Lupatino e Flacio Illirico: Alcune precisazioni," in *L'umanesimo e l'Istria,* 37–61; idem, "Francesco Patrizi and the 'Double Rhetoric,'" *New Literary History* 14 (1982–83): 539–51; idem, "Le teorie del Delminio e del Patrizi e i trattatisti d'arte fra '500 e 600," in *Cultura e società nel Rinascimento tra riforme e manierismi,* ed. V. Branca and C. Ossola (Florence, 1984), 249–70. On the poetics of Patrizi, see also Weinberg, *A History of Literary Criticism,* 765–86; Hathaway, *Age of Criticism,* 9–20, 43–45, 48–49, 72–74, 413–20, and passim.

270. For the general problem of music in the culture of the Italian Renaissance, see the fundamental study of P. O. Kristeller, "Music and Learning in the Early Italian Renaissance," *Journal of Renaissance and Baroque Music* 1 (1947): 255–74. For the relation of Patrizi to Renaissance musical humanism, Vincenzo Galilei, and Giovanni de' Bardi, see D. Aguzzi-Barbagli, "Francesco Patrizi e l'umanesimo musicale del Cinquecento," in *L'umanesimo e l'Istria,* 63–90.

271. Gabriele Paleotti, *Discorso intorno alle immagini sacre e profane* (Bologna, 1582): "Sempre la immagine presuppone una cosa anteriore." This remark has been described as indicative of the main position taken at the epistemological level by Paleotti in his treatise on painting. It has been said also that this view on art is analogous to the fundamental approach assumed by Castelvetro. See Barilli, *Poetiche e la critica d'arte,* 559.

272. Francesco Patrizi, *Della poetica,* ed. D. Aguzzi-Barbagli (Florence, 1969–71), 1:8.

273. On Patrizi and his relation with contemporary philosophers see P. O. Kristeller, "Patrizi," in *Eight Philosophers of the Italian Renaissance,* 110–26.

274. Patrizi developed an interest in Platonism at an early age, and, following the advice of a Franciscan friar, he read Ficino's *Platonic Theology.* See Patrizi's autobiographical letter to Baccio Valori in Francesco Patrizi, *Lettere ed opuscoli inediti,* ed. D. Aguzzi-Barbagli (Florence, 1975), 45–51.

275. One of the elements that demonstrates Patrizi's polemical interest in

Aristotle during the earlier part of his activity is his choice to translate almost exclusively Greek authors belonging to the Platonic, Neoplatonic, and even pseudo-Platonic traditions. His *Discussiones paripateticae*, published in 1571 and enlarged in 1581, contain a philosophical critique of Aristotle. In another work he tried to prove that the Aristotelian doctrines are in conflict not only with Plato but also with the Catholic church. See P. O. Kristeller, "Patrizi," 115, 176; and Muccillo, *La vita e le opere di Aristotele*, passim.

276. In 1553 Patrizi published *La città felice*, a short essay in the genre of utopian literature; in this volume he included a *Discorso della diversità de' furori poetici*, devoted to the discussion of the Platonic concept of furor. In the same volume appeared the *Lettura sopra il sonetto del Petrarca: La gola, il sonno e l'ociose piume*, in which the analysis focused upon the power of the language and the structural harmony of the sonnet. The volume containing the poem *Eridano* (1557) includes the prose essay *Sostentamenti del verso eroico*, in which Patrizi explained his invention of a new heroic verse of thirteen syllables and examined various problems related to poetics. In the *Discorso*, published in the volume *Le rime di Messer Luca Contile* (Venice, 1560). Patrizi spoke about themes popular in Neoplatonic speculation, e.g., beauty and love. For Patrizi's discussions of problems of poetics during the earlier period of his activity see Weinberg, *History of Literary Criticism*, 272–73; Bolzoni, *L'universo dei poemi possibili*, 26–52.

277. The original editions of Patrizi's treatises on poetry are *Della poetica di Francesco Patrici la deca istoriale* (Ferrara, 1586); *Della poetica di Francesco Patrici la deca disputata* (Ferrara, 1586). The manuscripts of the posthumous five *deche* remained unknown in the funds of the Biblioteca Palatina of Parma until they were identified by Kristeller in 1949. The recent edition of *Della poetica* by Aguzzi-Barbagli includes the *deche* published by the author and those left in manuscript form. For further information on the composition of Patrizi's treatise, see Patrizi, *Della poetica*, 1:xvi–xxi.

278. Patrizi, *Della poetica*, 2:29; 3:203.

279. Ibid., 2:8–9.

280. Ibid., 2:332.

281. Ibid., 2:174.

282. Ibid., 2:284.

283. Ibid., 2:361.

284. Ibid., 2:365.

285. Ibid., 2:213.

286. Ibid., 3:53.

287. Ibid., 3:228.

288. Bolzoni, *L'universo dei poemi possibili*, 31.

31 ⌘ HUMANISM AND RHETORIC
John Monfasani

ROM ONE PERSPECTIVE THE HISTORY OF RENAISSANCE RHETORIC
is the story of the recovery of classical texts and the integration of
classical rhetoric within contemporary education and practice.[1] By
their own account Renaissance humanists strove to recapture classical
eloquence. They scoffed at medieval Latin, rejected medieval rhetorical
practice, and condemned the dominance of logic in the medieval university arts curriculum.[2] At the same time, they proposed a new educational
program, the *studia humanitatis,* which focused on classical literature
and made rhetoric, not logic, the chief art of discourse.[3] Classical rhetoric
was central to the enterprise because, humanists believed, it held the key
to classical eloquence. As the Spanish humanist Juan Luis Vives explained
when discussing the best authorities in rhetoric:

> But since we do not now have a people speaking Latin or Greek, it
> would be difficult to think up new rules for expression in those lan-
> guages. The old rules will do, along with some universal ones
> drawn from nature and applicable to all languages.[4]

On the other hand, the Renaissance also gave birth to a view of
rhetoric that, despite the humanist credentials of its proponents,
amounted to a denial of the very principles of classical rhetoric. Four-
teenth- and fifteenth-century humanists produced remarkably few *Rhetorics*. Indeed, until the end of the fifteenth century only one large-scale
humanist *Rhetoric* appeared, George of Trebizond's *Rhetoricorum libri
V.*[5] But in the sixteenth century, at the very time that humanist classicism
succeeded in penetrating almost every aspect of European intellectual life
and humanist rhetorical manuals flooded the market, many humanists
rejected the theoretical structure of classical rhetoric and returned to a
medieval understanding of the purposes and content of the art. The
medievalist Étienne Gilson once praised medieval rhetoric for its narrow
pragmatism: "Fortunately, no age was more conscious than was the
Middle Ages of the ends it was pursuing and of the means needed to
attain them. . . . It possessed not only its own eloquence, but also its own
Rhetorics."[6] He could have said the same of much Renaissance rhetoric.

Because humanists were by definition students of classical antiquity, we can hardly speak of a conflict between classicists and modernists. Rather, in the Renaissance, an integralist approach to the classical tradition stood opposed to a pragmatic one. Some humanists believed they could revive the full classical art of rhetoric. Others tried to adapt classical rhetoric to contemporary practices and values. Mutations of either tendency abounded. But despite compromises the tension between classical integralism and contemporary pragmatism became, in the end, the leitmotif of Renaissance rhetoric.

This schizophrenia was in large measure geographic. Simply put, humanism was a natural growth in Italy, but an importation everywhere else. Italian humanists as a group were more consistently integralists in rhetoric than their northern counterparts because an integralist approach better reflected their cultural traditions. So while both Italy and the North participated in the recovery and absorption of classical rhetoric, the pragmatic reworking of that tradition enjoyed its greatest success outside Italy.

In what follows I make no attempt to be comprehensive. There were easily more than a thousand authors in rhetoric in the Renaissance and more than three times that number of treatises.[7] Moreover, the range of subjects and authors in which one could trace the influence of rhetoric is virtually endless. Consequently, because of my own limitations and interests, I shall concentrate on major rhetorical authorities and trends, and give special attention to Latin texts and fifteenth-century Italy.

*   *   *

To understand Renaissance rhetoric we must first look at medieval rhetoric. The Latin Middle Ages had at hand a good stock of classical rhetoric. The major Latin manuals—Cicero's *De inventione,* pseudo-Cicero's *Rhetorica ad Herennium,* and Quintilian's *Institutiones oratoriae* (albeit in an incomplete text)—were generally available after the revival of classical learning in the eleventh century.[8] Furthermore, Cicero's *Topica* and fragmentary versions of his *De oratore* and *Orator* were also known.[9] Some scholars even had access to Cicero's *Partitiones oratoriae.*[10] In the thirteenth century, Greek works of rhetoric were translated, namely, Aristotle's *Rhetoric,* pseudo-Aristotle's *Rhetorica ad Alexandrum,*[11] and Demetrius Phalereus's *De elocutione.*[12] Although the latter two texts hardly circulated, Aristotle's *Rhetoric* enjoyed a wide diffusion. Moreover, medieval readers had access to late antique works that contained much classical rhetoric. They were Victorinus's commentary on Cicero's *De inventione,* part of Grillius's commentary on the same, Martianus Capella's *De nuptiis Philologiae et Mercurii,* Cassiodorus's *Institutiones,* and book 4 of Boethius's *De differentiis topicis*.[13] Indeed, in the eleventh and twelfth centuries, the two classical *Rhetorics* attributed to Cicero (*De inventione* and *Rhetorica ad Herennium*) attracted so much interest that they demonstrably became the objects of study and commentary in the schools of northern and central France.[14]

So the difference between medieval and Renaissance rhetoric had nothing essential to do with the amount of classical rhetoric available. Rather, the difference lay in the view each period took of the use and value of rhetoric. Feudal society had little sympathy for the secular oratorical culture of antiquity and, therefore, limited need of the art that served that oratorical culture and had been a fundamental part of classical education. In the Middle Ages rhetoric suffered a severe demotion. It lost its educational preeminence first to grammar and then, from the thirteenth century on, to logic. Commentaries usually indicate instruction in the schools. So the eleventh- and twelfth-century commentaries on the two *Rhetorics* attributed to Cicero prove that these works were studied in the northern schools. Yet it is symptomatic of medieval interests that though some Ciceronian orations, the *Declamations* of Seneca, and the *Declamations* of pseudo-Quintilian were available, no medieval commentary on them survives.[15] Indeed, most of Cicero's extant orations were ignored in the Middle Ages and had to be discovered in the Renaissance.[16] Even at the height of the twelfth-century classical revival, the leading medieval humanist, John of Salisbury, did not refer to a single Ciceronian oration in his famous defense of "eloquence," the *Metalogicon*,[17] nor, I might add, in his other major works, the *Policraticus* and *Letters*.[18] In the great wave of translation from Greek from the twelfth century on, the only secular Greek oration translated was the pseudo-Isocratean *Ad Demonicum,* and it was viewed as a text in ethics rather than in oratory.[19] In the various educational and encyclopedic schemes produced by medieval scholars, rhetoric consistently received limited attention.[20] After the twelfth century, as the grammatical culture of the cathedral schools gave way to the new university arts curriculum dominated by Aristotelian logic and physics, rhetoric's place in higher learning shrank even further. Commentaries on the Ciceronian *Rhetorics* simply stopped being written in northern Europe.[21] Rhetoric became conspicuous by its absence from the arts requirements of northern universities.[22] The attempt of the eleventh- and twelfth-century northern scholars to teach classical rhetoric in the context of grammatical studies had collapsed before the advance of the scientific curriculum of thirteenth-century scholasticism.

By contrast, the medieval dismemberment of the classical art to meet contemporary needs was a brilliant success. This fragmentation took two guises. One was to use classical rhetoric for essentially nonrhetorical purposes. I have already mentioned the pseudo-Isocratean *Ad Demonicum* serving as a text in ethics. The same happened to Aristotle's *Rhetoric*.[23] Medieval scholars also found Aristotle's *Rhetoric* useful as a text in psychology, since it is the only place in which Aristotle discusses the emotions.[24] In antiquity, rhetorical invention and dialectics shared the argumentative techique of the *topoi*. But in the thirteenth century, as classical rhetoric fell by the wayside, the new logical manuals took over exclusive instruction in *topoi*.[25] To be sure, rhetorical *topoi* continued to contribute to literature. As George Kennedy remarks, "Ernst R. Curtius's important book, *European Literature and the Latin Middle Ages,* can be read as a history of the devices of style and exposition and of the rhetorical topics in which medieval authors exulted."[26] But the fact remains that topical invention as a part of rhetoric had a minuscule place in medieval university education. When topics were taught, they were taught as part of logic, not rhetoric. Mnemonics, the fourth part of classical rhetoric, took on independent life in works that drew on the classical rhetorical manuals for most of their contents but had little or nothing to do with rhetoric in purpose or inspiration.[27] However, it was the second part of classical rhetoric, style, that proved the most vitally useful. In fact, the Middle Ages especially conceived of the classical art in terms of style, viewing rhetoric as a source of prose and verse *colores* and *exornationes*. The precepts on tropes, figures, and rhythms in the classical manuals were exploited for this purpose by the medieval rhetorical manuals, in particular, by the manuals on the art of writing verse (*ars poetriae*),[28] by those on the art of preaching (*ars praedicandi*),[29] and by those on the most diffused form of formal rhetoric in the Middle Ages, the art of letter writing (*ars dictaminis*).[30] These medieval *Rhetorics* appropriated or adapted other rules and divisions of classical rhetoric, including instruction on invention. But in cannibalizing the classical art, they replaced it. Like Humpty Dumpty, classical rhetoric had suffered a great fall. So the initial goal of the humanists was to put all the pieces together again.

*   *   *

Renaissance humanism began in Italy, and, as far as rhetoric was concerned, Italian humanists generally remained faithful to their initial inspiration. And well they might, for the origins of humanism are intimately connected with Italian medieval rhetoric. In a seminal essay published in 1945, Paul Oskar Kristeller explained the relationship:

> The [early Italian] humanists were not classical scholars who for
> personal reasons had a craving for eloquence, but, vice versa, they

were professional rhetoricians, heirs and successors of the medieval rhetoricians, who developed the belief, then new and modern, that the best way to achieve eloquence was to imitate classical models, and who thus were driven to study the classics and to found classical philology. . . . The humanistic movement did not originate in the field of philosophical or scientific studies, but it arose in that of grammatical and rhetorical studies. The humanists continued the medieval tradition in these fields . . . but they gave [them] a new direction toward classical standards and classical studies, possibly under the impact of influences received from France after the middle of the thirteenth century.[31]

The medieval rhetorical tradition from which the Renaissance humanists emerged was that of the *ars dictaminis*. Whereas most of the known pre-thirteenth-century medieval commentaries on the Ciceronian *Rhetorics* emanated from northern Europe,[32] the narrow and intensely practical art of letter writing (primarily public letters) was exclusively the creation of Italy in the eleventh century.[33] The urban setting and the continuation of certain classical traditions, such as instruction in law and a linkage of law and rhetoric,[34] created in Italy needs and interests not immediately felt in the rest of Europe. By the middle of the thirteenth century the *ars dictaminis* became a staple in the arts curriculum of the Italian universities.[35] The lawyers and the notaries who studied *dictamen*, along with the *dictatores* and grammarians who taught it, constituted a large class of educated laymen professionally interested in the cultivation of eloquence. Not by chance, early Italian prose and poetry had close ties to the notarial and legal professions of medieval Italy.[36] Matteo de' Libri's thirteenth-century *Summa dictaminis* piquantly illustrates the continuity between medieval *dictamen* and Renaissance humanism by providing its readers with examples of *consolatoria* and *invectiva*, two favorite rhetorical genres of the humanists.[37] What was missing in Libri's work was a humanist's dedication to classical models. In the twelfth century, however, French grammarians took up *dictamen* and characteristically tried to incorporate into the art more classical lore than was usual in the Italian manuals.[38] The cross-pollination of Italian and French traditions of *dictamen* is a field that merits exploration, but it is at least clear that in the course of the thirteenth century, as the classical element receded in French grammatical instruction, Italian *dictatores* and grammarians became increasingly receptive to classical influences. By the fourteenth century, Italian grammarians at the University of Bologna such as Giovanni del Buonandrea and his student Bartolino de Benincasa were not only prime students of twelfth-century French commentaries on

Cicero's *Rhetoric,* but seemingly also the only people writing new commentaries on the *Rhetorics.*[39] Fourteenth-century Bolognese teachers of *dictamen* such as Giovanni del Virgilio, who corresponded with Dante, and Pietro da Moglia ("Pietro della Retorica"), the teacher of Coluccio Salutati, also made a career of lecturing on classical authors.[40] For this pattern of jurists and notaries pursuing classical studies, we may quote Roberto Weiss's classic essay of 1947, *The Dawn of Humanism in Italy:*

> It has just been suggested that lawyers had a large part in the launching of humanist activities. Let us then turn to the biographies of early humanists for confirmation. Padua: Lovato dei Lovati, Geremia da Montagnone, Rolando da Piazzola were judges while Albertino Mussato was a notary. Venice: in that town humanism started in the Ducal chancery, and all its leading exponents were notaries. Verona: Benzo d'Alessandria was a notary. Guglielmo da Pastrengo who continued his tradition was a jurist. . . . Florence: Geri d'Arezzo and Francesco da Barberino were both doctors of civil law. Naples: Paolo da Perugia and Barbato da Sulmona were both notaries, and the former was also well known for his legal studies.[41]

By the late thirteenth century the Italian rhetorical tradition had entered its "prehumanistic" stage, combining a professional concern for eloquence with a growing interest in classical literature. Petrarch (1304–1374), the son of a notary and once a student of law at Bologna, was the first brilliant exponent of this new Italian classicism.[42] Petrarch raised the humanist movement to a level of self-consciousness it might not otherwise have possessed by the mid-fourteenth century, but he was hardly the unique creator of the movement.

Medieval Italy possessed still another special characteristic in respect to rhetoric. As Alfredo Galletti and Paul Oskar Kristeller have pointed out,[43] from at least the eleventh century the Italian cities maintained a lively tradition of secular oratory. In the early thirteenth century, a leading *dictator,* Boncompagno of Signa, gave over one chapter of his *Rhetorica novissima* to speeches in public assemblies (*contiones*). Boncompagno condemned the *contionandi officium* as beneath the dignity of the educated, but admitted that "the practice of speechmaking thrives in the towns and hamlets of Italy because of excessive liberty."[44] Nonetheless, one generation later, the most important Italian *dictator,* Guido Faba, composed not only model letters, but also model speeches.[45] Again, in the mid-thirteenth century, the transplanted northern scholar Jacques de Dinant wrote at Bologna an *ars arengandi* that was a synopsis of the

Rhetorica ad Herennium, especially apropos delivery.[46] Jacques obviously saw the "art of haranguing" as something needed by his Italian pupils—rightly so, since we have various collections of vernacular and Latin *aringhe* from the Italian Middle Ages.[47] Medieval Italy produced a substantial literature of speeches at marriages, funerals, academic occasions, ambassadorial visits, political assemblies, judicial proceedings, and various other functions and ceremonies of public officials. The reason that Italian humanists grasped the oratorical nature of rhetorical instruction and remained so faithful to that conception of the art is that the traditions of their society prompted such an approach. Of the fourteenth-century prehumanists, Rolando da Piazzola was famous for his oratory,[48] and even Petrarch has left us a small corpus of orations.[49]

Whereas northern scholasticism had overwhelmed the earlier medieval French combination of grammar and classical study, Italian classicism closely tied to rhetorical concerns eventually transformed European culture. But it would be a mistake to connect virtually everything produced by humanists to a rhetorical impulse. The *studia humanitatis* contained more than rhetoric, and the humanists were more than rhetoricians.[50] Though collectively sharing an interest in rhetoric, individual humanists were moved by a great range of different interests.[51] In what follows I shall not attempt to trace rhetorical influences in every nook and cranny of the humanist enterprise, but focus on the humanists' technical writings.

*   *   *

One of the first feats of Italian humanism was the recovery of the extant classical Latin texts in oratory, epistolography, and rhetoric. Indeed, the Italians had essentially completed the task by 1430. The recovery of the Greek rhetorical tradition, by contrast, took much longer, and in the end owed as much to the work of transalpine humanists as it did to Italian scholarship.[52]

Petrarch inaugurated the Renaissance revival of classical rhetoric at Liège in 1333 when he discovered Cicero's oration *pro Archia*.[53] Fittingly, *pro Archia* was also Petrarch's first classical find. In 1350 Petrarch received from Lapo da Castiglionchio another four Ciceronian orations he had not known previously.[54] By the end of the fourteenth century anonymous scholars had unearthed yet two more orations of Cicero (*pro Quinctio* and *pro Flacco*).[55] In 1407 Leonardo Bruni uncovered six orations of Cicero;[56] and then between 1415 and 1417, while searching in northern Europe, Poggio Bracciolini discovered yet ten more.[57] In the 1420s Cicero's *Oratio pro Fonteio* also came to light, probably by the efforts of Cardinal Giordano Orsini.[58] Thus, as Sabbadini noted,[59] when

Giovanni Andrea Bussi published the first edition of the Ciceronian orations in 1471, he was able to bring together all but one of the extant Ciceronian orations. Apart from Cicero, the other major Latin oratorical finds in the Renaissance were the discovery of the *XII Panegyrici latini*, including Pliny the Younger's, by Giovanni Aurispa at Mainz in 1433,[60] and the unearthing of Seneca the Elder's *Suasoriae et controversiae*, apparently by Nicholas of Cusa, in the first half of the fifteenth century.[61]

Petrarch also stands at the start of the recovery of classical epistolography. In 1345 Petrarch discovered in the chapter library of Verona three collections of Cicero's letters: *ad Atticum* in sixteen books, *ad Brutum* in two books, and *ad Quinctum fratrem* in one book.[62] In the last decade of the fourteenth century all sixteen books of Cicero's other extant collection, *ad familiares,* were discovered in a manuscript at Vercelli; we know of one copy made for Coluccio Salutati.[63] The letters of Sidonius Apollinaris and Symmachus were certainly available by the early fourteenth century.[64] But Pliny the Younger's letters were only known in a collection of a hundred letters until a corpus of eight books of his letters was shown to Guarino of Verona at Verona in 1419.[65] Some eighty years later at Paris, the Franciscan friar Gioconda of Verona discovered the extant ten books of Pliny's letters.[66] Seneca's moral epistles as well as the letters of church fathers such as Augustine, Jerome, and Ambrose had circulated widely in the Middle Ages.

Poggio Bracciolini began the recovery of Latin rhetorical texts in 1416 when he discovered at the monastery of St. Gall in Switzerland Asconius Pedianus's commentary on five Ciceronian orations and a complete text of Quintilian's *Institutiones oratoriae.*[67] Cicero's *De optimo genere oratorum* (the preface to his lost translation of Demosthenes's *On the Crown*), a work almost unknown to the Middle Ages and never mentioned by Petrarch,[68] seems to have become generally available in Italy in the first decades of the fifteenth century.[69] Then, in 1421, Bishop Gerardo Landriani of Lodi found in the library of his own cathedral a manuscript containing Cicero's *Brutus* as well as the complete text of the *De oratore* and *Orator.*[70] With Landriani's find, all the extant rhetorical works of Cicero had been discovered. In 1421 or earlier Niccolò Niccoli gained possession of the text of three *rhetores Latini minores,* namely, Rutilius Lupus's *Schemata lexeos,* Aquila Romanus's *De figuris sententiarum et elocutionis,* and Priscian's *Praeexercitamenta.*[71] The last was a translation of Hermogenes's *Progymnasmata* and may have had some circulation in the Middle Ages;[72] the first two opuscules, however, were true finds and were not even printed until 1519. As late as 1433 humanists were treating new manuscripts of Chirius Consultus Fortunatianus's *Ars rhetorica* as something of a find, though the text had been known to

Petrarch and was used by George of Trebizond in his *Rhetoric*, published in 1433–34.[73] Thereafter the only new Latin rhetorical sources added by the humanists were Tacitus's *Dialogus de oratoribus*, which Enoch of Ascoli brought to Rome in 1455,[74] and three *rhetores Latini minores:* Iulius Severianus, whose *Praecepta artis rhetoricae* came to light in Italy sometime before 1462 but was not printed before 1556,[75] and Iulius Rufinianus and Sulpicius Victor, both of whom were discovered in a now lost manuscript by Beatus Rhenanus and printed by him in 1521.[76]

The Renaissance recovery of the Greek rhetorical tradition was a more complex affair. Italian humanists craved the oratory found in Greek sources and eagerly sought it in unusual places. For instance, Leonardo Bruni translated the speeches of Odysseus, Achilles, and Phoenix in book 9 of the *Iliad*.[77] Italian humanists made a cottage industry of excerpting in translation the historian Dio Cassio as a source of Greek eloquence: Battista Guarino rendered Mark Antony's speech over Caesar; Giovanni Aurispa, Philiscus's speech to Cicero; and Lauro Quirini and Andreas Brentius, the speeches of Julius Caesar.[78] What is even more bizarre, fifteenth-century humanists made a best seller of a set of purported orations of Aeschines, Demades, and Demosthenes forged by one of their own.[79]

Greek texts had not only to be translated, but also obtained and edited. By the early sixteenth century Italian humanists and émigré Greek scholars had brought to Italy and edited almost all of the known classical Greek rhetorical texts. So at least in this sense the recovery of the classical Greek rhetorical tradition was primarily the achievement of fifteenth- and early sixteenth-century Italy. Yet fifteenth-century Italians proved highly selective in their appreciation of Greek oratory. They chose to disseminate by translation only a relatively small part of the rich cache of Greek texts to which they had access. As a result, much of classical Greek rhetoric, oratory, and epistolography became available in Latin for the first time only in the sixteenth century.

Demosthenes is a case in point. By the early 1420s, Leonardo Bruni had rendered into Latin seven orations (*On the Crown, Philippics* 1–4, *On the Peace,* and *On the Chersonese*) along with Aeschines's *On the Crown* and, as a historical companion piece, Philip of Macedon's letter to the Athenians.[80] If we view *On the Crown* as a political speech, though delivered before a jury, then Bruni had created a Latin corpus of exclusively political speeches of Demosthenes. In the 1440s Rinuccio Aretino translated four other political orations (*Olynthiac* 1–3, *On Philip's Letter*) and even added a rendering of the decrees in Demosthenes's *On the Crown* which Bruni had omitted.[81] In 1470, to arouse the princes of Italy to the Turkish threat, Cardinal Bessarion retranslated the first

Olynthiac.[82] No doubt translations of other Demosthenean orations were made in the Quattrocento of which I am ignorant, but they could not have had wide diffusion. Indeed, even Rinuccio Aretino's translation of *Olynthiac* 1–3 no longer survives. Quattrocento Italians systematically ignored Demosthenes's numerous forensic orations. What is equally revealing is that between 1400 and the early sixteenth century at least six different scholars prepared translations of *On the Crown,* and a seventh, Theodore Gaza, demonstrably lectured on the text.[83] Lack of interest, not resources or ability, dictated the fifteenth-century concentration on Demosthenes's political speeches and most especially on the masterpiece Cicero himself had once translated, the *Oration on the Crown.* The early humanists simply were not as interested in studying or imitating the other items in Demosthenes's *oeuvre.* In 1504, Aldo Manuzio in Venice published Demosthenes's complete works. Henceforth the Greek text of all the orations as well as the letters were easily available. In the course of the sixteenth century, well-known northern humanists such as Philipp Melanchthon, Joachim Camerarius, Christopher Hegendorff, and Johann Lonicer, joined the Italians in translating Demosthenes.[84] Nonetheless, not until 1549 were all of Demosthenes's orations gathered together in a single Latin corpus translated by the German scholar Jerome Wolf.[85]

Isocrates's Renaissance *fortuna* was similar to that of Demosthenes. The first half of the fifteenth century saw a great rush of translation. But Italians concentrated on a few favorites (for instance, there were six versions of *Ad Demonicum* and four of *Ad Nicoclem*), and left the bulk of the Isocratean corpus to be translated in the next century.[86] Yet, even after the first edition of the orations edited by the Greek scholar Marcus Musurus for the Aldine Press appeared in 1513, we find the same group of moralizing orations by Isocrates retranslated and reprinted time and time again.[87] Isocrates's moral sententiousness as well as his pure style made him a favorite of schoolmasters.[88] All the Isocratean orations were translated into Latin for the first time in 1528 by the German humanist Johann Lonicer, and then again in 1548 by Jerome Wolf.[89]

The other Greek orators experienced nothing like the popularity of Demosthenes and Isocrates. In the fifteenth century Francesco Filelfo translated two orations by Lysias and two by Dio Chrysostom.[90] Leonardo Bruni wrote a celebrated imitation of Aelius Aristides's Panathenaic oration.[91] Niccolò Perotti translated Aristides's speech on the earthquake at Smyrna and Libanius's eulogy of Julian the Apostate.[92] Other Quattrocento humanists also contributed translations of Aristides, Libanius, Lysias, and Dio Chrysostom, but these translations reflected no broad interest in the particular orators, nor did they achieve any notable popularity.[93] The sixteenth century brought no radical change in the pattern. Probably as an exercise in Greek, Erasmus made a translation of three orations of Libanius. His translation was reprinted a number of times.[94] Yet even after the edition of the Greek text of Libanius in 1517 by the émigré Greek Soterianus Capsalis, Erasmus's translation of Libanius inspired few imitators.[95] In 1515 Aldo Manuzio issued in three volumes his edition of the Greek orators (including Aeschines, Antiphon, Aristides, Gorgias, Isaeus, Isocrates, and Lysias, but not Dio Chrysostom),[96] but only very gradually was this corpus translated into Latin in the course of the next hundred years.[97]

In favoring Demosthenes and Isocrates humanists were spontaneously following Byzantine school tradition. But their interest in Greek oratory did not extend to medieval Greek oratory. The only substantial body of Byzantine oratory translated in the fifteenth century were the orations of Cardinal Bessarion, and he himself, along with his protégé, Niccolò Perotti, made these translations.[98] In the next century, speeches of some other Byzantine authors were printed and even translated, but the primary motive in these instances seems to have been religious, scientific, or historical rather than rhetorical.[99] The irony, of course, is that with its classicism and concentration on declamation and epideictic prose, Byzantine oratory bore a remarkable resemblance to the oratory Renaissance humanists themselves practiced.[100]

Neither did the humanists have much interest in Byzantine rhetorical manuals and commentaries, despite the patent classicism of these texts. No Renaissance scholar bothered to translate any of the medieval commentaries on Hermogenes which the Byzantine émigré Demetrius Ducas had included in his great edition of the *Rhetores graeci* published by the Aldine press in 1508–9.[101] And very few other Byzantine rhetorical texts were edited, let alone translated, in the Renaissance.[102]

More surprisingly, only gradually and under prodding from their Greek teachers did humanists begin to accept even the specifically classical textbooks of rhetoric preserved by the Byzantine tradition. Hermogenes, the mainstay of the Byzantine rhetorical tradition, did have his doctrines disseminated in the fifteenth century, but, as we shall see, this diffusion was almost exclusively due to the fact that George of Trebizond incorporated so much of Hermogenes into his own *Rhetoric*. The other major classical authors of the Byzantine tradition—Aphthonius, Aristotle, Demetrius Phalareus, Dionysius of Halicarnassus, pseudo-Longinus, and Theon—had relatively little influence in the Quattrocento; and of these only Aphthonius (whose rhetorical exercises, the *Progymnasmata*, were translated by Rudolf Agricola and Giovanni Maria Cattaneo)[103] and Aristotle enjoyed great success in the sixteenth century. Theodore Gaza had translated several chapters of Dionysius of

Halicarnassus's *Techne* in the 1440s, but the first Latin edition containing the full *Techne* and the critical essays did not appear until the *opera omnia* of 1586.[104] Hermogenes took on a second life in the sixteenth century because of enthusiasm for him on the part of Johann Sturm and a few other scholars,[105] but he never came near displacing Cicero and Quintilian as the central rhetorical authorities of the Renaissance; and the further one recedes from the sixteenth century, the less evidence one has of the study of Hermogenes in the schools.[106] The opposite, however, is true of some other rhetorical texts preserved by the Byzantine tradition, specifically Aristotle's *Rhetoric* and *Poetics*, Demetrius Phalareus's *De elocutione*, and pseudo-Longinus's *On the Sublime*. Initially, in receiving these texts, the Latins also absorbed a Byzantine perception of their value. As a result, the Renaissance had to rediscover these texts twice: first by receiving them from the Byzantine tradition in the fifteenth century, and then by looking at them again with fresh eyes in the sixteenth.

In the Latin Middle Ages, Aristotle's *Rhetoric* had almost ceased to function as a textbook in rhetorical education, and his *Poetics* was barely known.[107] For the Byzantines, though, both works were rhetorical texts, but of a rather minor sort.[108] In the first half of the fifteenth century Leonardo Bruni claimed Aristotle for the humanists by retranslating Aristotle's *Politics, Nicomachean Ethics,* and *Economics,* as well as integrating Aristotelian principles into his own writings.[109] Yet he did not translate the *Rhetoric* and probably did not even have a Greek manuscript of the *Poetics*.[110] The first Renaissance translation of the *Rhetoric* was that of George of Trebizond in the mid-1440s. But even Trebizond in his preface treated the work as primarily a text in psychology; and Trebizond's own *Rhetoric* owed relatively little to Aristotle's *Rhetoric*.[111] In 1478 Ermolao Barbaro the Younger made a new translation of the *Rhetoric*, but it was not printed until 1544.[112] So Trebizond's remained the only widely diffused humanist translation in the fifteenth century. (George's contemporary, Francesco Filelfo, made a new rendering of the pseudo-Aristotelian *Rhetorica ad Alexandrum*.) At the end of the fifteenth century the first Renaissance translator of the *Poetics*, Giorgio Valla, disregarded Aristotle's work in his own *Poetics*.[113] When Aldo Manuzio published the first edition of the Greek text of Aristotle's work in 1495–98, he left out both the *Rhetoric* and the *Poetics*. Instead these works appeared as two lesser items in the massive Aldine edition of the *Rhetores graeci* 1508–9, which was a publication dominated by the chief authorities of the Byzantine rhetorical tradition,[114] namely Hermogenes of Tarsus and his commentators. However, during the sixteenth century both the *Rhetoric* and the *Poetics* began to occupy a central place in their respective spheres.[115] Eight new translations of the *Rhetoric* and six humanist commentaries and paraphrases appeared before 1600.[116] Aristotle became commonly cited in the rhetorical textbooks, and one standard Jesuit manual, Cyprianus Soarez's *De arte rhetorica libri tres ex Aristotele, Cicerone, et Quintiliano,* made this fact clear by its very title.[117]

Demetrius Phalareus's *De elocutione* has a similar history.[118] First edited in the Aldine *Rhetores graeci* of 1508–9, this work was first printed in 1540 in the translation made by Marcantonio Antimacho. Thereafter it enjoyed a fairly regular run of editions, translations, and commentaries. Eventually Demetrius, a minor authority in Byzantium, was far more popular in the Latin West than the Byzantine mainstay, Hermogenes.

Finally, the sixteenth century began the "discovery" of pseudo-Longinus's *On the Sublime,* which the Byzantines had ignored and which did not even enter the Aldine *Rhetores graeci.* Francesco Robortello edited the Greek text in 1554, and two translations followed in the next twenty years. But not until long after, in the wake of Nicolas Boileau's translation and commentary of 1674 and 1693, did *On the Sublime* become "one of the central texts in literary theory and criticism."[119]

Greek letter collections attracted early attention in the Renaissance.[120] In the first half of the Quattrocento Rinuccio Aretino translated a whole group of Greek epistolographers: pseudo-Brutus, pseudo-Hippocrates, and individual letters attributed to Diogenes Pythagoricus and Euripides.[121] Theodore Gaza subsequently retranslated pseudo-Brutus.[122] Francesco Griffolini made a popular rendering of pseudo-Phalaris; and the Greek monk Athanasius Chalkeopoulus added a translation of pseudo-Crates.[123] In the 1470s Francesco Zambeccari translated 109 authentic letters of Libanius and then, *mirabile dictu,* forged another 430 letters to make a corpus of 539 Libanian letters in Latin.[124] Francesco Filelfo translated some letters of pseudo-Diogenes and Apollonius of Tyana,[125] while his younger contemporary Antonio Bonfini rendered the letters of Philostratus.[126] Both Leonardo Bruni and Marsilio Ficino translated Plato's letters.[127] Hence, a very representative number of Greek letter collections had already been translated when the Greek émigré Marcus Musurus edited his famous corpus of Greek epistolographers for the Aldine press in 1499.[128] In the sixteenth century, after various scholars had translated other individual Greek epistolographers, such as Synesius in 1559 and Aelian in 1556,[129] the French humanist Jacques Cujas (1522–1590) brought the process to culmination by reediting and translating the whole Musuran corpus of epistolographers in an edition that appeared posthumuously in 1606.[130]

Because Julius Victor's *Rhetoric,* which contains a chapter *De epistolis,* was not discovered until the eighteenth century, the only classical manuals in epistolography available in the Renaissance were four Greek works.[131] I know of no major use of these Greek texts in a fifteenth-century manual, but in the first half of the sixteenth century, in his extraordinarily popular *De conscribendis epistolis,* Erasmus did draw upon pseudo-Demetrius's *typi epistolarii,* a fact that seems to have escaped the attention of Erasmus's modern editor.[132] But despite Erasmus's use of pseudo-Demetrius, Latins were slow in translating the Greek epistolographic manuals. We have seen that Demetrius Phalareus's *De elocutione,* which contains a section on letter-writing, first appeared in Latin dress in 1540. Subsequently, the epistolographic section was excerpted by a number of translators.[133] Earlier, in 1501, Pontico Virunio had edited pseudo-Libanius's *Characteres epistolici,* but his translation was published only posthumously in 1525.[134] At least three other Latin versions followed by 1557, none of which achieved any notable diffusion.[135] Johann Hartung published an edition and translation of the pseudo-Proclean recension of the same work in 1548; four years later Ioannes Sambucus edited an expanded version with translation, which was combined with the epistolographic section of Demetrius's *De elocutione* in later printings.[136] Pseudo-Demetrius's *Typi epistolarii* made its appearance as early as the Aldine Greek epistolographers of 1499, but was not translated until Sambucus joined it to his version of pseudo-Libanius in 1552.[137] So in the second half of the sixteenth century Greek epistolographic manuals did enjoy a certain currency. Except for Demetrius's *De elocutione,* however, interest in these Greek manuals seems to have died out after about 1630.[138]

Finally, we need to note the diffusion of Greek patristic oratory in the Renaissance. The Latin Middle Ages had access to some Greek patristic oratory, such as the sermons of St. Gregory Nazianzus and St. John Chrysostom. But in the fifteenth century Ambrogio Traversari, George of Trebizond, and others began what would become in the Reformation an avalanche of patristic translations and editions.[139] By the middle of the century, all the orations of Sts. Basil, Gregory Nazianzus, Gregory of Nyssa, and John Chrysostom, to mention just the most important patristic preachers, were available in Latin *opera omnia* as well as in translations of individual sermons and series of sermons.[140] Recent scholarship has shown how secular rhetorical theory affected preaching in the Renaissance.[141] What is now needed is an examination of the ways and the extent to which Latin as well as Greek patristic models influenced contemporary sacred and even secular oratory.[142]

*   *   *

Despite the ever-increasing flood of new classical sources, fifteenth-century humanist rhetoric was, in a way, a conservative movement. The social functions of Italian humanists in the schools and chanceries corresponded to those of thirteenth- and fourteenth-century Italian rhetoricians.[143] Humanist oratory flourished in genres already practiced in medieval Italy.[144] And by treating the *Rhetorica ad Herennium* as the prime text of rhetorical instruction, Quattrocento humanists also maintained a school tradition that in Italy went back to at least the late thirteenth century.[145] In the first decades of the fifteenth century, the influential humanist teacher Gasparino Barzizza lectured on the *Rhetorica ad Herennium* at Padua and Pavia and even utilized for the task earlier commentators such as Bartolino de Benincasa.[146] We have from the 1430s George of Trebizond's complaint against contemporary teachers of rhetoric who still depended on Bartolino and even the older commentary of Alain.[147] One of the most famous humanist teachers, Guarino of Verona, sedulously kept the *Rhetorica ad Herennium* as the mainstay of rhetorical instruction at his school in Ferrara, and his son Battista seems to have continued the practice well into the second half of the century.[148] George of Trebizond, who himself had written a larger and in many ways better *Rhetoric,* lectured on the *Rhetorica ad Herennium* at Rome in the 1460s.[149] Even doubts at the end of the century about the Ciceronian paternity of the *Rhetorica ad Herennium* did not change this pattern. In a *quaestio* of 1491, Raffaele Regio rejected the Ciceronian authorship of the work.[150] But even though Regio implied (wrongly, I believe) that Lorenzo Valla (d. 1457) had once held the same position and even though in the 1460s Angelo Decembrio had warmly defended its Ciceronian paternity, it cannot be said that Regio was riding a wave of suspicion.[151] Just the year before, Girolamo Capiduro had published the massive lecture notes on the *Rhetorica ad Herennium* of his teacher Giorgio Valla, which gave no hint of any difficulty with the attribution.[152] In 1493, two years after Regio's attack, another humanist teacher, Antonio Mancinelli, vigorously defended Cicero's authorship when he published a commentary on the first book of the *Rhetorica ad Herennium*.[153] In 1496 Francesco Maturazzo published a commentary on the whole work, and simply ignored Regio's theory.[154] Although leading sixteenth-century scholars such as Piero Vettori and Adrien Turnèbe denied the Ciceronian attribution,[155] if the number of printings and commentaries listed by John O. Ward is any indication, the popularity of the *Rhetorica ad Herennium* in Italian and transalpine schools continued unabated to the end of the sixteenth century.[156]

In respect to Cicero's authentic rhetorical writings, we have a good deal of evidence for the continued study in and outside of Italy of *De inventione* and Victorinus's commentary on it.[157] As for *De oratore,* even before the discovery of a complete copy in 1421, Gasparino Barzizza had already heavily glossed it.[158] Though not suited to be a school text, *De oratore* was reproduced in a large number of manuscripts and early printed editions.[159] The Quattrocento historian Flavio Biondo viewed its discovery as the doctrinal and inspirational turning point in the reemergence of classical eloquence.[160] Indeed, he excused Petrarch's stylistic weaknesses because he lacked this and other Ciceronian texts.[161] In a sense, Lorenzo Valla's grandiose claims for rhetoric in the mid-Quattrocento and Mario Nizolio's reassertions of the same claims in the next century are the logical culminations of Cicero's description of the orator in *De oratore* as the true universal man.[162] In the second half of the fifteenth century Ognibene Leoniceno wrote what seems to have been the first of a series of full-scale Renaissance commentaries on *De oratore.*[163] For Cicero's other rhetorical writings, Giorgio Valla commented on the *Topica,*[164] while Vittore Pisano published a commentary on the *Orator* in 1492.[165] The *Partitiones oratoriae,* however, seems never to have achieved in Italy the success as a school text that it would eventually enjoy in northern Europe under the influence of Johann Sturm.[166]

Cicero's one rival as the chief teacher of classical rhetoric was Quintilian. In the Renaissance as today, the *Institutiones oratoriae* was the single most comprehensive authority on the classical art. But its massive size and the intention of its author never suited it as a text for young students. Teachers, however, found it invaluable. In 1428, hardly more than a decade after Poggio Bracciolini discovered a complete *Institutiones,* Lorenzo Valla shook the Ciceronian bias of his fellow humanists by asserting Quintilian's superiority as an authority on style and rhetoric.[167] A few years later George of Trebizond wrote a new summa of classical rhetoric to supplant Quintilian's, but even he willy-nilly found himself borrowing from the Roman schoolmaster.[168] Fifteenth-century manuscripts and early printed editions of Quintilian abound.[169] Lorenzo Valla incorporated verbatim whole sections of the *Institutiones* into his *Dialectica.*[170] Well-known Quattrocento humanists such as Giovanni Andrea Bussi, Giovanni Antonio Campano, Angelo Poliziano, and Raffaele Regio edited the *Institutiones,* while Lorenzo Valla, Pomponio Leto, and Raffaele Regio glossed it; in the sixteenth century a plethora of commentators and editors elucidated the text.[171] One regularly finds borrowings from Quintilian in sixteenth-century rhetorical manuals; and when Petrus Ramus attempted to set rhetoric on a new basis, he fittingly refuted not only Cicero, but also Quintilian as the second pillar of the classical tradition.[172]

Because of such authority Quattrocento humanists produced few

Rhetorics of their own. Indeed, by their own principles, where better could they find the rules of classical eloquence than in the classical manuals? As a consequence, they tried not to supplant Cicero or Quintilian, but rather to write various kinds of epitomes of the classical art or to do original work in areas in which the classical tradition was not rich, namely, in commentaries or in the field of letter writing. The first two important Renaissance authorities in rhetoric, Gasparino Barzizza and Antonio Loschi, illustrate these developments.

Petrarch wrote no work of technical rhetoric, and as early as the first decade of the fifteenth century humanists had rejected him as a model of style.[173] Thus, the honor of being the first great humanist master of rhetoric fell to a much younger man, Gasparino Barzizza, schoolteacher at Pavia, Padua, and Milan in the last decade of the fourteenth century and the first three decades of the fifteenth century. Apart from his school lectures on the *Rhetorica ad Herennium* and annotations on *De oratore,* there have survived three important rhetorical pieces from Barzizza's pen. At the start of his treatise *De compositione,* Barzizza explained that *compositio,* that is, the stylistic placement of words, was an essential part of every *perfecta elocutio.* Drawing his precepts from Cicero, Quintilian, and Martianus Capella, Barzizza tried to bring contemporary *compositio* in line with classical standards.[174] Even more important was Barzizza's collection, *Epistolae ad exercitationem accommodatae,* set in ancient Rome. Barzizza inculcated classical epistolography by having students read fictive letters supposedly exchanged by classical figures.[175] Likewise, Barzizza's equally successful *Exampla exordiorum* was set in antiquity and offered the student a rich store of elegant openings for letters and speeches that would cover a very wide range of situations (for example, *de rebus quae pertinent ad rem publicam, de novis, de divitiis,* and so on) and which drew also on classical examples (such as Cicero's *Oratio pro Q. Ligario* for an example of *insinuatio*).[176] Contemporary and later humanist commentators unanimously praised the elegance of Barzizza's style and attributed to him the first effective teaching of Ciceronian style in the Renaissance. A modern scholar, Remigio Sabbadini, has remarked on the superior elegance and correctness of Barzizza's Latin in *De compositione* when compared even to Valla's in the *Elegantiae.*[177] Apropos Barzizza's model letters, Sabbadini has this to say: "All in all they have a correctness, a scrupulousness [in imitating Ciceronian style] of which one encounters no examples before Barzizza and very few after him until one reaches Paolo Cortesi [1465–1510]."[178] Barzizza earned the epithet Sabbadini applied to him: "primo apostolo" of Renaissance Ciceronianism.

Ciceronianism had unequivocally taken hold in northern Italy by the

1420s. Although by his own practice and precepts Barzizza was not a rigid Ciceronian if we define a rigid Ciceronian as someone unwilling to use any word or phrase not sanctioned by Cicero,[179] he did once recommend Cicero as the unique model of imitation.[180] In 1426, four years before Barzizza's death, the young George of Trebizond, while teaching in Vicenza, advised a student to adapt the *sententiae* extracted from Cicero and Aristotle to the *verba Ciceronis*.[181] But like Barzizza, George of Trebizond was not a rigid Ciceronian. In the cited passage, instead of advocating Cicero as the sole model of imitation, he was arguing against a method of imitation that indiscriminately mixed styles by stringing together tacit quotations from different authors. He himself did not hesitate to use non-Ciceronian terms when the need arose.[182] And even though he considered Cicero the supreme prose stylist, he still proposed Livy as the model of historical prose.[183]

In the Renaissance, the close study of classical oratory became an essential part of rhetorical education. The man who began this development was young Antonio Loschi in Pavia. Between 1392 and 1396, a decade before Poggio Bracciolini discovered Asconius's commentary on Cicero's orations, Loschi published his *Inquisitio super XI orationes Ciceronis*.[184] Loschi's work was significant not only because he had made classical orations the object of commentary for the first time since antiquity (Barzizza was so impressed by Loschi's achievement that he himself began to lecture on Cicero's orations at Padua),[185] but also because he had done so strictly in terms of classical rhetorical categories. In comparison, Asconius Pedianus's commentary is strictly grammatical and historical. Loschi believed that classical oratory embodied the precepts found in the classical manuals of rhetoric and that an analysis which utilized the categories of the manuals would reveal the wellsprings of Ciceronian eloquence. Consequently, in addition to explaining the historical setting (*argumentum*), style, and arguments of the eleven orations, he also analyzed the *causae genus, constitutiones,* and *dispositio* that each oration contained. For Loschi such an analysis was not an exercise in antiquarianism, but an eminently practical way to grasp and teach classical eloquence. Illustrating the fact that the humanists were the successors of the medieval Italian *dictatores,* Loschi later in his career wrote a new formulary for the papal chancery.[186]

In the mid-Quattrocento Flavio Biondo praised Loschi as the man who "primus et solus . . . in orationibus Ciceronis commentatus est." [187] *Solus* is inaccurate, for in 1413, following in Loschi's traces, another north-Italian humanist, Sicco Polenton, published his *Argumenta super aliquot orationibus et invectivis Ciceronis*.[188] Despite an emphasis on the historical setting (*argumentum*), Polenton did not omit to discuss the *constitutiones* and *dispositio* of the orations. Although Polenton's analysis was not as detailed as Loschi's, he did treat sixteen orations left untouched by Loschi. His contemporary Guarino of Verona commented on Cicero's *pro Sex. Roscio,*[189] while George of Trebizond sometime about 1440 published a very extensive commentary on Cicero's *pro Ligario*[190] and perhaps had even commented on Cicero's *Philippics.*[191] In 1477 George's commentary on the *pro Ligario*, Asconius Pedianus's commentaries, Loschi's *Inquisitio*, and Polenton's *Argumenta* were printed together as a corpus of Ciceronian commentary, and then reprinted about 1497.[192] Toward the end of the century Italian humanists such as Giorgio Merula, Filippo Beroaldo the Elder, and Francesco Maturazzo took to writing commentaries on Cicero's orations,[193] to be followed in the next century by northern scholars such as François du Bois (Franciscus Sylvius), Philipp Melanchthon, Bartholomäus Steinmetz (Bartholomaeus Latomus), Petrus Ramus, and Johann Sturm.[194] In the 1530s began the publication of massive volumes containing commentaries on all of Cicero's orations by fifteenth- and sixteenth-century scholars.[195] And while Quattrocento rhetorical commentaries focused primarily on Cicero, Greek scholars drew attention to Greek oratory. I have already mentioned Theodore Gaza's commentary on Demosthenes's *On the Crown.*[196] At the end of the century Marcus Musurus wrote a rhetorical commentary on several orations of Isocrates.[197] In the sixteenth century some Italian and northern scholars, such as Aldo Manuzio the Younger, Francesco Ciceri, Philipp Melanchthon, and Jerome Wolf, turned to the same task.[198] But it is clear from the much smaller number of commentaries on Greek orators that although teachers like Philipp Melanchthon and Johann Sturm quoted Greek passages in their manuals of rhetoric, the study of Greek oratory never seriously challenged the preeminence of Cicero in the schools.

Frequent quotation of Cicero's speeches was, in fact, a characteristic of the one great Quattrocento *Rhetoric*, George of Trebizond's *Rhetoricorum libri V,* published at Venice in 1433–34.[199] George exemplified his rhetorical precepts by quoting or citing time and again all but three of the then-known orations of Cicero. But the value of his *Rhetoric* went beyond its generous Ciceronian exemplification. George's was the greatest summa of classical rhetoric since Quintilian, and it eventually earned a place in the Renaissance as a "classic" source to be cited alongside the works of Cicero, Quintilian, and Aristotle. In restoring rhetoric to its full five classical parts (invention, disposition, memory, action, and style), he synthesized not only the classical Latin tradition of rhetoric, including the doctrines of *rhetores Latini minores* such as Fortunatianus and Martianus Capella, but also the Greek tradition as represented by Dionysius of Halicarnassus, Maximus the Philosopher, and, most especially, Hermogenes of Tarsus. George incorporated into his *Rhetoric* almost the whole of the Hermogenean corpus. Today, Hermogenes is best known for his complex system of stylistic categories, namely, the seven "forms" with their thirteen subdivisions and six competent factors, which provided a far more sophisticated and subtle tool of stylistic analysis than the hoary Latin division of high, low, and middle styles.[200] But no less innovative was George's section on invention. He enormously expanded the traditional contents of rhetorical invention by combining the teachings of Cicero, pseudo-Cicero, Quintilian, and Fortunatianus with one another and with the new and very substantial system of Hermogenes. Furthermore, he brought into rhetoric the dialectical *topoi* as found in Boethius's *De topicis differentiis* and the *Summulae logicae* of Peter of Spain. In brief, George had prepared a *Rhetoric* that could compete with the manuals of the logicians in teaching argumentation. The natural culmination of George's expansion of rhetorical argumentation was his *Isagoge dialectica,* published about 1440. The *Isagoge* was the first humanist manual of logic and the natural companion to the *Rhetoric,* teaching just that modest amount of logic which orators and people in general needed. With George of Trebizond's *Rhetoric* and *Isagoge,* humanists could threaten scholastics on their own ground as the main teachers of argumentation.[201]

But did George really expect his students to absorb the great mass of classical lore on judicial and political oratory in his *Rhetoric* when in point of fact humanist oratory, as he himself admitted, was by and large restricted to the third part of classical eloquence: the epideictic style (speeches in praise or blame of individuals, localities, institutions, a way of behaving, academic subjects, and so forth)?[202] The answer is yes. George lived in the first full flush of the discovery of Cicero's *De oratore* and its portrayal of the orator as the leader of society; he was unquestionably inspired by Hermogenes's description of the supreme orator as *deinos,* as the master of every societal situation; he had written and eventually published his *Rhetoric* in the Venetian republic, where political and judicial oratory was possible; he had published his *Isagoge dialectica* in or near the Republic of Florence; he had immersed himself in the writings of Cicero and the Greek and Roman historians with all their examples of oratorical effectiveness; and, finally, he was locked, as he himself acknowledged, in a competition with scholastic masters like Paul of Pergola to prove to the sons of the Italian elite that rhetoric was more useful than scholastic logic and philosophy "in deliberations and trials."[203] Time would show George's dream of reviving the full rhetorical culture of antiquity to be chimerical. All this rhetorical instruction did

not produce in the Renaissance a literature of polished political and judicial oratory.[204] Nonetheless, as we shall see, into the second half of the
sixteenth century many Italian manualists maintained George's vision of
rhetorical instruction. Indeed, George's contemporary and sometime rival, Lorenzo Valla, had an even more radical approach.

Valla never wrote a *Rhetoric,* but his *Dialectica* in effect reduced
logic to a subdivision of rhetoric.[205] Valla charged that the dialecticians
had falsified logic because they had falsified language; unlike the orators
and rhetoricians, the dialecticians had strayed from the *usitatissima verborum consuetudo,*[206] and created a mass of fictive abstractions and categories. Dialectics, Valla insisted, was in essence "a matter indeed short
and easy," merely a form of confirmation and refutation. Confirmation
and refutation, in turn, were subdivisions of invention, and invention
was one of the five parts of rhetoric. Moreover, rhetorical confirmation
and refutation compassed argumentative forms outside the purview of
dialectics, namely, enthymemes, epichiremes, and arguments from probability.[207] Indeed, agreeing with Cicero and Quintilian that orators had
to teach, please, and move,[208] Valla noted that logicians needed only to
teach. Therefore logic truly was a simple affair and, in essence, a subsidiary of the larger and far more complex province of rhetoric. Whereas
George of Trebizond viewed his *Isagoge dialectica* as excerpting for rhetorical purposes the complex logic of late scholasticism, Valla considered
all logic a mere subdivision of rhetoric, and not a very large one at that.
Fittingly, Valla rounded out his new comprehensive logic by including a
large section on topical invention, quoting verbatim for a full thirty-five
pages not Aristotle's *Topica,* but the relevant part of Quintilian's *Institutiones oratoriae.*[209]

Neither George's *Isagoge dialectica* nor Valla's *Repastinatio dialectice* enjoyed any brilliant success in fifteenth-century Italy. George's manual never penetrated the university curriculum, but remained, instead, a
text of humanist private tutors.[210] Valla's work circulated even less.[211]
Only in the sixteenth century, when "discovered" by northern humanists,
did either text begin to exercise a wide influence. In Italy, for the rest of
the century, evidence of humanist activity in logic is slight. At Florence,
the Byzantine émigré John Argyropoulos composed a brief *Compendium
de formis ratiocinandi,* which had minimal diffusion.[212] He also lectured
on Aristotle's logical works, as did the philologist Angelo Poliziano.[213]
Giorgio Valla wrote a treatise *De expedita ratione argumentandi* and
included a section on logic in his encyclopedia of learning, *De expetendis
ac fugiendis opus.*[214] Explicitly ignoring supposition theory and other
scholastic logical developments, Giorgio Valla presented a simplified
logic and tried, at the same time, to be as comprehensive as possible. He

took his section on the *topoi* in part from Cicero's *De inventione*.[215] Later northern humanists thought well of the work. Johann Caesarius, Peter Schade (Peter Mosellanus), and Philipp Melanchthon all glossed it.[216] But Giorgio Valla's treatise stands isolated in the general development of Quattrocento humanism after George of Trebizond and Lorenzo Valla.

Quattrocento *Rhetorics* after George of Trebizond's tended to provide synopses of the classical manuals while attempting some adaptation. For instance, Giorgio Valla's section on rhetoric in his *De expetendis et fugiendis rebus* summarizes classical Latin lore, including the status doctrine, but at the end adds four sections not found in the Ciceronian manuals or Quintilian: *De scribenda historia, De dialogo, De genere epistolico,* and *De imitatione*.[217] A law student at Pavia, Giovanni Battista Castellio, criticized the classical manuals as too prolix, but his solution was merely a précis ("epitoma seu breviarium") of rhetorical invention based on Cicero and Fortunatianus.[218] Jacopo Publicio of Florence recapitulated the full classical art in his *Ars orandi,* except that he omitted disposition and memory while adding a section on punctuation. But he also wrote a separate *ars memorandi* and, to complete the trilogy, an *ars epistolandi,* which smacked of the medieval *ars dictaminis* with lists of proper salutations and modes of address.[219] The *Nova rhetorica,* or *Margarita eloquentiae,* which the Franciscan friar Lorenzo Guglielmo Traversagni finished at Cambridge in 1478, may reflect the much more pragmatic approach of the North.[220] Ignoring most of the classical material on forensic argumentation, he concentrated on demonstrative oratory as useful for preaching and filled his text with examples from, and citations of, the Bible and the church fathers. Aurelio Lippo Brandolini, active in Rome in the 1480s, took a different tack in his *De ratione scribendi libri tres*.[221] Since he despaired of contemporary oratory ever returning to classical standards,[222] he postulated that written work, and specifically the letter, had become the only relevant sphere for classical rhetoric. But apart from memory and delivery, he still rehearsed the whole classical art, including the status doctrine, on the grounds that different parts of the classical orations could be useful to different kinds of letters. He even included a discussion of preaching, which, like Traversagni, he especially viewed as a form of demonstrative oratory;[223] and, like Aristotle before him, he gave over a large section of his work to a treatment of the emotions, where among other things he offered advice on what to say when composing a consolation. In his popular (twelve editions by 1495) *Novum epistolarium* of 1477 Giammario Filelfo not only gave many sample letters, but also covered the five parts of the classical oration, including delivery, which he admitted letter writing did not need.[224] Toward the end of the century the Roman schoolmaster Giovanni Sulpizio followed Brandolini and Filelfo by publishing an *ars epis-tolandi* that incorporated almost the full classical art of rhetoric. Sulpizio not only equated the parts of a letter to the six parts of the classical oration, but also taught in summary fashion the five parts of classical rhetoric, including delivery, memory, and invention in the *genus iudiciale* and *genus deliberativum*.[225]

If Brandolini and Sulpizio expanded the art of letter writing to encompass almost all of classical rhetoric, another very popular text, Niccolò Perotti's *Rudimenta grammaticae,* shrank the same art to a sub-division of grammar. The *Rudimenta* concludes with a brief section on letter writing, which—in comparison to the medieval *artes dictaminis* and contemporary *artes epistolandi*—is remarkable for its simplicity.[226] In another section of his work, Perotti expanded the domain of grammar to include figures of speech, an area usually reserved for the rhetorical manuals.[227] Equally representative of this link between grammar and let-ter writing is the *Ars epistolandi* of Francesco Negri, a teacher at Padua in the 1480s and an author of a *Grammar.* In his very popular *Ars epis-tolandi* (at least twenty-four editions before 1501) Negri described a great variety of letters, but he also added at the end thirty rules of "ele-gance" that really were of a grammatical nature and were reprinted sepa-rately in the sixteenth century.[228] Even Agostino Dati's grammatical work on classical usage, the *Elegantiolae,* contained some tips on letter writing and therefore, with some reason, was sometimes later joined to treatises on letter writing.[229]

But perhaps the most attractive Quattrocento work on letter writing was Niccolò Sagundino's (Nicholas Secundinus's) little *De epistolari di-cendi genere,* which used Hermogenean precepts on style, and inculcated clarity, brevity, and decorum.[230] With its stress on style rather than fig-ures, modes of address, salutations, lists of different kinds of letters, and the like, Secundinus's little piece resembles the elegant late sixteenth-century manual on letter writing of Justus Lipsius, who was also influ-enced by Hermogenes.[231] The inelegance of Secundinus's own style and perhaps the unfamiliarity of Latins with his Greek precepts and examples probably prevented the work from being better appreciated.

It is obvious that from Barzizza at the beginning of the century to Sulpizio at the end humanist work on rhetoric, aside from commentaries, gravitated toward letter writing. But unlike their discussions of judicial and deliberative oratory, in the field of letter writing the humanists practiced what they preached. In the high tide of twelfth-century human-ism, letter collections of individual authors enjoyed a golden age.[232] As Giles Constable remarks: "At no other time in the Middle Ages or be-tween antiquity and the nineteenth century was the gentlest 'art' more

assiduously cultivated or were letters more carefully written and collected."[233] The spread of the *ars dictaminis* with its formularies and
model letters seems to have stifled the impulse for personal letter collections. From the thirteenth century onward in the North the best-known
collections contained the letters of administrators and bureaucrats and
therefore functioned as formularies.[234] But beginning in the later fourteenth century with Petrarch, the discoverer of Cicero's letters, Renaissance humanists restored the cult of letter collections. Many humanists,
such as Petrarch, Ambrogio Traversari, Poggio Bracciolini, Francesco Filelfo, Angelo Poliziano, and, in the sixteenth century, Erasmus, published
collections of their letters, while some, such as Guarino of Verona, were
fortunate enough to have others do the same for them at least in manuscript.[235] And quite apart from letter collections of individual authors,
Renaissance manuscripts are replete with thousands upon thousands of
miscellaneous letters of many different authors, as humanists elevated the
letter to a favorite literary genre to be used for many purposes and therefore worth preserving singularly and in groups in either miscellaneous or
thematic collections.

The style of humanist orations, letters, and treatises was, of course,
as classical as humanists could make them. But what was classical style?
From the early fifteenth century Ciceronianism had dominated humanist
imitation of style.[236] But in the second half of the century a reaction set
in. Without really replacing Ciceronianism, scholars such as Giorgio
Valla[237] and Angelo Poliziano[238] argued for an eclectic approach to imitation and called for writers to cultivate their own individual styles. A
more peculiar development at the end of the century was the emergence
of Apuleianism as represented by such important figures as Paolo Cortesi
at Rome and Filippo Beroaldo the Elder at the University of Bologna.
Taking as their model the late antique author Apuleius, the Apuleians
cultivated a style that was obscure, suffused with archaic and rare words,
careless of balanced or periodic sentence structure, and willing to appropriate pell-mell phrasing and vocabulary of different periods, genres, and
styles of Latin literature.[239] However, by the second decade of the sixteenth century the only serious question in imitation of Latin prose once
more focused on Ciceronianism. At Rome in 1512–13 the count of Mirandola, Gianfrancesco Pico, and the Ciceronian champion from Venice,
Pietro Bembo, reenacted the controversy between Poliziano and Cortesi.
Pico's and Bembo's exchange of letters *De imitatione* proved very popular, going through sixteen printings between 1518 and 1652.[240] But it
was really Erasmus's devastating burlesque of Ciceronianism at Rome,
the dialogue *Ciceronianus,* published in 1528, that made Ciceronianism
a Europewide issue.[241] Not by chance the second and third printings of

the Pico–Bembo exchange followed in 1530. In 1531 Julius Caesar Scaliger published at Paris the first of his two orations in refutation of Erasmus;[242] and at Lyons in 1535 Etienne Dolet issued his *Dialogus de imitatione Ciceroniana adversus Desiderium Erasmum Roterodamum*.[243] Dolet then published his *Linguae latinae commentarii* (1536–38; based mainly on Cicero) and a collection of *Formulae* of, again, mainly Ciceronian usage (1539).[244] But the most successful text to come out of the controversy was undoubtedly Mario Nizolio's *Observationes in M. T. Ciceronem*, or, to use the title it was subsequently given, *Thesaurus Ciceronianus*, of 1535, which was a dictionary based exclusively on Cicero. So prized was this work that it went through at least seventy editions by 1620.[245] Cicero, to be sure, continued to be a model of style throughout the Renaissance and beyond (the great nineteenth-century author John Henry Newman considered him his only teacher of style[246]); but after the mid-sixteenth century Ciceronianism came to be understood especially as denoting not merely an adherence to Ciceronian diction but also a preference for a fulsome oratorical style as distinct from a plain or, as a major anti-Ciceronian, Justus Lipsius, put it, "Laconic" style, which, in fact, meant different things to different critics and which was believed to be best represented by other classical authors, such as Seneca and Tacitus.[247]

In sum, in recovering and absorbing virtually the full classical heritage in rhetoric, Quattrocento Italy produced little innovation save in letter writing, where the Latin classical tradition did not have much to offer by way of instruction. In any event, Italian humanists strove mightily to classicize the art of letter writing in content, style, and structure, even going as far as to transfer to letter writing almost the whole panoply of classical rhetoric. Aurelio Brandolini, who was raised in Naples and was living in Rome when he wrote his treatise on rhetoric, might despair of ever reforming contemporary oratory, but a Venetian civil servant such as Nicholas Secundinus could still believe that Italy would produce new Ciceros, Catos, Crassuses, and other great orators if only peace descended upon the land.[248] The same faith inspired Antonio Loschi, George of Trebizond, Lorenzo Valla, and the commentators on the Ciceronian *Rhetorics*. The desire to imitate classical eloquence accounted for the humanist mania for writing and delivering orations as well as for the various debates on imitation. Lorenzo Valla and, to a lesser extent, George of Trebizond expanded the content of rhetoric to take in logic. But by and large Italian humanists respected the difference between the two disciplines and left logic to the scholastics.

*   *   *

Northern humanism took a different tack, and it did so almost from the start. When the Dutch scholar Rudolf Agricola (1444–1485) crossed into Italy about 1469, he was already a trained scholastic,[249] and though Italy taught Agricola Greek and the cult of classical eloquence, in some important respects he never really lost his northern sensibilities. In Agricola's mind the paradigmatic orator was a teacher, a *magister,* and not specifically a political leader, a *dux populi* in Valla's phrase. The result was a peculiarly northern approach to oratory, his *De inventione dialectica libri III,* which Agricola began at Ferrara in the later 1470s and finished after he returned to the North in 1479.

The significance of *De inventione dialectica* lies more in its conception than in its content. In it Agricola discussed dialectical *topoi,* argumentation, the parts of an oration, how to make a speech pleasing, various means of achieving copiousness, ways of affecting emotions, and disposition. But what really mattered was that he stood on its head the classical dictum that orators must move, please, and teach. Lorenzo Valla had argued from this dictum to the view that rhetoric encompassed logic, since the logician merely taught while the orator did the same and much more. Agricola, however, apparently following St. Augustine's *De doctrina christiana* (4.27–28), insisted that teaching was the fundamental task of a speaker and that the *officia* of moving and pleasing were merely subsidiary.[250] Thus, in Agricola's work, logic, which had the specific task of teaching, retained primacy over rhetoric. Accepting a Stoic idea found in Cicero's *Topica* and Boethius's *De topicis differentiis,*[251] Agricola divided logic (*ratio disserendi*) into invention, which is prior and deals with the *topoi,* and judgment, which is concerned with the syllogism.[252] The very fact that Agricola did not bother to treat judgment was a telling indication that in his scheme it was quite minor compared to invention (in contrast to the Stoics, who concentrated on judgment). And rightly so, since Agricola justified writing *De inventione* on the grounds that almost everything we "learn" involves probability (and therefore is best developed by dialectical *topoi*) rather than certainty (what enters the domain of the syllogism and scientifically demonstrated truth).[253] But the decisive factor in Agricola's scheme was his equation of dialectical with rhetorical *topoi.*[254] Since these *topoi* were at root the same, logic, not rhetoric, best treated them. Agricola explicitly endorsed the Stoic analogy of the difference between logic and rhetoric as that between the closed and the open hand.[255] In other words, rhetoric differed from logic merely in that it presented more prettily and loosely what logic had demonstrated in strict fashion. Agricola left no doubt about this interpretation when discussing *delectatio,* one of the *officia* of the orator.[256] True, he admitted, delectation was the terrain of the orator, but the pleasure of a speech derived both from its content (*res*), which appeals to the mind, and from its rhetorical accoutrements, which appeal to the senses. The former, the substance of the speech, was the responsibility of the *dialecticus*.

Agricola had rhetoricized logic; but he had also devalued rhetoric, making it an appendage of logic. His ideas found little favor in Italy. Italian scholastics retained control of logical instruction at the universities throughout the Renaissance; and the leading Italian rhetoricians continued to view rhetoric as a training in argument. But in the North, especially after the Reformation had weakened or destroyed scholasticism, Agricola became the rage of the northern schoolteachers. *De inventione* seems to have dropped from sight after Agricola completed it. Not even Alexander Hegius, an admirer and compatriot of Agricola, argued for a peculiarly Agricolan conception of logic when he published his *Dialogi* on logic in 1503.[257] But between 1515, when it was first printed, and 1563 no less than forty-seven editions of either the complete text of Agricola's prolix work or epitomes of it appeared, an average of one edition every year in northern Europe, but not one in Italy.[258] Even apart from Bartholomew Latomus's and Jean Voyer's (Ioannes Visorius's) epitomes, students of the text soon had at their disposal commentaries by Alard of Amsterdam, Ioannes Matthaeus Phrissemus, and Reinardus Hadamarius. Agricola's *De inventione* was manifestly an adaptation of Italian humanism that suited the North.

*   *   *

The same cannot be said of other early transalpine works in rhetoric. Guillaume Fichet, a doctor of theology, teacher of rhetoric, and promoter of Italian humanism at Paris,[259] complained in 1470 that George of Trebizond's *Rhetoric* was so popular at Paris that a sect of *Giorgiani* had sprung up at the university.[260] We can identify Fichet's own manuscript of George's *Rhetoric* as well as a second manuscript that circulated at Paris.[261] The next year, and with considerable fanfare, Fichet published his own *Rhetoric*.[262] It was a large work covering the five classical parts of rhetoric, but offering not much more than a bald compilation of definitions and precepts drawn from the classical Latin manuals and George of Trebizond with hardly any exemplification by quotation of classical authors. It evoked scarce interest and never was reprinted. Four years later Fichet's colleague at the University of Paris, Guillaume Tardif, published a *Compendium rhetoricae artis et oratoriae facultatis* based on Cicero and Quintilian that fared a little better, going through a second edition, but apparently having little circulation beyond Paris.[263]

Others at Paris took a different approach. Toward the end of the century Jacques Lefèvre d'Etaples and his circle set about reforming education at the university.[264] They wrote fresh manuals of logic and published writings and translations of the Italian humanists that they considered useful for the reform of education at Paris, including George of Trebizond's *Isagoge dialectica,* Barzizza's *De compositione,* Dati's *Elegantiolae,* and Negri's *Grammar.*[265] This stress on logical and grammatical works assumed that the classical manuals were sufficient in rhetoric, and certainly, as has been seen, editions of and commentaries on classical *Rhetorics* were frequent throughout the sixteenth century in northern Europe.[266]

But, like the fifteenth-century Italians, the early northern humanists especially cultivated the art of letter writing.[267] The Netherlands alone produced at least thirteen *ars epistolandi* in the Renaissance.[268] One fifteenth-century northern scholar, writing under the pseudonym of Agostino Dati, published a popular summary of rhetoric entitled *Rhetoric minor,* but which was for the most part nothing other than an *ars epistolandi.*[269] In 1492 the German humanist Conrad Celtis published an innovative *Modus epistolandi,* which categorized all letters as either divine or secular, subdivided the latter more by tone than by content (*grave, severa, ardua, difficilia,* and so on), and treated the individual letter by a novel five-part scheme: *principium, causa, narratio, enumeratio* (ending), and *character* (punctuation).[270] The treatise reflects Celtis's teaching at the University of Leipzig, as does his *Epitoma in utramque Ciceronis Rhetoricam,* which was first published in conjunction with the treatise on letter writing as a comprehensive text in rhetoric. The later *Methodus conscribendarum epistolarum* of Christopher Hegendorff, by contrast, divides letters according to the three categories of the classical oration (judicial, political, and epideictic) before parading a multitude of examples before the reader.[271] But amid the great multiplicity of *artes epistolandi* written by northern humanists, unquestionably the most successful in terms of editions was Erasmus of Rotterdam's *Opus de conscribendis epistolis,* the first version of which was completed by 1498, before being published in a definitive edition in 1522 and revised in 1534.[272] Just in the period 1522–40 alone some fifty-five editions appeared, four in Italy, two in Spain, and the remaining forty-nine in northern Europe, especially Paris and the Rhineland. Erasmus's work was a bestseller in the North because he himself was one of the most pragmatic of humanists, who knew how to adapt humanist classicism to contemporary conditions. The *Opus,* a very large work, running to 275 pages in the modern critical edition, was in a very real sense Erasmus's *Rhetoric,* as he reworked classical rhetoric to suit what he perceived to be the practical rhetorical needs of the day. The range of his writings shows that he had scarce interest in reviving the full oratorical culture of antiquity. The only secular oratorical genre he favored by translation and imitation was declamation, an art form especially cultivated during the empire, when opportunities for political oratory had been stifled.[273] Erasmus wrote another massive work of technical rhetoric, *De duplici copia verborum et rerum* of 1512, which offered bountiful precepts on how to amplify a theme or idea and therefore was well suited to letters and declamations.[274] In the *Opus* Erasmus insisted that a letter could support a wide, really infinite, variety of subjects and the many different styles appropriate to those subjects. Revealing how much in his mind the letter had replaced the oration as the prime instrument of rhetoric, he said that all letters could be fitted into one of the three classical oratorical genera (legal, political, epideictic) or a new fourth one, the familiar. He subdivided these genera into many species, before discussing and exemplifying all of them. As in the old *artes dictaminis*, he also spent a lot of time on salutations, modes of address, and ending formulas. The *Opus* could have used more instruction on invention and rhetorical figures, but Erasmus's *De copia* can be seen as a companion work filling that lacuna to an extent. Indeed, in 1499, soon after finishing the first version of his work on letter writing, Erasmus wrote to a friend that he planned to add to it four other treatises: *De copia, De amplificationibus, De argumentationibus,* and *De schematibus.*[275] From the start Erasmus had envisaged his art of letter writing as the core of a complete art of rhetoric. One may argue that in some respects Aurelio Brandolini anticipated Erasmus by several decades. However, whereas Erasmus's work was an instant success, Brandolini's experienced no significant circulation in his native Italy and was first printed only in the middle of the sixteenth century in northern Europe.[276]

Like Erasmus's *Opus,* Juan Luis Vives's *De epistolis conscribendis* of about 1533 fitted within a pattern of other texts by its author.[277] In *De disciplinis,* published in 1531 (consisting of *De causis corruptarum artium* and *De tradendis disciplinis*), Vives had condemned Lorenzo Valla's *Repastinatio dialectice* as intemperate and filled with errors, mocked the pretension of Quintilian and others that rhetoric encompassed ethical education, denied that rhetoric had a right to teach invention, memory, or even delivery, and insisted that only *elocutio* was proper to rhetoric.[278] In all these matters Vives was only being consistent, because he also accepted the Agricolan division of dialectic into judgment and invention and Zeno's simile of the closed and open hands for the relationship of dialectic and rhetoric.[279] Indeed, at the start of *De epistolis* Vives argued that invention was really a function of prudence rather than art.[280] In his largest work of rhetoric, *De ratione dicendi* (1532), he did not even have a heading for invention;[281] but he did dedicate a separate logical treatise, the *Liber de instrumento probabilitatis,* to topical invention.[282] In *De ratione dicendi* Vives reshaped the traditional rhetorical manual. He treated *elocutio* in its first part, but to a lesser degree and in a different format than traditionally found in the rhetorical manuals. While book 2 offered general advice on persuasion and the emotions of the audience, Vives gave over all of book 3 to genres (narration, history, apologia, commentaries, translations, and so on). He simply had no use for the classical division of rhetoric into the three *genera dicendi.* Delivery never came up. As for Erasmus, so too for Vives rhetoric was really literary rather than oratorical training. In contrast to Erasmus, however, Vives kept his epistolary treatise relatively brief, because he did not view the letter as virtually a universal genre for any subject. Indeed, contrary to Erasmus—who objected to attempts by doctrinaire classicizers to limit the size and range of style appropriate to a letter—Vives gave over a chapter of his treatise precisely to the theme of brevity as a prime characteristic of the good letter. Vives's *De epistolis conscribendis* never came close to matching the popularity of Erasmus's *Opus,*[283] but it does represent a significant counter-current in northern humanist epistolography. An important later example of this more classicizing attitude toward letter writing is the concise *Epistolica institutio* which the great Flemish classicist Justus Lipsius dictated in 1587.[284] Lipsius reasserted Vives's view on brevity; but no less significantly, under the influence of Hermogenes and other Greek authorities, he also made simplicity and elegance the appropriate qualities of a letter. In short, he wished to bring Renaissance letter writing into closer approximation to classical models and instruction, as opposed to Erasmus's brilliant synthesis of humanism and the medieval dictatorial tradition.

*   *   *

Erasmus's *Opus* represented a pragmatic adaption of classical rhetoric in a way that did not seriously touch on the question of rhetoric's relationship to logic. But, as has been seen, his fellow Dutchman, Rudolf Agricola, had already taken up that issue in the previous century, even though his *De inventione* only began to exercise a wide influence after first being printed in 1515. One sign of this influence is how it colored Juan Luis Vives's own highly influential survey of learning, *De disciplinis.* Another very important avenue of Agricolan influence was the teaching of Philipp Melanchthon, the Lutheran *Praeceptor Germaniae.* In 1519, Melanchthon published the first edition of his *Rhetorica* and followed it the next year with the first version of his *Dialectica.*[285] Unlike George of Trebizond, whose *Isagoge dialectica* was a companion piece to his *Rhetorica,* Melanchthon worked under a different understanding of the relation between the two arts. As he explained in the later editions of both works, rhetoric added the ornament of *elocutio* to the *inventa* of dialectic.[286] Rhetoric was merely the art of "correctly speaking ornately." Dialectic, by contrast, was "the art of arts, the science of sciences," just as, Melanchthon explicitly acknowledged, the thirteenth-century logician Peter of Spain had described it. More specifically, dialectics was "the art of teaching." In addition to categories, propositions, syllogisms, and fallacies, Melanchthon's *Dialectica* also treated at length the *loci argumentorum* found in the classical *Rhetorics*. Conversely, his *Rhetoric* dropped the *loci*, or *topoi*, as more appropriately handled in dialectics. Although his *Dialectic* and *Rhetoric* did not change radically, Melanchthon actually shows the influence of Agricola to a greater extent in the later editions of 1529 and 1531 of these works than in those of 1519 and 1520. In fact, in the first edition of the *Rhetoric*, even though he endorsed the Zenian simile and though he referred the reader to Agricola and to Erasmus's *De copia* for the *loci communes,* he did not define rhetoric as merely the art of "recte ornate dicendi." However, from the start Melanchthon strove to adapt rhetoric to contemporary needs. He kept the three classical oratorical *genera causarum*—including the judicial *causa* and its accompanying statusdoctrine—and he added a fourth, the *genus didascalicum,* which clearly was the most important for him as being appropriate for preaching (in the first edition he made the *genus didacticum* a subdivision of the demonstrative genus); he dropped two of the three classical parts of rhetoric, namely, memory and delivery, as superfluous to the contemporary situation; and he worked mightily to apply his teaching on status and *elocutio* to religious themes and examples.

In the decades after 1518 Melanchthon's manuals went through many editions and exercised a broad influence in northern Europe. His synthesis of ancient rhetoric, Agricolan logic, and religious purpose was carried on in the late sixteenth cetury by followers such as David Chytraeus.[287] In his *Praecepta rhetoricae inventionis* of 1558 Chytraeus included the *status iuridicalis* of the classical *Rhetorics* as well as the Melanchthonian *genus didascalion* while constantly trying to show how his precepts could apply to religious texts.[288] Quite in keeping with the character of Melanchthon's school, in his essay *De ratione discendi* Chytraeus praised the first of the humanist *Dialectics*, George of Trebizond's *Isagoge dialectica,* for its concise treatment of judgment, but complained about its omission of topical invention.[289] Nevertheless, the best clue to the spreading influence of the Agricolan conception of logic and rhetoric is the *fortuna* of George of Trebizond's *Isagoge dialectica*. This work enjoyed a respectable circulation in Quattrocento Italy with more than fifteen manuscripts and one incunable extant. The circle of Jacques Le-

Jacques Lefèvre d'Etaples showed some interest in printing it in the first fifteen years of the sixteenth century. But beginning in 1516 printings of the *Isagoge* multiplied at a startling rate in northern Europe, with forty-nine editions appearing before the end of 1567, which is virtually the same as the number of editions of Agricola's *De inventione* in these years.[290] Agricola had posited a two-part logic of invention and judgment, but he himself had left a handbook only for invention. So in the craze for Agricolan logic that swept the North after 1515, schoolmasters in logic adopted George of Trebizond's little *Isagoge* as the companion piece on judgment to Agricola's *De inventione*. The irony, of course, is that George had written his opuscule as a supplement to a full-scale rhetoric that taught invention and argumentation, and not as a logic that appropriated these subjects from rhetoric.

After the 1550s the printings of George's and Agricola's works petered out, not, however, because the northern teachers had rejected the Agricolan conception of logic and rhetoric, but rather because they had now carried that conception a step farther and needed new textbooks for the purpose. The critical figure in this development was the Parisian master Petrus Ramus.[291] Ramus was obsessed with method, with a way of teaching an art quickly and efficiently. His answer was a universal topical logic, which proceeded from the most comprehensive category of an art to its most narrow, usually by a series of dichotomies, and everywhere he tried to simplify and reduce to essentials. In logic he followed Agricola and divided it into invention and judgment, the former splitting off into artificial and inartificial, the latter into axioms and notions, and so forth. Rhetoric consisted of *elocutio* and *pronuntiatio*, as the whole classical system of the rhetorical *topoi*, status doctrine, disposition, and memory fell out of rhetoric, to be taken up, except for memory, by logic. More radically than Agricola, who never wrote a *Rhetoric*, Ramus had reduced the content of rhetoric to a level even smaller than it had in the Middle Ages, when at least rhetoric was identified with the very important *ars dictaminis*. Ramus and his colleague Omer Talon published their first *Logics* and *Rhetorics* in the 1540s, and from that point on transformed the way these arts were taught and understood in much of Europe for the next century. Father Walter Ong has counted 253 editions of the *Logic* and 125 editions of the *Rhetoric* in their various revisions, adaptations, and translations, not including the many separate commentaries and various occasional pieces relevant to the two arts written by Ramus and Talon.[292] After Ramus's death in the massacre of St. Bartholomew's Day, 1572, his *Logic* was rarely printed at Paris, but his *Rhetoric* still had a following there, and both works were frequently reprinted and adapted elsewhere, for example in Switzerland, the Netherlands, the

British Isles, and most of all Germany. Calvinists especially favored these works, but he had followers among other Protestant denominations and among Catholics as well. Only in Italy did he make no impression.

While Agricola, Erasmus, Melanchthon, and Ramus were working their counter-revolution in humanist rhetoric, others strove to develop and even expand the classicizing rhetoric of the Italian Quattrocento. About 1498 Iacob Locher (Philomusus) published a *Compendium rhetorice,* which epitomized the classical manuals and George of Trebizond.[293] But even he tried to innovate with a separate section on funeral oratory. Among northern scholars of the first half of the sixteenth century one might mention the schoolteachers Johannes Rivius and Johannes Caesarius, both of whom wrote a *Logic* (first editions 1529 and 1532, respectively)[294] and a *Rhetoric* (of 1539 and 1532, respectively).[295] Their logical handbooks include topical invention not within the context of an Agricolan two-part logic, but rather as part of a comprehensive treatment of logic. Their *Rhetorics,* moreover, retain the classical five parts of rhetoric as well as the status doctrine.

But without question the most important classicizing authority on rhetoric in northern Europe in the sixteenth century was Johann Sturm.[296] Born in Luxembourg in 1507 and trained in the Netherlands, Sturm is usually credited with popularizing Agricolan logic at Paris after his arrival in 1529 (the first two Parisian editions of *De inventione* are from that year). Whether Sturm had any connection with these editions, the fact that he was an advocate of Agricola is not surprising, in view of his background. What is more interesting is his devotion to Hermogenes of Tarsus. Within two years of his arrival Greek editions of Hermogenes were printed at Paris with many copies having interleaved blank folios, obviously for the purpose of note-taking by students attending lectures on the text. From a very early point in his career Sturm saw Hermogenes as the means of expanding the content of Latin rhetoric. Eventually he translated the whole Hermogenean corpus into Latin, and then added massive commentaries based on his lectures.[297] In 1538 Sturm transferred to Strasbourg. The next year he published two very important works, the *Partitiones dialecticae* and *In partitiones oratorias Ciceronis dialogi.*[298] Their titles unequivocally broadcast Sturm's special predilection for "division." Sturm began the *Partitiones oratoriae* with a seminal discussion of method, which he defined as a quick and easy way of teaching an art. There were three such ways: synthesis, analysis, and division, the last of which was Sturm's favorite, and the inspiration for which he found in the opening passages of Hermogenes's treatise *On Status.*[299] As he says at the start of his own work, Sturm was already teaching the method of division in Paris before he came to teach at Strasbourg.[300] The even more famous Parisian master Petrus Ramus, began publishing only four years later. Contemporaries recognized the connection,[301] as does the modern authority on Ramus, Walter J. Ong, S.J., who discussed Sturm and Hermogenes in his book.[302] In the *Partitiones oratoriae* proper Sturm blended Hermogenes with Cicero and even Aristotle (Sturm later published a translation and commentary on Aristotle's *Rhetoric*). Sturm covered all five of the classical parts of rhetoric in the *Partitiones oratoriae*. In the companion *Partitiones dialecticae* Sturm once again reasserted the full classical range of rhetoric, specifically acknowledging in this work of dialectic that rhetoric had the responsibility of *invenire* et *disponere* as well as of *elocutio, memoria,* and *pronuntiatio.*[303] Although he divided dialectic into three parts ("in inveniendo, iudicando, et collocando"), the two books of the first edition concentrated, in good Agricolan fashion, on topical invention—including the Aristotelian categories—in book 1 and on judgment (the syllogism) in book 2. In the later four-book version of the *Partitiones oratoriae*, Sturm gave some more attention to *collocatio* (toward the end of book 4), but actually devoted most of the two new books to other topics: book 3 to the principles of proof, where he also discussed method and Hermogenes's theory of status; and book 4 to sophistical argumentation.[304] So even though Sturm accepted Agricola's system of logic, he vigorously reasserted the classical content and domain of rhetoric. At his school in Strasbourg and in his influential works of pedagogical theory Sturm made rhetoric, dialectic, and the study of oratory the culminating subjects of the curriculum.[305] In a late work, the *Linguae latinae resolvendae ratio* of 1573, after praising the uses of *eloquentia,* Sturm lashed out against the Jesuits, a new "race of men" clever in the way they conceal their snares.[306] Sturm went on to attribute some of the acumen of the Jesuits to their study of the medieval theologians whom Protestant humanists had condemned, but who were acute dialecticians. However, in attacking the Jesuits Sturm was confronting not only theological rivals, but also educational competitors, whose stress on the classics and rhetorical training came remarkably close to the education Sturm himself advocated. Indeed, the Jesuits themselves openly acknowledged Sturm as a major Protestant pedagogue whose influence they wished to eliminate at least as far as their own students were concerned.[307]

Without question, the Jesuits created the most successful school system of the early modern period, with 306 colleges in 1608 and more than 600 colleges by 1710 in Europe, America, and even the Far East.[308] In the master plan, the *Ratio studiorum,* of the Jesuit colleges, rhetoric held a privileged place as the culminating subject in the curriculum after grammar and "the humanities."[309] Not only was great stress laid on declamation and other oratorical practices, but the rhetoric the Jesuits taught was essentially classical in structure. A leading textbook in the Jesuit colleges, *De arte rhetorica libri tres ex Aristotele, Cicerone, et Quintiliano praecipue deprompti* by Cyprianus Soarez, S.J. (first printed in 1562), was premised on the view that rhetoric was the art of persuasion and not merely of style ("Rhetoricae officium est dicere apposite ad persuasionem, finis persuadere dictione"). It covered the five classical parts of rhetoric, taught judicial along with deliberative argumentation, and discussed both the status doctrine and topical invention.[310] Sturm had an admiration for Hermogenes that the Jesuits did not share. As a consequence, no one since George of Trebizond had been as innovative in expanding the doctrinal content of classical rhetoric in Latin education. The Jesuits, by contrast, were far more successful amongst Catholics than Sturm amongst Protestants in insuring that rhetoric retained its full classical dress and educational prestige. For all his influence, an integralist such as Sturm or, to take a major English example, Thomas Wilson—whose Ciceronian *Arte of Rhetorique* first appeared in 1553[311]—simply faced too much competition in Protestant lands from Melanchthon, Ramus, and other humanist pragmatists. Indeed, both Sturm and Wilson were themselves avowed Agricolans in dialectic and therefore open to the charge of inconsistency in their espousal of the complete classical art of rhetoric. Even in his *Rhetorique*, Wilson equated invention with logic and distinguished the orator from the logician by the way he embellished what the logician argued in "plaine teachyng."[312]

*   *   *

Religion and rhetoric also interacted in preaching, the most universal form of contemporary oratory.[313] Writing in the late fifteenth century, Guglielmo Traversagni and Aurelio Brandolini had both taught how to integrate classical rhetoric and sacred oratory.[314] Both found the *genus demonstrativum* the most appropriate model for preachers. An early northern humanist *ars predicandi* was Johann Reuchlin's *Liber congestorum de arte praedicandi* of 1504.[315] Modeling his treatise on the classical manuals, Reuchlin divided the art of preaching into three parts—invention, memory, and delivery—and the sermon into four parts—beginning, scriptural texts, division, and confirmation. His *divisio* recalls one of the chief characteristics of the medieval *artes praedicandi,* namely, their complex division of themes at the start of the sermon. Although he ignored the status doctrine, Reuchlin did incorporate the three secular *genera dicendi* (*iudiciale, deliberativum, demonstrativum*) into his work and gave generous attention to topical invention. Interestingly, he did not consider *elocutio* as having any place in an *ars praedicandi.* Erasmus, by contrast, did. After mulling it over for decades, in 1535, at the very end of his life, he produced his *Ecclesiastes,* or *De ratione concionandi.*[316] Although in the opening section he stressed the prerequisite moral condition and the natural gifts of a preacher, Erasmus filled his massive treatise with precepts inspired largely by the classical manuals of rhetoric. For instance, early in book 2 he described invention as very much the product of natural prudence, yet he then proceeded to teach in most of the book the *topoi* and argumentation, including a section on the status doctrine. All of the last book (book 4) treats religious topics, or, as Erasmus called them, *tituli.* He explicitly took classical deliberative oratory as the prime model of preaching (rather than the judicial and epideictic genera), divided the sermon according to the six parts of the classical oration, treated disposition, memory, and delivery, and (unlike Reuchlin) paid generous attention to the figures and tropes of *elocutio.* In a sense baptizing Aristotle, he was concerned with teaching the emotions proper to Christian piety and the means of arousing them. He of course disapproved of the complex system for dividing the theme employed in the medieval sermon. More interestingly, he also condemned the traditional invocation of the Virgin after the exordium, complaining that preachers saluted the mother of God "with greater reverence" (*religio*) than God Himself.[317] From the first comments on the qualifications of a preacher to the final *tituli,* Erasmus unremittingly poured into the *Ecclesiastes* his theological views and opinions on contemporary religious issues and practice. Therefore it is not surprising, to take one example, that he vigorously attacked the Lutheran doctrine of justification when explaining how to preach on morals.[318]

Perhaps it was in reaction to Erasmus's monumental work that in 1540 Reuchlin's more neutral treatise was reprinted in an edition of Lutheran preaching manuals that included among others Philipp Melanchthon's *Ratio brevis sacrarum concionum tractandarum* compiled by Melanchthon's student and Luther's former amanuensis Viet Dietrich.[319] The *Ratio brevis* seems first to have been published in 1535, the same years Erasmus's *Ecclesiastes* appeared. For Melanchthon the sermon consisted of eight parts modeled on the six parts of secular classical orations (*exordium, narratio, propositio, argumentio, confirmatio, ornamenta, amplicatio, epilogus*). But Melanchthon, or his compiler Dietrich, organized the subject matter of sermons by a system of *themata simplicia* and *themata composita* that harkens back to the medieval manuals. Like Reuchlin, Melanchthon ignored *elocutio;* but he also dropped memory and delivery and did not equate the system of *themata* with the topical invention of secular oratory. He did find, however, the secular *genus deliberativum* useful for sacred oratory and gave some examples of how it could apply. The same edition of 1540 contained the *Formula compendiaria de formandis sacris concionibus* of the Lutheran theologian Johann Hoech (Johannes Hepinus or Aepinus), who also studied at Wittenberg.[320] Hepinus divided preaching into three genera—*didacticum, demonstrativum, deliberativum*—and provided the reader with a system of appropriate *loci* and examples. Hepinus had replaced the *genus iudiciale* with the *genus didacticum,* which Melanchthon had popularized and which ultimately can be traced back to Agricola. Since Melanchthon's teaching at Wittenberg was the bond linking Dietrich's compilation of the *Ratio brevis* and Hepinus's piece, it was fitting that the edition of 1540 contained Melanchthon's brief *De officiis concionandi dissertatio.* This opuscule was really a supplement to his *Rhetoric* and *Dialectic,* which was suffused with religious examples.[321] Melanchthon listed three genera of sermons, *didacticum, epitrepticum ad credendum, paraeneticum ad mores,* but really only expounded the *genus didacticum.* Since in his *Rhetoric* Melanchthon made teaching the prime *officium* of the orator, this concentration on teaching when speaking of the preacher's *officia* is not surprising. As we have seen, his pupil Hepinus made *didacticum* the first of his three genera of sermons.

The first Italian manual on preaching to break with the medieval *artes praedicandi* was Alfonso Zorrilla's *De sacris concionibus recte formandis formula* published at Rome in 1543. As John O'Malley has shown, Zorrilla did not so much write an original work as plagiarize wholesale the treatises of Reuchlin, Dietrich, Melanchthon, and Hepinus.[322] By the end of the century, Catholic authors entered the market with fresh treatises that did not replicate the medieval or Lutheran *artes.* In *L'arte del predicare* (1562) the Franciscan preacher Luca Baglioni frequently cited Cicero, and for good reason, since he wanted the sermon to follow closely the structure of the classical oration (for instance, on exordium he discusses *capitatio benevolentiae* and *insinuatio*).[323] In general he imitated as much as he could the classical manuals. His *bête noire* was medieval sermon practice. So on the division Baglioni made sure to condemn the interminable division of themes in the medieval sermons, which, he said, "fa nausea alli moderni ascoltanti."

Some of the most popular early Counter-Reformation preaching manuals were produced in Spain. One of them, Diego de Estella's *De modo concionandi,* published in 1576, was not derived from any tradition, consisting mainly of general rules and not corresponding in its structure and content to the classical manuals.[324] But the same is not true of the very popular *Ecclesiasticae rhetoricae sive de ratione concionandi libri sex* of the Dominican Luis de Granada (1504–1588), which was also published in 1576 and which shows the influence of both classical and contemporary northern rhetorical theory.[325] Fray Luis divided the sermon according to the six parts of the classical oration, accepted the five classical parts of rhetoric, and—save for memory, which he did not teach—went into each one at great length. He followed Aristotle in including a section on the emotions as part of rhetoric, and he found the classical precepts for the genres of demonstrative and deliberative oratory eminently suitable for sermons. He only discarded the *genus iudiciale* as not applicable. In good Melanchtonian fashion, however, he had much to say about the new *genus didascalicum* and was much exercised to distinguish rhetoric and dialectic. The latter, he explained, had the duty of teaching and dealt with speculative matters in the schools; the former had to move and please, and treated practical things before a popular audience. He quoted Zeno's simile of the closed and open hands as reflecting the relation between the two disciplines (book 2, chapter 2). Yet he kept the *loci* and argumentation as parts of rhetoric, and therefore did not follow the northern tendency of reducing rhetoric to style.

Cardinal Carlo Borromeo much admired Granada's manual and recommended it to Counter-Reformation preachers.[326] Indeed, the *De ecclesiastica rhetorica* published a few years earlier, in 1574, by a member of his circle, Agostino Valerio, went even further than Granada in incorporating classical precepts into the modern preaching manual. Like Baglioni before him, Valerio made sure to include *elocutio,* with the treatment of invention (he believed deliberative oratory the most appropriate model) and the emotions taking up the rest of his book.[327] Ludovico Carbone, who wrote separate treatises on rhetorical invention, disposition, and style, published in 1595 his *Divinus orator vel de rhetorica divina libri septem,* which was in many respects more classical still, as Carbone drew on a greater range of classical authors, including Hermogenes, and taught fully the five classical parts of rhetoric, including the status doctrine in invention.[328] So even in comparison to their Spanish coreligionists the Italian authors of Counter-Reformation preaching manuals remained remarkably integralist in their approach to classical rhetoric.

*   *   *

We can see a similar classicizing pattern in sixteenth-century Italian *Rhetorics.* By mid-century authors such as the Florentine Bartolomeo Cavalcanti (*La retorica,* first edition 1555) and the Venetian Girolamo Mascher (*Il fiore della retorica,* first edition 1560) were writing in Italian, but otherwise continued the Quattrocento tradition of classicizing rhetoric.[329] Not only did both teach the full classical art, but Cavalcanti also gave a substantial defense of the importance to contemporary life of the status doctrine. If one reads Francesco Sansovino's *Della rhetorica* (1543), Daniele Barbaro's *Della eloquenza* (1557), Antonio Maria Conti's (Marcantonio Maioragio's) *De eloquentia dialogus* (1582), and Gian Denores' *Breve trattato dell'oratore,* just to mention the opuscules gathered in a modern edition by Bernard Weinberg, there cannot be any doubt that by and large sixteenth-century Italian authors continued to believe, teach, and preach that, in Conti's words, "eloquentia civitates gubernari."[330] The new century did bring changes, though. Hermogenes was more widely used, especially his system of stylistic forms, for example, by Cavalcanti and Barbaro.[331] Guilio Camillo Delminio (ca. 1485–1544), whom Sturm had known at Paris in the late 1520s and had considered even then somewhat bizarre,[332] made Hermogenes's stylistic forms a central part of his universal system of invention, the *Idea del teatro.*[333] However, it was not Hermogenes but Aristotle who now became an almost ubiquitous source.[334] Cavalcanti, for instance, constantly cited him, and even tried to prove that his *Rhetoric* contained the status doctrine, since it was inconceivable that the greatest rhetorical authority would be lacking in this respect.[335] In another form of innovation, Gian Denores, in his most substantial work on rhetoric, *Della rhetorica* (1584, in two books), tried a new organization of the material, placing *argumentatione* in book 1 and *dispositione* and *elocutio* in book 2. He also taught at the start his peculiar "wheels" of arguments, by the manipulation of which one was supposed to be able to invent and relate arguments in all three *genera dicendi.* Camillo's *Theatrum* may have been an influence here. Finally, in an appendix Denores analyzed the *artificio* of twenty orations of various authors, including some of his own.[336]

However, probably no text better exemplifies the continuity of fifteenth- and sixteenth-century Italian rhetoric than Mario Nizolio's *De veris principiis et vera ratione philosophandi contra pseudophilosophos,* published in 1553, more than a hundred years after the first redaction of Lorenzo Valla's *Repastinatio dialectice et philosophie.*[337] Like many modern students of Renaissance rhetoric, Nizolio had a special interest in style; indeed, justly or not, later generations viewed him as the arch-Ciceronian.[338] Yet, the culminating book of his life had little to do with style. Rather, it was about something far more basic, namely, the place of rhetoric in society and culture as a whole. After all, *elocutio* was only one of the five parts of classical rhetoric. Nizolio had read Agricola, Melanchthon, Vives, and perhaps Ramus on the content and value of rhetoric.[339] He rejected them all. For Nizolio rhetoric was the one universal art encompassing all that could be said or thought.[340] Like Valla, he was an extreme nominalist (he explicitly confessed his desire to defend the medieval nominalist philosopher William of Ockham[341]), and spent much of *De principiis* refuting, on the basis of grammar and correct linguistic usage, what he considered to be the mistaken realism of Aristotelian logic and metaphysics. Sharing, however, in the growing appreciation by humanists of Aristotle's work in other fields, he endorsed the Stagirite's writings on rhetoric, poetics, ethics, politics, and zoology.[342] Nizolio emphatically condemned Zeno's simile of the closed and open hands as reflecting the relation between logic and rhetoric.[343] He argued that logic was a subsection of rhetoric.[344] Thus, not only did topical invention belong properly to rhetoric rather than logic, but rhetorical instruction in argumentation was, in fact, more comprehensive and sophisticated than anything found in textbooks of logic. Whereas one could be a tongue-tied philosopher, the true orator, of necessity, *teste Cicerone,* must join in his person both wisdom and eloquence, and therefore be the embodiment of the best that a culture can produce.[345]

*   *   *

Nizolio's was an extreme position, not shared by other contemporary commentators on rhetoric. Sperone Speroni in his *Dialogo della rettorica* (published in 1542) gave oratory dominance not over all learning (its concern was not the discovery and strict demonstration of scientific truth), but, because of its capacity to persuade and lead the multitude on the basis of probability and verisimilitude, only over civil affairs.[346] For Speroni rhetoric stood at the foundation of the republic because "the orator's art, governance, practices, and words are eminently civil matters (*cose propriamente cittadinesche*)."[347] Another contemporary, the Platonist Francesco Patrizi, in his *Dialoghi della retorica,* first published in 1560, pared down the value of rhetoric even further, wondering if it had any subject proper to it and arguing that it was unnecessary in a republic governed by law. But even he recognized a good eloquence emanating from wisdom and had to admit that even though useless for the wise (*savi*), rhetoric nonetheless held sway over the ignorant *plebe.*[348] Knowing how to speak (*possente a dire*) may belong to rhetoric, but knowing how to think (*possente a sapere*) was the province of dialectic.[349]

But a better counterpoise to Nizolio and, indeed, to the whole integralist tradition in rhetoric is the Englishman Francis Bacon, writing in the first decades of the seventeenth century. Prophet of and propagandist for the new science, Bacon was no friend of Ramism;[350] he rejected the bloodless prose advocated by the ancient Stoics and admired by some Ramists,[351] and was himself adept at manipulating the traditional rhetorical tropes and figures.[352] Nonetheless, Bacon mocked the fulsome prose of the Ciceronians, the obsession of Renaissance rhetoricians with style at the cost of substance, and the *infinita et anxia opera* Sturm and others of his ilk lavished on Cicero's and Hermogenes's rhetorical works.[353] Rhetoric was ornamentation; it served the imagination the way dialectic served the intellect; rhetoric worked *per prestigias verborum*, and its task was to fill the imagination with images to supplement reason.[354] Like the Italian Platonist Patrizi, Bacon observed rhetoric from the perspective of another discipline, in this case, science. Just as the Renaissance humanists had rebelled against the narrowly scientific and philosophical curriculum of medieval scholasticism, so too now Renaissance science and philosophy were attempting to put rhetoric in a distinctly subordinate place within education and learning as a whole. Already in the late fifteenth century, Giovanni Pico della Mirandola had defended the philosophical culture and the scientific terminology of medieval scholastics against Ermolao Barbaro.[355] *Pace* Valla and Nizolio, it was not humanist rhetoric, but the new science that vanquished medieval Aristotelianism; and it was the cult of the new science and the attempts to replicate its methods and values in other disciplines that would over time most challenge the prestige and worth not only of the classical rhetoric revived by the Renaissance humanists, but also of the literary culture that was at the base of humanist education.[356]

NOTES

1. The best introduction are the articles by various authors in J. J. Murphy, ed., *Studies in the Theory and Practice of Renaissance Eloquence* (Berkeley, 1983), which contains a useful select bibliography of secondary literature. For primary bibliography a start has been made in idem, *Renaissance Rhetoric: A Short Title Catalogue of Works on Rhetorical Theory from the Beginning of Printing to A.D. 1700, with Special Attention to the Holdings of the Bodleian Library, Oxford. With a Select Basic Bibliography of Secondary Works on Renaissance Rhetoric* (New York, 1981); see B. Vickers's review in *Quarterly Journal of Speech* 69 (1983): 441–44, and 70 (1984): 335–38. Overviews of the literature are to be had in B. Vickers, "On the Practicalities of Renaissance Rhetoric," in *Rhetoric Revalued*, ed. Vickers (Binghamton, NY, 1982), 133–41; D. P. Abbot, "The Renaissance," in *The Present State of Scholarship in Historical and Contemporary Rhetoric*, ed. W. B. Horner (Columbia, MO, 1983), 75–100; and J. Fafner, "Wege der Rhetorikgeschichte," *Rhetorica* 1 (1983): 75–91. Old but still worth reading is C. S. Baldwin, *Renaissance Literary Theory and Practice: Classicism in the Rhetoric and Poetic of Italy, France, and England, 1400–1600* (New York, 1939), 39ff. See also W. S. Howell, *Logic and Rhetoric in England, 1500–1700* (Princeton, 1956). A work of large breadth and insight is G. A. Kennedy, *Classical Rhetoric and Its Christian and Secular Tradition from Ancient to Modern Times* (Chapel Hill, 1980). Finally, L. A. Sonnino, *A Handbook to Sixteenth-Century Rhetoric* (London and New York, 1968)

provides a guide to contemporary technical terms, but she fails to give their classical sources.

2. A famous expression of this attitude, especially apropos logic, is attributed to Niccolò Niccoli in Leonardo Bruni's *Ad Petrum Paulum Histrum Dialogus,* in *Prosatori latini del Quattrocento,* ed. and trans. E. Garin (Milan, 1952), 44ff. See N. W. Gilbert, "The Early Italian Humanists and Disputation," in *Renaissance Studies in Honor of Hans Baron,* ed. A. Molho and J. Kirschner (Florence, 1971), 201–26. For a condemnation of traditional oratorical practice in the three classical types of discourse (judicial, deliberative, epideictic) see Aurelio Lippo Brandolini's preface to his *De ratione scribendi libri tres* written in Rome in the late fifteenth century (I used the edition of Frankfurt am Main, 1568, 6–7): "whatever eloquence there is in this age, is exercised purely in writing. The practice of public speaking has almost completely disappeared. For the system [*ratio*] of accusing and defending is utterly destroyed and extinct. Judgments in the councils of other cities are delivered in the native and common tongue; here (in Rome) in our consistory [*colloquium*] they are delivered briefly and in not very good Latin. Sermons are well-nigh always said in the vernacular. Only a rather small number of eulogies of saints and the deceased are given in Latin, and these have been changed by those called friars from the ancient oratorical style to a certain new and barbarous format [i.e., the thematic sermons]."

3. See P. O. Kristeller, "Humanism and Scholasticism in the Italian Renaissance," *Byzantion* 17 (1944–45): 346–74; reprinted in his *Studies in Renaissance Thought and Letters,* 2 vols. (Rome, 1956–85), 1:553–83; *Renaissance Thought: The Classic, Scholastic, and Humanist Strains* (New York, 1961), 92–119; and *Renaissance Thought and Its Sources,* ed. M. Mooney (New York, 1979), 85–105. All three books contain other important articles on humanism and rhetoric.

4. Juan Luis Vives, *De tradendis disciplinis* 4.3, first published in 1531. The Latin text can be read in Vives, *Opera omnia* (Valencia, 1785), 6:358. I adapted the translation of F. Watson in *Vives: On Education* (Edinburgh, 1903; reprinted Totowa, NJ, 1971), 183.

5. See J. Monfasani, *George of Trebizond: A Biography and a Study of His Rhetoric and Logic* (Leiden, 1976), 239ff.

6. E. Gilson, "Michel Menot et la technique du sermon médiéval," in his *Les idées et les lettres* (Paris, 1932), 93–154, at 95.

7. See Murphy, *Renaissance Rhetoric: A Short Title Catalogue* (see also his "One Thousand Neglected Authors: The Scope and Importance of Renaissance Rhetoric," in *Studies in the Theory,* ed. Murphy, 20–36). E. J. Polak plans a bibliography of medieval and Renaissance treatises on letter-writing. See also J. J. Murphy, "Rhetoric in the Earliest Years of Printing, 1465–1500," *Quarterly Journal of Speech* 70 (1984): 1–11, who points out that of about thirty-five thousand incunable editions only four hundred were in rhetoric, in other words, only a shade more than one percent.

8. In general see J. J. Murphy, *Rhetoric in the Middle Ages: A History of Rhe-

torical Theory from Saint Augustine to the Renaissance (Berkeley, 1974), 106ff., 123ff.

9. In addition to ibid., 122–23, see also J. O. Ward, "From Antiquity to the Renaissance: Glosses and Commentaries on Cicero's *Rhetorica*," in *Medieval Eloquence,* ed. J. J. Murphy (Berkeley, 1978), 25–67, at 54; see also Ward's dissertation, "*Artificiosa Eloquentia* in the Middle Ages" (Ph.D. diss., University of Toronto, 1972), passim; and R. Sabbadini, *Le scoperte dei codici latini e greci ne' secoli XIV e XV,* 2 vols. (Florence, 1905–14; reprinted Florence, 1967), 2:115 and 209.

10. Murphy, *Rhetoric in the Middle Ages,* 117 (for Thierry of Chartres and the *Partitiones oratoriae*).

11. For Aristotle's *Rhetoric* see Murphy, *Rhetoric in the Middle Ages,* 90ff. Of the *Rhetorica ad Alexandrum* there were definitely two medieval translations and perhaps even a third, of which only a fragment remains; see *Aristoteles latinus. Codices,* ed. G. Lacombe et al. (Rome, 1939), 1:78–79; and M. Grabmann, *Guglielmo di Moerbeke O.P. il traduttore delle opere di Aristotele* (Rome, 1946), 116–19.

12. *A Medieval Latin Version of Demetrius' De elocutione,* ed. B. B. Wall (Washington, DC, 1937); and B. Weinberg, "Demetrius Phalereus," in *Catalogus Translationum et Commentariorum, Mediaeval and Renaissance Latin Translations and Commentaries* (henceforth CTC), ed. P. O. Kristeller, F. E. Cranz, and V. Brown, 6 vols. to date (Washington, DC, 1960–), 2:21–41.

13. See Ward, "From Antiquity to the Renaissance," 37–38; and Murphy, *Rhetoric in the Middle Ages,* 43–44, 64ff.

14. Ward, "From Antiquity to the Renaissance," 33ff.

15. A perception recently confirmed by J. O. Ward, "Renaissance Commentators on Ciceronian Rhetoric," in *Studies in the Theory,* ed. Murphy 127–73, at 146ff.

16. See note 53 below.

17. See the index of C. I. Webb's edition (Oxford, 1929).

18. The *Policraticus,* ed. C. I. Webb, 2 vols. (Oxford, 1909), does have tacit quotations of an oration (the *pro Ligario*) but taken from Augustine's *De civitate dei* (2:264.23). The *Letters,* ed. W. J. Miller, H. E. Butler, and C. N. L. Brooke, 2 vols. (Oxford, 1955–79), 2:64–65, quote tacitly *in Catalin.* 1.1.

19. For the literature on this translation see L. Gualdo Rosa, *La fede nella Paideia: Aspetti della fortuna europea di Isocrate nei secoli XV e XVI* (Rome, 1984), 16ff.

20. See Monfasani, *George of Trebizond,* 245, n. 8; R. McKeon, "Rhetoric in the Middle Ages," *Speculum* 17 (1942): 1–32, at 10 and passim; and for the Arabic and Jewish tradition I. Twersky, "*Ars Rhetorica* as Reflected in Some Jewish Figures of the Italian Renaissance," in *Jewish Thought in the Sixteenth Century,* ed. B. D. Cooperman (Cambridge, MA, 1983), 1–22, at 2–5. But note Kristeller's point (*Renaissance Thought and Its Sources,* 232)

that in subordinating rhetoric and dialectic to logic, medieval classifiers of the arts understood "logic in the broader sense of *philosophia rationalis* or *sermocinalis,* while reserving for logic in the narrower sense the term dialectic."

21. Ward, "From Antiquity to the Renaissance," 61.
22. E.g., in the curriculum formulated by papal legates for Paris in the mid-fourteenth century; see *Chartularium Universitatis Parisiensis* (Paris, 1894), 3:145. Murphy, *Rhetoric in the Middle Ages,* 95, n. 21, comments: "While records of medieval university curricula are of course fragmentary . . . the pattern in respect to rhetoric is nevertheless quite clear. It is a pattern of omission." See also the trenchant comments of P. Delhaye, "La place des arts libéraux dans les programmes scolaires du XIIIᵉ siècle," in *Arts libéraux et philosophie au Moyen Âge* (Montreal, 1969), 161–73. For more recent literature see P. O. Lewry, "Rhetoric at Paris and Oxford in the Mid-Thirteenth Century," *Rhetorica* 1 (1983): 45–63.
23. See Kristeller, *Renaissance Thought: The Classic, Scholastic, and Humanist Strains,* 40, 149, n. 19; and Murphy, *Rhetoric in the Middle Ages,* 97ff; and idem, "The Scholastic Condemnation of Rhetoric in the Commentary of Giles of Rome on the *Rhetoric* of Aristotle," in *Arts libéraux,* 833–41. See also Ward, "From Antiquity to the Renaissance," 55, for a list of some scholastic commentators on the *Rhetoric.*
24. See Kristeller and Murphy, cited in the previous note.
25. See Monfasani, *George of Trebizond,* 246 n. 11 and 276 n. 139; and *The Cambridge History of Later Medieval Philosophy,* ed. N. Kretzmann, A. Kenny, J. Pinborg, and E. Stump (Cambridge, 1982), 273ff.
26. Kennedy, *Classical Rhetoric,* 194.
27. H. Hajdu, *Das Mnemotechnische Schrifttum des Mittelalters* (Vienna, 1936); P. Rossi, *Clavis universalis: Arti mnemoniche e logica combinatoria da Lullo a Leibniz* (Milan, 1960), 7ff; F. A. Yates, *The Art of Memory* (London, 1966; reprinted Middlesex, 1969), 63ff.
28. For an overview see Murphy, *Rhetoric in the Middle Ages,* 135ff. See also Kristeller, *Renaissance Thought and Its Sources,* 319–20, n. 32 for more bibliography.
29. See Murphy, *Rhetoric in the Middle Ages,* 194ff.; Kristeller, *Renaissance Thought and Its Sources,* 236–37; and Gilson, "Michel Menot." The classic collection of texts is that of T.-M. Charland, O.P., *Artes praedicandi: Contribution à l'histoire de la rhétorique au Moyen Âge* (Paris and Ottawa, 1936). A special class of sermon is discussed in D. L. D'Avray and M. Tausche, "Marriage Sermons in *Ad Status* Collections of the Central Middle Ages," *Archives d'histoire doctrinale et littéraire du Moyen Âge* 47 (1980): 71–119, who report sermons by clerics in northern Europe. However, in Italy by the early Renaissance, if not earlier, laymen frequently delivered marriage orations; see F. Brandileone, *Saggi sulla storia della celebrazione del matrimonio in Italia* (Milan, 1906).
30. See E. J. Polak, "Dictamen," in *Dictionary of the Middle Ages* (New York,

1984), 4:173–77; Murphy, *Rhetoric in the Middle Ages*, 269ff.; and C. S. Baldwin, *Medieval Rhetoric and Poetic* (New York, 1928), 219ff.

31. Kristeller, "Humanism and Philosophy," in *Studies in Renaissance Thought*, 560–61; *Renaissance Thought and Its Sources*, 90–91.

32. Ward, "From Antiquity to the Renaissance," 35–38.

33. See Polak, "Dictamen"; C. H. Haskins, *Studies in Medieval Culture* (Oxford, 1929), 170–92; and Murphy, *Rhetoric in the Middle Ages*, 202ff.

34. See H. Rashdall, *The Universities of Europe in the Middle Ages*, ed. F. M. Powicke and A. B. Emden (Oxford, 1936), 1:99ff.

35. A good survey is H. Wieruszowski, "*Ars dictaminis* in the Time of Dante," in her *Politics and Culture in Medieval Spain and Italy* (Rome, 1971), 359–77. See also R. G. Witt, "Medieval *Ars Dictaminis* and the Beginnings of Humanism: A New Construction of the Problem," *Renaissance Quarterly* 35 (1982): 1–35.

36. For example, the earliest Italian literary prose is to be found in manuals of the thirteenth-century Bolognese *dictator* Guido Faba (see note 45 below); the first school of Italian poetry is connected with the bureaucrats of Frederick II's chancery in southern Italy; many early Italian poets, such as Jacopone da Todi and Cino da Pistoia, were jurists.

37. P. O. Kristeller, "Matteo de' Libri, Bolognese Notary of the Thirteenth Century, and His *Artes Dictaminis*," in *Miscellanea Giovanni Galbiati* (Milan, 1951), 2:283–320, at 288. Another thirteenth-century Italian *dictator*, Boncompagno da Signa, gave over a chapter of his *Rhetorica novissima* to a discussion of invectives (ed. A. Gaudenzi in *Bibliotheca iuridica medii aevi: Scripta anedota glossatorum* [Bologna, 1892] 2:249–97).

38. See the literature cited in notes 33 and 35 above.

39. Ward, "From Antiquity to the Renaissance," 60–61. See also S. Karaus Wertis, "The Commentary of Bartolinus de Benincasa de Canulo on the *Rhetorica ad Herennium*," *Viator* 10 (1979): 283–310; J. R. Banker, "The *Ars Dictaminis* and Rhetorical Textbooks at the Bolognese University in the Fourteenth Century," *Medievalia et Humanistica* n.s. 5 (1974): 153–68; and idem, "Giovanni di Bonandrea and Civic Values in the Context of the Italian Rhetorical Tradition," *Manuscripta* 18 (1974): 3–20.

40. See G. Billanovich, "Giovanni del Virgilio, Pietro da Moglio, Francesco da Fano," *Italia medioevale e umanistica* 6 (1963): 203–34, and 7 (1964): 277–324, esp. 289–98; idem, "Petrarca, Pietro da Moglio e Pietro da Parma," *Italia medioevale e umanistica* 22 (1979): 367–95, esp. 371–72; and P. O. Kristeller, "Un *Ars dictaminis* di Giovanni del Virgilio," *Italia medioevale e umanistica* 4 (1961): 181–200.

41. R. Weiss, *The Dawn of Humanism in Italy* (London, 1947), 5–6.

42. See P. O. Kristeller, "Petrarcas Stellung in der Geschichte der Gelehrsamkeit," in *Italien und die Romania in Humanismus und Renaissance: Festschrift für Erich Loos zum 70. Geburtstag*, ed. K. W. Hempfer and E. Straub (Wiesbaden, 1983), 102–21.

43. A. Galletti, *L'eloquenza* (Milan, 1938); P. O. Kristeller, *Renaissance*

Thought: The Classic, Scholastic, and Humanist Strains, 104; and *Renaissance Thought and Its Sources,* 236–38.

44. See Kristeller, "Matteo de' Libri, Bolognese Notary," 296.

45. His *Arenge* are a collection of *exordia* for speeches by public officials (see C. H. Faulhaber, "The *Summa dictaminis* of Guido Faba," in *Medieval Eloquence,* 85–111, at 88), while his *Parlamenti ed epistole* (Faulhaber, 90; ed. A. Gaudenzi, *I suoni, le forme e le parole dell'odierno dialetto della città di Bologna* [Turin, 1889], 127–60) contains Italian speeches, including judicial speeches. (no. 69ff.).

46. A. Wilmart, "L'*Ars arengandi* de Jacques de Dinant avec un appendice sur ses ouvrages *De dictamine,*" in his *Analecta Reginensis* (Vatican City, 1933), 113–51; concerning this author see also E. J. Polak, *A Textual Study of Jacques de Dinant's Summa dictaminis* (Geneva, 1975).

47. See Galletti, *L'eloquenza;* Kristeller, *Renaissance Thought: The Classic, Scholastic, and Humanist Strains;* and idem, *Renaissance Thought and Its Sources.* A good review of extant thirteenth-century *dicerie* is E. Vincenti, "Matteo dei Libri e l'oratoria pubblica e privata nel '200," *Archivio glottologico italiano* 54 (1969): 227–37. An interesting combination of moral and rhetorical instruction (especially on delivery) is the *Liber de arte loquendi et tacendi* of the thirteenth-century jurist Albertano da Brescia, which was found useful enough to be printed five times in the fifteenth century (for the text see T. Sundby, *Della vita e delle opere di Brunetto Latini,* trans. R. Renier [Florence, 1884], 475–506; for more recent literature see M. Ferrari, "Intorno ad alcuni sermoni inediti di Albertano da Brescia," *Atti dell'Istituto Veneto di scienze, lettere ed arti* 109 [1950–51]: 69–93). As Kristeller (*Renaissance Thought and Its Sources,* 237), reminds us, Boncampagno da Signa's *Rhetorica novissima* for law students was a textbook in oratory, not letter writing.

48. Weiss, *Dawn of Humanism,* 8.

49. Kristeller, "Petrarcas Stellung," 111–12.

50. Works emphasizing rhetorical inspiration in humanist activities are H. Gray, "Renaissance Humanism: The Pursuit of Eloquence," *Journal of the History of Ideas* 24 (1963): 497–514; J. E. Seigel, *Rhetoric and Philosophy in Renaissance Humanism* (Princeton, 1968); and N. S. Struever, *The Language of History in the Renaissance* (Princeton, 1970).

51. E.g., to stay in the Quattrocento, George of Trebizond, a professional rhetorician, defended scholastic philosophers and theologians and medieval translators against their humanist critics (see Monfasani, *George of Trebizond,* 154–56), and Giovanni Pico della Mirandola, despite his exquisite humanist credentials, rejected rhetorical values when they came in conflict with what he considered more important philosophical considerations (see Q. Breen, "Giovanni Pico della Mirandola on the Conflict of Philosophy and Rhetoric," *Journal of the History of Ideas* 13 [1952], 384–426; reprinted in his *Christianity and Humanism,* ed. N. P. Ross [Grand Rapids, MI, 1968], 3–38). Much of the humanist endeavor, such as Ciriaco d'Ancona's antiquarianism or Angelo Poliziano's philology, is difficult to

explain in terms of a primary rhetorical impulse.

52. We shall have a comprehensive picture of the process of the recovery and study of classical texts in the Renaissance when the CTC is completed (see note 12 above). Also of enormous value when finished will be the *Index Aureliensis* (Geneva), a union catalog of sixteenth-century printings currently up to the letter *C*.

53. P. de Nolhac, *Pétrarque et l' humanisme*, 2 vols. (Paris, 2d ed. 1907; reprinted 1965), 1:221; Sabbadini, *Le scoperte*, 1:27. De Nolhac, 1:219: "Petrarque semble avoir créé très rapidement autour de lui un mouvement de recherche des ouvrages de Cicéron." R. Sabbadini, *Storia e critica di alcuni testi latini* (Padua, 2d ed. 1971), 19, listed the Ciceronian orations "note prima delle nuove scoperte," by which he meant primarily the discoveries of Poggio in the early fifteenth century, and therefore after Petrarch. Of the extant fifty-eight Ciceronian orations, less than half seem to have been known before Petrarch, i.e., *In Catilinam* 1–4, *Philippicae* 1–14 (but in truncated form and counted as thirteen orations), some of the seven Verrine orations (Petrarch only knew one, according to de Nolhac, 1:252) the three Caesarean orations (*pro Marcello, pro Ligario, pro Deiotaro*), the two *post reditum* (*ad Quirites* and *ad senatum*), the *pro Cluentio* (in a fragmentary version), and the *pro Caelio*.

54. De Nolhac, 1:224; Sabbadini, *Le scoperte*, 1:27, 2:168, 210. The four orations were the *pro Milone, pro Plancio, pro Sulla*, and *de imperio Cn. Pompei*.

55. Sabbadini, *Le scoperte*, 2:172 and 211.

56. Ibid., 1:75; 2:210: *pro Balbo, pro Sestio, pro Caelio, in Vatinium, de responsis haruspicum*, and *de domo sua*. The first three orations could already be found in MS Verona, Capit. 155, compiled in 1329 (ibid., 2:96).

57. Ibid., 1:77, 81–82, 84 (addendum), 2:211; idem, *Storia e critica*, 23–27: *pro Q. Roscio Amerino, pro L. Murena, pro Caecina, in Pisonem, pro Rabirio perduellonis reo, pro Rabirio posthumo, pro S. Roscio comoedo, de lege agraria* 1–3. The first two orations the French scholar Jean of Montreuil had already seen in the previous century in the Cluny manuscript that was also Poggio's source (Sabbadini, *Le scoperte*, 1:84 [addendum], 2:73–74, 211; idem, *Storia e critica*, 17–18).

58. Sabbadini, *Le scoperte*, 1:127, 2:211–12; idem, *Storia e critica*, 39.

59. Sabbadini, *Le scoperte*, 1:127. Bussi also included the pseudo-Ciceronian fifth *in Catilinam*, which was known from at least 1439 onward.

60. Ibid., 1:116; 2:243; Giovanni Aurispa, *Panégyriques latins*, ed. and trans. E. Galletier, 2 vols. (Paris, 1949), 1:xxxviii ff.

61. Sabbadini, *Le scoperte*, 1:112, 2:250.

62. In addition to de Nolhac, *Pétrarque et l'humanisme*, 1:255ff.; Sabbadini, *Le scoperte*, 1:26–27, 2:213; and idem, *Storia e critica*, 53ff., now see P. L. Schmidt, "Die Rezeption des römischen Freundschaftsbriefes (Cicero-Plinius) im frühen Humanismus (Petrarca-Coluccio Salutati)," in *Der Brief im Zeitalter der Renaissance*, ed. F. J. Worstbrock (Weinheim, 1983), 25–59, at 27ff., for the history of these letters in the early Renaissance.

63. Sabbadini, *Le scoperte*, 1:34, 72, 74–75, 2:214; R. G. Witt, *Hercules at the Crossroads: The Life, Works, and Thought of Coluccio Salutati* (Durham, NC, 1983), 299–300; and Schmidt, "Die Rezeption," 36–37.

64. Sabbadini, *Le scoperte*, 2:252.

65. Ibid., 1:96; 2:242; idem, *Storia e critica*, 263–73; and R. A. B. Mynors, in the introduction to his edition of Pliny's *Epistularum libri decem* (Oxford, 1963), ix–xi.

66. Sabbadini, *Le scoperte*, 1:164, 212, 2:242–43; and Pliny, *Epistularum*, Mynors, xviii–xix. The first edition was that produced by Aldo Manuzio in 1508.

67. Sabbadini, *Le scoperte*, 1:78, 255–56, 2:202–3, 247–48. Poggio's was really a rediscovery, since Nicholas de Clemanges had access to a complete Quintilian before 1397 (ibid., 2:84–85).

68. De Nolhac, *Pétrarque et l'humanisme*, 1:253, n. 4.

69. Sabbadini, *Le scoperte*, 2:209. Except for two from the eleventh century, the earliest manuscripts are fifteenth-century (see Cicero, *L'Orateur, Du meilleur genre d'orateurs*, ed. and trans. A. Yon [Paris, 1964], 107).

70. Sabbadini, *Le scoperte*, 1:100, 2:209.

71. Ibid., 1:86–87, 2:202, 249, 263. For the scarcity of the first two of these works before printing see *Rhetores latini minores*, ed. K. Halm (Leipzig, 1863; reprinted Frankfurt am Main, 1964), vii, 3, 23.

72. Cf. Murphy, *Rhetoric in the Middle Ages*, 131.

73. Sabbadini, *Scoperte*, 1:101–2, 104, 116, 186, 2:224; but see G. Billanovich, "Il Petrarca e i retori latini minori," *Italia medioevale e umanistica* 5 (1962): 103–64, at 111 and 134ff.; and Monfasani, *George of Trebizond*, 271, 280, 286, 289 n. 191.

74. Sabbadini, *Le scoperte*, 1:108–9, 2:254; and Tacitus, *Dialogus de oratoribus*, ed. A. Gudeman (Amsterdam, 2d ed. 1967), 111ff.

75. Sabbadinni, *Le scoperte*, 1:130, 2:251; *Rhetores latini minores*, ed. Halm, vii, 354.

76. Sabbadini, *Le scoperte*, 1:171; 2:249, 253; *Rhetores latini minores*, ed. Halm, vi–vii, ix–x.

77. *Leonardo Bruni Aretino. Humanistisch-philosophische Schriften mit einer Chronologie seiner Werke und Briefe*, ed. H. Baron (Leipzig and Berlin, 1928; reprinted Wiesbaden, 1969), 132, 172. As Brian Vickers has pointed out to me, Quintilian (2.17.8) praised the *Iliad* for containing the three *genera dicendi*. See also Aulus Gellius, 7.14.

78. For Battista Guarino's translation of Mark Antony's speech, see J. Monfasani, "The Byzantine Rhetorical Tradition and the Renaissance," in *Studies in the Theory*, ed. Murphy, 174–87, at 178; for Giovanni Aurispa's translation of Philiscus's speech, see *Il carteggio di Giovanni Aurispa*, ed. R. Sabbadini (Rome, 1931), 174; and P. O. Kristeller, *Iter Italicum, a Finding List of Uncatalogued or Incompletely Catalogued Humanistic Manuscripts of the Renaissance in Italian and Other Libraries*, 3 vols. to date (Leiden and London, 1963–83), 2:*ad indicem* "Philiscus"; for Lauro Quirini's translation of Caesar's speech, see, e.g., ibid., 245, cod. Marc. lat. XIV, 7

(4319); for Andreas Brentius's translation of Caesar's speech see, e.g., ibid., 416, cod. Vatican, Ottob. lat. 1205.

79. See L. Bertalot, *Studien zum italienischen und deutschen Humanismus,* ed. P. O. Kristeller, 2 vols. (Rome, 1975), 2:246–47.
80. *Leonardi Bruni Aretino,* ed. Baron, 108, 128, 131, 171. Bruni translated *On the Crown* in 1407; he dedicated the corpus sometime after 1421.
81. D. P. Lockwood, "De Rinucio Aretino Graecarum litterarum interprete," *Harvard Studies in Classical Philology* 24 (1913): 51–109, at 55, 84–88.
82. See J. Monfasani, *"Bessarion Latinus," Rinascimento* 2d ser. 21 (1981): 165–209, at 180.
83. See Monfasani, "Byzantine Rhetorical Tradition," 177, 180.
84. An omnibus edition of these various translations appeared at Basel about 1545.
85. At Basel for Ioannes Oporinus. On Wolf see L. Gualdo Rosa, *Aspetti,* 168–75 and passim.
86. See Gualdo Rosa, *Aspetti,* 41, for a list of translations up to 1460. For the Italian study of Isocrates up to 1600, see ibid., 19–81.
87. Ibid. 112ff. for a handy list. For instance, ignoring unpublished translations, I counted fourteen different translations of *Ad Demonicum* and thirteen of *Ad Nicoclem* printed in the sixteenth century, most of which were then reprinted many times. Gualdo Rosa's book is an invaluable guide to the Renaissance *fortuna* of Isocrates.
88. E.g., because they viewed *Ad Demonicum* as primarily a moral text, Nikola of Majine in the fifteenth century and Joachim Camerarius in the sixteenth had no hesitation in omitting a passage which they viewed as detracting from that purpose; see Gualdo Rosa, ibid., 47.
89. For Wolf see note 85 above; for Lonicer see A. Horawitz, "Johann Lonicer," *Allgemeine Deutsche Biographie* 19 (1884): 158–63; and Gualdo Rosa, *Aspetti,* passim.
90. See A. Calderini, "Ricerche intorno alla biblioteca e alla cultura greca di Francesco Filelfo," *Studi italiani di filologia classica* 20 (1913): 204–424, at 287–89, 342. Filelfo translated Lysias's *Adv. Erastothenem* and *Epithaphios,* and Dio's *Ad Ilienses* and *De Troia non capta* (omitted by Calderini; first printed in 1492: *Gesamtkatolog der Wiegendrucke,* no. 8370).
91. H. Baron, *The Crisis of the Early Italian Renaissance,* 2 vols. in 1 (Princeton, rev. ed. 1966), 192ff.; idem, *From Petrarch to Leonardo Bruni* (Chicago, 1968), 102–37, 151–71, 217–63, where the text is edited.
92. G. Mercati, *Per la cronologia della vita e degli scritti di Niccolò Perotti, arcivescovo di Siponto* (Rome, 1925), 70ff.
93. Without making any pretense to completeness, I have come across the following translations. Carlo Valgulio: Aristides's *Ad Rhodienses,* and *De concordia,* and Dio Chrysostom's *Ad Nicomedenses* and *De concordia* (all printed); Gregorio Tifernate: Dio Chrysostom's *De regno* (printed); Benedetto Bursa: Libanius's *Defensio Archidami* (see *Collectanea Trapezuntiana* ed. J. Monfasani [Binghamton, NY, 1984], 146); Cincio de' Rustici:

Aristides's *In laudem Bacchi* (MSS Laur. Gadd. 90, 42; Vat. lat. 1883); Andrea Brenta: Lysius's *Epithaphios* (MS Vat. lat. 6855).

94. Erasmus, *Opus epistolarum,* ed. P. S. Allen, H. M. Allen, and H. W. Garrod, 12 vols. (Oxford, 1906–58), 2:390.

95. Apart from Erasmus's translation of three of Libanius's declamations and apart from Libanius's introductions which one finds in various editions of Demosthenes's orations, I know of no translation of Libanius until Féderic Morel's edition of the *opera omnia* at Paris in 1627.

96. In three volumes. The other orators of the Aldine edition were Alkidamantos, Andocides, Dinarchus, Lycurgus, Lesbonactes, and Herodes.

97. Eighty orations of Dio Chrysostom in Latin appeared at Venice in 1585 published by Girolamo Zenaro. Apart from Demosthenes and Isocrates and some translations of Lysias (by René Guillon and Andrew Downes [Andreas Dunaeus]) and Aeschines's *On the Crown,* the earliest printed translation of the other orations in the *Rhetores graeci* I know is that of Alfonso Miniato, whose rendering of Antiphon and Isaeus appeared at Antwerp in 1618, and of Josse van der Heyden, whose version of thirty-three orations of Lysias was first published at Hanover in 1619; see I. A. Fabricius, *Biblioteca graeca,* ed. G. C. Harles (Hamburg, 1791), 2:745 ff.

98. See Monfasani, *"Bessarion Latinus."*

99. For instance, the summaries of the Greek orators' speeches in the translated acts of the Council of Ferrara–Florence published in 1526 (see E. Legrand, *Bibliographie hellénique ou description raisonnée des ouvrages publiés en grec par des grecs aux XVe et XVIe siècles,* 4 vols. [Paris, 1885–1906; reprinted Paris, 1962], 3:305 ff.), or Themistius's orations translated by Henri Estienne and published in 1552 (see Themistius, *Orationes,* ed. G. Downey [Leipzig, 1965], xiii).

100. See the comments of G. Kristos, *Studies in Byzantine Rhetoric* (Thessalonica, 1973), 1 and passim; and of Kennedy, *Classical Rhetoric,* 197.

101. See Legrand, *Bibliographie,* 1:82 ff.

102. See Monfasani, "Byzantine Rhetorical Tradition," 182–83.

103. See *Index Aureliensis* (Geneva, 1966), 1:4:15 ff., as well as G. Ballistreri, "Cattaneo (Cataneo) Giovanni Maria (Mario)," *Dizionario biografico degli italiani,* 22 (Rome, 1979), 468–71, and L. Spitz, *The Religious Renaissance of the German Humanists* (Cambridge, MA, 1963), 35.

104. See R. Sabbadini, *Il carteggio di Giovanni Aurispa* (Rome, 1931), 168 ff.; and Monfasani, "Byzantine Rhetorical Tradition," 179. The 1589 *opera* appeared at Frankfurt, edited by Friedrich Sylburg.

105. See below; also Monfasani, "Byzantine Rhetorical Tradition," 183–84; and A. M. Patterson, *Hermogenes and the Renaissance: Seven Ideas of Style* (Princeton, 1970), passim, but esp. the bibliography, 219–20.

106. There were no new translations of Hermogenes after Gaspar Laurentius's published in 1614, and no editions between 1644 and 1790. See Patterson, 220; and Hermogenes of Tarsus, *Opera,* ed. H. Rabe (Leipzig, 1912), xxv.

107. See E. N. Tigerstedt, "Observations on the Reception of the Aristotelian

Poetics in the Latin West," *Studies in the Renaissance* 15 (1968): 7–24; and D. Aguzzi-Barbagli, "Humanism and Poetics," Chapter 30 in this volume.

108. See Monfasani, "Byzantine Rhetorical Tradition," 185, for some of the literature.

109. See E. Garin, "Le traduzioni umanistiche di Aristotele nel secolo XV," *Atti e memorie dell'Accademia Fiorentina di scienze morali: La Colombaria* n.s. 2 (1947–50): 55–104.

110. Angelo Poliziano in the second half of the century is the first Italian known to have studied the Greek text; see Tigerstedt, "Observations," 11.

111. See Monfasani, *George of Trebizond*, 270–71, 289.

112. P. O. Kristeller, "Un codice padovano di Aristotele postillato da Francesco ed Ermolao Barbaro . . . ," in his *Studies in Renaissance Thought*, 337–53, at 342; and E. Bigi, "Barbaro, Ermolao," *Dizionario biografico degli italiani* (Rome, 1964), 6:96–99, at 97.

113. Tigerstedt, "Observations," 15ff.

114. See Legrand, *Bibliographie*, 1:82ff.

115. For the *Poetics*, see Aguzzi-Barbagli's essay in this volume.

116. See F. E. Cranz, *A Bibliography of Aristotle Editions, 1501–1600*, ed. C. B. Schmitt (Baden-Baden, 2d ed. 1984), 220–21, where four Italian translations are also recorded.

117. See below.

118. B. Weinberg, "Demetrius Phalareus," in CTC, 2:27–41.

119. B. Weinberg, "ps. Longinus," ibid., 193–98.

120. For a bibliography of early printed editions of Greek letter collections see C. C. Clough, "The Cult of Antiquity: Letters and Letter Collections," in *Cultural Aspects of the Italian Renaissance: Essays in Honor of Paul Oskar Kristeller*, ed. C. C. Clough (Manchester and New York, 1976), 33–67, at 56–58.

121. Lockwood, "De Rinuccio Aretino," 52, 55–56, 60–61, 78–83, 88–93.

122. E.g., MS Vatican, Urb. lat. 1159, fols. 60v–67r, contains this translation.

123. Griffolini's translation was first printed at Rome in 1468–69 (Hain, no. 12874); Chalkeophilus's at Paris about 1474 (*Gesamtkatolog der Wiegendrucke*, no. 7819).

124. See R. Foerster, *Francesco Zambeccari und die Briefe des Libanius* (Stuttgart, 1878).

125. Calderini, "Ricerche," 300ff.

126. See G. Rill, "Bonfini (Bonfinius, de Bonfinis), Antonio," *Dizionario biografico degli italiani*, 12 (Rome, 1970), 28–30.

127. For Bruni's partial translation see *Leonardo Bruni, Aretino*, ed. Baron, 137–38, 174; for Ficino see P. O. Kristeller, *Supplementum Ficinianum*, 2 vols. (Florence, 1937), vol. 1, cxlvii ff.

128. See Legrand, *Bibliographie*, 1:51ff.

129. The German humanist Thomas Kirchmaier (Naogeorgus) published a Latin version of Synesius's letters at Basel in 1558; another German, Sebastian Guldenbeck, had his version of Aelianus's letters appear in the *opera* of

Aelianus edited by Conrad Gesner in 1556 at Zurich (see the *Index Aurelianesis* [Baden-Baden, 1965], 1.1:83, no. 100.773).

130. On Cujas's edition (Geneva, 1606), see Fabricius, *Bibliotheca graeca,* 662ff.

131. See J. Sykutris, "Epistolographie," in *Real-Encyclopädie der classischen Altertumswissenschaft,* Supplementband (Stuttgart, 1931) 5:185ff., esp. 189–90.

132. See Erasmus, *Opera omnia Des. Erasmi Roterodami,* 13 vols. to date (Amsterdam, 1969–), 1.2:153–579; *De conscribendis epistolis,* ed. J. C. Margolin, 312ff.

133. Weinberg, "Demetrius Phalareus," 36, 38–40.

134. Libanius, *Opera,* 9, ed. Foerster, 21ff.

135. Ibid., 23–25.

136. Weinberg, "Demetrius Phalareus, 36; Libanius, *Opera,* ed. Foerster, 23–25. For the origin of pseudo-Libanius, Proclus, and Demetrius see J. Sykutris, "Proklos *Peri epistolimaiou charakteros,*" *Byzantinisch-neugriechische Jahrbucher* 7 (1930): 108–18.

137. See the introduction of V. Weichert to his edition of *Demetrii et Libanii qui feruntur Typoi epistolikoi et epistolimaioi charakteres* (Leipzig, 1910), xviii ff.

138. Neither Foerster nor Weichert records any editions between this date and the nineteenth century.

139. See C. L. Stinger, *Humanism and the Church Fathers: Ambrogio Traversari (1386–1439) and Christian Antiquity in the Italian Renaissance* (Albany, NY, 1976); and Monfasani, *Collectanea Trapezuntiana,* 710ff.

140. See J. Baur, *Jean Chrysostome et ses oeuvres dans l'histoire littéraire* (Louvain, 1907); A. C. Way, "S. Gregorius Nazianzenus," in CTC 2:43–192, esp. 127ff.; Monfasani, *Collectanea Trapezuntiana,* 713–14, 728.

141. See J. W. O'Malley, S.J., *Praise and Blame in Renaissance Rome: Rhetoric, Doctrine, and Reform in the Sacred Orators of the Papal Court, ca. 1450–1521* (Durham, NC, 1979); and J. M. McManamon, S. J., "Renaissance Preaching: Theory and Practice: A Holy Thursday Sermon of Aurelio Brandolini," *Viator* 10 (1979): 355–73.

142. For instance, one finds numerous references to the Fathers as examples of Christian eloquence in the sources cited by M. Fumaroli in his *L'age de l'eloquence: Rhétorique et "res literaria" de la Renaissance au seuil de l'époque classique* (Paris, 1980). But one would like to know how much and in what ways Renaissance preachers followed patristic models.

143. Kristeller, *Renaissance Thought and Its Sources,* 93. Cf. F. Novati, *La giovinezza di Coluccio Salutati* (Turin, 1888), 66ff.

144. Kristeller, *Renaissance Thought and Its Sources,* 237–38.

145. See Ward, "From Antiquity to the Renaissance," 36, 60–61; idem, "Renaissance Commentators," 132ff.

146. R. G. G. Mercer, *The Teaching of Gasparino Barzizza with Special Reference to His Place in Paduan Humanism* (London, 1979), 91–92; G. W. Pigman III, "Barzizza's Studies of Cicero," *Rinascimento* n.s. 21 (1981): 121–63, at 128ff.

147. Monfasani, *George of Trebizond*, 263–64, 370–71 (George's Latin attack is translated by Ward, "Renaissance Commentators," 130).

148. R. Sabbadini, *La scuola e gli studi di Guarino Guarini Veronese* (Catania, 1896); reprinted in *Guariniana*, ed. M. Sancipriano (Turin, 1964), 93 ff.; Ward, "Renaissance Commentators," 131 and passim.

149. See the note in MS Rome, Biblioteca Casanatense, 417, reported in Monfasani, *Collectanea Trapezuntiana*, 47.

150. Regio's critique is in the form of a letter dated 18 September 1491, and was the first printed in an undated (1492?) collection of Regio's opuscules (*Repertorium Bibliographicum* no. 13809). See F. Marx, ed., *Incerti auctoris de ratione dicendi ad C. Herennium libri IV* (Leipzig, 1894; reprinted Hildesheim, 1966), 61 ff.

151. Ibid. In his *Repastinatio dialectice et philosophie*, which he worked on into the last years of his life, Valla recognized the Ciceronian authorship of the *Rhetorica ad Herennium;* see the edition by G. Zippel, 2 vols. (Padua, 1982), 1:17.18, 284.27, and 321.16. For Decembrio, see his *De politia litteraria*, 1.10 (pp. 55–64 in the Basel, 1562 edition).

152. Capiduro explains in the preface that his commentary reflects Valla's lectures; the first edition was accompanied by Victorinus's commentary on Cicero's *De inventione* (Hain, no. *5081). See Ward, "Renaissance Commentators," 143–44.

153. His preface is dated Venice, 6 November 1493. I used the second edition of 1496 (*Gesamtkatalog der Wiegendrucke*, no. 6729); see Ward, "Renaissance Commentators," 143; and Marx, ed., *Incerti auctoris*, 64.

154. In the same edition of 1496 cited in the previous note; see Ward, "Renaissance Commentators," 143.

155. Marx, ed., *Incerti auctoris*, 66.

156. Ward, "Renaissance Commentators," 128 ff.

157. Ibid., 141–47.

158. Mercer, *Teaching of Gasparino Barzizza*, 73–75, 78.

159. Ward, "Renaissance Commentators," 149–51, 154–55.

160. *Italia illustrata* (Basel, 1531), 346, in the section on the Romagna.

161. Ibid.

162. See below.

163. I consulted the edition of Venice, 1497 (*Gesamtkatalog der Wiegendrucke*, no. 6753). See Ward, "Renaissance Commentators," 147, 150.

164. Ward, ibid. I consulted the edition of Venice, 1485 (*Gesamtkatalog der Wiegendrucke*, no. 6908).

165. See *Gesamtkatalog der Wiegendrucke*, no. 6756.

166. Ward, "Renaissance Commentators," 150, mentions a commentary by Giorgio Valla, but otherwise I see no great Italian interest in the text.

167. See G. Mancini, *Vita di Lorenzo Valla* (Florence, 1891), 52 ff.; M. Fois, *Il pensiero cristiano di Lorenzo Valla nel quadro storico-culturale del suo ambiente* (Rome, 1969), 31 ff.; and S. Camporeale, *L. Valla, umanesimo e teologia* (Florence, 1972), 89 ff.

168. Monfasani, *George of Trebizond*, 289, and index.

169. See J. Cousin, *Recherches sur Quintilien: Manuscrits et éditions* (Paris, 1975), 169–70.

170. See the *index fontium* in Lorenzo Valla, *Repastinatio,* ed. Zippel, for Quintilian in general but especially for 5, 8ff.

171. See the bibliography of editions in Cousin, *Recherches sur Quintilien,* 171ff.; and Ward, "Renaissance Commentators," 158ff.

172. See Petrus Ramus, *Scholae in liberales artes,* ed. W. J. Ong, S.J. (Hildesheim, 1970), 319ff. Ong remarks, p. xiii*, that in the *Rhetoricae distinctiones in Quintilianum* "Ramus denounces over and over again Quintilian's 'many inane rules.' "

173. See R. Sabbadini, *Storia del ciceronianismo e di altre questioni letterarie nell'età della Rinascenza* (Turin, 1886), 9ff.; and D. Quint, "Humanism and Modernity: A Reconsideration of Bruni's *Dialogues," Renaissance Quarterly* 38 (1985): 423–45.

174. See *Gasparini Barzizii Bergomatis et Giuniforti filii opera,* ed. J. A. Furietti, 2 vols. (Rome, 1773), 1:1–14; Sabbadini, *La scuola,* 72–73; Mercer, *Teaching of Gasparino Barzizza,* 93–94; Monfasani, *George of Trebizond,* 265–66; and for an epitome R. P. Sonkowsky, "A Fifteenth-Century Rhetorical Opusculum," in *Classical, Mediaeval and Renaissance Studies in Honor of B. L. Ullman,* ed. C. Henderson, Jr., 2 vols. (Rome, 1964), 2:259–81.

175. I consulted the edition of Padua, 1483; see Mercer, *Teaching of Gasparino Barzizza,* 98.

176. Barzizza, *Opera,* ed. Furietti, 1:220–336; see Mercer, *Teaching of Gasparino Barzizza,* 96–98.

177. Sabbadini, *Storia del ciceronianismo,* 14.

178. Ibid., 16.

179. Ibid., 14–16; Pigman, "Barzizza's Studies of Cicero," 124–25.

180. Pigman, "Barzizza's Studies of Cicero," 124; and idem, "Barzizza's Treatise on Imitation," *Bibliothèque d'humanisme et Renaissance* 44 (1982): 341–52, where, e.g., one reads (p. 350, line 49): "Qui vult imitari, Ciceronem non relinquat" (I added comma).

181. See Monfasani, *Collectanea Trapezuntiana,* 232, sect. 30.

182. See Monfasani, *George of Trebizond,* 292.

183. See George of Trebizond, *Rhetoricum libri V* (Venice, 1523), fol. 84r.

184. I used the edition of Venice, 1477 (*Gesamtkatalog der Wiegendrucke,* no. 2739). For bibliography on Loschi, see Monfasani, *George of Trebizond,* 265; and more recently M. L. King, "Goddess and Captive: Antonio Loschi's Poetic Tribute to Maddalena Scrovegni (1389), Study and Text," *Medievalia et Humanistica* n.s. 10 (1981): 107–27. A good discussion of Loschi's work is Pigman, "Barzizza's Studies of Cicero," 130ff. The eleven orations Loschi analyzed are: *pro Pompeio, pro Milone, pro Plancio, pro Sulla, pro Archia, pro Marcello, pro Ligario, pro Deiotaro, pro Cluentio, pro Quinctio,* and *pro Flacco.*

185. Pigman, "Barzizza's Studies of Cicero," Mercer, *Teaching of Gasparino Barzizza,* 93.

186. See L. von Pastor, *History of the Popes from the Close of the Middle Ages,* trans. F. I. Antrobus et al. (London and St. Louis, 1891), 1:171.

187. *Italia illustrata* (Venice, 1510), fol. 105r, in the section on the Veneto.

188. I used the edition of Venice, 1477. No monograph on Polenton exists. Polenton treated the *post reditum in senatu, post reditum ad Quirites, pro domo sua, pro Coelio, pro Balbo, de haruspicum responsis,* the pseudo-Ciceronian *antequam iret in exilum, pro Sestio, in Vaticinium, de provinciis consularibus, in Catilinam* 1–4, and the exchange of speeches between pseudo-Sallust and pseudo-Cicero.

189. Sabbadini, *La scuola,* 90.

190. Monfasani, *George of Trebizond,* 38–39, 46–47, 292–93; and idem, *Collectanea Trapezuntiana,* 463–64.

191. *Collectanea Trapezuntiana,* 759–60.

192. See note 184 above.

193. Ward, "Renaissance Commentators," 150ff.

194. Ibid.

195. One finds a sampling of these editions in Monfasani, *Collectanea Trapezuntiana,* 463–64 and 759–60.

196. See above at note 83.

197. Gualdo Rosa, *Aspetti,* 73ff.

198. For Cicero and Wolf see ibid., 76ff. and 168ff.; for Melanchthon see his commentaries on Demosthenes in his *Opera omnia,* ed. H. E. Bindseil, vol. 17 (Halle, 1852).

199. For what follows see chapters 9–11 of my *George of Trebizond.*

200. See Patterson, *Hermogenes and the Renaissance,* who unaccountably ignores George of Trebizond. A more particularized study is F. Tateo, "La 'bella scrittura' del Bembo e l'Ermogene del Trapezunzio," in *Miscellanea di studi in onore di Vittore Branca* (Florence, 1983), 3:717–32.

201. For humanist logic in general, see C. Vasoli, *La dialettica e la retorica dell-'umanesimo* (Milan, 1968); and W. Risse, *Die Logik der Neuzeit* (Stuttgart, 1964), vol. 1.

202. To be sure, the humanists classicized the traditional forms, for instance, funeral oratory; see J. M. McManamon, "Innovation in Early Humanist Rhetoric: The Oratory of Pier Paolo Vergerio (the Elder)," *Rinascimento* n.s. 22 (1982): 3–32. Leonardo Bruni's panegyric of Florence about 1400 is an example of classicizing in another traditional form (see the literature cited in note 91 above). For epideictic prose in general, see T. C. Burgess, "Epideictic Literature," in *Studies in Classical Philology* 3 (1902): 89–261. A typical humanist oratorical collection is described by L. Bertalot, "Eine Sammlung Paduaner Reden des XV. Jahrhunderts," in his *Studien zum italienischen und deutschen Humanismus,* ed. P. O. Kristeller, 2 vols. (Rome, 1975), 2:209–35. For a survey of humanist oratory see V. Rossi, *Il Quattrocento* (Milan, 6th ed. 1956), 150–61, 166–68.

203. See Monfasani, *George of Trebizond,* 297–99.

204. This is not to say, of course, that law students did not study rhetoric; see, for example, R. J. Schoeck, "Lawyers and Rhetoric in Sixteenth-Century

England," in *Studies in the Practice,* ed. Murphy, 274–91. There developed, moreover, in the sixteenth century a literature of humanistic logic fit for lawyers; see V. Piano Mortari, "Dialettica e giurisprudenza: Studi sui tratti di dialettica legale del sec. XVI," *Annali di storia del diritto* 1 (1957): 293–401. A key figure in this development was the German teacher Christopher Hegendorff.

205. In addition to Valla, *Repastinatio,* ed. Zippel, and the authorities cited in note 201 above, see also Camporeale, *L. Valla,* 33ff.; and my review essay of Zippel's edition in *Rivista di letteratura italiana* 2 (1984): 177–94.

206. *Repastinatio,* ed. Zippel, 1:24.14–15.

207. Ibid., 1:175, 2:447.

208. Ibid., 1:176, lines 4ff. See, e.g., Cicero, *Orator* 69; *De oratore* 2.115, 121, 310; and Quintilian 8, pref. 7; 12, 2.11 and 10.59.

209. See the *index fontium* in *Repastinatio,* ed. Zippel.

210. See Monfasani, *George of Trebizond,* 328ff.

211. See Zippel's introduction to *Repastinatio* for the manuscripts and early printed editions.

212. See Vasoli, *La dialettica,* 100–15.

213. See ibid., 116–31 for Poliziano. Argyropoulos also translated Aristotle's logical works.

214. I used the Venice, 1540 edition of *De expedita ratione* and the Venice, 1501 edition of *De expectandis et fugiendis rebus* (vol. 2, fols. AA8v ff. contains *De dialectica*). See Vasoli, *La dialettica,* 132–44. I am not persuaded by Vasoli's argument that Lorenzo Valla strongly influenced Giorgio.

215. *De expedita ratione,* fol. 131r ff.

216. For Mosellanus, see the 1540 edition cited in note 214 above; for Caesarius and Melanchthon, see Vasoli, *La dialettica,* 134.

217. Vol. 2, fols. HH3r–KK3v in the edition of Venice, 1501.

218. I used the edition of Pavia, ca. 1498.

219. I used the edition of Venice, 1485 (*Repertorium Bibliographicum* no. 13546): *Artes orandi, epistolandi, memorandi.*

220. I used the edition of St. Albans, 1480. The first edition appeared the previous year. In 1480, at Paris, Traversagni also wrote an epitome of this work; see R. H. Martin (with a section by J. E. Mortimer), "The 'Epitome Margaritae Eloquentiae' of Laurentius Gulielmus de Saona," *Proceedings of the Leeds Philosophical and Literary Society* 14.4 (1971): 99–187. For literature see Monfasani, *George of Trebizond,* 261, and Ward, "Renaissance Commentators," 166–67.

221. I used the edition of Frankfurt, 1568. For bibliography on Brandolini, see A. Rotondò, "Brandolini, Aurelio Lippo," *Dizionario biografico degli italiani* (Rome, 1972), 14: 26–28; and O'Malley, *Praise and Blame,* 44–50, and index; and McMannon, "Renaissance Preaching."

222. See note 2 above.

223. See O'Malley, *Praise and Blame,* and McMannon, "Renaissance Preaching."

224. I used the edition of Basel, 1495 (Hain no. 12479).

225. I used the collection of *artes epistolandi* published by Josse Bade (Iodocus Badius Ascensius) at Paris in 1508, fols. 6v–22r. The first edition apparently was that of Rome, ca. 1490 (Hain no. 15157).

226. I used the Venice, 1486 edition of Perotti's *Grammar* (Hain no. 12676). For Perotti see Chapter 29, "Renaissance Grammar," in this volume.

227. See fols. i8v ff. of the Venice, 1486 edition.

228. I used the edition of Modena, 1490 (Hain no. 11865). An example of the separate publication of the thirty rules is the edition of 1508 cited in note 225 above. For the twenty-four editions before 1501 see Hain nos. 11863ff.

229. Dati's was an extraordinarily popular work, with more than a hundred editions before 1501 (*Gesamtkatalog der Wiegendrucke,* nos. 8033ff.). I used the Parisian edition of 1508 published by Josse Bade. For the sections relevant to letter writing see capitula 207–11. One *ars epistolandi* with which Dati's work was joined was that of pseudo-Lorenzo Valla, which was first printed at Venice by Cristoforo de' Pensi in 1503 in the collection entitled *Laurentii Vallensis oratoris clarissimi opuscula quaedam ...* (for a description see *Laurentii Valle Epistole,* ed. O. Besomi and M. Regoliosi [Padua, 1984], 85–86).

230. I used the autograph manuscript lat. XIII, 62 (= 4418), fols. 37r–46r, of the Biblioteca Marciana, Venice. There was one edition at Naples in 1472; see P. Mastrodimitris, *Nikolaos ho Sekoundinos (1406–1464). Bios kai ergon* [in Greek] (Athens, 1970), 193ff.

231. See below at note 284.

232. On this topic see G. Constable, *Letters and Letter Collections* (Turnhout, 1976).

233. *The Letters of Peter the Venerable,* ed. G. Constable, 2 vols. (Cambridge, MA, 1967), 1:1.

234. Constable, *Letters and Letter Collections,* 36ff.

235. For Guarino's failure to collect his own letters, see R. Sabbadini's introduction to his edition of the *Epistolario* (Venice, 1915), 1:iv. For Renaissance letter collections in general, see Clough, "Cult of Antiquity." See also H. Harth, "Poggio Bracciolini und die Brieftheorie des 15. Jahrhunderts. Zur Gattungsform des humanistischen Briefs," in *Brief im Zeitalter der Renaissance,* ed. Worstbrock, 81–99; and B. Marx, "Zur Typologie lateinischer Briefsammlungen in Venedig vom 15. zum 16. Jahrhundert," ibid., 118–54.

236. The literature on humanist stylistic imitation has been collected by G. W. Pigman, III, "Versions of Imitation in the Renaissance," *Renaissance Quarterly* 33 (1980): 1–32; and J. D'Amico, "The Progress of Renaissance Latin Prose: The Case of Apuleianism," *Renaissance Quarterly* 37 (1984): 351–92.

237. See his chapter on imitation, fol. K 3r–v, in *De rhetorica,* cited in note 214 above.

238. Poliziano especially made his views known in his controversy with Paolo Cortesi; see Sabbadini, *Il Ciceronianismo,* 32ff.

239. D'Amico, "Progress of Renaissance Latin Prose."

240. See *Le epistole "De imitatione" di Giovanfrancesco Pico della Mirandola e di Pietro Bembo*, ed. G. Santangelo (Florence, 1954). For Bembo, see the notice by C. Dionisotti in the *Dizionario biografico degli italiani* (Rome, 1966), 8:133–51. For Pico see C. B. Schmitt, *Gianfrancesco Pico della Mirandola (1469–1533) and His Critique of Aristotle* (The Hague, 1967), esp. 200–201.

241. Now available in a critical edition by P. Mesnard in Erasmus, *Opera omnia* (Amsterdam ed.), 1.2:581–710. Useful for the sixteenth-century phase of the controversy are also T. Simar, *Christophe de Longueil, humaniste (1488–1522)* (Louvain, 1911), 97ff.; and the introduction of Q. Breen to his edition of Mario Nizolio's *De veris principiis et vera ratione philosophandi contra pseudophilosophos*, 2 vols. (Rome, 1956).

242. See Sabbadini, *Il Ciceronianismo*, 68–69; V. Hall, "Life of Julius-Caesar Scaliger (1484–1558)," *Transactions of the American Philosophical Society* 40 (1950): 83–170, at 94–114; and Fumaroli, *L'age de l'eloquence*, 110, 452–54, and index.

243. See Sabbadini, *Il Ciceronianismo*, 69ff.; Fumaroli, *L'âge de l'eloquence*, 110ff., and R. C. Christie, *Etienne Dolet: The Martyr of the Renaissance 1508–1546, a Biography* (London, 1899), 195ff.

244. See Christie, *Etienne Dolet*, 228ff., and 268ff.

245. See Nizolio, *De veris principiis*, ed. Breen, and G. Pagani, "Mario Nizolio ed il suo lessico ciceroniano," *Accademia Nazionale dei Lincei, Rendiconti*, 5th ser. 2 (1893): 554–75, and his Appendix, 914–16. Pagani lists the editions in his "Gli ultimi anni di Mario Nizzoli," ibid., 897–922, at 914–16.

246. *Letters and Diaries of John Henry Newman*, ed. C. S. Dessain and T. Gornall (Oxford, 1973), 242, in a letter of 13 April 1869.

247. See R. Adolph, *The Rise of Modern Prose Style* (Cambridge, MA, 1968), who is a corrective to M. W. Croll, whose influential articles are collected in *Style, Rhetoric, and Rhythm: Essays by Morris W. Croll*, ed. J. M. Patrick and R. O. Evans (Princeton, 1966). But now see for English developments B. Vickers, "The Royal Society and English Prose Style: A Reassessment," in *Rhetoric and the Pursuit of Truth: Language Change in the Seventeenth and Eighteenth Centuries* (Los Angeles, 1985), 1–76. For French developments, see Fumaroli, *L'âge de l'eloquence*, 78ff., 254ff., and passim (see also Vickers's comments in the review cited in note 1 above). See also D. Shuger, "Morris Croll, Flacius Illyricus, and the Origin of Anti-Ciceronianism," *Rhetorica* 3 (1985): 269–84.

248. Fol. 43v of the cited manuscript (see n. 230, above).

249. See Vasoli, *La dialettica*, 147ff.; W. J. Ong, S.J., *Ramus, Method, and the Decay of Dialogue* (Cambridge, MA, 1983), 95ff.; Risse, *Logik der Neuzeit*, 19ff. I used the edition of Strasbourg, 1521.

250. Strasbourg, 1521 edition, fol. 1r–v; for Valla see note 208 above.

251. Cicero, *Topica*, 2; Boethius, *De topicis differentiis*, 1, *ad init*. See E. Stump's useful *Boethius's De topicis differentiis* (Ithaca, 1978).

252. Strasbourg, 1521 edition, fol. 3r–v.

253. Ibid., fols. 1v–2r: "Exiqua enim portio eorum quae discimus certa et immota est, adeoque si Academiae credimus, hoc solum scimus, quod nihil scimus."

254. Ibid., fols. 92v ff.

255. Ibid., fol. 74r.

256. Ibid., fols. 112v ff.

257. See Risse, *Logik der Neuzeit,* 22–23, who assumes, but without citing evidence, a specifically Agricolan influence in Hegius's discussion of method.

258. I rely on the listing of editions in W. J. Ong, S.J., *Ramus and Talon Inventory* (Cambridge, MA, 1958), 534ff. I do include in my count editions nos. i and ii, because Ong rightly views them as suspect.

259. See P. O. Kristeller, "An Unknown Humanist Sermon on St. Stephen by Guillaume Fichet," in *Mélanges Eugène Tisserant* (Vatican City, 1964), 459–97; F. Simone, "Guillaume Fichet retore ed umanista," *Memorie della Reale Accademia delle scienze di Torino* 2d ser. 69.2 (1939): 103–44.

260. See Monfasani, *George of Trebizond,* 321.

261. See Monfasani, *Miscellanea Trapezuntiana,* 44 for MS lat. 16224 of the Bibliothèque Nationale and MS 629 of the University of Paris.

262. For a discussion of this unique edition (Hain no. 7057) see Kristeller, "An Unknown Sermon," 472.

263. I have not read this work and am dependent for my information on F. Simone, "Robert Gaguin ed il suo cenacolo umanistico," *Aevum* 13 (1939): 410–76, at 440–54.

264. For what follows see *The Prefatory Epistles of Jacques Lefèvre d'Etaples and Related Texts,* ed. E. F. Rice, Jr. (New York and London, 1972), and the bibliography there cited, especially xxiv, n. 37.

265. Lefèvre's colleague, Josse Clichtove, published a variant version of Barzizza's work in 1498 (ibid., 51ff.) and included in his edition of Dati also Negri's thirty rules of elegance drawn from his *ars epistolandi* (see note 228 above).

266. A leading printer of classical texts at Paris was the humanist Josse Bade (Badius Ascensius), concerning whom see P. Renouard, *Bibliographie des impressions et des oeuvres de Josse Badius Ascensius, imprimeur et humaniste (1462–1535),* 3 vols. (Paris, 1908; reprinted New York, 1964).

267. In addition to Clough, "Cult of Antiquity," see A. Gerlo, "The *Opus de conscribendis epistolis* of Erasmus and the Tradition of the *Ars epistolica,*" in *Classical Influences on European Culture,* A.D. 500–1500, ed. R. R. Bolgar (Cambridge, 1971), 103–14; J. Rice Henderson, "Erasmus on the Art of Letter-Writing," in *Studies in the Theory,* ed. Murphy, 331–55; and M. Fumaroli, "Genèse de l'epistolographie classique: Rhétorique humaniste de la lettre, de Pétrarque à Juste Lipse," *Revue d'histoire littéraire de la France* 78 (1978): 886–905; the articles in *Briefe im Zeitalter der Renaissance,* ed. Worstbrock. I have not seen *Quaderni di retorica e poetica* 1 (1985), which contains the proceedings of a congress in 1983 on "la lettera familiare."

268. Gerlo, "*Opus de conscribendis epistolis* of Erasmus" 113, who lists Men-

niken, Schut, Erasmus, Despauterius, Vives, Langhveldt (Macropedius), Vibotius, Magnus de Ramlot, du Four, Verepaeus, Vladeraccus, Gramaye, and Justus Lipsius.

269. I counsulted pseudo-Dati in the edition of Cologne, Ulrich Zell, ca. 1470 (*Repertorium Bibliographicum* no. 6018).

270. See *De vita et scriptis Conradi Celtis Protucii*, ed. E. Klüpgelius, 2 vols. in 1 (Freiburg im Breisgau, 1827), 21–28; I used the collection *artes epistolandi* of 1568 cited for Brandolini in note 2 above, 371ff.

271. Edition of Frankfurt am Main, 1568 (see note 2 above), 391ff.

272. See Erasmus, *De conscribendis epistolis*, ed. Margolin, 1.2:153–579 of the Amsterdam *Opera omnia*. See also Rice Henderson, "Erasmus on the Art of Letter-Writing"; and J. Chomarat, *Grammaire et rhétorique chez Erasme*, 2 vols. (Paris, 1981), 2:1003ff.

273. For a good discussion of Erasmus's attitude toward this genre see Chomarat, *Grammaire et rhétorique chez Erasme*, 2:931ff.

274. Ibid., 2:731ff.

275. Ibid, 2:712.

276. The first edition of Brandolini was that of Basel, 1549; see O'Malley, *Praise and Blame*, 44, n. 17. All the sixteenth-century editions were printed in the north; see Rotondò, "Brandolini, Aurelio Lippo."

277. See Vives's *Opera omnia*, 2:263–314. On p. 311 a sample letter is dated 1533. See J. Rico Verdu, *La retorica española de los siglos XVI y XVII* (Madrid, 1973), 220ff.

278. See Vives, *Opera omnia*, 6:151, 155ff., and 340.

279. Ibid., 6:111, 155, 346, 354. See also Risse, *Logik der Neuzeit*, 37–39; and Vasoli, *La dialettica e la retorica*, 230–46.

280. Vives, *Opera omnia*, 2:265.

281. Ibid., 2:93–237.

282. Ibid., 3:82–120.

283. For instance the National Union Catalog (Pre-1956 Imprints) lists only six sixteenth-century editions in America. The British Library catalog lists only two editions.

284. I used the edition of Antwerp, 1614, which carries the title *Epistolica institutio, excepta dictantis eius ore, anno MDLXXXVII, mense Iunio*. See Fumaroli, *L'âge de l'eloquence*, 152ff. and idem, "Genèse de l'epistolographie classique."

285. See the introduction to the edition of these texts in Melanchthon's *Opera omnia*, ed. K. G. Bretschneider (Halle, 1846), 13:414 and 508. Bretschneider made the final version of each text the basis of his edition. In vol. 20, he edited the first version of the *Dialectic*, which carries the title *Compendaria dialectices ratio*. Since he used the question-and-answer format in the last version, Melanchthon called it *Erotematum dialectices*. I also consulted the first edition of the *Rhetoric*, entitled *De rhetorica libri tres*, in the printing of Cologne, 1521.

286. *Opera omnia*, 13:515, which is the text of the final version of the *Erotematum, dialectices*. In an earlier version (entitled *De dialectica;* I used the

Wittenberg, 1536 edition) he wrote: "Inter dialecticen et rhetoricam hos interest ... quod dialectica nudam causam brevibus verbis et tanquam punctis designat, rhetorica addit elocutionem inventis a dialectica et velut ornamentis verborum et sententiarum vestit." And in the first edition (*Opera omnia*, 20:711) he said: "[Dialectica] a Rhetoricis discrepat, quod haec splendidam magis et ad captum popularem orationem instruunt, dialectica<m> certam et exactam adornant et plane indicem orationis rhetoricae seu amussim."

287. For literature on him see the *Neue Deutsche Biographie* 3 (1956): 254.

288. I consulted the edition of Wittenberg, 1582.

289. Fol. H5r–v of the 1564, Wittenberg edition.

290. For Agricola, see note 249 above. For Trebizond see Monfasani, *Collectanea Trapezuntiana*, 473ff.; and idem, *George of Trebizond*, 333ff.

291. The standard work on Ramus is now Ong, *Ramus, Method* (despite its McLuhanite ideology). But also see Risse, *Logik der Neuzeit*, 122ff.; and Vasoli, *La dialettica e la retorica*, 333ff.

292. See Ong, *Ramus and Talon Inventory*, editions nos. 1–17, 58–182, 237–472; see also idem, *Ramus, Method*, 295ff.

293. I examined an undated edition at Yale University. Concerning Locher, see the notice in the *Neue Deutsche Biographie* 14 (1984): 743–44, by P. Ukena; and J. H. Overfield, *Humanism and Scholasticism in Late Medieval Germany* (Princeton, 1984), 185 ff. and passim.

294. I used the Venice, 1559 edition of Caesarius's *Dialectica* and the Augsburg, 1539 edition of Rivius's *De dialectica libri VI*. On Caesarius see Vasoli, *La dialettica e la retorica*, 260ff.; and Risse, *Logik der Neuzeit*, 25. For Rivius see Risse, *Logik der Neuzeit*, 47.

295. I used the Paris, 1542 edition of Caesarius and the Augsburg, 1539 edition of Rivius.

296. See A. Schindling, *Humanistische Hochschule und Freie Reichsstadt. Gymnasium und Akademie in Srassburg* (Wiesbaden, 1977), especially chap. 5, 162ff.; Vasoli, *La dialettica e la retorica*, 310ff.; N. W. Gilbert, *Renaissance Concepts of Method* (New York, 1960), index; and Ong, *Ramus, Method*, 232ff.

297. See Patterson, *Hermogenes and the Renaissance*, 219.

298. I consulted the editions of Paris, 1539 and Strasbourg, 1560 of the *Partitiones dialecticae* (the first edition was Strasbourg, 1539) and the editions of Strasbourg, 1539 and Strasbourg, 1549 of his dialogues on Cicero's *Partitiones oratoriae*.

299. See Monfasani, *George of Trebizond*, 325ff., which corrects Ong concerning Hermogenes.

300. On p. 8 of the 1549 edition: "Sed ex te Luteciae didici partiendi methodum. . . ."

301. In an unsigned preface to Ramus's *Scholae in liberales artes* (probably by the publisher Eusebius Episcopus; see Ong, *Ramus, Method*, 336, n. 6) we read (fol. a2v of the Basel, 1569 edition): "Hos dialecticos tam insignes tamque amabiles Ioannes Sturmius ex Agricolae schola Lutetiam Pari-

siorum primus attulit academiamque academiarum principem incredibili tam insperatae utilitatis desiderio inflammavit."

302. *Ramus, Method,* 230ff., but see note 299 above.

303. Fol. 3r in the Strasbourg, 1560 edition.

304. On Sturm's dialectic see Risse, *Logik der Neuzeit,* 41ff.

305. See Schindling, *Humanistische Hochschule,* 162ff.; and T. W. Baldwin, *William Shakespere's Small Latine and Lesse Greeke,* 2 vols. (Urbana, IL, 1914), 1:285ff.

306. I used the edition of Strasbourg, 1581, pp. 138ff.

307. See, for example, F. de Dainville, *La naissance de l'humanisme moderne* (Paris, 1960), 94. In this work and in his *L'education des Jésuites (XVIᵉ–XVIIIᵉ siècles)* (Paris, 1978), Dainville frequently compared Sturm's educational methods and curriculum to that of the Jesuit *Ratio studiorum.*

308. H. Boehmer, *The Jesuits: An Historical Study,* trans. P. Zeller Strodach (Philadelphia, 1928), 110.

309. In addition to Dainville, *La naissance* and idem, *L'éducation,* see also A. Battistini, "I manuali di retorica dei Gesuiti," in *La Ratio studiorum: Modelli culturali e pratiche educative dei Gesuiti in Italia tra Cinque e Seicento,* ed. G. P. Brizzi (Rome, 1981), 77–120.

310. See L. Flynn, S.J., "The *De arte rhetorica* of Cyprian Soarez, S.J.," *Quarterly Journal of Speech* 42 (1956): 356–74; and idem, "Sources and Influences of Soarez' *De arte rhetorica,*" *Quarterly Journal of Speech* 43 (1957): 257–65. Flynn counted 410 references to Cicero, 119 to Quintilian, and 37 to Aristotle. I consulted the editions of Paris, 1573 and Cologne, 1593. An edition significant for its late date, location, and content is that of Mexico City, 1693, which was a summary accompanying the text of twelve orations Cicero "ad usum gymnasorum Societatis Iesu." The first Mexican edition of this summary seems to have appeared in 1623. See also Rico Verdu, *La retorica española,* 212ff.

311. I used the facsimile reprint of the 1553 edition published at Gainesville, Florida, 1962, with an introduction by R. H. Bowers.

312. See ibid., 18, 37. See Howell, *Logic and Rhetoric,* 12ff. and 98ff.

313. See J. W. O'Malley, "Content and Rhetorical Forms in Sixteenth-Century Treatises on Preaching," in *Studies in the Theory,* ed. Murphy, 238–52. H. Caplan and H. H. King have provided useful bibliographical surveys: "Latin Tractates on Preaching: A Book-List," *Harvard Theological Review* 42 (1949): 185–206, at 187–95 for the sixteenth century; and in the vernacular languages: "French Tractates on Preaching: A Book-List," *Quarterly Journal of Speech* 36 (1950): 296–325, at 297–98; "Italian Treatises on Preaching: A Book-List," *Speech Monographs* 16 (1949): 243–52, at 244: "Spanish Treatises on Preaching: A Book-List," *Speech Monographs* 17 (1950): 161–70, at 161–62; and "Dutch Treatises on Preaching: A List of Books and Articles," *Speech Monographs* 21 (1954): 236–47 (no sixteenth-century imprints).

314. See note 220 above for Traversagni and note 221 for Brandolini.

315. I used the collection of northern *artes praedicandi* printed at London in 1570 (Reuchlin, Dietrich, Melanchthon, Hepinus), the first edition of which appeared in 1540. See J. W. O'Malley, "Lutheranism in Rome 1542–1543—The Treatise by Alfonso Zorilla," *Thought* 54 (1979): 262–73, reprinted as item X in his *Rome and the Renaissance: Studies in Culture and Religion* (London, 1981). For Reuchlin's treatise, see J. Benzing, *Bibliographie der Schriften Johannes Reuchlin* (Vienna, 1955), 23–24; and G. R. Evans, "The *Ars Praedicandi* of Johannes Reuchlin (1455–1522)," *Rhetorica* 3 (1985): 99–105.

316. Still to be read in vol. 5, cols. 767–1100, of Erasmus's *Opera omnia* edited by Jean LeClerc, 10 vols. (Leiden, 1703–6; reprinted London, 1962). See Chomarat, *Grammaire et rhétorique chez Erasme*, 2:1052ff.

317. *Opera*, ed. LeClerc, 5:873C.

318. Ibid., 5:1070D.

319. The work is anonymous in the edition, but is identified by Caplan and King, "Latin Tractates," 194. The work was not accepted into Melanchthon's modern *opera omnia*. But see K. Hartfelder, *Philip Melanchthon als Praeceptor Germaniae* (Berlin, 1899; reprinted Neeuwkoop, 1964), 593, an. 1535. For literature on Dietrich see the *Lexikon für Theologie und Kirche* 3 (1959): 387; "Dietrich, Veit (Vitus Theodorus oder Theodoricus)," in the *Allgemeine Deutsche Biographie* 5 (1875): 196–97.

320. See *The New Schaff-Herzog Encyclopedia* 1 (1949): 59.

321. See above at notes 264ff. See also J. Dyck, "The First German Treatise on Homiletics: Erasmus Sarcer's *Pastorale* and Classical Rhetoric," in *Studies in the Theory*, ed. Murphy, 221–37. I have been unable to see U. Schnell, *Die homiletische Theorie Philipp Melanchthons* (Berlin, 1968).

322. See O'Malley, "Lutheranism in Rome."

323. I used the first edition of Venice, 1562; see Fumaroli, *L'âge de l'eloquence*, 136.

324. I used the edition of Verona, 1732 of Diego de Estella's treatise.

325. I used the Spanish translation in the *Biblioteca de autores españoles*, 11 (Madrid, 1945): *Obras de Fray Luis de Granada*, 488–642. For an interesting comparison between Granada's work and the *Rhetorica christiana* of Diego Valadés, which did include memory, see E. J. Palomera, S.J., *Fray Diego Valadés o.f.m. evangelizador humanista de la nueva España* (Mexico City, 1962). See also A. Martí, *La preceptiva retórica española en el siglo de oro* (Madrid, 1972), 95ff.

326. Fumaroli, *L'âge de l'eloquence*, 143. See also O'Malley, "Lutheranism in Rome," and Martí, *La preceptiva retorica*, 196ff.

327. I used the edition of Verona, 1732. See Fumaroli, *L'âge de l'eloquence*, 142.

328. I read Carbone's treatise in the edition of Venice, 1595.

329. For Cavalcanti see the notice in the *Dizionario biografico degli italiani* (Rome, 1979), 22:611–17, by C. Mutini. I used the Venice, 1559 of the *Retorica*.

330. *Trattati di poetica e retorica del Cinquecento*, ed. B. Weinberg, 4 vols. (Bari,

1970–74), 1:451–67 (Sansovino); 2:141–61 (Conti) and 335–451 (Barbaro); 3:101–34 (Denores).

331. For Cavalcanti, see the edition of Venice, 1559, 329ff.; for Barbaro see the previous note.

332. See Sturm, *Linguae latinae resolvendae ratio,* Strasbourg, 1581, 3–5. Sturm did not think much of Camillo's *Theatrum.* Sturm also adds that Camillo was "imperitus linguae Graecae."

333. For bibliography see Monfasani, *George of Trebizond,* 324; and C. Vasoli, "Considerazioni su alcuni temi retorici di Giulio Camillo Delminio," in *Retorica e poetica,* ed. D. Goldin and G. Folena (Padua, 1979), 243–57.

334. For an indication of the spreading influence of the *Rhetoric* in a related field see B. Weinberg, *A History of Literary Criticism in the Italian Renaissance,* 2 vols. (Chicago, 1961), index (Aristotle, *Rhetoric*).

335. *La Retorica,* Venice, 1559, 24–25.

336. For the edition, see Legrand, *Bibliographie,* 4:268–69. For bibliography on Denores, see Weinberg, *Trattati,* 3:491–92.

337. The critical edition is Nizolio, *De veris principiis,* ed. Breen. See also Pagani, "Mario Nizzoli filosofo," 716–74; Vasoli, *La dialettica e la retorica,* 603–32; P. Rossi, "La celebrazione della rettorica e la polemica antimetafisica nel *De principiis* di Mario Nizolio," in *La crisi dell'uso dogmatico della ragione,* ed. A. Banfi (Milan, 1953), 99–121; and idem, "Il *De principiis* di Mario Nizolio," *Archivio di filosofia* 3 (1953): 57–92.

338. See Breen's introduction to *De veris principiis,* 1:xx–xxi.

339. Nizolio cited Agricola, Vives, and Melanchthon numerous times in *De veris principiis,* but was silent on Ramus; see Vasoli, *La dialettica e la retorica,* 611; and Breen's comment in *De principiis,* 2:177 n. 37.

340. *De veris principiis,* ed. Breen, 2:33ff., 91ff.

341. Ibid., 1:65.

342. Ibid., 1:22; 2:80.

343. Ibid., 2:53. Oddly enough, at several points Nizolio spoke of Zeno as if he predated Aristotle, e.g., 2:27, 29.

344. Ibid., 2:49ff.

345. Ibid., 2:31ff., esp. 36.

346. See Monfasani, *George of Trebizond,* 331–32.

347. Fol. 154v of the Venice, 1543 edition.

348. Monfasani, *George of Trebizond,* 331–32; and E. Garin, "Nota su alcuni aspetti delle retoriche rinascimentali e sulla 'Retorica' del Patrizi," *Archivio*

349. *di filosofia* 3 (1953): 7–56, at 35–36.

350. See, for example, his *De augmentis scientiarum,* published in 1623, book 6, chap. 2 (*The Works of Francis Bacon,* ed. J. Spedding, R. L. Ellis, and D. D. Heath [London, 1858; reprinted Stuttgart-Bad Cannstatt, 1963], 1:663); cf. his *Advancement of Learning,* book 2 (*Works of Francis Bacon,* 3:403), which was completed in 1603, but which lacks the specific attack on Ramus's "unica methodus." See L. Jardine, *Francis Bacon: Discovery and the Art of Discourse* (Cambridge, 1974), 171, 175n.

351. *Advancement,* book 2 (*Works of Francis Bacon,* 3:410); *De augmentis,* book 6, chap. 3 (1:672).
352. See B. Vickers, *Francis Bacon and Renaissance Prose* (Cambridge, 1968).
353. *Advancement of Learning,* book 1 (*Works of Francis Bacon,* 3:282–84); *De augmentis,* book 6, chap. 3 (1:450–51).
354. *De augmentis,* book 6, chap. 3 (*Works of Francis Bacon,* 1:670–71); and less powerfully in *Advancement of Learning,* book 2 (3:408–10); see Jardine, *Francis Bacon,* 216ff. For a somewhat different perspective see J. P. Zappen, "Science and Rhetoric from Bacon to Hobbes: Responses to the Problem of Eloquence," in *Rhetoric 78: Proceedings of "Theory of Rhetoric, an Interdisciplinary Conference,"* ed. R. L. Brown and M. Steinmann, Jr. (Minneapolis, 1979), 399–419.
355. See Breen, "Giovanni Pico della Mirandola."
356. There is much to be done on this educational issue; see, for instance, S. IJsseling, *Rhetoric and Philosophy in Conflict,* trans. P. Dunphy (The Hague, 1976), 60ff.

32 &. HUMANISM AND HISTORY
Donald R. Kelley

H ISTORY EMERGING FROM HUMANISM IS ACTUALLY MY THEME, for as Eugenio Garin has observed, "The modern conception of history appeared on the terrain of humanist 'philology' at just the point where 'consciousness' of the 'novelty' of humanism arose." [1] The "Renaissance" itself reflected a new perspective and awareness of a "middle age" between antiquity and modernity, while humanism raised history to the level of a liberal art, that is, one of the *studia humanitatis*. History also had important links with the other four of these humanities. Along with "method" it represented one of the two parts of the art of grammar, and indeed "historical sense" (*sensus historicus*) was equivalent to literal or grammatical as distinguished from figurative interpretation. With rhetoric history had even closer ties, since it was likewise devoted to concrete, causal, and didactic description (adding only the further criterion of truth); and as "philosophy teaching by example" it could also be seen as a branch of moral philosophy. History was of course normally contrasted with poetry; but there was a historical connection, since many Renaissance authors came to believe that history had originally emerged from poetic forms. In these and other ways the study of history illustrated and conformed to the "encyclopedic" aspirations of Renaissance humanism and especially of that scholarly aspect of humanism called philology.

This concept has become not only commonplace but perhaps also too commonplace, for in some ways it reflects the rhetorical hyperbole of humanists more than the historical circumstance that the much-deprecated "middle age" before the fourteenth century revival had its own sense of "history" both as a form of thought and as a literary genre. Medieval authors carefully distinguished between annals, chronicles, and history; had their own ideas of historical truth, which they distinguished from prophecy as well as from fable and poetry; and developed their own methods of investigation, authentication, and criticism. They also had sophisticated notions of "tradition" and of cultural change (for example, under the guise of "reformation," "renovation," the "translation of Empire and of learning," of periodization, and even of anachronism). Nor were they in a sense unaware of the "humanist" values of historical study.

"History," wrote Henry of Huntingdon in the twelfth century, "is the major mark of distinction between rational beings and brutes."[2]

* * *

Yet it remains true that no authors before the fourteenth century displayed the self-conscious literary posturing and critical nostalgia characteristic of Petrarch, who is as seminal a figure in the humanist conception of history, as of philology in general. "Among the many subjects that interested me I dwelt especially upon antiquity," he wrote, "for our own age has always repelled me, so that, had it not been for the love of those dear to me, I should have been born in any other period than our own. In order to forget my own time, I have continually striven to place my self in spirit in other ages."[3] And so indeed he did in his famous letters to Cicero, Quintilian, Varro, Livy, and Homer (not to mention Cola di Rienzo). This feigned correspondence is filled with a curious combination of excitement (at contact with their manuscript remains) and melancholy (at the destruction wrought by time to their reputations as well as to their works). How "mangled and mutilated" was the copy of Quintilian's *Institutes of Oratory* that came into Petrarch's hands! "I recognize therein the hand of time—the destroyer of all things," he lamented, from "the land of the living ... on the very first day of our becoming acquainted"—that is, his discovery of the manuscript—which, to show the vividness of Petrarch's sense of history, was "on the 7th of December, in the 1350th year of him whom thy master [Augustus] preferred to persecute rather than to profess."[4] And to Livy he wrote: "I should wish (if it were permitted from on high) either that I had been born in thine age or thou in ours. . . . As I read I seem to be living in the midst of [Scipio, Brutus, Cato, Nero, and others] not with the thievish company of today, among whom I was born under an evil star." Cicero was his chosen model, though Petrarch deplored the activism that had distracted Cicero from his literary pursuits. It was indeed Petrarch's discovery of Cicero's letters to Atticus that had inspired his imaginary correspondence with the ancients—symbolizing in his own very personal way one of the tasks of humanism from that time on.

Behind this sentimental pose Petrarch was in fact capable of impressive historical criticism, perhaps best illustrated in his exposure of a forged Austrian donation, allegedly made by Caesar to the Habsburgs but filled with a variety of ludicrous anachronisms, including ignorance of Caesar's style (always third person, for example) and of the Roman calendar.[5] To historical writing as such Petrarch's contributions were marginal, but again he showed an almost unprecedented sense of the special demands of historical study, which he set apart not only from mere chronicle but also from disputatious scholasticism, which he abhorred in any case. As he remarked in the preface to his *De viris illustribus,* "I am neither the peacemaker among conflicting historians nor the collector of every minute fact; but rather, I am the copier of those whose verisimilitude or greater authority demands that they be given great credence."[6] He registered his particular approval of Cicero's "first law of history," which was to tell the truth and, what is more, the whole truth, although he added that for didactic purposes his Lives of the ancients were highly selective and artful. Other exhibitions of Petrarch's historical skills include his *Rerum memorandum libri IV,* his epic poem *Africa,* and his critical notes on the text of Livy. What Petrarch accomplished for history in general was to establish Latin antiquity as a cultural and political ideal and to make it an object of historical study rather than the living but sadly degenerate tradition it had been for Dante: "What is all history but the praise of Rome?"[7]

On such grounds Petrarch created not only a scholarly tradition but also a legend—as the first (*il primo,* Leonardo Bruni called him) to open the way to a true understanding of history. Aside from Boccaccio, Coluccio Salutati was the first Petrarchist in this sense, and he continued to emphasize the central place of history in political as well as ethical terms. Than history, he wrote, "nothing is more elegant, . . . nothing more capable of moving while delighting the spirit."[8] This refrain was continued by Bruni, who was Salutati's successor as Florentine chancellor as well as champion of good letters, which he expanded by his pioneering study of Greek authors. "First among such studies I place history," he declared, ". . . for it is our duty to understand the origins of our own history and its development, and the achievements of Peoples and Kings." The aim of such study, he added, was both to enlarge political foresight and to draw moral examples. "Thus," he concluded, "history renders us both wiser and more moderate."[9]

Bruni established the model of humanist historiography in his *Historia florentini populi,* which occupied him from at least 1416 until his death in 1444. If his literary inspiration came from Livy and Thucydides, his perspective was more immediately fashioned in the crucible of recent Florentine experience, especially the long conflict with Milan and the attendant "crisis" of the early fifteenth century, which reinforced his republican commitments and led him beyond the largely moral preoccupations of Petrarch to the social and political concerns associated with what has been called "civic humanism." Following Salutati (who had made his own discovery of Cicero's familiar letters), Bruni praised Cicero precisely as one who illustrated the ideal of a life at once active and contemplative. Bruni also embraced the Ciceronian view of history as a repository of lessons (*plena exemplorum historia*) to be memorialized and imitated or avoided. As he wrote in the preface to his masterwork: "History . . . involves at the same time a long continuous narrative, causal explanation of each particular event, and appropriately placed judgments on certain issues."[10] The public good and great deeds of the Florentine past had hitherto been neglected, Bruni continued; "I have decided, therefore, to write the known history of this city, not only for my own time but for earlier ages as far as they can be studied." In Livian style, then, he began *ab urbe condita* ("from the founding of the city"), except that he displayed a characteristic humanistic impatience with such "fables" as those of Trojan origins and Carolingian restoration. According to Bruni, Florence had been an Etruscan settlement and later a military colony under Sulla—a thesis that satisfied the demands both of historical criticism and of republican ideology.

Having disposed of the crucial problem of origins, Bruni went on to describe the loss of both civil liberty and classical literature, as Cicero's republic was replaced by Caesar's empire and as the empire itself collapsed under pressures of invading barbarians and usurping popes. His sources included classical authors and medieval chroniclers such as Orosius, Paul the Deacon, and especially Bruni's Florentine predecessors, the brothers Villani and Goro Dati; but in keeping with his theory of translation, that Ciceronian Latin provided the most complete expression of reality, he transmuted and in a way homogenized his uneven and disparate authorities in a classicist-rhetorical solvent.[11] In keeping with Ciceronian convention, too, he devoted particular attention to individual psychology, often presenting his interpretation of motives and policies through the ancient devices of orations or dialogues. Yet throughout this fusion of classical form and medieval substance his theme remained the rise of Florence to greatness, which is to say republican liberty and humanist culture—and of course military success.

Medieval darkness descended on the Roman–Florentine tradition with the fall of the western empire in 476, and there were no glimmers of light until after the defeat of the Lombards in 774. "From the time when the liberty of the Italian people was recovered," Bruni wrote in his biography of Petrarch (referring to this event), "the cities of Tuscany and elsewhere began to revive, and to take up classical studies, and somewhat to refine the coarse style," especially from the time of Dante. It was in this social and political context that Petrarch, through his recovery of Cicero, could become "the first . . . to restore to light the ancient elegance of style, which was lost and dead."[12] It was in this context, too, that Bruni expanded Petrarchan self-understanding to include the political ideals and historical perspective of civic humanism. Florentine "liberty" and "virtue" (*virtus,* in a sense not far removed from Machiavellian *virtù*) did not survive the century, but Brunian history, as the chief teacher of prudence, practical wisdom, was preserved in the tradition of humanist historiography from Bruni to Machiavelli and beyond.

In terms of both the art of history and what has been called "the myth of Florence"[13] Bruni's work was an inspiration to later generations. Among practitioners of Brunian history were two of his successors in the chancery, Poggio Bracciolini and Bartolomeo della Scala, and various vernacular historians, including Francesco Guicciardini and Scipione Ammirato as well as Machiavelli. Poggio was a great humanist scholar in his own right; and his *Historiae florentini populi,* a continuation of Bruni's but narrower in scope, was a relatively minor work, assembled in the last years of his life (1455–59). While Bruni modeled his book on Livy, Poggio chose rather to follow the lead of Sallust; and his concern was largely with military and diplomatic affairs from the mid-fourteenth century. He also devoted considerable attention to psychological factors, especially anger and the drive for power, and likewise emphasized the didactic value of his work. Less successful was the *Historia florentinorum* of Scala, who began again with origins but who had not even reached the fourteenth century before his death in 1497. Other products of the Florentine school included a history of the First Crusade by Benedetto Accolti, another Florentine chancellor (1458–64); a history of Pisa by Giannozzo Manetti; several works by Matteo Palmieri; a history of the Italian wars and another on ancient Rome by Bernardo Rucellai; and others. But none of these works before the time of Machiavelli and Guicciardini surpassed, and few equaled, the standard set by Bruni.

*   *   *

In the course of the fifteenth century this new style of historiography—erudite, eloquent, elitist—attracted a growing number of practitioners outside of Florence. It also attracted a growing audience through the new art of printing, which (providentially, to the humanists' way of thinking) appeared just in time to carry their cultural message.[14] Among the most distinguished were two historians of Venice, Bernardo Giustiniani (1408–1489) and Marcantonio Coccio (known as Sabellico, ca. 1436–1506), who during the 1480s both wrote histories of the Serenissima, again *ab urbe condita* in a Livian and Brunian fashion, though without the same critical ability. Giustiniani had the characteristic humanist fascination with origins but remained satisfied with the old Trojan theory combined with the view, taken by Sabellico as well, that the *prisci Veneti* came from Gaul. Yet in political terms he regarded Venice as heir of the Roman Empire; and indeed he described Venetian history as a synthesis

of those two concepts which Florentines assumed to be opposed—
imperium and *libertas*—a balance maintained by an ancient and continuous tradition of nobility and institutional order. Sabellico, a student of
Pomponio Leto and an admirer of Flavio Biondo, was more successful,
and indeed his history had virtually official status. Florence's longtime
rival Milan also found a number of scholars to celebrate its ancient splen-
dors and modern successes, including Bernardino Corio's *Patria historia*
(1509), a humanist effort despite its vernacular form; and so did the
Kingdom of Naples, whose most notable historians were Giovanni Pontano and Lorenzo Valla. This fashion in historiography was followed
with varying degrees of fidelity and success by several of the smaller Italian states, including Genoa, Siena, Mantua, and Ferrara.

The proliferation and publication of such books and their classical
models in the late fifteenth century testify to the popularity of humanist
historical writing but only indirectly to the increasing depth and breadth
of historical studies in general. For it was the work not of official historiographers, publicists, or local antiquarians but of a few unconventional
scholars eager, in the spirit of Petrarch, to explore new areas or to apply
new methods. The vision of history that was emerging a century after
Petrarch's death was transformed by several factors: discoveries of classical manuscripts by Poggio and others and consequent new influences,
such as those of Tacitus and Polybius; accumulating labors in archaeology, topography, and related fields, such as the history of language, literature, art, law, and institutions; the central place given to history by
educators like Guarino and Vittorino da Feltre; and especially the techniques of historical, "grammatical," and conjectural criticism that lay at
the roots of the great western tradition of "philology" and historical
science.[15] The continuity of this tradition is neatly illustrated by a manuscript of Livy, which was successively examined and emended by Petrarch and Lorenzo Valla, whose criticisms, declarations, and general
perspective provided a model for generations of scholars concerned with
historical reconstruction and expression.[16]

From several angles Lorenzo Valla appears to be the dominant figure
of fifteenth-century historical studies, although his contribution to historiography was modest and flawed. Valla led assaults on the past from
various directions, his efforts including critical notes on the New Testament as well as on Livy, analyses of the texts of classical Roman law (the
"fathers of jurisprudence," Petrarch had called these authors), translations of Herodotus and Thucydides, and especially his writings on the
Latin language, representing the main thrust of his attempt to restore
Romanitas—ancient civilization as a whole—again exhibiting the Petrarchan combination of aesthetic and historical motives, of *elegantia*

242 DONALD R. KELLEY

and *philologia*. Valla's basic ideological theme was that, through Latin language and civil law, the Romanist tradition he represented still ruled: although political power had vanished, "yet we reign still, by this more splendid sovereignty, in a great part of the world." [17] Of course the barbarians continued to threaten, and Valla provided both a defense against the enemies of good letters and an implicit justification for historical scholarship in his *Disputationes dialecticae*, which was a humanist critique of degenerate Aristotelian philosophy. In general the effect of Valla's argument was to reject the inhuman categories of scholasticism (predicaments, transcendentals, and the rest) in favor of those of ordinary language (*usus hominum*), that is to say the "historical sense" of grammar and the "elegance" of rhetoric, which was his own "profession."

It was essentially this train of thought that led Valla to contradict Aristotle's commonly accepted judgment that history was inferior to—that is, less philosophical than—poetry. "History is more robust than poetry," Valla wrote, "because it is more truthful. It is oriented not toward abstraction but toward concrete truth, . . . teaching by example"; and he repeated the maxim of Cicero that "without history one remains always a child." [18] Valla's own most famous and most exemplary contribution to historical truth was surely his declamation against the Donation of Constantine, which was at once a critique of a particular canonist forgery (made on historical and philological as well as legal grounds) and a general attack on papal tradition—"not only against the dead," as he put it, "but the living also . . . and the authorities." [19] The only "authority" to Valla was that of "antiquity" as a whole, and even that only as interpreted by philological experts. What gives Valla a central place in the history of history in general is not his somewhat commonplace *Historiarum Ferdinandi regis Aragoniae libri tres* or even his polemical exchanges with Bartolomeo Facio about the nature of history, but rather his efforts at textual criticism, most notably his historical notes on the New Testament, his philological study of Roman law, and his critique of ecclesiastical tradition, which had a powerful impact on Protestant scholarship and perspective.

The major figure in humanist historiography before Guicciardini was surely Flavio Biondo (1392–1463), who to a remarkable degree combined the best qualities of Bruni and Valla with Livian narrative and Varronian erudition. Inclining toward the latter was his *Roma instaurata* (1443–46), devoted to the topography of ancient Rome and to the monuments of the Christian city as well; his *Italia illustrata* (1448–53), a geographical and historical survey of the fourteen regions of the peninsula based on extensive travel and observation; and his *Roma triumphans* (1452–59), a ground-breaking study of ancient institutions dedicated to his fellow historian Aeneas Silvius Piccolomini and including a short essay on legal history, *De militia et jurisprudentia*. In discussing the body of the city, he explained, one should not neglect its soul, that is to say its system of laws—like history itself a comprehensive reflection of human, or national, wisdom.[20] But Biondo's major work was his magisterial *Historiarum ab inclinatio romanorum imperii decades,* perhaps the most influential view of postclassical and medieval European history before its most famous descendant, the perhaps derivatively entitled *Decline and Fall of the Roman Empire* by Edward Gibbon, who likewise found his inspiration among the Roman ruins.

Biondo's book purported to survey the entire sweep of medieval European history—that *medium aevum* which Petrarch had perceived and the next century named—starting with the invasion of Rome by the Goths in 410.[21] He began, in other words, with that crisis of late antiquity which had inspired Augustine's *City of God* and the historiographical supplement by Orosius; and while Biondo could attain neither the depths of Augustine's insights nor the breadth of Orosius's geographical vision, he did pursue in unprecedented detail Bruni's theme of the collapse and revival of the Roman tradition. The work divides into four "decades" of books, the first reaching to the beginning of the Carolingian Empire, the second to 1410 (thousandth anniversary of the sack of Rome), the third to 1439, and the last, containing only two books, to 1441, the sections on his own century having been composed first. Neither focus nor subject is consistent, but the overall theme is clear: the replacement of the declining pagan *respublica* by the emergent *orbis christianus,* and of the caesars by Christ as *imperator;* and it is reflected in his system of dating, which changes significantly from *ab inclinatione imperii* to *anno Domini*. His horizons are Europewide, and he has a more coherent view of Italy as a community of cities, but his remarks about areas outside are scattered and increasingly infrequent, especially concerning his own age. To some extent this restriction may have been the result of his gloomy view of *praesens tempus,* especially after the outbreak of the Great Schism in 1378, but partly it was his inability to master the depressing pattern of interstate conflict in the fifteenth century and the wars that dominated his narrative.

Yet Biondo made an impressive effort to utilize an extraordinary range of sources (more than fifty), including not only familiar medieval chronicles but also writings (especially letters) of Dante and Petrarch, papal privileges and registers, canon law and of course archaeological and epigraphic material; and he tried to discuss cultural as well as political and military affairs. He tried also, however fitfully and awkwardly, to achieve a Ciceronian style; and perhaps most importantly he displayed a political point of view that gave direction as well as distinctiveness to his narrative. He had positive things to say about the new urban growth of northern Italy as well as the ancient empire. The principal civilizing mission he followed, however, was neither Bruni's civic humanism nor the imperialism of Bruni's Milanese and Venetian counterparts; rather, like Valla in his last years, it was that of the Roman church and so, unfashionably, of medieval tradition.

There were other medievalists who owed less to the humanist movement. One was Bartolomeo Sacchi (Platina), although his *Lives of the Popes*, extending to the pontificate of Paul II, was ostensibly aimed at "urging men to prudence, fortitude, modesty, and all the other human virtues." [22] The book was filled with enough scandalous revelations to be even more influential in the next century, through the Protestant adaptation of Robert Barnes as well as the edition and continuation by Onufrio Panvinio. Another genre was the universal world chronicle, which originated with Eusebius and Jerome and which also received new life in the hands of Protestants in the sixteenth century. Fifteenth-century collections having at least some connection with humanism included the world chronicle of St. Antonino of Florence, the *Enneades* of Sabellico, and to some extent the German chronicle of Hartmann Schedel, all of which had recourse to the old Augustinian (and Orosian) pattern of six ages and Four World Monarchies. Perhaps the most popular of all such attempts to write history not *ab urbe* but *ab orbe condito* was the *Supplementum chronicarum* of Jacopo Filippo of Bergamo, though among Protestants the *Chronicon carionis* was most authoritative, especially after receiving the humanist and Lutheran endorsement of Philipp Melanchthon.[23]

One of the most famous products of the Roman tradition, though it belongs to the category of contemporary history or memoirs, was the *Commentarii* of Biondo's friend Aeneas Silvius Piccolomini, humanist, diplomat, and (during the period covered by this work, 1458–64) Pope Pius II.[24] Aeneas Silvius was contentious, a bit vain and eccentric in a fashion not unlike that of Petrarch, with whom he also shared the humanist obsession with fame as a literary form of immortality. Drawing on a lifetime of travel and diplomatic experience, Pius II dealt with a variety of political matters, ranging from the Italian scene to France and the empire to the problem of the crusade; but the papacy remained the most constant focus, his own omnivorous interests the basis of selection, and a vivid and highly personal style the mode of discourse. Humanist attitudes were displayed prominently in this work and others, notably his abridgment of Biondo's *Decades*, his history of Bohemia and of Emperor Frederick III, and a famous letter on Germany that established an important link between Italian and northern humanism.

Related to, though not fully integrated with, humanist historiography was the work of "antiquarians," who went beyond the literary sources and methods of the Brunian school. Their motto was perhaps best expressed in the verse of Poliziano about

the wonderful faith of history reborn,
the wonderful second dawning of Rome.[25]

Ciriaco d'Ancona was one of the first to practice the art of *antiquitates* in order "not only to raise from the depths monuments which have been destroyed, but also to bring the names of cities back into the light."[26] Epigraphy had been born in the age of Petrarch, perhaps most notably with the commentary by his sometime friend Cola di Rienzo on the Capitoline inscription of the ancient *lex regia;* and it was developed further by Biondo and his sixteenth-century disciples, including Alessandro d'Alessandro, Carlo Sigonio, Onufrio Panvinio, and Fulvio Orsini. Numismatics was another embryonic humanist discipline, studied in a literary fashion by Guillaume Budé and more technically by Enea Vico, who unearthed coins of formerly unknown Roman emperors. In the period of the Counter-Reformation, Christian antiquity likewise was subjected to archaeological study according to the attitudes and methods of humanism.[27]

Most significant in the convergence of conventional history and antiquities was the study of Roman law, especially pursued through the examination of the famous Florentine manuscript of Justinian's Digest by such "grammarians" as Angelo Poliziano, Alessandro d'Alessandro, Lodovico Bolognini, Pietro Crinito, Budé, and Antonio Agustín.[28] The central figure in the emergence of "legal humanism" was Andrea Alciato, whose disciples at the University of Bourges formed a school (the socalled *mos gallicus iuris docendi*) on the basis of his literary and historical approach. Commentaries by Alciato, Budé, Ulrich Zasius, and others on the Digest title *De origine iuris* led to more systematic investigation of legal history, including eventually the whole European legal tradition arising and diverging from Roman law as well as pre-Justinianian law going back to the Twelve Tables. The reconstruction of legal antiquity was carried on by a distinguished line of humanist scholars, including Johann Oldendorp, Carlo Sigonio, Bishop Jean du Tillet, François Baudouin, and especially Jacques Cujas. It should be added that analogous humanist assaults were directed at canon and feudal law, the sources of which were also incorporated into historiography, thus helping to give it a social and cultural dimension that it "classically" lacked.

＊　　＊　　＊

Like the classicist movement itself, the new-style historiography emerged relatively late in Germany, and it was informed by competitive and often invidious motives. The first scholar to address the subject was Peter Luder, self-styled *poeta et historiographus* who taught at Heidelberg in 1456; and about the same time the effects of humanism could be seen in the old chronicle tradition, notably in Sigismund's work on Augsburg, fabulous and uncritical as it was. Perhaps most important for a critical view of German history and certainly for the rehabilitation of German culture was the contemporaneous discovery of Tacitus's *Germania,* which was passed on to German humanism by Aeneas Silvius, whose own book of that title was also seminal.[29] Tacitus had emphasized the indigenous, unmixed character of the Germans, the purity of their morals and economic relations, and the liberal and democratic nature of their political institutions; and these perceptions provided the ideological base for German historiography as well as a vehicle for critical scholarship and for the exposure of legends, such as that of Trojan origins. Important in another way was Biondo's *Italia illustrata,* both as a model of historical-topographical writing and as a challenge to German national sentiment. In response to it Conrad Celtis and some of his colleagues labored to produce a *Germania illustrata* to justify and to magnify their own tradition. "Let us be ashamed, noble gentlemen," he declared, "that certain modern historians (who, publishing new *Decades,* boast that they have equalled the ancient Roman Empire) should speak of our most famous leaders merely as 'the barbarians' . . . in order to . . . disparage the reputation of us Germans."[30]

Contemporaneously, Jacob Wimpheling lamented that the Germans had not joined the Romans, Venetians, English, French, and other peoples in producing a national history, and in 1505 he published the first humanist history of Germany. Wimpheling's *Epitome rerum germanicarum usque ad nostra tempora* was so dominated by Celtis's counsel that it might seem to be closer to Bruni's *Laudatio Florentinae urbis* than to his history of Florence, except for its adherence to chronological order. He cast Germanic origins back to Homeric times, thus declaring them to antedate Rome herself. He went on to celebrate notable events and personalities, including Ariovistus, "first king of the Germans," various victories over foreign kings, and the fortunes of the German empire from Charlemagne; and he ended with a survey of German cultural triumphs, especially the invention of printing.[31] More critical, certainly more in line with Italian models, were the pioneering books of Albert Krantz on the Saxons and the Wends, which also took up the problem of Germanic origins, dismissing again Trojan "fables," though retaining others.[32] Influenced by Biondo and Aeneas Silvius, he also published studies of Scandanavian history. Very soon, of course, German humanist historiography was swept up in the maelstrom of the Reformation, although historical writing in humanist style continued to flourish, most notably in Johann Aventine's writings on Bavarian history and Beatus Rhenanus's *Rerum germanicarum libri tres* (1531), which was fully abreast of modern scholarship and critical methods.[33] While celebrating German antiquity and some of its myths—"the German people have always lived in total liberty," he declared proudly—he rejected the popular forgery of Annius of Viterbo that would push it back to the offspring of Noah.

In France the new historiography also arrived rather late, and it was even more closely associated with the old chronicle tradition, powerfully represented in the fifteenth century by Thomas Basin, Georges Chastellain, Philippe de Comines (or Commynes), and the ongoing *Grandes chroniques* of Saint-Denis. The mythico-historical link between French and classical culture was suggested in the famous formula, the "translation of learning" (the *translatio studii*) accompanying the *translatio imperii* of Charlemagne as king of the "French," which the Saint-Denis chronicles cited almost verbatim from Chrétien de Troyes: "in the city of Athens philosophy formerly resided, and in Greece the glory of chivalry. Then from Greece it passed from Rome, from Rome to France. God grant that it be kept there to the glory of His name, which lives and rules throughout eternity."[35] This general theme, and even such supporting anecdotes as the founding of the University of Paris by Charlemagne, were retained by humanist authors, though they displayed skepticism about grosser legends, such as that of Trojan origins.

Of the new history in France the first example was Robert Gaguin, a former member of the circle of Guillaume Fichet, who had been responsible for the introduction of printing into France in 1470 and who had enjoyed a long career as diplomat and scholar.[36] Like Wimpheling a decade later, Gaguin lamented his countrymen's neglect of their history and proposed to remedy the situation through his own *Compendium super francorum gestis* of 1495, prefaced by a letter by Erasmus (his first published work) likening Gaguin to Livy. In fact, Gaguin's book was a hastily assembled narrative derived mostly from the chronicles of Saint-Denis, though he dropped some of the fables (such as Charlemagne's crusade), made use of some documentary sources (such as the Pragmatic Sanction of Bourges), and of course trumpeted the basic national message, which was that neither the kings nor the culture of France was in any way inferior to Rome's. In fact his effort was already being superseded by an Italian scholar who had come to France in 1483 and had begun work on French antiquities much in the spirit of Biondo, his principal model and (though often unacknowledged) source.

Paolo Emilio, often regarded as the first official historiographer of France, in any case received official support for the project of composing a national history; and his *De rebus gestis francorum,* like Gaguin's work, was often cited as a legal authority.[37] Though basically a narrative history in Italian style, this book of "Paul-Emile" was based on extensive ethnographic, philological, and topographical investigations, venturing into the comparative study of institutions, discussion of social and religious customs, and other monographic subjects. It was the judgment of Erasmus that Paolo Emilio's work was distinguished more by its eloquence than by its accuracy, and yet it certainly marked an advance over Gaguin's book in terms both of form and of content and especially of the "scissors-and-paste" method characteristic of so many Renaissance historians (not including Biondo). Paolo Emilio's work exhibited both a wider range and a more critical use of sources; and it at least tried to present a synthesis of its materials rather than a mere assemblage of uneven sources followed singly and eclectically. Both books were popular during the sixteenth century, enjoying many editions and French translations, but it was Paolo Emilio's book that became the model and major authority and indeed furnished the official image of the French monarchy for generations. It was also the nucleus of the great tradition of vernacular historiography down to the nineteenth century.

In England Paolo Emilio's counterpart was also an Italian émigré and a still more distinguished humanist. Polydore Vergil, before arriving in England in 1502, had already shown his attachment to a historical point of view with the publication of his *De rerum inventoribus* (1499), a kind of historical encyclopedia, which also set down his conception of history.[38] For Vergil, Moses was the "inventor" of history, but the discipline itself was a wholly human enterprise, concerning the actions and deeds of men and the causes and effects thereof (*consilia, causae, dictae, factae, casus et exitus*). By 1502 he had finished the first books of his *Anglica historia* and dedicated it to Henry VII.[39] Vergil built upon a chronicle tradition as rich as the French and was perhaps more strongly affected by it than he thought, in terms not only of chronology but also of such monkish subjects as droughts, floods, harvests, and miracles. Aside from such habits, Vergil was a worthy graduate of the humanist school, priding himself on his eloquent Latin and including orations in classical style. He took a skeptical view of the problem of English origins, especially the Trojan and Arthurian legends, and indulged in numerous critical asides not only on his sources and moral lessons but also on such degenerate institutions as English universities, monasteries, and the profession of common law. The work began with a discussion of geographical context, proceeded by devoting one book to each king, and fell into large divisions of pre- and post-Conquest. Before the complete version was published in the year of Vergil's death (1555) it had become, like Paolo Emilio's, the principal authority for English history during the sixteenth century, though it also provoked some hostile reactions.

From the late fifteenth century the new Latinate historiography was Europewide, extending from Sicily and Scandinavia and from the Iberian peninsula to Russia.[40] Many contributors were ecclesiastical authors who had only superficial contacts with humanism; others enrolled very deliberately in this school, such as Juan Margarit y Pau, who devoted himself to pre-Visigothic history under the direct influence of Bruni, Biondo, and Aeneas Silvius; and Albert Krantz, who did the same for Scandinavia and Russia. Some were Italians who undertook to write of other nations, among them Antonio Bonfini and Filippo Buonaccorsi (Callimachus Experiens), who composed histories of Hungary and Poland. Humanist historians were outspoken in their contempt for medieval antecedents—the "new history," Vergil called it scornfully—and so for example Biondo could reject Geoffrey of Monmouth as outdoing "the dreams of the drunken or the feverish." Admittedly, however, such criticism was often undertaken on grounds not so much of historical truth as of the rhetorical device of critical rejection (the *topos anasceua*) or some ideological consideration such as national honor or antiquity (and so, for example, Krantz could reject the notion of Trojan origins for Swabia while accepting it for France), and the humanists were quite capable of introducing their own mythical constructs.

In general the achievement of humanist historiography down to the sixteenth century was twofold. First it was to Latinize, if not classicize, the medieval past by dissolving, as it were, its uneven and "barbaric" sources in a solvent of Neociceronian, Neolivian, or Neotacitean prose, by giving it some coherence and continuity through establishment or imputation of causal relationships, through literary devices such as orations and dialogues, and through extracting moral and political lessons from this reconstructed past. Second, it proclaimed and sometimes practiced an ideal of truth and scholarly standards—*fides et eruditio* was Erasmus's formula and *certissima philosophia* that of Alciato—which placed historical writing on a basis of secular learning rather than theological convention and random chronology.[41] These accomplishments were made, it should be further noted, in the first age of print culture; and from this circumstance arose other consequences of major significance for the study of history: the development of new methods and research tools, the beginning of cooperative scholarship and a public domain of historiography that could expand in qualitative as well as quantitative terms, the proliferation of new specializations and so-called "auxiliary sciences," the unprecedented flourishing of history as a form of popular entertainment and propaganda, and (for good or ill) the formulation of common issues to investigate and to debate.

*   *   *

The study of history was always shaped by contemporary political and social pressure, and never as extensively as in the early sixteenth century. As the historical perspective of Bruni had been fashioned in the "crisis of the early Italian Renaissance," so that of his intellectual descendants Machiavelli and Guicciardini was in many ways the product of the crisis—or rather the calamity—of Italy occurring in the wake of the wars set off by the French invasions of 1494 and 1498.[42] The historiographical practice, largely vernacular, of the members of this generation of '94 was directed not so much to problems of cultural provenance and pedigree but rather to the particular political predicament facing the Italian states, and especially Florence, from the last quarter of the fifteenth century. The "causes" of the Italian wars were discussed by Rucellai, Comines, and others before Guicciardini's exhaustive treatment; but of course there were many more issues attendant on this ancient question—problems of counsel, formation of policy, marshaling support, social control, constitutional management, diplomatic relations with other states, and in general a whole constellation of topics tied to what has been called the "vision of politics on the eve of the Reformation." Such was the context not only of the "calamity of Italy" but also of a new phase of humanist historiography emerging from the old tradition of so-called civic humanism.

Of this particular calamity and general crisis Niccolò Machiavelli was the most significant intellectual product, observer, and interpreter— as of what we might call the vision of history in this same period he was a pioneering and seminal exponent. The other primary source of his historical work was the classical tradition, and indeed he carried further the dual enterprise that Bruni had begun a century earlier. In *Il principe* and the *Arte della guerra* Machiavelli endorsed the humanist recommendation that history should occupy a central place in education, especially that of a prince, though his arguments were political and military rather than moral and philosophical. In his *Discorsi sopra la prima deca di Tito Livio* he tried more comprehensively to ransack ancient history and modern experience for political lessons. "Whoever considers the past and the present will readily observe that all cities and all peoples are and ever have been animated by the same desires and the same passions; so that it is easy, by diligent study of the past, to foresee what is likely to happen in the future in any republic, and to apply those remedies that were used by the ancients, or . . . to devise new ones from the similarity of the events."[43] This idea was the starting point for Machiavelli's famous "new route," which was to do for statecraft what had been done for so many other fields, that is, give it a firm historical foundation. In fact, by taking Roman history as a model or experience Machiavelli was only continuing more purposefully what Dante and Petrarch had begun, except that his aim was not to "praise" but rather to criticize and learn from Rome.

In 1520 Machiavelli seized the opportunity to write the history of his own city for the ruling Medici family. In the subsequent *Historie Fiorentine* he set himself directly in the tradition of Bruni and Poggio, though he began by complaining that, despite their exact treatment of foreign affairs, "upon the subject of civil discord and internal strifes they had been entirely silent, or had written far too briefly concerning them."[44] So it was that Machiavelli turned to the "most remarkable" subject of political dissensions and their consequences for Florentine social life and constitutional order. Following Biondo, he began with the descent of Germanic tribes into the Roman Empire and then, following Bruni, took up specifically Florentine origins; and he ended with the death of Lorenzo de' Medici in 1492 just on the threshhold of another and no less destructive wave of "barbarian" invasions. Like Bruni, Machiavelli prized above all the republican liberty of Florence; but like Biondo he was forced in his narrative to trace the decline of that liberty, especially through the interfering policies of the popes, the rise of factions, and the ruin of the nobility (hence civic capacity for self-defense) and more fundamental class conflict. Like Bruni, too, Machiavelli celebrated the superiority of republican excellence (*virtù;* Latin *virtus*), but experience along with a broader view of history had taught that republican government was the most unstable of all. This was the basic lesson of Florentine and Roman history—and the political predicament underlying Machiavelli's advice for the Prince.

We must not make a caricature of Machiavelli's view of history. He was quite aware that predictions, like policies, were never infallible and that, as he remarked in the *Discorsi,* "we never know the whole truth about the past." Yet he could find no better guide, and he did his utmost to formulate a systematic interpretation of historical change. In the history of Florence it was expressed in various general comments (not unlike those of Bruni or Comines) on political psychology, patterns of social conflict and factionalism, the conditions of political *virtù,* and trajectory of political *fortuna.* In the *Discorsi* it took the more general form of a commentary on the famous (but newly revived) Polybian theory of constitutional cycles (*anacyclosis*), in which "monarchy becomes tyranny; aristocracy degenerates into oligarchy; and the popular government lapses readily into licentiousness," all because of the weakness of human nature, especially in social groups, and an endless alteration of generations. "Such is the circle which all republics are destined to run through," Machiavelli concluded.[45] "Tend to run through," we should perhaps amend, for such unqualified naturalism really does justice neither to Machiavelli's social psychology nor certainly to his concrete appreciation of the historical process.

Guicciardini, Machiavelli's younger and politically more eminent friend, shared many of his assumptions and views. "Past events throw light upon the future," Guicciardini opined in his *Ricordi*, "because the world has always been the same as it now is. . . . Things accordingly repeat themselves, but under changed names and colors, so that it is not everyone who can recognize them."[46] Yet Guicciardini, too—though deeply disillusioned by the calamity that had victimized him and Machiavelli as well as their city—had a subtler conception of historical change and indeed criticized his colleague for his tendency to jump to conclusions. Guicciardini tried twice to write the history of Florence, but even more than Machiavelli he was a man of the generation of '94; and his masterwork, the *Storia d'Italia*, started just where Machiavelli's history ended—with the "calamity of Italy," following the death of Lorenzo de' Medici, which for Machiavelli likewise marked the beginning of Italy's ruin. Like Gibbon's, Guicciardini's theme, though cast "within living memory," was epic— "rich for its variety and extent, and full of appalling disasters, for Italy has suffered for many years every kind of calamity that may vex mortals either through the just wrath of God or through the impious and wicked actions of their fellow men."[47] It was also carried out with unprecedented breadth of vision and depth of research, especially in archival sources, including those of the Giucciardini family.

With astonishing control of massive detail and multiple story lines, Guicciardini's narrative described and analyzed the first four years of the Italian wars starting in 1494, showing the policies and ambitions of the barbarians and his countrymen's weakness and progressive loss of mastery. In this pioneering effort of national synthesis Guicciardini provided a broad range of political analyses, character sketches, and descriptions of negotiations and actions, making full use of humanist forms and conventions, including orations. Although he did not scruple to invoke supernatural signs and events to enhance the drama of the Italian calamity, his focus was always human psychology and interaction. Yet like Machiavelli he well realized that the way of the fox had in the last extremity always to yield to the way of the lion, and as he remarked about the events of the spring of 1494: "More important than the speeches of the ambassador and the replies they received were the preparations by land and sea which were being made everywhere." Violence and injustice were the real protagonists of Guicciardini's story from this point, and the lessons he drew from his observations and investigations were even more pessimistic than Machiavelli's. It is perhaps because of this lack of idealism, combined with his acumen and mastery of detailed narrative in humanist form, that Guicciardini has been judged by some as the greatest historian between Tacitus and Gibbon.[48]

Machiavelli and Guiccardini set a style—or rather, in the tradition of Thucydides, Polybius, and Tacitus, they revived a style—of analytical, political narrative that has been continuallly practiced since the sixteenth century, beginning with their own Florentine epigones, including Francesco Vettori, Filippo Nerli, Bernardo Segni, Jacopo Nardi, Benedetto Varchi, Donato Gianotti, Scipione Annunciato, and other interpreters of Florentine history in the postrepublican period. It was a form that, still under the influence of humanism, was practiced variously around Guicciardini's time by Johann Sleidan in Germany, Jacques-Auguste de Thou in France, and William Camden in England, to mention only the most distinguished. The connections between history and political science were also reinforced by other scholars, for instance by Machiavelli's likeminded French contemporary Claude de Seyssel, another product of '94.[49] Seyssel also followed a humanist impulse and believed that of all ancient literature "history is the most profitable," and one result was a series of translations of historians, including Thucydides (based on Valla's Latin version), along with his own history of Louis XII and, most famously, his *Monarchie de France,* a sort of French counterpart to Machiavelli's *Principe* with even more historical parallels, from Venetian as well as Roman history. Like Machiavelli and Guicciardini, Seyssel thought that the first aim of historical study was "to understand causes and effects," which has always been the premise of political narrative.

*   *   *

In the sixteenth century the "new learning" implied religious heresy as much as humanist learning; and this implication suggests another crisis—or rather "calamity"—which, though hardly noticed by Italian political historians, had even more lasting consequences. The Protestant Reformation, which orthodox critics preferred to regard as the Lutheran "scandal" and which even Machiavelli saw only as a "pretext" for monkish troublemaking, produced even more unsettling shifts of perspective, since it called into question almost the whole of Christian tradition. Under Lutheran influence history was again viewed not *ab urbe* but *ab orbe condito,* according to the old Augustinian scheme and the "four world monarchies" (Medes, Persians, Greeks, and Romans), ending with the "translation of the empire to the Germans." In his preface to Robert Barnes's (evangelical version of Platina's) *Vitae romanorum pontificum* Luther acknowledged the didactic value of historical studies, but it was Philipp Melanchthon who most effectively introduced the humanist conception into Protestant doctrine, especially in his preface to the very popular *Chronica carionis.*[50] "Without history," Melanchthon was fond of quoting from Cicero, "one remains forever a child"; and this conviction became a major premise in his educational reforms of the universities of Protestant Germany. In other Protestant confessions, including Calvinism, history was increasingly prized not only to celebrate the pedigree of "true religion," for instance in martyrologies, but also as a weapon in the endless doctrinal controversies of that age.[51]

The first great exponent of Lutheran historiography was Johann Sleidan, author of an enormously popular textbook of universal history, *De quatuor summis imperiis* (Englished a century later as *The Key to History*), and of the official history of the Lutheran Reformation. Educated as a humanist, Sleidan admired and indeed translated into Latin works of Froissart, Comines, and Seyssel; and he carried their style of political analysis into his own major work, which he privately referred to as a "history of the restored church." Epic in theme, European in scope, annalistic in method, and based on extraordinary archival researches, Sleidan's *De statu religionis et republicae Carlo Quinti Caesari commentarii* carried the dual stories of political conflict and the expansion of evangelical religion from 1517 to his death in 1556. He tried to preserve classical forms, though they were often overwhelmed by documentation and by his efforts to discuss social and ideological factors beyond the narrower focus of political historians like Guicciardini, whom he in some ways resembles. Lutheran partisanship did not prevent Sleidan from maintaining a frankness and a fidelity to Cicero's "first law of history" that many critics found excessive, and he was forced to compose an "apology" for his history, in which he proclaimed his devotion both to *vera religio* and to *vera historia.* "If mine is not true history," he wrote, "then there is no such thing as a credible political history (I except sacred histories)."[52]

In a longer perspective Lutheranism entailed a general critique of Christian tradition, like humanism beginning with an idealized antiquity, which in this case was to say the "primitive church"; and it envisaged a wholly spiritual heritage, as contrasted with the corrupt "human traditions" of the Roman church. Yet for this very reason Protestant historians were licensed to discuss human history, including that of the church, in purely secular terms. What is more, they were able to subject it to the severest sort of historical criticism, Valla himself becoming a particularly useful model. So it was that Protestant historiography, in theory as well as practice, was able to advance the cause of humanist scholarship, though not without building up its own heroic legends, as in the fabricated intellectual hagiography of Matthias Flacius Illyricus called *Catalogus testium veritatis*. Most impressive is the monumental *Centuries* assembled by Flacius and his Magdeburg colleagues, which grouped together and discussed central topics of ecclesiastical history—persecutions, doctrines, ceremonies, miracles, and politics, among others— according to commonplaces corresponding to the *loci communes* of the reformed logic of Melanchthon and other humanists and similar to the historical method being developed contemporaneously by Jean Bodin.[53] On the other side of what one historian has called the "confessional iron curtain" the great response was the equally monumental compilation by Cesare Baronio, the *Annales ecclesiastici,* which massively reasserted Catholic tradition, and did so neither *ab orbe* nor *ab urbe* but *ab Incarnatione.*

The great classic of ecclesiastical history was surely Paolo Sarpi's *Istoria del Concilio Tridentino* (1619), the "Iliad of our times" as he regarded it. Sarpi enjoyed a classical education before joining the Servites and tried to unite sacred history with humanist form.[54] As a Venetian (and critic of the Interdict of 1606) Sarpi sympathized with many goals of evangelical reformers, criticizing indulgences and indeed, in his *History of Benefices,* the corrupting effects of ecclesiastical property in general; and he admired and followed Sleidan in his writing on the sixteenth century. Supporting "reformation," he lamented the "deformation" endorsed by the Council of Trent, which "brought about the greatest corruption of the Church since the name of 'Christian' was first heard." Among more theological protests Sarpi ridiculed the Tridentine fathers for claiming the authority of the Holy Ghost for the Vulgate version when this endorsement was explicitly denied by the translator himself, St. Jerome. In dramatic and often ironic or humorous fashion he depicted the dramatic battles of the Tridentine fathers as well as the political and religious "causes" of· the council, yet with the utmost respect for the virtues of historical accuracy (though this was denied and denounced voluminously by his nemesis Sforza Pallavicino). Many details he included against his own sense of relevance on the grounds that "some sharp mind will perhaps discover in [them] something important which I was not aware of."

While being used as a weapon of controversy in this age of confessional strife, history continued to be celebrated in classical style, especially through an increasingly popular sixteenth-century genre called the "art of history" (*ars historica,* analogous to the Horatian *ars poetica*), which originated in letters, educational treatises, and prefaces to historical works. In these works the emphasis was on the writing of history and its essential properties, which included elegance and form as well as truth and utility, causal analysis, and explanation in terms of times, places, circumstances, and persons.[55] These arguments were developed by a number of authors in the fifteenth century, including Guarino, Valla, Bartolomeo della Fonte, and Giovanni Pontano, before being discussed in a series of systematic treatises in the middle and later sixteenth century, beginning with Sperone Speroni in 1542 and especially with Francesco Robortello in 1548. The central issue was still whether Aristotle was right when he judged poetry to be more philosophical than history, though increasingly important was the Polybian criterion (*norma Polybiana,* in the words of Uberto Foglietta) of objective truth as well as "pragmatic" value. Valla had long before upheld the superiority of history over philosophy on these grounds, but sixteenth-century authors went further. In his contribution to the *ars historica,* for example, Francesco Patrizi argued that if the task of the philosopher was to understand causes, that of the historian was to understand both causes and effects, so he had a better grasp of the truth (*cognizione del vero*).[56] For Patrizi history was an autonomous, if a rather eclectic science.

The humanist "art of history" persisted into the seventeenth century, asking the same old questions: Is history an art or a science? What are its divisions, its standards and rules, its uses? In Italy the literary tradition was maintained, as it was in Spain. The commonplace character of this genre, unchanging into the nineteenth century and with recognizable descendants even today, can be seen in the treatise of Luis Cabrera de Córdoba devoted to "the understanding and writing of history." "I have described the importance of history and of the good historian," he writes, "the qualities he must have and those of authentic and complete history [*perfecta historia*] and how they may be acquired."[57] In the work of German methodologists such as Gerardus Vossius and Bartolomäus Keckermann the tendency was to rearrange the materials of history according to Ramist, or at least Ramoid bifurcating logic and so to shift the emphasis from the writing to the reading of history, though it must be added that "history" for these writers suggested empirical knowledge (*cognito singularium* in Keckermann's phrase) rather than understanding in temporal perspective.

In France the shift of emphasis to historical knowledge (rather than the narrative art) was even more conscpicuous, and it was much reinforced by a fruitful marriage between history and law. The "methods" of history of François Baudouin and especially Jean Bodin tried to bring together a number of classical, Christian, and modern concepts and practices—the pragmatic political history associated with Polybius and (for Bodin) Machiavelli, the universal perspective of Augustinian (and Lutheran) *historia sacra,* the developments of modern techniques of historical criticism and authentication, and especially the accommodation of geographic, institutional, and social factors associated with "legal science."[58] With Bodin and disciples like Pierre Droit de Gaillard and Henri de La Popelinière history achieved not only recognition as a science but a position "above all sciences" as the source of all human disciplines; thus it was joined to the investigation of human culture as a whole and was not merely the "new route" taken by Bodin, and Machiavelli before him, toward political science. For these authors, moreover, history implied the human rather than the physical aspect of creation—*res civiles* rather than *res naturales,* according to the distinction made in Baudouin's method of history, and civil rather than natural history in the more famous Baconian formula.[59]

More significant for the study of history than this rhetoric and theorizing were the scholarly developments of the later sixteenth century made possible by the mutual reinforcement of the humanist impulse and the new art of printing, which itself, according to Budé, was "the restitution and perpetuation of antiquity."[60] Among the most conspicuous results were the publication and correction of classical (and, increasingly, medieval) authors and collections of sources, not to speak of bibliographical aids such as Conrad Gesner's *Bibliotheca universalis* (1545), which included a topically arranged listing of histories "in general," followed by chroniclers, historiographers, antiquarians, and contributors to the genre *de viris illustribus.* Through a sort of transvaluation of classicism, philological investigations were also undertaken into the sources of medieval history; and among the fruits of this were Simon Schard's *Illustration of Ancient Germany,* concerning Tacitus and later commentaries (including works of Wimpheling, Conrad Peutinger, Celtis, and Aeneas Silvius), and Pierre Pithou's *Annals and Histories of France,* containing works from the eighth century through the tenth. Although they were fascinated with printing, sixteenth-century scholars did not turn away from the treasures of manuscript culture. Baudouin called attention to the riches that the Vatican archives must hold for the historian, while Jean du Tillet began the systematic ransacking of the royal archives to enhance the "defense and illustration" of France already being carried on in literary ways. A work of the next century by Baldassare Bonifacio celebrated and offered a brief historical survey of the archivist tradition in general.[61]

The late sixteenth and seventeenth centuries were the heroic age, too, of modern "criticism," of that *ars critica* which aimed not only to "emend" texts through reason and erudition in the fashion of Poliziano and Budé but to bring about the "restitution" of antiquity as a whole. Among the giants of this enterprise were Isaac Casaubon, whose translation of Polybius was a major contribution to the "royal science" of politics as well as to historiography; Justus Lipsius, "professor of history and jurisprudence" at Leiden; and especially Joseph Justus Scaliger, whose great *Opus de emendatione temporum* laid the foundation for the modern science of chronology.[62] These men and their colleagues established on a solid footing the scholarly tradition culminating in the work of Mabillon, Muratori, and the *Monumenta Germaniae Historica*. If the driving force of this tradition was religious conviction, its substance continued to be the product of the humanist impulse—that science of philology whose fruits are not only too numerous to mention but also too various to be comprehended from one point of view.

*   *   *

In the sixteenth and seventeenth centuries latinate historiography continued to flourish in all parts of Europe, as did its vernacular imitations; and among its most renowned practitioners were medieval historians like Juan de Mariana, William Camden, and George Buchanan as well as writers with a more universal reach like Paolo Giovio and Jacques-Auguste de Thou, just to mention a few whose fame survived them. De Thou was surely the most admired and remained a model of eloquence and impartiality through the Enlightenment, gaining praise from both Voltaire and Gibbon and chosen by Dr. Johnson as a text worthy of translation despite the heroic scale of his analysis (almost five thousand folios for sixty-one years). De Thou's *Historia sui temporis* began in 1546 and covered the period of the religious wars and the aftermath in extraordinary detail and international depth in a Polybian and Tacitean style, chronologically arranged and ornamented with biographical sketches (in effect obituary notices) of notable figures.[63] The embarrassing frankness with which he treated sensitive partisan issues brought him under the threat of censorship and led him to write an apology for objective and nonpartisan narrative that included religious as well as political matters and which did not ignore the terrible evils of the age. There were other distinguished historians of de Thou's generation in France—La Popelinière, Jean de Serres, Bernard du Haillan, Nicolas Vignier, and François Belleforest among them—but none of these vernacular historians, and probably no other European historian writing in Latin, matched the influence of de Thou down to the nineteenth century.

National historians continued to follow the Livian model, especially those who were supported as court historians—royal historiographers—beginning with Paolo Emilio and a series of vernacular historians including du Haillan, de Serres, and François Eudes de Mézeray, founders of a sort of guild of the "artisans of glory," devoted to the ideological interests of the monarchy.[64] There were also other more specialized efforts to plumb the remote past—antiquarianism in the style of Biondo but aimed at resurrecting "barbarian" antiquity. The pioneering *collections pour servir à l'histoire* published by du Tillet, Pithou, Schard, and others provided not only a scholarly basis for a fuller narrative but also an ideological arsenal for works of historical interpretation, perhaps most notably in François Hotman's notorious *Francogallia*, which sought to celebrate and in a sense to ressurect the "ancient constitution of France" as his Protestant colleagues had harkened back to the ideal of the primitive church. Although Hotman opposed a supposedly purifying Germanism to a supposedly corrupt Romanism in his interpretation of the course of French history, and although he was moved by partisan (religious as well as political) motives, he was still adhering to the humanist program: back to the sources![65]

Historical studies gained breadth as well as depth and political acumen during the sixteenth century, as illustrated by the penetration of historical notions into other disciplines. A central concern originating in the humanist program was language itself, and the infiltration of historical attitudes into this field was one of the conditions for the advance of the science of philology in this period. Insights into the history of the Latin language were provided in Valla's *Elegantiae*, in Erasmus's *De copia verborum*, and Pietro Crinito's *De honesta disciplina*, among other works written in the tradition of Varro; and indeed the famous quarrels over "Ciceronianism" and the "corrupt" Latin of medieval authors presupposed a historical view of linguistic change.[66] The same interests carried over into studies of the vernaculars and inspired such efforts as those of Etienne Pasquier and Claude de Fauchet in literary history. Another incipient but recognizable genre was legal history, which emerged especially from commentaries on the Digest title "On the Origin of Civil Law." Here the pioneering work of Aymar de Rivail's *Historia juris civilis* established the pattern of Roman history by joining the primary sources of law with the Polybian cycle of change (*anacyclosis*): the *leges regiae* of the monarchical period, the *senatusconsulta* of the aristocratic period, and the *plebiscita* of the popular period before the establishment of the empire; and his *Historia juris pontificii* provided a similar survey of canon law.[67] Valentinus Foster and others continued this investigation into the medieval and modern periods. More generally, the impact of jurisprudence was to widen the vision of history to include institutional and social materials and to extend it geographically to reinforce humanist interests in universal history. "Historical studies must be placed upon a solid foundation of law, and jurisprudence must be joined in history" is the way that Baudouin expressed this enrichment of the conventional "art of history."[68] When combined also with a universal perspective, a Eusebian concern for religious matters, and a Polybian interest in pragmatic political explanation, history could become truly catholic—truly "integral and perfect."

Other areas were opened up to historical investigation and interpretation. Viewing the general progress of what he called "Design," Giorgio Vasari studied the accomplishments of Renaissance painters, sculptors, and architects and so laid the foundation of art history. Louis Le Roy, regius professor of Greek in Paris, offered sketches of the history both of philosophy and of political thought from ancient times in connection with his translations of Plato and Aristotle.[69] History itself was historicized in certain contributions to the *ars historica,* beginning with that of Bartolomeo della Fonte, including that of Bodin, and culminating in that of La Popelinière, whose *Histoire des histoires, avec l'Idée de l'histoire accomplie* represents perhaps the most comprehensive of all humanist formulations of the "new history" of the Renaissance.[70] La Popelinière recognized a four-stage pattern in the development of historiography: first a period of "natural history," that is, oral tradition and myth; second a period of "poetic history" (anticipating the famous views of Vico); then "continuous history," including simple chronicles and annals; and finally a kind of civilized history, which added eloquence and an awareness of causation to the narration of facts—the level actually achieved by humanist historiography.

The fifth stage, envisioned by La Popelinière's *histoire accomplie,* had not yet been attained; but it was discussed by various scholars pursuing a broad cultural ideal, among them Le Roy, du Haillan, and Gaillard and of course La Popelinière himself, whose "design for a new history of the French" derived from the humanist view that "all the sciences, arts, and other human inventions originate in history," and that historians ought also to consider geography, forms of government, the crown and its various institutions and legal organization, social classes, and religion.[71] Perhaps the most serious and concrete contribution toward such a design of "perfect history" was undertaken by that "Montaigne" of history, Etienne Pasquier, whose *Recherches de la France* touched not only on legal and institutional antiquities, such as the history of universities, the Parlement, and the Gallican church, but also on art, literature, and even popular culture.[72] In this lifetime search for the "spirit" of French society and culture Pasquier was also joined by his colleague Claude de Fauchet and by Nicolas Vignier. To these scholars hardly anything was alien; and in many ways, in reach if not in grasp, they represent the fulfillment of the humanist conception of history, at least in a national context.

What this work suggests above all is that most grandiose aspect of the humanist legacy, which might be called the encyclopedic impulse. The humanist movement had begun in a sense as a celebration of the ancient *enkyklios paideia* with special emphasis on the humanities; and it was led in its mature stages to survey and to appreciate the totality of the arts and the sciences in a large historical perspective—a perspective that opened also on the future and perhaps favored the moderns over the ancients. Rudimentary examples include Polydore Vergil's *De rerum inventoribus,* which surveyed the origins and "inventors" of disciplines, and on the negative side Juan Luis Vives's *De causis corruptarum artium,* which offered skeptical critiques of the inadequacy of human disciplines, including the deceptions of history itself. More comprehensive was Christophe Milieu's *De scribenda universitatis rerum historia,* which discussed the universality of history in terms even more encyclopedic than those of Baudouin a decade later.[73] For Milieu *historia* encompassed nature but more importantly human culture, and this historical manifestation of humanity Milieu divided into three categories: *prudentia,* which included the practical or technical arts necessary for human sustenance; *principatus,* which referred to social and political organization (essentially, the history of the states); and most extensively *sapientia,* which classically meant wisdom ("the knowledge of things divine and human") but which came to imply both the "encyclopedia" of arts and sciences and "culture" in an anthropological sense (as later and more famously used by Vico), including literature (*literatura*) in a general sense including history itself.

Perhaps the most successful attempt to realize this ideal in historiographical terms was made by Le Roy, Budé's disciple and biographer. The encyclopedic vision that Budé had applied to philology, Le Roy transferred to universal history; and the result was what one scholar called "the first treatise devoted to the history of civilization."[74] Le Roy's *De la vicissitude ou variété des choses en l'univers*—"and," as the title continues, "the concurrence of arms and letters by the first and most illustrious nations of the world since civilization began until the present"—was a

262 DONALD R. KELLEY

comparative study of world cultures, especially the "heroic ages," according to a pattern that was cyclical (the biological trajectory already applied by Seyssel to France and by Polydore Vergil to England) on a national level but progressive in universal terms (one of the central themes being the intellectual and technical superiority of the moderns to the ancients). Although he began by celebrating the achievements of philology—to which indeed he had devoted his own life—he laid stress on novelty, especially "the new seas, new types of men, manners, laws, and customs" of the modern age.

In the seventeenth century the "new Philosophy that cast all into doubt" concentrated much of its skepticism on the historical attitudes associated with the humanist tradition. For Bacon "history" continued to suggest little more than the data that, according to the empirical method, were to be shaped by reason, while Galileo, like Descartes, had only contempt for those "memory-experts" who, thinking as well as looking backward, were as remote as possible from philosophy.[75] In his own way Leibniz, too, tried to subsume historical by natural knowledge. "To judge history distinctly, one may compare it to the body of an animal," he wrote. "The parts of history correspond thus: chronology to bones, genealogy to nerves, hidden motives to invisible spirits, useful examples to juices, and the details of circumstances to the whole mass of human flesh."[76] In that conceptual war which Ernst Troeltsch found dominant in seventeenth-century thought, naturalism seemed in many ways to be victorious over historicism.

In other ways, however, humanist scholarship continued to prevail, most notably in the work of scholars like Selden, du Cange, and Mabillon, which represented the culmination of Renaissance "philology." For such critical minds history continued to be prized as a special and independent form of knowledge—indeed as science in its own right and even a vocation (a "profession," in the term applied by Milieu, La Popelinière, and others). As much as reason itself history was, for humanists more elaborately than for Henry of Huntingdon, a distinguishing feature of humanity. About "that fretful animal we call man," Daniel Heinsius, in his essay on the value of history, wrote that "he would be free from the limits of time and space. . . . He would gather into one focus the immeasurable great vastness of ages and generations. . . . History renders man contemporary with the universe."[77] It is one of the most important bequests made by humanism to the modern world.

NOTES

1. *Rinascimento* 1 (1950): 97, review of F. Simone, *La coscienza della rinascità negli umanisti francese* (Rome, 1949). In general see H. Baron, "Das

Erwachsen des historischen Denkens im Humanismus des Quattrocento,"
Historisches Zeitschrift 147 (1932): 5–20; A. Buck, *Das Geschichtsdenken
der Renaissance* (Krefeld, 1957); P. Burke, *The Renaissance Sense of the
Past* (London, 1969); W. K. Ferguson, *The Renaissance in Historical
Thought* (Cambridge, MA, 1948); P. Joachimsen, *Geschichtsauffassung
und Geschichtsschreibung in Deutschland unter dem Einfluss des Human-
ismus* (Leipzig, 1910); D. R. Kelley, *Foundations of Modern Historical
Scholarship: Language, Law, and History in the French Renaissance* (New
York, 1970); N. S. Struever, *The Language of History in the Renaissance*
(Princeton, 1970); R. Weiss, *The Renaissance Discovery of Classical An-
tiquity* (Oxford, 1969). The most recent and most comprehensive survey is
E. Cochrane, *Historians and Historiography in the Italian Renaissance*
(Chicago, 1981), essential also for bibliography.

2. Henry of Huntingdon, *The Chronicle,* trans. T. Forester (London, 1853),
xxvii. And see, among others, G. Ladner, "Die mittelalterliche Reform-Idee
und ihr Verhältnis zur Idee der Renaissance," *Mitteilungen des Instituts für
österreichische Geschichtsforschung* 40 (1952): 41–59; R. Renucci, *L'aventure de l'humanisme européen au Moyen-Âge* (Paris, 1953); M. Schulz, *Die
Lehre von der historischen Methode bei den Geschichtsschreibern des Mittelalters* (Berlin, 1909); J. Spörl, *Grundformen hochmittelalterlichen Geschichtsanschauung* (Munich, 1935); W. J. Brandt, *The Shape of Medieval
History* (New Haven, 1966); M. T. Clanchy, *From Memory to Written Record* (London, 1979); and J. Knape, *Historie in Mittelalter und früher
Neuzeit* (Baden-Baden, 1984).

3. "Letter to Posterity," in *Petrarch, the First Modern Scholar and Man of
Letters,* ed. J. H. Robinson and H. W. Rolfe (New York, 1898), 64. And see
W. Handschin, *Petrarch als Gestalt der Historiographie* (Basel, 1964); E.
Kessler, "Geschichtsdenken und Geschichtsschreibung bei Francesco Pe-
trarca," *Archiv für Kulturgeschichte,* 51 (1969): 109–36; T. E. Mommsen,
"Petrarch's Conception of the 'Dark Ages,' " *Medieval and Renaissance
Studies,* ed. E. F. Rice, Jr. (Ithaca, 1959), 106–29; and P. de Nolhac, *Pétr-
arque et l'humanisme* (Paris, 2d ed. 1907; reprint, 1965).

4. *Letters to Classical Authors,* trans. M. Cosenza (Chicago, 1910), 84, 100ff.;
and see G. Billanovich, "Petrarch and the Textual Tradition of Livy," *Journal of the Warburg and Courtauld Institutes* 14 (1951): 137–208.

5. E. H. Wilkins, *Petrarch's Eight Years in Milan* (Cambridge, MA, 1958),
226.

6. "Petrarch's Prefaces to *De viris illustribus,*" trans. B. Kohl, *History and
Theory* 13 (1974): 139.

7. Mommsen, "Petrarch's Conception," 122. Cf. H. J. Erasmus, *The Origins
of Rome in Historiography from Petrarch to Perizonius* (Assen, 1962), and
W. Rehm, *Der Untergang Roms im abendländischen Denken* (Leipzig,
1930).

8. "Letters in Defense of Liberal Studies," in *Humanism and Tyranny,* ed. E.
Emerton (Cambridge, MA, 1925), 290–377; and see also B. L. Ullman, *The
Humanism of Coluccio Salutati* (Padua, 1963).

9. *De studiis et litteris,* in *Leonardo Bruni Aretino. Humanistisch-philosophische Schriften mit einer Chronologie seiner Werke und Briefe,* ed. H. Baron (Leipzig and Berlin, 1928; reprint, Wiesbaden, 1969), 169.

10. *Humanism and Liberty,* ed. and trans. R. N. Watkins (Columbia, SC, 1978). On Bruni see H. Baron, *The Crisis of the Early Italian Renaissance,* 2 vols. in 1 (Princeton, rev. ed. 1966) and *From Petrarch to Leonardo Bruni* (Chicago, 1968); and B. L. Ullman, "Leonardo Bruni and Humanistic Historiography," in his *Studies in the Italian Renaissance* (Rome 2d ed., 1973); C. C. Bayley, *War and Society in Renaissance Florence* (Toronto, 1961); and more generally E. Cochrane, *Historians and Historiography;* E. Fueter, *Geschichte der neueren Historiographie* (Berlin, 3d ed. 1963); D. Hay, *Annalists and Historians* (London, 1977); and D. J. Wilcox, *The Development of Florentine Humanist Historiography in the Fifteenth Century* (Cambridge, MA, 1969); also J. E. Seigel, *Rhetoric and Philosophy in Renaissance Humanism* (Princeton, 1968); and F. Vegas, "La concezione della storia dell-'umanesimo alla Controriforma," *Grande antologia filosofica,* ed. M. F. Sciacca, et al. (Milan, 1964), 10:1–59.

11. See L. Green, *Chronicle into History* (Cambridge, 1972).

12. "Vita di Petrarca," in *Leonardo Bruni Aretino,* ed. Baron, 64.

13. See Cochrane, *Historians and Historiography;* and Wilcox, *Development of Florentine Humanist Historiography.*

14. Besides Cochrane and Fueter, *Geschichte der neueren Historiographie,* see B. Reynolds, "Latin Historiography, A Survey 1400–1600," *Studies in the Renaissance* 2 (1955):7–66; and P. H. Labalme, *Bernardo Giustiniani: A Venetian of the Quattrocento* (Rome, 1969). J. W. Thompson, *A History of Historical Writing* (Chicago, 1942), discusses many minor writers but must be used with caution.

15. A. Grafton, *Joseph Scaliger; A Study in the History of Classical Scholarship* (Oxford, 1983); and W. H. Woodward, *Studies in Education During the Age of the Renaissance, 1400–1600* (Cambridge, 1906; reprinted New York, 1967); also P. Burke, "A Survey of the Popularity of Ancient Historians, 1450–1700," *History and Theory* 5 (1966): 135–52; and J. Jehasse, *La renaissance de la critique* (Saint-Etienne, 1976).

16. See above, note 4.

17. *Elegantiae latinae linguae,* preface, in *Opera omnia,* ed. E. Garin (Turin, 1962), 1:4; and see Kelley, *Foundations of Modern Historical Scholarship,* chap. 2, and E. Gaeta, *Lorenzo Valla: Filosofia e storia nell'umanesimo italiano* (Naples, 1955); also L. Janick, "Lorenzo Valla: The Primacy of Rhetoric and the De-Moralization of History," *History and Theory* 12 (1973): 389–404.

18. *De rebus a Ferdinando rege et maioribus eius gestis,* in *Opera omnia,* ed. Garin, 2:6.

19. *The Treatise of Lorenzo Valla on the Donation of Constantine,* ed. and trans. C. B. Coleman (New Haven, 1922), 21; and see J. Levine, "Reginald Pecock and Lorenzo Valla on the Donation of Constantine," *Studies in the Renaissance* 20 (1973): 118–43.

20. Flavio Biondo, *Scritti inediti e rari,* ed. B. Nogara (Rome, 1927), 138.
21. *Historiarum ab inclinatione Romanorum imperii decades* (Venice, 1483); and see D. Hay, "Flavio Biondo and the Middle Ages," *Proceedings of the British Academy* 45 (1959): 97–125; and F. Gilbert, "Biondo, Sabellico, and the Beginnings of Venetian Official Historiography," in *Florilegium Historiale: Essays Presented to Wallace K. Ferguson,* ed. J. G. Rowe and W. H. Stockdale (Toronto, 1971), 275–93; also L. Varga, *Das Schlagwort vom "Finsteren Mittelalter"* (Baden, 1932), and Ferguson, *Renaissance in Historical Thought.*
22. Bartolomeo Sacchi, *Historia de vitis pontificum romanorum,* ed. Onofrio Panvinio (Venice, 1562), fol. 1; Robert Barnes, *Vitae romanorum pontificum* (Basel, n.d.); and in general M. Miglio, *Storiografia pontificia del Quattrocento* (Bologna, 1975).
23. C. A. Patrides, *The Grand Design of God* (London, 1972).
24. *Memoirs of a Renaissance Pope: The Commentaries of Pius II,* trans. F. A. Gragg, ed. L. C. Gabel (New York, 1959).
25. Angelo Poliziano, *Opera omnia* (Basel, 1553), 621.
26. Besides Weiss, *Renaissance Discovery,* see C. Mitchell, "Archaeology and Romance in Renaissance Italy," *Italian Renaissance Studies,* ed. E. F. Jacob (London, 1960), 455–83; E. Mandowsky and C. Mitchell, *Pirro Ligorio's Roman Antiquities* (London, 1963); and F. Saxl, "The Classical Inscription in Renaissance Art and Politics," *Journal of the Warburg and Courtauld Institutes* 4 (1940–41):19–46.
27. S. Bertelli, *Ribelli, libertini e ortodossi nella storiografia barocca* (Florence, 1973).
28. Besides Kelley, *Foundations,* see D. Maffei, *Gli inizi dell'umanesimo giuridico* (Milan, 1956); H. E. Troje, *Graeca leguntur* (Cologne, 1971); and E. Viard, *André Alciat, 1492–1550* (Paris, 1926); also R. Metz, "La contribution de la France à l'étude du decret de Gratien," *Studia gratiana* 2 (1954):495–518. And see below, note 67.
29. E. C. Scherer, *Geschichte und Kirchengeschichte an den deutschen Universitäten* (Freiburg im Breisgau, 1927); F. L. Borchardt, *German Antiquity in Renaissance Myth* (Baltimore, 1971); H. Tiedemann, *Tacitus und das Nationalbewusstsein der deutschen Humanisten* (Berlin, 1913); E. L. Etter, *Tacitus in der Geistesgeschichte des 16. und 17. Jahrhunderts* (Basel, 1966); R. Buschmann, *Das Bewusstsein der deutschen Geschichte bei den deutschen Humanisten* (Göttingen, 1930); P. Joachimsen, "Tacitus im deutschen Humanismus," *Neue Jahrbücher für das klassische Altertum, Geschichte und deutschen Literatur* 17 (1911): 697–717; and K. Schellhase, *Tacitus in Renaissance Political Thought* (Chicago, 1976); also the fundamental collection in Simon Schardius, *Historicorum opus,* vol. 1, *Germaniae illustrationem continet* (Basel, 1574).
30. Cited by G. Strauss, *Sixteenth-Century Germany, Its Topography and Topographers* (Madison, WI, 1959), 21; see also L. W. Spitz, *Conrad Celtis: The German Arch-Humanist* (Cambridge, MA, 1957); and Joachimsen, *Geschichtsauffassung.*

31. Jacob Wimpheling, *Epitome rerum germanicarum* (Strasbourg, 1505).
32. Albert Krantz, *Saxonia* (Cologne, 1520), and *Wandalia* (Cologne, 1519). There is no critical study of this important historian.
33. Beatus Rhenanus, *Rerum germanicarum libri tres* (Basel, 1531), 3; and cf. idem, *In P. Cornelium, Tacitum Annotationes* (Lyons, 1542). Beatus also lacks a modern critical study.
34. See P. Archambault, *Seven French Chroniclers* (Syracuse, 1974); H. Baumann, *Die Geschichhtsschreiber Philippe de Commynes und die Wirkung seiner politischen Vorstellung in Frankreich um die Mitte des 16. Jahrhunderts* (Munich, 1982); and S. Kinser, introduction to *The Memoirs of Philippe de Commynes*, trans. I. Cazeaux (Columbia, SC, 1969); also J. Voss, *Das Mittelalter im historischen Denken Frankreichs* (Munich, 1973).
35. *Grans chroniques de France* (Paris, 1837), 4; and see G. Spiegel, *The Chronicle Tradition of Saint-Denis* (Leiden, 1978).
36. J. P. Bodmer, "Die französische Historiographie des Spätmittelalters und die Franken," *Archiv für Kulturgeschichte* 45 (1963):91–118.
37. C. Vivanti, "Paulus Aemilius condidit historias?" *Annales* 19 (1964):1117–24, and K. Davies, "Some Early Drafts of the *De Rebus Gestis Francorum* of Paulus Aemilius," *Medievalia et Humanistica* 12 (1958):99–110.
38. Polydore Vergil, *De rerum inventoribus* (Basel, 1536), 49.
39. D. Hay, *Polydore Vergil* (Oxford, 1952).
40. See above, notes 10 and 14.
41. See *Le lettere di Andrea Alciato giureconsulto*, ed. G. L. Barni (Florence, 1953), 222, and M. P. Gilmore, "*Fides et Eruditio:* Erasmus and the Study of History," *Teachers of History: Essays in Honor of Lawrence Bradford Packard*, ed. H. S. Hughes and M. P. Gilmore (Ithaca, 1954), 9–27; and A. Bonilla y San Martín, *Luis Vives y la filosofía del renascimiento* (Madrid, 1929), vol. 2.
42. See especially F. Gilbert, *Machiavelli and Guicciardini: Politics and History in Sixteenth-Century Florence* (Princeton, 1965), and R. von Albertini, *Das florentinische Staatsbewusstsein im Übergang von der Republik zum Prinzipat* (Bern, 1955). Cf. J. H. Hexter, *The Vision of Politics on the Eve of the Reformation* (New York, 1973), and E. Hassinger, *Empirisch-rationaler Historismus* (Munich, 1978).
43. Niccolò Macchiavelli, *The Discourses*, 3.43. For further bibliography here, as elsewhere, see Cochrane, *Historians and Historiography*.
44. Machiavelli, *History of Florence*, trans. W. Dunne (New York, 1901), intro. See also F. Gilbert, "Machiavelli's Istorie Fiorentine," in *Studies on Machiavelli*, ed. M. P. Gilmore (Florence, 1972), and his introduction to *History of Florence* (New York, 1960); M. Phillips, "Machiavelli, Guicciardini and the Tradition of Vernacular Historiography," *American Historical Review* 84 (1979): 86–105; and P. Bondella, *Machiavelli and the Art of Renaissance History* (Detroit, 1973).
45. *Discourses*, 1.2.
46. Francesco Guicciardini, *Ricordi*, trans. N. H. Thomson (New York, 1949), 71.

47. Francesco Guicciardini, *History of Italy,* trans. C. Grayson (New York, 1964), 85. And see M. Phillips, *Francesco Guicciardini: The Historian's Craft* (Toronto, 1977), and idem, "The Disenchanted Witness: Participation and Alienation in Florentine Historiography," *Journal of the History of Ideas* 44 (1983): 191–206; and V. Caprariis, *Francesco Guicciardini: Dalle politica alla storia* (Florence, 1950).

48. J. R. Hale, intro. to Guicciardini, *History of Italy,* vii.

49. Claude de Seyssel, *The Monarchy of France,* ed. D. R. Kelley and trans. J. H. Hexter (New Haven, 1981). Cf. "Exordium" to his translation of Justin, *Histoire* (Paris, 1559), trans. ibid., 163, and the edition of J. Poujol, *La Monarchie de France* (Paris, 1961).

50. *Chronica carionis* (Wittenberg, 1580), preface by Melanchthon (1558), and Luther, "Preface to Galaenus Capella's History," in *Works,* ed. and trans. L. Spitz (Philadelphia, 1960), 34:275. In general see E. Menke-Glückert, *Geschichtsschreibung der Reformation und Gegenreformation* (Leipzig, 1912); P. Fraenkel, *Testimonia Patrum: The Function of Patristic Argument in the Theology of Philipp Melanchthon* (Geneva, 1961); H. Brettschneider, *Melanchthon als Historiker* (Insterberg, 1880); J. M. Headley, *Luther's View of Church History* (New Haven, 1963); H. Lilje, *Luthers Geschichtsanschauung* (Zurich, 1932); E. Schäfer, *Luther als Kirchenhistoriker* (Gütersloh, 1897); and esp. A. G. Dickens and J. M. Tonkin, *The Reformation in Historical Thought* (Cambridge, MA, 1985).

51. See H. Berger, *Calvins Geschichtsauffassung* (Zurich, 1955); Bertelli, *Ribelli, libertini e ortodossi;* and P. Polman, *L'elément historique dans la controverse religieuse du XVIe siècle* (Gembloux, 1932); also P. Bietenholz, *History and Biography in the Works of Erasmus of Rotterdam* (Geneva, 1966).

52. Johann Sleidan, "Apology for His History," in *General History of the Reformation* (London, 1689); and see D. R. Kelley, "Johann Sleidan and the Origins of History as a Profession," *Journal of Modern History* 12 (1980):573–98; A. G. Dickens, "Johann Sleidan and Reformation History," in *Reformation, Conformity and Dissent,* ed. R. B. Knox (London, 1977), 17–43; and I. Vogelstein, *Johann Sleiden's Commentaries* (Lanham, MD, 1986).

53. See especially H. Scheible, *Die Entstehung der Magdeburger Zenturien* (Güttersloh, 1966); also C. K. Pullapilly, *Caesar Baronius, Counter-Reformation Historian* (South Bend, IN, 1975).

54. Paolo Sarpi, *History of Benefices and Selections from History of the Council of Trent,* trans. P. Burke (New York, 1967); and see W. Bouwsma, *Venice and the Defense of Republican Liberty* (Berkeley, 1968).

55. See G. Cotroneo, *I trattatisti dell'"Ars historica"* (Naples, 1971); R. Landfester, *Historia magistra vitae* (Geneva, 1972); and *Theoretiker humanistischer Geschichtsschreibung,* ed. and intro. E. Kessler (Munich, 1971), reproducing essential texts; also Giorgio Spini, "The Art of History in the Counter Reformation," in *The Late Italian Renaissance, 1525–1630,* ed. E. Cochrane (New York, 1970), 91–133; G. H. Nadel, "The Philosophy

of History before Historicism," in *Studies in the Philosophy of History,* ed. G. H. Nadel (New York, 1965), 49–73; F. Lamprecht, *Zur Theorie der humanistischen Geschichtsschreibung* (Winterthur, 1950); C. Trinkaus, "A Humanist's Image of Humanism: the Inaugural Orations of Bartolommeo della Fonte," *Studies in the Renaissance* 7 (1960):90–147; B. Reynolds, "Shifting Currents in Historical Criticism," *Journal of the History of Ideas* 14 (1953): 471–92; and D. R. Kelley, "Faces in Clio's Mirror," *Journal of Modern History* 47 (1975):679–90, and 54 (1982):320–26.

56. Francesco Patrizi, *Della historia dieci dialoghi* (Venice, 1560), 7, in Kessler, "Geschichtsdenken und Geschichtsschreibung"; and see P. M. Arcari, *Il pensiero politico di Francesco Patrizi da Cherso* (Rome, 1935).

57. Luis Cabrera de Córdoba, *De historia para entenderla y escribirla,* ed. S. M. Diaz (Madrid, 1948), intro. Cf. A. Seifert, *Cognitio historica. Die Geschichte als Namengaberin der frühneuzeitliche Empirie* (Berlin, 1976), chap. 5.

58. See Kelley, *Foundations;* J. H. Franklin, *Jean Bodin and the Sixteenth-Century Revolution in the Methodology of Law and History* (New York, 1963); J. L. Brown, *The Methodus . . . of Jean Bodin* (Washington, DC, 1939); A. Klempt, *Die Säkularisierung der universalhistorischen Auffassung* (Göttingen, 1960); *Jean Bodin: Verhandlungen der internationalen Bodin Tagung,* ed. H. Denzer (Munich, 1973); La *"République de Jean Bodin: Atti del convegno di Perugia* (Florence, 1981); *Jean Bodin: Actes du Colloque Interdisciplinaire,* 2 vols. (Angers, 1985). G. Huppert, *The Idea of Perfect History* (Urbana, IL, 1970). C. G. Dubois, *La conception de l'histoire en France au XVIe siècle* (Paris, 1977); also J. H. Preston, "Was There an Historical Revolution?" *Journal of the History of Ideas* 38 (1977):353–64; and see below.

59. François Baudouin, *De institutione historiae universae* (Strasbourg, 1561), l; M. Erbe, *François Bauduin (1520–1573)* (Gütersloh, 1978); and M. Turchetti, *Concordia o toleranza?* (Geneva, 1984).

60. Guillaume Budé, *De l'institution de prince* (Paris, 1547), 63; also in C. Bontems et al., *Le prince dans la France des XVIe et XVIIe siècles* (Paris, 1965).

61. Baldassare Bonifacio, *De archivis* (Venice, 1632), and in general see Kelley, *Foundations,* and above, note 29.

62. See Jehasse, *Renaissance de la critique;* Grafton, *Joseph Scaliger;* and V. A. Nordman, *Justus Lipsius als Geschichtsforscher und Geschichtslehrer* (Helsinki, 1932).

63. S. Kinser, *The Works of Jacques-Auguste de Thou* (The Hague, 1966). On the national traditions see F. S. Fussner, *The Historical Revolution* (New York, 1962); F. J. Levy, *Tudor Historical Thought* (San Marino, CA, 1967); A. B. Ferguson, *Clio Unbound* (Durham, NC, 1979); B. S. Alonso, *Historia de la historiografía española,* 3 vols. (Madrid, 1944–50); H. R. von Srbik, *Geist und Geschichte vom deutschen Humanismus bis zur Gegenwart,* 2 vols. (Munich, 1950–51); and more generally E. Breisach, *Historiography: Ancient, Medieval, and Modern* (Chicago, 1983), with further bibliography.

64. O. Ranum, *Artisans of Glory* (Chapel Hill, NC, 1980).

65. François Hotman, *Francogallia*, ed. R. E. Giesey, trans. J. H. M. Salmon (Cambridge, 1972); and D. R. Kelley, *François Hotman* (Princeton, 1973). Also see below, note 72.

66. See A. Bernardini and G. Righi, *Il concetto di philologia e di cultura classica* (Bari, 1953), and below.

67. E. von Moeller, *Aymer du Rivail, Der erste Rechtshistoriker* (Berlin, 1907), and D. R. Kelley, "The Rise of Legal History in the Renaissance," *History and Theory* 9 (1970): 174–94.

68. Baudouin, *De institutione*, 89.

69. Louis Le Roy, *De l'origine, antiquité, progrès, excellence, et l'utilité de l'art politique* (Paris, 1553); and idem, "L'origine, progrès et perfection de la philosophie . . . ," in *Le Phedon de Platon* (Paris, 1553); and see W. Gundersheimer, *The Life and Works of Louis Le Roy* (Geneva, 1966), and below, note 74.

70. Henri de La Popelinière, *Histoire des histoires, avec l'Idée de l'histoire accomplie* (Paris, 1599); and see D. R. Kelley, "History as a Calling: The Case of la Popelinière," in *Renaissance Studies in Honor of Hans Baron*, ed. A. Molho and J. Kirschner (Florence, 1971), 773–89; G. W. Sypher, "La Popelinière's *Histoire de France*," *Journal of the History of Ideas* 24 (1963): 41–54; and M. Yardeni, "La conception de l'histoire dans l'oeuvre de La Popeliniere," *Revue d'histoire moderne et contemporaine* 11 (1964):109–26; also C. Vivanti, "Alle origine della idea di civiltà, Le scoperte geografiche e gli scritti di La Popelinière," *Rivista storica italiana* 74 (1962):225–47.

71. Henri de La Popelinière, "Le dessein de l'histoire nouvelle des françois," in *Idée de l'histoire*, 401ff.; Le Roy, *Consideration sur l'histoire françois et universelle de ce temps* (Paris, 1568), and "Project ou dessein du royaume de France . . . ," in *Exhortation aux François pour vivre en concorde* (Paris, 1579). Cf. Nicolas Vignier, *Bibliothèque historiale* (Paris, 1582).

72. See D. Thickett, *Estienne Pasquier* (London, 1980); R. Bütler, *Nationales und universales Denken im Werke Etienne Pasquiers* (Basel, 1948); J. Espiner-Scott, *Claude Fauchet* and her supplementary thesis containing unpublished documents (Paris, 1938); also P. Ronzy, *Un humaniste italianisant, Papire Masson (1554–1611)* (Paris, 1924); and more generally H. Baron, "The *Querelle* of the Ancients and the Moderns as a Problem for Renaissance Scholarship," *Journal of the History of Ideas* 20 (1957): 3–22, and J. Schlobach, *Zyklentheorie und Epochenmetaphorik* (Munich, 1980).

73. See Kelley, *Foundations*, 129.

74. A. Le Franc, "Le traité 'De la vicissitude ou variétaté' des choses de Louis le Roy e sa veritable date," *Mélanges Lanson* (Paris, 1922), 115. Louis Le Roy, *De la vicissitude ou variété des choses en l'univers* (Paris, 1584), fol. 215, echoing themes appearing in his own G. *Budaei viri clarissimi vita* (Paris, 1540); see above note 69 and in general S. Kinser, "Ideas of Temporal Change and Cultural Process in France, 1470–1535," *Renaissance Studies in Honor of Hans Baron*, ed. Molho and Kirschner, 703–55.

75. See Seifert, *Cognitio historica;* L. F. Dean, "Francis Bacon's Theory of Civil

History Writing," *Literary History* 8 (1941): 161–83; and cf. Galileo, *Dialogue Concerning the Two Chief World Systems,* trans. S. Drake (Berkeley, 1953), 113.

76. Leibniz, cited in Thompson, *History of Historical Writing,* 2:100; and cf. E. Troeltsch, *Der Historismus and seine Probleme* (Tübingen, 1922), 104.

77. Daniel Heinsius *The Value of History,* trans. G. Robinson (Cambridge, MA, 1943), 10–11.

33 ❧ HUMANISM AND MORAL PHILOSOPHY
Paul Oskar Kristeller

MORAL PHILOSOPHY, UNLIKE THE OTHER PHILOSOPHICAL DIS-
ciplines (logic, natural philosophy, metaphysics), was considered a part of the *studia humanitatis* and was therefore closely
associated with the humanist movement. A considerable part of the
moral literature of the Renaissance was written by humanists, or by laymen with a humanist training, and practically all writers on moral subjects were influenced by humanism. The connection of this literature with
humanism accounts for several of its peculiar features. Many, if not all,
of the humanists were teachers, so that their moral thought was strongly
centered on the education of the young. The humanists considered classical antiquity their major guide and model in thought and literature, and
their moral writings are accordingly studded with quotations from Greek
and Roman authors, with episodes from classical history and mythology,
with ideas and theories derived from ancient philosophers and writers.
Finally, the humanists were professional rhetoricians, that is, writers and
critics, who wished not only to say the truth, but to say it well, according
to their literary taste and standards. They believed in the ancient rhetorical doctrine that a professional speaker and writer must acquire and
show skill in making any idea that is related to his chosen topic plausible
to his public. Consequently, an idea is often expressed in phrases that aim
at elegance rather than at precision, and many times, especially in a dialogue or in a speech, opinions may be defended with vigor and eloquence
that are appropriate for the occasion, but do not express the author's
final or considered view.[1]

✳   ✳   ✳

Moral teaching is often contained in literary genres cultivated by the
humanists where a modern reader might not expect to find it. The humanists inherited from the ancient and medieval grammarians and literary critics the view that moral instruction is one of the main tasks of the
poet. Hence there is a moral or even moralistic note in some of the poetry
they wrote, and in the interpretation they gave of the ancient poets in the

classroom and in their published commentaries. The humanists also followed ancient and medieval theory and practice in their belief that the orator and prose writer is a moral teacher and ought to adorn his compositions with pithy sentences quoted from the poets or coined by himself. To facilitate his task, a humanist would gather quotations and sentences in a commonplace book, and some writers would publish collections of sentences, proverbs, or historical anecdotes from which an author could freely quote on the appropriate occasion. Plutarch's *Apophthegmata,* in humanist translations, enjoyed great popularity for this reason, and Erasmus's *Adagia,* collected from many ancient sources and revised and enlarged several times by the author, was printed and used, though not always quoted, for several centuries.

Finally, another branch of study cultivated by the humanists, history, had moral significance for them. The humanists shared the view of many ancient and medieval authors that one of the tasks of historiography is to teach a moral lesson. Much Renaissance historiography is sustained by this belief. In the same way, the extensive biographical literature produced during the period is often animated by the desire to supply the reader with models worthy of imitation. The medieval Lives of saints provided a precedent, since they too were written to provide the reader with models of pious conduct. But it makes a difference whether the persons whose lives are described as models of human conduct are Christian saints or ancient statesmen and generals, philosophers and poets, contemporary princes, citizens, or artists. The Renaissance continued to produce biographies of the saints, but it left a much larger number of secular biographies. The lives of famous ancients as written by Petrarch and other humanists were clearly intended to provide models for imitation, since classical antiquity was for the humanists the admired model in all fields of human endeavor. No wonder that in a famous humanist controversy the relative superiority of the Romans Scipio and Caesar served as a basis for discussing the merits of republican and monarchical governments. When Machiavelli in his *Discourses on Livy* holds out the institutions and actions of the Roman republic as a model to his contemporaries, he follows the practice of his humanist predecessors, and he states his underlying assumption more clearly than any of them had done: human beings are fundamentally the same at all times, and therefore it is possible to study the conduct of the ancients, to learn from their mistakes and from their achievements, and to follow their example where they were successful.

If we turn from these humanist writings in which a moral or moralistic interest appeared to those works which deal explicitly with moral philosophy, we may notice the favorite genres used for this kind of literature. Most important are the treatise and the dialogue, and later on, the essay. More marginal forms are the oration and the letter, the most widespread forms of humanist literature, which at times serve to express moral ideas. The letter was especially popular with the humanists, as it allowed them to express their views in a personal and subjective fashion, although they considered letter-writing a branch of literature and gave the same polished elegance to their letters as to their other literary compositions. To these genres we might add the collections of sentences, proverbs, and commonplaces.

The language of these writings was usually Latin, but the use of the vernacular appears especially in Tuscany during the fifteenth century and becomes more widespread in the rest of Italy and of Europe during the sixteenth. The choice of language indicated the reading public to which an author wished to address a particular work. Latin writings were intended for an international audience of scholars and of educated alumni of humanist schools, while within a particular country or region works in the vernacular were read chiefly by a middle class of ladies, businessmen, and artisans who were able to read and eager to be entertained and instructed, but who usually knew no Latin and lacked a humanist school education or a university training.[2]

*   *   *

The existence of this large body of moral literature written by humanists and popularizers, and of the still larger body of humanist learning and literature, is in itself a significant historical phenomenon. We are confronted with a vast body of secular learning, nourished from ancient sources and contemporary experience and basically independent of, though not entirely unrelated to, the medieval traditions of scholastic philosophy and science, theology and law. As a part of this learning, or derived from it, there is a body of moral thought that is never opposed to religious doctrine—often explicitly harmonized with it—existing side by side with religious doctrine and claiming for its domain wider and wider areas of human life and experience. There are several medieval precedents for such secular moral thought, but they were different and more limited in scope. Certain moralists like Cicero, Seneca, and Boethius had enjoyed a continuous popularity throughout the Middle Ages, and medieval grammarians had tried to provide moral interpretations of ancient poets such as Ovid and Vergil. This tradition was apparently absorbed by Renaissance humanism in its beginnings in the fourteenth century. When Aristotle's writings were all translated into Latin and adopted as textbooks of philosophy at Paris and other universities during the thirteenth century, his *Ethics*—along with his *Politics*, his *Rhetoric*, and the *Economics* attributed to him—was expounded in the classroom. A number of commentaries on these works owe their origin to this teaching tradition, although the course on ethics was an elective rather than a required course and was considered less important than logic or natural philosophy. Thus Aristotle's doctrines of the virtues and of the supreme good, and also his theory of the passions as presented in the *Rhetoric,* were well known to students of philosophy and to many others. When the humanists took over much of the teaching of ethics in the fifteenth century and wrote general treatises on moral subjects, they continued to use the Aristotelian writings, which recommended themselves by their topical completeness and the wealth of their detail; and the humanists often tended to follow his views though they might interpret them in a different way or combine them with theories derived from other sources. Finally, in the later Middle Ages there had developed a code of moral conduct for knights, that is, for a privileged class of laymen, and this code found its literary expression in lyrical poetry, in romances in verse and prose, and in a few theoretical treatises. The moral literature of the Renaissance was similarly intended for laymen rather than for clerics. Yet aside from its heavy classical equipment, which had been lacking in the medieval literature of the knights, it was written by and for a different class of people: it had a different political, economic, and social foundation.

Renaissance humanism, which began in Italy toward the very end of the thirteenth century at the earliest, cannot be explained as a delayed but direct result of the economic and political development of the city communities that began in the eleventh century. For even a theory of a "cultural lag," whatever that may mean, does not seem to supply the missing link, as there was, after all, a distinctive tradition of learning and literature in twelfth- and early thirteenth-century Italy that was not humanistic. At the same time, it was an urban, not a feudal society that provided at least the background of Renaissance civilization. The Renaissance humanists wrote their moral works for their fellow scholars, for their students, and for an elite of businessmen and of urbanized noblemen who were willing to adopt their cultural and moral ideals. During the sixteenth century, ever wider circles of the middle class seem to have taken an interest in this literature.

Political theory was traditionally a part of ethics or a supplement to it, and the Renaissance moralists took a strong and sometimes a primary interest in political theory. The nature of their political ideas varied a good deal according to circumstances. There was a tradition of civic and republican humanism, especially in Florence and to a lesser degree in Venice, the historical significance of which has been emphasized by Hans

Baron and other scholars. Yet much Renaissance political thinking developed also along monarchical lines, especially during the sixteenth century. Both Machiavelli and Thomas More were also linked to the humanistic movement.

Aside from the political treatises, the moral literature of the Renaissance addressed itself mainly to the private individual. In such works the political and economic realities of the day are taken more or less for granted, and the purpose of the moral treatise is to give theoretical or practical instruction to the individual, especially to the young. The lines between decency and success are not always as clearly drawn as one might wish, and as a result, the word virtue came to have a curious ambiguity. It meant moral virtue, to be sure, but Machiavelli's virtue stood more for the strong character that assured political success, and the "virtuoso" was distinguished by intellectual and social skill rather than by moral excellence.

At this point, it might be well to consider the variety of meanings of the term "moral thought," both for the Renaissance and in its wider applications. When we speak of the morals of a person or a period, we think primarily of actual behavior and assume that this behavior expresses some conscious or unconscious convictions, though it may be quite contrary to the professed ideals of the person and of the time. In this respect the Renaissance, and especially the Italian Renaissance, enjoys a dubious reputation. In the popular view, which seems to find support in John Addington Symonds and other historians, the Italian Renaissance was a period of political ruthlessness, of crimes of violence and passion; and the glittering melodrama of dagger and poison seems to provide an appropriate foil for the admired beauty of Renaissance poetry and painting. Examples of crime and cruelty were numerous in the Renaissance, in Italy and elsewhere, as they are in other periods of history, including the Middle Ages and our own century. But not all the stories and anecdotes that found their way from the Renaissance chroniclers and gossip writers into modern textbooks of history are well documented, and those we can accept were probably as distasteful to their own time as to ours. Moreover, it would be quite wrong to assume that such misdeeds dominated the picture of public or private life during the Renaissance. There were a great many decent people whose conduct agreed with the highest moral standards.

Yet, ignoring the actual conduct of people during the Renaissance or whatever secret or unexpressed thought may have guided them, and examining those moral ideas which we find more or less explicitly stated in the literature of the period, we find that moral subjects were discussed in a variety of ways. An author may describe the actual moral customs and manners of his time, either through examples, as is often done in narrative literature, or through a discussion of their general traits, without explicitly setting forth any standards of how people should behave. He may also, however, try to guide the conduct of people, especially of his younger readers, by prescribing how they should behave. Description and prescription are often confused in modern discussions of moral and social problems, and they cannot always be kept apart in Renaissance literature; but it would help proper understanding of such discussions if the distinction were clearly kept in mind. In the literature that emphasizes the prescriptive aspect and tends to set standards for the young, we must distinguish between those authors who are mainly concerned with rules of prudence and expediency, and teach their readers how to behave in order to get along with other people and to have a successful career, and those who emphasize honesty and moral decency regardless of their practical consequences. In works of the latter kind there is often a mixture of ethical theory, which properly belongs to philosophy, and of moral exhortation and persuasion, which belongs to oratory and tends toward edification. Finally, there is the literature of strictly philosophical ethics, which intends to set forth general principles of moral thought and is prescriptive only in an implicit way or by deducing rules of conduct from those general principles. This literature may take the form of systematic handbooks of ethics or of monographic treatises that deal with specific topics in ethics.

All these types are present in the moral literature of the Renaissance, and it would be very wrong to say that any of them is limited to a particular phase of the period. However, the literature of the fifteenth and early sixteenth centuries is more frequently concerned with moralistic prescription and edification. As the sixteenth century progresses, rules of expediency and descriptions of manners and customs tend to prevail. One gets the impression of a more settled society in which standards of conduct and manners are well established and the main task of the young man is not to acquire valid ethical principles through independent critical thinking but rather to assure his success by learning how to adjust to life—that is, to the accepted modes of moral thought and conduct. This literature gains in historical and psychological interest what it loses in ethical solidity, and it leads the way toward such famous examples of seventeenth-century literature as Gracian, La Bruyère, or La Rochefoucauld.

*   *   *

In contrast to the books of manners stand the philosophical treatises on ethics that supply whatever theoretical structure and systematic thinking on moral problems there was during the Renaissance. Because of the general direction of Renaissance humanism, most though not all of their subject matter is derived from classical sources. The authors known during the Middle Ages, especially Aristotle, Cicero, and Seneca, continue to be important and in some ways become even more important, as there is a great effort to interpret and to apply their writings in great detail. Equally important are some other sources of ancient moral philosophy made available for the first time by humanist scholarship. These new sources include most of the writings of Plato and the Neoplatonists, Stoic authors such as Epictetus and Marcus Aurelius, Skeptics like Sextus Empiricus, and Epicureans like Lucretius. Diogenes Laertius supplied new information on several schools of ancient thought, especially on Epicurus. Of equal, if not even greater importance, were a number of popular ancient moralists not identified with any particular school of philosophy, such as Xenophon and Isocrates, Plutarch and Lucian. The number both of their translations and of the quotations taken from them shows that they were among the favorite sources of Renaissance humanists.

The impact of these various sources and schools on the moral thought of the Renaissance was varied and complex. Moreover, the history of moral thought during the Renaissance is related to, but not identical with, the history of philosophy. Only a part of the moral literature of the period came from philosophers in the technical sense of the word, or was systematic in content. At the same time, some of the most important philosophers of the Renaissance, and even entire groups and schools of Renaissance philosophy, such as the Aristotelians, the Platonists, and the philosophers of nature, were not interested primarily in ethics but made their major contributions to other parts of philosophy, especially logic, metaphysics, and natural philosophy. With these qualifications, we may say that there was a solid body of Aristotelian ethics throughout the Renaissance period. Its most obvious expressions are the numerous editions, translations, commentaries, and summaries of Aristotle's ethical writings (among which the *Eudemian Ethics* now took its proper place for the first time), and of their ancient and medieval interpreters. This literature has not been sufficiently explored, and we are just beginning to learn more about it. However, it may safely be said of the Aristotelian ethics what has become apparent about Renaissance Aristotelianism in general: it continues in many ways the traditions of medieval Aristotelianism, which were very much alive at the universities, in Italy as elsewhere. But there was also among the humanists a strong tendency to recapture the genuine thought of Aristotle apart from its supposed distortions by medieval translators and commentators. Finally, there were all kinds of combinations on the part of Aristotelian philosophers, who tried to reconcile and synthesize what seemed to be valuable in the scholastic and humanistic interpretations of Aristotle. In the study of ethics, as in other disciplines, the main contribution of the humanists to Aristotelian studies was to supply new translations based on a better philological understanding of the Greek text. This achievement is more important than one might suspect. For in an author as difficult and elusive as Aristotle, whose every word was (and still is) considered by many thinkers as the ultimate source and authority of philosophical truth, a different translation may be equivalent to a different philosophy. Moreover, whereas the medieval scholastics treated Aristotle pretty much in isolation, the humanist Aristotelians read and interpreted Aristotle in close conjunction with the other Greek philosophers and writers. On the whole, the humanist Aristotelians were primarily interested in Aristotle's ethical writings. Leonardo Bruni translated and summarized only Aristotle's *Ethics, Politics,* and *Economics,* while Francesco Filelfo wrote a summary of ethics based on Aristotle. Ermolao Barbaro the Younger, though not limited to Aristotle's ethical writings, favored them in his lectures and in a summary of ethics. Philipp Melanchthon, Luther's colleague, wrote several treatises on ethics, in which Aristotle's doctrine is preferred to that of other ancient philosophers, and it was due to Melanchthon's influence that the Reformed universities of Protestant Germany continued to base their teaching of philosophy on the works of Aristotle.

As a result of this widespread study of Aristotle, practically every writer of the period was acquainted with the main doctrines of Aristotelian ethics and was inclined to adopt them or at least to discuss them. Aristotle's views that the supreme good of man must include a minimum of external advantages and that the contemplative life is the highest goal of human existence are as familiar in the moral literature of the Renaissance as are his distinction between moral and intellectual virtues, his definition of the moral virtues as habits and as means between two opposite vices, and his detailed descriptions of individual virtues and vices.

Plato's influence on Renaissance moral thought is much more limited than Aristotle's, in spite of the well-known role played generally by Platonism in Renaissance philosophy. Plato's early dialogues, to be sure, deal with moral topics and were widely read in school, mainly in courses of Greek. Yet we do not find any system of ethics based primarily on Plato, as so many were on Aristotle, due partly to the unsystematic character of Plato's writings. More important, the leading Platonists of the Renaissance, like their late ancient and medieval predecessors, were interested in questions of metaphysics and cosmology rather than of ethics. They were not so much concerned with specific moral problems or theories but tended to reduce all ethical questions to the single task of attaining the contemplative life. Some of their specific theories that are relevant to moral thought will be mentioned later. The most important and widespread contribution of Platonism to the subject is the theory of love, based on the *Symposium* and *Phaedrus,* which was to constitute the subject matter of poems and lectures and of a special branch of prose literature. Among the moralists not committed to any special school of philosophy, quotations and borrowings from Plato were frequent and became increasingly so after the rise of Florentine Platonism during the second half of the fifteenth century.

Stoic ethics, as expressed in the writings of Seneca and discussed in Cicero's philosophical works, had been a familiar ingredient of medieval moral thought and continued to exercise a widespread influence during the Renaissance, when the writings of these Roman authors became even more popular than they had been before. The Stoic view that the supreme good of man consisted of virtue alone and that to secure virtue all passions must be thoroughly eradicated was generally known and often approved. Some Stoic theories appealed even to thinkers, such as Pietro Pomponazzi, who cannot be labeled as Stoic philosophers in their general orientation. Yet in contrast to this popular and eclectic Stoicism based on Cicero and Seneca, which permeated the moral thought of the fifteenth and early sixteenth century, it was only during the latter part of the sixteenth century that the Greek sources of ancient Stoicism became better known and that systematic attempts were made to restate Stoic philosophy (and especially Stoic ethics) in its original purity. The distinguished humanist Justus Lipsius compiled from the ancient sources a valuable handbook of Stoic ethics that was to enjoy great popularity during the seventeenth century, and the French writer Guillaume du Vair gave a more literary expression to the same doctrine. Most Renaissance humanists found Stoic ethics uncongenial on account of its rigidity. The great vogue of pure Stoicism came only in the seventeenth century. In order to understand this later appeal, we must remember that the Stoics are rigorous only in their emphasis on the difference between virtue and vice, but reserve a very large area of human life to the things they call morally indifferent. Where questions of virtue and vice are not involved the Stoic sage is allowed and even encouraged to follow expediency. With virtue and vice often limited to a few ultimate decisions, the sway of expediency becomes very large indeed; and the Stoic moralist, while continuing to be rigorous in theory, may turn out to be lax, if not selfish, on most practical questions. The same may happen to the Platonist (and to the mystic), as soon as he has to act on matters unrelated to the life of contemplation.

The ethics of Epicurus, which proposed intellectual pleasure as the chief end of human life, was widely known and frequently discussed in the Renaissance. Most humanists rejected Epicurean ethics and were more or less influenced by Cicero's unsympathetic account of that doctrine. Yet gradually the more favorable presentation of Epicurus in the works of Lucretius and Diogenes Laertius became better known, and Epicurus's emphasis on intellectual pleasure was more fully appreciated. Thus Epicurean ethics was endorsed by a few humanists, such as Lorenzo Valla and Cosimo Raimondi, and some of its tenets made an impression on thinkers whose general outlook was very different—for example, Marsilio Ficino.

Finally, ancient Skepticism had a number of followers in the Renaissance, especially in the sixteenth century, when the writings of Sextus became more widely known. The main appeal of Skepticism was in its claim that by abandoning all rigid doctrines and opinions we free ourselves from unnecessary worries and are left to face only the unavoidable necessities of life. If we wish to have a standard for our conduct, we should follow the customs of our country, at least in all matters that concern other people. In this way the boundaries between moral standards and established manners tend to be blurred, although there may remain a realm of personal and individual life in which we may think and do as we please. Skepticism in matters of reason is by no means incompatible with religious faith, as the example of Augustine may show; consequently this position had many more followers during the sixteenth century than is usually realized. The chief expression of this skeptical ethics is found in some of the essays of Montaigne and in the writings of his pupil Pierre Charron.[3]

*   *   *

The influence of ancient ethics on the Renaissance is not limited to an acceptance of the main systematic theories of antiquity by some Renaissance thinkers. The constant use of specific ancient ideas or sentences or examples in the discussion of moral topics is more widespread. This eclectic use of ancient material, for which some favorite author such as Cicero could serve as a classical model, is especially characteristic of the humanists and their popular followers. In this way, particular ideas or sentences taken from a particular philosopher, such as Plato or Aristotle, were indiscriminately combined with those of other philosophers who held a very different position on major questions or with those of ancient moralists like Isocrates, Lucian, or Plutarch, who cannot even be credited with a coherent systematic position in philosophy. Thus the sharp boundaries between philosophical concepts or theories derived from different sources tend to vanish. Furthermore, Renaissance humanists were not as interested as modern scholars are in emphasizing the distinctive traits of various periods, schools, and writers of antiquity or in playing up one against the other. They tended to admire ancient literature in all its periods and representatives (though some authors were more admired than others), and to be syncretistic as well as eclectic; that is, they liked to harmonize the views of various classical authors and to extract from their writings a kind of common wisdom that could be learned, imitated, and utilized.

The numerous classical quotations that characterize most humanist treatises and even the essays of Montaigne, and which are apt to bore and annoy the modern reader, were not vain displays of empty erudition, though they might often serve this purpose. The quotations served as authorities—as confirmations of the validity of what the author was trying to say. Quotations from recognized authors were counted by ancient theorists of rhetoric among the forms of proof that an orator was supposed to produce. Augustine had emphasized the authority of Scripture as a chief source of theological discourse, and during the Middle Ages not only theology but each discipline of knowledge employed its standard authorities, along with rational arguments, in support of its theories. For a Renaissance humanist, a sentence from a classical writer served as such an authority, and if he added to his quotation what seems to us an arbitrary interpretation, he merely did what his predecessors and contemporaries also had done. In a period in which the emphasis is on authority and tradition, originality asserts itself in the adaptation and interpretation of the tradition. Moreover, there may be some originality even in the choice of one's quotations. It makes a difference whether an author keeps quoting the same passages that had been quoted by his predecessors or for the first time introduces new quotations, singling them out from their context and, as it were, discovering their significance.

The frequency of quotations and of commonplaces repeated in the moral literature of the Renaissance gives to all but its very best products an air of triviality that is often very boring to the modern critical reader, especially when he is acquainted with the ancient sources from which the quotations are drawn and in which they seem to have a much more subtle and precise meaning. It we want to do justice to these Renaissance writers we must try to understand the circumstances under which they wrote and the purposes they had in mind. Whenever many books of the same type are written, most of them are bound to be dull and mediocre, and only a few will stand out by reason of their authors' intellectual or literary merits. Human inventiveness seems limited and repetition is the rule rather than the exception, even where no direct copying or plagiarism is involved. After all, no single reader was expected to read all the treatises on the same topic, just as a modern student will not read more than one or two textbooks on the same subject. Each treatise is addressed to its own readers and must supply to them the same amount of general information that other readers may derive from other works on the same topic. This necessity is even more present with orations, which were delivered on only a single occasion and were published only incidentally, when they happened to be very successful. An oration is composed to entertain and edify its audience by adapting general ideas to the occasion. While it was the custom in Florence to have each incoming group of magistrates treated to a speech in praise of justice, it was not very important that the orator should produce new or profound ideas about the meaning of justice—it was his job to impress his listeners with their duty to follow justice in the administration of their office. This task was surely of great practical importance for the city as a whole. Since the oration was a principal form of humanist literature, the example might be applied to its other branches. Each moral treatise had to exhort and edify its readers by instructing them in matters of great practical and human importance, which was in most instances more valuable than the presentation of novel or original thoughts. In other words, we should not approach the average moral literature of the Renaissance with excessive expectations as to its depth or originality, but with an awareness of its limited purposes and a recognition that it was well suited to these objectives.

*   *   *

The frequency of ancient ideas and quotations in the moral writings of the Renaissance humanists, and of humanist literature in general, raises another question that has been the subject of much debate: what was the attitude of the Renaissance humanists toward Christianity, and in what sense and to what extent were they inclined toward paganism? The charge of paganism was made against the humanists by some theologians of their own time, and it has been repeated by a number of modern historians, some of whom have turned the charge into praise. There were, however, very few attempts to revive the pagan religions of classical antiquity, although this attempt has been alleged by contemporaries and by modern scholars in a few instances. Although much was made of pagan mythology in the poetry and also in the prose treatises of the period, it was not intended to replace the use of Christian religious thought and imagery but to supplement it. In most instances it was no more than a literary ornament sanctioned by ancient precedent. Where it served a more serious intention, its use was justified by allegory—by attributing to the pagan stories a hidden meaning that was in accordance with Christian truth. This attitude culminates in Giovanni Pico della Mirandola's notion of a poetic theology, that is, of a philosophical and theological truth that could be discovered through the allegorical interpretation of pagan poetry and mythology. Yet the main impact of "paganism" on Renaissance moral thought consists in its heavy indebtedness to ancient philosophical ideas. The task of assimilating the moral and philosophical thought of the ancients into Christianity presented itself to the church fathers and again to many medieval thinkers. From these earlier attempts, the Renaissance differed at least in degree, if not in kind. The church fathers tended to fit Christianity into the ancient modes of thought that had been previously familiar to them and to their contemporaries. The humanists wanted to adapt classical ideas to a previously accepted Christian view of the world. Nevertheless, the affinity between the humanists and the church fathers has been stressed with some justification by modern historians like Giuseppe Toffanin, and the humanists themselves were to some extent aware of this affinity. For when they defended "poetry," that is, humanist learning and the reading of the pagan authors, against the theological critics of their own time, they cited the precedent of the church fathers. No doubt Bruni's translation of the letter in which Basil, one of the Fathers, defended the reading of pagan poets by a Christian youth owed its tremendous popularity to this issue. There were many humanists who were not concerned with religious or theological problems and did not touch on them in their writings. Those who did, and they were important, never undertook a general critique of the religious tradition such as appeared in the eighteenth century. They usually praised the Bible and the church fathers as the Christian classics and attacked scholastic theology as a barren distortion of original Christian doctrine and piety. A few of them attacked the weaknesses they observed in the church of their time, especially in monasticism. When the humanists wrote about moral subjects, either they tried to combine and harmonize ancient and Christian ideas in the manner of Erasmus, or they discussed moral topics on a purely classical and secular basis—without indicating any hostility toward Christianity, but rather taking for granted the compatibility between the two, as was done by Leon Battista Alberti and many other Italian humanists. In the sixteenth century, after the Protestant and Catholic reformations, humanist scholars and moralists could be found among the followers of both major camps, as well as among those who favored some of the smaller heretical movements or who tried hard to keep aloof from the religious struggle. It is clear once more that Renaissance humanism as a whole cannot be identified with a particular set of opinions or convictions, but is, rather, characterized by a cultural ideal and a range of scholarly, literary, and intellectual interests that the individual humanist was able to combine with a variety of professional, philosophical, or theological convictions.[4]

* * *

If we try to survey in more concrete detail the moral thought of the Renaissance period, it seems best to focus on the chief genres and themes of this literature, rather than on the ideas of individual writers and thinkers. The character of this literature, with its uncertain position between philosophical and popular thought, its dependence on classical sources, and its widespread eclecticism and triviality, seems to call for such an approach.

The most technical type of Renaissance literature on moral topics is the general treatise on ethics that was usually written for the use of students. Because Aristotle was and remained the chief basis of university instruction in the philosophical disciplines, many general treatises on ethics take the form of commentaries on Aristotle's *Nicomachean Ethics* and *Politics*, or of introductions, paraphrases, and summaries of those works. In the fifteenth century, the commentary of Donato Acciaiuoli and the *Compendium* of Ermolao Barbaro the Younger deserve mention; and in the sixteenth century there was Francesco Piccolomini, a Paduan, and a few other scholars such as Alessandro Piccolomini, who composed a handbook of Aristotelian ethics in Italian, indicating by this very fact that he was addressing himself to a broader educated public. Outside of Italy, the introductions of Jacques Lefèvre d'Etaples to Aristotle's writings on moral philosophy and Melanchthon's ethical writings represent the most influential attempts to restate Aristotle's ethics—especially his belief that the natural goods contribute to the supreme good of happiness and that the moral virtues are means between two opposite extremes—and to harmonize this natural ethics with the teachings of Scripture. John Case's moral questions on Aristotle, which originated in Oxford, are important as a rare example of a type of literature that must have flourished also at the English universities to a greater degree than is usually realized. More eclectic but still largely Aristotelian are the handbooks of Francesco Filelfo and of Sebastian Fox Morcillo. An early and very popular introduction to ethics, Leonardo Bruni's *Isagogicon moralis disciplinae*, follows Aristotle in the discussion of the moral and intellectual virtues, but advances a somewhat eclectic view on the supreme good. He bases the ultimate end of human life mainly on virtue but also grants some importance to external advantages and thus stays close enough to

Aristotle's position, but at the same time he claims that this view is essentially identical with those of the Stoics and Epicureans. The most consistent attempt to present Stoic ethics in a systematic handbook was made by Justus Lipsius toward the end of the sixteenth century. Its major effects were to be felt only during the following century.

Aside from such handbooks of ethics, there are a number of more informal humanist treatises and dialogues in which the central topic of ancient ethics, that is, happiness or the supreme good, is discussed. Whereas Petrarch had blamed Aristotle for his belief that man may attain his ultimate end during the present life, an attitude echoed by Bartolomeo Facio and others, many writers identified the goal of life with the knowledge and enjoyment of God but thought that this goal could be attained during the present life, at least by some people and for some time. This view was held especially by the leading Platonist, Marsilio Ficino, who wrote several short treatises on it. Bartolomeo Sacchi (Platina) stresses endurance and wisdom in a Stoic sense, and Pietro Pomponazzi approaches Stoicism rather than the view of Aristotle when in his treatise on immortality he defines moral virtue as the task peculiar to human beings, and emphasizes that this virtue is its own reward, just as wickedness is its own punishment. Also the Epicurean view that pleasure is the supreme good found its defenders. The most famous of them, Lorenzo Valla, considered Epicureanism as the best among the pagan philosophies but endorses as his own view a kind of Christian Epicureanism in which the pleasures of the present life are abandoned for the sake of the pleasures, both physical and spiritual, that are promised in a future life to the faithful Christian.

A number of humanistic treatises deal with individual virtues, a subject that occupies a large part of Aristotle's *Ethics* and now is singled out for monographic treatment. Several of the virtues are discussed in the moral treatises of the Neapolitan humanist Giovanni Pontano, such as courage, magnanimity, or prudence. Attempts to define the respective virtues are accompanied by a variety of moral rules and examples, and the concern is as much with stylistic elegance and moral edification as with precise philosophical definitions or distinctions. Similar treatises were written by several Italian and other humanist writers.

A whole literature was dedicated to the highest virtue, wisdom, which was identified either with the attainment of pure knowledge, or with moral and practical ability in the affairs of life. The latter tendency culminated in Pierre Charron, theologian and skeptical philosopher of the early seventeenth century. Analogous treatises were written on some specific vices, such as ingratitude or avarice. There is a famous treatise on avarice by Poggio Bracciolini, in which some of the beneficial effects of this vice also are mentioned in a way that some historians have tended to link with the spirit of modern capitalism.[5]

*   *   *

The humanist movement was closely identified with a reform of the program and curriculum of the secondary schools. Many of the humanists were professional tutors or schoolteachers, and it was through the training offered in the schools that most of the educated persons of the Renaissance period were influenced by humanist ideas, which they then carried into the larger spheres of public and professional life. Hence it was natural that the humanists would be very much concerned with the tasks and problems of education. The treatises on the education of the young form a large and important genre of humanist prose, and thanks to these treatises Renaissance humanism occupies as prominent a place in the history of educational theory as in that of educational practice.

The most influential early treatises were by Pier Paolo Vergerio the Elder and Leonardo Bruni, to which we may add the treatise on education attributed to Plutarch that was translated by Guarino of Verona, who along with Vittorino da Feltre was the most famous and successful humanist teacher in fifteenth-century Italy. Other influential educational treatises were written by Maffeo Vegio and by Aeneas Silvius Piccolomini, a prominent humanist who pursued an ecclesiastical career and finally became pope under the name of Pius II. Outside of Italy, educational treatises were written by many humanists such as Erasmus and Juan Luis Vives, by Jacob Wimpfeling and Joachim Camerarius in Germany, and by Roger Ascham in England. These treatises were written either for the young students themselves or for the parents of prospective students to convince them of the value of a humanist education. A good deal of attention is paid to the praise of Greek and Latin literature, study of which formed the core of humanist instruction, and to the value of such an education for the future citizen or statesman. Often the author would offer actual reading lists, discussing the merits and educational value of specific classical authors and their different works. Aside from the genuine concern for a ruling class thoroughly imbued with a cultural heritage of unquestioned intellectual importance, the humanist educators laid much stress on the moral value inherent in the study of ancient literature, history, and philosophy. Through the reading of the classical authors, the student was to acquire a fund of moral ideas, sentences, and examples that would give him the necessary preparation to face the tasks of his own life. In stressing the moral value of a classical education, the humanists effectively countered the charge made by some theologians that the reading of the pagan poets and writers would corrupt the morals of the young. The humanists knew, of course, that there was much in ancient literature that could not stand muster before a strict Christian censor, and many of them did not hesitate to emulate it in prose and verse, pleading like Catullus that their life was pure though their verse might be licentious. Yet they knew how to distinguish between a literature written by and for adults and the requirements of the education of the young. In their treatises on education they would usually omit from their reading list those ancient writings which gave rise to moral criticism, and Erasmus added the pointed remark that we should be careful not to imbibe the manners of the ancients along with their literature. In this way, the humanists managed to link their cultural ideals very closely with the moral aspirations of their time and to make their educational program acceptable to all but the most narrow-minded theologians.

The actual human ideal of the Renaissance has often been characterized as that of the *uomo universale,* the universal man, or to use a modern phrase, the well-rounded personality. We rarely encounter this slogan in the literature of the period, but the actual life of such persons as Leon Battista Alberti or Leonardo da Vinci seems to illustrate a quest for excellence in a great variety of pursuits, and the educational treatises of the time envisage a person who would achieve reasonable distinction in physical and artistic, intellectual and practical activities. This emphasis on breadth is also apparent in another large branch of literature that is concerned not with education in general but with the training of particular groups or classes of society.

A large number of treatises is dedicated to the education or the description of the good prince, and this literature has attracted a great deal of attention among historians of literature and of political thought. The "mirror of princes" was an important branch of literature during the later medieval centuries, and it has been shown that the ideal of the Christian king, based on Germanic customs and theological theories, was gradually transformed under the impact of the study of Roman law and of Aristotle's *Politics.* In fifteenth-century Italy, monarchical states were firmly established in Naples and Milan, and on a smaller scale, in Piedmont, Ferrara, and Mantua, not to speak of the numerous tiny and ephemeral principalities. It is against this background that the treatises on the best prince by humanists like Platina or Pontano and others must be understood. Important new sources for these treatises were several works of Isocrates and Plutarch that were widely diffused in a number of different translations. These humanist treatises were largely theoretical and gave much space to a list of the virtues that the prince should possess and to ancient examples of good conduct. It is characteristic that the tone of these treatises is secular rather than religious and that the reward promised to the good prince is everlasting fame rather than blessedness in a future life. The quest for fame was a central concern of the humanists and of their contemporaries, and the power of its appeal may be discovered in many episodes and writings of the period.

Another topic discussed in these treatises was the relation between virtue and expediency, and the authors usually concluded with Cicero that the most virtuous course of action is also in the long run the most advantageous. It has been pointed out by Allan Gilbert, Felix Gilbert, and other scholars that Machiavelli's *Prince,* though original in its extreme realism and its exclusive stress on expediency, is linked in its themes and problems with the late medieval and early humanist literature on the best prince. In the sixteenth century, the establishment of strong national monarchies outside of Italy forms the background for an important series of humanist treatises by Guillaume Budé, Johannes Sepulveda, and others. The most famous is Erasmus's *Education of a Christian Prince,* which is explicitly introduced as a counterpart of Isocrates's treatise *Ad Nicoclem,* which Erasmus had translated. The prince is expected to read a number of ancient writers, in addition to the Bible. Among his suggestions for the administration of the state, Erasmus reminds the ruler that he is merely a member of the state, that his rule rests basically on the consent of the people, and that the public welfare is the only standard of the laws. Erasmus wants to limit the death penalty to extreme cases and urges the rulers to submit their quarrels to arbitration, advocating on religious grounds the ideal of universal peace, a subject that he treated again elsewhere.[6]

*   *   *

In fifteenth-century Italy, the ideal of republican liberty was as much alive as that of the monarchical state, as many humanist writings show. The Roman republic was as much a model for imitation as the Roman Empire, and it was no coincidence that the superiority of Scipio, interpreted as a symbol of republican virtue, was defended by Poggio, a Florentine citizen, against the claims of Caesar that were supported by Guarino, a subject of the marquess of Ferrara. The comparison of different constitutions in the works of Plato, Aristotle, and Polybius found parallels in the writings of Francesco Patrizi, Aurelio Brandolini, and Machiavelli— who in his actual political career and in his *Discourses on Livy* attested his preference for the republican form of government. When Florentine political liberty was being undermined by the Medici regime, Alamanno Rinuccini wrote, but probably did not publish, his *De libertate.* Historians often exaggerate the significance of the fact that many of the city republics of the twelfth and thirteenth century succumbed to various forms of despotism during the fourteenth and fifteenth. The Venetian republic, ruled by its tightly restricted but responsible and educated nobility, became more powerful than ever, and was considered, on account of its wealth and stability, as a model by many political writers. The Florentine republic, which showed much less stability and underwent a variety of changes and revolutions, maintained its power and independence against several attacks from the outside and acquired, especially in the fifteenth century, a cultural and artistic predominance that was recognized throughout Italy and Europe. When Florence was threatened during the late fourteenth and early fifteenth centuries by the repeated attacks of the Visconti princes of Milan, who were expanding their rule over large areas of northern and central Italy, Florence mobilized against them her intellectual as well as her material resources. In this political crisis, many Florentine humanists emphasized the ideals of the republican state and of the responsible citizen called to govern that state. Hans Baron in a series of studies has forcefully described this civic humanism, which flourished in Florence during the first half of the fifteenth century, and it certainly deserves attention as one of the most impressive phases of Renaissance humanism, even though it would be quite mistaken to identify Renaissance humanism as a whole with this Florentine civic humanism. There was a good deal of "despotic humanism" even in fifteenth-century Italy, and it would be quite impossible to include under the heading of "civic humanism" the entire political literature of the Renaissance period, let alone the large body of humanist literature that was not concerned with political problems at all. Florentine civic humanism found its best expression in the writings of Leonardo Bruni, Leon Battista Alberti, and Matteo Palmieri. Humanist learning is presented by them as serving the active life of the citizen involved in the affairs of his business and of his republic. He will not only occupy his leisure with the reading of the best authors, but will follow in his own life and activities the examples and precepts offered in their writings. It was not always mentioned but evidently understood that the prominent citizen was often called upon to deliver speeches, or to compose letters, of public importance, and that his humanist training would give him the necessary literary ability to accomplish these tasks with sufficient distinction to earn a good reputation for himself and for his city. Florentine history between 1434 and 1537 was characterized by a gradual transition from a republican form of government to the monarchy of the Medici—a development that was slowed and sometimes interrupted by strong resistance on the part of the followers of the republican tradition. The political strife among the various parties was accompanied by literary controversy, as often happens, and the decline and fall of the Florentine republic thus produced a long series of political treatises defending the republican form of government and expounding the best ways to give it stability and perfection.

All Italian cities, whether their government was republican or monarchical, had a class of noble families of feudal or commercial antecedents. Its political influence varies greatly from place to place. In Venice, the nobles were the ruling class that monopolized all public office. In Naples, the feudal nobility possessed large landed property and traditional privileges, but the kings tended to reduce these privileges and to build a modern monarchy and a bureaucracy of trained persons directly responsible to them, just as the kings of England, France, and Spain were to do in the sixteenth century. In Florence, the older families were divided into bitterly opposed factions, and depending on the regime prevailing at a specific time, some of them were excluded from office or even exiled, while others shared the administration of the republic with able persons of more modest origins. Everywhere, regardless of their political position, the families of the nobility managed to maintain a good deal of wealth and social prestige, and their style of life served as model for the newcomers who established themselves through business enterprises or political careers or even through professional success. However, with the exception of Naples and possibly Rome, this nobility was no longer feudal in character but thoroughly urbanized, and hence may be called more appropriately a patriciate. The humanists succeeded in gaining this important class for their cause, educated their children, and impressed upon them the conviction that they needed a good education by humanist standards to be worthy of their social status. Moreover, the humanists cherished the ambition of attaining for themselves a comparable social position, and at least some of them succeeded. For the trained humanist could have a career as chancellor or secretary of princes and republics, and thus be able to contribute his share, along with the much larger body of lawyers, to what was to be called in later centuries the *noblesse de robe*. Against this background, it is quite understandable why the humanists of the fifteenth century were interested in the problem of nobility and why they should focus on the question whether nobility is or should be based on birth or on personal merit. The question had been discussed by a few late medieval authors, and some of them had already emphasized the role of personal merit as a basis of nobility. In the fifteenth century, there was a whole series of treatises *De nobilitate,* in which this problem is investigated further. In the treatises by Poggio Bracciolini, Buonaccorso da Montemagno, Platina, and the interesting dialogue of Cristoforo Landino, the thesis that nobility rests on virtue is strongly defended. The problem is treated in typically humanist fashion in the work of Buonaccorso da Montemagno, which enjoyed tremendous popularity. Two Romans compete for the hand of a noble woman and support their claims in elaborate speeches, one of them praising his illustrious ancestry, the other his personal achievements. The author does not tell us which of the two married the girl, but the greater force seems to be in the second speech, which defends the claims of merit. The tendency apparent in these treatises has led many scholars to consider the preference for personal merit as against inherited nobility as typical of Renaissance humanism. This claim is to some extent justified, but not entirely so. The authors of the treatises I have mentioned were for the most part Tuscans. We should not overlook the fact that the claims of the Neapolitan nobility were defended by one of its members who was himself a humanist, Tristano Caracciolo, and those of the Venetian nobility by Lauro Quirini, another well-known humanist who happened to be a Venetian nobleman himself. It is apparent once more how difficult it is to identify humanism as a whole with any particular set of opinions, though these opinions may be held by some of its representatives. The common denominator is always not a set of opinions, but a cultural and educational ideal.[7]

*   *   *

Another group of significant Renaissance moral treatises tries to describe, and to propose for imitation, the human ideal of the perfect citizen, magistrate, courtier, or gentleman. It is the ideal of a member of the ruling class, apart from its political connotations, held out as a model for young and old people alike. This genre, represented in the fifteenth century by some treatises of Alberti, Platina, and others, became especially important in the sixteenth. The most famous work of the group, Baldassare Castiglione's *Book of the Courtier,* was translated into several languages and found imitators all over Europe. This work, which has great stylistic merit and occupies an important place in the history of Italian prose literature, clearly envisages a member of the aristocracy and reflects many of the personal traits of its author, who was active as a diplomat for many years in the service of the princes of Mantua and of the papal curia. Castiglione's *Courtier* represents a human ideal of great breadth; it might be said to reflect the concept of the universal man, and it clearly exercised a civilizing influence on the ruling classes of Renaissance Europe. Aside from the traditional knightly virtues of courage and physical prowess, the courtier is expected to have polished manners, to be an able participant in elegant conversation, to have a good literary education, and to be moderately accomplished in the arts of painting, music, and dance. An English counterpart is Sir Thomas Elyot's *Boke*

Named the Governour, in which moral and religious considerations play a somewhat larger role. Later in the century, the emphasis shifts more and more to a description of manners practiced in good society and to the requirements of polite conversation. Giovanni della Casa's *Galateo* and Stefano Guazzo's book *On Civil Conversation* were widely read, translated, and imitated, and form the core of a large literature in all languages, usually described as books of courtesy, of conduct, or of manners. Louis Wright has shown that for England this literature more and more addressed itself not only to the members of the aristocracy, but also to the middle class of merchants and professionals who were eager to strengthen their social position by imitating the manners of the older ruling class. This literature prepares the way for the treatises on the perfect gentleman that were to be composed in the seventeenth century. Yet it also contains a good many prudential rules and seems to be intended partly for the young man of talent and modest means who is trying to get ahead in life and make a career. The straight preaching of moral virtues, so prominent in the early humanist treatises, occupies in these later works less and less space, though the possession of these virtues is taken more or less for granted.[8]

*   *   *

Aside from the generalized treatises on the ideal courtier or gentleman, many were written on the duties of persons who occupied a particular status or practiced a particular profession. There were books on the duties of a magistrate or ambassador or even on the duties of a bishop, in which moral prescriptions were combined with advice concerning the practical conduct of affairs. In the extensive literature of treatises on art that was written during the Renaissance period, the technical rules of the craft were embellished with moral advice for the artist. What Cicero and Quintilian had required of the orator, namely that he should combine moral stature and a general education with the technical competence appropriate for his profession, was now applied to all other professions, especially to that of the artist. The painter, the sculptor, and the architect not only acquired a higher social status and prestige than they ever possessed before or afterward, they also tended to combine artistic skill with literary, scholarly, and scientific interests and competence—as we may see in the writings of Alberti, Piero della Francesca, Leonardo, Dürer, Michelangelo, and Rubens—and hence to appropriate for their profession the moral claims advanced originally by the humanist scholars.

One of the chief innovations brought about by the Protestant Reformation was the abolition in Protestant countries of monastic orders, which had played such an important role during the Middle Ages and which retained and even increased their importance in the modern Catholic world. The radical move of the Reformers was preceded, as is well known, by centuries of medieval attacks on the vices and shortcomings of the monks and friars, charges that were at least in part justified and which the Catholic Reformation of the sixteenth century tended to obviate. The humanists contributed their share to the critique of monasticism. Valla and others wrote against the monks, and Erasmus in his *Praise of Folly* poured a good deal of ridicule upon them. Yet it should be noted that Erasmus in this work did not spare any class of contemporary society, not even his own, the grammarians and rhetoricians; elsewhere he insists that the pious life was not a monopoly of the monastic orders, asserting an ideal of lay piety that he inherited from the "Modern Devotion," the Dutch mystic movement in whose schools he had received his first education. Yet he nowhere advocates the abolition of the orders. Among the earlier Italian humanists, we find several writers and scholars of distinction, such as Petrarch, Coluccio Salutati, and Ermolao Barbaro the Younger, who actually came out in praise of the monastic life, and there were many learned monks, such as Ambrogio Traversari, who took a significant part in the humanist movement. Again it would be wrong to identify humanism as a whole with one or the other opinion on this important question.

A good deal has been written by Jacob Burckhardt and others about the place of women in Renaissance society. Women had not yet acquired an important place in professional life, and their activities were still largely confined to the house and the family. Yet within this limited range they were respected, and at least a few of them—especially the daughters of princes, noblemen, and scholars—received a literary and scholarly education and distinguished themselves as patrons of learning, or even as scholars and writers in their own right. Thus it is significant that one of the most important humanist treatises on education, Leonardo Bruni's *De studiis et litteris,* was dedicated to a woman. A number of treatises by fifteenth-century humanists deal with the family and with marriage, and hence have a good deal to say about the moral and practical duties of the housewife and mother. Famous and influential specimens of this literature are Francesco Barbaro's *De re uxoria* and Alberti's treatise *Della famiglia.* The former emphasizes moral advice, and the latter contains suggestions on the way the wife of a wealthy citizen is supposed to assist her husband and to govern the household, servants, and children. In the sixteenth century, Castiglione in his *Courtier* devotes a special section of his work to the court lady, the female counterpart of his male subject, and Vives composed a significant treatise *On the Education of a Christian Woman.* Later in the century, in Italy as elsewhere, a whole series of treatises was written on the conduct of women, in which prudential rules played a large part, and some advice was even offered on how to dress and how to use cosmetics.[9]

* * *

A large segment of literature extending from the end of the fifteenth to the end of the sixteenth century deals with the subject of love. A famous medieval example had been Andreas Capellanus's book on courtly love, in which the customs of French chivalry received a more theoretical, though not a more philosophical, expression than in the lyric and epic poetry of the period. More philosophical was the lyric poetry of Guido Cavalcanti, Dante, and their contemporaries in Italy; and the prose speculation on love began with Dante's *Vita nuova* and *Convivio* as well as with the commentaries on Cavalcanti's obscure poem. This whole literature was given a new impulse and direction by Marsilio Ficino, the head of the Platonic Academy of Florence, and one of the leading Platonists of the Renaissance. He supplied to western readers the first complete translations of Plato's *Symposium* and *Phaedrus* (parts of which had already been translated by Leonardo Bruni), and also published important commentaries on these two dialogues. In particular, the commentary on the *Symposium* became very famous. Basing himself primarily on Plato but transforming his doctrine under the influence of other philosophical, theological, and literary traditions, Ficino understood the love for another human being as a preliminary form and disguise of the basic love that each human being has for God and that finds its fulfillment only in the direct enjoyment and knowledge of God—a goal that is reached during the present life by only a few persons and for a short time, but which will be attained forever in the future life by those who have aspired to it while on Earth. Without rejecting sexual and earthly love, Ficino praises above all the pure and celestial love, that is, the mutual affection and friendship between two persons who are dedicated to the contemplative life and hence recognize that their mutual relationship is founded on the love each of them has for God. This divine love Ficino claimed to define according to the teachings of Plato, hence he coined a term that was to become famous as well as ridiculous, calling it "Platonic" or "Socratic love." The doctrine of Platonic love constitutes only a small, though important, part of Ficino's philosophical system, but it enjoyed a wide popularity apart from the rest of his work, especially among poets and moralists. The notion of Platonic love was taken over and adapted by many poets, including Lorenzo de'Medici and Michelangelo. Moreover, Ficino's commentary on Plato's *Symposium* became the fountainhead of a whole literature of love treatises, in Italy and elsewhere, in which the philosophical notion of Platonic love was repeated, developed, and sometimes distorted. The authors of these treatises include distinguished philosophers, such as Pico della Mirandola, Leone Ebreo (Judah ben Isaac Abravanel, from whom Spinoza seems to have borrowed his notion of the intellectual love of God), Francesco Patrizi, and Giordano Bruno, as well as famous writers like Pietro Bembo and Castiglione. For the last book of Castiglione's *Courtier* deals precisely with Platonic love along the lines defined by Ficino, and through this work the theory attained a very wide diffusion indeed. In the later treatises, the original link between Platonic love came to be a hypocritical disguise for refined sexual passion, or an empty game fashionable in good society. However, we should understand that originally it had a serious philosophical meaning, and that a good deal of serious talk and writing on love in the sixteenth century was shaped by the Platonist "philosophy of love." [10]

*   *   *

Another typically humanist fashion in which the various forms of human life were discussed during the fifteenth and sixteenth centuries was the so-called comparison (*paragone*). Ancient rhetoric had insisted that it was the task of the orator to praise and to blame, and the praise of some virtue or quality was often combined with the blame of its contrary. To show their skill, orators even composed mock praises of bad or ridiculous things, such as tyranny or baldness, and it was against this literary background and based on such models that Erasmus wrote his admirable *Praise of Folly*. Rhetorical contests left their traces in medieval Latin and vernacular poetry where the contrast between winter and spring, youth and old age are common themes. In humanist literature, the rhetorical contest between two contrasts or rivals was a favorite sport, and we have encountered several examples already: the comparison between Scipio and Caesar, between republic and monarchy, and Buonaccorso's comparison between nobility by birth and by merit. In the same way, the merits and relative superiority of various arts, professions, or ways of life were frequently discussed. There are treatises on "arms and letters" debating the advantages of the military and the literary lives. Leonardo da Vinci seriously argued that painting was superior to the other arts and sciences, and Michelangelo was consulted on the question of whether painting or sculpture was superior. The humanist defense of poetry, of which we have spoken before, took the form of attacking other learned disciplines, as in Petrarch's invectives against a physician. There was a whole literature on the relative merits of medicine and of law that had its roots in the rivalry of the university faculties and in which distinguished humanists such as Salutati and Poggio took an active part.

Salutati sided with the jurists because the law had a greater significance for the life of the citizen and of the state. Several historians would like to consider this position as a typically humanist one, but it happens that Poggio, no less a humanist than Salutati, voted in this contest in favor of medicine.

The argument used by Salutati in this discussion and on other occasions touches on another more serious issue, the relative merits of the contemplative and of the active life. The distinction occurs already in Aristotle, who tends, along with most ancient philosophers, to consider the life of contemplation, rather than that of action, to be most perfect and desirable. A notable exception was Cicero, the Roman statesman, who insisted on the political duties of the responsible citizen. During the Middle Ages, the life of contemplation was usually associated with the monastic ideal and was more or less persistently praised. In the Renaissance, we hear again several voices in praise of the active life, such as those of Salutati, Bruni, Alberti, and Palmieri, and these views have been emphasized by Hans Baron and other scholars as an important aspect of their civic humanism. Eugene Rice goes even further and treats the emphasis on the active life in these humanists, in some sixteenth-century writers and in Pierre Charron, as an important development leading away from the monastic ideal of the Middle Ages to a worldly and practical orientation of the modern age. Although it is significant that, from the fifteenth century on, the active life was finding more partisans among the writers of the age, the monastic life also had its defenders among the humanists, as we have seen, and even Salutati, one of the chief protagonists of the active life, wrote a whole treatise in praise of the monastic life, a fact that has puzzled several of his interpreters. Moreover, the ideal of the theoretical or contemplative life became dissociated during the Renaissance from the specific ideal of monasticism, and rather identified with the private existence of the scholar, writer, and scientist, no doubt under the influence of ancient philosophy; and this secularization of the contemplative life seems to me no less characteristic of the Renaissance (and of modern times) than the simultaneous emphasis on the claims of the active life. This tendency appears already in Petrarch's praise of solitude, and it is in this sense that the Platonists of the Florentine Academy praised the life of contemplation, which occupied a central place in their philosophy. The most famous document in which the question is debated is Cristoforo Landino's *Camaldulensian Disputations,* a dialogue in which the active life is defended by Lorenzo de' Medici and the contemplative life by Leon Battista Alberti—and the victory seems to go to the latter. In the sixteenth century, Pomponazzi considers the theoretical life as superior but uses the practical life to define the end of man, as this life is peculiar to man and all human beings are able to have a part in it. In Montaigne there is a strong, though by no means exclusive, emphasis on the solitary life of contemplation, and most other philosophers take its superiority for granted, whereas the popular moralists insist on the needs and claims of the active life. Far from being resolved in the sixteenth century, the question is still with us. Whereas many writers decry the "ivory tower" of the intellectual, others would still insist on the right of the scholar, artist, or scientist to concentrate on his peculiar task. The rival claims of the active and contemplative life seem to illustrate a perennial human problem, and there seems to be no permanent answer to it; each time, each profession, and each person will have to find a viable compromise.

Another similar question that was widely debated in Renaissance thought was the relation between the intellect and the will, or between knowledge and love. This question overlaps that of the contemplative and active life, but is not entirely identical with it. Some partisans of the contemplative life, for example, Petrarch, would still place will and love above intellect and knowledge, since they consider the willing of the good and the love of God as a part, and even as the most important part, of the contemplative life. The problem occupies a very important place in the history of western thought. It has been rightly asserted that the concept of will is absent from ancient Greek philosophy. Plato, Aristotle, and other Greek thinkers know a conflict between reason and desire, but they inherited from Socrates the conviction that reason is capable by its own power to know the good, to put it into practice, and to overcome the resistance of any contrary desire. In the Christian view, this Greek belief in the independent power of reason was far too optimistic. In order to overcome his native propensity to evil brought about by Adam's fall, man needed the grace of God. On the basis of this Christian conception, Augustine formulated his notion of the will. Aside from his faculty of knowing, man has an independent faculty of willing. It is the will that was corrupted by Adam's fall, and which must be purified by divine grace if we are to attain the good. Medieval thought inherited from Augustine this distinction between will and intellect, and the relative merits of these two faculties became the subject of important discussions, with Thomas Aquinas among others emphasizing the superiority of the intellect, whereas John Duns Scotus and other "voluntarists" insisted, in accordance with Augustine, on the superiority of the will. This question, in spite of its scholastic origin, continued to occupy the humanists. Both Petrarch and Salutati favored the superiority of the will. In the Platonic Academy of Florence, the problem was evidently a favorite topic of debate, as we may learn from Ficino's correspondence and from a treatise by one of his pupils, Alamanno Donati. Ficino himself apparently changed his view on the matter in the course of his life, favoring at first the superiority of the intellect but insisting in his later writings on the importance of the will and of love for the soul's ascent to God. His arguments show that the concept of will could be associated with the life of contemplation no less than with that of action.[11]

*   *   *

Renaissance thought was interested not merely in moral rules of conduct or in the specific ways of life that an individual might choose according to his status or profession, but also in the general situation in which human beings find themselves on Earth, in the chief forces determining this situation, and in the place man and his world occupy within the larger universe. There has been a widespread belief that Renaissance humanists held an optimistic view of life and were prone to enjoy this world without caring as much for the future life after death as their medieval predecessors had. It is true that the concern with earthly life and its problems tended to increase from medieval to modern times. Nevertheless we must try to avoid exaggerated opinions. Even in Lorenzo de' Medici's famous lines, "Let him be happy who so desires, for we are not sure of the next day," which used to be quoted as the quintessence of the Renaissance view of life as frivolous and superficial, we have learned to hear melancholy undertones. Historians like Ernst Walser and Charles Trinkaus have shown that the writers of the period were keenly aware of the miseries and ills of our earthly existence. Sickness and poverty, exile and imprisonment, the loss of friends and relatives were a common experience, and when Poggio and other humanists wrote about the misery of the human condition, they had no difficulty collecting ancient and modern examples to illustrate the frail and transitory state of earthly happiness. Lest we think that some classes of men are untouched by the miseries that befall the common lot, the humanists wrote special treatises about the unhappiness of scholars and of courtiers, and especially of princes. These treatises were full of examples from history, and they were intended to warn their readers not to trust their happiness and to comfort the unhappy with the record of the ills suffered by others that were worse than their own. This chorus of lament may seem to be out of tune with many real and imagined traits of the period, but it is nearly universal. The Platonic philosopher Ficino invokes the shade of Heraclitus to weep at the misery of men, as he would laugh with Democritus at their folly.

This feeling that man has to suffer many vicissitudes and that the events of his life, whether good or bad, are largely beyond his control was interpreted by the writers and thinkers of the period in a variety of ways that were not always consistent with one another but which lend a common note to the literature of the Renaissance. Divine providence was stressed by the theologians and never denied by any other thinkers, but popular and philosophical writers frequently played with the notions of fortune and fate.

The concept of chance was repeatedly discussed by ancient philosophers and played a role in the thought of Aristotle, and especially in that of Epicurus. In the moral thought of late antiquity, chance was given an important part in human affairs, and its power was even personified and worshiped as the goddess Tyche or Fortuna. During the Christian Middle Ages, Fortuna remained pretty much alive, not as a goddess, to be sure, but as an allegory and as an instrument of God. In the Renaissance the power of Fortuna was again very often mentioned. She appears in emblems and allegorical pictures as well as in the writings of the period. Statesmen and businessmen hoped that this blind and arbitrary power would bring them success, and Machiavelli devoted some striking pages to the description of her role in history and politics.

Many thoughtful persons were not satisfied with this whimsical rule of Fortuna over human affairs, but believed instead, or additionally, in the power of an inexorable fate. The view that all earthly events were rigidly determined by an unbroken chain of antecedent causes had been held by the ancient Stoics, and it was revived in a more or less modified form by Pomponazzi and other thinkers. Still more widespread was the belief in astrology, an elaborate system that presented itself as a science and tried to tie all earthly events, with the help of detailed but flexible rules, to the influence of the stars. The system, which had passed from the Babylonians into late antiquity and was transmitted through the Arabs to medieval Europe, was usually opposed by the theologians but was supported by the philosophers and scientists. During the Renaissance, astrology had a few opponents, such as Petrarch and Pico, but on the whole its prestige rose higher than ever before, among both scholars and laymen. The belief that all human affairs were governed by the motions of the stars was satisfactory to many people because it seemed to give some significance and regularity to the vicissitudes of life. The astrologers claimed to be able to predict the future of persons and countries, and in their passionate desire to know and to control their future, people were as little disturbed as in other times by the inherent contradiction in prophecy (for how can I change the future to my advantage if it is dependent on unchangeable laws, and how can I predict the future if I or others can do anything about it?) and as willing to forget the numerous predictions that were not confirmed by the outcome.

Different from the belief in fate is the theological doctrine of predestination, which also played an important part in the discussions of the period. Augustine had emphasized against the Pelagians that not only all earthly events but even our own moral choices and actions were fore-ordained by divine forethought and will, and the problem of how pre-destination can be reconciled with human free will gave rise to many difficulties in medieval theology and philosophy. The problem came to the fore with the Protestant Reformers, Luther and Calvin, who com-pletely denied free will, something neither Augustine nor his medieval successors had clearly done. The question was of importance also to sec-ular thinkers before the Reformation, as the examples of Lorenzo Valla and Pietro Pomponazzi show. Valla argued that it was easy to reconcile divine foreknowledge with human free will but considered the relation-ship between God's will and human freedom as a mystery of faith. Pom-ponazzi gave an intricate defense of predestination as well as of fate, but his attempt to make free will appear compatible with both of them seems neither clear nor convincing.

The concepts of fortune, of fate, and of predestination express in different ways and on different levels the feeling that human life is gov-erned by divine and natural powers over which we have no control and to which we must submit more or less helplessly. Yet most Renaissance thinkers did not stop with the assertion of these superhuman powers, but tried in some way to uphold and defend the power of man over his own destiny, in the face of fortune and fate. The attempt is in itself significant even where it seems to be inconsistent or unsuccessful. Already the an-cient Stoics, the most outspoken proponents of rigid fate, had struggled to assert the role of human freedom within a system of complete deter-minism. The later Stoics found their solution in the view that the wise man, while enduring patiently the external circumstances of his life, which he is unable to change, is entirely free in his thought and in his moral attitude. In a more popular fashion, they opposed the power of reason and virtue to that of fortune and claimed for the wise man an inner victory even when he may seem to be outwardly defeated. This is the keynote also of much humanist thinking and writing on the subject. In his extremely influential treatise on the remedies of good and bad fortune Petrarch opposes reason to the passions in good Stoic manner and exhorts his readers to overcome through virtue the hold that good and bad fortune alike have on our minds. Salutati also opposes vir-tue and wisdom to fate and fortune. The recurrent theme in Alberti's moral writings is the victory of virtue over fortune, and Ficino restates the same view, adding a Neoplatonic note by basing moral virtue on the life of contemplation. After having described the power of fortune, Ma-chiavelli also insists that the prudent statesman is able to overcome, or at least to modify, the power of fortune. Guillaume Budé teaches his readers to despise the external circumstances of life, which fortune may give or take away. Just as these thinkers wish to oppose the power of fortune, Pico della Mirandola made a strenuous effort to oppose the power of fate. His elaborate attack against astrology was actually a defense of human freedom, and the arguments that he uses show very clearly that his attitude was prompted by moral and religious as well as by scientific considerations. This same concern for man's moral autonomy was to prompt such humanist thinkers as Erasmus and Sepulveda to defend free will against Luther's exclusive doctrine of predestination.[12]

*   *   *

The themes and ideas that I have briefly discussed may illustrate the way in which Renaissance thinkers were preoccupied with moral and human problems. It has often been asserted that Renaissance thought, in contrast with medieval thought, was man-centered, not God-centered, or—to quote a rather unfriendly remark of Etienne Gilson—that the Renaissance was the Middle Ages minus God. Such statements are obviously exaggerated, since Renaissance thought as a whole was anything but indifferent to God, and since hardly any thinker of the period denied the existence of God, however his conception of God may have differed from various forms of religious orthodoxy. Yet the humanists who have attracted most of the attention of Renaissance historians were interested primarily in moral problems, frequently to the exclusion of theology and metaphysics, of natural philosophy and other learned disciplines. The very name "humanities," which they adopted for their studies, emphasized their concern with man in a programmatic fashion. No wonder that they were inclined to stress the importance of human problems and to extol the place of man in the universe. Already Petrarch argues in his treatise *On His Own and Other People's Ignorance* that it does not help us to know the nature of animals unless we also know the nature of man, and in his famous letter describing his ascent of Mont Ventoux he opposes his admiration for the human soul to the impression made upon him by mountains and the sea. It is significant that the latter passage is woven out of quotations from Seneca and Augustine, for the Renaissance doctrine of the dignity of man was nourished in many ways by classical and Christian sources. In the fifteenth century, the excellence of man was the theme of special treatises by Giannozzo Manetti and others. Especially in Manetti's treatise, the dignity of man is based not only on his biblical similarity to God, but above all on his varied achievements in the arts and sciences, which are described at great length. This favorite humanist theme then received a more metaphysical treatment at the hands of the Platonic philosophers. Marsilio Ficino dedicated several books of his chief work, the *Platonic Theology*, to man's achievements in the sciences and in government, emphasizing the universality of his knowledge and of his aspirations. When he restates the Neoplatonic conception that the universe is made of several degrees of being that extend from God at the summit to the corporeal world at the bottom, he intentionally revises the scheme in order to assign a privileged place in its center to the rational soul of man, thus making it the bond and knot of the universe, second in dignity only to God himself. Pico della Mirandola went even further. In the famous *Oration*, which deals only in its first half with the dignity of man, and in other writings, he states that man does not occupy any fixed place in the universal hierarchy, but can freely choose his place in it. For he has no fixed nature but possesses all the gifts that had been distributed singly among the other creatures. Thus man is capable of leading many forms of life from the lowest to the highest. Pico's view is echoed in Vives's *Fable on Man;* man is introduced here as an actor capable of playing the roles of all other creatures. The central position of man in the universe, halfway between animals and angels, is accepted also by Pomponazzi as a sign of man's excellence. Thus we may say that under the impact of a humanist tradition, systematic philosophers as different from each other as the Florentine Platonists and Pomponazzi assigned to man a privileged position in their conception of the universe. The emphasis on man's universal skill in the arts and sciences was to recur in Francis Bacon's notion of the reign of man over nature, and thus there is an echo of the Renaissance glorification of man in the ideology that still underlies the technological aspect of modern natural science.

However, even on this issue, which seems to be so close to the heart of Renaissance humanism, the period does not speak to us with a single voice. Even in the fifteenth century, Pope Innocent III's treatise *On Contempt for the World*, which constituted the foil and starting point of Manetti's work, was widely read and had its imitators. In the sixteenth century, a strong reaction against the excessive glorification of man may be noted. In the Protestant Reformers there was a tremendous emphasis on the depraved nature of man, and this view was probably expressed in conscious protest against the current stress on his dignity. Also Montaigne, otherwise so far removed from the theology of the Reformers and so close to humanist thought, goes a long way in his *Apology of Raymond de Sebond* to criticize the unfounded opinions on man's privileged place in the universe, and to insist on his humble position and on the vanity of his aspirations.

This Renaissance concern for man and his place in the universe may also account for the great prominence given during that period to the question of the soul's immortality. The notion that the individual human soul is immortal had been strongly defended by Plato and the Neoplatonists, whereas Aristotle and other ancient philosophers held ambiguous or contrary opinions. Augustine had adopted the Neoplatonic view, and he was followed by all medieval Christian thinkers. With Renaissance Platonism, the question assumed a central importance that it had never had before. Ficino actually designed his *Platonic Theology* around this problem and tried to demonstrate the immortality of the soul against the Aristotelians by a variety of arguments. This emphasis on immortality appealed to a large number of poets, philosophers, and theologians, and it is tempting to assume that it was under Platonist influence that the immortality of the soul was adopted at the Lateran Council in 1513 as an official dogma of the Catholic church. When the leading Aristotelian philosopher, Pietro Pomponazzi, set out to show that personal immortality cannot be demonstrated by reason, he not only accepted it as an article of faith, but also stressed that the human soul, even according to reason, is immortal at least in some respect (*secundum quid*), on account of its high place among the material forms. Moreover, by returning to the problem many times in published treatises and unpublished questions and lectures, Pomponazzi showed how much he was puzzled by the question and how great an importance he attributed to it. Nonetheless, his treatise of 1516 gave rise to a large number of written attacks on his position by philosophers and theologians, and the question continued to be debated beyond the end of the sixteenth century. The statement that Renaissance students were interested in problems of the soul rather than of nature, often repeated after the nineteenth-century French scholar Renan, is based on the misinterpretation of an episode in which a group of students wanted to hear a course on Aristotle's *On the Soul* rather than on his *Meteorology*, but it contains a grain of truth that may well be based on better evidence.

It might be in order to indicate very briefly at this point in what ways the moral thought of the humanists, even though it was primarily concerned with individual conduct, also led to broader social, political, and humanitarian ideals. The theory of friendship occupied an important place in the ethics of Aristotle, Epicurus, and Cicero, and its value is very often stressed in the letters and other writings of the humanists. In the Florentine Academy, the concept of friendship is closely associated with those of Christian and Platonic love, and Ficino liked to think that the members of his academy were bound to one another and to himself, their common master, by a tie of Platonic friendship, thus forming a close community after the model of the ancient schools of philosophy.

In political thought, not only were the humanists concerned with the education of princes and magistrates, or with the relative merits of republican and monarchical government, but some of the Renaissance thinkers began to reflect on ideal commonwealths more perfect than the ones in existence. Thomas More's *Utopia,* a highly original work in spite of its obvious indebtedness to Plato's *Republic,* was the first of an important genre that was to flourish down to the eighteenth century. Its example was followed by Tommaso Campanella, Bacon, and many lesser writers. The influence of this utopian literature on social and political reforms in modern times has been generally recognized. Another contribution to social reform was Vives's treatise on assistance to the poor, written at a time when the responsibility for public relief was taken over by the cities in the Low Countries.

No less important was the contribution of Renaissance thought to the development of the ideal of religious toleration. This ideal arose first in the fifteenth century against the background of medieval controversy with Judaism and Islam and of the echoes of patristic polemics against ancient paganism. In the sixteenth century, the problem acquired a new poignancy in the face of religious dissent, persecution, and war within western Christendom. Without abandoning a belief in the superiority of his own religion, Nicholas of Cusa advocated perpetual peace and toleration among the different creeds dividing mankind. Ficino praised the solidarity and fellowship of all human beings and insisted that religion was natural to man, and that all religions, though different in their practices and in the degree of their perfection, contained a common core of truth and expressed in some way the worship of the one true God. Moreover, Ficino maintained that there was a basic harmony between the true, Christian religion and the true, Platonic philosophy; and he accepted the apocryphal writings attributed to Zoroaster, Hermes Trismegistus, Orpheus, and Pythagoras as witnesses of an early pagan theology and philosophy that prepared the way for Plato and his followers, in the way that the Old Testament foreshadowed the New. These notions added a new and explicit force to the general humanist belief in the wisdom of the ancients and its compatibility with Christian religious teaching, and they exercised an enormous influence during the sixteenth century. Equally important were the ideas of Pico della Mirandola, who went even farther. According to him, all known philosophies and religions contained some elements of truth, and he proposed to defend in a public disputation nine hundred theses taken principally from ancient and medieval, Arabic and Jewish philosophers and theologians. In particular, he maintained that the writings of the Jewish kabbalists represented an ancient oral tradition and were in agreement with the teachings of Christianity. In the second part of his famous oration, which was actually composed as an introductory speech for his projected disputation, Pico eloquently expresses his belief in the universality of truth, in which every philosopher and theologian participates to a greater or lesser degree. A hundred years later, in his famous *Sevenfold Conversation,* which was widely circulated in manuscript but not printed until recent times, Jean Bodin defends the claims of all the different religions. In the seventeenth century, Herbert of Cherbury laid the ground for deism by describing a natural religion consisting of the common core of all the various human creeds.[13]

*   *   *

In spite of these broad and interesting ramifications, the moral thought of the Renaissance was fundamentally individualistic in its outlook. Of course, the term individualism has several meanings, and its applications to the Renaissance have aroused a good deal of controversy among historians. It cannot be denied that outstanding human individuals are found in other periods of history, including the Middle Ages, or that medieval nominalism emphasized the reality of the individual physical thing. When we speak of Renaissance individualism, the term should be understood in a different way. Above all, Renaissance thought and literature are extremely individualistic in that they aim, to a degree unknown to the Middle Ages and to most of ancient and modern times, at the expression of individual, subjective opinions, feelings, and experiences. Every humanist took himself very seriously and thought that everything he had heard and seen was eminently worth recording. Treatises on highly abstract subjects are intermixed with personal stories, gossip, flattery, and invective to a degree and in a manner of which a modern scholar, like his ancient or medieval predecessors, would be thoroughly ashamed. Hence the widespread Renaissance preference for the letter as a form of literary expression, in which the author may speak in the first person; for the biography, in which another person is vividly delineated in all his concrete qualities; and for the diary and autobiography, in which both of these traits are in a way combined. The rise of portrait painting in the visual arts seems to indicate the same general tendency. In a curious way, this individualism is blended in both art and literature with a strong classicism and formalism that might seem to be incompatible with it, but actually contributes to it a special color and physiognomy. Where moral precepts are involved, the literature is of course full of the most general rules, but these rules are addressed to the effort of the individual person, just as they are based on individual historical examples. This subjective and personal trait pervades most humanist literature, and it is apparent already in its first great representative, Petrarch.

He vents his opinions, his likes and dislikes, his scruples and preoccupations, whereas objective statements on general problems are rather rare and incidental even in his philosophical writings. When we come to the end of the Renaissance, this subjective and personal character of humanist thought finds its most conscious and consummate philosophical expression in the *Essais* of Michel de Montaigne. Montaigne had received a humanist education, he knew Latin before he knew French, and his quotations from ancient authors, especially Plutarch and Seneca, fill many pages of his writings. The essay, in the form that he created and bequeathed to later centuries, is written in the first person, like the humanist letter, and is equally free in its style and structure: we might call the essay a letter written by the author to himself. Montaigne shared with the humanists his exclusive preoccupation with moral questions, his lack of interest in logic and metaphysics and the other learned disciplines, as well as his dislike for the scholastic type of learning. His philosophical position, though flexible, shows the impact of ancient Skepticism and, to a lesser extent, of Stoicism. He wrote on a variety of moral topics, often starting from classical examples or sentences. He would always refer to his personal experience and draw the lesson for himself. His skepticism, from which he excepted only his religious faith, was prompted by observation and experience. He knew how complex and changeable all human affairs are. Circumstances alter all the time, and so do our moods. Most of his thoughts were prompted by introspection. What all humanists actually felt but did not express in so many words, he stated most bluntly and clearly, namely, that he intends to talk primarily about himself and that his own individual self is the chief subject matter of his philosophizing. "Authors communicate themselves to the public by some peculiar and strange quality; I, for the first time, through my entire self, as Michel de Montaigne, not as grammarian or poet or lawyer. If the world complains that I speak too much of myself, I complain that the world does not think only of itself" (*Essais*, 3.2). Yet by making of his personal way of talking a philosophical program, by elevating introspection and the observation of actual human conduct to the rank of a conscious method, Montaigne had already passed beyond the boundaries of humanist thought and literature and was leading the way toward the psychological study of moods and manners that was to characterize the moral literature of the seventeenth century.[14]

* * *

While a scholar may be concerned with the complexities of a historical period he is trying to understand, the layman and the student look for a broad synthesis that selects and emphasizes those aspects of the past which are significant for them and for their time, and constitute, as it were, a contribution to contemporary civilization. Such a view seemed easy when there was an unquestioned faith in the present and future status of our civilization, and in its steady and almost inevitable progress. In our own time, this faith has been shattered in many ways. There is no doubt notable progress in technology and in the natural sciences, and there is a good deal of hope for social and political progress, as there should be, since such progress depends at least in part on our efforts, and hence is our own responsibility. Yet the future is not completely under our control and is, at least to that extent, uncertain. There is constant change but no steady progress in a variety of fields, and a growing awareness that every gain, though necessary and desirable, may have to be paid for by some loss. The present—shifting, complex, and inconsistent— ceases to be a firm measure for selecting what is significant in the past. Concentration on the present and rejection of the past are actually widespread at this moment, but such attitudes are lacking in wisdom and are not likely to last very long. Philosophers, linguists, critics of the arts and of literature, and practitioners of the social sciences often treat present realities as if they were absolutes, valid for all times and places, and as if there were no alternatives. This outlook is narrow and provincial, and one of the tasks of historical scholarship, so widely ignored, is to broaden our outlook, to open our eyes to the achievements of the past, even where they differ from our own. In historical recollection, we may vicariously relive what is gone because it is intrinsically significant, and hence we can understand it. And by thus preserving it, we keep it available for the future, which may still make a use of it that we cannot now foresee. The study of history is highly important in any living tradition, and we like to think of ourselves as heirs of such a tradition, which we call western civilization. If the future belongs to a broader world culture, which will contain many strands other than those of the western tradition, we still think and hope that it will include what we consider to be the best in the heritage of western civilization.

If we look back on the moral thought of Renaissance humanism for part of this heritage, some of its most general traits will become apparent. Many of them are related to the social and professional situation in which most of the humanist writers found themselves. As scholars and writers professionally concerned with the study of history and of the classics, as well as with moral problems, they were thoroughly influenced by the form and ideas of ancient literature and philosophy, but at the same time eager to give expression to their personal feelings and experiences. As a result of their work and efforts through several centuries, the subject matter of the humanities was established as a branch of secular learning that included moral philosophy as distinct from, but not necessarily opposed to, theology and the natural sciences. It represented a peculiar combination of literature and scholarship that tended to disintegrate in the following centuries, but it left a double heritage that has more or less survived to the present day and that seems very much worth preserving. By contrast, there are the historical and philological branches of knowledge that have greatly extended the range of their subject matter and refined the instruments of their research (as an echo of their origin in Renaissance humanism they are still called in old-fashioned French and Italian, the moral sciences). But there is also a Renaissance tradition of literary culture that is not limited to formal techniques but is concerned with broad human and philosophical problems, without accepting the limitations (and/or responsibilities) of professional philosophy. This latter tradition was revived by nineteenth-century Romanticism and has recently found an influential representative in George Santayana, the American philosopher. After having surveyed the contributions made by Renaissance humanism to moral thought, some of them modest and trivial, we cannot help concluding with the hope that its double heritage, scholarly and literary, though now threatened by the onslaught of several competing forces, may survive in the future.

NOTES

1. E. Garin, *L'umanesimo italiano* (Bari, 1952), trans. by P. Munz as *Italian Humanism: Philosophy and Civic Life in the Renaissance* (New York, 1965); P. O. Kristeller, *Renaissance Thought and Its Sources,* ed. M. Mooney (New York, 1979); C. Trinkaus, *Adversity's Noblemen: The Italian Humanists on Happiness* (New York, 1940; rev. ed. 1965); idem, *In Our Image and Likeness: Humanity and Divinity in Italian Humanist Thought* 2 vols. (Chicago, 1970); idem, *The Scope of Renaissance Humanism* (Ann Arbor, MI, 1983); *The Renaissance Philosophy of Man,* ed. E. Cassirer, P. O. Kristeller, and J. H. Randall (Chicago, 1948).
2. For the writings of the humanists, see G. Voigt, *Die Wiederbelebung des classischen Alterthums,* ed. M. Lehnerdt, 2 vols. (Berlin, 3d ed. 1893); V. Rossi, *Il Quattrocento* (Milan, 1933, and later editions). For their historical writings, see E. Cochrane, *Historians and Historiography in the Italian Renaissance* (Chicago, 1981).
3. E. F. Cranz, *A Bibliography of Aristotle Editions, 1501–1600* (Baden-Baden, 1971); C. B. Schmitt, *Aristotle and the Renaissance* (Cambridge, MA, 1983). J. C. Nelson, *The Renaissance Theory of Love: The Context of Giordano Bruno's Eroici Furori* (New York, 1958); J. Hankins, "Latin Translations of Plato in the Renaissance" (Ph.D. diss., Columbia University, New York, 1984). L. Zanta, *La renaissance du stoïcisme au XVIe siècle* (Paris, 1914); J. L. Saunders, *Justus Lipsius* (New York, 1955); G. Abel, *Stoizismus and fruehe Neuzeit* (Berlin, 1978). Lorenzo Valla, *De vero fal-*

soque bono, ed. M. Lorch (Bari, 1970). R. H. Popkin, *The History of Scepticism from Erasmus to Spinoza* (Berkeley, rev. ed., 1979).

4. G. Toffanin, *Che cosa fu l'umanesimo* (Florence, 1929); idem, *Storia dell-'umanesimo,* 3 vols. (Bologna, 1950), English trans. be E. Gianturco *History of Humanism* (New York, 1954). Kristeller, *Renaissance Thought and Its Sources,* chap. 4; E. Wind, *Pagan Mysteries in the Renaissance* (New York, rev. ed. 1968).

5. E. F. Rice, Jr., *The Renaissance Idea of Wisdom* (Cambridge, MA, 1958).

6. *Vittorino da Feltre and Other Humanist Educators,* ed. W. H. Woodward (Cambridge, 1897; reprinted with intro. by E. F. Rice, Jr., New York, 1963); W. H. Woodward, *Studies in Education During the Age of the Renaissance, 1400–1600* (Cambridge, 1906; reprinted New York, 1967).

7. H. Baron, *The Crisis of the Early Italian Renaissance,* 2 vols. (Princeton, 1955; rev. ed. in one volume, 1966); idem, *Humanistic and Political Literature in Florence and Venice at the Beginning of the Quattrocento* (Cambridge, MA, 1955).

8. L. B. Wright, *Middle-Class Culture in Elizabethan England* (Chapel Hill, 1935).

9. *Beyond Their Sex: Learned Women of the European Past,* ed. P. A. Labalme (New York, 1980).

10. Nelson, *Renaissance Theory of Love.*

11. P. O. Kristeller, "The Active and the Contemplative Life in Renaissance Humanism," in *Arbeit, Musse, Meditation, Betrachtungen zur Vita activa und Vita contemplativa,* ed. B. Vickers (Zurich, 1985), 133–52. On will and intellect, see Kristeller, *Medieval Aspects of Renaissance Learning,* ed. and trans. E. P. Mahoney (Durham, NC, 1974), 81–90; and Kristeller, "A Thomist Critique of Marsilio Ficino's Theory of Will and Intellect," in *Harry Austryn Wolfson Jubilee Volume, English Section II* (Jerusalem, 1965), 463–94.

12. See E. Walser, *Gesammelte Studien zur Geistesgeschichte der Renaissance* (Basel, 1952); Trinkaus, *Adversity's Noblemen;* idem, *In Our Image and Likeness;* idem, *Scope of Renaissance Humanism;* A. Perosa, *Giovanni Rucellai ed il suo Zibaldone,* vol. 1. (London, 1960).

13. See Kristeller, *Renaissance Thought and Its Sources;* Trinkaus, *Adversity's Noblemen;* idem, *In Our Image and Likeness;* idem, *Scope of Renaissance Humanism.*

14. D. M. Frame, *Montaigne's Discovery of Man* (New York, 1955).

C HUMANISM AND THE PROFESSIONS

34 HUMANISM AND JURISPRUDENCE
Richard J. Schoeck

THE TITLE OF THIS ESSAY IS DELIBERATELY AMBIVALENT: IT points both to the interests of studying humanists active in juris- prudential studies during the Renaissance and to the double effects of humanism on legal studies and of legal studies on humanistic ones. I hope that this essay, which is designed for the nonspecialist in the history of law or of jurisprudence, will also permit a quick introduction into a number of closely related questions. I propose, therefore, to begin with a survey of the people who studied and taught law; to move next to some aspects of the study of law during the Renaissance; to consider the books and libraries of Renaissance lawyers; to glance at the contribution of legal scholars to the development of theories of textual criticism; and, finally to conclude with some reflections on the importance for human- istic studies of the field of jurisprudence.[1]

The area, as I wrote in 1971, is impossibly large. "It is, indeed (to use an old metaphor), a vast sea. And if so distinguished an historian as F. W. Maitland could write, 'having wetted the soles of my feet on the shores of the mediaeval *oceanus iuris,* I know a little of the profundity and immensity of a flood that exceeds my depth and my gaze,' I can claim only to have caught a glimpse, a distant glimpse, of its expanse and not plumbed enough of its depth."[2]

The implications for our full understanding of humanism in the Ren- aissance period are very great, and because by the nature of legal studies in France the symbiosis between humanism and jurisprudence was par- ticularly strong, I shall concentrate largely on France.

* * *

In spite of the mounting attack on the Italian method of studying the law (the *mos italicus,* discussed in the third part of this essay) by humanist critics like Lorenzo Valla, the prestige of the professional university teachers of law remained high. Indeed, As Myron Gilmore states (for the Italian universities):

> At Bologna, at Padua, at Pavia, at the University of Pisa, reconstituted after 1472, the lawyers enjoyed the greatest position and had by far the largest number of followers. In the official rolls of the University of Pisa in the period from 1472 to 1525 we find that 101 appointments were made in civil law, 71 in canon law, whereas there were but 13 in theology.[3]

Much the same was apparently true not only in Italian universities but also in the French universities with strong law faculties, such as Orléans and Montpellier. At Paris, to be sure, the faculty of theology remained strong in the sixteenth century. It follows that in the Italian universities the salaries of the law faculties were high, even "out of proportion to what was earned in any other area of academic life."[4]

More students studied law in the Renaissance universities than any other discipline, and we may well ponder today the fact that the young men of the Renaissance spent so many of their formative years studying Roman and canon law. On the Continent, to speak now generally:

> Many of the great figures of literature from Petrarch to Montaigne had studied the law even though they afterwards revolted against it, and we should not forget that Luther at least began the study of the law before his conversion and that Calvin spent years studying the Roman law under the best masters of France and Italy. Under these conditions the methods, the attitudes, and the incidental opinions of the law professors take on an importance far transcending their technical instruction. In many ways they contributed to forming the mind and style of their age.[5]

Reinforcing this importance of the law professors was the force of the scope of legal studies, which included all that we would now consider the domain of political science, as well as the substance of other social sciences.

From these and other facts about the study of law and the legal profession during the Renaissance, Gilmore offers a few "tentative" generalizations: that the lawyers not only reflected but contributed to the growth of a secular attitude; that among the lawyers discussion of the correct method of studying the law led some to be more receptive to the reformers—for, "after all, the latter proposed to teach the Christian texts in the same way in which the lawyers were expounding the *corpus iuris.*"[6] To these generalizations we might add the following: that some of the authority of the priest was shifted to the lawyers, that the study of ancient legal texts was necessarily interdisciplinary, and that the fraternity of legal scholars in Europe was indeed international, allowing, to be sure, for division between the followers of the *mos italicus* and the *mos gallicus.*

*   *   *

There were, as is well known, two dominant schools of legal study for the Roman (or civil) law: *mos italicus* and *mos gallicus,* and it was predominantly with the latter that humanists were associated and to which they contributed. But until Erasmus's generation the *mos italicus* was the established system of education and mode of interpretation, and the style favored by practitioners. Late medieval legal studies in Italy had been dominated by Bartolo of Sassoferrato (1314–1357), whose opinions had almost the authority of judicial decisions and were much sought by rulers and courts—leading to the widespread practice in Italy and France of writing and publishing *consilia.* Formerly known as postglossators,[7] Bartolo and his followers were less interested in a historial understanding of the original context or growth of Roman law than in the establishment and application[8] of a system of principles derived from the *Corpus iuris civilis* of Justinian, which in their view still had the force of *de jure* law in a still-existent Roman Empire.[9] In the widely read *De modo studendi* (1472), the question of Giovanni Battista de Caccialupo (ca. 1420–ca. 1485), speaks to the prestige of Bartolo, for in calling Bartolo the mirror, father, and lamp of the civil law, he asked: "Who would deny that Bartolus is the first, or prince, in civil law?"[10] As Watson summarily puts it: "What is called the 'Reception of Roman Law' owes a very great deal to him and his pupil, Baldus de Ubaldi [c. 1320–1400]."[11]

Humanist reaction to the university tradition of teaching Roman law began as early as Petrarch, who had deplored the lack of interest by civilian legists in the beginnings of Roman law and in jurisprudence before Justinian;[12] and Ambrogio Traversari (1386–1439) advised the study and imitation of the "ancient" jurisconsults, rather than the "new" commentators like Bartolo. But it was Lorenzo Valla (1407–1457), an early humanist and a scholar devoted to philology, who attacked Bartolo—along with his pupil Baldo and their predecessor Accursius[13]—for speaking a barbarous language. Valla's judgment of Bartolo was reinforced by the immense popularity and authority of his *Elegantiae linguae latinae,* which, between 1471 and 1536, appeared in more than fifty editions and was endorsed by Erasmus. Yet the school of Bartolo still continued to dominate legal teaching in Italian universities in the sixteenth century.[14]

The reaction against the Bartolists began in Italy but was carried to its fullest in France. Before the end of the fifteenth century, Angelo Poliziano proposed a critical edition of the celebrated Florentine edition of the *Pandects* (see below),[15] and Andrea Alciato (1492–1550) was applying a sense of history and a kind of literary criticism to the understanding of the great texts of Roman law. In France a little earlier than Alciato, Guillaume Budé, the great French humanist and legal scholar, had published his *Annotationes in Pandectas;* these texts established a new school of humanistic jurisprudence.[16] The *mos italicus* worked with a system of principles derived from the *Corpus iuris civilis,* applying techniques of scholasticism; the *mos gallicus* was historical in its effort to understand the text in its context, and it applied all of the resources of the new philological approaches of Valla, Poliziano, and other humanists.[17]

Less known than Alciato, Claudius Cantiuncula (ca. 1490–1549) studied law at Louvain and in 1517 moved to Basel, where he soon made contact with Erasmus.

> In his Basel writings Cantiuncula expounded the relationship between secular and canon law, but he also committed himself firmly to juristic humanism, the study of Latin legal sources, and the methodology of legal scholarship usually described as the *mos gallicus.* Glosses, commentaries, and repertories were to be avoided "as if they were poisoned fruits and vain dreams."[18]

It was Cantiuncula who, in letters written between 1518 and 1520 to Budé and Cornelius Agrippa of Nettesheim, added Alciato's name to those of Ulrich Zasius and Budé, calling them "a 'triumvirate' responsible for a new era in jurisprudence."[19] And Erasmus, who so strongly influenced Cantiuncula's thinking on equity[20] and whose *Adagia* was so remarkably used and reworked by Alciato in his emblems (written after 1523 but first published in 1531), characterized Alciato as "the ablest jurist in the ranks of the orators and the best orator in the ranks of the jurists" (in 1528); and again, in a later edition of the *Adages* he referred to Alciato as "the ornament in this age, not only of civil law, but of all studies."[21]

Guillaume Budé (1468–1540) was remarkable in several respects: he learned Greek without a teacher, and he studied classical learning without a first-rate supporting library; further, he was that "new type of man of letters in that he was not a member of the clergy but a married man." [22] Beginning with the translation of four treatises of Plutarch into Latin (from about 1503 to 1504), he established a landmark in the study of law with his *Annotationes in quattuor et viginti pandectarum libros* (1508), working as a philologist to get beneath the layers of glosses, which often obscured the meaning of the original text, in order to tackle the broad questions of the origin and nature of law from the first books of the *Digest* (or *Pandects*).[23] His *De asse et partibus ejus* (1515, with a second edition in 1516) is perhaps even more remarkable, for, departing from a law of the *Digest,* Budé aimed at rediscovering the value of all measures and monies of antiquity, thereby leading to reflections on social injustices and on abuses of the church. It was *De asse* that led to frequent comparison between Erasmus and Budé, with Budé often being thought the preeminent humanist of the age. The letter by Budé to Thomas More in the parerga of *Utopia,* commenting on the abuses of contemporary law and especially on misuses of the natural law, is consequently an important document in the interpretation of More's treatise by contemporary humanist jurists.

In Basel there was a circle of humanist jurisprudence of which Erasmus was a member, and the influence of this circle upon his thought, especially during the years of residence in Basel in the 1520s, is notable;[24] and there are others who merit reading and study. Boniface Amerbach (discussed below) was notable for mediating between the two *mores* of legal studies, proclaiming that position in his inaugural lecture of 1525. He so much insisted on following the principle of equity (ἐπιείκεια) in the elaboration of new laws that he was hailed as "magister epieikeias in iure nostro."

Thus while the *mos italicus* and the *mos gallicus* were reconciled in the work of Amerbach, or later of Jean Bodin, their practitioners often quarreled with each other. Jean Bodin (ca. 1530–1596) began with a commitment to the *mos gallicus,* being a student of law at Toulouse (where in 1559 his oration gave an account of the *translatio studii* from Italy to France); but he ended by returning to a respectful study and use of the *mos italicus.*[25] It would be reasonable to say that a number of the humanistic jurists of the Renaissance never lost their respect for the master-jurists of the Italian tradition who had so skillfully applied the Roman law to contemporary practice; and in any case the hostility that had existed between the two *mores* seems to have died down by the end of the sixteenth century. Rabelais, to be sure, found glossators and postglossators prime targets for his satire, especially in the *Tiers livre;* and Montaigne kept a distance from the details of the law in his *Essais.*[26]

The study of canon law in the fifteenth century was not notably original, being marked by the addition of another "book" to the canon, the publication of the *Extravagantes communes* at the end of the fifteenth century, which opened up a new series of *commentaria, repetitiones, consilia,* and the like. But the Councils of Pisa and Constance called for the expertise of canonists to deal with the general problems of schism and papal or conciliar supremacy, as well as with the wars against Turks and Saracens and the problems of the New World.[27] As noted, jurisconsults like Baldo, and Alciato later, also wrote on the canon law. There was also much interest in points of contact and conflict between the canon and the civil law: Bartolo of Sassoferrato, for example, wrote a *Tractus inter ius canonicum et civile,* and there were other treatises on *Contradictiones, Viatorium utriusque iuris, Concordantiae iuris civilis et canonici,* and a *Repertorium utriusque iuris.* The uses of canon law in pastoral and diocesan theological and disciplinary matters are marked by a large number of *summae confessorum* (or cases or conscience), with the two Franciscan works of Angelo de Clavisio and Giovanni Battista Trovamala—the *Summa Angelica* and the *Summa Rosella,* respectively—having wide currency; and there were other summas by members of other religious orders.[28]

There was less interest in the textual problems of the canon law, perhaps in part because the collection of church legislation—now first called the *Corpus iuris canonici,* by analogy with the *Corpus iuris civilis*—had been so recently established by Jean Chappuis and Vitalis de Thebes (between 1499 and 1502) for the Parisian printers Rembolt and Guering. (Chappuis, by the way, also edited a number of classical texts.) This collection, with its chronological limit of 1484, contained the authenticated collections (the *Decretals, Sext,* and *Clementines*) and the private collection of Gratian (the *Decretum*), together with the newly published *Extravagantes.* But perhaps the relative lack of interest in the text of the canon law was due also to the fact that almost immediately at the beginning of the Reformation there were attacks on the canon law by Luther and others, which often included a symbolic burning of the books themselves; and criticism of the *Corpus iuris canonici* was not encouraged among those who accepted its jurisdiction. Reform of the canon law was to have been taken up by the Fifth Lateran Council (1512), but nothing was accomplished. After the Council of Trent (which ended in 1563), Pope Pius IV decided to revise and reissue as an official text the Chappuis *Corpus,* and toward this end in 1566 he established a commission of cardinals to verify the authenticity of the texts in the *Decretum.* Some scholarship on the canon-law text continued; yet while scholarship in fifteenth-century canon law textual problems has been studied by Brian Tierney and some others, that of the sixteenth century has been too much neglected. At the end of the sixteenth century, Pierre

Pithou, a royal legist in France (see below), began to work on an edition of canon law that would make use of both Catholic and Protestant histories as well as of classical sources; this work, which included critical notes on the text, was published posthumously by his brother François in Paris in 1637.[29]

It is well to remind ourselves that the study of law on the Continent included both canon and civil law. No one could be thought expert in one unless at home in the other: "And of the two it was the Canon Law which had the more important function in the formation of a great jurist, according to the current adage, *Canonista sine legibus parum valet, legista sine canonibus nihil.*"[30] As I have written elsewhere, any modern attempt to understand fifteenth- or sixteenth-century history or political thought without considering the theories and discussions of the canonists is incomplete, if not fruitless; for the influence of the canon law before the Reformation was immensely far-reaching and significant.[31] Yet there has been no wide-ranging study of the cultural interests of canonists in the Renaissance period, no systematic study of their libraries (on which see the next section of this essay). I would expect that the humanistic content of the canonists' libraries would differ significantly from those of civilians, and that the libraries of lawyers of the *mos gallicus* would have markedly greater representation of humanistic texts than those of the *mos italicus.*[32]

*   *   *

If we take France as an example—because the *mos gallicus* was strongest there, and the impact of humanism correspondingly greater—the increase in lawyers' libraries during the Renaissance was dramatic both in absolute numbers, jumping manyfold from 1500 to 1550, and in comparison with the libraries of ecclesiastics, which clearly outnumbered all others from 1480 to 1500 but had fallen to a third the number of lawyers' libraries by the second half of the sixteenth century.[33] The implications of these figures are of prime importance in any examination of the evidence for studies of humanism and jurisprudence: first, lawyers had by 1600 become the strongest class of lay intellectuals, and their steady book-buying must be counted as a kind of patronage of much scholarship; and second, for study of the intellectual and professional interests of the lawyers a knowledge of their wider book interests is vital.

Independent both of the universities and of the ecclesiastical hierarchy (with whom, however, they were often linked by marriage), the new magistracy quite dramatically made their contribution as leaders in the Parlement and elsewhere during the sixteenth century, as they had not done in the fifteenth. In France, the growth of this new and self-conscious intellectual class, Kelley emphasizes,

> may be measured not only by the number and nature of published books but also by the increase of private libraries. Naturally attracted to controversy but covetous of scholarly renown, these cultivated advocates divided their attention between the ideological needs of the monarchy and the growing public appetite for learning of all sorts.[34]

Their model as a titan of philology was Budé, the greatest French humanist of the age of Erasmus, whose *Pandects* and *De asse* were still widely celebrated; but their model legal scholar, teacher, and colleague was Jacques Cujas, "with whom all of them (except for Fauchet) had studied and corresponded."[35] His magnificent collection of at least two hundred manuscripts was open to friends and scholars, as was in England the library of Sir Robert Cotton, the antiquarian-scholar; such was the custom of Renaissance scholars and lovers of books, citizens all, as it were, in a republic of letters with its sense of international, cosmopolitan scholarship.[36]

Perhaps the most extraordinary collection of the age was that of the Dupuy family, now the Collection Dupuy in the Bibliothèque Nationale, Paris; for it was rich in its original documents, transcripts of other manuscripts and archival materials, and above all in its collections of letters by scholars like Joseph Justus Scaliger, which so richly manifest the interworkings of legal scholars with scholars in other fields—or, rather, the extent to which legal history, with its insistence on the study of the texts of Roman and canon law in their historical contexts, was seen to be a part of the larger study of history and humanism. There was in fact a republic of letters.[37]

But there were many other libraries: in France, those of Pierre Pithou and Jacques-Auguste de Thou, for example. Pierre Pithou (1539–1596), who was

> the profoundest scholar of the lot, was a constant source of inspiration and information to his contemporaries. He offered scholarly counsel and books from his great family library to Cujas, Loisel, Fauchet, and other members of his circle, including De Thou, Barnabe Brisson, Nicolas Vignier, and the younger Scaliger, and to such foreign scholars as Bonifacius Amerbach, Josias Simler, Theodore Zwinger, Isaac Casaubon, and William Camden.[38]

For England there was the great Cottonian library, rich in Anglo-Saxon
and other antiquities; and other libraries were building as well. The famous library of Sir Edward Coke might well be compared with those of
contemporary French lawyers, but there would be the significant difference that Coke's library contained relatively few books on Roman and
canon law.

The beloved books of these learned lawyers became a standard for
collation, and the marginalia of the books of Claude Dupuy, Joseph Justus Scaliger, and others offer what has been called a *modus modernus:*
"Waves of notes printed in minute type break on all sides of a small
island of text set in large roman," and these notes are characteristically
then surrounded by minute marginalia by the scholar-owner of the
book.[39]

The story of lawyers' libraries in France is paralleled in other countries, and the libraries of the university teachers of the civil law at Oxford
and Cambridge tell similar stories, for one finds many editions of Erasmus and other humanists in those libraries. But this story is yet to be told
in careful detail, and the larger history of lawyers' libraries in the Renaissance needs much further study.

*   *   *

The development of the theory of textual criticism is far too complex to
treat in small compass, nor can I here outline the role of humanistic
scholarship and attempt to relate that role to the parallel concern of legal
scholars to establish better texts for the civil and canon law. Yet at least
an indication must be provided for a sketch of humanism and jurisprudence in the Renaissance period.

The first century of printing was a great age for the printing of all
ancient texts, but all too often the first edition of a classical author was
little more than an attempt, however careful, to transcribe a manuscript
(usually humanist) chosen as the copy for the printer.[40] Indeed, Kenney
has charged that "the Italian humanists of the fourteenth and fifteenth
centuries may well have inflicted more damage on classical texts by their
efforts at correction than they removed," and this damage was of course
incorporated into the earliest printed texts.[41]

The great advance is to be found in the figure of Angelo Poliziano
(1454–94), celebrated not only by Erasmus as representing the best of
bonae litterae but even by that most hypercritical of scholars, Joseph
Justus Scaliger, who recorded his admiration for only three (Theodore
Gaza, Giovanni Pico della Mirandola, and Poliziano), "inter eos omnes
qui bonas litteras suscitarunt in Italia" ("among all those who awakened
the liberal arts in Italy").[42] Though not alone in his perceptions of the
stemmatic relationships of manuscripts, it is to Poliziano that modern

textual scholarship is indebted for blazing the trail in understanding the line of descent of manuscripts and the importance therefore of collation.[43] Poliziano's early death at forty left unpublished a commentary on the *Digest*, and there is much else still to see light.[44]

Between Poliziano and the great textual editors and scholars of the sixteenth century lies the work of Pietro Vettori and other Italian scholars studying the texts of the Roman law, and their work was drawn upon by the sixteenth-century classical scholars.[45]

There was also the figure of Erasmus, whose great folio editions of the New Testament and the church fathers—and a goodly number of editions of Cicero, Seneca, and other classical authors—dominated the sixteenth century. Kenney has recently rehearsed his limitations, and they do not need to be listed here; but what does need to be kept in mind is the all-too-frequent habit of sixteenth-century writers and editors of leaving final corrections to the printer,[46] for this explains much in Erasmus's proneness to *errata*. But, that having been said, we cannot slight the immense prestige of Erasmus as the humanist-editor, and the relation of his editorial work (with so much of his "message" being communicated in his prefatory letters) to his great activity as a publicist for humanism; for decades of texts and editions in the sixteenth century follow in the footsteps of Erasmus. And there is implicit in Erasmus's work at least the core of a more modern theory of the text and textual transmission.

But as early as 1521 in Florence, Pietro Vettori and a small group of associates built upon the foundations of Poliziano, apparently on their own mastering Poliziano's method:

> Vettori's Florentine associates specialized in legal studies. The doyen of the group, and the man responsible for its chief original discovery, was Lelio Torelli, the legal adviser to Cosimo I. But the Spanish lawyer Antonio Agustín first won public attention for their work. These men applied Poliziano's genealogical method to the manuscripts of the *Digest*.[47]

Eventually these methods were applied to patristic texts and even to the Bible itself.[48]

The work of this group of lawyers provided the foundation for the more advanced classical scholarship later in the sixteenth century.

＊   ＊   ＊

In 1581 Alberico Gentili began to teach at Oxford, having been exiled from Italy because of his Protestantism. This event marks the strengthening of Roman law studies in England, and perhaps a rededication of those studies on a level comparable to the best scholarship of Europe at that time. Alberico Gentili (1552–1608) was a doctor of civil law from Perugia; in 1588 he published *De jure belli commentatio prima,* revised in 1598 as *De jure belli libri tres,* a landmark in the science of international law. Gentili maintained that international law should manifest the actual practice of civilized nations, though it should be guided by moral considerations; he rejected the authority of the church while using canon as well as civil law. Hugo Grotius's more widely recognized *De jure belli ac pacis* (1625) built upon the foundations laid by Gentili's work.[49] At the same time, much of the best of French humanistic and jurisprudential thought had been carried to England by Huguenots, among whom must be signaled the deeply learned Isaac Casaubon (1559–1614)—the master of "Adversaria" (of which there are sixty volumes in the Bodleian Library) and of commentaries and notes (on Strabo, Theophrastus, Suetonius, Polybius, and others).[50]

The point is that such remarkable examples demonstrate how international scholarship at its best often tends to be; and I have not even touched upon the great interplay of humanism and jurisprudence in Dutch scholarship, notably that of Hugo Grotius (1583–1645)—who was a pupil of Scaliger at Leiden and "the greatest and most catholic-minded *homo politicus* in the series of Dutch scholars."[51] And the thread through much of the scholarship that I have been discussing was an Erasmian spirit of catholicity of learning and belief: nationalism too often has been the enemy of the republic of letters.

The concluding essay of Gilmore's *Humanists and Jurists* is on the learned and dutiful Boniface Amerbach (1495–1562), whose friendships and personal relations span several countries and generations. He may well serve as an epitome of the interplay of humanism and jurisprudence in the Renaissance and Reformation. Trained in the liberal arts at the humanist school in Sélestat, which owed much to the intellectual and spiritual ideals of the Brethren of the Common Life, and further schooled in Latin and Greek at Basel (B.A. 1511 and M.A. 1512), Amerbach studied law under Zasius at Freiburg, who was already a follower of the *mos gallicus,* though he had reservations about Budé's use of it.[52] Amerbach then moved to Avignon, where from 1520 to 1523 he studied under Cesare Ripa and Alciato. It is striking that Amerbach had the independence to mediate between the two *mores*—being in fundamental sympathy with the *mos gallicus* but recognizing the excessive claims and practices of some of its followers, and making "abundant use of the Italian glossators and commentators who focused more closely on the practical legal needs of contemporary city republics." For Amerbach was a practicing attorney as well as a legal scholar, and he wrote more than a hundred *consilia* for private and public clients, including an opinion on a case between the duke of Brunswick and the city of Goslar.[53] He was also one who insisted on following the principle of equity (ἐπιείκεια) as a guideline in the making of new laws; "the growing interest of Erasmus in equity doubtless owes much to his friendship with Amerbach and his participation in the Basel circle of jurisprudence during the 1520s."[54] The legal heir and executor of Erasmus's will, Amerbach contributed much to making Basel a stronghold of Erasmian culture and tolerance. A voracious collector, his rich library, which included many books with dedicatory inscriptions, is now a part of the library at the University of Basel. As has already been noted, he was himself a student of Zasius and Alciato, he had Montaigne as a pupil, and he was a friend of Pithou and many other foreign scholars.

Against the well-known 1519 portrait of Boniface Amerbach by Hans Holbein, which presents an intense and eager young man, there is the portrait by Jacob Clauser of 1557: "Here," Gilmore writes, "is the syndic of the council, the university professor, the administrator of Erasmus' trusts. For him there will be no sudden revelation."[55] Yet surely we may read in the change from 1519 to 1557, and in the development portrayed, something of the slow and painful acquisition of wisdom gained by the humanists of the century, whether they lived through the religious conflicts of the 1520s and 1530s or the religious wars and the St. Bartholomew's Massacre (1572) of the second half of the century, for "in all these complicated attempts that men must make to adapt to varying circumstances the rules of law and the rules of the Evangel, the attainment of Truth will be a slow process, the product of a continuing dialogue from which there cannot be excluded the voices of the past."[56] Perhaps therein is the summing up of many lifetimes of intense scholarly dedication—the life of Erasmus and of many other humanists and jurists.

NOTES

1. See R. J. Schoeck, "Neo-Latin Legal Literature," in *Acta conventus neo-latini lovaniensis*, ed. J. IJsewijn and E. Kessler (Munich, 1973), 577–88. A compact introduction is provided by M. P. Gilmore, *Humanists and Jurists: Six Studies in the Renaissance* (Cambridge, MA, 1963). For a detailed study of legal and historical disciplines in sixteenth-century France, see D. R. Kelley, *Foundations of Modern Historical Scholarship: Language, Law, and History in the French Renaissance* (New York, 1970). There are excellent studies of Alciato, Budé, and Zasius, and of the problem of the reception of the Roman law, in *Pédagogues et juristes: Congrès du Centre d'Études Supérieures de la Renaissance de Tours 1960* (Paris, 1963). There is also my

uneven survey, "Recent Scholarship in the History of Law," *Renaissance Quarterly* 20 (1967): 279–91.

2. Schoeck, "Neo-Latin Legal Literature," 577.

3. Gilmore, *Humanists and Jurists,* 64–65.

4. Ibid., 66.

5. Ibid., 67–68. The study of law was a primary avenue to other careers at royal and other courts as well as in the universities.

6. Ibid., 83–84. In his excellent introduction to *Roman Legal and Constitutional History,* W. Kunkel has written that "indeed humanism and the spread of learned jurisprudence were only individual elements of one and the same phenomenon: the growth of a worldly learning, drawn from the models of classical antiquity, which replaced the medieval culture dominated by the traditions of the church and more or less reserved to the clergy" (trans. J. M. Kelly [Oxford, 2d ed. 1973], 187).

7. The most famous glossators of the first half of the thirteenth century were Azo and Accursius, and the collection of previous glosses, with a reconciliation of differing interpretations, was made by Accursius and usually called the *glossa ordinaria.* A writer of commentaries rather than a glossator, Bartolo dominated legal studies after the fourteenth century. See H. Kantorowicz, *Studies in the Glossators of the Roman Law* (Cambridge, 1938).

8. That is, Bartolo and his followers by use of the scholastic method of analysis set about applying Roman law to contemporary problems. See C. N. Woolf, *Bartolus of Sassoferrato: His Position in the History of Medieval Political Thought* (Cambridge, 1913); and L. M. Mladen, "Bartolus the Man," *Annals of the New York Academy of Sciences* 314 (1978): 311–48. The two-volume collection of studies on the influence of Bartolo in Geneva, Basel, Belgium, and elsewhere—*Bartolo de Sassoferrato* (Milan, 1962)—contains some admirable work.

9. Bartolo's repertorium of Roman law was printed with his *consilia* as *Repertorium Bartoli* (*Repertorium aureum,* Lyons, 1485, 1510), and it is noteworthy that there was an eleven-volume edition of his *Commentaria* as late as 1547 (Lyons).

10. See the enthusiastic paper of Mladen, "Bartolus the Man."

11. A. Watson, *The Law of the Ancient Romans* (Dallas, 1970), 98.

12. Petrarch, *Familiares,* 20, ep. 4.

13. See Woolf, *Bartolus of Sassoferrato;* and Mladen, "Bartolus the Man." See further, D. Maffei, *Gli inizi dell'umanesimo giuridico* (Milan, 1956). For an excellent summary introduction, see M. P. Gilmore, "The Lawyers and the Church in the Italian Renaissance," in *Humanists and Jurists,* 61–86; and H. E. Troje, "Die Literatur des gemeinen Rechts unter dem Einfluss des Humanismus," in *Handbuch der Quellen und Literatur der neuren europäischen Privatrechtsgeschichte,* ed. H. Coing, vol. 2, *1500–1800* (Munich, 1974); and his *Graeca leguntur* (Cologne, 1971).

14. I have noted above (note 9) the continuing printing of Bartolo in the sixteenth century, which was done both in France and in Italy. See further titles in the British Museum Catalogues of Books Printed in France and in Italy

to 1600. Certainly the school of Bartolo continued to dominate legal teaching, as Gilmore has stated (*Humanists and Jurists,* 29); see also Kelley, *Foundations,* 39–43.

15. See F. Buonamici, *Il Poliziano giureconsulto* (Pisa, 1863) and Gilmore, *Humanists and Jurists,* 32; A. Grafton, *Joseph Scaliger: A Study in the History of Classical Scholarship,* vol. 1, *Textual Criticism and Exegesis* (Oxford, 1983), 54, is misleading on this point.

16. On Alciato, see P. E. Viard, *André Alciat 1492–1550* (Paris, 1926); and the excellent summary by V. W. Callahan in *Contemporaries of Erasmus,* ed. P. G. Bietenholz and T. B. Deutscher, 3 vols. (Toronto, 1984–86), 1:23–26. On Budé, see L. Delaruelle, *Guillaume Budé, les origines, les débuts, les idées maîtresses* (Paris, 1907), and the incisive entry by M. M. de la Garanderie in *Contemporaries of Erasmus,* ed. Bietenholz and Deutscher, 1:212–17. The questions arising from the two *mores* are studied by G. Astuti, *Mos italicus et mos gallicus nei dialoghi "de iuris interpretibus" di Alberico Gentili* (Bologna, 1937); and G. Kisch, *Humanismus und Jurisprudenz: Der Kampf zwischen mos italicus und mos gallicus an der Universität Basel* (Basel, 1955).

17. See Gilmore, *Humanists and Jurists,* 33. There is much in Kelley, *Foundations,* passim, and much more in the several studies of G. Kisch: *Humanismus und Jurisprudenz; Erasmus und die Jurisprudenz seiner Zeit: Studien zum humanistischen Rechtsdenken* (Basel, 1960); *Claudius Cantiuncula: Ein Basler Jurist und Humanist des 16. Jahrhunderts* (Basel, 1970).

18. *Contemporaries of Erasmus,* ed. Bietenholz and Deutscher, 1:259–60.

19. Ibid., 1:24.

20. G. Kisch has studied the question of Erasmus's thinking on jurisprudence in considerable detail, *Erasmus und die Jurisprudenz.* He has shown that Cantiuncula, in formulating his doctrine of equity, followed Erasmus closely in using the same citations and examples. See also *Contemporaries of Erasmus,* ed. Bietenholz and Deutscher, 1:259–61; and Kisch, *Claudius Cantiuncula.*

21. See Callahan in *Contemporaries of Erasmus,* ed. Bietenholz and Deutscher, 1:25.

22. Thus de la Garanderie in *Contemporaries of Erasmus,* ed. Bietenholz and Deutscher, 1:213. It is notable that in England Thomas More was also a striking example of this new type of man (see, in these volumes, Chapter 17, "Humanism in England").

23. *Contemporaries of Erasmus,* ed. Bietenholz and Deutscher, 1:214.

24. See above, note 20.

25. See the studies of R. E. Giesey and M. Reulos in *Jean Bodin: Verhandlungen der internationalen Bodin Tagung,* ed. H. Denzer (Munich, 1973); and the papers by M. Reulos and R. J. Schoeck in *Jean Bodin: Actes du colloque interdisciplinaire,* 2 vols. (Angers, 1985).

26. On Rabelais, see E. Nardi, *Rabelais e il diritto romano* (Milan, 1962); and, more generally, P. Petot, "Le droit privé français au XVIᵉ siècle et l'human-

isme," in *Umanesimo e scienza politica—Atti del congresso internazionale di studi umanistici,* ed. E. Castelli (Milan, 1951).

27. See the summary of A. D. de Sousa Costa in *New Catholic Encyclopedia,* 3:46; and W. Plöchl, *Geschichte des Kirchenrechts,* 3 vols. (Vienna, 1953–59), vol. 3.

28. These *summae confessorum* were used by Thomas More and satirized by Rabelais. For the situation in England, see R. J. Schoeck, "Canon Law in England on the Eve of the Reformation," *Medieval Studies* 25 (1963): 125–47.

29. See P. Cimetier, *Les sources du droit ecclésiastique* (Paris, 1930); and L. E. Boyle in *New Catholic Encyclopedia,* 4:348, on the term "Corpus iuris canonici." C. H. Lefebvre, who has written extensively on canon law—see *Histoire du droit et des institutions de l'église en Occident,* ed. G. Le Bras et al. (Paris, 1965), esp. vol. 7—has summarized the influence of Roman law on canon law in *New Catholic Encyclopedia,* 3:50–53. The standard scholarly edition is that of A. Friedberg, *Corpus iuris canonici,* 2 vols. (Leipzig, 1879–81). On Pithou's work, see Kelley, *Foundations,* 263.

30. See P. E. Hughes, *Reformation in England,* 3 vols. (New York, 5th ed., 1963), 1:73.

31. Schoeck, "Canon Law in England," 147.

32. See the work on Fauchet, Le Caron, and others discussed by Kelley, *Foundations,* 248 and note. For France, the standard study of the great libraries and collections is still L. Delisle, *Le cabinet des manuscrits de la bibliothèque imperiale,* 3 vols. (Paris, 1868–81), vol. 1.

33. L. Febvre and H.-J. Martin, *L'apparition du livre* (Paris, 1958; reprinted 1971), 368. See also R. Doucet, *Les bibliothèques parisiennes au XVᵉ siècle* (Paris, 1956); and Kelley, *Foundations,* 244.

34. Kelley, *Foundations,* 244. See also the studies of Delachenal and Rousselet, cited by Kelley, 245, note.

35. Kelley, *Foundations,* 246.

36. See R. J. Schoeck on the republic of letters, introduction to *Sir Thomas Browne, Special Number* of *English Language Notes* (1982). See also P. Dibon and T. Gregory, "Presentation," *Nouvelles de la république des lettres* 1 (1981): 7–11. For England, see S. Jayne, *Library Catalogues of the English Renaissance* (Berkeley, 1956), especially the section on private libraries, 93ff. See L. A. Knafla, "The Influence of Continental Humanists and Jurists on English Common Law in the Renaissance," in *Acta conventus Neolatini Bononiensis* (Binghamton, NY, 1985), 60–71; and R. J. Schoeck, "The Libraries of Common Lawyers in Renaissance England," *Manuscripta* 6 (1962): 155–67. It is an irony that the *mos italicus* had its roots in the thirteenth-century law schools of Orléans and one or two others, and that the *mos gallicus* had its roots among Italian scholars. Further, sixteenth-century humanistic jurists spent significant periods of time in Italy conferring with Italian scholars like Pietro Vettori and examining manuscripts. Letters and documents in the Collection Dupuy (Bibliothèque Nationale)

testify to the impact of their Italian travels on Claude Dupuy, Scaliger, and others.

37. A little-studied connection between the common law in England and the Roman and civil law of all Europe is that of the natural law tradition; on this, see E. Barker, *Traditions of Civility* (Hamden, CT, 1967; reprint of 1948); and A. P. d'Entrèves, *Natural Law* (London, 1951). The natural law is not so much a legal transplant—in the terms and concepts of A. Watson, *Legal Transplants* (Edinburgh, 1974)—as it is a *peregrinus:* nowhere at home, yet everywhere to be found. For this reason the addition of Budé's letter to the second (Paris) edition of More's *Utopia,* with its vigorous commentary on the validity but misuses of natural law, is striking indeed. In the vast and still-growing literature on the traditions of natural law, relatively little has been done with concepts of natural law during the Renaissance, in discussions of which civilians, canonists, and common lawyers all made a contribution.

38. Kelley, *Foundations,* 247.

39. Grafton, *Joseph Scaliger,* 17. L. A. Knafla has studied the annotations, and from them the uses made of his books in successive phases of study and legal development by Sir Thomas Egerton, Lord Ellesmere (1540–1617): "The Law Studies of an Elizabethan Student," *Huntington Library Quarterly* 32 (1969): 221–40; he has also studied the implications of Egerton's studies of the classics and civil law in his *Law and Politics in Jacobean England* (Cambridge, 1977), ch. 1. On Egerton's connection with humanists, see note 49, below.

40. See L. D. Reynolds and N. G. Wilson, *Scribes and Scholars* (Oxford, 2d ed. 1974), chap. 6; and E. J. Kenney, *The Classical Text* (Berkeley, 1974). I have tried to offer a somewhat different emphasis in "The Humanistic Concept of the Text: Text, Context, and Tradition," in *Proceedings of the Patristic, Medieval, and Renaissance Conference 1982* (Villanova, PA, 1985), 13-31.

41. Kenney, *Classical Text,* 3.

42. *Scaligerana, Thuana, Perroniana, Tithoena, et Colomesianna,* ed. P. Desmaizeaux (Amsterdam, 1740), 242. See Kenney, *Classical Text,* 5; and I. Maïer, *Ange Politien: La formation d'un poète humaniste, 1469–1480* (Geneva, 1966).

43. Kenney, *Classical Text,* 10–11.

44. See Grafton, *Scaliger,* 54. On Poliziano, see further G. Saitta, *Il pensiero italiano nell'umanesimo e nel Rinascimento,* 3 vols. (Florence, 2d ed. 1961); and A. D. Scaglione, "The Humanist as Scholar and Politian's Conception of the *Grammaticus,*" *Studies in the Renaissance* 8 (1961): 49–70.

45. See Troje, *Graeca leguntur;* and Grafton, *Scaliger,* chap. 2, for a recent summary.

46. Kenney, *Classical Text,* 50–51.

47. See Grafton, *Scaliger,* 53, 63.

48. Ibid., 65.

49. Like Bodin, Gentili took a critical attitude toward the excessive literary and

antiquarian emphases of the followers of Cujas, the "Cujacians," as Gentili called them. See D. R. Kelley, "The Development and Context of Bodin's Method," in *Jean Bodin,* ed. Denzer, 129. Pithou was one who in this battle took the side of his mentor, Cujas (ibid., n. 16). It is to be noted that Egerton (see note 39, above) was a patron of Gentili, along with a number of English humanists. See V. B. Heltzel, "Sir Thomas Egerton as Patron," *Huntington Library Quarterly* 11 (1948): 115–24.

50. M. Pattison, *Isaac Casaubon 1559–1614* (Oxford, 2d ed. 1892).

51. R. Pfeiffer, *History of Classical Scholarship from 1300 to 1850* (Oxford, 1976), 126.

52. I must quote a letter of Amerbach, written when he returned to Basel in 1524 and giving his reactions to lectures on the civil law at Basel by Johann Sichard, successor to Cantiuncula:

> I see many around me who do not fear to undertake such a task, although they have hardly opened the *Pandects* and scarcely know the names of the various problems they are expected to elucidate. We have such a one at Basel now, the successor of our Claudius [Cantiuncula], a man who, although he is not unlearned in the Latin language, is nevertheless completely unskilled in legal science which he never practiced. He undertakes the interpretation of the *Pandects* as if he were explaining a comedy of Terence or Plautus with all the glosses and interpreters cast aside.

(Quoted by Gilmore, *Humanists and Jurists,* 156, who translated it from *Die Amerbachkorrespondenz,* 5 vols. ed. A. Hartmann [Basel, 1942–58], vol. 2, no. 962). These opinions are more formally expressed in Amerbach's *Defensio interpretum iuris civilis,* delivered in 1525 on beginning his professorship at Basel: text in Hartmann, 3:554–64 and discussed by Kisch, *Humanismus und Jurisprudenz,* 79–97.

53. *Contemporaries of Erasmus,* ed. Bietenholz and Deutscher, 1:43.

54. Ibid., 1:43. See Kisch, *Erasmus und die Jurisprudenz,* 379.

55. Gilmore, *Humanists and Jurists,* 176 (where both portraits are given).

56. Ibid., 177.

35 ❧ ITALIAN HUMANISM AND SCHOLASTIC THEOLOGY
Charles Trinkaus

T HE ITALIAN HUMANISTS, AND MANY NORTHERN HUMANISTS AS well, were trained as grammarians and rhetoricians and many of them developed—as an adjunct to their studies of Greek and Latin letters in accord with their grammatical and rhetorical precepts—a pioneering mastery of a new discipline, which yet precariously survives: classical philology.[1] Certainly it was their most enduring scholarly contribution, an activity swiftly applied to the study of the modern vernaculars as well, which has given rise to the multiplicity of literature departments in the modern university. Possibly next in importance was the humanist contribution to the discipline of history,[2] or perhaps rather to modern historical consciousness,[3] little though my contemporary colleagues like to recognize this ancestry.

But I write as a historian whose interest is in understanding the past and not in tracing disciplinary ancestries and contributions. The Italian and European humanists, on whom my mentor Lynn Thorndike set me to work with his well-known virulent lack of enthusiasm, I have wanted to view as originating and functioning within the highly developed and strongly institutionalized late medieval cultures. I have considered these humanists to be motivated by the needs, problems, and fashions of their culture not only to acquire the humanistic disciplines—which were after all medieval disciplines, though less flourishing than theology, natural philosophy, law, or medicine—but also, if only defensively, to demonstrate and to justify the importance of the humanities for dealing with the more urgent problems of their cultures.

In fact, humanism as a historical movement would seem incomprehensible in its scope and dynamic if it had not been characterized by an activistic, problem-solving mode of operation and self-justification. And it is indicative of the still potently surviving and self-cherishing modernism of contemporary Anglo-American scholarship that it sees the activist role of humanism as directed most significantly toward the imitation and revival of ancient civic and republican structures and virtues, to mention only Hans Baron, John Pocock, and Quentin Skinner.[4] The civic humanism syndrome, for all its attractiveness and partial verity, remains

committed to the great historical myth generated by the humanists themselves (though propagated far more in the eighteenth century) of the closing down of the darkened medieval centuries through the renewal of
antiquity by the fifteenth-century revivers of the liberal arts who did not
yet know they were the humanists.

While I am aware that the humanists did in fact make an important
contribution both to the political ideologies of the Italian city-states and
later of the European monarchies and to the modern political thinking
that was emerging in the sixteenth and seventeenth centuries, it is too
often forgotten that they lived under the aegis of the church as well as
under that of the political regimes, amid societies operated by highly
trained clerical administrators, both theologians and canonists, by
equally trained and skilled lawyers serving church, state, and mercantile
dealings, in communities in which the physical and spiritual needs of
individuals were administered by medics, parish priests, and the mendicant and monastic orders. The humanists knew themselves as Christians
and as much members of the *respublica christiana* as of the secular regimes. As medieval scholars had before them, they faced the problem of
pagan learning and of how its study related to Christian doctrine.

The classical literary tradition had provided the basis of early medieval Christian learning and had to be reconciled with Christian teaching
by a variety of methods, a problem that continued into the twelfth century. The scholastic movement, which evolved about this time, was initially based on the study of Boethius and his translations. But it found its
center in Aristotelian logical, physical, and metaphysical texts. How
Christian scholars could use Aristotle and his Greek and Arabic commentators licitly, and when illicitly, were questions that gave rise to well-
known controversies over this issue that raged through the twelfth,
thirteenth, and fourteenth centuries (as they also have raged retrospec-
tively in the nineteenth and twentieth!). Later the question of how Renaissance humanists, beginning with Albertino Mussato, or else with
Petrarch, Boccaccio, Coluccio Salutati, and others, should deal with classical writers was complicated by the charge of theologians that these
humanists' Christianity and that of their pupils was sure to be contami-
nated with false beliefs and outrageous morals through reading Homer,
Vergil, and Ovid. The humanists responded, as they were bound to do,
by questioning the purity of doctrine of those who read Aristotle, not to
mention Averroës. On a primary defensive or apologetic level, then, the
humanists reacted critically to attacks from clerical sources, some of
which were monastic, and not mendicant or scholastic. But, as it seems
to me, to stress only this conflict would be a very superficial way to deal
with the problem of the relationship of humanism and medieval,

especially scholastic, theology: for to begin with it leaves aside the positive reasons for the origins of humanistic consciousness. And, more importantly, it ignores the character of more mature humanistic thinking concerning the relationship of the *studia humanitatis* to the Christian religion, a faith to which they all adhered and which they wished to promote with varying degrees of fervor.

*   *   *

Petrarch not only was very influential in the development of humanism but also provides the historians with important insights as to the motivation for the revival of classical studies and for their application to the existing cultural and religious situations. Petrarch was no more sensitive to the complexities of earthly existence than many another man, layman or religious or cleric, in his age. What he did that rendered him unique was to discover the cultural and literary modes present within the inherited resources of classical culture with which to articulate the ambiguities of life in this world and to set forth, tentatively at least, remedies. But for Petrarch, as for most men living then, the solution of earthly problems should in no way be separate from any soul's eternal destiny. Clearly enough to him, though he proposed things men could do, the reception of the divine grace to do them alone brought salvation. But with the reception of grace, or with the acceptance of this insight concerning grace, came the acceptance of one's own misery and the motivation, as well as the possible stance, needed to live with it here and now. This acceptance of the actuality of misery and the possibility of grace was better than the condition of being hopelessly and helplessly driven and tossed by the vain and fruitless goals of urban greed and vanity. What then was this stance and what chance was there of a man assuming it, and from where in the arsenal of earthly historical culture could one find modes of effecting it?

Petrarch's initial impulse, which he never entirely abandoned, was that of withdrawal. Since he was unwilling to take the full step of becoming a monk, as his brother Gherardo had, though admiring many aspects of religious life, Petrarch invented a rural, literary solitude for himself and practiced it at Vaucluse for a number of years. But while rejecting the diverse and destructive effects of earthly urban life, he could not condemn it totally. It was an actuality with which mankind had to live in this world. He looked around, therefore, for partial, reparative solutions, and projected the ideal of the Christian layman deeply concerned with his own spiritual destiny, participating as unscathed as he could in social life while retaining his integrity and his piety.[5] This ideal, that by some recent scholars has been labeled "lay piety," should indeed be related to the developing lay religious movements of the fourteenth and fifteenth centuries, tertiaries and penitential confraternities.

Petrarch did not rest content with this passive solution, however: searching for some more positive mode of dealing with the situation, he embraced Ciceronian rhetoric. He did not discover rhetoric simply in this context, for he had long studied and admired Cicero; but it came to him that rhetoric, rather than the dialectical moral philosophy of the scholastics, should be the cultural instrument taken from the ancients. Teaching what was logically argued was not enough. Deep, meditative experience alone could penetrate and move the soul toward Christian virtue, and this only with the aid of grace. Such is the message of the *Secretum*. But rhetoric added onto meditation was an instrument directed to moving and arousing not simply man's intellect but his affections as well. Language itself could be used in such a way as to become affectively therapeutic, arousing a viator from his despair over the vagaries of his earthly *fortuna,* calming him and placing in perspective his earthly triumphs. Significantly, Petrarch did not consider this stance anti-intellectual. He cast himself in the role of moral therapist for the affective excesses in reacting to earthly vicissitude in his *De remediis utriusque fortunae,* personifying his rhetorical counsels in a figure called *Ratio.*[6]

Cicero's rhetoric became Petrarch's model for his own conception of the role of the Christian scholar and teacher, which in turn became paradigmatic; but he never forgot that Cicero was not a Christian. This point he makes clear in his *De otio religioso,* rejecting Cicero's pagan teaching that virtue was in one's own power, whereas fortune was in the hands of others: "God . . . shut off the road to truth to him which a little later he deemed suitable to open to us"; and excepting from his praise of Cicero in his *De ignorantia* all that was not Christian.[7] Petrarch also never forgot that he was a poet, for poetry was the other and perhaps major mode of affecting the situation of mankind that he took from ancient literary practice. But projecting his own poetic images, he transformed and reconstituted those of the ancient poets, extracting from them what Thomas Greene has called his "sub-texts."[8]

Petrarch's connections with the scholastic theology of his day were marginal. Although he attacked the puerility of the contemporary vogue for dialectic, condemned the natural philosophers who sought to elevate their science to a spiritual one, and proclaimed the uselessness of the study of Aristotle because it gave a knowledge unable to help save a soul, he avoided direct references to scholastic theology, though making it clear that he preferred Augustine to the medieval theologians. He considered the Augustinian Luigi Marsili as a kind of protégé, and Marsili, whose education was supervised by Gregory of Rimini, may well have imbibed that thinker's nominalistic tendencies along with Petrarch's classicism, which he seems to have propagated through the discussions he sponsored at Santo Spirito. His writings, such as have survived, are too few and fragmentary to permit interpretation. But Petrarch clearly sided with those who emphasized the primacy of the will; he found in Cicero's *Academica* grounds for doubt about universals; his metaphysics, if he had any, was an amalgam of Augustine and Seneca but with his interest totally focused on experience rather than ontology. Most telling to my mind was his atomistic view of human relations. If Seneca believed that there is an innate sense of justice in any individual, Petrarch did not.[9] Thomas Aquinas, by contrast, quite clearly shared this Stoic view. What I am suggesting is that from his own sources and intellectual development rather than in any direct or acknowledged way, wrestling, perhaps, with many of the same problems, Petrarch entertained a number of the positions that have been held to be characteristic of those fourteenth-century scholastics who were critical of the so-called *via antiqua*. Petrarch pursued his own *via antiqua* of classical letters, but it was not the scholastic one. Except for their wretched dialectical chattering, which he ceaselessly mocked, his views were closer to those of the scholastic *via moderna*. Saying this, I am aware of how fragmented our conceptions of late scholasticism have become and how perilous it is to generalize.

* * *

Coluccio Salutati, who knew or corresponded with such figures as Biagio de' Pelacani and Pietro Alboini of Mantua, was more explicit in his relations to scholasticism.[10] If Petrarch dealt with the common issues of late medieval culture in his own innovative humanistic way, Salutati took note of the scholastic positions and sought to incorporate them into his humanism. As we know, and both Berthold Ullman and Ronald Witt would confirm it, Salutati was not only broad and varied in his concerns but shifting and even self-contradictory in his statements.[11] I would argue that there was nonetheless a unity between his secular political preoccupations and his ethical/religious ones; moreover, he supported both of them by his humanistic rhetorical and poetic interests and practice.

Salutati's employment of scholastic theology, though not of its *sed contra* mode of presentation, comes in his *De fato, fortuna et casu* and his *De nobilitate legum et medicine,* both now published in critical editions.[12] In *De nobilitate,* which is an important effort to undermine the metaphysical basis of the natural philosophy employed by the medical profession both in their education and in the justification of their practice, Salutati, notary and civil servant that he was, upholds the epistemological superiority of the innate conception of human justice that underlies the practice of the lawyer and humanist. Even more important is his exposition and defense of the primacy of the will over the intellect, for the humanly invented and practiced elements of culture are more important and valid than those resting on the epistemologically shaky foundations of science with which the physician operates. For Salutati the will is so much more powerful and determinant of human behavior than the intellect that it not only distorts and obscures but actually dictates human thought and ideas. Although this view is not the basis on which scholastics such as John Duns Scotus and a notable number of fourteenth- and fifteenth-century scholastics defended the primacy of the will, it is significant that Salutati both parallels and exceeds them in his position.[13]

The primacy of the will is closely related to the two central arguments of De fato, which are also directed against a physical notion of causation not so much undermined as quarantined in this work. Salutati's major emphases are first the power and reality of divine providence flowing from the all-powerful divine will and then the totally compatible actuality, power, and freedom of the human will. Much of his argumentation here is directed against contemporary scholastic discussions of God's knowledge of future contingents and whether this foreknowledge in any way inhibits human freedom of the will. Parallel to this argument on behalf of human purpose and activity as an integral part and element of divine providence—the true mode, as he sees it, in which man functions in the image and likeness of God—Salutati argues the compatibility of divine predestination and human salvation, but holds that God has divine prescience only, and not the direction, of human actions bringing on damnation.[14] In these arguments concerning the primacy of the will, the harmony of divine providence and human freedom, and the responsibility of divine predestination for human salvation and human action foreknown but not willed by God, Salutati seems to be following Duns Scotus for the first two and Giles of Rome for the last. This point has been made on the basis of similarity of argument, not by direct citation. He apparently did have a manuscript containing Scotus that has disappeared, and he definitely possessed manuscripts of Giles.[15] Salutati's acquaintance with, if not thorough study of, many scholastic theologians of both the thirteenth century and his own is attested by Ronald Witt's rich study. Witt at one point declares: "Less fastidious, more ecumenical than his predecessor [Petrarch], Salutati willingly sought help wherever he could find it, betraying no reluctance to using terminology, ideas, and at times even the words of eminent scholastics."[16]

For my own approach what seems significant is not whether he was influenced by or utilized Giles, Scotus, any of the fourteenth-century post-Ockhamists whom he knew, or works then available in Florence, but rather the energy with which both Petrarch and Salutati—and, as we shall see, Lorenzo Valla as well—sought to emphasize human will and activity and at the same time divine grace and predestination. This combination of positions, which rhetorically rather than dialectically trained thinkers might more easily espouse, does seem to correspond to a very deep religious piety and a heightened encouragement and incitement to human activity in so many areas; so much so that these two attitudes were dominant characteristics of the period of the Renaissance, and, let me hasten to add, what could equally properly be called the late Middle Ages as well. Salutati, like Petrarch, was attempting to promulgate a rhetorical and poetic theology modeled on Augustine. But he was far more conversant with contemporary and earlier scholastic writings than Petrarch seems to have been and did not spurn the ideas of many of them. Like Petrarch, however, he did reject the dialectical and *sed contra* modes of argumentation and found Ciceronian rhetoric a more effective methodological guide. In his controversies in the last months of his life (1405–6), with Giovanni Dominici and with his erstwhile protégé, Poggio Bracciolini, Salutati upheld poetics and the liberal arts as the only legitimate features of ancient invention suitable for the Christian writer to borrow.[17]

*   *   *

Poggio, as a young man in controversy with his mentor, seems to have projected many of the same positions he later assumed in his invectives against Lorenzo Valla. An acerbic man of overpowering pessimism and even cynicism about his fellows, he was yet a pious Christian and an admirer of Thomas Aquinas. Although the scholastics might want to learn how to translate and write from the study of rhetoric, Poggio seems to have had no basic quarrel with their positions and to have assumed a general compatibility between Aristotelian and Stoic ethics and the ethics of Christianity. In all three he assumed an unenforceable morality of restriction. Petrarch and Salutati had emphatically argued the fundamental incompatibility of classical and Christian morals, as Valla would also do.[18]

Perhaps Leonardo Bruni—more explicit than Poggio, though less acute and radical—found it possible to reconcile even Epicurean with Stoic and Peripatetic ethics and advocate the classical texts of at least the last two as suitable for a Christian education and life. Though not uncritical of Epicurus elsewhere, in his *Isagogicon moralis disciplinae* and his *De studiis et litteris* he recognized that the differences in the Stoic and Aristotelian definitions of virtue could be transcended; he found that moderate Epicureanism stressed mental pleasure rather than physical and was thus close to the Peripatetics. A Christian should study Scripture and read the Latin Fathers, especially Lactantius, for a knowledge of religion, but for leading a moral life he exclusively advocates the study of the classical moralists, finding contemporary scholastic writing vulgar and confused. In refuting a "severe" critic who would forbid reading classical poets he replies: "But Plato and Aristotle read them; if you would put yourself above them in moral seriousness or the knowledge of things, I would not tolerate it. Do you think you perceive something that they did not see? 'I am a Christian,' he said. Did they live according to their own custom? as if indeed virtue and moral seriousness were not then the same as they are now."[19]

Leonardo Bruni's attitude toward scholasticism, which he studied himself as a young man, is best characterized by his translation of Aristotle's *Nicomachean Ethics*. He undertook this work to correct the lack of eloquence and mistranslation of words in the thirteenth-century scholastic translation made by Robert Grosseteste and revised by William of Moerbeke. He persisted in thinking that, because Cicero had said so, Aristotle had to be an elegant writer and that the scholastics, by ignoring eloquence, actually made their thinking incommunicable. There is little evidence that he rejected scholastic doctrine, essentially agreeing in his emphasis on Aristotle's ethics with the thirteenth-century moderate Aristotelians such as St. Thomas or Albertus Magnus. He was following the precedents of Petrarch and Salutati in condemning the so-called "sophistry" of the British scholastics, mocking the strange-sounding names Ferabrich, Bucer, Occam, Suisset.[20]

It is very probable that Valla had Bruni in mind in his refutation of Stoicism in *De vero bono*. In the first version, called *De voluptate*, the spokesman for Stoicism was Leonardo Bruni. Valla was equally critical of Stoic and Aristotelian ethics in this dialogue, and he linked Aristotle and Stoicism together, as Bruni had.

The fact that Poggio engaged in a polemic with Salutati over some of the same issues that came up later in his attack on Valla,[21] and that the nominal subject of the first polemic, the comparison of the greatness of Petrarch and Cicero, was also a central theme of Bruni's *Dialogi ad Petrum Paulum Istrum*, suggests the possibility of linking Salutati with Valla on one side and Bruni with Poggio on the other side of a basic split among the humanists over the relationship of ancient thought to that of the humanists' own epoch as well as to that of the scholastics. I would claim that Poggio and Bruni, together with various other humanists up to and including the sixteenth-century "Ciceronians," constituted a party of ancients, whereas Salutati and Valla, who argued for a development of culture in their own age beyond that of antiquity, were moderns.[22] One must immediately insert in this line of thinking, however, the qualifications that all humanists admired at least some of the ancients, that the thought of all of these figures retained strongly individual characteristics, that each developed and changed in the course of his career, and that there were basic inconsistencies in the positions of any of them.

*   *   *

It has been argued by Mario Fois in his comprehensive study of Lorenzo Valla's Christian thought in its historical context, that Bruni and Poggio were in some ways comparable to the scholastics he calls "integral Aristotelians," meaning figures such as Siger of Brabant and Boethius of Dacia who wished to study Aristotle autonomously and not strain to find a synthesis or an analogy of his ideas with Christian doctrine.[23] Lorenzo Valla, by contrast, believed that there had to be complete concordance between the Christian religion and the culture of his contemporaries. Christian thought, that is to say theology, should be based on St. Paul and on those Fathers (preeminently Jerome) who looked to the Scripture and carefully avoided introducing pagan classical philosophy into their theology. Salvatore Camporeale agrees with Fois's interpretation, and I concur in it as well.[24]

Valla has presented probably the greatest problem of interpretation of all the humanists because of a seeming paradox in his intellectual activity. He was the strictest and fiercest defender of Christianity as it could be established by careful philological analysis of Scripture, and he was the most advanced and skillful literary and linguistic scholar among the humanists prior to Angelo Poliziano. His textual emendations and his comprehension of textual meanings were so precise that it was assumed that he was a great admirer and advocate of classical culture. He was, as far as its technical linguistic skills and literary power were concerned; but he was not, as far as its ideas and values were concerned. In other words, possessing the advanced language skills of the generation of Poggio and Leonardo Bruni (the latter was Valla's Latin teacher and "emendator"), he carried these farther and introduced a new linguistic, semantic, and historical precision into them. At the same time, he reverted to, or rather continued the strong Christian commitment of Petrarch and Salutati, which carried with it strict limitations on aspects of ancient ideas and values that could be accepted or in some way amalgamated with the medieval Christian tradition. Bruni and Poggio, without yielding up their Christian faith, had instead detached their studies of the classics from Christianity and (especially Bruni) pursued them autonomously. It is this fact that gives some plausibility to Fois's suggested parallelism between their positions and the scholastic "integral Aristo-telians," actually meaning those who were once misnamed "Averro-ists." [25]

Valla took Petrarch's and Salutati's somewhat inconsistent stances with regard to Christianity and classical culture and brought them to a stricter and more defined conclusion. He regarded the broad acceptance of the ideas and values of classical texts—not just those of the ancient moralists but of classical literature generally—by his humanist contem-poraries as a malignant contamination of Christian thought. Even more radically, he came to consider the entire scholastic theological enterprise as a travesty and a great generator of heresy. He did not distinguish among the various phases of scholasticism, but condemned it all root and branch from Boethius on. Boethius was the thinker whom he regarded as the chief culprit in infiltrating Greek philosophy into Christian thought. He also believed that Augustine was not entirely innocent in this regard, though his theology was Neoplatonic, not Aristotelian, and Augustine was no scholastic. But Valla, despite his criticisms of Augus-tine, was also influenced by him more than he, and some modern schol-ars, would care to admit. Anselm, Abelard, and Thomas Aquinas were also guilty of this tendency to assimilate classical philosophy, as were the great figures of the thirteenth century and of the late scholastic age. Nonetheless, as Camporeale has shown, Valla's position was remarkably close to certain twelfth- and thirteenth-century critics of this trend,[26] and, I would suggest, to aspects of the Condemnations of 1277.

The consequence of this two-sided pattern of development, which emerged early in his career and continued to deepen over time, has been a drastic distortion of his views. Valla's perspective has seemed contra-dictory both to his contemporaries and to modern historians, and he has even been accused of advocating the most far-reaching revival of ancient pagan morality, specifically, vulgar Epicureanism, and of masking this daringly libidinous outlook by a pretended Christian piety. Charged with heresy by the Neapolitan Inquisition and by Poggio in his own time, he was fitted by modern scholars into the same category of "libertinism" that inspired Ernst Renan's notorious study of Averroists and Averroism.

Valla's first blow in what was actually a considered campaign si-multaneously to purge Christian culture of its pagan contaminations by both humanists and scholastics was his *Comparatio Ciceronis et Quin-tilianis,* a lost work written in 1428 when he was twenty-one. Campo-reale has attempted to reconstruct his positions from Valla's commentary on Quintilian's *Institutio oratoria.* What has emerged from his studies is the extraordinary extent to which Valla unearthed from Quintilian criti-cal historical, cultural, and linguistic insights of a more systematic nature than those which had been derived from Cicero. In his subsequent works, Valla transformed Quintilian's rhetoric into a historical-rhetorical vision of human culture that could be integrated into a new *theologia rhetorica*. The same philological, rhetorical, and historical methods were applied to reconstructing the foundations of Christianity by a return *ad fontes* and to understanding human culture by the empirical and analytic study of language and history.[27]

Valla's worst-interpreted work was his second one, first entitled *De voluptate,* then *De vero bono* and *De vero falsoque bono* through its three and possibly four redactions. The yearning of readers to find some sort of anticipation of modern personal liberties in Valla and to make of him a paradigm of Renaissance values has been so strong that the claim that his very vivid defenses of pleasure, bodily beauty, and sexual liberty, as well as a kind of absolute individualism, represented his authentic views and not those of his imagined Epicurean still persists. Perhaps there is some justification for this contention because Valla was far more perturbed by Stoic and Peripatetic moralism posing as Christian piety than he was by simple sensuality. But truth for Valla was based on revelation, clarified by the precise determination of the content of the divine Word in Scripture and reinforced by experience. The Creation, the Fall, the Advent, the Incarnation, and the Atonement were literal occurrences brought about by divine will and not to be doubted. The pagan classical world and its culture was the product of a time of forgetting of the truths revealed to Adam at his creation; the spiritual ignorance of the pagan world followed upon the Fall and lasted until the Advent. Since men could not then understand that salvation and beatitude were to become open to them, they responded to the impulses of their impaired nature. They pursued the gratifications available to them in this life, which was to Valla more admirable than the attempt to erect false gods and to pretend that happiness could come from virtuous activity of the soul, as Aristotle and the Stoics proclaimed. His depiction of the pursuit of virtue and the pursuit of pleasure in the classical culture of pre-Christian times reveals, to my mind, a profound insight concerning the nature of ancient *paideia* in both its material and its spiritual aspects.[28]

How could mankind transcend or escape from its entrapment in the Christless, worldly culture of antiquity, which survived into his own time? Only by scrapping the false values embedded in ancient philosophy and now so intertwined with modern Christian theology. Moreover, those false values were embodied in the historic transformation of the church itself into a new imperial body at the time of Constantine and Sylvester and reinforced by the infamous forged Donation. Popes should return to their true role as the heirs of St. Peter and the vicars of Christ rather than imperial temporal rulers. Theologians should study and expound Scripture.[29]

Christians should use the only legitimate part of the heritage to the Christian world from antiquity, the invention of the arts, meaning not only the literary and language arts of the *studia humanitatis* and the mathematical arts of the quadrivium, but also the arts of music, painting, sculpture, and architecture. Thus the famous preface to the fourth book of his *Elegantiae,* from which I shall quote three excerpts illustrating this point:[30]

> I do not wish to make a comparison of philosophy and eloquence at this point, showing which is more able to do harm. Many have spoken on this subject, showing that philosophy hardly accords with the Christian religion and that all heresies have been derived from philosophical sources. Rhetoric, by contrast, has nothing that is not laudable, so that as you invent and dispose you give bones and nerves to speech, as you ornament you introduce flesh and color, and finally, as you commit to memory and pronounce properly, you contribute spirit and action. Do I believe that it can harm anyone, except him who neglects the other matters, and especially true wisdom and the virtues, as Jerome did? Do I think this art will ever do something harmful? Certainly no more than painting, sculpting, engraving, and (as I speak of the liberal arts) music. And if from those who sing well, paint well, sculpt well, and from the other arts also, much service and beauty can be added to holy things, so that they almost seem born for this purpose, certainly much more is gained from the eloquent.
>
> Who was more eloquent than Jerome? Who more practiced in oratory? Although he often wished to conceal it, he was most solicitous, most studious, most experienced in speaking well. . . . For after he had nourished his tender years with the most salubrious food of holy Scripture and made his own the powers of that once despised knowledge, now placed beyond danger, he returned to the reading of the Gentiles, both because he wished now to acquire eloquence and in order that by approving their good sayings he might condemn their bad. All the other Fathers did the same, both the Latin and the Greek: Hilary, Ambrose, Augustine, Lactantius, Basil, Gregory [Nazianzus], Chrysostom, and many others who in every age dressed those precious gems of the divine Word in the gold and silver of eloquence. And indeed in my view, if anyone approaches the task of writing in theology, it matters little whether he

brings any other ability to it or not, for almost nothing else contributes. But he who is ignorant of eloquence I consider entirely
unworthy of speaking concerning theology.

Not the languages of the Gentiles, not grammar, not rhetoric, not
dialectic and their other arts are to be condemned, since the
Apostles wrote in Greek, but the dogmas, the religions, the false
beliefs concerning the effects of the virtues through which we ascend to heaven. Moreover, these other arts and sciences are placed
in a neutral position where they can be used well or badly. Therefore, I pray, let us strive to reach, or at least come close, to the
point to which those luminaries of our religion arrived.

Salvatore Camporeale has given a beautifully insightful analysis of
this preface in his *Lorenzo Valla, Between the Middle Ages and the Renaissance: The Encomium of St. Thomas Aquinas.*[31] As he points out,
Valla, in his praise of Thomas's saintliness, places his theology lower in
the scale of value than any of the Fathers named above, and indeed,
names the same ones. He would place Aquinas at about the same level
as the late Greek Father John Damascenus.[32] Camporeale compares
Thomas's argument for the compatibility of classical philosophy in his
Expositio super librum Boethii De Trinitate with Valla's conception of
the value of the arts, especially rhetoric, as a base for Christian theology.
In the first case the argument is that human reason can arrive at the
probability of certain positions that are compatible with Christian doctrine. The truths of revelation are absolute and unquestionable, while the
comparable truths of reason are merely similitudinous and hypothetical.
Nevertheless they have value.[33] Against this claim Valla argues in the
Encomium, in the preface to his *De libero arbitrio,* as well as in the
passage cited above, the incompatibility of philosophy and theology.
Camporeale shows the extent to which Valla follows Quintilian in reducing philosophy to rhetoric, especially *Institutio oratoria* book 12, chapter
2, which Valla extensively glossed. Quintilian said:

I would wish that a certain Roman whom I am teaching to be a
wise man would show himself to be a truly civil man, not by secret
disputations but by experiencing and acting upon matters. . . . The
life of the orator should be conjoined with the knowledge of divine
and human matters. . . . Oh may that time come when some orator, as perfect as we would wish him, will vindicate that proud art
[of the philosophers] to himself . . . and bring it back once again
into the body of eloquence.

Of the three branches of philosophy Quintilian recognized, the last or "rational" philosophy deals entirely with words and is fully part of rhetoric. Valla agreed and carried out this ideal in his *Dialectica,* a handbook of logic as subsumed under rhetoric. The moral branch of philosophy, Quintilian said, "is entirely suitable (*accommodata*) to the orator." Finally, "the natural branch [of philosophy], since it is as much richer for the practice of speaking as it is stronger in spirit in divine and human affairs, ought to be part of eloquence." For Valla, as Camporeale shows, natural philosophy would be reduced to experimental science and moral philosophy to moral practice. Ethics thus becomes the prevailing customs of any culture. The relationship of words and things, which involves dialectic—though it is very comprehensive in Valla's view—is totally managed within the theoretical and practical understandings of rhetoric.[34]

Valla's *Repastinatio philosophiae et dialecticae* has recently appeared in a definitive edition by Gianni Zippel.[35] It is in this work that his thought may be seen both to oppose and to parallel that of scholastic philosophy in its three medieval branches of theology, dialectic, and natural philosophy. The second and third books deal with dialectic in a way that Valla thought would be a useful guide for the rhetorician. Alan Perreiah recently argued that Valla's logic was that of the pre-fourteenth century, the *logica vetus,* and that he does not deal with the greatly expanded *logica nova* of Peter of Spain, Paul of Venice, and others.[36] There is, however, no doubt that Valla was aware of these writers and this development, for he mentioned them by name along with Albertus Magnus, Albert of Saxony, Ralph Strode, and William of Ockham in a letter to Giovanni Serra (*Epistolae* 13).[37] Zippel indexes these and other authors where there is a parallel statement in Valla's text. I would agree with John Monfasani's judgment concerning Perreiah's observation that the complications of late medieval logic seemed irrelevant to Valla, whose purpose was to criticize and restructure only those parts which he wished to incorporate as a part of rhetorical invention, namely *confirmatio* and *confutatio,* which he could find in the older logic.[38]

However, it is book 1 of the *Dialectica* that is of greater interest for this discussion. First of all, Valla attempted to simplify and undermine Aristotelian metaphysics, reducing essence and being to *res,* and Aristotle's ten predicaments to three: substance, quality, and action. All three would be in some way present in any *res.* Moreover, quality and action were observable and therefore namable and discussable, whereas substance was only the abstract underlying assumption that the *res* existed. The similarity of this position to Ockham's has been noted, but I would again agree with Monfasani that Valla, even though he probably knew of it in Ockham, something that cannot be documented, was capable of arriving at it on his own.[39] It is in the first redaction of book 1 that he made two assertions concerning the Trinity which he removed or modified in his later two redactions. He sees the Trinity as a single *res*, which has the three qualities associated by Augustine with the three members: memory or power in the Father, intellect in the Son, and love or will in the Spirit. In his *Elegantiae* Valla had discussed the term *persona*, which the Latins used and which he preferred to the Greek *hypostasis*. It was usage, according to Valla, that should determine meaning. From an analysis of the Gospel account of the baptism of Christ, and from paintings, he draws the conclusion that the Spirit proceeds from the Son and not from the Father and the Son. Valla's solution of the *Filioque* question, which was being settled in the opposite way at the Council of Ferrara–Florence, probably contemporaneously with Valla's composition of this passage, proved to be unorthodox. Let me quote, however, what he said on "person": "Indeed *person* in God, which is translated from the person of man, I distinguish from substance better than the philosophers, so I call it quality, no less properly, as I believe, than those who call the three persons three natures or three substances. Not that I say that Father and Son and Holy Spirit are solely qualities, but that they are distinguished from each other by quality."[40]

Regardless of the question of orthodoxy, the passage illustrates his method of taking verbal usage, whether in texts or in conversation, as the literal criterion of reality, and of his defining reality as meaning. Since language differs from culture to culture and over time, as he frequently argued, meaning is both probabilistic and ethnocentric. Victoria Kahn, in a recent and brilliant article, attempts to resolve the paradox of Valla's criticism of scholastic dialectical and metaphysical theology by arguing that it rests on probability and the imposition of relativistic points of view on absolute truth. It is in his *Dialogue on Free Will* that, as she argues, he puts forth his solution. *Suadere* and *persuadere* mean *facere fidem*, rhetoric as the willed act to produce the willed assent of faith in the reader or listener. Will is seen as the motivator of actions in place of the scholastic dialectic of necessity and contingency, in the case both of divine will and grace and of human free choice and action. Moreover, will is separated from cognition or understanding, which will always be relative and probabilistic. As Kahn shows, Valla turns from the lengthy dialectical discourse concerning divine foreknowledge and human volition which ends in a dilemma to an exhortation of faith based on St. Paul: "We do not know the cause of this matter [divine will]. Of what consequence is it? We stand by faith and not by the probability of reason."[41] Thus Valla, while he argues that rhetoric is more useful than metaphysics and dialectic in persuading of the truth of divine matters, holds that, like Thomas's analogies, rhetoric, too, is a similitude, and in the end only charity brings forth faith in the revealed truths of Scripture. A person must pass from Augustine's realm of the useful to the realm of love, joy, and beatitude, as Valla first argued in *De vero bono*. Virtue is a matter of the will or the affect, not of prudence and reason.[42]

Yet the reason of rhetoric and philology must enter into the understanding of Scripture, and Valla's *Collatio Novi Testamenti*, and even more his revised *Adnotationes in Novum Testamentum*, showed the way of the new theology to Erasmus and others. But in the end, however purged and precise our knowledge of Scripture becomes, it is our faith that sustains our understanding. As Camporeale, Kahn, and I have argued, Valla believed that human free will itself must be accepted as an act of faith corresponding to our experience, and that freedom of the will is not contradicted by divine predestination, a position that may be believed in, not understood. So Erasmus also believed and argued, though he did not understand Valla as believing it. Neither did Luther, who also wrongly agreed that Valla did not believe in freedom of the will, and who agreed with what he wrongly thought Valla believed.

Thus I may, not surprisingly, conclude that at least that one current of Italian humanism which sought to engage in theologizing—that of Petrarch, Salutati, and Valla—arrived at its destination in the biblical scholarship and theologizing of Erasmus. And, as we should be aware, it probably ended there.

*   *   *

But there is another aspect of this humanistic move toward the deployment of the arts in the service of the holy: the vision that human consciousness and invention are at work in the realm of man's religious beliefs and activities, as in all other fields of human endeavor. Man cannot know God except in the inspired utterances and projections of the humanly inscribed Scriptures, and they are also, like a ritual, a shaping and a construction of man's knowledge or man's sense of the presence or shape of his God. If we cannot know how man beatified enters into his heavenly reward, says Valla, let us imagine it:

> What more could God have promised us than that we shall be given in this life whatever good things we wish for, if only we ask for them? And in the future life more than we dare to ask, more than we are capable of thinking, will be reserved for us. . . . If, then, the happiness that is promised us is greater than the mind can conceive and is of such a kind that it cannot fall under the powers of the intellect, it will be in vain that it is attempted to picture

it. . . . Nevertheless it will be worthwhile for us to attempt to imagine it. . . . For what is it then that keeps us from seeking divine
things except that through a desperate and pestiferous hardness we
do not believe what we have not seen? And hence when we do not
believe what is preached concerning the future kingdom, we do not
seek that which we consider false. . . . Instead of imitating such
men, we ought to make them imitators of us, attempting to in-
struct them in certain pleasant ways in the faith they lack. For if
we place before them by a certain imagination these things that do
not fall before our eyes, will we not supply a certain great strengthening of faith and a kind of surety and what is similar to a mira-
cle? Although faith would be a certain vacuum if indeed we saw
the things that are promised, it nevertheless thus acquires the greatest powers if we see the very things that are promised. I will attempt, therefore, as I have promised, to give what I am accustomed
to turn over in my mind an imagined existence.

Whereupon Valla draws his account of the triumphant entrance of the
soul into heaven and its gracious welcome by the Savior, Jesus Christ.[43]

In this statement we find the humanist rationale both for the religious works of art that depict by invention and convention the world of
intertwined human and divine destiny and for the invented dramatic en-
actment of the relationship of the human and the divine through the
sacraments and rituals and festival dramas of Renaissance Christianity.

The world of religion, declares Valla, is invented and depicted by
man, not because it is not there, for the transcendent conviction of our
faith asserts that it is, but because we cannot know it except propheti-
cally and allegorically. And the attempt to demonstrate its presence and
nature by the organon or logical instruments of philosophy is sheer folly,
not wisdom. Therefore, it is the conjectural arts of persuasion and imitation—linguistic, visual, auditory, dramatic—that are our true instruments for instructing and deepening our faith.

How these arts may be seen to work, as Valla argued it, is to be
found in his beautiful *Sermon on the Mystery of the Eucharist:*

O ineffable, not only mystery, but gift given to mortals, for although we are equal with the angels in that we and they possess
Jesus Christ, yet in this way we ought to be considered superior,
because out of our own mouth, which is not permitted to angels,
this sacrament and mystery is wrought. . . . He is truly called
Emanuel, God with us, because he is more with us than with the
angels. Nor only from this fact, namely, that he is more similar to

us than to the angels, but from another it may also be known,
which God reveals to pious and not disbelieving minds, that just as
he transforms that bread, so he transforms us in the day of judgment into God.[44]

Finally let us recall that in the first, philosophical book of his *Repastinatio philosophiae et dialecticae,* in its earliest redaction, Valla likens God
and man to the light and heat and radiation of the sun in analogy to the
Holy Trinity and the trinity of the human soul. But man operates on his
external world as God does in his creation.

And to stay with the same comparison, just as a flame seizes and
devours and renders into ashes the material by which it is fed, so
the soul is nourished in learning and hides what it perceives within
itself and transfigures it in its own heat and light, so that it paints
others rather than being painted by them. And as the sun paints its
image in polished and smooth things and does not receive their images in itself, so the soul, advancing into exterior things by its own
light, projects and depicts a certain image of its memory, intellect,
and will.[45]

So not only the world of the divine but also the external world of nature
and man are continually being reinvented and redepicted by the active,
creative mind and imagination of man himself. And man operates in this
fashion because he has been created in the image and likeness of God,
who is thus invented and depicted by holy men themselves.

NOTES

On the relation of humanism and Christian thought in general the following are
particularly relevant: C. Angelieri, *Il problema religiosa del Rinascimento* (Florence, 1952); A. Birkenmaier, "Der Streit des Alonso von Cartagena mit Leonardo Bruni Aretino," *Beiträge zur Geschichte der Philosophie des Mittelalters*
20.5 (Münster, 1922): 129–210; W. J. Bouwsma, "The Two Faces of Humanism: Stoicism and Augustinianism," *Itinerarium Italicum: The Profile of the Italian Renaissance in the Mirror of Its European Transformations,* ed. H. A.
Oberman and T. A. Brady, Jr. (Leiden, 1975), 3–60; Q. Breen, *Christianity and
Humanism: Studies in the History of Ideas,* ed. N. P. Ross (Grand Rapids, MI,
1968); A. Buck, "Das Problem des christlichen Humanismus in der italienischen
Renaissance," in *Sodalitas Erasmiana* (Naples, 1949), 181–92; S. I. Camporeale,
O.P., *L. Valla, umanesimo e teologia* (Florence, 1972); idem, *Da Lorenzo Valla
a Tommaso Moro: Lo statuto umanistico della teologia* (Pistoia, 1973), also in

Memorie Domenicane n.s. 4 (1973): 9–105; idem, *L. Valla, tra Medioevo e Rinascimento, Encomium sancti Thomae—1457* (Pistoia, 1977), also in *Memorie Domenicane* n.s. 7 (1976): 3–190; P. Courcelle, "Pétrarque entre Saint Augustin et les Augustins du XIVᵉ siècle," *Studi petrarcheschi* 7 (1961): 51–71; J. F. D'Amico, *Renaissance Humanism in Papal Rome: Humanists and Churchmen on the Eve of the Reformation* (Baltimore, 1983); M. Fois, S.J., *Il pensiero cristiano di Lorenzo Valla nel quadro storico-culturale del suo ambiente* (Rome, 1969); E. Garin, "Problemi di religione e filosofi nella cultura fiorentina del Quattrocento," in his *La cultura filosofica del Rinascimento italiano* (Florence, 1961), 127–42; idem, "Desideri di riforma nell'oratoria del Quattrocento," ibid., 166–82; idem, "Dialettica e retorica dal XII al XVI secolo," in his *L'età nuova: Ricerche di storia della cultura dal XII al XVI secolo* (Naples, 1969), 43–79; idem, "Il francescanesimo e le origini del Rinascimento," ibid., 113–36; idem, "La cultura fiorentina nella seconda metà del Trecento e i 'barbari Britanni,'" ibid., 139–77; idem, "Dante nel Rinascimento," ibid., 179–213; P. O. Kristeller, "Augustine and the Early Renaissance," *Studies in Renaissance Thought and Letters*, 2 vols. (Rome, 1956–85), 1:355–72; idem, "Humanism and Scholasticism in the Renaissance," ibid., 553–83, also in *Renaissance Thought and Its Sources*, ed. M. Mooney (New York, 1979), 85–105; idem, "Renaissance Philosophy and the Medieval Tradition," ibid., 106–33; idem, *Medieval Aspects of Renaissance Learning*, ed. E. P. Mahoney (Durham, NC, 1974); U. Mariani, *Il Petrarca e gli Agostiniani* (Rome, 1946); R. McKeon, "Renaissance and Method in Philosophy," in *Studies in the History of Ideas* (New York, 1935), 3:37–114; H. A. Oberman, "Some Notes on the Theology of Nominalism with Attention to Its Relation to the Renaissance," *Harvard Theological Review* 53 (1960): 47–76; J. W. O'Malley, S.J., *Praise and Blame in Renaissance Rome* (Durham, NC, 1979); idem, *Rome and the Renaissance: Studies in Culture and Religion* (London, 1981); B. Smalley, *English Friars and Antiquity in the Early Fourteenth Century* (Oxford, 1960); C. L. Stinger, *Humanism and the Church Fathers: Ambrogio Traversari (1386–1439) and Christian Antiquity in the Renaissance* (Albany, NY, 1976); idem, *The Renaissance in Rome: Ideology and Culture in the City of the Popes, 1443–1527* (Bloomington, IN, 1985); C. Trinkaus, *In Our Image and Likeness: Humanity and Divinity in Italian Humanist Thought*, 2 vols. (London and Chicago, 1970), esp. part 1: "Human Existence and Divine Providence in Early Humanist Moral Theology"; idem, *The Poet as Philosopher: Petrarch and the Formation of Renaissance Consciousness* (New Haven, 1979); idem, *The Scope of Renaissance Humanism* (Ann Arbor, MI, 1983); *The Pursuit of Holiness in Late Medieval and Renaissance Religion*, ed. C. Trinkaus and H. A. Oberman (Leiden, 1974); B. L. Ullman, *The Humanism of Coluccio Salutati* (Padua, 1963); D. Weinstein, *Savonarola and Florence: Prophecy and Patriotism in the Renaissance* (Princeton, 1970); R. G. Witt, *Hercules at the Crossroads: The Life, Works, and Thought of Coluccio Salutati* (Durham, NC, 1983). See Chapter 32 in this volume, "Humanism and History."

1. See G. Billanovich, "Petrarch and the Textual Tradition of Livy," *Journal of*

the *Warburg and Courtauld Institutes* 14 (1951): 137–208. See Chapter 28 in this volume, "Quattrocento Humanism and Classical Scholarship."

2. E. Cochrane, *Historians and Historiography in the Italian Renaissance* (Chicago, 1981).

3. E. Panofsky, *Renaissance and Renascences in Western Art* (Stockholm, 1960; New York, 1969).

4. H. Baron, *The Crisis of the Early Italian Renaissance*, 2 vols. in 1 (Princeton, rev. ed. 1966); J. G. A. Pocock, *The Machiavellian Moment: Florentine Political Thought and the Atlantic Republican Tradition* (Princeton, 1975); Q. Skinner, *Foundations of Modern Political Thought*, vol. 1, *The Renaissance* (Cambridge, 1978). See Chapter 7 in these volumes, "The Significance of 'Civic Humanism' in the Interpretation of the Italian Renaissance."

5. See Trinkaus, *Poet as Philosopher*, chap. 3: "Petrarch's Critique of Self and Society."

6. Ibid., chap. 4: "*Theologia Poetica* and *Theologia Rhetorica* in Petrarch's *Invectives*." See also K. Heitmann, *Fortuna und Virtus: Eine Studie zu Petrarcas Lebensweisheit* (Cologne, 1958).

7. See Trinkaus, *In Our Image and Likeness*, 43, 46 and chap. 1 ("Petrarch: Man Between Despair and Grace") generally.

8. T. M. Greene, *The Light in Troy: Imitation and Discovery in Renaissance Poetry* (New Haven and London, 1982), chap. 5 ("Petrarch and the Humanist Hermeneutic").

9. *In Our Image and Likeness*, chap. 1. N. Gilbert has pointed to evidence in *De ignorantia* that Petrarch had read commentaries on the *Ethics*.

10. See *In Our Image and Likeness*, chap. 2, where I emphasize Salutati's efforts to deal explicitly with contemporary scholastic issues from a humanist perspective. See also Garin, "La cultura fiorentina nella seconda metà del Trecento," 141–66, and especially the appendix: "A proposito di Coluccio Salutati," 167–77.

11. Ullman, *Humanism of Coluccio Salutati;* Witt, *Hercules at the Crossroads*.

12. Coluccio Salutati, *De nobilitate legum et medicine*, ed. E. Garin (Florence, 1947); idem, *De fato, fortuna et casu*, ed. C. Bianca (Florence, 1985).

13. *In Our Image and Likeness*, 64–65 and passim.

14. Ibid., 76–97.

15. On these parallels, see ibid.; Ullman, *Humanism of Coluccio Salutati*, on Scotus, 139, 204; on Giles (Aegidius), 182, 183, 204, 207, 265; Witt, *Hercules at the Crossroads*, on Scotus, 316–28, 345.

16. Witt, *Hercules at the Crossroads*, 424.

17. *Epistolario di Coluccio Salutati*, ed. F. Novati, 5 vols. (Rome, 1891–1911), 4:137–38, 215–16.

18. For this interpretation of Poggio, see *In Our Image and Likeness*, 258–70. On Poggio and Thomas, see Camporeale, *L. Valla tra Medioevo e Rinascimento*, 6–7.

19. *Leonardo Bruni Aretino. Humanistisch-philosophische Schriften mit einer Chronologie seiner Werke und Briefe*, ed. H. Baron (Leipzig and Berlin, 1928; reprinted Wiesbaden, 1969), 18: "At Plato et Aristoteles legebant!

quibus si te aut gravitate morum aut intelligentia rerum anteponis, nullo modo feram. An tu te aliquid discernere putas, quod illi non viderint? 'Christianus—inquit—sum.' At illi forsan suo more vixerunt? Quasi vero honestas gravitasque morum non tunc eadem fuerit, quae nunc est!"

20. Baron notes an agreement and a disagreement with Thomas in Bruni's interpretation of Aristotle in his *Isagogicon moralis disciplinae,* ed. Baron, 36f. and 40. Bruni's mockery of the "sophists" is the well-known passage in his *Dialogus ad Petrum Paulum Histrum,* in *Prosatori latini del Quattrocento,* ed. E. Garin (Milan, 1952), 58.

21. *Epistolario,* 4:126–45, 158–70.

22. I have developed this thesis in "Humanistic Dissidence: Florence vs. Milan, or Poggio vs. Valla," forthcoming in the *Acta* of the Villa I Tatti Conferences on Milan and Florence. See also idem, "*Antiquitas* versus *Modernitas*: An Italian Humanist Polemic and Its Resonance," *Journal of the History of Ideas* 48 (1987): 11–21.

23. See Fois, *Il pensiero cristiano,* 19–20, 128, where he makes this comparison; 49–62 for his discussion of "Aristotelismo integralista."

24. Fois's judgment is best stated in his concluding chapter, "Una spiritualità di Lorenzo Valla?" 622–40, esp. 625, 630. See Camporeale in *L. Valla tra Medioevo e Rinascimento,* 38–40, 44–48.

25. See note 23, above.

26. Camporeale, *L. Valla tra Medioevo e Rinascimento,* 59–61, names Peter Damian, Bernard of Clairvaux, the Victorines, and especially Jean de Saint-Gilles and Eudes de Châteauroux, who said theologians "seipsos vendunt filiis Grecorum, id est philosophis." See also ibid., 77–79.

27. Camporeale, ibid., 40–44.

28. *In Our Image and Likeness,* 105–50.

29. See Lorenzo Valla, *The Treatise of Lorenzo Valla on the Donation of Constantine,* ed. and trans. C. B. Coleman (New Haven, 1922; reprinted New York, 1971), 182.

30. *Prosatori latini del Quattrocento,* ed. Garin, 616–22; my translation.

31. Camporeale, *L. Valla tra Medioevo e rinascimento,* 102–13.

32. Ibid., 38–54.

33. Ibid., 61–79.

34. Ibid., 40–44; see also 113–16.

35. Lorenzo Valla, *Repastinatio dialectice et philosophie,* ed. G. Zippel, 2 vols. (Padua, 1982). The important first redaction is in vol. 2, also the indexes.

36. A Perreiah, "Humanistic Critiques of Scholastic Dialectic," *Sixteenth-Century Journal* 13 (1982): 3–22.

37. Lorenzo Valla, *Epistole,* ed. O. Besomi and M. Regoliosi (Padua, 1984), 201.

38. J. Monfasani, review of *Laurentii Valle Repastinatio dialectice et philosophie,* ed. Zippel, in *Rivista di letteratura italiana* 2 (1984): 177–94 at 192–93.

39. Ibid., 191.

40. *In Our Image and Likeness,* 155, 382.

41. V. Kahn, "The Rhetoric of Faith and the Use of Usage in Lorenzo Valla's *De libero arbitrio,*" *Journal of Medieval and Renaissance Studies* 13 (1983): 91–109.

42. *In Our Image and Likeness,* 126–43, 156–62.

43. Ibid., 143–45, 378–79, from *De vero falsoque bono,* now in the translation of that work by M. Lorch and A. K. Hieatt (New York, 1977), 285–89. Translations are mine, with comparisons to Lorch and Hieatt.

44. *In Our Image and Likeness,* 633–38, 838–40; my translation.

45. Ibid., 154–56, 164, 386–87; my translation.

36 &· HUMANISM AND PRE-REFORMATION THEOLOGY
John F. D'Amico

T
HE RELATION BETWEEN RENAISSANCE HUMANISTS AND CHRISTIAN theology was an indirect one.[1] Humanists need not have dealt with the theological problems of their day in any extended way. Since humanism was a literary-pedagogical movement based on the recovery of ancient culture, it would have been possible and valid for humanists to have avoided theological matters and most aspects of religious thought by defining their studies in a narrow fashion. It could have been accomplished by emphasizing philology and pedagogy to the exclusion of any religious overtones in their teachings. Almost from the outset, however, Renaissance humanists dealt to a greater or lesser extent and selectively with important theological topics in a manner that complemented the literary foundations of humanism. When dealing with religious and theological material, the humanists first had to defend their right to discuss those matters which had been monopolized by the professional theologians and the members of the religious orders, and then to show that their recourse to antique models in no manner compromised the religious sincerity of their undertaking or the orthodoxy of their teachings.

Once some humanists had determined to deal with theological questions, they had to find a bridge that could unite their literary and philosophical interests to standard theology. That bridge was moral philosophy.[2] The humanists interpreted moral philosophy in a manner that could be easily assimilated into their literary rhetorical culture. The ideal of the ancient orator who expressed his *humanitas* with eloquence provided the humanists with a model to use in aiding fellow citizens to live a moral life without withdrawing from the world. But to offer moral advice required a clear understanding of society's religious and theological ideals. Humanists as moral counselors to the urban laity of communal Italy expanded their area of concern to criticize the professional theology of the later Middle Ages for not addressing the realities of this Italian world. On a more positive note, they had to move to a general redefinition of those elements which were most valid for the Christian learned in ancient culture and inhabiting an urban environment filled with temptations.

Humanists dealt with theology as part of the cultural world they wished to reform according to the precepts abstracted from their study of antiquity. Theology, as a component of moral philosophy, had to be brought into conformity with humanist ideals generally. This process required a reassessment of the medieval theology developed by the monks and the mendicant friars, which served a clerical environment. The critical issue was not to propose new doctrines but rather to alter the attitudes and deeds of men. Humanists meant to change attitudes and affect action. Consequently, we should not expect to find in humanist theological thought a complete dogmatic exposition; rather we find on the one hand a critique of method—language, logic, and presentation—and on the other hand an emphasis on those topics with theological features that relate directly to moral action but did not receive any extended treatment from the professional theologians. When humanists did discuss standard theological questions, such as free will, they did so with little concern for the dogmatic ideas developed in the Middle Ages.

Two terms popularized by Charles Trinkaus provide a basic orientation for appreciating humanist thought and its various emphases. They are *theologia rhetorica* or rhetorical theology and anthropological theology. Both refer to the particular humanistic quality in Renaissance religious thought. *Theologia rhetorica* is the presentation of theological concepts in an eloquent fashion so as to move the will of the hearer or reader to embrace them more fully and easily.[3] It is, therefore, a clear development from the principles of ancient rhetoric. Rhetorical theology displays the full blending of theology with humanistic educational principles. The second term, anthropological theology, refers to the humanists' "concern with God and religion [which] was inseparable from their concern with man in his other-worldly destiny and his this-worldly condition."[4] In sum, humanists balanced the principles laid down for securing salvation with the difficulties they realized people experienced on Earth living with their families and in society. Humanists understood the tensions implicit for any Christian who maintained an active life in the world, and they formed their theological ideas to meet this dilemma. Humanists, even when they were clerics, did not write for professional theologians or for monks insulated from the daily tribulations of secular life. Their audiences consisted of men who had to strive for salvation among the competing demands of merchant, political, and professional life where temptations could not be avoided and where moral pressures were constant. The ideal of St. Francis of Assisi—giving all to the poor and serving only God—clashed with the need of a man to feed his family and serve his state. The Franciscan ideal was not rejected, but it could not be accepted unchanged as a valid model for men with familial and civic responsibilities.[5]

Related to these themes was the humanists' search for a pure Latin style, which affected the way they expressed their theology.[6] Since they were not professional theologians with university degrees, the humanists wished to purge theology of the corrupt Latin and neologisms that had become standard in late medieval scholasticism, with its heavy dependence on inelegant translations of Greek Aristotelian philosophy. On occasion the humanist concern for proper Latinity led to excesses. Some writers transposed Christian ideas and terms into classical approximations; they referred to God the Father as Jupiter, to heaven as Olympus, to the saints as heroes and gods. Such procedures were merely a device to bring theology into conformity with humanist classical values and not a rejection or belittling of Christianity. The better the Latin, the humanists argued, the more appealing the message itself became, especially to those Christians who lacked training in professional theology.

Humanists were equally dissatisfied with the strong reliance on metaphysics in contemporary theology. Humanists saw little value in theologians speculating on the invisible world of theoretical constructs when they should be urging men to do good and avoid evil. While few humanists were capable of providing a thorough critique of the metaphysical basis of scholasticism, they generally subscribed to the intentions of such criticisms. Metaphysics, argued the humanists, was not only useless to men in their real condition of life but also destructive of a true understanding of Christian teachings. (These criticisms extended to other elements of medieval philosophy, such as Averroistic natural philosophy, which ignored moral philosophy and taught determinism.)[7]

One other term should be considered before turning to a fuller consideration of humanist theology. It is traditional to use the term "Christian humanism" to designate those humanists who directed their work to theological and biblical questions, and especially to use the term in reference to Erasmus and his *philosophia Christi* and to those humanists who were influenced by him and accepted his lead both in criticizing the medieval church and its practices and in offering a new moral philosophy based on a humanist reading of Christian sources.[8] The term, however, is problematic and is too easily contrasted to a "pagan" or "non-Christian" humanism, which does a disservice to the humanists and confuses modern historiography.[9] The idea that there was a "Christian" as opposed to a "pagan" humanism is anachronistic, and any term that continues this dichotomy should be used with great caution. The essential task is to determine how humanists actively joined their study of

Christian theology and history with their major emphasis on the recovery of classical values. Not all humanists did, but they were nevertheless humanists. Further, not all writers who utilized humanist elements in their theology (such as humanist rhetorical principles) were humanists. One must be careful not to use the term "Christian humanism" in such a way as to make divisions where they did not exist.

By whatever term we wish to designate it, there was a definite strain of Renaissance humanism that actively sought to discuss both traditional and new theological questions. Such interest in theology naturally risked opposition from the professional theologians and conservative churchmen. But humanist theology, as will be seen, was not simply a rejection of perceived excesses of scholastic theology. Humanism was able to find within its recovery of the ancient past, especially rhetoric, the means to present its own particular view of Christian thought, and this theology grew throughout the fifteenth century, ending only with the twin blows of the Reformation and the Counter-Reformation.

*   *   *

As in most matters relating to the development of Renaissance humanism, Petrarch early set the standard.[10] He was torn on the one hand between the literary attractions of the ancient writers—above all Cicero—and their cultural ideals, and on the other religious anxiety, which he felt from living in a world in which moral action seemed to be so difficult and religious justification beyond human attainment. In his concern for the literary and moral values of the ancient Latin writers, Petrarch found the Latin used by the scholastic theologians unacceptable and the questions they discussed useless. He saw in scholasticism generally a concern for topics with no practical significance, and which, instead of helping man to live a moral life in a world beset by temptations, could distract a Christian from the Christian message.[11]

Petrarch found the answer to the criticisms he had directed against contemporary theology in his study of the early church fathers, above all in his reading of Augustine of Hippo.[12] Petrarch's Augustine was a very different character from the medieval theologian. The medieval Augustine was the great dogmatic theologian. But Petrarch saw in Augustine a man who had suffered from the same moral dilemmas he experienced; both had tried to deal with them through increased study and knowledge, and had come to realize the fatuousness of such an enterprise. This psychological sensitivity on Augustine's part made him Petrarch's perfect classical-Christian model.

Like Augustine, Petrarch had come close to despairing of acting morally and achieving salvation. The search through competing philosophical schools did not supply either with the answers they required. In order to deal with this frustration Petrarch rejected the scholastics' emphasis on the distinction between God's power and mercy and advocated a modified fideism. Faith seemed to offer the only way to unburden the Christian from the sense of sin and its punishment. Above all, Petrarch used the Augustinian idea of voluntarism in opposition to the intellectualism that had characterized much of medieval scholasticism. He agreed with Augustine that the will was the source of both the motivation to act morally and the psychological weakness that prevented a man from doing good. To move the will was, therefore, more important than to inform the intellect. Only the will can lead a man to preparation, and only the will can offer the most secure means of achieving salvation. Faith is dependent on the will and not on the intellect. Grace, which is necessary for salvation, comes as a result not of knowledge but of faith. This emphasis on the will brings to the fore the question of the relation between Petrarch's humanism and the late medieval scholastic theology of nominalism.[13]

Charles Trinkaus, following the lead of such historians of late medieval scholasticism as Heiko Oberman, has noted the similarity between humanism and nominalism on the question of the will and the problems in theology and psychology resulting from it.[14] Trinkaus has emphasized that voluntarism was a natural part of humanist rhetoric, since it was the will that the orator sought to influence. The affective qualities of humanism could only be successful when they moved the will. Voluntarism was a natural complement to the revived rhetoric that marked humanism.

Voluntarism also marked the nominalist theology of the fourteenth and fifteenth centuries, especially as represented in the work of William of Ockham.[15] In part this nominalism was a function of new epistemological doctrines, partly the continuance of the Augustinian tradition and, finally, partly a reaction to the Aristotelian-intellectualist thought of the Thomists, though not necessarily directed against Aquinas personally. Nominalist theologians despaired of arriving at any knowledge of God through reason on both epistemological and theological grounds; one could know God only through the direct revelation of Scripture and not through any scrutiny of the created world. Since knowledge acquired through the study of the physical world and deductive reason could not offer any aid in learning of God or heaven, the Christian must reject the intellect as the primary faculty in his search for salvation and justification. The will, therefore, must be the faculty that may lead man to salvation.

This concentration on the will paralleled the nominalists' separation of God's power into absolute and ordinate, the *potentia absoluta* and the *potentia ordinata*. God's absolute power signifies his ability to do all things without any check; it represents his full divine power. But God has established a set procedure by which his creatures could depend on the regularity of creation and on his fidelity to his promises, which is his ordinate power. This distinction was not meant as a dialectical relationship but rather as a statement of the two sides of God's power. Through his covenant with God man can depend on the procedures established through Scripture and the church as sufficient in his search for salvation. Knowledge of these rules for salvation cannot be grasped by man's reason; a Christian must have faith in what God has presented through revelation and follow his commandments. In this the will plays the primary role of reacting to God's plan.[16]

This similar response to the problem of knowledge and the means of acquiring salvation in both nominalism and humanism represented a common reaction to the intellectualism of scholasticism. There was in this matter no direct influence of nominalism on Petrarch's humanism, but rather the same problem eliciting the same reaction. (Although the Franciscans did follow in part Ockham's teachings, there was no great Ockhamite influence in Italy outside the order.) This similarity of response indicates that Petrarch's formulation of the antithesis between will and intellect, faith and reason, reflected a Europewide phenomenon. Petrarch found in his humanism and his particular interpretation of Augustine a solution to his dilemma.

Coluccio Salutati (1331–1406), chancellor of the city of Florence and leader of the Florentine humanist community, followed Petrarch's lead by providing a synthesis of humanist and scholastic ideas.[17] Like Petrarch, Salutati looked to Augustine as his model for understanding the importance of the will in man's actions. Salutati especially emphasized the distinction between the active will the passive intellect and found the former superior. The active life rather than the contemplative life can provide man with the means of embracing the divine. It necessitates on man's part the task of choosing right action; hence, he has to possess free will. There is, however, an implicit contradiction between man's free will and God's sovereign power. Salutati's solution to this tension was to accept the implicit dilemma but to stress man's duty to act freely and be responsible for his actions.

Like Petrarch, Salutati argued that the *studia humanitatis* offered the best preparation for the Christian's life in a social context.[18] Classical historical theory blended with Christian ideas to form the moral man, anxious to act morally and to understand through action and not passively. Humanism had allowed Salutati to emphasize those elements in the Christian tradition—above all Augustinian voluntarism—which supported the rhetorical basis of humanist education. He did not wish to propose a new dogmatic theology but rather an interpretation of Christianity that would offer a more immediately applicable morality for the active, civic man.

*   *   *

Scholastic theology had dominated religious thought and education for two centuries, and although there were elements in the church that opposed its philosophical-Aristotelian foundations in general, it had established itself as the official theology. It is only to be expected that the scholastics were unwilling to have their ideas and procedures rejected and a new, non-Aristotelian and nonphilosophical theology take their place. The humanists' advocacy of the ancient writers defined the first phase of the conflict, in which the scholastics rejected the classical-pagan basis of rhetoric and the *studia humanitatis* as a substitute for traditional medieval education and scholastic procedures.

A clear indication of the nature of the scholastic attack can be seen in the work of Giovanni Dominici (1357–1419), a Dominican friar and later bishop and cardinal, who was active in Florence at the same time Salutati was directing that city's humanist community. Dominici issued a series of attacks on the humanists and their educational theory as dangerous to Christian morality, since it was based on pagan models.[19] Dominici made his criticisms most systematically in his treatise *Lucula noctis,* which was directed against Salutati and his circle in Florence. Outside of Florence, a similar assault on humanism as unchristian occurred in Rome, and the humanist Francesco da Fiano (ca. 1350–ca. 1425) specifically countered it by arguing that the study of the classical authors did not endanger a Christian's faith.[20]

Without doubt the most significant of the early Quattrocento answers to the charge that humanism was incompatible with Christian truth was proposed by Leonardo Bruni (ca. 1370–1444), Salutati's most famous protégé.[21] In responding to charges that irreligion and paganism result from the reading and study of classical authors, Bruni turned to the fathers of the church as the source for his defense. Bruni made use of the Greek Father, Basil the Great, and his famous *Letter on Reading Gentile Literature.*[22] Basil had argued that any writing that teaches morality should be studied, including the classics of pagan literature. By invoking the great Greek theologian and bishop, Bruni found the perfect response (and one that would find an echo in humanist thought throughout the Renaissance), and, as had Petrarch, turned to the fathers of the church as normative models. In a sense Bruni initiated the great rediscovery and use of the church fathers, which was perhaps Renaissance humanism's greatest contribution to theology.[23]

The fathers of the church, Greek and Latin, appealed to the humanists because they embodied those values the scholastics had rejected, or at least ignored: rhetoric and eloquence. The Fathers were part of the ancient literature that the humanists were in the process of reviving. They had been educated in the literary ideals that the humanists proposed as models and they had believed that this education could be the basis for expressing theological ideas in an attractive manner. In the hands of Basil the Great, Gregory of Nazianzus, Jerome, or Augustine of Hippo, no one could argue, as did some scholastics, that eloquence and the cultivation of good letters were distractions to religion and threats to orthodoxy. Further, medieval theologians had had only limited knowledge of the Greek Fathers, while scholastic theologians even shunned those Latin Fathers, such as Tertullian, who did not display the philosophical characteristics they appreciated. Other Fathers, such as Origen, were treated only selectively by the scholastics.[24]

In turning to the Fathers, the humanists found major allies in their struggle with what they judged to be the barbarities and irrelevancies of scholastic theology. The Fathers had not cluttered their theology and moral teachings with philosophical theories and inelegant language which distracted the Christian's attention from the plain message of Scripture. Rather they had offered a rhetorical presentation of doctrine meant to move the believer to accept these ideas. The Fathers presented a rhetorical framework rather than an Aristotelian-metaphysical one. To the humanist theologians the Fathers' language was a beautiful idiom free of philosophical neologisms and useless speculations.

If the Fathers were to be fully exploited, however, their writings had to be made available either in the original or in translations. The humanists, with their knowledge of the Greek and Latin languages and literatures, began to provide the reading public with translations of important patristic texts. Bruni began the process with his translations of Basil the Great, and he had many followers. Adding to the urgency of this endeavor was the intersection of humanist interest in classical learning with the general desire among Christians for a religious reform within the church. Pope Nicholas V (1447–55), for example, felt that the greater dissemination of Greek texts, patristic as well as classical, would aid in the rejuvenation of the clergy and the church in general. He commissioned new translations of various Greek patristic writings. Ambrogio Traversari (ca. 1386–1439), the Camaldolese humanist and leader of Florentine humanists, translated various Greek Fathers as part of a general reform of the church.[25] Humanist translations continued to appear throughout the fifteenth and sixteenth centuries. Even those Latin versions which had been available through the Middle Ages were refashioned to fit the humanists' literary standards.

The Fathers provided the humanists with an orthodox model for a rhetorical theology, and the perfect support they needed in dealing with any criticism of their theological interests as well as a general defense for their study and utilization of the classical writers. The best example was Lorenzo Valla (1407–1457).[26] His critical ability made him a major opponent and critic of scholasticism and of Aristotelian philosophy in general. In an oration in honor of St. Thomas Aquinas delivered on the saint's feast day, Valla was able to employ his knowledge of ancient languages and patristic theology as a means of criticizing Aquinas and scholastic theology in general.[27] His argument was basically that outlined above, that the ancient Fathers had enjoyed the education that the humanists now proclaimed as befitting a Christian. Their rhetorical education made the Fathers the best expositors of the Christian message, while Aquinas and the other scholastics were too involved in philosophical subtleties to present Christian truth in an appealing form. Underlying this criticism was Valla's belief that language and not metaphysics was the key to truth.

Perhaps Valla's most famous work was his *De falso credita et ementita Constantini donatione declamatio* (1442).[28] The *Declamatio* proved through philological methods that Constantine did not surrender the western empire to the papacy when he established his new capital at Constantinople. In addition to being a brilliant piece of literary and textual criticism, the treatise also sought to offer a means of church reform by exposing its excessive involvement in secular affairs and by demonstrating the false historical premises for this involvement. Valla thus demonstrated the value of humanist philology and historical thought to reform of the church and Christian society.

But Valla was more than a critic. He moved humanist theology farther than his predecessors by providing a basis for the study of sacred Scripture.[29] Scripture, of course, had provided the foundation for medieval theological speculation, but under the general influence of scholasticism, dialectics and philosophy had reshaped its basic methodology; Scripture became a study explicable only through the rubrics of Aristotle. While there were medieval thinkers who did not accept this procedure, it nevertheless became the professional theological means of biblical exegesis. Valla used humanistic literary values to offer an alternative means of interpreting the divine word. If language, as Valla claimed, created the matrix for valid understanding,[30] then it followed that the words of salvation must be properly understood. To understand what Christ said,

Scripture must be read like any other text; it must be criticized and revised according to the laws of grammar. Above all, the original language of the New Testament must be scrutinized and rendered into good, clear, and accurate Latin. The Vulgate, therefore, had to be criticized and brought into agreement with the principles of philology; the basic translation used in medieval theology was no longer acceptable as the authoritative text from which to expound the faith.

Valla demonstrated how he wished to revive Scripture in his *Collatio Novi Testamenti* (1443), which he dedicated in a subsequent redaction entitled *Adnotationes Novi Testamenti* to Pope Nicholas V[31] (and which Erasmus published in 1505). In it he emended specific passages in the New Testament. Basing his new renderings on the original Greek as well as on the rules for good Latin style, he suggested alternative translations for words and phrases. In most cases Valla's changes are merely the substitution of a better word, tense, voice, or preposition for that found in the Vulgate, while at other times he offered more extensive rewritings. In the *Collatio* Valla was able to provide a basis for the critical understanding of Scripture, a project carried much further two generations later by Erasmus.

It is hardly to be expected that the humanist claims to biblical expertise would go unquestioned by the professional scholastic theologians. What, they argued, could the humanists bring to the study of Scripture but literary credentials, which constitute no guarantee of theological expertise? The humanists, however, had a response to this attack. Aurelio Brandolini (1454–1497), a well-known poet and orator and in later life an Augustinian friar, was one who felt that he did indeed possess the credentials necessary for scriptural exposition.[32] His arguments in favor of humanist translation of Scripture are a good example of the type of arguments the humanists used to uphold their theological claims. Brandolini maintained that the humanists had a right to discuss and translate Scripture because their literary education made them the best spokesmen for Christian doctrine. If they had to change the language of the Vulgate in order to make Scripture clearer, then they were merely following in the tradition established by the Apostles, who had adapted their language to fit their audiences, and of Jerome, who went beyond them in changing the very language of Scripture. The words of Scripture, therefore, had to be adapted to the needs and literary tastes of the audience and not treated as fixed. The humanists maintained that they could provide Latin-reading people with a compelling rendition of God's word, and that Scripture should be brought into conformity with the perfected latinity of the humanists, thereby enabling the educated public to appreciate it on more than one level.

Generally the humanists did not turn their attention to Scripture as a whole. Hebrew scholarship was not, after all, part of the humanist educational program, and, consequently, the humanists' religious concerns did not center on the Old Testament. Indeed, there was a definite bias against Hebrew scholarship among some humanists. Bruni, for example, rejected the study of Hebrew as an uncultured enterprise.[33] In general, this attitude seems to have been dominant among the majority of Italian humanists. Still, other humanists did study Hebrew as part of a program of scriptural translation. The most famous Italian Hebrew scholar was Giannozzo Manetti (1396–1459), a rich Florentine whose wide-ranging interests make him one of the most fascinating—and under-studied—humanists of the mid-fifteenth century.[34] Like Brandolini, Manetti defended his attempt to produce a new translation of Scripture. Yet even Manetti placed most of his emphasis on the Greek New Testament.

*   *   *

Although Manetti's biblical studies would have assured him a prominent place in the history of humanist theology, he has another claim to prominence. Manetti gave expression to one of the most important of humanist themes, that of the dignity of man.[35] No single topic so perfectly epitomized the humanist approach to God and man as this one. It permitted a humanist to bring together both classical and Christian themes into a unity that expressed their attitude toward man in the world. The need to assure the Christian that he was performing valuable service while carrying out his civic duties led the humanists to present man as a positive actor in the cosmos, to praise human potential without becoming involved in detailed discussion of the theological character of human action and free will.

Manetti was, without doubt, the most famous proponent of the theme of the dignity of man. But he was not alone, and this topic appeared in different forms throughout the Renaissance. Significantly, this most representative of humanist theological themes was an extension of certain patristic ideas. The fathers of the church had carefully employed certain classical *topoi* as a means of establishing the distinctive qualities of man and of emphasizing his worth as the subject of salvation.[36] Any presentation of the dignity of man was especially dependent, in both its patristic and its humanist manifestations, on the study of Neoplatonic writings. Neoplatonism thus provided the humanist writers with a body of material that the medieval theologians, unlike their patristic predecessors, knew only at second hand and in very diluted form. The humanist recovery and use of the Neoplatonic texts constituted an important element in their theological thought.

One can overestimate the importance of the Neoplatonic revival among the humanists. As Paul Oskar Kristeller, Renaissance Neoplatonism's most famous modern student, has emphasized, Neoplatonism, like Aristotelianism, belongs to a special philosophical tradition independent of humanism.[37] Still, the recovery of the Platonic and Neoplatonic writings would have been impossible without the humanists' emphasis on the need to study Greek and to utilize it in cultural reform. Not surprisingly, the beginning of the Neoplatonic renaissance had a strongly religious and theological cast to it. It was at the unionist Council of Ferrara–Florence (1438–45) that many Italian humanists, especially the Florentines, first came into contact with a living Neoplatonic tradition, that of the Byzantine scholars around the Neoplatonic propagandist George Gemistus Pletho (1355–1450).[38] Pletho used Neoplatonic philosophy as part of a non-Christian cultural revival. He hoped to replace orthodox Christianity with the cosmological scheme of Neoplatonism. While this intention was not taken up in the West, his advocacy of the study of Neoplatonism, and that of his disciples, most notably Cardinal Bessarion, had a positive effect on many humanists and marks the beginnings of Renaissance Neoplatonism.

The Florentine humanists were inspired by Pletho's example to study the Neoplatonic writings and disseminate them to the culturally advanced. The leader of this endeavor was the *de facto* ruler of Florence, Cosimo de' Medici (1389–1464). As part of a program to popularize Neoplatonism, Cosimo commissioned a young scholar, Marsilio Ficino (1433–1499), to begin the process of translating the major Platonic and Neoplatonic writings into Latin.[39] This translation activity was to occupy Ficino for the rest of his life. Ficino felt, however, that it was necessary not only to translate Plato and his major commentators, but also to provide for his contemporaries expositions of Neoplatonism's meaning.

Ficino was convinced that Neoplatonism was in essential agreement with Christianity and that it could provide the Christian with valuable aid in understanding divine matters. There was, therefore, a unity to knowledge in Ficino's teachings, and Platonic philosophy was a key to discovering it. The universe was a carefully graded set of hierarchies that could lead the diligent searcher to an appreciation of the unity of creation and the glories of the creator. Significantly, Ficino was the first Christian to compose a treatise on the Christian religion; his *De christiana religione* was first published in 1474, and was being written at the same time that Ficino was at work on his most important treatise, the

Theologia platonica, which was first printed in 1482.[40] No man was more convinced of the value of the new humanistic enterprise to the Christian's striving to find salvation through knowledge.

Ficino stands in tangential relationship to humanism; he used his humanistic training to help clarify a variety of philosophical and theological topics. Unlike most humanists, however, he felt that metaphysics was an essential element in obtaining truth and vital for all men to study. Still, his work was of such a wide compass that he offered some themes the humanists—especially the poets—found to be very valuable to their literary enterprises. The idea of a *theologica poetica* combined certain literary and philosophical ideas in a way that was to be most productive in humanist literature.[41]

Ficino offered the fullest account of Neoplatonism in the Renaissance. In his reading of it, there was room for magic and astrology, both interpreted in a beneficial manner and as part of the general scheme of creation. But he was not the only man who sought to disseminate the new, or at least purer, form of Platonic thought. Among the Greeks who had come to Florence to attend the council was Bessarion (1403–1472). He identified himself so fully with the unionist sentiments among the Greeks that he had to flee his native Greece and take refuge in Italy.[42] His unionist feelings, however, won him the support of the pope, and he eventually became a cardinal and a prime contender for the papal throne. His long residence in Rome allowed him to assemble around him a number of Greek and Italian scholars who were especially devoted to the study and propagation of Plato's thought.

* * *

Close to Ficino in his desire to utilize a variety of unfamiliar sources of knowledge in the service of Christianity was Giovanni Pico della Mirandola (1463–1494).[43] Pico, like Ficino, had a tangential relationship to humanism. He was educated in the humanist tradition but went beyond it by attempting to bring into his purview a wide variety of learning the humanists generally ignored. Pico was a student of the Aristotelian scholastic philosophers and theologians as well as of the ancient Greek and Latin thinkers. Moreover, he extended his work to include the hermetic and kabbalistic writings, in his belief that all these sources of knowledge could be utilized to establish the truth of Christianity.

Pico did not subscribe to one of the basic humanist tenets underlying their treatment of theology, the cultivation of classical Latin as the language for discourse. In a famous epistolary controversy with the humanist and philologist Ermolao Barbaro the Younger (1453–1493), Pico denied that the classical Latin the humanists advocated was superior to the Latin the scholastics had invented.[44] Indeed, Pico denied the humanists' claim to be the arbiters of language. He judged the humanist search for the perfect linguistic form a danger to the underlying metaphysical content of philosophy. In this discussion Pico established his independence of certain humanist principles, but he did not reject the entire inheritance of Quattrocento humanism.

Justifying Pico's investigation of various traditions of knowledge was the desire to find the point at which truth united differing systems, especially the Platonic and Aristotelian philosophies.[45] This search for unity was basic to humanist theology in general. The humanist tendency was to see in theology not a body of set metaphysical doctrines but a series of concentric religious themes from various sources united in a rhetorical form that could be used in producing a functional morality.

Pico's clearest theological assertion of unity is his *Heptaplus,* a type of commentary on the Creation story in the book of Genesis.[46] In it he tries to show that the Creation story in Scripture is in accord with the Greek view of nature and the physical world. Central to both the classical philosophers' universe and the biblical account is man. He is the middle point between the physical and spiritual worlds and the image of God. Anthropomorphic ideas were fundamental to the view of man as a microcosm of the universe and as God's spiritual image. Both of these ideas were Neoplatonic in inspiration and had been introduced into Christianity and made popular by the fathers of the church.

But Pico's theology went beyond an emphasis on classical and biblical sources. He devoted much of his time to scholastic, kabbalistic, and hermetic writings. These interests would prove most problematic for Pico and all interpreters of his thought. The extent to which Pico's procedure of bringing together a variety of philosophical, theological, and mystical tendencies was unacceptable to the general humanist community as well as to the scholastic theologians can be seen in the fate of his famous *Nine Hundred Theses.*

In 1487 Pico announced his intention to debate with all comers nine hundred propositions he had extracted from classical, scholastic, kabbalistic, and hermetic sources.[47] The perceived arrogance of the challenge turned many individuals who were generally favorable to Pico's intellectual enterprise against him. The humanists felt that it was a sign of Pico's pride and desire for fame that he would attempt to undertake such a vast task; they judged the attempt a waste of time, since the questions to be discussed were further manifestations of metaphysical barrenness. The scholastic theologians, however, interpreted the propositions Pico intended to defend as heretical, since some of the scholastic theses were debatable or had been considered objectionable by the majority of theologians. Pico was, in fact, condemned by a specially appointed papal commission dominated by scholastic theologians, and it was only through the good offices of Lorenzo de' Medici that he avoided being imprisoned.

The most famous element of the planned debate was the oration, in humanistic form, that Pico intended to use as an introduction to the enterprise. This so-called *Oration on the Dignity of Man* brought together the diverse strands that made up the humanist theme of the dignity of man.[48] The oration became a classic statement of humanist theology and stood in many ways in contrast to the nonhumanistic theses Pico intended to debate.

The oration and the proposed theses for discussion did not represent Pico's final theological position. The last years of his short life were spent in Florence, where he came under the influence of the Dominican theologian and reformer Girolamo Savonarola (1452–1498).[49] Under Savonarola's guidance Pico moved away from the search for the unity of truth in Christian and non-Christian sources which had characterized his early years, and he seems to have accepted, at least in part, a more fundamentalist conception of Christianity, one that rejected the theories of the philosophers and emphasized Scripture as the sole basis for truth. It was also in these years in Florence that Pico issued his treatise on astrology, *Disputationes contra astrologiam divinatricem* (1494).[50] Less an attack on all aspects of astrology, the work was meant to deny the predictive quality of astrology as incompatible with the Christian teachings on free will.

Close to Pico in these last years was his nephew, the philosopher Gianfrancesco Pico della Mirandola (1469–1533).[51] The younger Pico's work was very different from the early thrusts of his famous uncle, but more in keeping with what Pico had come to accept in Florence. Gianfrancesco Pico rejected the search for the unity of truth, turning away from the eclectic path to wisdom his uncle believed would show the unity of Christian truth through all knowledge. Rather, Gianfrancesco displayed a skeptical attitude toward human reason and a fideistic theological stance, which in part harkened back to Petrarch but also demonstrated certain new elements in Renaissance humanist thought. While in later life the younger Pico was to issue a major attack on Aristotelian philosophy, in his early years, under the influence of Savonarola, he was more devoted to the theological problems of faith and the limits of human knowledge.

The two Picos were not the only Renaissance thinkers attracted to the fundamentalist message of Savonarola.[52] Many humanists had come to doubt the proposition that they could arrive at a true understanding of Christian truth by continuing to devote their energies to studying the ancient past. The result was the development of a skeptical attitude toward human reason and study which came to prominence in the last years of the Quattrocento and the first decades of the Cinquecento.[53] This skepticism was not simply or even primarily an attack on humanist learning, which had not tried to answer the more profound theological questions or to offer a complete critique of human epistemology. In great part the skepticism and fideism that became significant were directed at the continued claims of scholasticism to interpret theology through philosophy. Nevertheless, humanism came to share in the crisis of faith and reason that typified the decades before the Reformation.

The place of humanism in this skeptical-fideistic reaction can be seen in the work of two representatives, Gianfrancesco Pico and Cardinal Adriano Castellesi da Corneto (1458–ca. 1522). Pico, as noted, had the model of his uncle to react against. The major element in his skeptical thought, however, was directed against the philosophy of Aristotle and its claims to truth. Pico also denied the cult of antiquity that characterized humanism, but this rejection was usually in a specifically literary context, while his rejection of Aristotle was broader and formed a more complete program. Castellesi, who was a prominent curial cardinal and diplomat, was also well known as a proponent of Ciceronian Latin style and had a minor reputation as a Hebrew scholar. In his treatise, *De vera philosophia* (1504), he used the writings of the four Latin doctors of the Church—Augustine, Jerome, Ambrose, and Gregory the Great—to deny the ability of human reason to understand truth and to affirm the need for faith if man were to be saved.[54] While there are occasional broadsides issued against humanist learning, the bulk of the text questioned the dominance of elements of Aristotelian philosophy in Christian thought and did not constitute a general attack on humanist learning and thought. This skepticism was by no means limited to humanists. The authors of the famous *Libellus ad Leonem decem,* two Camaldolese monks from Venice, Paolo Giustiniani and Pietro Quirini, also called for a limit to the study of ancient philosophy and literature, because they might endanger the soul's—especially priests' souls—search for salvation.[55] The suspicion of human learning expressed by these writers was to a great extent a result of the advances made both by philosophy and by literature in turning away from certain traditional medieval themes and authors and exploiting more fully the classical heritage. Nevertheless, it did mark a crisis in the humanist movement just as external factors, such as the Reformation, put pressure on it in other directions.

*   *   *

By the beginning of the sixteenth century humanist thought had come to terms with the dominant form of Christian theology, scholasticism. Indeed, there was a definite movement to follow the work of Thomas Aquinas in theological matters. Aquinas had always enjoyed greater popularity among the humanists than had the other scholastic theologians. His major appeal to the humanists lay in the relative clarity of his theological discussions and expositions. To an extent the humanists actively propagated the cult of Thomas. In Rome a series of humanist orators celebrated his fame. If Valla could compare Aquinas unfavorably to the Greek Fathers, other humanists could see in his work and life a more secure exposition of Christian truth than in those of other theologians.[56] This acceptance of Aquinas as the clearest exponent of scholastic theology remained even when humanists rejected the school that developed around his teachings and the general character of scholasticism. Aquinas was for the humanist theologians a guide who could be depended on for his theological orthodoxy but also one who would not lead them into complicated and ultimately, in their eyes, useless theological and metaphysical sidetracks. The imperative of action, the need for a theology that held closely to the rhetorical base of humanist thought, was always primary in the minds of humanist writers.

Humanist theology did not remain simply an appendix to Thomist thought. The humanists had succeeded in producing by the beginning of the sixteenth century a body of theological work that was very much their own, whatever similarities it might have had with traditional scholasticism in some particulars. The humanist concern for patristic literature was still very much a part of humanist theology. New editions of Latin and Greek Fathers were constantly appearing, along with new or revised translations of the Greek works. Indeed, a study of the church fathers was a part of the humanist theological ideal which had some effect on the use of the Fathers among the scholastics. While the study of patristic literature was also a source of comparison with the ancient and contemporary churches, the acceptance of the Fathers was still strongly imbued with the rhetorical and moral ideals of humanist thought. Some humanists also tried to integrate their literary activities with their theological studies. They would offer to their humanist audience a theology rewritten in humanist fashion. There were degrees of this rewriting; some humanists merely cleaned up the language of theology while others sought completely to translate theological ideas into faultless humanist, usually Ciceronian, Latin. The most extreme example of this latter view was Paolo Cortesi's (1465–1510) "commentary" on Peter Lombard's textbook *Liber sententiarum,* a text in which all theological vocabulary was translated into Ciceronian approximations.[57] While Cortesi's undertaking might seem excessive, he felt that he was making the traditional teachings of the church more acceptable to the educated laymen and clerics and thereby bringing together humanist and scholastic education.

Reform is a topic inseparable from general humanist theological thought.[58] The humanists were as aware of the problems facing the church as were their clerical or lay contemporaries, indeed in some cases even more aware. Indeed, as professional rhetoricians and teachers they took their task as moral critics very seriously and often voiced criticisms of the church. At least in the Italian setting, such criticisms of the church were never meant to be interpreted as calls for its overthrow. In general, humanist reform thought emphasized personal amelioration rather than institutional change. The humanists, like their contemporaries, could not conceive of Christianity outside the particular setting of Roman Catholicism. As noted, the humanists did not primarily use the fathers of the church as means of criticizing the church, although they sometimes did so. Their study of ancient political practice and history had not left the humanists capable of making essential criticisms of the institutions they lived under and served. Whether in church or state, the humanists wished to offer particular proposals for amelioration rather than any revolutionary ideology.

How successful the humanists were in producing a theological attitude acceptable to the professional theologians can be seen in the use of humanist motifs by such scholastic thinkers as the Augustinian hermit Egidio of Viterbo (1465–1532) and the Dominican theologian Tommaso da Vio, called Cajetan (1469–1534).[59] Both men had had the normal scholastic education of their orders, but in later life they came to use in their theology elements that were borrowed from the humanists: the need to investigate the fathers of the church, to understand the ancient philosophers more fully, to exploit the full potential of Christian history, and to write their works in a less dialectic and more rhetorical manner in order to make them more effective to their readers, especially when they were discussing Scripture. In neither case was humanist theology a primary component of their thought, though Giles was more closely connected to humanists generally. Humanism did contribute to making their thought more contemporary.

Italian humanist theology grew essentially as a response to the Italian situation and the humanist classical values. Italian humanists really knew little of the theological traditions in the more advanced scholastic centers such as Oxford and Paris. Churchmen educated in these northern European centers could be found in Italy, especially at the *studia generalia* of the religious orders and at the Roman curia, but generally they had little influence outside their limited clerical circles. Neither were the scholastic texts in Italian libraries capable of sparking the humanists to study them. The weakness of the scholastic traditions in Italy and the special conditions surrounding humanist scholarship in the various Italian courts and republics gave to the humanists interested in theological questions a freedom of action that was not enjoyed, or at least not as fully, by their northern European contemporaries. Further, humanist theology in Italy had grown without much concern for the charges of heresy that some conservatives issued against it; they answered these complaints by reference to the church fathers and continued to do what they had done before. As the Reformation changed the levels of discourse and raised questions about the humanist contribution to the Lutheran movement, however, this freedom of thought and debate in Italy also declined. Nevertheless, it was not completely lost in the years when the fight against Luther consumed more and more Catholic attention. Even during the 1530s, when the Roman church was ending any chance of reconciliation, a humanist theologian such as Cardinal Jacopo Sadoleto (1477–1547) could still produce theological and biblical expositions betraying the humanist concern with moral action, rhetoric, and Christian history. Further, in the sixteenth century a new emphasis on evangelicalism developed in Italy.[60] But these emergences represented a final flowering of a declining plant.

*　　*　　*

The situation in northern Europe was very different from that of Italy in the fifteenth century, yet the concern for the theological and moral dimensions of humanist thought were as strong as, if not stronger than, in Italy.[61] Scholasticism had a much stronger position in northern European universities than in Italy, and the humanists had to deal with professional theologians in their areas of strength. In part, northern European humanism was an import from Italy. There had been centers of the study of ancient literature in a number of northern European intellectual centers, but they had not developed the full concern for classical antiquity that came to characterize Italian humanism. Scholastic thought and medieval education remained strong, and humanism could not easily displace them. Nevertheless, after a slow beginning, humanism made important inroads into the universities and became the intellectual avant-garde in northern Europe as it had in Italy.

It is traditional to emphasize a sharp conflict between humanism and scholasticism in the various universities. Recent scholarship, however, has cautioned us to refrain from such facile generalizations. There were points of conflict, but in general there were fewer than historians have maintained. While disagreements over courses in the universities occurred, they were minor, and in general the humanists were successful in bringing their new educational ideals partially into the universities. While the northern European humanists had to contend with a more firmly entrenched scholasticism, they did so with a great deal of success.[62]

In general the early phase of humanism's penetration into northern Europe concentrated on literary, moral, pedagogical, and historical topics. The first Italian humanist teachers were very much literary figures and gave to their German or French students a taste of the purified Latin the Italians had made central to their study of antiquity. It was only over time that the philosophical and theological consequences of humanism became clear to northern students, and when it did they gladly used these aspects in dealing with the dominant scholasticism.

Perhaps the most famous of early northern European humanist theologians was Nicholas of Cusa (1401–1464).[63] Nicholas, like his Italian contemporaries, brought together many themes in his theology. Further, like Petrarch he was preoccupied with the question of the relation between human knowledge and religious truth. He rejected the claims of human reason in dealing with divine matters and emphasized the limits of human reason and learning. He enjoyed contrasting the simplicity of faith to the uncertainty and tentativeness of human reason and knowledge, doing so most fully in his *De docta ignorantia* (1440).[64]

Nicholas was educated by the Brethren of the Common Life, a reformed religious order in the Rhineland that sought to inspire a more direct spirituality and which gave much consideration to education. Through the Brethren Nicholas was brought into contact with the vital spirituality called the "Modern Devotion," which sought a more immediate spirituality than that available through the scholastics.[65] Further, he came to know the teachings of the Rhenish mystical thinkers of the fourteenth century, such as Meister Eckhart. This background combined with his study of Augustine of Hippo, pseudo-Dionysius the Areopagite, and St. Bernard to give his thought a distinctive character.

Certain elements in Nicholas's thought were taken up by two other early northern humanists who spent time in Italy: Jacques Lefèvre d'Etaples (ca. 1460–1536) and John Colet (ca. 1466–1519). Both were influenced by the Neoplatonism and Hellenism originating in Italy, which they experienced at first hand in trips to Florence and other Italian cities and to which they tried to adapt their theological thought. Further, both men had great influence in their respective countries and helped to spark a new attitude in northern European religious thought.

Jacques Lefèvre d'Etaples brought together a wide variety of intellectual trends in his work.[66] There were several stages in his career, ranging from philosophical reform to mystical theology. He was early active in trying to remove medieval scholastic additions from the works of Aristotle and provide the scholarly world with clear renderings of the philosopher's words. Like other humanist Aristotelians, such as Leonardo Bruni, Lefèvre emphasized the compatibility of Aristotle's moral philosophy with Christianity and rejected scholastic commentaries based on poor translations. Concern for Latin style led him to champion the literary doctrines of the Italian humanists. At the same time he was influenced by the type of metaphysics expounded by Ficino and Pico della Mirandola. In addition, he found in early Christian and mystical writings a valid means of moving closer to Christian truth. This combination of interests and influences led him to publish editions of Aristotle's writings with commentaries, a variety of church fathers, mystical writers such as pseudo-Dionysius the Areopagite, and Nicholas of Cusa. He had great influence among students and professors at the University of Paris, where he taught. As he grew older, however, Lefèvre increasingly emphasized biblical studies, and he was especially active in trying to offer to the reader a clearer version of the words of God, a procedure analogous to his treatment of Aristotle. He was a supporter of the reform-minded bishop of Meaux, Guillaume Briçonnet, whom he aided in reforming his diocese. As part of his contribution, Lefèvre translated into French the New Testament and the Psalms in 1521.[67] In 1530 he issued a complete translation of the Bible. His evangelical work and his championing of doctrines resembling those of Martin Luther led to his scrutiny by the Catholic authorities in France, but support from the king and his sister, the queen of Navarre, saved him from any persecution.

John Colet was less important for his own works than for the effect he had on Desiderius Erasmus.[68] Colet's development was not unlike that of Lefèvre. He had spent some time in Italy and had come under the influence of Ficino. But Colet was not really interested in philosophical topics; rather, he was anxious to rid Scripture of the excesses of medieval exegesis. He was, however, strongly influenced in his treatment of Scripture by his study of Neoplatonic writers, above all pseudo-Dionysius the Areopagite. Colet wrote several expositions of Scripture that especially applied the Dionysian model to Paul's Epistles.[69] His study of Scripture was allied to a critical attitude toward what he and his contemporaries considered the excesses and deficiencies of the late medieval church.

*   *   *

Erasmus represented the fullest development of northern European humanism, and his thought was the model for many of his contemporaries.[70] While the Reformation affected Erasmus's attitudes toward the church and certain doctrines and caused him to become more conservative in the last years of his life, we may deal with his thought up to the Reformation as a unity. No other sixteenth-century thinker was more desirous than he of using humanist education and morality in the service of a religious and ecclesiastical reform.

Much of Erasmus's early work on religion was influenced by his years in the monastery.[71] He felt that the monastic life was too often inimical to humanist scholarship and a deep morality, and he tried to emphasize in his writings the importance of learning for the Christian in combating monastic and scholastic excesses and integrating humanism and Christianity. In this view he naturally turned to the writings of Jerome and Augustine and extracted from them and from other early Christian writers an educational system that incorporated the humanistic emphasis on classical learning and the need for a special Christian morality. But until his first visit to England in 1499, when he met Colet and entered Colet's circle of friends and admirers, especially Thomas More, Erasmus was more concerned with establishing his fame as a humanist poet than as a moral and ecclesiastical reformer.

Colet helped Erasmus to appreciate the full dimensions of the scriptural texts. Colet was primarily interested in the moral meaning of Scripture, and Erasmus followed Colet in this direction in his own work. But Colet realized that Erasmus could do more for scriptural studies than simply restate his own ideas, and he urged his Dutch friend to study the original texts of the New Testament as a means of understanding what Christ and the Apostles had taught and of offering a clearer teaching for his contemporaries. While Colet provided Erasmus with a basis for a deeper appreciation of scriptural truth, he could not offer a method to find and express this truth, since he lacked the scholarly tools to deal with the original texts. However, Erasmus discovered in a monastery a copy of Valla's *Adnotationes* and published it in 1505, and this text offered him the model he required to engage in scriptural work.[72]

Erasmus, however, did not begin his scriptural studies without extensive preparation. His mastery of Latin was universally acknowledged, and after his trip to England he set about mastering Greek. Like his Italian humanist predecessors and contemporaries, he also understood the need to study the fathers of the church if he were to understand properly what the Christian message was and above all how to express it in good Latin.[73] This goal led Erasmus to seek out and study the writings of several of the Latin and Greek Fathers. Erasmus's first love among the Fathers was Jerome, whose Latin style seemed to incorporate both learning and piety. Beginning with Jerome, Erasmus began a career as patristic editor, which resulted in the publication of editions of Jerome, Augustine, Ambrose, Hilary, and other Latin and Greek writers. His study of the Fathers led Erasmus to emphasize the words of Scripture and to avoid the allegorizing that had marked medieval exegesis. Erasmus had come fully to appreciate the value of humanist training in explaining the pure Christian message.

This emphasis on good humanistic learning as a basis for understanding Scripture and on a clean reading of Christ's words as the means of leading a moral life was encapsulated in the phrase *philosophia Christi*.[74] This "philosophy," Erasmus believed, was necessary for his contemporaries in their striving to overcome the evils that afflicted society and the church and to return to a Christian morality. It ignored doctrine in favor of morality. Erasmus saw in the doctrinal teachings of contemporary theologians a decidedly unchristian approach to Christianity, one that substituted logical and philosophical distinctions for the truth of Scripture.

The second decade of the sixteenth century marked the high point of Erasmus's fame and influence, as can be seen in the popularity of his two most important publications of that period, his *Praise of Folly* and his edition of the Greek New Testament. *Folly* was a direct attack on the immorality of European society and the defects of the church. Using irony to make his points, Erasmus contrasted the monks' and scholastic theologians' false humility and learning with a true Christian life based on evangelical truth. The success of the work at lampooning the monks and the scholastic theologians (among other groups) made them Erasmus's implacable enemies and established him as the leader of the religious reformers.

The edition of the Greek New Testament was a milestone in biblical scholarship. In it Erasmus brought to bear his enormous knowledge of classical literature and a sensitive appreciation of linguistic nuance. He benefited from his reading of Valla but also went beyond him in the sophistication of his treatment of the Greek and Latin texts. While the work contained many errors in the Greek text, a fact his opponents gleefully exposed and which he partly corrected in later editions, it made available the original text of the New Testament to a scholarly world anxious to receive it.

How extraordinary Erasmus's edition of the Greek New Testament was can be seen in a comparison with the Complutensian Bible sponsored by the Spanish Cardinal Ximenes de Cisneros.[75] The Complutensian Bible included the Hebrew, Greek, and Aramaic versions of the Old Testament as well as the Greek New Testament and the Vulgate translation. But its editors did not challenge the accepted Vulgate version of key texts, rather providing the traditional readings. Erasmus, by contrast, allowed the Greek text to be his guide. If the Greek said something different from the Latin translation, then Erasmus tried to show how the text should be translated in order to express the proper meaning. This application of literary critical methods to the sacred texts was a scandal to the conservative theologians, who argued that the accepted meaning should be preferred to any reading based on the Greek text, that is, that the Latin tradition was a better guide than literary criticism combined with the schismatic Greek tradition. Erasmus defended his critical procedure in a series of *Annotationes* and continued to apply his growing knowledge of Greek and of biblical and patristic literature to later editions.

Certainly the most famous of Erasmian emendations of the New Testament was his retranslation of the opening of the Gospel according to St. John.[76] The Vulgate "In principio erat verbum" Erasmus rejected because it did not convey the dynamism of the Greek *logos*. Further, the translation made little sense. Rather, Erasmus argued that a better translation would be *sermo*, which implied a more active understanding of Christ's message. Indeed, Erasmus felt that *oratio* would be an even more appropriate reading but rejected it on the ground that its feminine gender would lead to a series of new theological controversies. In emending the translation Erasmus had properly understood the patristic teaching on this passage and wanted to bring to his readers a clearer understanding of the active quality of the original.

Erasmus influenced his followers to devote their time and scholarship to patristic and biblical studies. Just as he produced the fullest version of his *philosophia Christi*, however, events were occurring that would undermine his calculated attempt to reform society and the church and substitute a pure morality and simple Christian love for disputatious theology. The Reformation made it impossible for Erasmus's message to be communicated clearly. While he at first welcomed the Lutheran critique of the church, the growing stridency of Luther and his Catholic opponents led him to a defensive posture that ultimately caused him to propose more conservative readings of church tradition and critical scholarship.

The effects of the Reformation on those associated with Erasmus can be seen in the patristic scholarship of his closest follower, the humanist historian and editor Beatus Rhenanus (1485–1547).[77] Beatus had studied with Lefèvre d'Etaples before coming under Erasmus's influence in 1514. He devoted his scholarly work to advancing both humanist scholarship and Erasmian morality. In 1521 he produced the first edition of Tertullian. In this edition he attacked the Roman papacy for usurping power in the church and denied many of the scholastic theologians' doctrines. Like Erasmus he found in the Fathers the perfect means by which to expose what he considered the errors of the Roman church. When producing this edition, Beatus had come under the influence of Martin Luther, and he felt that his scholarship was most fittingly applied to the criticism of the church. In time Beatus, like Erasmus, was to reject the Lutheran reform and give a more conservative reading to the Christian past, but in 1521 he felt that Erasmus had found his fulfillment in Luther.

The Reformation marks a proper terminal point for any consideration of humanist theology. The humanists did not stop their theological work with the Reformation, and on both sides of the confessional divide humanists could be found expressing their respective churches' theologies. Biblical and patristic studies increased in importance as a result of the Reformation as all groups sought support for their views in Scripture and in the Fathers. Nevertheless, the quality of humanist theology changed. The Reformation and the Counter-Reformation were more concerned with dogmatic theology than were the humanists, who were pushed aside by the professional theologians. Humanist theology, especially as represented by Erasmus, increasingly came to be viewed as a threat to the theologian's traditional teaching authority. Thus did humanist theological reflection end where it had begun.

NOTES

1. The most important work on the religious thought of the Renaissance humanists is Charles Trinkaus, *In Our Image and Likeness: Humanity and Divinity in Italian Humanist Thought*, 2 vols. (Chicago, 1970). Trinkaus discusses in detail and with great learning and sensitivity the major humanist theological writers. A valuable supplement to his major work is his collected essays, *The Scope of Renaissance Humanism* (Ann Arbor, MI, 1983). Although humanist theology is not his major interest, the various writings of Paul Oskar Kristeller provide a fundamental background for any understanding of humanist theology; see his *Studies in Renaissance Thought and Letters*, 2 vols. (Rome, 1956–85), *Renaissance Thought: The Classic, Scholastic, and Humanist Strains* (New York, 1961), and *Medieval Aspects of Renaissance Learning* (Durham, NC, 1974). See the collected essays in *The Pursuit of Holiness in Late Medieval and Renaissance Religion*, ed. C. Trinkaus and H. A. Oberman (Leiden, 1974). See also the bibliographical essays of J. W. O'Malley, S.J., "Recent Studies in Church History, 1300–1600," *Catholic Historical Review* 55 (1969): 394–437, and C. Trinkaus, "Humanism, Religion, Society: Concepts and Motivations of Some Recent Studies," *Renaissance Quarterly* 29 (1976): 676–713. See for Northern Europe L. W. Spitz, *The Religious Renaissance of the German Humanists* (Cambridge, MA, 1963).

2. See Paul Oskar Kristeller, "Humanism and Moral Philosophy," Chapter 33 in this volume.
3. See Trinkaus, *In Our Image and Likeness*, index.
4. Ibid., 4.
5. See H. Baron, "Franciscan Poverty and Civic Wealth as Factors in the Rise of Humanistic Thought," *Speculum* 13 (1938): 1–37.
6. On Renaissance Latin, see J. IJsewijn, *Companion to Neo-Latin Studies* (Amsterdam, 1977), and J. F. D'Amico, "The Progress of Renaissance Latin Prose: The Case of Apuleianism," *Renaissance Quarterly* 37 (1984): 351–92.
7. See E. Garin, *Italian Humanism: Philosophy and Civic Life in the Renaissance*, trans. P. Munz (New York, 1965), 24–27.
8. See for "Christian Humanism," A. Weiler, "The Christian Humanism of the Renaissance and Scholasticism," *Concilium* 27 (1967): 29–46.
9. The best example of this is to be found in L. von Pastor's *History of the Popes from the Close of the Middle Ages*, trans. F. I. Antrobus et al. (London and St. Louis, 1891–1910), vol. 1.
10. See in these volumes the section "Petrarch and the Humanist Traditions." For his theology see Trinkaus, *In Our Image and Likeness*, 3–50.
11. See his attack "On his own Ignorance and that of many Others" in *The Renaissance Philosophy of Man*, ed. E. Cassier, P. O. Kristeller, and J. H. Randall (Chicago, 1948), 47–133.
12. See in these volumes Chapter 5, "Petrarch, Augustine, and the Classical Christian Tradition."
13. On nominalism, see the review essay by W. J. Courtenay, "Nominalism and Late Medieval Religion," in *Pursuit of Holiness*, ed. Trinkaus and Oberman, 26–59. See Chapter 35 above, "Humanism and Scholastic Theology."
14. See H. A. Oberman, *The Harvest of Medieval Theology: Gabriel Biel and Late Medieval Nominalism* (Cambridge, MA, 1963); and Trinkaus, *In Our Image and Likeness*, 60–61, 332–33.
15. See G. Leff, *William of Ockham: The Metamorphosis of Scholastic Discourse* (Manchester, 1975).
16. See Oberman, *Harvest of Medieval Theology*, especially 30–56.
17. See R. G. Witt, *Hercules at the Crossroads: The Life, Works, and Thought of Coluccio Salutati* (Durham, NC, 1983); also Garin, *Italian Humanism*, 29–33; and Trinkaus, *In Our Image and Likeness*, 51–102.
18. See Trinkaus, *In Our Image and Likeness*, 555–62.
19. See G. Ronconi, "Giovanni Dominici e le dispute sulla poesia nel primo umanesimo," in *Dizionario critico della letteratura italiana* (Turin, 1973), 2:11–17, and P. Denley, "Giovanni Dominici's Opposition to Humanism," in *Religion and Humanism*, ed. K. Robbins (Oxford, 1981), 103–14.
20. See H. Baron, *The Crisis of the Early Italian Renaissance: Civic Humanism and Republican Liberty in an Age of Classicism and Tyranny*, 2 vols in 1 (Princeton, rev. ed. 1966).
21. Ibid., passim.
22. See L. Schucan, *Das Nachleben von Basilius Magnus "Ad adolescen-*

tes": *Ein Beitrag zur Geschichte des christlichen Humanismus* (Geneva, 1973).

23. See A. Buck, "Der Rückgriff des Renaissance-Humanismus auf die Patristik," in *Festschrift Walther von Wartburg*, ed. K. Baldinger (Tübingen, 1968), 1:153–75.

24. For Basil, see Schucan, *Nachleben von Basilius;* for Gregory, see Sister A. C. Way, "S. Gregorius Nazianzenus," in *Catalogus Translationum et Commentariorum, Medieval and Renaissance Latin Translations and Commentaries,* ed. P. O. Kristeller, F. E. Cranz, and V. Brown, 6 vols. to date (Washington, DC, 1960–), 2:43–192; for Jerome, see E. F. Rice, Jr., *Saint Jerome in the Renaissance* (Baltimore, 1985); for Tertullian, see J. F. D'Amico, "Beatus Rhenanus, Tertullian, and the Reformation: A Humanist's Critique of Scholasticism," *Archiv für Reformationsgeschichte* 21 (1980): 37–63; for Origen, see M. Schär, *Das Nachleben des Origines im Zeitalter des Humanismus* (Basel, 1979); and D. P. Walker, *The Ancient Theology: Studies in Christian Platonism from the Fifteenth to the Eighteenth Century* (Ithaca, NY, 1972). See also H. B. Wicher, "Gregorius Nyssenus," in *Catalogus Translationum et Commentariorum,* 5:1–250.

25. See for Nicholas and Rome, C. L. Stinger, "Greek and Patristics and Christian Antiquity in Renaissance Rome," in *Rome in the Renaissance: The City and the Myth,* ed. P. A. Ramsey (Binghamton, NY, 1982), 153–69. For Traversari, see A. Corsano, *Per la storia del Rinascimento religioso in Italia: Dal Traversari a G. F. Pico* (Naples, 1935); and C. L. Stinger, *Humanism and the Church Fathers: Ambrogio Traversari (1386–1439) and Christian Antiquity in the Italian Renaissance* (Albany, NY, 1976).

26. For Valla, see in these volumes Chapter 13, "Lorenzo Valla," and the sources cited there; more specifically for his theology, see M. Fois, S.J., *Il pensiero cristiano di Lorenzo Valla nel quadro storico-culturale del suo ambiente* (Rome, 1969); G. Di Napoli, *Lorenzo Valla: Filosofia e religione nell' umanesimo italiano* (Rome, 1970); Trinkaus, *In Our Image and Likeness,* 103–70; S. I. Camporeale, *L. Valla, umanesimo e teologia* (Florence, 1972); E. Marino, O.P., "Umanesimo e teologia (a proposito della recente storiografia su Lorenzo Valla)," *Memorie Domenicane* n.s. 3 (1972): 198–218.

27. The oration is available in English translation in *Renaissance Philosophy: New Translations,* ed. L. A. Kennedy (The Hague, 1973), 10–31. For the oration, see H. H. Gray, "Valla's *Encomium of St. Thomas Aquinas* and the Humanist Conception of Christian Antiquity," in *Essays in History and Literature Presented by the Fellows of the Newberry Library to Stanley Pargellis,* ed. H. Bluhm (Chicago, 1965), 37–51; J. W. O'Malley, S.J., "Some Renaissance Panegyrics of Aquinas," *Renaissance Quarterly* 27 (1974): 174–92; S. I. Camporeale, "L. Valla, tra Medioevo e Rinascimento, Encomium Sanctae Thomae—1457," *Memorie Domenicane* n.s. 7 (1976): 3–190, and published separately (Pistoia, 1977).

28. See W. Setz, *Lorenzo Vallas Schrift gegen die konstantinische Schenkung. De falso credita et mentita Constantini donatione. Zur Interpretation und Wirkungsgeschichte* (Tübingen, 1975).

29. See, in general, S. Garofalo, "Gli umanisti italiani del secolo XV e la Bibbia," *La Bibbia e il concilio di Trento* (Rome, 1947), 338–75, and Trinkaus, *In Our Image and Likeness,* 563–614.

30. See H.-B. Gerl, *Rhetorik als Philosophie: Lorenzo Valla* (Munich, 1974).

31. See Lorenzo Valla, *Collatio Novi Testamenti,* ed. A. Perosa (Florence, 1970); see also J. H. Bentley, *Humanists and Holy Writ: New Testament Scholarship in the Renaissance* (Princeton, 1983), 32–69.

32. See Trinkaus, *In Our Image and Likeness,* 601–13.

33. Ibid., 578–81.

34. Ibid., 571–601; also for Manetti, see A. de Petris, "Le teorie umanistiche dell' tradurre e l'*Apologeticus* di Giannozzo Manetti," *Bibliothèque d'humanisme et Renaissance* 37 (1975): 15–32; idem, "L'*Adversus Judeos et Gentes* di Giannozzo Manetti," *Rinascimento* 16 (1976): 193–205, and idem, "Giannozzo Manetti and His *Consolation,*" *Bibliothèque d'humanisme et Renaissance* 41 (1979): 493–525; and G. Fioravanti, "L'apologetica anti-guidaica di Giannozzo Manetti," *Rinascimento* 23 (1983): 3–32.

35. Trinkaus, *In Our Image and Likeness,* 230–58.

36. See Ibid., 179–99, and E. Garin, "La *dignitas hominis* e la letteratura patristica," *La Rinascita* 1 (1938): 102–46.

37. See P. O. Kristeller, "Renaissance Platonism," in *Renaissance Thought: The Classic, Scholastic, and Humanist Strains,* 48–69.

38. See J. Gill, S.J., *The Council of Florence* (Cambridge, 1959), and idem, *Personalities of the Council of Florence* (New York, 1964). For Pletho, see F. Masai, *Pléthon et le platonisme de Mistra* (Paris, 1956).

39. See P. O. Kristeller, *The Philosophy of Marsilio Ficino,* trans. V. Conant (New York, 1943); A. B. Collins, *The Secular Is Sacred: Platonism and Thomism in Marsilio Ficino's Platonic Theology* (The Hague, 1974); A. T. Canavero, "S. Agostino nella teologia platonica di Marsilio Ficino," *Rivista di filosofia neo-scolastica* 7 (1978): 626–46.

40. See Marsilio Ficino, *Théologie platonicienne de l'immortalité des âmes,* ed. and trans. R. Marcel, 3 vols. (Paris, 1964).

41. See Trinkaus, *In Our Image and Likeness,* 683–721.

42. See L. Labowski, "Bessarion," *Dizionario biografico degli italiani* (Rome, 1967): 9:686–96.

43. See E. Monnerjahn, *Giovanni Pico della Mirandola: Ein Beitrag zur philosophischen Theologie des italienischen Humanismus* (Wiesbaden, 1960); H. de Lubac, *Pic de la Mirandole* (Paris, 1975); G. Di Napoli, *Giovanni Pico della Mirandola e la problematica dottrinale del suo tempo* (Rome, 1965); *L'opera e il pensiero di Giovanni Pico della Mirandola nella storia dell'umanesimo: Convegno internazionale,* 2 vols. (Florence, 1965). See also W. G. Craven, *Giovanni Pico della Mirandola, Symbol of His Age: Modern Interpretations of a Renaissance Philosopher* (Geneva, 1981).

44. See the translations in Q. Breen, "Giovanni Pico della Mirandola on the Conflict of Philosophy and Rhetoric," *Journal of the History of Ideas* 13 (1952): 384–412, see also H. H. Gray, "Renaissance Humanism: The Pursuit of Eloquence," *Journal of the History of Ideas* 24 (1963): 497–514.

45. See the translation of Pico's "On Being and the One," in Pico della Mirandola, *On the Dignity of Man, On Being and the One, Heptaplus,* ed.
P. J. W. Miller (Indianapolis, 1965), 37–45.

46. Ibid., 65–174.

47. For the debate, see Di Napoli, *Giovanni Pico della Mirandola,* chaps. 2 and
3; de Lubac, *Pic de la Mirandole,* chap. 2; *Une controverse sur Origène à
la Renaissance: Jean Pic de la Mirandole et Pierre Garcia,* ed. and trans. H.
Crouzel, S.J. (Paris, 1977); *Conclusiones sive Theses DCCCC,* ed. B. Kieszkowski (Geneva, 1973); J. F. D'Amico, "Paolo Cortesi's Rehabilitation of
Giovanni Pico della Mirandola," *Bibliothèque d'humanisme et Renaissance*
44 (1982): 37–51.

48. *On the Dignity of Man,* 3–34.

49. See P. Rocca, *Giovanni Pico della Mirandola nei suoi rapporti di amicizia
con Gerolamo Savonarola* (Ferrara, 1964).

50. See Pico della Mirandola, *Disputationes adversus astrologiam divinitricem,*
ed. and trans. E. Garin, 2 vols. (Florence, 1946).

51. See C. B. Schmitt, *Gianfrancesco Pico della Mirandola (1469–1533) and
His Critique of Aristotle* (The Hague, 1967).

52. See D. Weinstein, *Savonarola and Florence: Prophecy and Patriotism in the
Renaissance* (Princeton, 1970).

53. In addition to Schmitt, *Gianfrancesco Pico della Mirandola,* see also R. Popkin, *The History of Scepticism from Erasmus to Spinoza* (Berkeley, rev. ed.,
1979); C. B. Schmitt, *Cicero Scepticus: A Study of the Influence of the Academia in the Renaissance* (The Hague, 1972).

54. For Castellesi, see J. F. D'Amico, *Renaissance Humanism in Papal Rome:
Humanists and Churchmen on the Eve of the Reformation* (Baltimore,
1983), chap. 7.

55. See F. Gilbert, "Cristianismo, umanesimo e la bolla 'Apostolici Regiminis'
del 1513," *Rivista storica italiana* 79 (1967): 976–90.

56. See Collins, *The Secular Is Sacred,* and P. O. Kristeller, "Thomism and the
Italian Thought of the Renaissance," in his *Medieval Aspects of Renaissance
Learning,* 29–91.

57. See D'Amico, *Renaissance Humanism in Papal Rome,* chap. 6.

58. See the bibliography in ibid., chap. 9.

59. See J. W. O'Malley, S.J., *Giles of Viterbo on Church and Reform: A Study
in Renaissance Thought* (Leiden, 1968); and "Egidio da Viterbo O.S.A. e il
suo tempo," *Studia augustiniana historica* 9 (1983): 68–84.

60. See R. Douglas, *Jacopo Sadoleto, 1477–1547: Humanist and Reformer*
(Cambridge, MA, 1959), and for later developments, see E. A. Gleason,
"On the Nature of Sixteenth-Century Italian Evangelism: Scholarship,
1953–1978," *Sixteenth-Century Journal* 9 (1978): 3–26.

61. See A. Renaudet, *Préréforme et humanisme à Paris pendant les premières
guerres d'Italie, 1494–1517* (Paris, 2d ed. 1953); Spitz, *Religious Renaissance;* S. E. Ozment, *The Age of Reform: 1250–1550* (New Haven, 1980);
see also the bibliographical reviews of F. Oakley, "Religious and Ecclesiastical Life on the Eve of the Reformation," in *Reformation Europe: A Guide*

to Research, ed. S. E. Ozment (St. Louis, 1982), 5–32, and J. D. Tracy, "Humanism and Reformation," ibid., 33–57. Although it deals with the period after the one under consideration, see also the fundamental work of L. Febvre, *The Problem of Unbelief in the Sixteenth Century: The Religion of Rabelais,* trans. B. Gottlieb (Cambridge, MA, 1982).

62. See J. H. Overfield, "Scholastic Opposition to Humanism in Pre-Reformation Germany," *Viator* 7 (1976): 391–420; idem, *Humanism and Scholasticism in Late Medieval Germany* (Princeton, 1984), and C. G. Nauert, Jr., "The Clash of Humanists and Scholastics: An Approach to Pre-Reformation Controversies," *Sixteenth-Century Journal* 4 (1973): 1–18.

63. For Nicholas of Cusa see the recent study of P. M. Watts, *Nicolaus Cusanus, a Fifteenth-Century Vision of Man* (Leiden, 1982).

64. See *On Learned Ignorance,* trans. G. Heron (London, 1954).

65. See R. R. Post, *The Modern Devotion: Confrontation with Reformation and Humanism* (Leiden, 1968).

66. See in addition to Renaudet, *Préréforme et humanisme, The Prefatory Epistles of Jacques Lefèvre d'Etaples and Related Texts,* ed. E. F. Rice, Jr. (New York and London, 1972). See in these volumes Chapter 20, "Humanism in France."

67. See G. Bedouelle, *Lefèvre d'Etaples et l'intelligence des Ecritures* (Geneva, 1976).

68. See E. F. Rice, Jr., "John Colet and the Annihilation of the Natural," *Harvard Theological Review* 45 (1952): 141–63; P. A. Duhamel, "The Oxford Lectures of John Colet: An Essay in Defining the English Renaissance," *Journal of the History of Ideas* 14 (1953): 493–510; L. Miles, *John Colet and the Platonic Tradition* (London, 1962); S. R. Jayne, *John Colet and Marsilio Ficino* (Oxford, 1963); C. A. L. Jarrot, "Erasmus' Annotationes and Colet's Commentaries on Paul: A Comparison of Some Theological Themes," in *Essays on the Works of Erasmus,* ed. R. L. DeMolen (New Haven, 1978), 125–44. See in these volumes Chapter 17, "Humanism in England."

69. See now *John Colet's Commentary on First Corinthians,* ed. and trans. B. O'Kelly and C. A. L. Jarrott (Binghamton, NY, 1985).

70. See in these volumes Chapter 23, "Desiderius Erasmus."

71. See E. F. Rice, Jr., "Erasmus and the Religious Tradition, 1495–1499," *Journal of the History of Ideas* 11 (1950): 387–411.

72. See A. Rabil, Jr., *Erasmus and the New Testament: The Mind of a Christian Humanist* (San Antonio, TX, 1972); and Bentley, *Humanists and Holy Writ.*

73. For Erasmus as a patristic scholar, see D. Gorce, "La patristique dans la réforme d'Erasme," in *Festgabe Joseph Lortz,* ed. E. Iserloh and P. Manns, 2 vols. (Baden-Baden, 1958), 1:233–76; C. Béné, *Erasme et Saint Augustin ou Influence de Saint Augustin sur l'humanisme d'Erasme* (Geneva, 1969); G. Chantraine, S.J., "Erasme et Saint Basile," *Irenikon* 52 (1979): 451–93; J. C. Olin, "Erasmus and the Church Fathers," in his *Six Essays on Erasmus* (New York, 1979), 33–48.

74. See the translation of the "Paracelsis," which elucidates the "Philosophy of Christ," in *Renaissance Philosophy,* ed. and trans. A. B. Fallico and H. Shapiro (New York, 1969), 2:149–62.
75. See Bentley, *Humanists and Holy Writ,* for comparisons.
76. See M. O'Rourke Boyle, *Erasmus on Language and Method in Theology* (Toronto, 1977); relatedly, see eadem, *Rhetoric and Reform: Erasmus' Civil Dispute with Luther* (Cambridge, MA, 1983).
77. See D'Amico, "Beatus Rhenanus, Tertullian and the Reformation" for details.

37 ᐁ HUMANISM AND THE PROTESTANT REFORMATION
Lewis W. Spitz

T
HE BRILLIANT, THOUGH ERRATIC, FRIEDRICH NIETZSCHE DE-
scribed Luther as "a vengeful, unlucky priest who brought to
shame the one cleverly refined beautiful brilliant possibility—Caesar Borgia as pope." (*Der Anti-Christ,* aph. 61). Of course, history was
not Nietzsche's strong point, for Cesare Borgia, duke of Valentinois and
Romagna and son of Pope Alexander VI, died in 1507 under trying circumstances, roughly a decade before the posting of the Ninety-five Theses by Martin Luther. Nevertheless, Nietzsche's thought does point up
the fact that one school of writers in the historiographical tradition from
Jacob Burckhardt's time to the present has seen Renaissance and Reformation, humanism and Protestantism, as antithetical. Another interpretive tradition has paired Renaissance and Reformation as twin sources of
modernity, a view that has led to the periodization of history into ancient,
medieval, and modern, with the modern beginning with the Renaissance.
The debate over the relation between the two historic movements was
given classical expression in the writings of Wilhelm Dilthey, who saw
the Reformation as the religious expression of the Renaissance, and Ernst
Troeltsch, for whom the Reformation represented the revival of other-
worldly religiosity, antithetical both to the artistically ennobled naturalism of the Renaissance and to the secularized, scientized culture of
modern times.[1] The role of humanism in the Reformation and the effects
of Protestantism on humanism require a closer examination than they
usually receive from cultural historians.

The term humanism is a protean concept, which has been used in
varying modalities. The word has been associated in a general way with
the rationalist and humanitarian concerns of the Enlightenment, with the
"second humanism" of Wilhelm von Humboldt, who made reason and
experience the sole touchstones of truth; with a variety of intellectual
movements from the "new humanism" of the twentieth century, which is
radically anthropocentric and antireligious; and even with the "progressive humanism" of the Communists. It has been claimed by the Neo-
thomists at one extreme and the existentialists at the other. The term itself
is of relatively recent origin, for a German philologist, F. J. Niethammer,

coined the term in 1808 in order to describe a concept of secondary education that favored classical studies as the core of the curriculum. *Umanesimo* or *Humanismus* subsequently entered the scholarly and popular literature on the Italian and northern Renaissance, the form of humanism that Luther and the reformers encountered and that had such a formative influence on them. Renaissance humanism was itself not a simple and static cultural phenomenon, but gradually metamorphosed over the course of three hundred years, from the mid-fourteenth to the mid-seventeenth century. It was an intellectual movement initially and primarily literary and philological in nature, rooted in the love of and desire for the rebirth of classical antiquity in both form and norm.[2] Humanism associated ethical norms with aesthetic forms, the good with the beautiful, in a manner reminiscent of Plato. In looking backward toward classical antiquity, the humanists were not merely antiquarians, but they represented a certain way of assessing classical antiquity and relating it to the present. The term "humanism" was a derivative of the *studia humanitatis* or the liberal arts, those studies "worthy of a free man." This idea is said to have been largely inherited from Cicero, who believed that the orator or poet was best suited to teach the *humaniora* or humane studies. A humanist in the fifteenth century meant a student of the humanities in that classical context. Renaissance humanism contributed tremendously to the Reformation, and the Reformation, in turn, provided for the continuity of humanism into the seventeenth century or longer.

By the year 1517 humanism as a significant cultural movement at the forefront of thought was well established in the Germanies, in France, and in England, though perhaps to a lesser extent. The view that humanism was in the North derived largely from indigenous sources has lost ground in the scholarly opinion of the past two decades, so that the importance of Italian humanism for the North must be taken even more seriously.[3] Humanism was transmitted early and continuously to the Holy Roman Empire, at least as early as the conciliar period and throughout the fifteenth century to the time of Peter Luder, Samuel Karoch, and Rudolf Agricola, the father of German humanism, who died in 1485. Erasmus was indulging in a historical hyperbole when he made statements such as: "It was Rudolf Agricola who first brought with him from Italy some gleam of a better literature," or, "Agricola could have been the first in Italy had he not preferred Germany." Nevertheless, Agricola served not only as mentor, but also as a symbol to the so-called high generation of German humanists such as Conrad Celtis, Johann Reuchlin, Ulrich von Hutten, Conrad Mutian, Willibald Pirckheimer, and the rest.[4] Humanism penetrated courts and cities, and, though it met stronger resistance at the universities, it was well established in several

German universities such as Heidelberg, Erfurt, and Wittenberg before Luther became a student of the arts and law. Similarly the course of French humanism has been charted with greater precision by scholars of recent vintage. In the past century historians were apt to date the French Renaissance from the time of the invasion of Italy by Charles VIII (1494), but it is now established that French humanism was building up throughout the fifteenth century and by Calvin's time was already a well-represented cultural force, not only at the court of François I but in the universities, including one major approach to the study of the law, to which Calvin was introduced with powerful effect. Similarly, historians now appreciate the impact of Italian humanism even in England during the Quattrocento, so that the English scene in the study of classical culture was not so dismal then as has often been supposed. As English humanism entered the upper strata of English thought during that century it was not regarded as a new intellectual system that was incompatible with scholasticism. Most English humanists became ecclesiastical officials or civil servants, clerics being the mainstay of the governmental officialdom, the diplomatic corps, and the universities. As in the case of Germany and France, there was a continuous exchange of churchmen, diplomats, merchants, students, and artists between England and Italy throughout the century. It is not possible here to document the extent of these contacts, but appreciating the fact of their existence makes the emergence of John Colet and Thomas More and the reception of Erasmus seem less phenomenal than once supposed. Humanism was a well-established phenomenon and cultural force in each of the major countries that became Protestant.[5]

*   *   *

The magisterial reformers—Luther, Ulrich Zwingli, Calvin—benefited significantly from humanist learning, as did a small number of the radical reformers and a significant number of the Catholic reformers. Without the humanists and without humanism there would not have been a Reformation such as we know from history and from our own experience. Luther viewed the revival of learning in the Renaissance as a kind of John the Baptist that heralded the coming of the resurgence of the Gospel.[6] Zwingli not only was tutored by a learned uncle in the languages but also studied at Maximilian's University of Vienna, possibly with Conrad Celtis, the German archhumanist; read Erasmus assiduously and perhaps to his detriment; and mastered the art of rhetoric and much humanist or classical learning.[7] So did Joachim Vadian, reformer of St. Gallen.[8] Calvin has often been feted as a young humanist, and his early edition of Seneca's *De clementia* continues to be an object of wonder.[9] One should note also that a number of the Anabaptist reformers, especially among the Swiss Brethren, such as Conrad Grebel, were quite well-educated university men, who knew their patristic writings as well as many classical texts.[10] Among the evangelical humanists such as Michel Servet and Sébastien Castellio, the influence of humanist learning is also immediately apparent. Not always was such humanist input conducive to evangelical soundness, for it may be that although Erasmus lost the exchange with Luther on the freedom or bondage of the will with respect to man's ability to love God above all things and to believe in Christ as Redeemer on the basis of natural reason, he won the war with his rationalist and spiritualist approach to questions of biblical interpretation and understanding of the Sacrament, as reflected in Zwingli's and the reformed as well as the Anabaptist and spiritualist or evangelical-rationalist teachings. When humanism and Protestantism are considered, all too often attention is focused on the Luther–Erasmus exchange rather than on the broad exchange of influences and the counterpoint between humanism and Protestantism and, indeed, between humanism and Christianity whether Protestant or Catholic.

Protestantism was indebted to humanism on many grounds, but above all for the humanistic emphasis on the importance of the classical languages and scholarship. The importance of the languages for biblical studies, patristic learning, and classical erudition can scarcely be overestimated. Second, the humanists' emphasis on education was essential to the reformers' program for the opening of Scripture to the masses and for the elevation of the leaders of the evangelical movement to a position comparable to that of the most learned clergy of the traditional religion. Education was needed also for the lay leaders of the church and for the bureaucrats of the territorial states and the Protestant cities, Lutheran and Calvinist, and in due course for the Anglicans and Puritans. Third, the humanist emphasis on rhetoric, poetry, and history was of the essence for the Protestant movement. Clearly the stress on the spoken word of the Gospel and on preaching of the Word was central to the Protestants, who had much to learn from the humanists. Poetry was closely related to the rhetorical emphasis on *affectus,* and music became a major conveyor of the Gospel message and mover of emotion, which along with reason moved the will of man. History, so assiduously cultivated by the humanists, became for the reformers a mainline interest on two levels and for two reasons. The reformers were interested in history on two levels, of course, secular and sacred. They were also interested and, in fact, deeply concerned with history as a support for their essentially experiential rather than sapiential approach to religion or faith. For them biblical history told the story of God's people, not merely the history of old Israel and of the spiritual Israel—the church—but of individual believers and heroes of the faith. Such history provided case studies of the way God deals with man, and secular history reveals in retrospect the *locutia* of God having spoken and acted in history.

In terms of theology proper there was a marked difference between evangelical theology and the religious assumptions both of the classical world and of Christian humanism, particularly in anthropology and soteriology. The reformers' Christology contrasted strongly with the Christocentrism of the Christian humanists. For the reformers Christ served as *exemplar*, demonstrating the way that God deals with man, grinding him down into the dust of death but raising him up again to eternal life. Christ was not merely an *exemplum*, a nice model to be followed in leading the Christian life. As long as they remained merely Christian humanists, without undergoing a conversion to the evangelical view, even the most religious of the humanists could scarcely grasp the depths of the sin-and-grace, law-and-gospel, life-and-death antinomies of biblical theology. Despite the theological shift effected by the Protestants, a change that Aristotle would characterize as a true *Metabasis eis allo genos* ("transformation from one dimension to another"), they were appreciative of humanist culture and viewed the life of the mind and higher culture as a sphere of faith's works just as were all other areas of life, and in so doing they legitimized religiously the humanists' achievements in the world of thought and learning. The reformers contributed to classical learning through the work of their own savants, they broadened its influence on a larger segment of the population, they provided for the continuity of humanist disciplines through education, they perpetuated many humanist values and liberal arts education into modern times, and so they gave to humanism a new and longer life than it might otherwise have enjoyed.

*   *   *

Plutarch once observed that in criticizing lectures the auditor should improve upon them like Plato on Lysias and should not be as the Lacedaemonians said of Philip of Macedon: for on hearing that Philip had razed Olynthus to the ground, they said, "Yes, but to create a city as good is beyond the man's power." Luther, along with most Protestant reformers, was very critical of the schooling they had received from the elementary level right through their scholastic university studies. Luther in his *Appeal to the Municipalities of Germany* (1523), a writing that in the sphere of education was as important as his *Address to the Christian Nobility* (1520) in the area of general church reform, declared that his own schooling had been a disaster and that the schools needed radical change. He wrote that the schools "once were a hell and purgatory, in which we were tormented with the grinding cases and tenses and yet learned less than nothing despite all the flogging, trembling, anguish and misery we suffered at the hands of our brutal school masters. . . . How much I regret now that I did not read more poets and historians, and that nobody taught them to me. Instead, I was obliged to read at great cost, toil, and detriment to me the [scholastic] philosophers and sophists, from which I have had all I can do to purge myself." [11] Of that treatise Felix Rayther correctly observed that the whole little book is a eulogy of languages, for the state needs *rhetores* and *poetae*. "If it is necessary, dear sirs, to expend annually such great sums for firearms," Luther wrote to the councilmen, "for roads, bridges, dams, and countless similar things, in order that a city may enjoy temporal peace and prosperity, why should not at least as much be devoted to the poor needy youth?" [12] Luther's private correspondence is replete with admonitions to promote education and encouragement to pastors and teachers to devote themselves to improving the schools. In a letter to Jakob Strauss at Eisenach, April 1524, he wrote: "I beg you to do your utmost in the cause of the training of the youth. For I am convinced that the neglect of education will bring the greatest ruin to the Gospel. This matter is the most important of all." [13] In his *Sermon on the Estate of Marriage* (1519), he assured parents that they can please God, Christendom, the entire world, themselves, and their children in no better way than by educating their children. In his *Sermon on Keeping Children in School* (1530), he insisted that the civil authorities have a right to compel people to send their children to school. "It is true that it would be hard for me to ride in armor," he wrote. "But on the other hand, I should like to see the rider who could sit for a whole day and look in a book, even if he did not have to be concerned, write, or think. Ask a chancellor, preacher, or rhetorician what work writing and speaking are; ask a schoolteacher what labor teaching and educating youths are. The quill is light, that is true . . . but in this case the most noble parts of the human body are active here and do the most work, the best member (the head), the most noble member (the tongue), and the loftiest labor (speech), whereas in the case of the others either the fist, foot, back, or some similar member works along, and they can cheerfully sing joyously or joke freely, from which a writer must desist. Three fingers do it (they say of writing), but the entire body and soul are involved in the work." [14]

Luther was the first reformer to advocate universal compulsory education for boys and girls, for at least a number of grades, and if the boys had ability, and nature "had not denied them sense and wit," they should be encouraged and enabled to continue regardless of wealth and birth up to the university level. He was very likely the first person in the history of the world to do so. His motive was primarily religious but not exclusively so, for his thought was both humanistic and civic. "The prosperity of a country," he wrote in his *Address to the Municipalities,* "depends, not on the abundance of its revenue, nor on the strength of its fortifications, nor on the beauty of its public buildings, but it consists in the number of cultivated citizens, in its men of education, enlightenment and character." [15] That he favored education in order to provide bureaucrats for the government of the territorial states is an assertion that especially a social historian might assent to without heavy documentation. The magisterial reformers were fortunate to have as their successors men worthy of them. Calvin chose Theodore de Beze, a happy choice. Zwingli was followed by Heinrich Bullinger, a providential event, for Zwingli had not anticipated a change of authoritative venue when the Zurichers set out to battle against tremendous odds on his fateful day. Luther's successor was the least of all surprises, for it naturally proved to be Philipp Melanchthon, his associate through many years of reformatory effort. With respect to humanist education, Melanchthon, Johann Reuchlin's grandnephew, be it remembered, was even more zealous than Luther.

Luther himself never overcame a certain nonchalance and sense of irony about the achievements of worldly culture. In his transition period, when he was doing his *Lectures on Romans,* he wrote in his *Corollarium,* 7.6:

> It is not the most learned, who read much and many books, who are the best Christians. For all of their books and all of their knowledge is "letter" and death for the soul. No, they are the best Christians who really with complete free will translate into action what the others read in books and teach to others. But they cannot act in that complete freedom if they do not through the Holy Spirit possess love. Therefore, one must fear for our times when, thanks to the multiplicity of books, men become very learned to be sure, but completely unlearned for Christ.

Subsequently Luther freed himself from some of his monkish inhibitions with respect to classical culture and reached a climax in his humanistic identification in 1519, when for a time he referred to himself as Eleutherios, the liberated one and the liberator. Even then he chose a moniker that could be either humanistic or biblical, for the pun on his own name was surely derived from John 8:31–36 and 1 Corinthians 9:19. Luther never confused the liberal arts, with all that they have to offer for this brief moment of time between the eternities of nontime, with the means of grace. He took an active part—in fact, played the role of initiator and leader—in the reform of his own university in favor of the humanistic liberal arts, for he found that students who came to the theological faculty with a background in dialectic and traditional disciplines were poorly equipped for theological studies. He instituted a curriculum that stressed languages and rhetoric instead.[16] The revised course of studies at Wittenberg, much like the humanistic curriculum introduced a short time thereafter at Louvain, served as a model for many new Protestant foundations as well as for those universities which were reformed along Protestant and humanist lines.[17]

If Luther was important for initiating the drive toward universal compulsory public education for all children and for his role in the reform of university education, his coworker Philipp Melanchthon merits credit for the important innovations in secondary education initiated under Protestantism. The *praeceptor germaniae* wrote an impressive number of tracts on behalf of humanistic studies and had a hand in the founding and development of the secondary schools that became preparatory academies for students destined for the universities or to serve church and state in some lesser capacity.[18] In Germany they were called *gymnasia* and in France developed into the *lycées*. In such orations as his *Oration in Praise of a New School* (1526), Melanchthon waxed eloquent with such passages as this: "For what else brings greater benefits to the whole human race than letters? No art, no work, not, by Hercules, the very fruits born of the earth, not, finally, this sun, which many have believed is the author of life, is as necessary as the knowledge of letters!" He was insistent that the ultimate end that education is to serve is not private virtue alone but the interest of the whole commonwealth. For religion itself to be rightly taught implies as a necessary precondition sound instruction in good letters.

No doubt the educator who most adequately fulfilled Melanchthon's vision of the ideal educator was Johann Sturm of Strasbourg, one of his students. Sturm not only wrote some prolix but nevertheless influential treatises, arguing the case for humanistic studies, he was also the director of one of the Protestant gymnasia, which became a model for many others, especially in the Calvinist areas of France, through the influence of Claude Baduel and of Calvin himself. Sturm influenced England directly through his close relation with Roger Ascham, the renowned English educator and tutor to Queen Elizabeth I, who even named one of his children John Sturm Ascham.[19]

In a second surge of Protestantism, the Genevans picked up the theme of compulsory universal attendance at free public schools. At

Guillaume Farel's insistence the General Council in Geneva met on 21 May 1536, and with uplifted hands the citizens pledged themselves to abandon idolatry, live by the Word of God—and to maintain a school to which all would be obliged to send their children and in which the children of the poor would receive a free education. "Thus," says Eugène Choisy, "was born the free and compulsory public school."[20] Could this claim be a slight Gallic exaggeration? The influence of Calvinist educational ideals in France and the story of the Calvinist academies has not as yet been told in detail and as a unified account, though we now have an excellent monograph on public schools in Renaissance France.[21]

A more obvious example of the impact of Protestantism on education is the case of Scotland, where Calvinism triumphed in Scottish Presbyterianism. John Knox, who pronounced Geneva "the most perfect school of Christ that ever existed on earth," was a prime mover. *The First Book of Discipline* (1560) laid out a plan for an educational system that set the goals, which were not fully realized until the 1890s. It envisioned a national education system in which, first, every church reader was to teach the rudiments of religion and education; second, every town church was to have a schoolmaster to teach Latin grammar; and third, every city, especially towns of the superintendent, was to establish a college of liberal arts with honest stipends for the masters. Then, it declared in words reminiscent of Melanchthon's, at the age of twenty-four the learner must be recovered to serve the church or commonwealth unless he is found to be needed as a reader in his college or university. Calvin had difficulty in setting up four colleges in Geneva, and the Scottish Presbyterians had to keep at the problem constantly. In 1616 they called again for a school in every parish, and eighty years later, 1696, an "Act for Settling Schools" once again attempted to set up a parochial system of education throughout Scotland. At the time of the Reformation in Scotland the revenues of the church, a mere eighty thousand pounds, were to go to the clergy, to education, and to the poor, but there was much resistance on the part of the landed aristocrats and wealthier clansmen. Lord Erskine, for example, refused to subscribe to the *Book of Discipline,* whereupon John Knox exclaimed: "Small wonder, for if the poor, the schools and the ministry of the kirk had its own, his kitchen would lack two-thirds and more of what he now unjustly possesses!"[22]

The nature of the impact of the English Reformation on education is still very much under discussion. Traditionally scholars have held to a positive assessment, and the assertion has been made that the dissolution of the monasteries made available wealth partially reinvested in education. For centuries Edward VI, and his counselors, were considered to be patrons of education; but revisionists assert that of the three hundred

Latin schools that were in existence in 1535, nearly all were swept away under Henry VIII and Edward VI, or plundered and damaged. The Puritans reasserted the necessity for universal compulsory education in England. Robert Cleaver, for example, in 1598 argued for the education of all children so that "they may read the word of God to their comfort and instruction to salvation." Finally, when Johann Amos Comenius in the seventeenth century demanded universal education, writing "let none therefore be excluded unless God denied him sense and intelligence," he was closing the historical circuit, for Comenius was the last senior bishop of the *Unitas fratrum* or Bohemian Brethren, forced into exile by the victory of the Counter-Reformation in Jan Hus's Bohemia.

Not only did the reformers throughout the movement advocate universal compulsory public education, which naturally was to include religious instruction, thus broadening the base of education beyond the Italian humanist ideal of education for the social and intellectual elite, but they reemphasized the need for the liberal arts for the truly educated person. They advocated at the university level the arts or classical curriculum, Plato's royal science. They stressed the need at the secondary level for preparation in the languages and sciences that would make that kind of classical education possible. Luther was enthusiastic: "Education is a divine gift to be seized upon by all." Luther was not reticent about expressing the practical value of the liberal arts. "The fine liberal arts," he wrote, "invented and brought to light by learned and outstanding people—even though those people were heathen—are serviceable and useful to people for this life." [23] When Margrave Georg of Brandenburg undertook the reformation of his territory, he asked Luther for advice on how to proceed. On 18 July 1529 Luther replied that he should establish one or two universities where not only the holy Scripture but also law and all sorts of arts would be taught. "From these schools," he explained, "learned men could be taken to serve as preachers, pastors, secretaries, councilors, and in other capacities for the whole principality. For this purpose the income of monasteries and foundations should be set aside for the purpose of maintaining good, learned men in the schools of honest salaries, viz., two theologians, two jurists, one professor of medicine, one mathematician, and four or five men for logic, rhetoric, etc." [24] Learning cannot be promoted as well in solitude as in a university, he argued, for association with other scholars provides incentive and example. Education, however, provides a source of personal and private pleasure and satisfaction. [25]

That Luther took his Vergil and Plautus into the monastery with him is well known. That he considered the rediscovery of the sciences and languages by the Renaissance humanists as providential, and that he saw the classical and biblical languages as the scabbard in which the word of God is sheathed, is all well known. He advocated the reading of Terence and Plautus in the schools in nonbowdlerized texts, so that the pupils would encounter life realistically. He urged that languages, history, singing, instrumental music, and all branches of mathematics be taught to children. But a somewhat less-known passage spells out Luther's advice on the proper assembling of a good library, including classical works:

> My advice is not to huddle together indiscriminately all sorts of books and to look only to their number and quantity. I would make a selection of books. There is no need of collecting the commentaries of all jurists, the sentences of all theologians, the questions of all philosophers, and the sermons of all monks. In fact, I would throw out such dung and furnish my library with the right sort of books, consulting with scholars as to my choice.
>
> First of all, the library should contain Holy Scripture in Latin, Greek, Hebrew, German, and in whatever other languages it may be available. Then there should be the best and oldest commentaries, if I could find them, in Greek, Hebrew and Latin. Then books that aid us in acquiring the languages, such as the poets and orators, no matter whether heathen or Christian, Greek or Latin, for these are the books from which one must learn grammar. Then should come books about the liberal arts and all the other arts; and finally also books of law and medicine, though here, too, a judicious choice of texts is necessary.
>
> Among the chief books, however, should be chronicles and histories in whatever language they may be had. For they are of wondrous value for understanding and guiding the course of the world, and especially for noting the wonderful works of God.[26]

If Luther took the lead in reforming university education at Wittenberg, his friend Melanchthon helped to develop the regulations that became normative and served as a model for all universities in Germany influenced by the Reformation, the *Leges academiae* of 1545. Melanchthon's orations from his inaugural lecture of 1518, *De corrigendis adolescentiae studiis,* on improving the studies of the young, through such orations as his *Encomium eloquentiae,* and through the addresses delivered at the founding of the new humanistic evangelical academies, consistently decried the spreading depreciation of classical culture, and urged the continued cultivation of the classics. His style of advocacy for the study of the classics was duplicated and in part imitated by other

Protestant reformed educators. Peter Schade (Petrus Mosellanus, 1493–1524) at the University of Leipzig, for example, delivered *An Oration Concerning the Knowledge of Various Languages Which Must Be Esteemed*. Ulrich Zwingli in his treatise *Of the Upbringing and Education of Youth in Good Manners* followed the promptings of his hero Erasmus, as well as some of the discourses of the church fathers on education. A friend of Melanchthon and Luther, Joachim Camerarius (1500–1574), who became a professor at Nuremberg, Tübingen, and Leipzig and a leader in the reform of university education at the latter two places, was a professor of classical Greek and the author of more than 150 treatises. He was an impassioned advocate of classical learning, as is reflected in such addresses as his *Oration on the Study of Good Letters and the Arts and of the Greek and Latin Languages* and his *Oration Concerning the Cultivation of Piety and Virtue by the Studies of Good Arts*. Camerarius himself translated Homer, Theocritus, Demosthenes, Sophocles, Lucian, and many other classical authors. One cannot help but be impressed with the fact that these reformers found the classics to be of value at all levels of education. In his *Instructions for the Visitors* sent to the local parishes to look into conditions, Luther together with his colleagues recommended that in the first division pupils be taught the Lord's Prayer, the creed, Donatus, and Cato; in the second, Aesop, Peter Mosellanus's *Paedagogica*, selections from the *Colloquies* of Erasmus, Terence, Plautus, doctrine, and the Bible; in the third, music, Vergil, Ovid, Cicero, composition, dialectic, rhetoric, and spoken Latin. Luther was innovative as an educator, urging a three-track system. "When the children have become well-versed in grammar," he wrote, "one should select the most gifted and form a third group." [27] He had an eye for the gifted children and their potential for society. "But the exceptional pupils who give promise of becoming skilled teachers, preachers, or holders of other spiritual offices," he insisted, "should be kept at school longer or altogether devoted to a life of study." [28] From the elementary level, then, through the university curriculum, the classics were recommended and used along the lines advocated by the humanist educators.

The Catholic apologist and historian Florimond de Raemond, who wrote at the end of the sixteenth century, argued that Strasbourg rather than Geneva had been the first and foremost gateway for heresy into France. The major reformer there was Martin Bucer, who was keenly interested in pedagogy and considered the school to be the *primarium membrum Ecclesiae*.[29] Not only did Calvin benefit from his two-year experience at Strasbourg, but others did likewise, such as the educator Claude Baduel, who went from there to Geneva and eventually on to become the reformer of education and refounder of the academy in Nîmes. The founding of the *Schola genevensis*, which developed into the University of Geneva, has been called the first external manifestation of the definitive triumph of the Calvinist idea, so that it was from that point that Geneva became the Protestant Rome and began to make universal history.[30] At the school's opening Calvin's fairly brief remarks and Theodore de Beze's *Address at the Solemn Opening of the Academy in Geneva* suggested the way in which the reformers would combine religion with humanistic classical culture. The distribution of the twenty-seven weekly lectures indicates the emphasis given: three on theology, eight on Hebrew, three on Greek ethics, five on Greek orators and poets, three on physics or mathematics, and five on dialectic or rhetoric. The influence of the Genevan academy, fused at times with that of the Haute École of Strasbourg—as in the case of the Académie de Lausanne—was determinative for the many reformed academies in France. By the beginning of the seventeenth century France and the smaller states around it that were later absorbed into the kingdom had eight Reformed academies, quite a sizable number considering the fact that the whole kingdom had only fifteen universities.[31] Moreover, the Genevan academy served as a model for many universities outside of France, for it contributed to the renewal of the Scottish universities of St. Andrews and Edinburgh, it was copied by Heidelberg University in the Palatinate when it turned Calvinist, and it influenced the founding of the University of Leiden in 1575 by William of Orange and of the Herborn Academy founded in 1584.[32]

One final comment on Prostestantism and humanistic education is in order. Much has been said about the humanist teacher, tutors in a tradition represented in ancient times by such mentors to princes as Seneca and Quintilian, schoolmasters and educational theorists such as Vittorino da Feltre, Pier Paolo Vergerio the Elder, Guarino of Verona, Battista Guarino, or Leonardo Bruni. The reformers added a new dimension to the dignity and esteem of the teacher, for they emphasized the divine vocation of the teacher. Next to preaching the Gospel as a pastor of the whole congregation, the noblest calling was that of teacher to the young.

There was a discrepancy between the reformers' highest idealistic vision of what could be accomplished through church reform and education and their more realistic and at times disappointed expectations. Moreover, it is not surprising that actual achievements in education often fell far short even of their minimal expectations and wishes. Nevertheless, when due allowances are made for failures, education in the Protestant areas of Europe did make tremendous advances. Though it took until the nineteenth century, Scotland and three German territorial estates were the first to eliminate illiteracy, and classical studies flourished in the centuries that followed the Reformation, with Switzerland and Germany becoming the main centers for the study of Hebrew Scripture and language.[33]

*   *   *

The battle of the *viae* in the universities in late medieval times and the struggle between scholasticism and humanism during the Renaissance period have been wildly exaggerated. It is easier to define scholasticism and humanism in the abstract than it is to specify which person followed the one or the other discipline. There were half-scholastic humanists and half-humanist scholastics, and the conflicts at the universities were as often as not about who should be given which chairs than about the intellectual differences involved. It is true that the reformers across the board emphasized the utility of rhetoric and the value of poetry over that of dialectic or logic—a natural reaction to the scholastic preoccupation with syllogistic reasoning and the invasion of theology by the philosophy of Aristotle. To deemphasize the dialectical approach to theology Luther had suspended the university disputations, but then in the early 1530s restored them as having a certain value for training in apologetics and clear thinking. Similarly the young Melanchthon took a humanist line on dialectic. His first edition of the *Loci* or theological commonplaces is free of traditional dialectic, for he is devoted to humanistic rhetoric, follows the Topics of Aristotle rather than the Analytics, and takes his cue from Cicero and Quintilian. However, his later edition of the *Loci*, much larger and longer, is once again replete with technical terms drawn from traditional dialectic. Bearing these qualifications in mind, it is possible to assert that the reformers found rhetoric more in harmony with their scriptural concerns and biblical approach to religious truth.[34]

Luther once wrote to Georg Spalatin that he could see no utility in using dialectic in theology and did not believe that it could be anything else but a hindrance to the Gospel. Luther believed that the Scriptures themselves were fundamentally rhetorical, played on emotion, employed fine figures of speech, used stories to illustrate lessons, and nowhere were composed of labyrinthine syllogisms or dialectical proofs. His emphasis on the *verbum evangelii vocale* or spoken word of the Gospel underlines the affinity he felt between rhetorical expression and the spoken Word as the carrier of the good news of salvation. The church was there before the Gospels were committed to writing. When the good news is preached, confessed, or related, the Word of God is spoken. "The church," he declared, "is a mouth-house, not a pen-house."[35] As for the humanists, dialectic may convince intellectually on a certain plane, but rhetoric moves one to action. Hutten and Luther agreed that what one knows mentally which does not lead one to action, one does not really know.[36] The reformers' preference for rhetoric over dialectic reflects in a way a certain affinity to the humanists' anthropology, at least their definition of man borrowed from the Greeks as *Zoon logikon echon,* a living being having the power of speech.[37] The humanists saw man as less intellective, with the *ratio* in control of reflection and conclusion, than did the main-line scholastics, and the reformers, too, emphasized man as the *totus homo,* man as body, soul, and spirit, not compartmentalized. Man is wholly either rightly related to God or remains alienated from God. The Gospel does not merely change minds, but moves the heart, and for the reformers as for humanist rhetoricians, speaking with synecdoche, the heart stands for the whole man including his emotions. That rhetoric as a discipline became a valuable instrument for Protestant preachers and evangelizers is underlined by the recent studies of Reformation homiletics.[38]

The attempt has been made to relate the reformers' doctrine of *vivificatio* (vivification) of the sinner by the Holy Spirit to the rhetorical art of moving the affections (*ars movendi affectus*). In Luther one encounters many sentences such as "Revive me according to thy word" or "Christ's words not only have the power to teach, but also the power to move within." For Luther Christ is the model teacher and the ultimate orator, who instructs, delights, alarms, moves to action. The line of separation between humanist rhetorical theory and the Protestant use of the spoken Word of the gospel is a very thin one indeed, at least on the surface. The critical difference is, of course, that for the reformers the Word as gospel is the means of grace, whether preached or associated with the Sacrament, through which the Holy Spirit brings man from spiritual death to life. For all the power of the spoken word to move emotions, only the Holy Spirit can work faith and trust in the heart. Words are the external instrument through which internal change affecting the body, soul, and spirit of man is accomplished.

The emphasis on the value of rhetoric remained constant throughout the Reformation period. Melanchthon declared that much ruin happened to the church through the decline of grammar. He wrote a volume on rhetoric and in his oration *Encomium eloquentiae* or *Declamation on the Absolute Necessity of the Art of Speaking to Every Kind of Study* he praised rhetoric for its utility in service to church and state. His rhetoric text, *De rhetorica libri tres* (1519), followed along the lines of Rudolf Agricola's *De inventione,* linking German humanism and the Reformation. At Strasbourg the educator Johann Sturm wrote a variety of rhetorical works, including *De amissa dicendi ratione libri duo* (Lyons, 1542). The phenomenally productive Joachim Camerarius wrote a highly successful *Elementa rhetoricae* (Basel, 1541), published in many editions. Melanchthon had, after all, declared the two aims of classical study to be to stimulate *linguae cultum* and *ad vitae rationes formandas*. It is not possible in brief scope to trace the course of rhetoric through the subsequent course of Protestantism, but perhaps a single instance will suffice to illustrate the point. Laurence Chaderton, the Puritan head of Emmanuel College in Cambridge, made an eloquent statement on the importance of rhetoric and declared that "it teacheth truly to discern proper speeches from those that are tropical and figurative."[39] The tradition persisted well into modern times, including the most venerable of American university curricula and traditions.

A brief comment is called for on poetry as another instrument for moving the *affectus* or feelings of people. As is well known, Luther, the hymnodist, thought that song and music together had near-magical powers that approached those of the Word of God. Calvin's cherishing of Clement Marot (d. 1544), who resided at the court of François I and rewrote selected Psalms into hymn form, is well known. Perhaps he owed his sense of poetry as well as of literary style to Mathurin Cordier, the Rouen priest who had taught him so much about humanism. The savant Camerarius saw fit to write a biography not only of Melanchthon, but also of Eobanus Hessus (1488–1540) sometimes described as the first if not the foremost evangelical poet.

*   *   *

From Petrarch with his newly recovered sense of the past or of his distance from antiquity, through Valla and the Renaissance historians to the beginning of the sixteenth century, history loomed increasingly large in the consciousness of western man. T. S. Eliot referred to culture as "the incarnation of religion," or "lived religion."[40] The Christian religion, like the Jewish, is quintessentially historical. Protestant theology and religious belief alike reemphasized certain dimensions of the faith that had been forgotten or half-forgotten in the church, lost in the Neoplatonic clouds and in the varieties of labyrinthine dialectic. Protestant theology emphasized the concrete, the historical, the experiential rather than the sapiential. History moved into a new prominence in the mind of western man, history as the study of and reflection on past actuality. The Renaissance humanists had moved away from the mere annals and chronicles level of history characteristic of much medieval historical writing, that which was not at the other extreme of metahistory. The humanists stressed the pragmatic value of history, history as philosophy teaching by example. The reformers took up this view of the value of history but pressed on to stress history as evidence of the *locutia* of God, God having spoken, and the quality of *egisse*, God having acted in history. Moreover, on both sides of the theological divide, history became a weapon in controversy, which added to the urgency of its study.

Already at the time of the Leipzig debate in 1519 Luther had occasion to regret his historical deficiencies, for he spent weeks cramming on the history of the early church councils and the patristic writings. In his later years he tried to repair his deficiencies by reading history, with Melanchthon's encouragement. Luther related how even on the journey to Torgau, a time of high political tension between the princes and the emperor, he discussed history with Melanchthon at length. Between 1555 and 1560 Melanchthon gave lectures on world history, and he also edited Johann Carion's *Weltchronik* for publication. A comparison of Luther's various prefaces to historical works such as Caspar Hedio's *Chronicle* (1539) and Johann Cuspinian's *Caesares* (1541) with Melanchthon's *Introduction to the Chronicon* reveals the consanguinity of their views on history. Twenty years after the Leipzig debate Luther remarked that he had at that time not been well versed in history and had attacked the institution of the papacy a priori on the basis of the Scriptures, but that he now understood the correspondence of history with the Scriptures and could attack the papacy a posteriori.[41] The year after the Leipzig debate Luther had been led by his reading of Hutten's edition published by Schöffer of Lorenzo Valla's *De falso credita et ementita Constantini Donatione Declamatio* to conclude that the papacy was the Antichrist. In 1537 he wrote his own sharp attack on the "monstrous fraud" of the Donation of Constantine, using historical arguments.[42]

Luther's deepening interest in history is reflected in the various prefaces he wrote for historical works: Spalatin's edition of consolatory sentences from the lives of the saints, Robert Barnes's lives of the Roman pontiffs, Johann Kymaus's account of the council at Gangro, Galeazzo Capella's (1487–1537) history of the Sforzas, an edition of Jerome's letter to Evangrium, *De potestate*, Georg Major's Lives of the Fathers, a document of Popes Adrian IV and Alexander III against Emperor Frederick Barbarossa. These prefaces reveal that Luther shared the humanists' passion for the entire sweep of history as well as their interest in contemporary history, and that he shared their pragmatic predilection for drawing moral lessons from history. He stressed that histories should not be "cold and dead" but should serve moral ends.[43] In these prefaces, and most explicitly in the foreword to Galeazzo Capella's history of the reign of Francesco II Sforza, duke of Milan, Luther declares histories to be precious for they are nothing else "than a demonstration, recollection, and sign of divine action and judgment, how He upholds, rules, obstructs, prospers, punishes, and honors the world, and especially men, each according to his just desserts, evil or good."[44] In that same year, 1538, Melanchthon published a dialogue on Arminius and Tacitus on the Germans, which may have piqued Luther's interest in the Germans further.[45] In his later years Luther constructed a chronological outline of world history for his own use, the *Supputatio annorum mundi* (1541) or *Reckoning of the Years of the World*.[46] Inspired perhaps by Eusebius, whom he admired, he did three columns of events and dates for eastern, western, and German history and worked out the parallel traditions of biblical history and secular events down to his own day.

Among the ancient historians Luther's favorite was Livy, and he expressed regret that Livy had not written the Carthaginian side of the story as well as that of Rome. Like Celtis, Hutten, and other German humanists, Luther was much preoccupied with Tacitus, fascinated with his picture of the Germans as "noble savages" and of their vices as well. Suetonius and Sallust were also favorites for their accounts of Nero and imperial conspiracies. He was less interested in the Greek historians. In his *Address to the Christian Nobility of the German Nation* (1520), he urged that professorships of history be established in the universities; but there is no evidence that he took concrete steps as a university reformer to found them, for history continued to be subsumed under rhetoric and law.[47]

Various emphases in Luther's view of history are related to those of Renaissance humanism, and some introduce novelty. He was, of course, no philosopher of history, and his convictions developed out of his theological premises. Henri Strohl asserted that Luther's concept of an active and lively God, whose immanence and immediate presence are taken for granted in history, was new to the intellectual scene in the early sixteenth century.[48] "Sic enim ludit sapientia dei in orbe terrarum" ("Thus does the wisdom of God play in the world"), wrote Luther. Humanist historians had been attracted to the role of the individual in history. Luther pressed farther in this direction and developed a fascinating "hero in history" theory that reflected his own view of God. In his Genesis commentary Luther said of God, "Deus est heroicus sine regula!" ("God is a hero without compare!")[49].

In an absolute sense only God can be a true hero, but in a relative sense men, too, can achieve the status of the heroic makers of history. These men of action Luther calls heroes—*Helden, Wundermänner, Wunderleute*—and they serve God's purposes, however unwittingly. He created a "heroic hierarchy" in which he ranked people in accordance with the amount of Spirit in them. The biblical heroes began with Christ and ran the gamut downward from David and Abraham. The secular heroes included many classical figures such as Hercules, Achilles, Agamemnon, Hannibal, and Scipio, Cicero, Cyrus, Themistocles, Alexander, Augustus, Vespasian, and Naaman, with some figures such as Samson bridging religious and secular realms in his heroics. The number of heroes increases as he approaches his own time, but there are naturally also antiheroes. The most problematical are those unlikely people, such as the Virgin Mary, who seem to be chosen for special roles in history precisely because they are unlikely candidates. Here understanding "inner history" or salvation history proves to be the only resolution of the paradox. Luther's commentary on the *Magnificat* is the text that most directly struggles with the problem, explaining that the great *coram deo* are not necessarily the great *coram mundo!*[50] He brings out yet another dimension of the historical problem as seen theologically, the relation of the *deus absconditus* in nature and in history to the *deus revelatus* of Scripture. Luther's treatment of the *Magnificat* makes plain that for him God remains strangely abscondite, hidden in revelation. That he would choose this lowly maiden, of a despised people, from an obscure town in lowly Galilee defies all reason and must nevertheless (*Dennoch!*) be humbly accepted on trust. This dimension of inner history is an affront also to "religion," a rebuff to *theologia gloriae*, the birth of the *theologia crucis!* Luther's theological understanding of history conditioned the historical writing of Protestantism and introduced a dimension foreign to the approach of most humanist historiography.[51]

The German humanists had given a place of special honor to history. In his Heidelberg address Peter Luder praised rhetoric and poetry, but he gave the first place of importance to the study of history. From the fifteenth century to the seventeenth this emphasis on the importance of the study of history for human culture remained a constant in the Protestant tradition. From Felix Fabri, Sigismund Meisterlin, Lorenz Blumenau, Hartmann Schedel, Conrad Celtis, Jacob Wimpheling, Johannes Nauclerus, and other humanists through a long line of Protestant historians the humanist style of historiography prevailed, though the Protestants ever sought to espy the footsteps of God in history. Melanchthon based his *Chronicon* on Carion's simpler version of world history and did revealing prefaces to the histories of Caspar Hedio and Johann Cuspinian. Sebastian Franck's German chronicle of 1538 was intended "to point out the true kernel and main themes of our history." His was not a cultural nationalistic history, but rather an attempt to fill in the void left by the neglect of the Germans by the classical authors, and to respond to the defamation of Italian humanist historians. Notable among those detractors was Marcantonio Coccio (Sabellico), who also attracted Luther's attention. Johann Sleidan wrote on his *Commentarii de statu religionis et rei publicae Germanorum Carolo V. Caesare* until shortly before his death in 1556, a work depicting the German nation at its height under Charles V with a mission to the world, which proved to be an immensely popular theme.[52] Flacius Illyricus used history for apologetic purposes and gave it a distinctly polemical cast in his *Catalogue of the Witnesses of Truth* (1556) and the *Magdeburg Centuries* (1559ff.). These works precipitated a polemical response, of course, by such popular Catholic apologists as Florimond de Raemond and such learned scholars as Cesare Baronio (1538–1607), who spent thirty years gathering unpublished material in Vatican archives for his *Annales ecclesiastici a Christo nato ad annum 1198,* a reply to the *Magdeburg Centuries*. The Protestant historiographical line reaches down to the pragmatic church histories by Veit Ludwig von Seckendorff, a polemicist opposed by the Jesuit Louis Maimbourg, Johann Lorenz Mosheim, and the Helmstedt and Göttingen schools in the seventeenth and eighteenth centuries.

Calvin was too involved in churchmanship to write history himself, so that his treatise on relics is the closest approximation to critical history.[53] He was theologically involved in historical thinking along biblical lines, of course, seeing prefiguration in the Old Testament pointing forward and history moving on to the Eschaton. As he wrote to Charles V, the Reformation was a movement independent of human will so that he must go along with God's design and not oppose it. His successor as leader in Geneva, Theodore de Beze (1517–1605), professor of Greek in Lausanne and pastor and professor in Geneva, did some significant historical work, a *Vie de Calvin,* and an *Histoire ecclésiastique des églises réformées,* more a compilation of materials than an organic or analytical history. The tradition of polemical and pragmatic church histories persisted in the Calvinist tradition, carried along in a cacophonous dialogue with Jesuit and other polemical Catholic historians. In the French cultural milieu the study of legal history contributed to historical consciousness in a fundamental way.[54] It is not possible, nor is it necessary in order to make the point, to relate the ongoing concern with history in the Puritan and Anglican traditions where the debt to the humanist preoccupation with history continued to influence the Protestant intellectual ethos.

*   *   *

The historical interest in antiquity contributed to the continuous and growing interest in and knowledge of Christian antiquity and patristic writing. That Italian humanists were involved in the revival of Christian antiquity, as in the case of Ambrogio Traversari, for example, is coming to be increasingly appreciated. Erasmus, the prince of the northern humanists, of course, devoted his life's work to editions not only of the classics, but of the church fathers as well, such as Jerome (1516), Cyprian (1520), pseudo-Arnobius (1522), Hilary (1523), Ambrose (1527), Augustine (1528), Irenaeus (1526), Chrysostom (1530), Basil (1532), and a number of others. He recorded that his "mind was in such a glow" as he read Jerome! His editions were supplemented by Protestant scholars, and new Lives of the Fathers and patristic studies continued to expand during the subsequent century. One needs perhaps to be reminded that the church fathers in rethinking the universe in Christian terms incorporated much of the cultural good of the classical world in an overarching harmony. Their attitude was selectively but overwhelmingly positive toward the achievements of classical philosophy, history, and literature. Julian's effort to forbid Christians access to and the right to cite from classical authors failed. Gregory Nazianzus exulted: "By this measure Julian showed himself in advance to be conquered. He wished to overcome the Christians in a spiritual struggle, but robbed them in advance of their weapons. That is as though a champion were to challenge all men to a duel except the strong. He could, to be sure, forbid the Christians to speak Greek, but he could not keep them from speaking the truth."

Neither did the hostility of Tertullian to the classics prevail. Calling Plato a "grocery store of all heretics" and the philosophers the "patriarchs of heresy," Tertullian blamed them for the gnostic heresy and denied that they were inspired by an *anima naturaliter christiana*. In *De praescriptione*, 6, he decried the influence of Aristotle on Christian theology: "Unhappy Aristotle, who introduced dialectic for the benefit of heresy, the great master in building up and tearing down, ambiguous in its sentences, forced in its conjectures, ruthless in its arguments; a burden for itself, it discourses on everything so as not to have discoursed on anything." The more positive attitude toward the classics prevailed in Justin Martyr, Basil, Clement of Alexandria, Origen, Augustine, and a near patristic consensus. Justin Martyr argued in the *Apologia*, 1.46, "If Christ is the word of God himself, then he was that from eternity; then the Logos was eternal; then the Jewish conception of God was the absolute Reason from which also Greek wisdom came, then also Heraclitus and Socrates were Christians." His views were reminiscent of Philo's metaphor of the spoiling of the Egyptians for the appropriation of pagan cultural goods. Basil in his treatise "To the Youth, on How One Should Read the Classics" argued along the same lines as Plato, Plutarch, or

Seneca as to the utility of expounding the old poets. In the *Stromata*, 1.5, Clement of Alexandria wrote: "Philosophy educated the Greek people for Christ just as the law did the Hebrews. Thus philosophy was a forerunner insofar as it prepared the way for him who would be enlightened by Christ. It is a schoolmaster for Christ." Origen, whose standing as an orthodox churchman has been rehabilitated by the Roman Catholic church only in our own day, could write in the second *praefatio* of his *De principiis:* "That alone is to be accepted as truth which differs in no respect from ecclesiastical and apostolic tradition," and yet plead with his readers: "I beseech you then to draw from Greek philosophy such things as are capable of being encyclic or preparatory studies to Christianity, and from geometry and astronomy such things as will be useful for the exposition of holy Scriptures, or order that what the sons of the philosophers say about geometry, music, grammar, rhetoric, and astronomy, that they are handmaidens of philosophy, we may say of philosophy itself in relation to Christianity." Finally, Augustine himself in his *De doctrina christiana* declared most boldly: "If perchance those who are called philosophers have spoken things true and agreeable to our faith, especially the Platonists, not only are they not to be feared, but they should be appropriated from them as from unjust possessors for our own use."

It has perhaps been useful to rehearse some representative samples of patristic attitudes toward the classics, because the Fathers are considerably less known to today's readers than they were to the literate population of the Renaissance and Reformation period. That Petrarch recommended the Fathers as models and "princes" to be read and emulated in their way of life comes as no surprise to all who have come to realize that the Renaissance was not a revival of pagan antiquity, but had its deeply traditional Christian dimensions.[55] Typical of the magisterial reformers' appreciation of the church fathers was that of Philipp Melanchthon, whose understanding of the life of the one holy church through the centuries underlined the continuity in the line of great teachers from the prophets to the evangelists, apostles, church fathers, spokesmen of truth in the medieval period, and those in the latter days of humanism and reform. He articulated this idea with passion in his funeral oration over Luther: "After the apostles comes a long line, inferior, indeed, but distinguished by the divine attestations: Polycarp, Irenaeus, Gregory of Neocaesarea, Basil, Augustine, Prosper, Maximus, Hugo, Bernard, Tauler and others. And though these later times have been less fruitful, yet God has always preserved a remnant; and that a more splendid light of the gospel has been kindled by the voice of Luther cannot be denied."[56] John Calvin and other reformers achieved a knowledge of the church fathers that benefited from the emphases of Christian humanism but went well beyond the reach of the Italian humanists in that area of ancient thought.[57] The *testimonia patrum* continued to be valued all through the period, in the sacramental debates of Anglicans and Puritans, for example. Along with their utility as witnesses to the positions held in the early church, the Fathers provided reassurance to the reformers that the solution of the basic problem need not be religion or culture, religion without culture, or culture without religion, but religion and culture, each in its proper sphere and acceptably related to the other. As Paul Tillich once expressed his views: "Religion is the substance of culture and culture the form of religion."[58] Although the proposition is debatable for our times, unless one denatures religion with neologisms and idealist substitutes for historical content, as Tillich was wont to do, the statement applies to the early modern period of European history, when humanism and Protestantism flowed together to form the mainstream of higher culture.

*   *   *

The problem of continuity or change is one of the perennial subjects on which historians exercise their ingenuity. When the discussion becomes tedious, as is often the case, readers are no doubt moved to agree with Lord Acton, when he wrote: "Better one great man than a dozen immaculate historians." Such problems are best discussed in a concrete historical setting such as the present one, the continuity of humanism through the Reformation period and the change that it underwent as it became allied with religious and sectarian interests. This discussion has necessarily been more suggestive than definitive, for a full discussion or a real history of the past actuality involved would require volumes. It has not been possible, for example, to include even in passing the radical Reformation, which is unfortunate for a number of reasons. Some of the Anabaptist leaders, particularly the Zurich group at the outset and some of those in the Netherlands as well, were educated men not only schooled in university learning, but "spiritualized" under the influence of Erasmianism. One thinks of Conrad Grebel, for example. Moreover, a good number of the spiritualists and evangelical humanists, a better term than "evangelical rationalists," were by way of humanist learning and overall educational achievement a match for the magisterial reformers. One thinks of Servet or Castellio by way of example. Nevertheless, when the dust had settled by the end of the sixteenth century over 90 percent of all Protestants—a conservative estimate, for perhaps 98 percent would be more accurate—were members of the four major confessions: Lutheran, Reformed, Calvinist, or Anglican. Anabaptism had nearly died out by the end of the century, to be reawakened in another manifestation in the century following. Though small in numbers, the radical reformers across the spectrum from the sectarian groups to the mystical and idealistic individual thinkers had an influence on the modern world of outsized proportions, and classical or humanist ideas made their contribution also there.

One extreme position on the matter of humanism and Protestantism is held by those who have seen the two as being in an essentially antithetical position, analogous to those who see largely a contrast between Renaissance and Reformation. A gross caricature of this position is the book of H. A. Enno van Gelder of the Royal Netherlands Academy of Sciences, *The Two Reformations in the 16th Century: A Study of the Religious Aspects and Consequences of Renaissance and Humanism* (The Hague, 1961). Van Gelder describes a second reformation, which he calls the major Reformation. The latter developed under the influence of the Renaissance and humanism, which caused a wider and deeper gap between the groups of those who were or who were not affected by it, since it was here a question of two completely different views of religion in general. These two views were the theological one and the philosophically ethical one, a Christian one compared with a classical one, an older compared with a more modern view. Van Gelder concludes that the origin of this major Reformation is to be found in Italy in the fifteenth century, that it extended in the sixteenth century over the whole of Europe and was destined, more than the other religious Reformation, to dominate cultural life in these regions. What is usually indicated as a middle path, preserving a happy mean between Catholicism and the Reformation, was in reality a thoroughly specific view of the Christian religion, a third path deviating more from the medieval point of view and leading more directly to the civilization of the modern period than Protestantism did. Van Gelder is not entirely mistaken, and yet his model does not fit the historical reality very conveniently.

The Reformation was a more immediately powerful historical force than was the Renaissance and its doctrines a more radical and powerful solvent of medieval orthodoxy than was Christian humanism. Humanism was partially subsumed under the religious drive of the Reformation and thereafter moved along with powerful sectarian streams.[59] But thanks to the magisterial reformers, who not only bestowed an *imprimatur* upon it, but understood the promotion of higher culture, too, as a *negotium cum Deo* (cooperative undertaking with God) humanism through approbation and amalgamation with religious reform received a broader, deeper, and longer-lasting impact upon modern European and western culture. As an intellectual movement humanism enjoyed an impressive continuity and tremendous influence on modern cultural developments, only very rarely independently of religious forces. The idea of discontinuity, a sharp break or disjunction between Renaissance humanism and Reformation religion is a historiographical convenience that reinforces unfortunate secular and modernist prejudices at the expense of historical veracity. The *Carmina Burana* in the twelfth century expressed nostalgia for the olden days when "florebat olim studium" ("study formerly flourished"). One can understand why men of the "late Reformation" or those living through the seventeenth-century crises would look back to the golden age of the Renaissance and the heroic age of the Reformation and regret their fate at being born in their own times. Actually the knowledge of the three philosophies expressed in three languages, Latin, Greek and Hebrew, was much more highly developed later in the century than when northern humanism made its first amateurish linguistic and literary efforts.

There was undoubtedly a certain loss of verve and spontaneity in humanistic writings as they became increasingly humanistic studies of the schools, but that loss was not nearly as total as some suppose. Cicero's definition of the best life—that for the learned and erudite man to live is to think—gained the agreement of an ever-growing number of people, as humanist ideals moved out from the courts and universities to a broader spectrum of the middle-class population. It is difficult to conceive of the Elizabethan age in England, of Shakespeare, without both the advantage of classical inheritance mediated through the humanism of a Protestant century and the intense earnestness about religious questions introduced and transmitted by Protestantism. If, as some have argued, the age of Elizabeth was the real English Renaissance, that French humanism after the traumas of the religious wars culminated in the French Enlightenment, and that the eighteenth-century Weimar culture of the Germanies represented the culmination of the civilization of old Europe, before the disintegrating forces of industrialization, democratization, and mass societies characteristic of the modern world set in, then the amalgam of humanism and Protestantism may well be both appreciated and celebrated.

The Protestants through their educational programs, as was true also of the Catholics, provided for the preservation of humanist culture and for its continuity. Even the resurgence of Aristotelian dialectic in the theological and philosophical faculties of the universities did not lead to the suppression of the characteristic humanist intellectual interests and disciplines: rhetoric, poetry, drama, moral philosophy, history, Platonism, and natural philosophy or science. Many external or social factors can be adduced to explain the pattern of dispersion and the varying fortunes of humanist culture during the three centuries that followed that first union of humanism and Protestantism. Commercial activity is said to have shifted away from central Europe, Italy, and the empire to the Atlantic seaboard, though there has been some revision regarding the extent of decline in the old centers of culture such as Venice. Political fortunes varied; as particularism grew more powerful in the empire, France became involved in civil wars, England underwent its revolutions, and the duels for hegemony between England and Spain or England and France, the rise of the Netherlands, all had an enormous impact on the cultural developments of the time. But despite all of the economic, political, and social pressures, the cultural alliance of humanism and Protestantism remained a powerful and constructive force in the life of western man.

It is not possible to elaborate here on the points of theological tension regarding anthropology and theology proper, between humanism and evangelical theology.[60] But it is interesting to note that the very year in which Luther made his stand—1521—saw the birth of "evangelical humanism" with the publication of Melanchthon's *Loci communes rerum theologicarum*. The *Loci* created for theology a new scholarly method that was quickly acknowledged and widely accepted, combining rhetoric and biblical content. He constantly reworked this volume, much as Calvin continuously revised the *Institutes*, creating a more elaborate statement but never departing from the humanist rhetorical premises. It became programmatic for theology and a statement approving the humanist approach to learning and culture, and its influence lasted for much more than a century.[61] The concern of the reformers, just as that of most humanists, was for church, commonwealth, and culture.

NOTES

1. W. Dilthey, "Auffassung und Analyse des Menschen im 15. und 16. Jahrhundert," in his *Gesammelte Schriften* (Stuttgart, 1940), 2:39–42, 53–63; E. Troeltsch, "Renaissance und Reformation," in his *Gesammelte Schriften* (Tübingen, 1925), 4:261–96.
2. P. Joachimsen, "Der Humanismus und die Entwicklung des deutschen Geistes," *Deutsche Vierteljahrsschrift für Literaturwissenschaft und Geistesgeschichte* 8 (1930): 419–80. The distinguished biographer of Vadian, the reformer of St. Gallen, declared Joachimsen's definition given here as the first clear formulation of the concept: W. Näf, "Aus der Forschung zur Geschichte des deutschen Humanismus," *Schweizer Beiträge zur Allgemeinen Geschichte* 2 (1944): 214.
3. R. Weiss, *The Spread of Italian Humanism* (London, 1964), addresses the problem of diffusion.
4. E. Bernstein, *German Humanism* (Boston, 1983), provides the very best

overview available in English. *German Humanism and the Reformation,* ed. R. P. Becker (New York, 1982), supplies most interesting texts in English. The best analysis in brief compass is that of E. Meuthen, "Charakter und Tendenzen der deutschen Humanisten," in *Säkulare Aspekte der Reformationszeit,* ed. H. Angermeier (Munich, 1983), 217–66.

5. On the matter of the spread of diffusion of Italian Renaissance humanism to the rest of Europe north and west of the Alps, see the *Festschrift* in honor of P. O. Kristeller, *Itinerarium Italicum: The Profile of the Italian Renaissance in the Mirror of Its European Transformations,* ed. H. A. Oberman and T. A. Brady, Jr. (Leiden, 1975). Also of special value are the essays by E. F. Jacob, "Christian Humanism," in *Europe in the Late Middle Ages,* ed. J. Hale et al. (London, 1965), 437–65; and C. Trinkaus, "Humanism, Religion, Society: Concepts and Motivations of Some Recent Studies," *Renaissance Quarterly* 29 (1976): 676–713. See also W. Kölmel, *Aspekte des Humanismus* (Westfallen, 1981), but not without reading the most acerbic review by R. N. Watkins, *Renaissance Quarterly* 35 (1982): 593–95. See also L. W. Spitz, "Humanismus/Humanismusforschung," in *Theologische Realencyklopädie,* ed. M. Greschat (Berlin, 1986), 15, *Lieferung* 5, 639–61.

6. *Weimar Ausgabe, Briefwechsel* (Weimar, 1933), no. 596, 3:50, lines 23–25. Luther's reference to the Renaissance revival of language and literature was originally published in a collection of letters addressed to the first Protestant poet—and some hold the greatest—of the first generation, Eoban Koch (Eobanus Hessus), *De non contemnendis studiis humanoribus futuro theologo maxime necessariis.* . . .

7. The most careful examination of Zwingli's move through Christian humanism to his discovery of St. Paul in Romans and his transformation beyond Erasmianism into a dedication to reform is that of W. H. Neuser, *Die reformatorische Wende bei Zwingli* (Neukirchen-Vluyn, 1977), 38–74.

8. See W. Näf's great volume: *Vadian und seine Stadt St. Gallen,* vol. 1, *Humanist in Wien* (St. Gallen, 1944), and vol. 2, *Bürgermeister und Reformator von St. Gallen* (St. Gallen, 1957). Vadian's statue to this day dominates the marketplace in St. Gallen.

9. There is naturally very little scholarly agreement regarding the significance of Calvin's *Commentary on Seneca's De clementia.* To reach one's own opinion one should see the translation with the introduction and notes by F. L. Battles and A. M. Hugo (Leiden, 1969), published for the Renaissance Society of America.

10. G. H. Williams, *The Radical Reformation* (Philadelphia, 1962), 93: "Grebel, a radical leader from a patrician family, was a humanist of refinement."

11. Luther, "To the Councilmen of all Cities in Germany that They Establish and Maintain Christian Schools," *Luther's Works,* 45, *The Christian in Society,* vol. 2, ed. W. I. Brandt (Philadelphia, 1962), 369–70, trans. A. T. W. Steinhaeuser, rev. W. I. Brandt.

12. Ibid., 350.

13. *D. Martin Luthers Werke. Kritische Gesamtausgabe. Briefwechsel* (Weimar,

1933), 3:276, lines 17–19. K. Holl, "Die Kulturbedeutung der Reformation," in *Gesammelte Aufsätze zur Kirchengeschichte*, vol. 1, *Luther* (Tübingen, 1932), 518: "Jedermann musste mindestens dahin gebracht werden, dass er die Bibel zu lesen und selbständig Belehrung aus ihr zu schöpfen vermochte." In his book, *The Doctrines of the Great Educators* (London, 1937), R. R. Rush argues that it was only on religious grounds that the Protestant faith in the universal education of the people could at that time be based. See also *A History of Religious Educators*, ed. E. L. Towns (Grand Rapids, MI, 1975).

14. The old classic work by F. V. N. Painter is still worth reading, *Luther on Education* (St. Louis, 1889). The most recent excellent work containing relevant essays is *Luther and Learning: The Wittenberg University Luther Symposium*, ed. M. J. Harran (Selinsgrove, PA, 1985). The citation from *A Sermon on Keeping Children in School* is to be found in *Luther's Works*, 46, *The Christian in Society*, vol. 3, ed. R. Schultz (Philadelphia, 1967), 249, in another translation.

15. *Luther's Works*, 45, 355–56.

16. H. Junghans, *Der junge Luther und die Humanisten* (Weimar, 1984), discusses the humanists in Luther's environment, his relation to humanists, the rhetorical observations in his *Dictata super Psalterium*, and his emphasis on the Word of God. The bibliography is very thorough. See also Junghans's two studies, "Der Einfluss des Humanismus auf Luthers Entwicklung bis 1518," *Luther Jahrbuch* 37 (1970): 37–101; and "Luther als Bibelhumanist," *Luther. Zeitschrift der Luther-Gesellschaft*, 1 (1982): 1–9. See also the excellent work of J. H. Overfield, *Humanism and Scholasticism in Late Medieval Germany* (Princeton, 1984), and *Die Humanisten in ihrer politischen und sozialen Umwelt*, ed. O. Herding and R. Stupperich (Bonn, 1976).

17. See *University and Reformation: Lectures from the University of Copenhagen Symposium*, ed. L. Grane (Leiden, 1981).

18. W. Maurer analyzes Melanchthon as a humanist, *Der junge Melanchthon*, 2 vols. (Göttingen, 1967–69). See also P. Fraenkel and M. Greschat, *Zwanzig Jahre Melanchthonstudium* (Geneva, 1967).

19. For Sturm and his school, see A. Schindling, *Humanistische Hochschule und Freie Reichsstadt. Gymnasium und Akademie in Strassburg* (Wiesbaden, 1977).

20. J. T. McNeill, *The History and Character of Calvinism* (New York, 1954), 135. See also Q. Breen, *John Calvin: A Study in French Humanism* (Grand Rapids, MI, 2d ed. 1968); and A. Biéler, *The Social Humanism of Calvin* (Richmond, VA, 1968).

21. G. Huppert, *Public Schools in Renaissance France* (Urbana, IL, 1984).

22. F. Farman, *Landmarks in the History of Education* (New York, 1952), 147.

23. *Weimar Ausgabe. Schriften*, 48:29; trans. in *What Luther Says: An Anthology*, ed. and trans. E. M. Plass (St. Louis, 1959), 1:450.

24. Ibid., *Briefwechsel* 5: 120.

25. Ibid., *Schriften*, 30^{II}: 565.

26. Ibid., 15: 51f. Scholars have in recent years given more attention to the role of libraries as a tool for recapturing the mindset of the literate classes in early modern times. See, for example, G. Strauss, "The Mental World of a Saxon Pastor," in *Reformation Principle and Practice: Essays in Honor of Arthur Geoffrey Dickens,* ed. P. N. Brooks (London, 1980), 157–70; B. Moeller, "Die öffentlichen Bibliotheken in Deutschland und die Reformation," summarized in *University and Reformation,* ed. Grane, 32–34, and in full in a publication of the Göttingen Akademie der Wissenschaften under the title "Die Entstehung der Ratsbibliotheken in Deutschland."

27. *Weimar Ausgabe. Schriften* 26: 239, lines 29ff.

28. Ibid. 15: 47, line 13.

29. See E.-W. Kohls, *Die Schule bei Martin Bucer in ihrem Verhältnis zu Kirche und Obrigkeit* (Heidelberg, 1963).

30. C. Borgeaud, *Histoire de l'Université de Genève,* vol. 1, *L'Académie de Calvin (1559–1798)* (Geneva, 1900), 81.

31. R. Stauffer, "Calvinism and the Universities," in *University and Reformation,* ed. Grane, 76–90, 87.

32. Ibid., 76–77.

33. See J. M. Kittelson, "Luther on Education for Ordination," *Lutheran Theological Seminary Bulletin,* 65 (1985): 27–44.

34. R. Lorenz, *Die unvollendete Befreiung vom Nominalismus. Martin Luther und die Grenzen hermeneutischer Theologie bei Gerhard Ebeling* (Gütersloh, 1973).

35. *Weimar Ausgabe. Schriften,* 10ᴵᴵ: 2, line 48.

36. Ibid., *Tischreden,* 2, no. 2199a. Luther argues the value of logic and rhetoric for fitting people for life.

37. See the article by L. W. Spitz, "Luther, Humanism and the Word," *Lutheran Theological Seminary Bulletin* 65 (1985): 3–26, and n. 15 for bibliography on rhetoric and the Word. See also Q. Breen, "John Calvin and the Rhetorical Tradition," in his *Christianity and Humanism: Studies in the History of Ideas,* ed. N. P. Ross (Grand Rapids, MI, 1968), 107–29; and B. Girardin, *Rhétorique et théologique: Calvin et le commentaire de l'Epître aux Romains* (Paris, 1979).

38. U. Nembach, *Predigt des Evangeliums: Luther als Prediger, Pädagoge und Rhetor* (Neukirchen-Vluyn, 1972), 117–74, on Luther's homiletical method measured against rhetorical principles and the advice of Quintilian on counseling people. See also M. Doerne, "Luther und die Predigt," *Luther. Mitteilungen der Luthergesellschaft* 22 (1940): 36–77.

39. M. Curtis, *Oxford and Cambridge in Transition, 1558–1642* (Oxford, 1959), 206. Regrettably the whole Pierre de la Ramée (Peter Ramus) polemic and its place in French Protestantism must be passed over here.

40. T. S. Eliot, *Notes Towards the Definition of Culture* (London, 1948), 15, 33, 67–82.

41. *Weimar Ausgabe. Schriften,* 50: 5. See J. M. Headley, *Luther's View of Church History* (New Haven, 1963), 51. See the chapter in E. B. Fryde,

Humanism and Renaissance Historiography (London, 1983), "The Revival of a 'Scientific' and Erudite Historiography in the Earlier Renaissance," 3–31.

42. *Einer aus den hohen Artikeln des päpstlichen Glaubens, genannt Donatio Constantini.*

43. *Weimar Ausgabe. Schriften,* 43: 418.

44. Ibid. 50, 383–85; trans. in *Luther's Works,* 34 (Philadelphia, 1960), 275–78.

45. Philipp Melanchthon, *Arminius dialogus Huttenicus, continens res arminii in Germania gestas. P. Cornellii Taciti, de moribus et populis Germaniae libellus. Adiecta est brevis interpretatio appellatiorum partium Germaniae* (Wittenberg, 1938); *Corpus Reformatorum,* ed. C. G. Bretschneider and H. E. Bindseil (Halle, 1851), 17: 611–38 at 611.

46. *Supputatio annorum mundi. 1541, 1545, Weimar Ausgabe. Schriften* 52¹: 22–184, 679.

47. W. Elert, *Morphologie des Luthertums* (Munich, 1958), 1:426, n. 2, discusses the question as to whether or not Luther and then Melanchthon wished to establish chairs for historians, which would have been an advance over Italian universities. See D. K. Bauer, *Die Wittenberger Universitätstheologie und die Anfänge der deutschen Reformation* (Tübingen, 1928), 80–98: "Die Bereicherung der Wittenberger Theologie durch die Geschichte." The pioneering work still of value was E. Schäfer, *Luther als Kirchenhistoriker* (Gütersloh, 1897).

48. H. Strohl, *L'évolution religieuse de Luther* (Strasbourg, 1922), 161ff.

49. *Luther's Works,* 13, 172: God himself has "the fear-inspiring, stern, strict spirit of a hero." For Calvin's understanding of history, see H. Berger, *Calvins Geschichtsauffassung* (Zurich, 1955).

50. H. W. Beyer, "Gott und die Geschichte nach Luthers Auslegung des *Magnificat,*" *Luther Jahrbuch* 21 (1939): 110–34, writing on God and history in Luther's exegesis of the *Magnificat,* properly distinguished between "outer history," dealing with external goods or riches, wisdom, and power; and "inner history" or history within history, the real actuality that transpires inside a person such as Mary, a relation between God and the human being. But he does not bring out the dimension that did not escape Luther, namely, the importance to world history of the "inner history" also for the "external history" of mankind.

51. See the two excellent studies of faith and history in Luther: H.-W. Krumwiede, *Glaube und Geschichte in der Theologie Luthers. Zur Entstehung des geschichtlichen Denkens in Deutschland* (Göttingen, 1952); and H. Zahrnt, *Luther deutet Geschichte. Erfolg und Misserfolg im Licht des Evangeliums* (Munich, 1952).

52. In 1761 Heinrich Schütz wrote a critical commentary on the many works that were based on Sleidan's *opus* or even tangentially related to it. See W. Kögl, *Studien zur Reichsgeschichtsschreibung deutscher Humanisten* (Vienna, 1972), dissertation, 16–18, n. 37.

53. John Calvin, *Three French Treatises,* ed. F. M. Higman (London, 1970), 46, refers to a work on the beginnings of critical history in the Middle Ages: A. Lefranc, "Le traité des reliques de Guibert de Nogent, et les commencements de la critique historique au Moyen Âge," in *Études d'histoire du Moyen Âge, dédiées à Gabriel Monod* (Paris, 1896), 285–306. I owe this reference to Bruce Tolley.

54. See D. R. Kelley, *Foundations of Modern Historical Scholarship: Language, Law, and History in the French Renaissance* (New York, 1970).

55. See, for example, Petrarch's *De otio religioso,* in which he points to the Fathers as models, and the excellent analysis by C. Trinkaus, "Humanist Treatises on the Status of the Religious: Petrarch, Salutati, Valla," *Studies in the Renaissance* 11 (1964): 7–45, at 16, reprinted in his *The Scope of Renaissance Humanism* (Ann Arbor, MI, 1983), 195–236; and in his *In Our Image and Likeness: Humanity and Divinity in Italian Humanist Thought* (Chicago, 1970), 2:651–62, at 655–60. On the other hand, some humanists such as Ermolao Barbaro the Younger resisted the idea of directing their energies toward the Fathers: *Epistolae, orationes, carmina,* ed. V. Branca (Florence, 1943), ep. 72, 1:92. Luther once commented in the *Table Talks* that there is far more wisdom in Aesop than in Jerome!

56. Philipp Melanchthon, "Funeral Oration Over Luther," in *The Protestant Reformation,* ed. L. W. Spitz (Englewood Cliffs, NJ, 1966), 70. On Melanchthon's impressive knowledge of patristic authors, see P. Fraenkel, *Testimonia Patrum: The Function of Patristic Argument in the Theology of Philipp Melanchthon* (Geneva, 1961).

57. A major work on Calvin and the church fathers awaits its author, but an exemplary monograph is B. Warfield, *Calvin and Augustine* (Philadelphia, 1956). See also L. Nixon, *John Calvin's Teachings on Human Reason* (New York, 1963). H. R. Van Til, *The Calvinistic Concept of Culture* (Grand Rapids, MI, 1959), includes such challenging essays as "Augustine, the Philosopher of Spiritual Antithesis and Cultural Transformation." The scholarly world awaits with keen anticipation the publication of W. Bouwsma's Calvin studies, for his mastery of Renaissance culture, keen perception of the Stoic and Augustinian elements in humanist thought, and deep appreciation of Calvin's theological wisdom will lend great authority to his analysis.

58. P. Tillich, *The Protestant Era* (Chicago, 1938), 57.

59. On the continuity of humanism in confessional alliance with Lutheranism, see M. P. Fleischer, *Späthumanismus in Schlesien. Ausgewählte Aufsätze* (Munich, 1984). Also of interest is H. Schöffler, *Deutsches Geistesleben zwischen Reformation und Aufklärung: Von Martin Opitz zu Christian Wolff* (Frankfurt am Main, 3d ed. 1974).

60. The theological differences and varying emphases between Christian humanism and evangelical theology with respect to anthropology and theology proper are spelled out by E. Wolf, "Reformatorische Botschaft und Humanismus," in *Studien zur Geschichte und Theologie der Reformation. Festschrift für Ernst Bizer,* ed. L. Abramowski and J. F. G. Goeters (Neukirchen, 1969), 97–119.

61. W. Maurer, "Melanchthons *Loci communes* von 1521 als wissenschaftliche Programmschrift," *Luther Jahrbuch* 27 (1960): 1–50. Joachimsen, "Humanismus und die Entwicklung," 475, said of the *Loci communes:* "Das Ergebnis ist eine Theorie der inneren Erfahrung, die ganz auf die reformatorische abgestellt ist und sich anheischig macht, diese Erfahrung in eine logische Deduktion von allgemein gültigem Charakter zu verwandeln."

D &. HUMANISM, THE ARTS, AND SCIENCE

38 &. HUMANISM AND ART
David Cast

W E SHOULD BEGIN WITH DEFINITIONS. THE WORD HUMANISM in this title refers to a particular movement—described in many other places in these volumes—that took shape in Italy in the late fourteenth century and spread then throughout Europe, both the Protestant North and the Catholic South.[1] And the word art refers to the visual arts, specifically the higher, nondecorative arts: painting, sculpture, architecture, or all that Leon Battista Alberti had in mind when, in the preface to the Italian version of his treatise *De pictura* (1436), he spoke of the "laudable deeds" of Brunelleschi the architect; Donatello, Ghiberti, and Luca della Robbia the sculptors; and Masaccio the painter. This sense is not what the word art necessarily meant in the Renaissance. In one context, art (*ars*) was a general type of action, an activity based on knowledge in the Aristotelian sense,[2] and something, as Leonardo Bruni suggested, that could be compared then to wisdom (*sapientia*), knowledge (*scientia*), prudence (*prudentia*), or intelligence (*intelligentia*).[3] The word *ars* could also mean, as it did for Quintilian, a technique, or all that can be learned, as opposed to talent (*ingenium*), which denotes all that cannot be learned, but merely improved or developed.[4] In using the words art and humanism in this way, I am suggesting a contrast. The word art is used in the modern meaning, but in a way only partly familiar in the Renaissance. The word humanism is employed in a way quite distinct from modern usage but with a meaning true for any literate person in the Renaissance.

The word humanism was an invention of the early nineteenth century. But in the Renaissance there were the "humanist" studies, the *studia humanitatis,* and it was the humanists, the *umanisti*—a term of student slang similar to that for other university teachers, *legistà, cannonistà*—who taught this new discipline. The *studia humanitatis* were made up of a specific set of subjects: grammar, rhetoric, history, poetry, and moral philosophy, but not natural philosophy or metaphysics or law or medicine, which had been the main topics of study in medieval universities and schools. This difference is important. The *studia humanitatis* were concerned with wisdom (*sapientia*), and for the humanists, whether we think of early scholars like Coluccio Salutati or Bruni or later figures like John Colet, Erasmus, or Cardinal Jacopo Sadoleto, wisdom meant human wisdom and human actions, the will, prudence, what men do as thinking, active members of society, concerned always with the improvement of the self and of the very society that gives individuals their strength and virtues. The purpose of the *studia humanitatis* was simple: to show how to live nobly, to achieve happiness (*beatitudo*) or, as one humanist put it, to live well and honestly.

To achieve this was to achieve *humanitas*. Above *humanitas,* the condition of man, was *divinitas,* the condition of God. At the other end of the line was *feritas* or *immanitas* (wildness), and it was this condition, that of the willful rather than the willing creature, the person or animal outside rather than in society, that we should always try to avoid; such a warning is found, for example, in Petrarch.[5] Humanism was concerned first with ethics, and then, of course, with the classics, and the classics read in two ways: first as ancient texts—philology was an important part of humanist training—and second, as part of the material for the study of ethics—ancient writers told, with often marvelous richness, just how certain moral problems might be defined, described, and resolved.

It is necessary then to recognize the particular technique of the humanists. In their arguments—and here a contrast might be set with a text like the *Summa theologia* of Aquinas—the humanists proceeded less by logic than by what they called example. And to prove an argument meant gathering examples to support a conclusion and make it persuasive, instead of providing an analysis or using logic to move from certain premises to certain conclusions. As Lorenzo Valla said so crisply, to the humanists *oratio* (speech) was as important as *ratio* (reason). And it was in this kind of *oratio* that antiquity could be of use, providing so many instances of examples—or what Francis Bacon called "Similitudes and Instances Conformable and Parallels."[6] Two descriptions of humanism can perhaps make this method clear. The late Latin writer Aulus Gellius noted that the correct meaning of the word *humanitas*—it is interesting that he has to make this point—is something precise, that it does not mean just friendliness but something more akin to what he calls an education and training in the liberal arts, both of which come from reading.[7] It is a short step in meaning, if not in time, from this definition to what Matteo Palmieri said about the *studia humanitatis* in his widely read book, *Della vita civile* (1432–36), that they are a rounding out of the virtues that come from the Greeks[8]—that is to say, ethics based on the model of the past.

*   *   *

But what does a program of this kind have to do with the visual arts? The connections between Renaissance architecture and the literary traditions of humanism have long been recognized; we need only refer here to Rudolf Wittkower's important book, *Architectural Principles in the Age of Humanism*. But painting and sculpture are, in some ways, quite distinct from architecture. They do not have such immediately identifiable principles or parts, no such absolute forms as circles and squares, or elements, like pilasters and architraves and lintels, that can be named and thus caught by the language available to the humanists. And yet also, more importantly, painting and sculpture in the Renaissance, engaged as they were with depiction, or what the English humanist George Puttenham called in 1589 "the visible representation of the thing,"[9] would seem to be concerned more with epistemology than with ethics, that is to say, more with the idea of representation itself than with any moral actions of the kind espoused by the humanists. And yet, at one level, of course there was a connection between the activities of the humanists and the forms of Renaissance painting and sculpture. But it is one that we have to look for very carefully if we do not take it to be self-evident. It is with this less obvious connection that I am concerned here. After the work of Rudolf Wittkower, it is not necessary for me to concern myself much with architecture; my main subjects, then, will be painting and sculpture. And in talking about them I depend a great deal on two recent studies by Michael Baxandall, *Giotto and the Orators* and *Painting and Experience in Fifteenth-Century Italy.*

We can recognize immediately the difficult nature of these connections. In any general account of the Renaissance, the visual arts now occupy an honored place, and names like Leonardo, Raphael, and Michelangelo are given great acclaim. But humanists, especially in the fifteenth century, said very little about art—especially perhaps painting and sculpture—and even the little they did say is often marked by hesitancy and questions. Are the visual arts a useful medium for moral instruction? And if set against poetry and prose, are they capable of true discrimination or subtlety? And was art, in the humanist sense, a learned activity? It was, after all, a trade and a manual activity, and artists, like cobblers, sold the products of their trade in shops. And what did it matter if paintings and reliefs began to represent subjects of clear classical meaning or if they included such learned elements as Greek and Latin inscriptions? Artists were ill-born—only a few, like Baldassare d'Este or Giovanni Boltraffio or Francesco Melzi, came of better families. They were poorly educated, rough, sometimes shrewd, high-spirited, but ill at ease in what then passed for polite society. Botticelli, so reported a contemporary (albeit an angry one), was barely able to read or write. Then what did it matter if his paintings contained a Venus?[10]

The effect of such comments should not be ignored. And to balance them—if we are concerned with the question of how much artists knew—we must remember that information, even in the bookish society of the Renaissance, might be passed on by mere word of mouth. Botticelli's studio, so a contemporary tells us, was always full of people ready to talk about everything; and there must have been among these visitors many who were literate and could impart the fruits of their literacy to Botticelli. But, in the end, the hesitation of the humanists about art was surely more than social prejudice, something based on what we can perhaps call the limits of language. For what was there that could be said, within humanism, about the properties of art, of matters like space, color, or depiction? There were some humanists and educated people, we may be sure, won over by friendship or by the nature of their own sensibilities, who took an interest in the arts: Alberti is the great example. And, of course, from the time of Ristoro d'Arezzo in the thirteenth century, there was an ever more open admiration for the complexities of art and for beauty, that mysterious element which was spoken of by connoisseurs and by *dilettanti*.[11] Perhaps in casual conversation the humanists talked easily of art; perhaps they knew even what we now call the shop talk of artists. But within their favored and primary discipline, the humanists were not generally able to talk directly or precisely about the virtues of art, of subjects like color, or light, or perspective, of the particular mode of representation of painting and sculpture in the Renaissance. Perhaps literacy was a barrier. Faced with the image of St. Jerome by Pisanello, the humanist Guarino of Verona was all too ready to call on conventions he knew. I keep silent, he remarked, rather than let my voice "break loutishly in on one who contemplates God and the Kingdom of Heaven"[12]—a play on the idea of the potential life in the image that goes back through Petrarch to antiquity.[13] Unarmed with such phrases, Duke Ercole d'Este of Ferrara, looking at the still unfinished paintings of the *Triumphs of Caesar* by Mantegna, was quieter. "They pleased him much" was all that Silvestro Calandra could report back in 1486 to his master, Marquess Francesco Gonzaga.[14]

We have not reached, however, the end of the story. The humanists generally chose not to speak precisely of the visual arts. But, by a not completely paradoxical process, it was from within the general moral language of humanism that those who so wished could construct an account of the idea of the artist, which served in time to work first to the credit of individual artists and then to art itself. Humanist language had its limits; but seen in this light, it also had some particular benefits.

It is necessary here to generalize. Renaissance art took as its subject the human figure, and the human figure seen in two ways: first, literally, the figure with a certain structure, occupying space (Figure 38-1), and second, more abstractly, the figure as a token of measurement and proportion that could, in the end, serve as a guide for all the proportion embodied in a work of art (Figure 38-2). These claims are true even in as abstract an art as architecture, for the figure was the implied element in all the parts of architectural design, whether by analogy—as with the column—or from the correspondence that could so easily be suggested between the perfection of the body in its parts and the perfection of the universe (the module, the golden section; see Figure 38-3). In painting or sculpture, the figure, seen as in the flesh, standing solidly on the ground—a quality of figures by Masaccio that Vasari praised—was a perfect vessel for all that artists could encompass, in the fullest sense of the word, expressing by their art, in epistemological terms, the validity of the world of the senses, and in moral terms, the notion of humanness, of community, of shared actions and thoughts.

The Renaissance was, of course, a Christian culture, and most Renaissance art had religious subjects. But if the Renaissance artist was concerned with God, it was the God who became man, the Word as Flesh, rather than God as mystery, a God whose nature could be approached only through the paradox of the Trinity. Christ is the subject of Renaissance art, but Christ usually with others, acting upon them, ministering, preaching (as in Figure 38-1); or he is shown in scenes of his childhood, or we see the moment of the Annunciation to Mary, the mother of God (Figure 38-4). And when we move from Christ to his apostles and the saints, they too are generally shown in action, in clear, comprehensible narrative (see again Figure 38-1). This idea of narrative was the underlying reason for the development of perspective; for perspective quite explicitly maps out relationships, the place of figure against figure (see, for example, Figure 38-2). It was also this idea of narrative that encouraged the naturalistic style of Renaissance art, a style that invited the spectator to draw into what he saw in the art the experiences of his life, a style that chose to emphasize the comparability between the image and the world, between the image and what might be called the general perception of the world beyond the images. The ikon, the isolated devotional image of the medieval church, asked for adoration. But Renaissance paintings with their clear spaces, their narratives, their

Figure 38-1. Masaccio, The Tribute Money (1425). Santa Maria del Carmine, Florence. Alinari.

Figure 38-2.   Piero della Francesca, Madonna and Saints with Angels Adored by Federigo da Montefeltro *(1472). Milan, Brera. Alinari.*

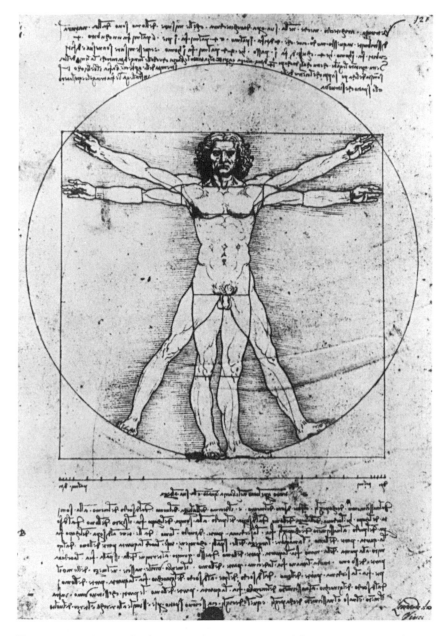

Figure 38-3. *Leonardo da Vinci*, The Proportions of the Human Figure after Vitruvius. *Drawing (1492), Accademia, Venice. Alinari.*

Figure 38-4. Alesso Baldovinetti, Annunciation *(1450). Uffizi, Florence. Alinari.*

apparently common forms, urged the viewer to trust his ordinary perceptions, perhaps to go beyond them, but to do so without abandoning all
that he seemed to know before he came to the image.

In all this attempt to embody the ordinary in form classical art was
important, for it supplied the Renaissance artist—as classical literature
supplied the writers—with a whole host of examples of the same intention. For the figures themselves there were the great classical statues, the

Apollos and the Venuses; for the figures in action there were the sarcoph-
agi or the scenes on cameos, vases, or reliefs; and for architecture there
were the buildings that could be found all over Italy, but above all, of
course, in Rome. For some elements of art, like color or perspective, the
artist had no such practical models from the past. But even there, if he
knew his Pliny, the artist could call on the authority of antiquity. Were
there not some details on what classical artists did with color in the stories of Apelles? And as Ghiberti noted, is it not clear from the story of
the dispute of Protogenes and Apelles and the drawing of the lines that
ancient artists were also concerned with the schemes of perspective? [15]

As we have seen, Renaissance art was concerned with the figure,
often an individual figure like the *St. George* of Donatello (Figure 38-5),
the *David* of Michelangelo (Figure 38-6). And indeed since the nineteenth century it has been suggested that the Renaissance was the first
great period of what might be called individualism. But we must be careful; there are of course great single figures in Renaissance art—especially
in sculpture. But the truest model of the Renaissance is the image of
many figures acting together, in concert and to a common purpose. And
the idea of the person in the Renaissance did not lead to a solipsistic
account of reality or a belief in what we might call, as against the idea
of universals, the exclusive truth of particular things. In the Renaissance,
a concern with the material and sensible world did not mean that the
intangible world was slighted; a concern with a particular figure did not
imply that the idea of society or community was ignored. In the end the
art of the Renaissance was not involved with anything that might be
termed an individualist imagery; the portrait, for example, appears at
this time, but the portrait seems always to be intended to show the person as a type—the *Gattamelata* by Donatello shows Erasmo da Narni
both as a Roman general and a "leonine" temperament (Figure 38-7) or
the person as a member of a group or of a community—the famous men
of Florence in the painting by Masaccio of the dedication of Santa Maria
del Carmine or something like Giovanni Basso della Rovere and his family in the *Baptism of Christ* by Perugino in the Sistine Chapel (Figure
38-8).

*   *   *

It is perhaps in such terms that we might choose to describe the concerns
of Renaissance art. But are there any expressions from the Renaissance
of similar preoccupations? Two hints can be found; one, appropriately
enough, in Alberti, the other in a text by the humanist Naldo Naldi.

At the beginning of his treatise *De pictura* (1436), Alberti made
some general remarks about the relation that exists between painting—

Figure 38-5. Donatello, Sculpture of the St. George Tabernacle *(1415–17). Or San Michele, Florence.*

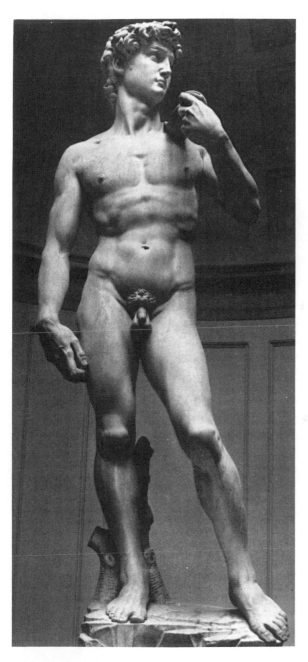

Figure 38-6.   Michelangelo, David (1501–4). Accademia, Florence.

Figure 38-7.   Donatello, Equestrian Monument of Erasmo da Narni, il Gattamelata *(1447–53). San Antonio, Padua.*

and by implication, sculpture—and the physical and sensible world. Art
uses mathematics, he noted, which his own account of perspective
shows. But art is not mathematics, because mathematics measures forms
in the mind alone, divorced from matter. "We, however, [i.e., we as pu-
tative artists] . . . who wish to talk of things that are visible, will express
ourselves with a fatter Minerva."[16]

In either Latin (*pinguiore Minerva*) or Italian (*più grassa Minerva*)
this phrase "a fatter Minerva" is curious, but it had some classical authority. Minerva was, of course, one of the patrons of art, and thus she
could easily stand for art itself. Here, however, she is a fat Minerva, a
clumsy Minerva (to act *pingui Minerva,* as Cicero wrote, is to act clum-
sily), even a rustic, illiterate Minerva (here the phrase can be compared
to gross Minerva, *crassa Minerva,* of the *Priapea* or the gross Muse,
crassiore Musa, of Quintilian).[17] The phrase Alberti used has been translated in a number of ways as "more sensate wisdom," "a more down-to-
earth inspiration," "in cruder terms." But whatever these differences it is

Figure 38-8.   Perugino, Baptism of Christ. *Detail, fresco (1481), Sistine Chapel, Rome. Alinari.*

generally clear what Alberti meant, namely, that art is not simple matter, or pure reason, but something between matter and mind. Art, then, may be called Minerva, Reason, but a Minerva who partakes of her natural— and for humanists, familiar—opposite, Nature. And if the phrase Alberti used was somewhat awkward, it was something that could stand against what other, earlier writers had said. The scholastics had much to say on substance. John Duns Scotus, for example, had emphasized the notion of "thisness" (*haeccitas* or what in the seventeenth century Ralph Cudworth would call *haeccitie*), using this term to argue against a Platonic possibility of universals and on behalf of a description of knowledge that saw knowledge as coming from nothing more than sensory experience. Alberti could not use this notion, for what he was trying to describe and define was an art that contained both *haeccitie* and the idea of universality, both the material and the intangible world. The phrase about Minerva was the best he could do; but it served his purpose if only because it was new and had behind it true classical credentials.

A second and more direct notion of art can be found in the preface to the Life of Giannozzo Manetti written by Naldo Naldi, about 1450. Naldi is speaking of wisdom, the humanist *sapientia*. Wisdom is not simple philosophy, he writes, for as philosophers we perceive things only mentally and spiritually. Wisdom is closer to history, for in history—and here is the key phase—just as in painting, we grasp the world both through our cognition and through our senses and are thus led to moral action, action that is not merely the result of reflection but is admitted to us "through sense and participation."[18] Painting, then, like history, is concerned with action and response. Neither the work of art nor the text of history is distant; they are things we can act through, learning in this way how, as striving moral persons, we should work against evil, which all too often confounds the lazy man. Naldi used the simple word action (*actio*). Alberti was fond of verbs like "to use onself" (*adoperarsi*), "to exercise oneself" (*exercitarsi*); and at one point in *Della famiglia* he crowned this whole idea of performance with a metaphor: we are brought into life, he wrote, like a ship that is not meant to rot in port but to furrow long paths in the sea.[19]

Naldi, in speaking of history, was thinking of the new humanist history rather than the bare chronicles of the medieval scribe. The humanist historian was steeped in antiquity and, like the orator, was taken up with persuasion, defining and selecting examples of the moral life, teaching what was good and what was bad. *Istoria,* then, held a special place in the humanist canon, and it is striking to see this very word used by Alberti in another passage in which he is talking seriously about art; the *istoria,* he says, being the most important part of painting. Dante had used the term *istoria* to refer to the theme or subject of a work.[20] And it is not difficult to find examples in the fourteenth and fifteenth centuries of the word being used in this way. Alberti seems to have meant something else. For him the simple theme of a work was covered by the term *inventio,* which was, as for classical writers, the first part of oratory, before arrangement, diction, memory, and delivery. What Alberti says about the *istoria* occurs in the midst of a description of the most individual qualities of a painting, namely, composition. Indeed, Alberti adds to his account of the *istoria* something of what he said about composition, that the *istoria* is all the parts of the bodies: part of the body is the member, part of the member is the surface. It seems, then, that for Alberti the *istoria* involves both the theme of a painting and the expression of the theme in the painting. It is persuasion and persuasion of a truth. And here we might think of what Cicero said when he placed *istoria* between *fabula* (story) and *argumentum* (argument), or what Salutati said when he noted that history, like a story, was concerned with a figurative language but a figurative language that was true.[21]

In medieval Latin, the word *istoria* could mean allegory. In Alberti's time, *istoria* seems to have meant not just a subject, but a subject that involved action. Thus, in the documents describing Donatello's *Cantoria*, with its free and centerless actions (Figure 38-9), the word *inventio* is used.[22] And Bruni in his recommendations for the subjects of the baptistery doors was careful to call them *istorie*, saying that the representation of a true *istoria* would involve on the part of the artist (and then the viewer) an understanding of both the persons and the actions shown (Figure 38-10). It was in this way, then, that the word *istoria* could be used in a document of 1446 referring to scenes from the life of St. Peter, commissioned for the Bigallo in Florence; or, to move beyond Italy, by a German humanist who called subjects on the walls of the old Rathaus in Nuremberg, from classical writers like Aulus Gellius, Plutarch, and Valerius Maximus, the "historien." In this context, in the context of rhetorical persuasion, form and content might be taken as one. And if, as time went on, more and more attention was indeed given by connoisseurs to the idea of beauty itself, such beauty or embellishment could also be justified in practical terms. Petrarch noted in his account of poetry that beauty transfixes us with its hidden darts, impelling us toward the kind of virtue that poetry—and painting—are concerned to represent.[23] Why work hard on what Alberti called the *istoria*? So that we can communicate this virtue, or as Alberti put it, so that what we have in our private papers can be put in its correct position in the work for public exhibition. Paintings, Alberti continued, should be large; painting itself should charm both the eyes and the mind of the spectator. Then it can persuade him.[24]

*   *   *

These texts suggest something of what the humanists noted about painting and sculpture. But in fact it seems that there was more for them to say about art in a somewhat different context, namely, in the history they established for culture in general, culture here taken in the widest meaning to include all that men do in the making of things. Culture, for the humanists, was tied to the history of politics, and politics then was important not only for itself but also for what it could represent of all human action. Within politics, one issue was of supreme importance, that of liberty, or opportunity, or what Alamanno Rinuccini meant when he spoke of "doing and making what one wants."[25] Liberty was the prerequisite for culture, the humanists emphasizing here the notion of suc-

Figure 38-9. Donatello, Cantoria (1433–39). Museo dell'Opera del Duomo, Florence.

Figure 38-10.   Ghiberti, Flagellation. *Baptistery, north doors (1416–19), Florence. Alinari.*

coring and nurturing. As Athens showed, freedom and art go together, as did Rome—though here it was, for Florentines, the Rome of the Republic that was praiseworthy, not the Rome of the Empire. Like Athens and Rome, Florence was a perfect republic in which all men were in sympathy and all opportunities were realized, or, as Buonaccorso da Montemagno put it, "so many hearts come together in one heart, so many wills in one will, so many powers in one power." [26] The fruit of the political freedom in Florence was the Renaissance. Its outward sign was the beauty of the city, its inward sign, the magnificence of Florentine poetry. Why was it, Filippo Villani asked, that no true poetry was written in the Middle Ages, at least after the time of Claudian? It was because the Catholic church began to regard the imagination as pernicious and vain, and thus poetry lay prostrate without honor or dignity. Why then the triumph of the Renaissance? It was because in Italy there was once again a system of government that respected the natural temperament of man, his simple zeal for virtue, his fear of death and the many other parts of his character that made him fallible and frail but optimistic. A government that allows man to fulfill his innate nature will be a government that encourages art.[27]

The art of the Renaissance was based on antiquity, but this idea of one source did not limit the freedom of artists or poets. For artistic action in the Renaissance was not seen as copying, but as imitation. To copy was to lose dignity, to act unfreely—which, as Petrarch noted, had been the fault of the scholastics.[28] But to imitate was to do something quite different in spirit; it was to act freely, to select—or as one humanist put it, to retain—a sense of oneself. The past, then, was not a burden; for modern man, free and emboldened as he was, could borrow just what he wanted from antiquity and do so exceedingly well, surpassing, as Alberti said, what antiquity had done. For Petrarch the idea of perfect imitation could be expressed by the metaphor of the bee who gathers up the fruit of all the flowers and transforms it into honey.[29] For Matteo Palmieri this idea could be substantiated from a story in Cicero about Zeuxis who had been able to bring together for a picture of Venus (or Helen) the parts of all the lovely women of Croton and make then a yet more lovely image.[30]

Set as they were, by temperament and profession, within a linguistic tradition, many of the humanists judged the health of a society by language alone, speaking of it as a complete model of the ideas of community and freedom. This model could be extended. At one point in his essay on the dignity of man, Giannozzo Manetti set down a list of all the objects man makes with his intelligence, all the things that, in his words, are his. Naturally Manetti includes language, "that great and subtle artifice." But he then extends the catalog to include a range of more practical actions that have the same value as language, activities like the making of houses, towns, cities, buildings, or works of sculpture and paintings.[31] It was only reasonable that Manetti should have wished to speak about buildings, for, like every Florentine, he stood in the shadow of Brunelleschi's great new dome of the Florentine cathedral. If such an extension of the idea of virtue was easy, it was significant. For then the visual arts, like poetry, could stand as demonstrations of virtue, virtue being, as Alberti said in his treatise *Della famiglia*, "nature itself, complete and well-formed."[32] Most of the citizens who had been celebrated in national biographies were professional men or poets, but artists began to be included. Villani had noted the names of Cimabue, Giotto, Stefano Fiorentino, Taddeo Gaddi, and Maso di Banco. Antonio Manetti, whose work is partly a translation of Villani, reserved half his biographies for artists: Donatello, Lorenzo di Bartolo, Masaccio, Fra Angelico, Filippo Lippi, Uccello, and Luca della Robbia. After Manetti were to come texts like the *Libro di Antonio Billi* (1481–1530), the *Anonimo della Magliabecchiana* (1537–42), and the incomparable book of Giorgio Vasari, *Lives of the Painters, Sculptors, and Architects,* first published in 1550.

In this book Vasari set down an account of the rediscovery and progress of art, which was based on the then familiar idea that Italy, and above all Florence, in allowing men to develop their talents, had thereby produced the most perfect art yet known. Republicanism had been the cause for this flowering in the early Renaissance. But for Vasari, now dedicating his book as he did to two powerful princes, Cosimo I, grand duke of Florence, and the short-lived Pope Julius III, it was the great patron who could take the place of the republic, the patron with the stimulus of his money and his honor. It was politic to say so, but antiquity, as ever, lent Vasari his example. A society can become inclined to ease, as Aristotle wrote, and thus good to the arts.[33] Such a moment, Horace thought, was the period of Ennius, the moment in Rome just after the Punic Wars.[34] But neither riches nor peace were in themselves enough; the patron is also needed who uses his riches (which are basically vile) to do truly wonderful things. "Honor nourishes art" was an old phrase. Think of the soil when it is dry, wrote Federigo Zuccaro in 1601. "So remains the student if he does not drink in the dew and rain of grace, the protection of princes." [35]

Man is born with a desire to do something great. This appetite is strong, yet it is one that requires constant attention and encouragement if it is to come to action. Within each person the desire for action was called emulation, and it was the capacity for emulation that for humanists was the most important quality of the good pupil. At the level of social action, such an appetite expressed itself as a love of glory, and if classical writers had thought long and hard about glory, so now did the humanists, glory being the social reward of true virtue. Poets and writers thus have a solemn responsibility when they speak of this person or that; for the hope of glory can lead men to the greatest deeds. Those who are driven by genius and learn a science, Vasari wrote of Benedetto da Maiano, can lead themselves on under the stimulus of glory, moving from a mortal to an immortal glory. It had been true for Giotto; it was true even for Michelangelo.

Vasari is important: for what his book represents is the summary of the humanist account of culture and the arts, a summary set down just before the development of the Venetian school of writing of Pietro Aretino, Paolo Pino, and Lodovico Dolce, or of the Neoplatonists like Federigo Zuccaro, Gregorio Comanini, and Vincenzo Danti. The scheme of Vasari's history, with its idea of decline, revival, and flowering, came from a pattern familiar since Petrarch. And his accounts of the development of artists was borrowed, if indirectly, from humanist teachers like Guarino of Verona and Pier Paolo Vergerio the Elder. The ancient Romans had loved art, which was clear, Vasari noted, from the number and beauty of the monuments that survive from Rome, especially from the time of the Republic. If art was carried out under the emperors, it often lacked true invention. To support this contention Vasari cited the Arch of Constantine, which used fragments taken from other buildings. Worse yet was to come with the Visigoths, the Vandals, the Ostrogoths, and, at the end, the Lombards. At this time, not knowing better, men simply copied the awkward clumsy style of the Byzantine artists (Vasari is speaking here only of painting and sculpture). Yet, help was on its way. In 1016—Vasari is precise, but wrong—the Pisans began to build a new cathedral under the guidance of a certain Greek architect, Buschetto of Dulichium. This new cathedral was magnificent and resplendent, and its presence served to inspire all architects and sculptors in Italy. One detail had to be added to make the account complete. Some time toward the middle of the thirteenth century, heaven took pity on the talented men Italy had still always produced—however much they languished—and led them back to the true standard of art, namely, antiquity. These new artists were able to distinguish between what was good and bad; they knew what true imitation consisted of, so that art began to progress and advance. Thus began, with Cimabue, the rich and ever increasingly perfect art of the Renaissance.

Vasari knew what the qualities or properties of this perfect art were, and he could list them: rule, order, proportion, design, style. But what he wrote in the *Lives,* through the form of biographies, was, in true humanist fashion, less an account of art than of the moral choices made by artists, that led them to their works, to what Alberti had called their "laudable actions." A Life (a *vita*) as opposed to a description (a *descrizione*) was a moral accounting in which, as in Plutarch, the person is judged, compared, praised, or blamed. The text of Vasari was not a commentary; Annibal Caro suggested such a title, thinking probably of Ghiberti's *Commentary.* Nor was it, as the Olivetan Don Miniato Pitti suggested, a simple history. It was a sequence of *vite,* of true and full lives, judged and summarized. And for those artists still living, whose careers could not yet be judged, Vasari wrote what he called descriptions.

A life is more important, for the life and the work of the true artist are in perfect moral balance. Emulation is good, Vasari wrote; but too much competition, such as that found among the Bolognese artists, led them from the true way, so that all they were concerned with was crushing their rivals. Morto da Feltro was as eccentric in his life as in his inventions and the grotesques he painted. Domenico Puligo was talented, but he was led away by the pleasures of the world, working more for gain than glory, so that what he did, while often well drawn and well colored, did not develop. Jacopo l'Indaco, being fond of amusements, was a charming gossip, never worked except when he was obliged to, and though he had skill, hated discipline. Was it not to be expected then that a serious artist like Michelangelo would tire of him?

Against such examples there were the great artists, great in their work, great for the quality of their moral discernment, their education, their response to the older art, their reckoning of their own ambition, their behavior toward patrons and other artists. Here Raphael was the perfect example. He had rare gifts; he was gracious, excellent, modest, humane, and gentle—so much so that even animals loved him, not to speak of men. What Vasari could say of him covers all the parts of art:

> For this, O Painting, you may consider yourself fortunate in having had an artist who, by his genius and character, raised you above the Heavens. Blessed are you to have seen your disciples brought together by the instruction of such a man, uniting the arts and the virtues, in which Raphael compelled the greatness of Julius II and the generosity of Leo, men occupying the highest dignity, to treat him with familiarity and practice every kind of liberality, so that by their favor and the money they gave him, he was able to do great honor to himself and to his art. Happy also were those who served under him, because all who imitated him were on a safe road, and so those who imitate his labors in art will be rewarded by the world, as those who copy his virtuous life will be rewarded in heaven.[36]

This passage invokes almost all the notions dear to the humanists: virtue, the importance of the patron, models, just rewards, imitation. In the most profound way a work of art was a moral self-portrait, the perfect work revealing the perfect judgment of the artist, the bad work revealing all that was bad in his powers of discrimination. The ideal of the perfect artist depended on the classical model of perfection—so too did that of the bad artist, resting on what Horace had called the mad poet, the good poet upside down, an artist then who, like the bad poet, had imagination (*ingenium*), but lacked judgment (*iudicium*) or technique (*ars*).[37]

In the Renaissance an identity was early assumed between the mind and character of the artist and his art. Thus Brunelleschi could speak of a bad painter who turned out works of art as mad as himself;[38] and Vasari, in a phrase he cut from the second edition of the *Lives,* could say that since medieval sculptors had foolish (*tondi*) minds, so their sculpture was foolish.[39] It had been common since antiquity to say that an artist must first experience in his own soul the emotions he wished to represent in his image; Alberti repeated this claim as a prescription he deemed necessary to make the *istoria* vivid and direct. But the idea of the work of art as a self-portrait is about the development of the artist, the record of the parts of his own progress by which, if all went well, his first disposition was trained and guided to standards that were true and noble. Such a notion could be placed in a Christian context or in a Neoplatonic one. What Vasari wrote depended, perhaps, on these ideas, but it was also a more commonsense notion, concerned, as all humanism was, with the idea of moral choice, and the identity of judgment in one area of life with all the other aspects of behavior. The virtues of painting and sculpture, like design and composition, are peculiar to art. But the virtues that the artist brings to his work in all the decisions he has to make are, like prudence, a part of his general moral equipment. If virtue is, as Alberti suggested, nature "completed," this completion required the most profound moral exercise. This point of view accounts for the moral preambles Vasari appends to almost all the *Lives;* the dignity and importance of the artist; and at the conclusion of his work the significance, both intrinsic and exemplary, of what the artist produces in his own work, and of the society, whether a republic or a benevolent dukedom, in which the artist was able to work.

*   *   *

The relationship of humanism and art was at once less direct and more important than it might at first seem. About art itself, humanists had little to say, about the artist a degree more. And about the visual arts as a part of general culture, there was much that they discussed, much that could be used by those wishing to speak up for art and for artists. We may think of these remarks as a range of possibilities; some, which served to accommodate art within the accepted culture, may be mentioned.

The painting as an exemplum. Alberti mentioned two subjects appropriate for painting (and by extension, sculpture), both taken from antiquity and both charged with high moral significance. The first was that of the Calumny of Apelles, a theme that invoked Envy and Calumny, the disruption of language and society; the other was that of the Three Graces, a perfect model of pure liberality, true community.[40] We can refer back to what was said about the exemplum. Rhetoric was concerned with affect rather than with reason, for logic does not have the power to move men to action. It was for this reason that orators would talk of legends of human action. In this context the sympathy to the viewer implied by clear narrative and by the formal patterns of Renaissance art had their place, inviting a human response, suggesting what could be done. This situation would be as true for a religious painting as for one that took more secular or classical topics as its subject.

The painting as ecphrasis. Persuasion, as classical writers recognized, is manipulative, most effective when self-effacing. The metaphors used by both classical and Renaissance writers often borrowed their images from the visual arts. Quintilian used the term *color* to emphasize this idea, *color* being the particular aspect granted a subject by the control an orator has.[41] In antiquity, the rhetorical description of a work of art was called an ecphrasis, a kind of proleptic simile by which all that is to follow is foreshadowed. The ecphrasis must be lively or have what Erasmus called *evidentia,* which he described as being a way of portraying a thing in color "so that we seem to have painted the scene rather than described it."[42] All art should have beauty (*venustas*). But such beauty is what Alberti called grace (*gratia*) and delightfulness (*amoenitas*), which are recognized parts of rhetoric, the way ideas are presented and made persuasive.

Classical subjects. The gradual appearance in Renaissance art of classical subjects is an expression of the general progress of humanism. But classical subjects were still generally rare before the seventeenth century, and they were often set down by artists barely capable of knowing the idea in its literary form. The example of Botticelli has been noted. The first examples we have of the theme of Cupid and Psyche were done in the 1490s in Ferrara at the palace of Belriguardo. But the artists, whoever they were, must have been mere journeymen compared with Raphael, who did a cycle on this same subject at the Villa Farnesina in the late 1510s, enriched now with all that contemporary humanists could add. After Raphael came Titian, after Titian Rubens, and then the great tradition of seventeenth- and eighteenth-century allegories and narratives, done by artists familiar with the general content of classical texts.

The artist as a learned figure. As Albrecht Dürer was supposed to have said: "An intelligent man without learning is like an unpolished mirror."[43] Yet, which artists could be learned, for, as Leonardo said of himself, were they not all men without letters? What we can see, how-

ever, is a gradual evolution of the *idea* of the learned artist. One author
tried hard to portray Brunelleschi as learned and as held in esteem by
learned men; but all Brunelleschi read was the Bible and Dante, which is
also all Michelangelo knew. Raphael, however, was more learned, trav-
eling with such scholars as Andrea Navigero and Agostino Beazzano to
Tivoli, taking into his home the humanist Fabio Calvo, who translated
Vitruvius for him.[44] However far this image was from the truth, the figure of the learned artist was one that could then be called up by supporters of the arts. Writing in 1642, Philip Angel listed in his *Lof der
Schilderkonst* some forty-seven learned artists, many from antiquity, but
some also from nearer his own time: Dürer, Leonardo, Hans Sebald
Beham.

The artist as well-born. Most artists were from the artisan class;
some, like Brunelleschi, Masaccio, and Leonardo, were the sons of notaries and were thus of higher birth. It is with the record of Michelangelo's supposed parentage—and its recognition by those more truly a part
of the lineage—that we see an example of the particular progress of the
artist's position in the Renaissance. Ascanio Condivi said that Michelangelo's first Florentine ancestor was Messer Simone dei Conti of Canossa,
podestà or mayor of Florence in 1250. Michelangelo seems to have believed this claim; so, too, more importantly, did Count Alessandro of
Canossa, and in a letter of 1520 he went so far as to speak of Michelangelo as a close relative.[45] Such matters were important. Michelangelo
was much concerned to have noblemen as pupils. But it was Leonardo
who came closest to this ideal, with pupils such as Melzi and Boltraffio,
Melzi in particular being from a very notable family.

The importance of the patron. The patron came to occupy a particular and important place in later humanist writing; he was the stimulus,
the guide, the encourager. Yet, if one aspect of patronage was the encouragement of virtue, the other was decorum. The notion that it was
appropriate for men to gain glory through their support of art was familiar in antiquity. During the Renaissance a somewhat richer and more
elaborate account of patronage was developed in relation to the Aristotelian idea of *magnificentia. Magnificentia* was a measure of propriety.
The will of Erasmo da Narni, Il Gattamelata, specifically required that
his tomb be honorable and in keeping with his *magnificentia.*[46] To Giovanni Sabadino degli Arienti, in his praise of Ercole d'Este, *magnificentia*
is first spoken of as spending that is sumptuous and grand. But it is also
akin to liberality, and thus a token of the range of moral authority a
prince has over his people—a benevolent authority, granted to him by
the very subjects who enjoy the rewards of his kindness and encourage-

ment.[47] *Magnificentia* was much commented upon in the Renaissance, and the many discussions served to justify the prince and to encourage in him the idea of commissioning works of art and of supporting individual artists. The great rulers of antiquity had been patrons of value. So, too, had been many more recent princes, like Robert of Naples who helped Giotto; and Charles V who, like Alexander the Great and Apelles, showered his favors on Titian.

Progress, newness. It was clear to learned and unlearned alike that a new form of art was being created during the Renaissance in Italy—in painting, sculpture, and architecture. Alberti said so quite boldly in the Italian preface to *De pictura*, noting that his contemporaries were uncovering arts and sciences unheard of before. The same idea is reflected in more ordinary discourse. We find it, for example, in a legal declaration of 1449 by the Paduan painter Niccolò Pizzolo, who spoke of a recent style of painting that could be compared to the work of a painter who knew nothing but rough work.[48] We see it in a contract of 1471 for Tommaso Soderini, in which it is clearly noted that Lorenzo di Bicci should replace an old work with one done in the new style.[49] Humanists were able to give all such natural remarks—for indeed the new painting was in a new style—a proper context. The terms of the language used might vary. In his eulogy of Giotto, Villani said that he had followed the new direction indicated by Cimabue, leaving behind the old—meaning here the Greek or Byzantine style. The full context for such actions was defined in Rudolf Agricola's Life of Petrarch when he said that Petrarch had called men back to the severer standards of the past and led the way for all who followed.[50] The same was said of Mantegna by Camillo Leonardi: he opened up the light and showed all who came after him what the rules and reasons for painting are.[51]

The artist as a divine figure. The development of disposition, of virtue, was, as many humanists said, an act that raised the artist almost to the level of a hero. Artists had been called divine as early as the thirteenth century. The epithet "divine" was applied to Michelangelo in 1516 by Lodovico Ariosto.[52] And if Ariosto was affected here by intimations of a Neoplatonic tradition, he was swayed by humanism and by that part of humanist discourse which gave pride of place to men who were virtuous—who, in Albertian terms, completed their nature. Angelo Poliziano was prepared to call Lorenzo de' Medici divine for his virtues; why then not Michelangelo?

The artist as fictor. Vasari made it clear, in everything he wrote in the *Lives*, that the development of the artist was a moral journey. It drew on a range of qualities much lauded by humanists—*actio, studium, prudentia, exercitatio, diligentia.* To each his own virtue. The artist was, like all men, following a particular human talent, his capacity for making, or, as Alberti put it, for constituting things, just as nature is a constituter.[53] At an earlier moment, as in someone like Isidore of Seville, the making of a painting was seen in purely logical terms as a fashioning, and thus a kind of fiction or deceit. In the Renaissance the idea of fiction was regarded more positively. The painter was like the poet who, as the name itself shows, is a maker: "This is ποιέω," wrote Gianmaria Filelfo, "from which is said 'ποιητής.' "[54] The painter works, like the poet, from the forms conceived in his mind, an idea found as early as 1436 in Pier Candido Decembrio. Thus his power and responsibility are immense. Like the poet, he can grow "to another nature," bringing forth forms that might even challenge the world God had made.

Ingenium, iudicium, acumen. In his work the artist might use his invention. Brunelleschi is called the inventor and controller of the cupola of the cathedral of Florence.[55] But more specifically he uses his shrewdness, his *acumen.* This term, suggested perhaps by classical writers, was used by Giannozzo Manetti to praise Brunelleschi for the cupola.[56] Or the artist used his *ingenium* (his talent), that which, as opposed to *ars,* could not be learned. This word was frequently used with reference to artists. It is found in Villani's praise of Giotto and in what was said of Brunelleschi's achievement at Santa Maria degli Angeli.[57] And if we think here of the model humanism could provide in these contexts, it is notable that Manetti's description of Brunelleschi as "a man of wonderful genius" is close to Bruni's earlier description of Petrarch as "a man no less great in virtue than in genius."[58] In time, the word *ingenium* came to be understood as judgment (*iudicium*), a faculty, as Alberti made clear, close to reason.[59] It was this reasoning, this proper use of all his talents and capacities, that made the artist a moral being and his art a moral performance.

*   *   *

We come back to Vasari. It was from within a range of ideas and examples such as the ones just outlined that his account of the artist was possible. The ideal for the humanist was happiness, what has often been called freedom from care. For Vasari it was the development of ability and tranquility, or what he called, in his Life of Baldassare Peruzzi, virtue, quiet, and peace of mind.[60] This quality was a gift of heaven, but also an achievement that justified the praise of the artist. Not everyone agreed with Vasari. Vincenzo Borghini, his close friend and adviser during the years he was at work on the *Lives,* believed that biography should concern itself only with public individuals, not with lower people who work with their hands. The purpose of your work, he wrote in a letter of 1545, is not to tell us of the lives of these artists but of their works.[61] What importance is it to know of Baccio d'Agnolo or Pontormo? An answer was offered by Francesco Patrizi when he said that the artist was as much a public person as was a prince or statesman, displaying his value—and his virtue—by contributing to the life of the community. But the position of the artist was hardly secure, even in 1550, for he could still be excluded from serious society and kept beyond the pale of truly cultured men. His works might be admired by some; he himself was all too often ignored. One late instance of this ostracism shows the problem in familiar terms. The Florentine painter Bernardino Pocetti was much praised by some for his virtue. But when Grand Duke Ferdinand I asked him why he spent so much time with people so far below him in propriety and social behavior, his answer was sharp: "I wonder if all that *virtù* which Your Highness so kindly concedes to me would be enough to make them regard me as more than a servant, because not every nobleman values *virtù* as highly as nobility." Pocetti, we may be sure, was right.[62]

The expression of such ideals in the visual arts was difficult. There could, of course, be images of patronage, the patron shown accepting the artist or defending him against a host of evils: Envy, Ignorance, and the like. On occasion, the moral judgement of the artist became a topic. One such instance—for which we still have a preliminary drawing (Figure 38-11)—was a design, done in the late sixteenth century by Raffaellino da Reggio, for the facade of a house in the Campo Marzio, Rome, that belonged to the architect Francesco da Volterra.[63] Below is a motto: "Virtue rises to heaven"; in the middle Virtue with Hercules and Genius; at the top the Mountain of Virtue. All of these images were familiar to humanists. Another image on this same subject was one by Philip Uffenbach (Figure 38-12), signed and dated 1631. At the bottom is Poverty; to the side are Juno and Pallas Athena; in the middle is the artist, φιλό-τεχνος (a Platonic word), gazing up at the figure of Fame who is obviously lending him strength and fortitude for the battles ahead.

*   *   *

But iconography is no more than a symptom. If we wish to mark the true significance of humanism for the development and encouragement of the visual arts, we must come back to the forms of this art. Vasari can help us in what he says about some works of Masaccio and Donatello, Bartolomeo della Scala in what he says about the dome of the Florentine cathedral. For what such descriptions preserve is something of the critical life that existed around these objects and which, in time, became part of their meaning. The images are those of the Santa Croce *Annunciation* by

Figure 38-11. Raffaellino da Reggio, design for house facade. Drawing (1570), private collection, England.

Donatello (Figure 38-13), the *Consecration of the Church of Santa Maria del Carmine* in Florence (Figure 38-14), and the dome of Santa Maria dei Fiori in Florence (Figure 38-15). It should be noted that the account by Scala has been questioned in relation to a number of details,[64] that the drawings usually associated with the Masaccio composition refer in all probability to a work by Domenico Ghirlandaio,[65] and that the work by Donatello was indeed not the first important project he completed.[66] What these texts speak of is a sequence of Renaissance and humanist virtues: magnificence, innate ability, fame, the idea of community, ability, skill, reason, narrative, and, of course, the models of antiquity. They form a suitable ending. Scala writes:

> The temple, which was dedicated to Mary the Liberator from that day on, proceeded from small beginnings to such splendid magnitude that it can contend with any buildings in magnificence and decoration. . . . Above all else, the vault is to be admired, since its size surpasses all possibility of requiring wooden scaffolding.

Figure 38-12.   Philip Uffenbach, Allegory *(1631). Städelsches Kunstinstitut, Frankfurt am Main.*

However, Filippo Brunelleschi, an architect of great genius, discovered a system shortly before our time whereby it was easily completed without any supporting formwork at all. . . . In praise of his genius Brunelleschi received the honor of public burial. His marble effigy is near the entrance of the right-hand portal with a carefully composed epigram attesting to what we have said. Carlo Marsuppini, the renowned poet, composed the epigram.[67]

Vasari writes of Donatello:

But the work that made his name and brought him into notice was an Annunciation in *macigno* stone, placed at the altar and chapel of the Cavalcanti in Santa Croce, for which he made an ornament in the grotesque manner, the base varied and twisted and the pediment a quarter-circle, adding six infants bearing festoons, who seem to be afraid of the height, and to be reassuring themselves by embracing each other. But he showed especial genius and art in the figure of the Virgin, who, affrighted at the sudden appearance of the angel, moves her person timidly and sweetly to a modest reverence, turning with beautiful grace to the one who salutes her, so

Figure 38-13. Donatello, Annunciation Tabernacle *(1428–33). Santa Croce, Florence.*

Di Masaccio.

Figure 38-14. *After Masaccio,* Consecration of Santa Maria del Carmine, *Florence. Drawing (1424), Folke-stone Museum and Art Gallery, England. Photo courtesy of Kent County Museum Service.*

Figure 38-15.   Brunelleschi, dome. Santa Maria dei Fiori (1420–36), Florence.

that her face displays the proper humility and gratitude due to the bestower of the unexpected gift. Besides this, Donato showed a mastery in the arrangement of the folds of the drapery of the Madonna and the angel, and by a study of the nude he endeavored to discover the beauty of the ancients which had remained hidden for so many years. He gave evidence of so much facility and art in this work that design, judgment and skilled use of the chisel could produce nothing finer.[68]

About Masaccio Vasari writes:

While he was engaged upon this work, the consecration of the Carmine church took place, and, as a memorial of this, Masaccio painted the scene as it occurred, in *verde terra* and *chiaroscuro,* in the cloister over the door leading to the convent. There he drew the portraits of a great number of citizens in mantle and hood who are taking part in the procession, including Filippo di ser Brunellesco in sabots, Donatello, Masolino da Panicale, who had been his master, Antonio Brancacci, who employed him to do the chapel, Niccolò da Uzzano, Giovanni di Bicci de' Medici and Bartolommeo Varlori, which [portraits] are also in the house of Simon Corsi, a Florentine nobleman, by the same hand. He also drew there Lorenzo Ridolfi, then ambassador to the Florentine Republic in Venice, and not only did he draw all these notable persons from life, but also the door of the convent, and the porter with his keys in his hand. The work possesses many perfections, for Masaccio's knowledge enabled him to put five or six people in a row upon the piazza, judiciously diminishing them in proportion as they recede, according to the point of view, a truly marvellous feat, especially as he has used his discretion in making his figures not all of one size, but of various stature, as in life, distinguishing the small and stout from the tall and the slender, all foreshortened in their ranks with such excellence that they would not look otherwise in real life.[69]

The forms of Renaissance painting and sculpture might, at first glance, seem self-evident. For are they not a simple representation of that most obvious of subjects, the world we see around us, the world in which we labor with the tasks of human existence? But nothing is self-evident about representation. And if the artists of the Renaissance, the painters and sculptors, chose to encompass within their art references to what we might choose to call ordinary perception, this choice involved, on their part, an immensely important idea. In large part the impulse to work with this manner of representation depended upon what, with a purposefully loose phrase, we might call the tenor of the age. And to describe this age and its character we might refer to the emphasis within Christianity on the particular humanity of Christ and the idea of the Word as Flesh. Humanism was an expression of just this same impulse, set within the world of learning and letters. And if it was not immediately sympathetic to the visual arts, it served in time in a number of important ways to identify and describe a set of ideas and possibilities from which the visual arts could benefit. I have tried to give a list of these concepts. Perhaps the forms of Renaissance art would have been as they were without humanism. But humanism surely served to confirm the progress of these arts and lend them a measure of credibility that could only help them in their progress. It might not seem as strong a connection as we might have hoped for, but it is enough.

NOTES

1. Any understanding of the relation between Renaissance art and contemporary philosophies must begin from the following studies: E. Cassirer, *The Individual and the Cosmos in Renaissance Philosophy* (1927), trans. M. Domandi (New York, 1963); P. O. Kristeller, "The Modern System of the Arts: A Study in the History of Aesthetics," *Journal of the History of Ideas* 12 (1951): 496–527, and 13 (1952): 17–46, reprinted in *Renaissance Thought II: Papers on Humanism and the Arts* (New York, 1965); E. Panofsky, *Idea* (1924), trans. J. J. S. Peake (Columbia, SC, 1968); C. Trinkaus, "Humanism," *Encyclopedia of World Art* (New York, 1962–82), 7:702–34; R. Wittkower, *Architectural Principles in the Age of Humanism* (London, 1949). A number of studies on the arts have appeared recently, among which the following should be consulted: M. Baxandall, *Giotto and the Orators: Humanist Observers of Painting in Italy and the Discovery of Pictorial Composition, 1350–1450* (Oxford, 1971); E. H. Gombrich, "The Leaven of Criticism in Renaissance Art," in *Art, Science, and History in the Renaissance,* ed. C. S. Singleton (Baltimore, 1967), 3–42, reprinted in Gombrich's *The Heritage of Apelles: Studies in the Art of the Renaissance* (Ithaca, NY, 1976); E. F. Van der Grinten, *Elements of Art Historiography in Medieval Texts: An Analytic Study* (The Hague, 1969); L. Jardine, *Francis Bacon: Discovery and the Art of Discourse* (Cambridge, 1974); R. Klein, *Form and Meaning: Writings on the Renaissance and Modern Art* (1970), trans. M. J. Wieselter and L. Wieselter (New York, 1980). See the special note at the end of these notes.
2. Aristotle, *Nicomachean Ethics,* 6.3, 1139b 15.
3. Leonardo Bruni, *Epistolarum libri VIII,* ed. L. Mehus (Florence, 1741), 2:140.
4. Quintilian, 2.14.5; 10.2.12.
5. *Francesco Petrarca: Prose,* ed. G. Martellotti et al. (Milan, 1955), 292.

6. Lorenzo Valla, *De dialectica libri III* (Paris, 1530), 1.9; Francis Bacon, *Novum organum*, 4.247.

7. Aulus Gellius, 13.17.

8. Matteo Palmieri, *Della vita civile*, ed. S. Battaglia (Bologna, 1944), 33.

9. George Puttenham, *The Art of Englishe Poesie* [1589] ed. E. Arber (London, 1869), 250.

10. Giorgio Vasari, *Vite*, ed. G. Milanesi (Florence, 1878–85), 3:321. For the text that speaks of the visitors to Botticelli's studio—it is referred to as an academy of loungers (*un academia di scioperati*)—see *Le Giornale di Ser Lorenzo Violi*, fol. 41, as quoted in R. Lightbown, *Sandro Botticelli: Life and Works* (Berkeley, 1978), 1:169, document 13.

11. Ristoro d'Arezzo, *Della composizione del mondo* (1282), ed. E. Narducci (Milan, 1864), 257, book 8, chap. 4

12. Guarino of Verona, *Epistolario*, ed. R. Sabbandini, 3 vols. (Venice, 1915–19), 1:154–57.

13. Petrarch, *Familiares*, 16.2.

14. P. Kristeller, *Andrea Mantegna* (London, 1901), 483.

15. Lorenzo Ghiberti, *I commentari*, ed. O. Morisani (Naples, 1947), 25.

16. Alberti, *De pictura*, 1.1; *On Painting*, ed. and trans. J. R. Spencer (New Haven, 1956).

17. Cicero, *De amicitia*, 19; *Carmina Priapea*, 3.10, ed. F. Buecheler (Berlin, 1904), 139; Quintilian, 1.10.28.

18. L. Muratori, ed. *Rerum italicarum scriptores* (Milan, 1723–51), 20:527.

19. Leon Battista Alberti, *Opere volgari*, ed. C. Grayson (Bari, 1960–73), 1:49.

20. Dante, *Purgatory*, 10.71.

21. Cicero, *De inventione*, 1.19.270; Coluccio Salutati, *Epistolario*, ed. F. Novati (Rome, 1891–1911), 1:196.

22. G. Poggi, *Il Duomodi* (Florence, 1909), 257f.

23. Petrarch, *Familiares*, 1.9.

24. Alberti, *De pictura*, 2.35; 2.41; 3.60–61.

25. Alamanno Rinuccini, "Alamanno Rinuccini, *Dialogus de libertate*," ed. F. Adorno, *Atti e memorie dell'Accademia Toscana di scienze e lettere "La Columbaria"* 22 [n.s. 8] (1957): 280.

26. *Prose di Buonaccorso da Montemagno*, ed. G. B. C. Giuliari (Bologna, 1874), 44.

27. Filippo Vilanni, *Liber de civitatis Florentine famosis civibus*, ed. G. C. Galletti (Florence, 1847), 8.

28. P. de Nolhac, *Pétrarque et l'humanisme* (Paris, 2d ed. 1907), 2:89.

29. Petrarch, *Familiares*, 1.8.

30. Palmieri, *Della vita civile*, 77–79.

31. Giannozzo Manetti, *De dignitate et excellentia hominis* (1452), ed. E. R. Leonard (Ithaca, NY, 1964), 113.

32. Alberti, *Opere volgari*, 1:63.

33. Aristotle, *Politics*, 8.6, 1341a 29.

34. Horace, *Epistolae*, 2.1.162.

35. *Scritti d'Arte di Federigo Zuccaro*, ed. D. Heikamp (Florence, 1961), 116.

36. Vasari, *Vite*, 4:385.
37. Horace, *Ars poetica*, 453f.
38. A. Parronchi, "Le 'misure dell' occhio' secondo il Ghiberti," *Paragone* 133 (1961): 47.
39. Vasari, *Vite*, 1:333.
40. Alberti, *De pictura*, 53.
41. Quintilian, 10.1.116.
42. Erasmus, *De copia*, 2.177E, in *Collected Works of Erasmus: Literary and Educational Writings*, vol. 2, ed. C. R. Thompson (Toronto, 1978), 577.
43. *Dürers schriftlicher Nachlass*, ed. H. Rupprich (Berlin, 1956–70), 1:326.
44. *Raffaello nei documenti*, ed. V. Golzio (Rome, 1936), 42, 281.
45. *Il carteggio di Michelangelo*, ed. G. Poggi (Florence, 1967), 2:245.
46. G. Eroli, *Erasmo Gattamelata da Narni, suoi monumenti e sua famiglia* (Rome, 1876), 344.
47. *Art and Life at the Court of Ercole d'Este: The "De triumphis religionis" of Giovanni Sabadino degli Arienti*, ed. W. Gundersheimer (Geneva, 1972), 50.
48. *Renaissance Art*, ed. C. Gilbert (New York, 1970), 84.
49. Vasari, *Vite*, 2:86, note 5.
50. L. Bertalot, "Rudolf Agricolas Lobrede auf Petrarch," *La Bibliofilia* 30 (1928): 384.
51. Kristeller, *Andrea Mantegna*, 483.
52. Lodovico Ariosto, *Orlando furioso*, canto 23. See also L. Steinberg, *Michelangelo's Last Paintings* (New York, 1975), 57.
53. Alberti, *Della famiglia*, 1.45.
54. *Le vite di Dante, Petrarca e Boccaccio, scritto fino al secolo XVI*, ed. A. Solerti (Milan, 1904), 177.
55. C. Guasti, *La cupola di Santa Maria del Fiore* (Florence, 1867), 71.
56. Giannozzo Manetti, *De dignitate et excellentia hominis*, 2.710 (p. 86).
57. Antonio Manetti, *The Life of Brunelleschi*, ed. H. Saalman, trans. C. Engass (University Park, PA, 1964), 102–3.
58. Solerti, *Le vite di Dante*, 288.
59. Alberti, *De re aedificatori*, 9.5.
60. Vasari, *Vite*, 4:589.
61. K. Frey, *Der literarische Nachlass Giorgio Vasaris* (Munich, 1923–30), 2:102.
62. *Notizie de' professori del disegno da Cimabue in qua (1681–1728)*, ed. F. Baldinucci (Florence, 1845–57), 3:147–49.
63. On the works of art illustrated and discussed in the final pages of this essay, see Gaspare Celio, *Memoria dei nomi dell'artefici delle pitture che sono in alcune chiese, facciate, e palazzi di Roma* (1638), ed. E. Zocca (Milan, 1967), 147 (Raffaellino da Reggio); C. Gilbert, "The Drawings Associated with Masaccio's *Sagra*," *Storia dell'arte* n.s. 1.2 (1969): 260–78; H. W. Janson, *The Sculpture of Donatello* (Princeton, 1962), 103–7; H. Saalman, *Brunelleschi: The Cupola of Santa Maria del Fiore* (London, 1980), 13–15;

E. Schilling, *Städelsches Kunstinstitut: Frankfurt am Main: Katalog der deutschen Zeichnungen* (Ansbach, 1973), 1:90, no. 548 (Uffenbach).

64. See Saalman, *Brunelleschi,* 13.
65. See Gilbert, "Drawings Associated with Masaccio's *Sagra,*" 260.
66. See Janson, *Sculpture of Donatello,* 103.
67. Bartolomeo della Scala, *Historia florentinorum,* 23.
68. Vasari, *Vite,* 2:397.
69. Ibid., 2:295.

Special note: The following article, which deals in a most interesting way with many of the issues discussed in my essay, was received too late to be used: G. B. Canfield, "The Florentine Humanists' Concept of Architecture in the 1430s and Filippo Brunelleschi," in *Scritti di storia dell'arte in onore di Federigo Zeri,* ed. M. Natale (Venice, 1984), 1:112–21.

39 ₰ HUMANISM AND MUSIC
Claude V. Palisca

WHEREAS FOR LITERATURE, ARCHITECTURE, SCULPTURE, PAINTing, and theater there were actual ancient Greek and Roman models that could be imitated by writers and artists of the fifteenth and sixteenth centuries, of ancient Greek and Roman music there were only a few hymns from the Hellenic period that no one then took the trouble to transcribe completely from their Greek letter notation. The several codices containing four hymns set to music (and a fifth lacking musical notation) were in private Italian libraries from the early fifteenth century on, but the hymns received no attention until Girolamo Mei sent a copy of them to Vincenzo Galilei in a letter of about 1579. This letter is not preserved, but a previous one is, in which Mei describes the notation, provides the tables of Alypius for deciphering it, and gives an account of his sources for the hymns.[1] Galilei published the hymns in their original notation and the tables, but no transcriptions appeared until some years later.[2] There were, therefore, no audible models for musicians to imitate.

Until fairly recently, as a consequence, music historians dismissed the relevance of humanism and ancient music to the music of the Renaissance.[3] The Renaissance in music was seen as a rebirth of musical activity sponsored in part by Italian patrons but essentially an achievement of northern composers, some of whom traveled to Italy.[4]

D. P. Walker in a pioneering essay in 1941 objected to the narrow interpretation of the influence of antiquity on the music of this period.[5] Although he acknowledged that there were no performable examples of ancient Greek music that could have served as models, he argued that there could be indirect imitation, because the ancient writers left sufficient descriptions and theoretical formulations to give those bent on reviving the ideals of ancient music a clear goal.

The flame of antiquity thus passed from purely musical to literary sources, from sounding music to the literature and theory about it. For the humanism that touched music was a literary and scientific humanism and not a strictly musical one. Its history, dynamics, sources, and many of the personalities are those familiar to students of humanism in general.[6] The ancient writings revived by the humanists, some of them of general interest, such as Plato's *Republic* or Athenaeus's *Deipnosophists*, others specifically musical, such as Ptolemy's *Harmonics,* affected musical practice in several ways. They described the ancient music itself and through these descriptions put before the modern reader a vision of a musical object different from what he experienced in his day. This reader, to be sure, was rarely a musician, more often a poet or patron who was in no position to realize such a vision, but he could stimulate musicians to aspire to it. Or the ancient writings described the marvelous effects music had on the morals and feelings of listeners, leading modern readers to long for a return to a music that had such power. The more technical ancient literature on music, almost all of it eventually translated into Latin, reached musicians themselves and told them of compositional procedures, scales, tunings, poetic meters, relationships between text and music that presented new options for artistic creation and performance. There was a lag, naturally, between the recognition of the potential of an antique model or device and its application, but once a path of communication was established between humanists and musicians, the experimentation with antique devices spread to every recess of musical activity. Eventually almost every ancient ideal and manifestation found a modern counterpart.

Thus there was a practical side to the mainly literary-theoretical humanist movement in music. The practical, which is what has most often passed for "musical humanism," was not so much humanism as a response to humanism. If it is correct to label "humanist" the scholar in the Renaissance who edited or translated a Greek rhetorical treatise and studied and taught its doctrine, but not necessarily the ambassador who applied that doctrine to composing letters and speeches, then the humanist in music similarly was the scholar who transmitted ancient learning, while the composer or even theorist who applied or reacted to that knowledge was not necessarily a humanist. Yet both form part of the picture of humanism in music. This distinction has not always been kept clear by those who have written about music in the Renaissance. This essay will deal mainly with humanist activity that affected musical practice, and only minimally with the practice itself.

Several waves or stages of humanist influence can be discerned in the musical thought of the Renaissance. They were not isolated chronologically, of course, but overlapped considerably. In the fifteenth century there was a pervasive revival of the doctrine contained in the arithmetical and musical treatises of Boethius, which transmit a mainly Pythagorean musical philosophy and theory expounded by the late Greeks Nicomachus and Ptolemy. Overlaying this tradition toward the end of the fifteenth century was a Neoplatonic revival for which Marsilio Ficino was largely responsible. In the last decade of the century there was a sudden flurry of translation of and commentary on the technical Greek musical treatises of late antiquity—those of Bacchius, Ptolemy, Aristides Quintilianus, and Cleonides. An older treatise possibly by Euclid and a more recent Byzantine synthesis by Bryennius of around 1300, as well as the *Problems* attributed to Aristotle, were also part of this corpus of "scientific" works on music that gained the attention of western musical writers at this time. In the early sixteenth century the interest of the humanists turned toward reforming modern music and reviving the *ethe* and moral power of the Greek modes and genera. This effort was inspired particularly by pseudo-Plutarch's musical treatise, which was published in translation at this time. Concurrently a growing awareness of the links among grammar, rhetoric, and music led to an intense exploration of the possibilities of wedding music more intimately with words. Aristotle's *Poetics* injected into this ferment the idea of imitation as the goal of the arts. Toward the end of the sixteenth century the interest in dramatic theory and in the revival of ancient tragedy penetrated musical discussions.

There were, then, several successive layers of humanist thought, and they may be characterized as (1) metaphysical, (2) mathematical-scientific-theoretical, (3) moral-ethical, (4) rhetorical-grammatical, (5) mimetic, and (6) dramatic. Although these phases may be distinguished categorically and chronologically, they combined and operated on one another, and, once injected into the stream of humanist thought, continued to infect every aspect of it.[7]

*   *   *

It will strike a student of the Renaissance as strange that Boethius should have needed a revival. After all, he was one of the most widely read authors throughout the Middle Ages. But this popularity was based on his *Consolation of Philosophy* and his compendia and commentaries on dialectical works. Manuscript copies of his musical treatise were also everywhere, but few musicians read it, for its contents were of little relevance to their concerns, which were the singing of plainchant, the making of counterpoint, and the notation of measured music. When Johann Legrense (Johannes Gallicus) of Namur, who had been trained in music in France, encountered Boethius in the school of Vittorino da Feltre at Mantua, he exclaimed that only then did he begin to understand the true nature of this art. In his treatise, *Ritus canendi,* Gallicus showed that he had learned, probably from Vittorino, that Boethius in his *De institutione musica* had translated a Greek work, later identified as having been written by Nicomachus of Gerasa.[8] In the absence at this time—in the mid-fifteenth century—of other Greek technical works on music, Gallicus highly valued this indispensable link to ancient learning. Nicomachus of Gerasa (Syria), on whose work Boethius based the first four of his five books on music, was active in the early second century of the Christian era and wrote on arithmetic, geometry, and music with a Pythagorean orientation.[9]

The inclusion in the concept of music of the three kinds—*mundana* or cosmic music; *humana*, or the harmony of the human soul and body; and *instrumentalis*, man-made sounding music for voices or instruments—is true to the Pythagorean tradition, though the threefold division may have originated with Boethius. It was adopted by almost all of the early Renaissance musical writers. *Musica mundana* was the harmony of the cosmos, at once the force that held the universe together and the unheard music made by the revolving celestial bodies.[10] Boethius presented two contrasting systems, one based on Nicomachus, in which the planets, sun, and moon were likened to the seven strings of the lyre, Saturn giving off the lowest pitch and the moon the highest, and the other derived from Cicero, who thought of the highest sphere, that of the stars, as producing the shrillest tone, while the moon held to the lowest. Renaissance writers early began to modify the Pythagorean doctrine. Ugolino of Orvieto (ca. 1380–1457) in his *Declaratio musice discipline*[11] completed in Ferrara between 1430 and 1435, subordinated cosmic music to the higher harmony of the celestial hierarchy of angels, proclaiming without end, *Sanctus, Sanctus, Sanctus*. Celestial harmony was the ground for all music, cosmic, human, and instrumental, and from it flowed all consonance. It permitted the parts of the soul to act together in harmony, and it was the celestial harmony that a musician imitated when he offered his songs to the Lord. This Christian spiritualization of cosmic harmony was continued by Giorgio Anselmi (before 1386–ca. 1440/43), who combined it with elements from Socrates's myth of Er reported in Plato's *Republic*. In place of Socrates's sirens, who sang on each of the rims that whirled around Necessity and the three Fates, Anselmi located various hosts of angels: the Angels, Archangels, Virtues, Powers, Principalities, Dominations, Thrones, Cherubim, and Seraphim.[12] Anselmi, whose sophistication about astronomy and musical combinations did not permit him to accept the vague analogies of his predecessors, took pains to explain how such a diversity of motions and sounds could produce a music sweet and satisfying to the ear. He is important also in the context of musical humanism, because his exposition was the basis of a better-known account of cosmic music, in the *Theorica musice* (1492) of Franchino Gaffurio (1451–1522),[13] one of the most frequently cited musical books of the entire Renaissance. Gaffurio was not content merely to copy Anselmi, however, for he integrated into his

account ingredients from Boethius and Macrobius, and in his final theoretical work, *De harmonia musicorum instrumentorum opus,* finished in
1500 but not published until 1518, he swept away the Christian overlay
and adopted a Neoplatonic cosmology based on Plato's *Timaeus,* Ficino's
Compendium in Timaeum, and the treatise *De musica* of Aristides Quintilianus, translated for him by Francesco Burana.[14]

Ficino, by making the *Timaeus* accessible through his translation
and commentary, gave the speculation about cosmic harmony a fresh and
fruitful new direction. Cosmic harmony ceased to be a representation of
the world in eternal balance; it became a play of forces that had moral
consequences and could influence and be influenced by men and demons.
This view was made possible by Plato's notion of a world-soul in a number of ways analogous to the planetary system. Through the world-soul,
the individual human soul could aspire to participate in heavenly harmony and absolute virtue. The soul and the celestial "cithara" thus vi-
brate to the same ratios. In a key passage that paraphrases Ficino's
translation of Plato, Gaffurio sums up this musical philosophy:

> Harmony, which has motions that are congruent and akin to the
> wanderings of our soul, was given by the Muses to men who use
> them with sagacity, not for pleasure devoid of reason, as is now
> seen to be its usefulness, but so that we may calm through it the
> dissonant revolutions of the soul and render it a harmony conso-
> nant within itself. Rhythm, too, was dedicated to this purpose, so
> that we might very aptly temper an immoderate character lacking
> grace in us.[15]

In Gaffurio's late thought the Muses replaced the angels as the founts of
harmony and controllers of the cosmic music. In a famous figure that
Gaffurio published in both his *Practica musice*[16] and his *De harmonia,*[17]
the Muses are shown to be correlated with certain planetary bodies, musical modes, and notes of the scale (see Figure 39-1).[18] The hierarchies of
angels are absent, and the modes are not the plainchant modes but the
ancient *tonoi,* as described by Boethius and Bryennius, with Hypermix-
olydian on top and Hypodorian at the bottom. Aristides Quintilianus
(fourth century) offered Gaffurio the means for expanding his conception
of cosmic harmony. Music or consonance controls the periodicity of the
moon, of the seasons, of births, and of fevers. It mediates between public
bodies and between individual people to serve peace and friendship.[19] To
Gaffurio, who was choirmaster of the cathedral of Milan, cosmic and
human harmony were not purely metaphysical concepts; they were at
the core of music's power. In his dedication of the *Practica musice* to

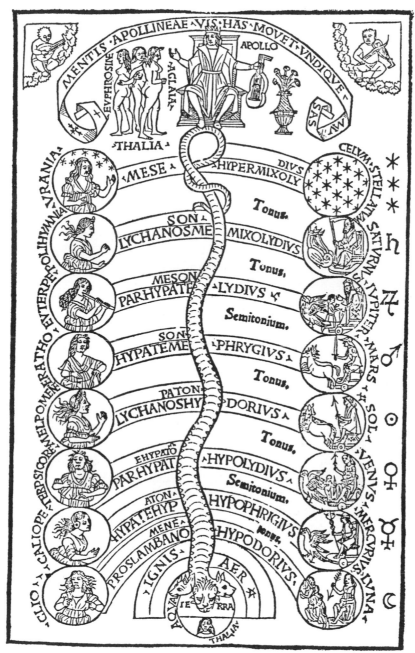

Figure 39-1. The harmonious union of the Muses, Strings, Modes, and Planets. From Franchino Gaffurio, Practica musice (Milan, 1496), frontispiece.

Duke Lodovico Maria Sforza (Il Moro), Gaffurio invokes both *musica mundana* and *musica humana:*

> If we believe Plato, who said that the world soul consists of musical melody, I surely do not see why it should be doubted that any other living thing possessing a soul, which, it is clear, is a gift of heaven, is also affected by and rejoices in harmonies congruent with its own nature, since it is well known that one is inclined toward something like oneself.

All souls, then, are imbued with harmony, and they derive pleasure from music that answers to the harmony in themselves. We may assume that Gaffurio conceived cosmic music as the model upon which all earthly music was fashioned.

Skepticism about the music of the spheres was expressed already in the fifteenth century. Johannes Tinctoris (ca. 1435–ca. 1511) rejected the idea in the dedication of his *Liber de arte contrapuncti* to King Ferrante I of Sicily. He leaned upon Aristotle, who vigorously denied the existence of any sound, real or potential, in the heavens.[20] Francisco de Salinas (1513–1590), in his *De musica libri septem* (1577), also cited Aristotle but proceeded to develop his own resolution of the difficulties. He admitted that there was a harmony in celestial movements, as also in the parts of the soul, but it was an architecture of numerical proportions that had nothing to do with sounding music, which addressed the sense of hearing and not the intellect.[21]

The most rigorous refutation was that by Giovanni Battista Benedetti (1530–1590), an Aristotelian commentator who wrote on mathematics, physics, and music. Although Benedetti admitted that there was order in the velocities, magnitudes, distances, and influxes of the celestial bodies, the quantities did not fit the proportions of musical harmony. Ptolemy found no harmonic intervals in the aspects of the sky. If the celestial orbs are distant from one another, they are separated by a vacuum, which does not transmit sound. If they are contiguous, they must be so polished that they produce no friction and no sound. If it was a question of a spherical body moving speedily around its own axis, moreover, it too would not make any sound, because it would not displace another body.[22]

Despite increasing doubts about celestial harmony, the notion continued to exert its fascination, particularly on poets and dramatists. A splendid multimedia celebration of musical cosmology was the first Intermedio of the entertainments of 1589 for the wedding in Florence of Grand Duke Ferdinand de' Medici and Christine of Lorraine. The verses were written by Giovanni Bardi, who was partial to Neoplatonic philosophy, and Ottavio Rinuccini. The action is a dramatization of the myth of Er. At the center of the stage, surrounded by the Planets, is a cloud bearing Necessity and the three Fates, who invite the Sirens to climb upward and join the Planets in song. All then unite in praising the wedding couple. Cosmic harmony is presented as a myth, among others in succeeding intermedi, all illustrating the power of music—the singing contest of the Muses and Pierides; the battle between Apollo and the Python; the story of Arion, threatened by mutineers, appealing for help in song and saved from drowning by the dolphins; and the granting of music by the Muses to humanity. In associating the harmony of the spheres with these other myths Bardi relegated it to the realm of fiction.

*　　*　　*

The Pythagorean, Platonic, and Neoplatonic traditions also dominated speculative music theory in the early Renaissance. The fundamental Pythagorean principles are met again and again, whether as professions of faith or as targets for attack. Pythagoreans doubted the reliability of the ear as an instrument for judging consonance or intonation. The science of harmonics, they believed, must be based on number and is consequently a branch of mathematics. Intervals may be classified according to the ratios of the string lengths of the component tones. Two genres of ratios yield consonances: the multiple and the superparticular. Not all ratios belonging to these genres, only those expressible by the first four numbers, are admitted to the circle of consonances. There are five, of which three are formed from multiple ratios—octave ($2:1$), octave-plus-fifth ($3:1$), double octave ($4:1$)—and the other two are formed from superparticular ratios—fifth ($3:2$) and fourth ($4:3$). The basis of the diatonic scale associated with the Pythagoreans, first described by Plato,[23] utilizes the difference between the fifth and the fourth, namely a whole tone, as the building block of the scale ($3:2 \div 4:3 = 9:8$). A fourth will contain two of these and a remainder or limma: $4:3 \div (9:8 \times 9:8) = 256:243$. When taken in descending order, two tones and a limma form the four-note module known as the tetrachord. Tetrachords are joined, sometimes through a linking whole tone, to form the heptachord, octachord, and larger scales.

One of the limitations of this system discovered by the early Pythagoreans is that a cycle of twelve fifths is larger than a cycle of seven octaves by a small interval. The two cycles—or, properly speaking, spirals—miss coinciding in a unison by the amount called the comma, $524,288:531,441$. Six whole tones exceed an octave by the same comma. Also in the Pythagorean canon was the observation that a superparticular ratio, such as the whole tone, 9:8, cannot be divided into two equal parts. By an equal division is meant one yielding a ratio, which, multiplied by itself, equals the ratio being divided. Thus 2:1 × 2:1 is 4:1, that is, an octave added to an octave makes a double octave. Conversely, the double octave may be equally divided by extracting the square root of its ratio 4:1, giving 2:1, the size of its component halves. But the square root of a superparticular ratio will always be a surd, for example the equal "halves" of the interval 9:8 are each $3/2\sqrt{2}$. Such irrational proportions were excluded from music by the Pythagoreans. The musical theorists who followed the Pythagoreans adopted these principles.[24]

Early Renaissance authors did not necessarily associate these principles with Pythagoras or his followers. Pythagoras's name is usually cited early in a treatise as the inventor of music or discoverer of the ratios of the consonances. Typically the legend of the blacksmith's shop is recounted. Almost everyone depended on the embroidered version of the story told by Boethius,[25] which goes as follows. By divine will Pythagoras happened to pass a blacksmith shop, from which came diverse sounds of apprentices hammering, sounds that blended in consonance. After observing the smithies, he theorized that the diversity of pitches was caused by the strength of those hammering. But on testing the theory by having them exchange hammers he was forced to admit that he was wrong. He then examined the weights of the hammers and found that one that weighed twice as much as another sounded with it an octave. Comparing the other weights, he discovered that two in the ratio of 3:2 produced the fifth, and weights in the ratio of 4:3 produced the fourth. By this means he determined the ratios of the consonances. After returning home, he made further tests. He attached weights to strings, blew on pipes of various lengths, and filled and partly filled glasses with water and struck them with a copper or iron rod. In all these experiments the same ratios caused the same consonances.

Gaffurio took over the account from Boethius but noted that Josephus attributed the discovery to Jubal, who is shown in a famous woodcut as overseeing the six smithies, five of them swinging hammers weighing 4, 6, 8, 12, and 16 pounds. In accordance with the account by Boethius, three other woodcuts show Pythagoras coaxing the same consonances from bells, water glasses, strings with weights attached, and pipes (see Figure 39-2). Both Boethius and Gaffurio introduced the legend to show that because of the inadequacy of the hearing when confronted with a multitude of sensations, only the reason coupled with accurate observation and measurement can establish the true relationships of tones. Yet neither author gave evidence of observation, measurement, or reasoning thereon. Neither attempted to demonstrate

Figure 39-2. *The discovery of the ratios of the consonances by Jubal and Pythagoras. From Franchino Gaffurio,* Theorica musice *(Milan, 1492).*

anything geometrically, mathematically, or by logical induction or deduction.

Of the four woodcuts in Gaffurio's figure, only the last represents phenomena that are verifiable. If pipes 4, 6, 8, 9, 12, and 16 units long are otherwise equal, the sequence of intervals that Gaffurio aimed to illustrate, a series comparable to *A E a b e a'* will result when they are blown. The other four cases—hammers, bells, glasses partly filled with water, and strings stretched by weights—will not yield these intervals.

With hammers, the pitch emitted depends more on the metal struck than on the hammers. With bells and water glasses the relationships are complex. In the case of weights attached to strings the frequency will vary as the square of the weights. The one medium with which Gaffurio had direct experience—the single stretched string—is not brought into the account, although its division would support the series of ratios he wished to demonstrate.

The accounts of the hammers exhibit some of the trappings of scientific research and demonstration; yet they are transparent appeals to authority and legend and cannot be considered scientific expositions at all. In contrast to Gaffurio's recounting of the hammer legend, his treatment of the mechanics of sound and consonance is quite sophisticated and relies on one of the most enlightened ancient sources, notably the *Paraphrases* by Themistius (fl. ca. A.D. 317–338) on Aristotle's *De anima* in the Latin translation of Ermolao Barbaro the Younger.[26]

Aristotle had challenged the Platonic view that the air struck by the sounding object was the same as that which reached the ear. Rather the percussions causing the sound were transmitted from one particle of air to the next, eventually moving the air next to the ear. Themistius noted, following Aristotle, that the notions of grave and acute were assigned to sounds by analogy with touch, and elucidated this point by saying that the acute voice stabs the air and pungently wounds it, while the grave tone hits bluntly and spreads as it hits. Whereas the acute sound moves the sense a great deal and quickly, the grave sound moves it little and slowly.[27] Gaffurio depended on Themistius also to explain the mechanism of hearing. The nature of the ear is akin to that of air in that the ear is congenitally filled with air, which is excited by the air outside and transmits the motion to little sensitized tinders inside a tissue of little bread baskets (*paniculae*) filled with air. The outside and inside air are continuous, which explains why animals do not hear by their other bodily parts.[28]

Gaffurio made no attempt to reconcile the Aristotelian and Pythagorean-Platonic traditions in his *Theorica musice*. The split became more intense in Gaffurio's last treatise, *De harmonia*, in which he turned to a wider variety of Greek sources, often eclectic themselves. One such source was the *Harmonics* of Ptolemy, translated for him by Niccolò Leoniceno.[29] Ptolemy offered an alternative to Pythagorean tuning, one better suited to current polyphonic musical practice, which utilized consonances not recognized by the Pythagoreans, namely, major and minor thirds and sixths. In the Pythagorean tuning they were harsh-sounding, the major thirds, for example, being too large. Gaffurio described this tuning, which Ptolemy called syntonic diatonic. It is also known as "just intonation," because besides pure fifths and fourths, thirds and sixths also were in their acoustically most perfect size (the major and minor third in the ratios 5:4 and 6:5 instead of the Pythagorean 81:64 and 32:27). Yet Gaffurio could never bring himself to accept this departure from Boethian authority.

The mathematician Bartolomé Ramos de Pareja (ca. 1440–after 1491) in 1482 had proposed a tuning similar to Ptolemy's syntonic-diatonic as a practical strategy.[30] Ramos appears not to have read any of the Greek sources directly, but, like Gallicus and Gaffurio, had studied Boethius closely. Although he began his book by paying tribute to Boethius, Ramos proceeded to overturn completely the Pythagorean system. Slyly constructing a string division that would improve the tuning of the imperfect consonances, he proposed it simply as a method that anyone moderately educated would easily understand. Only toward the end of the book did he make it plain that his imperfect consonances had simpler ratios than those of the Pythagorean system, namely 5:4 and 6:5 for the major and minor thirds, and 5:3 and 8:5 for the major and minor sixths.[31]

Although Ramos was a mathematician, he proposed the new tuning as a practical strategy. It was not until Lodovico Fogliano's treatise, *Musica theorica* (1529), that the imperfect consonances in the just tuning received a logically developed defense. Fogliano (d. ca. 1539) was exceptionally well qualified to deal with questions of Greek musical theory. He combined skill as a singer and composer with a thorough knowledge of Greek. Fogliano based his chapters on sound, consonance, and hearing on Aristotle's *De anima* and *Physics* and espoused the method of his *Posterior Analytics*. Fogliano acknowledged that numbers, that is, ratios, determined the intervals of music; however, insofar as music consisted of sound, which was caused by motion, it was not a mathematical but a natural phenomenon. This fact located music as a science in an intermediate position between the mathematical and natural sciences.[32]

Being natural phenomena, consonance and dissonance should be determined by sense experience. Fogliano demonstrates this point through Aristotelian physics, psychology, and logic. First he analyzes the interaction of the sounding body and the air. Sound is caused, he shows, by the rapid condensation and expansion of air set off by a percussion or by the movement of a firm body in a fluid one.[33] Three things concur in the generation of sound: that which violently expels the air, the air violently expelled, and the motion of the expulsion. None of these three is formally the cause of sound. The agent expelling the air and the air itself are bodies, species of the genus substance. But sound is an occurrence, not a substance. Sound is also not the motion or the expulsion of the air, because it is a special object of the sense, not an object common to all senses.[34] Since motion is a "common sensible," whereas sound is a "sensible particular," Fogliano argues, motion of air cannot be sound. Fogliano thus moves away from Aristotle's position, which was that sound was motion, toward the view that it is an effect of motion. Fogliano concludes that sound is a sensible quality arising from the violent motion of the air, is commensurate with it in that it lasts as long as the motion, and has the potential of altering the sense. Both sound and hearing being natural potentials, the hearing has the perfect and definitive cognition of consonance and dissonance.

Freed of the necessity of determining the limits of consonance by numerical definition, Fogliano proposed a new enumeration and classification of consonances. He limited the consonances to seven within the octave, for after the octave they seemed to return as if by a cyclical motion, just as numbers do after ten. The seven consonances, then, were: minor third, major third, fourth, fifth, minor sixth, major sixth, and octave. Fogliano limited the perfect consonances to the octave and fifth. The rest were imperfect, including the fourth, which had traditionally been a perfect consonance.[35]

Fogliano applied his empirical methodology to the tuning of the practical musical scale. Contrasted to the usual mathematical method of dividing the monochord, his, he insisted, was done in "a new way, almost according to the sense, and materially" (novo modo quasi secundum sensum: et materialiter).[36] Like Ramos's monochord, Fogliano's permitted not only pure fifths and fourths, as in the Pythagorean tuning, but also pure major and minor thirds.

Fogliano's ideas were given prominence (though not credit) in the most widely read musical treatise of the sixteenth century, Le istitutioni harmoniche of Gioseffo Zarlino (1517–1590). Zarlino accepted many of Fogliano's conclusions, but the empirical methodology did not suit his rationalistic tendencies. For example, if Fogliano was content to accept just intonation on the grounds of oral experience, Zarlino, not confident of the judgment of the senses, had to find rational arguments and authority for the classification of consonances and the determination of their proper ratios. So Zarlino devised numerical criteria that did not contradict the ear: he conceived a sacred precinct of consonance, the senario—the set of numbers from one to six—to contain the realm of consonance.[37] Six, he pointed out, is the first perfect number, meaning that it is the sum of all the numbers of which it is a multiple, that is, one, two, and three. Any two numbers from one to six yield the ratio of either a simple or composite consonance. The only tuning system that permitted both imperfect and perfect consonances to be formed of ratios with the first six numbers was Ptolemy's syntonic-diatonic, the same tuning that was sponsored by Fogliano, who did not give it a name or identify its source. Zarlino appealed to the authority of Ptolemy, who consistently followed the principle that reason and sensation should both be satisfied when one theorized about music. Zarlino utilized the translation made by Antonio Gogava of Ptolemy's *Harmonics,* which was later published together with other translations.[38] Zarlino was too pragmatic a musician to insist on the just consonances for instrumental music, however. He recognized that it was not possible to tune a chromatic keyboard so that every fifth, fourth, and third was in a ratio of the senario. He was willing to admit compromises in tuning these intervals in instruments, provided vocal music remained pure. His faith in nature demanded that the ideal ratios be operative in the natural medium of voices:

> If it were true that in voices as well as instruments we hear only the consonances and intervals out of their natural ratios, it would result that those which are born of the true harmonic numbers would never reach actuality but would remain always potential. This potential would be futile and frustrated, for every potential that is not put in action is without utility in nature. And yet we see that God and nature never do anything in vain.[39]

One of the beneficiaries of the Gogava translations was Vincenzo Galilei (d. 1591), father of Galileo. Aided by the humanist literary critic and amateur musician, Giovanni Bardi de' Conti di Vernio (1534–1612), he embarked around 1570 on a project to reform modern music theory and practice on the basis of Greek theory and practice. He enlisted the help of, among others, another humanist, Girolamo Mei (1519–1594), who had been a pupil and collaborator of Pietro Vettori, and now, in Rome, was investigating the music of the ancients. Mei was dubious about the Ptolemaic tuning, because it favored the imperfect consonances, which Mei knew were not used as harmonies in Greek music, for his research showed him it was monophonic. In a lengthy letter that responded to a stack of questions with which Galilei had besieged him, Mei wrote a virtual treatise on ancient music[40] and enclosed a list of Greek sources he had studied to reach his conclusions. It contains nineteen ancient authors, one more than in a similar list sent ten years earlier to Vettori.[41]

> Notice of the writers on music that are still found today whom I have seen:

Aristoxenus, two books and a half or a little more, and perhaps half of the second book of the Rhythmics

Aristides Quintilianus, three books

Alypius with the signs that they used to notate the steps of all the modes and the tones in each genus, with I don't know how much missing at the end

Anonymous book without name printed under the name of Harmonic Introduction of Euclid, also found under the name of Cleoneda or Cleomede, one book

Baccheius Senior introduction, one book

Gaudentius introduction, one book

Emanuel Bryennius, three books

Nicomachus "Strazeno" introduction

Plutarch is printed

Ptolemy, three books

Porphyry on about a book and a half of the music [treatise] of Ptolemy

Psellus introduction. I am told that it is found also printed

Theon, brief compilation, one book

Racendito Josefo, compilation or compendium in one book

Several fragments by diverse authors without name

Ancient Latins:

St. Augustine

Boethius

Censorinus

Martianus Capella in the notes of his Philology.[42]

In none of these sources, Mei told Galilei, did he find any support for the principle of the senario, or evidence of the use of imperfect consonances. On the question of whether voices singing in harmony hold to just intonation, Mei suggested to Galilei an experiment in which two lute strings are tuned respectively to the Pythagorean and the syntonic tuning, and singing voices are tested against them.[43] Galilei may have carried out the experiment, for the same year he addressed a polemic letter to Zarlino correcting his resolution of the tuning question. He then proceeded to lay out his position in a dialogue dedicated to Count Bardi.[44]

Much of what Mei had reported to him in letters about ancient music is aired in the dialogue between the two interlocutors, Giovanni Bardi and Piero Strozzi.[45] Galilei, encouraged by Mei, who seems in turn to have been influenced by Benedetti's lectures on Aristotle's scientific tracts, took an increasingly empirical stance. He put in the mouth of Strozzi the statement, "I wish in those things which sensation can reach that authority always be set aside (as Aristotle says in the Eighth Book of the *Physics*), and with it the tainted reason that contradicts any perception whatever of truth."[46] The habit of testing by experiment the doctrines of even the most noted authorities led Galilei to discover that the ratios that were thought always to cause certain consonances did so only under certain circumstances. So, for example—contrary to what the Pythagoreans taught—the ratio of weights attached to strings had to be in quadruple and not in duple proportion to produce the octave.[47]

Another important influence on Galilei were the writings of Aristoxenus, whose *Harmonic Elements,* written about 300 B.C., were neglected in the early Renaissance because of this Aristotelian author's anti-Pythagorean bias. Galilei used the translation of Gogava and had it translated into Italian,[48] but also sought Mei's help in interpreting some difficult passages. Many of Aristoxenus's ideas had found their way into the treatises of the Pythagorean school, such as those of Nicomachus, Aristides Quintilianus, Ptolemy, and Boethius; but one important aspect of his thought that was rejected by all of them was the belief that a musical scale could be defined entirely by ear, without reference to intervallic ratios. Aristoxenus had divided the octave into equal semitones, so that twelve of them or six whole tones filled the octave exactly without the excess of a comma produced by the Pythagorean system. As a lutanist Galilei had experienced the equal division of the octave in placing frets around the fingerboard; theoretical corroboration for this practice encouraged him to adopt this tuning as the ideal one for both instrumental and vocal music, although he had to fight his inclination toward purely tuned consonances,[49] for none of the consonances in this tuning, besides the octave, is pure.

Zarlino's adherence to the syntonic-diatonic tuning was challenged even before the debate with Galilei by a highly respected commentator on Aristotle, the scientist and mathematician Giovanni Battista Benedetti. Apparently in response to a query from the composer Cipriano de Rore, who was then choirmaster of San Marco in Venice, Benedetti around 1563 explained why the syntonic-diatonic was not a practicable tuning for polyphonic music. Irrefutable calculations, applied to several examples of simple four-part music, showed that if singers kept to the pure tuning of perfect and imperfect consonances both in successive and simultaneous intervals, the pitch of the choir would rise or fall by minute amounts that would eventually add up to a semitone or more in one direction or the other.[50]

Benedetti, too, came to the conclusion that an equal temperament was needed, but his description of how to achieve it on a keyboard was too approximate to define the method as an equal temperament. In all fairness to Zarlino it must be said that he too had arrived at a temperament for keyboard instruments that equalized the Pythagorean comma error by subtracting two-sevenths of this comma from each fifth. For this purpose he employed an instrument, the Mesolabium, described by Eutocius in his commentary on Archimedes,[51] one of several geometric methods for finding mean proportionals described by the humanist Giorgio Valla.[52] Zarlino later used this same device for arriving at an equal temperament. By this time, in 1588, he too had read Aristoxenus and had been partly converted to the empirical camp.[53]

*   *   *

It is no accident that one of the earliest Greek works on music translated into Latin in the Renaissance was the treatise *De musica* attributed to Plutarch.[54] Moral philosophy, one of the subjects of the *studia humanitatis,* attracted a good deal of attention at the end of the fifteenth century. It was in the pursuit of this subject that Carlo Valgulio, secretary to Cardinal Cesare Borgia (son of Pope Alexander VI), encountered the Plutarch treatise on music, for it was usually incorporated in this author's *Moralia.* Apparently a devoted music lover, some years after translating Plutarch's *De virtute morum* and *Praecepta connubialia,*[55] Valgulio turned to the music treatise.[56] He accompanied it with an essay dedicated to a friend, Titus Pyrrhinus, a singer, whom he urged to find a new path that would lead music back to the moral and ethical kind practiced by the ancient Greeks and celebrated by Plutarch.

It is understandable that the pseudo-Plutarch treatise should have attracted Valgulio. Not a musician himself, he was less interested in the theory or practice of music than in its social, civic, and moral uses. The possibility that music could make men better and healthier was a revelation to him. Moreover, he could see a parallel between the decadence deplored by the interlocutors of Plutarch's dialogue and events in Valgulio's own time. Musicians were cultivating innovations and technical virtuosity at the expense of expressivity and ethical effect. The speakers in the dialogue, though critical of most recent music, offered many examples from more ancient times that could be emulated by modern musicians—the lost enharmonic and chromatic genera, the power of certain modes, the majestic and simple music that developed moral character, the laudable dedication to worship and to the praise of heroism and nobility. Valgulio responded sympathetically to the nostalgia expressed by Plutarch's interlocutors for a once powerful, now lost, art.

Valgulio's prefatory essay adopted Plutarch's moralistic and critical tone concerning the music of his own time. Valgulio lamented their music's decline and hoped his friend Tito could help return it to its former height:

> Theophrastus rightly said in the second book concerning music that the essence of music is the movement of the soul, driving away the evils and troubles that have invaded it. If music did not have this effect, that is, to draw the soul where it wants, it would become in essence nothing. I would lament here the music of our time, if it had not already been mourned as dead.

Valgulio was dazzled by the variety in antiquity of poetico-musical genres and their suitability to various social and religious functions. There were songs for praising gods, for honoring deeds of illustrious men or victors at Olympic games, nuptial songs, lyric odes, banquet and love songs, laments, prayers to drive away the plague, tragic and comic songs. The rhythms, rapidity of beat, melody, and instruments were chosen and composed to fit the matter expressed. Against this variety, yet simplicity, of ancient music, he found a monotonous complexity in that of his day. Valgulio recommended that his friend note Aristotle's classification of songs into three kinds—edifying, purgative, and recreational[57]—for some songs were moral and instilled virtue, others imbued the soul with divine spirit and purged men of fear and pity, and others were active.

Valgulio also knew the *Problems* of Aristotle,[58] which spoke illuminatingly of the music of the Greek tragedy. Besides Plutarch and Aristotle, Valgulio demonstrated that he gleaned information about Greek theatrical music also from plays of Aristophanes and from the scholia that appear in some manuscripts of his comedies. He also knew the commentary on Ptolemy's *Harmonics* by Porphyry, for he cited the defense quoted there of the theory that sound is a quality, not a quantity. From this point of view, Valgulio showed, the Aristoxenian opposition to numerical measurement in music was entirely valid, and the equal division of the octave perfectly feasible.

The pseudo-Plutarchan dialogue that Valgulio translated is perhaps the most informative concerning ancient Greek musical culture of any of the surviving Greek writings. It preserves fragments of treatises by Heracleides Ponticus, Glaucus of Reggio, Pratinas, Lamprocles of Athens, Aristoxenus, and various anonymi. Pseudo-Plutarch in Valgulio's translation was probably the most read of any of the Greek sources by the musical humanists of the Renaissance. Galilei drew much of the information on Greek musical practices in his *Dialogo* from this translation. Probably the most important passage for musicians of the sixteenth century was that in which the enharmonic was extolled as the noblest of the genera, favored by the ancients because of its majesty: "The musicians of our times, though, disdained completely the most beautiful genus of all and the most fitting, which the ancients cherished for its majesty and severity."[59] This statement more than anything promoted the mystique surrounding the chromatic and enharmonic that fueled Nicola Vicentino's crusade for the revival of these two lost genera in the 1550s.[60]

After Valgulio's often reprinted essay, it became common, particularly among churchmen, to mourn and ridicule the state of contemporary music. One of the most influential of such critiques is that of Bishop (later Cardinal) Jacopo Sadoleto in his dialogue on education, modeled on another spurious work of Plutarch, *De pueris educandis*. In it Jacopus addresses his son, Paulus, and tells him that he would not have him taught about modern music, that "common trivial harmony, which is entirely a pandering caress of the ear with sweetness and which consists of hardly anything but variation and running of notes."[61] Even when the text of a musical composition was moral and worthwhile, which was rare, it was obscured by "abruptly cutting and jerking the sounds in the throat—as though music were designed not to soothe and control the spirit but merely to afford a base pleasure to the ears, mimicking the cries of birds and beasts, which we should be sorry to resemble."[62] Musicians should follow the precept of Plato, which was that, of the three components of song—words, rhythm, and melody—"the words are by far the most important of the three, being the very basis and foundation of the rest."[63]

Another bishop around this time, according to his later confession, was thinking along the same lines. This was Bishop Bernardino Cirillo Franco, who did not write his thoughts down until twenty years later in 1549 in a letter addressed to "Ugolino Gualteruzzi."[64] He recalled that the ancients "created powerful effects that we nowadays cannot produce either with rhetoric or with oratory in moving the passions and affections of the soul."[65] The only music he has heard that produces such effects is that of the pavane and galliard. He would have the music of the church "framed to the fundamental meaning of the words, in certain intervals and numbers apt to move our affections to religion and pity." Modern musicians should recover the power of the modes and the enharmonic, chromatic, and diatonic genera. An ancient musician would have set the *Kyrie eleison* in the Mixolydian mode, evoking real contrition, whereas Bishop Cirillo was accustomed to hearing the Kyrie and Gloria in the same mode and in the same style. After the fashion of contemporary sculptors, painters, architects, and writers, composers should imitate the art of the ancients, who were able with music to make the lazy active, the angry calm, the dissolute temperate, to console the afflicted and to make happy the miserable.[66]

The idea that music should move the affections, as oratory and rhetoric were intended to do, was a new goal for composers. If one could unleash the power of musical rhetoric, as the humanists had led orators to exploit verbal rhetoric, the miraculous effects of ancient music could once again become common.

When Bishop Cirillo spoke of the Mixolydian mode, he had in mind the ancient mode, "by which anyone hearing it was immediately moved to tears, cries, and lamentation,"[67] not the church "Mixolydian," that is, the seventh of the plainchant modes, which Pietro Aron characterized as containing a mixture of lasciviousness, modesty, and mirth.[68] Composers and theorists were, in fact, being increasingly sensitive to the effects of the different modes or Tones, as witnessed by Gaffurio's injunction:

> Let the composer of a vocal piece strive to make the melody agree in sweetness with its words, so that when these are about love or a plea for death or some lament let him set and dispose mournful sounds so far as he can, as the Venetians do. What I believe will most contribute to this is to order the piece in the Fourth, Sixth, or even Second Tone, since these Tones are more relaxed and are known to produce this kind of effect easily. But when the words speak of indignation and rebuke, it is fitting to utter harsh and harder sounds, which are ascribed most often to the Third and Seventh Tones. To be sure, words of praise and modesty seek somehow intermediate sounds, which are properly ascribed to the First and Eighth Tones.[69]

For a fuller treatment of the powers of the individual modes Gaffurio sends the reader to his *De harmonia*, book 4, which, however, is about the Greek modes. This confusion of the plainchant with the Greek modes and the resulting misunderstandings about their ethical effects continued well into the sixteenth century.

Heinrich Glarean set out to redefine the plainchant modes in terms of polyphonic practice in his famous *Dodekachordon*,[70] in which he added to the eight traditional modes four more, named Aeolian, Hypoaeolian, Ionian, and Hypoionian, after those set forth by Aristoxenus.[71] Glarean sincerely believed that with his reordering and expansion of the modes, which took into account contemporary practices of transposition and added accidentals, or *musica ficta,* as it was called, he had recovered the ancient Greek tonalities. He was mistaken, for his twelve modes and the similarly named twelve *tonoi* of Cleonides were altogether different systems. Nonetheless, Glarean's ostentatiously documented association of the modern modes with the Greeks enhanced the prestige and vigor of the modern modes in the minds of many and attracted the attention of composers to their expressive potential. Zarlino, in a remarkable review of the history of modality, in which he exploited a vast library of Greek and Latin sources, showed the fallacy of linking the Greek and modern systems. As most of the pre-Glarean theorists had done, he refrained from giving the modes Greek ethnic names.[72] Indeed he seemed to want to put a distance between his own theory of the modes and the theory of Boethius and the ancients, to free himself from the burden of the past.

Whereas Zarlino never really understood the dynamics of the ancient *tonoi* and octave species, at the very moment he was writing his great work, two scholars were busy in Rome investigating the nature of the Greek tonal system. The two were Francisco de Salinas and Girolamo Mei. They worked independently; Mei finished his work, in four books, on the ancient modes in 1573, but it was never published.[73] Salinas published his great work, *De musica libri septem,* in 1577, and it contained three brief, though significant, chapters on the Greek *tonoi.*[74] Salinas was the first to distinguish in print between a mode, octave species, or *harmonia* and a *tonos.* By means of a *tonos* (his Latin translation was *tonus*) a melody could be raised or lowered to a different level of pitch without changing the intervallic configuration of the melody, that is, its octave species (the arrangement of tones and semitones in the octave scale). Through a change of *harmonia* or mode, a melody changes character, the sequence of tones and semitones—the octave species—is altered and with it "the affection of the soul" that it stirs in the listener.[75] Salinas based his interpretation largely on the *Harmonics* of Ptolemy, but he did not penetrate his theory sufficiently to appreciate the link Ptolemy made between the *tonoi* and octave species.

This subject, among other subtleties of the Greek system, was explored exhaustively by Mei. His conclusions were communicated to Galilei and Bardi. Galilei faithfully reported them briefly in his *Dialogo della musica antica,* particularly through a set of charts.[76] Bardi modified Mei's representation of Ptolemy's system somewhat in his "Discorso mandato a Caccini sopra la musica antica e 'l cantar bene," an essay that received limited circulation until it was published in the eighteenth century.[77] Giovanni Battista Doni also adopted many of Mei's ideas, though he arrived at an interpretation of Ptolemy's system that differs slightly from Mei's and is more consistent with recent scholarship.[78] Both Bardi and Doni experimented with the Greek modes in their own compositions and urged others to do the same, but composers generally showed rather little interest in the project. The net effect of the revision of modal theory that Zarlino, Mei, Salinas, and their successors brought about was to deprive the modern modal system of the authority of antiquity and to undermine its relevance to large-scale structure in musical composition. The decline of the modes as the basis of tonal organization, indeed, can be traced partly to this humanist activity.

*   *   *

When Bishop Bernardino Cirillo compared music to rhetoric he was affirming the strong link that had developed between music and the verbal arts. Throughout the Middle Ages music as a discipline was a component of the quadrivium of mathematical sciences, in which it was a companion to arithmetic, geometry, and astronomy. The trivium, by contrast, had no place for either music or poetry, for it consisted of grammar, rhetoric, and dialectic. In the early Renaissance the seven liberal arts were expanded and redefined. Coluccio Salutati conceived of poetry as a union of the quadrivium and trivium.[79] Angelo Poliziano joined poetics to the old trivium.[80] In these systems music as a speculative science was still grouped under the quadrivium, but practical music, which was really a branch of poetry, was not mentioned. Mei devised a system of "constructive arts" (*arti fattive*), based on Aristotle's *Poetics,* that recognizes visual, verbal, and musical media among the imitative arts.[81]

Of the arts of the trivium, grammar had the longest association with western music theory. Johannes dictus Cotto, around 1100, compared the *distinctiones* of Aelius Donatus (fourth century), namely, colon, comma, and period, to the pauses in plainchant that mark the divisions of the text and therefore the melody set to it.[82] Composers of the earliest polyphony, called organum, also observed this punctuation, but in the later Middle Ages, considerations of rhythmic structure, numerical proportions, and strictly musical temporal organization took precedence over fidelity to the grammatical construction of the text. With the growing recognition in the Renaissance of the natural alliance of music with the verbal arts, composers renewed their attention to the grammatical structure of the texts they set.

The most thorough application of classical grammar to musical composition was undertaken by Giovanni del Lago (ca. 1490–after 1543), a man greatly revered as an authority in Venetian circles in the first half of the sixteenth century but almost unknown to the public. Again it was Donatus who was invoked to guide the composer in selecting places in the text at which to make musical cadences of various degrees of finality. In addition he instructed the musician to be sensitive to the text on other levels: general mood, units of thought or sentences, punctuation, accentuation of words, and length of syllables; and in poetic texts the location of long syllables within a line, the place of caesuras, and scansion.[83] Significantly, del Lago was not content to stop with the structure of the text, but put its affective content at the very top of the conditions that should be observed, and he tied it to the choice of mode:

> Whenever learned composers have to compose a song they are accustomed to ask themselves conscientiously to what end they might be starting and composing it, that is, what affections of the soul they ought to arouse with the piece, thus in what mode it should be composed, for some are severe and sedate, some mournful and lamenting, others angry, or impetuous. So should the melodies of songs be diversely distinctive, some stirring people one way, some another.[84]

Del Lago's instructions reflect a sensitivity to a number of parameters of language that had been neglected by polyphonic composers in the fifteenth century. But the best composers of the previous generation had followed these rules, even though the textbooks then were silent about them. Josquin des Prez (ca. 1440–1521) is the most notable among these composers, and his manner of setting Latin texts in his late works was considered a model by del Lago's generation.[85]

Literary humanists may have exercised strong influence on composers directly, though the path of this influence has not so far been well documented. Its effect can be observed particularly in the Italian madrigal and shortly afterward in the Latin motet. Pietro Bembo identified sonic qualities in the poetry of Petrarch that could not help but inspire composers to try to match them. He characterized the two general qualities of sound: gravity (*gravità*) and pleasingness (*piacevolezza*).[86] The grave sound was suited to feelings of modesty, dignity, majesty, magnificence, and grandeur, while the pleasing sound expressed grace, sweetness, charm, smoothness, playfulness, and wit. Factors such as rhyme, rhythm, number of syllables, accents, combinations of long and short syllables, the sound of particular vowels and consonants affected the gravity or pleasingness of a verse or sentence of prose. D. T. Mace in 1969 put forth a theory that Bembo's way of reading Petrarch stimulated a new wave of madrigal writing in which these qualities of Petrarch's poetry inspired a variety of techniques that exploited the resources of the learned polyphonic medium developed in Franco-Netherlandish chansons and sacred music.[87]

Petrarch's highly musical verse owed a great debt to Vergil, in whose poetry Zarlino, who had probably read Bembo, found these same qualities:

> He adapts the sonority of the verse with such art that it truly seems that the sound of the words places before the eyes those things of which he speaks, so that where he speaks of love, one sees that he artfully chose smooth, sweet, pleasing sounds supremely welcome to the hearing. Where he needed to speak of warlike subjects, such as describing a naval encounter, a shipwreck, or similar things, where spilling of blood is involved, ire, disdain, unpleasantness, and every hateful thing, he chose hard, harsh, and displeasing words that terrify the listener.[88]

Zarlino showed that polyphonic music possessed parallel resources. Harshness and bitterness could be evoked by having vocal lines proceed by whole tone and major third, while feelings of grief and sorrow could be produced by semitone and minor-third movements. Similarly, certain simultaneous intervals, major thirds and sixths, were hard, while minor thirds and sixths were sweet and soft sounding.[89] Vicentino earlier made similar observations.[90] Zarlino and Vicentino were both disciples of Adrian Willaert (ca. 1490–1562), whose music bears out the effectiveness of these devices.

Bishop Cirillo's prophetic vision of a musical rhetoric more powerful than oratory was already on the way to realization when he wrote his letter-manifesto in 1549. Whether deliberately or unconsciously adopting a rhetorical approach, composers were approaching the task of bringing life to both secular and sacred words through music in a rhetorical manner. They chose musical devices for their capacity to convey the feeling and meaning of the words. Some of these devices were departures from normal usage, and were, consequently, analogous to figures of speech, which Quintilian defined as deliberate errors, divergences from direct and simple language for the sake of embellishment and effect.[91] Quintilian, indeed, was one of the authors most widely read by students of both language and music. Despite the obvious parallels between musical composition and rhetoric, or musical performance and oratory, little was said in writing about them until the end of the sixteenth century. A few isolated instances may be mentioned. Vicentino in 1555 urged freedom of tempo in performance on the grounds that we learn this technique from oratory:

the movement of the measure should be changed to slower or
faster according to the words. . . . The experience of the orator
teaches us to do this, for in his oration he speaks now loudly, now
softly, now slowly, now quickly, and thus greatly moves the listeners; and this manner of changing the measure has great effect on
the soul.[92]

An anonymous author of a counterpoint treatise of about 1570 preserved in Besançon speaks of four musical figures or ornaments of composition, the first of which is fugue, which he likens to the Greek musical
figure *plokē*. The other *figurae melopaejas,* he said, were *tonē, agogē,* and
petteia, which he translated *extensio, ductus,* and *pettia.* These musical
figures are enumerated by a number of Greek authors, including Cleonides, a translation of which by Giorgio Valla was available.[93] The concept
of melopoetics as the art of composition probably had a humanist origin.
In 1537 Nicholaus Listenius expanded the usual division of music into
theoretical and practical, adding a third part, "poetic." He may have
imitated the classification of Aristides Quintilianus, who divided the
practical art into composition (*christikon*) and performance (*exangelti-
kon*).[94] In teaching the art of laying out a composition, or *musica poetica,*
German authors increasingly adopted rhetorical terminology.[95] Thus
Gallus Dressler in 1563 proposed that a polyphonic composition should
follow the plan of an oration: *exordium, medium,* and *finis.*[96] The analogy to oratory was pursued most thoroughly by Joachim Burmeister,
who eulogized music as a higher form of oratory:

> Not Apelles, with the most accurate skill of his art, not Demos-
> thenes, not Cicero by the art of persuading, deflecting, moving and
> orating, would have better placed the burden of trouble and lamen-
> tation before the eyes, moved the ears, implanted these [feelings] in
> the heart than Orlandus [Lassus] did with his harmonic art.[97]

Burmeister gave pseudo-rhetorical names to many of the most used compositional devices, such as *mimesis* for the imitation of one vocal group
by another, or *noema* for note-against-note declamatory polyphonic setting, or *climax* for the modern sequence. Expressive devices, such as
"word painting" (*hypotyposis*), or expressive intervals (*pathopoeia*),
were also recognized as figures.[98]

Probably independently, Francis Bacon also dwelled on the parallels
between musical composition and rhetoric in several of his works,
among them, the *Advancement of Learning:* "Is not the precept of a
Musitian, to fall from a discord or harsh accord, vpon a concord, or

sweete accord, alike true affection? Is the Trope of Musicke, to auoyde or slyde from the close or Cadence, common with the Trope of Rhetoricke of deceyuing expectation?"[99] Here Bacon describes the suspension (Burmeister's *syncopa*) and the evaded cadence, for which Burmeister had no name and, surprisingly, did not even recognize. It is possible to analyze much of the repertory of the second half of the sixteenth century, most notably Italian madrigals and Latin motets, in terms of rhetorical figures. The rhetorical approach to composition became ever more deliberate and intense in the seventeenth century and received its fullest expression in German sacred music of the Baroque period.

*   *   *

The musician was not separate from the poet, nor the poet from the musician, for poets in those times being expert in music and musicians in poetry (as Strabo has it), the one and the other were called by these two names, musician and poet. This is evident from what Plutarch says.[100]

The ideal of the poet-composer-musician exerted a powerful fascination on Renaissance humanists.[101] Again it was Plutarch who launched this image, not by any direct statement to this effect, but simply by naming a multitude of poets who sang to the kithara or lyre, from Amphion and Linus to Terpander and Timotheus.[102] The madrigal, though it realized a close rapport between words and music, broke a tradition of singing to the strumming and plucking of a lyrelike instrument—usually the lira da braccio or lute—that was alive in Italy from Dante's time through the fifteenth century. When humanists spoke approvingly of music, it was usually in reference to such sung recitation of poetry.[103] Ficino claimed to have revived "Orphic singing to the lyre" and counted it among the principal achievements of Florentine culture in this, its golden age.[104]

The art of musically reciting verses did not die out in the sixteenth century, but it was eclipsed by polyphonic music in which the poet's diction was almost overwhelmed by a composer's complex and artful texture. Toward the end of the century, when both musicians and poets had become disillusioned with the artificiality of the polyphonic chanson and madrigal, a return to a simple songful projection of a poem that would move the listener through the inherent power of the verses and their rhythms and inflections became the goal of parallel movements in France and Italy. In France the crusade was led by Pontus de Tyard and Jean Dorat among the philosophers and scholars, Jean-Antoine de Baïf among the poets, and Claude Le Jeune and Jacques Mauduit among the musicians. In Italy the leaders were Bardi and Galilei on the theoretical side and Emilio de' Cavalieri, Jacopo Peri, and Giulio Caccini on the practical.

The French manifestation of the effort to join music and poetry in a more perfect union was the less radical of the two and had firmer roots in the early Renaissance. Tyard, who was deeply influenced by the Italian humanists, particularly Ficino, shared with them a preference for the musical projection of a poem by a single voice.

> If the purpose of music is to give such a melody to a text that whoever hears it is moved and lets himself be drawn to the affection of the poet, the composer who can adapt it to a single voice, seems to me better to achieve the sought for goal, for polyphonic music [*Musique figurée*] most often does not convey to the ears but a lot of noise, from which you do not get any vital feeling.[105]

Various experiments aimed at making poetry more musical or better suited to musical setting led eventually to a manner of composing verses as if French syllables possessed the same sort of quantity as was observed in classical Latin, or *vers mesurées à l'antique*.[106] When these verses were set to music in a style also called *vers mesurées,* the long syllables were usually assigned to note values twice as long as those set to the short syllables, with the result that successions of such values did not divide evenly into duple or triple measures. This allowed the antique meters to impress the listener unimpeded by the normal recurrence of stress and measure. The accompanying parts, whether vocal or instrumental, might divide some of the values into smaller notes, but they were not allowed to oppose the reigning meters.[107] Odes of Horace and Latin odes composed in imitation of them were sung in the German grammar schools in much this way as a means of drilling the pupils in the ancient meters. Some of these settings were published, beginning with those of Petrus Tritonius,[108] but it was not tried before with a vernacular. The French language, lacking quantity, offered great resistance to any consistent application of the classical meters. After a brief flowering the *vers mesurées* died out, but the irregular musical measures left their mark in the *air de cour* and the French recitative of the ballet and lyric theater.

The Italian experiment in wedding music and poetry had more lasting results, for it led to a new theatrical genre, opera. The emergence in Florence of the play set entirely to music in the last years of the sixteenth century is one of the most remarkable examples of scholarship inspiring artistic innovation and of theory blossoming into practice. There were, of course, many kinds of spectacles in Italy that joined music and theater before the musical pastorals of the 1590s: sacred representations, which were popular particularly in Florence, songs and sung recitations within plays, marvelous intermedi between the acts of plays in which the texts were set entirely to music, Latin tragedies with choruses set polyphonically, and madrigal comedies.[109] But music's function remained accessory and decorative. In the new musical pastorals it became the prime mover of the drama without destroying its integrity and momentum.

Humanist scholarship contributed two indispensable components: classical precedent for a drama that unfolded entirely in song, and a manner of singing dramatically on the stage. Both the poet of *Euridice* and the composer of the music for this pastoral, performed entirely in music in 1600, cited the example of the ancients in justifying their innovation. According to "the opinion of many," the ancient Greeks and Romans sang entire tragedies on the stage, Rinuccini and Peri argued in the prefaces and dedications of their printed editions. The "many" may not actually have been so many, for most literary scholars then as now believed that only some, not all, of an ancient tragedy was set to music. But there were a few who were convinced that an entire tragedy would have been performed musically, and one of them was the mentor to the Florentine Camerata: Mei.[110] He had expressed the opinion that the Greeks used music throughout their tragedies, the old comedy, and satyr plays in his *De modis musicis,* book 4. The active chorus, he believed, sang with melody and the rhythm of dance. The stationary chorus sang melody but not with the rhythm of dance, therefore in an unmeasured chant. The actors likewise sang without rhythm, but they were accompanied by the aulos. Mei based these beliefs partly on Aristotle's *Poetics* (6.2–3.1449b). Of the other evidence that Mei (and Patrizi) cited, the most persuasive was out of the pseudo-Aristotelian *Problems,* particularly problem 48 of section 19.[111] Here the Aristotelian author implied that the tragic choruses did not sing in the Hypodorian and Hypophrygian modes (Mei emended these to Dorian and Phrygian), because these modes had an active character and were more suited to the actors. The others, which had a plaintive and quiet character, were more suited to commoners who functioned in the choruses. Mei concluded from his reading in the Greek sources that three kinds of music, rhythmic choral song, unmeasured choral chanting, and sung recitation constituted the entire dramatic performance.

Peri in his preface claimed, moreover, that he had forged a new style of singing in imitation of the half-song, half-speech that was employed by actors on the ancient stage, "a melody that, elevated beyond ordinary speech, descended so much from the melody of song that it assumed an intermediate form." Peri reveals his classical sources by the technical language he applied to describe this new genre of song:

>I reflected that the sort of voice assigned by the ancients to song, which they called diastematic (as if to say sustained and suspended) could at times be hurried, and take a moderate course between the slow, sustained movements of song and the fluent and rapid ones of speech, and thus suit my purpose (just as the ancients, too, adapted the voice to reading poetry and heroic verses), approaching that other [voice] of conversation, which they called continuous.[112]

The distinction between the diastematic movement of the voice in song and continuous movement of the voice in speech is first found in the work of Aristoxenus,[113] and it was repeated by almost all of the Greek authors and reported also by Boethius. Aristides Quintilianus spoke in addition of a third kind of voice, used in reciting poems,[114] and Boethius was even more specific, when he said Albinus stated that "we read a heroic poem neither in a continuous flow as in prose nor in the sustained and more sluggish manner of voice as in song" but in an intermediate style.[115] Peri sought to imitate the more rapid and less pitch-conscious inflections of speech in which the voice slides over a range of pitches without stopping on any of them and to combine this imitation with the sustained discrete tones of a voice that pauses on stressed and sustained syllables. He achieved this goal extraordinarily well in his new style of speech-song. It is significant that Peri recognized this creative effort as an act of imitation, not only the imitation of the ancients, but the imitation of natural speech. For music, like poetry, was an imitation of action, as Aristotle taught. Thus Peri's new recitative style, as it was later called, was not only an intimate union of poetry and music but a marriage of creative intuition and humanist learning.

NOTES

1. Mei, letter to Galilei, 15 May 1579, ed. in *Girolamo Mei: Letters on Ancient and Modern Music to Vincenzo Galilei and Giovanni Bardi, a Study with Annotated Texts,* ed. C. V. Palisca (Stuttgart, 2d ed. 1977), 155–57, 162–64.

2. Vincenzo Galilei, *Dialogo della musica antica, et della moderna* (Florence, 1581), 92–97. Francesco Patrizi gave transcriptions of a few lines in *Della poetica, La deca istoriale* (Ferrara, 1586), ed. D. Aguzzi-Barbagli (Florence, 1969–71), vol. 1, book 6, 329–33. Ercole Bottrigari published some longer excerpts in *Il Melone* (Ferrara, 1602), 10–11. See U. Sesini, "Studi sull'-umanesimo musicale: Ercole Bottrigari," *Convivium* 13 (1941): 9–10. The best modern editions and transcription of the four hymns, including a fifth that lacks music, are in *Denkmäler altgriechischer Musik,* ed. E. Pöhlmann (Nuremberg, 1970), 13–21.

3. L. Schrade espoused this view in his "Renaissance: The Historical Conception of an Epoch," in *Kongress-Bericht der Internationale Gesellschaft für Musikwissenschaft, Utrecht 1952* (Amsterdam, 1953), 19–32.

4. In the most recent history of music in the Renaissance published in English, H. M. Brown states: "Studies of the Renaissance, from the time of Burckhardt and Huizinga on, have rightly centered on artistic, intellectual, and philosophical events in Italy. Music in the Renaissance, on the other hand, is a northern art, or at least an art by northerners." *Music in the Renaissance* (Englewood Cliffs, NJ, 1976), 4. Schrade had taken a similar stand in "Renaissance: The Historical Conception," p. 30: "In contrast to the bonae litterae and to the visual arts as well, the rebirth of music came to pass as an achievement of northern composers."

5. D. P. Walker, "Musical Humanism in the 16th and Early 17th Centuries," *Music Review* 2 (1941): 1–13, 111–21, 220–27, 288–308; 3 (1942): 55–71; translated into German as *Der musikalische Humanismus* (Kassel, 1949).

6. Indeed, a historian of philosophy, P. O. Kristeller, contributed one of the important early studies of the movement: "Music and Learning in the Early Italian Renaissance," *Journal of Renaissance and Baroque Music* (later named *Musica disciplina*) 1 (1947): 255–74.

7. An account of this evolution is given in C. V. Palisca, *Humanism in Italian Renaissance Musical Thought* (New Haven, 1986). This essay draws liberally on the findings laid out in greater detail in that book, but without further reference to it. Rather, the footnotes will point directly to primary sources, significant secondary sources, and directions for further reading.

8. See C. Bower, "Boethius and Nicomachus: An Essay Concerning the Sources of *De institutione musica*," *Vivarium* 16 (1978): 1–45.

9. See F. R. Levin, ed. "Nicomachus of Gerasa *Manual of Harmonics:* Translation and Commentary" (Ph.D. diss., Columbia University, New York, 1967).

10. There is an extensive literature on the "harmony of the spheres," as it is usually called. Studies mainly from the point of view of iconology and imagery are K. Meyer-Baer, *Music of the Spheres and the Dance of Death* (Princeton, 1970); and S. K. Heninger, Jr., *Touches of Sweet Harmony: Pythagorean Cosmology and Renaissance Poetics* (San Marino, CA, 1974). Concerning poetic uses of the concept see J. Hutton, "Some English Poems in Praise of Music," in *English Miscellany,* ed. M. Praz (Rome, 1951), 1:1–63; J. Hollander, *The Untuning of the Sky* (Princeton, 1961). Philosophical and scientific implications are considered in D. P. Walker, *Spiritual and Demonic Magic from Ficino to Campanella* (London, 1958), and *Studies in Musical Science in the Late Renaissance* (London and Leiden, 1978).

11. Ugolino of Orvieto, *Declaratio musice discipline,* ed. A. Seay, Corpus scriptorum de musica 7 (Rome, 1959).

12. Giorgio Anselmi, *De musica,* ed. G. Massera (Florence, 1961), 103–6.

13. Franchino Gaffurio, *Theorica musice* (Milan, 1492), book 1, chap. 1, fol. a4–a4v.

14. *Aristidis Quintiliani Musica e graeco in latinum conversa,* Verona, Bibl. capitolare, MS CCXL (201), fols. 1r–25v. Dated 15 April 1494.

15. Gaffurio, *Theorica musice,* book 1, chap. 1, fol. a5; Plato, *Timaeus,* 47c.

16. *Practica musice* (Milan, 1496).

17. Franchino Gaffurio, *De harmonia musicorum instrumentorum opus* (Milan, 1518), trans. C. A. Miller (Stuttgart, 1977).

18. There are several exhaustive commentaries on this figure, all listed in the best of them: J. Haar, "The Frontispiece of Gafori's *Practica musicae* (1496)," *Renaissance Quarterly* 27 (1974): 7–22.

19. These ideas are drawn from Aristides Quintilianus, *De musica* 3.13–14; see Aristides Quintilianus, *On Music in Three Books,* ed. and trans. T. J. Mathiesen (New Haven, 1983), 180–82.

20. Johannes Tinctoris, *The Art of Counterpoint,* trans. A. Seay (n.p., American Institute of Musicology, 1961), 13–14; Aristotle, *De caelo,* 2.9.292b.

21. Francisco de Salinas, *De musica libri septem,* (Salamanca, 1577; reprinted Kassel, 1958), book 1, chap. 1 (pp. 1–2).

22. Giovanni Battista Benedetti, *Diversarum speculationum mathematicarum & physicorum liber* (Turin, 1585), chap. 33 (pp. 190–91).

23. *Timaeus,* 36B.

24. For a reconstruction of ancient Pythagorean mathematical thought about music, see R. L. Crocker, "Pythagorean Mathematics and Music," *Journal of Aesthetics and Art Criticism* 22 (1963): 189–98, 325–35. An excellent survey of Pythagorean musical theory is C. A. Barbera, "The Persistence of Pythagorean Mathematics in Ancient Musical Thought" (Ph.D. diss., University of North Carolina, Chapel Hill, 1980).

25. Boethius, *De institutione musica,* 1.10–11.

26. Themistius, *Paraphraseos de Anima libri tres, interprete Hermolao Barbaro* (Paris, 1535), ed. R. Heinze (Berlin, 1899).

27. Ibid., 2:30, fol. 74.

28. Gaffurio, *Theorica musice,* 2:2; Themistius, *Paraphraseos,* 2:28, no. 81.

29. *Claudii Ptolomei Harmonicon interprete Nicolao Leoniceno . . . adhortatione et opera celeberrimi uiri Petri Barotii . . . ac Franchini Gafurii.* London, British Library, MS Harleian lat. 3306. Another copy, dated 1499, is in Vatican City, Biblioteca Apostolica Vaticana, MS vat. lat. 4570. Concerning this and other translations made for Gaffurio, see F. A. Gallo, "Musici scriptores graeci," in *Catalogus Translationum et Commentariorum: Mediaeval and Renaissance Translations and Commentaries,* ed. P. O. Kristeller, F. E. Cranz, and V. Brown (Washington, DC, 1976), 3:64–73.

30. Bartolomé Ramos de Pareja, *Musica practica* (Bologna, 1482; facsimile Bologna, 1969), [part 1], tractate 1, chap. 2, ed. J. Wolfe in *Publikationen der Internationalen Musikgesellschaft, Beihefte* 2 (Leipzig, 1901), p. 1.

31. Ibid., 3.2.3, Wolf ed., 98.

32. Lodovico Fogliano, *Musica theorica* (Venice, 1529), 1.1, fol. 1r–v. The notion that music lies midway between natural science and mathematics is from Aristotle, *Physics,* 2.2.194a.

33. Fogliano, *Musica theorica*, 2.2, fol. XVr.

34. Aristotle makes this distinction in *De anima*, 2.6: color is a special object of sight, sound of hearing, flavor of taste; movement, rest, number, figure, and magnitude, by contrast, are objects common to all the senses.

35. Fogliano, *Musica theorica*, 2.5, fol. XVIIr.

36. Ibid., 3.1, fol. XXXIIIr.

37. Gioseffo Zarlino, *Le istitutioni harmoniche* (Venice, 1558), book 1, chap. 15.

38. Antonio Gogava, *Aristoxeni . . . Harmonicorum elementorum libri iii . . . Cl. Ptolomaei Harmonicorum . . . lib. iii. Aristoteli de objecto auditus* (Venice, 1562).

39. Zarlino, *Istitutioni harmoniche*, 2:45.

40. Part of this letter, of 8 May 1572, was, in fact, later edited by Piero del Nero and published posthumously as *Discorso sopra la musica antica e moderna* (Venice, 1602; reprinted Milan, 1933).

41. Letter from Mei to Vettori, Rome, 21 February 1562, British Library MS Add. 10,268, fols. 224r–225r, printed in *Girolamo Mei*, ed. Palisca, 180–82.

42. For bibliographical notes concerning these authors and their works, see *Girolamo Mei*, ed. Palisca, 118–21, notes 58–77.

43. Letter from Mei to Galilei, Rome, 17 January 1578, in *Girolamo Mei*, ed. Palisca, 140.

44. Galilei, *Dialogo della musica antica*.

45. The dialogue is, of course, fictitious, but there is evidence that Mei's letters were the subject of weekly meetings during the year 1577 at Bardi's academy, later known as the Camerata. See J. W. Hill, "Oratory Music in Florence, I, *Recitar cantando*, 1583–1655," *Acta musicologica* 51 (1979): 111, n. 13.

46. Galilei, *Dialogo della musica antica*, 2.

47. Vincenzo Galilei, *Discorso intorno all'opere di messer Gioseffo Zarlino* (Florence, 1589), 103–4.

48. The translation is in Florence, Biblioteca Nazionale centrale, MSS Galileiani 8.

49. In the *Discorso intorno all'opere*, 113, Galilei says of the Aristoxenian solution: "No demonstrable distribution besides this one can be found among stable steps that is simpler and more perfect and more powerful, whether played or sung."

50. Benedetti, *Diversarum speculationum*, 278–80. For a summary of Benedetti's analysis, see C. V. Palisca, "Scientific Empiricism in Musical Thought," in *Seventeenth Century Science and the Arts*, ed. H. H. Rhys (Princeton, 1961), 113–18.

51. See J. M. Barbour, *Tuning and Temperament* (East Lansing, MI, 1953), 50; and P. L. Rose, *The Italian Renaissance of Mathematics* (Geneva, 1975), 48.

52. *De geometria*, 4.2, fols. u6r–xlr, in Giorgio Valla, *De expetendis et fugiendis rebus opus* (Venice, 1501), book 13.

53. See his Gioseffo Zarlino, *Sopplimenti musicali* (Venice, 1588), 4.20 (pp. 181–83); 4.30 (pp. 208–10). D. P. Walker has noted the increasing rapprochement between Galilei's and Zarlino's ideas in the course of their debate in *Studies in Musical Science,* 14–26.

54. At this time it was considered an authentic work of Plutarch; only later was this attribution challenged.

55. Brescia, 1497.

56. Published Brescia, 1507; reprints: Basel, 1530, Venice, 1532, Paris, 1555, 1557, 1566.

57. Aristotle, *Politics,* 8.7.1341b.

58. They had been published in a medieval Latin translation with a commentary by Pietro d'Abano, one of the founders of Paduan Aristotelian studies, in *Aristotelis problemata cum expositio* (Mantua, 1475).

59. Translated from Valgulio in *Plutarchi Chaeronei . . . Opuscula (quae quidem extant) omnia* (Basel, 1530), fol. 31v.

60. Nicola Vicentino, *L'antica musica ridotta alla moderna prattica* (Rome, 1555; facsimile ed. E. E. Lowinsky, Kassel, 1959). See H. W. Kaufmann, *The Life and Works of Nicola Vicentino* (Rome, 1966).

61. *De pueris recte instituendis* (Venice, 1533; Basel, 1538).

62. Jacopo Sadoleto, *De pueris,* trans. E. T. Campagnac and K. Forbes, *Sadoleto on Education* (London, 1916), 117.

63. *De pueris* (1533 ed.), fol. 42v. Plato, *Republic,* 3.399–400. This dictum of Plato was later cited by Johann Ott, *Missae tredecim* (Nuremberg, 1539), Zarlino (*Istitutioni* (1558), 4:32); and Giulio Cesare Monteverdi in the preface to Claudio Monteverdi's *Scherzi musicali* (Venice, 1607), trans. in *Source Readings in Music History,* ed. O. Strunk (New York, 1950), 407. Sadeleto's critique was also quoted by Galilei in his *Discorso intorno all'uso delle dissonanze,* ed. F. Rempp in *Die Kontrapunkttraktate Vincenzo Galileis* (Cologne, 1980), fol. 194v (p. 158).

64. So the letter is addressed in Aldo Manuzio, ed., *Lettere volgari di diversi nobilissimi huomini . . . Libro terzo* (Venice, 1564), 114, but according to O. Mischiati (review of L. Lockwood, *The Counter Reformation and Masses of V. Ruffo,* in *Rivista italiana di musicologia* 9 [1974]: 304), the addressee of the letter was really Ugolino Guastanezzi, who was employed by Ludovico Beccadelli, secretary of Cardinal Ranuccio Farnese. The letter is translated in *Palestrina, Pope Marcellus Mass,* ed. L. Lockwood (New York, 1975), 10–16.

65. *Palestrina,* ed. Lockwood, 11.

66. Ibid., 12–13.

67. Ibid., 11.

68. Pietro Aron, *Trattato della natura et cognitione di tutti gli tuoni di canto figurato* (Venice, 1525), chap. 25, fol. lr.

69. Gaffurio, *Practica musice,* 3.15.

70. Heinrich Glarean, *Dodekachordon* (Basel, 1547), trans. C. A. Miller (n.p., American Institute of Musicology, 1965).

71. Glarean's source was the Aristoxenian treatise, *Harmonic Introduction,* translated by Giorgio Valla in *Cleonidae harmonicum introductorium* (Venice, 1497).
72. *Istitutioni harmoniche,* 4.1–8. Although Zarlino adopted Glarean's twelve modes, and these chapters were obviously intended to refute Glarean's claim to have recovered the ancient Greek system, Glarean's name is never mentioned. See Zarlino, *On the Modes, Part Four of "Le istitutioni harmoniche," 1558,* trans. V. Cohen, ed. C. V. Palisca (New Haven, 1983).
73. *De modis musicis antiquorum,* Vatican City, Biblioteca Apostolica Vaticana, MS vat. lat. 5323.
74. Salinas, *De musica libri septem,* book 4, chaps. 11–13.
75. *De musica libri septem,* book 4, chap. 12 (pp. 198–99).
76. Galilei, *Dialogo della musica antica,* 57–60.
77. In G. B. Doni, *Lyra Barberina,* ed. A. F. Gori and G. B. Passeri (Florence, 1763), 2:233–48. A partial translation, omitting, however, the section on the *tonoi,* is in *Source Readings,* ed. Strunk, 290–301.
78. G. B. Doni, *Compendio dell Trattato de' generi e de' modi della musica* (Rome, 1635), 33–34.
79. Coluccio Salutati, *De laboribus Herculis,* ed. B. L. Ullman (Zurich, 1951), 18–20.
80. See B. Weinberg, *A History of Literary Criticism in the Italian Renaissance,* 2 vols. (Chicago, 1961), 1:3.
81. Letter to Vettori, 10 January 1560, London, British Library, MS Add. 10268, fol. 209. For his table in English translation see *Girolamo Mei,* ed. Palisca, 45.
82. *Hucbald, Guido, and John On Music: Three Medieval Treatises,* trans. W. Babb, ed. C. V. Palisca (New Haven, 1978), 70. See also E. Lippman, "The Place of Music in the System of the Liberal Arts," in *Aspects of Medieval and Renaissance Music,* ed. J. LaRue (New York, 1966), 545–59.
83. Giovanni del Lago, *Breve introduttione di musica misurata,* "Modo, & osseruatione di comporre qualunche concento," p. [39]. See D. Harrán, "The Theorist Giovanni del Lago," *Musica disciplina* 27 (1973): 107–51.
84. *Breve introduttione,* p. [39].
85. See the volume of studies containing the proceedings of the Josquin Congress in New York, 1971, *Josquin des Prez,* ed. E. E. Lowinsky (London, New York, and Toronto, 1976).
86. Pietro Bembo, *Prose della volgar lingua,* ed. M. Marti (Padua, 1967), book 1, 63ff.
87. D. T. Mace, "Pietro Bembo and the Literary Origins of the Italian Madrigal," *Musical Quarterly* 55 (1969): 65–86.
88. Zarlino, *Istitutioni harmoniche,* 1.2 (p. 5).
89. Ibid., 4.32; Vered trans., 95.
90. Vicentino, *L'antica musica,* 4.21, fols. 81v–82r.
91. Quintilian, *Institutio oratoria,* 9.3.3–4.
92. Vicentino, *L'antica musica,* book 4, chap. 42, fol. 94v.
93. *Cleonidae harmonicum introductorium* (Venice, 1497).

94. *De musica,* 1.5; Mathiesen trans., 76–77. Aristides's treatise was not available in a printed translation, but Giorgio Valla summed up this classification in his "De musica," 3.3, in *De expetendis.*

95. See G. Buelow, "Rhetoric and Music," in *New Grove Dictionary of Music and Musicians,* ed. S. Sadie (London and New York, 1980), 15:793–803.

96. Gallus Dressler, "*Praecepta musicae poeticae,*" ed. B. Engelke, *Geschichtsblätter für Stadt und Land Magdeburg* 49 (1914–15): 213–50.

97. Joachim Burmeister, *Musica autoschediastike* (Rostock, 1601), fols. A2v–A3. A later edition of this book, published as *Musica poetica* (Rostock, 1606), is reprinted, ed. M. Ruhnke (Kassel, 1955).

98. See C. V. Palisca, "*Ut oratoria musica:* The Rhetorical Basis of Musical Mannerism," in *The Meaning of Mannerism,* ed. F. W. Robinson and S. G. Nichols (Hanover, NH, 1972), 37–65; or Buelow, "Rhetoric and Music."

99. Francis Bacon, *The Tvvoo Bookes Of the Proficiencie and Aduancement of Learning diuine and humane* (London, 1605), fols. 21v–22r. A later version of this passage in *Sylva sylvarum* (London, 1627), 38, begins: "There be in *Musick* certain *Figures,* or *Tropes* almost agreeing with the *Figures* of *Rhetoricke,*" and he counts "fuges" among the figures.

100. Zarlino, *Istitutioni harmoniche,* 2.6 (p. 67).

101. Baïf's famous prefatory poem to Guillaume Costeley's *Musique* (Paris, 1570), echoes the same thought:

> Jadis Musiciens et Poëtes et Sages
> Furent mesmes auteurs; mais la suite des ages,
> Par le temps qui tout change, a separé les troys.

102. Plutarch, *De musica,* 3.1131–1132.

103. See N. Pirrotta, "Music and Cultural Tendencies in Fifteenth-Century Italy," *Journal of the American Musicological Society* 19 (1966): 146–61.

104. Letter to Paul of Middelburg, 13 September [1492] in *Epistolae* (Venice, 1495), book 12, fol. 186v. See also D. P. Walker, "Le chant orphique de Marsile Ficin," in *Musique et poésie au XVIᵉ siècle,* ed. J. Jacquot (Paris, 1954), 17–33.

105. Pontus de Tyard, *Solitaire second, ou Prose de la musique* (Lyons, 1555), 132; ed. C. M. Yandell (Geneva, 1980), 214.

106. For an excellent history of this development see F. A. Yates, *The French Academies of the Sixteenth Century* (London, 1947), 36–76.

107. E. E. Lowinsky has recently demonstrated that there was a connection between this style of musical setting and earlier experiments in Italy and Germany with ancient meters. See his "Humanism in the Music of the Renaissance," in *Medieval and Renaissance Studies,* ed. F. Tirro (Durham, NC, 1982), 87–220.

108. Petrus Tritonius, *Melopoiae sive harmoniae tetracenticae* (Augsburg, 1507). For a history of this genre see E. Weber, *Musique et théâtre dans les pays rhénans,* vol. 1, *Le musique mesurée à l'antique en Allemagne* (Paris, 1974).

109. See N. Pirotta and E. Povoledo, *Music and Theatre from Poliziano to Monteverdi,* trans. K. Eales (Cambridge, 1982).

110. Besides Mei at least two scholars published their opinion that the tragedy was sung in its entirety: Orazio Toscanella in *Precetti necesarii et altre cose utilissime* (Venice, 1562), fols. 82v–83r, and Francesco Patrizi in *Della poetica, La deca istoriale,* book 6, ed. Aguzzi-Barbagli, 1:309ff. For other contemporary views see B. R. Hanning, *Of Poetry and Music's Power: Humanism and the Creation of Opera* (Ann Arbor, MI, 1980), 15ff.

111. Mei sent Galilei an Italian translation of the entire problem, reflecting his emendations of the Greek text, in a letter of September (?) 1581 (in *Girolamo Mei,* ed. Palisca, 178–79). Galilei refers to Mei's emended text in *Dialogo,* 145. Patrizi cited in addition problems 6, 15, 30, and 31 of section 19, and gave full Italian translations of the last three of them as well as of 48.

112. Jacopo Peri, *Le musiche sopra l'Euridice* (Florence, 1601; reprinted Bologna, 1969).

113. *Harmonicorum elementorum,* 1.8.

114. *De musica,* 1.4. See the translation by Mathiesen, 76.

115. Boethius, *De institutione musicae,* 1.12.

40 ❧ HUMANISM AND SCIENCE
Pamela O. Long

THE STUDY OF THE NATURAL WORLD, WHAT WE CALL "SCIENCE," was termed "natural philosophy" in the premodern period. Natural philosophy, fundamentally Aristotelian in its assumptions and methodology, constituted a branch of philosophy. By 1700, however, "natural philosophy" had been transformed; a profound intellectual reorientation had occurred, a scientific revolution involving changes in the most basic assumptions of cosmology, physics, astronomy, biology, and almost every other branch of the study of nature, involving as well changes in methodology in which mathematics, precise measurement, experiment, and observation became centrally important. New questions had been asked, and new methods had been devised to answer those questions. As important, the development of scientific societies such as the Royal Society provided new social organizations within which scientific questions were openly considered.

The scientific revolution was preceded by a period of 150 years in which Renaissance humanism was an influential mode of thought. Nevertheless, historians have often denied or disputed the nature of the connection between humanism and the achievements of Copernicus, Kepler, Galileo, Gilbert, Vesalius, and other important figures of early modern science. Indeed, the nature of the scientific revolution itself has been the focus of intensive study and debate. Questions have been asked about whether it was in fact a revolution, or the more cumulative result of medieval developments in physics; whether it was influenced by Renaissance Neoplatonism, or by some other group of influences. The problem of what was traditional and what was innovative continues to be explored for many of the central works that form the basis of classical (seventeenth-century, Newtonian) science. The relationship of these scientific developments to their historical context, including the context of Renaissance humanism, is a central problem.[1]

An underlying dimension in the study of these issues has been the interpretive framework of historical periodization. Jacob Burckhardt's influential description of the Italian Renaissance as a period included (as

I am especially grateful for the valuable comments of E. F. Beall, Stanley Goldberg, William C. McNeill, Thomas B. Settle, and Alice Stroup, which have helped to improve this essay.

will be elaborated) a role for science. Many early twentieth-century historians, newly exploring the riches of medieval science, reversed Burckhardt's judgment, depicting Renaissance science as insignificant or in a state of decline; nevertheless, they often assumed the validity of his sharp separation of the Renaissance from the preceding centuries.[2] The interpretive structure of periodization still underlies many of the studies that concern the origins of classical science.

For example, Timothy J. Reiss has recently elaborated the thesis that a new discourse (analytico-referential) emerged in the sixteenth century out of the "parallel" discourses of the preceding epoch and was directly responsible for the new science of the seventeenth century. Though influenced by the work of Michel Foucault, Reiss argues against a sudden rupture and broadens the period during which he perceives one discourse replacing another. Yet for Reiss the rupture was so complete that "moderns" who use the analytico-referential discourse are incapable of truly comprehending their medieval predecessors. While he uses Thomas More's *Utopia* as an exemplary text in the inception of analytico-referential discourse, he has little to say about the humanist tradition and context in which More wrote.[3]

In contrast to the radical break posited by writers such as Foucault and Reiss, the German philosopher Hans Blumenberg sees the development of early modern science as part of the emergence of a new epoch, but one that maintains specific threads of continuity with the medieval past. In a series of complex and important writings, Blumenberg has elaborated in detail the crisis in medieval thought, which he suggests led to the possibility of a Copernicus, and indeed to the "modern age" as well. For him, the prehistory of Copernicanism is the history of the tension between the Greek philosophy of nature and the Christian view of an omnipotent and omnipresent God. One result was the freeing of theoretical curiosity, a development encouraged by the humanist belief in the dignity of man. Related to Blumenberg's argument for the essential "modernity" of Copernicanism is his thesis of the "legitimacy" of the "modern age" (meaning the epoch from the end of the Middle Ages to the present). He denies that modern notions of technical and scientific progress represent a transformation or "secularization" of medieval Christian ideas. Rather, he suggests that notions of cumulative progress in science and technology are derived directly from early modern experience. There is continuity as well, however, because problems and functions remain from the previous epoch and are "reoccupied" by new positions and beliefs, once the older notions lose their power to persuade.[4]

From the time of Burckhardt to the present, then, periodization has been a more or less obvious presence in interpretations of the origins of seventeenth-century science. It is a presence that has some relevance to the relationship of Renaissance humanism and science, because it has affected the delineation of subject matter itself. For instance, while Blumenberg sees early modern science as in some sense a result of the crisis engendered by a qualitatively different fourteenth-century nominalism, other scholars are still devoting considerable attention to the contribution of nominalism to that science.[5] Fourteenth-century nominalism (often viewed as late medieval) and Petrarchan humanism (usually considered early Renaissance) are both the focus of highly developed subspecialties. Nevertheless, although it is well known that Petrarch and William of Ockham were contemporaries, the interrelationships of their thought have been insufficiently explored.[6] Yet some of their shared values (such as their common inclination toward particularism as opposed to universalism) had important implications for the development of science. It may be that the bent toward particularism as a mental attitude preceded both humanist and nominalist modes of thought, instead of being derived from them. This question and others relevant to understanding the development of science could be illuminated by more often considering humanism and fourteenth-century nominalism as simultaneous developments in a common culture, rather than as beginning and end points, respectively, of two different epochs.

That this essay concerns the contribution of Renaissance humanism to science should not be taken to imply an underlying assumption of a Renaissance period that is sharply delineated from previous centuries. The fourteenth to seventeenth centuries were transitional and witnessed some profound changes in values and attitudes. My own view is that many (although not all) of the roots of this cultural transformation can be found in the High Middle Ages—for instance, in the rise of the cities and in their new urban populations; in the development of monied economies and of early forms of capitalism; and in the profound effects of the growth of literacy on literate and nonliterate alike.[7] Renaissance humanism was at once a result of these changes and a contributor of new attitudes. Its contribution to science lay most importantly in its dissemination of values. Neither was that contribution peripheral; new values and attitudes engendered many of the problems, questions, and methods that lay at the heart of the scientific revolution.

*   *   *

In his pivotal essay on the Italian Renaissance, Jacob Burckhardt included science as an important aspect of the new age. The Renaissance for him involved not only the discovery of man, but the discovery of the world as well. He believed that in this period, "the Italian mind . . .

turned to the discovery of the outward universe, and to the representation of it in speech and in form." Burckhardt had in mind the voyages of discovery and the related development of the geographical sciences. He postulated a concomitant interest in the natural world, pointing to the vivid descriptions of nature in the *Commentarii* of Aeneas Silvius Piccolomini (Pope Pius II). He contrasted what he believed to be the isolated achievements of such medieval thinkers as Roger Bacon to those of the Italian Renaissance in which "a whole people" took a "natural delight in the study and investigation of nature" at a time "when other nations" were "indifferent." Burckhardt noted the Italian interest in the collection and comparative study of plants and animals, evident in the princely courts and in the cities. He suggested that one practical result of the zoological studies associated with Renaissance menageries was the rationally guided domestic breeding of horses (with the goal of establishing desirable traits), first successfully achieved by Francesco Gonzaga.[8]

Burckhardt also believed that Italians were "the first among modern peoples by whom the outward world was seen and felt as something beautiful." Citing precedents in medieval Italian literature and in the work of Dante, he named Petrarch as the first for whom nature was truly significant, and for whom the enjoyment of nature was a natural accompaniment to intellectual pursuits. He suggested that the *Ascent of Mount Ventoux* was the most dramatic expression of the new appreciation of the natural world, and that the lyrical descriptions of the beauties of nature in the *Commentarii* of Aeneas Silvius constituted the most important fifteenth-century development of this Petrarchan tradition.[9] Burckhardt's treatment was neither extensive nor detailed, but it did allow the inference that the Italian Renaissance, and Renaissance humanism in particular, provided fertile soil for the development of science.

In the first decades of the twentieth century, historians of science decisively rejected Burckhardt's view of the development of science. Their studies emphasized the continuity between medieval science and the achievements of the scientific revolution in the seventeenth century, and denied or ignored possible contributions from Renaissance humanism. The French historian and physicist Pierre Duhem elaborated the thesis of a continuous scientific tradition from about 1200, which was known to both Leonardo da Vinci and Galileo, and which played an important role in the development of the latter's physics.[10] Anneliese Maier's studies on scholastic natural philosophy provided a critique of Duhem's tendency to view medieval authors as anticipators of specific aspects of Galilean science; with greater sensitivity to historical context, she delineated the fourteenth-century scholastic contribution in terms of a correspondence of conceptual approach.[11]

That early historians of science were deeply implicated in periodization is underlined by the work of Charles Homer Haskins, who wrote a basic text on the history of medieval science, and also authored an implicit assault on the Burckhardtian thesis in his elaboration of the twelfth-century Renaissance.[12] George Sarton's monumental *Introduction to the History of Science* ended in the fourteenth century. In his later work, he seems to modify his early negative assessment of Renaissance humanism. While accepting the notion of the Renaissance as a period, his work on Renaissance science was primarily concerned with texts and individuals, with little attention to interpretive issues of continuity and change.[13] At the same time, Lynn Thorndike's view of humanism remained negative. Was it not, he asked, "in part an easier way for princes and their sons who found the existing university requirements too harsh, and for those in general who preferred to write poems, letters, and orations, instead of following intricate arguments and arranging their own thought in a systematic, orderly manner?" Thorndike, who emphasized the continuing importance of scholastic thought in the fifteenth and sixteenth centuries, characterized humanism by "its emphasis on style rather than science, show rather than substance."[14]

John H. Randall, Jr., in *The School of Padua and the Emergence of Modern Science,* argued that the methods of Galilean science derived from the cooperative efforts of generations of Aristotelians in the universities of northern Italy. He contrasted the achievements of these men with the methodological work of the humanists, "who seem to have displayed all the customary ignorance and futility of revolutionaries and to have proposed new methods distinguished chiefly by the novelty of their ignorance." Randall believed that the concepts of mathematical physics developed by Galileo were deeply indebted to a long and productive critical evaluation of Aristotelian ideas, and that Galileo's scientific method was a result of "a fruitful critical reconstruction of the Aristotelian theory of science."[15] It was a reconstruction achieved by the very scholastic methods that the humanists had condemned.

More recently, this negative assessment of the humanist relationship to science has been revised, giving humanism a positive, albeit indirect role in the development of the scientific disciplines.[16] In part, this change has involved a revision of the view that seventeenth-century science was a direct derivation of fourteenth-century natural philosophy. The influence of Platonism and of Archimedes also achieved greater recognition, particularly after the work of Alexandre Koyré.[17] In addition, there has been more study of the relationship of humanists to the scientific disciplines, though it should be added that much remains to be done.[18] No one has denied that Renaissance humanists were primarily interested in rhetoric, grammar, moral philosophy, and history, rather than the natural sciences. Moreover, it is well known that many humanists vociferously opposed Aristotelian scholastic traditions, which had nurtured natural philosophy in the thirteenth and fourteenth centuries. Nevertheless, the humanists made positive contributions, the precise nature of which will be my concern in the remainder of this essay.

*   *   *

The humanist opposition to scholasticism involved a rejection of the unquestioned acceptance of Aristotle's authority, rather than a disapproval of the study of the natural sciences per se. Whether this criticism involved an accurate assessment is open to question. It is now understood that the scholastic method allowed significant modifications of ancient precepts. Yet both the scholastic reliance on ancient authors as the starting point for investigations into natural philosophy and the usually pedagogical context of scholasticism often mitigated against a thoroughgoing empiricism. Thus the humanist accusation, although not accurate, may have fruitfully encouraged alternate approaches to the study of the natural world.

The humanist critique of scholasticism can be illustrated with the writings of Petrarch. In his famous essay "On His Own Ignorance and That of Many Others," Petrarch ridiculed medieval and Aristotelian traditions in natural history by listing some of the more fantastic notions transmitted by those traditions—for example, "the sea urchin stops a ship, however fast she is driving along," and "the newborn bear has yet no shape." The great humanist was making the point that many traditional beliefs concerning the natural world were wrong, and further that they had not actually been investigated by those who were considered authorities. Only after criticizing the credulous acceptance of authority and lack of empirical investigation did Petrarch question the utility of knowing natural history at all while remaining ignorant of the nature of man.[19]

Petrarch heaped scorn upon those who worshiped the very name of Aristotle (he had in mind his "friends" against whom he was writing the invective): "Let them keep their exorbitant opinion of everything that regards them, and the naked name of Aristotle which delights many ignorant people by its four syllables." Describing conversations with these maligning "friends," Petrarch reported that when they raised "an Aristotelian problem or question concerning animals," he would remain silent, make a joke, or begin another subject. At times he would ask, however, how Aristotle could have known something "for which there is no reason and which cannot be proved by experience." Thereupon, his companions would look upon him as if he were "a blasphemer to require anything beyond his [Aristotle's] authority in order to believe it." Petrarch believed "that Aristotle was a great man who knew much, but he was human and could well be ignorant of some things, even of a great many things." [20] Moreover, he faulted the Peripatetic for his lack of knowledge concerning faith and immortality. He concluded that he had engendered the enmity of his companions because he did "not adore Aristotle." [21]

Unable to read Aristotle in the original Greek, Petrarch nevertheless criticized the style of the Latin translations, attributing their shortcomings to the "rudeness or to the envious dispositions" of the interpreters.[22] He pointed out that although much could be learned from books, much could also be learned outside them, and that, moreover, a great deal was known by men before Aristotle wrote. He reserved his harshest criticism for the commentators of Aristotle, suggesting that they adopted the works of others as if they were their own, and that they did not dare write anything original.[23] Elsewhere, Petrarch attacked the scholastics' use of the dialectical method.[24]

At no point did Petrarch's criticism become an attack on natural science. Rather it was a declaration against the unquestioning acceptance of authority and against the acceptance of "facts" without empirical verification. Indeed, the humanist emphasis on the particular and the individual was consistent with an acceptance of the empirical (in other words, the particular case as it is available to individual experience). Petrarch's criticism of Aristotelian natural philosophy thus accommodated his orientation toward individual man. Yet his contribution was essentially negative; it was limited to the criticism of contemporary science.

*   *   *

A more positive contribution to the development of science resulted from the association of humanists and artisans in the fifteenth century.[25] This association raised the status of handwork, since it associated craftsmen, who worked with their hands, with the more learned humanists who also had higher status. One consequence was that handwork, practice, experiment, and observation gained in prestige. In an age in which the theoretical disciplines were usually considered superior to the practical and were often without a firm empirical base, the resultant greater unity between theory and practice ultimately encouraged a greater empirical foundation in scientific work.

A central figure is Filippo Brunelleschi, the founder of the new Renaissance style in architecture. Brunelleschi was not only an architect who first discovered linear perspective, but an engineer and inventor as well. E. H. Gombrich has pointed out the close connection between his reform of architecture and the early humanist reform of Latin orthography, of which a particular proponent was Niccolò Niccoli. Brunelleschi's architectural designs embodied elaborate, mathematically proportionate relationships, and his elaboration of perspective combined knowledge of optics and of geometry. He was a theoretician who invented and built machines; he effectively combined theoretical and practical knowledge. It is significant that he developed his program of architectural reform in the context of the humanist reform of orthography as well as the humanist interest in antiquity.[26]

Brunelleschi's achievements were taken up and developed by one of the great humanists of the fifteenth century, Leon Battista Alberti. In his treatise *De pictura* (1435), Alberti transformed painting into a humanist discipline. He conceived it as a mathematical subject by virtue of its new tool of geometric perspective. He also gave it a rhetorical component; through its *istoria,* the painting should move the soul of the viewer. Alberti's writings were germane to science as well as to art. By means of his treatise he consolidated the Brunelleschian achievement in perspective and made the practical craft of painting mathematical. As a result, theory and practice were brought closer together, and the value of a mathematical approach to a problem was demonstrated. Alberti himself was a practitioner of painting, a designer of buildings, and a friend of other practitioners such as Brunelleschi and Donatello.[27]

Alberti's interest in practice extended to scientific subjects. He was a cartographer who made the most accurate map of Rome of its time, and he wrote a treatise on practical measurement (*Ludi matematici,* ca. 1450) that was indebted to late medieval mathematical writings, including the encyclopedic work, *Liber abbaci* (1202) by Leonardo Fibonacci. Thomas B. Settle has shown that a mathematics teacher, Ostilio Ricci, exposed the young Galileo to Alberti's treatise, and that it may well have influenced Galileo not only with respect to certain techniques of measurement, but in its attitude of appreciation for the simplicity and elegance of mathematical precision.[28]

The development of artists' perspective, to which Alberti made a fundamental contribution, may have been influenced by Ptolemy's *Cosmographia,* which arrived in Florence in 1400. It was brought there by the famous teacher of Greek, Manuel Chrysoloras, to be used as an additional text for the circle of humanists who were his students. In this work, Ptolemy discussed a method of projection that may have inspired the notion of constructing geometric perspective on a flat painter's surface. Painter's perspective in turn influenced the development of the science of cartography, important for navigation, as well as for travel by land. Probably influential in these developments was the learned Florentine, Paolo Toscanelli, friend of Brunelleschi and Alberti and knowledgeable in mathematics, geography, cartography, and optics. Brunelleschi's invention of perspective may well have been influenced by Toscanelli's advice. Toscanelli, whose ideas were known to Christopher Columbus, may also have influenced the latter in his ventures that led to the discovery of the West Indies.[29]

What we can recognize here are the results of an energetic social and intellectual community of humanists (interested in science and art as well as letters) and skilled artisans. It is this community that formed the social and cultural base for developments in artists' perspective, cartography, navigation, and optics. It is significant that the social base of humanism constituted the urban patriciate class, whose existence and development was intimately tied to commerce and banking, enterprises that encouraged an appreciation for precision and practical mathematics. It is perhaps not surprising that linear perspective, for example, was invented in such a milieu.[30]

*   *   *

The invention of perspective was influenced by ideas about vision inherited from ancient and medieval optical traditions. We know too little about Toscanelli, in whose imagination the science of optics and the technique of perspective were, presumably for the first time, joined. We know much more about Leonardo da Vinci, many of whose writings on optics and perspective are extant. Leonardo began as a painter, grounded in Albertian perspective. Gradually, he tested the assumptions of that perspective against his growing knowledge of scientific optics. Eventually, he realized that the visual pyramid (with the pinnacle at the eye and the base at the object) on which painters' perspective was based, did not represent the way in which the eye actually saw according to contemporary theories; the artist was not engaged in reproducing reality on a flat surface, but was merely using a technique. Coincident with these discoveries is the cessation of all geometric perspective from Leonardo's paintings, a fact that can be explained by his discovery of the differences between perception and representation.[31]

Leonardo was a scientist as well as an artist. His work in optics was both mathematical and empirical. Although historians do not consider him a founder of modern optical science, this judgment can be significant only if the present state of our knowledge becomes the criterion for judging the science of the past, a dubious historical procedure. Leonardo's was a complex and multifaceted genius that has never lent itself to facile generalizations concerning either the influences upon it or its results. Yet one of the most enduring features of his social and intellectual context was the humanism of the courts and cities in which he worked. He never mastered Latin. Nevertheless, he absorbed much through his associations with more "learned" humanists, who were supported by the same patrons who also provided his own subsistence. Leonardo was not a humanist, but he was, among other things, a product of the close interaction of humanist and artisan cultures, an interaction that had already been evident in Brunelleschi's Florence.[32]

The importance of Leonardo's humanist environment is evident in his anatomical work. His interest in the human body was initially an adjunct to his work as an artist. Whether or not Florentine artists such as the Pollaiuolo brothers studied flayed bodies as Vasari reported, their intense interest in human anatomy is manifest in their work. Leonardo's earliest anatomical drawings, which treated the skeletal and musculature systems, were related to his interest in painting. Later, his scientific interests prevailed. Performing his own dissections, he produced anatomical drawings that were far more accurate than any of their predecessors. The work of Martin Kemp has revealed the extent to which Leonardo's anatomical studies constituted an attempt to illustrate theories derived from ancient and medieval anatomical traditions. Particularly striking is the influence of Galen on his work after 1508, probably the result of Leonardo's association with Marcantonio della Torre, a professor of anatomy at Pavia who was engaged in the humanist task of attempting to replace traditional anatomical texts with the original writings of Galen. In spite of his traditionalism, Leonardo's work represents a leap beyond that of his predecessors, both because he understood the importance of direct observation through repeated dissections, and because he realized the significance of illustration for anatomy and developed new illustrative techniques.[33]

Another attempt to combine observed data with Galenic theory was made by Andreas Vesalius, who rejected many Galenic notions on the basis of observation in his *De humani corporis fabrica*, published in 1543. Yet Vesalius was also a careful student of Galen and by no means discarded all of the Greek anatomist's theories. Although he may not have known the drawings of Leonardo, he was working in the same tradition. Careful observation (a value that had been reinforced by the emphasis on realism in Renaissance art) and the diligent study of ancient anatomical theory (a result of the humanist enterprise) were joined in the work of both Leonardo and Vesalius. For the latter, the result was the partial rejection of Galen and the foundation of modern anatomy.[34]

*   *   *

The arrival in Florence and subsequent influence of Ptolemy's *Cosmographia,* and the dissemination of Galenic texts, exemplify one of the central contributions of humanists to science—the rediscovery and widespread dissemination of ancient scientific works. To recognize this contribution is not to deny the deep classicism of the medieval period. Medieval interest in ancient texts has again been underlined, for example by Nancy G. Siraisi, who has elaborated the interest in and use of the nonanatomical works of Galen (as well as other ancient authorities) by the thirteenth-century physician Taddeo Alderotti and his circle at the University of Padua.[35] Indeed, there is reason to view the humanist recovery of ancient texts as one part of a continuum that would include, for instance, the twelfth-century restoration of Aristotle.

Yet within this continuum, humanist contributions had several distinguishing characteristics that also constituted a contribution to the development of science. Their critical approach to the editing of texts (which marks the early stages of the modern philological method) was informed by their historicism; they attempted to bring ancient texts as close as possible to their original state and to rid them of their medieval accoutrements. The critical approach that allowed Lorenzo Valla to discredit the *Donation of Constantine* by pointing to its medieval Latin was as important to the development of science as it was to classical studies and literature.

For a text well known in the medieval period, Pliny the Elder's *Natural History,* Charles G. Nauert, Jr. has distinguished the humanist approach from that of medieval readers. He suggests that the latter used Pliny's important work "as a storehouse of useful information," an encyclopedia, "with little concern about the accuracy of the text." Humanists expanded this use. They studied Pliny's citations of earlier Greek and Roman authors who were otherwise unknown. They mined his work for classical scientific terminology. They devoted public lectures to the text, emphasizing textual and interpretive issues that had not ordinarily concerned medieval scholars. They were involved in the preparation of the earliest printed editions, an activity that resulted in important commentaries. It was in the context of this critical study of Pliny's text that the controversial issue of whether his information was scientifically accurate came to the fore.[36]

Humanists made available the science of antiquity to a greater extent than had been the case, due in part to their interest in and growing knowledge of Greek and their concomitant recovery of Greek texts. In part it was also because, at least initially, they were working outside of the universities. Their interest in ancient texts, while not encouraged by the needs of the university curriculum, was also not limited by the demands of that curriculum or by the satisfaction of those demands. Thus, the purview of their interest in ancient texts was quite broad and provided new emphases at a time that the curricula of the universities had been well established. By the late fifteenth century, as some recent studies concerning the University of Padua have emphasized, humanist textual work influenced the study of natural philosophy in the universities.[37]

In addition to the critical editing of known texts, humanists rediscovered works virtually unknown in the medieval period, such as the treatise *De rerum natura* of Lucretius (influential in the spread of atomism) and the medical work of Celsus. The humanist dissemination of ancient scientific works included a great work of translating—of Greek texts into Latin and of Latin texts into the vernacular languages. The advent of printing brought even wider distribution of these books. Particularly significant was the publication by Niccolò Tartaglia of the first Latin edition of Archimedes in 1543.[38]

The work of Paul Lawrence Rose has underscored the deep involvement of Renaissance humanists in mathematics. Rose detailed the humanist recovery and dissemination of ancient mathematical texts, including the works of Archimedes, Hero, Pappus, Apollonius, and Diophantus. He emphasized that it was classical texts that supplied Renaissance mathematicians with much of the technical knowledge upon which the scientific revolution was founded. He also demonstrated that mathematicians often went beyond their ancient texts to develop new concepts and ideas. One example of the importance of the humanist recovery of ancient mathematics is the influence of Archimedean statics (*On Floating Bodies* and *Equilibrium of Planes*) on the mechanics of Galileo. Humanist interest in mathematics included the extension of patronage to mathematicians, giving them the opportunity to study classical mathematical works collected in the great libraries of Florence, Rome, and Venice. The advent of printing found humanist mathematicians, such as Regiomontanus, enthusiastically involved in the even wider dissemination of mathematical knowledge.[39]

For another discipline, botany, Karen M. Reeds has shown that the recovery and translation of ancient texts—of Theophrastus, Dioscorides, Pliny, and Galen—was only one part of the humanist contribution. The fact was that corrupt botanical texts could not be corrected without the direct observation of the plants in question. Humanists such as Rudolf Agricola, Ermolao Barbaro the Younger, and Caspar Bauhin were following the advice of the ancients when they attempted to observe the flora anew. The botanical observations and collections of the humanists, and their delight in gardens, resulted in far more accurate botanical knowledge. It also represented a sharp departure from the scholastic tradition in which theoretical bias and disdain for the manual trade of pharmacy prevented medical students from recognizing even the most common herbs. The herbal by Otto Brunfels, *Herbarum vivae eicones* (1530), a result of this new orientation, was dramatically superior to medieval herbals. The introduction of botany into the medical curriculum can also be credited to the humanists. Indeed, humanist botanical knowledge, which gradually surpassed that of the ancients, was not acquired by rejecting classical texts, but by carefully studying and emending them.[40]

To a discussion of specific textual studies should be added a broader contextual note, namely, the growing confluence of methodology in some of the disciplines of humanism and in natural history. As Barbara J. Shapiro has elaborated, in the sixteenth century humanist disciplines such as law and history became closely linked to natural history. Historical scholarship, for instance, moved away from rhetorical traditions toward a concern for the verifiability of historical facts, a concern that at the same time became central to natural history. She notes the creation of a common ground "as some philosophers moved from logical to empirical modes of proof and some humanists moved from the rhetorically plausible to the empirically probable."[41]

*   *   *

The humanist promotion of contemporary scientific and technical treatises should perhaps be seen as one result of the growing concurrence of shared assumptions delineated by Shapiro. Technical literature is of particular interest, for there are relatively few western European writings about technology from the medieval period. They appear with increasing frequency from the fourteenth century and represent a large literature by the sixteenth.[42]

Technical literature is an important genre, which still requires much study with regard to both specific texts and the reasons for its expansion in this period. Although it was encouraged by printing, it cannot be explained thereby, because its proliferation preceded printing by more than a century. The universities engendered much scientific but little technical writing, the latter being beneath their theoretical concerns. Craft guilds, employing an apprenticeship system of training, utilized, developed, and transmitted much technology but did not produce technical writings. Part of the explanation for the appearance of a large technical literature is the decline of the guilds and the development of humanist patronage. As a patronage that encouraged the study and imitation not only of classical literature, but also of ancient arts and architecture, it engendered a closer association between theory and practice than had previously been the case. The military concerns of these patrons also encouraged writings on the military arts.[43] Artisans and engineers, aspiring to the rewards of humanist culture, in increasing numbers began themselves to write treatises.

The significance of humanist patronage for the production of scientific and technical literature has not been sufficiently recognized; the specific influence of that patronage needs much further study. It is possible here only to cite a few examples from the literature itself. Giovanni de' Dondi dall'Orologia (d. 1389) was a versatile scholar who taught medicine at Padua and Pavia, and he was a friend of Petrarch as well as a protagonist (for the ancients) in the early humanist "quarrel of the ancients and moderns." He also built an astrarium (which was eventually installed in the Castello Visconteo in Pavia by Duke Giangaleazzo Visconti) and wrote a treatise describing it.[44] Conrad Kyeser, a German physician, and Mariano Taccola, a Sienese notary, both wrote treatises on military and (in Taccola's case) other machines. The books were very different from each other and contained much that was original. That they were influenced at least to some extent by the humanist interest in ancient texts is suggested by their common indebtedness to Vegetius's treatise on military strategy, *Epitoma rei militaris*.[45] Robert Valturio's *Elenchus et index rerum militarum,* usually referred to as *De re militari* (written ca. 1455–60 and first published in 1472), is a compendium of ancient writings and Valturio's own comments and includes some discussion of military technology. Also indebted to Vegetius, it was dedicated to Valturio's patron, Sigismondo Pandolfo Malatesta of Rimini.[46] Later in the fifteenth century, Francesco di Giorgio (a Sienese trained as a painter who worked as an architect and military engineer in several humanist courts) wrote treatises on architecture and military engineering that were indebted to the Roman architect Vitruvius.[47] Francesco's contemporary, Luca Pacioli, wrote an encyclopedic work on practical mathematics and a Latin translation of Euclid's *Elements,* as well as the *Divina proportione,* a book inspired by Ficino and the Florentine Neoplatonists.[48]

In the sixteenth century, Andreas Vesalius's *De humani corporis fabrica* (1543), Georg Agricola's *De re metallica* (1556), Leonard Fuchs's *De historia stirpium* (1542), and Conrad Gesner's *Historia animalium*

(1551–58 and 1587) each represented a landmark in the history of its respective science. At the end of the century, Ulisse Aldrovandi (a Bolognese from a noble family who had studied Latin with the distinguished humanist Giovanni Gundolfo) produced a series of books, often beautifully illustrated, on botany, teratology, embryology, ichthyology, and ornithology, books that are notable for their attempt to substitute direct observation for traditional authority.[49] All of these works were influenced by a humanist tradition that encouraged the production of clearly written and finely illustrated treatises (in the vernacular languages as well as in Latin) on technical and scientific subjects.

Architectural writings were particularly important for the dissemination of ideas relevant to the development of science. *De architectura,* by the first century B.C. architect Vitruvius, was the only architectural work to survive from antiquity. In the fifteenth century it inspired the treatises of Alberti, Filarete, and Francesco di Giorgio; and in the sixteenth it became the focus of a series of translations and commentaries. Those of Cesare Cesariano (1521), Guillaume Philandrier (1544), Walther Ryff (1548), and Daniele Barbaro (1556) are the most important. These architectural writings repeatedly stressed a number of central themes: the importance of the unity of theory and practice; the notion that the universe was a uniform and mathematically harmonious entity; the necessity of precise measurement and the significance of practical mathematics; and finally, the idea that technical progress is possible, and that it is achieved through cooperation and the openness of knowledge. Each of these beliefs aided the development of science.[50]

No one reading the words of the great humanist, scholar, and Vitruvian commentator Daniele Barbaro can argue that humanism encompassed solely a bookish culture. Barbaro is discussing the construction of dials and clocks:

> I wish to warn those to whom these things will seem difficult, that if they believe they understand them well, without making a test, they will be easily deceived. Neither is it necessary to say that they are written obscurely, because in every experience there is difficulty where there has not been practice. And truly I can state that I have understood it, and this more through making and experimenting, than through reading.[51]

This passage is not an isolated example, but rather a typical sentiment, expressed again and again in the books of the Vitruvian tradition.

*   *   *

Humanism also influenced the development of science, particularly cosmology, through its propagation of Neoplatonism. The extent and nature of this influence has been disputed. Fundamental studies explicating the influence of Platonism on early modern science, such as those of E. A. Burtt and Alexandre Koyré,[52] have been countered by the observation that most Renaissance Platonists developed mystical and theological notions and were indifferent to science. But recent research has underlined the lack of a sharp division between what we would label "scientific" and "nonscientific" in the early modern period, and has shown that scientific innovators were also involved in studies that we would consider occult. Although it is clear that mystical and occult notions were not necessarily inimical to science in the early modern period, the relationship of these traditions to science is the subject of ongoing study and debate.[53]

Whatever the outcome of these studies, it is clear that Renaissance Platonism influenced cosmology. This influence can be illustrated by the work of Nicholas of Cusa, one of the most original philosophers of the fifteenth century and a theologian who wrote treatises on mathematics. Although the German-born Nicholas first received an education in scholastic science and theology at the University of Heidelberg, his intellectual development was decisively influenced by Italian humanism. He studied canon law at the University of Padua, where he befriended Paolo Toscanelli and the humanist educators Guarino of Verona and Vittorino da Feltre. Ordained as a priest around 1430, he spent his life in the service of the church, carrying out diplomatic and other missions for Eugenius IV, Nicholas V, and his friend the humanist Aeneas Silvius. His own search for classical texts led him to the discovery of Pliny's *Natural History* and twelve comedies of Plautus. Ernst Cassirer has called Nicholas the first western thinker to attain insight into the fundamental sources of Platonic doctrine. His mastery of Greek at the University of Padua, his association with humanists such as George Gemistus Pletho and Cardinal Bessarion, and his training in humanist philological criticism must all have contributed to his understanding of Platonic texts.[54]

Nicholas of Cusa's cosmology, which was engendered by theological concerns, can be contrasted to the Aristotelian cosmos of the fifteenth century. That Aristotelian cosmos contained two regions—the sublunar, composed of the four elements (earth, air, fire, water), and the celestial, consisting of the fifth quintessential element. At the center was the immobile Earth. Each element had its natural place vis-à-vis the Earth and the celestial sphere, and each possessed a natural striving to return to that place. There was, moreover, a hierarchy of elements; those closer to the Earth were considered more base than those with greater proximity to the quintessential sphere. It was a dualistic cosmos in which the sublunar and celestial spheres not only contained different elements, but were governed by different laws.

Nicholas's most important philosophical work, *De docta ignorantia* (1440), is a theology and a metaphysics, not a physics. Jasper Hopkins has pointed to the successive use of mathematical, metaphysical, and mystical language in the three books of the treatise.[55] If the aim of this succession was to bring the reader to a deep understanding of the unknowable quality of the divine, to learned ignorance, its requirements led to a rejection of fundamental aspects of the Aristotelian universe. Nicholas stressed mathematics as a tool for understanding, a Neoplatonic departure from the Aristotelian emphasis on quality. He replaced the hierarchical, fixed, Earth-centered Aristotelian universe with a boundless cosmos with no center and no circumference. Further:

> the earth, which cannot be the center, cannot be devoid of all motion. Indeed, it is even necessary that the earth be moved in such a way that it could be moved infinitely less. Therefore, just as the earth is not the center of the world, so the sphere of the fixed stars is not its circumference—although when we compare the earth with the sky, the former *seems* to be nearer to the center, and the latter nearer to the circumference. Therefore, the earth is not the center either of the eighth sphere or any other sphere.[56]

With the aid of a thought experiment, Nicholas elaborated by showing that our perceptions about the relationships of place are relative to our position.[57]

Nicholas of Cusa's humanist background is evident in another of his treatises, *Idiota: De sapientia, De mente, De staticis experimentis* (ca. 1450).[58] This work is cast in the humanist form of a dialogue in the Roman Forum between an unlearned man and an educated orator, who are later joined by a philosopher. It is the Idiota who leads the way to knowledge, first by rejecting the learning of his protagonists, which has been based on the authority of books. For him, wisdom can be found in the streets and the marketplace where ordinary weighing and measuring occur. Eventually, he leads the orator to the correct conception of God (a kind of learned ignorance) through mathematics. In the third book, *De mente,* a philosopher seeking knowledge about the mind from ancient books in Rome is found by the orator and led to the Idiota, who is busy making spoons in the Temple of Eternity. In the most important fifteenth-century vindication of the artisanal experience, the Idiota defends his "unworthy" occupation by claiming that the maker of spoons and pots is even closer to the Divine than the painter and others who imitate nature. There are no spoons in nature; likewise the divine creation was original, not imitative.[59] The relevance of Nicholas's viewpoint to science becomes evident in the fourth book, *De staticis experimentis*, which describes a series of experiments in practical measurement, including the determination of specific gravities, the measurement of the upward thrust of bodies immersed in liquid, and the assaying of metals. It is worth emphasizing that Nicholas's Platonism does not move him away from practical mathematics; to the contrary.

We can recognize in his work the influence of Socrates, both in his practical wisdom and in his knowledge of his own ignorance in the face of divine wisdom (see Plato, *Apology,* 21A–23B). Petrarch's diatribe against the unquestioning authority of books reverberates in his writings as well. Riccardo Gavagna's documentation of the influence of Vitruvius, along with his analysis of the similarities between the *De staticis experimentis* and Alberti's *Ludi matematici,* have elucidated other important aspects of Nicholas's humanist debt.[60]

After Nicholas of Cusa, Platonism was avidly promoted by Florentine humanists of the Platonic Academy in the second half of the fifteenth century. Their influence led other writers to conclusions that, though not identical to those of Nicholas, were just as destructive of the Aristotelian cosmos. In the 1470s, Marsilio Ficino translated the Hermetic corpus of writings—a group of Neoplatonic texts actually written in the second century of the Christian era, but believed to be the work of an ancient Egyptian living many centuries earlier, Hermes Trismegistus. Hermetic philosophy included the beliefs that the sun was the center of the universe, that the Earth revolved around the sun, and that the universe constituted a mathematical and musical harmony.[61]

Luca Pacioli's treatise of the 1490s, *Divina proportione,* elaborated a congruity between divine and earthly proportions. Although it was the opposite of Nicholas of Cusa's belief in the absolute separation between the divine and the earthly, Pacioli's notion was also derived from Platonism—from the Platonic notion that appearances were a reflection of the ideal, and the belief that the universe was fundamentally mathematical. That this point of view was not inimical to practical mathematics is suggested by his earlier compendium, the *Summa,* which included the first printed account of double-entry bookkeeping.[62] Francesco Giorgi, in his *De harmonia mundi* of 1525, described a universe constructed with mathematical and musical laws derived from a supreme law of musical harmony. Giorgi's involvement in the direction of two architectural projects points to the practical manifestation of his beliefs.[63] Ideas like

Pacioli's and Giorgi's, which were widely disseminated in the sixteenth century, offered an alternative to the bifurcated, geocentric Aristotelian cosmos. They also tended to reinforce a belief in the importance of mathematics, both as an approach to problems and as the key to understanding the cosmos. This belief in turn led to an emphasis on the importance of practical mathematics and precise measurement.

It was through a critique of Ptolemaic astronomy and geocentric cosmology that Copernicus in his *De revolutionibus* of 1543 saw the need to remove the Earth from the center of the universe and set it in motion revolving around the sun. For Copernicus the system was an accurate reflection of the physical world. Johann Kepler also believed that his work on the motion of the planets referred to actual physical events. Yet both men were fundamentally influenced by the Neoplatonism of the Italian humanists. They lived at a time when an alternative to the Aristotelian/Ptolemaic cosmos had been elaborated and widely disseminated. It was for them to provide the scientific basis for that alternative.

The humanist dissemination of Neoplatonism also affected the history of medicine and chemistry through the work of Paracelsus, an itinerant German medical practitioner whose combative personality frequently embroiled him in controversy. There is still a lack of consensus on his place in the history of medicine. He was influenced by popular culture and religion and was a vociferous advocate of experience as opposed to book learning in medicine. His biographer has emphasized, however, that his thought was also fundamentally indebted to the Neoplatonic, gnostic, kabbalistic, alchemical, astrological, and other sources revived by the humanists immediately before and during his lifetime.[64]

Paracelsus proselytized anti-Aristotelian views in both medicine and chemistry. He was influenced by Ficino and by the mystical tradition of the Jewish kabbalah, available to the Latin West through the humanist study of Hebrew. He attacked Galenic medicine, in which disease was believed to be the result of an imbalance of the four humors—phlegm, choler, melancholy, and blood. In place of this paradigm, he applied the Neoplatonic notions of macrocosm and microcosm to medicine. He saw the human body as a microcosm of everything in the universe, be it animal, vegetable, mineral, or spiritual. The role of the doctor was to bring remedies from the macrocosm to cure the diseases of the microcosm. Paracelsus concentrated on individual parts of the body, such as the liver, rather than upon the organic whole. He believed that disease came from outside the body instead of from an imbalance of the humors. As a consequence, he searched for specific remedies for specific diseases. To these advances in medicine he added a new orientation to chemistry, going beyond the traditional Greek elements (earth, air, fire, and water) to postulate three active principles, which he called sulfur, salt, and mercury. His work involved a new search for chemical remedies and a new emphasis on experiment, but it was also permeated with mystical and magical notions. Nevertheless, his Platonic orientation allowed him to offer alternatives to traditional medicine and chemistry in ways that proved productive to the further development of these disciplines.[65]

*　　*　　*

We can conclude, then, that the humanists made a profoundly important, though often indirect, contribution to early modern science. Beginning with Petrarch, they attacked the method of arguing from the authority of the ancients, particularly Aristotle. Their alliance with artists and artisans and their propagation of artists' perspective led to an increased appreciation for mathematics and at the same time to a growing respect for handwork and empiricism. Artists' perspective was enriched by, and in turn contributed to, the disciplines of cartography and optics. The humanist discovery and dissemination of ancient scientific texts, and the humanist stimulus for the writing of contemporary treatises on scientific and technical subjects, both contributed to growing knowledge in these areas. Humanist Neoplatonism propagated new cosmological views and new ideas in chemistry and medicine. As Eric Cochrane has pointed out, Galileo used humanist rather than scholastic modes of expression.[66] Galileo's adoption of the language of humanism is an indication of his indebtedness to it—not surprising in view of the humanist influence on European culture in the previous two centuries.

NOTES

1. Standard introductions to the history of science, written from very different points of view, are H. Butterfield, *The Origins of Modern Science: 1300–1800* (London, 2d ed. 1957); A. C. Crombie, *Augustine to Galileo* (London, 1952), reissued as *Medieval and Early Modern Science*, 2 vols. (New York, 2d ed. 1959); and E. J. Dijksterhuis, *The Mechanization of the World Picture*, trans. C. Dikshoorn (Oxford, 1961). Studies of Renaissance science and its cultural context include M. Boas, *The Scientific Renaissance: 1450–1630* (New York, 1962); E. Garin, *L'età nuova: Ricerche di storia della cultura dal XII al XVI secolo* (Naples, 1969), esp. 385–502; and his *Scienza e vita civile nel Rinascimento italiano* (Bari, 1965), English trans. by P. Munz as *Science and Civic Life in the Italian Renaissance* (Garden City, NY, 1969); H. Kearney, *Science and Change: 1500–1700* (New York, 1971); *Science and the Arts in the Renaissance*, ed. J. W. Shirley and F. D. Hoeniger (Washington, DC, 1985); C. Vasoli, *Profezia e ragione: Studi sulla cultura del Cinquecento e del Seicento* (Naples, 1974); W. P. D. Wightman, *Science and the Renaissance*, 2 vols. (Edinburgh and London, 1962); and

his *Science in a Renaissance Society* (London, 1972). See also C. B. Schmitt, "Recent Trends in the Study of Medieval and Renaissance Science," in *Information Sources in the History of Science and Medicine*, ed. P. Corsi and P. Weindling (London, 1983); and N. G. Siraisi, "Some Current Trends in the Study of Renaissance Medicine," *Renaissance Quarterly* 37 (1984): 585–600. The *Dictionary of Scientific Biography* is an indispensable reference for the life and work of individual scientists.

2. This point will be elaborated in greater detail below.

3. T. J. Reiss, *The Discourse of Modernism* (Ithaca, NY, 1982).

4. See particularly H. Blumenberg, *Die Kopernikanische Wende* (Frankfurt am Main, 1965); idem, *Die Genesis der kopernikanischen Welt* (Frankfurt am Main, 1975); and idem, *Die Legitimität der Neuzeit (erweiterte und überarbeitete Neuausgabe)*, 3 vols. (Frankfurt am Main, 1973–76), which was translated as *The Legitimacy of the Modern Age*, trans. R. M. Wallace (Cambridge, MA, and London, 1983). Helpful assessments of Blumenberg's work are K. Harries, "Copernican Reflections," *Inquiry* 23 (1980): 253–69; and the review essay of *Legitimacy* by M. Jay in *History and Theory* 24 (1985): 183–96.

5. For a recent discussion, see N. H. Steneck, "The Relevance of the Middle Ages to the History of Science and Technology," in *Science and Technology in Medieval Society*, ed. P. O. Long, *Annals of the New York Academy of Sciences* 441 (1985): 21–27.

6. The value of exploring those relationships can be seen in the illuminating essay by C. Trinkaus, "L'umanesimo italiano e la scienza del Rinascimento," in *Letteratura e scienza nella storia della cultura italiana*, Atti del IX congresso dell'Associazione Internazionale per gli Studi di Lingua e Letteratura Italiana (Palermo, 1978), 49–80.

7. For a brilliant elaboration of the latter topic, see B. Stock, *The Implications of Literacy* (Princeton, 1983).

8. *The Civilization of the Renaissance in Italy*, trans. S. G. C. Middlemore, 2 vols. (1929; reprinted New York, 1958), 2:279–92.

9. Ibid., 2:293–302.

10. P. Duhem, *Études sur Léonard de Vinci*, 3 vols. (Paris, 1906–13); and idem, *Le système du monde*, 10 vols. (Paris, 1913–59). For an excellent introduction to Duhem's career, see D. G. Miller, "Duhem, Pierre-Maurice-Marie," in *Dictionary of Scientific Biography* (New York, 1971), 4:225–33.

11. A. Maier, *Studien zur Naturphilosophie der Spätscholastik*, 5 vols. (Rome, 1949–58); and eadem, *Ausgehendes Mittelalter. Gesammelte Aufsätze zur Geistesgeschichte des 14. Jahrhunderts*, 3 vols. (Rome, 1964–77). For a recent introduction to her work and selected English translations, see *On the Threshold of Exact Science: Selected Writings of Anneliese Maier on Late Medieval Natural Philosophy*, ed. and trans. S. D. Sargent (Philadelphia, 1982).

12. C. H. Haskins, *Studies in the History of Mediaeval Science* (Cambridge, MA, 2d ed. 1927); and idem, *The Renaissance of the Twelfth Century* (Cambridge, MA, 1927). For recent assessments of the latter, see *Renais-*

sance and Renewal in the Twelfth Century, ed. R. L. Benson, G. Constable, and C. D. Lanham (Cambridge, MA, 1982).

13. In an early essay, "Science in the Renaissance," in *The Civilization of the Renaissance* (Chicago, 1929), 78–79, Sarton asserted that the artificiality of the humanists' Latin language accentuated "the artificiality and flimsiness of their intellectual life"; he also stressed the "antiscientific tendencies of the humanists." Cf. G. Sarton, *Six Wings: Men of Science in the Renaissance* (Bloomington, IN, 1957); and idem, *The Appreciation of Ancient and Medieval Science During the Renaissance (1450–1600)* (Philadelphia, 1955). For a recent appreciation of Sarton, see the issue of *Isis* devoted to him: 75 (1984): 7–62.

14. L. Thorndike, *Science and Thought in the Fifteenth Century* (New York, 1929), 13; and idem, *A History of Magic and Experimental Science* (New York, 1941) 5:5.

15. J. H. Randall, Jr., *The School of Padua and the Emergence of Modern Science* (Padua, 1961), 15–16. This book is a revised version of a paper that first appeared in the *Journal of the History of Ideas* 1 (1940): 177–206. Although Randall's thesis is no longer generally accepted, it inspired a continuing debate and a series of studies on Renaissance Aristotelianism. For a review of some of this literature, see C. B. Schmitt, *A Critical Survey and Bibliography of Studies on Renaissance Aristotelianism, 1958–1969* (Padua, 1971), 38–46. Studies on Paduan Aristotelianism are indebted to the work of B. Nardi—see especially *Saggi sull'Aristotelismo padovano dal secolo XIV–XVI* (Florence, 1958). A recent work that pays particular attention to the influence of Renaissance Aristotelianism on science is C. B. Schmitt, *Aristotle and the Renaissance* (Cambridge, MA, and London, 1983).

16. See E. Cochrane, "Science and Humanism in the Italian Renaissance," *American Historical Review* 81 (1976): 1039–57, to which this essay is indebted; M. Cottino-Jones, "Boccaccio e la scienza," in *Letteratura e scienza,* 356–70; V. de Caprio, "Il contributo del classicismo umanistico alla scienza: *Auctoritas* e *ratio* nella filologia di Lorenzo Valla," in *Letteratura e scienza,* 371–84; U. Dotti, "Petrarca e la scienza," in *Letteratura e scienza,* 345–55; D. B. Durand, "Tradition and Innovation in Fifteenth-Century Italy," and H. Baron, "Towards a More Positive Evaluation of the Fifteenth-Century Renaissance," and the discussions that follow these two articles in the *Journal of the History of Ideas* 4 (1943): 1–74; J. Gadol, "The Unity of the Renaissance: Humanism, Natural Science and Art," in *From the Renaissance to the Counter-Reformation: Essays in Honor of Garrett Mattingly,* ed. C. H. Carter (New York, 1965) 29–55; E. Garin, "Gli umanisti e la scienza," *Rivista di filosofia* 52 (1961): 261–78, reprinted in *L'età nuova,* 451–75; R. Klein, "Les humanistes et la science," *Bibliothèque d'humanisme et Renaissance* 23 (1961): 7–16; *Humanismus und Naturwissenschaften,* ed. R. Schmitz and F. Krafft (Boppard am Rhein, 1980); Schmitt, "Recent Trends"; Trinkaus, "L'umanesimo italiano"; and C. Vasoli, "The Contribution of Humanism to the Birth of Modern

Science," *Renaissance and Reformation* n.s. 3 (1979): 1–15; and the essays in his *Profezia e ragione.*

17. A. Koyré, *Études Galiléennes,* 3 vols. (Paris, 1939–40), trans. by J. Mepham as *Galileo Studies* (Atlantic Highlands, NJ, 1978); and idem, *From the Closed World to the Infinite Universe* (Baltimore, 1957).

18. Cf. Schmitt, "Recent trends," 226ff.

19. "On His Own Ignorance and That of Many Others," in *The Renaissance Philosophy of Man,* ed. E. Cassirer et al. (Chicago, 1948), 57–59. For a discussion of Petrarch's polemics and some modern interpretations of their import, see Dotti, "Petrarca e la scienza."

20. "On His Own Ignorance," 64, 73–74.

21. Ibid., 101.

22. Ibid., 102.

23. Ibid., 107–9.

24. "A Disapproval of an Unreasonable Use of the Discipline of Dialectic," in *Renaissance Philosophy,* ed. Cassirer et al., 134–39. Petrarch's criticism of Aristotle was carried on by his successors. For a later humanist critique, see C. B. Schmitt, *Gianfrancesco Pico della Mirandola (1469–1533) and His Critique of Aristotle* (The Hague, 1967), esp. 63–73.

25. Fundamental works on the importance of artisanal traditions to science in this period are J. Ackerman, "The Involvement of Artists in Renaissance Science," in *Science and the Arts in the Renaissance,* ed. Shirley and Hoeniger, 94–129; A. C. Keller, "Zilsel, the Artisans, and the Idea of Progress in the Renaissance," in *Roots of Scientific Thought,* ed. P. P. Wiener and A. Noland (New York, 1957): L. Olschki, *Geschichte der neusprachlichen wissenschaftlichen Literatur,* 3 vols. (Leipzig, 1919–22 and Halle, 1927); P. Rossi, *I filosofi e le macchine* (Milan, 1962), translated by S. Attanasio as *Philosophy, Technology, and the Arts in the Early Modern Era,* ed. B. Nelson (New York, 1970); C. Vasoli, "A proposito di scienza e technica nel Cinquecento," in his *Profezia e ragione;* E. Zilsel, "The Sociological Roots of Science," *American Journal of Sociology* 47 (1942): 544–62, and idem, "The Genesis of the Concept of Scientific Progress," in *Roots of Scientific Thought,* ed. Wiener and Noland, 251–75. Also relevant is M. Baxandall's *Painting and Experience in Fifteenth-Century Italy* (Oxford, 1972), a fascinating essay stressing the relation between theory and practice. It should be noted that scholars such as Olschki and Zilsel viewed artisan and humanist cultures as quite separate and denied any contribution from the humanists to science.

26. E. H. Gombrich, "From the Revival of Letters to the Reform of the Arts: Niccolò Niccoli and Filippo Brunelleschi," in *Essays in the History of Art Presented to Rudolf Wittkower,* ed. D. Fraser, H. Hibbard, and M. J. Lewine (London, 1967), 71–82. For Brunelleschi's importance for the development of science, see G. de Santillana, "The Role of Art in the Scientific Renaissance," in *Critical Problems in the History of Science,* ed. M. Clagett (Madison, WI, 1959), 33–65. For his engineering, see F. D. Prager and G.

Scaglia, *Brunelleschi: Studies of His Technology and Inventions* (Cambridge, MA, 1970).

27. An excellent introduction to Alberti's life and work is J. Gadol, *Leon Battista Alberti: Universal Man of the Early Renaissance* (Chicago, 1969).

28. T. B. Settle, "Ostilio Ricci, a Bridge Between Alberti and Galileo," *XIIe congrès international d'histoire des sciences: Actes* 3-B (Paris, 1968), 121–26. For a recent study of the *Ludi matematici*, see L. Vagnetti, "Considerazioni sui *Ludi matematici*," *Studi e documenti di architettura* 1 (1972): 175–259.

29. For a detailed discussion of these matters, see S. Y. Edgerton, Jr., *The Renaissance Rediscovery of Linear Perspective* (New York, 1975). Edgerton's thesis, elaborated in "The Renaissance Artist as Quantifier," in *The Perception of Pictures,* ed. M. A. Hagen, 2 vols. (New York, 1980), 1:179–212, that artist's perspective led to the invention of machines on paper and was a direct prerequisite of the scientific revolution has been disputed by M. S. Mahoney, "Diagrams and Dynamics: Mathematical Perspectives on Edgerton's Thesis," in *Science and the Arts in the Renaissance,* ed. Hoeniger and Shirley, 198–220.

30. See Baxandall, *Painting and Experience,* esp. 86–108; and W. van Egmond, "The Commercial Revolution and the Beginnings of Western Mathematics in Renaissance Florence: 1300–1500" (Ph.D. diss. Indiana University, Bloomington, 1976).

31. See J. S. Ackerman, "Leonardo's Eye," *Journal of the Warburg and Courtauld Institutes* 41 (1978): 108–46; and M. Kemp, "Leonardo and the Visual Pyramid," *Journal of the Warburg and Courtauld Institutes* 40 (1977): 128–49.

32. The best introduction to Leonardo and his work, M. Kemp, *Leonardo da Vinci: The Marvellous Works of Nature and Man* (Cambridge, MA, 1981), does justice to both the complexity and the unity of his achievements.

33. M. Kemp, " 'Il concetto dell'anima' in Leonardo's Early Skull Studies," *Journal of the Warburg and Courtauld Institutes* 34 (1971): 115–34. See also E. Panofsky, "Artist, Scientist, Genius: Notes on the Renaissance Dämmerung," in *The Renaissance: Six Essays* (New York, 1962), 123–82. For Vasari's remark, see Giorgio Vasari, *Le vite dei più eccellenti pittori, scultori e architetti,* ed. C. L. Ragghianti (Milan, 1942), 1:862.

34. A standard biography of Vesalius is C. D. O'Malley, *Andreas Vesalius of Brussels: 1514–1564* (Berkeley, 1964).

35. N. G. Siraisi, *Taddeo Alderotti and His Pupils: Two Generations of Italian Medical Learning* (Princeton, 1981), esp. 96–117 and passim. But see also J. L. Bylebyl, "Medicine, Philosophy, and Humanism in Renaissance Italy," in *Science and the Arts in the Renaissance,* ed. Hoeniger and Shirley, 27–49, which elaborates the influence of humanism on medicine in the late fifteenth and early sixteenth centuries.

36. C. G. Nauert, Jr., "Humanists, Scientists, and Pliny: Changing Approaches to a Classical Author," *American Historical Review* 84 (1979): 72–85.

37. See particularly E. P. Mahoney, "Philosophy and Science in Nicoletto Vernia and Agostino Nifo," and C. B. Schmitt, "Aristotelian Textual Studies at Padua: The Case of Francesco Cavalli," both in *Scienza e filosofia all' Università di Padova nel Quattrocento,* ed. A. Poppi (Padua, 1983), 135–202 and 287–314, respectively.

38. For an account of early printed editions of ancient and medieval scientific works, see Sarton, *Appreciation of Ancient and Medieval Science.* E. L. Eisenstein, *The Printing Press as an Agent of Change,* vol. 2 (Cambridge, 1979), has elaborated the importance of printing to the development of science in this period.

39. P. L. Rose, *The Italian Renaisance of Mathematics: Studies on Humanists and Mathematicians from Petrarch to Galileo* (Geneva, 1975).

40. K. M. Reeds, "Renaissance Humanism and Botany," *Annals of Science* 33 (1976): 519–42.

41. B. J. Shapiro, "History and Natural History in Sixteenth- and Seventeenth-Century England: An Essay on the Relationship Between Humanism and Science," in *English Scientific Virtuosi in the 16th and 17th Centuries* (Los Angeles, 1979), 1–55; and eadem, *Probability and Certainty in Seventeenth-Century England: A Study of the Relationships Between Natural Science, Religion, History, Law, and Literature* (Princeton, 1983), esp. 13 and 119–62.

42. For a discussion of early modern technical writings, see B. S. Hall, " 'Der Meister sol auch kennen schreiben und lesen': Writings About Technology ca. 1400–ca. 1600 A.D. and Their Cultural Implications," in *Early Technologies,* ed. D. Schmandt-Besserat (Malibu, CA, 1979), 47–58; and idem, "Giovanni de' Dondi and Guido da Vigevano: Notes Toward a Typology of Medieval Technical Writings," in *Machaut's World: Science and Art in the Fourteenth Century, Annals of the New York Academy of Sciences* 314 (1978): 127–42.

43. The importance of Venice for publishing sixteenth-century military writings has been elaborated by J. R. Hale, "Printing and Military Culture of Renaissance Venice," in his *Renaissance War Studies* (London, 1983), 429–70. See esp. 432–36 for the role of patronage in the production of this literature.

44. Giovanni de' Dondi, *Tractatus astrarii, Biblioteca Capitolare di Padova, cod. D. 39,* ed. A. Barzon, E. Morpurgo, A. Petrucci, and G. Fracescato (Vatican City, 1960). See also S. A. Bedini and F. R. Maddison, "Mechanical Universe: The Astrarium of Giovanni de' Dondi," *Transactions of the American Philosophical Society* n.s. 56.5 (1966) [monograph]; and N. W. Gilbert, "A Letter of Giovanni Dondi dall'Orologio to Fra' Guglielmo Centueri: A Fourteenth-Century Episode in the Quarrel of the Ancients and the Moderns," *Viator* 8 (1977): 299–346.

45. Conrad Kyeser aus Eichstatt, *Bellifortis,* ed. and trans. G. Guarg, 2 vols. (Düsseldorf, 1967); Mariano Taccola, *De machinis: The Engineering Treatise of 1449,* ed. G. Scaglia, 2 vols. (Wiesbaden, 1971); and F. D. Prager

and G. Scaglia, *Mariano Taccola and His Book "De ingeneis"* (Cambridge, MA, 1972).

46. F. Klemm, "Valturio, Roberto," *Dictionary of Scientific Biography* (New York, 1976), 13:567–68.

47. Francesco di Giorgio, *Trattati di architettura ingegneria e arte militare,* ed. C. Maltese, transcription by L. M. Degrassi, 2 vols. (Milan, 1957).

48. Luca Pacioli, *Summa de arithmetica, geometria, proportioni et proportionalità* (Venice, 1494); idem, *Euclid megarensis opera . . .* (Venice, 1509); and idem, *Divina proportione* (Venice, 1509).

49. See C. Castellani, "Aldrovandi, Ulisse," *Dictionary of Scientific Biography* (New York, 1970), 1:108–10; G. Olmi, *Ulisse Aldrovandi: Scienza e natura nel secondo cinquecento* (Trent, 1976); and S. T. Pattaro, *Metodo e sistema delle scienze nel pensiero di Ulisse Aldrovandi* (Bologna, 1981).

50. For an elaboration of some of these themes, see P. O. Long, "The Contribution of Architectural Writers to a 'Scientific' Outlook in the Fifteenth and Sixteenth Centuries," *Journal of Medieval and Renaissance Studies* 15 (1985): 265–98.

51. Daniele Barbaro, *I dieci libri dell'architettura di M. Vitruvio . . .* (Venice, 1556), 243 (my translation).

52. E. A. Burtt, *Metaphysical Foundations of Modern Science* (New York, 2d ed. 1932); Koyré, *Études Galiléenes* and *From the Closed World.*

53. See particularly F. A. Yates, *Giordano Bruno and the Hermetic Tradition* (London, 1964). For a selection of the numerous more recent discussions, see *Reason, Experiment, and Mysticism in the Scientific Revolution,* ed. M. L. Righini Bonelli and W. R. Shea (New York, 1975); *Occult and Scientific Mentalities in the Renaissance,* ed. B. Vickers (Cambridge, 1984), particularly the introduction, 1–55, by B. Vickers; and R. S. Westman and J. E. McGuire, *Hermeticism and the Scientific Revolution* (Los Angeles, 1977).

54. My discussion is dependent on Cassirer's fundamental treatment in *The Individual and the Cosmos in Renaissance Philosophy,* trans. M. Domandi (New York, 1963). An excellent introduction to Nicholas of Cusa's thought and to the recent scholarship is J. Hopkins, *A Concise Introduction to the Philosophy of Nicholas of Cusa* (Minneapolis, 1978).

55. J. Hopkins, *Nicholas of Cusa on Learned Ignorance: A Translation and Appraisal of De Docta Ignorantia* (Minneapolis, 1981), 41.

56. Ibid., 114–15.

57. Ibid., 115–16. To recognize the importance of Nicholas's cosmology as an alternative to the Aristotelian universe is not to suggest that he was a forerunner of Copernicus in the sense of dealing with the concrete problems and data of astronomy. Cf. Blumenberg, *Legitimacy,* 502ff.

58. The work is published in the Heidelberg Academy Edition of Nicholas of Cusa, *Opera omnia,* ed. L. Bauer (Leipzig, 1937), vol. 5. There is an English translation—*The Idiot in Four Books,* translated anonymously (London, 1650).

59. For the importance of this dialogue for the idea of creativity, see H. Blumenberg, " 'Nachahmung der Natur': Zur Vorgeschichte der Idee des schöpferischen Menschen," *Studium Generale* 10 (1957): 266–83.

60. R. Gavagna, "Un abbinamento editoriale del'500: Vitruvio e Cusano," *Rivista critica di storia della filosofia* 30 (1975): 400–410; and idem, "Cusano e Alberti a proposito del 'De architectura' di Vitruvio," *Rivista critica di storia della filosofia* 34 (1979): 162–76.

61. See Kearney, *Science and Change,* 37–41; W. Shumaker, *The Occult Sciences in the Renaissance: A Study in Intellectual Patterns* (Berkeley, 1972), 201–51; and F. A. Yates, "The Hermetic Tradition in Renaissance Science," in *Art, Science and History in the Renaissance,* ed. C. S. Singleton (Baltimore, 1967), 255–74.

62. See note 48. A good summary of Pacioli's career is S. A. Jayawardene, "Pacioli, Luca," *Dictionary of Scientific Biography* (New York, 1974), 10:269–72.

63. C. Vasoli, "Intorno a Francesco Giorgio Veneto e all 'armonia del mondo,' " in his *Profezia e ragione,* 129–405.

64. W. Pagel, *Paracelsus: An Introduction to Philosophical Medicine in the Era of the Renaissance* (Basel and New York, 2d ed. 1982), 39 and passim.

65. I am indebted to the useful discussion of Kearney, *Science and Change,* 114–25. For the influence of Paracelsus, see A. G. Debus, *The Chemical Philosophy: Paracelsian Science and Medicine in the Sixteenth and Seventeenth Centuries,* 2 vols. (New York, 1977). For some recent discussions that are not necessarily in agreement with one another or with the point of view presented here, see the articles in *Scienze credenze occulte livelli di cultura: Convegno Internazionale di Studi (Firenze 20–30 giugno, 1980),* Instituto Nazionale di Studi sul Rinascimento (Florence, 1982), 3–62; and B. Vickers, "Analogy Versus Identity," in *Occult and Scientific Mentalities,* ed. Vickers, 126ff. A valuable collection of essays on both Paracelsan and more traditional forms of medicine, *The Medical Renaissance of the Sixteenth Century,* ed. A. Wear, R. K. French, and I. M. Lonie (Cambridge, 1985), appeared too late to be used in the substantive part of this essay. It contains much of interest concerning the influence of humanism on sixteenth-century medicine.

66. Cochrane, "Science and Humanism," 1055–57. More recently, M. A. Finocchiaro, *Galileo and the Art of Reasoning: Rhetorical Foundations of Logic and Scientific Method* (Dordrecht, 1980), has provided a detailed analysis of the rhetorical form and content of Galileo's *Dialogue,* one that suggests a close parallel between the concerns of Galileo and those of the humanists. See further J. D. Moss, "Galileo's *Letter to Christina:* Some Rhetorical Considerations," *Renaissance Quarterly* 36 (1983): 547–76.

PART V

THE LEGACY OF HUMANISM

41 ❧ THE CULTURAL HERITAGE OF HUMANISM: AN OVERVIEW
Paul Oskar Kristeller

THE HISTORICAL IMPORTANCE OF RENAISSANCE HUMANISM CON-
sists above all in its own remarkable achievements and in its great
contributions to the civilization of its own time, some of which
have been described in the preceding chapters of these volumes. This
importance is further enhanced by the considerable impact, both direct
and indirect, that Renaissance humanism had on the seventeenth and
later centuries of western culture and which has been felt, at least in some
areas, until the recent past or even to the present day. This influence has
been as complex and diverse as humanism itself, which had a great number of different facets and hence cannot be brought under a single denominator. As a matter of fact, Renaissance humanism, when taken as a
whole, has no single counterpart in our own contemporary civilization,
and consequently its influence has been broken up into many different
aspects, whose common origin we can perceive only through a special
effort of historical understanding.[1]

I shall try to sum up very briefly the main contributions of Renaissance humanism (in doing which I cannot avoid repeating some of the
points made in previous chapters), and I shall then describe some of the
major areas in which the legacy of humanism was transmitted to later
centuries. We should keep in mind that during the fourteenth and early
fifteenth centuries humanism had its center in Italy and that it spread to
the rest of Europe, apart from a few earlier episodes, only during the
fifteenth century and especially during the sixteenth. Whereas early
Italian humanism had its own medieval antecedents (Italian and also
French),[2] northern humanism was much indebted to Italian influences
but assumed in each country some novel and different traits that reflected,
at least in part, the medieval traditions of that country and which were
different from those of the other countries and also of Italy.[3]

In order to avoid misunderstandings, we should remember that Renaissance humanism, in Italy and elsewhere, constituted only one sector
among many—though an important one—within the world of learning,
of the intellectual professions, and of the literary production during the
Renaissance period. The modern term "humanism," as I shall continue

to use it (disregarding the many other connotations that are currently associated with it), is derived from the Renaissance term "humanist," and this term is derived, as we know from several testimonies, from the "humanities," called the *studia humanitatis,* which included, according to contemporary definitions, the fields of grammar, rhetoric, poetry, history, and moral philosophy.[4] The *studia humanitatis,* taken in their proper meaning, did not include other areas of learning that were quite actively pursued at the same time, such as logic, metaphysics or natural philosophy, mathematics or medicine, jurisprudence or theology. They also did not include vernacular literature, the visual arts, or music, or the political, economic, or religious life and thought of the period. Nonetheless all these areas, though not a part of the domain of the humanists, came to be strongly influenced by humanism.

*   *   *

The specific place that the humanists occupied within Renaissance civilization is reflected in the subjects they studied and taught, in the professional and social positions they occupied, and in the range of their literary production.

Many humanists, though by no means all, were teachers at secondary schools or universities, and all of them were at least exposed as students to the humanist teaching offered at schools and universities. The subjects taught and studied by the humanists were the humanities as then understood: Latin and Greek grammar, which involved the ability to read and understand and to write (that is, to copy) the two classical languages; rhetoric and poetry, which covered the interpretation and translation of Latin and Greek prose writers and poets, and the ability to compose and to write in Latin prose and verse; history, which taught both the reading and understanding of ancient historians and the skill to write in Latin on historical subjects; and moral philosophy, which again involved the reading and interpretation of the ancient moralists and the ability to think and to write about themes and problems belonging to this field.[5]

Whereas teaching was always an important activity for many humanists, it was by no means the only professional or social career followed by them. Another career pursued by many was that of chancellor or secretary, in which their skills in composing Latin letters and orations were extremely useful.[6] We find many trained humanists in the chanceries of popes and bishops, of emperors, kings, and princes, of republics and towns; and these functions were sometimes combined with teaching duties inside the chancery or court or at the local schools or universities, and often with the task of writing the official history of the princely family or of the town that employed them. But humanistic study and education served not only as a professional training for future teachers or secretaries, but also as a favorite background for many other professional or practical careers. Among the persons who had enjoyed a humanist education, we find theologians, jurists, philosophers, physicians, mathematicians and other scientists, and even some artists and musicians who were to make use within their respective fields of the classical sources and ideas, style, and forms with which they had become familiar through their training. Finally, many persons prominent in public affairs, popes, cardinals, bishops, priests and other men of the church, abbots, monks and friars of many different orders, kings and princes, republican office-holders, patricians, bankers, and merchants were either humanists in their own right (including two popes) or were pupils or patrons of humanists, received the dedication of their works, and rewarded them for their efforts. To this broadly based influence may be added the important contribution made by the humanists to the production and diffusion of books. They were active as scribes and copied numerous manuscripts, more modestly for their own personal use and more sumptuously for libraries and collectors, transcribing not only classical texts and their own writings but also many other medieval and contemporary texts. The humanist scribe actually invented two types of script, in contrast to the Gothic script that had prevailed in the thirteenth and fourteenth centuries: the humanist or Roman book hand, an imitation of the Carolingian minuscule, which they mistook for an ancient Roman script, and the humanist cursive, which was a new modification and served as the basis for our Italic script.[7] Many humanists also served as librarians in charge of the newly formed collections and of some older ones. After the invention of printing around 1450 and its rapid diffusion from Germany to other countries including Italy, the humanists were actively involved in the new production and trade of books, sometimes as printers or publishers, more often as authors, editors, and proofreaders.[8] The printing of classical texts and of the writings of the humanists accounts for a significant sector, though by no means for the entire body, of the amazingly large book production of the late fifteenth and sixteenth centuries.

The literary production of the humanists, much of it found only in rare editions or manuscripts, reflects the range of their interests and activities.[9] It constitutes only one sector, though an important one, of the written output of the period, but it is large and diversified and rarely appreciated in its total wealth and complexity. Among the writings of the humanists, we find treatises on grammar and rhetoric; commentaries on and translations of ancient Greek and Latin authors; private and state

letters; political and ceremonial speeches; works on ancient history, mythology, law, and archaeology; historical works that deal more often with
medieval and contemporary than with ancient events; many biographies
of political and ecclesiastical figures, of scholars, writers, and artists; a
large and interesting group of treatises and dialogues on moral, educational, political, and religious subjects; and a vast amount of poetry of
all kinds, most of it in Latin. It is this contribution to Latin poetry and
literature that is often overlooked by those historians who emphasize
only the humanists' contribution to classical scholarship and to moral
thought. This omission leads to a distorted view of humanism as a
whole, for it is this literary contribution, apart from any philosophical
or scholarly pursuits, that occupies a major part or even the center of the
work of many minor and even some major humanists.

*   *   *

If we pass from the contributions of the humanists to the legacy they left
to later centuries, we may begin with their important and extensive,
though not always appreciated activities as classical scholars and as critical philologists.[10] They discovered the manuscripts of many ancient
Latin and Greek authors, copied and collated, edited and published
them, translated them from Greek into Latin and sometimes from Latin
into the vernacular, wrote commentaries on them, and tried, through a
careful study of the texts and of ancient monuments and inscriptions, to
arrive at an accurate and comprehensive knowledge of the ancient languages and of Greek and Roman literature and history. By comparing
and selecting the variant readings of different manuscripts, and by correcting and emending words and passages that seemed to be corrupt or
wrong in the manuscripts they used, the humanists made great advances
in the methods of textual criticism. They were also pioneers in the techniques of philological and historical criticism, recognizing that some
works attributed to ancient authors were actually composed by different
authors or even forged at a much later period, and by dating historical
events more correctly with the help of all available evidence.

The humanists thus were the predecessors, if not the founders, of
modern classical, philological, and historical scholarship as it is still
being pursued and developed in our time. Later centuries, especially the
seventeenth, nineteenth, and twentieth, have greatly improved and refined the methods used by the humanists and extended their research
from classical antiquity to other earlier and later periods of western history and to wide areas of other civilizations in different parts of the
world. Yet in spite of recent fashions and ideologies, the firm criteria of
textual and documentary evidence and of textual, philological, and his-

torical criticism, as they were first used by the humanists, are still valid and productive and will continue to be applied and further developed in a steady expansion of our knowledge of all periods and areas of history that happen to interest us.

As we have seen, the humanists were not only scholars, but also teachers. They were convinced that the study of the classical languages and literatures provided an indispensable basis for any serious scholarly endeavor, and also the best possible training for an educated and civilized person. It was the humanists, as well as other humanistically trained educators, both Catholic and Protestant, who formulated their program in various treatises on education, and who founded all over Europe many primary and secondary schools whose curriculum was centered around the study of Latin and Greek.[11] These schools, some of them private and many others sponsored by state or church authorities, continued to flourish and to train future scholars and political leaders up to the early decades of this century. It is only during the past few decades that they have declined in number, influence, and public attention, though they have by no means completely disappeared. For nearly five hundred years, the humanist school has provided all western countries with a large group of competent and educated citizens who, regardless of nationality, religion, or class, had a common literary background and a common standard of disciplined reasoning, thus assuring a certain continuity of thought and scholarship that did not exclude novelty or change where such change was called for as a result of new insights or discoveries.

Another contribution of the humanists, of a more modest kind, has actually survived to the present day and is likely to last also in the future and much longer than any other humanist achievement: the humanist script in both its forms, Roman and Italic. The humanists originated these forms of handwriting, rejecting the Gothic script that had been prevalent for some time before. The early printers imitated in their typefaces the various forms of contemporary handwriting and adopted along with the Gothic also the two humanist scripts. If the Gothic script has gradually disappeared from use, and if we now use only the Roman and Italic script and find it easier to read than the Gothic, this is ultimately due to the reform of handwriting that was introduced by the humanist scribes of the fifteenth century.[12]

*   *   *

The humanists were not only active as scholars, educators, and editors, but also as writers and poets. They wrote for the most part in Latin, and it was in part due to their efforts that Latin survived for several more centuries as a second language. It was used for literary purposes to the eighteenth century, for scientific and scholarly purposes even longer, and in some areas almost to the present day. Whereas a work in the vernacular surely had a much wider audience in the author's own country, a work written in Latin reached an international public of educated or learned readers who in most cases did not read any vernacular language except their own. The use of Latin, especially in classical scholarship, has survived until recent times, and even where it has disappeared from use, its long predominance is reflected in the persistent use of Latin terminology in all the sciences and in all other branches of learning. The use of Latin prose in letters, speeches, and state papers, and especially of Latin verse in epigrams, elegies, and eclogues, in epic and didactic poems, and in plays, survived in many countries well into the eighteenth or even into the early nineteenth century. Also works of history and of moral philosophy continued to be written in Latin. There were other factors besides humanism, however, that played a part in the survival of Latin. Many state papers and international documents continued to be written in Latin, especially in central and eastern Europe. University instruction continued to be given in Latin, and consequently many textbooks and other treatises intended for university students were published in Latin. Finally, the Roman Catholic church continued until very recent times to use Latin in its liturgy, in its theological instruction, and in its official documents. The extent to which the Latin used in modern times by state chanceries, by university scholars, and by the authorities of the Catholic church was indebted to humanist influences, in addition to medieval traditions, is a subject that would require further investigation and on which it is not possible to make a clear statement at this time.[13]

*   *   *

Another area of humanist influence that has received some recent attention but which would lend itself to much further investigation is the impact of Renaissance humanism on the various vernacular literatures before, during, and after the sixteenth century. The vernacular languages originated in oral and popular use and were but slowly and gradually adapted to written and literary purposes, and even later to prose than to poetry, to doctrinal than to narrative prose. The rise of vernacular literature differed from country to country, and it seems to have started later in Italy than in some other countries. The vernacular had to assert itself against the entrenched use of Latin, and also against the variety of local dialects that apparently for those accustomed to other dialects were as difficult to understand as Latin. The vernacular languages had to be transformed after the model of Latin before they could be used as vehicles of literature, and especially of learned prose literature. This transformation took place in Italy during the sixteenth century, and it was the humanists of the fifteenth century, especially in Tuscany, who played a significant role in this development, a fact that has been persistently denied or overlooked, due to certain traditional prejudices, partly purist and partly romantic. The vernacular language had to acquire a precise syntax and sentence structure as well as a pattern of literary style and rhetorical composition if it was to be used for a clearly reasoned discourse, and it needed an abstract and often technical terminology if it was to become the vehicle of learned discourse. All of these things were borrowed from Latin models and often acquired through vernacular translations of Latin writings, some of them scholastic but many more humanistic in character.[14] The vernacular literatures, to be sure, had developed by the time of the Renaissance, and were to develop in later times, a number of literary genres and topics that were quite different and often quite independent from ancient sources and traditions. Yet there are many instances, especially in the sixteenth century, in which humanist genres, and classical genres transmitted through the humanists, found their way into vernacular literatures, from the various forms of lyric and epic poetry to the play, and from the prose letter, speech, and history to the dialogue and treatise. Even in vernacular poems and stories where we might not expect it, the classical and humanistic influence appears in the borrowing of certain phrases, metaphors, and episodes, in the use of some favorite ideas (as the dignity of man in Marlowe's *Tamberlaine*), or in the adaptation of classical themes (as in Shakespeare's Roman plays).

*   *   *

A special place belongs to the humanists in the development of historiography and biography. Their numerous writings in this area, covering the history of Florence (Leonardo Bruni), Venice, and other cities, of England (Polydore Vergil) and other countries, and also of the Middle Ages (Flavio Biondo), were widely read, admired, and imitated and had a significant influence on later historiography. Long criticized as empty and rhetorical, the humanist historians have recently received more praise, both on account of their literary style and composition, and on account of their critical judgment and their rational treatment of the past.[15]

*   *   *

Humanist scholars were not only consummate practitioners in poetry, oratory, and historiography, but they were also concerned with the theory of poetics, of rhetoric, and of history. They echoed in part the theories of ancient authors, but also developed some new ideas in an attempt to explain classical theory and practice. Humanist treatises on poetics and their interpretations of Aristotle's *Poetics* have greatly influenced later literary criticism, as have their rhetorical theories, which have not yet been adequately studied, and their theory of history, which has received some scholarly attention.[16] The influence of the humanists in these areas may well be traced to such later thinkers as Vico, Baumgarten (the founder of modern aesthetics), and Hegel (the first systematic philosopher of history). Those modern thinkers who place history alongside nature, respect the contribution of the historical and philological disciplines to valid knowledge, and like to see philosophy associated not only with theology or with the natural and social sciences but also with the humanities, may find the ideas and attitudes of many Renaissance humanists quite congenial.

*   *   *

The large literature of humanist treatises and dialogues that has come down to us deals with a great variety of problems that belong for the most part to the realm of moral philosophy. They touch on such favorite themes as the ultimate good of human life, wisdom and the other virtues, pleasure, fate and freedom, the active and the contemplative life, the will and the intellect, the dignity and misery of man, the immortality of the soul, the unity of truth, and many other subjects.[17] In presenting different views, the humanists frequently draw on ancient, and occasionally on medieval, sources, but they contribute many interesting ideas of their own, and they usually indicate their own preference when presenting different views on the same subject. These treatises have rightly attracted the attention of recent intellectual historians, but their direct impact on later philosophers and moralists is hard to assess, even where they deal with the same problems, and it should probably be further investigated. There is no doubt that humanist ideas had a strong influence on many more systematic philosophers of the Renaissance, whether Platonists, Aristotelians, or independent thinkers, and that in turn these philosophers, whom we do not consider humanists in the strict sense of the word, had a strong and direct influence on later philosophers and transmitted to them some of the ideas and attitudes of humanist thought.

Another trait of humanist thought that finds expression in so many of their letters, biographies, and treatises, and probably culminates in Montaigne's *Essais* (a major humanist work, though written in French), is the highly personal and subjective note that pervades these writings and that is what Jacob Burckhardt means when he speaks of "individualism," a term that has often been misunderstood.[18] The humanists, and

Montaigne more than any other, think and write in terms of their own individual person and experience, not in terms of an incorporeal mind or of a pure reason common to all human beings, as do most ancient, medieval, and early modern philosophers. It is this personal attitude and approach that may prompt us to see a link, though not conscious or intended, between Renaissance humanism and modern existentialism.

*   *   *

No less significant than the direct legacy that the Renaissance humanists left to later centuries through their own work was the indirect influence they exercised through their impact on other areas of Renaissance learning and culture. If we begin with philosophy, in addition to moral philosophy, just discussed, we may single out the humanist attempts at a reform of logic which is associated with the names of Lorenzo Valla, Rudolf Agricola, Petrus Ramus, and Mario Nizolio. It was a logic that was influenced by rhetoric and that aimed at clarity of expression rather than at precision of thinking. We know that Nizolio was respected and edited by Leibniz, and that the Ramist school flourished for centuries in several Protestant countries, including early America.[19]

In the other branches of philosophy, and especially in metaphysics and natural philosophy, the official tradition of university instruction remained Aristotelian and scholastic well into the eighteenth century, whereas in the less official areas of philosophical thought, a variety of Neoplatonic, eclectic, and original ideas prevailed. The Aristotelian tradition was frequently criticized but not seriously challenged by the humanists. It was effectively attacked and eventually replaced by the physics of Galileo and the metaphysics of Descartes. Nevertheless, humanism went a long way to modify and transform this tradition. The humanist scholars went back to the Greek text of Aristotle, and they supplied new and supposedly better Latin translations for most of his writings. They also made available for the first time all the Greek commentaries on Aristotle and the botanical writings of his pupil Theophrastus. Even more incisive was the large body of non-Aristotelian Greek philosophy that the humanists added to the philosophical library of the period and of later periods. They introduced most of the works of Plato and the Neoplatonists, the major Greek sources of Stoicism, Epicureanism and Skepticism, and many other authors such as Plutarch and Lucian. As a result, many non-Aristotelian philosophical doctrines of antiquity were reexamined and restated. The broadened perspective led to a widespread eclecticism and syncretism that caused a fermentation and even confusion of thought, but it also helped to raise doubts about many conventional opinions for which there had been no alternative, and thus prepared the way for new and more solid constructions such as the great philosophical systems of the seventeenth and eighteenth centuries from Descartes to Kant.

*   *   *

The impact of humanism outside the humanities was not only felt in philosophy but also in all other areas of learning. Theology was deeply affected by the biblical and patristic studies of the humanists, who tried to apply to the New Testament and to the writings of the church fathers the same philological methods they had developed for the pagan classics. In the same way, the critical methods of history were applied to the history of the church. As has been rightly observed, Protestant and Catholic reformers alike were deeply affected by these new methods and perspectives, and it is becoming increasingly clear how large a proportion of Greek patristic literature was made known for the first time through the translations and editions due to humanist scholars. In the wake of humanist studies of Latin and Greek, the study of Hebrew, Syriac, and Arabic also made great progress among western scholars, especially during the sixteenth century, and thus new avenues were opened up for the study of the Old Testament, of the Koran, and of later Jewish and Arabic thought.[20]

In the field of jurisprudence, it was above all the textual study of the *Corpus iuris civilis* (which contained a number of Greek passages) that gradually led to a historical rather than a purely logical interpretation of the Roman law. This historical study of Roman law flourished especially in France during the sixteenth century.[21] As the Roman law, always valid in Italy and southern France, extended its domain to the German empire in the sixteenth century, its study remained an active scholarly pursuit for several centuries. This study remained important even after the Roman law had been abandoned, since the new law codes that replaced it, at least in continental Europe, reflected on many points its continuing influence.

The notable progress of the natural and other sciences was to a large extent due to new discoveries, observations, and theories, but it also owed something to humanist scholarship.[22] Many important Greek writings on mathematics, astronomy, geography, and medicine were translated for the first time during the fifteenth and sixteenth centuries. It was necessary to absorb completely the knowledge attained by the ancients before further progress could be accomplished.

In the area of political theory, which was considered a part of moral philosophy, the Renaissance produced a number of important thinkers.[23]

The long list includes Erasmus and Thomas More who were leading humanists, and Machiavelli and Jean Bodin who surely had enjoyed a humanist education. All of them were quite original, but it has also been shown that they were strongly indebted to classical sources, and for this and other reasons, humanism must receive a share of the credit for the great influence that these thinkers have exercised up to the present day.

Another indirect way through which humanist influences reached later times was through the arts. It was due to the humanist climate of their time that the great architects of the Renaissance (one of whom, Leon Battista Alberti, was himself a leading humanist) imitated the structure and decoration of the ancient buildings they saw and tried to follow the rules of Vitruvius. In a comparable way, the painters and sculptors of the time tried to follow the ancient standards of form and composition as they were known to them from available specimens and from literary sources. No less important was the frequent choice of classical subjects, historical, mythological, or allegorical, for major compositions and decorations. This classical tradition in the visual arts lasted until the early nineteenth century. It has disappeared from more recent art, and there may be no desire or good reason for reviving it. But we continue to admire the earlier works of art of which this classical element was a vital ingredient, and we must hence give a somewhat grudging tribute to the culture saturated with humanism that made this art possible.[24]

In the case of music, the classical influence is less apparent. There were attempts to revive ancient musical theories, but they were neither accurate nor practicable. But the Italian opera started out as an imaginary revival of ancient music and favored among its themes from the beginning, and for some time to come, some classical subjects, including the immortal theme of Orpheus and Eurydice.[25]

*   *   *

A last word may be in order concerning the role of Renaissance humanism in the long development that has led our civilization away from a predominant concern with religious problems toward an increasingly secular outlook. There has been a gradual trend that we may call the secularization of culture, but it should be realized that religious concerns are by no means absent from our contemporary world, and that lay culture and secular learning were never absent at any period of the Middle Ages. What we do observe is a gradual increase in the volume and importance of lay culture and of secular learning, which began in the high and later Middle Ages and which has been continued and accelerated in modern times. Renaissance humanism, with its emphasis on classical antiquity and with its great contributions to a scholarship, literature, and thought that were not religious in their content or origin, has undoubt-edly played a role in this development. But it shares this role with medie-val and modern philosophy, jurisprudence, and science, and with many other facets of modern culture. Renaissance humanism has rarely, if ever, led to a frontal attack on the religious beliefs prevalent at the time. It has rather extended and broadened in a number of fields the area of secular culture that was to coexist with the religious beliefs of the time and to open the way to a number of mutual influences.

*　　*　　*

I hope it has become apparent that during the centuries that followed the Renaissance and extending more or less to the present day, there has been, along with many new developments, a frequent and recurrent, if not continuous, influence of Renaissance humanism. I think this is one more reason for studying Renaissance humanism, that is, not only in its own right and in its relation to antiquity and the Middle Ages, but also in its impact on later centuries down to our own. I should go even fur-ther: just as our understanding of antiquity may be enriched by our knowledge of the way the Middle Ages and the Renaissance saw and interpreted it, so the modern understanding (and even misunderstanding) of the Renaissance and of humanism may help us to see more clearly certain aspects of it that might otherwise have escaped us. Our cultural tradition is rich and varied, and all of its components, large and small, famous or forgotten, may at any time be studied, newly apprehended, interpreted, combined with other elements and put to a fresh and novel use. It is this ongoing pursuit, along with other factors, which justifies, I hope, our life and work as scholars, and our attempts to keep the past and its culture available and interesting for changing generations of stu-dents and readers.

NOTES

1. P. O. Kristeller, *Renaissance Thought and Its Sources,* ed. M. Mooney (New York, 1979); idem, *Renaissance Thought and the Arts* (Princeton, 1980). E. Garin, *Italian Humanism: Philosophy and Civic Life in the Renaissance,* trans. P. Munz (New York, 1965); C. Trinkaus, *Adversity's Noblemen: The Italian Humanists on Happiness* (New York, 1940; rev. ed. 1965); *In Our Image and Likeness: Humanity and Divinity in Italian Humanist Thought,* 2 vols. (Chicago, 1970).

2. See Chapter 3 in these volumes, "Medieval Italian Culture and the Origins of Humanism as a Stylistic Ideal."

3. R. Weiss, *Humanism in England During the Fifteenth Century* (Oxford, 2d ed. 1957). Kristeller, *Renaissance Thought and the Arts,* chap. 3. See Chap-

ters 17 to 22 and 24 to 26 in these volumes on humanism outside of Italy.

4. A Campana, "The Origin of the Word 'Humanist,' " *Journal of the Warburg and Courtauld Institutes* 9 (1946): 60–73. Kristeller, *Renaissance Thought and Its Sources,* 98–99, 282–84. See chapters 29–33 in these volumes, on each discipline of the *studio humanitatis.*

5. See Chapter 27 in these volumes, "Humanism and Education."

6. H. Baron, *The Crisis of the Early Italian Renaissance,* 2 vols. (Princeton, 1955; rev. ed. in one volume, 1966). See Chapter 7 in these volumes, "The Significance of 'Civic Humanism' in the Interpretation of the Italian Renaissance."

7. B. L. Ullman, *The Origin and Development of Humanistic Script* (Rome, 1960). A. C. de la Mare, *The Handwriting of Italian Humanists* (Oxford, 1973).

8. R. Hirsch, *Printing, Selling and Reading, 1450–1550* (Wiesbaden, 1967); idem, *The Printed Word* (London, 1978). C. F. Bühler, *Early Books and Manuscripts* (New York, 1973); idem, *The Fifteenth-Century Book* (Philadelphia, 1960). E. L. Eisenstein, *The Printing Press as an Agent of Change,* 2 vols. (Cambridge, 1979).

9. Kristeller, *Renaissance Thought and the Arts,* chap. 1.

10. J. E. Sandys, *A History of Classical Scholarship,* 3 vols. (Cambridge, 3d ed. 1921), vol. 2. R. Pfeiffer, *History of Classical Scholarship from 1300 to 1850* (Oxford, 1976). R. Weiss, *The Renaissance Discovery of Classical Antiquity* (Oxford, 1969). See Chapter 28 in these volumes, "Quattrocento Humanism and Classical Scholarship."

11. *Vittorino da Feltre and Other Humanist Educators,* ed. W. H. Woodward (Cambridge, 1897; reprinted with intro. by E. F. Rice, Jr., New York, 1963); idem, *Studies in Education During the Age of the Renaissance, 1400–1600* (Cambridge, 1906; reprinted New York, 1967). See Chapter 27 in these volumes, "Humanism and Education."

12. See Chapter 27 in these volumes, "Humanism and Education."

13. Kristeller, *Renaissance Thought and the Arts,* chap. 7.

14. Ibid. See Chapters 19, 20, and 26 in these volumes, "Humanism in Spain," "Humanism in France," and "Humanism in . . . the Czech Lands," each of which deals with the relation of Latin humanist culture to the vernacular tradition.

15. E. Cochrane, *Historians and Historiography in the Italian Renaissance* (Chicago, 1981). See Chapter 32 in these volumes, "Humanism and History."

16. B. Weinberg, *A History of Literary Criticism in the Italian Renaissance,* 2 vols. (Chicago, 1961). E. Grassi, *Rhetoric as Philosophy* (University Park, PA, 1980). B. Reynolds, "Shifting Currents in Historical Criticism," in *Renaissance Essays from the Journal of the History of Ideas,* ed. P. O. Kristeller and P. P. Wiener (New York, 1968), 115–30. See Chapters 30, 31, and 32 in these volumes: "Humanism and Poetics," "Humanism and Rhetoric," and "Humanism and History."

17. See above, note 1; E. F. Rice, Jr., *The Renaissance Idea of Wisdom* (Cambridge, MA, 1958); and Chapter 33 in these volumes, "Humanism and Moral Philosophy."

18. J. Burckhardt, *The Civilization of the Renaissance in Italy,* trans. S. G. C. Middlemore (reprint, New York, 1954).

19. P. Miller, *The New England Mind,* 2 vols. (Cambridge, MA, 1939–53). W. J. Ong, S. J., *Ramus, Method and the Decay of Dialogue* (Cambridge, MA, 1983). N. W. Gilbert, *Renaissance Concepts of Method* (New York, 1960). See Chapter 31 in these volumes, "Humanism and Rhetoric."

20. See Chapters 15, 35, 36, 37, and 23 in these volumes: "The Italian Renaissance and Jewish Thought," "Italian Humanism and Scholastic Theology," "Humanism and Pre-Reformation Theology," "Humanism and the Protestant Reformation," and "Desiderius Erasmus."

21. D. R. Kelley, *Foundations of Modern Historical Scholarship: Language, Law, and History in the French Renaissance* (New York, 1970). See Chapter 34 in these volumes, "Humanism and Jurisprudence."

22. P. L. Rose, *The Italian Renaissance of Mathematics* (Geneva, 1975). See Chapter 40 in these volumes, "Humanism and Science."

23. Q. Skinner, *The Foundations of Modern Political Thought,* vol. 1, *The Renaissance* (Cambridge, 1978). See Chapter 7 in these volumes, "The Significance of 'Civic Humanism' in the Interpretation of the Italian Renaissance."

24. See Chapter 38 in these volumes, "Humanism and Art."

25. See Chapter 39 in these volumes, "Humanism and Music."

CONTRIBUTORS TO VOLUME 3

DANILO AGUZZI-BARBAGLI ("Humanism and Poetics") is Professor of Italian at the University of British Columbia, Vancouver, Canada. He is the editor of Francesco Patrizi's *Della poetica,* 3 vols. (1969–71) and of Patrizi's *Lettere opusculi inediti* (1975); he is the author of "Francesco Patrizi and Musical Humanism" (1983).

DAVID CAST ("Humanism and Art") is Associate Professor of the History of Art at Bryn Mawr College. He is the author of *The Calumny of Apelles: A Study in the Humanist Tradition* (1981).

JOHN F. D'AMICO ("Humanism and Pre-Reformation Theology") is Associate Professor of History at George Mason University. He is the author of *Renaissance Humanism in Papal Rome* (1983).

ANTHONY GRAFTON ("Quattrocento Humanism and Classical Scholarship") is Professor of History at Princeton University. He is the author of *Joseph Scaliger: A Study in the History of Classical Scholarship* (1983).

DONALD R. KELLEY ("Humanism and History") is Wilson Professor of History at the University of Rochester. He is the author of *Foundations of Modern Historical Scholarship: Language, Law and History in the French Renaissance* (1970) and, most recently, of *History, Law, and the Human Sciences* (1984), a collection of essays.

BENJAMIN G. KOHL ("Humanism and Education") is Professor of History at Vassar College. He has edited (with R. G. Witt) *The Earthly Republic: Italian Humanists on Government and Society* (1978), written an introduction and notes to Giovanni di Conversino da Ravenna's *Dragmalogia de eligibili vite genere* (1980), and, most recently, published *Renaissance Humanism, 1300–1500: A Bibliography of Materials in English* (1985).

PAUL OSKAR KRISTELLER ("Humanism and Moral Philosophy"; "The Cultural Heritage of Humanism: An Overview") is Frederick J. E. Woodbridge Professor of Philosophy Emeritus at Columbia University. His numerous books and articles largely determine the way in which Italian humanism is viewed today, and his *Iter Italicum* (3 vols. published, 3 more projected) continues to help define areas of research.

PAMELA O. LONG ("Humanism and Science") is an independent historian doing research at the Library of Congress in Washington. She is editor of *Science and Technology in Medieval Society* (1985) and author of "The Contribution of Architectural Writers to a 'Scientific Outlook' in the 15th and 16th Centuries" (1986).

JOHN MONFASANI ("Humanism and Rhetoric") is Professor of History at the State University of New York at Albany. He is the author of *George of Trebizond: A Biography and a Study of His Rhetoric and Logic* (1976) and the editor of *Collectanea Trapezuntiana* (1984).

CLAUDE V. PALISCA ("Humanism and Music") is Henry L. and Lucy G. Moses Professor of Music at Yale University. He is the author of *Humanism in Italian Renaissance Musical Thought* (1985).

W. KEITH PERCIVAL ("Renaissance Grammar") is Professor of Linguistics at the University of Kansas. He has written "The Grammatical Tradition and the Rise of the Vernaculars" (1975), "The Place of the 'Rudimenta grammatices' in the History of Latin Grammar" (1981), and other articles related to Renaissance grammar.

ALBERT RABIL, JR. (Editor) is Distinguished Teaching Professor of Humanities, State University of New York, College at Old Westbury. He is the author of *Erasmus and the New Testament* (1972), one of the translators of *Erasmus' Paraphrases of Romans and Galatians* (1983), and author and editor of *Knowledge, Goodness, and Power: The Debate over "Nobility" Among Quattrocento Italian Humanists*, 2 vols. (forthcoming).

RICHARD J. SCHOECK ("Humanism and Jurisprudence") is Professor of English and Humanities at the University of Colorado at Boulder. He is editor of *Editing Sixteenth-Century Texts* (1966) and of a number of other volumes, and author of *The Achievement of Thomas More* (1976), *Intertextuality and Renaissance Texts* (1984), and many articles on English and French humanism and jurisprudence during the Renaissance.

LEWIS W. SPITZ ("Humanism and the Protestant Reformation") is William R. Kenan, Jr. Professor of History at Stanford University. He is the author of *The Religious Renaissance of the German Humanists.* (1963) and, most recently, of *The Protestant Reformation 1517–1559* (1985).

CHARLES TRINKAUS ("Italian Humanism and Scholastic Theology") is Professor of History Emeritus, University of Michigan. He is the author of *Adversity's Noblemen* (1941, 1965), *In Our Image and Likeness*, 2 vols. (1970), *The Poet as Philosopher: Petrarch and the Formation of Renaissance Consciousness* (1979), and *The Scope of Renaissance Humanism* (1983), a collection of his essays.

BIBLIOGRAPHY FOR VOLUMES 1–3

The following bibliography contains every item noted in the 41 preceding essays, under four headings: (1) Primary Sources: Anthologies; (2) Primary Sources: Individual Authors; (3) Secondary Sources: Collections of Essays and Reference Works; and (4) Secondary Sources: Individual Authors. Authors of articles and books are not cited in the index except in those cases in which an issue is addressed in the notes.

PRIMARY SOURCES: ANTHOLOGIES

Abel, E., ed. *Analecta ad historiam renascentium in Hungaria litteratum spectantia* (Budapest, 1880).
Arnaldi, F. et al., eds., *Poeti latini del Quattrocento* (Milan, 1964).
Baldinucci, F., ed., *Notizie de' professori del disegno da Cimabue in qua (1681–1728),* 7 vols. (Florence, 1845–57).
Basetti-Sani, F., ed., *The Earliest Lives of Dante,* trans. J. R. Smith (New York, 1963).
Becker, R. P., ed., *German Humanism and the Reformation* (New York, 1982).
Boksenboim, Y., ed., *Letters of the Carmi Family, Cremona, 1570–77* [Hebrew] (Tel Aviv, 1983).
Burke, P., ed., *The Renaissance Sense of the Past* (London, 1969).
Cassirer, E., P. O. Kristeller, and J. H. Randall, eds., *The Renaissance Philosophy of Man* (Chicago, 1948).
Charland, T.-M., O.P., ed., *Artes praedicandi: Contribution à l'histoire de la rhétorique au Moyen Âge* (Paris and Ottawa, 1936).
Chartularium Universitatis Parisiensis, 5 vols. (Paris, 1889–1954): vols. 1–2 (1889–97) ed. H. Denifle and E. Chantelain; vols. 3–4 (1935–42) ed. C. Samaran and E. A. Van Moe; vol. 5 (1954) ed. A. L. Gabriel and G. Boyce.
Codex diplomaticus langobardiae (Turin, 1873).
Desmaizeaux, P., ed., *Scaligerana, Thuana, Perroniana, Tithoena, et Colomesiana* (Amsterdam, 1740).
Drei, G., ed., *Le carte degli archivi parmensi dei secoli X–XII,* 3 vols. (Parma, 1924–50).
Emerton, E., ed., *Humanism and Tyranny: Studies in the Italian Trecento* (Cambridge, MA, 1925; reprinted Gloucester, MA, 1964).
Emler, J., ed., *Regesta diplomatica nec non epistolaria Bohemiae et Moraviae,* 2 (Prague, 1882): letters of Henry of Isernia.
Fallico, A. B. and H. Shapiro, eds. and trans., *Renaissance Philosophy,* vol. 1,

The Italian Philosophers (New York, 1967); vol. 2, *The Transalpine Thinkers* (New York, 1969).

Friedberg, A., ed., *Corpus iuris canonici*, 2 vols. (Leipzig, 1879–81).

Garin, E., ed., *Educazione umanistica in Italia* (Bari, 1971).

———, *Filosofi italiani del Quattrocento* (Florence, 1942).

———, *Prosatori latini del Quattrocento* (Milan, 1952).

Gilbert, C., ed., *Italian Art, 1400–1500: Sources and Documents* (Englewood Cliffs, NJ, 1980).

———, *Renaissance Art* (New York, 1970).

Gligo, V., ed., *Govori protiv Turaka* [*Orations Against the Turks*] (Split, 1983).

Gloria, A., ed., *Codice diplomatico padovano dal secolo sesto a tutto l'undecimo* (Padua, 1877).

Gortan, V. and V. Vratović, eds., *Hrvatski latinisti, Croatici auctores qui Latine scripserunt*, 2 vols. (Zagreb, 1969–70).

Grosz, J. and W. A. Boggs, eds. and trans., *Hungarian Anthology: A Collection of Poems* (Toronto, 2d ed., 1966).

Halm, K., ed., *Rhetores latini minores* (Leipzig, 1863); reprinted Frankfurt am Main, 1964).

Halm, S. F., ed., *Collectio monumentorum veterum et recentium ineditorum*, 2 vols. (Brunswick, 1724–26).

Kardos, T., ed., *Régi magyar drámai emlékek* [*Monuments of Early Hungarian Drama*], 2 vols. to date (Budapest, 1960–).

Kennedy, L. A., ed., *Renaissance Philosophy: New Translations* (The Hague, 1973).

Kessler, E., ed., *Theoretiker humanistischer Geschichtsschreibung* (Munich, 1971).

King, M. L. and A. Rabil, Jr., eds., *Her Immaculate Hand: Selected Works by and About the Women Humanists of Quattrocento Italy* (Binghamton, NY, 1983).

Kohl, B. G. and R. G. Witt, with E. B. Welles, eds., *The Earthly Republic: Italian Humanists on Government and Society* (Philadelphia, 1978).

La Penna, A., ed., *Scholia in P. Ovidi Nasonis Ibin* (Florence, 1959).

Laporta, A., ed., *Otranto 1480* (Lecce, 1980).

Mahl, M. and H. Koon, eds., *The Female Spectator: English Women Writers Before 1800* (Bloomington, IN, 1977).

Manuzio, Aldo, ed., *Lettere volgari di diversi nobilissimi huomini . . . Libro terzo* (Venice, 1564).

Martène, E. and U. Durand, eds., *Veterum scriptorum ac monumentorum historicorum, dogmaticorum, moralium, amplissima collectio*, vol. 3 (Paris, 1724).

Marx, F., ed., *Incerti auctoris de ratione dicendi ad C. Herennium libri IV* (Leipzig, 1894; reprinted Hildesheim, 1966).

Mitis, T., ed., *Bohuslavi Hasisteinii Farrago poematum* (Prague, 1570).

Nugent, E. M., ed., *The Thought and Culture of the English Renaissance: An Anthology of Tudor Prose, 1481–1555* (Cambridge, 1956).

Palisca, C. V., ed., *Hucbald, Guido and John on Music: Three Medieval Treatises,* trans. W. Babb (New Haven, 1978).

Pasqui, U., ed., *Documenti per la storia della città di Arezzo nel medio evo,* vol. 1, *650–1180* (Florence, 1899).

Penna, M., ed., *Prosistas castellanos del siglo XV* (Madrid, 1959).

Perosa, A. and J. Sparrow, eds., *Renaissance Latin Verse: An Anthology* (Chapel Hill, 1979).

Pini, V., ed., *Multiplices epistole que diversis et variis negotiis utiliter possunt accomodari* (Bologna, 1969).

Poggi, G., ed., *Il carteggio di Michelangelo,* 5 vols. (Florence, 1967–83).

Pöhlmann, E., ed., *Denkmäler altgriechischer Musik* (Nuremberg, 1970).

Polívka, J., ed., *Dvě povidky v české literatuře XV. století* [*Two Novelle in Czech Literature of the Fifteenth Century*] (Prague, 1889).

Ponte, G., ed., *Il Quattrocento* (Bologna, 1966).

Porcacchi, Thomaso, ed., *Lettere di XIII huomini illustri* (Venice, 1565).

Rabil, A., ed., *Knowledge, Goodness, and Power: The Debate over "Nobility" Among Quattrocento Italian Humanists—A Reader* (forthcoming).

Rockinger, L., ed., *Briefsteller und Formelbücher des eilften bis vierzehnten Jahrhunderts* (Munich, 1863).

Ross, J. B. and M. McLaughlin, eds., *The Portable Renaissance Reader* (New York, 1953).

Rupprich, H., ed., *Humanismus und Renaissance in den deutschen Städten und an den deutschen Universitäten* (Leipzig, 1935; reprinted Darmstadt, 1964 and 1965).

Scolari, A., ed., *Scritti di varia letteratura e critica* (Bologna, 1937).

Solerti, A., ed., *Le vite di Dante, Petrarca e Boccaccio, scritto fino al secolo XVI* (Milan, 1904).

Spitz, L. W., ed., *The Protestant Reformation* (Englewood Cliffs, NJ, 1966).

Stechow, W., ed., *Northern Renaissance Art, 1400–1600* (Englewood Cliffs, NJ, 1966).

Strunk, O., ed., *Source Readings in Music History* (New York, 1950).

Tateo, F., ed., *Gli umanisti e la guerra otrantina: Testi dei secoli XV e XVI* (Bari, 1982).

Thompson, D. and A. E. Nagel, eds. and trans., *The Three Crowns of Florence: Humanist Assessments of Dante, Petrarca, and Boccaccio* (New York, 1972).

Torelli, P., ed., *Le carte degli archivi reggiani fino al 1050* (Reggio nell'Emilia, 1921).

——, *Regestro mantovano* (Rome, 1914).

Travitsky, B., ed., *The Paradise of Women: Writings by Englishwomen of the Renaissance* (Westport, CT, 1981).

Truhlář, J., ed., *Dva Listáře humanistické: (a) Dra. Racka Doubravského, (b) M. Václava Píseckého z Doplňkem listáře Jana Šlechty ze Všehrd* [*Two Humanist Letter Collections: (a) Dr. Racko Doubrausky, (b) M. Vaclav Pisecky with an Edition of the Collected Letters of Jan Šlechta ze Všehrd*] (Prague, 1897).

Valentinelli, G., ed., *Bibliotheca manuscripta ad S. Marci Venetiarum,* 6 vols. (Venice, 1868–73).

Vicini, E. P., ed., *Regestro della chiesa cattedrale di Modena*, Regesta chartarum Italiae 16 (Rome, 1931) and 21 (Rome, 1936).

Watkins, R. N., ed. and trans., *Humanism and Liberty: Writings on Freedom from Fifteenth-Century Florence* (Columbia, SC, 1978).

Weinberg, B., ed., *Trattati di poetica e retorica del Cinquecento*, 4 vols. (Bari, 1970–74).

Whitcomb, M., ed., *Sourcebook of the Renaissance* (New York, rev. ed. 1903).

Woodward, W. H., ed., *Vittorino da Feltre and Other Humanist Educators* (Cambridge, 1897; reprinted with intro. by E. F. Rice, Jr., New York, 1963).

Zeno, A., ed., *Degl'istorici delle cose veneziane, i quali hanno scritto per pubblico decreto*, 10 vols. in 11 (Venice, 1718–22).

PRIMARY SOURCES: INDIVIDUAL AUTHORS

Abravanel, Judah ben Isaac (Leone Ebreo), *Leone Ebreo: Dialoghi d'amore*, ed. C. Gebhardt (Heidelberg, 1924); *The Philosophy of Love*, trans. F. Friedberg-Seeley and J. H. Barnes (London, 1937); *Yehudah Abravanel, Siḥot al ha-Avavah* [Hebrew edition], trans. and ed. M. Dorman (Jerusalem, 1983).

Adalbertus, Samaritanus, *Praecepta dictaminum*, ed. F.-J. Schmale, *Monumenta Germaniae historica*, Quellen zur Geistesgeschichte des Mittelalters 3 (Weimar, 1961).

Aedicollius, Servatus, "Una nuova testimonianza della fortuna petrarchesca nei Paesi Bassi," ed. G. Mezzanotte, *Humanistica Lovaniensia* 29 (1980): 166–75.

Agricola, Rudolf, *De inventione dialectica/Lucubrationes* (Cologne, 1539; facsimile, Nieuwkoop, 1967).

Alberico de Monte Cassino, *Flores rhetorici*, ed. D. M. Inguanez and H. M. Willard (Monte Cassino, 1938).

Albertano da Brescia, *Liber de arte loquendi et tacendi*, in *Della vita a delle opere di Brunetto Latini*, ed. T. Sundby, trans. R. Renier (Florence, 1844), 475–506.

Alberti, Leon Battista, *The Family in Renaissance Florence*, trans. R. N. Watkins (Columbia, SC, 1969).

———, *On Painting*, ed. and trans. J. R. Spencer (New Haven, 1956).

———, *Opere volgari*, ed. C. Grayson, 3 vols. (Bari, 1960–73).

Alciato, Andrea, *Le lettere di Andrea Alciato giureconsulto*, ed. G. L. Barni (Florence, 1953).

Alcuin of York, *Opusculum primum: Grammatica*, in *Patrologia latina* 101 (Paris, 1863), 849–902.

Alessandro, Alessandro d', *Geniales dies* (Lyons, 1673).

Alexander of Villedieu, *Das doctrinale des Alexander de Villa-Dei*, ed. D. Reichling (Berlin, 1893).

Amerbach, Boniface, *Die Amerbachkorrespondenz*, ed. A. Hartmann, 5 vols. (Basel, 1942–58).

Ammirati, Scipione, *Opuscoli del Signor Scipione Ammirato*, 3 vols. (Florence, 1642).

———, *Il Rota overo dell'imprese dialogo* (Naples, 1562).

Andreis, Franjo Trankvil, *Krvava rijeka* [*Bloody River*], ed. N. Kolumbić (Zagreb, 1979).

Andrelini, Fausto, *Publi Fausti Andrelini Amores sive Livia,* ed. G. Tournay-Thoen (Brussels, 1982).

Anselm of Besate, *Gunzo: Epistola ad Augienses und Anselm von Besate: Rhetorimachia,* ed. K. Manitius, *Monumenta Germaniae historica,* Quellen zur Geistesgeschichte des Mittelalters 2 (Weimar, 1958).

Anselmi, Giorgio, *De musica,* ed. G. Massera (Florence, 1961).

Arévalo, Rodrigo Sánchez de, "*De arte, disciplina et modo alendi et erudiendi filios, pueros et juvenes,*" ed. A. Keniston, *Bulletin hispanique* 32 (1930): 193–217.

Arezzo, Ristoro d', *Della composizione del mondo,* ed. E. Narducci (Milan, 1864).

Aristides Quintilianus, *On Music in Three Books,* ed. and trans. T. J. Mathiesen (New Haven, 1983).

Aristoteles Latinus XXXIII. De arte poetica. Translatio Guillelmi de Moerbecke, ed. L. Minio-Paluello (Leiden, 1968).

Aristotle, *The Poetics,* trans. D. S. Margoliouth (London, 1911).

Arnauld, Antoine and Claude Lancelot, *Grammaire générale et raisonnée* (Paris, 1660).

Aron, Pietro, *Trattato della natura et cognitione di tutti gli tuoni di canto figurato* (Venice, 1525).

Ascham, Roger, *The Scholemaster,* ed. L. V. Ryan (Ithaca, NY, 1967); ed. R. J. Schoeck (Toronto, 1966).

Atto of Vercelli, *Capitulare,* in *Patrologia latina* 134 (Paris, 1853), 27–52.

Augustine, *Confessions,* trans. W. Watts (Cambridge, MA, 1919); trans. J. K. Ryan (Garden City, NY, 1960).

———, *Earlier Writings,* ed. and trans. J. H. S. Burleigh (Philadelphia, 1958).

———, *On Christian Doctrine,* trans. D. W. Robertson (New York, 1958).

Aurispa, Giovanni, *Il carteggio di Giovanni Aurispa,* ed. R. Sabbadini (Rome, 1931).

———, *Panégyriques latins,* ed. and trans. E. Galletier, 2 vols. (Paris, 1949).

Bacon, Francis, *Sylva sylvarum* (London, 1627).

———, *The Tvvo Bookes Of the Proficiencie and Aduancement of Learning diuine and humane* (London, 1605).

———, *The Works of Francis Bacon,* ed. J. Spedding, R. L. Ellis, and D. D. Heath, 14 vols. (London, 1858–74; reprinted Stuttgart-Bad Cannstatt, 1963).

Bade, Josse, *Horatii Flacci poemata: Cum commentariis eruditissimorum grammaticorum reconditissimis: Antonii Mancinelli Jodoci Badij Ascensii & Joannis Britannici* (Milan, 1518).

———, *La nef des folles: Stultiferae naves de Josse Bade,* ed. C. Béné and O. Sauvage (Grenoble, 1979).

———, *Quinti Horatii Flacci opusculum aureum* (Paris, 1500): exegetical work on the *Ars poetica.*

Barbaro, Daniele, *I dieci libri dell'architettura di M. Vitruvio . . .* (Venice, 1556).

Barbaro, Ermolao the Elder, *Orationes contra poetas (with Epistolae)*, ed. G. Ronconi (Florence, 1972).

Barbaro, Ermolao the Younger, *Castigationes Plinianae et in Pomponium Melam*, ed. G. Pozzi (Padua, 1973).

————, *De coelibatu, De officio legati*, ed. V. Branca (Florence, 1969).

————, *Epistolae, orationes, carmina*, ed. V. Branca (Florence, 1943).

————, *Themistii Paraphraseos de Anima libri tres, interprete Hermolao Barbaro* (Paris, 1535), ed. R. Heinze (Berlin, 1899).

Barbaro, Francesco, *Centotrenta lettere inedite di Francesco Barbaro precedute dall'ordinamento critico cronologico dell'intero suo epistolario*, ed. R. Sabbadini (Salerno, 1884).

————, *De re uxoria liber*, ed. A. Gnesotto in *Atti e memorie della R. Accademia di Scienze, Lettere ed Arti in Padova* n.s. 32 (1916): 6–105; preface and second part trans. in *Earthly Republic*, ed. Kohl, Witt, and Welles (q.v.), 177–228.

————, *Diatriba praeliminaris in duas partes divisa ad Francisci Barbari et aliorum ad ipsum epistolae ab anno Christi 1425 ad annum 1453*, ed. A. M. Quirini, 2 vols. (Brescia, 1741–43).

Barlaam, *Opera*, in *Patrologia graeca* 151 (Paris, 1865), 1243–1364.

Barlaeus, Caspar, *Caspar Barlaeus: From the Correspondence of a Melancholic*, ed. and trans. F. F. Blok (Assen, 1976).

Barnes, Robert, *Vitae romanorum pontificum* (Basel, n.d. [1520s]).

Barozzi, Pietro, *Il vescovo Pietro Barozzi e il trattato "De factionibus extinguendis,"* ed. F. Gaeta (Venice, 1958).

Bartolus, *Repertorium Bartoli* (Lyons, 1485).

Barzizza, Gasparino, *De compositione*, ed. R. Sonkowsky (Chapel Hill, 1959).

————, *Epilogus ac summa praeceptorum*, ed. R. Sonkowsky in *Classical, Medieval and Renaissance Studies in Honor of B. L. Ullman* (q.v.), 2:268–76.

————, *Gasparini Barzizii Bergomatis et Guiniforti filii opera*, ed. J. A. Furietti, 2 vols. (Rome, 1773).

Barzizza, Guiniforte, *Gasparini Barzizii Bergomatis et Guiniforti filii opera*, ed. J. A. Furietti, 2 vols. (Rome, 1773).

Basset, Mary, *St. Thomas More's History of the Passion*, ed. P. H. Hallett (London, 1944).

Baudouin, François, *De institutione historiae universae* (Strasbourg, 1561).

Bebel, Heinrich, *De laudibus atque philosophia germanorum in opuscula nova* (Strasbourg, 1508).

————, *Heinrich Bebel nach seinem Leben und Schriften*, ed. G. Zapf (Augsburg, 1802; facsimile, Leipzig, 1973).

Beccadelli, Antonio (Panormita), *Liber rerum gestarum Ferdinandi regis*, ed. G. Resta (Palermo, 1968).

————, *Ottanta lettere inedite del Panormita tratte dei codici milanesi*, ed. R. Sabbadini (Catania, 1910).

Bembo, Pietro, *Prose della volgar lingua*, ed. M. Marti (Padua, 1967).

Benci, Francesco, *Ab Aqua Pendente e Societate Iesu orationes XXII* (Rome, 1590).

Bene of Florence, *Bene Florentini Candelabrum,* ed. G. C. Alessio (Padua, 1983).

Benedetti, Giovanni Battista, *Diversarum speculationum mathematicarum & physicorum liber* (Turin, 1585).

Beni, Paolo, *Disputatio* (Padua, 1600).

Beroaldo, Filippo the Elder, *Annotationes centum* [*Gesamtkatalog der Wiegendrucke* 4113] (Bologna, 1488).

——, *Annotationes in commentarios Servii Virgiliani Commentatoris* [*Gesamtkatalog der Wiegendrucke* 4115] (Bologna, 1482).

Béthune, Evrard de, *Eberhardi Bethuniensis Graecismus,* ed. J. Wrobel (Breslau, 1887).

Biondo, Flavio, *Historiarum ab inclinatione Romanorum imperii decades* (Venice, 1483).

——, *Scritti inediti e rari,* ed. B. Nogara (Rome, 1927).

Birkenmaier, A., "Der Streit des Alonso von Cartagena mit Leonardo Bruni Aretino," in *Vermischte Untersuchungen zur Geschichte der mittelalterlichen Philosophie* (Münster, 1922), 129–210 (includes edition of Cartagena's tract and Bruni's responses).

Boccaccio, Giovanni, *Il comento alla Divina commedia e gli altri scritti intorno a Dante,* ed. D. Guerri, 3 vols. (Bari, 1918).

——, *De mulieribus claris,* in *Tutte le opere di Giovanni Boccaccio,* ed. V. Branca (Verona, 2d ed., 1970), vol. 10; *Concerning Famous Women,* trans. G. Guarino (New Brunswick, NJ, 1963).

——, *Esposizioni sopra la "Comedia" di Dante,* ed. G. Padoan (Milan, 1965).

——, *Genealogie deorum gentilium libri,* ed. V. Romano, 2 vols. (Bari, 1951).

——, *On Poetry: Being the Preface and the Fourteenth and Fifteenth Books of Boccaccio's "Genealogia deorum gentilium,"* trans. C. G. Osgood (Indianapolis, 1956).

——, *Opere minori,* ed. A. F. Massera (Bari, 1928).

——, *Opere minori in volgare,* ed. M. Marti, 4 vols. (Milan, 1969–72).

——, *Tutte le opere,* ed. V. Branca, 10 vols. (Milan, 1964–83).

Boncompagno, *Breviloquium di Boncompagno da Signa,* ed. G. Vecchi (Bologna, 1954).

——, *Liber de obsidione Ancona (a. 1173),* ed. G. C. Zimolo, in Muratori, *Rerum italicarum scriptores* n.s. 6 (Bologna, 1937).

——, *Rhetorica novissima,* ed. A. Gaudenzi in *Bibliotheca juridica medii aevi: Scripta anedota glossatorum* 2 (Bologna, 1892), 249–97.

Bonfini, Antonio, *Rerum Hungaricarum decades quattor,* ed. I. Sambucus (Basel, 1568; Frankfurt, 1581).

Bonifacio, Baldassare, *De archivis* (Venice, 1632).

Borghesi, Diomede, *Oratione intorno a gli onori et ai pregi della poesia e della eloquenze* (Siena, 1596).

Bracciolini, Poggio, *Opera omnia,* ed. R. Fubini, 4 vols. (Turin, 1964–69).

——, *Two Renaissance Book Hunters: The Letters of Poggius Bracciolini to Nicolaus de Niccolis,* ed. and trans. P. W. G. Gordon (New York, 1974).

Brandolini, Aurelio Lippo, *De ratione scribendi libri tres* (Frankfurt am Main, 1568).

Breen, Q., "Giovanni Pico della Mirandola on the Conflict of Philosophy and Rhetoric," *Journal of the History of Ideas* 13 (1952): 384–412; reprinted in his *Christianity and Humanism* (Grand Rapids, MI, 1968), 11–38.

Britannico of Brescia, Giovanni, *Horatii Flacci poemata: Cum commentariis eruditissimorum grammaticorum reconditissimis: Antonii Mancinelli Jodoci Badij Ascensii & Joannis Britannici* (Milan, 1518).

Brown, Edward, *A Brief Account of Some Travels in Hungaria, Servia, Bulgaria, Macedonia, Thessaly, Austria, Styria, Carinthia, Carniola and Friuli. As also Some Observations on the Gold, Silver, Copper, Quick-Silver Mines, Baths, and Mineral Waters in Those Parts* (London, 1673).

Bruni, Leonardo Aretino, *Dialogues to Pier Paolo Vergerio*, in *Three Crowns of Florence*, ed. and trans. Thompson and Nagel (q.v.), 19–52.

———, *Epistolarum libri VIII*, ed. L. Mehus, 2 vols. (Florence, 1741).

———, *Humanistich-philosophische Schriften mit einer Chronologie seiner Werke und Briefe*, ed. H. Baron (Leipzig and Berlin, 1928; reprinted Wiesbaden, 1969).

———, *Rerum suo tempore gestarum commentarius*, in *Rerum italicarum scriptores* 19.3, ed. C. di Pietro (Bologna, 1926).

———, *War and Society in Renaissance Florence: The "De militia" of Leonardo Bruni*, ed. C. C. Bayley (Toronto, 1961).

Bruto, Pietro, *Epistola contra Judeos* [*Gesamtkatalog der Wiegendrucke* 5658] (Vicenza, 1477).

———, *Victoria contra Judaeos* [*Gesamtkatalog der Wiegendrucke* 5659] (Vicenza, 1489).

Budé, Guillaume, *De l'institution du prince* (Paris, 1547).

———, *De transitu Hellenismi ad Christianismum* (Paris, 1535; facsimile with trans. by M. Lebel, Sherbrooke, 1973).

Bunić, Jakov, *Otmica Kerbera, Kristov život i djela (Odabrani odlomci)* [*Rape of Cerberus, The Life of Christ, and Works (Selections)*], ed. B. Glavičić (Zagreb, 1978).

Buonaccorso da Montemagno, *Prose di Buonaccorso da Montemagno*, ed. G. B. C. Giuliari (Bologna, 1874).

Burmeister, Joachim, *Musica autoschediastike* (1601), published as *Musica poetica* (1606), the latter reprinted, ed. M. Ruhnke (Kassel, 1955).

Bury, Richard de, *Philobiblon*, ed. and trans. E. C. Thomas and M. Maclagan (Oxford, 1960).

Calderini, Domizio, *Commentarioli in Ibyn Ovidii* [*Repertorium Bibliographicum* 4242] (Rome, 1474).

———, *Elucubratio in quaedam propertii loca quae difficiliora videantur* (Brescia, 1476).

———, *Lampas, sive fax artium liberalium, hoc est, thesaurus criticus*, ed. J. Gruter, 6 vols. (Frankfurt, 1602–12).

Calvin, John, *Commentary on Seneca's "De clementia,"* trans. F. L. Battles and A. M. Hugo (Leiden, 1969).

———, *Three French Treatises*, ed. and trans. F. M. Higman (London, 1970).

Campanella, Tommaso, *Poetica*, ed. L. Firpo (Rome, 1944).

Canter, Jacob, *Dialogus de solitudine (c. 1491)*, ed. B. Ebels-Hoving (Munich, 1981); corrections by J. IJsewijn in *Wolfenbütteler Renaissance Mitteilungen* 8 (1984): 30–32.

Capriano, Giovanni Pietro, *Della vera poetica libro uno* (Venice, 1555).

Carafa, Diomede, *Tractato dello optimo cortesano*, ed. G. Paparelli (Salerno, 1971).

Cartagena, Alonso de, *Defensorium unitatis christianae*, ed. P. M. Alonso (Madrid, 1943).

———, *"Oracional" de Alonso de Cartagena*, ed. S. Gonzalez-Quevedo Alonso (Valencia and Chapel Hill, 1983).

———, *La retórica de M. Tullio Cicerón*, ed. R. Mascagna (Naples, 1969).

———, *Un tratado de Alonso de Cartagena sobre la educación y los estudios literarios*, ed. J. N. H. Lawrance (Barcelona, 1979).

Cassiodorus, *Institutiones*, ed. R. A. B. Mynors (Oxford, 1937).

Castelvetro, Lodovico, *La poetica d'Aristotele vulgarizzata e sposta*, ed. W. Romani, 2 vols. (Bari, 1979).

Celio, Gaspare, *Memoria dei nomi dell'artefici delle pitture che sono in alcune chiese, facciate, e palazzi di Roma* [1638], ed. E. Zocca (Milan, 1967).

Celtis, Conrad, *Briefwechsel*, ed. H. Rupprich (Munich, 1934).

———, *De vita et scriptis Conradi Celtis Protucii*, ed. E. Klügelius, 2 vols. in 1 (Freiburg im Breisgau, 1827).

———, *Opera Hrosvita . . . a Conr. Celte inventa* (Nuremberg, 1501).

Cereta, Laura, "Critical Edition of Unpublished Materials in the Cereta Corpus," in A. Rabil, Jr., *Laura Cereta: Quattrocento Humanist* (Binghamton, 1981), pt. 3.

———, *Laurae Ceretae brixiensis feminae clarissimae epistolae jam primum e manuscriptis in lucem productae*, ed. G. F. Tomasini (Padua, 1640).

Cespedes, Baltasar de, *El maestro Baltasar de Cespedes y su "Discurso de las letras humanas,"* ed. G. de Andres (El Escorial, 1965).

Cicero, *L'Orateur, Du meilleur genre d'orateurs*, ed. and trans. A. Yon (Paris, 1964).

Cinzio, Giambattista Giraldi, *Scritti estetici*, 2 vols. (Milan, 1864).

Cipico, Kariolan (Coriolanus Cepio), *O Azijskom ratu* [*About the Asian War*], ed. and trans. V. Gligo (Split, 1977).

Clarke, Samuel, *The Lives of Sundry Eminent People in This Later Age*, 2 vols. (London, 1683).

Colet, John, *Commentary on First Corinthians*, ed. and trans. B. O'Kelly and C. A. L. Jarrott (Binghamton, 1985).

Colonna, Francesco, *Francesco Colonna, biografia e opere*, ed. M. T. Casella and G. Pozzi, 2 vols. (Padua, 1959).

Commynes, Philippe de, *The Memoirs of Philippe de Commynes*, trans. I. Cazeaux (Columbia, SC, 1969).

Conrad von Mure, *Die Summa de arte prosandi des Konrad von Mure*, ed. W. Kronbichler (Zurich, 1968).

Contarini, Francesco, *De rebus in Hetruria a Senensibus gestis cum adversus*

Florentinos, tum adversus Ildibrandinum petilianensam Comitem, libri tres, ed. G. M. Bruto (Venice, 1623; reprint of Lyons, 1562).

Conte, Matteo, *Le osservationi grammaticali e poetiche della lingua italiana del Signor Matteo Conte di San Martino e di Vische* (Rome, 1555).

Conversini, Giovanni, *Dragmalogia de eligibili vite genere,* ed. and trans. H. L. Eaker, intro. and notes B. G. Kohl (London and Lewisburg, PA, 1980).

Córdoba, Luis Cabrera de, *De historia para entenderla y escribirla,* ed. S. M. Diaz (Madrid, 1948).

Corio, Bernardino, *Storia di Milano,* ed. A. M. Guerra (Turin, 1978).

Correa, Tommaso, *Globus canonum et arcanorum linguae sanctae ac Divine Scripturae* (Rome, 1586).

Cortesi, Paolo, *De hominibus doctis,* ed. G. Ferraù (Palermo, 1979).

———, *De hominibus doctis dialogus,* ed. and trans. M. T. Graziosi (Rome, 1973).

Costeley, Guillaume, *Musique* (Paris, 1570).

Crassus, Peter, *Petri Crassi defensio Heinrici IV regis,* ed. L. de Heinemann, in *Monumenta Germaniae historica 1: Libelli de lite* (Hanover, 1891).

Damian, Peter, *Epistolarum libri octo,* in *Patrologia latina* 144 (Paris, 1867), 205–498.

———, *Opusculum octavum: De parentelae gradibus,* in *Patrologia latina* 145 (Paris, 1867), 191–208.

———, *Sancti Petri Damiani Sermones,* ed. I. Lucchesi (Turnhout, 1983).

Dandolo, Marco, *Catena seu expositio graecorum patrum in psalmos: In Psalterium expositionum collectio e graeco in latinum versa M. D. interpreta* (Venice, Bibl. Marciana, cod. Lat. I.33 [2133]).

Daniello, Bernardino, *La poetica* (Venice, 1536).

David ben Judah, *Ein ha-Koreh,* ed. P. Perreau, in *Hebraeische Bibliographie* 8 (1865): 64–65.

Decembrio, Angelo, *Politiae literariae libri septem* (Augsburg, 1540).

Decembrio, Pier Candido, *Opuscula historica,* ed. A. Butti, F. Fossati, and G. Petraglione, *Rerum italicarum scriptores* 20.1 (Bologna, 1925–58).

Decsi, János, *Az Caius Crispus Sallustiusnak két historiája* [*Two Stories of Caius Crispus Sallustius*], ed. A. Kurz (Budapest, 1979).

Delmedigo, Elijah, *Beḥinat da-Dat* [*Examination of the Faith*], ed. J. J. Ross (Tel Aviv, 1984).

Delmonio, Giulio Camillo, *Due trattati dell'Eccellentissimo M. Iulio Camillo: L'uno delle materia che possono venir sotto lo stile dell'eloquente: L'altro della imitatione* (Venice, 1544).

———, *Il secondo tomo dell'opere di M. Giulio Camillo* (Venice, 1560).

Demetrius Phalereus, *A Medieval Latin Version of Demetrius' De elocutione,* ed. B. B. Wall (Washington, DC, 1937).

Dolce, Lodovico, *La Poetica d'Horatio tradotto per Messer Lodovico Dolce* (Venice, 1535).

Domenichi, Domenico dei, *De reformationibus romanae curiae* (Brescia, 1495).

Dominici, Giovanni, *Lucula noctis,* ed. E. Hunt (Indianapolis, 1940).

Donato, Antonio, *Vitae ducum venetorum* (Bibl. Marciana, cod. Lat. X, 145 [3533], fols. 79–93).

Donato, Girolamo, *Contra Caroli regis Francorum in senatum venetum calumnias apologia*, in D. Malipiero, *Annali veneti dall'anno 1457 al 1500*, ed. A. Sagredo, *Archivio storico italiano* 7.1–2 (1843–44): 443–63.

Dondi, Giovanni de', *Tractatus astrarii, Biblioteca Capitolare di Padova, cod. D. 39*, ed. A. Barzon, E. Morpurgo, A. Petrucci, and G. Fracescato (Vatican City, 1960).

Doni, Giovanni Battista, *Compendio del Trattato dei generi e dei modi della musica* (Rome, 1635).

———, *Lyra Barberina*, ed. A. F. Gori and G. B. Passeri (Florence, 1763).

Dorp, Martin, *Martini Dorpii Naldiceni Orationes IV cum Apologia et litteris adnexis*, ed. J. IJsewijn (Leipzig, 1986).

Dressler, Gallus, "Praecepta musicae poeticae," ed. B. Engelke, *Geschichtsblätter für Stadt und Land Magdeburg* 49 (1914–15): 213–50.

Dürer, Albrecht, *Dürers schriftlicher Nachlass*, ed. H. Rupprich, 3 vols. (Berlin, 1956–70).

Ennius, *The Tragedies of Ennius: The Fragments*, ed. H. D. Jocelyn (Cambridge, 1967).

Enrico da Settimello, *Elegia*, ed. G. Cremaschi (Bergamo, 1949).

Erasmus, Desiderius, *The Adages of Erasmus*, ed. and trans. M. M. Phillips (Cambridge, 1964).

———, *Ciceronianus*, ed. P. Mesnard, ASD 1.2 (1971), 581–710; *The Imitation of Cicero*, trans. I. Scott (New York, 1910); "Essai sur le 'Ciceronianus' d'Erasme, avec une édition critique," ed. and trans. J.-G. Michel (Ph.D. diss., University of Paris, 1951); *Il Ciceroniano o dello stile migliore*, ed. and trans. A. Gambaro (Brescia, 1965).

———, *Collected Works of Erasmus*, 22 vols. to date (Toronto, 1974–), cited as CWE.

———, *The Colloquies of Erasmus*, trans. C. R. Thompson (Chicago, 1965); critical ed. ASD 1.3 (1972).

———, *The Correspondence of Erasmus*, trans. R. A. B. Mynors, 9 vols. to date (Toronto, 1974–).

———, *De libero arbitrio*: critical editions ed. J. Walter, *Quellenschriften zur Geschichte des Protestantismus*, 8 vols. (Leipzig, 1904–10), vol. 8 (reprinted 1935); and AS 4:1–195, with a German translation; *Luther and Erasmus: Free Will and Salvation*, ed. and trans. E. G. Rupp et al. (London, 1969).

———, *Desiderius Erasmus: Christian Humanism and the Reformation*, ed. J. C. Olin (New York, 1965).

———, *Desiderius Erasmus: Concerning the Aim and Method of Education*, ed. W. H. Woodward (New York, 1904; reprinted 1964).

———, *Desiderius Erasmus Roterodamus Ausgewählte Werke*, ed. A. Holborn and H. Holborn (Munich, 1933).

———, *The Education of a Christian Prince*, trans. L. K. Born (New York, 1936; reprinted 1964).

————, *The Enchiridion of Erasmus,* trans. R. Himelick (Bloomington, IN, 1963).

————, *Erasmi opuscula,* ed. W. K. Ferguson (The Hague, 1933).

————, *Erasmus and Cambridge,* ed. H. C. Porter, trans. D. F. S. Thomson (Toronto, 1963).

————, *Erasmus von Rotterdam Ausgewählte Schriften,* ed. W. Welzig, 8 vols. (Darmstadt, 1967–80), cited as AS.

————, *Un inédit d'Erasme: La première version du nouveau testament copiée par Pierre Meghen 1506–1509,* ed. H. Gibaud (Angers, 1982).

————, *Julius Excluded from Heaven,* trans. P. Pascal, ed. J. K. Sowards (Bloomington, IN, 1968).

————, *Opera omnia,* ed. Jean LeClerc, 10 vols. (Leiden, 1703–6; facsimile, London, 1962).

————, *Opera omnia Des. Erasmi Roterodami,* 18 vols. to date (Amsterdam, 1969–), cited as ASD.

————, *Opus espitolarum Des. Erasmi Roterodami,* ed. P. S. Allen, H. M. Allen, and H. W. Garrod, 12 vols. (Oxford, 1906–58).

————, *Paraclesis:* critical edition, AS 139–49; trans. in *Christian Humanism,* ed. Olin, 92–106.

————, *Paraphrases of Romans and Galatians,* ed. R. D. Sider, trans. J. Payne, A. Rabil, Jr., and W. S. Smith, Jr., CWE 42 (Toronto, 1984).

————, *The Poems of Desiderius Erasmus,* ed. C. Reedijk (Leiden, 1956).

————, *The Praise of Folly,* ed. and trans. C. H. Miller (New Haven, 1979); critical ed. ASD 4.3 (1979).

————, *Vies de Jean Vitrier et de John Colet,* ed. and trans. A. Godin (Angers, 1982).

Faba, Guido, *Parlamenti ed epistole,* in *I suoni, le forme e le parole dell'odierno dialetto delle città di Bologna,* ed. A Gaudenza (Turin, 1889), 127–60.

————, *Summa dictaminis,* ed. A. Gaudenza, *Il Propugnatore* n.s. 3.1 (1890): 287–338, 3.2 (1890): 345–93.

Fabrini, Giovanni, *L'opere d'Orazio poeta lirico comentate da Giovanni Fabrini da Fighine in lingua vulgare toscana* (Venice, 1566).

Facio, Bartolomeo, *Invectiva in Laurentium Vallam,* ed. E. I. Rao (Naples, 1978).

Fausto, Vittore, *Hoc pugillari Terentius numeris concinatus, et L. Victoris Fausti De comoedia libellus* (Venice, 1515).

Fedele, Cassandra, *Clarissimae feminae Cassandrae Fidelis venetae epistolae et orationes posthumae,* ed. G. F. Tomasini (Padua, 1636).

Ferrariis, Antonio de (Galateo), *Epistole,* ed. A. Altamura (Lecce, 1959).

Ficino, Marsilio, *Epistolae* (Venice, 1495); *The Letters of Marsilio Ficino,* trans. by members of the Language Department of the School of Economic Science, London, 3 vols. (London, 1975–81; New York, 1985).

————, "Marsilio Ficino's Commentary on Plato's *Symposium,*" ed. and trans. S. R. Jayne, *University of Missouri Studies* 19 (1944): 1–235.

————, *Opera omnia,* 2 vols. (Basel, 2d ed. 1576; reprinted Turin, 1959).

————, *Supplementum Ficinianum,* ed. P. O. Kristeller, 2 vols. (Florence, 1937).

———, *Théologie platonicienne de l'immortalité des âmes*, ed. and trans. R. Marcel, 3 vols. (Paris, 1964).

Filelfo, Francesco, *Cent-dix lettres grecques de François Filelfe*, ed. E. Legrand (Paris, 1892); trans. into Italian by A. Agostinelli and G. Benaducci (Tolentino, 1902).

———, special edition of *Atti e memorie della R. Deputazione di storia patria per la provincia della Marche* 5 (1901): 459–535, a bibliographical contribution by A. Benaducci; and 535ff., containing many unpublished and rare texts of Filelfo's.

———, *Testi inediti e rari di Cristoforo Landino e Francesco Filelfo*, ed. E. Garin (Florence, 1949).

Fogliano, Lodovico, *Musica theorica* (Venice, 1529).

Fonte, Bartolommeo della, "The Unknown Quattrocento Poetics of Bartolommeo della Fonte," ed. C. Trinkaus, *Studies in the Renaissance* 13 (1966): 95–122.

Fox, Richard, *Letters of Richard Fox, 1486–1527*, ed. P. S. Allen and H. M. Allen (Oxford, 1929).

Foxe, John, *The Acts and Monuments of John Foxe*, ed. G. Townsend, 8 vols. (reprint New York, 1965).

Fracastoro, Girolamo, *Naugerius sive de poetica dialogus*, trans. R. Kelso, intro. M. W. Mundy (Urbana, IL, 1924).

———, *Opera omnia* (Venice, 1555).

Frachetta, Girolamo, *Dialogo del furore poetico* (Padua, 1581).

Francesco da Fiano, "Il *Contra oblucutores et detractores poetarum* di Francesco da Fiano," ed. I. Taù, *Archivio italiano per la storia della pietà* 4 (1965): 256–350.

———, "Un opuscolo inedito di Francesco da Fiano in difesa della poesia," ed. M. L. Plaisant, *Rinascimento* 2d ser. 1 (1961): 119–62; and ed. I. Taù, *Archivio italiano per la storia della pietà* 4 (1965): 256–350.

Fuller, Thomas, *The History of the Worthies of England*, ed. P. A. Nuttall, 3 vols. (reprint New York, 1965).

Gaffurio, Franchino, *De harmonia musicorum instrumentorum opus*, trans. C. A. Miller (Stuttgart, 1977).

———, *Theorica musice* (Milan, 1492).

Galilei, Galileo, *Dialogue Concerning the Two Chief World Systems*, trans. S. Drake (Berkeley, 1953).

Galilei, Vincenzo, *Dialogo della musica antica, et della moderna* (Florence, 1581).

———, *Discorso intorno all'opere di messer Gioseffo Zarlino* (Florence, 1589).

———, *Discorso intorno all'uso delle dissonanze*, ed. F. Rempp in *Die Kontrapunkttraktate Vincenzo Galileis* (Cologne, 1980).

Gambara, Lorenzo, *Tractatio* (Rome, 1576); modern edition in *Trattati di poetica e retorica del Cinquecento*, ed. B. Weinberg (q.v.), 3:205–34.

Garcia, Pedro, *Une controverse sur Origène à la Renaissance: Jean Pic de la Mirandole et Pierre Garcia*, ed. and trans. H. Crouzel, S.J. (Paris, 1977).

Georg von Peuerbach, "Aus dem Briefwechsel des grossen Astronomen Georg von Peuerbach," ed. A. Czerny, *Archiv für österreichische Geschichte* 72 (1888): 281–332.

George of Trebizond, *Collectanea Trapezuntiana: Texts, Bibliographies, and Documents of George of Trebizond*, ed. J. Monfasani (Binghamton, 1985).

——, *Rhetoricorum libri V* (Venice, 1523).

Ghiberti, Lorenzo, *I Commentari*, ed. O. Morisani (Naples, 1947).

Giordano da Terracina, *Un certame dettatorio tra due notai pontifici (1260): Lettere inedite di Giordano da Terracina e di Giovanni da Capua*, ed. P. Sambin (Rome, 1955).

Giorgi, Francesco di, *Trattati di architettura ingegneria e arte militare*, ed. C. Maltese, transcription by L. M. Degrassi, 2 vols. (Milan, 1957).

Giovanni da Capua, *Un certame dettatorio tra due notai pontifici (1260): Lettere inedite di Giordano da Terracina e di Giovanni da Capua*, ed. P. Sambin (Rome, 1955).

Giovanni da Cermenate, *Historia Iohannis de Cermenate (sec. XIV)*, ed. L. A. Ferrai (Rome, 1889).

Giovio, Paolo, *Elogia doctorum virorum*, trans. F. A. Gragg (Boston, 1935).

Giraldi, Lilio Gregorio, *Dialogi duo de poëtis nostrorum temporum* (Florence, 1551).

——, *Historiae poetarum tam Graecorum quam Latinorum Dialogi decem* (Basel, 1545).

Guistiniani, Bernardo, *De origine urbis venetiarum rebusque gestis a Venetis libri quindecim*, in *Thesaurus antiquitatum et historiarum Italiae*, ed. J. G. Graevius, 5.1 (Leiden, 1722), 1–172.

Glarean, Heinrich, *Dodekachordon* (Basel, 1547), trans. C. A. Miller (n.p., American Institute of Musicology, 1965).

Gogava, Antonio, *Aristoxeni . . . Harmonicorum elementorum libri iii . . . Cl. Ptolemaei Harmonicorum . . . lib. iii. Aristoteli de objecto auditus* (Venice, 1562).

Gravina, Vincenzo, *Della ragione poetica libri due* (Rome, 1708).

Gregory VII, Pope, *Das Register Gregors VII*, ed. E. Caspar in *Monumenta Germaniae historica*, Epistolae selectae 2.1–2 (Berlin, 1920–23).

Grifoli, Jacopo, *Lucinianensis orationes variae variis in locis habitae* (Venice, 1557).

——, *Q. Horatii Flacci Liber de arte poetica Iacobi Grifoli Lucinianensis interpretatione explicatus* (Florence, 1550).

Guarico, Pomponio, *Super arte poetica Horatii* (Rome, 1541).

Guarino of Verona, *Epistolario di Guarino Veronese*, ed. R. Sabbadini, 3 vols. (Venice, 1915–19).

Guicciardini, Francesco, *History of Italy*, trans. C. Grayson (New York, 1964).

——, *Ricordi*, trans. N. H. Thomson (New York, 1949).

Gunzo of Novara, *Epistola ad Augienses und Anselm von Besate: Rhetorimachia*, ed. K. Manitius, *Monumenta Germaniae historica*, Epistolae 2 (Weimar, 1958), 19–57.

Haneron, Anthonius, "Magistri Anthonii Haneron (c. 1400–1490) Opera Grammatica et Rhetorica," ed. J. IJsewijn-Jacobs, *Humanistica Lovaniensia*

24 (1975): 29–68; 25 (1976): 1–83 (edition of the *Syntax*), 284 (a correction by M. Haveals); 27 (1978): 10–17; to be continued with an edition of *De epistolis brevis.*

Harrison, William, *The Description of England,* ed. G. Edelen (Ithaca, NY, 1968).

Hassenstein, Bohuslav Lobkowitz, *Epistolae: Accedunt epistolae ad Bohuslaum scriptae,* ed. A. Potuček (Budapest, 1946).

———, *Listář Bohuslava Hasištejnského z Lobkovic* [*Correspondence of Bohuslav Hasištejnský of Lobkovice*], ed. J. Truhlář (Prague, 1892).

———, *Scripta moralia, Oratio ad Argentinenses, Memoria Alexandri de Imola,* ed. B. Ryba (Leipzig, 1937).

———, *Spisy Bohuslava Hasištejnského z Lobkovic, Svazek I. Spisy prosaické* [*Writings of . . . Lobkovic, vol. 1, Prose Writings*], ed. B. Ryba (Prague, 1933).

Hegius, Alexander, "Alexander Hegius (d. 1498), *Invectiva in modos significandi,*" ed. J. IJsewijn, *Forum for Modern Language Studies* 7 (1971): 229–318; corrections in *Humanistica Lovaniensia* 22 (1973): 334–35.

Heinsius, Daniel, *The Value of History,* trans. G. Robinson (Cambridge, MA, 1943).

Heltai, Gáspár, *Cancionale, azaz historias énekes könyv* [*Cancionale, or A Collection of Poems for Singing*] (Kolossvar, 1574; facsimile, 1962).

———, *Halo,* ed. P. Köszeghy (Budapest, 1979).

———, *Historia inclyti Matthiae Hunyadis* (Cluj, 1565).

Henry of Huntingdon, *The Chronicle,* trans. T. Forester (London, 1853).

Hermogenes of Tarsus, *Opera,* ed. H. Rabe (Leipzig, 1912).

Hillel ben Shemu'el of Verona, *Sefer Tagmule ha-Nefesh* [*The Book of the Rewards of the Soul*], ed. J. Sermoneta (Jerusalem, 1981); a second volume is forthcoming.

Honorius III, Pope, *Epistolae saec. XIII e regestis pontificum romanorum selectae,* ed. C. Rodenberg, *Monumenta Germaniae historica,* Epistolae 1 (Berlin, 1883).

Hotman, François, *Francogallia,* ed. R. E. Giesey, trans. J. H. M. Salmon (Cambridge, 1972).

Hucbald, Guido, and John on Music: Three Medieval Treatises, trans. W. Babb, ed. C. V. Palisca (New Haven and London, 1978).

Hutten, Ulrich von, *On the Eve of the Reformation,* trans. F. G. Stokes, intro. H. Holborn (New York, 1964).

Isolella of Cremona, Petrus de, *Une grammaire latine inédite du XIIIe siècle,* ed. C. Fierville (Paris, 1886).

Janus of Paris, Aulus, *A. Iani Parrhasii Cosentini in Q. Horatii Flacci Artem poeticam commentaria locupletissima* (Naples, 1531).

Jennaro, Pietro Jacopo de, *Rime e lettere,* ed. M. Corti (Bologna, 1956).

John of Jandun, *Quaestiones super libros physicorum* (Venice, 1488).

John of Salisbury, *Letters,* ed. W. J. Millor and H. E. Butler, rev. C. N. L. Brooke, 2 vols. (London and New York, 1955–79).

———, *Metalogicon,* ed. C. I. Webb (Oxford, 1929).

———, *Policraticus,* ed. C. I. Webb, 2 vols. (Oxford, 1909).

Kotruljić, Benko (Benedetto Cotrugli), *Della mercatura et del mercante perfetto* (Venice, 1573; reprinted Zagreb, 1975).

Krantz, Albert, *Saxonia* (Cologne, 1520).

——, *Wandalia* (Cologne, 1519).

Kyeser, Conrad, *Bellifortis*, ed. and trans. G. Guarg, 2 vols. (Düsseldorf, 1967).

Landino, Cristoforo, *Disputationes Camaldulenses*, ed. P. Lohe (Florence, 1980).

——, *Scritti critici e teorici*, ed. R. Cardini, 2 vols. (Rome, 1974).

——, *Testi inediti e rari di Cristoforo Landino e Francesco Filelfo*, ed. E. Garin (Florence, 1949).

Landulph Junior, *Landulfi de Sancto Paulo Historia mediolanensis*, ed. L. Bethmann and P. Jaffé, *Monumenta Germaniae historica*, Scriptores 20 (Hanover, 1868).

Landulph Senior, *Landulphi Senioris Mediolanensis historiae libri quatuor*, ed. A. Cutolo (Bologna, 1942).

Lanfranc of Bec, *The Letters of Lanfranc Archbishop of Canterbury*, ed. H. Clover and M. Gibson (Oxford, 1979).

La Popelinière, Henri de, *Histoire des histoires, avec l'Idée de l'histoire accomplie* (Paris, 1599).

Latimer, Hugh, *Selected Sermons of Hugh Latimer*, ed. A. G. Chester (Charlottesville, VA, 1968).

Latini, Brunetto, *Della vita e delle opere de Brunetto Latini*, ed. T. Sundby (Florence, 1884).

Lefèvre d'Etaples, Jacques, *The Prefatory Epistles of Jacques Lefèvre d'Etaples and Related Texts*, ed. E. F. Rice, Jr. (New York and London, 1972).

Leon, David Messer, *Kevod Ḥakhamim [Honor Due to Scholars]* (Berlin, 1899; reprinted Jerusalem, 1970).

Leon, Judah Messer, *Sefer Nofet Ẓufim*, ed. R. Bonfil (Jerusalem, 1980); *The Book of the Honeycomb's Flow*, trans. I. Rabinowitz (Ithaca, NY, 1983).

Le Roy, Louis, *Considération sur l'histoire françois et universelle de ce temps* (Paris, 1568).

——, *De la vicissitude ou variété des choses en l'univers* (Paris, 1584).

——, *De l'origine, antiquité, progrès, excellence, et l'utilité de l'art politique* (Paris, 1553).

——, *G. Budaei viri clarissimi vita* (Paris, 1540).

——, "L'origine, progrès et perfection de la philosophie . . . ," in *Le Phédon de Platon* (Paris, 1553).

——, "Projet ou dessein du royaume de France . . . ," in *Exhortation aux François pour vivre en concorde* (Paris, 1579).

Liburnio, Niccolò, *Le Seluette di Messer Nicolao Lyburnio* (Venice, 1513).

Lily, William, *A Shorte Introduction of Grammar by William Lily*, ed. V. J. Flynn (London, 1945).

Lionardi, Alessandro, *Dialogi di Messer Alessandro Lionardi Della inventione poetica* (Venice, 1554).

Lombardo, Bartolomeo, *Vincentii Madii Brixiani et Bartholomaei Lombardi Veronensis in Aristotelis librum de poetica communes explanationes* (Venice, 1550).

Lorenzo Palmireno, Juan, *Vocabulario del humanista* (Valencia, 1569).

Loschi, Antonio, "Goddess and Captive: Antonio Loschi's Poetic Tribute to Maddalena Scrovegni (1389), Study and Text," ed. M. L. King, in *Medievalia et Humanistica* n.s. 10 (1981): 107–27.

Lovati, Lovato dei, *De Senecae tragoediarum lectione vulgate*, ed. R. Peiper (Breslau, 1893).

Lovisini, Francesco, *In Librum Q. Horatii Flacci de arte poetica commentarius* (Venice, 1554).

Lucena, Juan de, *Antologia de humanistas españoles*, ed. A. M. Arancón (Madrid, 1980), 171–239.

———, *Opúsculos literarios*, ed. A. Paz y Mélia (Madrid, 1892).

———, *Testi spagnoli del secolo XV*, ed. G. M. Bertini (Turin, 1950), 97–182.

Lupus Servatus (Lupus of Ferrières), *Correspondance*, ed. and trans. L. Levillain, 2 vols. (Paris, 1927–35).

Luther, Martin, *Weimar Ausgabe: Schriften*, 58 vols.; *Briefwechsel*, 13 vols.; *Tischreden*, 6 vols.; *Deutsche Bibel*, 12 vols. (Weimar, 1883–).

———, *What Luther Says: An Anthology*, ed. and trans. E. M. Plass, 3 vols. (St. Louis, 1959).

———, *Works, American Edition*: vols. 1–30 ed. J. Pelikan; vols. 31–55 ed. H. T. Lahmann (St. Louis and Philadelphia, 1955–).

Luther and Erasmus: Free Will and Salvation, trans. and ed. E. G. Rupp, A. N. Marlow, P. S. Watson, and B. Drewery (London, 1969).

Machiavelli, Niccolò, *History of Florence*, trans. W. Dunne (New York, 1901).

———, *The Prince and the Discourses*, intro. M. Lerner (New York, 1950).

Macrobius, *Commentary on the Dream of Scipio*, trans. W. H. Stahl (New York, 1952).

Maggi, Vincenzo, *Vincentii Madii Brixiani et Bartholomaei Lombardi Veronensis in Aristotelis librum de poetica communes explanationes* (Venice, 1550).

Maio, Giuniano, *De maiestate*, ed. F. Gaeta (Bologna, 1956).

———, *Opera omnia soluta oratione composita* (Venice, 1518).

Maioragio, Marcantonio, *In tres Aristotelis libros de arte rhetorica* (Venice, 1572).

———, *Orationes et praefationes omnes* (Venice, 1582).

Malatesta, Giuseppe, *Della nuova poesia* (Verona, 1589).

Maldonado, Juan, *Paraenesis ad litteras: Juan Maldonado y el humanismo español en tiempos de Carlo V*, ed. J. Alcina Rovira, intro. E. Asensio (Madrid, 1980).

Mancinelli, Antonio, *Horatii Flacci poemata: Cum commentariis eruditissimorum grammaticorum reconditissimis: Antonii Mancinelli Jodoci Badij Ascensii & Joannis Britannici* (Milan, 1518).

Manetti, Antonio, *The Life of Brunelleschi*, ed. H. Saalman, trans. C. Engass (University Park, PA, 1964).

Manetti, Giannozzo, *De dignitate et excellentia hominis*, ed. E. R. Leonard (Ithaca, NY, 1964).

———, *Two Views of Man: Pope Innocent III and Giannozzo Manetti*, ed. and trans. B. Murchland (New York, 1966).

————, *Vitae Socratis et Senecae*, ed. A. de Petris (Florence, 1979).

Marnix, Philippe de, *Oeuvres de Ph. de Marnix de Sainte Aldegonde*, pt. 2, *Correspondance et mélanges*, ed. A. Lacroix, 6 vols. (Paris, 1857–60).

Marulić, Marko, *Zbornik Marka Marulica, 1450–1950* [*A Collection on Marko Marulić, 1450–1950*] (Zagreb, 1950).

Marullus, Michael, *Michaelis Marulli Carmine*, ed. A. Perosa (Zurich, 1951).

Massini, Filippo, *Lettioni dell'estatico insensato* (Perugia, 1588).

Matamoros, Alonso García de, *Apologia pro adserenda hispanorum eruditione*, ed. J. López de Toro (Madrid, 1943).

Mazzoni, Jacopo (pseud. Donato Rofia), *Della difesa della Comedia di Dante* (Cesena, 1587).

Mei, Girolamo, *Discorso sopra la musica antica e moderna*, ed. Piero del Nero (Venice, 1602; reprinted Milan, 1933).

————, *Letters on Ancient and Modern Music to Vinzenzo Galilei and Giovanni Bandi: A Study with Annotated Texts*, ed. C. V. Palisca (Stuttgart, 3d ed. 1977).

Melanchthon, Philipp, *Arminius dialogus Huttenicus, continens res arminii in Germania gestas. P. Cornellii Taciti, de moribus et populis Germaniae libellus. Adiecta est brevis interpretatio appellatiorum partium Germaniae* (Wittenberg, 1938).

————, *Declamationes*, ed. K. Hartfelder (Berlin, 1891).

————, *Opera omnia*, ed. K. G. Bretschneider and H. E. Bindseil, 28 vols. (Halle, 1834–60).

Mendoza, Don Iñigo López de (Marqués de Santillana), *Obras de Don Iñigo López de Mendoza*, ed. J. Amador de los Ríos (Madrid, 1852).

————, *Marqués de Santillana: Prose and Verse*, ed. and trans. T. B. Trend (London, 1940).

Menechini, Andrea, *Delle lodi della poesia d'Omero et di Virgilio* (Venice, 1572).

Minturno, Antonio Sebastiano, *De poeta* (Venice, 1559); *L'arte poetica* (Venice, 1564).

Mithridates, Flavius (Guglielmo Raimondo Moncada), *Sermo de Passione Domini*, ed. C. Wirszubski (Jerusalem, 1963).

Mocenigo, Filippo, *Universales institutiones ad hominum perfectionem* (Venice, 1581).

Modius, Franciscus, "Un poème inédit de François Modius sur l'éducation du prince humaniste," ed. J. IJsewijn, *Latomus* 25 (1966): 570–83.

Montaigne, Michel de, *The Complete Essays of Montaigne*, trans. D. M. Frame (Stanford, 1965).

Monte, Pietro del, *Monarchia in qua generalium conciliorum materia de potestate prestantia et excellentia Romani pontificis et imperatoris plenissime discutitur* (Rome, 1537).

Montreux, Nicolas de, *Sophonisbe*, ed. D. Stone, Jr. (Geneva, 1976).

Morata, Olimpia, *Olympiae Fulviae Moratae foeminae doctissimae ac plane divinae orationes, dialogi, epistolae, carmina, tam Latina quam Graeca*, ed. C. S. Curione (Basel, 3d ed. 1570).

————, *Opere*, ed. L. Caretti, *Deputazione provinciale ferrarese di storia patria,*

Atti e memorie n.s. 2 (1954), pt. 1 (*Epistolae*) and pt. 2 (*Orationes, dialogi et carmina*).

More, Thomas, *The Correspondence of Sir Thomas More*, ed. E. F. Rogers (Princeton, 1947).

———, *St. Thomas More: Selected Letters*, ed. E. F. Rogers (New Haven, 2d ed. 1967).

———, *Utopia*, ed. E. Surtz, S.J. (New Haven, 1964).

Morosini, Paolo, *De aeterna temporalique Christi generatione in judaice improbationem perfidiae* [*Repertorium Bibliographicum* 10924] (Padua, 1473).

———, *De fato seu praescientia divina et liberi humani arbitrii libertate* (Bibl. Apostolica Vaticana, cod. Vat. Lat. 13157).

———, *Defensio venetorum ad Europae principes contra obtrectatores* and *De rebus ac forma reipublicae venetae*, both in *Bibliotheca Manuscripta ad S. Marci Venetiarum*, ed. G. Valentinelli, 6 vols. (Venice, 1868–73), 3:189–229 and 3:231–64, respectively.

Mosellanus, Peter, *Paedologia* (Leipzig, 1521); trans. R. F. Seybold (Urbana, IL, 1927).

Mussato, Albertino, *Ecerinide*, ed. L. Padrin (Bologna, 1900).

Muzio, Girolamo, *Rime diverse* (Venice, 1551).

Nebrija, Antonio de, *De vi ac potestate litterarum* (Salamanca, 1503).

———, *Gramática de la lengua castellana*, ed. A. Quilis (Madrid, 1980).

Nemesius of Emesa, *De natura hominis*, in *Patrologia graeca* 40 (Paris, 1858), 503–818.

Newman, John Henry, *Letters and Diaries of John Henry Newman*, ed. C. S. Dessain and T. Gornall (Oxford, 1973).

Nicholas of Cusa, *The Idiot in Four Books*, trans. anonymously (London, 1650).

———, *Nicholas of Cusa on Learned Ignorance: A Translation and an Appraisal of De Docta Ignorantia* (Minneapolis, 1981); and *On Learned Ignorance*, trans. G. Heron (London, 1954).

———, *Opera*, 3 vols. (Paris, 1514; facsimile, Frankfurt am Main, 1962).

———, *Opera omnia*, 17 vols. (Leipzig, 1932–84).

Nicomachus of Gerasa, "Nicomachus of Gerasa *Manual of Harmonics:* Translation and Commentary," ed. F. R. Levin (Ph.D. diss., Columbia University, New York, 1967).

Nizolio, Mario, *De veris principiis et vera ratione philosophandi contra pseudophilosophos*, ed. Q. Breen, 2 vols. (Rome, 1956).

Nogarola, Isotta, *Isottae Nogarolae Veronensis opera quae supersunt omnia, accedunt Angelae et Zeneverae Nogarolae epistolae et carmina*, ed. E. Abel, 2 vols. (Budapest, 1886).

Nores, Giason de, *Discorso di Iason Denores intorno a que principi, cause et accrescimenti, che la comedia, la tragedia et il poema heroico ricevono dalla philosophia morale e civile e da governatori delle repubbliche* (Padua, 1586).

———, *In epistolam Q. Horatii Flacci de arte poetica Iasonis de Nores Ciprij ex quotidianis Tryphonis Gabrielij sermonibus interpretatio* (Venice, 1553).

Ortel, Abraham, *Album amicorum*, facsimile text in Pembroke College, Cambridge, by J. Puraye (Amsterdam, 1969).

Ortiz, Alfonso, *Diálogo sobre la educación del principe Don Juan, hijo de los reyes católicos*, trans. G. M. Bertini (Madrid, 1983).

Ovid, *Publi Ovidi Nasonis Ibis*, ed. A. La Penna (Florence, 1957).

Pacioli, Luca, *Divina proportione* (Venice, 1509).

———, *Euclid megarensis opera* . . . (Venice, 1509).

———, *Summa de arithmetica, geometria, proportioni et proportionalità* (Venice, 1494).

Palencia, Alfonso de, *Cronica de Enrique IV*, in *Biblioteca de autores españoles*, 3 vols. (Madrid, 1973–75), vol. 1.

———, *Dos tratados de Alfonso de Palencia*, ed. M. M. Fabié (Madrid, 1876).

———, "Una lletra d'Alfons de Palencia a Vespasiá da Bisticci," ed. A. Mundo, in *Studi di bibliografia e di storia in onore di Tammaro de Marinis*, 3 vols. (Verona, 1964), 3:271–81.

———, *Quarta decas hispaniensium gestarum ex annalibus suorum dierum*, ed. J. López de Toro (Madrid, 1970).

Paleotti, Gabriele, *Discorso intorno alle immagini sacre e profane* (Bologna, 1582).

Palestrina, *Pope Marcellus Mass*, ed. L. Lockwood (New York, 1975).

Palmieri, Matteo, *Della vita civile*, ed. S. Battaglia (Bologna, 1944).

Pannonius, Janus, *Jani Pannonii poemata*, ed. Samuel Teleki (Utrecht, 1774).

Papias of Lombardy, *Elementarium* (Milan, 1476).

Paracelsus, *Selected Writings*, ed. J. Jacobi, trans. N. Guterman (London, 1951).

Pareja, Bartolomé Ramos de, *Musica practica* (Bologna, 1482; facsimile Bologna, 1969), ed. J. Wolf in *Publikationen der Internationalen Musikgesellschaft, Beihefte* 2 (Leipzig, 1901).

Parthenio, Bernardino, *Della imitatione poetica di M. Bernardino Parthenio* (Venice, 1560).

Patrizi, Francesco, *Della poetica, La deca istoriale*, ed. D. Aguzzi-Barbagli, 2 vols. (Florence, 1969–71).

———, "F. Patrizi, Emendatio in libros suos Novae philosophiae," ed. P. O. Kristeller, *Rinascimento* 10 (1970): 215–18.

———, *Lettere ed opuscoli inediti*, ed. D. Aguzzi-Barbagli (Florence, 1975).

Pazzi, Alessandro dei, *Aristotelis poetica per Alexandrum Paccium patritium florentinum in latinum conversa; eadem graece* (Venice, 1536).

Pedemonte, Francesco Filippo, *Ecphrasis in Horatii Flacci Artem poeticam* (Venice, 1546).

Peri, J., *Le musiche sopra l'Euridice* (Florence, 1601; reprinted Bologna, 1969).

Perleoni, Giuliano, *Compendio di Sonecti et altre Rime de varie texture, intitolato lo Perleone, recolte tra le opere antiche e moderne de l'humile discipulo et imitatore devotissimo de' vulgari poeti Giuliano Perleonio dicto Rustico Romano* (Naples, 1492).

Perotti, Niccolò, *Niccolò Perotti's Version of the Enchiridion of Epictetus*, ed. R. P. Oliver (Urbana, IL, 1954).

Persius Flaccus, Aulus, *Auli Persii Flacci Satirarum liber*, ed. O. Jahn (Leipzig, 1843).

Peter of Blois, *Epistolae*, in *Patrologia latina* 207 (Paris, 1855), 1–560.

Peter the Venerable, *The Letters of Peter the Venerable,* ed. G. Constable, 2 vols. (Cambridge, MA, 1967).

Petrarch, Francesco, "La *Collatio laureationis* del Petrarca," ed. C. Godi, *Italia medioevale e umanistica* 13 (1970): 1–27.

———, *Le familiari,* ed. V. Rossi, 4 vols. (Florence, 1933–42).

———, *Invective contra medicum,* ed. P. G. Ricci, trans. (Italian) D. Silvestri (Rome, 1950); also *Invettive contro un medico,* ed. M. Schiavone (Milan, 1972).

———, *Letters from Petrarch,* ed. and trans. M. Bishop (Bloomington, IN, 1966).

———, *Letters on Familiar Matters, I–VIII,* trans. A. S. Bernardo (Albany, NY, 1975).

———, *Letters on Familiar Matters, IX–XVI,* trans. A. S. Bernardo (Baltimore, 1982).

———, *Letters to Classical Authors,* trans. M. Cosenza (Chicago, 1910).

———, *The Life of Solitude,* trans. J. Zeitlin (Urbana, IL, 1924).

———, "L'orazione del Petrarca per Giovanni il Buono," ed. C. Godi, *Italia medioevale e umanistica* 8 (1965): 73–83.

———, *Petrarch's Correspondence,* ed. E. H. Wilkins (Padua, 1960).

———, *Petrarch, the First Modern Scholar and Man of Letters,* ed. J. H. Robinson and H. W. Rolfe (New York, 1898).

———, *Petrarch: Selected Sonnets, Odes, and Letters,* ed. and trans. T. G. Bergin (New York, 1966).

———, *Petrarch's 'Africa,'* trans. T. G. Bergin and A. S. Wilson (New Haven, 1977).

———, "Petrarch's Prefaces to *De viris illustribus,*" trans. B. Kohl, *History and Theory* 13 (1974): 132–44.

———, *Phisicke Against Fortune,* trans. T. Twayne (London, 1579; reprinted Delmar, NY, 1980); trans. of *De remediis fortunae.*

———, *Prose,* ed. G. Martellotti, P. G. Ricci, E. Carrara, and E. Bianchi (Milan, 1955).

———, *Scritti inediti di Francesco Petrarca,* ed. A. Hortis (Trieste, 1874).

———, *Secret,* trans. W. H. Draper (London, 1911).

———, *Testament,* ed. T. E. Mommsen (Ithaca, NY, 1957).

———, *The Triumphs of Petrarch,* trans. E. H. Wilkins (Chicago, 1962).

Pflug z Rabštejna, Jan, *Dialogus,* ed. B. Ryba (Prague, 1946).

———, *Disputacio,* ed. B. Ryba (Budapest, 1942).

Piccolomini, Aeneas Silvius, *Aeneae Silvii De liberorum educatione,* ed. J. S. Nelson (Washington, DC, 1940).

———, *Der Briefwechsel des Eneas Silvius Piccolomini . . . ,* ed. R. Wolkan, 4 vols. (Vienna, 1909–18).

———, *Enea Silvio Piccolomini Papst Pius II: Ausgewählte Texte aus seinen Schriften,* ed. B. Widmer (Basel, 1960).

———, *Memoirs of a Renaissance Pope: The Commentaries of Pius II,* trans. F. A. Gragg, ed. L. C. Gabel (New York, 1959).

——, *Tractatus de liberorum educatione,* Fontes rerum Austriacarum 61, 62, 67, 68 (1909–18).

Piccolomini, Alessandro, *Annatationi di M. Alessandro Piccolomini nel libro della Poetica d'Aristotele* (Venice, 1575).

——, *Il libro della Poetica d'Aristotele tradotto di greca lingua in volgare da M. Alessandro Piccolomini* (Siena, 1572).

Pico della Mirandola, Giovanfrancesco, *Le epistole "De imitatione" di Giovanfrancesco Pico della Mirandola e di Pietro Bembo,* ed. G. Santangelo (Florence, 1954).

Pico della Mirandola, Giovanni, *Conclusiones sive Theses DCCCC,* ed. B. Kieszkowski (Geneva, 1973).

——, *Une controverse sur Origène à la Renaissance: Jean Pic de la Mirandole et Pierre Garcia,* ed. and trans. H. Crouzel, S.J. (Paris, 1977).

——, *De hominis dignitate,* ed. E. Garin (Florence, 1942).

——, *Disputationes adversus astrologiam divinitricem,* ed. and trans. E. Garin, 2 vols. (Florence, 1946).

——, *On the Dignity of Man, On Being and the One, Heptaplus,* ed. P. J. W. Miller (Indianapolis, 1965).

——, *Opera omnia,* ed. Gianfrancesco Pico della Mirandola, 2 vols. (Bologna, 1496, many times reprinted).

Pigna, Giovanni Battista, *Poetica horatiana* (Venice, 1561).

Pino, Bernardino, *Discorso intorno al componimento della comedia de' nostri tempi* (Venice, 1578).

Pletho, George Gemistus, *Traité des lois,* ed. C. Alexandre and A. Pelissier (reprinted Amsterdam, 1966).

Pliny the Younger, *Epistularum libri decem,* ed. R. A. B. Mynors (Oxford, 1963).

Poliziano, Angelo, *La commedia e l'Andria di Terenzio,* ed. R. L. Roselli (Florence, 1973).

——, *Commento inedito alle Selve di Stazio,* ed. L. Cesarini Martinelli (Florence, 1978).

——, *Della congiura dei Pazzi (Coniurationis commentarium),* ed. A. Perosa (Padua, 1958).

——, *Epigrammi greci,* ed. A. Ardizzoni (Florence, 1951).

——, *Miscellaneorum centuria prima,* ed. H. Katayama (Tokyo, 1981).

——, *Miscellaneorum centuria secunda,* ed. M. Pastore Stocchi and V. Branca (Florence, 1972).

——, *Opera omnia* (Basel, 1553).

——, *Le selve e La strega,* ed. I. del Lungo (Florence, 1925).

——, *The "Stanze" of Angelo Poliziano,* trans. D. Quint (Amherst, MA, 1979).

——, *Sylva in scabiem,* ed. A. Perosa (Rome, 1954).

Pontano, Giovanni, *Carmina,* ed. J. Oeschger (Bari, 1948).

——, *De immanitate,* ed. L. Monti Sabia (Naples, 1970).

——, *I dialoghi,* ed. C. Previtera (Florence, 1943).

Possevini, Antonio, *Societatis Iesu tractatio de poesi et pictura ethnica, humana et fabulosa collata cum sacra* (Rome, 1593).

Pozzo, Paride del, *Libellus syndacatus officialium* (Naples, 1485).

Pray, Georgius, *Annales regum Hungariae*, 5 vols. (Vienna, 1763–70).

Propertius, *The Elegies of Propertius*, ed. H. E. Butler and E. A. Barber (Oxford, 1933).

pseudo-Boethius, *De disciplina scolarium*, ed. O. Weyers (Leiden, 1976).

pseudo-Demetrius, *Demetri et Libanii qui feruntur Typoi epistolikoi et epistolimaioi charakteres*, ed. V. Weichert (Leipzig, 1910).

pseudo-Libanius, *Demetri et Libanii qui feruntur Typoi epistolikoi et epistolimaioi charakteres*, ed. V. Weichert (Leipzig, 1910).

pseudo-Longinus, *De sublime*, ed. G. Martano (Bari, 1965).

Puteanus, Erycius, *Suada Attica sive Orationum selectarum syntagma* (Leiden, 1623).

Puttenham, George, *The Art of Englishe Poesie*, ed. E. Arber (London, 1869).

Quintilian, *Institutio oratoria*, trans. H. E. Butler, 4 vols. (Cambridge, MA, 1961–66).

Quirini, Lauro, *Lauro Quirini umanista*, ed. V. Branca et al. (Florence, 1977).

Racine, Jean, *Principes de la tragédie*, ed. E. Vinaver (Manchester and Paris, 1951).

Raffaelo, *Raffaello nei documenti*, ed. V. Golzio (Rome, 1936).

Raimondi, Cosimo, *Defensio Epicuri*, in *Filosofi italiani del Quattrocento*, ed. E. Garin (Florence, 1942), 133–49.

Ramus, Petrus, *Rhetoricae distinctiones in Quintilianum ad Carolum Lotharingum cardinalem* (Paris, 1559).

———, *Scholae in liberales artes*, ed. W. J. Ong, S.J. (Hildesheim, 1970).

Ratherius of Verona, *Synodica*, in *Patrologia latina* 136 (Paris, 1853), 553–68.

Reuchlin, Johann, *De verbo mirifico, 1494; De arte cabalistica, 1517* (facsimile, Stuttgart-Bad Cannstatt, 1964).

———, *Johannes Reuchlins Briefwechsel*, ed. L. Geiger (Stuttgart, 1875; facsimile Hildesheim, 1962).

Reusner, Nicolaus, *Hodoepicorum sive itinerarium totius fere orbis libri VII* (Basel, 1580).

Rhenanus, Beatus, *In P. Cornelium Tacitum Annotationes* (Lyons, 1542).

———, *Rerum germanicarum libri tres* (Basel, 1531).

Ricci, Bartolomeo, *De imitatione libri tres* (Venice, 1545).

Riccobaldo of Ferrara, *Compendium romanae historiae*, ed. A. T. Hankey, 2 vols. (Rome, 1984).

Riccobono, Antonio, *Aristotelis liber de poetica ab Antonio Riccobono . . . latine conversus* (Venice, 1589).

———, *Poetica Antonii Riccoboni poeticam Aristotelis per paraphrasim explicans & nonnullas Ludovici Castelvetrij captiones refellens. Eiusdem ex Aristotele ars comica* (Vicenza, 1585).

Rinuccini, Alamanno, "Alamanno Rinuccini, *Dialogus de libertate*," ed. F. Adorno, *Atti e memorie dell'Accademia Toscana di scienze e lettere "La Colombaria"* 22 [n.s. 8] (1957): 265–303.

Robortelli, Francesco, *Francisci Robortelli Utinensis in librum Aristotelis De arte poetica explicationes* (Florence, 1548).

Rolandino of Padua, *Cronica facta Marchie tarvisine,* ed. A. Bonardi (Città di Castello, 1905–6); *The Chronicles of the Trevisan March,* trans. J. R. Berrigan (Lawrence, KS, 1980).

Rubeanus, Crotus, *On the Eve of the Reformation,* trans. F. G. Stokes, intro. H. Holborn (New York, 1964).

Sabadino, Giovanni, *Art and Life at the Court of Ercole d'Este: The "De triumphis religionis" of Giovanni Sabadino degli Arienti,* ed. W. Gundersheimer (Geneva, 1972).

Sacchi, Bartolomeo (Platina), *Historia de vitis pontificum romanorum,* ed. Onofrio Panvinio (Venice, 1562).

———, *Liber de vita Christi ac omnium pontificum,* ed. G. Gaida (Città di Castello, 1913–32).

Sadoleto, Jacopo, *De pueris,* trans. E. T. Campagnac and K. Forbes, in *Sadoleto on Education* (London, 1916).

Salinas, Francisco dei, *De musica libri septem* (Salamanca, 1577; reprinted Kassel, 1958).

Salutati, Coluccio, *De fato, fortuna et casu,* ed. C. Bianca (Florence, 1985).

———, *De laboribus Herculis,* ed. B. L. Ullman (Zurich, 1951).

———, *De nobilitate legum et medicine,* ed. E. Garin (Florence, 1947).

———, *Epistolario di Coluccio Salutati,* ed. F. Novati, 5 vols. (Rome, 1891–1911).

———, *Il trattato "De tyranno" e lettere scelte,* ed. F. Ercole (Bologna, 1942).

———, "Letters in Defense of Liberal Studies," in *Humanism and Tyranny,* ed. E. Emerton (Cambridge, MA, 1925; reprinted Gloucester, MA, 1964), 290–377.

Salviati, Lionardo, *Il Lasca dialogo* (Florence, 1583).

Sambucus, Ioannes, *Emblemata* (Antwerp, 1964; facsimile, Budapest, 1982).

Sánchez de las Brozas, Francisco, *Minerva* (Salamanca, 1587).

Sannazaro, Jacopo, *Opere volgari,* ed. A. Mauro (Bari, 1961).

Sansovino, Francesco, *Sette libri di satire* (Venice, 1560).

Sarpi, Paolo, *History of Benefices and Selections from History of the Council of Trent,* trans. P. Burke (New York, 1967).

Scaliger, Julius Caesar, *De causis linguae latinae* (Lyons, 1540).

———, *Poetices libri septem* (Lyons, 1561).

Schardius, Simon, *Historicorum opus,* vol. 1, *Germaniae illustrationem continet* (Basel, 1574).

Segni, Agnolo, *Ragionamento di M. Agnolo Segni gentilhuomo fiorentino sopra le cose pertinenti alla poetica* (Florence, 1581).

Segni, Bernardo, *Rettorica e Poetica d'Aristotele tradotte di greco lingua in volgare da M. Alessandro Piccolomini* (Siena, 1572).

Segni, Lothario dei (Pope Innocent III), *On the Misery of the Human Condition,* trans. M. M. Dietz, ed. D. R. Howard (Indianapolis, 1969).

Seyssel, Claude de, *The Monarchy of France,* ed. D. R. Kelley, trans. J. H. Hexter (New Haven, 1981).

Sidney, Philip, *Sir Philip Sidney's Defense of Poesy,* ed. L. Loens (Lincoln, NE, 1970).

Šižgorić, Juraj (Georgius Sisgoreus Sibenicensis), *De situ Illyriae et civitate Sibenici*, ed. M. Šrepel, in *Gradja za povijest književnosti Hrvatske* [*Sources for the History of Croatian Literature*] 2 (1899): 1–13; *O smještaju Ilirije i o gradu Šibeniku* [*On the Location of Illyria and the City of Šibenik*], ed. V. Gortan (Šibenik, 1981).

Sleiden, Johann, "Apology for His History," in *General History of the Reformation* (London, 1689).

Starkey, Thomas, *A Dialogue Between Reginald Pole and Thomas Lupset by Thomas Starkey*, ed. K. M. Burton (London, 1948).

Stojković, Ivan (Johannes de Ragusio), *Tractatus de ecclesia* (reprinted Zagreb, 1983).

Strozzi, Giovambattista, *Orazioni et altre prose* (Rome, 1635).

Sylvester, János, *Grammatica hungaro-latina*, facsimile of 1539 edition, foreword T. A. Sebeok (Bloomington, IN, 1968).

Taccola, Mariano, *De machinis: The Engineering Treatise of 1449*, ed. G. Scaglia, 2 vols. (Wiesbaden, 1971).

Taccone, Baldassare, *L'Atteone e le rime di Baldassare Taccone*, ed. F. Bariola (Florence, 1888).

Tacitus, *Dialogus de oratoribus*, ed. A. Gudeman (Amsterdam, 2d ed. 1967).

Tardi, György, *Historia Szikszoniensis* (Bratislava, 1588).

Tasso, Torquato, *Discorsi dell'arte poetica e del poema eroico*, ed. L. Poma (Bari, 1964).

———, *Prose diverse*, ed. C. Guasti, 2 vols. (Florence, 1875).

Tebalducci, Lorenzo Giacomini, *Orationi e discorsi* (Florence, 1597).

Themistius, *Orationes*, ed. G. Downey (Leipzig, 1965).

———, *Paraphraseos De anima libri tres, interprete Hermolao Barbaro*, ed. R. Heinze (Berlin, 1899).

Theodoret of Cyrene, *Theodoriti Cyrensis episcopi de curatione Graecarum affectionum libri duodecim Zenobio Acciaolo interprete* (Paris, 1519).

Thomas of Capua, *Die Ars dictandi des Thomas von Capua*, ed. E. Heller, 2 vols. (Heidelberg, 1928–29).

Thurot, C., *Extraits de divers manuscrits latins pour servir à l'histoire des doctrines grammaticales au Moyen Âge* (Paris, 1869; reprinted Frankfurt, 1964).

Tinctoris, Johannes, *The Art of Counterpoint*, trans. A. Seay (n.p., American Institute of Musicology, 1961).

Tinódi, Sebestyén, *Cronica*, intro. B. Varjas (Budapest, 1959).

Tomitano, Bernardino, *Ragionamenti della lingua toscana ... dell'eccellente medico e filosofo Bernardino Tomitano* (Venice, 1545).

Tortelli, Giovanni, *Ioannis Tortellii Arretini Commentaris grammatica de orthographia dictionum e Graecis tractarum* (Vicenza, 1480).

Toscanella, Orazio, *Precetti necessari sopra diverse cose pertinenti alla grammatica, poetica, retorica, historia, loica, et ad altre facoltà* (Venice, 1562).

Traversari, Ambrogio, *Ambrosii Traversarii generalis Camaldulensium aliorumque ad ipsum et ad alios de eodem Ambrosio latinae epistolae*, ed. L. Mehus, 2 vols. (Florence, 1759).

Trissino, Giangiorgio, *La Pωetica di M. Giωvan Giorgiω Trissinω* (Vicenza, 1529).

———, *La quinta e la sesta divisione della poetica del Trissino* (Venice, 1562).

———, *La Sofonisba con note di Torquato Tasso,* ed. F. Paglierani (Bologna, 1884).

Tritonius, Petrus, *Melopoiae sive harmoniae tetracenticae* (Augsburg, 1507).

Tyard, Pontus de, *Solitaire second, ou Prose de la musique,* ed. C. M. Yandell (Geneva, 1980).

Ugolino da Orvieto, *Declaratio musice discipline,* ed. A. Seay (Rome, 1959).

Urso, *Regesta della chiesa di Pisa,* ed. N. Caturegli (Rome, 1938).

Valla, Giorgio, *De expetendis et fugiendis rebus opus* (Venice, 1501).

Valla, Lorenzo, *Antidotum primum,* ed. A. Wesseling (Amsterdam, 1978).

———, *Apologus,* ed. S. Camporeale, in *L. Valla, umanesimo e teologia* (Florence, 1972), 503–34.

———, *Collatio Novi Testamenti,* ed. A. Perosa (Florence, 1970).

———, *De dialectica libri III* (Paris, 1530).

———, *De falso credita et ementita Constantini Declamatio,* ed. W. Schwahn (Leipzig, 1928); *The Treatise of Lorenzo Valla on the Donation of Constantine,* trans. C. B. Coleman (New Haven, 1922).

———, *De libero arbitrio,* ed. M. Anfossi (Florence, 1934); "On Free Will," trans. C. Trinkaus in *The Renaissance Philosophy of Man,* ed. Cassirer et al. (q.v.), 155–82; and in *Renaissance Philosophy,* vol. 1, *The Italian Philosophers,* ed. Fallico and Shapiro (q.v.), 40–65.

———, *De vero falsoque bono,* ed. M. Lorch (Bari, 1970); *On Pleasure,* trans. A. K. Heiatt and M. Lorch (New York, 1979).

———, *Epistole,* ed. O. Besome and M. Regoliosi (Padua, 1984).

———, *Gesta Ferdinandi regis Aragonum,* ed. O. Besomi (Padua, 1974).

———, *In Bartholomeum Facium ligurem recriminationes libri IV,* ed. M. P. Regoliosi (Padua, 1982).

———, *Opera omnia,* ed. E. Garin, 2 vols. (Turin, 1962).

———, *The Profession of the Religious,* ed. and trans. O. Z. Pugliese (Toronto, 1985), 17–61.

———, *Repastinatio dialectice et philosophie,* ed. G. Zippel, 2 vols. (Padua, 1982).

———, *Scritti filosofici e religiosi,* trans. G. Radetti (Florence, 1953).

Varano, Costanza, *C. Varaneae Sfortiae Pisauri Principis orationes et epistolae,* ed. T. Bettinelli, in *Miscellanea di varie operette* 7 (Venice, 1743), 295–330.

———, Letters and Orations, in *Catalogus codicum manuscriptorum qui in Bibliotheca Riccardiana Florentiae adservantur . . . ,* ed. G. Lami (Livorno, 1756), 145–50.

Varchi, Benedetto, *Lezzioni di M. Benedetto Varchi* (Florence, 1590).

Vasari, Giorgio, *Le vite dei più eccellenti pittori, scultori e architetti,* ed. C. L. Ragghianti (Milan, 1942); *The Lives of the Painters, Sculptors and Architects,* trans. W. Gaunt, 4 vols. (New York and London, 1927; rev. ed. 1963).

Vegio, Maffeo, *De educatione liberorum et eorum claris moribus, libri sex,* books

1–3 ed. Sister M. W. Fanning (Washington, DC, 1933); books 4–6 ed. A. S. Sullivan (Washington, DC, 1936).

———, *Elencho delle opere: Scritti inediti,* ed. L. Raffaele (Bologna, 1909).

Vergerio, Pier Paolo, *De ingenuis moribus,* ed. A. Gnesotto, *Atti e memorie della R. Accademia di scienze, lettere ed arti, Padova* n.s. 34 (1918); trans. in *Vittorino da Feltre and Other Humanist Educators,* ed. Woodward (q.v.), 93–118.

Vergil, Polydore, *De rerum inventoribus* (Basel, 1536).

Vespasiano da Bisticci, *Le vite,* ed. A. Greco, 2 vols. (Florence, 1970–74); *Renaissance Princes, Popes and Prelates,* trans. W. George and E. Waters (New York, 1963).

Vettori, Pietro, *Commentarii in primum librum Aristotelis de arte poetarum* (Florence, 1560).

Vicentino, Nicola, *L'antica musica ridotta alla moderna prattica* (Rome, 1555; facsimile ed. E. E. Lowinsky, Kassel, 1959).

Vida, Marco Girolamo, *The Christiad: A Latin–English Edition,* ed. and trans. G. C. Drake and C. A. Forbes (Carbondale, IL, 1978).

———, *De arte poetica libri III* (Rome, 1527); ed. and trans. R. G. Williams (New York, 1976).

Vignier, Nicolas, *Bibliothèque historiale* (Paris, 1582).

Villani, Filippo, *Liber de civitatis Florentine famosis civibus,* ed. G. C. Galletti (Florence, 1847).

Villalón, Cristóbal de, *El scholastico,* ed. R. J. N. Kerr (Madrid, 1967).

———, *Ingeniosa comparación entre lo antiguo y lo presente* (Madrid, 1898).

Villena, Don Enrique de, *Arte de Trovar,* ed. F. J. Sánchez Cantón (Madrid, 1923).

———, *La primera versión castellana de la "Eneida" de Virgilio,* ed. and trans. R. Santiago Lacuesta (Madrid, 1979).

———, *La traducción de la Divina comedia atribuida a D. Enrique de Aragón: Estudio y edicion del "Inferno,"* ed. J. A. Pascual Rodríguez (Salamanca, 1974).

———, *Tratado de la consolación,* ed. D. C. Carr (Madrid, 1976).

Viperano, Giovanni Antonio, *De poetica libri tres* (Antwerp, 1579).

———, *De scribendis virorum illustrium vitis sermo* (Perugia, 1570).

Vitéz, Ivan (Ioannes de Zredna), *Opera quae supersunt,* ed. I. Boronkai (Budapest, 1980).

Vives, Juan Luis, *Juan Luis Vives: Arbeitsgespräch ... Wolfenbüttel ... 1980,* ed. A. Buck (Hamburg, 1981).

———, *Opera omnia,* 8 vols. in 7 (Valencia, 1782–90).

———, *Vives: On Education,* trans. F. Watson (Edinburgh, 1903; reprinted Totowa, NJ, 1971).

Vrančić, Antun (Antonius Verantius), *Monumenta Hungariae historica, Scriptores: Verancsics Antal,* vols. 2–6, 9, 10, 19, 20, 25, 26, 32 (Budapest, 1857–75).

Walter of Châtillon, *Galteri de Castellione, Alexandreis,* ed. M. L. Colker (Padua, 1978).

Wannemaker, Philippus, *Triumphus litteratorum, in quo Borromeianae virtutis imago* (Milan, 1611).
Wimpheling, Jacob, *Epitome rerum germanicarum* (Strasbourg, 1505).
Wipo, *Tetralogus, Die Werke Wipos,* ed. H. Bresslau (Hanover, 3d ed. 1915).
Zarlino, Gioseffo, *Le istitutioni harmoniche* (Venice, 1558).
―――, *On the Modes, Part Four of "Le institutioni harmoniche," 1558,* trans. V. Cohen, ed. C. V. Palisca (New Haven, 1983).
―――, *Sopplimenti musicali* (Venice, 1588).
Zuccaro, Federigo, *Scritti d'arte di Federigo Zuccaro,* ed. D. Heikamp (Florence, 1961).

SECONDARY SOURCES: COLLECTIONS OF ESSAYS AND REFERENCE WORKS

Actes du congrès Erasme, 1969 (Amsterdam and London, 1971).
Anuario de estudios medievales 7 (1970–71): *La investigación de la historia hispanica del siglo XV: Problemas y cuestiones* (special issue).
Arts libéraux et philosophie au Moyen Âge (Montreal and Paris, 1969).
Atti del congresso di studi sull'età aragonese (Bari, 1969).
Atti del convegno di studi su Angelo Colocci (Jesi, 1972).
Ati del convegno di studi su Giangiorgio Trissino (Vicenza, 1980).
Bartolo de Sassoferrato, 2 vols. (Milan, 1962).
Benda, K., ed., *Magyarország történeti kronológiaja* [*Hungary's Historical Chronology*], 4 vols. to date (Budapest, 1983–).
Bennassar, B. et al., *Inquisición española: Poder político y control social,* trans. J. Alfaya (Barcelona, 1981).
Ben Sasson, H. H. and S. Ettinger, eds., *Jewish Society Through the Ages* (New York, 1971).
Benson, R. L., G. Constable, and C. D. Lanham, eds., *Renaissance and Renewal in the Twelfth Century* (Cambridge, MA, 1982).
Bernardo, A. S., ed., *Francesco Petrarca, Citizen of the World* (Padua and Albany, NY, 1980).
Bertelli, S. and G. Ramakus, eds., *Essays Presented to Myron P. Gilmore,* 2 vols. (Florence, 1978).
Bibliographie internationale de l'humanisme et de la Renaissance (Geneva, 1966–) annually since 1966.
Bietenholz, P. G. and T. B. Deutscher, eds., *Contemporaries of Erasmus,* 3 vols. (Toronto, 1984–86).
Billanovich, G. and G. Frasso, eds., *Il Petrarca ad Arquà* (Padua, 1975).
Boehm, L. and E. Raimondi, eds., *Università, accademie e società scientifiche in Italia e in Germania dal Cinquecento al Settecento* (Bologna, 1981).
Bolgar, R. R., ed., *Classical Influences on European Culture, A.D. 500–1500* (Cambridge, 1971).
―――, *Classical Influences on European Culture, A.D. 1500–1700* (Cambridge, 1976).
Bontems, C. et al., *Le Prince dans la France des XVIᵉ et XVIIᵉ siècles* (Paris, 1965).

Brahmer, M., ed., *Italia, Venezia e Polonia tra umanesimo e Rinascimento* (Wroclaw, 1967).

Branca, V., ed., *Giorgio Valla tra scienza e sapienza: Studi di G. Gardenal, P. Landucci Ruffo, C. Vasoli* (Florence, 1981).

———, *Umanesimo europeo ed umanesimo veneziano* (Florence, 1963).

——— and S. Graciotti, eds., *L'umanesimo e l'Istria* (Florence, 1983).

Brezzi, P. and M. Lorch, eds., *Umanesimo a Roma nel Quattrocento* (Rome and New York, 1984).

Buck, A., ed., *Biographie und Autobiographie in der Renaissance* (Wiesbaden, 1983).

———, *Die Rezeption der Antike* (Hamburg, 1981).

——— and K. Heitmann, eds., *Die Antike-Rezeption in den Wissenschaften während der Renaissance* (Weinheim, 1983).

Carter, C. H., ed., *From the Renaissance to the Counter-Reformation: Essays in Honor of Garrett Mattingly* (New York, 1965).

Chastel, A. et al., *The Renaissance: Essays in Interpretation* (London and New York, 1982).

La civiltà veneziana del Quattrocento (Florence, 1957).

La civiltà veneziana del Rinascimento (Florence, 1958).

La civiltà veneziana del Trecento (Florence, 1956).

Clough, C. C., ed., *Cultural Aspects of the Italian Renaissance: Essays in Honor of Paul Oskar Kristeller* (Manchester and New York, 1976).

Cochrane, E., ed., *The Late Italian Renaissance, 1525–1630* (New York, 1970).

The Complete Works of Raphael (New York, 1969): essays by various writers.

Congrès international d'histoire des sciences, 3-B (1968).

Cooperman, B. D., ed., *Jewish Thought in the Sixteenth Century* (Cambridge, MA, 1983).

Coppens, J., ed., *Scrinium Erasmianum*, 2 vols. (Leiden, 1969).

Dąbrowski, J., ed., *Krakowskie odrodzenie. Referaty z konferencji naukowej Towarzystwa milošników historii i zabytków Krakowa z września 1953* [*Cracow Renaissance: Papers Presented at the Scholarly Conference at the Society of Friends of the History and Monuments of Cracow, Sept. 1953*] (Cracow, 1954).

Delisle, L., ed., *Le cabinet des manuscrits de la Bibliothèque impériale* (Paris, 1868).

DeMolen, R. L., ed., *Essays on the Works of Erasmus* (New Haven, 1978).

———, *The Meaning of the Renaissance and Reformation* (Boston, 1974).

Denzer, H., ed., *Jean Bodin: Verhandlungen der internationalen Bodin Tagung* (Munich, 1973).

Dictionary of Scientific Biography, 15 vols. and an index volume (New York, 1970–80).

Di Napoli, G., ed., *L'opera e il pensiero di Giovanni Pico della Mirandola nella storia dell'umanesimo: Convegno internazionale*, 2 vols. (Florence, 1965).

Dizionario biografico degli italiani, 30 vols. to date (Rome, 1960–84).

Dorey, T. A., ed., *Erasmus* (London, 1970).

Dorman, M. and Z. Levy, eds., *The Philosophy of Love of Leone Ebreo* [Hebrew] (Haifa, 1985).

Durand, D. B. et al., discussion of science in the Renaissance, *Journal of the History of Ideas* 2 (1943): 1–74.

Farenga, P., G. Lombardi, A. G. Luciani, and M. Miglio, eds., *Scrittura, biblioteche e stampa* (Vatican City, 1980).

Florence and Venice: Comparisons and Relations, acts of two conferences at the Villa I Tatti, 1976–77, 2 vols. (Florence, 1979–80).

French, R. K. and I. M. Lonie, eds., *The Medical Renaissance of the Sixteenth Century* (Cambridge, 1985).

Garin, E., ed., *Il pensiero pedagogico dell'umanesimo* (Florence, 1958).

Gesamtkatalog der Wiegendrucke, 7 vols. and 4 fasc. of vol. 8 (Stuttgart, 2d ed. 1968–76).

Gilmore, M. P., ed., *Studies on Machiavelli* (Florence, 1972).

Grane, L., ed., *University and Reformation: Lectures from the University of Copenhagen Symposium* (Leiden, 1981).

Gundersheimer, W. L., ed., *French Humanism, 1470–1600* (New York, 1969).

Hacker, J., ed., *Mehkarim be-Sifrut ha-Kabbalah [Researches in the Literature of the Kabbalah]* (Tel Aviv, 1976).

Hale, J. R., ed., *Renaissance Venice* (London, 1973).

Hannay, M., ed., *Silent but for the Word: Tudor Women as Patrons, Translators, and Writers of Religious Works* (Kent, OH, 1985).

Harran, M. J., ed., *Luther and Learning: The Wittenberg University Luther Symposium* (Selinsgrove, PA, 1985).

Helton, T., ed., *The Renaissance: A Reconsideration of the Theories and Interpretations of the Age* (Madison, WI, 1961).

Henderson, C., Jr., ed., *Classical, Mediaeval and Renaissance Studies in Honor of B. L. Ullman,* 2 vols. (Rome, 1964).

Herding, O. and R. Stupperich, eds., *Die Humanisten in ihrer politischen und sozialen Umwelt* (Bonn, 1976).

Holotík, L'. and A. Vantuch, eds., *Humanizmus a renasancia na Slovensku v. 15.–16. storočí [Humanism and Renaissance in Slovak Lands in the 15th and 16th Centuries]* (Bratislava, 1967).

Hubertus Goltzius en Brugge 1583–1983 (Brugge, 1983).

IJsewijn, J., ed., *Roma Humanistica: Studia in honorem . . . J. Ruysschaert* (Louvain, 1985).

———— and G. Verbeke, eds., *The Late Middle Ages and the Dawn of Humanism Outside Italy* (Louvain, 1972).

———— et al., *Acta conventus neo-latini Lovaniensis* (Louvain, 1973).

Irmscher, J., ed., *Renaissance und Humanismus in Mittel- und Osteuropa. Eine Sammlung von Materialen,* 2 vols. (Berlin, 1962).

Jacob, E. F., ed., *Essays in Later Medieval History* (Manchester, 1968).

————, *Italian Renaissance Studies* (London, 1960).

Jean Bodin: Actes du colloque interdisciplinaire d'Angers, 2 vols. (Angers, 1985).

Juric, S., ed., *Jugoslaviae scriptores latini recentioris aetatis,* part 1, *Opera scriptorum latinorum natione Croatorum usque ad annum MDCCCXLVII typis edita;* vol. 1, *Index alphabeticus;* vol. 2, *Index sistematicus;* addenda, *Ad tomos I et II additamentum I* (Zagreb, 1968–82).

Kardos, T. and S. V. Kovács, eds., *Janus Pannonius tanulmányok* [*Janus Pannonius Studies*] (Budapest, 1975).

Kingdon, R. M., ed., *Transition and Revolution: Problems and Issues of European Renaissance and Reformation History* (Minneapolis, MN, 1974).

Kohl, B. G., *Renaissance Humanism, 1300–1550: A Bibliography of Materials in English* (New York, 1985).

Kretzmann, N., A. Kenny, J. Pinborg, and E. Stump, eds., *The Cambridge History of Later Medieval Philosophy* (Cambridge, 1982).

Kristeller, P. O., F. E. Cranz, and V. Brown, eds., *Catalogus Translationum et Commentariorum, Medieval and Renaissance Latin Translations and Commentaries,* 6 vols. to date (Washington, DC, 1960–).

Kristeller, P. O. and P. P. Wiener, eds., *Renaissance Essays from the Journal of the History of Ideas* (New York, 1968).

Labalme, P. A., ed., *Beyond Their Sex: Learned Women of the European Past* (New York, 1980).

Lacombe, G. et al., *Aristoteles latinus. Codices,* 2 vols. (Rome, 1939–55).

Lampe, G. W. H., ed., *The Cambridge History of the Bible* (Cambridge, 1969).

LaRue, J., ed., *Aspects of Medieval and Renaissance Music* (New York, 1966).

Le Bras, G. et al., *Histoire du droit et des institutions de l'église en Occident* (Paris, 1965).

Leiden University in the Seventeenth Century: An Exchange of Learning (Leiden, 1975).

Letteratura e scienza nella storia della cultura italiana, Atti del IX congresso dell'Associazione Internazionale per gli Studi di Lingua e Letteratura Italiana (Palermo, 1978).

Levi, A. H. T., ed., *Humanism in France at the End of the Middle Ages and in the Early Renaissance* (Manchester and New York, 1970).

Lewis, C. T. and C. Short, eds., *A Latin Dictionary* (Oxford, 1879; reprinted 1962).

Lisio, P. A. de and C. Martelli, eds., *Dal progetto al rifiuto* (Salerno, 1979).

Lloyd-Jones, H., ed., *History of Classical Scholarship* (London, 1982).

Lowinsky, E. E., ed., *Josquin des Prez* (London, New York, and Toronto, 1976).

Maddison, F., M. Pelling, and C. Webster, eds., *Essays on the Life and Work of Thomas Linacre, c. 1460–1524* (Oxford, 1977).

Magyar Irodalmi Lexikon [*Hungarian Literary Dictionary*], 3 vols. (Budapest, 1965).

Mahoney, E. P., ed., *Philosophy and Humanism: Festschrift for Paul Oskar Kristeller* (New York, 1976).

Martines, L., ed., *Violence and Civil Disorder in Italian Cities, 1200–1500* (Berkeley, 1972).

Medioevo e Rinascimento: Studi in onore di Bruno Nardi, 2 vols. (Florence, 1955).

Milano nell'età di Ludovico Il Moro: Atti del convegno internazionale 28 febbraio–4 marzo 1983, 2 vols. (Milan, 1983).

Miscellanea di studi in onore di Vittore Branca, 4 vols. in 6 (Florence, 1983).

Molho, A. and J. A. Tedeschi, eds., *Renaissance Studies in Honor of Hans Baron* (Dekalb, IL, 1971).

Momenti e problemi di storia dell'estetica (Milan, 1959).

Murphy, J. J., ed., *Medieval Eloquence* (Berkeley, 1978).

———, *Studies in the Theory and Practice of Renaissance Eloquence* (Berkeley, 1983).

Oberman, H. A., ed., *Luther and the Dawn of the Modern Era* (Leiden, 1974).

——— and T. A. Brady, Jr., eds., *Itinerarium Italicum: The Profile of the Italian Renaissance in the Mirror of Its European Transformations* (Leiden, 1975).

Odrodzenie w Polsce. Materiały sesji naukowej PAN, 25–30 października 1953 roku [*Renaissance in Poland: Materials of the Scholarly Session of the Polish Academy of Sciences, 25–30 October 1953*], 5 parts in 7 vols. (Warsaw, 1955–58).

O'Kelly, B., ed., *The Renaissance Image of Man and the World* (Columbus, OH, 1966).

Ozment, S. E., ed., *Reformation Europe: A Guide to Research* (St. Louis, 1982).

Padoan, G., ed., *Petrarca, Venezia, e il Veneto* (Florence, 1976).

Patrizi, Francesco (Franjo Petrić): Conference papers dealing with his thought published in a special issue of *Prilozi za istraživanje hrvatske filozofske baštine* [*Contributions to Research into the Croatian Philosophical Heritage*] 5 (1979).

Pédagogues et juristes: Congrés du Centre d'Études Supérieures de la Renaissance de Tours 1960 (Paris, 1963).

Pedro Martínez de Osma: Homenaje en el V centenario de su muerte (Soria, 1980).

Perez Villaneuva, J., ed., *La Inquisición española: Nueva visión, nuevos horizontes* (Madrid, 1980).

Perosa, A., ed., *Mostra del Poliziano* (Florence, 1955).

Perotti, Niccolò: two special issues devoted to his thought: *Res publica litteraria* 4 (1981) and 5 (1982).

Pertusi, A., ed., *La storiografia veneziana fino al secolo XVI: Aspetti e problemi* (Florence, 1970).

Petrarca e la Lombardia (Milan, 1904).

Platon et Aristote à la Renaissance, XVIᵉ colloque international de Tours (Paris, 1976).

Poppi, A., ed., *Scienza e filosofia all'Università di Padova nel Quattrocento* (Padua, 1983).

Quaderni di retorica e poetica (1985). Proceedings of a congress in 1983 on "la lettera familiare."

Rabb, T. K. and J. E. Seigel, eds., *Action and Conviction in Early Modern Europe: Essays in Memory of E. H. Harbison* (Princeton, 1969).

Ramsey, P. A., ed., *Rome in the Renaissance: The City and the Myth* (Binghamton, NY, 1982).

Realencyclopädie der classischen Altertumswissenschaft, 34 vols. and 15 suppl. vols. and index, ed. A. F. von Pauly, G. Wissowa, W. Kroll, K. Mittelhaus, and

K. Ziegler (Stuttgart, 2d ed. 1893–1970; last three suppl. vols. and index, Munich, 1973–78).

Redondo, A., ed., *L'humanisme dans les lettres espagnoles* (Paris, 1979).

La Renaissance et la Reformation en Pologne et en Hongrie . . . (1450–1650) (Budapest, 1962).

Renaissance Reconsidered: A Symposium (Northampton, MA, 1964).

Repertorium bibliographicum, 2 vols. in 4 (Stuttgart, 1826–38): list of incunabula.

La "Republique" de Jean Bodin: Atti del convegno di Perugia (Florence, 1981).

Righini Bonelli, M. L. and W. R. Shea, eds., *Reason, Experiment, and Mysticism in the Scientific Revolution* (New York, 1975).

Robbins, K., ed., *Religion and Humanism* (Oxford, 1981).

Rochon, A., ed., *Les écrivains et le pouvoir en Italie à l'époque de la Renaissance* (Paris, 1973).

Rowe, J. G. and W. H. Stockdale, eds., *Florilegium Historiale: Essays Presented to Wallace K. Ferguson* (Toronto, 1971).

Rubinstein, N., ed., *Florentine Studies* (Evanston, IL, 1968).

Saggi sulla cultura veneta del Quattrocento e Cinquecento (Padua, 1971).

Santoro, Marco, ed., *Il libro a stampa, I Primordi* (Naples, 1970).

Sarton, George: *Isis* 75 (1984) devoted to his work.

Scaglione, A., ed., *Francis Petrarch, Six Centuries Later* (Chapel Hill and Chicago, 1975).

Schalk, F., ed., *Petrarca 1304–1374. Beiträge zu Werk und Wirkung* (Frankfurt, 1975).

Schallaburg, '82, Matthias Corvinus und die Renaissance in Ungarn (Schallaburg, 1982).

Schmitz, R. and F. Krafft, eds., *Humanismus und Naturwissenschaften* (Boppard am Rhein, 1980).

Scienze credenze occulte livelli di cultura: Covegno internazionale di studi (Firenze 20–30 giugno, 1980), Istituto Nazionale di Studi sul Rinascimento (Florence, 1982).

Scolari, A., ed., *Scritti di varia letteratura e critica* (Bologna, 1937).

Sharratt, P., ed., *French Renaissance Studies, 1540–1570* (Edinburgh, 1976).

Shirley, J. W. and Hoeniger, F. D., eds., *Science and the Arts in the Renaissance* (Washington, DC, 1985).

Singleton, C. S., ed., *Art, Science, and History in the Renaissance* (Baltimore, 1967).

Smith, G. C., ed., *Elizabethan Critical Essays*, 2 vols. (Oxford, 1904).

Söter, I., ed., *A magyar irodalom története* [*History of Hungarian Literature*], 6 vols. (Budapest, 1964–66).

Spitz, L. W., ed., *The Northern Renaissance* (Englewood Cliffs, NJ, 1972).

Stone, L., ed., *The University in Society,* 2 vols. (Princeton, 1974–75).

Storia della cultura veneta, 5 vols. in 8 (Vicenza, 1976–84).

Storia di Milano, 17 vols. (Milan, 1953–66).

Storia di Napoli, 11 vols. in 15 (Naples, 1967–78).

Studi su Antonio de Ferrariis (Galatone, 1970).

Thompson, J. W., et al., *The Civilization of the Renaissance* (Chicago, 1929).

Towns, E. L., ed., *A History of Religious Educators* (Grand Rapids, MI, 1975).

Trend, J. B. and Loews, H., eds., *Isaac Abravanel, Six Lectures* (Cambridge, 1937).

Trezzini, G. B. et al., *Tra Latino e Volgare: Per Carlo Dionisotti* (Padua, 1974).

Trinkaus, C. and H. A. Oberman, eds., *The Pursuit of Holiness in Late Medieval and Renaissance Religion* (Leiden, 1974).

Tuñón de Lara, M., ed., *Historia de España* (Madrid, 1982), vols. 4–5.

Twersky, I. and B. Septimus, eds., *Jewish Thought in the Seventeenth Century* (Cambridge, MA, 1987).

Umanesimo e Rinascimento: Studi offerti a Paul Oskar Kristeller (Florence, 1980).

Università, Accademie e società scientifiche in Italia e in Germania dal Cinquecento al Settecento (Bologna, 1981).

VI Centenario della morte di Giovanni Boccaccio: Mostra di manoscritti, documenti e edizioni. Firenze—Biblioteca Medicea Laurenziana, 22 maggio–31 agosto 1975, 2 vols. (Certaldo, 1975): catalog.

Vickers, B., ed., *Occult and Scientific Mentalities in the Renaissance* (Cambridge, 1984).

———, *Rhetoric Revalued* (Binghamton, NY, 1982).

Vielhaber, G. and G. Indra, eds., *Catalogus codicum Plagensium manuscriptorum* (Linz, 1918).

Vivanti, C., ed., *Storia dell'Italia, Annali 4, Intellettuali e potere* (Turin, 1981).

Wear, A., R. K. French, and I. M. Lonie, eds., *The Medical Renaissance of the Sixteenth Century* (Cambridge, 1985).

Westman, R. S. and J. E. McGuire, eds., *Hermeticism and the Scientific Revolution* (Los Angeles, 1977).

Williams, K., ed., *Twentieth-Century Interpretations of the Praise of Folly* (Englewood Cliffs, NJ, 1966).

Worstbrock, F. J., ed., *Der Brief im Zeitalter der Renaissance* (Weinheim, 1983).

Zbornik radova o Federiku Grisogonu [*A Collection of Works About Federik Grisogono*] (Zadar, 1974).

SECONDARY SOURCES: INDIVIDUAL AUTHORS

Abati Olivieri Giordani, A. degli, *Notizie di Battista Montefeltro moglie di Galeazzo Malatesta signore di Pesaro* (Pesaro, 1782).

Abbott, D. P., "The Renaissance," in *The Present State of Scholarship in Historical and Contemporary Rhetoric*, ed. W. B. Horner (Columbia, MO, 1983), 75–100.

Abel, G., *Stoizismus und frühe Neuzeit* (Berlin, 1978).

Ábel, J., *Magyarországi humanisták és a Dunai Tudós Társaság* [*Hungarian Humanists and the Sodalitas Danubiana*] (Budapest, 1880).

Abellán, J. L., *Historia crítica del pensamiento español*, 4 vols. (Madrid, 1979–85).

Abercrombie, N., *St. Augustine and Classical French Thought* (Oxford, 1938).

Abrams, M. H., *The Mirror and the Lamp: Romantic Theory and the Critical Tradition* (Oxford, 1974).

Ackerman, J. S., "Leonardo's Eye," *Journal of the Warburg and Courtauld Institutes* 41 (1978): 108–46.

Ács, P., "A magyar irodalmi nyelv két elmélete: az Erazmista és a Balassi-követö" ["Two Theories on the Hungarian Literary Language: The Erasmists and the Balassi Followers"], *Reneszánsz füzetek* 53 (1983): 391–403.

Adams, R. P., *The Better Part of Valor: More, Erasmus, Colet and Vives on Humanism, War and Peace, 1496–1535* (Seattle, 1962).

Adolph, R., *The Rise of Modern Prose Style* (Cambridge, MA, 1968).

Ady, C. M., *A History of Milan Under the Sforza*, ed. E. Armstrong (London, 1907).

Agnelli, G., *Olimpia Morata* (Ferrara, 1892).

Aguzzi-Barbagli, D., "Un contributo di Francesco Patrizi alle dottrine rinascimentali sull'amore," *Yearbook of Italian Studies* 2 (1972): 19–50.

———, "Francesco Patrizi e l'umanesimo musicale del Cinquecento," in *L'umanesimo e l'Istria*, ed. Branca and Graciotti (q.v.), 63–90.

Ajo y Sainz de Zuñiga, C. M., *Historia de las universidades hispánicas*, 2 vols. (Madrid, 1957).

Albertini, R. von, *Das florentinische Staatsbewusstsein im Übergang von der Republik zum Prinzipat* (Bern, 1955).

Alekseev, M. P., *Javlenie gumanizma v literature i publicistike drevnej Rusi (XVI–XVII vv.)* [*The Phenomenon of Humanism and Renaissance in the Literature and Public Statements of Old Rus' XVI–XVII C.*] (Moscow, 1958).

Alessio, G. C., "Appunti sulla diffusione manoscritta di Virgilio nel Mezzogiorno d'Italia," in *Atti del convegno virgiliano di Brindisi* (Perugia, 1983), 361–81.

———, "Brunetto Latini e Cicerone (e i dettatori)," *Italia medioevale e umanistica* 22 (1979): 123–69.

Allen, C. G., "The Sources of Lily's Latin Grammar," *Library* 5th ser. 9 (1954): 85–100.

Allen, P. S., *The Age of Erasmus* (Oxford, 1914).

Alonso, B. S., *Historia de la historiografía española*, 3 vols. (Madrid, 1944–50).

Altamura, A., *La letteratura dell'età angioina* (Naples, 1952).

———, *Studi e ricerche di letteratura umanistica* (Naples, 1956).

———, *L'umanesimo nel Mezzogiorno d'Italia* (Florence, 1941).

———, "La letteratura volgare," in *Storia di Napoli*, 11 vols. in 15 (Naples, 1967–78), 4:501–72.

Altmann, A., "*Ars Rhetorica* as Reflected in Some Jewish Figures of the Italian Renaissance," in *Jewish Thought in the Sixteenth Century*, ed. Cooperman (q.v.), 1–22.

———, "Expressions of the Uniqueness of the Jewish People During the Period of the Renaissance" [Hebrew], *Sinai* 76 (1975): 36–46.

Amaturo, R., *Francesco Petrarca* (Rome, 1980).

Anastos, M., "Some Aspects of Byzantine Influence in Latin Thought," in *Twelfth-Century Europe and the Foundations of Modern Society* (Madison, WI, 1961), 138–49.

Andreas, W., *Deutschland vor der Reformation: Eine Zeitenwende* (Stuttgart, 1932).

Andrés, G. de, *El maestro Baltasar de Céspedes y su "Discurso de las letras humanas"* (El Escorial, 1965).

Andrés, M., "Las facultades de teología españolas hasta 1575: Cátedras diversas," *Anthologica annua* (1972): 123–78.

Andrews, A., "The 'Lost' Fifth Book of the Life of Paul II by Gaspare of Verona," *Studies in the Renaissance* 17 (1970): 7–45.

Angelieri, C., *Il problema religiosa del Rinascimento* (Florence, 1952).

Angelis, V. de, *Papiae elementarium: Littera A* (Milan, 1977).

Arcari, P. M., *Il pensiero politico di Francesco Patrizi da Cherso* (Rome, 1935).

Archambault, P., *Seven French Chroniclers* (Syracuse, 1974).

Arnaldi, G., "Alle origini dello Studio di Bologna," in *Le sedi della cultura nell'Emilia Romagna: L'età comunale* (Milan, 1984).

Arnold, K., *Johannes Trithemius (1462–1516)* (Würzburg, 1971).

Artz, F. B., *Renaissance Humanism, 1300–1550* (Kent, OH, 1966).

Asaf, S., "From the Hidden Treasures of the Library in Jerusalem" [Hebrew], *Minhah le-David: Kovez Ma'amarim be-Hokhmat Yisra'el R. David Yellin* [*Present to David: A Collection of Essays in Jewish Thought in Honor of David Yellin*] (Jerusalem, 1935), 226–28.

Aschback, J. R. von, *Geschichte der Wiener Universität und ihre Humanisten*, 3 vols. (Vienna, 1865–88; reprinted Vienna, 1965).

Asensio, E., "El erasmismo y las corrientes espirituales afines, conversos, franciscanos, italianizantes," *Revista de filología española* 36 (1952): 31–99.

Astuti, G., *Mos italicus et mos gallicus nei dialogi "de iuris interpretibus" di Alberico Gentili* (Bologna, 1937).

Auer, A., *Die vollkommene Frömmigkeit des Christen* (Düsseldorf, 1954).

Auerbach, E., "Sermo humilis," *Romanische Forschungen* 64 (1952): 304–64; 66 (1954): 1–64.

Avilés, M., "La teología española en el siglo XV," in *Historia de la teología española* (Madrid, 1983), 1:495–577.

Baekelants, L. and R. Hoven, *Bibliographie des oeuvres de Nicolas Clénard 1529–1700*, 2 vols. (Verviers, 1981).

Baer, Y., *A History of the Jews in Christian Spain*, 2 vols. (Philadelphia, 1961–66).

Baere, S. de, "Hadrianus Junius' *Nomenclator omnium rerum* als deutsches Wörterbuch. Sprache und Quellen" (Ph.D. diss., University of Ghent, 1981).

Bahner, W., *La linguistica española del Siglo de Oro*, trans. J. Munárriz Peralta (Madrid, 1966).

Bainton, R. H., *Erasmus of Christendom* (New York, 1969).

———, *Women of the Reformation from Spain to Scandinavia* (Minneapolis, 1977).

———, *Women of the Reformation in France and England* (Minneapolis, 1973; repr. Boston, 1975).

———, *Women of the Reformation in Germany and Italy* (Minneapolis, 1971).

Balázs, J., *Sylvester János és kora* [*János Sylvester and His Time*] (Budapest, 1957).

Baldwin, C. S., *Medieval Rhetoric and Poetic* (New York, 1928).

———, *Renaissance Literary Theory and Practice: Classicism in the Rhetoric and Poetic of Italy, France, and England, 1400–1600* (New York, 1939).

Baldwin, T. W., *William Shakespere's Small Latine and Lesse Greeke*, 2 vols. (Urbana, Il, 1914).

Ballistreri, G., "Bonaccorso da Pisa," *Dizionario biografico degli italiani*, 30 vols. to date (Rome, 1960–84), 11:464–65.

———, "Cattaneo (Cataneo), Giovanni Maria (Mario)," *Dizionario biografico degli italiani*, 30 vols. to date (Rome, 1960–84), 22:468–71.

Balogh, J., *A müvészet Mátyás király udvarában* [*Art at the Court of King Matthias*], 2 vols. (Budapest, 1966).

Bán, I., "Adalékok Balassi-versértelmezésekhez" ["Contributions to the Analysis of Balassi Poems"], *Studia litteraria* 17 (1979): 14–24.

Banker, J. R., "The *Ars Dictaminis* and Rhetorical Textbooks at the Bolognese University in the Fourteenth Century," *Mediaevalia et Humanistica* n.s. 5 (1974): 153–68.

———, "Giovanni di Bonandrea and Civic Values in the Context of the Italian Rhetorical Tradition," *Manuscripta* 18 (1974): 3–20.

———, "Giovanni di Bonandrea's *Ars dictaminis* Treatise and the Doctrine of Invention in the Italian Rhetorical Tradition of the Thirteenth and Early Fourteenth Centuries" (Ph.D. diss., University of Rochester, 1972).

Barbera, C. A., "The Persistence of Pythagorean Mathematics in Ancient Musical Thought" (Ph.D. diss., University of North Carolina, Chapel Hill, 1980).

Barberi Squarotti, G., "Le poetiche del Trecento in Italia," in *Momenti e problemi di storia dell'estetica* (Milan, 1959), 255–324.

Barboran, E., *Girolamo Fracastoro e le sue opere* (Verona, 1897).

Barbour, J. M., *Tuning and Temperament* (East Lansing, MI, 1953).

Barilli, R., *Poetica e retorica* (Milan, 1969).

———, "Le poetiche e la critica d'arte," in *Il Cinquecento: Dal Rinascimento alla Controriforma* (Bari, 1973), 506–71.

Barker, E., *Traditions of Civility* (Hamden, CT, 1967; reprint of 1948).

Baron, H., *The Crisis of the Early Italian Renaissance: Civic Humanism and Republican Liberty in an Age of Classicism and Tyranny*, 2 vols. (Princeton, 1955; rev. ed. in one volume, 1966).

———, *From Petrarch to Leonardo Bruni: Studies in Humanistic and Political Literature* (Chicago, 1968).

———, *Humanistic and Political Literature in Florence and Venice at the Beginning of the Quattrocento: Studies in Criticism and Chronology* (Cambridge, MA, 1955).

———, "Cicero and the Roman Civic Spirit in the Middle Ages and the Early Renaissance," *Bulletin of the John Rylands Library* 22 (1938): 72–97.

———, "Das Erwachsen des historischen Denkens in Humanismus des Quattrocento," *Historisches Zeitschrift* 147 (1932): 5–20.

————, "Franciscan Poverty and Civic Wealth as Factors in the Rise of Humanistic Thought," *Speculum* 13 (1938): 1–37.

————, "Leonardo Bruni: 'Professional Rhetorician' or 'Civic Humanist'?" *Past and Present* 36 (1967): 21–37.

————, "Moot Problems of Renaissance Interpretation: An Answer to Wallace K. Ferguson," *Journal of the History of Ideas* 19 (1958): 26–34.

————, "The *Querelle* of the Ancients and the Moderns as a Problem for Renaissance Scholarship," *Journal of the History of Ideas* 20 (1957): 3–22.

————, "Secularization of Wisdom and Political Humanism in the Renaissance," *Journal of the History of Ideas* 21 (1960): 131–50.

————, "Towards a More Positive Evaluation of the Fifteenth-Century Renaissance," *Journal of the History of Ideas* 4 (1943): 21–49.

Baron, S. W., *A Social and Religious History of the Jews,* 18 vols. (New York, 2d ed. 1952–83), 13:159–205: "Humanism and Renaissance."

Barozzi, L. and R. Sabbadini, *Studi sul Panormita e sul Valla* (Florence, 1891).

Barré, H., *Les homéliaires carolingiens de l'école d'Auxerre* (Vatican City, 1962).

Barzilay, I., *Between Faith and Reason: Anti-Rationalism in Italian Jewish Thought, 1250–1650* (The Hague and Paris, 1967); reviewed by J. Sermoneta in *Kiryat Sefer* 45 (1970): 539–46 (Hebrew).

Bataillon, M., *Erasmo y el erasmismo,* trans. C. Pujol (Barcelona, 1977).

————, *Erasmo y España,* trans. A. Alatorre (Mexico, 1950).

————, *Estudios sobre Bartolomé de las Casas,* trans. J. Coderch and J. A. Martínez Schrem (Barcelona, 1976).

Battistella, A., "Un inventario d'un maestro friuliano del Quattrocento," *Memorie storiche foroguiliesi* 21 (1925): 139–59.

Battistini, A., "I manuali di retorica dei Gesuiti," in *La Ratio studiorum: Modelli culturali e pratiche educative dei Gesuiti in Italia tra Cinque e Seicento,* ed. G. P. Brizzi (Rome, 1981), 77–120.

Bauch, G., *Die Rezeption des Humanismus in Wien* (Breslau, 1903).

Bauer, D. K., *Die Wittenberger Universitätstheologie und die Anfänge der deutschen Reformation* (Tübingen, 1928).

Baumann, H., *Die Geschichtsschreiber Philippe de Commynes und die Wirkung seiner politischen Vorstellung in Frankreich um die Mitte des 16. Jahrhunderts* (Munich, 1982).

Baur, J., *Jean Chrysostome et ses oeuvres dans l'histoire littéraire* (Louvain, 1907).

Baxandall, M., *Giotto and the Orators: Humanist Observers of Painting in Italy and the Discovery of Pictorial Composition, 1350–1450* (Oxford, 1971).

————, *Painting and Experience in Fifteenth-Century Italy* (Oxford, 1972).

Bayerle, G., "The Compromise at Zsitvatorok," *Archivum Ottomanicum* 6 (1980): monograph.

Bayley, C. C., *War and Society in Renaissance Florence: The "De militia" of Leonardo Bruni* (Toronto, 1961).

Beck, H. G., "Intellectual Life in the Late Byzantine Church," *Handbook of Church History* 4 (1968): 505–12.

Bečka, J. and E. Urbánková, *Katalogy knihoven kolejí Karlový university* [*Catalogs of College Libraries in the Caroline University*] (Prague, 1948).

Becker, M. B., *Florence in Transition,* 2 vols. (Baltimore, 1967–68).

Bedini, S. A. and F. R. Maddison, "Mechanical Universe: The Astrarium of Giovanni de' Dondi," *Transactions of the American Philosophical Society* n.s. 56.5 (1966): monograph.

Bedouelle, G., *Lefèvre d'Etaples et l'intelligence des Ecritures* (Geneva, 1976).

———, *Le Quincuplex Psalterium de Lefèvre d'Etaples: Un guide de lecture* (Geneva, 1979).

Bell, S. G., "Medieval Women Book Owners: Arbiters of Lay Piety and Ambassadors of Culture," *Signs* 7 (1982): 742–68.

Belladonna, R., "Pontanus, Machiavelli and a Case of Religious Dissimulation in Early Sixteenth-Century Siena (Carli's *Trattati nove della prudenza*)," *Bibliothèque d'humanisme et Renaissance* 37 (1975): 377–85.

Beltrán de Heredia, V., *Bulario de la Universidad de Salamanca,* 3 vols. (Salamanca, 1966).

———, *Cartulario de la Universidad de Salamanca,* 3 vols. (Salamanca, 1970).

Béné, C., *Erasme et Saint Augustin ou Influence de Saint Augustin sur l'humanisme d'Erasme* (Geneva, 1969).

Benedictis, L. de, *Della vita e della opere di Bernardino Tomitano* (Padua, 1903).

Benesch, O., *The Art of the Renaissance in Northern Europe* (London, rev. ed. 1965).

Benito Ruano, E., *Los orígenes del problema converso* (Barcelona, 1976).

Bentley, J. H., *Humanists and Holy Writ: New Testament Scholarship in the Renaissance* (Princeton, 1983).

Benzing, J., *Bibliographie der Schriften Johannes Reuchlin* (Vienna, 1955).

Berceiro, I., "La biblioteca del conde de Benavente a mediados del siglo XV y su relación con las mentalidades y usos nobiliarios de la época," *En la España medieval: Estudios en memoria del Professor D. Salvador de Moxó,* ed. M. A. Ladero Quesada, 3 vols. (Madrid, 1982), 2:135–45.

Berger, H., *Calvins Geschichtsauffassung* (Zurich, 1955).

Bergin, T. G., *Boccaccio* (New York, 1981).

Berkowitz, D. S., *Humanist Scholarship and Public Order* (Washington, DC, 1984).

Bermejo Cabrero, J. L., "Orígenes del oficio de cronista real," *Hispania* 145 (1980): 395–409.

———, "Los primeros secretarios de los reyes," *Anuario de historia del derecho español* 49 (1979): 187–286.

Bernardini, A. and G. Righi, *Il concetto di philologia e di cultura classica* (Bari, 1953).

Bernardo, A. S., *Petrarch, Laura and the "Triumphs"* (Albany, NY, 1974).

———, *Petrarch, Scipio and the "Africa": The Birth of Humanism's Dream* (Baltimore, 1962).

———, "Petrarch's Attitude Toward Dante," *PMLA* 70 (1955): 488–517.

Bernardo, F. di, *Un vescovo umanista alla corte pontificia: Giannantonio Campano (1429–1477)* (Rome, 1975).

Bernstein, E., *German Humanism* (Boston, 1983).

Berrigan, J. R., *The Chronicles of the Trevisan March* (Lawrence, KS, 1980).

Berschin, W., *Griechisch-lateinisches Mittelalter* (Bern, 1980).

Bertalot, L., *Studien zum italienischen und deutschen Humanismus*, ed. P. O. Kristeller, 2 vols. (Rome, 1975).

———, "Rudolf Agricolas Lobrede auf Petrarch," *La Bibliofilia* 30 (1928): 382–404.

Bertelli, S., *Ribelli, libertini e ortodossi nella storiografia barocca* (Florence, 1973).

Bertini, G. M., "Un diálogo humanístico sobre la educación del principe Don Juan," in *Fernando el Católico y la cultura de su tiempo* (Zaragoza, 1961), 37–62.

Bertola, M., *I due primi registri di prestito della Biblioteca Apostolica Vaticana* (Vatican City, 1942).

Bertoni, G., *Il duecento* (Milan, 1930).

———, "Nota su Vincenzo Maggi," *Giornale storico della letteratura italiana* 96 (1930): 325–27.

Berzero, G., "Girolamo Savonarola," in *Orientamenti culturali; Letteratura italiani; I Minori* (Milan, 1969), 1:743–67.

Besomi, O., "Dai *Gesta Ferdinandi regis Aragonum* del Valla al *De orthographia* del Tortelli," *Italia medioevale e umanistica* 9 (1966): 75–121.

Beyer, H. W., "Gott und die Geschichte nach Luthers Sulegung des *Magnificat*," *Luther Jahrbuch* 21 (1939): 110–34.

Bezzola, R. R., *Les origines et la formation de la littérature courtoise en Occident (500–1200)*, pt. 1, tome 1, *La tradition impériale de la fin de l'antiquité au XIᶜ siècle* (Paris, 1958).

———, *Les origines et la formation de la littérature courtoise en occident (500–1200)*, pt. 2, tome 1, *La société féodale et la transformation de la littérature de cour* (Paris, 1960).

Biéler, A., *The Social Humanism of Calvin* (Richmond, VA, 1968).

Bietenholz, P., *History and Biography in the Works of Erasmus of Rotterdam* (Geneva, 1966).

Bigi, E., *La cultura del Poliziano e altri studi umanistici* (Pisa, 1967).

———, "Ambrogini, Angelo (Poliziano)," *Dizionario biografico degli italiani*, 30 vols. to date (Rome, 1960–84), 2:691–702.

———, "Barbaro, Ermolao," *Dizionario biografico degli italiani*, 30 vols. to date (Rome, 1960–84): The Elder, 6:95–96; The Younger, 6:96–99.

———, "Il Poliziano critico," *La rassegna della letteratura italiana* 58 (1954): 367–76.

Bignami-Odier, J., *La bibliothèque vaticane de Sixte IV à Pie IX* (Vatican City, 1973).

Billanovich, Giuseppe, *Petrarca letterato*, vol. 1, *Lo scrittoio del Petrarca* (Rome, 1947).

———, *La tradizione del testo di Livio e le origini dell'umanesimo*, vol. 1, *Tradizione e fortuna di Livio tra medioevo e umanesimo*, pt. 1 (Padua, 1981).

————, "Da Livio di Raterio al Livio del Petrarca," *Italia medioevale e umanistica* 2 (1959): 103–78.

————, "Giovanni del Virgilio, Pietro da Moglio, Francesco da Fiano," *Italia medioevale e umanistica* 6 (1963): 203–34; 7 (1964): 277–324.

————, "Petrarca e gli storici romani," in *Francesco Petrarca, Citizen of the World*, ed. Bernardo (q.v.), 100–14.

————, "Il Petrarca e i retori latini minori," *Italia medioevale e umanistica* 5 (1962): 103–64.

————, "Il Petrarca, il Boccaccio, Zanobi da Strada e le tradizioni dei testi della cronaca di Ugo Falcando e di alcune vite dei Pontefici," *Rinascimento* 4 (1953): 17–24.

————, "Petrarca, Pietro da Moglio e Pietro da Parma," *Italia medioevale e umanistica* 22 (1979): 367–95.

————, "Petrarch and the Textual Tradition of Livy," *Journal of the Warburg and Courtauld Institutes* 14 (1951): 137–208.

————, "Pietro Piccolo da Monforte tra il Petrarca e il Boccaccio," in *Medioevo e Rinascimento: Studi in onore di Bruno Nardi*, 2 vols. (Florence, 1955), 1:3–76.

————, "Terenzio, Ildemaro, Petrarca (Tav. I–VII)," *Italia medioevale e umanistica* 17 (1974): 1–60.

————, "Tra Dante e il Petrarca," *Italia medioevale e umanistica* 8 (1965): 1–44.

————, "La tradizione del "Liber de dictis philosophorum antiquorum" e la cultura di Dante, del Petrarca e del Boccaccio," *Studi petrarcheschi* 1 (1948): 111–23.

———— and M. Ferraris, "Le Emendationes in T. Livium del Valla e il Codex Regius di Livio," *Italia medioevale e umanistica* 1 (1958): 245–64.

Billanovich, Guido, "Il preumanesimo padovano," in *Storia della cultura veneta*, 5 vols. in 8 (Vicenza, 1976–84), 2:19–110.

————, "*Veterum vestigia vatum* nei carmi dei preumanisti padovani: Lovato Lovati, Zambono di Andrea, Albertino Mussato e Lucrezio, Catullo, Orazio (*Carmina*), Tibullo, Properzio, Ovidio (*Ibis*), Marziale, Stazio (*Silvae*)," *Italia medioevale e umanistica* 1 (1958): 155–243.

Billanovich, M., "Benedetto Bordon e Giulio Cesare Scaligero," *Italia medioevale e umanistica* 11 (1968): 187–256.

Birkenmaier, A., "Der Streit des Alonso von Cartagena mit Leonardo Bruni Aretino," *Beiträge zur Geschichte der Philosophie des Mittelalters* 20 (1922): 129–210.'

Birnbaum, M. D., *Humanists in a Shattered World: Croatian and Hungarian Latinity in the Sixteenth Century* (Los Angeles, 1985).

————, *Janus Pannonius: Poet and Politician* (Zagreb, 1981).

Black, R., *Benedetto Accolti and the Florentine Renaissance* (Cambridge, 1985).

Blade, M. K., *Education of Italian Renaissance Women* (Mesquite, TX, 1983).

Blau, J. L., *The Christian Interpretation of the Cabala in the Renaissance* (Port Washington, NY, 1944, reprinted 1965).

Bloch, H., "Monte Cassino's Teachers and Library in the High Middle Ages," in *La scuola nell'Occidente latino dell'alto medioevo* (Spoleto, 1972), 563–605.

Bludau, A., *Die beiden ersten Erasmus-Ausgaben des Neuen Testaments und ihre Gegner* (Freiburg, 1902).

Bluher, K. A., *Seneca in Spanien. Untersuchungen zur Geschichte der Seneca-Rezeption in Spanien vom 13 bis 17 Jahrhundert* (Munich, 1969), Spanish trans. revised and expanded, *Séneca en España*, trans. J. Conde (Madrid, 1983).

Blum, R., *La biblioteca della Badia Fiorentina e i codici di Antonio Corbinelli* (Vatican City, 1951).

Blumenberg, H., *Die Genesis der kopernikanischen Welt* (Frankfurt am Main, 1975); assessment of Blumenberg: K. Harries, "Copernican Reflections," *Inquiry* 23 (1980): 253–69.

———, *Die kopernikanische Wende* (Frankfurt am Main, 1975).

———, *Die Legitimität der Neuzeit (erweiterte und überarbeitete Neuausgabe)*, 3 vols. (Frankfurt am Main, 1973–76); *The Legitimacy of the Modern Age*, trans. R. M. Wallace (Cambridge, MA and London, 1983); review essay, M. Jay, *History and Theory* 24 (1985): 183–96.

———, "'Nachahmung der Natur': Zur Vorgeschichte der Idee des schöpferischen Menschen," *Studium generale* 10 (1957): 266–83.

Blunt, A., *Artistic Theory in Italy, 1450–1600* (Oxford, 1940; reprinted 1966).

Boas, M., *The Scientific Renaissance: 1450–1630* (New York, 1962).

Bobbio, A., "Seneca e la formazione spirituale e culturale del Petrarca," *La bibliofilia* 43 (1941): 224–91.

Bober, P. P., "The 'Coryciana' and the Nymph Coryciana," *Journal of the Warburg and Courtauld Institutes* 40 (1977): 223–39.

Bodmer, J. P., "Die französische Historiographie des Spätmittelalters und die Franken," *Archiv für Kulturgeschichte* 45 (1963): 91–118.

Boehmer, H., *The Jesuits: An Historical Study*, trans. P. Zeller Strodach (Philadelphia, 1928).

Bogges, W. F., "Aristotle's Poetics in the Fourteenth Century," *Studies in Philology* 67 (1970): 278–94.

Boháček, M., "Literatura středověkých právních škol v rukopisech Kapitulní knihovny Olomoucké" ["The Literature of Medieval Legal Schools in the Manuscripts of the Chapter Library of Olomouc"], *Rozpravy Československe Akademie věd* 70, no. 7 (Prague, 1960), 87pp.

Bohatec, J., *Budé und Calvin: Studien zur Bedankenwelt des französischen Frühhumanismus* (Graz, 1950).

Boissier, G., *Ciceron et ses amis* (Paris, 13th ed. 1905).

Bolgar, R. R., *The Classical Heritage and Its Beneficiaries* (Cambridge, 1954).

Bolzoni, L., *L'universo dei poemi possibili: Studi su Francesco Patrizi* (Rome, 1980).

———, "Il 'Badoaro' di Francesco Patrizi e l'Accademia Veneziana della Fama," *Giornale storico della letteratura italiana* 158 (1981): 71–101.

———, "Ercole e i pigmei, ovvero Controriforma e intellettuali neoplatonici," *Rinascimento* 21 (1981): 285–96.

————, "La poesia e le 'imagini dei sognati' (Una risposta inedita del Patrizi al Cremonini)," *Rinascimento* 19 (1979): 171–88.

————, "La 'Poetica' del Patrizi e la cultura veneta del primo Cinquecento," in *L'umanesimo e l'Istria,* ed. Branca and Graciotti (q.v.), 19–35.

————, "La 'Poetica' di Francesco Patrizi da Cherso: Il progetto di un modello universale della poesia," *Giornale storico della letteratura italiana,* 151 (1974): 357–82; 152 (1975): 33–56.

————, "Il segretario neoplatonico (F. Patrizi, A. Querenghi, V. Gramigna)," in *Centro Studi Europa delle Corti: La Corte e il "Cortegiano"* (Rome, 1980), 2:133–69.

Bondella, P., *Machiavelli and the Art of Renaissance History* (Detroit, 1973).

Bonfil, R., *Ha-Rabbanut be-Italyah bi-Tekufat ha-Renesance* [*The Rabbinate in Italy in the Period of the Renaissance*] (Jerusalem, 1979).

————, "Change in Cultural Patterns of Jewish Society in Crisis: The Case of Italian Jewry at the Close of the Sixteenth Century," in *The Transformation of Jewish Society in the Sixteenth and Seventeenth Centuries,* forthcoming.

————, "Cultura e mistica a Venezia nel '500," in *Gli ebrei e Venezia,* ed. G. Cozzi (Milan, 1987), 469–509, 543–48.

————, "Expressions of the Uniqueness of the Jewish People During the Period of the Renaissance" [Hebrew], *Sinai* 76 (1975): 36–46.

————, "The Historian's Perception of the Jews in the Italian Renaissance: Towards a Reappraisal," *Revue des études juives* 143 (1984): 59–82.

Boni, M., "Note ai *Rerum memorandarum libri,*" *Studi petrarcheschi* 2 (1949): 167–81.

Bonilla y San Martín, A., *Fernando de Córdoba (1425?–1486?) y los orígenes del Renacimiento filosófico en España: Episodio de la historia de la lógica* (Madrid, 1911).

————, *Luis Vives y la filosofía dei Renacimiento,* 3 vols. (Madrid, 1929).

————, "Un aristotelico del Renacimiento: Hernando Alonso de Herrera y su breve disputa de ocho levadas contra Aristotil y sus secuaces," *Revue hispanique* 50 (1920): 61–196.

————, "Erasmo en España," *Revue hispanique* 17 (1907): 379–548.

Bonita, V. A., "The Saint Anne Altar in Sant'Agostino: Restoration and Interpretation," *Burlington Magazine* 124 (1982): 268–80.

Bonner, S. F., *Education in Ancient Rome: From the Elder Cato to the Younger Pliny* (Berkeley, 1977).

Bonnet, J., *Vie d'Olympia Morata: Épisode de la Renaissance et de la Réforme en Italie* (Paris, 3d ed. 1856).

Borchardt, F. L., *German Antiquity in Renaissance Myth* (Baltimore, 1971).

Borgeaud, C., *Histoire de l'Université de Genève,* vol. 1 *L'académie de Calvin (1559–1798)* (Geneva, 1900).

Borsa, M., "Correspondence of Humphrey Duke of Gloucester and Pier Candido Decembrio," *English Historical Review* 19 (1904): 509–26.

————, "Pier Candido Decembrio e l'umanesimo in Lombardia," *Archivio storico lombardo* 20 (1893): 5–75, 338–441.

574 BIBLIOGRAPHY FOR VOLUMES 1-3

——, "Un umanista vigevanesco del secolo XIV," *Giornale ligustico* 20 (1893): 81–111.

Borsetto, L., "Il fiuto di Prometeo: Struttura e scrittura nei *Poeticorum libri* di M. G. Vida," *Rassegna della letteratura italiana* 85 (1981): 93–108.

Bosco, U., *F. Petrarca* (Milan, 1956).

——, "Il Petrarca e l'umanesimo filologico," *Giornale storico della letteratura italiana* 119 (1942): 1–55.

Bouterwek, F., *Historia de la literatura española*, trans. J. Gómez de la Cortina and N. Hugalde de Mollineda (Madrid, 1829).

Bouwsma, W. J., *Venice and the Defense of Republican Liberty: Renaissance Values in the Age of the Counter-Reformation* (Berkeley, 1968).

——, "The Renaissance and the Drama of Western History," *American Historical Review* 84 (1979): 1–15.

Bower, C., "Boethius and Nicomachus: An Essay Concerning the Sources of *De institutione musica*," *Vivarium* 16 (1978): 1–45.

Branca, V., *Boccaccio medievale* (Florence, 1956).

——, *Boccaccio: The Man and his Works,* trans. R. Monges (New York, 1976).

——, *Poliziano e l'umanesimo della parola* (Turin, 1983).

——, "Ermolao Barbaro e l'umanesimo veneziano," in *Umanesimo europeo e umanesimo veneziano*, ed. Branca (q.v.), 193–212.

——, "L'umanesimo veneziano alla fine del Quattrocento: Ermolao Barbaro," in *Storia della cultura veneta*, 5 vols. in 8 (Vicenza, 1976–84), 3.1:123–75.

Brandileone, F., *Saggi sulla storia della celebrazione del matrimonio in Italia* (Milan, 1906).

Brandt, W. J., *The Shape of Medieval History* (New Haven, 1966).

Brann, N. L., *The Abbot Trithemius (1462–1516): The Renaissance of Monastic Humanism* (Leiden, 1981).

——, "Conrad Celtis and the 'Druid' Abbot Trithemius: An Inquiry into Patriotic Humanism," *Renaissance and Reformation/Renaissance et réforme* n.s. 3, o.s. 15 (1979): 16–28.

——, "Was Paracelsus a Disciple of Trithemius?" *Sixteenth Century Journal* 10 (1979): 71–82.

Bravo Garcia, A., "Sobre las traducciones de Plutarco y de Quinto Curcio Rufo hechas por Pier Candido Decembrio y su fortuna en España," *Cuadernos de filología clásica* 12 (1977): 143–85.

Breen, Q., *Christianity and Humanism: Studies in the History of Ideas*, ed. N. P. Ross (Grand Rapids, MI, 1968).

——, *John Calvin: A Study in French Humanism* (Grand Rapids, MI, 2d ed. 1968).

——, "Giovanni Pico della Mirandola on the Conflict of Philosophy and Rhetoric," *Journal of the History of Ideas* 13 (1952): 384–412.

——, "John Calvin and the Rhetorical Tradition," in his *Christianity and Humanism* (q.v.), 107–29.

Breisach, E., *Historiography: Ancient, Medieval, and Modern* (Chicago, 1983).

Breitenbürger, G., *Metaphora. Die Rezeption des aristotelischen Begriffs in den Poetiken des Cinquecento* (Kronberg, 1975).

Brentano, R., *Two Churches: England and Italy in the Thirteenth Century* (Princeton, 1968).

Bresslau, H., *Handbuch der Urkundenlehre für Deutschland und Italien* (Leipzig, 1912), vol. 1.

Brettschneider, H., *Melanchthon als Historiker* (Insterberg, 1880).

Brickman, B., "An Introduction to Francesco Patrizi's Nova de universis philosophia" (Ph.D. diss., Columbia University, New York, 1941).

Brink, C. O., *Horace on Poetry*, 3 vols. (Cambridge, 1971–82).

Brink, J. R., *Female Scholars: A Tradition of Learned Women Before 1800* (Montreal, 1980).

Brinkschulte, E., *J. C. Scaliger's kunsttheoretische Anschauungen* (Bonn, 1913).

Brooke, T., *A Literary History of England*, ed. A. C. Baugh (New York, 1948).

Brown, A., *Bartolomeo Scala (1430–1497), Chancellor of Florence: The Humanist as Bureaucrat* (Princeton, 1979).

Brown, A. J., "The Date of Erasmus' Latin Translation of the New Testament," *Transactions of the Cambridge Bibliographical Society* 8:4 (1984): 351–80.

Brown, H. M., *Music in the Renaissance* (Englewood Cliffs, NJ, 1976).

Brown, J. L., *The Methodus ad Facilem Historiarum Cognitionem of Jean Bodin: A Critical Study* (Washington, DC, 1939).

Brown, P. M., "Una grammatichetta inedita del Cavalier Lionardo Salviati," *Giornale storico della letteratura italiana* 133 (1956): 544–72.

———, "I veri promotori della 'rassettatura' del 'Decamerone' nel 1582," *Giornale storico della letteratura italiana* 134 (1957): 314–32.

———, "Manoscritti e stampe delle poesie edite ed inedite del Cavalier Lionardo Salviati," *Giornale storico della letteratura italiana* 146 (1969): 530–49.

Browning, R., "Byzantine Scholarship," *Past and Present* 28 (1964): 3–30.

Brucker, G., *The Civic World of Early Renaissance Florence* (Princeton, 1977).

———, *Florentine Politics and Society, 1343–1378* (Princeton, 1962).

———, *Renaissance Florence* (Berkeley, rev. ed. 1983).

———, "A Civic Debate on Higher Education (1460)," *Renaissance Quarterly* 34 (1981): 517–33.

———, "Florence and Its University, 1348–1434," in *Action and Conviction in Early Modern Europe*, ed. Rabb and Seigel, (q.v.), 220–36.

———, "Tales of Two Cities: Florence and Venice in the Renaissance," *American Historical Review* 88 (1983): 599–616.

Bruère, R. T., "Lucan and Petrarch's *Africa*," *Classical Philology* 56 (1961): 83–99.

Brugnoli, G., "La 'Praefatio in Suetonium' del Poliziano," *Giornale italiano di filologia* 10 (1957): 211–20.

Brummer, H. H. and T. Janson, "Art, Literature and Politics: An Episode in the Roman Renaissance," *Konsthistorisk Tidskrift* 45 (1976): 79–93.

Bryce, J., *Cosimo Bartoli (1503–1572): The Career of a Florentine Polymath* (Geneva, 1983).

Buck, A., *Das Geschichtsdenken der Renaissance* (Krefeld, 1957).

————, *Italienische Dichtungslehren vom Mittelalter bis zum Ausgang der Renaissance* (Tübingen, 1952).

————, "Das Problem des christlichen Humanismus in der italienischen Renaissance," in *Sodalitas Erasmiana* (Naples, 1949), 181–92.

————, "Der Rückgriff des Renaissance-Humanismus auf die Patristik," in *Festschrift Walther von Wartburg*, ed. K. Baldinger (Tübingen, 1968), 1:153–75.

————, "Dichtung und Dichter bei Cristoforo Landino. Ein Beitrag zur Dichtungslehre des italienischen Humanismus," *Romanische Forschungen* 58–59 (1947): 233–46.

————, "Die Rangstellung des Menschen in der Renaissance," *Archiv für Kulturgeschichte* 42 (1960): 61–75.

————, "Über einige Deutungen des Prometheus-Mythos in der Literatur der Renaissance," in *Romanica: Festschrift G. Rohlfs* (Halle, 1958), 86–96.

Bucko, V., *Mikuláš Oláh a jeho doba* [*Miklós Oláh and His Time*] (Bratislava, 1940).

Budd, F. E., "A Minor Italian Critic of the Sixteenth Century: Jason Denores," *Modern Language Review* 22 (1927): 421–34.

Buelow, G., "Rhetoric and Music," in *New Grove Dictionary of Music and Musicians*, ed. S. Sadie, 20 vols. (London and New York, 1980), 15:793–803.

Bueno De Mesquita, D. M., "Cane, Facino," *Dizionario biografico degli italiani*, 30 vols. to date (Rome, 1960–84), 17:791–801.

————, "Cappelli, Pasquino de'," *Dizionario biografico degli italiani*, 30 vols. to date (Rome, 1960–84), 18:727–30.

Buhler, C. F., *Early Books and Manuscripts* (New York, 1973).

————, *The Fifteenth-Century Book* (Philadelphia, 1960).

Bullough, D. A., "Le scuole cattedrali e la cultura dell'Italia settentrionale prima dei comuni," *Vescovi e diocesi in Italia nel medioevo (sec. IX–XIII)* (Padua, 1964), 111–43.

Buonamici, F., *Il Poliziano giureconsulto* (Pisa, 1863).

Burckhardt, J., *The Civilization of the Renaissance in Italy*, trans. S. G. C. Middlemore, 2 vols. (1929; reprinted New York, 1954).

Burdach, K., *Aus Petrarchas älstesten deutschen Schülerkreise* (Berlin, 1929).

————, *Vom Mittelalter zur Reformation*, 3 vols. (Halle, 1893–1926).

Burgess, T. C., "Epideictic Literature," *Studies in Classical Philology* 3 (1902): 89–261.

Burke, P., "A Survey of the Popularity of Ancient Historians, 1450–1700," *History and Theory* 5(1966): 134–52.

Bursill-Hall, G. L., *A Census of Medieval Latin Grammatical Manuscripts* (Stuttgart, 1981).

Burtt, E. A., *Metaphysical Foundations of Modern Science* (New York, 2d ed. 1932).

Buschmann, R., *Das Bewusstsein der deutschen Geschichte bei den deutschen Humanisten* (Göttingen, 1930).

Bush, D., *The Renaissance and English Humanism* (Toronto, 1939).

Bütler, R., *Nationales und universales Denken im Werke Etienne Pasquiers* (Basel, 1948).

Butterfield, H., *The Origins of Modern Science: 1300–1800* (London, 2d ed. 1957).

Bylebyl, J. L., "Medicine, Philosophy, and Humanism in Renaissance Italy," in *Science and the Arts in the Renaissance*, ed. Shirley and Hoeniger (q.v.), 27–49.

Cabanelas, D., *Juan de Segovia y el problema islámico* (Madrid, 1952).

Cagni, G. M., *Vespasiano da Bisticci e il suo epistolario* (Rome, 1969).

Calcaterra, C., *Nella selva del Petrarca* (Bologna, 1942).

———, "Il Petrarca e il Petrarchismo," in *Problemi ed orientamenti critici di lingua e di letteratura italiana*, ed. A. Momigliano, 5 vols. in 6 (Milan, 1948–59), 3:167–273.

Calderini, A., "I codici milanesi delle opere di F. Filelfo," *Archivio storico lombardo* 37 (1915): 335–411.

———, "Ricerche intorno alla biblioteca e alla cultura greca di Francesco Filelfo," *Studi italiani di filologia classica* 20 (1913): 204–424.

Calderini, R., *A. S. Minturno, vita e opere* (Aversa, 1921).

Cammelli, G., *I dotti bizantini e le origini dell'umanesimo*, 3 vols. (Florence, 1951–54).

Campana, A., "Il carteggio di Vitale e Pacifico di Verona," *Atti del congresso internazionale di diritto romano e di storia del diritto, Verona 27–28–29/ix/ 1948*, 4 vols. (Milan, 1951–53), 1:269–80.

———, "The Origin of the Word 'Humanist,'" *Journal of the Warburg and Courtauld Institutes* 9 (1946): 60–73.

———, "Poema antimalatestiano di un umanista spagnolo per Pio II," in *Atti del convegno storico Piccolominiano* (Ancona, 1964–65), 189–218.

———, "Riccobaldo da Ferrara," *Enciclopedia dantesca*, 6 vols. (Rome, 1970–78), 3:908–10.

Campbell, L. B., "A Note on Scaliger's Poetics," *Modern Philology* 20 (1922–23): 375–78.

Camporeale, S. I., *L. Valla, umanesimo e teologia* (Florence, 1972).

———, "Da Lorenzo Valla a Tommaso Moro: Lo statuto umanistico della teologia," *Memorie Domenicane* n.s. 4 (1973): 9–101; and published separately (Pistoia, 1973).

———, "L. Valla, tra Medioevo e Rinascimento, Encomium Sanctae Thomae—1457," *Memorie Domenicane* n.s. 7 (1976): 3–190; and published separately (Pistoia, 1977).

Canavero, A. T., "S. Agostino nella teologia platonica di Marsilio Ficino," *Rivista di filosofia neo-scolastica* 7 (1978): 626–46.

Canfield, G. B., "The Florentine Humanists' Concept of Architecture in the 1430s and Filippo Brunelleschi," in *Scritti di storia dell'arte in onore di Federigo Zeri*, ed. M. Natale, 2 vols. (Venice, 1984), 1:112–21.

Cantimori, D., *Umanesimo e religione del Rinascimento* (Turin, 1975).

Cantin, A., *Les sciences séculières et la foi: Les deux visages de la science au jugement de S. Pierre Damien (1007–1072)* (Spoleto, 1975).

Capelli, A., "Guiniforte Barzizza, maestro di Galeazzo Maria Sforza," *Archivio storico lombardo* 21 (1894): 399–432; appendix of documents, 433–42.

Capello, G., "Maestro Manfredo e maestro Sion: Grammatici vercellesi del Duecento," *Aevum* 17 (1943): 45–70.

Caplan, H., *Mediaeval "Ars Praedicandi"* (Ithaca, 1934).

———, *Mediaeval "Artes Praedicandi": A Supplementary Handlist* (Ithaca, 1936).

———, *Of Eloquence: Studies in Ancient and Medieval Rhetoric,* ed. A. King and H. North (Ithaca, NY, 1970).

——— and H. H. King, "Latin Tractates on Preaching: A Book-List," *Harvard Theological Review* 42 (1949): 185–206; "French Tractates . . . ," *Quarterly Journal of Speech* 36 (1950): 296–325; "Italian Treatises . . . ," *Speech Monographs* 16 (1949): 243–52; "Spanish Treatises . . . ," *Speech Monographs* 17 (1950): 161–70; "Dutch Treatises . . . ," *Speech Monographs* 21 (1954): 236–47.

Caprariis, V. de, *Francesco Guicciardini: Dalla politica alla storia* (Florence, 1950).

Caprio, V. de, "L'area umanistica romana (1513–1527)," *Studi romani* 29 (1981): 321–35.

———, "Il contributo del classicismo umanistico alla scienza: *Auctoritas* e *ratio* nella filologia di Lorenzo Valla," in *Letteratura e scienza nella storia della cultura italiana* (q.v.), 371–84.

———, "Intellettuali e mercato del lavoro nella Roma medicea," *Studi romani* 29 (1981): 29–46.

———, "Retorica e ideologia nella Declamatio di L. Valla sulla Donazione di Constantino," *Paragone* 338 (April 1978): 35–56.

Cardini, R., *La critica del Landino* (Florence, 1973).

Carini, A. M., "Le postille del Tasso al Trissino," *Studi tassiani* 7 (1957): 31–73.

Carpi, D., "R. Judah Messer Leon and His Activity as a Doctor" (Hebrew), *Michael* 1 (1973): 277–301; republished in abbreviated form in English as "Notes on the Life of Rabbi Judah Messer Leon," in *Studi sull'ebraismo italiano in memoria di Cecil Roth* (Rome, 1974), 37–62.

Cartault, A., *À propos du Corpus Tibullianum: Un siècle de philologie latine classique* (Paris, 1906).

Casacci, A., "Gli *Elegantiarum libri* di Lorenzo Valla," *Atene e Roma* 2d ser. 7 (1926): 187–203.

Casciano, P., "Appunti grammaticali di Lorenzo Valla," *Annali dell'Istituto Universitario Orientale di Napoli* 2–3 (1980–81): 233–67.

Casella, M. T. and G. Pozzi, *Francesco Colonna, biografia e opere,* 2 vols. (Padua, 1959).

Caspari, F., *Humanism and the Social Order in Tudor England* (Chicago, 1954); reviewed by R. J. Schoeck in *Catholic Historical Review* 41 (1955): 206–7.

Cassirer, E., *The Individual and the Cosmos in Renaissance Philosophy,* trans. M. Domandi (New York, 1963).

Cassuto, U., *Gli ebrei a Firenze nell'età del Rinascimento* (Florence, 1918); Cassuto, M. D. [Hebrew name], *Ha-Yehudim be-Firenzi bi-Tekufat ha-Renesans,* trans. from Italian by M. Hartum (Jerusalem, 1967).

———, *Un rabbino fiorentino del secolo XV* (Florence, 1908).

Cast, D., *The Calumny of Apelles: A Study in the Humanist Tradition* (New Haven, 1981).

Castellani, C., "Aldrovandi, Ulisse," *Dictionary of Scientific Biography,* 16 vols. (New York, 1970–80), 1:108–10.

Castro, A., *El pensamiento de Cervantes* (Madrid, 1925).

Castro, F., *El manuscrito apologetico de Alfonso de Zamora* (Madrid, 1950).

Cátedra, P. M., "Enrique de Villena y algunos humanistas," *Academia literaria Renacentista* 3 (1983): 187–203.

Cattaneo, E., "Le riforme del secolo XI e XII," *Archivio storico lombardo* 87 (1960): 21–27.

Cecconi, E., *Studi sul concilio di Firenze* (Florence, 1869).

Cella, S., "Recenti studi sul Patrizi," *Pagine istriane* 8–9 (1980): 11–22.

Cencetti, G., "*Studium fuit Bononie,*" *Studi medievali* 3d ser. 7 (1966): 781–833.

———, "Sulle origini dello studio di Bologna," *Rivista storica italiana* 6th ser. 5 (1940): 248–58.

Cerone, F., "La politica orientale di Alfonso d'Aragona," *Archivio storico per le provincie napoletane* 27 (1902): 3–93, 384–456, 553–634, 794–852; 28 (1903): 154–212.

Cerreta, F. V., *Alessandro Piccolomini letterato e filosofo senese del Cinquecento* (Siena, 1960).

———, "An Account of the Early Life of the Accademia degli Infiammati in the Letters of Alessandro Piccolomini to Benedetto Varchi," *Romanic Review* 48 (1957): 253–64.

———, "Alessandro Piccolomini on the Poetics of Aristotle," *Studies in the Renaissance* 4 (1957): 139–68.

Cesarini Martinelli, L., "In margine al commento di Angelo Poliziano alle *Selve* di Stazio," *Interpres* 1 (1978): 96–145.

———, "Note sulla polemica Poggio–Valla e sulla fortuna delle *Elegantiae*," *Interpres* 3 (1980): 29–79.

Cessi, R., *Storia della Repubblica di Venezia,* 2 vols. (Milan, 1944).

Chabod, F., *Scritti sul Rinascimento,* 2 vols. (Turin, 1967).

Chambers, D. S., *The Imperial Age of Venice, 1380–1580* (London and New York, 1970).

———, "The Economic Predicament of Renaissance Cardinals," *Studies in Medieval and Renaissance History* 3 (1966): 289–313.

Chambers, M. C. E., *The Life of Mary Ward,* 2 vols. (London, 1882).

Chantraine, G., S.J., "Erasme et Saint Basile," *Irenikon* 52 (1979): 451–93.

Charlton, H. B., *Castelvetro's Theory of Poetry* (Manchester, 1913).

Chastel, A., *Art et l'humanisme à Florence au temps de Laurent le Magnifique: Études sur la Renaissance et l'humanisme platonicien* (Paris, 1959).

———, *Marsile Ficin et l'art* (Paris, 1954).

———, *The Sack of Rome, 1527,* trans. B. Archer (Princeton, 1983).

Chatillon, J., "Les écoles de Chartres et de Saint-Victor," *La scuola nell'Occidente latino del alto medioevo* 19 (1972): 795–839.

Chester, A. C., "The New Learning: A Semantic Note," *Studies in the Renaissance* 2 (1955): 139–47.

Chiappetti, P. M., *Vita di Costanza Varano* (Jesi, 1871).

Chomarat, J., *Grammaire et rhétorique chez Erasme*, 2 vols. (Paris, 1981).

———, "Grammar and Rhetoric in the Paraphrases of the Gospels by Erasmus," *Erasmus of Rotterdam Society Yearbook* 1 (1981): 30–68.

Christie, R. C., *Etienne Dolet: The Martyr of the Renaissance, 1508–1546, a Biography* (London, 1899).

Cimitier, P., *Les sources du droit ecclésiastique* (Paris, 1930).

Cinquino, J., "Coluccio Salutati Defender of Poetry," *Italica* 26 (1953): 131–35.

Cioni, M., "Woman and Law in Elizabethan England with Particular Reference to the Court of Chancery," in *Tudor Rule and Revolution: Essays for G. R. Elton from His American Friends*, ed. D.Guth and J. McKenna (New York, 1982).

Cipolla, C., "Studi su Ferreto de' Ferreti," *Giornale storico della letteratura italiana* 6 (1885): 103–12.

Čiževskij, D., *Comparative History of Slavic Literature*, trans. R. N. Porter and M. P. Rice (Nashville, TN, 1971).

Claes, F., *Lijst van Nederlandse woordenlijsten en woordenboeken gedrukt to 1600* (Nieuwkoop, 1974).

Clanchy, M. T., *From Memory to Written Record* (London, 1979).

Clark, A. C., "Ciceronianism," in *English Literature and the Classics*, ed. G. G. Stuart (Oxford, 1912), 118–45.

Clark, K., *The Drawings by Sandro Botticelli for Dante's Divine Comedy* (New York, 1976).

Classen, P., "Burgundio von Pisa," in *Sitzungsberichte der Heidelberger Akademie der Wissenschaften, Philosophisch-historische Klasse* (Heidelberg, 1974), fasc. 4.

Clements, R., "Literary Theory and Criticism in Scaliger's Poemata," *Studies in Philology* 51 (1954): 561–84.

———, "The Peregrine Muse," *North Carolina University Studies in the Romance Languages and Literatures* 31 (1959): monograph.

Closa Farrés, J., "La difusión hispana de la *Ars menor* de E. Donato en los siglos XVI y XVII," *Anuario de filología* 3 (1977): 47–80.

———, "Notas sobre la difusión medieval hispana del Arte menor de Elio Donato," *Anuario de filología* 2 (1976): 37–67.

Clough, C. C., "The Cult of Antiquity: Letters and Letter Collections," in *Cultural Aspects of the Italian Renaissance*, ed. Clough (q.v.), 33–67.

Cochrane, E., *Florence in the Forgotten Centuries, 1527–1800: A History of Florence and the Florentines in the Age of the Grand Dukes* (Chicago, 1973).

———, *Historians and Historiography in the Italian Renaissance* (Chicago, 1981).

———, "Science and Humanism in the Italian Renaissance," *American Historical Review* 81 (1976): 1039–57.

———, "The Transition from Renaissance to Baroque: The Case of Italian Historiography," *History and Theory* 19 (1980): 21–38.

Codoñer, C., "Las Introductiones latinae de Nebrija: Tradición e inovación," *Academia literaria renacentista* 3 (1983): 105–22.

Cohen, J., *The Friars and the Jews* (Ithaca, NY, 1982).

Colish, M., "Eleventh-Century Grammar in the Thought of St. Anselm," in *Arts libéraux et philosophie au Moyen Âge* (Montreal and Paris, 1969), 785–95.

Collenuccio, P., *Compendio de la istoria del regno di Napoli,* ed. A. Saviotto (Bari, 1928).

Collins, A. B., *The Secular Is Sacred: Platonism and Thomism in Marsilio Ficino's Platonic Theology* (The Hague, 1974).

Collodo, S., "Temi e caratteri della cronachista veneziana in volgare del Tre-Quattrocento (Enrico Dandolo)," *Studi veneziani* 9 (1967): 127–51.

Colorni, V., "Note per la biografia di alcuni dotti ebrei vissuti a Mantova nel secolo XV," *Annuario di studi ebraici* 1 (1935): 172–75.

Constable, G., *Letters and Letter Collections* (Turnhout, 1976).

Contarini, G. B., *Anecdota Veneta* (Venice, 1757).

Cooper, L. and A. Gudeman, *A Bibliography of the Poetics of Aristotle* (New Haven, 1928).

Coq, D., "Une édition ignorée de Thierry Martens: Les *Constitutiones synodales episcopatus Atrebatensis* (Louvain, c. 1500/1501)," in *Hellinga Festschrift* (Amsterdam, 1980), 85–88.

Corsano, A., *Per la storia del Rinascimento religioso in Italia: Dal Traversari a G. F. Pico* (Naples, 1935).

———, "Studi sul pensiero del tardo Rinascimento: G. C. Scaligero," *Giornale critico della filosofia italiana* 37 (1958): 34–63.

Cortese, D., "Sisto quatro: Papa antoniano," *Il Santo* 7 (1972): 211–81.

Corti, M., "Il codice bucolico e l'Arcadia di Jacopo Sannazaro," *Strumenti critici* 2 (1968): 141–67.

———, "L'impasto linguistico dell'*Arcadia,*" *Studi di filologia italiana* 22 (1964): 593–619.

———, "Rivoluzione e reazione stilistica nel Sannazaro," in *Metodi e fantasmi* (Milan, 1969), 305–23.

Cosenza, M., *Biographical and Bibliographical Dictionary of Italian Humanists of the World of Classical Scholarship, 1300–1800,* 5 vols. (Boston, 2d ed. 1962), suppl. vol. 6 (Boston, 1967).

Costamagna, G. and M. Amelotti, *Alle origini del notariato italiano* (Rome, 1975).

Costanzo, M., *Dallo Scaligero al Quadrio* (Milan, 1961).

Costello, W. T., *The Scholastic Curriculum in Early Seventeenth-Century Cambridge* (Cambridge, MA, 1958).

Cotroneo, G., *I trattatisti dell' "Ars historica"* (Naples, 1971).

Cottino-Jones, M., "Boccaccio e la scienza," in *Letteratura e scienza nella storia della cultura italiana* (q.v.), 356–70.

Courcelle, P., *Late Latin Writers and Their Greek Sources,* trans. H. W. Wedeck (Cambridge, MA, 1969).

———, "Pétrarque entre Saint Augustin et les Augustins du XIVᵉ siècle," *Studi petrarcheschi* 7 (1961): 51–71.

Cousin, J., *Recherches sur Quintilien: Manuscrits et éditions* (Paris, 1975).

Cozzi, G., "Federico Contarini, un antiquario veneziano tra Rinascimento e

Controriforma," *Bollettino dell'Istituto storico per la storia e cultura veneziana* 3 (1961): 190–221.

Cracco, G., *Società e stato nel medioevo veneziano, secoli XII–XIV* (Florence, 1967).

Cranz, F. E., *A Bibliography of Aristotle Editions, 1501–1600* (Baden-Baden, 1971), ed. C. B. Schmitt (Baden-Baden, 2d ed. 1984).

Craven, W G., *Giovanni Pico della Mirandola, Symbol of His Age: Modern Interpretations of a Renaissance Philosopher* (Geneva, 1981).

Cremaschi, G., *Stefanardo da Vimercate: Contributo per la storia della cultura in Lombardia nel sec. XIII* (Milan, 1950).

Crevatin, G., "Scipione e la fortuna del Petrarca nell'umanesimo," *Rinascimento* 17 (1977): 3–30.

Croce, B., *La Spagna nella vita italiana durante la Rinascenza* (Bari, 5th ed. 1968).

———, *Storia di Napoli* (Bari, 1953).

———, "M. Marullo Tarcaniota: Le elegie per la patria perdute e altri suoi carmi," in his *Poeti e scrittori del pieno e tardo Rinascimento* (Bari, 1945), 1:269ff.

Crocker, R. L., "Pythagorean Mathematics and Music," *Journal of Aesthetics and Art Criticism* 22 (1963): 189–98, 325–35.

Croll, M. W., *Style, Rhetoric, and Rhythm: Essays by Morris W. Croll*, ed. J. M. Patrick and R. O. Evans (Princeton, 1966).

Crombie, A. C., *Augustine to Galileo* (London, 1952); reissued as *Medieval and Early Modern Science*, 2 vols. (New York, 2d ed. 1959).

Cronia, A., "Inchiesta Petrarchesca in Czechoslavacchia, Contributi bibliografici," *L'Europa orientale* n.s. 15 (1935): 164–79.

———, "Relazioni culturali tra Ragusa e l'Italia negli anni 1358–1526," *Atti e memorie della società Dalmata di Storia Patria* 1 (1926): 1–39.

Crosby, R., "Oral Delivery in the Middle Ages," *Speculum* 2 (1936): 88–110.

Cruciani, F., "Il teatro dei Ciceroniani," *Forum italicum* 41 (1980): 356–77.

Csapodi, C. and K. Csapodi Gardonyi, *Bibliotheca Corviniana* (New York, 1969; 2d ed. 1978).

Curtis, M., *Oxford and Cambridge in Transition, 1558–1642* (Oxford, 1959).

Curtius, E. R., *European Literature in the Latin Middle Ages* (New York, 1963).

———, "Die Lehre von den drei Stilen in Altertum und Mittelalter," *Romanische Forschungen* 64 (1952): 66–69.

———, "Theologische Poetik im italienischen Trecento," *Zeitschrfit für Romanische Philologie* 60 (1940): 1–15.

Dahan, G., "Notes et textes sur la poétique au Moyen Âge," *Archives d'histoire doctrinale et littéraire du Moyen Âge* 55 (1981): 171–239.

Dainville, F., de, *La naissance de l'humanisme moderne* (Paris, 1960).

———, *L'éducation des Jésuites (XVIᵉ–XVIIIᵉ siècles)* (Paris, 1978).

Dalzell, A., "The *Forma Dictandi* Attributed to Albert of Morra and Related Texts," *Mediaeval Studies* 39 (1977): 440–65 [many bibliographical references.]

D'Amico, J. F., *Renaissance Humanism in Papal Rome: Humanists and Churchmen on the Eve of the Reformation* (Baltimore, 1983).

———, "Beatus Rhenanus, Tertullian, and the Reformation: A Humanists's Critique of Scholasticism," *Archiv für Reformationsgeschichte* 21 (1980): 37–63.

———, "Contra divinationem: Paolo Cortesi's Attack on Astrology," in *Renaissance Studies in Honor of Craig Hugh Smyth*, 2 vols. (Florence, 1985), 1:281–91.

———, "Paolo Cortesi's Rehabilitation of Giovanni Pico della Mirandola," *Bibliothèque d'humanisme et Renaissance* 44 (1982): 37–51.

———, "Papal History and Curial Reform in the Renaissance: Raffaele Maffei's *Breuis Historia* of Julius II and Leo X," *Archivum historiae pontificiae* 18 (1980): 157–210.

———, "The Progress of Renaissance Latin Prose: The Case of Apuleianism," *Renaissance Quarterly* 37 (1984): 351–92.

——— and K. Weil-Garris, *The Renaissance Cardinal's Ideal Palace: A Chapter from Cortesi's "De Cardinalatu"* (Rome, 1980).

Damiens, S., *Amour et intellect chez Léon l'Hébreu* (Toulouse, 1971).

Davies, K., "Some Early Drafts of the *De Rebus Gestis Francorum* of Paulus Aemilius," *Medievalia et Humanistica* 12 (1958): 99–110.

Davis, C. T., *Dante's Italy and Other Essays* (Philadelphia, 1984).

———, "Education in Dante's Florence," *Speculum* 40 (1965): 415–35.

Davis, J. C., *The Decline of the Venetian Nobility as a Ruling Class* (Baltimore, 1962).

D'Avray, D. L. and M. Tausche, "Marriage Sermons in *Ad Status* Collections of the Central Middle Ages," *Archives d'histoire doctrinale et littéraire du Moyen Âge* 47 (1980): 71–119.

Dazzi, M., *Leonardo Giustiniani, poeta populare d'amore* (Bari, 1934).

———, *Il Mussato preumanista, 1261–1329: L'ambiente e l'opera* (Venice, 1964).

———, "Il Mussato storico," *Archivio veneto* 6 (1929): 359–471.

Deakins, R. L., *The Tudor Dialogue* (Cambridge, MA, 1980).

Dean, L. F., "Francis Bacon's Theory of Civil History Writing," *Literary History* 8 (1941): 161–83.

Debus, A. G., *The Chemical Philosophy: Paracelsian Science and Medicine in the Sixteenth and Seventeenth Centuries*, 2 vols. (New York, 1977).

Deferrari, R. J., "St. Ambrose and Cicero," *Philological Quarterly* 1 (1922): 142.

Dejob, C., *De l'influence du Concile de Trente sur la littérature et les beaux arts chez les peuples catholiques* (Paris, 1884).

Delaruelle, L., *Guillaume Budé, les origines, les débuts, les idées maîtresses* (Paris, 1907).

Delhaye, P., "La place des arts libéraux dans les programmes scolaires du XIIIᵉ siècle," in *Arts libéraux et philosophie au Moyen Âge* (Montreal and Paris, 1969), 161–73.

Delisle, L., *Le cabinet des manuscrits de la Bibliothèque impériale*, 3 vols. (Paris, 1868–81).

Delumeau, J., *Vie économique et sociale de Rome dans le seconde moitié du XVIe siècle*, 2 vols. (Paris, 1957).

Denifle, H., *Die Entstehung der Universitäten des Mittelalters bis 1400* (Berlin, 1885; reprinted Graz, 1936).

Denley, P., "Giovanni Dominici's Opposition to Humanism," in *Religion and Humanism*, ed. K. Robbins (Oxford, 1981), 103–14.

Desgraves, L., "Contribution à la bibliographie des éditions de J. Despauterius (d. Comines, 1520) aux XVIe et XVIIe siècles," *Mémoires Société d'Histoire de Comines Warneton et de la Région* 7 (1977): 385–402.

Devereux, E. J., *Renaissance English Translations of Erasmus: A Bibliography to 1700* (Toronto, 1983).

Diano, C., "Francesco Robortello interprete della catarsi," in *Aristotelismo padovano e filosofia aristotelica: Atti del XII congresso internazionale di filosofia* (Florence, 1960), 71–79.

Dibon, P. and T. Gregory, "Présentation," *Nouvelles de la république des lettres* 1 (1981): 7–11.

Di Camillo, O., *El humanismo castellano del siglo XV* (Valencia, 1976).

Di Cesare, M. A., *Bibliotheca Vidiana: A Bibliography of Marco Girolamo Vida* (Florence, 1974).

———, *Vida's Christiad and Vergilian Epic* (New York, 1964).

Dickens, A. G., "Johann Sleiden and Reformation History," in *Reformation, Conformity and Dissent*, ed. R. B. Knox (London, 1977), 17–43.

——— and J. M. Tonkin, *The Reformation in Historical Thought* (Cambridge, MA, 1984).

Dijksterhuis, E. J., *The Mechanization of the World Picture*, trans. C. Dikshoorn (Oxford, 1961).

Diller, A., "Greek Codices of Palla Strozzi and Guarino Veronese," *Journal of the Warburg and Courtauld Institutes* 24 (1961): 313–21.

Dilthey, W., "Auffassung und Analyse des Menschen im 15. and 16. Jahrhundert," in his *Gesammelte Schriften*, 12 vols. (Leipzig, 1921–58), 2:39–63.

Di Napoli, G., *Giovanni Pico della Mirandola e la problematica dotttrinale del suo tempo* (Rome, 1965).

———, *Lorenzo Valla: Filosofia e religione nell'umanesimo italiano* (Rome, 1971).

Dionisotti, C., *Geografia e storia della letteratura italiana* (Turin, 1967).

———, "Appunti su Leone Ebreo," *Italia medioevale e umanistica* 2 (1959): 409–28.

———, "Bembo, Pietro," *Dizionario biografico degli italiani*, 30 vols. to date (Rome, 1960–84), 8:133–51.

———, "Calderini, Poliziano e altri," *Italia medioevale e umanistica* 11 (1968): 151–85.

———, "Dante nel Quattrocento," *Atti del Congresso Internazionale di Studi Danteschi*, 2 vols. (Florence, 1965), 1:360–78.

———, " 'Lavinia venit litora': Polemica virgiliana di M. Filetico," *Italia medioevale e umanistica* 1 (1958): 283–315.

———, "Niccolò Liburnio e la letteratura cortigiana," in *Rinascimento europeo e Rinascimento veneziano*, ed. V. Branca (Florence, 1967), 26–37.

Di Stefano, G., "Per la fortuna di Valerio Massimo nel Trecento: Le glosse di Pietro da Monteforte e il commento di Dionigi da Borgo San Sepolcro," *Atti dell'Accademia di Scienze di Torino, Classe di Scienze morali* 96 pt. 2 (1961–62): 272–314.

Ditt, E., "Pier Candido Decembrio, Contributo alla storia dell'umanesimo italiano," *Memorie del Reale Istituto Lombardo* 24 (1931): 21–108.

Diurni, G., *L'Expositio ad librum papiensem e la scienza guiridica preirneriana* (Rome, 1976).

Doerne, M., "Luther und die Predigt," *Luther. Mitteilungen der Luthergesellschaft* 22 (1940): 36–77.

Donnet, D., "L'humaniste malinois Varennius et la tradition grammaticale byzantine," *Belgisch Tijdschrift voor Filologie en Geschiedenis* 55 (1977): 93–105.

———, "La *Syntaxis* de Jean Varennius et les *Commentarii* de Guillaume Budé," *Humanistica Lovaniensia* 22 (1973): 103–35.

Dorsch, T. S., "Two English Antiquaries: John Leland and John Stow," *Essays and Studies* n.s. 12 (1959): 18–35.

Dotti, U., "Aspetti della tematica petrarchesca, I: Umanesimo e poesia in Petrarca," *Letterature moderne* 9 (1959): 582–90.

———, "La formazione dell'umanesimo nel Petrarca," *Belfagor* 33 (1968): 532–63.

———, "Petrarca e la scienza," in *Letteratura e scienza nella storia della cultura italiana* (q.v.), 345–55.

Doucet, R., *Les bibliothèques parisiennes au XVIᵉ siècle* (Paris, 1956).

Douglas, R., *Jacopo Sadoleto, 1477–1547: Humanist and Reformer* (Cambridge, MA, 1959).

Drake, S., *Galileo Studies: Personality, Tradition, and Revolution* (Ann Arbor, MI, 1970).

Dresdner, A., *Kultur und Sittengeschichte der italienischen Geistlichkeit im 10. und 11. Jahrhundert* (Breslau, 1890).

Dressler, F., *Petrus Damiani: Leben und Werk* (Rome, 1954).

Dubois, C. G., *La conception de l'histoire en France au XVIᵉ siècle* (Paris, 1977).

Duhamel, P. A., "The Oxford Lectures of John Colet: An Essay in Defining the English Renaissance," *Journal of the History of Ideas* 14 (1953): 493–510.

Duhem, P.-M.-M., *Études sur Léonard de Vinci*, 3 vols. (Paris, 1906–13).

———, *Le système du monde*, 10 vols. (Paris, 1913–59).

Dunston, A. J., "Pope Paul II and the Humanists," *Journal of Religious History* 7.4 (1973): 287–306.

———, "A Student's Notes on Lectures by Giulio Pomponio Leto," *Antichthon* 1 (1967): 86–94.

———, "Studies in Domizio Calderini," *Italia medioevale e umanistica* 11 (1968): 71–150.

Durand, D. B., "Tradition and Innovation in Fifteenth-Century Italy," *Journal of the History of Ideas* 4 (1943): 1–20.

Dvornik, F., *The Slavs in European History and Civilization* (New Brunswick, NJ, 1962).

Eckhardt, S., "Balassi Bálint írói szándeka" ["Bálint Balassi's Literary Aims"], *Itk* 62 (1958): 337–49.

Eco, U., *Il problema estetico in Tommaso d'Aquino* (Milan, 1970).

Edgerton, S. Y., Jr., *The Renaissance Rediscovery of Linear Perspective* (New York, 1975).

———, "The Renaissance Artist as Quantifier," in *The Perception of Pictures*, ed. M. A. Hagen, 2 vols. (New York, 1980), 1:179–212.

Eisenstein, E., *The Printing Press as an Agent of Change: Communications and Cultural Transformations in Early Modern Europe*, 2 vols. (Cambridge, 1979).

Elert, W., *Morphologie des Luthertums*, 2 vols. (Munich, 1931–32; reprinted 1958).

Eliot, T. S., *Notes Towards the Definition of Culture* (London, 1948).

Ellinger, G., *Geschichte der neulateinischen Literatur Deutschlands im sechzehnten Jahrhundert*, vol. 3, pt. 1, *Geschichte der neulateinischen Lyrik in den Niederlanden vom Ausgang des fünfzehnten bis zum Beginn des siebzehnten Jahrhunderts* (Berlin, 1933).

Engelbert, P., "Zur Frühgeschichte des Bobbieser Skriptoriums," *Revue bénédictine* 78 (1968): 220–60.

Entrèves, A. P. d', *Natural Law* (London, 1951).

Erasmus, H. J., *The Origins of Rome in Historiography from Petrarch to Perizonius* (Assen, 1962).

Erbe, M., *François Bauduin (1520–1573)* (Gütersloh, 1978).

Erdmann, C., *Studien zur Briefliteratur Deutschlands im elften Jahrhunderts* (Leipzig, 1938).

Eroli, G., *Erasmo Gattamelata da Narni, suoi monumenti e sua famiglia* (Rome, 1876).

Errera, C., "Le *Commentationes Florentinae de exilio* di Francesco Filelfo," *Archivio storico italiano* 5th ser. 5 (1890): 193–227.

Esch, A., "Dal medioevo al rinascimento: Uomini a Roma dal 1340–1450," *Archivio della Società Romana di Storia Patria* 94 (1971): 3–10.

———, "Florentiner in Rom 1400: Namenverzeichnis der ersten Quattrocento-Generation," *Quellen und Forschungen aus italienischen Archiven und Bibliotheken* 51 (1972): 476–525.

Espiner-Scott, J., *Claude Fauchet* (Paris, 1938).

Etter, E. L., *Tacitus in der Geistesgeschichte des 16. und 17. Jahrhunderts* (Basel, 1966).

Evans, G. R., "The *Ars Praedicandi* of Johannes Reuchlin (1455–1522)," *Rhetorica* 3 (1985): 99–105.

Fabricius, I. A., *Bibliotheca graeca*, ed. G. C. Harles, 2 vols. (Hamburg, 1791).

Facciolatus, J., *De Gymnasio patavini* (Padua, 1752).

Fafner, J., "Wege der Rhetorikgeschichte," *Rhetorica* 1 (1983): 75–91.

Fahy, C., "Three Early Renaissance Treatises on Women," *Italian Studies* 11 (1956): 30–55.

Fakhry, M., "Philosophy and Scripture in the Theology of Averroes," *Medieval Studies* 30 (1968): 78–89.

Fanelli, V., *Ricerche su Angelo Colocci e sulla Roma cinquecentesca* (Vatican City, 1979).

Faral, E., *Les arts poétiques du XIIe et du XIIIe siècle* (Paris, 1924).

Farinelli, A., *Spagna e Italia*, 2 vols. (Turin, 1929).

Farman, F., *Landmarks in the History of Education* (New York, 1952).

Farris, G., *Eloquenza e teologia nel "Prooemium in librum primum sententiarum" di Paolo Cortesi* (Savona, 1972).

———, "Teologia e paolinismo in L. Valla," *Studium* 68 (1973): 671–83.

Fasoli, G., "Ancora un'ipotesi sull'inizio dell'insegnamento di Pepone e Irnerio," in his *Scritti di storia medievale* (Bologna, 1974), 567–81.

Febvre, L., *The Problem of Unbelief in the Sixteenth Century: The Religion of Rabelais*, trans. B. Gottlieb (Cambridge, MA, 1982).

——— and H.-J. Martin, *L'apparition du livre* (Paris, 1958; reprinted 1971).

Fedalto, G., *Simone Atumano monaco di studio* (Brescia, 1968).

Feld, M. D., "Sweynheym and Pannartz, Cardinal Bessarion and Neoplatonism: Renaissance Humanism and Two Early Printers' Choice of Texts," *Harvard Library Bulletin* 30.3 (1982): 282–335.

Feliciangeli, B., "Notizie sulla vita e sugli scritti di Costanza Varano-Sforza (1426–1447)," *Giornale storico della letteratura italiana* 12 (1894): 1–75.

Fenigstein, B., *Leonardo Giustiniani 1383?–1446), venetianischer Staatsmann, Humanist und Vulgärdichter* (Halle am S., 1909).

Ferguson, A. B., *Clio Unbound* (Durham, NC, 1979).

Ferguson, W. K., *The Renaissance in Historical Thought* (Cambridge, MA, 1948).

———, "The Interpretation of Italian Humanism: The Contribution of Hans Baron," *Journal of the History of Ideas* 19 (1958): 14–25.

Fernandez Alvarez, M., *La sociedad española del Renacimiento* (Salamanca, 1970).

Ferrari, M., " 'In Papia conveniant ad Dungalum' (Tav. I–III)," *Italia medioevale e umanistica* 15 (1972): 1–52.

———, "Intorno ad alcuni sermoni inediti di Albertano da Brescia," *Atti dell'Istituto Veneto di Scienze, Lettere ed Arti* 109 (1950–51): 69–93.

———, "Note su Claudio di Torino 'Episcopus ab ecclesia damnatus,' " *Italia medioevale e umanistica* 16 (1973): 291–308.

Ferrarino, P., "La prima, e l'unica, *Reductio omnium artium ad philologiam:* Il *De nuptiis Philologiae et Mercurii* di Marziano Capella e l'apoteosi della filologiae," *Italia medioevale e umanistica* 12 (1969): 1–7.

Ferraro, R. M., *Giudizi critici e criteri estetici nei "Poetices libri septem" (1561) di Giulio Cesare Scaligero rispetto alla teoria letteraria del Rinascimento* (Chapel Hill, 1971).

Ferraù, G., *Pontano critico* (Messina, 1983).

Ferroni, G., "La teoria classicistica della facezia da Pontano a Castiglione," *Sigma* 13 (1980): 69–96.

Festa, N., "L'*Africa* poema della grandezza di Roma nella storia e nella visione profetica di Francesco Petrarca," *Annali della cattedra petrarchesa* 2 (1931): 39–67.

Fialová, A., "Znojemský rukopis Dantový *Monarchie*" ["The Manuscripts of Dante's *De monarchia* from Znojem"], *Listy filologiké* 3 (1955): 52–56.

Field, A., "Cristoforo Landino's First Lectures on Dante," *Renaissance Quarterly* 39 (1986): 16–48.

———, "An Inaugural Oration by Cristoforo Landino in Praise of Virgil," *Rinascimento* 21 (1981): 235–45.

———, "A Manuscript of Cristoforo Landino's First Lectures on Virgil, 1462–63 (Codex 1368, Biblioteca Casanatense, Rome)," *Renaissance Quarterly* 31 (1978): 17–20.

———, "The 'Studium Florentinum' Controversy, 1455," *History of Universities* 3 (1983): 31–59.

Filipović, V., "Osnovi etičko-filozofske orijentacije Marka Marulića" ["The Foundations of the Ethical-Philosophical Orientation of Marko Marulić"], *Prilozi za istraživanje hrvatske filosofske baštine* [*Contributions to Research into the Croatian Philosophical Heritage*] 9 (1983): 3–22.

Finlay, R., *Politics in Renaissance Venice* (New Brunswick, NJ, 1980).

———, "Venice, the Po Expedition, and the End of the League of Cambrai, 1509–1510," *Studies in Modern European History and Culture* 2 (1976): 37–72.

Finocchiaro, M. A., *Galileo and the Art of Reasoning: Rhetorical Foundations of Logic and Scientific Method* (Dordrecht, 1980).

Fioravanti, G., "L'apologetica anti-giudaica di Giannozzo Manetti," *Rinascimento* 2d ser. 23 (1983): 3–32.

Firpo, L., "Filosofia italiana e Controriforma," *Rivista di filosofia* 46 (1950): 150–73; 47 (1951): 30–47.

Fissore, G. C., "Cultura grafica e scuola in Asti nei secoli IX e X," *Bollettino dell'Istituto Italiano per il Medioevo* 85 (1974–75): 17–51.

Fitz, L., "What Says the Married Woman? Marriage Theory and Feminism in the English Renaissance," *Mosaic* 13 (1980): 1–22.

Fleischer, M. P., *Späthumanismus in Schlesien. Ausgewählte Aufsätze* (Munich, 1984).

Flitner, A., *Erasmus im Urteil seiner Nachwelt: Das literarische Erasmus-Bild von Beatus Rhenanus bis zu Jean LeClerc* (Tübingen, 1952).

Flodr, M., "Olomoucká Kapitulní knihovna a její inventáře na počátku 15. stoleti" ["The Chapter Library of Olomouc and Its Inventories at the Beginning of the 15th Century"], *Sborník prací Filosofické fakulty Brněnské university* 7 (1958): 76–97.

Flynn, L., S.J., The *De arte rhetorica* of Cyprian Soarez, S.J.," *Quarterly Journal of Speech* 42 (1956): 356–74.

———, "Sources and Influences of Soarez' *De arte rhetorica*," *Quarterly Journal of Speech* 43 (1957): 257–65.

Flynn, V. J., "The Grammatical Writings of William Lily," *Papers of the Bibliographical Society of America* 37 (1943): 85–113.

Foerster, R., *Francesco Zambeccari und die Briefe des Libanius* (Stuttgart, 1878).

Foffano, T., "La costruzione di Castiglione Olona in un opuscolo inedito di Francesco Pizolpasso," *Italia medioevale e umanistica* 3 (1960): 153–87.

Fois, M., S.J., *Il pensiero cristiano di Lorenzo Valla nel quadro storico-culturale del suo ambiente* (Rome, 1969).

Folena, G., *La crisi linguistica del Quattrocento e l'Arcadia del Sannazaro* (Florence, 1952).

Folts, J. D., "In Search of the 'Civic Life': An Intellectual Biography of Poggio Bracciolini (1380–1459)" (Ph.D. diss., University of Rochester, 1976).

Forster, L., *Dichten in fremden Sprachen* (Munich, 1974).

——, *The Icy Fire: Five Studies in European Petrarchism* (Cambridge, 1969).

——, "On Petrarchism in Latin and the Role of Anthologies," *Acta conventus neo-latini lovaniensis*, ed. J. IJsewijn and E. Kessler (Louvain and Munich, 1973), 235–44.

Foster, K., *Petrarch: Poet and Humanist* (Edinburgh, 1984).

Fraenkel, P., *Testimonia Patrum: The Function of Patristic Argument in the Theology of Philipp Melanchthon* (Geneva, 1961).

—— and M. Greschat, *Zwanzig Jahre Melanchthonstudium* (Geneva, 1967).

Fraknói, V., *Egy magyar jezsuita a XVI. században* [*A Hungarian Jesuit of the Sixteenth Century*], Katolikus Szemle (Budapest, 1888).

——, *Hazai és külföldi iskoláztatás a XVI, században* [*Local and Foreign Education of Hungarian Students in the Sixteenth Century*] (Budapest, 1873).

Frame, D. M., *Montaigne's Discovery of Man* (New York, 1955).

Franceschini, E., *Studi e note di filologia latina medioevale* (Milan, 1938).

——, "Battista Montefeltre Malatesta, signora di Pesaro," *Studia oliveriana* 6 (1958): 7–43.

——, "Leonardo Bruni e il 'vetus interpres' dell'*Etica a Nicomaco*," in *Medioevo e Rinascimento: Studi in onore di Bruno Nardi* (q.v.), 1:299–319.

——, "La Poetica di Aristotele nel secolo XIII," *Atti del R. Istituto Veneto di Lettere, Scienze ed Arti* 94 (1935): 523–48.

Franičević, M., *Povijest hrvatske renesansne književnosti* [*A History of Croatian Renaissance Literature*] (Zagreb, 1983).

Franklin, J. H., *Jean Bodin and the Sixteenth-Century Revolution in the Methodology of Law and History* (New York, 1963).

Franzheim, L., "Das Gymnasium Tricoronatum und sein Lateinunterricht um die Mitte des 16. Jahrhunderts," *Jahrbuch Kölnischen Geschichtsvereins* 48 (1977): 139–50.

Frati, L., "Le polemiche umanistiche di Benedetto Morandi," *Giornale storico della letterature italiana* 75 (1920): 32–39.

Freccero, J., "Dante's Ulysses, From Epic to Novel," in *Concepts of the Hero in the Middle Ages and the Renaissance* (Albany, NY, 1975), 101–19.

Frede, C. de, *I lettori di umanità nello Studio di Napoli durante il Rinascimento* (Naples, 1960).

——, "Biblioteche e cultura di medici-filosofi napoletani del '400," *Gutenberg Jahrbuch* (1969): 89–96.

Freimann, A., "Paulus de Heredia als Verfasser der kabbalistischen Schriften

Igeret-ha-sodot und Galie Raze," in *Festschrift zum siebzigsten Geburtstage Jacob Guttmanns* (Leipzig, 1915), 206–9.

Frey, K., *Der literarische Nachlass Giorgio Vasaris*, 2 vols. (Munich, 1923–30).

Fried, J., *Der Entstehung des Juristenstandes im 12. Jahrhundert. Zur sozialen Stellung und politischen Bedeutung gelehrter Juristen in Bologna und Modena* (Cologne and Vienna, 1974).

Friedman, J., *The Most Ancient Testimony* (Athens, OH, 1983).

Friedman, M., "The Influence of Humanism on the Education of Girls and Boys in Tudor England," *History of Education* 25 (1985): 57–70.

Friedrich, H., *Montaigne* (Bern, 1949).

Fryde, E. B., *Humanism and Renaissance Historiography* (London, 1983).

Fubini, R., "Antonio da Rho," *Dizionario biografico degli italiani*, 30 vols. to date (Rome, 1960–84), 3:574–77.

———, "Biondo, Flavio," *Dizionario biografico degli italiani*, 30 vols. to date (Rome, 1960–84), 10:536–57.

———, "Intendimenti umanistici e riferimenti patristici dal Petrarca al Valla," *Giornale storico della letteratura italiana* 95 (1974): 521–78.

———, "Tra unamesimo e concili: Note aggiunte a una publicazione recente su Francesco Pizolpasso (1370–1443)," *Studi medievali* 3d ser. 7 (1966): 322–70.

Fuchs, F., *Die höheren Schulen von Konstantinopel im Mittelalter* (Leipzig, 1926; reprinted Amsterdam, 1964).

Fueter, E., *Geschichte der neueren Historiographie* (Berlin, 3d ed., 1963).

Fuiano, M., *Insegnamento e cultura a Napoli nel Rinascimento* (Naples, 1971).

———, *Maestri di medicina e filosofia a Napoli nel Quattrocento* (Naples, 1973).

———, "La Scuola del Pucci e Antonio Seripando," *Atti dell'Accademia Pontaniana* n.s. 19 (1970): 197–292.

Fumaroli, M., *L'âge de l'eloquence: Rhétorique et "res literaria" de la Renaissance au seuil de l'époque classique* (Paris, 1980).

———, "Genèse de l'epistolographie classique: Rhétorique humaniste de la lettre, de Pétrarque à Juste Lipse," *Revue d'histoire littéraire de la France* 78 (1978): 886–905.

Funkenstein, A., "Changes in the Patterns of Christian Anti-Jewish Polemics in the Twelfth Century" [Hebrew], *Zion* 33 (1968): 125–44.

Fussner, F. S., *The Historical Revolution* (New York, 1962).

Gabotto, F., "L'attività politica di Pier Candido Decembrio," *Giornale ligustico* 20 (1893): 161–99, 241–80.

——— and A. Badini-Confalonieri, *Vita di Giorgio Merula* (Alessandria, 1893).

Gabriel, A. L., *The Medieval Universities of Pécs and Pozsony* (Frankfurt am Main, 1969).

Gadol, J., *Leon Battista Alberti: Universal Man of the Early Renaissance* (Chicago, 1969).

———, "The Unity of the Renaissance: Humanism, Natural Science and Art," in *From the Renaissance to the Counter-Reformation: Essays in Honor of Garrett Mattingly*, ed. C. H. Carter (New York, 1965), 29–55.

Gaeta, F., *Lorenzo Valla: Filologia e storia nell'umanesimo italiano* (Naples, 1955).

———, "La 'leggenda' di Sigismondo Malatesta," in *Studi malatestiani* (Rome, 1978), 159–95.

———, "Recenti studi su L. Valla," *Rivista della storia della chiesa in Italia* 29 (1975): 560–77.

Galasso, G., *Mezzogiorno medievale e moderno* (Turin, 1965).

Gall, F., *Die Insignien der Universität Wien* (Vienna, 1965).

Gallegos Barnes, A., *Juan Lorenzo Palmireno (1524–1579)* (Zaragoza, 1982).

Galletti, A., *L'eloquenza* (Milan, 1938).

———, "La ragione poetica di Albertino Mussato e i poeti teologi," in *Scritti vari in onore di R. Renier* (Turin, 1912), 331–59.

Gallick, S., "*Artes Praedicandi:* Early Printed Editions," *Mediaeval Studies* 39 (1977): 477–89.

Galliver, H., "Agathius Guidacerius, 1477–1540: An Early Hebrew Grammarian in Rome and Paris," *Historia Judaica* 2.2 (1940): 85–101.

Gallo, F. A., "Musici scriptores graeci," in *Catalogus,* ed. Kristeller, Cranz, and Brown (q.v.), 3:64–73.

Garandarie, M.-M. de la, *Christianisme et lettres profanes (1515–1535)* (Paris, 1976).

Gargan, L., *Cultura e arte nel Veneto al tempo del Petrarca* (Padua, 1978).

Garin, E., *La cultura filosofica del Rinascimento italiano* (Florence, 1961; reprinted 1979).

———, *L'educazione in Europa* (Bari, 1957).

———, *L'età nuova: Ricerche di storia della cultura dal XII al XVI secolo* (Naples, 1969).

———, *Giovanni Pico della Mirandola, vita e dottrina* (Florence, 1936).

———, *Italian Humanism: Philosophy and Civic Life in the Renaissance,* trans. P. Munz (New York, 1965).

———, *La letteratura degli umanisti,* in *Storia della letteratura italiana,* vol. 3, *Il Quattrocento e l'Ariosto* (Milan, 1965), 7–353.

———, *Medioevo e Rinascimento* (Bari, 1966).

———, *Portraits from the Quattrocento,* trans. V. A. Velen and E. Velen (New York, 1972).

———, *Science and Civic Life in the Italian Renaissance,* trans. P. Munz (Garden City, NY, 1969).

———, "La cultura a Milano alla fine del Quattrocento," in *Milano nell'età di Ludovico Il Moro* (Milan, 1983), 1:21–28.

———, "La cultura milanese nella prima metà del XV secolo," in *Storia di Milano* (Milan, 1955–56), 6.4:546–608.

———, "La diffusione della 'Poetica' di Aristotele dal secolo XV in poi," *Rivista critica di storia della filosofia* 28 (1973): 447–51.

———, "La *dignitas hominis* e la letteratura patristica," *La Rinascita* 1 (1938): 102–46.

———, "*Enoelecheia* e *Entelecheia* nelle discussioni umanistiche," *Atene e Roma,* 3d ser. 5 (1937): 177–87.

———, "L'età Sforzesca dal 1450 al 1500," in *Storia di Milano* (Milan, 1955–56), 7.4:540–97.

———, "Filologia e poesia in Angelo Poliziano," *La rassegna della letteratura italiana* 58 (1954): 349–66.

———, "Nota su alcuni aspetti delle retoriche rinascimentali e sulla 'Retorica' del Patrizi," *Archivio di filosofia: Testi umanistici sulla retorica* (Rome, 1953), 7–47.

———, "Poliziano e il suo ambiente," in *Ritratti di umanisti* (Florence, 1967), 131–62.

———, "La *Retorica* di Leonardo Bruni," in *Dal Rinascimento all'Illuminismo: Studi e ricerche* (Pisa, 1970), 21–42.

———, "Ricerche sulle traduzioni di Platone nella prima metà del secolo XV," *Medioevo e Rinascimento: Studi in onore di Bruno Nardi* (q.v.), 1:361–63.

———, "Le traduzioni umanistiche di Aristotele nel secolo XV," *Atti e memorie dell'Accademia Fiorentina di scienze morali: La Colombaria* n.s. 2 (1947–50): 55–104.

———, "Gli umanisti e la scienza," *Rivista di filosofia* 52 (1961): 261–78; reprinted in his *L'età nuova* (q.v.), 451–75.

Garnett, R., "A Laureate of Caesar Borgia," *English Historical Review* 17 (1902): 15–19.

Garofalo, S., "Gli umanisti italiani del secolo XV e la Bibbia," *La Bibbia e il concilio di Trento* (Rome, 1947), 338–75.

Gasquet, Cardinal, *Cardinal Pole and His Early Friends* (London, 1927).

Gastaldelli, F., "Note sul codice 619 della Biblioteca capitolare di Lucca e sulle edizione del *De arithmetica compendiose tractata* e della *Summa dialectice artis*," *Salesianum* 39 (1977): 693–702.

Gaudenzi, A., "Sulla cronologia delle opere dei dettatori bolognesi da Boncompagno a Bene di Lucca," *Bollettino dell'Istituto storico italiano* 14 (1895): 85–174.

Gavagna, R., "Un abbinamento editoriale del '500: Vitruvio e Cusano," *Rivista critica di storia della filosofia* 30 (1975): 400–410.

———, "Cusano e Alberti a proposito del *De architectura* di Vitruvio," *Rivista critica di storia della filosofia* 34 (1979): 162–76.

Gavazzuti, G., *Lodovico Castelvetro* (Modena, 1903).

Geanakoplos, D. J., *Byzantine East and Latin West* (Oxford, 1966).

———, *Greek Scholars in Venice: Studies in the Dissemination of Greek Learning from Byzantium to the West* (Cambridge, MA, 1962); republished as *Byzantium and the Renaissance* (New Haven, 1978).

———, *Interaction of the "Sibling" Byzantine and Western Cultures in the Middle Ages and Italian Renaissance (330–1600)* (New Haven, 1976).

———, "The Byzantine Recovery of Constantinople from the Latins in 1261: A Chrysobull of Emperor Michael Palaeologus in Favor of Hagia Sophia," in *Continuity and Discontinuity in Church History: Essays to G. Williams*, ed. F. Church and T. George (Leiden, 1979), 104–17.

———, "The Career of the Little-Known Renaissance Greek Scholar Nicholas Leonicus Tomaeus and the Ascendancy of Greco-Byzantine Aristotelianism at

Padua University (1497)," Δώρημα στὸν I. Καραγιαννόπουλο, Byzantina 13 (1985): 357–72.

———, "The Discourse of Demetrius Chalcondyles on the Inauguration of Greek Studies at the University of Padua in 1463," Studies in the Renaissance 21 (1974): 18–44.

———, "Erasmus and the Aldine Academy of Venice," Greek, Roman and Byzantine Studies 3 (1960): 107–34.

———, "The Italian Renaissance and Byzantium: The Career of the Greek Humanist-Professor John Argyropoulos in Florence and Rome (1415–87)," in Conspectus of History, 8 vols. (Muncie, IN, 1974–82), 1:12–28.

———, "A Reevaluation of the Influences of Byzantine Scholars on the Development of the Studia Humanitatis, Metaphysics, Patristics, and Science in the Italian Renaissance (1361–c. 1531)," in Proceedings of the Patristic, Medieval, and Renaissance Conference, 3 vols. (Villanova, PA, 1978), 3:1–25.

———, "St. Basil, Christian Humanist of the Three Hierarchs and Patron Saint of Greek Letters," Greek Orthodox Theological Review 25 (1980): 94–102.

———, "Theodore Gaza, a Byzantine Scholar from the Palaeologan 'Renaissance' in the Italian Renaissance," Medievalia et Humanistica n.s. 12 (1984): 61–81.

Gee, J. A., The Life and Works of Thomas Lupset (New Haven, 1928).

Geffen, M. D., "Faith and Reason in Elijah Delmedigo's Beḥinat ha-Dat and the Philosophic Backgrounds of His work" (Ph.D. diss., Columbia University, New York, 1970).

———, "Insights into the Life and Thought of Elijah Delmedigo Based on His Published and Unpublished Works," Proceedings of the American Academy of Jewish Research 41–42 (1973–74): 69–86.

Gehl, P. F., "From Monastic Rhetoric to Ars Dictaminis: Traditionalism and Innovation in the Schools of Twelfth-Century Italy," American Benedictine Review 34 (1983): 33–47.

Geiger, L., Renaissance und Humanismus in Italien und Deutschland (Berlin, 1882).

———, "Der alteste römische Musenalmanach," Vierteljahrschrift für Kultur und Literatur der Renaissance 1 (1886): 145–61.

Giernaert, N., Vlaamse Kunst op Perkament (Brugge, 1981).

Gentile, G., Storia della filosofia italiana fino a Lorenzo Valla (Florence, 2d ed. 1962).

Gentile, S., "In margine all'epistola De divino furore di Marsilio Ficino," Rinascimento 23 (1983): 33–77.

Gerardi, E. N., "Lo Apologetico del Savonarola e il problema di una poesia cristiana," Rivista di filologia neoscolastica 44 (1952): 412–30.

Gerbi, A., La natura delle nuove indie (Milan, 1975).

Gerézdi, R., Janus Pannoniustól Balassi Bálintig [From Janus Pannonius to Bálint Balassi] (Budapest, 1968).

———, A magyar világi lira kezdetei [The Beginnings of Vernacular Poetry in Hungary] (Budapest, 1962).

———, Váradi Péter [Péter Váradi] (Budapest, 1942).

Gerl, H.-B., *Rhetorik als Philosophie: Lorenzo Valla* (Munich, 1974).

Gerlo, A., "The *Opus de conscribendis epistolis* of Erasmus and the Tradition of the *Ars epistolica*," in *Classical Influences on European Culture, A.D. 500–1500*, ed. Bolgar (q.v.), 103–14.

———— and H. D. L. Vervliet, *Bibliographie de l'humanisme des anciens Pays-Bas, avec un répertoire bibliographique des humanistes et poètes néolatins* (Brussels, 1972); ten-year suppl. covering 1972–82 (Brussels, 1985).

Gerosa, P. P., *Umanesimo cristiano del Petrarca: Influenza agostiniana attinenze medievali* (Turin, 1966).

Gerulaitis, L. V., *Printing and Publishing in Fifteenth-Century Venice* (Chicago and London, 1976).

Giannini, A., "Il libro X dei *Pensieri diversi* di A. Tassoni e 'La ingeniosa comparación de lo antiguo y lo presente,' " *Revue hispanique* 41 (1917): 635–72.

Gianturco, G., "La poetica di Girolamo Fracastoro," *Logos* (1932): 1–16.

Gibson, M. T., *Lanfranc of Bec* (Oxford, 1978).

Gigante, M., "La civiltà letteraria," in *I Bizantini in Italia* (Milan, 1982), 615–51.

Gilbert, F., *Machiavelli and Giucciardini: Politics and History in Sixteenth-Century Florence* (Princeton, 1965).

————, *The Pope, His Banker and Venice* (Cambridge, MA, 1980).

————, "Bernardo Rucellai and the Orti Oricellari: A Study on the Origins of Modern Political Thought," *Journal of the Warburg and Courtauld Institutes* 12 (1949): 101–31.

————, "Biondo, Sabellico, and the Beginnings of Venetian Official Historiography," in *Florilegium Historiale . . .* , ed. Rowe and Stockdale (q.v.), 275–93.

————, "Cristianismo, umanesimo e la bolla *Apostolici Regiminis* del 1513," *Rivista storica italiana* 79 (1967): 976–90.

Gilbert, N. W., *Renaissance Concepts of Method* (New York, 1960).

————, "The Early Italian Humanists and Disputation," in *Renaissance Studies in Honor of Hans Baron*, ed. Molho and Kirschner (q.v.), 201–26.

————, "A Letter of Giovanni Dondi dall'Orologia to Fra' Guglielmo Centueri: A Fourteenth-Century Episode in the Quarrel of the Ancients and the Moderns," *Viator* 8 (1977): 299–346.

————, "Renaissance Aristotelianism and Its Fate: Some Observations and Problems," in *Naturalism and Historical Understanding: Essays on the Philosophy of John Herman Randall, Jr.* (Buffalo, 1967), 42–52.

Gil Fernandez, L., *Panorama social del humanismo español (1500–1800)* (Madrid, 1981).

————, "El humanismo español del siglo XVI," *Estudios clásicos* 51 (1966): 211–97.

————, "Nebrija y el menester del gramático," *Academia literaria renacentista* 3 (1983): 53–64.

Gill, J., S.J., *The Council of Florence* (Cambridge, 1959).

————, *Eugenius IV: Pope of Christian Reunion* (Westminster, MD, 1961).

————, *Personalities of the Council of Florence* (New York, 1964).

Gilmore, M. P., *Humanists and Jurists: Six Studies in the Renaissance* (Cambridge, MA, 1963).

——, "Beroaldo, Filippo, senior," *Dizionario biografico degli italiani*, 30 vols. to date (Rome, 1960–84), 9:382–84.

——, "*Fides et Erudito*: Erasmus and the Study of History," *Teachers of History: Essays in Honor of Lawrence Bradford Packard*, ed. H. S. Hughes and M. P. Gilmore (Ithaca, 1954), 9–27.

——, "More's Translation of Gianfrancesco Pico's Biography," in *L'opere e il pensiero di Giovanni Pico della Mirandola nella storia dell'umanesimo* (Florence, 1965), 1:301–4.

——, "The Renaissance Conception of the Lessons of History," in *Facets of the Renaissance*, ed. W. H. Werkmeister (New York, 2d ed. 1963), 73–101; reprinted in his *Humanists and Jurists* (q.v.), 1–37.

Gilson, E., *Les idées et les lettres* (Paris, 1932).

——, "Michel Menot et la technique du sermon médiéval," in his *Les idées et les lettres* (Paris, 1932), 93–154.

Girardin, B., *Rhétorique et théologique: Calvin et le commentaire de l'Epître aux Romains* (Paris, 1979).

Girgensohn, D., "Wie wird man Kardinal? Kuriale und ausserkuriale Karrieren an der Wende des 14. zum 15. Jahrhundert," *Quellen und Forschungen aus italienischen Archiven und Bibliotheken* 57 (1977): 138–62.

Giuliano, O., *Allegoria, retorica e poetica nel 'Secretum' del Petrarca* (Bologna, 1977).

Gleason, E. A., "On the Nature of Sixteenth-Century Italian Evangelism: Scholarship, 1953–1978," *Sixteenth-Century Journal* 9 (1978): 3–26.

Gnoli, D., *Un giudizio de lesa romanità sotto Leone X* (Rome, 1891).

——, *La Roma di Leone X* (Milan, 1938).

Godin, A., *Erasme et Origène* (Paris, 1983).

Goffis, C. F., "Il sincretismo lucreziano-platonico negli *Hymni naturales* del Marullo," *Belfagor* 24 (1969): 386–417.

Goldthwaite, R. A., *The Building of Renaissance Florence* (Baltimore, 1980).

Goleniščev-Kutuzov, I. N., *Gumanizm u vostočnyx slavjan (Ukraina i Belorussija)* [*Humanism Among Eastern Slavs: Ukraine and White Russia*] (Moscow, 1963).

——, *Ital'janskoe vozroždenie i slavjanskie literatury XV i XVI vekov* (Moscow, 1963); *Il Rinascimento italiano e le letterature slave dei secoli XV e XVI*, trans. S. Graciotti and J. Křesálková, 2 vols. (Milan, 1973).

Göllner, C., *Turcica. Die europäischen Türckendrucke des XVI. Jahrhunderts*, 4 vols. (Bucharest, 1961–78).

Gombrich, E. H., *The Heritage of Apelles: Studies in the Art of the Renaissance* (Ithaca, NY, 1976).

——, "Botticelli's Mythologies: A Study in the Neoplatonic Symbolism of His Circle," in *Symbolic Images: Studies in the Art of the Renaissance II* (London, 1972), 31–81.

——, "From the Revival of Letters to the Reform of the Arts: Niccolò Niccoli and Filippo Brunelleschi," in *Essays in the History of Art Presented to Rudolf*

Wittkower, ed. D. Fraser, H. Hibbard, and M. J. Lewine (London, 1967), 71–82.

González, J., *El maestro Juan de Segovia y su biblioteca* (Madrid, 1954).

Gonzalez-Quevedo Alonso, S., "Alonso de Cartagena, una expresión de su tiempo," *Critica hispanica* 1 (1982): 1–20.

Gorce, D., "La patristique dans la réforme d'Erasme," *Festgabe Joseph Lortz,* ed. E. Iserloh and P. Manns, 2 vols. (Baden-Baden, 1958), 1:233–76.

Gordon, D. J., *The Renaissance Imagination,* ed. S. Orgel (Berkeley, 1975).

Gortan, V. and V. Vratović, *Hrvatski latinisti [Croatian Latinists],* 2 vols. (Zagreb, 1969).

———, "The Basic Characteristics of Croatian Literature," *Humanistica Lovaniensia* 20 (1971): 37–64.

———, "Trmeljne značajke hrvatskog latinizma" ["The Fundamental Signification of Croatian Latinism"], *Forum* 8 (1969): 606–36.

Gothein, P., *Francesco Barbaro (1390–1454): Frühhumanismus und Stattskunst in Venedig* (Berlin, 1932).

———, "Zaccaria Trevisan," *Archivio veneto* 5th ser. 21 (1937): 28–30, 47–49.

Gottleib, E., *"Or Olam* of R. Elhanan Sagi Nahor" [Hebrew], *Michael* 1 (1973): 144–68.

Grabmann, M., *Guglielmo di Moerbeke O.P. il traduttore delle opere di Aristotele* (Rome, 1946).

Graetz, H., *History of the Jews,* trans. B. Löwy et al., 6 vols. (Philadelphia, 1891–98; reprinted 1974); *Divrei Yemei Yisra'el,* ed. and trans. S. P. Rabinowitz, 10 vols. (Warsaw, 1890–99; reprinted 1916); Hebrew edition has augmented bibliography.

Graevius, J. G., *Thesaurus antiquitatum et historiarum Italiae* (Leiden, 1722).

Grafton, A., *Joseph Scaliger: A Study in the History of Classical Scholarship* (Oxford, 1983).

———, "On the Scholarship of Politian and Its Context," *Journal of the Warburg and Courtauld Institutes* 40 (1977): 150–88.

Grassi, E., *Einführung in philosophische Probleme des Humanismus* (Darmstadt, 1986).

———, *Heidegger and the Question of Renaissance Humanism* (Binghamton, NY, 1983).

———, *Rhetoric as Philosophy* (University Park, PA, 1980).

Gray, H. H., "Renaissance Humanism: The Pursuit of Eloquence," *Journal of the History of Ideas.* 24 (1963): 497–514.

———, "Valla's *Encomium of St. Thomas Aquinas* and the Humanist Conception of Christian Antiquity," in *Essays in History and Literature Presented by the Fellows of the Newberry Library to Stanley Pargellis,* ed. H. Bluhm (Chicago, 1965), 37–51.

Green, L., *Chronicle into History* (Cambridge, 1972).

Greene, D. H., "Lady Lumley and Greek Tragedy," *Classical Journal* 36 (1941): 537–47.

Greene, T. M., *The Light in Troy: Imitation and Discovery in Renaissance Poetry* (New Haven and London, 1982).

Greenfield, C. C., *Humanist and Scholastic Poetics, 1250–1500* (Lewisburg, PA, 1981).

Gregorovius, F., *History of the City of Rome in the Middle Ages,* trans. from the 4th German ed. by A. Hamilton (London, 1900–1902), vols. 5–8.

Gregory, T., "La 'Apologia ad censuram' di Francesco Patrizi," *Rinascimento* 4 (1953): 89–104.

———, "La 'Apologia' e le 'Declarationes' di Francesco Patrizi," in *Medioevo e Rinascimento: Studi in onore di Bruno Nardi* (q.v.), 1:387–442.

Grendler, P. F., *Critics of the Italian World, 1530–1560: Anton Francesco Doni, Nicolò Franco, and Ortensio Lando* (Madison, WI, 1969).

———, *The Roman Inquisition and the Venetian Press, 1540–1605* (Princeton, 1977).

Griffiths, G., "Leonardo Bruni and the Restoration of the University of Rome (1406)," *Renaissance Quarterly* 26 (1973): 1–10.

Griggio, G., "Tradizione e rinnovavamento nella cultura del Galateo," *Lettere italiane* 26.4 (1974): 415–33.

Grossman, M., *Humanism in Wittenberg, 1485–1517* (Nieuwkoop, 1975).

Gualazzini, U., *Ricerche sulle scuole pre-universitarie del medioevo* (Milan, 1943).

———, "La sculoa pavese, con particulare riguardo all'insegnamento del diritto," in *Atti del 4° congresso internazionale di studi sull'alto medio evo* (Spoleto, 1969), 35–73.

Gualdo, G., "Francesco Barbaro," *Dizionario biografico degli italiani,* 30 vols. to date (Rome, 1960–84), 6:101–3.

Gualdo Rosa, L., *La fede nella Paideia: Aspetti della fortuna europea di Isocrate nei secoli XV e XVI* (Rome, 1984).

———, "Ciceroniano o Cristiano? A proposito dell'orazione *De morte Christi* di Tommaso Fedra Inghirami," in *Roma humanistica,* ed. J. IJsewijn (q.v.), 52–64.

Guardia, A. della, *La "Politia litteraria" di Angelo Decembrio e l'umanesimo a Ferrara nella prima metà del secolo XV* (Modena, 1910).

Guasti, C., *La cupola di Santa Maria del Fiore* (Florence, 1867).

Gulyás, P., *A könyvnyomtatas Magyarországon a XV. és XVI. században* [*Printing in Hungary in the Fifteenth and Sixteenth Centuries*] (Budapest, 1931).

Gundersheimer, W., *The Life and Works of Louis Le Roy* (Geneva, 1966).

———, "Bartolommeo Goggio: A Feminist in Renaissance Ferrara," *Renaissance Quarterly* 23 (1980): 175–200.

Guttmann, J., *Philosophies of Judaism* (Garden City, NY, 1966).

———, "Elia del Medigo's Verhältnis zu Averroës in seinem Bechinat Ha-Dat," in *Jewish Studies in Memory of Israel Abrahams* (New York, 1927), 192–208.

Haar, J., "The Frontispiece of Gafori's *Practica musicae* (1496)," *Renaissance Quarterly* 27 (1974): 7–22.

Haebler, K., *The Study of Incunabula,* trans. L. E. Osborne (New York, 1933).

Hajdu, H., *Das Mnemotechnische Schrifttum des Mittelalters* (Vienna, 1936).

Hale, J. R., *Florence and the Medici: The Pattern of Control* (London, 1977).

———, *Renaissance War Studies* (London, 1983).

Hall, B. S., " 'Der Meister sol auch kennen schreiben und lesen': Writings About Technology ca. 1400–ca. 1600 A.D., and Their Cultural Implications," in *Early Technologies*, ed. D. Schmandt-Besserat (Malibu, CA, 1979), 47–58.

———, "Giovanni de' Dondi and Guido da Vigevano: Notes Toward a Typology of Medieval Technical Writings," in *Machaut's World: Science and Art in the Fourteenth Century, Annals of the New York Academy of Sciences* 314 (1978): 127–42.

Hall, V., "Life of Julius-Caesar Scaliger," *Transactions of the American Philosophical Society* 40 (1950): 86–170.

———, "Preface to Scaliger's *Poetices libri septem*," *Modern Language Notes* 40 (1945): 445–543.

———, "Scaliger's Defense of Poetry," PMLA 63 (1948): 1125–30.

Hallman, B. M., *Italian Cardinals, Reform, and the Church as Property, 1492–1563* (Berkeley, 1985).

Hamilton, Dom A., *The Chronicle of the English Augustinian Canonesses Regular of the Lateran at St. Monica's in Louvain*, 2 vols. (London, 1904).

Hampe, K., *Beiträge zur Geschichte der letzten Staufer* (Leipzig, 1910).

Handschin, W., *Petrarch als Gestalt der Historiographie* (Basel, 1964).

Hanka, V., "České prvotisky" ["Czech Incunables"], *Časopis českého museum* 26.3 (1852): 109–26; 26.4 (1852): 62–111.

Hankey, A. T., "Riccobaldo of Ferrara, Boccaccio and Domenico di Bandino," *Journal of the Warburg and Courtauld Institutes* 21 (1958): 208–26.

Hankins, J., "Latin Translations of Plato in the Renaissance" (Ph.D. diss., Columbia University, New York, 1984).

Hanning, B. R., *Of Poetry and Music's Power: Humanism and the Creation of Opera* (Ann Arbor, MI, 1980).

Hanus, J. J., "Frantiska Petrarky: Knihy o lekarstvi proti stesti a nestesti—prelozil Řehoř Hrubý z Jeleni a vydal r. 1501 v Praze" ["The Books *De remediis* by Francesco Petrarch—translated by Řehoř Hrubý of Jeleni and published in Prague in 1501"], *Časopis Musea Království českého* 36 (1862): 161–74.

Harbison, E. H., *The Christian Scholar in the Age of the Reformation* (New York, 1956).

Hardison, O. B., "The Orator and the Poet: The Dilemma of Humanist Literature," *Journal of Medieval and Renaissance Studies* 1 (1971): 33–44.

Hardt, M., *Die Zahl in der Divina Commedia* (Frankfurt am Main, 1973).

Harrán, D., "The Theorist Giovanni del Lago," *Musica disciplina* 27 (1973): 107–51.

Hartfelder, K., *Philipp Melanchthon als Praeceptor Germaniae* (Berlin, 1899; reprinted Neeuwkoop, 1964).

Harvey, S., "The Cooke Sisters: A Study of Tudor Gentlewomen" (Ph.D. diss., Indiana University, Bloomington, 1981).

Haskins, C. H., *The Renaissance of the Twelfth Century* (Cambridge, MA, 1927).

———, *Studies in Medieval Culture* (Oxford, 1929).

———, *Studies in the History of Mediaeval Science* (Cambridge, MA, 2d ed. 1927).

Hassinger, E., *Empirisch-rationaler Historismus* (Munich, 1978).

Hathaway, B., *The Age of Criticism: The Late Renaissance in Italy* (Ithaca, NY, 1962).

Hay, D., *Annalists and Historians* (London, 1977).

——, *Polydore Vergil* (Oxford, 1952).

——, "Flavio Biondo and the Middle Ages," *Proceedings of the British Academy* 45 (1959): 97–125.

——, "Renaissance Cardinals," *Synthesis* (Bucharest) 3 (1976): 35–46.

Hazlitt, W. C., *The Venetian Republic, Its Rise, Its Growth, and Its Fall, A.D. 409–1797*, 2 vols. (London, 4th ed., 1915).

Headley, J. M., *Luther's View of Church History* (New Haven, 1963).

Heath, T., "Logical Grammar, Grammatical Logic, and Humanism in Three German Universities [viz., Freiburg-im-Breisgau, Ingolstadt, Tübingen]," *Studies in the Renaissance* 18 (1971): 9–64.

Heesakkers, C. L., "Foundation and Early Development of the Athenaeum Illustre at Amsterdam," *Lias* 9 (1982): 3–18.

Heiberg, J. B., "Beiträge zur Geschichte Georg Vallas und seiner Bibliothek," *Centralblatt für Bibliothekswesen* 16 (1896): 1–129.

Heireman, K., *Tentoonstelling Dirk Martens 1473–1973* (Aalst, 1973).

Heitmann, K., *Fortuna und Virtus: Eine Studie zu Petrarcas Lebensweisheit* (Cologne, 1958).

——, "Insegnamenti agostiniani nel *Secretum*," *Bibliothèque d'humanisme et Renaissance* 22 (1960): 34–43.

Heller, E., "Der kuriale Geschäftsgang in den Briefen des Thomas von Capua," *Archiv für Urkundenforschung* 13 (1935): 198–318.

Heltzel, V. B., "Sir Thomas Egerton as Patron," *Huntington Library Quarterly* 11 (1948): 115–24.

Heninger, S. K., Jr., *Touches of Sweet Harmony: Pythagorean Cosmology and Renaissance Poetics* (San Marino, CA, 1974).

Hercigonja, E., *Nad iskonom hrvatske knjige* [*At the Source of Croatian Books*] (Zagreb, 1983).

Herrick, M. T., *The Fusion of Horatian and Aristotelian Criticism, 1531–1555* (Urbana, IL, 1946).

——, *Italian Comedy in the Renaissance* (Urbana, IL, 1960).

——, *Italian Tragedy in the Renaissance* (Urbana, IL, 1965).

Hexter, J. H., *The Vision of Politics on the Eve of the Reformation* (New York, 1973).

Hilary, R. B., "The Appointments of Pope Pius II," *Catholic Historical Review* 64 (1978): 33–35.

Hill, J. W., "Oratory Music in Florence, I, *Recitar cantando*, 1583–1655," *Acta musicologica* 51 (1979): 246–67.

Hirsch, R., *The Printed Word* (London, 1978).

——, *Printing, Selling and Reading, 1450–1550* (Wiesbaden, 1967).

Hobson, A., "The Printer of the Greek Editions *In Gymnasio Mediceo ad Caballinum Montem*," in *Studi di biblioteconomia e storia del libro in onore di Francesco Barberi* (Rome, 1976), 331–35.

Hoffman, C. F., Jr., "Catherine Parr as a Woman of Letters," *Huntington Library Quarterly* 23 (1960): 349–67.

Hoffman, H., "Zum Register und den Briefen Papst Gregors VII," *Deutsches Archiv* 32 (1972): 86–130.

Hofmann, W. von, *Forschungen zur Geschichte der kurialen Behörden vom Schisma bis zur Reformation*, 2 vols. (Rome, 1914).

Hogrefe, P., *Tudor Women: Commoners and Queens* (Ames, IA, 1975).

Holborn, H., *Ulrich von Hutten and the German Reformation*, trans. R. H. Bainton (New Haven, 1937).

Holl, K., "Die Kulturbedeutung der Reformation," *Gesammelte Aufsätze zur Kirchengeschichte*, vol. 1, *Luther* (Tübingen, 1932).

Hollander, J., *The Untuning of the Sky* (Princeton, 1961).

Holmes, G., *The Florentine Enlightenment, 1400–1450* (New York, 1969).

Holtzmann, W., "*Eine oberitalienische ars dictandi,*" *Neues Archiv für deutsche Geschichte* 46 (1926): 34–52.

———, "Laurentius von Amalfi, ein Lehrer Hildebrands," *Studi gregoriani* 1 (1947): 207–36; republished in *Beiträge zur Reichs- und Papstgeschichte des hohen Mittelalters* (Bonn, 1957), 9–33.

Honecker, M., "Nikolaus von Cues und die griechische Sprache," *Sitzungsberichte der Heidelberger Akademie der Wissenschaften, Philosophisch-historische Klasse* 28 (Heidelberg, 1938), fasc. 2.

Hood, S. J. R., "The Impact of Protestantism on the Renaissance Ideal of Women in Tudor England" (Ph.D. diss., University of Nebraska, Lincoln, 1977).

Hook, J., *The Sack of Rome, 1527* (London, 1972).

Hopkins, J., *A Concise Introduction to the Philosophy of Nicholas of Cusa* (Minneapolis, 1978).

Horák, F., "Five Hundred Years of Czech Printing," in *Pět století českého knihtisku* [*Five Hundred Years of Czech Printing*] (Prague, 1968), 115–52.

Horawitz, A., *Der Humanismus in Wien* (Leipzig, 1883).

———, "Johann Lonicer," *Allgemeine Deutsche Biographie* 19 (1884): 158–63.

Horváth, I. *Balassi költészete történeti poétikai megközelítésben* [*The Poetry of Balassi in a Historical Poetical Approach*] (Budapest, 1982).

———, "Az eszményi Balassi-kiadás koncepciója" ["The Concept of an Ideal Balassi Edition"], *Itk* 74 (1972): 209–306; and *Reneszansz füzetek* 35 (1977): 613–31.

Horváth, J., *A reformáció jegyében* [*In the Sign of the Reformation*] (Budapest, 1953).

———, *Az irodalmi műveltség megoszlása: A Magyar humanizmus* [*The Distribution of Book Learning: Hungarian Humanism*] (Budapest, 1954).

Houlbrooke, R. A., *The English Family, 1450–1700* (New York, 1984).

Hoven, R., *Bibliographie de trois auteurs de grammaires grecques . . . Adrien Amerot, Arnold Oridryus, Jean Varennius* (Aubel, Belgium, 1985).

——— and J. Hoyoux, *Exposition: Le livre scolaire au temps d'Erasme et des humanistes* (Liège, 1969).

Howell, W. S., *Logic and Rhetoric in England, 1500–1700* (Princeton, 1956).

Hrkać, S., "Nikola Modruški," *Prilozi za istraživanje hrvatske filozofske baštine*

[*Contributions to Research into the Croatian Philosophical Heritage*] 2 (1976): 145–56.

Hübsch, A., "Elia Delmedigo's Bechinath ha-dath und Ibn Roschd's Fael ul-maqal," *Monatschrift für Geschichte und Wissenschaft Judenthums* 31 (1882): 555–63; 32 (1883): 28–46.

Hughes, P. E., *Reformation in England*, 3 vols. (New York, 5th ed. 1963).

Huillard-Bréholles, J. L. A., *Historia diplomatica Friderici secundi*, 6 vols. (Paris, 1852–61).

———, *Vie et correspondance de Pierre de la Vigne* (Paris, 1865).

Huizinga, J., *Erasmus and the Age of Reformation* (New York, 1957).

Hull, S. W., *Chaste, Silent and Obedient: English Books for Women, 1475–1640* (San Marino, CA, 1982).

Hunger, H., *Die hochsprächliche profane Literatur der Byzantiner* (Munich, 1978).

Hunt, A. J., "Three New Incunables with Marginalia by Politian," *Rinascimento* 2d ser. 24 (1984): 251–59.

Huppert, G., *Les bourgeois gentilshommes* (Chicago and London, 1977).

———, *The Idea of Perfect History* (Urbana, IL, 1970).

———, *Public Schools in Renaissance France* (Urbana, IL, 1984).

Husik, I., *Judah Messer Leon's Commentary on the "Vetus Logica"* (Leiden, 1906).

Huszti, J., *Janus Pannonius* (Budapest, 1931).

Hutton, J., *The Greek Anthology in Italy to the Year 1800* (Ithaca, NY, 1935).

———, "John Leland's *Laudatio pacis*," *Studies in Philology* 58 (1961): 616–26.

———, "Some English Poems in Praise of Music," in *English Miscellany* 2 (1951): 1–63.

Hyma, A., *The Christian Renaissance: A History of the "Devotio Moderna"* (Hamden, CT, 2d ed. 1965).

Ianziti, G., "The First Edition of Giovanni Simonetta's 'De rebus gestis Francisci Sfortiae commentarii': Questions of Chronology and Interpretation," *Bibliothèque d'humanisme et Renaissance* 44 (1982): 137–47.

Idel, M., "Between the Concept of Sefirot as Essence and Instrument in Kabbalah in the Renaissance Period" (Hebrew), *Italia* 3 (1982): 89–111.

———, "The Epistle of R. Isaac of Pisa (?) in Its Three Versions" [Hebrew], *Kovez al Yad* n.s. 10 [20] (1982): 163–214.

———, "Kabbalah and Ancient Theology in R. Isaac and Judah Abravanel" (Hebrew), in *The Philosophy of Love of Leone Ebreo,* ed. M. Dorman and Z. Levy (Haifa, 1985).

———, "The Magical and Neoplatonic Interpretations of the Kabbalah in the Renaissance," in *Jewish Thought in the Sixteenth Century,* ed. B. Cooperman (q.v.), 186–242.

———, "Major Currents in Italian Kabbalah Between 1560 and 1660," *Italia Judaica* 2 (1986): 243–62.

———, "Particularism and Universalism in Kabbalah 1480–1650," in *The*

Transformation of Jewish Society in the Sixteenth and Seventeenth Centuries, forthcoming.

———, "Sources of the Image of the Circle in the *Dialoghi d'Amore*" [Hebrew], *Iyyun* 28 (1978): 156–66.

———, "The Study Program of R. Yohanan Alemanno" [Hebrew], *Tarbiz* 48 (1979): 303–31.

———, "Two Books on Christian Kabbalah of Professor Chaim Wirszubski" [Hebrew], *Eshkolot* n.s. 4 [11] (n.d.): 98–103.

IJsewijn, J., *Companion to Neo-Latin Studies* (Amsterdam, 1977; 2d ed. 1987).

———, "Annales theatri Belgo-Latini: Inventaris van het Latijns toneel uit de Nederlanden," *Album Gilbert Degroote* (Brussels, 1980), 41–55.

———, "Cauletum: Les choux d'Erasme et d'Horace," *Moreana* 20 (1983): 17–19.

———, "The *Declamatio Lovaniensis de Tutelae severitate:* Students Against Academic Authority at Louvain in 1481," *Lias* 3 (1976): 5–31.

———, "Haneron," *Die deutsche Literatur des Mittelalters: Verfasserlexikon,* 5 vols. (Berlin, 1933–55), 3:431–35.

———, "Lo storico e grammatico Matthaeus Herbenus di Maastricht, allievo del Perotti," *Res publica litterarum* 4 (1981): 93–122.

———, "Theatrum Belgo-Latinum: Het Neolatijns toneel in de Nederlanden," in *Academiae Analecta: Mededelingen van de Koninklijke Academie voor Wetenschappen, Letteren en Schone Kunsten van België, Klasse der Letteren* 43.1 (1981): 69–114.

——— and P. Lefevre, "Collatio de laudibus Facultatum Lovanii saeculo XV (1435?) habita, nunc primum typis edita," in *Zetesis: Bijdragen . . . Professor Dr. E. De Strijcker* (Antwerp, 1973), 416–35.

IJsseling, S., *Rhetoric and Philosophy in Conflict,* trans. P. Dunphy (The Hague, 1976).

Isaac, M.-T., *Les livres manuscrits de l'abbaye des Dunes* (Aubel, 1984).

Iványi, B., *Könyvek, könyvtárak, könyvnyomdák Magyarországon, 1331–1600* [*Books, Libraries, and Printing Presses in Hungary, 1331–1600*] (Budapest, 1937).

Jacob, E. F., *Essays in Later Medieval History* (Manchester, 1968).

———, "Christian Humanism," in *Europe in the Late Middle Ages,* ed. J. Hale et al. (London, 1965), 437–65.

Jacobs, E., "Francesco Patrizi und seine Sammlung griechischer Handschriften," *Zentralblatt für Bibliothekswesen* 25 (1908): 19–47.

Jacoby, F., "Zur Entstehung der römischen Elegie," *Rheinisches Museum für philologie* n.s. 60 (1905): 38–105.

Janick, L., "Lorenzo Valla: The Primacy of Rhetoric and the De-Moralization of History," *History and Theory* 12 (1973): 389–404.

Janson, H. W., *The Sculpture of Donatello* (Princeton, 1962).

———, "The Image of Man in Renaissance Art: From Donatello to Michelangelo," in *The Renaissance Image of Man and the World,* ed. B. O'Kelly (Columbus, OH, 1966), 77–102.

Jardine, L., *Francis Bacon: Discovery and the Art of Discourse* (Cambridge, 1974).

———, *Still Harping on Daughters: Women and Drama in the Age of Shakespeare* (Totowa, NJ, 1983).

———, "Lorenzo Valla and the Intellectual Origins of Humanist Dialectic," *Journal of the History of Philosophy* 15 (1977): 143–64.

Jayawardene, S. A., "Pacioli, Luca," *Dictionary of Scientific Biography,* 16 vols. (New York, 1970–80), 10:269–72.

Jayne, S. R., *John Colet and Marsilio Ficino* (Oxford, 1963).

———, *Library Catalogues of the English Renaissance* (Berkeley, 1956).

Jehasse, J., *La renaissance de la critique* (Saint-Etienne, 1976).

Jennings, M., "Monks and the *Artes Praedicandi* in the Time of Ranulph Higden," *Revue bénédictine* 86 (1976): 119–28.

Jireček, J. C., "Der ragusanische Dichter Šiško Menčetić," *Archiv für slavische Philologie* 19 (1897): 22–89.

Joachimsen, P., *Geschichtsauffassung und Geschichtsschreibung in Deutschland unter dem Einfluss des Humanismus* (Leipzig, 1910).

———, "Der Humanismus und die Entwicklung des deutschen Geistes," *Deutsche Vierteljahrsschrift für Literaturwissenschaft und Geistesgeschichte* 8 (1930): 419–80.

———, "Tacitus im deutschen Humanismus," *Neue Jahrbücher für das klassische Altertum, Geschichte und deutschen Literatur* 17 (1911): 697–717.

Jordan, C., "Feminism and the Humanists: The Case of Sir Thomas Elyot's *Defence of Good Women*," *Renaissance Quarterly* 36 (1983): 181–201.

Julow, V., "A Balassi-strofa ritmikaja es eredetenek kerdese" ["The Rhythm and Origin of the Balassi Stanza"], *Studia litteraria* 9 (1970): 39–49.

Junghans, H., *Der junge Luther und die Humanisten* (Weimar, 1984).

———, "Der Einfluss des Humanismus auf Luthers Entwicklung bis 1518," *Luther Jahrbuch* 37 (1970): 37–101.

———, "Luther als Bibelhumanist," *Luther. Zeitschrift der Luther-Gesellschaft* 1 (1982): 1–9.

Jurić, Š., "Aus der Geschichte des koratischen Wiegendrucks," *Beiträge zur Inkunabelkunde* 6 (1983): 68–90.

Jurilli, A., "La fortuna editoriale delle opere di Virgilio nell'Italia meridionale fino al XVIII secolo," in *Atti del convegno virgiliano di Brindisi* (Perugia, 1983), 66–69.

———, "Problemi lessicali nell'*Esposizione del Pater Noster* di Antonio Galateo," *Lingua e storia di Puglia* 9 (1980): 45–58.

Kagan, R., *Students and Society in Early Modern Spain* (Baltimore and London, 1974).

Kahn, V., "The Rhetoric of Faith and the Use of Usage in Lorenzo Valla's *De libero arbitrio*," *Journal of Medieval and Renaissance Studies* 13 (1983): 91–109.

Kai-Kee, E., "Social Order and Rhetoric in the Rome of Julius II (1503–1513)" (Ph.D. diss., University of California, Berkeley, 1983).

Kaiser, W., *Praisers of Folly: Erasmus, Rabelais, Shakespeare* (Cambridge, MA, 1963).

Kallendorf, C., *Latin Influences on English Literature from the Middle Ages to the Eighteenth Century: An Annotated Bibliography of Scholarship, 1949–1979* (New York, 1982).

Kamalic, P. I., *F. Patrizi nella cultura e sopratutto nella poetica cinquecentesca* (Frieburg, 1930).

Kamen, H., *La inquisición española*, trans. E. Obregón (Madrid, 1965).

Kantorowicz, E., "An Autobiography of Guido Faba," *Medieval and Renaissance Studies* 1 (1943): 253–80.

———, "The Sovereignty of the Artist," in *Selected Studies* (Locust Valley, NY, 1965), 352–65.

Kantorowicz, H., *Studies in the Glossators of the Roman Law* (Cambridge, 1938).

Karaus Wertis, S., "The Commentary of Bartolinus de Benincasa de Canulo on the *Rhetorica ad Herennium*," *Viator* 10 (1979): 283–310.

Kardos, T., *A magyarországi humanizmus kora* [*The Period of Humanism in Hungary*] (Budapest, 1955).

———, "A regi magyar szinjatszas nehany kerdesehez" ["On Some Problems of Early Hungarian Theater"], *Magyar Tudományos Akadémia Irodalom-történeti, Osztály* 7 (1955): 16–64.

Kastner, E., "Cultura italiana alla corte transilvana nel secolo XVI," *Corvina* 2 (1922): 40–56.

Kaufman, G., "Juan Luis Vives on the Education of Women," *Signs* 3.4 (1978): 891–96.

Kaufmann, H. W., *The Life and Works of Nicola Vicentino* (Rome, 1966).

Kearney, H., *Science and Change: 1500–1700* (New York, 1971).

Keightley, R. G., "Alfonso de Madrigal and the *Chronici Canones*," *Journal of Medieval and Renaissance Studies* 7 (1977): 225–48.

Keller, A. C., "Montaigne on the Dignity of Man," *PMLA* 72 (1957): 43–54.

———, "Zilsel, the Artisans, and the Idea of Progress in the Renaissance," in *Roots of Scientific Thought*, ed. P. P. Wiener and A. Noland (New York, 1957).

Kelley, D. R., *Foundations of Modern Historical Scholarship: Language, Law, and History in the French Renaissance* (New York, 1970).

———, *François Hotman* (Princeton, 1973).

———, *History, Law and the Human Sciences: Medieval and Renaissance Perspectives* (London, 1984).

———, "Faces in Clio's Mirror," *Journal of Modern History* 47 (1975): 679–90; 54 (1982): 320–26.

———, "History as a Calling: The Case of La Popelinière," in *Renaissance Studies in Honor of Hans Baron*, ed. Molho and Kirschner (q.v.), 773–89.

———, "Johann Sleidan and the Origins of History as a Profession," *Journal of Modern History* 12 (1980): 573–98.

———, "The Rise of Legal History in the Renaissance," *History and Theory* 9 (1970): 174–94.

Kemp, M., *Leonardo da Vinci: The Marvellous Works of Nature and Man* (Cambridge, MA, 1981).

——, " 'Il concetto dell'anima' in Leonardo's Early Skull Studies," *Journal of the Warburg and Courtauld Institutes* 34 (1971): 115–34.

——, "Leonardo and the Visual Pyramid," *Journal of the Warburg and Courtauld Institutes* 40 (1977): 128–49.

Keniston, A., "A Fifteenth-Century Treatise on Education by Bishop Rodericus Zamorensis," *Bulletin hispanique* 32 (1930): 193–217.

——, "Notes on the *De liberis educandis* of Antonio de Nebrija," *Homenaje a R. Menéndez Pidal*, 3 vols. (Madrid, 1925), 3:126–41.

Kennedy, G. A., *The Art of Persuasion in Greece* (Princeton, 1963).

——, *Classical Rhetoric and Its Christian and Secular Tradition from Ancient to Modern Times* (Chapel Hill, 1980).

Kenney, E. J., *The Classical Text* (Berkeley, 1974).

Kerecsényi, D., "Nicolas Olah," *Nouvelle revue de Hongrie* 2 (1934): 277–87; republished in his *Válogatott írásai [Selected Writings]* (Budapest, 1979).

Kessler, E., "Geschichtsdenken und Geschichtsschreibung bei Francesco Petrarca," *Archiv für Kulturgeschichte* 51 (1969): 109–36.

Kibre, P., *Scholarly Privileges in the Middle Ages* (Cambridge, MA, 1962).

Kieszkowski, B., "Les rapports entre Elie Delmedigo et Pic de la Mirandole (d'après le ms. lat. 6508 de la Bibliothèque Nationale)," *Rinascimento* 2d ser. 4 (1964): 41–91.

King, M. L., *Venetian Humanism in an Age of Patrician Dominance* (Princeton, 1986).

——, "Goddess and Captive: Antonio Loschi's Poetic Tribute to Maddalena Scrovegni (1389), Study and Text," *Medievalia et Humanistica* n.s. 10 (1981): 103–27.

——, "Personal, Domestic, and Republican Values in the Moral Philosophy of Giovanni Caldiera," *Renaissance Quarterly* 28 (1975): 535–74.

——, "The Religious Retreat of Isotta Nogarola," *Signs* 3 (1978): 807–22.

——, "A Study in Venetian Humanism at Mid-Quattrocento: Filippo da Rimini and His *Symposium de paupertate* (Study and Text)," *Studi veneziani* n.s. 2 (1978): 75–96; 3 (1979): 141–86; 4 (1980): 27–44.

——, "Thwarted Ambitions: Six Learned Women of the Early Italian Renaissance," *Soundings* 59 (1976): 280–300, bibliography 301–4.

Kinser, S., *The Works of Jacques-Auguste de Thou* (The Hague, 1966).

——, "Ideas of Temporal Change and Cultural Process in France, 1470–1535," *Renaissance Studies in Honor of Hans Baron*, ed. Molho and Kirschner (q.v.), 703–55.

Kirner, G., "Contributo alla critica del testo delle *Epistolae ad familiares* di Cicerone (1.IX–XVI)," *Studi italiani di filologia classica* 9 (1901): 400–406.

Kisch, G., *Claudius Cantiuncula: Ein Basler Jurist und Humanist des 16. Jahrhunderts* (Basel, 1970).

——, *Erasmus und die Jurisprudenz seiner Zeit: Studien zum humanistischen Rechtsdenken* (Basel, 1960).

————, *Humanismus und Jurisprudenz: Der Kampf zwischen mos italicus und mos gallicus an der Universität Basel* (Basel, 1955).

Kittelson, J. M., "Luther on Education for Ordination," *Lutheran Theological Seminary Bulletin* 65 (1985): 27–44.

Klaniczay, T., *A mult nagy korszakai [Great Epochs of the Past]* (Budapest, 1973).

————, *A reneszánsz és a barokk [Renaissance and Baroque]* (Budapest, 1961).

Klausner, J., "Don Judah Abravanel and His Philosophy of Love" (Hebrew), *Tarbiẓ* 3 (1931): 67–98.

Klein, R., *Form and Meaning: Writings on the Renaissance and Modern Art*, trans. M. J. Wieselter and L. Wieselter (New York, 1980).

————, "Les humanistes et la science," *Bibliothèque d'humanisme et Renaissance*, 23 (1961): 7–16.

Kleinhans, A., "De vita et operibus Petri Galatini, O.F.M., scientiarum biblicarum cultoris (c. 1460–1540)," *Antonianum* 1 (1926): 145–78.

Klemm, F., "Valturio, Roberto," *Dictionary of Scientific Biography*, 16 vols. (New York, 1970–80), 13:567–68.

Klempt, A., *Die Säkularisierung der universalhistorischen Auffassung* (Göttingen, 1960).

Klette, T., "Die griechischen Briefe des Franciskus Philelphus. Nach den Handschriften zu Mailand (Trivulziana) und Wolfenbüttel. Mit ergänzenden Notizen zur Biographie Philelphos und der Gräcisten seiner Zeit," *Beiträge zur Geschichte und Litteratur der Italienischer Gelehrterenaissance* 3 (1890): 98–180.

Klibansky, R., *The Continuity of the Platonic Tradition . . . with Plato's Parmenides* (Millwood, NY, 1982).

————, E. Panofsky, and F. Saxl, *Saturn and Melancholy* (New York, 1964).

Klimes, P., *Bécs és a magyar humanizmus [Vienna and Hungarian Humanism]* (Budapest, 1934).

Kloos, R. M., "Petrus de Prece und Konradin," *Quellen und Forschungen aus italienischen Archiven und Bibliotheken* 34 (1954): 88–108.

Knafla, L. A., *Law and Politics in Jacobean England* (Cambridge, 1977).

————, "The Influence of Continental Humanists and Jurists on English Common Law in the Renaissance," *Acta conventus neolatini Bononiensis* (Binghamton, NY, 1985), 60–71.

————, "The Law Studies of an Elizabethan Student," *Huntington Library Quarterly* 32 (1969): 221–40.

Knape, J., *Historie in Mittelalter und früher Neuzeit* (Baden-Baden, 1984).

Koch, A. C. F., *The Year of Erasmus' Birth and Other Contributions to the Chronology of His Life* (Utrecht, 1969).

Kögl, W., *Studien zur Reichsgeschichtsschreibung deutscher Humanisten* (Vienna, 1972).

Kohls, E.-W., *Die Schule bei Martin Bucer in ihrem Verhältnis zu Kirche und Obrigkeit* (Heidelberg, 1963).

————, *Die Theologie des Erasmus*, 2 vols. (Basel, 1966).

Kohut, K., *Las teorías en España y Portugal durante los siglos XV y XVI* (Madrid, 1973).

———, "Der Beitrag der Theologie zum Literaturbegriff in der Zeit Juans II. von Kastilien," *Romanische Forschungen* 89 (1977): 183–226.

———, "El humanismo castellano del siglo XV: Replanteamiento de la problemática," *Actas del séptimo congreso de la Asociación de Hispanistas,* ed. G. Bellini, 2 vols. (Rome, 1982), 2:639–47.

Kolendić, P., "Krunisanje Ilije Crijevića u akademiji Pomponija Leta" ["The Crowning of Ilija Crijević in the Academy of Pomponio Leto"], *Zbornik radova Instituta za proučavanje književnosti SANU* [*Collection of the Works of the Institute for the Study of Literature: Serbian Academy of Sciences and Arts*] 10 (1951): 65–95.

Kölmel, W., *Aspekte des Humanismus* (Westfallen, 1981); reviewed by R. N. Watkins, *Renaissance Quarterly* 35 (1982): 593–95; and by A. Rabil, Jr., *Bibliothèque d'humanisme et Renaissance* 44 (1982): 707–11.

Koltay-Kastner, J., "Bornemissza Péter humanizmusa" ["Péter Bornemissza the Humanist"], *Itk* 57 (1953): 91–124.

Kolumbić, N., *Hrvatska književnost od humanizma do manirizma* [*Croatian Literature from Humanism to Mannerism*] (Zagreb, 1980).

———, "Hrvatski humanizam i Franjo Trankvil Andreis" ["Croatian Humanism and Franjo Trankvil Andreis"], in *Franjo Trankvil Andreis, Krvava rijeka* [*Franjo Trankvil Andreis, Bloody River*], ed. N. Kolumbić (Zagreb, 1979), 303–32.

Kombol, M., *Povijest hrvatske književnosti do narodnog preporoda* [*History of Croatian Literature up to the National Revival*] (Zagreb, 2d ed. 1961).

Königsberger, D., *Renaissance Man and Creative Thinking: A History of Concepts of Harmony, 1400–1700* (Atlantic Highlands, NJ, 1979).

Könneker, B., *Wesen und Wandlung der Narrenidee im Zeitalter des Humanismus: Brant, Murner, Erasmus* (Wiesbaden, 1966).

Köppen, U., *Die "Dialoghi d'amore" des Leone Ebreo in ihren französischen Übersetzungen* (Bonn, 1979).

Körbler, D., "Iz mladih dana triju humanista Dubrovcana 15. vijeka" ["The Youth of Three Fifteenth-Century Ragusan Humanists"], *Rad JAZU* [*Works of the Yugoslav Academy of Sciences and Arts*] 206 (1915): 218–52.

Kordić, I. N., "Novija literatura o Matija Vlačiću" ["Most Recent Literature on Matthias Flacius"], *Prilozi za istraživanje hrvatske filozofske baštine* [*Contributions to Research into the Croatian Philosophical Heritage*] 9 (1983): 219–28.

Kottman, K. A., *Law and Apocalypse: The Moral Thought of Luis de Leon (1527–1591)* (The Hague, 1972).

Kovács, S. V., "A Dózsa háboru humanista éposza" ["The Humanist Epic of the Dózsa Uprising"], *Itk* 63 (1959): 451–73.

Koyré, A., *Études Galiléennes,* 3 vols. (Paris, 1939–40); *Galileo Studies,* trans. J. Mepham (Atlantic Highlands, NJ, 1978).

———, *From the Closed World to the Infinite Universe* (Baltimore, 1957).

Krasić, S., "Šibenski humanist Ivan Polikarp Severitan i njegova politička misao"

["Ivan Polikarp Severitan, a Humanist of Šibenik, and His Political Thought"], *Prilozi za istraživanje hrvatske filozofske baštine* [*Contributions to Research into the Croatian Philosophical Heritage*] 3 (1977): 7–78.

Krautter, K., *Philologische Methode und humanistische Existenz: Filippo Beroaldo und sein Kommentar zum Goldenen Esel des Apuleius* (Munich, 1971).

Kretschmayr, H., *Geschichte von Venedig,* 3 vols. (Gotha, 1920; reprinted Darmstadt, 1964).

Kristeller, P., *Andrea Mantegna* (London, 1901).

Kristeller, P. O., *The Classics and Renaissance Thought* (Cambridge, MA, 1955).

———, *Eight Philosophers of the Italian Renaissance* (Stanford, 1964).

———, *Iter Italicum, a Finding List of Uncatalogued or Incompletely Catalogued Humanistic Manuscripts of the Renaissance in Italian and Other Libraries,* 3 vols. to date (Leiden and London, 1963–83).

———, *Medieval Aspects of Renaissance Learning,* ed. and trans. E. P. Mahoney (Durham, NC, 1974).

———, *The Philosophy of Marsilio Ficino,* trans. V. Conant (New York, 1943).

———, *Renaissance Concepts of Man* (New York, 1972).

———, *Renaissance Thought and Its Sources,* ed. M. Mooney (New York, 1979).

———, *Renaissance Thought and the Arts: Collected Essays* (Princeton, 1980).

———, *Renaissance Thought: The Classic, Scholastic, and Humanist Strains* (New York, 1961).

———, *Renaissance Thought II: Papers on Humanism and the Arts* (New York, 1965).

———, *Studies in Renaissance Thought and Letters,* 2 vols. (Rome, 1956–85).

———, "The Active and the Contemplative Life in Renaissance Humanism," in *Arbeit, Musse, Meditation, Betrachtungen zur Vita activa und Vita contemplativa,* ed. B. Vickers (Zurich, 1985), 133–52.

———, "Un *Ars dictaminis* di Giovanni del Virgilio," *Italia medioevale e umanistica* 4 (1961): 181–200.

———, "The Contributions of Religious Orders to Renaissance Thought and Learning," *American Benedictine Review* 21 (1970): 1–55; reprinted in his *Medieval Aspects of Renaissance Learning* (q.v.), 3–25.

———, "The European Diffusion of Italian Humanism," *Italica* 39 (1962): 1–20; reprinted in *Studies in Renaissance Thought and Letters* (q.v.), 2:147–65.

———, "Florentine Platonism and Its Relation with Humanism and Scholasticism," *Church History* 8 (1939): 201–11.

———, "Giovanni Pico della Mirandola and His Sources," in *L'Opera e il pensiero di Giovanni Pico della Mirandola nella storia della umanismo,* 2 vols. (Florence, 1965), 1:35–142.

———, "A Latin Translation of Gemistos Pletho's *De fato* by Johannes Sophianos dedicated to Nicholas of Cusa," in *Nicolò Cusano agli inizi del mondo moderno: Atti del congresso internazionale in occasione del V centenario della morte di Nicolò Cusano Bressanone, 1964* (Florence, 1970), 175–93.

———, "Marsilio Ficino as a Man of Letters and the Glosses Attributed to Him in the Caetani Codex of Dante," *Renaissance Quarterly* 36 (1983): 1–47.

————, "Matteo de' Libri, Bolognese Notary of the Thirteenth Century, and His *Artes Dictaminis,*" in *Miscellanea Giovanni Galbiati,* 3 vols. (Milan, 1951), 2:283–320.

————, "Music and Learning in the Early Italian Renaissance," *Journal of Renaissance and Baroque Music* 1 (1947): 255–74; reprinted in *Renaissance Thought II* (q.v.), 142–62.

————, "Il Petrarca, l'umanesimo e la scolastica," *Lettere italiana* 7 (1955): 367–88.

————, "Petrarchas Stellung in der Geschichte der Gelehrsamkeit," in *Italien und die Romania in Humanismus und Renaissance: Festschrift für Erich Loos zum 70. Geburtstag,* ed. K. W. Hempfer and E. Straub (Wiesbaden, 1983), 102–21.

————, "Petrarch's 'Averroists': A Note on the History of Aristotelianism in Venice, Padua, and Bologna," *Bibliothèque d'humanisme et Renaissance* 14 (1952): 59–65.

————, "Renaissance Aristotelianism," *Greek, Roman and Byzantine Studies* 6 (1965): 157–74.

————, "The Scholastic Condemnation of Rhetoric in the Commentary of Giles of Rome on the *Rhetoric* of Aristotle," in *Arts libéraux et philosophie au Moyen Âge* (Montreal, 1969), 833–41.

————, "A Thomist Critique of Marsilio Ficino's Theory of Will and Intellect," in *Harry Austryn Wolfson Jubilee Volume, English Section II* (Jerusalem, 1965), 463–94.

————, "An unknown Humanist Sermon on St. Stephen by Guillaume Fichet," in *Mélanges Eugène Tisserant* (Vatican City, 1964), 459–97.

Kristos, G., *Studies in Byzantine Rhetoric* (Thessalonica, 1973).

Krstic, K., "Humanizam kod Juznih Slavena" ["Humanism Among the South Slavs"], *Enciklopedija Jugoslavije,* 8 vols. (Zagreb, 1955–71), 4:287–300.

Krumwiede, H.-W., *Glaube und Geschichte in der Theologie Luthers. Zur Entstehung des geschichtlichen Denkens in Deutschland* (Göttingen, 1952).

Kunkel, W., *Roman Legal and Constitutional History,* trans. J. M. Kelly (Oxford, 2d ed. 1973).

Kuspit, D. B., "Melanchthon and Dürer: The Search for the Simple Style," *Journal of Medieval and Renaissance Studies* 3 (1973): 177–202.

Kustas, G., "The Function and Evolution of Byzantine Rhetoric," *Viator* 1 (1970): 55–73.

————, "Studies in Byzantine Rhetoric," *Theologia* 45 (1975): 413ff.

Labalme, P. H. *Bernardo Giustiniani: A Venetian of the Quattrocento* (Rome, 1969).

————, "Venetian Women on Women: Three Early Modern Feminists," *Archivio veneto* 5th ser. 197 (1981).

Laboa, J. M., *Rodrigo Sánchez de Arévalo, Alcaide de Sant'Angelo* (Madrid, 1973).

Labowsky, L., *Bessarion's Library* (Rome, 1979).

————, "Bessarion," in *Dizionario biografico degli italiani,* 30 vols. to date (Rome, 1960–84), 9:686–96.

———, "Bessarion Studies," *Medieval and Renaissance Studies* 5 (1961): 108–62.

———, "Il Cardinale Bessarione e gli inizi della biblioteca Marciana," in *Venezia e l'oriente fra tardo Medio Evo e Rinascimento,* ed. A. Pertusi (Venice, 1966), 159–82.

Ladero Quesada, M. A., "Aristocratie et régime seigneurial dans l'Andalousie du XVe siècle," *Annales: Économies, sociétés, civilisations* 6 (1983): 1346–68.

Ladner, G., "Die mittelalterliche Reform-Idee und ihr Verhältnis zur Idee der Renaissance," *Mitteilungen des Instituts für österreichische Geschichtsforschung* 40 (1952): 41–59.

Laistner, M. L. W., *Thought and Letters in Western Europe, A.D. 500–900* (Ithaca, NY, 2d ed., 1957).

Lamprecht, F., *Zur Theorie der humanistischen Geschichtsschreibung* (Winterthur, 1950).

Lancetti, V., *Della vita e degli scritti di Girolamo Vida* (Naples, 1904).

Landfester, R., *Historia magistra vitae* (Geneva, 1972).

Lane, F. C., *Venice: A Maritime Republic* (Baltimore, 1973).

Lapesa, R., *La obra literaria del Marqués de Santillana* (Madrid, 1957).

Larner, J., *Culture and Society in Italy, 1290–1420* (London, 1971).

Lawrance, J. N. H., "Nuño de Guzmán and Early Spanish Humanism: Some Reconsiderations," *Medium aevum* 51 (1982): 55–86.

Lazzari, A., "Un umanista romagnolo alla corte d'Ercole II d'Este, B. Ricci da Lugo," *Atti e memorie della Deputazione ferrarese di storia patria* 13 (1913): 3–240.

Lazzarini, L., *Paolo de Bernardo e i primordi dell'umanesimo in Venezia* (Geneva, 1930).

———, "Amici del Petrarca a Venezia e Treviso," *Archivio veneto* 5th ser. 14 (1933): 1–14.

———, "Un libro su Francesco Barbaro," *Archivio storico italiano* 7th ser. 20 (1933): 97–104.

Lazzarini, V., *Rimatori veneziani del secolo XIV* (Padua, 1877).

———, "La seconda ambasceria di Francesco Petrarca a Venezia," in *Miscellanea di studi pubblicati in onore di Guido Mazzoni,* 2 vols. (Florence, 1907), 1:173–83, summary of an otherwise unknown oration by Petrarch.

Lee, E., *Sixtus IV and Men of Letters* (Rome, 1978).

Lee, R. W., "Ut Pictura Poesis: The Humanistic Theory of Painting," *Art Bulletin* 22 (1940): 197–269.

Lefevre, R., "Fiorentini a Roma del '400: I Dati," *Studi romani* 20 (1972): 186–97.

Leff, G., *William of Ockham: The Metamorphosis of Scholastic Discourse* (Manchester, 1975).

Lefranc, A., "Le traité *De la vicissitude ou varietaté des choses* de Louis Le Roy et sa veritable date," in *Mélanges Lanson* (Paris, 1922), 109–20.

———, "Le traité des reliques de Guibert de Nogent, et les commencements de la critique historique au Moyen Âge," in *Études d'histoire du Moyen Âge, dédiées à Gabriel Monod* (Paris, 1896), 285–306.

Le Goff, J., "Alle origine del lavoro intellettuale in Italia: I problemi del rapporto fra la letteratura, l'università e le professioni," *Letteratura italiana*, vol. 1, *Il letterato e le istituzioni* (Turin, 1982), 649–79.

Legrand, E., *Bibliographie hellénique ou description raisonnée des ouvrages publiés en grec par des grecs aux XVe et XVIe siècles*, 4 vols. (Paris, 1885–1906; reprinted Paris, 1962).

Lehmberg, S. E., *Sir Thomas Elyot: Tudor Humanist* (Austin, TX, 1960).

Leicht, P. S., "Documento toscani dei secoli XI–XII," *Bollettino senese di storia patria* 16 (1909): 174–90.

———, "Ideali di vita dei veneziani del Cinquecento," *Archivio veneto* 5th ser. 14 (1933): 217–31.

Lempicki, S., *Renesans i Humanizm w Polsce. Materialy do Studiów [Renaissance and Humanism in Poland: Research Materials]* (Cracow, 1952).

Lencek, R. L., "At the Roots of Slavic Cultural History," in *Părvi Meždunaroden kongres po bălgaristika Sofija, 23 maj–3 juni 1981. Dokladi. Plenarni dokladi* (Sofija, 1982), 29–53.

———, "Humanism in the Slovene Lands," *Nationalities Papers* 7 (1979): 155–70.

Lentini, A., "Alberico," *Dizionario biografico degli italiani*, 30 vols. to date (Rome, 1960–84), 1:696.

Lentzen, M., *Studien zur Dante Exegese C. Landinos* (Cologne and Vienna, 1971).

Leopardi, G., *Zibaldone di pensieri*, ed. F. Flora, 2 vols. (Milan, 1937; 7th ed. 1967).

Lesley, A. M., *All the Wisdom of Solomon: The Jewish Humanist Movement in Italy, 1450–1600* (forthcoming).

———, "Hebrew Humanism in Italy: The Case of Biography," *Prooftexts* 2 (1982): 163–78.

———, "The Place of the *Dialoghi d'amore* in Contemporaneous Jewish Thought," in *Volare alla divina bellezza: Ficino and Renaissance Neoplatonism*, ed. O. Z. Pugliese and K. Eisenbichler (forthcoming).

———, "The Song of Solomon's Ascents: Love and Human Perfection According to a Jewish Associate of Giovanni Pico della Mirandola" (Ph.D. diss., University of California, Berkeley, 1976).

Lesne, E., *Les livres, 'scriptoria' et bibliothèques du commencement du VIIIe à la fin du XIe siècle: Histoire de la propriété ecclésiastique en France*, 6 vols. (Lille, 1910–43).

Levin, C., "Advice on Women's Behavior in Three Tudor Homilies," *International Journal of Women's Studies* 6 (1983): 176–85.

Levine, J., "Reginald Pecock and Lorenzo Valla on the *Donation of Constantine*," *Studies in the Renaissance* 20 (1973): 118–43.

Levy, F. J., *Tudor Historical Thought* (San Marino, CA, 1967).

———, "The Making of Camden's *Britannia*," *Bibliothèque d'humanisme et Renaissance* 26 (1964): 70–97.

Lewis, C. S., *English Literature in the Sixteenth Century, Excluding Drama* (Oxford, 1954).

Lewry, P. O., "Rhetoric at Paris and Oxford in the Mid-Thirteenth Century," *Rhetorica* 1 (1983): 23–42.

Libby, L. J., "Venetian History and Political Thought After 1509," *Studies in the Renaissance* 20 (1973): 7–45.

Lida de Malkiel, M. R., *Juan de Mena, poeta del prerenacimiento español* (Mexico, 1950).

———, *La tradición clásica en España* (Barcelona, 1975).

Lightbown, R., *Sandro Botticelli: Life and Works*, 2 vols. (Berkeley, 1978).

Lilje, H., *Luthers Geschichtsanschauung* (Zurich, 1932).

Lintilhac, E., "Un coup d'état dans la république des lettres: Jules-César Scaliger fondateur du 'Classicisme' cent ans avant Boileau," *La nouvelle revue* 64 (1890): 333–46, 528–47.

Lippman, E., "The Place of Music in the System of the Liberal Arts," in *Aspects of Medieval and Renaissance Music*, ed. LaRue (q.v.), 545–59.

Liscu, M., *Étude sur la philosophie morale chez Ciceron* (Paris, 1950).

Lisio, P. A. de, *Gli anni della svolta* (Salerno, 1976).

———, *Studi sull'umanesimo meridionale* (Naples, 1973).

Liva, A., *Notariato e documento notarile a Milano dall'alto medioevo alla fine del settecento* (Rome, 1979).

Lixačev, D. S., *Razvitie russkoj literatury X–XVII vekov. Èpoxi i stili* [*Development of Russian Literature 10th–17th Centuries: Periods and Styles*] (Leningrad, 1973).

Lobel, E., *The Medieval Latin Poetics* (New York, 1972).

———, "The Medieval Latin Poetics," *Proceedings of the British Academy* 17 (1931): 309–34.

Lockwood, D. P., "De Rinucio Aretino Graecarum litterarum interprete," *Harvard Studies in Classial Philology* 24 (1913): 51–109.

Logan, G. M., "Substance and Form in Renaissance Humanism," *Journal of Medieval and Renaissance Studies* 7 (1977): 1–34.

Logan, O., *Culture and Society in Venice, 1470–1790: The Renaissance and Its Heritage* (London and New York, 1972).

Long, P. O., "The Contribution of Architectural Writers to a 'Scientific' Outlook in the Fifteenth and Sixteenth Centuries," *Journal of Medieval and Renaissance Studies* 15 (1985): 265–98.

Longère, J., *Oeuvres oratoires de maîtres Parisiens au XIIᵉ siècle*, 2 vols. (Paris, 1973).

———, *La prédication médiévale* (Paris, 1983).

Longpré, P. E., "Les distinctiones de Fr. Thomas de Pavia, O.F.M.," *Archivum franciscanum historicum* 16 (1923): 3–33.

López de Toro, J., "Jorge de Trebisonda traducido por Alonso Ortiz de Castro," in *Studi in onore di Riccardo Filangieri*, 3 vols. (Naples, 1959), 2:129–31.

———, "El primer tratado de pedagogía en España (1453)," *Boletín de la Universidad de Granada* 5 (1933): 259–75; 6 (1934): 153–71; 7 (1935): 195–218.

López Martínez, N., "La biblioteca de D. Luis de Acuña en 1496," *Hispania* 78 (1960): 81–110.

López Piñero, J. M., *Ciencia y técnica en la sociedad española de los siglos XVI y XVII* (Barcelona, 1979).

López Rueda, J., *Helenistas españoles del siglo XVI* (Madrid, 1973).

Lorch, M., *Valla's Defense of Life: A Theory of Pleasure* (Munich, 1985).

Lorenz, R., *Die unvollendete Befreiung vom Nominalismus. Martin Luther und die Grenzen hermeneutischer Theologie bei Gerhard Ebeling* (Gütersloh, 1973).

Lorenzi, G., *Cola Montano, studii storici* (Milan, 1875).

Lowinsky, E. E., "Humanism in the Music of the Renaissance," in *Medieval and Renaissance Studies*, ed. F. Tirro (Durham, NC, 1982), 87–220.

Lowry, M. J. C., *The World of Aldus Manutius: Business and Scholarship in Renaissance Venice* (Ithaca, NY, 1979).

———, "The 'New Academy' of Aldus Manutius: A Renaissance Dream," *Bulletin of the John Rylands University Library of Manchester* 58 (1976): 378–420.

———, "Two Great Venetian Libraries in the Age of Aldus Manutius," *Bulletin of the John Rylands University Library of Manchester* 57 (1974): 128–66.

Lubac, H. de, *Pic de la Mirandole* (Paris, 1975).

Lucas, C., *De l'horreur au "lieto fine": Le contrôle du discours tragique dans le théâtre de Giraldi Cinzio* (Rome, 1984).

Lucchesi, G., *Per una vita di san Pier Damiani: Componenti cronologiche e topografiche*, 2 vols. in 1 (Cesena, 1972).

Luck, G., "Marullus und sein dichterisches Werk, Versuch einer Würdigung," *Arcadia* 1 (1966): 31–49.

Luhrman, G. J., "C. L. Pasius, T. Linacre, J. C. Scaliger en hun beschouwing van het werkwoord: Een kritisch-vergelijkende studie omtrent XVI^{de} eeuwse taalkundige theorievorming" (inaugural diss. Groningen University, 1984).

Lulvès, J., *Die Summa cancellariae des Johan von Neumarkt* (Berlin, 1891).

Lungo, I., del, *Florentia: Uomini e cose del Quattrocento* (Florence, 1897).

Lupi, S., "Il *De sermone* di G. Pontano," *Filologia romanza* 2 (1955): fasc. 8.

Luzzatto, G., *Storia economica di Venezia dall'XI al XVI secolo* (Venice, 1961).

———, *Studi di storia economica veneziana* (Padua, 1954).

Maas, C. W., *The German Community in Rome, 1378–1525* (Rome, 1981).

Mace, D. T., "Pietro Bembo and the Literary Origins of the Italian Madrigal," *Musical Quarterly* 55 (1969): 65–86.

Machiels, J., "Johannes Dullaert, Gent, c. 1480–Parijs, 10 September 1513," in *Professor R. L. Plancke 70. Getuigenissen en Bijdragen* (Ghent, 1981), 69–96.

Mack, P., "Valla's Dialectic in the North: A Commentary on Peter of Spain by Gerardus Listrius," *Vivarium* 21 (1983): 58–72.

MacKay, A., *Spain in the Middle Ages: From Frontier to Empire, 1000–1500* (New York, 1977).

Maffei, D., *Alessandro d'Alessandro, giureconsulto e umanista* (Milan, 1956).

———, *Gli inizi dell'umanesimo giuridico* (Milan, 1956).

Mahdi, M., "Averroes on Divine Law and Human Wisdom," in *Ancients and*

Moderns: Essays on the Tradition of Political Philosophy in Honor of Leo Strauss, ed. J. Cropsey (New York and London, 1964), 114–31.

Mahoney, E. P., "Philosophy and Science in Nicoletto Vernia and Agostino Nifo," in *Scienza e filosofia all'Università di Padova nel Quattrocento,* ed. Poppi (q.v.), 135–202.

Mahoney, M. S., "Diagrams and Dynamics: Mathematical Perspectives on Edgerton's Thesis," in *Science and the Arts in the Renaissance,* ed. F. D. Hoeniger and J. W. Shirley (Washington, DC, 1985), 198–220.

Maier, A., *Ausgehendes Mittelalter. Gesammelte Aufsätze zur Geistesgeschichte des 14. Jahrhunderts,* 3 vols. (Rome, 1964–77).

———, *On the Threshold of Exact Science: Selected Writings of Anneliese Maier on Late Medieval Natural Philosophy,* ed. and trans. S. D. Sargent (Philadelphia, 1982).

———, *Studien zur Naturphilosophie der Spätscholastik,* 5 vols. (Rome, 1949–58).

Maier, B., "Agnolo Poliziano," in *Orientamenti culturali. Letteratura italiana. I maggiori* (Milan, 1969), 300–305.

———, "La poetica di Girolamo Fracastoro," *Annali dell'Università di Trieste* 19 (1949): 29–55.

Maïer, I., *Ange Politien: La formation d'un poète humaniste, 1469–1480* (Geneva, 1966).

———, *Les manuscrits d'Ange Politien* (Geneva, 1965).

Mainardi, G., "Il Travesio, il Barzizza e l'umanesimo pavese," *Bollettino della Società Pavese di Storia Patria* 52 (1953): 13–25.

Maitre, L. *Les écoles épiscopales et monastiques en Occident avant les universités (768–1180)* (Paris, 2d ed. 1924).

Major, J. M., *Sir Thomas Elyot and Renaissance Humanism* (Lincoln, NE, 1964).

Malaguzzi-Valeri, F., *La corte di Lodovico Il Moro,* 4 vols. (Milan, 1913–23).

Mallet, M., *The Borgias* (London, 1969).

Manacorda, G., *Benedetto Varchi, l'uomo, il poeta, il critico* (Pisa, 1903).

———, *Storia della scuola in Italia,* 1 vol. in 2 pts. (Milan, 1913).

Manaresi, C., *I placiti del regum italicum* (Rome, 1955).

Mancini, G., *Vita di Lorenzo Valla* (Florence, 1891).

———, "Giovanni Tortelli: Cooperatore di Niccolò V nel fondare la Biblioteca vaticana," *Archivio storico italiano* 78.2 (1920): 161–268.

Mandowsky, E. and Mitchell, C., *Pirro Ligorio's Roman Antiquities* (London, 1963).

Mann, M., *Erasme et les débuts de la Réforme française* (Paris, 1934).

Mansfield, B., *Phoenix of His Age: Interpretations of Erasmus, 1550–1750* (Toronto, 1979); a second volume to cover the period since 1750 is underway.

Maravall, J. A., *Antiguos y modernos* (Madrid, 1966).

———, *Carlo V y el pensamiento político del Renacimiento* (Madrid, 1960).

———, *Estado moderno y mentalidad social,* 2 vols. (Madrid, 1972).

———, "La diversificación de modelos del Renacimiento: Renacimiento francés y Renacimiento español," *Cuadernos hispano-americanos* 390 (1980): 551–614.

———, "Los *hombres de saber* o letrados y la formación de su conciencia estamental," in *Estudios de historia del pensamiento español* (Madrid, 1967), 345–80.

———, "El prerenacimiento del siglo XV," *Academia literaria renacentista* 3 (1983): 17–36.

Marchesi, C., *Bartolomeo della Fonte (Bartholomaeus Fontius): Contributo alla storia degli studi classici in Firenze nella seconda metà del Quattrocento* (Catania, 1900).

Marchetti, V. and G., Patrizi, "Castelvetro, Ludovico," *Dizionario biografico degli italiani*, 30 vols. to date (Rome, 1960–84), 22:8–21.

Mare, A. de la, *The Handwriting of Italian Humanists*, vol. 1 (Oxford, 1973).

Margolin, J.-C., *Douze années de bibliographie erasmienne (1950–1961)* (Toronto, 1977).

———, *L'humanisme en Europe au temps de la Renaissance* (Paris, 1981).

———, *Neuf annés de bibliographie erasmienne (1962–1970)* (Toronto, 1977).

———, *Quatorze années de bibliographie erasmienne (1936–1949)* (Toronto, 1977).

Mariani, U., *Il Petrarca e gli Agostiniani* (Rome, 1946).

Mariétan, J., *Problème de la classification des sciences d'Aristote à Saint Thomas* (Paris, 1901).

Marinis, T. de, *La biblioteca napoletana dei re d'Aragona*, 4 vols. (Milan, 1947–52), Supplemento, 2 vols. (Verona, 1969).

Marino, E., O.P., "Umanesimo e teologia (a proposito della recente storiografia su L. Valla)," *Memorie domenicane* n.s. 3 (1972): 198–218.

Maritain, J., *Art et scholastique* (Paris, 1935); *Art and Scholasticism and the Frontiers of Poetry*, trans. J. W. Evans (South Bend, IN, 1974).

Marius, R., *Thomas More* (New York, 1984).

Marrou, H. I., *A History of Education in Antiquity*, trans. G. Lamb (New York, 1956).

Marsh, D., *The Quattrocento Dialogue* (Cambridge, MA, 1980).

———, "Grammar, Method, and Polemic in Lorenzo Valla's *Elegantiae*," *Rinascimento* 19 (1979): 91–116.

Martelli, M., "La semantica di Poliziano e la *Centuria secunda* del Rinascimento," *Rinascimento* 2d ser. 13 (1973): 21–84.

Martellotti, G., *Dante e Boccaccio e altri scrittori dall'umanesimo al romanticismo* (Florence, 1983).

———, "Barzizza, Gasperino," *Dizionario biografico degli italiani*, 30 vols. to date (Rome, 1960–84), 7:34–39.

———, "Barzizza, Guiniforte," *Dizionario biografico degli italiani*, 30 vols. to date (Rome, 1960–84), 7:39–40.

———, "La difesa della poesia nel Boccaccio e un giudizio su Lucano," *Studi sul Boccaccio* 4 (1967): 265–79.

———, "In margine ai *Trionfi* e al *De viris*," *Studi petrarcheschi* 2 (1949): 95–99.

————, "Linee di sviluppo dell'umanesimo petrarchesco," *Studi petrarcheschi* 2 (1949): 51–80.

————, "Petrarca e Cesare," *Annali della R. Scuola Superiore di Pisa* 16 (1942): 149ff.

————, "Sulla composizione del *De viris* e dell'*Africa*," *Annali della R. Scuola Superiore di Pisa* 10 (1941): 247–62.

————, "L'umanesimo del Petrarca," *Il veltro*, 14.1–2 (1980): 71–82.

Martí, A., *La preceptiva retórica española en el siglo de oro* (Madrid, 1972).

Martin, A. von, *Coluccio Salutati und das humanistische Lebensideal* (Berlin, 1916).

————, *Coluccio Salutati's Traktat "Vom Tyrannen." Eine kulturgeschichtliche Untersuchung nebst Textedition* (Berlin, 1913).

Martin, R. H, "The *Epitome margaritae eloquentiae* of Laurentius Gulielmus de Saona," *Proceedings of the Leeds Philosophical and Literary Society* 14 (1971): 99–187.

Martines, L., *Power and Imagination: City-States in Renaissance Italy* (New York, 1979).

————, *The Social World of the Florentine Humanists, 1390–1460* (Princeton, 1963).

Masai, F., *Pléthon et le platonisme de Mistra* (Paris, 1956).

Massalongo, R., "Alessandro Benedetti e la medicina veneta del Quattrocento," *Atti del R. Istituto Veneto di Scienze, Lettere ed Arti* 76.2 (1916–17): 197–259.

Mastrodemetris, P., *Nikolaos Sekoundinos (1406–1444). Bios kai ergon* [in Greek] (Athens, 1970).

Matheeussen, C., "À propos d'une lettre inconnue de Despautère," *Lias* 4 (1977): 1–11.

Mattei, R. de, "Ammirato, Scipione," *Dizionario biografico degli italiani*, 30 vols. to date (Rome, 1960–84), 3:1–4.

Maurer, W., *Der junge Melanchthon*, 2 vols. (Göttingen, 1967–69).

————, "Melanchthons *Loci communes* von 1521 als wissenschaftliche Programmschrift," *Luther Jahrbuch* 27 (1960): 1–50.

Maylender, M., *Storia delle accademie d'Italia*, 5 vols. (Bologna, 1926–30).

Mazza, A., "L'inventario della *parva libraria* di Santo Spirito e la biblioteca del Boccaccio," *Italia medioevale e umanistica* 9 (1966): 1–74.

Mazzacurati, G., *La crisi della retorica umanistica nel Cinquecento: Antonio Riccobono* (Naples, 1961).

————, "Prologo e promemoria sulla 'scoperta' della Poetica (1500–1540)," in *Conflitti di cultura nel Cinquecento* (Naples, 1977), 1–41.

Mazzocco, A., "Biondo Flavio and the Antiquarian Tradition" (Ph.D. diss., University of California, Berkeley, 1973).

McConica, J. C., *English Humanists and Reformation Politics Under Henry VIII and Edward VI* (Oxford, 1965).

McDonald, W. C., "Maximilian I of Habsburg and the Veneration of Hercules: On the Revival of Myth and the German Renaissance," *Journal of Medieval and Renaissance Studies* 6 (1976): 139–54.

McKeon, R., "Renaissance and Method in Philosophy," in *Studies in the History of Ideas*, 3 vols. (New York, 1918–35), 3:37–114.

——, "Rhetoric in the Middle Ages," *Speculum* 17 (1942): 1–32.

McManamon, J. M., S. J., "The Ideal Renaissance Pope: Funeral Oratory from the Papal Court," *Archivum historiae pontificae* 14 (1976): 5–70.

——, "Innovation in Early Humanist Rhetoric: The Oratory of Pier Paolo Vergerio (the Elder)," *Rinascimento* n.s. 22 (1982): 3–32.

——, "Pier Paolo Vergerio (the Elder) and the Beginnings of the Humanist Cult of Jerome," *Catholic Historical Review* 71 (1985): 353–71.

——, "Renaissance Preaching, Theory and Practice: A Holy Thursday Sermon of Aurelio Brandolini," *Viator* 10 (1979): 355–73.

McMullen, N., "The Education of English Gentlewomen, 1540–1640," *History of Education* 6 (1977): 87–101.

McNeil, D. O., *Guillaume Budé and Humanism in the Reign of Francis I* (Geneva, 1975).

McNeill, J. T., *The History and Character of Calvinism* (New York, 1954).

Medin, A., "Raffaele Regio a Venezia, epigrammi per la sua morte," *Archivio veneto tridentino* 4th ser. 1 (1922): 237–44.

Meiss, M., "Toward a More Comprehensive Renaissance Palaeography," in *The Painter's Choice: Problems in the Interpretation of Renaissance Art* (New York, 1976), 151–75.

Melamed, A., "Rhetoric and Philosophy in *Sefer Nofet Zufim* of R. Judah Messer Leon" [Hebrew], *Italia* 1 (1978): 7–38.

Melczer, W., "Platonisme et Aristotélisme dans la pensée de Léon l'Hébreu," in *Platon et Aristote à la Renaissance* (Paris, 1976), 293–306.

Memola, A. A., *Catalogo delle opere di Antonio de' Ferrariis (Galateo)* (Lecce, 1982).

Menapace-Brisca, L., "La retorica di F. Patrizio o del platonismo antiaristotelico," *Aevum* 26 (1952): 434–61.

Meneghel, R., "La *Leandride* di Giovanni Girolamo Nadal," *Italia medioevale e umanistica* 16 (1973): 163–78.

Menéndez Pelayo, M., *Poetas de la corte de Don Juan II* (Madrid, 1943).

Mengaldo, P. V., "La lirica volgare del Sannazaro e lo sviluppo del linguaggio poetico rinascimentale," *Rassegna delle letteratura italiana* 66 (1962): 436–82.

Mengozzi, G., *Ricerche sull'attività della scuola da Pavia nell'alto medioevo* (Pavia, 1924).

Menke-Glückert, E., *Geschichtsschreibung der Reformation und Gegenreformation* (Leipzig, 1912).

Mercati, G., *Per la cronologia della vita e degli scritti di Niccolò Perotti, arcivescovo di Siponto* (Rome, 1925).

——, "Tre dettati universitari dell'umanista Martino Filetico sopra Persio, Giovenale et Orazio," in *Classical and Mediaeval Studies in Honor of Edward Kennard Rand*, ed. L. W. Jones (New York, 1938), 221–30.

Mercer, R. G. G., *The Teaching of Gasparino Barzizza with Special Reference to His Place in Paduan Humanism* (London, 1979).

Meter, J. H., *The Literary Theories of Daniel Heinsius* (Assen, 1984).

Metz, R., "La contribution de la France à l'étude du decret de Gratien," *Studia gratiana* 2 (1954): 495–518.

Meuthen, E., "Charakter und Tendenzen der deutschen Humanisten," in *Säkulare Aspekte der Reformationszeit*, ed. H. Angermeier (Munich, 1983), 217–66.

Meyendorff, J., *A Study of Gregory Palamas* (London, 1964).

Meyer-Baer, K., *Music of the Spheres and the Dance of Death* (Princeton, 1970).

Michiel, D., *Elogio di Costanza da Varano* (Venice, 1807).

Miele, L., *Saggi galateani* (Naples, 1982).

———, "Per una rilettura dell'*Esposizione del Pater* di A. de Ferrariis Galateo," *Esperienze letterarie* 9.4 (1984): 39–55.

———, "Tradizione ed 'esperienza' nella precettistica politica di Diomede Carafa," *Atti dell'Accademia Pontaniana* n.s. 24 (1976): 1–11.

———, "Tradizione letteraria e realismo politico nel *De principe* del Pontano," *Atti dell'Accademia Pontaniana* n.s. 32 (1983): 301–21.

Miglio, M., *Storiografia pontificia del Quattrocento* (Bologna, 1975).

Milano, A., *Storia degli ebrei in Italia* (Turin, 1963).

Milburn, A. R., "Leone Ebreo and the Renaissance," in *Isaac Abravanel: Six Lectures*, ed. J. B. Trend and H. Loewe (Cambridge, 1937), 131–57.

Miles, L., *John Colet and the Platonic Tradition* (London, 1962).

Miller, D. G., "Duhem, Pierre-Maurice-Marie," in *Dictionary of Scientific Biography*, 16 vols. (New York, 1970–80), 4:225–33.

Miller, P., *The New England Mind*, 2 vols. (Cambridge, MA, 1939–53).

Minio-Paluello, L., "Guglielmo di Moerbecke traduttore della 'Poetica' di Aristotele (1278)," *Rivista di filosofia neo-scolastica* 39 (1947): 1–17.

Minoia, M., *La vita di Maffeo Vegio umanista lodigiano* (Lodi, 1896).

Miola, A., "Su un umanista milanese lettore di retorica nello Studio di Napoli," *Atti della Società Italiana per il Progresso delle Scienze* (Naples, 1910), 897–99.

Mirković, M., *Matija Vlačić Ilirik* (Zagreb, 1960).

Misch, G., *Autobiographie in Altertum* (Leipzig, 1907).

Mischiati, O., review of L. Lockwood, *The Counter Reformation and Masses of V. Ruffo*, in *Rivista italiana di musicologia* 9 (1974): 304.

Mitchell, B., *Rome in the High Renaissance: The Age of Leo X* (Norman, OK, 1973).

Mitchell, R. J., *The Laurels and the Tiara: Pope Pius II, 1405–1464* (Garden City, NY, 1962).

Mladen, L. M., "Bartolus the Man," *Annals of the New York Academy of Sciences* 314 (1978): 311–48.

Moeller, B., "The German Humanists and the Reformation," in *Imperial Cities and the Reformation*, ed. H. C. E. Midelfort and M. U. Edwards, Jr. (Philadelphia, 1972), 19–38.

Moeller, E. von, *Aymer du Rivail, Der erste Rechtshistoriker* (Berlin, 1907).

Mohler, L., *Kardinal Bessarion als Theologe, Humanist, und Staatsmann*, 3 vols. (Paderborn, 1923–42).

Moldaenke, G., *Schriftverständnis und Schriftdeutung im Zeitalter der Reformation*, vol. 1, *Matthias Flacius Illyricus* (Stuttgart, 1936).

Molhuysen, P. C., *Bronnen tot de geschiedenis der Leidsche Universiteit*, 7 vols. (The Hague, 1913–24).

Momigliano, A. D., "Polybius' Reappearance in Western Europe," in *Polybe, Entretiens sur l'antiquité classique* 20 (Vandoeuvres, 1974), 345–72.

Mommsen, T. E., "Petrarch and the Decoration of the Sala virorum illustrium in Padua," *Art Bulletin* (1952): 95–116.

———, "Petrarch's Conception of the 'Dark Ages,' " in *Medieval and Renaissance Studies*, ed. E. F. Rice, Jr. (Ithaca, 1959), 106–29.

Monfasani, J., *George of Trebizond: A Biography and a Study of His Rhetoric and Logic* (Leiden, 1976).

———, "*Bessarion Latinus*," *Rinascimento* 2d ser. 21 (1981): 165–209.

———, "The Byzantine Rhetorical Tradition and the Renaissance," in *Studies in the Theory and Practice of Renaissance Eloquence*, ed. Murphy (q.v.), 174–87.

———, review of *Laurentii Valle Repastinatio dialectice et philosophie*, ed. Zippel, in *Rivista di letteratura italiana* 2 (1984): 177–94.

Monnerjahn, E., *Giovanni Pico della Mirandola: Ein Beitrag zur philosophischen Theologie des italienischen Humanismus* (Wiesbaden, 1960).

Monnier, P., *Le Quattrocento*, 2 vols. (Paris, 2d ed., 1912).

Montera, P. de, *L'humaniste Napolitain Giovanni Carbone et ses poésies inédites* (Naples, 1935).

Monteverdi, A., "Orazio nel medioevo," *Studi medievali* 7 (1934): 162–80.

———, "Pier Candido Decembrio in Italia romana, Lombardia romana," *Istituto di Studi Romani* 1 (1938): 171–94.

Monti Sabia, L., "Esegesi critica e storia del testo nei Carmina del Pontano (a proposito di Parth. I.13 e II.12)," *Annali della Facoltà di Lettere e Filosofia dell'Università di Napoli* 12 (1969–70): 219–35.

———, "L'estremo autografo di Giovanni Pontano," *Italia medievale e umanistica* 23 (1980): 293–314.

———, "Ricerche sulla cronologia del *Dialoghi* del Pontano," *Annali della Facoltà di Lettere e Filosofia dell'Università di Napoli* 10 (1962–63): 247–312.

———, "L'umanitas di Elisio Calenzio alla luce del suo epistolario," *Annali della Facoltà di Lettere e Filosofia dell'Università di Napoli* 11 (1964–68): 175–251.

Moore, E., *Studies in Dante, First Series, Scripture and Classical Authors in Dante* (Oxford, 1896; reprinted with intro. by C. Hardie, Oxford, 1969).

Moro, D., "Tre note per la biografia di Antonio Galateo," *Esperienze letterarie* 4.3 (1979): 81–102.

———, "I Turchi ad Otranto (1480–81)," *Quaderni dell'Istituto Nazionale di Studi sul Rinascimento Meridionale* 3 (1986): 99–121.

Morsolin, B., *Giangiorgio Trissino: Monografia d'un gentiluomo letterato del secolo XVI* (Florence, 1894).

Mortara, M., "Expurgated Passages in the Printed *Sefer Behinat ha-Dat*" [Hebrew], *Ozar tov* (Hebrew supplement to *Magazin für die Wissenschaft des Judenthums*) 1 (1878): 082–084.

Moss, J. D., "Galileo's *Letter to Christiana:* Some Rhetorical Considerations," *Renaissance Quarterly* 36 (1983): 547–76.

Mousnier, R., *Les institutions de la France sous la monarchie absolue, 1598–1789*, 2 vols. (Paris, 1974–80).

Moxó, S. de, "La elevación de los *letrados* en la sociedad estamental del siglo XIV," in *XII semana de estudios medievales* (Pamplona, 1976), 183–215.

Muccillo, M., "La storia della filosofia presocratica nelle 'Discussiones Peripateticae' di Francesco Patrizi da Cherso," *La cultura* 13 (1975): 48–105.

———, "La vita e le opere di Aristotele nelle 'Discussiones peripateticae' di Francesco Patrizi da Cherso," *Rinascimento* 22 (1981): 53–119.

Muir, E., *Civic Ritual in Renaissance Venice* (Princeton, 1981).

———, "Images of Power: Art and Pageantry in Renaissance Venice," *American Historical Review* 84 (1979): 16–52.

Müller, E., *Peter von Prezza, ein Publizist der Zeit des Interregnums* (Heidelberg, 1913).

Munnynck, M. de, "L'esthetique de Saint Thomas d'Aquin," in *San Tommaso d'Aquino: Pubblicazione commemorative del sesto centenario della canonizzazione* (Milan, 1923).

Murphy, J. J., *Medieval Rhetoric: A Select Bibliography* (Toronto, 1971).

———, *Renaissance Rhetoric: A Short Title Catalogue of Works on Rhetorical Theory from the Beginning of Printing to A.D. 1700, with Special Attention to the Holdings of the Bodleian Library, Oxford. With a Select Basic Bibliography of Secondary Works on Renaissance Rhetoric* (New York, 1981); review by B. Vickers, *Quarterly Journal of Speech* 69 (1983): 441–44 and 70 (1984): 335–38.

———, *Rhetoric in the Middle Ages: A History of Rhetorical Theory from Saint Augustine to the Renaissance* (Berkeley, 1974).

———, "Rhetoric in the Earliest Years of Printing, 1465–1500," *Quarterly Journal of Speech* 70 (1984): 1–11.

Mutini, C., "Cavalcanti, Bartolomeo," *Dizionario biografico degli italiani*, 30 vols. to date (Rome, 1960–84), 22:611–17.

Mycue, D., "Founder of the Vatican Library: Nicholas V or Sixtus IV?" in *Libraries and Culture: Proceedings of the Library History Association* 4th ser. (Austin, TX, 1981), 121–33.

Nadel, G. H., "The Philosophy of History Before Historicism," in *Studies in the Philosophy of History*, ed. G. H. Nadel (New York, 1965), 49–73.

Nader, H., *The Mendoza Family in the Spanish Renaissance, 1350–1550* (New Brunswick, NJ, 1979).

Näf, W., *Vadian und seine Stadt St. Gallen*, vol. 1, *Humanist in Wien* (St. Gallen, 1944); vol. 2, *Bürgermeister und Reformator von St. Gallen* (St. Gallen, 1957).

———, "Aus der Forschung zur Geschichte des deutschen Humanismus," *Schweizer Beiträge zur Allgemeinen Geschichte* 2 (1944): 221–26.

Nardi, B., *Saggi sull'Aristotelismo padovano dal secolo XIV–XVI* (Florence, 1958).

————, "Letteratura e cultura veneta del Quattrocento," in *Saggi sulla cultura veneta del Quattrocento e Cinquecento* (Padua, 1971), 3–43.

————, "La mistica averroistica e Pico della Mirandola," in *Umanesimo e Machiavellismo,* ed. E. Castrelli (Padua, 1949), 55–74.

Nardi, E., *Rabelais e il diritto romano* (Milan, 1962).

Nauert, C. G., Jr., *Agrippa and the Crisis of Renaissance Thought* (Urbana, IL, 1965).

————, "The Clash of Humanists and Scholastics: An Approach to Pre-Reformation Controversies," *Sixteenth-Century Journal* 4 (1973): 1–18.

————, "Humanists, Scientists, and Pliny: Changing Approaches to a Classical Author," *American Historical Review* 84 (1979): 72–85.

Nauwelaerts, M. A., *Latijnse School en Onderwijs te 's Hertogenbosch tot 1629* (Tilburg, 1974).

————, "La correspondance de Simon Verepaeus (1522–1598)," *Humanistica lovaniensia* 23 (1974): 271–340.

Negri, R., "Benci, Francesco," *Dizionario biografico degli italiani,* 30 vols. to date (Rome, 1960–84), 8:192–93.

Nelson, J. C., *The Renaissance Theory of Love: The Context of Giordano Bruno's Eroici Furori* (New York, 1958).

Nelson, W., "The Scholars of Henry VII," in *John Skelton* (New York, 1939), 4–39.

Nembach, U., *Predigt des Evangeliums: Luther als Prediger, Pädagoge und Rhetor* (Neukirchen-Vluyn, 1972).

Nemeskürty, I., "Bornemissza stilusa" ["The Style of Bornemissza"], *Itk* 59 (1955): 23–35.

Németh, G., "Balassi Bálint és a török költészet" ["Bálint Balassi and Turkish Poetry"], *Magyar Szazadok* 3 (1948): 80–100.

Netanyahu, B., *Don Isaac Abravanel: Statesman and Scholar* (Philadelphia, 1953).

Neuser, W. H., *Die reformatorische Wende bei Zwingli* (Neukirchen-Vluyn, 1977).

Neve, F., "Mémoire historique et littéraire sur le Collège des Trois-Langues à l'Université de Louvain (Brussels, 1856).

Nibley, H., "New Light on Scaliger," *Classical Journal* 37 (1942): 391–95.

Niccolai, F., *Pietro Vettori* (Florence, 1912).

Nieto, J. C., *Juan de Valdes and the Origins of the Spanish and Italian Reformation* (Geneva, 1970).

Nixon, L., *John Calvin's Teachings on Human Reason* (New York, 1963).

Nolhac, P. de, *Erasme en Italie* (Paris, 1898).

————, *Petrarque et l'humanisme,* 2 vols. (Paris, 2d ed. 1907).

Nonni, C., "Contributi allo studio della commedia umanistica *La Poliscena,*" *Arcadia: Accademia letteraria italiana* 6 (1975–76): 393–451.

Nordman, V. A., *Justus Lipsius als Geschichtsforscher und Geschichtslehrer* (Helsinki, 1932).

Noreña, C. G., *Juan Luis Vives* (The Hague, 1970).

————, *Studies in Spanish Renaissance Thought* (The Hague, 1975).

Norpoth, L., "Zur Biobibliographie und Wissenschaftslehre des Pietro d'Abano," *Kyklos: Jahrbuch für Geschichte und Philosophie der Medizin* 3 (1930): 292–353.

Novák, A., *Czech Literature,* trans. P. Kussi, ed. with a supplement by W. E. Harkins (Ann Arbor, 1976).

——, "Dějiny české literatury" ["History of Czech Literature"], in *Československá vlastivěda, Díl VII. Písemnictví* [*Czechoslovak Book of Knowledge on Czechoslovakia*] (Prague, 1933), 7–208.

Novak, B. C., "Giovanni Pico della Mirandola and Jochanan Alemanno," *Journal of the Warburg and Courtauld Institutes* 45 (1982): 125–47.

Novati, F., *La giovinezza di Coluccio Salutati* (Turin, 1888).

——, "Aneddotti viscontei," *Archivio storico lombardo* 4th ser. 10 (1908): 193–216.

Oberdorfer, A., "Di Leonardo Giustiniani umanista," *Giornale storico della letteratura italiana* 56 (1910): 107–20.

Oberman, H. A., *The Harvest of Medieval Theology: Gabriel Biel and Late Medieval Nominalism* (Cambridge, MA, 1963).

——, "Some Notes on the Theology of Nominalism with Attention to Its Relation to the Renaissance," *Harvard Theological Review* 53 (1960): 47–76.

Odebrecht, B., "Die Briefmuster des Henricus Francigena," *Archiv für Urkundenforschung* 14 (1936): 231–61.

O'Donnel, J. R., "Coluccio Salutati on the Poet Teacher," *Medieval Studies* 22 (1960): 240–56.

Ogilvy, J. D. A., *Books Known to Anglo-Latin Writers from Aldhelm to Alcuin* (Cambridge, MA, 1936).

Olin, J. C., "Erasmus and the Church Fathers," in his *Six Essays on Erasmus* (New York, 1979), 33–48.

Oliver, R. P., "Giovanni Tortelli," in *Studies Presented to David Moore Robinson,* ed. G. E. Mylonas, 2 vols. (St. Louis, 1951–53), 2:1257–71.

——, " 'New Fragments' of Latin Authors in Perotti's *Cornucopiae*," *Transactions of the American Philological Association* 78 (1947): 376–424.

Olmedo, F. G., *Nebrija (1441–1522) debelador de la barbarie, comentador eclesiástico, pedagogo-poeta* (Madrid, 1942).

——, *Nebrija en Salamanca* (Madrid, 1944).

Olmi, G., *Ulisse Aldrovandi: Scienza e natura nel secondo Cinquecento* (Trent, 1976).

Olschki, L., *Geschichte der neusprachlichen wissenschaftlichen Literatur,* 3 vols. (Leipzig, 1919–22 and Halle, 1927).

O'Malley, C. D., *Andreas Vesalius of Brussels: 1514–1564* (Berkeley, 1964).

O'Malley, J. W., S.J., *Giles of Viterbo on Church and Reform: A Study in Renaissance Thought* (Leiden, 1968).

——, *Praise and Blame in Renaissance Rome: Rhetoric, Doctrine, and Reform in the Sacred Orators of the Papal Court, ca. 1450–1521* (Durham, NC, 1979).

——, *Rome and the Renaissance: Studies in Culture and Religion* (London, 1981).

————, "Egidio de Viterbo, O.S.A. e il suo tempo," *Studia augustiniana historica* 9 (1983): 68–84.

————, "Erasmus and the History of Sacred Rhetoric: The *Ecclesiastes* of 1535," *Erasmus of Rotterdam Society Yearbook* 5 (1985): 1–29.

————, "The Feast of Thomas Aquinas in Renaissance Rome: A Neglected Document and Its Impact," *Rivista di storia della chiesa in Italia* 35 (1981): 1–27.

————, "Lutheranism in Rome 1542–1543—The Treatise by Alfonso Zorrilla," *Thought* 54 (1979): 262–73.

————, "Recent Studies in Church History, 1300–1600," *Catholic Historical Review* 55 (1969): 394–437.

————, "Some Renaissance Panegyrics of Aquinas," *Renaissance Quarterly* 27 (1974): 174–92.

Ong, W. J., S.J., *Ramus and Talon Inventory* (Cambridge, MA, 1958).

————, *Ramus, Method and the Decay of Dialogue* (Cambridge, MA, 1983).

Onofri, L., "Sacralità, immaginazione e proposte politiche: La *Vita* di Niccolò V di Giannozzo Manetti," *Humanistica Lovaniensia* 28 (1979): 27–77.

O'Rourke Boyle, M., *Erasmus on Language and Method in Theology* (Toronto, 1977).

————, *Rhetoric and Reform: Erasmus' Civil Dispute with Luther* (Cambridge, MA, 1983).

Overfield, J. H., *Humanism and Scholasticism in Late Medieval Germany* (Princeton, 1984).

————, "Scholastic Opposition to Humanism in Pre-Reformation Germany," *Viator* 7 (1976): 391–420.

Ozment, S. E., *The Age of Reform: 1250–1550* (New Haven, 1980).

————, *When Fathers Ruled: Family Life in Reformation Europe* (Cambridge, MA, 1983).

Padley, G. A., *Grammatical Theory in Western Europe, 1500–1700* (Cambridge, 1976).

Pagani, G., "Mario Nizolio ed il suo lessico ciceroniano," *Accademia Nazionale dei Lincei, Rendiconti* 5th ser. 2 (1893): 554–75, 897–922.

Pagden, A. R. D., "The Diffusion of Aristotle's Moral Philosophy in Spain, ca. 1400–ca. 1600," *Traditio* 31 (1975): 287–313.

Pagel, W., *Paracelsus: An Introduction to Philosophical Medicine in the Era of the Renaissance* (Basel and New York, 2d ed. 1982).

Pagliara, P. M., "La Roma antica di Fabio Calvo: Note sulla cultura antiquaria e architettonica," *Psicon* 8–9 (1977): 65–87.

Painter, F. V. N., *Luther on Education* (St. Louis, 1889).

Pajnić, E., *Antun Medo, dubrovački filozof šesnaestog stoljeća* [*Antun Medo, a Sixteenth-Century Ragusan Philosopher*] (Zagreb, 1980).

Palermino, R. J., "Platina's History of the Popes" (M.Litt. thesis, University of Edinburgh, 1973).

————, "The Roman Academy, the Catacombs and the Conspiracy of 1468," *Archivum historiae pontificiae* 18 (1980): 117–55.

Palisca, C. V., *Humanism in Italian Renaissance Musical Thought* (New Haven, 1986).

———, "Scientific Empiricism in Musical Thought," in *Seventeenth Century Science and the Arts*, ed. H. H. Rhys (Princeton, 1961), 113–18.

———, "*Ut oratoria musica:* The Rhetorical Basis of Musical Mannerism," in *The Meaning of Mannerism*, ed. F. W. Robinson and S. G. Nichols (Hanover, NH, 1972), 37–65.

Palomera, E. J., S.J., *Fray Diego Valadés o.f.m. evangelizador humanista de la nueva España* (Mexico City, 1962).

Palumbo, P., "Giangiorgio Trissino," in *Orientamenti culturali. Letteratura italiana. I minori*, 4 vols. (Milan, 1961–62): 2:873–89.

Pandžić, B., "Vida y obra de Jorge Dragišić," *Studia Croatia* 11 (1970): 114–31.

———, "Zivot i djela Jurja Dragišića" ["Life and Works of Juraj Dragišić"], *Dobar pastir* [*The Good Shepherd*] 26 (1976): 3–27.

Pane, R., *Andrea Palladio* (Turin, 1961).

Panizza, L., "Textual Interpretation in Italy, 1350–1450: Seneca's Letter I to Lucilius," *Journal of the Warburg and Courtauld Institutes* 46 (1983): 40–62.

Panofsky, E., *Albrecht Dürer*, 2 vols. (Princeton, 1943).

———, *Idea*, trans. J. J. S. Peake (Columbia, SC, 1968).

———, *Renaissance and Renascences in Western Art* (Stockholm, 1960; New York, 1969).

———, "Artist, Scientist, Genius: Notes on the Renaissance Dämmerung," in *The Renaissance: Six Essays* (New York, 1962).

Paparelli, G., "La disputa delle arti," in *Feritas, humanitas, divinitas* (Florence, 1960), 49–66.

———, "Umanesimo e paraumanesimo napoletano: D. Carafa," in *Da Dante al Seicento* (Salerno, 1971), 71–107.

Paratore, E., "Cicerone attraverso i secoli," *Marco Tullio Cicerone* (Florence, 1961), 235–53.

Pardo, M., "Le 'Batalla campal de los perros contra los lobos' d'Alfonso de Palencia," *Mélanges offerts à Pierre Le Gentil* (Paris, 1973), 587–603.

Paré, G., A. Brunet, and P. Tremblay, *La renaissance au XIIe siècle: Les écoles et l'enseignement* (Paris and Ottawa, 1933).

Parenti, G., "Pontano o dell'allitterazione: Lettura di Parthenopoeus I.7," *Rinascimento* n.s. 15 (1975): 89–110.

Parronchi, A., "Le 'misure dell'occhio' secondo il Ghiberti," *Paragone* 133 (1961): 18–48.

Partner, P., *The Papal States Under Martin V* (London, 1958).

———, *Renaissance Rome, 1550–1559: A Portrait of a Society* (Berkeley, 1977).

———, "Papal Financial Policy in the Renaissance and Counter-Reformation," *Past and Present* 88 (1980): 17–62.

Pasquali, G., *Storia della tradizione e critica del testo* (Florence, 2d ed. 1952).

Pasquazi, S., *Rinascimento ferrarese* (Caltanisetta, 1957).

Pastine, L., "Antonio Loschi umanista vicentino," *Rivista d'Italia* 18 (1915): 831–79.

Pastor, L. von, *History of the Popes from the Close of the Middle Ages*, trans. F. I. Antrobus et al. (London and St. Louis, 1891–1910), vols. 1–11.

Pastor, P., "Papal Financial Policy in the Renaissance and Counter-Reformation," *Past and Present* 88 (1980): 17–62.

Pastorello, E., *Bibliografia storico-analitica dell'arte della stampa a Venezia* (Venice, 1933).

Patera, A. and A. Podlaha, *Soupis rukopisů knihovny Metropolitní kapituly pražské* [*Description of Manuscripts of the Metropolitan Chapter Library of Prague*], 2 vols. (Prague, 1910–22).

Patrides, C. A., *The Grand Design of God* (London, 1972).

Patridge, L. and R. Starn, *A Renaissance Likeness: Art and Culture in Raphael's 'Julius II'* (Berkeley, 1980).

Pattaro, S. T., *Metodo e sistema delle scienze nel pensiero di Ulisse Aldrovandi* (Bologna, 1981).

Patterson, A. M., *Hermogenes and the Renaissance: Seven Ideas of Style* (Princeton, 1970).

———, "Tasso and Neoplatonism: The Growth of His Epic Theory," *Studies in the Renaissance* 18 (1971): 105–33.

Pattin, A., "Reinerus van Sint-Truiden, rector van de Latijnse school te Mechelen (c. 1370) en commentator van Boethius' *De consolatione philosophiae*," *Tijdschrift voor Filosofie* 44 (1982): 298–319.

Pattison, M., *Isaac Casaubon 1559–1641* (Oxford, 2d ed. 1892).

Pavlovskis, Z., *The Praise of Folly: Structure and Irony* (Leiden, 1983).

Paz y Mélia, A., "Biblioteca fundada por el conde de Haro," *Revista de archivos bibliotecas y museos* 1 (1897): 18–24, 60–66, 156–63, 225–62, 452–62; 4 (1900): 335–45, 661–67; 6 (1902): 198–208, 372–82; 7 (1902): 51–55.

Pellegrin, E., *La bibliothèque des Visconti et des Sforza* (Paris, 1955).

Pellegrini, F., *Fracastoro* (Trieste, 1948).

Penna, M., *Exposición de la biblioteca de los Mendoza del Infantado* (Madrid, 1958).

Percival, W. K., "Antonio de Nebrija and the Dawn of Modern Phonetics," *Res publica litterarum* 5 (1982): 221–32.

———, "The Grammatical Tradition and the Rise of the Vernaculars," *Current Trends in Linguistics* 13 (1975): 231–75.

———, "The Historical Sources of Guarino's Regulae grammaticales: A Reconsideration of Sabbadini's Evidence," *Civiltà dell'umanesimo: Atti del VI, VII, VIII Convegno del Centro di Studi Umanistici "Angelo Poliziano"* (Florence, 1972), 263–84.

———, "The Place of the *Rudimenta grammatices* in the History of Latin Grammar," *Res publica litterarum* 4 (1981): 233–64.

———, "Textual Problems in the Latin Grammar of Guarino Veronese," *Res publica litterarum* 1 (1978): 241–54.

Percopo, E., "Gli scritti di G. Pontano," *Archivio storico per le provincie napoletane* 62 (1937): 222–25.

Perles, J., *Beiträge zur Geschichte der hebräischen und aramäischen Studien* (Munich, 1884).

———, "Les savants juifs à Florence à l'époque de Laurent de Médicis," *Revue de études juives* 12 (1886): 245–57.

Perosa, A., *Giovanni Rucellai ed il suo Zibaldone* (London, 1960), vol. 1.

———, "Contributi e proposte per la pubblicazione delle opere latine del Poliziano," in *Poliziano e il suo tempo: Atti del VI convegno internazionale di studi sul Rinascimento* (Florence, 1957), 89–100.

———, "Documenti di polemiche umanistiche," *Rinascimento* 2d ser. 1 (1950): 178–82.

———, "Due lettere di Domizio Calderini," *Rinascimento* 2d ser. 13 (1973): 3–20.

———, "Febris: A Poetic Myth Created by Poliziano," *Journal of the Warburg and Courtauld Institutes* 9 (1946): 74–95.

———, "Studi sulla tradizione delle poesie del Poliziano," in *Studi in onore di U. E. Paoli* (Florence, 1956), 539–62.

Perotto Sali, L., "L'opusculo inedito di Giorgio Merula contro i *Miscellanea* di Angelo Poliziano," *Interpres* 1 (1978): 146ff.

Perreiah, A., "Humanistic Critiques of Scholastic Dialectic," *Sixteenth-Century Journal* 13 (1982): 3–22.

Perry, T. A., *Erotic Spirituality: The Integrative Tradition from Leone Ebreo to John Donne* (University, AL, 1980).

Persico, T., *Diomede Carafa, uomo di stato e scrittore del secolo XV* (Naples, 1899).

Pertusi, A., *Leonzio Pilato fra Petrarca e Boccaccio* (Venice, 1964).

———, "*Erotemata*: Per la storia e le fonti delle prime grammatiche greche e stampe," *Italia medioevale e umanistica* 5 (1962): 321–51.

———, "Le fonti greche del 'De gestis, moribus et nobilitate civitatis venetiarum' de Lorenzo de Monacis, cancelliere di Creta (1388–1428)," *Italia medioevale e umanistica* 8 (1965): 162–211.

———, "Leonzio Pilato a Creta prima del 1358–59; Scuole e cultura a Creta durante il secolo XIV," *Kretika Chronika* 15–16 (1961–62): 363ff.

Pesenti, G., "Alessandra Scala, una figuriana della Rinascenza fiorentina," *Giornale storico della letteratura italiana* 85 (1925): 241–67.

Petot, P., "Le droit privé français au XVIe siècle et l'humanisme," in *Umanesimo e scienza politica—Atti del congresso internazionale di studi umanistici*, ed. E. Castelli (Milan, 1951), 347–51.

Petrie, J., *Petrarch: The Augustan Poets, the Italian Tradition and the Canzoniere* (Dublin, 1983).

Petris, A. de, "L'*Adversus Judeos et Gentes* di Giannozzo Manetti," *Rinascimento* 16 (1976): 193–205.

———, "Giannozzo Manetti and His *Consolation*," *Bibliothèque d'humanisme et Renaissance* 41 (1979): 493–525.

———, "Le teorie umanistiche dell'tradurre e l'*Apologeticus* di Giannozzo Manetti," *Bibliothèque d'humanisme et Renaissance* 37 (1975): 15–32.

Petrucci, A., "Libro, scritture e scuole," *La scuola nell'Occidente latino dell'alto medioevo* 19 (1972): 313–37, discussion, 363–81.

Petrucci, F., "Calco, Tristano," *Dizionario biografico degli italiani*, 30 vols. to date (Rome, 1960–84), 16:537–41.

————, "Corio, Bernardino," *Dizionario biografico degli italiani,* 30 vols. to date (Rome, 1960–84), 29:75–78.

Pfeiffer, R., *History of Classical Scholarship from 1300 to 1850* (Oxford, 1976).

Pflaum, H., *Die Idee der Liebe, Leone Ebreo* (Tübingen, 1926).

Phillips, M., *Francesco Guicciardini: The Historian's Craft* (Toronto, 1977).

————, "The Disenchanted Witness: Participation and Alienation in Florentine Historiography," *Journal of the History of Ideas* 44 (1983): 191–206.

————, "Machiavelli, Guicciardini and the Tradition of Vernacular Historiography," *American Historical Review* 84 (1979): 86–105.

Phillips, M. M., *Erasmus and the Northern Renaissance* (London, 1949; rev. ed. 1981).

Piano Mortari, V., "Dialettica e giurisprudenza: Studi sui tratti di dialettica legale del sec. XVI," *Annali di storia del diritto* 1 (1957): 293–401.

Picha, A., "Das wissenschaftliche Leben und der Humanismus in Krummau im 15. Jahrhundert," *Mitteilungen des Vereines für Geschichte der Deutschen in Böhmen* 42 (1904): 67–77.

Pieri, P., "L'arte militare italiana della seconda metà del secolo XV negli scritti di Diomede Carafa," in *Ricordi e studi in memoria di Francesco Flamini* (Naples, 1931), 87–103.

————, "Il *Governo et exercitio de la militia* di Orso degli Orsini e i *Memoriali* di Diomede Carafa," *Archivio storico per le provincie napoletano* n.s. 19 (1933): 99–125.

Piggott, S., "William Camden and the Britannia," *Proceedings of the British Academy* 37 (1951): 199–217.

Pigman, G. W., III, "Barzizza's Studies of Cicero," *Rinascimento* n.s. 21 (1981): 123–63.

————, "Barzizza's Treatise on Imitation," *Bibliothèque d'humanisme et Renaissance* 44 (1982): 341–52.

————, "Versions of Imitation in the Renaissance," *Renaissance Quarterly* 33 (1980): 1–32.

Pinborg, J., *Die Entwicklung der Sprachtheorie im Mittelalter* (Münster and Copenhagen, 1967).

————, *Logik und Semantik im Mittelalter: Ein Überblick* (Stuttgart-Bad Cannstatt, 1972).

Pines, S., "Scholasticism After Thomas Aquinas in the Teachings of Hasdai Crescas and His Predecessors," *Israel Academy of Sciences and Humanities Proceedings* 1 (1967): 101 pp.

Pirnát, A., "A magyar reneszánsz dráma poétikája" ["The Poetic Properties of Hungarian Renaissance Drama"], *Reneszánsz füzetek* [*Booklets on the Renaissance*] 1 (1969): 527–55.

Pirrotta, N., "Music and Cultural Tendencies in Fifteenth-Century Italy," *Journal of the American Musicological Society* 19 (1966): 146–61.

Plöchl, W., *Geschichte des Kirchenrechts,* 3 vols. (Vienna, 1953–59).

Pocock, J. G. A., *The Machiavellian Moment: Florentine Political Thought and the Atlantic Republican Tradition* (Princeton, 1975); and review essay by J. H. Hexter, *History and Theory* 16 (1977): 306–37.

————, "*The Machiavellian Moment* Revisited: A Study in History and Ideology," *Journal of Modern History* 53 (1981): 49–72.

Poggi, G., *Il Duomodi* (Florence, 1909).

Polak, E. J., *A Textual Study of Jacques de Dinant's Summa Dictaminis* (Geneva, 1975).

————, "Dictamen," in *Dictionary of the Middle Ages,* 9 vols. to date (New York, 1982–), 4:173–77.

Polívka, J., *Dvě povidky v české literatuře XV. století* [*Two Novelle in Czech Literature of the 15th Century*] (Prague, 1889).

Polman, P., *L'élément historique dans la controverse réligieuse du XVIᵉ siècle* (Gembloux, 1932).

Pontieri, E., *Ferrante d'Aragona, re di Napoli* (Naples, 2d ed. 1969).

Popkin, R. H., *The History of Scepticism from Erasmus to Spinoza* (Berkeley, rev. ed., 1979).

Poppi, M., "Un'orazione del cronista Lorenzo de Monacis per il millenario di Venezia (1421)," *Atti dell'Istituto Veneto di Scienze, Lettere ed Arti* 131 (1972–73): 463–97.

————, "Ricerche sulla vita e cultura del notaio e cronista veneziano Lorenzo de Monacis, cancelliere cretese (ca. 1351–1428)," *Studi veneziani* 9 (1967): 153–86.

Portoghesi, P., *Rome in the Renaissance*, trans. P. Sanders (London, 1977).

Post, R. R., *The Modern Devotion: Confrontation with Reformation and Humanism* (Leiden, 1968).

Powicke, M., "William Camden," *Essays and Studies* n.s. 1 (1948): 67–84.

Prager, F. D. and G. Scaglia, *Mariano Taccola and His Book "De ingeneis"* (Cambridge, MA, 1972).

Prati, P. da, *Giovanni Dominici e l'umanesimo* (Rome, 1965).

Pražák, E., "Český překlad Platonovy *Politeie* z 15. století" ["The Fifteenth-Century Czech Translation of Plato's *Statesman*"], *Listy filologické* 9 (1961): 102–8.

Preger, W., *Matthias Flacius Illyricus und seine Zeit*, 2 vols. (Erlangen, 1859–61; 2d ed. 1964).

Preston, J. H., "Was There an Historical Revolution?" *Journal of the History of Ideas* 38 (1977): 353–64.

Preston-Dargan, E., "Trissino a Possible Source for the Pléiade," *Modern Philology* 13 (1916): 685–88.

Prete, S., *Observations on the History of Textual Criticism in the Medieval and Renaissance Periods* (Collegeville, MN, n.d.).

Proto, E., "Sulla poetica di G. G. Trissino," *Studi di letteratura italiana* 6 (1944–46): 197–298.

Pullapilly, C. K., *Caesar Baronius, Counter-Reformation Historian* (South Bend, IN, 1975).

Purnell, F., "Francesco Patrizi and the Critics of Hermes Trismegistus," *Journal of Medieval and Renaissance Studies* 6 (1976): 155–78.

Questa, C., *Per la storia del testo di Plauto nell'umanesimo*, vol. 1, *La "recensio" di Poggio Bracciolini* (Rome, 1986).

Quint, D., "Humanism and Modernity: A Reconsideration of Bruni's *Dialogues*," *Renaissance Quarterly* 38 (1985): 423–45.

Quintanilla Raso, M. C. and M. A. Ladero Quesada, "Biblioteca de le alta nobleza castellana en el siglo XV," in *Livre et lecture en Espagne et en France sous l'ancien régime* (Paris, 1981), 47–59.

Rabikauskas, P., S. J., *Diplomatica pontifica (Praelectionum lineamenta)* (Rome, 1972).

———, "Chancellerie apostolique," in *Dictionnaire de droit canonique*, 7 vols. (Paris, 1924–65), 3:465–71.

Rabil, A., Jr., *Erasmus and the New Testament: The Mind of a Christian Humanist* (San Antonio, TX, 1972).

———, *Knowledge, Goodness and Power: The Debate over "Nobility" Among Quattrocento Italian Humanists—Ancillary Text*, forthcoming.

———, *Laura Cereta: Quattrocento Humanist* (Binghamton, NY, 1981).

Raby, F. J. E., *A History of Christian-Latin Poetry from the Beginnings to the Close of the Middle Ages* (Oxford, 2d ed. 1953).

———, *A History of Secular Latin Poetry in the Middle Ages*, 2 vols. (Oxford, 2d ed. 1957).

Radding, C., *A World Made by Men: Cognition and Society 400–1200* (Chapel Hill, 1985).

Rademaker, C. S. M., *Life and Work of Gerardus Johannes Vossius (1577–1649)* (Assen, 1981).

Radetti, G., "L'epicureismo nel pensiero umanistico del Quattrocento," *Grande antologia filosofica*, 31 vols. (Milan, 1954–78), 6:839–961.

———, "Le origini dell'umanesimo civile fiorentino nel Quattrocento," *Giornale critico della filosofia italiana* 38 (1959): 98–122.

Raimondi, E., "Alcune pagine del Petrarca sulla dignità umana," *Convivium* 19 (1947): 376–93.

Rallo Asunción, A., *Antonio de Guevara en su contexto renacentista* (Madrid, 1979).

Randall, J. H., Jr., *The School of Padua and the Emergence of Modern Science* (Padua, 1961).

Ranum, G., *Artisans of Glory* (Chapel Hill, NC, 1980).

Rao, E. J., "Alfonso of Aragon and the Italian Humanists," *Esperienze letterarie* 4.1 (1979): 43–52.

Raponi, N., "Barbavara, Francesco," *Dizionario biografico degli italiani*, 30 vols. to date (Rome, 1960–84), 6:141–42.

Rashdall, H., *The Universities of Europe in the Middle Ages*, ed. F. M. Powicke and A. B. Emden, 3 vols. (Oxford, 1936).

Re, N. del, *La Curia Romana* (Rome, 1972).

Redondo, A., *Antonio de Guevara et l'Espagne de son temps* (Geneva, 1976).

Reeds, K. M., "Renaissance Humanism and Botany," *Annals of Science* 33 (1976): 519–42.

Reeves, J.-B., O. P., "St. Augustine and Humanism," in *A Monument to St. Augustine*, ed. M. C. D'Arcy (London, 1930), 123–51.

Rehm, W., *Der Untergang Roms im abendländischen Denken* (Leipzig, 1930).

Reiss, T. J., *The Discourse of Modernism* (Ithaca, NY, 1982).

Rekers, B., *Benito Arias Montano* (Leiden, 1972).

Renaudet, A., *Erasme et l'Italie* (Geneva, 1954).

——, *Préréforme et humanisme à Paris pendant les premières guerres d'Italie, 1494–1517* (Paris, 2d ed. 1953).

Renouard, A. A., *Annales de l'imprimerie des Alde,* 3 vols. (Paris, 3d ed. 1834).

Renouard, P., *Bibliographie des impressions et des oeuvres de Josse Badius Ascensius, imprimeur et humaniste (1462–1535),* 3 vols. (Paris, 1908; reprinted New York, 1964).

Renucci, R., *L'aventure de l'humanisme européen au Moyen Âge* (Paris, 1953).

Resta, G., *L'epistolario del Panormita, Studi per un'edizione critica* (Messina, 1954).

——, "Beccadelli, Antonio," *Dizionario biografico degli italiani,* 30 vols. to date (Rome, 1960–84), 7:400–406.

——, "Introduzione" to Antonio Beccadelli (Panormita), *Liber rerum gestarum Ferdinandi regis* (Palermo, 1968).

Reynolds, B., "Latin Historiography: A Survey, 1400–1600," *Studies in the Renaissance* 2 (1955): 7–66.

——, "Shifting Currents in Historical Criticism," *Journal of the History of Ideas* 14 (1953): 471–92; reprinted in *Renaissance Essays from the Journal of the History of Ideas,* ed. Kristeller and Wiener (q.v.), 115–30.

Reynolds, E. E., *Margaret Roper, Eldest Daughter of St. Thomas More* (London, 1960).

Reynolds, L. D. and N. G. Wilson, *Scribes and Scholars* (Oxford, 2d ed. 1974).

Ricci, C., *Sophonisbe dans la tragédie classique italienne et française* (Turin, 1904).

Rice, E. F., Jr. *The Renaissance Idea of Wisdom* (Cambridge, MA, 1958).

——, *Saint Jerome in the Renaissance* (Baltimore, 1985).

——, "Erasmus and the Religious Tradition, 1495–1499," *Journal of the History of Ideas* 11 (1950): 387–411.

——, "The Humanist Idea of Christian Antiquity: Lefèvre d'Etaples and His Circle," *Studies in the Renaissance* 9 (1962): 126–60.

——, "John Colet and the Annihilation of the Natural," *Harvard Theological Review* 45 (1952): 141–63.

Rice Henderson, J., "Erasmus on the Art of Letter-Writing," *Studies in the Theory and Practice of Renaissance Eloquence,* ed. Murphy (q.v.), 331–55.

Richardson, B., "Notes on Machiavelli's Sources and His Treatment of the Rhetorical Tradition," *Italian Studies* 26 (1971): 24–48.

Riché, P., *Les écoles et l'enseignement dans l'Occident chrétien de la fin du Ve siècle au milieu du XIe siècle* (Paris, 1979).

Rico, F., *Nebrija frente a los bárbaros: El canon de gramáticos nefastos en las polémicas del humanismo* (Salamanca, 1978).

——, *Vida u obra de Petrarca: Lectura del "Secretum"* (Chapel Hill, NC, 1974).

——, "Precisazioni di cronologia Petrarchesca: Le 'Familiares' VIII.ii–v, e i rifacimenti del 'Secretum,' " *Giornale storico della letteratura italiana* 105 (1978): 481–525.

———, "Un prólogo al Renacimiento español: La dedicatoria de Nebrija a las *Introduciones latinas* (1488)," in *Seis lecciones sobre la España de los siglos de Oro, Homenaje a M. Bataillon,* ed. P. M. Piñero Ramírez and R. Reyes Cano (Seville, 1981), 61–85.

Rico Verdu, J., *La retorica española de los siglos XVI y XVII* (Madrid, 1973).

Ridruejo, E., "Notas romances en gramáticas latino-españolas del siglo XV," *Revista de filología española* 59 (1977): 47–80.

Rill, G., "Bonfini (Bonfinius, de Bonfinis), Antonio," *Dizionario biografico degli italiani,* 30 vols. to date (Rome, 1960–84), 12:28–30.

Risse, W., *Die Logik der Neuzeit* (Stuttgart, 1964).

Rizzo, S., *Il lessico filologico degli umanisti* (Rome, 1973).

Robathan, D. M., "Flavio Biondo's *Roma instaurata,*" *Medievalia et Humanistica,* n.s. 1 (1970): 203–16.

Robb, N. A., *Neoplatonism of the Italian Renaissance* (London, 1935).

Robertis, D. de, "M. Marullo Tarcaniota," in *Storia della letteratura italiana,* 9 vols. (Milan, 1965–69), 3:556–66.

Roberts, P. B., *Stephanus de Lingus-Tonante: Studies in the Sermons of Stephen Langton* (Toronto, 1981).

Robey, D., "Humanism and Education in the Early Quattrocento: The *De ingenuis moribus* of P. P. Vergerio," *Bibliothèque d'humanisme et Renaissance* 42 (1980):27–58.

Robin, D., "A Reassessment of the Character of Francesco Filelfo (1398–1481)," *Renaissance Quarterly* 36 (1983): 202–24.

———, "Unknown Greek Poems of Francesco Filelfo," *Renaissance Quarterly* 37 (1984): 173–206.

Robins, R. H., *A Short History of Linguistics* (London and New York, 2d ed. 1979).

Robinson, I. S., *Authority and Resistance in the Investiture Contest: The Polemical Literature of the Late Eleventh Century* (Manchester, 1978).

Rocca, P., *Giovanni Pico della Mirandola nei suoi rapporti di amicizia con Gerolamo Savonarola* (Ferrara, 1964).

Rodocanachi, E., *Le pontificat de Jules II, 1503–1513* (Paris, 1928).

———, *La première Renaissance de Rome au temps de Jules II et Léon X* (Paris, 1912).

Rogers, K., *The Troublesome Helpmate: A History of Misogyny in Literature* (Seattle, 1966).

Romanin, S., *Storia documentata di Venezia,* 10 vols. (Venice, 1853–61).

Romanini, A. M., "Averlino (Averulino), Antonio, detto Filarete," *Dizionario biografico degli italiani,* 30 vols. to date (Rome, 1960–84), 4:662–67.

Romero, I. O., *Floresta de gramática, poética y retórica en Nueva España (1521–1767)* (Mexico, 1980).

Romero de Lecea, C., *Antecedentes de la imprenta y circunstancias que favorecieron su introducción en España* (Madrid, 1972).

Ronca, U., *Cultura medioevale e poesia latina d'Italia nei secoli XI e XII,* 2 vols. (Rome, 1892).

Ronconi, G., *Le origini delle dispute umanistiche sulla poesia* (Rome, 1975).

———, "Francesco da Fiano, *Contra oblucutores et detractores poetarum* a cura di I. Taù," *Studi sul Boccaccio* 3 (1965): 403–11.

———, "Giovanni Dominici e le dispute sulla poesia nel primo umanesimo," *Dizionario critico della letteratura italiana,* 3 vols. (Turin, 1973), 2:11–17.

Ronzy, P., *Un humaniste italianisant, Papire Masson (1554–1611)* (Paris, 1924).

Rosa, D. de, *Coluccio Salutati: Il cancelliere e il pensatore politico* (Florence, 1980).

Roscoe, W., *The Life and Pontificate of Leo the Tenth,* 2 vols. (London, 1910).

Rose, P. L., *The Italian Renaissance of Mathematics: Studies on Humanists and Mathematicians from Petrarch to Galileo* (Geneva, 1975).

———, "The Academia Venetiana, Science and Culture in Renaissance Venice," *Studi veneziani* 11 (1969): 191–242.

———, "Humanist Culture and Renaissance Mathematics: The Italian Libraries of the Quattrocento," *Studies in the Renaissance* 20 (1973): 46–105.

——— and S. Drake, "The Pseudo-Aristotelian *Questions in Mechanics* in Renaissance Culture," *Studies in the Renaissance* 18 (1971): 65–104.

Rosenberg, C., "Cenni biografici di alcuni rabbini et letterati della Communità Israelitica di Ancona," *Saggio degli scritti in lingua ebraici degli Eccelentissimi Rabbini Vivanti et Tedeschi* d.v.m. (Casale, Monferato, 1932), V–XLVIII.

Rosenberg, S., "Logic and Ontology in Jewish Philosophy of the Fourteenth Century" (Hebrew with English summary; Ph.D. diss., Hebrew University, Jerusalem, 1974).

Rosenthal, F. J. E., "Yohanan Alemanno and Occult Science," in *Prismata: Naturwissenschaft geschichtliche Studien: Festschrift für Willy Hartner* (Wiesbaden, 1977), 349–61.

Rosmini, C. dei, *Vita di Francesco Filelfo da Tolentino,* 3 vols. (Milan, 1808).

Ross, D. O., Jr., *Backgrounds to Augustan Poetry: Gallus, Elegy and Rome* (Cambridge, 1975).

Ross, J. B., "The Emergence of Gasparo Contarini: A Bibliographical Essay," *Church History* 41 (1972): 22–45.

———, "Venetian Schools and Teachers, Fourteenth to Early Sixteenth Century: A Survey and a Study of Giovanni Battista Egnazio," *Renaissance Quarterly* 29 (1976): 521–66.

Rossi, P., *Clavis universalis: Arti mnemoniche e logica combinatoria da Lullo a Leibniz* (Milan, 1960).

———, *I filosofi e le macchine* (Milan, 1962); *Philosophy, Technology, and the Arts in the Early Modern Era,* trans. S. Attanasio, ed. B. Nelson (New York, 1970).

———, "La celebrazione della rettorica e la polemica antimetafisica nel *De principiis* di Mario Nizolio," in *La crisi dell'uso dogmatico della ragione,* ed. A. Banfi (Milan, 1953), 99–221.

———, "Il *De principiis* di Mario Nizolio," *Archivio di filosofia* 3 (1953): 57–92.

——, "La negazione delle sfere e l'astrobiologia di Francesco Patrizi," *Il Rinascimento nelle corti padane: Società e cultura* (Bari, 1977), 401–37.

Rossi, V., *Il Quattrocento* (Milan, 1933, and later editions).

——, *Scritti di critica letteraria* (Florence, 1930).

——, "Un grammatico cremonese [Travesi] a Pavia nella prima età del Rinascimento," *Bollettino della Società Pavese di Storia Patria* 1 (1901): 16–46.

Roth, C., *The Jews in the Renaissance* (New York, 1959).

Rothschild, T. T., "The Concept of the Torah in the Thought of R. David Messer Leon" (Hebrew), *Meḥkarei Yerushalayim be-Maḥshevet Yisra'el* 2 (1981–82): 94–117.

——, "The Philosophy of R. David ben Judah Messer Leon" (Hebrew with English summary; Ph.D. diss., Hebrew University, Jerusalem, 1978).

——, Sefirot as the Essence of God in the Writings of David Messer Leon," *Association for Jewish Studies Review* 7–8 (1982–83): 409–25.

Rotondò, A., "Brandolini, Aurelio Lippo," *Dizionario biografico degli italiani*, 30 vols. to date (Rome, 1960–84), 14:26–28.

Ruberto, L., "Studi sul Poliziano filologo," *Rivista di filologia e d'istruzione classica* 12 (1884): 235–37.

Rubinstein, A. L., "Imitation and Style in Angelo Poliziano's *Iliad* Translation," *Renaissance Quarterly* 36 (1983): 48–70.

Rubió i Balaguer, J., *La cultura catalana del Renaixement a la Decadéncia* (Barcelona, 1964).

——, "Humanisme i Renaixement," *VIII congreso de historia de la Corona de Aragón V*, 3.2 (Valencia, 1973), 9–36.

Ruderman, D., *The Perfect Kinship: Kabbalah, Magic, and Science in the Cultural Universe of a Jewish Physician*, forthcoming.

——, *The World of a Renaissance Jew: The Life and Thought of Abraham ben Mordecai Farissol* (Cincinnati, OH, 1981).

——, "An Exemplary Sermon from the Classroom of a Jewish Teacher in Renaissance Italy," *Italia* 1 (1978): 7–38.

Rüdiger, W., *Pietro Vettori aus Florenz* (Halle, 1896).

Ruggiero, G., *Violence in Early Renaissance Venice* (New Brunswick, NJ, 1980).

Runciman, S., *The Last Byzantine Renaissance* (Cambridge, 1970).

Rupprich, H., *Die Frühzeit des Humanismus und der Renaissance in Deutschland* (Leipzig, 1938).

Rusconi, R., *Predicazione e vita religiosa nella società italiana da Carlo Magno alla controriforma* (Turin, 1981).

Rush, R. R., *The Doctrines of the Great Educators* (London, 1937).

Russell, P. E., *Traducciones y traductores en la península ibérica* (Bellaterra, 1985).

——, "Arms Versus Letters: Towards a Definition of Spanish Fifteenth-Century Humanism," in *Aspects of the Renaissance: A Symposium*, ed. A. R. Lewis (Austin, TX, 1967), 47–58; translated and expanded in his *Temas de la "Celestina" y otros estudios* (Barcelona, 1978), 207–39.

—— and A.R.D. Pagden, "Nueva luz sobre una versión española cuatrocentista de la *Etica a Nicomaco:* Bodleian Library MS Span. D.1," in *Homenaje a Guillermo Guastavino* (Madrid, 1974), 125–46.

Rutherford, W. G., *Scholia Aristophanica,* 3 vols. (London, 1896–1905).

Ruysschaert, J., "À propos des trois premières grammaires latines de Pomponio Leto," *Scriptorium* 15 (1961): 68–75.

———, "Les manuels de grammaire latine composés par Pomponio Leto," *Scriptorium* 8 (1954): 98–107.

Ryan, L. V., *Roger Ascham* (Stanford, 1963).

Ryan, M. B., "John of Salisbury on the Arts of Language in the Trivium" (Ph.D. diss., Catholic University of America, Washington, DC, 1958).

Ryba, B., *Soupis rukopisů Strahovské knihovny Památníků národního písemnictví v Praze. Strahovské rukopisy* [*Description of the Manuscripts of Strahov's Library, of Monuments of National Literature in Prague. Manuscripts Held at Strahov's Library*] (Prague, n.d.).

———, "K biografii humanisty Jana z Rabštejna" ["Two Biographies of the Humanist Jan z Rabštejna"], *Český časopis historický* 46 (1940): 260–72.

Saalman, H., *Brunelleschi: The Cupola of Santa Maria del Fiore* (London, 1980).

Sabatini, F., *Napoli angioine* (Naples, 1975).

Sabbadini, R., *Il carteggio di Giovanni Aurispa* (Rome, 1931).

———, *Classici e umanisti da codici Ambrosiani* (Florence, 1933).

———, *Da Dante al Leonardi* (Milan, 1904).

———, *Giovanni da Ravenna, insigne figura d'umanista (1343–1406)* (Como, 1924).

———, *Il metodo degli umanisti* (Florence, 1922).

———, *Le scoperte dei codici latini e greci ne' secoli: XIV e XV,* 2 vols. (Florence, 1905–14; reprinted Florence, 1967).

———, *La scuola e gli studi di Guarino Guarini Veronese* (Catania, 1896); reprinted in *Guariniana,* ed. M. Sancipriano (Turin, 1964), 93ff.

———, *Storia del ciceronianismo e di altre questioni letterarie nell'età della Rinascenza* (Turin, 1886).

———, *Storia e critica di alcuni testi latini* (Padua, 2d ed. 1971).

———, "Cronologia documentata della vita di Giovanni Lamola," *Propugnatore* n.s. 3 (1890): 417–36.

———, "Dei metodi nell'insegnamento della sintassi latina," *Rivista di filologia* 30 (1902): 304–14.

———, "Elementi nazionali nella teoria grammaticale dei Romani," *Studi italiani di filologia classica* 14 (1906): 113–25.

———, "Nuove notizie di Giovanni Lamola," *Giornale storico della letteratura italiana* 31 (1898): 244–45.

Saintsbury, G., *A History of Criticism and Literary Taste in Europe from the Earliest Texts to the Present Day* (Edinburgh and London, 1900–1904).

Saitta, G., *Il pensiero italiano nell'umanesimo e nel Rinascimento,* 3 vols. (Florence, 2d ed. 1961).

———, "La filosofia di Leone Ebreo," in *Storici antichi e moderni* (Venice, 1928).

————, "Il pensiero di Girolamo Fracastoro," *Atti dell'Accademia di Agricoltura, Scienze e Lettere di Verona* (1924): 155–93.

Salazar, A. M., "El impacto humanístico de las misiones diplomáticas de Alonso de Cartagena en la Corte de Portugal entre medioevo y renacimiento (1421–31)," in *Medieval Studies Presented to Rita Hamilton,* ed. A. Deyermond (London, 1976), 215–26.

Salvatore, N., *L'arte poetica di Marco Girolamo Vida* (Foligno, 1912).

Samaran, C., "Une *summa grammaticalis* du XIII* siècle avec gloses provençales," *Archivum latinitatis medii aevi* 31 (1961): 157–224.

Sánchez de la Brozas, F., *Minerva o de la propriedad de la lengua latina,* trans. F. Riveras Cárdenas (Madrid, 1976).

Sandonnini, T., *Lodovico Castelvetro e la sua famiglia* (Bologna, 1882).

Sandys, J. E., *A History of Classical Scholarship,* 3 vols. (Cambridge, 3d ed. 1921).

Santagata, M., *La lirica aragonese* (Padua, 1979).

Santayana, S. G., *Two Renaissance Educators: Alberti and Piccolomini* (Boston, 1930).

Santillana, G. de, "The Role of Art in the Scientific Renaissance," in *Critical Problems in the History of Science,* ed. M. Clagett (Madison, WI, 1959).

Santoro, C., *Gli Sforza* (Milan, 1968).

Santoro, Marco, *La stampa a Napoli nel Quattrocento* (Naples, 1984).

Santoro, Mario, *Fortuna, ragione e prudenza nella civiltà letteraria del Cinquecento* (Naples, 1967).

————, *Note umanistiche* (Naples, 1970).

————, *Uno scolaro del Poliziano a Napoli: Francesco Pucci* (Naples, 1948).

————, *Tristano Caracciolo e la cultura napoletana della Rinascenza* (Naples, 1957).

————, "La cultura umanistica," in *Storia di Napoli,* 11 vols. in 15 (Naples, 1967–78), 4.2:315–498.

————, "Il *De immanitate* testamento spirituale del Pontano," *Partenope* 1 (1960): 5–15.

————, "Machiavelli e l'umanesimo," *Cultura e società* 1 (1959): 21–43.

————, "Masuccio fra Salerno e Napoli," *Atti dell'Accademia Pontaniana* n.s. 11 (1962): 309–40.

————, "Panormita aragonese," *Esperienze letterarie* 9.4 (1984): 3–25.

————, "La polemica Poliziano-Merula," *Giornale italiano di filologia* 5 (1952): 212–33.

————, "Il Pontano e l'ideale rinascimentale del 'prudente,' " *Giornale italiano di filologia* 17 (1964): 29–54.

————, "Scienza e humanitas nell'opera del Galateo," *La Zagaglia* 2 (1960): 25–40, 50–63.

Sarton, G., *The Appreciation of Ancient and Medieval Science During the Renaissance (1450–1600)* (Philadelphia, 1955).

————, *Six Wings: Men of Science in the Renaissance* (Bloomington, IN, 1957).

————, "Science in the Renaissance," in *The Civilization of the Renaissance* (Chicago, 1929; reprinted New York, 1959), 75–95.

Sasso, G., " 'Florentina libertas' e rinascimento italiano nell'opera di Hans Baron," *Rivista storica italiana* 69 (1957): 250–76.

———, "Polibio e Machiavelli: Costituzione, potenza, conquista," *Giornale critico della filosofia italiana* 40 (1961): 51–86.

Saunders, J. L., *Justus Lipsius* (New York, 1955).

Saxl, F., "The Classical Inscription in Renaissance Art and Politics," *Journal of the Warburg and Courtauld Institutes* 4 (1940–41): 19–46.

Scaglia, G. and F. D. Prager, *Brunelleschi: Studies of His Technology and Inventions* (Cambridge, MA, 1970).

Scaglione, A. D., *Ars grammatica* (The Hague, 1970); reviewed by W. K. Percival in *Language* 51 (1975): 440–56.

———, "The Humanist as Scholar and Politian's Conception of the *Grammaticus*," *Studies in the Renaissance* 8 (1961): 49–70.

Scarpa, A., *Giangiorgio Trissino vicentino* (Vicenza, 1950).

Schäfer, E., *Luther als Kirchenhistoriker* (Gütersloh, 1897).

Schaller, H. M., "Die Kanzlei Kaiser Friedrichs II," *Archiv für Diplomatik; Schriftengeschichte, Seigel- und Wappenkunde* 3 (1957): 207–86; 4 (1958): 264–327.

Schar, M., *Das Nachleben des Origenes im Zeitlater des Humanismus* (Basel, 1979).

Schechter, S., "Notes sur Messer David Leon," *Revue des études juives* 24 (1892): 118–38.

Scheible, H., *Die Entstehung der Magdeburger Zenturien* (Gütersloh, 1966).

Schellhase, K., *Tacitus in Renaissance Political Thought* (Chicago, 1976).

Scherer, E. C., *Geschichte und Kirchengeschichte an den deutschen Universitäten* (Freiburg im Breisgau, 1927).

Schiff, M., *La bibliothèque du marquis de Santillane* (Paris, 1905).

Schilling, E., *Städelsches Kunstinstitut, Frankfurt am Main: Katalog der deutschen Zeichnungen*, 3 vols. (Ansbach, 1973).

Schindling, A., *Humanistische Hochschule und Freie Reichsstadt. Gymnasium und Akademie in Strassburg* (Wiesbaden, 1977).

Schio, G. da, *Sulla vita e sugli scritti di Antonio Loschi vicentino uomo di lettere e di stato, commentarii* (Padua, 1858).

Schlobach, J., *Zyklentheorie und Epochenmetaphorik* (Munich, 1980).

Schmitt, C. B., *Aristotle and the Renaissance* (Cambridge, MA and London, 1983).

———, *Cicero Scepticus: A Study of the Influence of the Academia in the Renaissance* (The Hague, 1972).

———, *A Critical Survey and Bibliography of Studies on Renaissance Aristotelianism, 1958–1969* (Padua, 1971).

———, *Gianfrancesco Pico della Mirandola (1469–1533) and His Critique of Aristotle* (The Hague, 1967).

———, "Aristotelian Textual Studies at Padua: The Case of Francesco Cavalli," in *Scienza e filosofia all'Università di Padova nel Quattrocento,* ed. Poppi (q.v.), 287–314.

————, "Perennial Philosophy from Agostino Steuco to Leibniz," *Journal of the History of Ideas* 27 (1966): 505–23.

————, "Prisca Theologia e Philosophia Perennis: Due temi del Rinascimento italiano e la loro fortuna," *Il pensiero italiano del Rinascimento e il tempo nostro* (Florence, 1970), 211–36.

————, "Recent Trends in the Study of Medieval and Renaissance Science," in *Information Sources in the History of Science and Medicine*, ed. P. Corsi and P. Weindling (London, 1983), 221–40.

————, "Towards a Reassessment of Renaissance Aristotelianism," *History of Science* 11 (1973): 159–93.

Schmitt, F. S., "Anselmo d'Aosta," *Dizionario biografico degli italiani*, 30 vols. to date (Rome, 1960–84), 18:387.

Schmitt, L., *Die deutsche Urkundensprache in der Kanzlei Kaiser Karls IV* (Prague, 1936).

Schmitt, W. O., "Die Ianua (Donatus)—Ein Beitrag zur lateinischen Schulgrammatik des Mittelalters und der Renaissance," *Beiträge zur Inkunabelkunde* 3d ser. 4 (1969): 43–80.

Schneider, E., *Das Bild der Frau im Werk des Erasmus* (Basel, 1955).

Schnell, U., *Die homiletische Theorie Philipp Melanchthons* (Berlin, 1968).

Schoeck, R. J., *The Achievement of Thomas More* (Victoria, BC, 1976).

————, *Intertextuality and Renaissance Texts* (Bamberg, 1984).

————, "Canon Law in England on the Eve of the Reformation," *Medieval Studies* 25 (1963): 125–47.

————, "The Humanistic Concept of the Text: Text, Context, and Tradition," *Proceedings of the Patristic, Medieval and Renaissance Conference 1982* (Villanova, PA, 1985), 13–31.

————, "Lawyers and Rhetoric in Sixteenth-Century England," in *Studies in the Theory and Practice of Renaissance Eloquence*, ed. Murphy (q.v.), 274–91.

————, "The Libraries of Common Lawyers in Renaissance England," *Manuscripta* 6 (1962): 155–67.

————, " 'Lighting a Candle to the Place': On the Dimensions and Implications of *Imitatio* in the Renaissance," *Italian Culture* 4 (1985): 123–43.

————, "Neo-Latin Legal Literature," in *Acta conventus neo-latini lovaniensis*, ed. J. IJsewijn and E. Kessler (Munich, 1973), 577–88.

————, "On the Spiritual Life of St. Thomas More," *Thought* 52 (1977): 324–27.

————, "Recent Scholarship in the History of Law," *Renaissance Quarterly* 20 (1967): 279–91.

————, "The School of More," in *New Catholic Encyclopedia*, 17 vols. (Washington, DC, 1967), 9:1142.

————, "Thomas More and the Italian Heritage of Early Tudor Humanism," in *Arts libéraux et philosophie au Moyen Âge* (Montreal and Paris, 1969), 1191–97.

Schöffler, H., *Deutsches Geistesleben zwischen Reformation und Aufklärung: Von Martin Opitz zu Christian Wolff* (Frankfurt am Main, 3d ed. 1974).

Scholem, G., "On the Knowledge about the Kabbalah in Spain on the Eve of the Expulsion" (Hebrew), *Tarbiz,* 24 (1954–55), 167–206.

——, "An Unknown Composition from Yohanan Alemanno" [Hebrew], *Kiryat Sefer* 5 (1928–29): 273–77.

——, "Zur Geschichte der Anfänge der Christlichen Kabbala," in *Essays Presented to Leo Baeck* (London, 1954), 158–93.

Schrade, L., "Renaissance: The Historical Conception of an Epoch," in *Kongress-Bericht der Internationale Gesellschaft für Musikwissenschaft, Utrecht 1952* (Amsterdam, 1953), 19–32.

Schucan, L., *Das Nachleben von Basilius Magnus "Ad adolescentes": Ein Beitrag zur Geschichte des christlichen Humanismus* (Geneva, 1973).

Schulz, M., *Die Lehre von der historischen Methode bei den Geschichtsschreibern des Mittelalters* (Berlin, 1909).

Schumann, R., *Authority and the Commune: Parma 833–1133 (Impero e comune, Parma 833–1133)* (Parma, 1973).

Schwarz, W., *Principles and Problems of Biblical Translation* (Cambridge, 1955).

——, "Studies in Luther's Attitude Towards Humanism," *Journal of Theological Studies* 6 (1955): 66–76.

Schwarzwald, J., *Bartol Djurdjević: Bibliografija izdanja 1544–1686 [Bartol Djurdjević: A Bibliography of Publications, 1544–1686]* (Zagreb, 1980).

Sciacca, G. M., *La visione della vita nell'umanesimo di Coluccio Salutati* (Palermo, 1954).

Scott, I., *Controversies over the Imitation of Cicero* (New York, 1910).

Screech, M. A., *Ecstasy and the Praise of Folly* (London, 1980).

Scrivano, R., *Cultura e letteratura nel Cinquecento* (Rome, 1966).

——, *Il manierismo nella letteratura del Cinquecento* (Padua, 1959).

——, "Bellincioni, Bernardo," *Dizionario biografico degli italiani,* 30 vols. to date (Rome, 1960–84), 7:687–89.

Secret, F., *Les kabbalistes chrétiens de la Renaissance* (Paris, 1964).

——, "L'Ensis Pauli de Paulus de Heredia," *Sefarad* 26 (1966): 79–102, 253–71.

——, "Pico della Mirandola e gli inizi della cabala cristiana," *Convivium* n.s. 25 (1957): 31–47.

——, "Qui était l'orientaliste Mithridate," *Revue des études juives* 16 [116] (1957): 96–102.

Seebohm, F., *The Oxford Reformers of 1498* (London, 1867).

Segarizzi, A., "Cenni sulle scuole pubbliche a Venezia nel secolo XV e sul primo maestro d'esse," *Atti del R. Istituto Veneto di Scienze, Lettere ed Arti* 75 (1915–16): pt. 2, 637–67.

——, "Francesco Contarini, politico e letterato veneziano del secolo XV," *Nuovo archivio veneto,* n.s. 12.2 (1906): 272–306.

——, "Niccolò Barbo, patrizio veneziano del secolo XV e le accuse contro Isotta Nogarola," *Giornale storico della letteratura italiana* 43 (1904): 39–54.

Seifert, A., *Cognitio historica. Die Geschichte als Namengaberin der frühneuzeitliche Empirie* (Berlin, 1976).

Seigel, J. E., *Rhetoric and Philosophy in Renaissance Humanism: The Union of Eloquence and Wisdom, Petrarch to Valla* (Princeton, 1968).

———, " 'Civic Humanism' or Ciceronian Rhetoric?" *Past and Present* 34 (1966): 3–48.

———, "The Teaching of Argyropoulos and the Rhetoric of the First Humanists," in *Action and Conviction in Early Modern Europe*, ed. Rabb and Seigel (q.v.), 237–60.

Seneca, F., *Venezia e Papa Giulio II* (Padua, 1962).

Sermoneta, J., "La dottrina dell'intelletto de la fede filosofica de Jehudah e Immanuel Romano," *Studi medievali* 3d ser. 6 (1965), 3–78.

———, "Hillel ben Shemu'el mi-Verona u-Mishnato ha-Pilosofit" (Ph.D. diss., Hebrew University, Jerusalem, 1965).

———, "Jehudah Ben Moshe Daniel Romano, Traducteur de Saint Thomas," in *Homage à Georges Vajda*, ed. G. Nahon and C. Touati (Louvain, 1980).

Serrano, L., *Los conversos Don Pablo de Santa María y Don Alfonso de Cartagena* (Madrid, 1942).

Sesini, U., "Studi sull'umanesimo musicale: Ercole Bottrigari," *Convivium, Rivista di lettere, philosophie e storia* 13 (1941): 1–25.

Settle, T. B., "Ostilio Ricci, a Bridge Between Alberti and Galileo," *XIIe congrès international d'histoire des sciences: Actes*, 3-B (Paris, 1968), 121–26.

Setton, K., "The Byzantine Background to the Italian Renaissance," *Proceedings of the American Philosophical Society* 100 (1956): 1–76.

Setz, W., *Lorenzo Vallas Schrift gegen die konstantinische Schenkung. De falso credita et ementita Constantini donatione. Zur Interpretation und Wirkungsgeschichte* (Tübingen, 1975).

Ševčenko, I., "Théodore Métochites, Chora et les courants intellectuels de l'époque," in *Art et société a Byzance sous les Paléologues* (Venice, 1971), 15–39.

Shapiro, B. J., *Probability and Certainty in Seventeenth-Century England: A Study of the Relationships Between Natural Science, Religion, History, Law, and Literature* (Princeton, 1983).

———, "History and Natural History in Sixteenth- and Seventeenth-Century England: An Essay on the Relationship Between Humanism and Science," in *English Scientific Virtuosi in the 16th and 17th Centuries* (Los Angeles, 1979), 1–55.

Shepard, S., "Scaliger on Homer and Virgil: A Study of Literary Prejudice," *Emerita* 29 (1961): 313–40.

Shepherd, S., *Amazons and Warrior Women: Varieties of Feminism in Seventeenth-Century Drama* (New York, 1981).

Sherrard, P., *Greek East and Latin West* (London, 1959).

Shuger, D., "Morris Croll, Flacius Illyricus, and the Origin of Anti-Ciceronianism," *Rhetorica* 3 (1985): 269–84.

Shulvass, M. A., *The Jews in the World of the Renaissance* (Leiden, 1973).

———, "The Disputes of Messer Leon with His Contemporaries and His Attempt to Exert His Authority on the Jews of Italy" [Hebrew], *Zion* 12 (1947): 17–23.

Shumaker, W., *The Occult Sciences in the Renaissance: A Study in Intellectual Patterns* (Berkeley, 1972).

Sicherl, M., *Johannes Cuno* (Heidelberg, 1978).

Sifler-Premec, L., "Miho Monaldi, dva dijaloga" ["Miho Monaldi, Two Dialogues"], *Prilozi za istraživanje hrvatske filozofske baštine* [*Contributions to Research into the Croatian Philosophical Heritage*] 7 (1981): 31–51.

Simar, T., *Christophe de Longueil, humaniste (1488–1522)* (Louvain, 1911).

Simone, F., *La coscienza della rinascità negli umanisti francese* (Rome, 1949).

———, *The French Renaissance: Medieval Tradition and Italian Influence in Shaping the Renaissance in France* (London, 1969).

———, "Guillaume Fichet retore ed umanista," *Memorie della Reale Accademia delle scienze di Torino* 2d ser. 69.2 (1939): 103–44.

———, "La notion d'encyclópedie: Élément caractéristique de la Renaissance française," in *French Renaissance Studies, 1540–1570,* ed. Sharratt (q.v.), 234–62.

———, "Robert Gaguin ed il suo cenacolo umanistico," *Aevum* 13 (1939): 410–76.

Simoniti, P., *Humanizem na Slovenskem in slovenski humanisti do srede XVI. stoletja* [*Humanism in Slovenia and Slovene Humanists Until the Mid-16th Century*] (Ljubljana, 1979).

Simonsohn, S., *History of the Jews in the Duchy of Mantua* (Tel Aviv, 1978).

———, "From the Letters of Solomon of Poggibonsi" (Hebrew), *Kovez Al Yad* 5, bk. 6, pt. 2 (1966): 381–417.

Siraisi, N. G., *Arts and Sciences at Padua: The Studium of Padua Before 1350* (Toronto, 1973).

———, *Taddeo Alderotti and His Pupils: Two Generations of Italian Medical Learning* (Princeton, 1981).

———, "Some Current Trends in the Study of Renaissance Medicine," *Renaissance Quarterly* 37 (1984): 585–600.

Sismondi, S. de, *Historia de la literatura española,* trans. L. de Figueroa and J. Amador de los Rios (Seville, 1841).

Sivo, V., "Le *Introdutiones dictandi* di Paolo Camaldolese," *Studi e ricerche dall'Istituto di Latina* 3 (Geneva, 1980).

Skinner, Q., *The Foundations of Modern Political Thought,* vol. 1, *The Renaissance* (Cambridge, 1978).

Skutch, O., *Studia Enniana* (London, 1968).

Šmahel, F., *Humanismus v době Poděbradské* [*Humanism in the Age of George of Poděbrady*] (Prague, 1963).

———, "Knihovna Jana z Rabštejna" ["The Library of Jan of Rabstejn"], in *Zápiský katedry československých dějin a archivního studia* (Prague, 1958), 93–113.

———, "Počátky humanismu na pražské universitě v době poděbradské" ["The Beginnings of Humanism at Prague University in the Age of George Poděbrady"], *Historia Universitatis Carolinae Pragensis* 1 (1960): 55–85.

Smalley, B., *English Friars and Antiquity in the Early Fourteenth Century* (Oxford, 1960).

————, *The Study of the Bible in the Middle Ages* (Oxford, 2d ed. 1952).

Smet, R. de, "Hadriani Barlandi (Hadriaan Beverland) *De prostibulis veterum.* Een kritische uitgave met inleiding en commentaar van het handschrift, BPL 1994" (Ph.D. diss., Vrije Universiteit, Brussels, 1984).

Šojat, Z., "Dragišićeva teorija volje" ["Dragišić's Theory of Will"], *Prilozi za istraživanje hrvtaske filozofske baštine* [*Contributions to Research into the Croatian Philosophical Heritage*] 2 (1976): 29–66.

Solmi, E., *Benedetto Spinoza e Leone Ebreo* (Modena, 1903).

Sonkowsky, R. P., "A Fifteenth-Century Rhetorical Opusculum," in *Classical, Mediaeval and Renaissance Studies in Honor of B. L. Ullman*, ed. Henderson (q.v.), 2:259–81.

Sonne, I., *Intorno alla vita di Leone Ebreo* (Florence, 1934).

————, "Eight Letters from Ferrara from the 16th Century" (Hebrew), *Zion* 17 (1952): 148–56.

————, "On the Question of the Original Language of the *Dialoghi d'amore* of Judah Abravanel" (Hebrew), in *Ẓiyyunim. Koveẓ le-Zikhrono shel Y. N. Simḥoni (Notes: A Collection in Memory of Y. N. Simḥoni)* (Berlin, 1928–29), 142–48.

————, "The Place of Kabbalah as a Means of Incitement of the Church in the Seventeenth Century" (Hebrew), *Bizaron* 36 (1957): 7–12, 57–66.

————, "Traces of the *Dialoghi d'Amore* in Hebrew Literature and the Printed Hebrew Translation" (Hebrew), *Tarbiẓ* 3 (1932): 287–313.

Sonnino, L. A., *A Handbook to Sixteenth-Century Rhetoric* (London and New York, 1968).

Soria, A., *Los humanistas de la corte de Alfonso el Magnánimo (según los epistolarios)* (Granada, 1956).

Sörös, P., *Jerosini Brodarics István [Stephanus Brodericus]* (Budapest, 1907).

Soudek, J., "Leonardo Bruni and His Public," *Studies in Medieval and Renaissance History* 5 (1968): 49–136.

Southern, R. W., *The Making of the Middle Ages* (New Haven, 1953).

Southey, C. A. B., *Olympia Morata, Her Times, Life, and Writings* (London, 1834).

Sowards, J. K., "Erasmus and the Education of Women," *Sixteenth Century Journal* 13 (1982): 77–90.

Sozzi, B. T., *Nuovi studi sul Tasso* (Bergamo, 1955).

Spencer, J. R., "Ut Rhetorica Pictura: A Study in Quattrocento Theory of Painting," *Journal of the Warburg and Courtauld Institutes* 20 (1957): 26–44.

Spiegel, G., *The Chronicle Tradition of Saint-Denis* (Leiden, 1978).

Spingarn, E. L., *Literary Criticism in the Renaissance* (New York, 1899).

Spitz, L. W., *Conrad Celtis: The German Arch-Humanist* (Cambridge, MA, 1957).

————, *The Religious Renaissance of the German Humanists* (Cambridge, MA, 1963).

————, *The Renaissance and Reformation Movements*, 2 vols. (Chicago, 1971).

————, "Luther, Humanism and the Word," *Lutheran Theological Seminary Bulletin* 65 (1985): 3–26.

Spivakovsky, E., *Son of the Alhambra: Diego Hurtado de Mendoza, 1504–1575* (Austin, TX, 1970).

Spongano, R., "Un capitolo di storia della nostra prosa d'arte," in *Due saggi sull'umanesimo* (Florence, 1964), 39–78.

Spörl, J., *Grundformen hochmittelalterlichen Geschichtsanschauung* (Munich, 1935).

Srbik, H. R. von, *Geist und Geschichte vom deutschen Humanismus bis zur Gegenwart*, 2 vols. (Munich, 1950–51).

Starn, R. "Florentine Renaissance Studies," *Bibliothèque d'humanisme et Renaissance* 32 (1970): 677–84.

Starrabba, R., "Guglielmo Raimondo Moncada Ebreo convertito siciliano del secolo XV," *Archivio storico siciliano* n.s. 3 (1878): 15–91.

Stäuble, A., "Francesco da Fiano in difesa della poesia," *Bibliothèque d'humanisme et Renaissance* 26 (1964): 256–59.

Stauffer, R., "Calvinism and the Universities," in *University and Reformation*, ed. Grane (q.v.), 76–90.

Stefanelli, R., *Boccaccio e la poesia* (Naples, 1978).

Steinberg, L., *Michelangelo's Last Paintings* (New York, 1975).

Steinschneider, M., *Letteratura delle donne* (Rome, 1880).

———, "Zur Frauen-literatur," *Israelitische Letterbode* 10 (1884): 88–105, 113–33, 139–47; 11 (1885): 52–92; 12 (1886): 63ff.

Steneck, N. H., "The Relevance of the Middle Ages to the History of Science and Technology," in *Science and Technology in Medieval Society*, ed. P. O. Long, *Annals of the New York Academy of Sciences* 441 (1985): 21–27.

Stephens, J. N., *The Fall of the Florentine Republic, 1512–1530* (New York, 1983).

Stevens, H. J., Jr., "Lorenzo Valla and Isidore of Seville," *Traditio* 31 (1975): 343–48.

Steyaert, F., "Puteanus Criticized by a Former Student, Nicolaus Burgundius," *Lias* 3 (1976): 131–38.

Stieber, J. W., *Pope Eugenius IV, the Council of Basel and the Secular and Ecclesiastical Authorities in the Empire: The Conflict over Supreme Authority in the Church* (Leiden, 1978).

Stinger, C. L., *Humanism and the Church Fathers: Ambrogio Traversari (1386–1439) and Christian Antiquity in the Italian Renaissance* (Albany, NY, 1976).

———, *The Renaissance in Rome: Ideology and Culture in the City of the Popes, 1443–1527* (Bloomington, IN, 1985).

Stock, B., *The Implications of Literacy* (Princeton, 1983).

Stock, P., *Better than Rubies: A History of Women's Education* (New York, 1978).

Stone, L., *The Family, Sex, and Marriage in England, 1500–1800* (New York, 1977).

Stow, K., *Catholic Thought and Papal Jewry Policy 1555–1593* (New York, 1977).

Strauss, G., *Historian in an Age of Crisis: The Life and Work of Johannes Aventinus, 1477–1534* (Cambridge, MA, 1963).

————, *Luther's House of Learning: Indoctrination of the Young in the German Reformation* (Baltimore and London, 1978).

————, *Nuremberg in the Sixteenth Century* (New York and London, 1966).

————, *Sixteenth-Century Germany, Its Topography and Topographers* (Madison, WI, 1959).

————, "The Mental World of a Saxon Pastor," in *Reformation Principle and Practice: Essays in Honor of Arthur Geoffrey Dickens*, ed. P. N. Brooks (London, 1980), 157–70.

Strnad, A. A., "Francesco Todeschini-Piccolomini: Politik und Mäzenatentum im Quattrocento," *Römische Historische Mitteilungen* 8–9 (1964–65): 101–425.

Strohl, H., *L'évolution religieuse de Luther* (Strasbourg, 1922).

Struever, N. S., *The Language of History in the Renaissance: Rhetoric and Historical Consciousness in Florentine Humanism* (Princeton, 1970).

Stump, E., *Boethius' De topicis differentiis* (Ithaca, 1978).

Sturm-Maddox, S., *Petrarch's Metamorphoses: Text and Subtext in the "Rime Sparse"* (Columbia, MO, 1985).

Surtz, E., S. J., *The Praise of Pleasure: Philosophy, Education, and Communism in More's Utopia* (Cambridge, MA, 1957).

Sutter, C., *Aus Leben und Schriften des Magisters Boncompagno* (Freiburg im Breisgau, 1894).

Svaboda, K., *L'esthétique de Saint Augustin et ses sources* (Brno, 1933).

Sykutris, J., "Epistolographie," in *Real Encyclopädie der classischen Altertumswissenschaft* (q.v.), Supplementband, 5:185–220.

————, "Proklos *Peri epistolimaiou charakteros*," *Byzantinisch-neugriechische Jahrbucher* 7 (1930): 108–18.

Symonds, J. A., *The Renaissance in Italy*, 7 vols. in 5 (New York, reprint 1960–64).

Sypher, G. W., "La Popelinière's Histoire de France," *Journal of the History of Ideas* 24 (1963): 41–54.

Székely, S., "Brodarics István élete es mü ködese" ["The Life and Work of István Brodarics"], *Történelmi Tár* (1888): 1:1–34, 2:225–62.

Szemes, J., *Oláh Miklós [Nicolaus Olahus]* (Esztergom, 1936).

Tadra, F., *Kanceláře a písaři v zemích českých za králů z rodu lucemburského Jana, Karla IV, a Václava IV (1310–1420) [Chancellors and Scribes in Czech Lands at the Time of the Kings of the Luxembourg Dynasty: John, Charles IV, Wenceslas IV (1310–1420)]* (Prague, 1892).

Tatakis, B., *'La philosophie byzantine* (Paris, 1949).

Tate, R. B., *Ensayos sobre la historiografía peninsular del siglo XV*, trans. J. Díaz (Madrid, 1970).

————, "Alfonso de Paléncia y los preceptos de la historiografía," *Academia literaria renacentista* 3 (1983): 37–64.

————, "Political Allegory in Fifteenth-Century Spain: A Study of the *Batalla campal de los perros contra los lobos* by Alfonso de Palencia (1423–92)," *Journal of Hispanic Philology* 1 (1977): 169–86.

Tateo, F., *Dialogo interiore e polemica ideologica nel "Secretum" del Petrarca* (Florence, 1965).

————, *Retorica e poetica fra Medioevo e Rinascimento* (Bari, 1960).

————, *Tradizione e realtà nell'umanesimo italiano* (Bari, 1967).

————, *L'umanesimo etico di Giovanni Pontano* (Lecce, 1972).

————, "La 'bella scrittura' del Bembo e l'Ermogene del Trapezunzio," in *Miscellanea di studi in onore di Vittore Branca* (Florence, 1983), 3:717–32.

————, "Diagnosi del potere nell'oratoria di un medico," in *Chierici e feudatari del mezzogiorno* (Bari, 1984), 1–20.

————, "La poetica di G. Pontano," *Filologia romanza* 6 (1959): 277–303, 337–69.

Tatham, E. H. R., *Francesco Petrarca, the First Modern Man of Letters: His Life and Correspondence,* 2 vols. (London, 1925–26).

Taylor, H. O., *Thought and Expression in the Sixteenth Century* (New York, 1920).

Theuerkauf, G., "Burchard von Worms und die Rechtskunde seiner Zeit," *Frühmittelalterliche Studien* 2 (1968): 144–61.

Thickett, D., *Estienne Pasquier* (London, 1980).

Thompson, C. R. *Translations of Lucian by Erasmus and St. Thomas More* (Ithaca, NY, 1940).

————, "Erasmus and Tudor England," *Actes du congrès Erasme* (q.v.), 29–68.

Thompson, I., "Manuel Chrysoloras and the Early Italian Renaissance," *Greek, Roman and Byzantine Studies* 7 (1966): 63–82.

Thompson, J. W., *A History of Historical Writing* (Chicago, 1942).

————, *The Literacy of the Laity in the Middle Ages* (Berkeley, 1939).

Thompson, M. G., C.S.J., "The Range of Irony in Three Visions of Judgment: Erasmus' *Julius Exclusus,* Donne's *Ignatius His Conclave,* and Lucian's *Dialogues of the Dead,*" *Erasmus of Rotterdam Society Yearbook* 3 (1983): 1–22.

Thomson, J. A. F., *Popes and Princes, 1417–1517: Politics and Popes in the Late Medieval Church* (London, 1980).

Thorndike, L., *A History of Magic and Experimental Science,* 8 vols. (New York, 1923–58).

————, *Science and Thought in the Fifteenth Century* (New York, 1929).

————, "Peter of Abano and Another Commentary on the *Problems* of Aristotle," *Bulletin of the History of Medicine* 29 (1955): 517–23.

Ticknor, G., *Historia de la literatura castellana,* trans. P. de Gayangos and E. de Vedia, 4 vols. (Madrid, 1851–56).

Tiedemann, H., *Tacitus und das Nationalbewusstsein der deutschen Humanisten* (Berlin, 1913).

Tigerstedt, E. N., "Observations on the Reception of the Aristotelian *Poetics* in the Latin West," *Studies in the Renaissance* 15 (1968): 7–24.

————, "The Poet as a Creator: Origins of a Metaphor," *Comparative Literature Studies* 4 (1968): 455–88.

Tillich, P., *The Protestant Era* (Chicago, 1938).

Timpanaro, S., *La genesi del metodo del Lachmann* (Padua, 2d ed., repr. 1985).

————, "Atlas cum compare gibbo," *Rinascimento* 2d ser. 2 (1951): 311–18.

Tirelli, V., "Gli inventari della biblioteca della cattedrale di Cremona (sec. X–

XIII) e un frammento di glossario latino del secolo X," *Italia medioevale e umanistica* 7 (1964): 1-76.

Tobolka, Z. V., *Dějiny československého knihtisku v době nejstarší* [*History of Czechoslovak Printing of the Oldest Period*] (Prague, 1930).

Todd, M., "Humanists, Puritans, and the Spiritualized Household," *Church History* 49 (1980): 18-34.

Toews, J. B., "Formative Forces in the Pontificate of Nicholas V," *Catholic Historical Review* 54 (1968-69): 261-84.

Toffanin, G., *Che cosa fu l'umanesimo* (Florence, 1929).

———, *La fine dell'umanesimo* (Turin, 1920).

———, *Giovanni Pontano fra l'uomo e la natura* (Bologna, 1938).

———, *Machiavelli e il tacitismo* (Naples, 1972).

———, *Storia dell'umanesimo,* 3 vols. (Bologna, 1950); *History of Humanism,* trans. E. Gianturco (New York, 1954).

———, "Pro Pio Madio," *La cultura* 10 (1931): 239-45.

Töllner, R., "Renata dissectionis ars. Vesals Stellung zu Galen in ihren wissenschaftsgeschichtlichen Voraussetzungen und Folgen," in *Die Rezeption der Antike,* ed. A. Buck (Hamburg, 1981), 85-95.

Tomalin, M., *The Fortunes of the Warrior Heroine in Italian Literature: An Index of Emancipation* (Ravenna, 1982).

Tomasović, M., *Zapisi o Maruliću i drugi komparatistički prilozi* [*Notes About Marulić and Other Comparativistic Contributions*] (Split, 1984).

Torre, A. della, *Paolo Marsi da Peschina: Contributo alla storia dell'Accademia Pomponiana* (Rocca S. Casciano, 1903).

———, *Storia dell'Accademia Platonica di Firenze* (Florence, 1902).

Torre, M. A. del, "Di alcuni problemi della 'Historia' in Francesco Patrizi," *Atti del XXIV congresso nazionale di filosofia,* 2 vols. (Rome, 1974), 2:387-95.

Tourney, G., "Francesco Diedo, Venetian Humanist and Politician of the Quattrocento," *Humanistica Lovaniensia* 19 (1970): 201-34.

Trabalza, C., *La critica letteraria nel Rinascimento* (Milan, 1915).

Tracy, J. D., *Erasmus: The Growth of a Mind* (Geneva, 1972).

———, *The Politics of Erasmus* (Toronto, 1978).

———, "Humanists Among the Scholastics: Erasmus, More and Lefèvre d'Etaples on the Humanity of Christ," *Erasmus of Rotterdam Society Yearbook* 5 (1985): 30-51.

Trame, R. H., *Rodrigo Sánchez de Arévalo, 1404-1470: Spanish Diplomat and Champion of the Papacy* (Washington, DC, 1958).

Trapp, J. B., "John Colet: His manuscripts and the Pseudo-Dionysius," in *Classical Influences on European Culture, A.D. 1500-1700,* ed. Bolgar (q.v.).

Traube, L., *Einleitung in die lateinische Philologie des Mittelalters* (Munich, 1911).

Traversari, D., *Ambrogio Traversari e i suoi tempi* (Florence, 1912).

Travitsky, B. S., "The New Mother of the English Renaissance: Her Writings on Motherhood," in *The Lost Tradition: Mothers and Daughters in Literature,* eds., C. Davison and E. M. Broner (New York, 1980), 33-43.

Trencsényi-Waldapfel, I., *Erasmus és magyar barátai* [*Erasmus and His Hungarian Friends*] (Budapest, 1941).

——, "Bornemissza Péter nyelvmüvészete" ["The Poetic Language of Peter Bornemissza"], *Nyugat* 24 (1931): 124–26.

Trexler, R. C., *Public Life in Renaissance Florence* (New York, 1980).

Trinkaus, C., *Adversity's Noblemen: The Italian Humanists on Happiness* (New York, 1940; rev. ed., 1965).

——, *In Our Image and Likeness: Humanity and Divinity in Italian Humanist Thought*, 2 vols. (Chicago, 1970).

——, *The Poet as Philosopher: Petrarch and the Formation of Renaissance Consciousness* (New Haven, 1979).

——, *The Scope of Renaissance Humanism* (Ann Arbor, MI, 1983).

——, "*Antiquitas* versus *Modernitas*: An Italian Humanist Polemic and Its Resonance," *Journal of the History of Ideas* 48 (1987): 11–21.

——, "Humanism," *Encyclopedia of World Art*, 16 vols. (New York, 1962–82), 7:702–34; reprinted in his *The Scope of Renaissance Humanism* (q.v.), 3–51.

——, "Humanism, Religion, Society: Concepts and Motivations of Some Recent Studies," *Renaissance Quarterly* 29 (1976): 676–713.

——, "Humanistic Dissidence: Florence vs. Milan, or Poggio vs. Valla," *Acta* of the Villa I Tatti Conference on Milan and Florence, forthcoming.

——, "A Humanist's Image of Humanism: The Inaugural Orations of Bartolommeo della Fonte," *Studies in the Renaissance* 7 (1960): 90–147; reprinted in his *The Scope of Renaissance Humanism* (q.v.), 52–87.

——, "L'umanesimo italiano e la scienza del Rinascimento," in *Letteratura e scienza nella storia della cultura italiana* (q.v.), 49–80.

——, "The Unknown Quattrocento Poetics of Bartolommeo della Fonte," *Studies in the Renaissance* 13 (1966): 40–95.

Tříška, J., *Literární činnost předhusitské university* [*Literary Activity of the Pre-Hussite University*] (Prague, 1967).

——, "Středověky literární Krumlov" ["The Medieval Literary Krumlov"], *Listy filologické* 9 (1961): 93–103.

Troeltsch, E., *Der Historismus und seine Probleme* (Tübingen, 1922).

——, "Renaissance und Reformation," in his *Gesammelte Schriften*, 4 vols. (Tübingen, 1912–61), 4:261–96.

Troje, H. E., *Graeca leguntur* (Cologne, 1971).

——, "Die Literatur des gemeinen Rechts unter dem Einfluss des Humanismus," in *Handbuch der Quellen und Literatur der neuren europäischen Privatrechtsgeschichte*, ed. H. Coing, vol. 2, *1500–1800* (Munich, 1974).

Trudel, J. P., *St. Augustin humaniste* (Trois Rivières, 1954).

Truhlář, J., ed., *Catalogus codicum manuscriptorum latinorum qui in C. R. Bibliotheca Publica atque Universitatis Pragensis asservantur*, 2 vols. (Prague, 1905–6).

——, *Humanismus a humanistě v Čechách za Krále Vladislava II* [*Humanism and Humanists Among Czechs at the time of King Ladislas II*] (Prague, 1894).

————, *Počátky humanismu v Čechách* [*The Beginnings of Humanism Among Czechs*] (Prague, 1892).

Tschiżewskij, D., *Die Renaissance und das ukrainische Geistesleben* (Berlin, 1929).

Turchetti, M., *Concordia o toleranza* (Geneva, 1984).

Turnbull, R., *Olympia Morata, Her Life and Times* (Boston, 1846).

Turóczi-Trostler, J., *Magyar irodalom-világirodalom* [*Hungarian Literature— World Literature*], 2 vols. (Budapest, 1961).

————, *A magyar nyelv felfedezése* [*The Discovery of Hungarian*] (Budapest, 1953).

Turyn, A., *Dated Greek Manuscripts of the 13th and 14th Centuries in the Libraries of Italy*, 2 vols. (Chicago, 1972).

————, *The MS Tradition of the Tragedies of Aeschylus* (New York, 1943).

————, *The MS Tradition of the Tragedies of Euripides* (Urbana, IL, 1957).

————, *The MS Tradition of the Tragedies of Sophocles* (Urbana, IL, 1952).

————, "Demetrius Triklinios and the Planudean Anthology," in *Festschrift N. Tomadakes* (Athens, 1973), 403–50.

Ubaldini, F., *Vita di Mons. Angelo Colocci*, ed. V. Fanelli (Vatican City, 1964).

Ullman, B. L., *The Humanism of Coluccio Salutati* (Padua, 1963).

————, *The Origin and Development of Humanistic Script* (Rome, 1960).

————, *Studies in the Italian Renaissance* (Rome, 2d ed., 1973).

———— and P. A. Stadter, *The Public Library of the Renaissance: Niccolò Niccoli, Cosimo de' Medici and the Library of San Marco* (Padua, 1972).

Ullman, W., *Medieval Foundations of Renaissance Humanism* (Ithaca, NY, 1977).

Ussani, V., "Gregorio VII scrittore nella sua corrispondenza e nei suoi dettati," *Studi gregoriani* 2 (1947): 341–59.

Vacalopoulos, A. E., *Origins of the Greek Nation: The Byzantine Period: 1204– 1461* (New Brunswick, NJ, 1970).

Vagnetti, L., "Considerazioni sui *Ludi matematici*," *Studi e documenti di architettura* 1 (1972): 175–259.

Vajda, G., *Isaac Albalag, Averroiste juif, traducteur et annotateur d'al-Ghazali* (Paris, 1960).

————, *Juda ben Nissim ibn Malka, philosophe juif marocain* (Paris, 1954).

————, *Recherches sur la philosophie et la kabbale dans la pensée juive du Moyen Âge* (Paris, 1962).

————, "Recherches sur la synthèse philosphico-kabbalistique de Samuel ibn Motot," *Archives d'histoire doctrinale et littéraire du Moyen Âge* 27 (1960): 29–63.

Valente, P. M., *L'ethique stoicienne chez Ciceron* (Paris, 1956).

Valentini, R., "Sul Panormita: Notizie biografiche e filologiche," *Rendiconti di R. Accademia dei Lincei* 16 (1907): 456–90.

Vallone, A., "Il latino di Dante," *Rivista di cultura classica e medioevale* 8 (1966): 184–92.

Van den Branden, L., E. Cockx-Indestege, and F. Sillis, *Bio-bibliografie van Cornelis Kiliaan* (Nieuwkoop, 1978).

Van den Oord, C. J. A., *Twee Eeuwen Bosch' Boekbedrijf 1450–1650* (Tilburg, 1984).

Van der Grinten, E. F., *Elements of Art Historiography in Medieval Texts: An Analytic Study* (The Hague, 1969).

Van Egmond, W., "The Commercial Revolution and the Beginnings of Western Mathematics in Renaissance Florence: 1300–1500" (Ph.D. diss., Indiana University, Bloomington, 1976).

Van Steenburghe, E., *Le Cardinal Nicolas de Cues* (Paris, 1920).

Van Til, H. R., *The Calvinistic Concept of Culture* (Grand Rapids, MI, 1959).

Varela, J., *Modos de educación en la España de la Contrarreforma* (Madrid, 1983).

Varga, L., *Das Schlagwort vom "Finsteren Mittelalter"* (Baden, 1932).

Varjas, B., "A Sárvár-Ujsziget nyomda betütipusai" ["The Types of the Sárvár-Ujsziget Press"], *Itk* 62(1958): 140–51.

———, "Heltai Gáspár a könyvkiadó" ["Gáspár Heltai, the Publisher"], *Reneszánsz füzetek* [*Booklets of the Renaissance*] 24 (1973): 291–314.

Vasoli, C., *La dialettica e la retorica dell'umanesimo* (Milan, 1968).

———, *Profezia e ragione: Studi sulla cultura del Cinquecento e del Seicento* (Naples, 1974).

———, "A proposito di Francesco Patrizi, Gian Giorgio Patrizi, Baldo Lupatino e Flacio Illirico: Alcune precisazioni," in *L'umanesimo e l'Istria*, ed. Branca and Graciotti (q.v.), 37–61.

———, "Aspetti dei rapporti culturali tra Italia e Spagna nell'età del Rinascimento," *Annuario dell'Istituto Storico Italiano per l'Età Moderna e Contemporanea* 29–30 (1977–78): 459–81; reprinted in *La cultura della corti* (Bologna, 1980), 13–37.

———, "Bruni, Leonardo," *Dizionario biografico degli italiani*, 30 vols. to date (Rome, 1960–84), 14:618–33.

———, "Considerazioni su alcuni temi retorici di Giulio Camillo Delminio," in *Retorica e poetica*, ed. D. Goldin and G. Folena (Padua, 1979), 243–57.

———, "The Contribution of Humanism to the Birth of Modern Science," *Renaissance and Reformation* n.s. 3 (1979): 1–15.

———, "Il *De pace fidei* di Niccolò da Cusa," in *Studi sulla cultura del Rinascimento* (Manduria, 1968), 122–79.

———, "Le *Dialecticae disputationes* del Valla e la critica umanistica della logica aristotelica," *Rivista critica di storia della filosofia* 12 (1957): 412–34; 13 (1958): 27–46.

———, "L'estetica dell'umanesimo e del Rinascimento," in *Momenti e problemi di storia dell'estetica* (Milan, 1959), 348–433.

———, "Francesco Patrizi and the 'Double Rhetoric,' " *New Literary History* 14 (1982–83): 539–51.

———, "Francesco Patrizi e la tradizione ermetica," *Nuova rivista storica* 45 (1980): 25–40.

———, "Note su Giorgio Valla e il suo 'Sistema' delle 'Arti' del discorso," *Interpres* 4 (1982): 247–61.

———, "Le teorie del Delminio e del Patrizi e i trattatisti d'arte fra '500 e '600," in *Cultura e società nel Rinascimento tra riforme e manierismi*, ed. V. Branca and C. Ossola (Florence, 1984), 249–70.

Vast, H., *Le Cardinal Bessarion* (Paris, 1878).

Vecchi, G., "Le Arenge di Guido Faba e l'eloquenza d'arte civile e politica due-centesca," *Quadrivium* 4 (1960): 65–69.

———, "Boncompagno," *Dizionario biografico degli italiani* 30 vols. to date (Rome, 1960–84), 11:722–25.

Vegas, F., "La concezione della storia dall'umanesimo alla Controriforma," *Grande antologia filosofica*, 31 vols. (Milan, 1954–78), 10:1–59.

Vermaseren, B. A., *De katholieke Nederlandsche Geschiedschrijving in de XVIe en XVIIe eeuw over den opstand* (Maastricht, 1941).

Viard, E., *André Alciat, 1492–1550* (Paris, 1926).

Vickers, B., *Francis Bacon and Renaissance Prose* (Cambridge, 1968).

———, "On the Practicalities of Renaissance Rhetoric," in *Rhetoric Revalued*, ed. Vickers (q.v.), 133–41.

———, "The Royal Society and English Prose Style: A Reassessment," in *Rhetoric and the Pursuit of Truth: Language Change in the Seventeenth and Eighteenth Centuries* (Los Angeles, 1985), 1–76.

Villa, C., " 'Denique Terenti dultia legimus acta . . . ': Una 'lectura Terenti' a S. Faustino di Brescia nel secolo IX," *Italia medioevale e umanistica* 22 (1979): 1–44.

——— and G. C. Alessio, "Tra commedia e Comedía," *Italia medioevale e umanistica* 24 (1981): 1–17.

Vinay, G., "Il Mussato e l'estetica medievale," *Giornale storico della letteratura italiana* 126 (1949): 113–59.

Vincenti, E., "Matteo dei Libri e l'oratoria pubblica e privata nel '200," *Archivio glottologico italiano* 54 (1969): 227–37.

Violante, C., "Anselmo da Baggio," *Dizionario biografico degli italiani*, 30 vols. to date (Rome, 1960–84), 18:399.

———, "Anselmo da Besati," *Dizionario biografico degli italiani*, 30 vols. to date (Rome, 1960–84), 18:408.

Viscardi, A., *Le origini* (Milan, 3d ed. 1957).

———, "Idee estetiche e letteratura militante nel Medioevo," in *Momenti e problemi di storia dell'estetica* (Milan, 1959), 231–52.

Vivanti, C., "Alle origine della idea di civiltà: Le scoperte geografiche e gli scritti di La Popelinière," *Rivista storica italiana* 74 (1962): 225–47.

———, "Paulus Aemilius condidit historias?" *Annales* 19 (1964): 1117–24.

Vocht, H. de, *History of the Foundation and the Rise of the Collegium Trilingue Lovaniense, 1517–1550*, 4 vols. (Louvain, 1951–55).

Vodnik, B., *Povijest hrvatske književnosti*, vol. 1, *Od humanizma do potkraj XVIII. stoljeća* [*History of Croatian Literature*, vol. 1, *Humanism to the End of the 18th Century*] (Zagreb, 1913).

Vogelstein, I., *Johann Sleiden's Commentaries* (Lanham, MD, 1986).

Voigt, G., *Enea Silvio de' Piccolomini, als Papst Pius II. und sein Zeitalter*, 3 vols. (Berlin, 1856–63).

———, *Die Wiederbelebung des classischen Alterthums*, ed. M. Lehnerdt, 2 vols.

(Berlin, 3d ed. 1893); *Il risorgimento dell'antichità classica*, trans. D. Valbusa, ed. G. Zippel, 3 vols. (Florence, 1888–97; reprint ed. E. Garin, Florence, 1968).

Volf, J., "Knihovna Hilaria z Litoměřic" ["The Library of Hilarius of Litoměřice"], *Český časopis historický* 81 (1907): 131–33.

Volpe, G. della, *Poetica del Cinquecento* (Bari, 1954).

Volpicella, L., *Federico d'Aragone e la fine del regno di Napoli nel 1501* (Naples, 1901).

Vorlander, D., "Olympia Fulvia Morata—eine evangelische Humanistin in Schweinfurt," *Zeitschrift für Bayerische Kirkengeschichte* 39 (1970): 95–113.

Voss, J., *Das Mittelalter im historischen Denken Frankreichs* (Munich, 1973).

Vossler, K., *Poetische Theorien in der Italienischen Frührenaissance* (Berlin, 1900).

Vratović, V., "Hrvatski latinizam u kontekstu hrvatske i evropske književnosti" ["Croatian Latinism in the Context of Croatian and European Literature"], in *Hrvatska književnost u evropskom kontekstu* [*Croatian Literature in a European Context*], ed. A. Flaker and K. Pranjić (Zagreb, 1978), 137–51.

———, "Pisma Antuna Vračića u okviru suvremene epistolografije evropske" ["The Letters of Antun Vrančić Within the Framework of Contemporary European Epistolography"], in D. Novakovic and V. Vratović, *S visina sve: Antun Vrančić* [*From the Heights, Everything: Antun Vrančić*] (Zagreb, 1979), 293–317.

Walker, D. P., *The Ancient Theology: Studies in Christian Platonism from the Fifteenth to the Eighteenth Century* (Ithaca, NY, 1972).

———, *Spiritual and Demonic Magic from Ficino to Campanella* (London, 1958).

———, *Studies in Musical Science in the late Renaissance* (London and Leiden, 1978).

———, "Le chant orphique de Marsile Ficin," in *Musique et poésie au XVIe siècle*, ed. J. Jacquot (Paris, 1954), 17–33.

———, "Ficino's Spiritus and Music," *Annales musicologiques* 1 (1951): 131–50.

———, "Musical Humanism in the 16th and Early 17th Centuries," *Music Review* 2 (1941): 1–13, 111–21, 220–27, 288–308; 3 (1942): 55–71.

Waller, G. F., "The Text and Manuscript Variants of the Countess of Pembroke's Psalms," *Review of English Studies* n.s. 26 (1975): 1–18.

Waller, M., *Petrarch's Poetics and Literary Theory* (Amherst, MA, 1980).

Walser, E., *Gesammelte Studien zur Geistesgeschichte der Renaissance* (Basel, 1932).

Waltzer, H., "Beziehungen des böhmischen Humanisten Johann von Rabenstein zu Bayern," *Mittheilungen des Instituts für österreichische Geschichtsforschung* 24 (1903): 630–45, text 637–43.

Ward, J. O., "*Artificiosa Eloquentia* in the Middle Ages" (Ph.D. diss., University of Toronto, 1972).

Warfield, B., *Calvin and Augustine* (Philadelphia, 1956).

Warnicke, R. M., *Women of the English Renaissance and Reformation* (Westport, CT, 1983).

Warren, L. C., *Humanistic Doctrines of the Prince from Petrarch to Sir Thomas Elyot: A Study of the Principal Analogues and Sources of "The Boke Named the Governour"* (Chicago, 1939).

Wartelle, A., *Inventaire des manuscrits grecs d'Aristote et de ses commentateurs* (Paris, 1963).

Waswe, R., "The 'Ordinary Language Philosophy' of Lorenzo Valla," *Bibliothèque d'humanisme et Renaissance* 41 (1979): 255–71.

———, "The Reaction of Juan Vives to Valla's Philosophy of Language," *Bibliothèque d'humanisme et Renaissance* 42 (1980): 595–609.

Watanabe, M., "Humanism in the Tyrol: Aeneas Sylvius, Duke Sigismund, Gregor Heimberg," *Journal of Medieval and Renaissance Studies* 4 (1974): 177–202.

Waterbolk, E. H., *Twee eeuwen Friese geschiedschrijving. Opkomst, bloei en verval van de Friese historiografie in de 16e en 17e eeuw* (Groningen, 1952).

Watson, A., *The Law of the Ancient Romans* (Dallas, 1970).

———, *Legal Transplants* (Edinburgh, 1974).

Watts, P. M., *Nicolaus Cusanus, a Fifteenth-Century Vision of Man* (Leiden, 1982).

Webber, E. S., "A Spanish Linguistic Treatise of the Fifteenth Century," *Romance Philology* 16 (1962): 32–40.

Weber, É., *Musique et théâtre dans les pays rhénans*, vol. 1, *Le musique mesurée à l'antique en Allemagne* (Paris, 1974).

Weiler, A., "The Christian Humanism of the Renaissance and Scholasticism," *Concilium* 27 (1967): 29–46.

Weinberg, B., *A History of Literary Criticism in the Italian Renaissance*, 2 vols. (Chicago, 1961).

———, "Argomenti di discussione letteraria nell'Accademia degli Alterati (1570–1600)," *Giornale storico della letteratura italiana* 131 (1954): 175–94.

———, "Badius Ascensius and the Transmission of Medieval Literary Criticism," *Romance Philology* 9 (1955): 209–16.

———, "Bartolomeo Maranta: nuovi manoscritti di critica letteraria," *Annali della Scuola Normale Superiore di Pisa* 24 (1955): 115–25.

———, "Castelvetro's Theory of Poetics," in *Critics and Criticism: Ancient and Modern*, ed. R. S. Crane (Chicago, 1952), 349–71.

———, "From Aristotle to Pseudo-Aristotle," *Comparative Literature* 5 (1952): 97–104.

———, "Nuove attribuzioni di manoscritti di critica letteraria del Cinquecento," *Rinascimento*, 2d ser. 3 (1952): 245–59.

———, "The Poetic Theories of Minturno," in *Studies in Honor of F. L. Shipley* (Washington, DC, 1942), 101–29.

———, "Robortello on the Poetics," in *Critics and Criticism: Ancient and Modern*, ed. R. S. Crane (Chicago, 1952), 319–48.

———, "Scaliger Versus Aristotle on Poetics," *Modern Philology* 39 (1942): 337–60.

———, "Translations and Commentaries of Longinus' *On the Sublime* to 1600: A Bibliography," *Modern Philology* 47 (1950): 145–51.

Weinstein, D., *Savonarola and Florence: Prophecy and Patriotism in the Renaissance* (Princeton, 1970).

———, "In Whose Image and Likeness? Interpretations of Renaissance Humanism," *Journal of the History of Ideas* 33 (1972): 165–76.

Weisheipl, J. A., "Classification of Sciences in Medieval Thought," *Medieval Studies* 25 (1965): 54–90.

Weiss, J. M., "*Ecclesiastes* and Erasmus: The Mirror and the Image," *Archiv für Reformationsgeschichte* 65 (1974): 83–108.

Weiss, R., *Humanism in England During the Fifteenth Century* (Oxford, 2d ed. 1957).

———, *Il primo secolo dell'umanesimo* (Rome, 1949).

———, *The Renaissance Discovery of Classical Antiquity* (Oxford, 1969).

———, *The Spread of Italian Humanism* (London, 1964).

———, *Un umanista veneziano: Papa Paolo II* (Venice, 1958).

———, "Andrea Fulvio antiquario romano (ca. 1470–1527)," *Annali della Scuola Normale Superiore di Pisa*, 2d ser. 28 (1959): 1–44.

———, "The Dawn of Humanism in Italy," *Bulletin of the Institute of Historical Research* 42 (1969): 1–16, originally published as a monograph (London, 1947).

———, "In obitv Vrsini Landredini: A Footnote to the Literary History of Rome Under Pope Innocent VIII," *Italia medioevale e umanistica* 2 (1959): 353–66.

———, "Lovato Lovati (1241–1309)," *Italian Studies* 6 (1951): 3–28.

———, "Poesie religiose di Francesco da Fiano," *Archivio italiano per la storia della pietà* 2 (1957): 199–206.

Wemple, S. F., *Atto of Vercelli: Church, State and Christian Society in Tenth Century Italy* (Rome, 1979).

Wertis, S. K., "The Commentary of Bartolinus de Benincase de Canulo on the *Rhetorica ad Herennium*," *Viator* 10 (1979): 283–310.

Westfall, C. W., *In This Most Perfect Paradise* (University Park, PA, 1974).

Westman, R. S. and J. E. McGuire, *Hermeticism and the Scientific Revolution* (Los Angeles, 1977).

White, H. C., *The Tudor Books of Private Devotion* (Madison, WI, 1951).

Whitfield, J. H., *Petrarch and the Renascence* (New York, 1965).

Wieruszowski, H., *Politics and Culture in Medieval Spain and Italy* (Rome, 1971).

———, "Rhetoric and the Classics in Italian Education of the Thirteenth Century," in her *Politics and Culture in Medieval Spain and Italy* (Rome, 1971), 589–627.

Wightman, W. P. D., *Science and the Renaissance*, 2 vols. (Edinburgh and London, 1962).

———, *Science in a Renaissance Society* (London, 1972).

Wilcox, D. J., *The Development of Florentine Humanist Historiography in the Fifteenth Century* (Cambridge, MA, 1969).

Wilhelm, R. M., "Vergil's Dido and Petrarch's Sophonisba," *Studies in Language and Literature*, ed. C. Nelson (Richmond, KY, 1976), 585–91.

Wilkins, E. H., *Life of Petrarch* (Chicago, 1961).

———, *The Making of the "Canzoniere" and Other Petrarchan Studies* (Rome, 1951).

———, *Petrarch's Eight Years in Milan* (Cambridge, MA, 1958).

———, *Studies in the Life and Works of Petrarch* (Cambridge, MA, 1955).

Williams, G. H., *The Radical Reformation* (Philadelphia, 1962).

Williams, R. G., "The Originality of Daniello," *Romanic Review* 15 (1924): 121–22.

Williamson, E., "Tasso's Annotations to Trissino's Poetics," *Modern Language Notes* 63 (1948): 153–58.

Wilmart, A., "L'*Ars arengandi* de Jacques de Diant avec un appendice sur ses ouvrages *De dictamine*," in his *Analecta reginensis* (Vatican City, 1933), 113–51.

Wilson, N. G., "A Chapter in the History of Scholia," *Classical Quarterly* 17 (1967): 244–56.

———, "The Church and Classical Studies in Byzantium," *Antike und Abendland* 16 (1970): 68–77.

Wind, E., *Pagan Mysteries in the Renaissance* (New York, rev. ed. 1968).

———, "The Revival of Origen," in *Studies in Art and Literature for Bella Costa Greene*, ed. D. Miner (Princeton, 1954), 412–24.

Winter, E., *Frühhumanismus: Seine Entwicklung in Böhmen und deren europäische Bedeutung für die Kirchenreformbestrebungen im 14. Jahrhundert* (Berlin, 1964).

Wirszubski, C., *Flavius Mithridates, Sermo de passione domini* (Jerusalem, 1963).

———, *Mekkubal Nozri Koreh Ba-torah* [A Christian Kabbalist Reads the Torah] (Jerusalem, 1977).

———, *Sheloshah Perakim be-Toledot ha-Kabbalah ha-Nozrit* [Three Chapters in the History of the Kabbalah] (Jerusalem, 1975).

———, "Flavius Mithridates" [Hebrew], *Israel National Academy for Sciences Proceedings* 1 (1966): 1–10.

———, "Flavius Mithridates' Christological Sermon" [Hebrew], in *Yiẓḥak Baer Jubilee Volume* (Jerusalem, 1960), 191–206.

———, "Francesco Giorgio's Commentary on Giovanni Pico's Kabbalistic Theses," *Journal of the Warburg and Courtauld Institutes* 37 (1974): 145–56.

———, "Giovanni Pico's Book of Job," *Journal of the Warburg and Courtauld Institutes* 32 (1969): 171–99.

———, "Giovanni Pico's Companion to Kabbalistic Symbolism," in *Studies in Mysticism and Religion Presented to Gershom G. Scholem* (Jerusalem, 1967), 353–62.

———, "Liber Redemptionis: An Early Version of the Kabbalistic Commentary on the Guide to the Perplexed of Abraham Abulafia in Its Latin Translation of

Flavius Mithridates" (Hebrew), *Israel National Academy of Sciences Proceedings* 3 (1970): 135–49.

Witt, R. G., *Coluccio Salutati and His Public Letters* (Geneva, 1976).

———, *Hercules at the Crossroads: The Life, Works, and Thought of Coluccio Salutati* (Durham, NC, 1983).

———, "Boncompagno on Grammar and Rhetoric," *Journal of Medieval and Renaissance Studies* 16 (1986): 1–31.

———, "Brunetto Latini and the Italian Tradition of *Ars Dictaminis*," *Stanford Italian Review* 3 (1983): 5–24.

———, "Medieval *Ars Dictaminis* and the Beginnings of Humanism: A New Construction of the Problem," *Renaissance Quarterly* 35 (1982): 1–35.

———, "On Bene of Florence's Conception of the French and Roman Cursus," *Rhetorica* 3 (1985): 77–98.

Wittkower, R., *Architectural Principles in the Age of Humanism* (London, 1949).

Wolf, E., "Reformatorische Botschaft und Humanismus," in *Studien zur Geschichte und Theologie der Reformation. Festschrift für Ernst Bizer,* ed. L. Abramowski and J. F. G. Goeters (Neukirchen, 1969), 97–119.

Wolff, M. J., "Die Theorie der italienischen Tragödie im 16 Jahrhunderts," *Archiv für das Studium der neueren Sprachen und Literaturen* 128 (1912): 161–83.

Wolfson, H. A., *The Philosophy of Spinoza,* 2 vols. (Cleveland and New York, 1958).

Woodbridge, F., "Boccaccio's Defence of Poetry in the XIVth Book of the Genealogiis," *PMLA* 13 (1925): 61–80.

Woodbridge, L., *Women and the English Renaissance: Literature and the Nature of Womanhood, 1540–1620* (Urbana, IL, 1984).

Woodward, W. H., *Studies in Education During the Age of the Renaissance, 1400–1600* (Cambridge, 1906; reprinted New York, 1967).

Woolf, C. N., *Bartolus of Sassoferrato: His Position in the History of Medieval Political Thought* (Cambridge, 1913).

Wright, L. B., *Middle-Class Culture in Elizabethan England* (Chapel Hill, 1935).

Yardeni, M., "La conception de l'histoire dans l'oeuvre de La Popelinière," *Revue d'histoire moderne et contemporaine* 11 (1964): 109–26.

Yates, F. A., *The Art of Memory* (London, 1966; reprinted Middlesex, 1969).

———, *The French Academies of the Sixteenth Century* (London, 1947).

———, *Giordano Bruno and the Hermetic Tradition* (London, 1964).

———, *The Occult Philosophy in the Elizabethan Age* (London, 1979).

———, "The Hermetic Tradition in Renaissance Science," in *Art, Science and History in the Renaissance,* ed. C. S. Singleton (Baltimore, 1967), 255–74.

Yates, L., "The Uses of Women to a Sixteenth Century Bestseller," *Historical Studies* 18 (1979): 422–34.

Yost, J. K., "The Value of Married Life for the Social Order in the Early English Renaissance," *Societas* 6 (1976): 25–39.

Zabughin, V., *Giulio Pomponio Leto: Saggio critico,* 3 vols. (Rome, 1909–12).

————, *Vergilio nel Rinascimento italiano da Dante a Torquato Tasso*, 2 vols. (Bologna, 1921).

Zaccaria, V., "L'epistolario di Pier Candido Decembrio," *Rinascimento* 3 (1952): 85–118.

————, "Pier Candido Decembrio e Leonardo Bruni," *Studi medievali* 3d ser. 2 (1967): 506–14.

————, "Pier Candido Decembrio traduttore della "Republica" di Platone," *Italia medioevale e umanistica* 2 (1959): 179–206.

————, "Sulle opere di Pier Candido Decembrio," *Rinascimento* 7 (1956): 13–74; additions and corrections, Kristeller, *Studies in Renaissance Thought and Letters* (q.v.), 2:561–65.

Zacchino, V., "Il *De educatione* di A. Galateo e i suoi sentimento antispagnuoli," in *Atti del congresso di studi sull'età aragonese* (Bari, 1969), 620–42.

Zahrnt, H., *Luther deutet Geschichte. Erfolg und Misserfolg im Licht des Evangeliums* (Munich, 1952).

Zambelli, P., "Agrippa von Nettesheim in den neueren kritischen Studien und in den Handschriften," *Archiv für Kulturgeschichte* 51 (1969): 264–96.

————, "Aneddoti patriziani," *Rinascimento* 7 (1967): 309–18.

Zanta, L., *La renaissance du stoïcisme au XVIe siècle* (Paris, 1914).

Zappen, J. P., "Science and Rhetoric from Bacon to Hobbes: Responses to the Problem of Eloquence," in *Rhetoric 78: Proceedings of "Theory of Rhetoric, an Interdisciplinary Conference,"* ed. R. L. Brown and M. Steinmann, Jr. (Minneapolis, 1979), 399–419.

Zeitlin, W., "Bibliotheca epistolographia," *Hebraeische Bibliographie* 22 (1919): 32–47.

Zetzel, J. E. G., "*Emendavi ad Tironem*: Some Notes on Scholarship in the Second Century A.D.," *Harvard Studies in Classical Philology* 77 (1973): 225–43.

————, "On the History of Latin Scholia," *Harvard Studies in Classical Philology* 79 (1975): 335–54.

Zielinski, T., *Cicero im Wandel der Jahrhunderte* (Leipzig, 3d ed. 1912).

Zika, C., "Reuchlin's *De verbo mirifico* and the Magic Debate of the Late Fifteenth Century," *Journal of the Warburg and Courtauld Institutes* 39 (1976): 104–38.

Zilsel, E., "The Genesis of the Concept of Scientific Progress," in *Roots of Scientific Thought*, ed. P. P. Wiener and A. Noland (New York, 1957), 251–75.

————, "The Sociological Roots of Science," *American Journal of Sociology* 47 (1942): 544–62.

Zimmels, B., *Leo Hebraeus, ein judischer Philosoph der Renaissance* (Breslau, 1886).

————, *Leone Hebreo: Neue Studien* (Vienna, 1892).

Zimmerman, S., "Juraj Dragišić kao filozof humanizma" ["Juraj Dragišić as a Philosopher of Humanism"], *Rad JAZU* [*Works of the Yugoslav Academy of Sciences and Arts*] 227 (1923): 59–79.

Zinberg, I., *A History of Jewish Literature,* ed. and trans. B. Martin (Cincinnati, OH, 1974), vol. 4.

Zippel, G., *Il Filelfo a Firenze (1429–1434)* (Rome, 1899).

———, "Note sulle redazioni della *Dialectica* di Lorenzo Valla," *Archivo storico per la province parmensi* 4th ser. 9 (1957): 301–15.

INDEX TO VOLUMES 1–3

References to volume numbers are set in italic type. Notes are cited only when they contain discussions of issues; otherwise, consult the Bibliography.